GROLIER

ENCYCLOPEDIA
OF KNOWLEDGE

Grolier Incorporated
Danbury, Connecticut

1993 Printing

ISBN 0-7172-5300-7 (complete set)
ISBN 0-7172-5311-2 (volume 11)

Printed and manufactured in the United States of America.

This publication is an abridged version of the *Academic American Encyclopedia*.

3 4 5 6 7 8 9 10

Kk

GERMAN-GOTHIC	RUSSIAN-CYRILLIC	CLASSICAL LATIN	EARLY LATIN	ETRUSCAN	CLASSICAL GREEK	EARLY GREEK	EARLY ARAMAIC	EARLY HEBREW	PHOENICIAN

K *K/k* is the 11th letter of the English alphabet. Both the letter and its position in the alphabet are derived from the Latin, which in turn came from the Greek by way of the Etruscan. The Greeks call the letter *kappa* and took its name, form, and position from a Semitic writing system in which the name of the sign was *kaph.*

In both Semitic and Greek writing systems the letter represents the sound *k,* a voiceless velar stop. Early Latin writing, under the influence of Etruscan, used three letters for this sound: *c* before *e* and *i, k* before *a,* and *q* before *u.* The use of *K/k* was eventually dropped, however, in favor of *C/c,* except for a few well-known and often-abbreviated words.

When the Latin alphabet was introduced into the British Isles, the letter *C/c* was used to write all *k* sounds (thus modern *kind* and *king* were *cynd* and *cyning* in Old English), but the use of *K/k* for this sound before *e, i,* or *y* was soon revived in English. As a consequence, almost all English words that have the spelling *K/k* before *a, o, u, l,* or *r* are of foreign origin (for example, *kangaroo, kosher, kumquat, blitzkrieg*). In modern English, initial *K/k* followed by *n* is silent, as in *knee* and *knot,* although earlier both sounds were pronounced, as they still are in German.

K2 K2 (formerly Godwin Austen) is the world's second highest peak and is located in northern Kashmir, Pakistan, in the KARAKORAM RANGE of the Himalayas. It has an elevation of 8,611 m (28,250 ft). It was the second peak to be measured in the 1856 survey of the Karakoram Range (hence, K2) and was originally named for its first surveyor, Henry Haversham Godwin-Austen (1834–1923). Numerous attempts to reach its snow- and glacier-covered summit failed until an Italian team, led by the geologist Ardito Desio, succeeded in 1954.

Kaaba Kaaba (Arabic, "a square building"), ISLAM's most sacred sanctuary and pilgrimage shrine, is located in the courtyard of the Great Mosque of MECCA. According to the Koran, the cubic-shaped structure was built by Adam according to a divine plan and rebuilt by Abraham and Ishmael. A trough in which they reputedly mixed mortar stands near the door and is a popular place of prayer. The Kaaba houses the Black Stone, the most venerated object for Muslims. Probably of meteoric origin, the stone is reputed to have been given to Ishmael by the angel Gabriel. All Muslims face toward the Kaaba during their daily prayers.

Kabalevsky, Dmitri [kah-buh-lef'-skee, duh-mee'-tree] The Soviet composer Dmitri Borisovich Kabalevsky, b. Dec. 30 (N.S.), 1904, d. February 1987, attended the Moscow Conservatory, then spent much of his life as a professor of composition there. He was appointed to the Ministry of Culture in 1954 and was named People's Artist in 1963. He wrote much educational music and several operas, including *Colas Breugnon* (1938), *The Family of Taras* (1950), *Nikita Vershinin* (1955), and *The Sisters* (1969). In addition to much music for film and occasional theater music, Kabalevsky's compositions include the orchestral suite *The Comedians,* two string quartets, a number of songs, four symphonies, and three concertos for piano, one for violin, and two for cello. His *Requiem* for two choruses, soloists, and orchestra won the Glinka Prize in 1966.

Kabbalah [kab-uh-lah'] *Kabbalah,* the Hebrew word for tradition, originally designated the legal tradition of JUDAISM, but it was later applied to the Jewish mystical tradition, especially the system of esoteric mystical speculation and practice that developed during the 12th and 13th centuries. The teachings of Kabbalah, as developed by the visionary Isaac ben Solomon LURIA, are credited with giving rise to the Sabbatean movement led by SABBATAI ZEVI.

Like every other Jewish religious expression, Kabbalah was based on the Old Testament revelation. The revealed text was interpreted with the aid of various hermeneutic techniques. Of the many methods available, the Kabbalists most frequently used three forms of letter and number symbolism: *gematria, notarikon,* and *temurah.*

The Kabbalists developed distinctive doctrines of creation and of redemption. Their doctrine of creation was built on a theory of emanations and asserted that the world derived from the transcendent and unknowable God (*En Soph*) through a series of increasingly material manifestations (*sephirot*). By the sin of Adam and the later sins of humankind, the immanent aspect of God, or the *Shekhinah* (divine presence), was exiled in the final *sephirah, malkhut* (kingdom). The sexual imagery of Kabbalah treats *Shekhinah* (the word is feminine in gender) as the female aspect of divinity; it symbolically expresses the idea of the restoration of harmony (*tikkun*) as the reunion of the male and female aspects of the divine, that is, as the reunion of divine transcendence and immanence.

The classic document of the Kabbalistic tradition, the *Zohar*, was compiled by Moses de León about 1290. A more systematic presentation of the basic doctrine is contained in Moses Cordovero's *Pardes rimmonim* (Garden of Pomegranates, 1548).

Kabuki [kah-boo'-kee]   Kabuki is a popular Japanese theater form in which stylized acting is combined with lyric singing, dancing, and spectacular staging. The characters with which the word *Kabuki* is written in fact mean song, dance, and acting.

The female entertainer Okuni first performed Kabuki dances and comic sketches in 1603. Since 1629, however, when women were banned from professional stages, both Kabuki and the puppet drama BUNRAKU have been performed only by men. In Tokyo, Ichikawa Danjuro I (1660–1704) created a bravura acting style for history plays, while in Kyoto the elegant actor Sakata Tojuro (1644–1709) created a gentle, comic style for romantic domestic plays. Bunraku plays were adapted for Kabuki actors in the 18th century, and dance plays were adapted from Kyogen and NO DRAMA in the 19th. Gangster plays, with thieves and murderers as heroes, were the invention of playwrights Tsuruya Namboku IV (1755–1829) and Kawatake Mokuami (1816–93). The classic Kabuki plays are still performed at commercial theaters in Japan, and some modern authors have tried to create new ones.

Following the custom of No drama, the all-day Kabuki program provides variety by alternating play types and acting styles. Walkways, revolving stages, elevators, trap doors, curtains, and rapid costume changes are used for theatrical effect. The female impersonator (*onnagata*) stylizes feminine traits into a half-real, half-artificial art. Actors use the *mie*, a pose, as the visual climax of a scene. Background music is selected from among some 500 melodies and rhythms.

Elaborate makeup and costumes are integral parts of Kabuki, a form of Japanese drama that evolved during the late 17th century and remains popular today. The Kabuki performance combines dance, mime, music, and melodrama.

Kabul [kuh-bool']   Kabul, the capital and the largest city of Afghanistan as well as the capital of Kabul province, is located on the Kabul River in the northeastern section of the country, about 80 km (50 mi) east of the border with Pakistan. The population is 1,424,400 (1988 est.). Manufactures include building materials, machinery, textiles, and processed food; in contrast, local craftspeople use methods that have changed little over thousands of years. The city has a university (1932).

Kabul (called Kabura by Ptolemy) has existed for more than 3,000 years. In AD 664 it was conquered by Arabs, and in the 13th century it was sacked by Genghis Khan. In 1504 the city was conquered by BABUR, under whom it was capital of the Mogul Empire until 1526. In 1773, Kabul became the capital of Afghanistan. Kabul was captured by the British in both 1842 and 1879 during the Afghan Wars. During the 1980s the city was a major Soviet military base.

kachina [kuh-chin'-uh]   A kachina is an ancestral spirit in the religion of the PUEBLO Indians of present-day Arizona and New Mexico. In certain ceremonies kachinas, or kachinam, are impersonated by masked dancers wearing colorful costumes. The HOPI believe that when a person dies his or her ghost may be metamorphosed into a kachina and live on as such in the underworld. A particular kachina does not, however, represent an individual but is instead a generalized mythical conception. No one knows how many different kachinas there are, but more than 250 have been identified. The kachinas are believed to spend half of every year in the Hopi villages, returning each July to underground dwelling places. The carved-wood kachina dolls of the Hopi and Zuñi are considered representations of the kachina spirits.

Kádár, János [kah'-dahr, yahn'-ohsh]   The Hungarian political leader János Kádár, b. May 26, 1912, d. July 6, 1989, became the Soviet-appointed premier of Hungary after the HUNGARIAN REVOLUTION of 1956 and remained in power until 1988. Following the Communist takeover in 1948, Kádár became minister of internal affairs and deputy chief secretary of the party. Imprisoned (1951–54) as a pro-Titoist, Kádár later joined Imre NAGY's reform government during the 1956 Hungarian uprising. He soon sided with the Soviets and formed a countergovernment. When the rebellion was put down, Kádár became premier and first secretary. His regime gradually introduced comparatively liberal domestic policies.

Kael, Pauline [kayl]   Pauline Kael, b. Petaluma, Calif., June 19, 1919, is a film critic whose sharp, analytical, sometimes eccentric opinions have won her a large following. She is particularly known for her reviews in the *New Yorker* (1968–91), which relate movies to wide-ranging aspects of culture as well as to the audience itself. Her collections of essays and reviews include *Deeper* *into Movies* (1973; National Book Award) and *5001 Nights at the Movies* (1982).

Kaesong [kay'-suhng]   Kaesong is a special city with provincial status in southwestern North Korea, near the 38th parallel (the demarcation line between North and South Korea). It has a population of 259,000 (1981 est.). An agricultural trade center, Kaesong is also noted for porcelain and for locally grown ginseng. The walled city (Songdor) was the capital of the Koryo dynasty from 938 until 1392. It was taken by North Korean forces during the Korean War, and the first truce talks were held there in 1951. Its special administrative status was attained when a military installation was built along the truce line.

Kaffir cat   The Kaffir cat, *Felis libyca*, also known as the African wildcat, closely resembles the domestic cat and is often regarded as its primary ancestor. The Kaffir cat is sometimes classified as a subspecies of the European wildcat, *F. sylvestris*. Its color ranges from yellowish gray to orangy brown, with narrow, dark stripes. It reaches about 65 cm (27 in) in length and weighs up to 4.5 kg (10 lb) or more.

Kafir [kaf'-ur]   The Kafir (Nuri) people occupy parts of the Hindu Kush in northern Pakistan and Afghanistan and number nearly 70,000. A Caucasoid people, they speak Kafiri—an Indo-European language—and subsist through agriculture, hunting, and the raising of livestock. Most Kafirs were forcibly converted to Islam in the late 19th century, but some still practice their traditional religion, which encompasses numerous gods and the practice of shamanism. The term *kafir* (Arabic for "infidel") was originally used to denote non-Muslims in a derogatory fashion. The name *Kafir* or *Kaffir* was also applied to the Xhosa peoples of southern Africa by early white settlers; it was later used in a pejorative sense by white South Africans to refer to all black Africans.

Kafka, Franz [kahf'-kah]   Franz Kafka, b. Prague, Bohemia (then belonging to Austria), July 3, 1883, d. June 3, 1924, is one of the most influential writers of this century. Kafka came from a middle-class Jewish family and grew up in the shadow of his domineering shopkeeper father. The feeling of impotence, even in his rebellion, was a syndrome that became a pervasive theme in his fiction. Kafka did well in the prestigious German high school in Prague and went on to receive a law degree in 1906. He soon found a position in the semipublic Workers' Accident Insurance institution, where he remained a loyal and successful employee until—beginning in 1917—tuberculosis forced him to take repeated sick leaves and finally to retire (1922). Kafka spent half his time after 1917 in sanatoriums and health resorts, his tuberculosis of the lungs finally spreading to the larynx.

Franz Kafka, a 20th-century Czech author, wrote such intense, symbolic tales as The Metamorphosis *(1915) and* The Trial *(1925), in which he portrays people as tormented by isolation and ineffectuality.*

None of Kafka's novels was printed during his lifetime, and it was only with reluctance that he published a fraction of his shorter fiction. This fiction includes *Meditation* (1913; Eng. trans., 1949), a collection of short prose pieces; *The Judgment* (1913; Eng. trans., 1945), a long short story written in 1912 that Kafka himself considered his decisive breakthrough (it tells of a rebellious son condemned to suicide by his father); and *The Metamorphosis* (1915; Eng. trans., 1961), dealing again with the outsider, a son who suffers the literal and symbolic transformation into a huge, repulsive, fatally wounded insect. *In the Penal Colony* (1919; Eng. trans., 1961) is a parable of a torture machine and its operators and victims— equally applicable to a person's inner sense of law, guilt, and retribution and to the age of World War I. *The Country Doctor* (1919; Eng. trans., 1946) is another collection of short prose. At the time of his death Kafka was also preparing *A Hunger Artist* (1924; Eng. trans., 1938), four stories centering on the artist's inability to either negate or come to terms with life in the human community.

Contrary to Kafka's halfhearted instruction that his unprinted manuscripts be destroyed after his death, his friend Max Brod set about publishing them and thus became the architect of his belated fame. The best known of the posthumous works are three fragmentary novels. *The Trial* (1925; Eng. trans., 1937) deals with a man persecuted and put to death by the inscrutable agencies of an unfathomable court of law. The Castle (1926; Eng. trans., 1930) describes the relentless but futile efforts of the protagonist to gain recognition from the mysterious authorities ruling (from their castle) the village where he wants to establish himself. *Amerika* (1927; Eng. trans., 1938) portrays the inconclusive struggle of a young immigrant to gain a foothold in an alien, incomprehensible country. In all these works the lucid, concise style forms a striking contrast to the labyrinthine complexities, anxiety-laden absurdities, and powerfully oppressive symbols of torment and anomie that are the substance of the writer's vision.

Kahn, Albert [kahn]   The American architect Albert Kahn, b. Rhaunen, Germany, Mar. 2, 1869, d. Dec. 8,

1942, was best known for his strikingly novel approach to factory design, especially for the assembly-line plants that he designed for the Ford Motor Company in the Detroit area. Kahn's buildings were the practical outcome of the ideas of Henry Ford (see FORD family), who revolutionized manufacture by combining all production under one roof. Kahn's Highland Park Plant, Detroit (1908–10), was the first truly autonomous industrial plant in the world. His River Rouge Plant, Detroit (begun 1917), was planned as a single-story structure, allowing the assembly line to proceed in a continuous flow from raw material to finished product.

Kahn, Louis

Louis Isadore Kahn, b. Estonia, Feb. 20 (N.S.), 1901, d. Mar. 17, 1974, was one of the major architects of the 20th century. He emigrated with his parents to Philadelphia in 1905 and studied architecture at the University of Pennsylvania. Kahn's first building to achieve international recognition was the Yale University Art Gallery, New Haven, Conn. (1952–54), built while he was professor of architecture at Yale (1947–57). From 1957 until his death he taught at the University of Pennsylvania, where he designed the Richards Medical Research Building, which was quickly recognized as a challenge to the INTERNATIONAL STYLE of modern architecture.

Kahn's buildings are thought to reveal his interest in mystical philosophy. They are characterized by bold, clearly defined shapes, which achieve a massive, monumental effect through the use of large blocks of concrete. Some of his most important buildings are the Salk Institute for Biological Studies, La Jolla, Calif. (1959–65); the library at Phillips Exeter Academy, Exeter, N.H. (1967–72); the Kimbell Art Museum, Fort Worth, Tex. (1966–72); and the Yale Center for British Art, New Haven (1969–74).

Kaifeng

[K'ai-feng] [ky'-fuhng] Kaifeng is a city in east central China in Henan province. It has a population of 450,000 (1982). Located on the Longhai Railroad and on several canals south of the Huang He (Yellow River), it is a shipping point for trade with the interior. Kaifeng is also an industrial center, with automotive, metallurgical, chemical, and food-processing plants. It served as the country's capital during the period of China's Five Dynasties (907–60) and then of the Northern Song Dynasty until 1127. From 1368 until 1954 it was the capital of Henan province. A colony of Chinese Jews lived in the city from at least the 12th century; few traces of it remained by the 19th.

Kaifu Toshiki

[ky'-foo' toh'-shih-kee] Kaifu Toshiki, b. Jan. 2, 1931, became prime minister of Japan on Aug. 8, 1989. Elected to successive terms in parliament from 1960, he served two terms as education minister. Kaifu, Japan's third prime minister in three months, was untainted by an influence-peddling scandal that forced Prime Minister TAKESHITA NOBORU to resign in June 1989. His successor, Uno Sosuki, stepped down after July elections in which his Liberal Democratic party (LDP) lost its

majority in the upper house of parliament for the first time in 35 years. Kaifu remained in office after LDP gains in the February 1990 elections.

Kaiser, Georg

[ky'-zur, gay'-ork] Georg Kaiser, b. Magdeburg, Germany, Nov. 25, 1878, d. June 4, 1945, was the leading dramatist among the German expressionists and a consistent experimenter and innovator of theater forms. Early in his career he dealt with themes of sexuality in *Die jüdische Witwe* (The Jewish Widow, 1911), school tyranny in *Rektor Kleist* (Headmaster Kleist, 1905), and impotence in *König Hahnrei* (King Cuckold, 1913). Then Kaiser turned to the expressionistic mode of excitement, energy, and emotion that characterized his greatest works: *Die Bürger von Calais* (The Citizens of Calais, 1914), *From Morn to Midnight* (1916; Eng. trans., 1920), and the extraordinary trilogy *The Coral* (1917; Eng. trans., 1929), *Gas I* (1918), and *Gas II* (1920; Eng. trans., 1924) where the characters are given abstract labels instead of names, the sets appear to come from the easel of a modern painter, and the enemy is an unreal, modern technology—the result of a civilization out of control.

Kaiser, Henry John

Henry John Kaiser, b. Sprout Brook, N.Y., May 9, 1882, d. Aug. 24, 1967, was a California industrialist who pioneered in the mass production of prefabricated cargo vessels during World War II. He had previously been a builder of dams and bridges including the Hoover Dam, the San Francisco–Oakland Bay Bridge, and the Grand Coulee Dam. During the war his shipyards built 1,460 vessels. After the war Kaiser Industries grew to include steel, cement, and aluminum plants. Kaiser was also a founder of the Kaiser-Frazer Corporation, an unsuccessful automobile manufacturer.

kala-azar   see LEISHMANIASIS

Kalahari Desert

[kah-lah-har'-ee] The Kalahari Desert, 260,000 km^2 (100,000 mi^2) in area, covers the western two-thirds of Botswana and adjoining areas of eastern Namibia and South Africa's Cape Province. It is mostly a flat tableland that was once covered by an inland sea. The most prominent surface features, all of them in Botswana, are the Okavango Swamp (a remnant of the inland sea), the Makgadikgadi Pans (an ancient drainage basin), and Lake Ngami. Much of the region is covered by sand. Flora consists of grasses and acacias typical of a steppe environment. Rainfall is light and erratic, decreasing from about 660 mm (26 in) per year in the northeast to 153 mm (6 in) in the southwest. Summers are very hot, and winters are cool. The Kalahari Gemsbok National Park, in South Africa, is a huge game preserve. Sparsely populated, the region is inhabited by nomadic KHOIKHOI, SAN (Bushmen), and TSWANA. It is believed that the first white men to cross the Kalahari were David Livingstone and W. C. Oswell in 1849.

Kalamazoo [kal-uh-muh-zoo'] Kalamazoo is a city in southwestern Michigan on the Kalamazoo River. It is the seat of Kalamazoo County and has a population of 80,277 (1990). In addition to its role as market center for the surrounding farms, Kalamazoo has industries engaged in the production of paper and the manufacture of drugs, clothing, musical instruments, and metal products. It is the seat of Western Michigan University (1903).

The site was a fur-trading post in the late 1700s; permanent settlement began in 1829. The city's name is Indian for "boiling water." The arrival of the Michigan Central Railroad in 1846 accelerated population growth in the area.

Kalb, Johann [kahlp, yoh'-hahn] Johann Kalb, b. June 29, 1721, d. Aug. 19, 1780, was a German-born officer, known as Baron de Kalb, in the Continental Army during the American Revolution. While serving in the French army, Kalb was sent (1768) to America on a secret mission to make observations for the French government. After his return to Paris, Kalb, the marquis de LAFAYETTE, and other American sympathizers were offered (1776) commissions by Silas DEANE. He became a major general, served at VALLEY FORGE (1777–78), and distinguished himself under Horatio GATES in the Carolina campaign. He was mortally wounded at the Battle of Camden.

kale [kayl] Kale is a nonheading leaf vegetable, *Brassica oleracea,* of the Cruciferae family. It is eaten cooked and is an excellent source of minerals and vitamins A and C. One of the oldest cultivated vegetables, kale closely resembles wild cabbage and may be the ancestor of all the common CABBAGE crops. It is hardy in cold weather—in fact, its flavor is improved after it has been touched by frost. Some types of kale are raised for cattle fodder and may grow more than 2.1 m (7 ft) in height. Garden kale usually grows to about 0.6 m (2 ft).

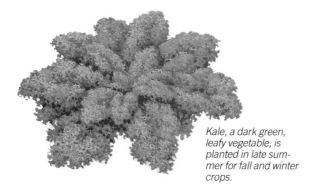

Kale, a dark green, leafy vegetable, is planted in late summer for fall and winter crops.

Kalevala [kah'-le-vah-lah] The *Kalevala,* Finland's national epic, is based on an oral tradition that dominat-ed the epic, lyric, magic, and aphoristic poetry of the Balto-Finnish peoples (Finns, Karelians, Votes, Estonians) for about 2,500 years. Characteristic of this poetry are trochaic tetrameter, alliteration, and parallelism. The *Kalevala* owes its existence to Elias Lönnrot (1802–84), a country doctor who compiled it from oral poetry collected principally in Karelia. The first edition, published in 1835, consisted of 12,078 lines arranged in 32 cantos. A later edition (1849) had 22,795 lines in 50 cantos. The 1849 edition has had an enormous impact on all the arts in Finland, particularly on the music of Jean Sibelius.

Kalgoorlie [kal-gur'-lee] Kalgoorlie, a famous mining town in south central Australia on the Nullarbor Plain, merged with Boulder in 1947 and is now officially known as Kalgoorlie-Boulder. Kalgoorlie has a population of 9,145; the population of the metropolitan area is 19,818 (1981). Kalgoorlie is located over huge gold deposits, and gold mining has long been the economic mainstay, although nickel deposits discovered in 1966 are now also economically significant. Other industries include engineering, brewing, and metal fabricating. Kalgoorlie was settled (1894) after gold was discovered (1893); the town was originally called Hannan's Find.

Kali [kah'-lee] Among the many metamorphoses of the wife of the Hindu god SHIVA is that of Kali (the Black One). She represents one facet of SHAKTI, the divine creative power or mother goddess, but also the power of destruction. The rituals of her cult, which is particularly strong among the lower castes in India, focus both on sensual pleasure and on fertility. The THUGS, an Indian subcaste, were devoted to Kali.

Kalidasa [kah-li-dah'-suh] India's foremost Sanskrit dramatist and poet Kalidasa flourished about AD 400 during the reign of Chandragupta II, the height of Indian classical civilization. The most famous of his three extant plays, *Shakuntala,* reveals his command of poetic language. The play is a dramatization of part of *the Mahabharata* and deals with King Dusyanta's love for the hermit girl Shakuntala, their parting, and their eventual reunion. The courtly comedy *Malavikagnimitra* (*Malavika and Agnimitra*) and the heroic *Vikramorvasiya* (*Vikrama and Urvashi*) show the author's sense of characterization and humor. Kalidasa's "nature" poetry culminated in *Meghaduta* (*Cloud Messenger*), in which a *yaksa* (exiled spirit) sends messages to his wife by a passing cloud. Its lyricism appealed to the early European romantics, particularly Schiller and Goethe. Kalidasa also wrote several court epics based on the legend of Rama.

Kaline, Al [kay'-lyn] Baseball Hall of Fame member Albert William Kaline, b. Baltimore, Md., Dec. 19, 1934, was a star right fielder for the American League's Detroit Tigers, for whom he played exclusively (1953–74). In his career, Kaline accumulated 3,007 hits, 1,583 runs batted in, 399 home runs, and a .297 batting average (AL leader in 1955, at .340). An excellent defensive player, he won 10 Gold Glove awards.

Kalinin [kuhl-yee'-neen] Kalinin (1985 est. pop., 438,000) is the capital of Kalinin oblast in the Russian republic of the USSR. It is situated on the upper Volga River and is served by the Moscow-Leningrad highway and railroad. Kalinin evolved as a diversified industrial city during the Soviet period, producing textiles and a wide range of machinery. Originally named Tver, it was the center of a separate Russian principality until absorbed by Moscow in 1485. In 1931 it was named for Mikhail I. Kalinin, an early Soviet president.

Kaliningrad [kuhl-yee'-neen-graht] Kaliningrad, a city in the Russian republic of the USSR, is situated on the Pregolya River near the Baltic Sea. It has a population of 401,000 (1989). Kaliningrad (formerly Königsberg) was the capital of the German province of East Prussia until 1945. After World War II, East Prussia was partitioned, with the northern half, including Königsberg, passing to the USSR and the southern half to Poland. The city was renamed for Soviet President Mikhail I. Kalinin in 1946.

Kaliningrad has been almost entirely rebuilt after near total destruction in the war. From a historic German city with distinctive Gothic architecture, it has been transformed into a Soviet manufacturing and fishing center producing railroad equipment, ships, and paper. It is the base for the Soviet Baltic fleet. Its port is linked by a deep-water canal with the outer Baltic port of Baltisk, formerly Pillau.

Königsberg grew around a castle built (1255) by the Teutonic Knights. It developed into a major trading center and joined the Hanseatic League in 1340.

Kamasutra [kah-muh-soo'-truh] The *Kamasutra* is a Hindu treatise on the art of love, composed sometime between the 1st and 4th centuries AD (Eng. trans., 1883). Written in Sanskrit, it is attributed to Vatsyayana, also known as Mallanaga. *Kama* is the Hindu word for love, pleasure, and sensual gratification; *sutra* are aphorisms. The work is partly a marriage manual, with specific sexual information, but its enormous influence stems from its wider discussion of women, courtship, and the place of erotic pleasure in the urbane life of a person of leisure.

Kamchatka Peninsula [kahm-chaht'-kuh] The Kamchatka Peninsula, part of the far eastern Russian republic of the USSR, extends about 1,200 km (750 mi) southward between the Sea of OKHOTSK and the BERING SEA, ending in Cape Lopatka, 11 km (7 mi) north of the KURIL ISLANDS. The peninsula has an area of 370,000 km² (140,000 mi²). Two great volcanic ranges, Sredinnyi and Vostochnyi, run from north to south, separated by the Kamchatka River valley.

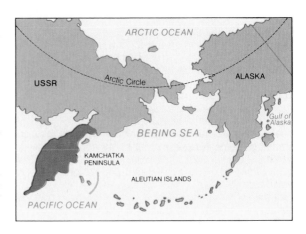

Petropavlovsk-Kamchatsky is the main settlement. The peninsula is sparsely populated. Lumbering, fur trapping, and fishing are the major economic activities. The peninsula is noted for its giant crabs. Some grains and potatoes are grown in the central valley. Kamchatka has oil, coal, and copper deposits, but little exploitation has taken place. The peninsula was visited (1697) by a Russian expedition under Vladimir Atlasov (d. 1711) and annexed to Russia.

Kamehameha (dynasty) [kah-may'-hah-may'-hah] Kamehameha was the name of the first five monarchs of the Hawaiian Islands (see HAWAII, state). **Kamehameha I**, b. *c.*1758, d. May 8, 1819, known as Kamehameha the Great, conquered most of the Hawaiian islands and by 1810 became ruler of a united Hawaii. He brought law and order and prosperity to his realm. He was succeeded (1819) by his son, **Kamehameha II**, also called Liholiho, 1797–1824. During Kamehameha II's reign the ancient Kapu system of laws and taboos was abolished, and in 1820 the first American missionaries were admitted to Hawaii.

Kamehameha II was succeeded (1825) by his brother, **Kamehameha III**, also called Kauikeouli, b. Mar. 7, 1814, d. Dec. 15, 1854. He permitted adoption (1840) of a charter making Hawaii a constitutional monarchy. Another landmark of his reign was the *Great Mahele* (1848), a policy that replaced the ancient feudal landholding system by giving land to the cultivator. In 1852 a new constitution granted suffrage to adult males and specified that the king must share power with a partially elected legislature.

Kamehameha III was succeeded by his nephew, Alexander Liholino, or **Kamehameha IV**, b. Feb. 9, 1834, d. Nov. 30, 1863. The king's brother, b. Dec. 11, 1830, d. Dec. 11, 1872, ascended the throne in 1863 as **Kamehameha V**. He abrogated (1864) the constitution of 1852 and promulgated instead a charter that strengthened royal power, weakened the legislature, and restricted suffrage. Kamehameha V died without an heir, thus ending the dynasty.

Kamenev, Lev Borisovich [kah'-min-yif, lyef buh-ree'-suh-vich] Lev Borisovich Kamenev, b. July 22 (N.S.), 1883, d. Aug. 24, 1936, was a Soviet political leader who briefly formed a ruling triumvirate with Joseph STALIN and Grigory ZINOVIEV in 1924. He joined the Russian Social Democratic Workers' party in 1901 and soon aligned himself with Vladimir Ilich LENIN in the split between the BOLSHEVIKS AND MENSHEVIKS. At the time of the RUSSIAN REVOLUTION of November 1917, Kamenev advocated a coalition of all the socialist parties. The triumvirate with Stalin and Zinoviev was formed on Lenin's death to exclude Leon TROTSKY from power. In 1925, however, Stalin began to ease out his colleagues; Kamenev was expelled from the party in 1927. In 1936 he was tried for treason in the first show trial of the GREAT PURGE and executed. He was posthumously rehabilitated in 1988.

Kaminaljuyú [kahm-ee-nuhl-hoo-yoo'] Kaminaljuyú, an archaeological site on the outskirts of Guatemala City and now largely encompassed by it, dominated the MAYA highlands during the Late Preclassic (300 BC–AD 300) and flourished in the Early Classic (AD 250–550). Early relief sculpture there contributed to the patterns followed by the Classic Maya, including low-relief portraiture and accompanying hieroglyphic inscriptions, but the Kaminaljuyú texts, unlike later Maya ones, cannot yet be read.

Archaeological investigations carried out in the 1930s revealed that during the Early Classic, pots found in tombs were made in a hybrid Maya-TEOTIHUACÁN style, with gods and lords figured in Maya style on cylinder tripods of Teotihuacán type. Teotihuacán often had been identified as the home of the later TOLTEC (fl. 9th–12th centuries), but this discovery confirmed the contemporaneity of the Maya and Teotihuacán.

Kamloops [kam'-loops] Kamloops is a city in southern British Columbia, Canada, at the confluence of the North Thompson and South Thompson rivers; it has a population of 61,773 (1986). The city attracts many visitors who hunt and fish amid the rugged scenery of the surrounding Cariboo region. Kamloops also serves the area's extensive lumbering, mining, ranching, and farming interests. Local industries include the manufacture of food products and wood and pulp processing.

The trading post of Fort Kamloops, earlier called *cume-loups* (Indian for "meeting of the waters"), was established there about 1812. The gold seekers of the 1850s, the coming of the "overlanders" (1862), and the arrival of the railroad (1885) contributed to the town's growth.

Kampala Kampala (1980 pop., 458,423), capital and largest city of Uganda, is the nation's commercial, financial, and industrial center. The city has rail and road connections to the rest of the country and to the Indian Ocean through Kenya. Port Bell on Lake Victoria and the

ENTEBBE airport, 34 km (21 mi) to the south, serve the city. Kampala is a processing center for livestock and agricultural products; exports include cotton, coffee, and sugarcane. Makerere University (1922) is located there. In 1890, Frederick, Lord LUGARD, chose the site as headquarters for the British East Africa Company. Kampala became capital of Uganda in 1962.

Kampuchea   see CAMBODIA

Kanchenjunga [kahn-chuhn-jung'-guh] Kanchenjunga, the third highest mountain in the world (8,598 m/ 28,208 ft) after Mount Everest and K2 (Godwin Austen), is located in the HIMALAYAS on the border between Nepal and Sikkim, 75 km (47 mi) northeast of the city of Darjeeling, in India. Its name, which means "Five Treasuries of the Great Snow" in Tibetan, refers to its five peaks, four of which are arranged symmetrically around the highest summit. Several attempts to climb the mountain have ended in fatal accidents, but in 1955 a British team led by Charles Evans almost reached the top. The party stopped 1.5 m (5 ft) below the summit out of respect for local religious traditions.

Kandahar [kan-duh-hahr'] Kandahar (Qandahar) is the seat of Kandahar province and the second largest city in Afghanistan, with a population of 225,500 (1988 est.). The commercial center for a fruit-growing and sheep-raising region, Kandahar has fruit-processing plants and textile mills. Trade in hides, tobacco, textiles, and carpets is also important. The city has many mosques; its imposing mausoleums include that of Ahmad Shah Durrani, who founded the Kandahar Afghan kingdom in 1747.

Allegedly founded by Alexander the Great in the 4th century BC, Kandahar was subsequently conquered by Arabs, Turks, Moguls, and Persians and was the capital of Afghanistan from 1747 to 1773.

Kandinsky, Wassily [kuhn-deen'-skee, vah-see'-lee] The Russian-born painter Wassily Kandinsky, b. Dec. 4 (N.S.), 1866, d. Dec. 13, 1944, is often regarded as the originator of ABSTRACT ART. In 1907 he exhibited with the German expressionist group Die BRÜCKE, and in 1909 he founded the New Association of Munich Artists. In 1910, Kandinsky executed his first abstract painting and wrote his famous theoretical study *Concerning the Spiritual in Art* (1912), developing his ideas about nonrepresentational painting, the psychological power of pure color, and the analogy between art and music. In 1911, Kandinsky, with August Macke, Franz Marc, and, later, Paul Klee, founded Der BLAUE REITER group. That same year Kandinsky and Marc published their theories of abstract art and in 1911 and 1912 held exhibitions of their work.

After teaching art in Moscow, Kandinsky moved (1921) to Germany once again and became a teacher at the Bauhaus in 1925. In 1926 he wrote *Point and Line*

The linear activity of Wassily Kandinsky's Improvisation 33 (Sketch for "Orient") *(1913) demonstrates that his abstract art continued to be based on images. The painting represents a reclining couple.*

to Plane, an analysis of geometric forms in art. During this decade Kandinsky's painting evolved from the more expressionistic and highly colored improvisations of his early work toward more precisely drawn and geometrically arranged compositions.

When the Bauhaus was closed (1933) by the Nazis, Kandinsky moved to Paris, where he lived for the rest of his life. His later works are arrangements of organically shaped forms resembling microscopic creatures. Kandinsky's paintings and theoretical writings exercised a strong influence on the subsequent development of modern art, especially on the development of ABSTRACT EXPRESSIONISM.

Kandy [kan'-dee]   Kandy, the capital of Kandy district, Sri Lanka, is located at an elevation of 490 m (1,600 ft) on the Kandy Plateau in the middle of the island, on the banks of the Mahaweli River. The city has a population of 130,000 (1986 est.). The surrounding area is mountainous and densely forested. The economy of the city and of the region is based primarily on tea and rice production. The inhabitants, mostly Sinhalese, are Buddhists. Kandy is the site of the University of Sri Lanka; the National Academy of Dance, where the Kandyan dance is taught; and the Dalada Maligawa, or Temple of the Tooth, where

a relic, allegedly a tooth of the Buddha, is kept.

Kandy, which dates from the early centuries AD, was the capital of the kingdom of Kandy, a Sinhalese domain, from 1592. It remained the last anti-British holdout until 1815, when the British finally succeeded in taking the region.

Kane, Paul   Paul Kane, b. Ireland, Sept. 3, 1810, d. Feb. 20, 1871, was a Canadian painter best known for his depictions of North American Indian life. Inspired by George Catlin's paintings of American Indians, Kane made (1845) a sketching trip among the Ojibwa tribe of the Lake Huron area, executing numerous portraits and genre works in the romantic tradition. Under the auspices of the Hudson's Bay Company, he journeyed (1846–48) to western Canada to paint the Indians and buffalo herds. Kane gained considerable fame through his 1848 exhibition in Toronto of 100 of these works. He wrote an account of these travels, *Wanderings of an Artist among the Indians of North America* (1859).

Kanem-Bornu [kah'-nem bohr'-noo]   Kanem-Bornu is the name applied to territories around Lake Chad (within modern Nigeria, Niger, Chad, and Cameroon) that were ruled from about 800 to 1846 by the Sefuwa line of kings. The original Sefuwa kings were probably nomad-warriors from the Sahara, but they ruled over large populations of farmers. An 11th-century *mai* (divine king) named Humai was converted to Islam. Thereafter, Muslim officials regulated the state's important long-distance trade across the Sahara.

The state was originally centered on the farming lands of Kanem, northeast of Lake Chad, but invasions by Saharan nomads caused the Sefuwa to move their capital to Bornu, on the lake's southwestern shore, probably in the 14th century. In the late 16th century Kanem-Bornu extended its dominion over the Hausa cities to the west. The Sefuwa dynasty died out in 1846, and the state fell in 1893 to the Sudanese conqueror Rabiyh Zubayr. In 1898, Kanem-Bornu was partitioned between the British, French, and German colonial spheres.

K'ang-hsi   see KANGXI

Kang Youwei (K'ang Yu-wei) [kahng yoo-wee]   Kang Youwei, b. Mar. 19, 1858, d. Mar. 31, 1927, was the dominant figure of the reform movement that briefly gained ascendancy in China following that country's humiliating defeat in the SINO-JAPANESE WAR of 1894–95. A Cantonese scholar, he published a series of books reinterpreting Confucian thought in such a way as to justify radical changes in the Chinese imperial system. In 1898 the Guang Xu emperor adopted Kang's program, issuing edicts covering such matters as the creation of a public school system, the modernization of the bureaucracy, the promotion of commerce and industry, and military reorganization. Dowager Empress CIXI (Tz'u-hsi), however, was enraged by this threat to old court ways. Backed by conservative officials, she imprisoned the emperor and abruptly ended the so-called "Hundred Days of Reform." Kang escaped abroad but returned to China in 1914.

kangaroo [kang-guh-roo']   A kangaroo is a marsupial mammal in the family Macropodidae. Typically, it has greatly enlarged hind legs, a strong, muscular tail, small forelegs, a relatively small head, and large ears. It usually moves in a hopping gait. The forepart of the kangaroo's stomach has been modified for the bacterial fermentation of plant cellulose, which makes that material digestible. Female kangaroos have an abdominal pouch for carrying their young, which are born in a rather undeveloped state. Although the period of gestation, or pregnancy, may be short, generally ranging from 27 to nearly 40 days, the young may spend a long period in the pouch; in the case of the red kangaroo, *Macropus rufus,* they remain nearly 8 months.

The 50 or more species of kangaroos are distributed from Tasmania and Australia proper to New Guinea and adjacent islands, and some have been introduced into New Zealand. The Macropodidae family is divided into two subfamilies, Macropodinae, containing the large and

In combat, a male red kangaroo grabs its opponent with its forearms and kicks the abdomen with its hind legs. Female red kangaroos are actually bluish gray in color.

small kangaroos (wallabies and wallaroos), and Potorinae, containing the small and primitive rat kangaroos.

The largest kangaroo, and the largest marsupial, is the gray kangaroo, *Macropus giganteus,* also called *M. major* or *M. cangaru,* which inhabits open forest or bushland in eastern Australia and Tasmania. It may stand more than 2 m (7 ft) tall, be 2.9 m (9.6 ft) long, including its tail, and weigh nearly 80 kg (200 lb). It can leap 1.5 m (5 ft) when moving at a slow pace and more than 9 m (30 ft) at high speeds. For short distances a gray kangaroo can travel at 48 km/h (30 mph). Gray kangaroos feed on grasses and other herbaceous material. The smallest kangaroo is the musky rat kangaroo, *Hypsiprymnodon moschatus,* of northeastern Australia, which grows to 33.5 cm (13 in) long, has a 17-cm (6.7-in) hairless tail, and weighs about 500 g (1 lb). Its limbs are nearly equal in size, and its foot structure is quite different from that of the other species.

kangaroo rat   Kangaroo rats are about 22 species of North American rodents of the genus *Dipodomys,* family Heteromyidae. They are found in arid areas west of the Missouri River from Canada to central Mexico. Kangaroo rats are stocky animals with long hind legs, short front legs, and a long tail, which is tufted at the tip. The hind legs are used for hopping, in the manner of kangaroos.

The small front feet are used to gather food, which is stuffed into two external, fur-lined cheek pouches, each with an opening in the skin near the side of the mouth. The largest kangaroo rats are 20 cm (8 in) long, plus a slightly longer tail, and weigh up to 140 g (5 oz). The coat is yellowish to dark brown, with white underparts and a white stripe on each side of the tail.

Kangaroo rats seldom or never drink, obtaining sufficient water from the breakdown of their food. Mating may occur at any time under favorable climatic conditions. Gestation is about 29 to 33 days, with usually 2 to 4 young to a litter.

Kangxi, Emperor of China (K'ang-hsi) [kahng'-shee'] Kangxi, b. May 4, 1654, d. Dec. 20, 1722, second QING (Manchu) emperor of China, is famous both for his astute management of civil and military affairs and for his patronage of scholars. Succeeding to the throne in 1661, he assumed personal rule in 1669.

Kangxi's armies pacified southern China (1673–81), conquered Taiwan (1683), and, led by the emperor himself, defeated the Dzungar Mongol chieftain Galdan in 1696. By 1720, Tibet was also under imperial control. In addition, the emperor established (1689) diplomatic relations with Russia and encouraged trade with the West. He tolerated Christian missionary activity in order to take advantage of the Jesuits' scientific knowledge. Kangxi patronized Chinese as well as Manchu scholars, who compiled such literary monuments as the Kangxi dictionary of the Manchu language, a geography of China, and an encyclopedia of 5,000 volumes.

Kano [kay'-noh] Kano, a city in northern Nigeria, lies about 860 km (535 mi) northeast of Lagos and has a population of 594,800 (1991 est.). For centuries it has been the most important commercial center of the savanna zone. Kano serves as a distribution center for skins, eggs, and livestock. Industries include textile milling, oil refining, printing, and brewing.

Tools found in Kano suggest that a Stone Age settlement existed there. A permanent city can be traced back about 1,000 years. From the 12th century, Kano was the center of one of the seven Hausa city-states. First visited by Europeans in the 1820s, it was captured by the British in 1903.

Kano (family of Japanese painters) see EITOKU; MOTONOBU

Kanpur [kahn'-pur] Kanpur, an industrial city in the state of Uttar Pradesh, northern India, lies on the right bank of the Ganges River about 400 km (250 mi) southeast of New Delhi. It has a population of 1,958,282 (1991). A booming industrial, rail, and trade center, Kanpur produces wool and cotton textiles and leather goods. The population is largely Hindu, but there are some Muslims and Sikhs. Kanpur University (1966) is located there.

Kanpur, originally a small village, was taken over by the British in 1801. Then known as Cawnpore, the village was the scene of a massacre during the INDIAN MUTINY (1857), when the entire British garrison and its dependents were killed by Indian rebels.

Kansa [kan'-saw] The Kansa, or Kaw, are North American Indians who speak a Siouan dialect closely related to the languages of the OSAGE and QUAPAW. According to their own tradition they originated in the east; they crossed the Missouri and ascended the Kansas until forced back by the CHEYENNE. When first encountered by white traders, they lived in a village of 130 earth lodges near Council Grove (Kansas) and numbered about 2,500. Clan membership appears to have been determined according to female ancestry. Women owned the lodges, took charge of sacred burial customs, and had considerable influence in village affairs. Young men established links with a variety of mysterious powers, or *wakans,* through the sacred rite of the vision quest. Traditions were maintained until the late 19th century despite intensive Christian missionary efforts. After ceding land in a peace treaty of 1825, they settled on a reservation in Kansas. In 1846 they ceded two million acres more for only $200,000. After their last bison hunt in 1873, they left the Neosho Valley for Indian Territory (present-day Oklahoma). In 1905 only 204 Kansa remained; by the late 1980s those living on the Kaw Reservation had increased to nearly 600.

Kansas Occupying the central position in the conterminous United States, Kansas is one of the nation's leading agricultural states. Though relatively large in area, it is not densely populated. Kansas is bordered by Nebraska, Missouri, Oklahoma, and Colorado. The area was first explored by Europeans with the Coronado expedition of 1541, but significant Anglo settlement did not occur until 1855. After a six-year struggle over the slavery issue, the "Sunflower State" entered the Union in 1861 on the free side. Today it is a prosperous, conservative, rural state with an economy well balanced between agriculture and industry. TOPEKA is the capital. The name *Kansas* is a Sioux word meaning "people of the south wind."

Land and Resources

Kansas has a reputation for flat topography, but this stereotype is correct only for the western quarter of the state; most of the land is rolling and hilly. The highest point, Mount Sunflower, in Wallace County in the west, is 1,231 m (4,039 ft); the lowest elevation is 207 m (679 ft) in Montgomery County in the southeast. The rock strata are arranged in the manner of shingles. The oldest rocks, Mississippian (345–320 million-year-old) limestones, outcrop only in the southeastern corner of the state. To the west newer surface materials are found, first Pennsylvanian and Permian (320–225 million-year-old) limestones and shales, then recent Cretaceous (135–65 million-year-old) and Quaternary (less than 2.5 million-year-

KANSAS

Land: Area: 213,110 km^2 (82,282 mi^2); rank: 15th. Capital: Topeka (1990 pop., 119,883). Largest city: Wichita (1990 pop., 304,011). Counties: 105. Elevations: highest—1,231 m (4,039 ft), at Mount Sunflower; lowest—207 m (679 ft), at Verdigris River.

People: Population (1990): 2,485,600; rank: 32d; density: 11.7 persons per km^2 (30.3 per mi^2). Distribution (1990): 69.1% urban, 30.9% rural. Average annual change (1980–90): +0.5%.

Government (1993): Governor: Joan Finney, Democrat. U.S. Congress: Senate—2 Republicans; House—2 Democrats, 2 Republicans. Electoral college votes: 6. State legislature: 40 senators, 125 representatives.

Economy: State personal income (1989): $41.5 billion; rank: 31st. Median family income (1989): $32,966; rank: 26th. Agriculture: income (1989)—$6.3 billion. Lumber production (1991, with Nebraska): 11 million board feet. Mining (nonfuel): value (1988)—$292 million. Manufacturing: value added (1987)—$12.9 billion. Services: value (1987)—$8.4 billion.

Miscellany: Statehood: Jan. 29, 1861; the 34th state. Nickname: Sunflower State; tree: cottonwood; motto: *Ad Astra per Aspera* ("To the Stars through Difficulties"); song: "Home on the Range."

Wild Native Sunflower

Western Meadowlark

old) deposits. The western two-thirds of Kansas is part of the GREAT PLAINS, the eastern third belongs to the Central Lowlands, and the tiny Mississippian outcrop is part of the Ozark Upland.

Wind-deposited soil, called loess, was deposited at the time of the last ice age, and it provides an excellent, stone-free medium for agriculture. Streams have dissected the plains in central Kansas to form the Blue and Smoky hills in the northern part of the area and the Gypsum Hills in the south; the latter contain scenic buttes and mesas.

The Central Lowlands portion of Kansas is commonly divided into four subregions. South of the Kansas River are the Osage Cuestas, a plains area broken by limestone escarpments exceeding 60 m (200 ft) in height. To the west, in a belt from Washington County to Cowley County, these escarpments become bolder and more frequent. Kansans call this area the Flint Hills, a name referring to a mineral commonly found in the limestone layers. Sandstone replaces limestone in the Chautauqua Hills, a small area along the Chautauqua-Montgomery County line. North of the Kansas River is the Till Plain, where the rock escarpments are masked by a layer of glacial debris. The terrain there is gently rolling. Soils in eastern Kansas are not quite as good as those in the west, because they have generally been subjected to leaching and erosion for a longer period of time. Humus-rich chernozems predominate in the glaciated area of the northeast.

Climate. Kansas's "big sky," dramatic sunsets, and great variability in temperature and precipitation are all important aspects of the regional personality. Because the state is remote from the moderating influences of oceans, it has a wide annual temperature range. The average January temperature is −1° C (30° F); the July average is 26° C (79° F). Diurnal ranges are also broad. Precipitation is highly variable. Average rainfall increases from 380 mm (15 in) in the extreme west to 1,140 mm (45 in) in the southeast. About 75% of the annual precipitation falls between April and September, but summer is often a moisture-deficient season because of high evaporation rates. Because precipitation is dependent on the chance meeting of moist air from the Gulf of Mexico and low-pressure systems, yearly totals are highly variable, especially in western Kansas. Thus, the region of greatest variability coincides with that of lowest average rainfall totals, and the combination produces doubled risks for local farmers. Sharply contrasting air masses frequently clash over the Kansas plains, bringing violent weather and adding to the variability.

Drainage. The Kansas (Kaw) River in the north and the ARKANSAS RIVER in the south drain most of the state. The Kaw is a short stream (275 km/170 mi) formed by the junction of the Smoky Hill and the Solomon and the Republican rivers; it enters the Missouri River at Kansas City. Principal tributaries of the long Arkansas River (2,348 km/1,459 mi) in Kansas are the Cimarron,

KANSAS

Major Urban Area

Federal/Recreation Area

Railroad

Interstate Highway System

U.S. or State Highway

County Boundary

County Seat

Spot Elevation

State capitals are underlined

City type size indicates relative importance

Meters	Feet
2000	6562
1000	3281
500	1640
200	656
	-656

Scale 1:3,012,000

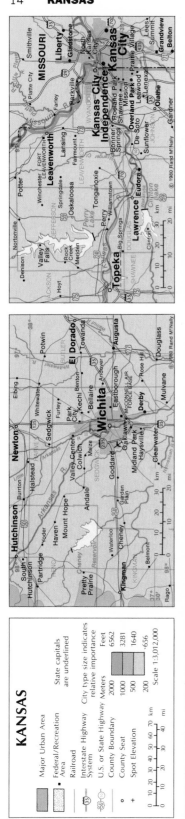

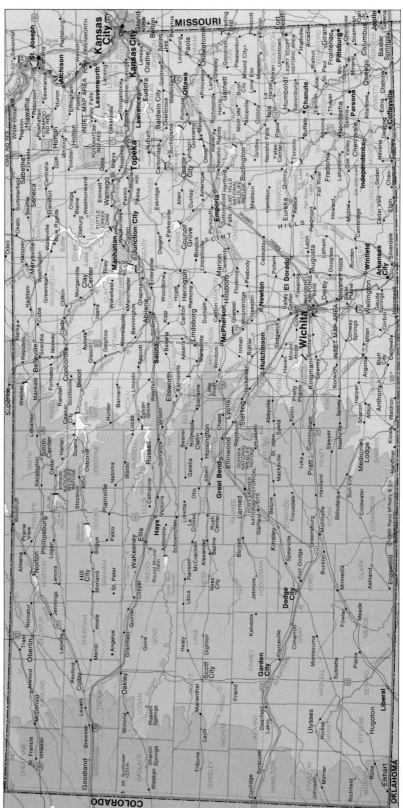

© 1980 Rand McNally & Co.

Neosho, and Verdigris. The Arkansas occupies an especially wide and fertile lowland from the Hutchinson area in the south central part of the state to the Oklahoma border. None of the Kansas waterways is used for navigation. The state has 20 major reservoirs and more than 70,000 farm ponds. Extensive groundwater reserves are being depleted by heavy irrigation.

Vegetation and Animal Life. Prairie vegetation was the dominant pattern encountered in Kansas by the first explorers. Blue grama and buffalo grass grew in the west, and taller bluestem species dominated elsewhere. Timber, especially cottonwoods, sycamores, and walnut trees, was common in the river valleys. Today oak, hickory, elm, hackberry, juniper, and other tree species are common in some areas. Animal life is highly diverse in Kansas and includes both woodland and grassland species. Pheasants are a popular game bird in the west, and antelope have recently been reintroduced there. Squirrels, raccoon, and deer occur in the east.

Resources. Petroleum and natural-gas deposits are widespread in the southern half of Kansas. The fields are in decline but still produce over half of the state's mineral output. Most of the oil and gas is shipped out of Kansas to power-manufacturing plants in states east of Kansas. Before World War II the state was, with Oklahoma and Missouri, a major producer of lead and zinc. Salt, from the Hutchinson area, and coal, in the southeast, are other resources.

People

The population density of Kansas is less than half the national average. Natural increase along with a net inmigration produced a modest growth rate from 1980 to 1990 of 5.2%, also well below the national norm of 10.2% (1980–90). About two-thirds of the population live in urban areas. These figures do not imply a lack of prosperity, however, for Kansas ranks above the national average in per capita income.

Most of the major cities in the state are located on early transportation routes, principally the Kaw Valley–Union Pacific line due west from KANSAS CITY and the path of the Santa Fe Railroad from ATCHISON through Topeka, Emporia, HUTCHINSON, and Garden City. A major exception is WICHITA, a city whose initial prosperity can be attributed more to promotion than to transportation advantages. Today, thanks principally to the petroleum and aircraft industries, Wichita is the largest city in the state, followed by Kansas City and Topeka.

Most early Kansans were born in Illinois, Indiana, Ohio, and Pennsylvania, but there was also an influential minority from New England. Today almost 6% of the people are blacks, many of whom are descendants of the "exodusters," former slaves who came to Kansas just after the Civil War. A substantial majority of church members in Kansas are Protestant. Roman Catholicism and the United Methodist church are the largest single denominations. Kansas has a small Jewish population.

Education. Education has always enjoyed a high level of local support. In the 1980s nearly 75% of adults had completed high school, and 7% were college graduates. There are more than 50 institutions of higher learning in Kansas. Six are state universities. The University of Kansas in Lawrence, with about 26,000 students, is known for its liberal arts program and medical school. Kansas State University in Manhattan enjoys national stature for its agricultural and other applied-science programs. Other

The cultivation of wheat, grown in each of Kansas's 105 counties, annually injects millions of dollars into the state economy. Although Kansas carries the image as agrarian heartland of the United States, manufacturing has superseded agriculture as the state's most important economic activity.

public universities are located in Emporia, Hays, Pittsburg, and Wichita. Significant libraries outside the universities are housed at the state historical society in Topeka and at the Eisenhower Library in Abilene.

Cultural Activity. Because Kansas lacks cities of great size, most cultural activities are concentrated in the universities. Notable art museums are at the University of Kansas and in Wichita; the State Historical Society in Topeka has a historical museum; and the University of Kansas has an excellent museum of natural history. Historical sites include various forts and stations along the Santa Fe and Oregon trails and on the Pony Express route, and John Brown Memorial Park in Osawatomie, containing the log cabin where the abolitionist John BROWN lived. An annual rodeo at Strong City in June attracts a large crowd. Local sports interest is concentrated on the two major universities and the professional teams in Kansas City, Mo.

Perhaps because of a low population density, local communications have always been well developed. A number of daily newspapers are published, led in circulation by the *Wichita Eagle-Beacon.* The state has several commercial television stations, along with many radio stations.

Economic Activity

The Kansas economy has been based on agriculture since settlement. Meat packing, milling, and processing of other food products are the leading industries. Warehouses exploit the state's central location, and transportation equipment is an important product.

Agriculture. Kansas ranks among the top ten U.S. states in the value of its total farm marketings and traditionally leads the nation in wheat production. Other leading crops include grain sorghum (a drought-resistant feed grain), hay crops, corn, and soybeans in southeastern Kansas, and irrigated crops of various types in the western half of the state. Through irrigation more corn is now grown in western than in eastern Kansas, and the irrigation acreage has increased rapidly.

In spite of Kansas's reputation as a wheat state, beef cattle are a more important part of the economy. Typically, cattle account for a greater share of the total agricultural receipts than does wheat. Cattle are found throughout the state, but the highest concentration occurs in the Flint Hills. Kansas cattle used to be shipped east for fattening and slaughter, but today the trend is to keep these operations in the cattle-producing areas. Feedlots are now common throughout the state, and meat packers are abandoning their large and antiquated facilities in cities such as Chicago and Kansas City in favor of smaller plants in places such as Dodge City and Emporia.

Manufacturing and Transportation. One of the nation's first natural-gas booms occurred in southeastern Kansas in the 1890s. Glass and portland-cement factories, zinc smelters, brick and tile works, and other concerns were attracted to the area in large numbers. The glass and zinc industries eventually left the area, but southeastern Kansas remains an area of small manufacturing cities. The production of transportation equipment is the state's leading industry, and Wichita manufactures about two-thirds of all American general-aviation aircraft. Nonelectrical machinery and chemicals production, coal and gas products, printing and publishing, and food processing are also leading industries.

Excellent transportation has always characterized this crossroads of the nation. Main lines of the Union Pacific

The grasslands of Kansas are dotted with oil pumps that provide wealth for the state. Kansas is a major producer of petroleum, natural gas, helium, and petroleum-related chemicals.

An auctioneer (right) acknowledges a bid at the Rezac Livestock Auction in Saint Marys, Kans. Livestock and related products are the state's most valuable agricultural commodities.

Wichita, located at the confluence of the Arkansas and Little Arkansas rivers, is the largest city in Kansas.

and Santa Fe railroads bisect the state, as do interstate highways 35 and 70.

Tourism. Kansas attracts some tourism dollars each year, mostly from people in transit to and from Colorado and the West. In recent years there has been a statewide debate over the merits of establishing a Prairie National Park somewhere in the Flint Hills. Proponents talk of capturing more tourist dollars and preserving a major natural ecosystem; opponents say that development would destroy the serenity of the prairie and that Kansas ranchers are already doing a good job of preserving the grasslands.

Energy. Most of the electrical power sold in Kansas annually is generated by coal- and gas-fired power plants. The state has one nuclear power plant, and many residents have explored the potentials of solar and wind power. These last two sources may be especially appropriate for Kansas, given the state's relatively high percentage of sunshine, its windy climate, and its dispersed population.

Government

Kansas is governed under its original constitution (1859), one of the oldest still in use. Legislators represent districts set up under the one-person–one-vote principle. The state senate has 40 members; the house of representatives has 125. Elected boards of commissioners head the 105 county governments. Local politics has traditionally been Republican because that party was initially associated with the free-state cause and with the popular Homestead Act of 1862; since statehood only a small number of Democratic governors have been elected. Notable Republican figures with Kansas roots include Alf Landon, 1936 presidential nominee, and Dwight Eisenhower. Pockets of Democratic strength are Wyandotte County, an urbanized, blue-collar area; Ellis County, a German Catholic center; and the coal-mining area of southeastern Kansas.

History

When Francisco Vásquez de CORONADO explored the area in 1541, Kansas was occupied primarily by Osage, Paw-

nee, and Kansa peoples. A Pueblo group, fleeing Spanish rule in New Mexico, occupied a site in western Kansas from about 1664 until 1730. (The Pueblo site and a Pawnee village in northern Kansas have now been restored.)

Kansas was part of the area claimed by France as Louisiana at the end of the 17th century. It was ceded to Spain in 1762, restored to France in 1800, and sold to the United States in 1803 in the Louisiana Purchase. Many of the famous expeditions to the West in the early 19th century passed through Kansas, including those of Zebulon Montgomery PIKE in 1806 and Stephen H. LONG in 1819–20. Reports from the Long party led to the erroneous use of the term "Great American Desert" to describe the plains region.

Primarily because of this image, Kansas was considered an unlikely place for Anglo settlement, and the government decided to use the land for reservations for displaced Indians from the East. Westward-bound migrants were passing through Kansas, however, on both the OREGON TRAIL and the SANTA FE TRAIL. Soon tremendous pressure developed to open Kansas itself for settlement, and in the early 1850s the Indians were moved to what became Oklahoma. Three small reservations in northeast Kansas are relics from that earlier time: the Potawatomi, the Kickapoo, and the Iowa-Sac-Fox.

The U.S. government opened Kansas to settlement in 1854 under the terms of the KANSAS-NEBRASKA ACT, which allowed the territory to determine its own position on slavery. The peopling of Kansas thus immediately became a national issue. Organizations like the EMIGRANT AID COMPANY promoted immigration by antislavery Northerners, while proslavery groups mounted a similar drive. The two groups of settlers established rival governments, violence erupted, and the territory soon became known as "Bleeding Kansas." After much controversy within both the territory and the U.S. Congress, the proposed proslavery LECOMPTON CONSTITUTION was rejected by the electorate, and Kansas entered the Union in 1861 under the terms of the Wyandotte Constitution (1859). Guerrilla raids continued along the Missouri-Kansas border throughout the Civil War.

A major land boom occurred in the 1870s, as adequate rainfall, good soil, postwar mobility, and rapidly expanding railroads brought thousands to the state, including many immigrants from Germany, Sweden, Russia, and elsewhere. One group, the German-Russian Mennonites, introduced the hard winter wheat that transformed Kansas agriculture.

Settlers dealt with the dry environment of the West much as they had with the humid East, plowing the land and establishing small farms. When especially dry conditions occurred in the 1930s, widespread winds blowing across thousands of acres of nearly unprotected soil produced the infamous Dust Bowl. Since the 1930s, improved tillage techniques, enlarged land holdings, increased use of irrigation, rural-to-urban migration, and other factors have improved the situation greatly.

Nineteenth-century Kansas was noted for its activism. Abolitionist concern was followed by major involvement in the temperance movement and Populist party. Populism ended as a formal political movement about 1900, but it brought about many innovations including federal grain inspection and stockyard regulation. More recently, the case of Brown v. Board of Education of Topeka, Kansas led to the 1954 Supreme Court ruling that racial segregation in the public schools was unconstitutional. At least one observer has called modern Kansas the "eclipsed state," contrasting past activity with present complacency. The state is certainly conservative politically and has a net out-migration of the young and highly educated. Other Kansans, however, believe that the state possesses what many Americans value today: smaller urban centers; clean air; an emphasis on self-reliance; and a reputation for good government and progressive education.

Kansas City, Mo., at the confluence of the Kansas and Missouri rivers, was settled in 1821 by French traders. The city's future was assured by the arrival (1865) of the railroad. Union Station (foreground) is a stately reminder of the railroad's importance.

Kansas City Two separate political units, Kansas City, Kans., in the northeastern part of its state, and Kansas City, Mo., on the western side of its state—each located on opposite banks of the Kansas River where it meets the Missouri River—comprise the Kansas City metropolitan area. Although separate politically, the two cities form one economic unit. Kansas City, Mo., has always been two or three times the size of its companion city in Kansas. The population of the former is 435,146; the latter has 149,767 inhabitants (1990). The population of the greater metropolitan area is 1,566,280. Kansas City, Kans., is the seat of Wyandotte County.

After the completion (1869) of the first bridge across the Missouri River, Kansas City became a transportation hub. Today it is a junction of rail, highway, and water routes and an inland port. From the end of the Civil War to the beginning of World War II the local economy was based primarily on the handling, processing, and marketing of grain and cattle. Kansas City, Kans., has the world's largest grain elevator. The leading industries today are flour milling, meat packing, automobile assembly, oil refining, printing, and the manufacturing of steel and aluminum products, airplane engines, furniture, apparel, agricultural equipment, and chemicals.

The city's educational institutions include the University of Kansas Medical Center (1899) and the University of Missouri at Kansas City (1963). The Nelson-Atkins Art Gallery, one of the nation's leading art museums, and an extensive municipal park system grace Kansas City, Mo.

The first permanent settlement at this river junction was a trading post established in 1821. A succession of small villages was founded in the decades that followed, but the prosperity they enjoyed as the beginning point for westward expeditions was continually interrupted by disease epidemics. Economic stability was ensured by the arrival of railroad lines in 1865. The name Kansas City became official in the Kansas settlement in 1886 and in the Missouri town in 1889. Recent industrial and commercial expansion has established both cities as the second largest in their respective states.

Kansas-Nebraska Act On May 30, 1854, the U.S. Congress passed the Kansas-Nebraska Act, establishing the territories of Kansas and Nebraska. This controversial legislation repealed the Missouri Compromise of 1820–21 and reopened the controversy over the extension of slavery in the western territories. The Missouri Compromise had prohibited slavery north of a line drawn at latitude 36° 30' through the Louisiana Purchase. Four early attempts to organize a single territory for the area west of Missouri and Iowa and north of the 36° 30' line failed in Congress.

In January 1854, Sen. Stephen A. Douglas of Illinois introduced a bill dividing the land into two territories, Kansas and Nebraska, and leaving the question of slavery to be decided by the settlers. This latter provision, known as popular sovereignty, enraged antislavery people, but after months of bitter debate, the bill passed. This solution did not defuse the slavery issue. Kansas was soon rent by conflict, and the sectional split between North and South was aggravated to a point that made reconciliation virtually impossible. The Republican party was founded by opponents of the act, and the United States was pushed further toward the CIVIL WAR.

Kansu see GANSU

Kant, Immanuel [kahnt, i-mahn'-oo-el] A pivotal force in the history of philosophy, the German philosopher Immanuel Kant, b. Apr. 22, 1724, d. Feb. 12, 1804, radically altered the nature of philosophic inquiry. Kant was born and educated in Königsberg, East Prussia, and taught at the university there from 1756 to the end of his life. During the years 1755–1781 he wrote a series of works that developed his growing criticism of Leibnizian and other rationalist philosophy (see RATIONALISM). By the time of his inaugural dissertation as professor (1770), he had declared a complete break with Leibnizian metaphysics.

Critical Period (1781–90). Between 1770 and 1781, Kant published very little. Between 1781 and 1790, however, he produced his most important works, representing the full development of his critical powers. In 1781 he published the CRITIQUE OF PURE REASON (Eng. trans., 1838), his most famous work. It is divided into two major parts: "The Transcendental Doctrine of the Elements," which deals with the sources of human knowledge, and the "Transcendental Doctrine of Method," which deals with the proper and improper uses of reason. Kant used the word *transcendental* to designate that method which examines the necessary but nonempirical conditions of knowledge. In 1785 he published *The Foundations of the Metaphysics of Morals* (Eng. trans., 1969) and, in 1787, *The Critique of Practical Reason* (Eng. trans., 1949), both of which examine moral philosophy. The third critique, *The Critique of Judgment* (1790; Eng. trans., 1895), deals with aesthetic and teleologic, or purposive, judgments.

Philosophy. From Kant's point of view, the philosophical traditions of both EMPIRICISM and rationalism had reached a "dark, confused, and useless" dead end. What he proposed was a radical, new synthesis in which he would incorporate both experience and reason without falling into the skepticism of the empirical school or the vast, unverifiable metaphysical structure of the rationalist school. The problem of knowledge, as he saw it, was how to connect the "is" of sense experience with the "must" of necessary and universal truth. His starting point was the distinction between analytic and synthetic judgments. An analytic judgment is one in which the predicate is contained in the subject—for instance, "Triangles have three sides." The truth of such a judgment can be known by an analysis of the subject. A synthetic judgment is one in which the predicate adds to or expands the subject— for instance, "Triangles were the earliest figures to be discovered in geometry." The truth of such a statement cannot be known through an analysis of the subject.

Immanuel Kant, an 18th-century German philosopher, achieved what he called a "Copernican revolution in philosophy," defining the limitations inherent in speculative philosophy. His works have had profound impact on Western thought. (Staatliches Kantgymnasium, Berlin.)

Kant also distinguished two ways in which judgments can be known: something is known *a priori* if it is neither derived from nor testable by sense experience; it is known *a posteriori* if it is derived from or testable by experience. Philosophers before Kant had held that analytic judgments were known *a priori* and that synthetic judgments were known *a posteriori*. Analytic *a priori* judgments were always and necessarily true—but true only about the meaning and relations of words, not about the world. Synthetic *a posteriori* judgments, on the other hand, were about the world—but they could only be contingent or probable truths. This meant that we could have no certain knowledge about experience, and Kant believed that we had such knowledge. Thus, he formulated this problem: "How are synthetic *a priori* judgments possible?" His solution, in essence, was that experience provides the content (the synthetic element) and the mind provides the structure (the *a priori* element) that determines the way in which the content will be organized and understood.

Kant calls the contribution of the mind a "category." He distinguishes four groups of categories by which the contents of experience are ordered: quantity, quality, relation, and modality. Examples of specific categories within these groups are space, time, causality, and substance. These categories are contentless and prescribe the structure only for objects of possible experience. Space, for example, is not something external to us but a structure in the mind that relates objects to one another. The active contribution of the mind gives meaning to the external material of experience. Whether things really are the way they appear to us is something we can never know, for all our knowledge comes prestructured through the filter of the mind. This is the basis for Kant's famous distinction between the unknowable *noumenon*, or thing-in-itself, and the *phenomenon*, or thing-as-it-appears.

Kant held that synthetic *a priori* judgments were possible in mathematics and physics but not in metaphysics. Thus, he thought it a mistake for metaphysicians to attempt to go beyond sense experience in order to define concepts such as God, freedom, or the immortal soul. All theoretical knowledge consists in applying the categories to perceptual material located in space and time, and these concepts lie outside the spatiotemporal categories. Such ideas have, for Kant, an indispensable function. Whereas most concepts have a "constitutive" function (they classify experience), concepts such as God, freedom, or soul have a "regulative" function: they guide us toward certain goals useful for science and ethics. They are held "as if" they were true.

In the moral sphere Kant says that he has denied knowledge to make room for faith. Because moral law cannot be justified by reason, it can only be obeyed for its own sake. Kant's ethical theory thus rests on the concept of duty. A good person acts out of duty, not because he or she fears punishment or hopes for reward or happiness, but only because it is his or her duty. Like other concepts, moral laws are only mental structures, so the primary moral law will be a contentless form of judgment that can be applied universally; Kant calls this the *categorical imperative*. The categorical imperative states that a person should "act in such a way that it is possible for one to will that the maxim of one's action should become a universal law." Kant gives the example of someone who borrows money, promises to repay it, but has no intention of doing so. If this were a universal law—that is, if everyone behaved this way—promises would be meaningless, and no one would lend money to anyone.

In his aesthetic theory, Kant holds that judgments that ascribe beauty to something, although they rest on feeling, do have a claim to validity and are not merely statements of taste or opinion. When a person judges something to be beautiful, imagination, perception, and understanding are in harmony; there is a harmony of the experienced object with mental structure. The concepts involved in such judgments are purpose and purposiveness.

Influence. Kant called his radical redefinition of philosophic problems and procedures a "Copernican revolution in philosophy." As Copernicus had reversed the way subsequent scientists thought about the relationship of the Earth and the Sun, so Kant reversed the way subsequent philosophers thought about the relationship of the world of experience and the mind. The mind is not shaped by the world of experience; rather, the world of experience is shaped by the patterns set by the mind.

Kantorovich, Leonid V.

[kuhn-tahr'-uh-vich, lay'-oh-need] The Soviet economist Leonid Vitalyevich Kantorovich, b. Saint Petersburg, Jan. 19 (N.S.), 1912, d. Apr. 7, 1986, won the Nobel Prize for economics (with Tjalling Koopmans) in 1975. Kantorovich gained fame in 1939–40 for a paper entitled "Mathematical Methods for the Organization and Planning of Production," which advocated a method of improving the Soviet system of central planning by applying the econometric tool of linear programming. His principal work is *Economic Calculation and the Use of Resources* (1959; Eng. trans., 1965). He was also coauthor (with G. P. Akilov) of *Functional Analysis* (2d ed., 1982).

Kaohsiung

(Gaoxiong) [gow'-shyoong'] Kaohsiung is a major seaport in southwestern Taiwan. The population is 1,374,561 (1990 est.). The city is a commercial and industrial center where chemicals, paper and food products, aluminum, and ships are manufactured. The main exports are rice, sugar, and fruit. Settled in the early 17th century, Kaohsiung was opened as a treaty port in 1863 and underwent major development as a port during the Japanese occupation (1895–1945) of Taiwan.

kaolinite   see CLAY MINERALS

kaon

[kay'-ahn] A kaon, or K-meson, is a FUNDAMENTAL PARTICLE classified as both a boson and a hadron; it has a mass between that of the electron and that of the proton. Four kaons exist: two electrically charged, K^+ and K^- (antiparticles of each other), and two neutral, K^0 and $\bar{K}^0$ (also a pair of antiparticles).

See also: MESON.

Kapital, Das

Das Kapital ("Capital," 3 vols., 1867, 1885, 1894; Eng. trans., 1886, 1907, 1909), a monumental politico-economic study written by Karl MARX and edited in part by Friedrich ENGELS, served as the theoretical basis of modern socialism and COMMUNISM. In it Marx attempted to show that the capitalist system contained the seeds of its own destruction. He assumed that the value of a product is determined by the amount of labor needed to produce it (the labor theory of value) and that the capitalist's profit depends on his or her ability to keep the worker's wages lower than the value of the goods he or she produces. Marx called the difference between the two amounts "surplus value." He predicted that competition among capitalists would lead to an inevitable decline in surplus value, causing a crisis in the system. From this would come a revolution that would replace capitalism with socialism.

Kaplan, Mordecai Menahem

[kap-luhn, mor-duh-ky] The American-Jewish philosopher, educator, and rabbi Mordecai Menahem Kaplan, b. Lithuania, June 11, 1881, d. Nov. 8, 1983, founded the Society for the Advancement of Judaism (1922) and the Jewish Reconstructionist Foundation (1940). He also served as dean of the Teachers Institute of the Jewish Theological Seminary of America (1931). Kaplan originated the concept of reconstructionism. He argued that Judaism is a dynamic civilization based on nationhood, not religion. Zionism and Israel, therefore, are central components of Judaism that serve to revitalize the pride of diaspora Jews.

kapok [kay'-pahk] The kapok is a large deciduous tree, *Ceiba pentandra,* family Bombacaceae, with spines on its branches and young trunks. The irregularly shaped tree has a wide-spreading crown and has prominent buttresses at its base. It is native to tropical Asia, although it is now grown throughout the tropics in both the New and the Old World. The flowers are white or rose and occur in dense clusters, usually blooming before the leaves appear. Each seed within the fruit is surrounded by a dense mat of cottony fibers. These fibers are almost pure cellulose, although unlike cotton fibers, they do not lend themselves to spinning. Buoyant, impervious to water, and with a low thermal conductivity, kapok fibers were extensively used for stuffing, padding, and insulation but have been somewhat replaced by synthetic fibers.

The kapok tree, a deciduous tree of the tropics, has seedpods that produce a floss still used for stuffing and clothing insulation. The seeds also yield an oil used in manufacturing soap.

Kaprow, Allan [kap'-roh] Allan Kaprow, b. Atlantic City, N.J., Aug. 23, 1927, is an American painter, assemblage artist, and art theorist who created the art form called HAPPENINGS. Kaprow experimented with collages and assemblages composed of nontraditional art materials such as straw, wadded newspapers, and flashing lights. Inspired by ABSTRACT EXPRESSIONISM's emphasis on the act of painting, Kaprow began (1957–58) to create environmental works that integrated space, materials, time, sound, color, and even spectators. Kaprow called these works happenings, and they were intended to inject spontaneity and improvisation into art. During the 1960s he devoted himself to creating and publicizing happenings and establishing them as a viable art form.

Kapteyn, Jacobus Cornelius [kahp-teen', yah-koh'-buhs kor-nay'-lee-uhs] Jacobus Cornelius Kapteyn, b. Jan. 19, 1851, d. June 18, 1922, was a Dutch astronomer who made the first major contributions since William and John Herschel to an understanding of the distribution and motions of the stars in the Milky Way galaxy. In a 13-year collaboration (1885–98) with Sir David Gill, he measured the position and brightness of almost a half-million stars. In 1902, Kapteyn discovered that stars do not move randomly but stream in two opposite directions. Kapteyn coordinated a worldwide effort to gather data on parallaxes, proper motions, and radial velocities of stars and used statistical methods to determine stellar distances. This work yielded the first approximation of the size and structure of the Milky Way.

Kapustin Yar [ka-poos'-tin yahr] Kapustin Yar, the Soviet Union's oldest space center (see BAIKONUR COSMODROME), lies several kilometers below Volgograd near the Volga River. The site of rocketry experiments in the 1930s and of ballistic-missile and early space tests in the 1940s and 1950s, its location was known to other nations but not publicly acknowledged by the Soviet Union until 1983.

Kara Kum [kar-uh-kum'] Kara Kum, a major desert of the USSR, lies east of the Caspian Sea, covering 60% of Turkmenia as well as the southwestern Kazakhstan. With an area of about 300,000 km^2 (116,000 mi^2), it extends approximately 965 km (600 mi) from east to west and 400 km (250 mi) from north to south. Its name means "black sands."

The low-lying Kara Kum is dominated by sand dunes. Sulfur is mined at Sernyy Zavod in central Turkmenia. Rainfall averages less than 255 mm (10 in) a year. The Tedzhen and Murgab rivers irrigate oases, as does water from the AMU DARYA, diverted along the 837-km (520-mi) Kara Kum Canal. Cereal grains are grown in the oases. Seminomadic herders of Turkmen (Turcoman) descent raise camels, sheep, and goats.

Karachi [kuh-rah'-chee] Karachi, the largest city and the major seaport of Pakistan, is situated on the Arabian Sea just northwest of the Indus River delta. The population is 5,180,562 (1981). Together with its suburbs, Karachi encompasses an area of 591 km^2 (228 mi^2). Karachi has grown rapidly because of its port and its industries. Manufactures include textiles (jute and cotton), footwear, food products, and handicraft items. A sophisticated road-, rail-, and air-route system makes the city an important transportation junction. Its port also serves landlocked Afghanistan. Migration from other parts of Pakistan and India has been significant since the two countries gained independence. The University of Karachi (1951) and several colleges and technical schools are located there.

Karachi was founded in 1729 on the site of a fishing village. During the 18th century it became a port and expanded rapidly. The British captured the city in 1839 and

The port city of Karachi, the former capital of Pakistan, retains its position as the major industrial and communications center.

annexed it to their Indian territories in 1842. By 1914 it was the largest grain-exporting port in the British Empire. It was the capital of independent Pakistan until 1959.

Karaites [kair'-uh-yts]   Karaites are members of a Jewish sect founded by Anan ben David in Babylonia in the 8th century AD. Their name (from the Hebrew *qara,* "to read") refers to the sect's concentration on the written Law (TORAH), as distinct from the majority of Jews' emphasis on the TALMUD and the rabbinic traditions (the Rabbanites). The Karaites avoided dealings with Rabbanites, forbade intermarriage, replaced Jewish liturgy by selected biblical readings, and developed an extensive polemic literature.

Karajan, Herbert von [kahr'-ah-yahn]   The Austrian Herbert von Karajan, b. Apr. 5, 1908, d. July 16, 1989, is acknowledged as one of the foremost conductors of his generation. He studied at the Salzburg Mozarteum and the Academy of Music in Vienna. His first appointment as conductor was at the opera house in Ulm, and he quickly became one of Germany's most prominent conductors. Although he had been a member of the Nazi party, after the war an Allied commission cleared him of charges of political collaboration. In 1955 he became conductor-for-life of the Berlin Philharmonic, a post he held for 35 years before resigning in 1989, primarily because of conflicts with the orchestra members. From 1957 to 1964 he was artistic director of the Vienna State Opera and he conducted at the Salzburg Festival from 1951.

Karakoram Range [kah-ruh-kohr'-uhm]   The Karakoram Range, a high (mean elevation: 6,096 m/20,000 ft) mountain range in the HIMALAYAS of Central Asia, extends 483 km (300 mi) southeast from the Pamir Knot in northern Kashmir to southwestern Tibet. The tallest peak,

K2, is the second highest mountain in the world (see K2). Young geologically, the Karakoram mountains emerged in the Cenozoic Era. Because of their steep slopes and alpine glaciers, the summits are almost inaccessible. The dry, harsh climate supports little vegetation or wildlife, but pastoral Tibetans inhabit the lower elevations.

Karamanlis, Konstantinos G. [kah-rah-mahn-lis']   Konstantinos G. Karamanlis, b. Feb. 23, 1907, is a conservative politician who served as premier and president of Greece. Karamanlis was elected to parliament in 1935 and entered the cabinet in 1946 as minister of labor. Appointed prime minister in 1955, Karamanlis formed his own party, the National Radical Union, and won three elections. He resigned as prime minister in 1963 and went into exile in France. After the fall (1974) of the military regime that had come to power in 1967, he returned to Greece and founded another party, New Democracy, which he led as prime minister from 1974 until 1980. Karamanlis held the presidency from 1980 to 1985 and was reelected to that post in 1990.

Karamzin, Nikolai Mikhailovich [kuh-ruhm-zeen', nee-kuh-ly' mee-ky'-luh-vich]   Nikolai Mikhailovich Karamzin, b. Dec. 12 (N.S.), 1766, d. June 3 (N.S.), 1826, is considered the greatest prose writer of 18th-century Russia. His *Letters of a Russian Traveler* (1790, 1801; Eng. trans., 1951), written after a trip (1789–90) to western Europe, is a monument of Russian literary sentimentalism. Karamzin also wrote a number of fictional works, the most famous of which is *Bednaia Liza* (Poor Liza, 1791–92). Appointed Russian historiographer in 1803, he concentrated thereafter on his great *Istoriya Gosudarstva Rossiyskogo* (History of Russia, 12 vols., 1819–29).

karate   SEE MARTIAL ARTS

Karelia [kuh-ree'-lee-uh]   Karelia is a region adjoining Finland in the northwestern USSR, politically constituted as the Karelian autonomous republic within the Russian republic of the USSR. Its area is 172,400 km^2 (66,546 mi^2). Its population is 792,000 (1989), of which about 11% are Karelians, a Finnish-speaking people. The capital is Petrozavodsk (1989 pop., 270,000). The area is heavily forested, and much of the land is covered with swamps. Karelia is a major supplier of wood and paper products, including prefabricated housing, furniture, skis, and paper.

In 1923, Karelia was constituted as an autonomous republic. After the USSR acquired borderlands from Finland as a result of the RUSSO-FINNISH WAR (1939–40), the new territory was combined with Karelia to form the Karelo-Finnish SSR. In 1956, however, it reverted to the status of an autonomous republic. The Karelian Isthmus, a neck of land linking the USSR and Finland, lies to the south of the Karelian autonomous republic, on the opposite side of Lake Ladoga. All but the southernmost section became part of Finland in 1917 but was ceded to the USSR in 1940. This region is now part of the Leningrad oblast of the Russian republic.

Karen   The Karen people of Burma, who numbered about 3,267,000 in the mid-1980s, are, with the Shans, one of the two largest non-Burmese ethnic groups in that country. A Karen state lies east of Rangoon along the Thai border, but only a minority of Karens live there; the rest are dispersed. Some speak a Karen dialect, and others have adopted Burmese. Although many leading Karens are Christians, the majority (about two-thirds) are Buddhist.

The influence of the Karens under British rule was out of proportion to their numbers. Many of them, especially those who were Christian, came to hold important positions in the colonial army, and they were disliked by the Burmese who led the nationalist movement that gained independence for Burma in 1948. Unwilling to submit to Burmese rule, the Karens rebelled unsuccessfully in 1949, and Karen insurgency has persisted since then.

Karinska, Barbara [kuh-rinz'-kuh]   Barbara Karinska, b. Russia, Oct. 3 (N.S.), 1886, d. Oct. 19, 1983, worked in Paris during the 1930s realizing the costume designs of such painters as Salvador Dalí and André Derain. She moved to New York in 1938, executed costumes for Broadway shows and the Metropolitan Opera, won an Academy Award (1948) for her costumes for the film *Joan of Arc*, and in 1948 became resident costume maker and designer for the new New York City Ballet (NYCB).

Karl-Marx-Stadt   see CHEMNITZ

Karloff, Boris [kahr'-lawf]   Although his name became synonymous with horror, Boris Karloff, b. Nov. 23, 1887, d. Feb. 2, 1969, was actually a tall, quiet, charming Englishman, originally named William Pratt, who after a wandering theatrical career became a Hollywood extra and was chosen to play the Frankenstein monster. His best films include *Frankenstein* (1931), *The Old Dark House* (1932), *The Mummy* (1932), *Bride of Frankenstein* (1935), *The Body Snatcher* (1945), and *The Raven* (1935, 1963).

Karlsruhe [kahrls'-roo-e]   Karlsruhe is an industrial city and inland port in Baden-Württemberg state, southwestern Germany. It lies about 65 km (40 mi) northwest of Stuttgart and is connected with the Rhine River to the west by a 6.5-km (4-mi) canal. The population is 268,300 (1987 est.). The city's industries include oil refining, metalworking, machinery construction, printing, chemical production, brewing, and food processing. Since 1956, Karlsruhe has been a center for nuclear research. The city is the seat of the Federal Supreme Court and the Federal Constitutional Court.

Established in 1715, Karlsruhe was laid out in a fan

shape, with streets lined by imposing neoclassical buildings radiating outward from the margrave's palace. The city was heavily bombed during World War II.

Karlstadt [kahrl'-shtaht]   The German theologian Andreas Rudolf Bodenstein, b. c.1480, d. Dec. 24, 1541, was later called Karlstadt (or Carlstadt) for his birthplace. He became a professor at the University of Wittenberg, where he played an important role in the early years of the Reformation. Karlstadt and Martin Luther together debated the Catholic apologist Johann Eck at Leipzig in 1519, but Karlstadt later became increasingly radical, favoring the destruction of religious images and reinterpretation of the Eucharist. In 1525, Luther directly criticized Karlstadt in his treatise *Against the Heavenly Prophets, on Images and Sacrament.*

karma [kahr'-muh]   Karma is a fundamental concept in all Indian religions. Its meaning has shifted through the centuries but has always revolved around the notion of action, especially religious or ritual action. In the early Brahmanical tradition (see HINDUISM), this meant primarily the act of sacrifice addressed to the gods, but later, particularly in BUDDHISM, the concept was mixed with moral notions and came to refer to acts, good or bad, that resulted in correspondingly positive or negative fruits either in this or in a future life. As such, karma also came to be viewed as a metaphysical principle, a law of karma, that bound beings to the cycle of rebirth (see TRANSMIGRATION OF SOULS).

Kármán, Theodore von [kahr'-mahn]   The Hungarian-born physicist Theodore von Kármán, b. May 11, 1881, d. May 7, 1963, received his Ph.D. from the University of Göttingen in 1908. From 1912 to 1929, while director of the Aeronautical Institute at the University of Aachen, he formulated a new law of turbulence that allowed the prediction of drag on the surface of aircraft and rockets, as well as permitting description of fluid flow in pipes.

In 1930, Kármán became director of the Guggenheim Aeronautical Laboratory at the California Institute of Technology, where he remained until 1949. He became a citizen of the United States in 1936. Later he cofounded the institute's Jet Propulsion Laboratory, a government-funded center for rocket research and space exploration. Aerodynamic work by Kármán and his students became the basis for the design of supersonic aircraft. His autobiography, *The Wind and Beyond* (1967), was edited posthumously by Lee Edson.

Karnak [kahr'-nak]   Karnak, a village on the Nile at the northern extremity of LUXOR, is the site of the greatest assembly of ancient temples in Egypt. They are spread over about 48 ha (120 acres) and range in date over about 2,000 years. By far the largest and most important is the temple of Amun (Amon). In origin, it probably dates back to the Old Kingdom (c.2686–2181 BC), but the earliest surviving building is a pavilion of Sesostris I (c.1971–1928 BC). Amun, called king of the gods, was the state god in the New Kingdom (c.1570–1085 BC). Vast quantities of booty from campaigns in Western Asia and Nubia paid for building the Amun temple and made its priesthood the richest religious organization in the land. Architecturally, the temple's most impressive element is the colossal Hypostyle Hall of Seti I (c.1318–1304 BC). Its walls are decorated with scenes carved in relief and hieroglyphic inscriptions that primarily depict religious ceremonies or record historical events.

Karnataka [kahr-nah-tah'-kah]   Karnataka (formerly Mysore) is a state located on the southwest coast of India. It has an area of 192,204 km² (74,210 mi²) and a population of 37,135,714 (1981); its capital city is BANGALORE. Coffee, tea, rice, sugarcane, cotton, and peanuts are the main crops. Gold, iron ore, manganese, bauxite, and copper are mined. The major industries include iron, steel, and machinery manufacturing, food processing, and cotton and silk textile manufacturing.

The area was controlled by a succession of Hindu dynasties from the 3d century BC, and later by both Hindu and Muslim rulers. In the mid-18th century, HYDER ALI, a Muslim, conquered the region. In 1767 the four Mysore Wars between Ali and the British began; they continued under Hyder Ali's son TIPPU SULTAN until 1799, when the victorious British assumed control. In 1947 the state of Mysore became part of independent India. In 1973 its name was changed to Karnataka.

Karpov, Anatoly [kahr'-pohf]   The Soviet Anatoly Yevgenievich Karpov, b. May 23, 1951, was world chess champion from 1975 to 1985. Karpov won the world junior championship in 1969 and a year later became the world's youngest international grand master. His game is noted for economy and precision. In 1975, Karpov was awarded the world championship by default, after Bobby Fischer refused to defend his title. In 1978 and again in 1981, Karpov retained the world title against Viktor Korchnoi. In 1985, however, he lost the title to Gary KASPAROV; he was beaten again by Kasparov in 1986, 1987, and 1990.

Karsavina, Tamara Platonovna [kur-sah'-veen-uh, tuh-mar'-uh pluh-toh-nohv'-nuh]   Tamara Platonovna Karsavina, b. Saint Petersburg, Mar. 10 (N.S.), 1885, d. London, May 26, 1978, was one of the greatest dancers of the BALLETS RUSSES DE SERGE DIAGHILEV. She entered (1902) the Maryinsky Ballet (now Kirov Ballet) as a soloist. From 1909, when she was given star roles, until 1912, Karsavina divided her time between the Maryinsky company and Diaghilev's touring group, where she was the frequent partner of Vaslav Nijinsky. Influenced by Mikhail Fokine's ideas of expressive dance, she excelled in his ballets, notably *Les Sylphides* (1909), *L'Oiseau de Feu* (The Firebird, 1910), and *Petrushka* (1911). After the Russian Revolution, Kar-

savina emigrated to the West, where she worked with Diaghilev in Paris and was for many years associated with the Royal Academy of Dancing in London.

Karsh, Yousuf [kahrsh, yoh'-zuf]   The Canadian photographer Yousuf Karsh, b. Mardin, Turkey, Dec. 23, 1908, specializes in revealing and dramatic portraits of prominent men and women. Using a battery of studio lights and a large view camera, he poses his subjects against a plain background and illuminates them in a way that emphasizes their psychological makeup. His portrait *Winston S. Churchill* (1941) not only made Karsh famous but became a symbol of British resistance to the Nazis. *Marian Anderson* (1948), *Jawaharlal Nehru* (1949), and *Ernest Hemingway* (1958) all embody his strong yet quiet style. Karsh's portraits have been collected in several books.

Yousuf Karsh is one of the leading photographers of the 20th century, renowned for portraits such as those of the American artist Georgia O'Keeffe (1956). (Karsh, Ottawa.)

Kasavubu, Joseph [kas-uh-voo'-boo]   Joseph Kasavubu, b. 1910 or 1917, d. Mar. 24, 1969, was the first president of the Congo republic (now Zaire). A teacher and junior civil servant under the Belgian government in the Congo, he became politically active during the 1940s. Initially, Kasavubu worked to reunify the Bakongo people. In 1955 he became a spokesman for Congolese independence.

When the Congo became independent in 1960, an uneasy coalition government was formed, with Kasavubu as president and Patrice LUMUMBA as premier. Later that year, Kasavubu had Lumumba removed from office. Kasavubu himself was toppled from power in 1965 by Gen. Joseph Mobutu (MOBUTU SESE SEKO).

Käsebier, Gertrude [kay'-ze-beer]   Gertrude Käsebier, b. Des Moines, Iowa, May 18, 1852, d. Oct. 12, 1934, a founding member (1902) of the avant-garde Photo-Secession group, began taking photographs in 1893 and opened a highly successful portrait studio in New York

City in 1897. Her evocative, soft-focused platinum prints far surpassed contemporary camera portraiture. As her business became larger and more commercial, however, her portrait work suffered the loss of careful composition and ingenuity. The resulting conflict with Alfred STIEGLITZ precipitated a break (1912) with the Photo-Secession.

Kashmir [kash-mir'] Kashmir is a mountainous region at the extreme north of the Indian subcontinent. The territory of about 223,000 km^2 (86,000 mi^2) is divided into the Indian state of Jammu and Kashmir (139,000 km^2/ 53,700 mi^2) and the Pakistani Azad (Free) Kashmir (83,800 km^2/32,400 mi^2). Its population is 5,987,389 (1981). Famous for its natural beauty, Kashmir is sometimes called the "Switzerland of India." Almost half the population lives in the fertile Vale of Kashmir (India).

The capitals of the Indian section are SRINAGAR in summer and Jammu in winter; the capital of the Pakistani Kashmir is Muzaffarabad. More than 65% of the inhabitants are Muslims. Hindus reside mostly in the south, around the city of Jammu. In the east is the region of Ladakh, where many of the people are of Tibetan ethnic stock and Buddhists.

Historically, Kashmir was part of the Indian kingdoms. During the Asokan period (273–232 BC), Buddhism was introduced; between the 9th and 12th centuries AD, the area was a center of Hindu culture. Muslim rule began in 1341 and initiated mass conversion to Islam. In 1846 the territory became the princely state of Jammu and Kashmir, belonging to British India. Since 1947 the state has been the object of several armed conflicts between India and Pakistan—India claiming the territory on historical and legal grounds, and Pakistan maintaining that this Muslim-majority state rightfully belongs to Pakistan (see INDIA-PAKISTAN WARS). The 1962 Chinese invasion of India resulted in the Chinese takeover of a northern, uninhabited section of Ladakh known as Aksai Chin. A "line of control," agreed on in 1972, divides the Indian and

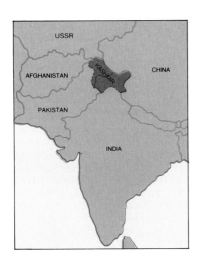

Kashmir, a former princely state, has become the focus of several international disputes since 1947 because of its politically strategic location in India and Pakistan, bordering Afghanistan and China.

Pakistani sections of Kashmir. Subsequent efforts to resolve the conflicting Indian, Pakistani, and Chinese territorial claims in Kashmir have met with little success.

Kasparov, Gary [kahs'-pah-rawf] The Soviet chess player Gary Kimovich Kasparov, b. Apr. 13, 1963, became the world champion in 1985 by defeating his countryman and then-champion Anatoly KARPOV. Kasparov became a grand master in 1980; his first challenge to Karpov came in 1984–85, when their match was halted inexplicably after 48 games, with Karpov retaining the title. In 1985, 1986, 1987, and 1990, however, Kasparov was victorious. His autobiography, *Fighting Chess*, was published in 1985.

Kassel [kah'-sul] Kassel (1987 est. pop., 185,400) is an industrial city in Hesse state, Germany. It is located on the Fulda River about 20 mi (32 km) west of the former border between West and East Germany. The city's manufactures include locomotives, automobiles, electrical machinery, synthetic textiles, and optical and precision instruments. Lignite is mined nearby. The city is also a transportation center and a river port.

Originally a Roman settlement, Kassel was chartered in 1180. The city flourished after the landgraves of Hesse established their residence there in 1277; in 1567 it became the capital of Hesse-Kassel. The city was heavily damaged during World War II, but most historic buildings were rebuilt. Notable among them are the Rathaus, the State Theater, and several 17th- and 18th-century castles.

Kassites [kas'-yts] The Kassites (or Cassites) were a nonnative population of the ancient Near East who infiltrated southern Mesopotamia from the Zagros Mountains of Iran in the 18th century BC. They were political masters of BABYLONIA for 500 years (c.1600–1100 BC). Between 1450 and 1200 BC, Kassite Babylonia interacted diplomatically with New Kingdom Egypt, the Hittite empire, and the Middle Assyrian kingdom.

Katanga see SHABA

Katayev, Valentin Petrovich [ka-ty'-yuhf, vuhl-yin-teen' pee-troh'-vich] Russian novelist Valentin Petrovich Katayev, b. Jan. 28 (N.S.), 1897, d. Apr. 12, 1986, has been called "the licensed humorist of the Soviets." *The Embezzlers* (1926; Eng. trans., 1928) deals with Soviet bank tellers who escape their drab jobs by taking along the cash; *Squaring the Circle* (1928; Eng. trans., 1934) is about two mismatched couples who exchange partners. *Time Forward!* (1932; Eng. trans., 1933), by contrast, is a serious novel about the building of a cement plant. His *Lonely White Sail* (1936; Eng. trans., 1937), a partly autobiographical novel, is the first in a series of four chronicling life in Odessa from 1910 through World War II. Personal reminiscences are the subject of his later books, *The Holy Well* (1965; Eng. trans., 1967), *The Grass of Oblivion* (1967; Eng. trans., 1970), and *A Mosaic of Life; or, The Magic Horn of Oberon* (1972; Eng. trans., 1976).

Katmai, Mount [kat'-my]   Mount Katmai is a 2,047-m (6,715-ft) volcano located on the Alaska Peninsula in southern Alaska. Katmai erupted in 1912, blowing off the top of the mountain and scattering volcanic ash to a depth of 300 mm (1 ft) in some areas as far as 160 km (100 mi) away. The wasteland it created became known as the VALLEY OF TEN THOUSAND SMOKES because of the steam vents that dot its surface. The area was declared a national monument in 1918. The crater measures 13 km (8 mi) in circumference and 1,130 m (3,700 ft) deep.

Katmandu [kaht-mahn-doo']   Katmandu, the capital of Nepal, is located in the southern foothills of the Himalayas. Its population is 235,160 (1981). Katmandu is the commercial and transportation center of Nepal; its economy is based on jute, sugar, hides, and textiles. A 1934 earthquake severely damaged the city, forcing the construction of new buildings. Historical landmarks include many Hindu temples and a palace housing a 1549 temple that is a pilgrimage site for Tibetan Buddhists. Tribhuvan University was established in 1959.

Katmandu (also spelled Kathmandu) was founded in 723. In 1768 the city was captured by Gurkha kings and became their capital.

Kato Takaaki [kah'-toh tah-kah-ah'-kee]   Kato Takaaki, b. 1860, d. Jan. 28, 1926, also called Kato Komei, was a leading Japanese statesman in the early 20th century. He began (1887) his political life as private secretary to OKUMA SHIGENOBU and, like Okuma, was associated throughout his career with the Mitsubishi business cartel.

Kato was twice ambassador to Great Britain (1894–99, 1908–13) and several times minister of foreign affairs (1900, 1906–08, 1913, 1914–15). In 1915 he sent the so-called Twenty-one Demands to China, calling for increased Japanese privileges in that country. As leader of the Kenseikei party after World War I, Kato became prime minister in 1924. He introduced universal male suffrage and reduced the power of the army but also suppressed political radicalism.

Katowice [kah-toh-veet'-se]   The city of Katowice (1988 est. pop., 368,600) is located in the Silesian coal-mining region of southwest Poland, about 120 km (75 mi) northwest of Kraków. Katowice is a major rail junction. Its industries include the manufacture of iron, steel, chemicals, textiles, and heavy machinery. Settled in the late 16th century, Katowice was annexed by Prussia in 1742. It became a part of Poland in 1921.

Katsura Taro [kaht'-soo-rah tah-roh']   Katsura Taro, b. 1847, d. Oct. 10, 1913, was a leading Japanese statesman in the period preceding World War I. A supporter of the MEIJI RESTORATION (1868), by which the shogunate was overthrown and the emperor restored to authority, Katsura rose to prominence as a protégé of the statesman YAMAGATA ARITOMO. He was minister of the army from 1898 to 1900.

As prime minister from 1901 to 1906, Katsura concluded an alliance (1902) with Britain and presided over Japan's victory in the RUSSO-JAPANESE WAR (1904–05). After a period in opposition to ITO HIROBUMI, he returned to office for a second term and carried out the annexation of Korea in 1910. A third term as premier lasted only seven weeks (December 1912 to February 1913) because of opposition to his armaments program and to the oligarchical basis of his power. Although he opposed the concept of party politics, Katsura contributed to the development of two-party politics in Japan.

katydid [kayt'-ee-did]   Katydids are stout-bodied grasshoppers of the family Tettigoniidae, order Orthoptera. They are usually green in color, with long, hairlike antennae, the front wings draped over the sides of the body, and a long, bladelike ovipositor (egg-laying tube) extending from the rear of the body in females. The raspy *katy-did* song is produced only by males and serves to attract females. The sound is made by rubbing together the roughened areas at the bases of the two front wings.

The bush katydid is also called a long-horned grasshopper because its antennae are as long as its body (4 cm/1.6 in).

Kauffmann, Angelica [kawf'-muhn, ahng-gay'-lee-kah]   The Swiss artist Angelica Kauffmann, b. Oct. 30, 1741, d. Nov. 5, 1807, was one of the most important neoclassical painters. Kauffmann became one of the founding members of the English Royal Academy of Art. In Britain she made a sizable income from the production of allegorical portraits as well as from her designs for the interiors of numerous houses, especially those designed by Robert Adam. In 1781 she married the Venetian painter Antonio Zucchi (1762–95) and settled in Rome, where she became (1795) the unofficial head of the Roman school of painting. Kauffmann painted more than 500 paintings during her lifetime, including numerous self-portraits and history paintings such as *Cornelia, Mother of the Gracchi* (1785).

Kaufman, George S. [kawf'-muhn] One of the most brilliant playwrights and directors in the history of Broadway, George Simon Kaufman, b. Pittsburgh, Pa., Nov. 16, 1889, d. June 2, 1961, left law school to become drama critic of the *New York Times* (1917–30) and retained that post after succeeding as a playwright. His first successful play, *Dulcy* (1921), was written with Marc CONNELLY, also his coauthor on *To the Ladies* (1922), *Merton of the Movies* (1922), *Beggar on Horseback* (1924), and *The Butter and Egg Man* (1925). With Edna FERBER, Kaufman wrote *The Royal Family* (1927), *Dinner at Eight* (1932), *Stage Door* (1936), and *The Land Is Bright* (1941). His best plays, *Once in a Lifetime* (1930), *You Can't Take It with You* (1936; Pulitzer Prize), and *The Man Who Came to Dinner* (1939), were joint ventures with Moss HART. He also collaborated with Morrie Ryskind on the book for the Gershwins' *Of Thee I Sing* (1932), with Howard Dietz and Arthur Schwartz on *The Band Wagon* (1931), with Ring Lardner on *June Moon* (1929), and with Alexander Woollcott on *The Dark Tower* (1933).

George S. Kaufman, an American playwright, comedy writer, and director, helped create some of the most popular plays and musicals of the 1930s.

Kaunas [kow'-nahs] Kaunas (1989 pop., 423,000) is the second largest city in Lithuania. It is situated at the juncture of the Neman and Neris rivers. Kaunas is an industrial center, with textile mills and diversified manufacturing. Part of its electric power is derived from the Kaunas hydroelectric station, upstream on the Neman.

First mentioned in the 11th century, the city has the remains of a castle, basilica, and church dating from the 14th and 15th centuries. Annexed by Russia in the third partition of Poland (1795), it was called Kovno and served as the provincial capital. From 1918 until 1940, Kaunas was the capital of independent Lithuania.

Kaunda, Kenneth D. [kown'-duh] Kenneth David Kaunda, b. Apr. 28, 1924, became the president of Zambia (formerly Northern Rhodesia) after it won independence from Great Britain in 1964. He was reelected in 1968, 1973, 1978, 1983, and 1988. Kaunda began his career as a teacher but in 1949 joined the anticolonial African National Congress and eventually became the leader of the independence movement. In the 1980s he focused chiefly on Zambia's huge foreign debt.

kauri pine [kow'-ree] The beautiful, massive kauri pine is a New Zealand cone-bearing evergreen tree, *Agathis australis*, of the family Araucariaceae. Although its maximum height may not exceed 46 m (150 ft), the diameter of the trunk may exceed 6 m (20 ft). The trunk yields high-quality wood. The kauri pine is also a source of kauri gum, or copal, used in varnishes, paints, and printing inks. The finest copal, however, is dug from the soil in fossil form. Plants grown commercially are usually the Australian *A. robusta*, the Queensland kauri.

Kautsky, Karl Johann [kowt'-skee] Karl Kautsky, b. Oct. 16, 1854, d. Oct. 17, 1938, was an influential German socialist theorist. A staunch Marxist, he founded (1883) the journal *Die neue Zeit*, which he edited until 1917, and was the author of much of the Erfurt program (1891), by which the German Social Democratic party upheld revolutionary Marxism. Kautsky opposed the revisionist theories of Eduard BERNSTEIN but later condemned the Bolshevik Revolution (1917) in Russia as antidemocratic. He lost influence after World War I.

Kaw see KANSA

Kawabata Yasunari [kah-wah'-bah-tah yah'-soo-nar-ee] Kawabata Yasunari, b. June 11, 1899, d. Apr. 16, 1972, was one of the greatest modern Japanese novelists and the first to receive (1968) the Nobel Prize for literature. Kawabata began his literary career as a standard-bearer for European expressionism in Japan, but his lyrical qualities soon came to the fore, beginning with "The Dancing Girl of Izu" (1926; Eng. trans., 1955) and continuing with *Snow Country* (1937–48; Eng. trans., 1956), *Thousand Cranes* (1952; Eng. trans., 1959), *The Sound of the Mountain* (1954; Eng. trans., 1970), and *The Old Capital* (1962; Eng. trans., 1987). His evocative, haunting descriptions, emphasis on setting as much as on character, and open-ended plots made him the most "Japanese" of modern writers. He died by his own hand.

Kawasaki [kah-wah-sah'-kee] Kawasaki is an industrial city in Japan, adjacent to Tokyo on the north and to Yokohama on the south. The city has a population of 1,157,005 (1989 est.). As one of Japan's leading centers of heavy industry, Kawasaki has many petrochemical, steel, oil-refining, and other industrial plants. Lying on Tokyo Bay, it is also a port city.

Founded about 1150, Kawasaki was a residential town for noblemen during the Tokugawa period (1603–1868). In the 1930s it developed as an industrial center, and after the mid-1950s it also became a bedroom community for the sprawling Tokyo-Yokohama metropolis.

Kawasaki disease   Kawasaki disease is an unusual childhood disease characterized by a rash, swollen lymph glands, and fever. First described in 1967 by Tokyo pediatrician Dr. Tomisaku Kawasaki, the disease strikes a few hundred children in the United States each year. Most cases pass without permanent ill effects, but in about 20 percent of the cases the walls of the coronary arteries are at least temporarily weakened. In about 1 percent of U.S. cases, this leads to heart attack and death. The cause of the disease is unknown, although some recent evidence suggests a RETROVIRUS.

Kay, John   The English engineer John Kay, b. July 16, 1704, d. 1764, invented the flying shuttle, which paved the way for power-loom WEAVING. Kay invented several minor textile improvements before patenting a carding (combing) machine and the flying shuttle in 1733. The shuttle, equipped with a mechanical attachment that sent it flying through the weft at the jerk of a cord, increased the speed of weaving and made it possible for a double width of cloth to be woven by one person.

kayaking   see CANOEING AND KAYAKING

Kaye, Danny   An American stage, film, and television comedian who developed scat singing into a fine art, Danny Kaye, b. Daniel David Kominsky, Brooklyn, N.Y., Jan. 18, 1913, d. Mar. 3, 1987, received his comedy training in the resort hotels of the Catskills. Here he met Sylvia Fine, who became his wife and the arranger of the special material that showcased his talent for dialects and patter songs. Their cooperation led to such strong Kaye vehicles as *The Court Jester* (1956) and *The Five Pennies* (1959). Kaye also starred in *The Secret Life of Walter Mitty* (1947) and *Hans Christian Andersen* (1952) and was known around the world for his work on behalf of UNICEF.

Kazakhstan [kah-zahk'-stan]   Kazakhstan was formerly one of the republics of the USSR, but it became independent in 1991. Bordered on the east by China, on the south by Kyrgyzstan, Uzbekistan, and Turkmenistan, on the west by the Caspian Sea, and on the west and north by Russia, the new republic has an area of 2,717,300 km^2 (1,049,155 mi^2) and a population of 16,793,100 (1991 est.). The capital is ALMA-ATA, with a population of 1,156,200 (1991 est.).

The topography of Kazakhstan is varied, with a predominance of lowland and upland plains and rolling hill country. High mountains occur only in the northeast, where the republic reaches into the ALTAI MOUNTAINS, and southeast, where it extends to the TIAN SHAN. The climate becomes progressively drier from north to south, as the natural vegetation changes from grassland steppe in the

north to desert with irrigated oases in the south. The lowlands are drained by the IRTYSH RIVER, the SYR DARYA, the URAL RIVER, the Tobol, and the Ishim River. In addition to bordering on the CASPIAN SEA, Kazakhstan includes part of the ARAL SEA and all of Lake Balkhash.

The Kazakh are in the minority, constituting 42% of the population. Traditionally a nomadic stock-herding group of Muslim religion and Turkic language, they still live principally in rural areas, with only one-quarter residing in cities. The ethnic Russians, 38% of the population, are concentrated in cities. Other large minorities are Ukrainians and ethnic Germans. The principal cities, in addition to Alma-Ata, are the coal-and-steel center of Karaganda (1989 pop., 614,000), Chimkent (393,000), Semipalatinsk (334,000), and Pavlodar (331,000).

Kazakhstan is a rich depository of mineral resources and industrial raw materials, development of which has given rise to a highly diversified mineral industry. The republic has large coal basins, which provide fuel for an important electric-power industry. Kazakhstan is a major producer of iron ore, nonferrous metals (chromite, copper, lead, zinc), bauxite for the aluminum industry, and other metals. Petroleum is now being produced, and the Tenghiz oil field on the Caspian Sea is estimated to be one of the world's largest. Agriculture and sheepherding remain major features of the economy. The BAIKONUR COSMODROME, a major space-launching center, continues to function.

Except for the southern margins, Kazakhstan was a sparsely populated region of nomadic herders until the Russians gained control in the mid-19th century. After the Bolshevik Revolution the region was constituted in 1920 as the Kirghiz ASSR, the name Kirghiz having been mistakenly applied to the Kazakh in the past. It was renamed Kazak (the original spelling) in 1925, and in 1936 its status was raised to that of full Soviet republic.

The newly independent Kazakhstan, under the leadership of its president, Nursultan Nazarbayev, has begun to assert its sovereignty in international affairs, but close relations to Russia remain the key to the country's future development.

Kazan [kuh-zahn']   Kazan, the capital of the Tatar autonomous republic in the Russian Federation is situated on the left bank of the Volga River and is a major river port. Its population is 1,107,300 (1991 est.). Although Kazan is nominally the capital of the TATARS, ethnic Russians outnumber Tatars in its population.

Kazan is an important industrial center, with diversified manufacturing including aircraft and machine tools, petroleum refining, chemical plants, and Russia's largest fur-dressing factory. The old town contains a kremlin, or fortress, built in the 16th century. Nearby is the 18th-century Cathedral of Saint Peter and Saint Paul. Kazan has a noted university dating from 1804.

The city was established in the early 15th century as the capital of the Tatar khanate of Kazan, one of the successor states of the GOLDEN HORDE. After its conquest by IVAN IV of Russia in 1552, Kazan developed into a military, administrative, and economic center of the Volga. It became a provincial capital in 1708. When a republic was established (1920) for the Tatar minority, Kazan became the capital.

Kazan, Elia [kuh-zan', eel'-yuh]   An American stage and film director, Elia Kazan (originally Kazanjoglous), b. Istanbul, Turkey, Sept. 7, 1909, to Greek parents, became a director after a brief career as an actor with New York's Group Theater in the 1930s. His greatest success was directing plays by Arthur Miller and Tennessee Williams, including *A Streetcar Named Desire* (1947) and *Death of a Salesman* (1949). He also directed the Academy Award–winning films *Gentleman's Agreement* (1947) and *On The Waterfront* (1954). His two autobiographical novels, *America, America* (1962) and *The Arrangement* (1967), were turned into films in 1963 and 1968.

Kazantzakis, Nikos [kah-zahnd-zah'-kees, nee'-kohs]   The Greek novelist, poet, and thinker Nikos Kazantzakis, b. Crete, 1883, d. Oct. 26, 1957, spent half his life in Germany, the USSR, and France. He also traveled widely throughout Europe, Japan, and Communist China. His career started out more philosophical and pedagogical than literary, and he came to the fore as a poet only in 1938 with his vast philosophical epic *The Odyssey: A Modern Sequel* (Eng. trans., 1958), which takes up the hero's story where Homer leaves off.

Even more successful were his novels, which he did not begin writing until after his 60th year. His first, *Zorba the Greek* (1946; Eng. trans., 1952; film, 1965), is the most popular. In it Kazantzakis embodies Bergsonian ideas of the *élan vital* in the exuberant figure of Zorba. His other novels are perhaps deeper, if less exuberant. *Freedom and Death* (1953; Eng. trans., 1956) deals with the concept of liberty told through the story of a dour resistance fighter in the Cretan struggle for independence from the Turks. *The Greek Passion* (1954; Eng. trans., 1954) is a reenactment of Christ's passion set in a Greek village. Kazantzakis also wrote the novels *The Last Temptation of Christ* (1955; Eng. trans., 1960; film, 1988) and *God's Pauper: Saint Francis of Assisi* (1956; Eng. trans., 1962), a large number of plays, and an autobiography, *Report to Greco* (1961; Eng. trans., 1965).

Kazin, Alfred [kay'-zin]   With the publication of *On Native Grounds: An Interpretation of Modern American Prose Literature* (1942), Alfred Kazin, b. Brooklyn, N.Y., June 5, 1915, established himself in the center of New York intellectual life. As literary critic, editor, and teacher, Kazin continued his examination of American writing with works such as *The Inmost Leaf* (1955), *Contemporaries* (1962), and *Bright Book of Life: American Novelists and Storytellers from Hemingway to Mailer* (1973). His autobiographical trilogy—*Walker in the City* (1951), *Starting Out in the Thirties* (1965), and *New York Jew* (1978)—evokes New York life from the 1920s through the 1970s.

Edmund Kean, an English tragedian, became a celebrity in 1814 with his memorable performance as Shylock at London's Drury Lane Theatre. Subsequent roles established him as England's finest dramatic actor.

Kean (family) [keen]   The Kean family was one of the most illustrious theatrical families in 19th-century England. Edmund Kean, b. London, Mar. 17, *c.*1787, d. May 15, 1833, became the greatest tragic actor of the period, excelling particularly in Shakespearean roles. His son, Charles John Kean, b. Waterford, Ireland, *c.*1811, d. Jan. 22, 1868, established himself as an actor during his father's lifetime and went on to become a notable manager and director. In 1842 he married another performer, the highly acclaimed actress Ellen Tree, b. Ireland, December 1805, d. Aug. 20, 1880, with whom he worked for the rest of his career.

Edmund Kean played Shylock at Drury Lane in 1814 and was immediately accepted as a major star. He excelled in portraying nobility—usually with a touch of malignancy, marked by outbursts of emotional, almost murderous, frenzy. Audiences enjoyed Kean's passionate, romantic style, but his wild exploits off the stage and bouts of drunkenness diminished both his popularity and skill.

Charles Kean contributed significantly to the English theater as both a manager and director. He began acting in 1827 and achieved fame in 1838 as Hamlet. Kean directed his first production, *Romeo and Juliet*, in 1841. He married Ellen Tree a year later. In 1848 he was appointed master of revels by Queen Victoria, and he also managed (1850–59) London's Princess's Theatre, where he staged productions notable for their historical authenticity. The increasing patronage of Victoria revived theatergoing as a respectable pastime. More than anyone else in England, Kean established the director as the theater's primary artist.

Ellen Tree Kean became a successful comedienne with her first performance at Covent Garden in 1823. Regarded as one of the best actresses of her time, she retired from the stage when her husband died.

Kearny, Philip [kar'-nee]   Philip Kearny, b. New York City, June 1, 1814, d. Sept. 1, 1862, was a Union general in the U.S. Civil War who became renowned for his courage and for the rapport he enjoyed with his men. A nephew of Stephen Watts Kearny, he joined (1837) the army as a lieutenant, went to Europe to study the French cavalry service, and served with French forces in Algeria (1840). He lost an arm in the Mexican War. At the beginning of the Civil War, Kearny commanded a New Jersey brigade in the Army of the Potomac. Later he was cavalry commander in the Peninsular Campaign and at Second Bull Run. He was killed when he unwittingly crossed enemy lines at Chantilly.

Kearny, Stephen Watts   Stephen Watts Kearny, b. Newark, N.J., Aug. 30, 1794, d. Oct. 31, 1848, led the U.S. forces that occupied New Mexico and pacified California in the Mexican War. Commissioned in the army in 1812, he won distinction during the War of 1812. A series of frontier assignments followed, including service in the Yellowstone expedition of 1825 and, after 1833, in the First Dragoons, for which he has been called the "father of the U.S. Cavalry."

Stationed at Fort Leavenworth at the beginning of the Mexican War, Kearny was given command of the Army of the West in May 1846. He entered New Mexico without resistance and organized a civil government. He then proceeded to California, guided by Kit Carson. Although wounded in the Battle of San Pascual near San Diego on Dec. 6–7, 1846, he linked forces with Commodore Robert F. Stockton and defeated the Mexicans at San Gabriel on Jan. 8, 1847. Kearny then briefly served as military governor of California. He subsequently went to Mexico, where he was military governor, first of Veracruz and then of Mexico City.

Keaton, Buster [keet'-uhn]   Joseph Francis "Buster" Keaton, b. Piqua, Kans., Oct. 4, 1895, d. Feb. 1, 1966,

This scene from The General *(1926) pictures Buster Keaton, the master of silent film comedy, in his typical role as an impassive loner and hero who triumphs over unbelievable odds.*

actor and director, was one of the giants of silent film comedy. Raised in a vaudeville family, Keaton entered the film industry in 1917 as a protégé of Fatty Arbuckle and quickly mastered film technique on both sides of the camera. A superb acrobat from youth, Keaton developed a keen appreciation for movie sight gags. In 1921, under the banner of his own company, he began his solo-starring career and refined his unique deadpan character—a loner caught in the flurry of modern life who somehow manages to triumph over even the most mind-boggling disasters. Such classic shorts as *One Week* (1920), *The High Sign* (1921), *The Boat* (1921), *Cops* (1922), and *The Balloonatic* (1923) led to feature films in which he expanded his highly individual comic views: *Our Hospitality* (1923), *The Navigator* (1924), *Seven Chances* (1925), *The General* (1926), and his cinematic tour de force, *Sherlock Jr.* (1924). He continued to work in films and television the rest of his life, but after his move to MGM in 1928, he never again exercised the creative control he had enjoyed in the silent era.

Keaton, Diane   The film actress Diane Keaton, b. Diane Hall in Los Angeles, Jan. 5, 1946, first came to notice in *The Godfather* (1972). It was as a comedienne, however, that Keaton became famous, playing opposite Woody Allen in a series of his movies during the 1970s, winning an Academy Award for *Annie Hall* (1977). The funny, kooky, half-awkward urban types in these films gave way to more dramatic roles in *Looking for Mr. Goodbar* (1977), *Interiors* (1978), *Reds* (1981), *The Little Drummer Girl* (1984), and *The Good Mother* (1988).

Keats, John [keets]   John Keats, one of England's greatest poets and literary theoreticians, together with Lord Byron and Percy B. Shelley, formed the second generation of British romantic poets (see ROMANTICISM). Noted for the rich, sensuous texture of his poetry and his ability to identify with and render the thing contemplated, Keats was also a strenuous thinker; in his letters he speculated on the nature of poetry and the poet and struggled with the problems of suffering and death.

Born in London, Oct. 31, 1795, the son of a livery stable keeper, Keats was orphaned while still a child and in 1811 was apprenticed to a surgeon. Influenced by his friend the poet Leigh Hunt, who encouraged him to write and also introduced him to many famous poets, Keats left surgery for poetry.

After writing several mediocre poems, Keats produced the remarkably assured sonnet "On First Looking into Chapman's Homer" (1816), followed by his ambitious allegory *Endymion* (1818). Written in the lush style of Hunt—which Keats soon rejected—this poem describes the poet's search for ideal beauty. After its publication, Keats was attacked as a member of Hunt's "Cockney School" of poetry in an article in *Blackwood's*. This and other severe attacks gave rise to the myth, embodied most notably in Shelley's elegy *Adonais* (1821), that Keats had been killed by criticism.

John Keats, one of the outstanding English romantic poets, appears in this study by a close friend, Joseph Severn.

Actually he died of tuberculosis, against which both he and his brother Tom had long struggled; in 1818, Tom died, and shortly afterward Keats became aware that he, too, had contracted the disease. His misery was exacerbated by his love for Fanny Brawne; because of his increasing ill health, marriage was impossible. Throughout this anguished time, however, Keats was producing his masterpieces. During 1819 alone he composed *The Eve of St. Agnes, La Belle Dame sans Merci, Lamia,* and the six great *Odes* (including "Ode on a Grecian Urn" and "Ode to a Nightingale") and reworked his unfinished epic *Hyperion* into *The Fall of Hyperion,* in which he examined his poetic career and rededicated himself to poetry.

By early 1820, Keats understood clearly that he was dying and in the fall traveled with his friend the painter Joseph Severn to Rome in an attempt to delay the workings of the disease. From there he wrote agonized letters lamenting his loss of love and the failure of his hopes of poetic excellence. He died on Feb. 23, 1821, in the house on the Spanish Steps that now forms a memorial to him and Shelley.

Keats's short poetic life is unprecedented in English literature; between the ages of 18 and 24 he wrote poems that rank with the greatest in the language. Taking in all the senses, they render the totality of an experience and catch the complexity of life in which pain and pleasure are inextricably joined. The theory that complements this poetry is expounded in his letters, in which he speculates on the truth of the imaginative world and proposes a theory of negative capability requiring that the poet open himself to all experience.

Keble, John [kee'-bul]   The English theologian and poet John Keble, b. Apr. 25, 1792, d. Mar. 29, 1866, is considered the founder of the OXFORD MOVEMENT. A fellow of Oriel College, Oxford, he was ordained in the Church of England in 1815. In 1827 he published a volume of poems, *The Christian Year,* which went through 95 editions during his lifetime and led to a professorship of poetry at Oxford (1831–41). In his poetry Keble exhibited fervent faith in the authority of the church and its sacraments, and he was believed by John Henry NEWMAN to have begun the Oxford movement with a sermon on "National Apostasy" preached on July 14, 1833.

keeshond [kays'-hahnd]   The keeshond is a Dutch breed of dog of the spitz type characterized by a dense, rough coat, erect ears, and a tightly curled tail carried over its back. It is a squarely built dog, standing about 46 cm (18 in) high at the shoulder and weighing up to 18 kg (40 lb). Its coat color is a mixture of gray and black, with a very pale gray undercoat. The keeshond was originally developed as a barge dog, accompanying the small vessels on the rivers and canals of Holland.

Kefauver, Estes [kee'-faw-vur, es'-teez]   Carey Estes Kefauver, b. Madisonville, Tenn., July 26, 1903, d. Aug. 10, 1963, was a U.S. senator from Tennessee whose investigations into organized crime in 1950–51 were nationally televised and created great public interest. A lawyer, Kefauver sat in the U.S. House of Representatives from 1939 to 1949 and in 1948 won election to the Senate. After chairing the Special Committee to Investigate Organized Crime in Interstate Commerce, Kefauver sought the Democratic nomination for president in 1952 but lost to Adlai E. Stevenson. He lost to Stevenson again in 1956, but he was the vice-presidential nominee. Despite his support for civil rights for African Americans, an anomalous position for a Southern politician in that era, Kefauver remained in the Senate until his death.

Keino, Kipchoge [kay'-noh, kip-choh'-gay]   Kipchoge Keino, b. Jan. 17, 1940, was the first great distance runner to come from Kenya, a country now known for its talented runners. In the 1964 Olympics he placed fifth in the 5,000-m (5,500-yd) run. The next year he ran the mile in 3 min 54.2 sec. At the 1968 Olympic Games he won the 1,500-m (1,650-yd) event with a world-record time of 3 min 34.9 sec. Keino won the 3,000-m (3,300-yd) steeplechase, an event in which he had little experience, at the 1972 Olympics. In 1973, Keino became a professional runner; he retired about 1975.

Keitel, Wilhelm [ky'-tuhl]   Wilhelm Keitel, b. Sept. 22, 1882, d. Oct. 16, 1946, was chief of the high command of the German Armed forces during World War II. Hitler's closest military advisor, he dictated the terms of the French surrender in 1940 and signed Germany's surrender to the Allies in May 1945. He was convicted of war crimes at the Nuremberg Trials and executed.

Kekkonen, Urho K. [kek'-oh-nen, oor'-hoh]   As president of Finland from 1956 to 1981, Urho Kaleva

Urho Kaleva Kekkonen was president of Finland for 25 years. He was first elected in 1956 and reelected in 1962 and 1968; in 1974, Parliament extended his third term by 4 years to 1978. He was then reelected to another 6-year term, but declining health caused his resignation in October 1981.

Kekkonen, b. Sept. 3, 1900, d. Aug. 31, 1986, pursued a policy of neutrality in international affairs, trying to maintain good relations with the West without antagonizing the neighboring USSR. Kekkonen was educated at the University of Helsinki and worked as a lawyer until he was elected to Parliament in 1936. He served as minister of justice (1936–37) and minister of the interior (1937–39). After the Russo-Finnish War, Kekkonen handled the resettlement of 420,000 refugees from Karelia, the territory ceded to the USSR. As leader of the Agrarian party (later renamed Center party), he was prime minister four times in the years 1950–56.

Kekulé von Stradonitz, Friedrich August [kay'-koo-lay fuhn strah'-doh-nits]

Friedrich August Kekulé von Stradonitz, b. Sept. 7, 1829, d. July 13, 1896, was a German chemist best known for his work on the structure of the BENZENE molecule. Kekulé's first important work was carried out in London in 1854, when he found thioacetic acid, the first known organic acid containing sulfur. In 1857 he deduced the key concept that carbon always forms four bonds and introduced the fundamentally important idea that carbon atoms can bond with one another. He became a professor at Ghent in 1858 and while there developed his benzene theory and wrote his famous textbook, *Lehrbuch der organischen Chemie* (Handbook of Organic Chemistry).

The structure of benzene was given by Kekulé in 1865 as a simple hexagon, and in 1866 he postulated a pair of structures differing in the location of the alternate double bonds. Later he showed that the two possible arrangements are identical, the benzene ring behaving as if there were oscillation between the double and single bonds, by which he anticipated the concept of RESONANCE of the early 1930s.

Keller, Gottfried [kel'-ur, gawt'-freet]

The stories of the Swiss author Gottfried Keller, b. July 19, 1819, d.

July 15, 1890, are among the best examples of the trend in German literature that came to be known as poetic realism. Keller set out to become a painter, then tried his hand at writing poetry, tragedy, and an autobiographical novel, *Green Henry* (1854–55; Eng. trans., 1960). The basis for Keller's renown, however, was his collection of village tales, *The People of Seldwyla* (1856; Eng. trans., 1931), which contains his best-known story, "Romeo und Julia auf dem Dorfe," an adaptation of the Shakespearean theme to a rural setting.

Keller, Helen

Helen Adams Keller, b. Tuscumbia, Ala., June 27, 1880, d. June 1, 1968, was an author, lecturer, and humanitarian whose unusual life and dedicated work had an international influence on the lives of the handicapped. She became blind and deaf at the age of 19 months through a damaging brain fever and could communicate only through hysterical laughter or violent tantrums. With the help of her teacher Anne Mansfield Sullivan, however, Keller learned to read braille and to write by using a special typewriter. Their early relationship was the subject of *The Miracle Worker*, a 1960 Pulitzer Prize–winning play and 1962 film by William Gibson. In 1904, Keller graduated with honors from Radcliffe College and began a life of writing, lecturing, and fund-raising on behalf of the handicapped.

Helen Keller graduated cum laude from Radcliffe College in 1904, despite being stricken, at the age of 19 months, by an illness that left her blind, deaf, and mute. Keller overcame these disabilities and spent her life writing and speaking to benefit the handicapped.

Kelley, Florence

Florence Kelley, b. Philadelphia, Sept. 12, 1859, d. Feb. 17, 1932, strove to improve industrial working conditions. A graduate (1882) of Cornell University, she later became a socialist and translated Friedrich Engels's *The Condition of the Working Class in England* (1887); in 1894 she earned a law degree from Northwestern University. A forceful advocate of protective wage and labor laws for women and an end to child labor, Kelley served as the first chief factory inspector in Illinois (1893–97) and, from 1899, as secretary of the National Consumers' League.

Kelley, William Melvin The novelist William Melvin Kelley, b. the Bronx, N.Y., Nov. 1, 1937, is well known for his understated, bitterly ironic, sharply intelligent stories of African-American lives. *A Different Drummer* (1962), regarded as his best novel, imagines the effect on a southern state of a sudden exodus of all its black citizens. *A Drop of Patience* (1965) follows the life of a blind musician, and *dem* (1967) attacks the myths white Americans live by. Kelley's novel *Dunfords Travels Everywheres* (1970) uses linguistic play and fantasy to explore the resemblances between a black writer in Paris and a black hustler in Harlem.

Kellogg, Frank B. Frank Billings Kellogg, b. Potsdam, N.Y., Dec. 22, 1856, d. Dec. 21, 1937, was an American politician and diplomat, best known as the sponsor of the KELLOGG-BRIAND PACT (1928). In 1904 he became a special counsel to the federal government in the antitrust suits against the General Paper Company and Standard Oil.

A Republican, Kellogg served in the U.S. Senate (1917–23), as ambassador to Britain (1924–25), and as secretary of state (1925–29). In the last office Kellogg not only promoted the Kellogg-Briand Pact, by which 62 nations renounced war, but also improved relations with Mexico and settled the TACNA-ARICA DISPUTE between Chile and Peru. He was awarded the 1929 Nobel Peace Prize. From 1930 to 1935, Kellogg served as a judge on the Permanent Court of International Justice in The Hague, Netherlands.

Kellogg, W. K. Will Keith Kellogg, b. Battle Creek, Mich., Apr. 7, 1860, d. Oct. 6, 1951, was the creator of Kellogg's Corn Flakes. As a young man he worked with his brother, Dr. John H. Kellogg, at the latter's Battle Creek Sanitarium, where they developed toasted wheat flakes and other vegetarian health foods. In 1906 he organized the Battle Creek Toasted Corn Flake Company and merchandised his product with heavy advertising. He added other breakfast foods to the company's line, making it the world's largest manufacturer of prepared cereals.

Kellogg-Briand Pact The Kellogg-Briand Pact was an agreement to renounce war as an instrument of national policy. It was signed in Paris by 15 nations on Aug. 27, 1928. Almost every country in the world soon joined the pact, which was hailed as an important step toward peace. Aristide BRIAND, the French foreign minister, led the way to this pact by proposing that France and the United States renounce war with each other. The U.S. secretary of state, Frank B. KELLOGG, then suggested that other nations be invited to pledge to settle all disputes peacefully. Because the pact did not provide for enforcement, it was useless in stopping undeclared wars, such as the Japanese invasion of Manchuria in 1931.

Yellow-Blue, *painted by the American artist Ellsworth Kelly in 1963, is an example of the hard-edge trend in abstract art. (Private collection.)*

Kelly, Ellsworth American abstract painter Ellsworth Kelly, b. Newburgh, N.Y., May 31, 1923, is a prominent figure in the so-called hard-edge movement, which developed in New York in the late 1950s. He is best known for large paintings composed of brilliant monochrome areas of color juxtaposed with two or three precisely edged and intensely colored two-dimensional images. Underlying this formula is an effort to demonstrate that the image and the field are interchangeable elements that can be interpreted as either figure or ground—as positive or negative space. In 1966, Kelly did a series of monochrome paintings arranged in pairs and began experimenting with geometrically shaped canvases that play shape and color against color.

Kelly, Emmett An American circus clown, Emmett Kelly, b. Sedan, Kans., Dec. 9, 1898, d. Mar. 28, 1979, became famous as Weary Willie, a sad-faced hobo in ragged clothing. Kelly first created Willie as a cartoon character in 1920 and later assumed the role with the Ringling Brothers circus, on television, and in films and Broadway shows. In contrast to the traditional white-faced clown, the laughter Willie provoked was directed more at life's pitfalls than at its pratfalls.

Kelly, Gene A dancer, singer, and actor whose cheerful manner and innovative dance sequences enlivened some of Hollywood's most memorable musicals, Eugene Curran Kelly, b. Pittsburgh, Pa., Aug. 23, 1912, turned choreography into a virile, athletic American art. Synthesizing ballet with the tattoo of tap, the rhythms of jazz, and a sense of fun and grace, he was at his best in *The Pirate* (1948), *On the Town* (1949), *An American in Paris* (1951), *Singin' in the Rain* (1952), and *Brigadoon* (1954). Kelly has also directed films, including *Hello*

Gene Kelly, a leading Hollywood dancer and actor during the 1940s and '50s, displays his athletic dancing style in the classic street scene from Singin' in the Rain *(1952).*

Dolly (1969), and was a principal in the MGM reprise *That's Entertainment* (1974).

Kelly, Grace Grace, Princess of Monaco, b. Philadelphia, Nov. 12, 1929, as Grace Patricia Kelly, d. Sept. 14, 1982, first achieved fame as an American film star. She appeared in *High Noon* (1952) and *High Society* (1956) and won an Academy Award for her performance in *The Country Girl* (1954). Her cold beauty and aristocratic bearing were perhaps most successfully exploited in three Alfred Hitchcock thrillers—*Dial M for Murder* (1954), *Rear Window* (1954), and *To Catch a Thief* (1955). Grace Kelly's acting career ended when she married Prince Rainier III of Monaco in 1956, but she remained an international celebrity until her death following an automobile accident.

Kelly, Ned Edward "Ned" Kelly, b. June 1855, d. Nov. 11, 1880, was Australia's most notorious bushranger and folk hero. After serving time in prison for stealing horses, he was later hunted for killing three policemen in Victoria. The Kelly gang—Ned, his brother Dan, and two friends—took to the bush, seizing a sheep station, robbing two banks, and capturing a hotel. Encased in roughly made armor, they eventually fought it out with the police. His companions were killed, and Ned Kelly was captured and hanged in Melbourne.

Kelmscott Press see MORRIS, WILLIAM

kelp Kelps are any of a number of genera of seaweeds belonging to the brown algae, division Phaeophyta, order Laminariales. Kelps tend to grow in large, offshore beds in the temperate oceans. They vary in size from 0.5 m (1.65 ft) up to 60 m (198 ft). Most kelps have three basic parts: the holdfast, stipe, and blade. The holdfast is a basal growth that secures the kelp to its substrate. The blade is the large, laminar portion of the plant that is the principal location of photosynthesis. The stipe is the stemlike portion connecting the holdfast to the blade. Reproduction involves ALTERNATION OF GENERATIONS, with the sporophyte generation dominant.

Kelps are important sources of detritus in the marine food chain. They are a source of potash, iodine, and alginic acid. Alginic acid is used for treating latex in tire manufacturing, in paints, in ice cream, and as a filler for confections. Kelps are used extensively as a food in the Far East because of their high mineral and vitamin content.

kelpie [kel'-pee] The Australian kelpie is a breed of dog whose primary function today is that for which it was originally bred—herding sheep in Australia. The breed is descended from Scottish shepherd dogs, most probably border collies, sent to Australia about 1870, with the likely infusion of dingo blood during the early stages of its development. The kelpie grows to 50 cm (20 in) high at the shoulder and weighs about 18 kg (40 lb). Its short, straight, harsh coat is usually black or black and tan; red, brown, and bluish gray also occur. The breed is placed in the Miscellaneous Class by the American Kennel Club.

The Australian kelpie is a medium-sized dog used primarily for herding sheep in Australia. It is considered an excellent stock dog. The kelpie's ancestry most likely includes the border collie and possibly the dingo, a wild dog native to Australia.

Kelsey, Henry [kel'-see] Henry Kelsey, c.1667–1724, was an English explorer of the Canadian west. In 1684 he joined the Hudson's Bay Company and was stationed at York Factory on Hudson Bay. His many expeditions included one (1690–92) into what is now Saskatchewan, and Kelsey was probably the first white man to see the western prairies, bison, and grizzly bears. Appointed governor of all the company's Hudson Bay posts in 1718, he made two attempts (1719, 1721) to find the Northwest Passage before being recalled (1722) to England.

Kelvin, William Thomson, 1st Baron [kel'-vin] The thermodynamics studies of the Scottish physicist William Thomson, b. June 26, 1824, d. Dec. 17, 1907, led to his proposal (1848) of an absolute scale of TEMPERATURE. The Kelvin absolute temperature scale, developed later, derives its name from the title—Baron Kelvin of Largs— that he received from the British government in 1892. Thomson also observed (1852) what is now called the Joule-Thomson effect—the decrease in temperature of a gas when it expands in a vacuum.

Thomson served as professor of natural philosophy (1846–99) at the University of Glasgow. One of his first projects was to calculate the age of the Earth, based on the rate of cooling of the planet—assuming it had once been a piece of the Sun. (His result—20 to 400 million years—was far short of the current estimate of 4.5 billion years.) Greatly interested in the improvement of physical instrumentation, he designed and implemented many new devices.

Kelvin scale The Kelvin, or absolute temperature, scale is defined so that 0 K is absolute zero, the coldest theoretical temperature (−273.15° C/−459.67° F), at which the energy of motion of molecules is zero. Each absolute degree is equivalent to a Celsius degree, so that the freezing point of water (0° C/32° F) is 273.15 K, and its boiling point (100° C/212° F) is 100° higher, or 373.15 K. The scale is named for the physicist William Thomson, 1st Baron of Kelvin, who first proposed an absolute temperature scale.

Kemble (family) [kem'-bul] Son of an itinerant actor-manager, **John Philip Kemble**, b. Feb. 11, 1757, d. Feb. 26, 1823, first appeared on the London stage in 1783 and was considered England's leading actor of his time. With his sister Sarah SIDDONS he practiced the "classical style." As manager (1803–17) of the Covent Garden, he turned it into the English-speaking world's leading theater. Faced with financial problems and Edmund KEAN's rivalry, he retired in 1817. His brother **Charles Kemble**, b. Nov. 25, 1775, d. Nov. 12, 1854, a noted Shakespearean actor, managed Covent Garden from 1817 to 1832, encouraging the use of historically accurate costumes and scenery.

Charles Kemble's eldest daughter, the beautiful **Fanny (Frances) Kemble**, b. Nov. 27, 1809, d. Jan. 15, 1893, was interested in a literary career but became an actress at Covent Garden in 1829, when her father was threatened with bankruptcy. Her three years there temporarily brought back the theater's prosperity, as she proved to be an accomplished comedic and tragic actress. She married the owner of a plantation in the United States; her *Journal of a Residence on a Georgian Plantation in 1838–1839* (1863) later gained fame for its harrowing account of slave life. Divorced, she resumed her career as a writer of plays, journals, and poems.

Kemp, Jack Jack French Kemp, b. Los Angeles, July 13, 1935, served in Congress (1971–89) as a Republican from upstate New York and then (1989–   ) as U.S. secretary of housing and urban development. He graduated (1957) from Occidental College and was a professional football quarterback for 13 years, becoming active in Republican politics. Kemp gained national prominence by championing supply-side economics. He ran unsuccessfully for his party's presidential nomination in 1988.

Kendall, Amos [ken'-dul] An influential American journalist, Amos Kendall, b. Dunstable, Mass., Aug. 16, 1789, d. Nov. 12, 1869, was a Democratic political figure for nearly 40 years. Kendall migrated to Kentucky, where he edited *Argus of Western America*, published in Frankfort. Breaking his allegiance to Henry Clay, Kendall campaigned for Andrew Jackson's election to the presidency in 1828. He became a leading member of Jackson's informal KITCHEN CABINET and reputedly wrote a number of Jackson's state papers. After serving as auditor of the Treasury, Kendall was postmaster general (1835–40) and instituted the pony-express service, originally between New York and Philadelphia, and the money-order system.

kendo see MARTIAL ARTS

Kennan, George F. [ken'-uhn] George Frost Kennan, b. Milwaukee, Wis., Feb. 16, 1904, a scholar and former U.S. diplomat, was known for advocating the policy of "containment" of Soviet expansionism. After graduating (1925) from Princeton University he entered the foreign service and became an expert on Russian affairs.

In an influential article in *Foreign Affairs* in 1947, Kennan called for the application of counterforce to contain the Soviet Union. Although this remained U.S. policy toward the USSR for decades, Kennan himself eventually turned away from U.S. COLD WAR policies; he opposed the Vietnam War. He had served briefly (1952) as U.S. ambassador to Moscow, then joined the Institute for Advanced Study in Princeton, N.J. He was also ambassador to Yugoslavia in 1961–63. Author of numerous works on history and foreign relations, including *American Diplomacy* (1951; rev. ed., 1985), Kennan published *Sketches from a Life* in 1989.

Kennedy (family) The Kennedy family of Massachusetts has achieved a prominence in American political life comparable only to that of the Adams family in the late 18th and early 19th centuries. In 1960, John F. KENNEDY was elected president of the United States. His term in office was cut short by assassination in November 1963, and the same fate befell his brother Robert F. KENNEDY when he campaigned for the Democratic nomination for the presidency in 1968. A third brother, Edward M. KENNEDY, remains an influential figure in the Democratic party.

The Kennedys, one of the most influential families in the American political arena, convened for a portrait photograph on Nov. 9, 1960, the day after John Fitzgerald Kennedy (standing, center) won election to the presidency.

These brothers came from a family of nine, the children of **Joseph Patrick Kennedy**, b. Sept. 6, 1888, d. Nov. 18, 1969, and **Rose Fitzgerald Kennedy**, b. July 22, 1890. The son of a Boston saloonkeeper turned politician, Joe Kennedy graduated from Harvard in 1912 and married (1914) Rose Fitzgerald, daughter of a mayor of Boston. A bank president at the age of 25, he made a fortune by investment in stocks, importing, shipbuilding, and moviemaking. He became chairman (1934–35) of the newly created Securities and Exchange Commission, head (1937) of the U.S. Maritime Commission, and then U.S. ambassador to Britain (1937–40). As ambassador he became known as an isolationist and a pessimist about Britain's chances of resisting Nazi German conquest.

Although Joe Kennedy never ran for elective office, he and his wife had great ambitions for their children. Set against a record of extraordinary talent and accomplishment, however, is a haunting recurrence of tragedy. The oldest son, Joseph P. Jr. (1915–44), was killed in wartime service over England. Rosemary (b. 1918), the oldest daughter, was mentally retarded. The next daughter, Kathleen (1920–48), died in an airplane crash in Europe. The assassinations of John, who had fulfilled his family's political ambition, and then of Robert, who inherited his mantle, continued the pattern of tragedy. The youngest of this generation is Edward Kennedy. The three other Kennedys of the same generation are Eunice (b. 1921), who married Sargent SHRIVER, director of the Peace Corps (1961–66) and ambassador to France (1968–70); Patricia (b. 1924), who was for a time married to the actor Peter Lawford; and Jean (b. 1928), who married businessman Stephen Smith.

The 28 cousins of the next generation—the children of John, Eunice, Patricia, Robert, Jean, and Edward—have shown promise but have also shared grief. In 1986, Robert's son Joseph II was elected to Congress from Massachusetts. Edward Jr. lost a leg to bone cancer in 1973, however, and Robert's son David died in 1984 of multiple-drug ingestion.

Kennedy, Anthony M.   Anthony McLeod Kennedy, b. Sacramento, Calif., July 23, 1936, was appointed to the U.S. Supreme Court by President Reagan on Nov. 11, 1987, and sworn in on Feb. 18, 1988. A graduate of Stanford University (1958) and Harvard Law School (1961), Kennedy had served 12 years as a U.S. Court of Appeals judge, acquiring a reputation as a legal conservative.

Kennedy, Cape   see CAPE CANAVERAL

Kennedy, Edward M.   Brother of President John F. Kennedy and U.S. senator Robert F. Kennedy, Edward Moore Kennedy, b. Boston, Feb. 22, 1932, is a leader of the liberal Democrats in the U.S. Senate. He entered Harvard, as had his brothers, but was suspended for cheating on an examination. After serving two years in the armed forces, he returned to Harvard and received his degree in 1956. With his brother John in the White House, "Teddy" was elected to John's Senate seat in 1962.

Ted Kennedy suffered a major political setback in the summer of 1969, when he drove his car off a bridge on Chappaquiddick Island, Mass. His companion, 28-year-old Mary Jo Kopechne, was drowned. He was later found guilty of leaving the scene of an accident; his explanations of the tragedy were unconvincing to many. Despite the accident, he was regularly reelected to the Senate. Although considered a strong potential contender for the Democratic presidential nomination, Kennedy declined to seek the nomination until 1980, when he challenged the incumbent, Jimmy Carter. Defeated by Carter in most of the primaries, Kennedy nonetheless remained in the race until the convention in August nominated Carter.

Kennedy, John F.   John Fitzgerald Kennedy, the 35th president of the United States (1961–63), was, at the age of 43, the youngest person and the first Roman Catholic ever elected to the presidency. His assassination in Dallas, Tex., in November 1963 provoked outrage and widespread mourning.

Early Life. Kennedy was born in Brookline, Mass., on May 29, 1917, a descendant of Irish Catholics who had immigrated to America in the 19th century. His father, Joseph P. Kennedy, was a combative businessman who became a multimillionaire, head of the Securities and Exchange Commission, and ambassador to Great Britain (see KENNEDY family).

Kennedy graduated from Choate School in Wallingford, Conn., briefly attended Princeton University, and then entered Harvard University in 1936. At Harvard he wrote an honors thesis on British foreign policies in the 1930s; it was published in 1940, the year he graduated, under the title *Why England Slept*. In 1941, shortly before the United States entered World War II, Kennedy joined the U.S. Navy. While on active duty in the Pacific in 1943, the boat he commanded—PT 109—was sunk by the Japanese. Kennedy performed heroically in rescuing his crew, but he aggravated an old back injury and

AT A GLANCE

JOHN FITZGERALD KENNEDY
35th President of the United States (1961–63)

Nicknames: "JFK"; "Jack"

Born: May 29, 1917, Brookline, Mass.

Education: Harvard College (graduated 1940)

Professions: Author, Public Official

Religious Affiliation: Roman Catholic

Marriage: Sept. 12, 1953, to Jacqueline Bouvier (1929–   )

Children: Caroline Bouvier Kennedy (1957–   ); John Fitzgerald Kennedy (1960–   ); Patrick Bouvier Kennedy (1963)

Political Affiliation: Democrat

Writings: *Why England Slept* (1940); *Profiles in Courage* (1956)

Died: Nov. 22, 1963, Dallas, Tex.

Buried: Arlington National Cemetery, Arlington, Va.

Vice-President: Lyndon Baines Johnson

contracted malaria. He was discharged in early 1945.

U.S. Representative and Senator. In 1946, Kennedy ran successfully for a Boston-based seat in the U.S. House of Representatives; he was reelected in 1948 and 1950. As a congressman he backed social legislation that benefited his working-class constituents. He also advocated a strong, anti-Communist foreign policy. In 1952, Kennedy challenged and defeated incumbent Republican senator Henry Cabot Lodge, Jr., and a year later, on Sept. 12, 1953, he married Jacqueline Bouvier (see ONASSIS, JACQUELINE BOUVIER KENNEDY).

Kennedy was a relatively ineffectual senator. During parts of 1954 and 1955 he was seriously ill with back ailments and therefore unable to play an important role in government. During his illness Kennedy worked on a book of biographical studies of American political heroes. Published in 1956 under the title *Profiles in Courage*, it won a Pulitzer Prize for biography in 1957. Like his earlier book on English foreign policy, it revealed his admiration for forceful political figures. This faith in activism was to become a hallmark of his presidency.

In 1956, Kennedy bid unsuccessfully for the Democratic vice-presidential nomination. Thereafter, he set his sights on the presidency. A cautious liberal on domestic issues, he backed a compromise civil rights bill in 1957 and devoted special efforts to labor legislation.

By 1960, Kennedy was but one of many Democratic aspirants for the party's presidential nomination. He put together, however, a well-financed, highly organized campaign and won on the first ballot. As a northerner and a Roman Catholic, he recognized his lack of strength in the South and shrewdly chose Sen. Lyndon B. JOHNSON of Texas as his running mate. Kennedy also performed well in a series of unprecedented television debates with his Republican opponent, Vice-President Richard M. NIXON. Kennedy promised tougher defense policies and progressive health, housing, and civil rights programs. His New Frontier, he pledged, would bring the nation out of its economic slump.

Presidency. Kennedy won the election, but by a narrow margin. He lacked reliable majorities in Congress. Primarily for these reasons, most of his domestic policies stalled on Capitol Hill. When advocates of racial justice picked up strength in 1962–63, he moved belatedly to promote civil rights legislation (see CIVIL RIGHTS ACTS). He also sought a tax cut to stimulate the economy. At the time of his assassination, however, these and other programs such as federal aid to education and MEDICARE remained tied up in Congress. It was left to his successor, President Johnson, to push this legislation through the more compliant congresses of 1964 and 1965.

Kennedy's eloquent inaugural address—in which he

exhorted the nation: "Ask not what your country can do for you—ask what you can do for your country"—sounded cold-war themes. Soon thereafter, the president acted on his anti-Communism by lending American military assistance to the BAY OF PIGS INVASION of Cuba in April 1961—and then took the blame for its total failure. Later in his administration he tried to diminish anti-Americanism in the Western Hemisphere by backing development projects under the Alliance for Progress, but the small sums involved had little impact. The Peace Corps program was developed with similar goals in mind (see ACTION).

Kennedy's chief adversary abroad was the Soviet leader Nikita Khrushchev. As early as June 1961 the two men talked in Vienna, but the meeting served only to harden Soviet-American hostility. Khrushchev then threatened to sign a treaty with East Germany that would have given the East Germans control over western access routes to Berlin. Kennedy held firm, and no such treaty was signed. The Soviets responded, however, by erecting a wall between East and West Berlin. Kennedy used the crisis to request from Congress, and to receive, greatly increased appropriations for defense.

By far the tensest overseas confrontation of the Kennedy years occurred with the CUBAN MISSILE CRISIS. In October 1962, U.S. intelligence discovered that the Russians were constructing offensive missile sites in Cuba. In response Kennedy ordered a naval and air quarantine on shipments of offensive weapons to Cuba. At first armed conflict seemed likely, but the Soviets pulled back and promised not to set up the missiles. The United States then said it would not attack Cuba.

As if chastened by this crisis, the most frightening of the cold war, the Soviets and Americans in 1963 signed a treaty barring atmospheric testing of nuclear weapons. Kennedy nevertheless remained as ready as before to stop Communist advances. He continued to bolster American defenses and stepped up military aid to South Vietnam, where revolutionary forces were increasingly active. By November 1963, the United States had sent about 16,000 military personnel to Vietnam. His administration also intervened in South Vietnamese politics by at least conniving at the overthrow of Ngo Dinh Diem in November 1963.

Assassination. While driving in a motorcade through Dallas, Tex., on November 22, 1963, Kennedy was shot in the head and died within an hour. President Johnson appointed the WARREN COMMISSION to investigate the assassination. It concluded that the killer, acting alone, was 24-year-old Lee Harvey OSWALD. No motive was established. Speculation about the assassination persisted, however. In 1978 a special Congressional committee concluded that "probably" Kennedy had been the victim of a conspiracy but that Oswald was the killer.

Kennedy, Robert F.   Robert Francis ("Bobby") Kennedy, b. Brookline, Mass., Nov. 20, 1925, d. June 6, 1968, younger brother of U.S. President John F. Kennedy, was U.S. attorney general (1961–64) and a U.S. senator (1965–68). Like his brother, he was assassinated.

Robert F. Kennedy served as attorney general of the United States during the presidency of his brother John F. Kennedy. Later he became (1965) a U.S. senator from New York, and in 1968 he campaigned for the Democratic nomination for president. On the night of his victory in the California primary, however, he was assassinated.

A 1951 graduate of the University of Virginia Law School, Kennedy was first a Justice Department lawyer and then the manager of his older brother's 1952 senatorial campaign. He became an assistant counsel to Sen. Joseph McCARTHY's Permanent Investigations Subcommittee in 1953. With one interruption to protest McCarthy's methods, he worked for the panel into 1956. From 1957 to 1959 Kennedy was chief counsel for the Senate Rackets Committee and exposed the underworld connections of Teamsters Union officials James Hoffa and Dave Beck.

In 1960, Bobby managed the presidential campaign of John Kennedy, earning a reputation for considerable ruthlessness as well as skill. Appointed attorney general in his brother's administration, he stressed civil rights enforcement and a drive against organized crime. He was subsequently criticized for his extensive use of wiretaps, including one on Martin Luther King, Jr. Kennedy was also a close advisor to his brother.

After President Lyndon B. Johnson declined to choose Kennedy as his 1964 running mate, the attorney general resigned and won a U.S. Senate seat from New York. He focused increasingly on the needs of poor minorities and, beginning in 1966, became a sharp critic of the Vietnam War. In March 1968, Kennedy announced his candidacy for the Democratic presidential nomination. On the night (June 4–5) of his victory in the California primary, however, Kennedy was fatally shot. His assassin, an immigrant from Jordan named Sirhan B. Sirhan, was arrested at the scene and later convicted of first-degree murder.

Kennedy, William   The American writer William Joseph Kennedy, b. Albany, N.Y., Jan. 16, 1928, has received critical acclaim for realistic fiction infused with an essentially comic spirit. In the novels *The Ink Truck* (1969), *Legs* (1975), *Billy Phelan's Greatest Game* (1978), *Ironweed* (1983; Pulitzer Prize; film, 1987), and *Quinn's Book* (1988), Kennedy evokes a powerful sense of time (1930s) and place (Albany) through fresh, vibrant language, an acute feel for setting, and a marvelous ear for conversation. Kennedy also writes short stories and has published a volume of essays, *O Albany!* (1983).

Kennedy Center for the Performing Arts

The John F. Kennedy Center for the Performing Arts, in Washington, D.C., was created by an act of Congress as a memorial to the slain president. The center officially opened on Sept. 8, 1971, with the world premiere of Leonard Bernstein's *Mass*. The center was financed by the federal government as well as by private and corporate contributions, and was furnished in part by generous gifts from countries thoughout the world. With a concert hall, opera house, several theaters, restaurants, and various spaces for exhibitions and conferences, the center has become a national cultural institution. The Performing Arts Library of the Library of Congress and the American Film Institute also operate from the center.

In 1983 the AMERICAN NATIONAL THEATER AND ACADEMY (ANTA) founded the American National Theater Company, which offered productions of new works until it was dissolved in 1986.

Kennedy Space Center

Kennedy Space Center (KSC) is the chief civilian space launch facility in the United States. It is located adjacent to Cape Canaveral Air Force Station at Cape Canaveral, Fla. The center began operation in 1951 as the Experimental Missile Firing Branch of the Army Ordnance Guided Missile Center in Huntsville, Ala. In 1960 these became, respectively, the Launch Operations Directorate and the Marshall Space Flight Center. The directorate was made the independent launch operations center in July 1962 and was renamed in 1963 for President John F. Kennedy, who had committed the United States to landing astronauts on the Moon before 1970.

Because of this commitment, larger space launch facilities were built on nearby Merritt Island and were incorporated as part of the space center in July 1965. New facilities, called Launch Complex 39, included a vehicle assembly building for vertical assembly of the SATURN V rocket, two launch pads, and a launch control center. A complex for administrative and operational support was also built.

In addition to sending men to the Moon and orbiting the first U.S. space station, Kennedy Space Center is responsible for smaller civilian launches that must use air force launch pads at the cape. The center was designated (1973) as the eastern launch site for the reusable SPACE SHUTTLE.

Kenosha

[kin-oh'-shuh]   Kenosha, the seat of Kenosha County, is a city in southeastern Wisconsin on Lake Michigan at the Pike River estuary. It has a population of 80,352 (1990). A manufacturing city of automobiles, metal parts, and furniture, it is also an important port on the St. Lawrence Seaway. Kenosha is the site of Carthage College (1847) and the University of Wisconsin Parkside

campus (1965). The city was founded in 1835; its name means "pike" in Potawatomi dialect.

Kensett, John Frederick

[ken'-set]   The American painter John Frederick Kensett, b. Cheshire, Conn., Mar. 22, 1816, d. Dec. 14, 1872, belonged to the HUDSON RIVER SCHOOL and was an important exponent of LUMINISM. He was trained as an engraver. In his early paintings Kensett used thick brushstrokes to depict dense forest scenes. By the mid-1850s, however, he was concentrating on typical Hudson River–school compositions in which broad expanses of shore, water, and sky are viewed from a height. The atmospheric haze enveloping these vistas produces the subdued and delicate color effects that are Kensett's trademark. The poetic rendering of fall colors in his *View Near Cozzens Hotel from West Point* (1863; New-York Historical Society, New York City) exemplifies his technical mastery, as does the limpid, almost magically still surface of the water in his *Lake George* (1869; Metropolitan Museum of Art, New York City).

Kent

Kent is a county in southeastern England on the English Channel. Its area is 3,711 km^2 (1,433 mi^2), and its population is 1,520,400 (1988 est.). Maidstone is the county town. The relief of Kent is dominated by the North Downs—long, low, chalk hills culminating in the white cliffs of DOVER. The rivers Thames, Medway, and Stour flow through the county.

Shipping is an important part of Kent's economy; ports are at Dover and Folkstone. Fruits (apples and cherries), hops and other grains, and truck-farm crops for London are grown. Grazing land for sheep and cattle is extensive. Paper, heavy machinery, cement, and chemicals are manufactured, and petroleum is refined on the Isle of Grain. Many resorts are located along the coast. Because of Kent's proximity to London, many of the towns are commuting suburbs. CANTERBURY is the seat of the primate of the Church of England.

Because of Kent's coastal location, it has been the site of many invasions into Britain, including those of the Romans (AD 43) and the Saxons and Jutes (5th century). The Jutes established the independent kingdom of Kent (5th–7th century). In 1170, Archbishop Thomas BECKET was murdered in Canterbury Cathedral, which became a major pilgrimage center during the Middle Ages. (See CANTERBURY TALES, THE.)

Kent, James

James Kent, b. near Brewster, N.Y., July 31, 1763, d. Dec. 12, 1847, was a U.S. jurist whose *Commentaries on American Law* (4 vols., 1826–30) made him known as "the American Blackstone." After graduating from Yale University, he studied law and was admitted to the bar in 1785. He practiced law in Poughkeepsie, N.Y., and then taught law at Columbia College, New York City, from 1794 to 1798. In 1798 he was appointed to the New York Supreme Court, becoming chief judge in 1804. In 1814 he was made chancellor of the

New York Court of Chancery, where his opinions contributed to development of the law of equity in the United States.

Kent, Rockwell   Rockwell Kent, b. Tarrytown Heights, N.Y., June 21, 1882, d. Mar. 13, 1971, was an American painter, printmaker, and writer whose theme was the vastness and grandeur of nature, and often the heroic loneliness of humans before it, as seen in *The Road Roller* (1909; Phillips Collection, Washington, D.C.). As a printmaker, Kent favored wood engravings; his style used marked contrasts of light and dark for dramatic effect, as in his *Northern Night* (1930; one version, Philadelphia Museum of Art). Kent is best known as the illustrator of numerous books, including a special edition (1930) of Herman Melville's *Moby-Dick*.

Kent, William   William Kent, b. *c.*1685, d. Apr. 12, 1748, was an English architect, decorator, and landscape gardener. As a landscapist he created the first English landscape garden at Stowe in Buckinghamshire; as a building architect he continued the neo-Palladian style (see Andrea PALLADIO) initiated by Inigo JONES. On a trip (1709–19) to Italy Kent met the architect Richard Boyle, 3d earl of BURLINGTON, who on returning to England employed Kent as a painter, furniture designer, and decorator. Their most notable collaboration was Chiswick House (begun 1725) in London. A neo-Palladian preoccupation with symmetrical design marks Kent's masterpiece, Holkham Hall, Norfolk (begun 1734), as well as his major architectural works.

Kentucky   Kentucky presents a mixture of both the Midwest and the South. The northern, more urban portion of the state, particularly the Ohio Valley corridor, is characterized by manufacturing and is oriented to the Midwest. Southern Kentucky tends to be rural in nature, concentrating on agriculture and mining; it is generally associated with the South. The state's abundant natural resources, scenic beauty, historic treasures, and proud people contrast with Kentucky's problems of poverty, poor housing, and low levels of education.

Kentucky is centrally located within the eastern United States, bordered by the seven states of Illinois, Indiana, Ohio, West Virginia, Virginia, Tennessee, and Missouri. Kentucky was once an Indian hunting ground. The name is believed to come from an Indian word meaning "prairie." White men had explored the area by 1750, but

---

AT A GLANCE

KENTUCKY

Land: Area: 104,665 km² (40,411 mi²); rank: 37th. Capital: Frankfort (1990 pop., 25,968). Largest city: Louisville (1990 pop., 269,063). Counties: 120. Elevations: highest—1,262 m (4,139 ft), at Black Mountain; lowest—78 m (257 ft), at the Mississippi River.

People: Population (1990): 3,698,969; rank: 23d; density: 35.2 persons per km² (91.2 per mi²). Distribution (1990): 51.8% urban, 48.2% rural. Average annual change (1980–90): +0.1%.

Government (1993): Governor: Brereton C. Jones, Democrat. U.S. Congress: Senate—1 Democrat, 1 Republican; House—4 Democrats, 2 Republicans. Electoral college votes: 8. State legislature: 38 senators, 100 representatives.

Economy: State personal income (1989): $51.2 billion; rank: 26th. Median family income (1989): $27,028; rank: 46th. Agriculture: income (1989)—$2.9 billion. Lumber production (1991): 553 million board feet. Mining (nonfuel): value (1988)—$345 million. Manufacturing: value added (1987)—$18 billion. Services: value (1987)—$9.9 billion.

Miscellany: Statehood: June 1, 1792; the 15th state. Nickname: Bluegrass State; tree: Kentucky coffee tree; motto: United We Stand, Divided We Fall; song: "My Old Kentucky Home."

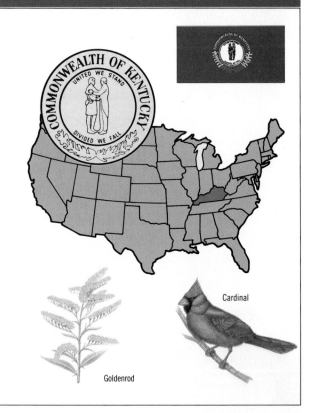

Cardinal

Goldenrod

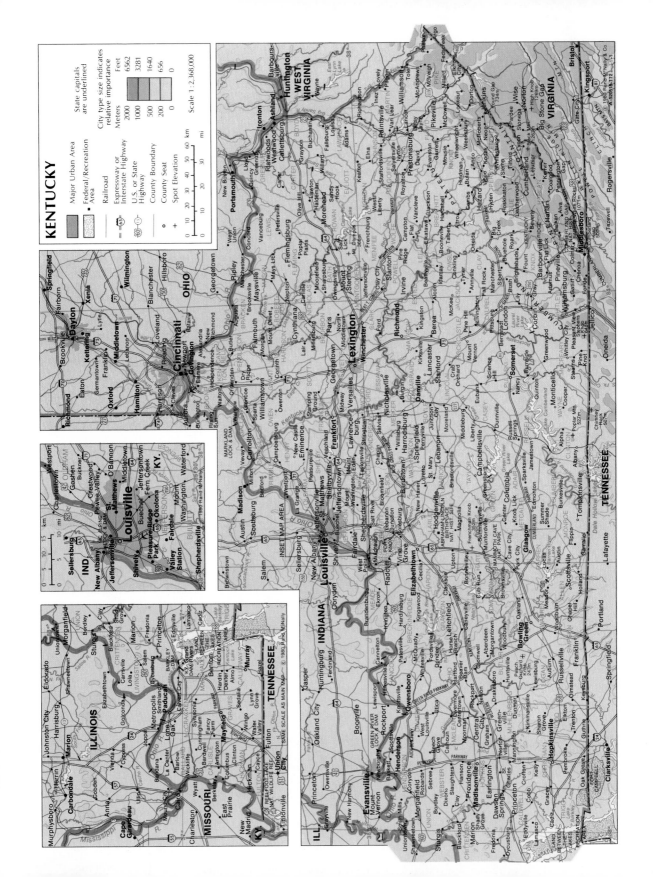

the first permanent settlement was not established until 1774 in Harrodsburg. In 1792, Kentucky separated from Virginia to become the 15th state.

Land

Kentucky shows diversity in its terrain. Considerable areas of plains, many hills, and a limited mountainous area in southeastern Kentucky, the highest part of the state, can be found in the state. Elevations generally decrease to the west and north, varying from 610 to 914 m (2,000 to 3,000 ft) in the southeast to between 122 and 183 m (400 and 600 ft) in the northwest and 396 m (1,300 ft) in the north. The highest point is Black Mountain, 1,262 m (4,139 ft), located near the Virginia border; the lowest elevation, 78 m (257 ft), is the Mississippi River along the state's western tip.

The state may be divided into six regions. The Pennyroyal region, named for a type of mint native to the area, is a flat-to-rolling limestone agricultural area at the heart of Kentucky. It extends nearly two-thirds of the distance across the state and accounts for about 30% of the total area.

To the east of the Pennyroyal, the Eastern Mountain and Coalfield claims more than 25% of the land. This part of the state, Kentucky's Appalachia, is characterized by vast coal resources, rugged terrain, and widespread poverty. North of the Pennyroyal is the Knobs, a narrow crescent-shaped belt of conical hills containing less than 10% of Kentucky's area. It surrounds the limestone-based Bluegrass region, centered on Lexington. The Bluegrass region covers about one-fifth of the state along the Ohio River. It is famous for its horse farms, tobacco, and cattle.

The Western Coalfield, more than 10% of the state, is a relatively rolling sandstone and shale area west of the Pennyroyal where agriculture and area stripping of coal takes place. To its west, the Jackson Purchase, 6% of Kentucky, is that region lying west of the Tennessee River which was bought from the Chickasaw Indians in 1818 by Andrew Jackson and former governor Isaac Shelby. It is characterized by large farms developed on unconsolidated floodplain deposits.

The state is geologically simple: rocks are sedimentary and consist primarily of limestones, sandstones, and shales. Rocks vary in age from the recent (less than 10,000 years) in the Jackson Purchase to more than 420 million years, found in the Ordovician limestones of the Bluegrass.

Soils are primarily woodland residual, but extensive areas possess alluvial and aeolian, or wind-borne, soils. The most fertile soils are associated with alluvial deposits along the Mississippi and Ohio rivers and their tributaries. The poorest soils are in the coalfield regions.

Climate. The climate is moderate but variable. Kentucky's weather is influenced by warm air from the Gulf of Mexico in summer and by cyclonic storms during winter. The west is slightly warmer than the east in summer, and the south is marginally warmer than the north in winter. Summer temperatures range from highs of 33° C (92° F) to lows of 17° C (62° F). Winter highs average 10° C (50° F) and lows −3° C (26° F).

Annual precipitation decreases from south to north, with northern Kentucky receiving an average of 1,016 mm (40 in) and southern Kentucky more than 1,270 mm (50 in). Much of the state's rainfall occurs between March and June. Severe storms can occur any time of the year but are most common from March to September. Kentucky averages six tornadoes yearly.

Cumberland Gap is a natural passageway through the scenic Cumberland Mountains of the Appalachians. Daniel Boone, with a group of pioneers, built (1775) the Wilderness Road through the gap, creating a route for western-bound settlers.

Drainage. Three streams mark Kentucky's western, northern, and eastern boundaries: the MISSISSIPPI, OHIO, and Big Sandy rivers. Other important streams include the CUMBERLAND, TENNESSEE, Green, Kentucky, Licking, and Salt rivers. Virtually all of Kentucky's streams flow from the south or southeast to the north or northeast and into the Ohio River.

Kentucky's best-known lakes include Cumberland (205 km²/79 mi²), Kentucky (194 km²/75 mi²), and Barkley (184 km²/71 mi²). Lakes Cumberland and Barkley were formed by damming the Cumberland River, while Kentucky Lake was formed on the Tennessee and is part of the TENNESSEE VALLEY AUTHORITY. The state's best-known natural water body is Reelfoot Lake, formed as a result of an 1811 earthquake. The most productive groundwater areas are in the Jackson Purchase, in the Ohio River floodplain, and in the Pennyroyal.

Vegetation and Wildlife. The state is about 48% tree covered. Dominant trees include oak, tulip poplar, hickory, beech, buckeye, maple, pine, cedar, and hemlock. Animal life consists largely of deer, rabbit, squirrel, opossum, raccoon, skunk, woodchuck, snake, and quail. Fish include crappie, bass, perch, catfish, and darters.

Resources. Kentucky's most abundant natural resources include reserves of bituminous coal, limestone, sand and gravel, and water and forest resources. Also present are reserves of natural gas, petroleum, oil shale, clay, and fluorspar.

People

Kentucky's population grew by more than the national average in the decade between 1970 and 1980, from 1980 to 1990, however, the growth rate was only 1%, far below the 10.2% for the nation as a whole. The farm population continues to decrease.

Kentucky has a relatively large rural and small-town population. Few cities are of significant size. The state has two large cities, LOUISVILLE and LEXINGTON, and one other city with a population in excess of 50,000—OWENSBORO. A number of other cities have more than 20,000 people, including Covington, Bowling Green, PADUCAH, Hopkinsville, Ashland, FRANKFORT, and Henderson.

The state's population is mostly white. African Americans form the largest nonwhite group, followed by persons of Spanish origin, who account for less than 1% of the state's population; Asian and Pacific Islanders; and American Indians. Of the state's foreign-born residents, most originated from Germany, the United Kingdom, Italy, and Canada.

Baptists constitute the largest religious group. Other large denominations are the Roman Catholics, Presbyterians, Methodists, and Disciples of Christ.

Education. Kentucky's first school opened in Harrodsburg in 1775, and the public school system was established in 1838. Higher education can be traced to the 1780 chartering of Transylvania Seminary, now Transylvania University. The state's largest school, the University of Kentucky, dates to 1865. The Kentucky community-college system, administered by the University of Kentucky, has branches located in several cities. In addition

Kentucky tobacco is as famous as Kentucky horses. The state ranks second after North Carolina in tobacco production.

to the state schools, a number of private institutions of higher education are located in Kentucky.

Many public libraries, along with college and specialized libraries, serve Kentucky. The largest library collections are found at the University of Kentucky, the University of Louisville, the Kentucky State Library, and the Louisville Public Libraries.

Culture. The J. B. Speed Art Museum is in Louisville. Examples of unique museums in the state include the John James Audubon Museum in Henderson and the Kentucky Derby Museum in Louisville. The state's three principal symphony orchestras are located in Louisville, Lexington, and Owensboro. One opera company and one resident theater are located in Louisville, and ballet companies are headquartered in Lexington and Louisville.

Historical Sites. Federal, state, and local historic attractions total about 2,000. Some of the more significant include reconstructed forts Harrod and Boonesboro; Cumberland Gap; the Abraham Lincoln and Jefferson Davis birthplaces; Ashland, home of Henry Clay; Federal Hill, known as Stephen Foster's "My Old Kentucky Home"; and the communities of Danville and Frankfort, the state capital.

Communications. Kentucky has a number of daily newspapers, including the influential *Louisville Courier-Journal*. There are also commercial television and radio stations and an educational television system in the state.

Economy

Manufacturing contributes far more to Kentucky's economy than agriculture and mining combined. Agriculture is

Many of the finest Thoroughbreds, standardbreds, and saddle horses in the United States have been bred in Kentucky. Most of the horse farms are located near Lexington in the Bluegrass region.

still important to the state, and Kentucky ranks among the leading U.S. states in the production of tobacco. Eastern Kentucky is highly dependent on coal mining and is the poorest region of the state. Beginning in the 1960s both the state and federal governments established poverty-combating programs in Kentucky's Appalachian region, but income has remained lower and unemployment higher in that area than elsewhere in the state.

Agriculture. Kentucky's agriculture is confined generally to the western two-thirds of the state. By far the most valuable crop is tobacco—primarily burley; the crop is grown in almost every county in the state. Also significant are corn, soybeans, and hay. Livestock is dominated by cattle with associated dairy products, hogs, horses, and poultry. Although Kentucky is a leader in hardwood production, forestry contributes relatively little to the state's economy except on a local level in eastern and southern Kentucky.

Mining. The only state with two distinct coalfields—the Appalachian in eastern Kentucky and the Eastern Interior in western Kentucky—Kentucky is the nation's leading bituminous-coal–producing state. Other leading mineral activities, by value of production, include stone, petroleum, natural gas, sand and gravel, and clay.

Manufacturing. Manufacturing in Kentucky is dominant along the Ohio River corridor between the Ashland-Catlettsburg area in northeastern Kentucky and the Paducah–Calvert City area in the extreme western part of the state. An additional manufacturing area is in Lexington. Louisville is the state's principal center of manufacturing; other important industrial cities are Owensboro and the Newport-Covington area. The leading types of manufacturing include metals (steel and aluminum), machinery, transportation equipment, chemicals, food (including Bourbon whiskey and other alcoholic beverages), tobacco products, and lumber and wood products.

Tourism. Four federal parks lie wholly or partly within the state: Mammoth Cave National Park, Cumberland Gap National Historical Park, Abraham Lincoln Birthplace National Historic Site, and Land Between the Lakes National Recreation Area. The Kentucky state park system supervises 17 areas, the newest of which is Kentucky Horse Park, near Lexington. Breaks Interstate Park is jointly operated by Kentucky and Virginia. Six areas are significant to tourism: the Kentucky and Barkley lakes area, the Mammoth Cave area, scattered locations in and near Daniel Boone National Forest, the Lake Cumberland area, Lexington and the Bluegrass area, and Louisville. The state has three Thoroughbred and four standardbred, or harness, racetracks. The best known include the Thoroughbred tracks at Churchill Downs in Louisville, site of the KENTUCKY DERBY, and Keeneland Race Course in Lexington, one of the country's most beautiful racing facilities. Also popular is the historic Red Mile in Lexington, site of many record-setting harness races. Rupp Arena, the nation's largest college basketball facility, is in Lexington.

Transportation. Kentucky has 112,651 km (70,000 mi) of highways. An extensive system of toll roads also crosses the state. Local roads, however, are considered poor when compared with those of adjacent states. The Mississippi and Ohio rivers and intrastate rivers provide 2,575 km (1,600 mi) of navigable waterway. In addition, 5,954 km (3,700 mi) of railroad track cross the state, and scheduled flights are provided to seven major airports. In all, 67 airports, including Greater Cincinnati International Airport in northern Kentucky and Standiford Field in Louisville, service the state.

Energy. Kentucky, with coal reserves presently estimated at 66 billion tons, will play a nationally important energy role in future years. At present coal provides more than 90% of the state's electric generating capacity. A total of 51 electric generating plants operate in the state; 33 are steam generating plants, 9 are hydroelectric plants, and 9 are internal-combustion plants. Kentucky has no nuclear generating plants.

Government and Politics

Kentucky is organized as a commonwealth rather than a state and operates under its fourth constitution, adopted in 1891. The governor is elected to a 4-year term. The legislature consists of 38 senators, elected for 4 years, and 100 representatives, elected for 2 years. The judiciary is composed of one court of justice, which, in turn, is composed of four courts: supreme, appeals, circuit, and district.

Kentucky has 120 counties, a number exceeded only by Texas and Georgia. Counties are governed by a fiscal court, composed of an elected judge-executive, who serves as county administrator, and three or more magistrates. Recently a new legal entity was approved by the legislature that permitted the city of Lexington and Fayette County to merge, thus forming a metropolitan government.

Politically, the state is dominated by Democrats, who have a two-to-one registration margin over Republicans.

Republican strength is greatest in a 15-county area in southeastern Kentucky.

Kentucky, "the Bourbon whiskey capital of the world," is conservative with the sale of alcoholic beverages. Of Kentucky's 120 counties, 84 totally prohibit alcoholic-beverage sales. These dry counties are located primarily in the rural, southern part of the state.

History

Indians established civilizations in Kentucky more than 13,000 years ago. When the first white people entered the area, it was being used as a hunting ground by the SHAWNEE and CHEROKEE Indians.

One of the early explorers, Dr. Thomas Walker, entered Kentucky after discovering Cumberland Gap in 1750. The gap provided a relatively easy route through the Cumberland Mountains, and in subsequent years countless explorers and settlers moved through it. One of the best-known explorers was the legendary Daniel BOONE, who arrived in 1767.

The first settlement of Fort Harrod, now known as Harrodsburg, was established by James Harrod in 1774. Boonesboro was settled in 1775 by Daniel Boone and his companions. Increased settlement brought pressures for statehood. The first constitution was approved in April 1792, and Kentucky became the 15th state on June 1, 1792. Frankfort was selected the state capital. The new state legislature adopted a strong STATE RIGHTS position when it adopted (1798) resolutions opposing the Alien and Sedition Acts (see KENTUCKY AND VIRGINIA RESOLUTIONS).

Between statehood and the Civil War, Kentucky increased its population from about 75,000 to more than 1 million. Slavery became the dominant social and political issue as the state expanded its farm production. An agricultural market downstream on the Mississippi River was assured by the Louisiana Purchase in 1803. The steamboat provided transportation on the Ohio River by 1815, and a rail system was developed before 1860.

A border state, Kentucky attempted to remain neutral during the Civil War but was unsuccessful because of its strategic location and the divided loyalties of its citizens. Farmers who used the Ohio and Mississippi rivers for transporting their produce wanted access to both waterways and the international port of New Orleans. If the South separated itself from the North, this free access would be impeded. On the other hand, influential plantation owners and state-rights advocates sided with the Confederacy. As a result, Kentuckians could be found in both Union and Confederate armies. Confederate forces invaded Kentucky in 1861. Most of the fighting within the state's boundaries, however, had ceased by 1863, after the Confederate army was driven out.

After the Civil War, the state changed economically and socially. Tobacco replaced hemp as the major agricultural crop. Coal mining was stimulated by the extension of rail lines into the coalfields of the eastern part of the state. Increased employment opportunities arose in manufacturing and services, and the major cities grew rapidly. After 1920 the state began a trend of marked decreases in rural population and growth in urban areas.

From World War II to the present, Kentucky has changed with the nation. Certain internal events, however, have had a particular impact on Kentucky's historic development. A modern highway system of interstate routes and an extensive toll-road network connecting all parts of the state have been established. The creation of the Kentucky Program Development Office and the authorization for the 15 Area Development Districts, beginning in 1968, showed serious efforts to plan for the state's future. Aggressive state involvement with industrial development and stimulation of tourism was begun. The state joined in the formation of the Appalachian Regional Commission in 1965 and obtained assistance from the Tennessee Valley Authority in the western part of the state. Higher education was upgraded through the creation of regional universities and community colleges. The state's judicial system was revamped in 1976, and the long-established pattern of out-migration appears to have been reversed recently.

In order to realize its potential, Kentucky must solve a number of problems: regional economic inequality; poor transportation in certain areas; widespread pollution, particularly with regard to the mining industry; and an agricultural base overly dependent on tobacco. Kentucky's future looks promising, however. Continued economic development is possible because of the state's advantages in energy, natural resources, transportation, water, scenery, and climate.

◼

Kentucky and Virginia Resolutions In 1798 the legislatures of Kentucky and Virginia adopted resolutions opposing the ALIEN AND SEDITION ACTS, which Congress, dominated by the FEDERALIST PARTY, had passed earlier in the year. The Democratic-Republicans (see DEMOCRATIC PARTY) regarded these acts as a dangerous denial of individual liberty. Although his authorship was not known at the time, Thomas JEFFERSON, then U.S. vice-president, had drafted (Nov. 16, 1798) the resolutions adopted in Kentucky, and James MADISON had authored Virginia's set (adopted Dec. 24, 1798).

The Kentucky Resolutions, the more radical of the two sets, declared specifically that the Alien and Sedition Acts were unconstitutional and that a state had the right to make that determination. An additional resolution passed by the Kentucky legislature in 1799 declared that formal NULLIFICATION was the proper remedy for a federal law that a state deemed unconstitutional. The Virginia Resolutions referred to the duty of a state to "interpose" its authority when the federal government assumed powers not granted by the Constitution. The resolutions were later viewed as the first significant statement of STATE RIGHTS.

◼

Kentucky coffee tree The Kentucky coffee tree, *Gymnocladus dioica*, is native to forests of the eastern United States—mostly west of the Appalachian Mountains. It is about 30 m (100 ft) in height and bears twice-compound leaves. Early settlers roasted the tree's seeds—contained in pods—as a coffee substitute.

Kentucky Derby   The Kentucky Derby, first run on May 17, 1875, is the most important and prestigious Thoroughbred horse race in the United States. Called "the run for the roses," it is held each year on the first Saturday in May at the 1-mi (1.6-km) Churchill Downs racetrack in Louisville, Ky.; it is the first and most acclaimed of the Triple Crown races (the others are the Preakness Stakes and Belmont Stakes). Each year more than 150,000 people attend this 1.25-mi (2-km) race for a field of up to about 20 three-year-old horses. Since the 1960s millions have watched the Derby on television. The winner's purse of some races has exceeded $500,000; the winner also receives a gold trophy. Some of the greatest racehorses in history have won the Derby: Sir Barton (1919), Gallant Fox (1930), War Admiral (1937), Whirlaway (1941), Citation (1948), Swaps (1955), Needles (1956), Secretariat (1973), Seattle Slew (1977), and Affirmed (1978).

Kenya [ken'-yuh]   Kenya, a republic of East Africa, is bordered by the Indian Ocean on the southeast, Somalia on the east, Ethiopia on the north, Sudan on the northwest, Uganda on the west, and Tanzania on the south. It is named for Mount KENYA, the highest point in the country and the second highest mountain in Africa. Kenya was a colony of Great Britain before becoming independent on Dec. 12, 1963.

Land and Resources

The only lowlands in Kenya are located in a narrow belt along the Indian Ocean. Inland are three upland areas, which include a belt of low plateaus in the east, the Kenya Highlands and the GREAT RIFT VALLEY in the west central regions, and the broad uplands of the Lake Victoria Basin in the west. The low eastern plateaus begin abruptly at the edge of the coastal plain and rise gradually westward to 1,525 m (5,000 ft) in the Yatta Plateau. West of the Yatta Plateau, the Kenya Highlands are divided by the spectacular tectonic trough of the eastern arm of the Great Rift Valley, which cuts across the highlands from north to south. The Kenya Highlands rise to more than 3,950 m (13,000 ft) in the Aberdare Range, which forms the steep eastern edge of the rift valley, and to more than 3,000 m (10,000 ft) in the Mau Escarpment, which forms the western edge; they rise to 5,199 m (17,058 ft) in Mount Kenya. The Great Rift Valley varies in width from about 50 to 65 km (31 to 40 mi), and the floor of the trough is 600 to 900 m (2,000 to 3,000 ft) below the surrounding landscape.

West of the highlands, elevations drop to about 1,200 m (4,000 ft) in the Lake Victoria Basin, which is part of a broad uplifted area between the eastern and western arms of the Great Rift Valley. The Lake Victoria Basin is composed of the Kericho Highlands in the south; the Nandi and Elgeyo plateaus in the north; the Kano Plain, on Lake VICTORIA's Kavirondo Gulf; and the Kisii and Luy-

AT A GLANCE

REPUBLIC OF KENYA

Land: Area: 582,646 km^2 (224,961 mi^2). Capital and largest city: Nairobi (1989 est. pop., 1,429,000).

People: Population (1990 est.): 24,639,261. Density: 42.3 persons per km^2 (109.5 per mi^2). Distribution (1986): 16% urban, 84% rural. Official language: Swahili. Major religions: traditional religions, Protestantism, Anglicanism, Roman Catholicism, Islam.

Government: Type: one-party state. Legislature: National Assembly. Political subdivisions: 7 provinces, Nairobi area.

Economy: GNP (1989 est.): $8.5 billion; $360 per capita. Labor distribution (1987): agriculture—78%; other—22%. Foreign trade (1988): imports—$1.8 billion; exports—$1.0 billion. Currency: 1 Kenya shilling = 100 cents.

Education and Health: Literacy (1985): 59% of adult population. Universities (1990): 4. Hospital beds (1987): 31,356. Physicians (1987) 3,071. Life expectancy (1990): women—67; men—62. Infant mortality (1990): 60 per 1,000 live births.

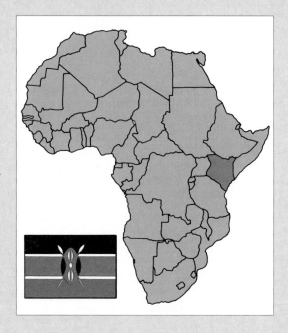

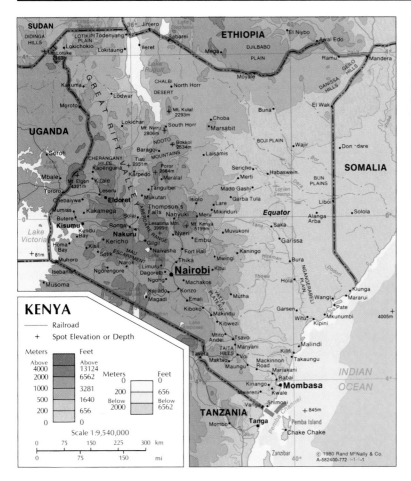

This large plantation on Kenya's coastal strip produces sisal, one of the nation's cash crops. Major agricultural exports include coffee, tea, and sugar.

la highlands, located to the south and north, respectively, of the Kavirondo Gulf.

Soils. Thin sandy soils cover about three-fourths of Kenya; because of dry climatic conditions, these soils are unsuitable or marginally suitable for agriculture. By contrast, the soils of the Lake Victoria Basin are generally of high agricultural potential, as are the rich volcanic soils of the Kenya Highlands.

Climate. Kenya's low-lying coastal plain has a humid equatorial type of climate characterized by little temperature variation from month to month. Inland the northern region has a semiarid climate with near-desert conditions in the drier areas. The higher inland regions receive more rainfall, and temperatures range from subtropical to temperate depending on elevation. The average annual temperature along the coast is 27° C (80° F), but in the Kenya Highlands it is only 14° C (57° F).

About three-fourths of Kenya is semiarid and receives less than 500 mm (20 in) of rain a year. Rainfall is greater in the narrow coastal belt near Mombasa and in the Kenya Highlands, where total precipitation varies from 900 to 1,525 mm (35 to 60 in). Most precipitation occurs during the rainy season from March to May.

Drainage. Kenya's principal river is the Tana. Western sections of Kenya are drained by the Nzoia and Kuja rivers. Lake Victoria, Lake RUDOLF, and other smaller lakes in the Great Rift Valley drain much of the interior.

Vegetation and Animal Life. Tropical savanna grasslands cover most of the low-altitude regions of Kenya; the savanna takes on a semidesert aspect in the dry northern areas. In the highlands, savanna predominates at lower altitudes, giving way to forest at higher elevations.

Herbivores, ranging in size from the small dik-dik to the eland, and carnivores, such as lions, leopards, and cheetahs, are abundant in Kenya, and large areas have been set aside as national parks and wildlife preserves. The principal national parks are Tsavo, Mount Kenya, Amboseli, and Aberdare. Poaching of protected species remains a major problem. Black rhinoceros, elephant, leopard, zebra, and giraffe populations are endangered despite a government ban on the sale of skins, tusks, and other hunting trophies.

People

Kenya's population is divided by language and culture into more than 40 different ethnic groups. The largest and traditionally the most important group politically is the KIKUYU. Other important Bantu-speaking peoples are the Kamba, the Luhya, and the Kisii. The Luo, a people of Nilotic origin, are the largest non-Bantu group. The second largest non-Bantu ethnic group comprises several tribes of Nilotic origin who have taken the name Kalenjin to indicate their common identity and cultural origins. The MASAI, a cattle-herding people, are also of Nilotic origin. Arabs and SWAHILI predominate in the coastal areas, and there are small numbers of nomadic Somali and Galla in northern sections of the nation. Several thousand Europeans and Asians live in Nairobi and other cities.

Language and Religion. Swahili, which became the official language of Kenya in 1974, is grammatically a Bantu language, although it is heavily influenced by Arabic and is written with the Roman alphabet. English is also an official language and is still widely used. Bantu and Nilo-Hamitic languages, consisting of numerous dialects associated with individual ethnic groups, predominate in the highlands.

Kenya has no official religion. The majority of Kenyans follow traditional religious practices, but about one-third of the population is Christian. Islam is prevalent in areas of Arab and Asian influence along the coast and among the nomadic tribes of the north.

Demography. The overall population density figure for Kenya obscures the fact that one-fifth of the country is occupied by more than 85% of the total population. The most densely populated areas are the Kenya Highlands and the Lake Victoria Basin. Some 70% of the urban population is concentrated in NAIROBI, the capital, and MOMBASA. Kenya has one of the highest rates of population growth in the world. Due to the high birthrate and low death rate, more than half the population is under the age of 15.

Education and Health. Kenya's educational goal is the provision of eight years of free primary education for all children, but only about 70% of school-age children attend classes. The University of Nairobi was founded in 1956. Rapid population growth has placed strains on health facilities and other social services, particularly in rural areas.

The Arts. Traditional oral histories have had a significant effect on literature in Kenya. Among the best-known contemporary authors are James NGUGI WA THOING'O, Muga Gicaru, and Josiah Kariuki. The Kamba are known for their wood carvings and the Kisii for soapstone carvings. Drums and plucked instruments provide musical accompaniment to traditional dancing. The principal cultural institutions are in Nairobi and include the National Museum, the Kenya Cultural Center, and the National Theater.

Economic Activity

The Kenyan economy is predominantly agricultural. Farming provides about 30% of the gross domestic product and accounts for about 65% of all export earnings. Due chiefly to pressures created by the rapidly growing population, Kenya now imports large quantities of food, particularly wheat. Unemployment is high, especially in urban areas.

Agriculture. About 45% of the area under cultivation is occupied by large farms. These large farms and cooperatives involving about 20% of all smallholders grow cash crops for export markets, and their income from farming is thus subject to the wide price swings associated with world trade in agricultural commodities. The most valuable cash crop is coffee, which is grown mainly in the Kenya Highlands on both large and small farms. Tea and coffee together accounted for 45% of all foreign exchange earnings in 1987. Corn (the chief subsistence crop), pyrethrum, and wheat are also grown in the highlands. Kenya is the world's leading producer of pyrethrum extract, which is used in the manufacture of pesticides. The principal crops grown on the coastal lowlands are sisal, cashew nuts, sugarcane, cotton, and rice. Stock raising is the chief activity in the three-fourths of Kenya that is too dry for cultivation.

Manufacturing and Energy. Kenya is the most highly industrialized nation in East Africa. Among the chief manufactured products are processed foods, textiles and clothing, and cement. Kenya has no coal or petroleum. There are hydroelectric plants along the Tano River and an oil-fired plant on the coast. About 10% of the nation's power supply is imported from Owen Falls Dam in Uganda. A geothermal plant, the first in Africa, began operation near Lake Naivasha in 1981.

Tourism. With its national parks and wildlife preserves and the added attractions of the Indian Ocean coast, Kenya draws more visitors than any other country in tropical Africa. In 1987, due to low world prices for tea and coffee, tourism was the largest foreign-exchange earner.

Transportation and Trade. In 1967, Kenya, Tanzania, and Uganda formed the East African Community (EAC). By 1977, however, the organization's once-flourishing customs unit, common market, and joint postal, air, rail, and telecommunications systems had collapsed due to political and economic differences between the three countries. Kenya suffered from the loss of the regional trade and transportation network in which it had provided the larger share of manufactured goods and services. A larger regional trade group, the Preferential Trade Area for Eastern and Southern Africa, began operations in 1984.

Kenya's principal exports are primarily agricultural products, as in the colonial period, but processed industrial goods are also economically important. The leading imports are petroleum, machinery and transportation equipment, and chemicals. Since the early 1970s, Kenya has generally had an unfavorable balance of trade and has borrowed to finance food imports for the growing urban population. A shortage of foreign exchange has led to restrictions on the import of raw materials and equipment by industry.

Government

Independence was achieved on Dec. 12, 1963, and in 1964, Kenya became a republic headed by a president. The country has a unicameral National Assembly; most of its members are elected by universal adult suffrage at least once every five years. Kenya effectively became a one-party state of the Kenya African National Union (KANU) in 1964, when the Kenya African Democratic Union (KADU)

Nairobi, the capital of Kenya since 1905, has expanded rapidly since its founding in 1899 and is today the nation's most populous city. Located in the highlands of southeastern Kenya, the city is a trade center for the agricultural produce of that fertile region.

joined KANU. In 1982 the constitution was changed to legalize Kenya's status as a one-party state.

History

Bantu tribes are believed to have migrated eastward and southward across the continent from West Africa and to have entered Kenya about 1,000 years ago. The Nilotic peoples began to enter from the north at about the end of the 15th century and were still migrating when the Europeans arrived. Arabs dominated the coastal areas from the 7th century until the Portuguese took possession of the coast following Vasco da GAMA's visit to Mombasa in 1498; they reestablished their control after the Portuguese were ousted in 1729. From then until 1963 the Arabs retained nominal control of the coastal regions, first as part of the sultanate of Muscat (Oman), and after 1861, when the Muscat empire was divided, as part of the sultanate of Zanzibar.

In the 1850s, Europeans explored the interior in search of the source of the Nile, and Christian missionaries began their efforts to convert the inhabitants and to end the Arabs' flourishing trade in slaves. The slave trade was ended by the sultan in 1873. In 1885, Karl Peters received a charter for his German East Africa Company and initiated a scramble among the European nations to establish colonies in East Africa. The Anglo-German agreements of 1886 recognized the sultan's authority over the coastal areas and placed the southern coastal strip (now Tanzania) in the German sphere of influence and the northern coastal strip (now Kenya) in the British sphere of influence. In 1887 the sultan leased the northern coastal strip to the Imperial British East Africa Company, and when that company was dissolved in 1895 the

British government established the East Africa Protectorate. The railroad from Mombasa to Nairobi and Lake Victoria was built in the last decade of the 19th century, and as white settlers began to enter Kenya, large areas of the Kenya Highlands—later known as the White Highlands—were subsequently alienated from the Africans and reserved for white-only settlement. In 1920 the interior regions were organized as the British crown colony of Kenya, whereas the coastal strip remained a British protectorate over lands nominally ruled by the sultan of Zanzibar.

The African population did not submit easily to British authority, and there were countless clashes between the two groups. The British appointed African chiefs and village headmen to carry out some administrative duties, but efforts to enlist black leaders into legislative bodies met with little success. An educated African elite began to emerge, however, from the schools established primarily by the Christian missionaries, and in 1944 black Kenyans, especially Kikuyu, concerned about their political future formed the Kenya African Union (KAU), which three years later came under the leadership of Jomo KENYATTA. In the early 1950s open revolt against the British took the form of a terrorist campaign against the settlers by the so-called MAU MAU movement. Jomo Kenyatta was imprisoned in 1953, but the terrorism continued and a state of emergency was in effect from 1952 to 1960.

In 1960 a constitutional change replaced the system of multiracial representation in the government with one of majority rule. Kenyatta was freed in 1961 and in May 1963 led the Kenya African National Union (KANU) in a decisive victory at the polls, thereby establishing black control of the government and paving the way for independence. Kenya became internally self-governing on

June 1, 1963, and full independence was achieved on Dec. 12, 1963, with Jomo Kenyatta as the first prime minister. On Dec. 12, 1964, Kenya became a republic and Kenyatta the first president. Kenyatta remained head of the highly centralized government until his death in August 1978. He was succeeded by his vice-president, Daniel arap MOI, a member of the Kalenjin minority. Moi, who ran unopposed in the 1979, 1983, and 1988 presidential elections, gradually reduced Kikuyu dominance of political life.

Since independence Kenya has followed a policy of nonalignment with a definite westward tilt. Kenya has been unusual among African nations in that private ownership and investment in land and industry have been actively encouraged. By the early 1980s, however, Kenya's once-flourishing economy was no longer able to keep pace with rapid population growth. Rural poverty and poor nutrition were widespread, and food shortages and unemployment led to unrest in urban areas. In 1982 economic woes and opposition to the legalization of the one-party state sparked an attempted coup against Kenya's government—the first in 19 years. Moi cracked down on dissent but faced growing opposition from students demanding an end to one-party rule and from the underground Mwakenya movement.

Jomo Kenyatta, an African nationalist and Kenyan political leader, became the first prime minister (1963) and, later, first president (1964) of Kenya following its establishment as a state independent of Great Britain.

Kenya, Mount

Mount Kenya, an extinct volcano in central Kenya, with an elevation of 5,199 m (17,058 ft), is Africa's second highest mountain, after KILIMANJARO. The crater is eroded and contains several small receding glaciers. Mount Kenya National Park includes the area above 3,290 m (10,800 ft) and most of the forested (cedar, bamboo) slopes below. The summit was first reached (1899) by the party of the British geographer Sir Halford Mackinder.

Kenyatta, Jomo

[ken-yah'-tuh, joh'-moh] Jomo Kenyatta (Kamau wa Ngengi), b. c.1891, d. Aug. 22, 1978, was the leader of Kenya's struggle for national independence and president of the Republic of Kenya from 1964 until his death. A Kikuyu, he became (1928) general secretary of the Kikuyu Central Association (KCA). In 1931 he went to London to represent the KCA at the Colonial Office and stayed there for 15 years. He studied anthropology at the London School of Economics.

Kenyatta returned to Kenya in 1946 to fight for *uhuru* (independence). After the bloody MAU MAU rebellion broke out, he was imprisoned in 1952 as the leader, a charge which he always denied. He was released in 1961 and became president of the opposition Kenya African Nationalist Union (KANU). With KANU's electoral victory in 1963 he became the first prime minister of self-governing Kenya and the president of the Republic of Kenya in 1964. As Kenya's unchallenged ruler, he maintained political stability, a fairly free press, pro-Western policies, and a prosperous mixed economy. He encouraged foreign private investment and greatly advanced public education

and health. Kenya, however, remained a one-party state with significant tribal divisions and rural poverty, and Kenyatta was unable to control corruption. He was succeeded as president by Daniel Arap Moi.

Kenzan

Ogata Kenzan, 1663–1743, a master ceramicist, firmly established pottery as one of Japan's major art forms. He opened (1699) his own kiln at Narutaki, where he produced pottery that until 1701 was decorated by his brother, the painter KORIN. From the location of the kiln in the northwest hills of Kyoto, he took the name Kenzan, or Northwest Mountain. Kenzan's Narutaki ceramics were highly valued for their superbly executed decorative designs. He also produced lacquer ware and small paintings that reflected his interests in literature, calligraphy, and Zen. Kenzan's assimilation of decorative painting into the potter's craft set a trend in Japanese ceramics that still thrives today.

Kepler, Johannes

[kep'-lur] The German astronomer Johannes Kepler, b. Dec. 27, 1571, d. Nov. 15, 1630, was the first strong supporter of the heliocentric theory of COPERNICUS and the discoverer of the three laws of planetary motion. He attended seminaries at Adelberg and Maulbronn before studying theology, philosophy, and mathematics at the University of Tübingen. At Tübingen, Kepler's scientific ability attracted the notice of the astronomer Michael Maestlin. Through Maestlin, Kepler became a supporter of the Copernican theory, although his teacher continued to expound officially the old Ptolemaic system. Kepler had planned to enter religious life, but he accepted a chair in mathematics and astronomy at Graz.

At the age of 24, Kepler published *Mysterium cosmo-*

Johannes Kepler, a German mathematician, formulated the three laws of planetary motion that bear his name by using the astronomical observations recorded by Tycho Brahe, for whom he worked briefly. Kepler was instrumental in the development of early telescopes.

graphicum (Cosmographic Mystery, 1596), in which he defended the Copernican theory and described his ideas on the structure of the planetary system. Influenced by the Pythagoreans, Kepler viewed the universe as being governed by geometric relationships that conform to the inscribed and circumscribed circles of the five regular polygons.

Although he was not a Copernican himself, Tycho BRAHE, the mathematician at the court of Emperor Rudolph II at Prague, was so impressed with Kepler's work that in 1600 he invited Kepler to come to Prague as his assistant. Confronted with the Catholic persecution of the Protestant minority in Graz, Kepler gladly accepted. When Brahe died the following year, Kepler was appointed his successor and thus inherited Brahe's scientific legacy.

This legacy included many accurate positional determinations of the planets, especially those of Mars. Kepler now embarked on an intensive study of the true orbits of the planets. Abandoning the ancient belief that the planets must move in perfect circles, Kepler concentrated on Mars. He proved that the orbit of Mars is an ellipse, with the Sun occupying one of its two foci. This, the first of Kepler's laws of planetary motion, appeared in *Astronomia nova* (New Astronomy) in 1609, with the second "law of areas" governing planetary velocity. The third law was published in 1619.

Among Kepler's numerous scientific contributions are an influential treatise on the theory of optics (1604), a treatise on optics as applied to telescope lenses (1611), a work offering physical explanations of the appearance of a nova in 1604, and an enthusiastic acceptance of and elaboration on Galileo's observations with a telescope (1610). His *Epitome astronomiae Copernicanae* (Introduction to Copernican Astronomy, 1618–21) became one of the most widely read treatises on astronomy in Europe. Kepler's last great work, known as the *Rudolphine Tables* (1627), was a widely used compilation of accurate tables of planetary motion.

The posthumous *Somnium* (Dream, 1634), on which Kepler labored until shortly before his death, describes a

journey to the Moon and discusses the existence of lunar inhabitants. A crucial link between the thought of Copernicus and that of Newton, Kepler was an important figure in the 17th-century scientific revolution.

Kepler's laws [kep'-lurz]

Formulated by the German astronomer Johannes Kepler, Kepler's laws of planetary motion describe the shape of the orbit, the velocities, and the distances of the planets with respect to the Sun. The laws were announced after Kepler's long and elaborate analysis of Tycho BRAHE's observations of the planets; they may be stated as follows: (1) the planets move in ellipses with the Sun at one focus; (2) the line joining the Sun and a planet sweeps out equal areas in equal intervals of time; (3) the square of the time of revolution of a planet divided by the cube of its mean distance from the Sun gives a number that is the same for all the planets. The second law, enunciated (1609) along with the first law, is known as the law of areas; the third law, announced in 1619, is sometimes referred to as the harmonic law.

Kepler's laws were generalized and corrected by Sir Isaac Newton so that they apply to any motion associated with the so-called two-body problem. In this problem two bodies are idealized as point masses, or small rigid spheres, and the motion of one about the other is subject to Newtonian mechanics (see LAWS OF MOTION) and to Newton's law of GRAVITATION; no force other than the mutual gravitational attraction is considered. The possible forms of motion in this problem are now called Keplerian motion.

Kepler's second law required no amendment by Newton; in the generalized form of the first law, however, orbits can be ellipses, parabolas, or hyperbolas. The amended third law applies only to elliptic orbits. Let a be the semimajor axis of the orbit of one body about the other, and P its period; let m_1 and m_2 be the masses of the two bodies and G the constant of gravitation. Then $P^2/a^3 = \pi G (m_1 + m_2)$.

The amended laws can be applied to a satellite revolving around a planet or to two stars that form a binary sys-

Johannes Kepler was the first to describe the planetary orbits as ellipses with the Sun at one of the two focal points (f_1 and f_2). Although a planet's speed varies, the line joining the Sun and a planet sweeps out equal areas (A_1 and A_2) in equal time periods, represented by the colored section of the orbit.

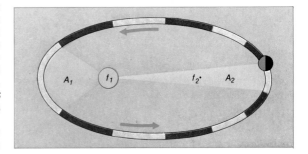

tem (see BINARY STARS). The amended third law is important in determining the masses of binary stars.

Kerala [ker'-uh-luh]   Kerala, a state on the Arabian Sea in southwestern India, is bordered on the north by Karnataka and on the east by Tamil Nadu. Kerala has a population of 25,453,680 (1981) and an area of 38,855 km² (15,005 mi²). The capital is Trivandrum, and the leading ports are COCHIN and Quilon. Most of the population speaks Malayalam, and most are Hindus. Kerala has a large Christian community (see MALABAR CHRISTIANS) and a substantial Muslim minority.

The land rises from the 580-km-long (360-mi) Malabar Coast to an alluvial plain, where rice, coconuts, cassava, and cashew nuts are grown. To the east, tea, rubber, coffee, and pepper plantations extend in the foothills of the Western GHATS. The mountains have forests of teak, ebony, and rosewood.

Kerala became a powerful state in the 9th century. Its history from the 15th to the 20th century was marked by Arab, Portuguese, Dutch, and British intervention. In the state elections of 1957, the Communist party won a majority, giving Kerala the first Communist government in the country. The Communists have participated in several governments since.

keratin   see HAIR; HOOF, NAIL, and CLAW

Kerensky, Aleksandr Fyodorovich [kuh-ren'-skee, uhl-yik-sahn'-dur fyoh'-dor-uh-vich]   Aleksandr Kerensky, b. Apr. 22 (N.S.), 1881, d. June 11, 1970, headed the Russian provisional government from July to October 1917, during the interim between the overthrow of the tsar and the Bolshevik Revolution. A lawyer and a democratic moderate, Kerensky joined the Socialist Revolutionary party in 1905 and was elected to the fourth DUMA in 1912. As premier, Kerensky was identified with Russia's abortive military offensive in World War I, which further weakened his shaky coalition government. In a vain effort to maintain control, Kerensky ordered Vladimir Ilich LENIN's arrest as well as that of the right-wing general Lavr KORNILOV. Beleaguered by radicals and reactionaries alike, he fled Russia in October. He lived in Paris until 1940, after which he settled in New York City.

Kern, Jerome   Jerome David Kern, b. New York City, Jan. 27, 1885, d. Nov. 11, 1945, was one of the most innovative composers for the American musical theater. His *Show Boat* (1927), with book and lyrics by Oscar Hammerstein II, marked the beginning of the musical play as distinguished from musical comedy. Among Kern's other successful musicals were *Sally* (1920), *Music in the Air* (1932), and *Roberta* (1933). He received Oscars for his film songs "The Way You Look Tonight" and "The Last Time I Saw Paris." His other songs include the classic "Ol' Man River," "Smoke Gets in Your Eyes," and "All the Things You Are."

kerosene [kair'-uh-seen]   Kerosene, also known as paraffin oil or coal oil, is a liquid hydrocarbon fuel commonly obtained from the fractional distillation of PETROLEUM. Originally used as a fuel for lamps, kerosene is now used primarily as a heating fuel, especially in domestic heating systems, and as an aviation fuel. It is also used as a solvent and thinner. The quality of kerosene is determined by its burning properties, which depend on the mixture of components present in the particular sample.

Because kerosene has a high boiling point (150–300° C/300–570° F), it shows no tendency to evaporate at room temperature and must therefore be encouraged to vaporize for most efficient combustion.

Stringent constraints are placed on the performance of kerosene when it is used as a fuel for aviation gas turbine engines. The most important constraints relate to thermal stability, so that the fuel can be heated to relatively high temperatures without leaving gummy deposits in the fuel system.

Kerouac, Jack [kair'-oo-ak]   The American writer Jack Kerouac, b. Jean Louis Kerouac, Lowell, Mass., Mar. 12, 1922, d. Oct. 21, 1969, became the leading chronicler of the BEAT GENERATION, a term he coined for a social and literary movement in the 1950s. After studying briefly at Columbia University, he achieved fame with his spontaneous and unconventional prose, particularly the novel *On the Road* (1957). After the success of this work, Kerouac produced a series of thematically and structurally similar novels, including *The Dharma Bums* and *The Subterraneans* (both 1958), *Doctor Sax* (1959), *Lonesome Traveler* (1960), and *Big Sur* (1962).

Kerr, Clark [kur]   Clark Kerr, b. Stony Creek, Pa., May 17, 1911, is a labor economist, arbitrator, and university administrator best known for his association with the University of California at Berkley (1949–67). In 1949 he vigorously protested the board of regents' policy requiring special loyalty oaths from university teachers and as president of the university (1958–67) he helped arrange a compromise solution to disputes between the state colleges and the university. He was president when the Berkeley Free Speech Movement inaugurated a period of turbulent student-administration relations in the mid-1960s. From 1967 to 1973 he was chairman of the Carnegie Foundation Commission on Higher Education, and since 1974 has been chairman of the Carnegie Council Policy Studies in Higher Education.

Kerr, Sir John Robert [kar]   Sir John Robert Kerr, b. Sept. 24, 1914, d. Mar. 24, 1991, was governor-general of Australia from 1974 to 1977. Previously he had been a lawyer and judge, serving (1972–74) as chief justice of the supreme court of New South Wales. As governor-general, because of a parliamentary deadlock, he took the unprecedented and controversial step of dismissing Prime Minister Gough WHITLAM's Labor government and dissolving Parliament in 1975.

Kerry   Kerry, a county in southwestern Ireland in MUNSTER province, is bounded by the Atlantic Ocean on the west and south and the River SHANNON on the north. It has an area of 4,701 km^2 (1,815 mi^2) and a population of 124,159 (1986). Tralee is the county seat. Three long, mountainous peninsulas give the coastline a rugged and picturesque appearance. Farming, stock breeding, and fishing are the major occupations. Tourism is also important because of Kerry's beautiful scenery, including Macgillicuddy's Reeks, Ireland's highest mountains, and the lakes of KILLARNEY. The area was ruled by the Fitzgeralds from the 13th century until the 16th century, when it became part of the Munster plantation.

Kerry blue terrier   The Kerry blue terrier, a native of Ireland, has apparently been known in County Kerry, southwestern Ireland, at least since the mid-19th century. The breed was not officially recognized until the 20th century—in 1922 by the English Kennel Club and in 1924 by the American Kennel Club. The Kerry, as its name indicates, is a "blue" dog, ranging from deep slate to light gray; it is born black, but solid black is unacceptable in the show ring. A medium-sized and long-legged terrier, it reaches 50 cm (19.5 in) high at the shoulder and about 18 kg (40 lb) in weight. Its coat is dense, wavy, soft, and silky.

Kertész, André   [kair'-tesh]   André Kertész, b. Budapest, Hungary, July 2, 1894, d. Sept. 27, 1985, was one of the inventors of modern PHOTOJOURNALISM. He moved to Paris in 1925 and three years later purchased a Leica miniature camera that enabled him to work with both speed and discretion. Kertész contributed photographs to the first French picture magazines, including *Vu*, where he formulated and edited his own stories. His

The Hungarian photographer André Kertész, a pioneer in modern photojournalism, took this photograph called Broken Bench *in New York City in 1962.*

ability to expose the significant details and communicate the essence of a subject directed the future trend of journalistic photography.

In the United States from 1936, Kertész earned a living as a free-lance magazine photographer until 1962, when he became sufficiently prosperous to photograph, for his own interest, subjects related to his early work. In his best-known images, of ordinary places, irrational elements are exposed so as to obtain a suddenly witty and unfamiliar situation.

Kesey, Ken   [kee'-zee]   The novelist and screenwriter Ken Kesey, b. La Junta, Colo., Sept. 17, 1935, is best known for his first novel, *One Flew over the Cuckoo's Nest* (1962; film, 1975), based on his experience as a hospital attendant. After *Sometimes a Great Notion* (1964; film, 1971), a saga of the Northwest, Kesey achieved notoriety as an LSD advocate and member of the Merry Pranksters, a group that toured the country in a school bus. *Demon Box* (1986) is a mixture of essays and short stories.

Kesselring, Albert   [kes'-ul-ring, ahl'-bairt]   Albert Kesselring, b. Nov. 20, 1885, d. July 16, 1960, was one of the leading German generals in World War II. After commanding air force operations in the conquest of Poland (1939) and the invasion of the Low Countries and France (1940), he was promoted to field marshal (June 1940). He then commanded the Luftwaffe in the Battle of Britain (August–October 1940) and on the Russian front (1941–42). As commander in chief of the German forces in Italy from 1943, he was responsible for the massacre of 335 Italian hostages in the Ardeatine Caves near Rome in 1944. In March 1945, Kesselring became supreme German commander on the Western front. He was sentenced to death by a British military court in 1947, a sentence that was later commuted to life imprisonment.

kestrel   see FALCON

ketone   [kee'-tohn]   Ketones are organic compounds that contain a carbonyl group (an oxygen atom doubly bonded to a carbon atom) bonded to two other organic groups. Closely related are ALDEHYDES, in which the carbonyl group is bonded to one organic group and one hydrogen atom. Ketones are commonly named by appending the suffix *-one* to a descriptive prefix, or by naming the groups attached to the carbonyl carbon atom. Thus the mixed ketone called methyl ethyl ketone ($CH_3COCH_2CH_3$) is also called butanone.

The first and simplest member of the ketone series, CH_3COCH_3, has the common name ACETONE and is by far the most important industrial ketone. More than one million tons of acetone are produced each year in the United States. Half of this amount is used for the synthesis of other chemicals such as methyl isobutyl ketone and methyl methacrylate. Methyl isobutyl ketone is used as a solvent for paints and lacquers; methyl methacrylate is used in PLASTICS. In the laboratory, ketones are prepared by oxidizing secondary ALCOHOLS.

The blood-ketone level in humans, normally low, increases in response to starvation, diabetes mellitus, or a high-fat, low-carbohydrate diet. This condition is known as ketosis. Dietary changes and, in diabetes, the administration of insulin usually correct the condition.

Kettering, Charles Franklin

Kettering, Charles Franklin [ket'-ur-ing] Charles Franklin Kettering, b. near Loudonville, Ohio, Aug. 29, 1876, d. Nov. 25, 1958, was an American engineer and inventor. He was also a cofounder of the Sloan-Kettering Institute for Cancer Research. While working at the National Cash Register Co., he designed (1905) the first electric cash register. In 1908 he developed an improved ignition system. In 1912 the Cadillac Division of General Motors turned to Kettering's newly formed Dayton Engineering Laboratories Company (Delco) for components that combined ignition, lighting, and the first practical electric self-starter. His starter system used a small, yet powerful, electric motor. Kettering became (1919) the director of research at General Motors and guided such projects as high-octane, knock-free gasoline and the lightweight two-cycle diesel engine (used to power locomotives).

kettledrum

kettledrum Kettledrums (*timpani*), which produce sounds of definite pitch, are the most important percus-sion instruments of the orchestra. They consist of a calf-skin or plastic sheet mounted on a hoop that is fitted over a hemispherical shell of brass or copper with a hole in the bottom to relieve the stress of concussion. The skin is tightened by screws, formed with T-shaped handles for efficiency. The player uses two sticks with heads ranging from hard (wooden) to soft (felt) that, along with the positioning of the stroke, can produce a gentle roll, a harsh, explosive effect, or any shade between. Kettledrums come in two basic sizes: one with a 28-in-diameter (71-cm) head and the other with a 25-in-diameter (63.5-cm) head.

Kettledrums originated in the Near East before AD 600. At first used only with trumpets, and carried on horses during displays of military pomp, kettledrums began to appear in opera and church orchestras during the 17th century.

Two kettledrums were standard in the 18th-century orchestra, three by the mid-19th century. Only rarely did their number exceed five. Hector Berlioz, however, used ten pairs in his *Requiem* (1837). A satisfactory tuning pedal was finally developed in the 20th century, making possible chromatic passages and even glissandi (rapid "sliding" of pitch).

Kew Gardens

Kew Gardens Kew Gardens, or the Royal Botanic Gardens, in Kew, near London, England, is one of the major botanical gardens in the world. It contains more than 40,000 different kinds of plants, with particularly noteworthy collections of Australian plants, succulents, tropical orchids, and ferns. The Gardens also has three museums, a taxonomy laboratory, an extensive library, and a large herbarium of dried species. Formerly a royal estate, Kew Gardens became a government institution in 1841.

key

key The term *key* in music has two meanings. (1) A key is that movable part of a keyboard or woodwind instrument which, when activated, produces the desired pitch. On keyboards (such as that of a piano or organ) each key corresponds to a string or pipe of different pitch; to sound a note the key is depressed. On woodwinds the keys open or close holes in the instruments, an action that shortens or lengthens the column of air vibrating in a tube, thus altering the pitch. (2) The key of a musical composition denotes the pitch (keynote) of its tonal center (TONALITY). A composition in the key of C, for example, has the note C as its tonal center.

Music has always had a tonal center, at least since medieval times, but the concept of tonality—of music being in a key—emerged only in the early 18th century with the dominance of the major-minor system and its accompanying key "signatures" (arrangements of sharps or flats at the beginning of a composition to indicate the key). Even though a piece may modulate or change its key (perhaps even its key signature) during its course, it normally returns to its original key and is considered to be in that key. Some 20th-century music is written in more than one key simultaneously (polytonality) or completely without key (ATONALITY).

Changing the pitch on a hand-tuned kettledrum (top right) involves turning the T-shaped screws that control the tension of the drum head. The pitch of the pedal kettledrum is controlled by moving the pedal (6), which controls six tuning rods (3). The tuning rods tighten or loosen their grip on the head (1), changing the tuning almost instantaneously. Other parts of the pedal drum include the flesh hoop and metal counterhoop (2), the shell (4), crown (5), and castor (7).

Key, Francis Scott   A Maryland lawyer and poet, Francis Scott Key, b. Carroll City, Md., Aug. 1, 1779, d. Jan. 11, 1843, wrote the words of The STAR-SPANGLED BANNER (1814), which became the U.S. national anthem by an act of Congress in 1931. Key also wrote other songs and verse as well as a study entitled *The Power of Literature and Its Connection with Religion* (1834).

Francis Scott Key, a lawyer and poet from Maryland, composed the lyrics to "The Star-Spangled Banner" in 1814, shortly after witnessing the British shelling of Baltimore's Fort McHenry. Key's patriotic verses, set to the melody of an old drinking song, became the national anthem of the United States in 1931.

Key West   Key West, Fla. (1990 pop., 24,832), is the southernmost city of the continental United States and the seat of Monroe County. The city is located approximately 95 km (60 mi) southwest of the Florida mainland, in the Florida Keys. Its economy is dependent on fishing, tourism, and U.S. naval installations. Key West was settled during the 1820s.

keyboard, computer   see COMPUTER

keyboard instruments   see MUSICAL INSTRUMENTS

Keynes, John Maynard [kaynz, may'-nurd]   John Maynard Keynes, b. June 5, 1883, d. Apr. 21, 1946, was one of the most influential economists in the 20th century. Keynes was educated at Eton and Cambridge. After service in the India Office and the Treasury, he became the principal British financial representative to the Paris Peace Conference that followed World War I. Resigning in protest at the reparations imposed on Germany, he published *The Economic Consequences of the Peace* (1919), which gave him an international reputation.

Keynes's classic work, *The General Theory of Employment Interest and Money* (1936), was his answer to the riddle of the Great Depression of the 1930s—that millions of people willing to work could not find employment. A central proposition of the *General Theory* is that times exist in a market economy when the total demand of consumers and investors may be insufficient to purchase all

John Maynard Keynes, perhaps the most influential economist of the 20th century, established his reputation with theories advocating government spending to relieve protracted unemployment.

the goods the society has produced. (Traditional economics had held that supply creates its own demand.) Business managers, finding that they cannot sell all they have on hand, will cut back on production and employment, and a depression will result. Keynes held that part of the solution during periods of high unemployment was for the government to increase the money supply, thus lowering interest rates and stimulating business investment. But Keynes also advocated an active government FISCAL POLICY of deficit spending on public works and other projects and the maintenance during depressions of an unbalanced budget to increase the aggregate demand for goods and services.

Keynes's opinions were a sharp departure from conventional economics, and his theory remains controversial. In the years after World War II, however, his views in one form or another became widely accepted among economists in England and the United States, while his critics were in the minority.

An intensely active man, Keynes returned to government service during World War II. In 1942 he was raised to the peerage as Baron Keynes of Tilton. He played an important role at the Bretton Woods Conference of 1944, which established the basis of the postwar international monetary system, and he negotiated the multibillion-dollar U.S. loan to Britain in 1945. Keynes is one of a handful of social scientists who, through their writings, have substantially affected the course of history.

See also: ECONOMY, NATIONAL.

keypunch   see COMPUTER

Keystone Kops   Virtually synonymous with silent-film comedy, Mack SENNETT's Keystone Kops were inspired bunglers whose slapstick antics concentrated on wild chases featuring an out-of-control paddy wagon and death-defying acrobatic stunts. Sennett explored the idea for the zany policemen at his Keystone studio in December 1912, and the original seven uniformed Keystone Kops made their formal debut in a two-reeler in 1914. Their most famous madcap leader was Ford Sterling.

KGB The KGB (*Komitet Gosudarstvennoy Bezopasnosti*, Committee for State Security) controls both the political and federal police and the intelligence and counterintelligence activities of the USSR. Founded in 1954, the KGB succeeded the NKVD (1934) and the MGB (1946) of the repressive Stalin era, and the earlier secret-police organizations the Cheka (1917) and the OGPU (1922). The KGB concentrates on INTELLIGENCE OPERATIONS and places less emphasis on its predecessors' policy of systematic terrorism. It also polices Soviet borders, operates prison camps and mental hospitals, and directs a large network of internal informers. It is estimated that in the 1980s the KGB employed 500,000 people. Unlike the earlier secret police organizations, which attained a degree of autonomy, the KGB is firmly controlled by the Communist party. Well-known leaders of the various Soviet security organizations have included Feliks DZERZHINSKY, Genrikh Yagoda, Nikolai Yezhov, Lavrenti BERIA, and Yuri V. ANDROPOV.

Khafre, King of Egypt [kah'-fruh] Khafre, also called Chephren, fl. 1st half of the 26th century BC, was the fourth king of the 4th dynasty (*c.*2613–*c.*2498 BC) of ancient Egypt. The son of Khufu, he built at Giza the second of the three Great Pyramids and the Great SPHINX, whose colossal facial image may be a representation of Khafre's features.

Khajuraho [kaj-rah'-hoh] Khajuraho, in north Madhya Pradesh, India, about 600 km (360 mi) southeast of New Delhi, is the site of a magnificent series of Hindu temples built by the Chandella Rajputs from about AD 950 to 1050. The complex originally contained 85 buff-colored sandstone and granite temples, of which about 25 remain today.

Each temple, set upon a lofty terrace, comprises a sequence of halls, foyers, and porches fused into a single architectural fabric and coordinated along a common axis. On the exterior, the pyramidal superstructures echo a natural mountain range, rising from the low, broad shapes of the porch in regular stages, peaking in the high, phallic form that covers the sanctum. The stone surfaces are animated with myriad representations of the gods and of erotic scenes, concrete demonstrations of the potency of the icon enshrined within.

khaki [kak'-ee] Khaki is a durable, yellowish or greenish brown, cotton or wool fabric. An excellent camouflage color, the fabric is in common use for military uniforms. Khaki was first used as a military color by the British army in India, in 1848 (the name is derived from the Hindi for *dusty*). It became the official color of British army uniforms and, eventually, of the military dress of many other countries. During World War I an olive tint was added to the khaki shade to help camouflage soldiers fighting on European battlegrounds.

Khalid, King of Saudi Arabia [kah'-leed] Khalid ibn Abd al-Aziz, b. Riyadh, 1913, d. June 13, 1982, became king of Saudi Arabia after the assassination (Mar. 25, 1975) of his half brother King FAISAL. Khalid was one of several dozen sons of Ibn Saud, who founded the Saudi kingdom in 1926. Preceded on the throne by his brothers Saud (1953–64) and Faisal (1964–75), he was said to be a self-effacing man who had played a conciliatory role among the royal princes. He was succeeded by his crown prince, FAHD ibn Abd al-Aziz.

Khalkhas [kal'-kuhz] The Khalkha people are the principal inhabitants of Outer MONGOLIA (the Mongolian People's Republic). Their language, spoken by one million people, represents several closely related dialects, all subsidiary to Altaic.

Khalkha society was traditionally based on nomadic patriarchal clans. A landowning nobility existed as a result of land grants received in exchange for military service. Tribes lived in herding camps that were moved from pasture to pasture several times a year. Traditionally shamanists or pagans, the Khalkha became Lamaist Buddhists in the 17th century.

Loose-knit Khalkha-Tatar tribal confederations, originating in 300 BC, became united under GENGHIS KHAN in the 13th century. On horseback, the MONGOLS conquered Central Asia, southern Russia, and eastern Europe. Their empire collapsed in the 1500s. Since 1920 the Khalkha people have been influenced by the USSR but resisted collectivization.

Kharkov [kar'-kuhf] Kharkov is the second largest city of Ukraine in the USSR, and the administrative center of Kharkov oblast. Located in northeast Ukraine, the city has a population of 1,611,000 (1989). Kharkov is one of the largest economic centers of the USSR and, after Moscow and Leningrad, the most important transport hub. It is situated at the confluence of the Kharkov, Lopan, and Udy rivers and the junction of eight rail lines; highways run north to Moscow, west to Kiev, and southeast to the Caucasus.

Kharkov is a modern industrial city that developed only during the second half of the 19th century. Its importance for the Soviet economy lies entirely in the manufacturing of diversified machinery products. Kharkov produces tractors, heavy electrical equipment, power-generating turbines, engines, and mining equipment. It is a major educational and industrial research center, with the Kharkov A. M. Gorky State University (1805) and technical schools training engineers for the city's industries.

Kharkov arose originally in 1656 as a military stronghold along the Russians' southern defense line against the Crimean Tatars. After the end of the 18th century, when Russia conquered the Crimea, Kharkov lost its military significance. Its modern industrial development was due to the rise of the coal and steel industry in the nearby DONETS BASIN and to the construction of railroads. After the Bolshevik Revolution, Kharkov served as the capital of the Ukraine from 1917 to 1934. The city was heavily damaged in World War II.

Khartoum

Khartoum [kar-toom'] Khartoum is the capital of Sudan and of Khartoum province. Situated at the confluence of the White and Blue NILE rivers, it is connected by bridges to the neighboring suburbs of OMDURMAN and Khartoum North. The population is 476,218 (1983), the majority of which is Arabic.

Khartoum is the commercial and transportation hub of the country. It has rail links to the north and west, and the two Nile rivers carry a large volume of traffic. Khartoum's industries include oilseed, gum-Arabic, and food processing; printing; and textile and glass manufacturing. The presidential palace and the parliament building are the principal landmarks. The University of Khartoum (1956) and a branch of Cairo University (1955) are there.

Khartoum, founded in 1821 by Muhammad Ali of Egypt, grew rapidly as a trade and military center. It was destroyed (1895) when the Mahdists massacred the Anglo-Egyptian garrison under Charles George GORDON. The city was recaptured (1898) by Lord KITCHENER, who rebuilt it to serve as the administrative center of Anglo-Egyptian Sudan. When Sudan became independent in 1956, Khartoum became the capital.

Khatchaturian, Aram

Khatchaturian, Aram [kah-chah-toor-yahn', uh-rahm'] Aram Khatchaturian, b. June 6 (N.S.), 1903, d. May 1, 1978, was a Soviet composer of Armenian birth best known outside the USSR for the "Sabre Dance" from his ballet *Gayane* (1942) and for two concertos—one for piano (1936), the other for violin (1940). Khatchaturian made use of Oriental melodic and rhythmic forms borrowed chiefly from Armenia, but also from neighboring Caucasian (Georgian and Azerbaijani) folk music. Brilliant orchestral coloring plays an important part in all his music, which includes popular choral songs, balalaika pieces, military marches, film and incidental music for plays, as well as compositions in classical forms.

Khazars

Khazars [kah'-zars] The Khazars, a Turkic people, created a commercial and political empire that dominated substantial parts of South Russia during much of the 7th through 10th centuries. During the 8th century the Khazar aristocracy and the *kagan* (king) were converted to Judaism. The Khazars established their capital at Itil (or Atil), in the Volga delta, and for four centuries thereafter this Jewish empire held the balance of power between the Christian BYZANTINE EMPIRE and the Muslim CALIPHATE. The Khazars controlled many of the trade routes to the Orient; and the fortified city of Sarkil on the lower Don River, built with Byzantine help, served as a crossroads to central Asia. During the late 10th and early 11th centuries an alliance of Byzantines and Russians broke the power of the Khazars in the Crimea. In 965, SVYATOSLAV I, duke of Kiev, decisively defeated the Khazar army.

Khiva

Khiva Khiva is a town in Khorezm oblast of Uzbekistan, USSR. Although it is of little importance today, its history goes back to the 6th century AD and it was a major city of Muslim Central Asia in medieval times. From the 16th to the 19th century it was the capital of the Khanate of Khiva, an Uzbek principality. Annexed by Russia in 1873, it was the capital of the Khorezm People's Soviet Republic from 1920 to 1924. Khiva's Ichan-Kala (Inner City) contains the 14th-century tomb of Seyid Ala-ud-Din, the Kunya-Ark fortress (17th century), the former palace of the khans (19th century), and many historic mosques and *madrasahs* (Islamic schools).

Khmer

Khmer see CAMBODIA; KHMER EMPIRE

Khmer Empire

Khmer Empire The Khmer Empire, which occupied contemporary Cambodia and parts of present-day Thailand, Laos, and Vietnam, existed between the 6th and 15th centuries.

The Khmers, whose descendants are today's Cambodians, are first known to have lived along the lower and middle Mekong River in northern Cambodia and southern Laos. Their capital was initially near Kompong Thom, but under King Yasovarman I (r. 889–900), it was moved to ANGKOR, which became a magnificent city whose architectural splendor was not subsequently equaled by other mainland Southeast Asian cultures. Khmer art, architecture, and culture were strongly Indian-influenced but included distinct local contributions.

The Khmers warred constantly with the adjacent Mon, Cham, Annamese, and Thai peoples. Their dominant role in continental Southeast Asia was ended by the Thais, coming out of southwest China, in the 14th and 15th centuries. Angkor was abandoned c.1434 and the capital moved to Phnom Penh.

Khmer Rouge

Khmer Rouge [kmair roozh'] The Khmer Rouge, or Cambodian Communist army, emerged as a significant rebel group during the late 1960s. With the aid of the North Vietnamese and the Viet Cong, the Khmer Rouge carried on a systematic war against the government of Prince NORODOM SIHANOUK and his successor, LON NOL. By 1970 the Khmer Rouge controlled about two-thirds of Cambodia. Despite massive economic and military aid from the United States—including bombing of Khmer Rouge positions—the Lon Nol government continued to lose territory. Phnom Penh, the capital, fell to the Khmer Rouge on Apr. 16, 1975.

A Communist government under President Khieu Samphan and Prime Minister POL POT was then established. It immediately implemented a program of radical social change in which entire city populations were evacuated to rural areas. It was charged with responsibility for the deaths of at least one million Cambodians before border clashes with Vietnam culminated early in 1979 with a full-scale Vietnamese invasion and the installation of a

Vietnamese-backed government in Phnom Penh. The Khmer Rouge, aided by China, retreated to remote villages along the Thai border and had the largest rebel army when Vietnamese troops withdrew in 1989.

Khoikhoi [koy'-koy]   The Khoikhoi are a southern African people who have often been called *Hottentot*. The latter name, used principally by white South Africans, now connotes a derogatory stereotype. A seminomadic pastoral people who were also hunters and gatherers, the Khoikhoi once inhabited the southern part of Namibia and parts of South Africa. They speak a Khoisan language noted for the four clicks—dental, alveolar, cerebral, and lateral—occurring in many words.

In 1650, when contacted by Dutch settlers, the total Khoikhoi population was an estimated 35,000–50,000. The largest political unit was the tribe, varying in size from 500 to 2,500 people. Traditionally, each tribe consisted of a federation of clans united by the institution of chieftainship. Each nuclear family occupied separate beehive-shaped huts. The Khoikhoi were monotheists and worshiped a celestial god.

As a result of European colonization the traditional Khoikhoi social system collapsed, and many Khoikhoi intermarried with the settlers, thus forming part of the Cape COLOUREDS. The Republic of South Africa now has fewer than 500 Khoikhoi-speakers. In Namibia more than 50,000 Khoikhoi were reported in the mid-1980s.

Khoisan language   see AFRICAN LANGUAGES

Khomeini, Ayatollah Ruhollah [koh-may-nee', roo-hoh'-lah]   The Ayatollah (Arabic, "Reflection of Allah") Ruhollah Khomeini (Ruhollah Hendi), b. Khomein, Iran, May 27, 1900?, d. July 3, 1989, became leader of Iran in 1979 by forcing the overthrow of the shah (see MUHAMMAD REZA SHAH PAHLAVI) and Prime Minister Shahpur Bakhtiar. The son of an ayatollah of the SHIITE sect, he studied theology and by 1962 was one of the six grand ayatollahs of Iran's Shiite Muslims. Exiled in 1963 for his

The Ayatollah Khomeini ruled Iran with an iron hand from 1979 until his death in 1989. He was succeeded as spiritual leader of Iran by Ali Khamenei, but temporal power passed to the new president, Hashemi Rafsanjani.

part in religious demonstrations against the shah, he was expelled from Iraq in 1978 and moved to France, where he emerged as the leader of the antishah movement. In January 1979, after the shah left Iran, he returned to lead the country, becoming *faqih* (supreme religious guide) of Iran's Islamic republic for life in December.

In his efforts to transform Iran into an Islamic state, Khomeini was hostile to the West. In November 1979 he supported militant students who invaded the U.S. embassy and precipitated the IRANIAN HOSTAGE CRISIS. Khomeini and other fundamentalist clerics imposed rigid censorship, executed members of the opposition, and banned Western customs. Khomeini used the IRAN-IRAQ WAR initiated by Iraq in 1980 to help unify the country, although he was less than successful in exporting his revolution and reluctantly accepted a cease-fire in the costly conflict in 1988. After his death, Iran remained a theocracy, although the constitution was revised to grant more power to the president.

Khorezm [kuh-rez'-uhm]   Khorezm (Khwarizm) is a historic region of the USSR located along the Amu Darya (Oxus River) south of the Aral Sea. From ancient times its rulers were known as the Khwarizm-shahs. In the late 12th and early 13th centuries, under the fourth Khwarizm-shah dynasty, Khorezm was the center of an empire that included most of Iran and Central Asia. From the 16th to the 19th century it was ruled by the Khanate of KHIVA. Annexed by Russia in 1873, it existed briefly as the Khorezm People's Soviet Republic from 1920 to 1924; today it is an oblast of Uzbekistan.

Khorsabad [kohr'-suh-bahd]   The village of Khorsabad, 20 km (12 mi) northeast of Mosul in Iraq, is the site of the ancient neo-Assyrian capital Dur Sharrukin (Fortress of Sargon). Founded (717 BC) by Sargon II of ASSYRIA (721–705 BC), it was virtually abandoned, unfinished, after his death.

The well-planned ancient city, almost 4 km^2 (1.5 mi^2) in area, was surrounded by a wall about 24 m (80 ft) thick, fortified with towers. The seven entrances were guarded by huge, winged human-headed bulls of carved stone. Little remains of the inner city. On the upper terrace of the citadel, together with temples and a ziggurat, stood Sargon's palace. Below were official residences and a temple to the god Nabu. Superb examples of Assyrian imperial art and architecture have been found at Khorsabad.

Khosru I, King of Persia [kahs-roo']   Khosru I, d. 579, called Chosroes in the West, succeeded his father, Kavad, as ruler of Sassanian Persia in 531. Khosru reformed the taxation of the Sassanian empire as well as its military and social structure. He successfully fought the Byzantine Empire, briefly occupying Antioch in 540, and in the east crushed the nomadic Hephthalites and established Sassanian hegemony over present-day Afghanistan. His troops conquered areas as far away as Yemen and the

Caucasus. A patron of learning, Khosru invited Greek philosophers to his court after their academy in Athens was closed in 529, and during his long reign many works were translated from Greek and Sanskrit into Persian.

Khrushchev, Nikita Sergeyevich

[kroos'-chef or krus-chawf', nyi-kee'-tuh syir-gay'-uh-vich] Nikita Sergeyevich Khrushchev, b. Apr. 17 (N.S.), 1894, d. Sept. 11, 1971, was first secretary of the Soviet Communist party from 1953 to 1964 and effective leader of the USSR from 1956 (premier from 1958) to 1964. According to his memoirs, he had a strict religious upbringing and became a revolutionary under the influence of one of his teachers. In 1918 he joined the Bolshevik party and fought in the Russian Civil War. Later, the party sent him to a technical institute.

Khrushchev rose steadily up the party ladder and in 1934 became a member of the Central Committee of the Soviet Communist party. Although increasingly influential, he was never an intimate associate of Joseph STALIN; he concentrated on technical rather than political matters. Perhaps for that reason he escaped the GREAT PURGE of the 1930s. As first secretary of the Ukrainian Communist party from 1938, he focused his attention on agriculture, in which he gained a reputation as an expert. After World War II he was brought again to Moscow, where he served in the Secretariat and the Politburo.

Khrushchev in the Post-Stalin Era. Stalin died on Mar. 5, 1953, and the resulting power vacuum was filled by a "collective leadership," consisting primarily of Khrushchev, Lavrenti BERIA, Nikoli BULGANIN, Georgy MALENKOV, Vyacheslav MOLOTOV, and Lazar Kaganovich. The collective leadership soon collapsed: Beria was executed later in the year, Malenkov was forced out in 1955, and by 1956, Khrushchev had become paramount in the party. At the 20th party congress that year, he gave his famous six-hour "secret speech" denouncing the "crimes of the Stalin era." In 1958, Khrushchev became premier as well as party secretary.

Khrushchev's Domestic Policies. Khrushchev set bold new economic goals for "overtaking the West" and the United States in particular. In 1954, under his supervision, vast new virgin lands were opened to cultivation, and the result was a dramatic increase in food production. Two outstanding harvests (1956, 1958) enabled him to push ahead with rapid industrial development, especially in the production of consumer goods. He also introduced administrative reforms and relaxed censorship, allowing some dissident intellectuals, like Aleksandr SOLZHENITSYN, to publish previously suppressed works. Problems soon developed, however. The good harvest years were followed by bad ones, his administrative changes led to much confusion, and his policy of more open discussion provoked new opposition. Dissidence grew along with popular frustration, as expectations outstripped accomplishments.

Foreign Affairs. Energy, ebullience, and lofty goals also characterized Khrushchev's foreign policy. After a dramatic reconciliation with President TITO of Yugoslavia in

Nikita Khrushchev achieved political supremacy in the USSR by 1956. His policies of "destalinization" at home and "peaceful coexistence" abroad eased relations with the West but antagonized China.

1955, he met with Western leaders at a Geneva summit conference that same year. He traveled to the United States in 1959 and 1960, the first Soviet leader to do so. His insistence on "peaceful coexistence" with the capitalist West did much to thaw the COLD WAR but also contributed to a rupture with the Communist government of China.

On the other hand, Khrushchev created the WARSAW TREATY ORGANIZATION in 1955, and the next year he presided over a brutal suppression of the HUNGARIAN REVOLUTION. Cuba represented both a triumph and a failure. Under Fidel CASTRO it became the first ally of the USSR in the Western Hemisphere, but during the CUBAN MISSILE CRISIS (1962) Khrushchev was forced to remove Soviet missiles from the island, with a great loss of face.

Khrushchev's Decline. Khrushchev's unorthodox policies had created opposition from the beginning, especially among the old-guard party members. As his failures began to mount, both domestically and internationally, his opponents in the Politburo gained strength and in October 1964 forced him out of office. He lived in quiet retirement until his death, but his years in power have had a lasting effect on the Soviet Union.

Khufu, King of Egypt

[koo'-foo] Khufu, or Cheops, fl. *c.*2680 BC, was the king of ancient Egypt who directed the construction of the Great Pyramid at Giza (see PYRAMIDS), the largest tomb-pyramid ever built. He was the son and successor of King Snefru, who founded the 4th dynasty (*c.*2613–2498). In 1954 remains of the 43-m (142-ft) funerary ship of Khufu were discovered near the Great Pyramid; a second boat was found in 1987. An ivory statuette found in the temple at Abydos and thought to depict Khufu is in the Egyptian Museum in Cairo.

Khyber Pass

[ky'-bur] The Khyber Pass, a strategically important pass, is on the border between Pakistan and Afghanistan. Cutting through the Safed Koh Range, it is 53 km (33 mi) long and 5 m to 5 km (15 ft to 3 mi) wide and reaches 1,067 m (3,500 ft) in elevation. The pass, controlled by Pakistan, links the cities of Peshawar, Pakistan, and Kabul, Afghanistan, by railroad, paved highway, and caravan route. For centuries the pass has been used by invaders into India. On the northwest frontier of British India, it was the scene of frequent fighting between British forces and local PATHAN tribes.

kiang [kih-ang'] The kiang, a wild ass and a member of the horse family, Equidae, lives on the Tibetan Plateau in Asia at altitudes of 4,100 to 4,800 m (13,500 to 16,000 ft). It is classified either as a separate species, *Equus kiang*, or as a subspecies of the Asiatic wild asses, *E. hemionus kiang*.

The kiang stands 14 hands high (142 cm/56 in) at the withers and weighs up to 400 kg (900 lb). It lives in herds of about five to several hundred. It has a black stripe down its back, and its coat varies from red in summer to brownish in winter.

Kiangsi see JIANGXI

Kiangsu see JIANGSU

kibbutz [kih-buts'] A kibbutz is one type of collective settlement in Israel whose members own or lease land together and practice farming. Agricultural work, cooking, and decision making are carried out in common. Children are raised by the community in many kibbutzim, seeing their own parents a few hours a day.

The first kibbutz (Degania) was founded in 1910 as an experiment by seven agricultural workers. Other kibbutzim soon followed; they played an important role in the Jewish settlement of Palestine as part of the international Zionist movement, which stressed the need to create agricultural roots in the Jewish homeland. These kibbutzim, run on principles that emphasized equality and the dignity of manual work, served both to accustom settlers to a raw country where group work was essential to survival and to settle territory in Palestine.

From the mid-1930s to 1945 growth of the kibbutzim was particularly rapid as European Jews fled persecution and the Nazi Holocaust. Kibbutz members were frequently in the vanguard of Jewish socialist thinking, and they continue to play an important political role in the government of modern Israel. Israel has nearly 300 kibbutzim, most of which own their own factories or processing plants. About 3% of the Israeli population live in kibbutzim.

Kickapoo [kik'-uh-poo] Noted as "great pedestrians" by the first French traders to meet this Algonquian-speaking Indian tribe of North America, the Kickapoo endured numerous relocations in their drive to remain free of white domination. Originally from central Michigan, by 1670 they had migrated to the portage of the Fox and Wisconsin rivers (southwestern Wisconsin), where they became closely allied with the SAUK and FOX. They were decimated by OJIBWA, OTTAWA, and POTAWATOMI attacks during the Fox wars in the early 18th century, but changing their affiliations they aided in the final conquest of

the ILLINOIS tribes, whereupon they settled south of present-day Peoria, Ill.

The Kickapoo adopted horses earlier than neighboring tribes and adapted themselves to the great belt of prairie lands stretching from central Illinois to northern Mexico. They supported the Shawnee chief TECUMSEH against the Americans in the War of 1812 and the Americans against the SEMINOLE in Florida a decade later. In 1852 a large number of Kickapoo migrated to Texas and later to Mexico. Other reservation groups are located in central Oklahoma, northeast Kansas, and Texas, where the Kickapoo number about 2,000 (1987 est.).

Kidd, Captain William Kidd, known as Captain Kidd, b. Scotland, c.1645, d. May 23, 1701, was a British pirate whose life has been much romanticized by literature. Kidd became a privateer and by 1690 was an affluent shipowner in New York. While engaged in a privateering mission off East Africa in 1696–97, he turned to piracy, capturing several ships. He returned (1699) to Oyster Bay, Long Island, thinking that his privateering commission would shield him from arrest. He was induced to sail to Boston, however, where he was detained and sent to London. Kidd was tried for piracy and murder and executed.

The disappearance of most of his booty gave rise to legends about Kidd and his buried treasure. The only treasure actually recovered was found on Gardiners Island, off Long Island, in 1699. Literary treatments of the Kidd legend include Edgar Allan Poe's *The Gold Bug* (1843).

Kidder, Alfred Vincent Alfred Vincent Kidder, b. Marquette, Mich., Oct. 29, 1885, d. June 11, 1963, was one of the most eminent American archaeologists of the early 20th century. Working in the southwestern United States and later in Mesoamerica, he developed the first truly systematic approach to American prehistory. A specialist in southwestern archaeology, in 1915 he began long-term investigations at the large Pecos pueblo in New Mexico. After his appointment to the Carnegie Institution of Washington in 1926, Kidder's interests shifted to Mesoamerica. He was active in Carnegie projects in the MAYA region, especially the KAMINALJUYÚ excavations near Guatemala City.

Kidder's work at Pecos led him to develop a classification system that served as a vital framework for later investigations of PUEBLO culture. His *Introduction to the Study of Southwestern Archaeology* (1924), a model of archaeological reasoning, had an enormous impact on the field. As director of the Carnegie investigations in Mesoamerica, Kidder produced a body of multidisciplinary research that is a major contribution to knowledge of the Maya.

kidnapping Kidnapping (from *kid* plus *napper*, thief) is carrying away a person against that person's will and often holding him or her for ransom. The ransom demanded is usually monetary, but kidnapping has also been used for political extortion—to draw attention to a cause or to demand the release of political prisoners. In the 1970s and '80s political kidnapping internationally was increasingly linked to various practitioners of TERRORISM.

After the kidnapping of Charles A. LINDBERGH's 20-month-old son in 1932, federal kidnapping laws with severe penalties were enacted in the United States. In most states the penalty for kidnapping for ransom is life imprisonment. A recent trend in the United States has been an increased number of kidnappings of their own children by parents involved in child-custody disputes.

kidney, artificial Artificial kidneys remove toxic wastes and fluids that build up in the blood of patients with impaired KIDNEY function. The procedure in blood filtering—termed *hemodialysis*—is employed in acute situations resulting from drug overdose, burns that can cause kidney shutdown, or circulatory shock following surgery. Chronic dialysis treatment is used by patients with end-stage renal failure, which results from disorders such as glomerulonephritis (an immunological reaction to a strep infection resulting in kidney inflammation). Chronic patients are treated for 4 to 6 hours, 3 times a week, on the average, usually for the rest of their lives or until a kidney transplant can be performed (see TRANSPLANTATION, ORGAN).

The artificial kidney was first used on humans in 1943 by Dr. Willem Kolff in the Netherlands. He used a drum apparatus with a cellophane membrane that rotated through a saline solution. Blood from the patient was allowed to flow, via tubing, through the closed membrane. Because the saline solution was on the external side, the processes of osmosis and diffusion removed waste products and fluids, respectively.

Since the 1940s the saline solution bath has been replaced by sophisticated machines that deliver a solution, dialysate, to the artificial organ and have a number of safety monitors. The artificial kidney was made presterilized, disposable, and commercially available in 1955, an innovation that led the way to chronic treatment programs. Such programs grew significantly after 1973, when the U.S. government passed legislation guaranteeing 80 percent reimbursement through Medicare to all patients. In the 1980s emphasis shifted to home dialysis. Continuous ambulatory peritoneal dialysis (CAPD), which uses a small, portable dialysis unit and allows patients greater movement, is less traumatic to the body, requires less time, and costs about 50 percent less than traditional dialysis.

In the late 1980s a natural kidney hormone, erythropoietin, became available in quantity through genetic engineering. Clinical trials have indicated that the protein can reverse the anemic condition observed in most dialysis patients.

kidney disease The kidneys are subject to numerous disorders. Some, present at birth, are called developmental and hereditary abnormalities; some arise as a result of uncontrolled cell growth and are called tumors. The majority of disorders, however, occur secondary to physiologic, anatomic, metabolic, or immunologic alterations within the body, or to toxic or infectious agents acquired from the environment. For instance, preliminary studies have shown a link between the overuse of two common painkillers, ibuprofen and acetaminophen, and kidney failure in some patients. Kidney disorders can be categorized according to the anatomic site they involve: those interfering with the blood flow of the kidneys, those directly damaging the nephrons (the functional units of the kidneys), and those obstructing the outflow of urine from the kidneys.

Developmental and Hereditary Abnormalities. Congenital abnormalities of size, shape, and number of the kidneys are quite common. These abnormalities cause problems only if they interfere with the passage of urine. A rather devastating hereditary condition is adult polycystic kidney disease. The kidneys become filled with large cysts, and the disease usually becomes apparent in the fourth or fifth decade of life.

A more unusual condition is hereditary nephritis, the most common variety being Alport's syndrome. Red blood cells and protein are present in the urine, deafness frequently develops, and progressive loss of renal function occurs. There are several hereditary renal tubular functional defects (the Fanconi syndrome) involving excretion of amino acids, monosaccharides, phosphate, and hydrogen ions; the Fanconi syndrome does not usually lead to renal failure. Cystinuria is an inherited disease that involves urinary excretion of abnormally high levels of certain amino acids. Patients have a tendency to develop kidney stones or bladder stones.

Tumors. The two important malignant tumors of the kidney are Wilm's tumor, which occurs primarily in the early years of life, and hypernephroma (renal cell cancer), which is more common in later years. Wilm's tumor occurs as a painful abdominal mass. Patients with hypernephroma have weight loss, weakness, and anemia. Surgical excision of these tumors is curative if it is done before they spread outside of the kidney.

Disorders of Renal Blood Flow. A decrease in renal blood flow may be secondary to primary events, including reduced cardiac output, decreased blood volume, or decreased blood pressure (hypotension). Correction of the primary event allows renal function to return to normal. Disease of the renal arteries or arterioles also reduces renal blood flow, thereby decreasing renal function. Toxemia of pregnancy and renal vein thrombosis also may cause renal failure.

Disorders Directly Damaging the Nephrons. Each nephron in the kidney is composed of a glomerulus and its tubule. Some diseases, such as glomerulonephritis, primarily attack the glomeruli; others attack the tubulointerstitial portions of the kidneys. Acute glomerulonephritis occurs one to three weeks after a streptococcal skin infection or an upper-respiratory-tract infection and is manifested by scanty urine, red blood cells in the urine, edema, hypertension, and impaired renal function. The majority of patients recover completely. Systemic diseases such as diabetes mellitus, multiple myeloma, and amyloidosis also may cause damage that can progress to renal failure.

The causes of tubulointerstitial disease of the kidneys are even more numerous. Acute tubular necrosis (cell death) is caused by toxic substances, circulating blood or muscle pigments, or shocklike states. Interstitial nephritis may be due to toxic agents, metabolic abnormalities, infectious diseases, hypersensitivity reactions to drugs, vascular lesions, obstruction of urine flow, tumors, or hereditary disorders.

Disorders Obstructing the Urine Outflow. Blockage of the outflow of urine leads to renal damage. Numerous types of lesions can cause obstruction, such as congenital malformations and hereditary disorders, infectious processes causing strictures, stones, and tumors. Bladder dysfunction due to a neurologic lesion and bladder outlet obstruction due to prostatic hypertrophy also are common.

When end-stage renal failure, that is, complete loss of excretory function, ensues, patients may be kept alive by hemodialysis (see KIDNEY, ARTIFICIAL) or by receiving a renal transplant. When kidney failure occurs, toxic wastes build up in the body and cause UREMIA. If untreated, death may result.

---

kidney stone   Stones, or calculi, commonly form in kidney tissue or the draining structures of the urinary tract as a result of diseases, infections, or problems of mineral excretion. The most common types of stones contain various combinations of calcium, magnesium, phosphorus, or oxalate. Kidney stones may form once without recurrence. In extreme cases they may enlarge to fill the entire draining structure of the kidney. Uric-acid stones complicate gout, and they occasionally develop in the absence of other manifestations of that disease. Less common types are due to inherited disorders. Recurrence of most stones can be prevented by therapy.

When a stone causes erosion of tissue, blood appears in the urine; when one lodges in the draining tubes, there may be severe pain in the flank extending to the lower abdomen and groin. Other complications include obstruction to urine flow, persistent infection of the kidneys, and progressive tissue damage with loss of kidney function.

Most solitary stones are passed in the urine, but others require medical treatment. Procedures now replacing traditional surgical removal include percutaneous removal, which employs a fiberoptic nephroscope to extract a stone through the skin. A noninvasive technique, LITHOTRIPSY, uses acoustic shock waves to break up kidney stones. To break up stones in the lower ureter, the canal between the kidney and the bladder, a laser light guided by optical fibers is used.

---

kidneys   The two kidneys are the major organs of excretion in vertebrates. Excess water, toxic waste products of metabolism such as UREA and URIC ACID, and inorganic salts are disposed of by the kidneys in the form of URINE. The kidneys are also largely responsible for maintaining the water balance of the body and the acidity (pH) of the blood (see EXCRETORY SYSTEM). The kidneys and associated organs that produce and eliminate urine are collectively called the urinary system. The kidneys also play important roles in other body activities, such as in releasing the protein erythropoietin—which stimulates the bone marrow to increase the formation of red blood cells—and in helping to control blood pressure. Some drugs or their breakdown products are eliminated through the kidneys.

Anatomy

Human kidneys are paired, reddish brown, bean-shaped structures about 11 cm (4.4 in) long. They are located in back of the body cavity, one on each side of the spine just above the waist. The kidneys are loosely held in place by a mass of fat and by fibrous tissue. The outer margin is convex, the inner border concave. On the inner surface is a slit, the hilus, through which pass the arteries, veins, nerves, and the renal pelvis, a funnellike structure. Urine from each kidney is collected in the renal pelvis and passes into a hollow tube, the ureter, which extends downward, emptying into the urinary bladder. A shorter, single tube, the urethra, eliminates urine from the bladder.

The cut surface of the kidney reveals two distinct areas: the cortex—a dark band along the outer border, about 1 cm (0.4 in) in thickness—and the inner medulla. The medulla is divided into 8 to 18 conical tissues termed renal pyramids. The apex of each pyramid, the papilla, extends into the renal pelvis, through which urine is discharged. The cortex arches over the bases of the pyramids (cortical arches) and extends down between each pyramid as the renal columns.

Nephrons. Each kidney contains at least 1 million microscopic structures called nephrons, or renal tubules. These are the urine-forming units. Each nephron has thin walls and is divided into a Bowman's capsule and a tubule. The nephron begins with a renal corpuscle, which is a granular body found in the cortex and is composed of the double-walled, cuplike Bowman's capsule. Each Bowman's capsule surrounds a tuft or knot of blood vessels called a glomerulus (pl. glomeruli). A winding, convoluted section of the nephron tubule extends from Bowman's capsule toward the medulla region of the kidney and is called the proximal convoluted tubule. This region is followed by Henle's loop, which extends into the medulla and loops back to the cortex. The final section, the distal convoluted tubule, is located near the proximal convoluted portion. It continues on to connect other tubules in a branching structure, the collecting tubules, which descend into the medulla and terminate at the papillae, thus conducting the urine to the renal pelvis.

Blood Circulation. Arterial blood enters the kidneys, at the hilus, by renal arteries, which subdivide into smaller and yet smaller arteries, and finally into afferent arterioles. They lead into the 30 to 40 capillary loops of each glomerulus. Blood is recollected from each glomerulus by the efferent arterioles, which are much smaller in diameter than the afferent arterioles and therefore create a relatively higher backup blood pressure in the capillaries of the glomerulus than in other capillaries of the body. This is significant in the efficient filtering function of the nephron. The efferent vessels divide into capillaries surrounding the tubules, thus supplying blood to the medulla. Eventually they rejoin into veins and exit through the renal hilus.

Urine Production

The initial site of urine production is the glomerulus. Arterial blood pressure drives a filtrate of plasma across the capillary walls of each glomerulus into the open space around the capillary tuft. The filtered plasma is collected in Bowman's capsule. Now called glomerular filtrate, it is mainly water but also contains salts, glucose, amino acids, nitrogenous wastes such as urea, and a small amount of ammonia. Proteins, fats, and cellular elements are filtered out so that they remain in the general blood circulation. In normal kidneys 100 to 140 ml (0.21 to 0.29 pt) of filtrate is formed each minute, for a total of about 170 l (180 qt) per day.

As the glomerular filtrate passes along the proximal convoluted tubule, most of its water content and some of its dissolved materials are reabsorbed into the blood of the surrounding capillaries. This process is highly selective.

Water, sodium and chloride ions, most of the bicarbonate, and all of the glucose are reabsorbed into the blood; products such as urea and ammonia remain in the tubule.

During the later stage, through Henle's loop and the distal convoluted tubule, most of the remaining filtrate is further selectively reabsorbed, so only about 1 percent of the volume of the original filtrate is finally excreted as urine.

The kidneys excrete 400 to 2,000 ml (0.84 to 4.2 pt) of urine or more per day; excretion varies in volume and composition depending on the needs of the host. The cells lining the tubules are under the influence of regulating factors such as the hormones aldosterone, antidiuretic hormone, parathyroid hormone, and atrial natriuretic factor.

The distal tubule regulates the overall acidity of the urine, and ultimately of the blood, by excretion of hydrogen ions. Ammonia combines with hydrogen to form ammonia ions that are secreted into the urine. The removal of hydrogen ions decreases the acidity.

All the blood glucose will be removed unless the blood

The kidneys filter out waste products from blood and maintain the salt and water balance of the body. A kidney has an outer cortex (1) and an inner medulla (2), which is divided into 8 to 18 segments known as pyramids (3). A renal artery (4) carries blood to the kidneys, and a renal vein (5) carries purified blood back into the general system. The nephron, which is the basic unit of the kidney, includes a glomerulus (6) that filters waste products from the blood. The waste products form a concentrated fluid (7) that passes through a descending tubule (8) to the loop of Henle (9) and into an ascending tubule (10). These tubules are surrounded by blood vessels that absorb and recycle water and salts from the fluid. A collecting tubule (11) carries the product, urine, from the nephron to the renal pelvis (12), which connects to a ureter (13).

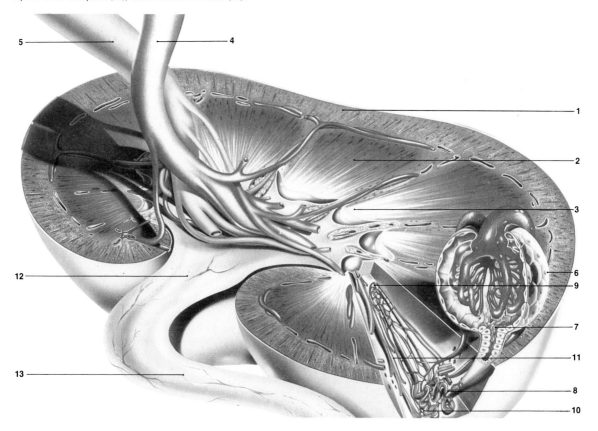

glucose exceeds normal concentrations by a considerable amount. Other mechanisms remove most, if not all, of the other solutes, such as sodium. Most of the sodium ions in kidney filtrate are transported back to the blood, but 3 to 5 g (0.1 to 0.17 oz) pass into the urine each day. As a result, most animals have strict salt requirements and must consume several grams of sodium chloride daily in order to live.

When excessive amounts of fluid are lost from the body, or when the blood pressure falls below normal, the kidneys release the enzyme renin into the blood, where it promotes the formation of angiotensin. Within minutes, angiotensin causes vasoconstriction, which increases blood pressure and stimulates the secretion of aldosterone.

Evolution of the Kidney

The structure of the nephron is basically the same in the kidneys of all vertebrates. The kidney has gone through a series of changes, however, in the course of evolution. In invertebrates, the excretory organ is a simple absorbing tubule called a nephridium. Among lower vertebrates, such as the fishes, there exists a primitive kind of kidney, called the holonephros, that consists of three to five kidney tubules near the heart. Most adult fishes and amphibians have a posterior kidney, or opisthonephros, containing a more complicated type of tubule. Adult reptiles, birds, and mammals have the most advanced form of kidney, called a metanephros.

It is generally believed that the kidney first evolved in the original vertebrates, which were freshwater life-forms. In keeping with the laws of OSMOSIS, there is a continual flow of water into the bodies of freshwater fish. Excess water must be disposed of once it has entered. When the nephron first evolved and developed, it became capable of reabsorbing glucose, salts, and other materials that otherwise would have been lost in pumping out surplus water.

In the case of freshwater fishes that returned to the sea and in the evolution of land animal forms (reptiles and birds), the situation became reversed: water conservation, rather than disposal, became the problem, and the nephron became a liability instead of an asset. This difficulty appears to have been solved during evolution in a number of ways. Nearly all marine teleosts (bony fishes) show more or less reduction in the number and size of glomeruli. These fishes also eliminate large amounts of salt through the gills, thus retaining fresh water. Retaining their large glomeruli, the marine elasmobranchs (sharks and rays) are similar to the freshwater teleosts in that they take in water and excrete copious amounts of urine.

The reptile-bird line, like the marine teleosts, reduced the glomerular system. Mammals adapted to dry land are able to conserve water by producing extremely concentrated urine.

See also: KIDNEY DISEASE.

Kiel [keel] Kiel is the capital of Schleswig-Holstein state in northern Germany. It is located about 90 km (55 mi) north of Hamburg, on the Kiel Fjord, where the Kiel Canal enters the Baltic Sea. Its population is 243,600 (1987 est.). Industries include shipping, shipbuilding, electrical engineering, food processing (especially fish), printing, and the manufacture of textiles and precision instruments. Christian Albrecht University (1665) is there. The naval base at Kiel was of major importance to Germany during both world wars.

First mentioned in the 10th century, Kiel was chartered in 1242 and became a member of the HANSEATIC LEAGUE in 1284. It was the seat of the powerful dukes of Holstein until 1773, when it came under Danish control. In 1866 it passed, with all of Holstein, to Prussia. Construction of the canal, linking the North and Baltic seas, began in 1887, and the canal began operating in 1895. The city was heavily bombed during World War II, but the damaged sections have been rebuilt.

Kierkegaard, Søren [kyair'-kuh-gawr, sur'-en] Søren Aabye Kierkegaard, b. May 5, 1813, d. Nov. 11, 1855, was a Danish philosopher and religious thinker whose reaction against the depersonalization of society and against the established church of Denmark took the form of brilliant literary and philosophical essays. He is regarded by philosophers today as a precursor of EXISTENTIALISM.

In 1841, Kierkegaard broke his marriage engagement for fear that he and his fiancée might lack common philosophic interests. Thereafter he lived a life of seclusion, devoted to writing. The impact on his career of the broken engagement, as well as his austere Lutheran upbringing and his melancholia, is evident in virtually everything he wrote thereafter.

Many of Kierkegaard's books, such as *Either/Or* (1843; Eng. trans., 1944) and *Philosophical Fragments* (1844; Eng. trans., 1936), were written under pseudonyms. He adopted this practice in order to avoid giving the impression that the views expressed in the books constituted any definitive religious position, or even that they necessarily represented his own position.

Kierkegaard's unifying theme was that there are three spheres of existence—the aesthetic, the ethical, and the religious—in constant tension. He found the first of these, personal aesthetic enjoyment, in the fickle search for pleasure that is essentially egoistic. The second, the ethical sphere, is not egoistic; rather, it is an impersonal ideal, a law based on reason rather than on personal preference and convenience. In this stage, life is not a series of separate moments of pleasure but a long-range project to be organized according to rational principles. These principles include not only the rules of ultimate self-interest but also the abstract principles of morality that describe what an individual ought to do. In the third stage, that of true religious choice, no automatic, rational decision procedure can be employed, but rather a "leap of faith" provides the grounds for decision. Thus, in *Fear and Trembling* (1843; Eng. trans., 1941), Kierkegaard retold the story of Abraham's dilemma in such a way as to present the two alternatives of an abstract ethical universal (the abstract rule that one should not kill one's child) and a concrete religious commitment (the unjustifiable but undeniable command of God to Abraham that he should slay Isaac).

Søren Kierkegaard, a 19th-century Danish philosopher and religious writer, sought to differentiate the religious, aesthetic, and ethical modes of life. His emphasis on subjective commitment to truth made him the forerunner of existentialism.

For Kierkegaard, the highest level of human life consists of recognizing the need for RELIGION as a subjective commitment to truth, as opposed to the Hegelian philosophy of pure thought. Kierkegaard attacked what he considered to be the sterile METAPHYSICS of G. W. F. HEGEL, who attempted to systematize the whole of existence and create an objective theory of knowledge. Kierkegaard's often repeated statement, "truth is subjectivity," should not be understood in the sense of a shallow individualism. Rather, it links truth with the subject instead of with its object, making the full communication of truth to other subjects impossible. Kierkegaard drew the only logical conclusion from his principle—that it is impossible to establish an objective system of doctrinal truths.

Kiesler, Frederick John [kees'-lur] The Austrian architect Frederick John Kiesler, b. Vienna, Sept. 2, 1896, d. Dec. 27, 1965, was a visionary "nonbuilding" architect noted for his development of freely flowing spaces in sculptured forms. His unorthodox approach to architecture was first expressed in a 1923 design for a City in Space, which he based on the principles of bridge building. In the late 1920s and early '30s he carried these ideas forward in designs for an Endless Theater and a House in Space, culminating eventually in his plan for an Endless House, which was exhibited (1959–60) at the Museum of Modern Art in New York City. According to Kiesler the rounded shapes of these revolutionary architectural forms could be created by applying a plastic substance, such as concrete, to a sculptured mesh of steel. Kiesler's avant-garde aesthetics were put to most direct use in his work as director of scenic design (1934–37) at the Juilliard School of Music, New York City.

Kiev [kee'-yuhf] Kiev, the third largest city of USSR, is the capital of Ukraine and the administrative center of Kiev oblast. Located in the north central Ukraine, it is on

the DNEPR RIVER. Kiev's population is 2,587,000 (1989). One of the largest industrial, cultural, and educational centers of the USSR, the city is also a major transport hub at the junction of railroads, highways, and the navigable Dnepr.

Contemporary City. The historical heart of Kiev, on the west bank of the Dnepr, is divided into the Upper Town, the city center with the main business street; Pechersk, to the south, with a noted 11th-century cave monastery and the government buildings; and Podol, to the north, the old commercial and Jewish district.

Kiev's important industries are situated mainly in Darnitsa, on the eastern side of the Dnepr. The principal manufacturing establishments produce ships, airplanes, motorcycles, cameras, synthetic fibers, building materials, and a wide range of machinery and metal products.

As the national center of the Ukraine, Kiev has a wide network of educational institutions, including the Ukrainian Academy of Sciences, Kiev State University (1834), and the Polytechnical Institute (1898). Cultural facilities include the Shevchenko Theater of Opera and Ballet and both Ukrainian and Russian drama theaters, as well as the Kiev State Historical Museum and museums of both Ukrainian and Russian fine arts. Historical sites are St. Sophia Cathedral, dating from 1037; the 11th-century Golden Gate; and the ruins of the 11th-century Kiev-Pechersk cave monastery, long an important pilgrimage site and now a museum. The Babi Yar monument (1976) marks a site where thousands of Jews and Soviet prisoners of war were massacred by the Germans during World War II.

History. One of the oldest cities in Europe, Kiev was probably founded by the 7th century and was first mentioned in 9th-century chronicles. It flourished from the 9th to the 12th century as a trade center and the capital of an early Russian state known as Kievan Russia (see RUSSIA/UNION OF SOVIET SOCIALIST REPUBLICS, HISTORY OF). Kiev was virtually destroyed by Mongol invaders in 1240. It fell under the rule of Lithuania (c.1362) and then Poland (1569) before passing to Russia in 1654. With the development of steam navigation on the Dnepr and the building of railroads, Kiev became an important financial and commercial city in the mid-19th century. Industrial development dates mainly from the Soviet period, especially after the capital of the Ukraine was moved there in 1934. German forces occupied the city from September 1941 to November 1943, and it suffered extensive damage.

Kigali [kee-gah'-lee] Kigali is the capital and commercial center of Rwanda, in central Africa (1981 est. pop., 156,700). An international airport and the École Technique Officielle Don Bosco (1956) are located there. Tin and tungsten are mined nearby.

Kikuyu [ki-koo'-yoo] The Kikuyu (Gikuyu) are an East African people of the Kenya highlands. They speak a Bantu language of the Benue-Congo subfamily of the Niger-Congo stock; in the mid-1980s they numbered more than 4,000,000. A farming people, they traditionally live in hilltop villages of dispersed homesteads. Political authority rests in a council of elders. Males are organized in age grades, progressing from initiation in adolescence to political office in mature adulthood. Descent is patrilineal, residence patrilocal. Polygyny is the general rule, with each wife having her own dwelling. Bride price is paid by the husband to the wife's people in the form of livestock.

The Kikuyu have long been subject to competition for land, first with neighboring Masai raiders and later with English settlers. By the mid-1900s many Kikuyu were working as laborers on European farms or in Nairobi. From 1952 to 1956, under the leadership of Jomo KENYATTA, the MAU MAU movement aimed at recovering land taken by Europeans, obtaining self-government for Africans, restoring traditional customs, and driving out all foreigners. Kenya's largest tribal group, the Kikuyu have continued to play a strong role in national affairs since Kenyan independence (1963).

Kilauea [kee-lah-way'-uh]   Kilauea is the world's largest active volcano crater. Part of MAUNA LOA, it is on south central Hawaii island in Volcanoes National Park. The summit of Kilauea reaches 1,247 m (4,090 ft), and the crater is 13 km (8 mi) in circumference. Kilauea's eruptions are generally in the form of molten lava lakes, with little escaping gas and few explosions.

Kildare [kil-dair']   Kildare is a county in eastern Ireland, located in Leinster province. It covers 1,694 km^2 (654 mi^2) and has a population of 116,247 (1986). Kildare is the county seat, but the county council meets at Naas. Most of the area is flat farmland. The principal crops are wheat, barley, oats, and root vegetables. Kildare is famous for racehorse breeding, and cattle raising is also important. Manufactures include textiles, paper products, and cutlery. Naas was the home of the kings of Leinster from the 2d to the 12th century. The town of Kildare grew up around a religious house founded in the 5th century.

Kilimanjaro [kil-ih-muhn-jah'-roh]   Kilimanjaro, the highest mountain in Africa, is a snow-covered inactive volcano on the plains of northeastern Tanzania close to the border with Kenya. It has two peaks: the taller, Kibo, is 5,895 m (19,340 ft) high, and the lower, Mawenzi, is 5,149 m (17,564 ft). Kibo and Mawenzi are connected by a ridge. The crater of Kibo, 2 km (1.2 mi) wide and up to 300 m (984 ft) deep, is covered by a thick, slowly decreasing ice cap.

The first Europeans to discover Kilimanjaro, the legendary burial place of King Solomon, were two German missionaries, Johannes Rebmann and Ludwig Krapf, in 1848. Their tales of a snow-covered peak near the equator, however, were not initially believed. Later two other Germans were the first to reach (1889) the Kibo summit.

Kilkenny [kil-ken'-ee]   Kilkenny (1986 pop., 73,186) is a county in Leinster province, southeastern Ireland. Its 2,061-km^2 (796-mi^2) area consists of hills and plains watered by the Barrow, Nore, and Suir rivers. Grains, vegetables, and livestock are raised, anthracite coal is mined, and brewing is a well-established industry. Kilkenny became part of Leinster province in 1210.

The county town, also named Kilkenny (Gaelic: Cill Choinnigh), has a population of 9,473 (1981). Saint Canice established a monastery there in the 6th century. Later the town was the capital of the kingdom of Ossory. From the Norman period until 1843, Kilkenny was divided into Englishtown and Irishtown, with much strife between the two. Anglo-Norman parliaments were held there from 1293 to 1408, and from 1642 to 1648 (during the English Civil War) Kilkenny was the capital of the Roman Catholic confederacy.

Killarney [kil-lar'-nee]   Killarney (1981 pop., 7,678) is the market town of County Kerry, southwestern Ireland. Many tourists are attracted by Killarney's mild climate and scenic location. The town is surrounded by lakes and mountains, with Macgillycuddy's Reeks—the highest mountains in Ireland—nearby and the Lakes of Killarney only 2.5 km (1.5 mi) away. Lace, shoes, woolens, and other light manufactures are produced. The cathedral (built 1846) was designed by Augustus Pugin.

Killy, Jean Claude [kee-leé, zhawn klohd]   Jean Claude Killy, b. Aug. 30, 1943, was a French downhill skier who, during the 1968 Winter Olympic Games in Grenoble, France, became only the second skier ever to win all three gold medals for men's Alpine skiing. Killy also won the World Championship combined titles in 1965 and 1966 and the World Cup in 1967 and 1968. He was world professional champion in 1972 and retired soon thereafter. Killy served as copresident of the Olympic organizing committee for the 1992 Winter Games, in Albertville, France.

Kilmer, Joyce [kil'-mur]   The poet and journalist Alfred Joyce Kilmer, b. New Brunswick, N.J., Dec. 6, 1886, d. July 30, 1918, is famous for his poem "Trees" (1914), a work full of sentiment and confused simile. Kilmer wrote war poems that were far better, such as "Rouge Bouquet" (1918). His collections include *Trees and Other Poems* (1914) and *Main Street and Other Poems* (1917). Kilmer died in battle during World War I.

kiln   A kiln is an oven or furnace designed to bake, dry, harden, or burn various materials. Low-temperature kilns are used to dry hops, cure tobacco, and season wood; high-temperature kilns may operate at temperatures up to 1,200° C (2,192° F) and are used to fire brick (see BRICK

AND BRICKLAYING) and pottery (see POTTERY AND PORCELAIN). In an intermittent kiln the material to be fired is loaded, and the temperature is raised to the required level for the necessary time; the kiln is then allowed to cool before the fired material is unloaded. In continuous kilns the firing temperature is maintained continuously. The material to be fired is drawn slowly into the firing zone, and then into gradually cooler areas so it can be removed. Rotary kilns, such as those used to make cement (see CEMENT AND CONCRETE), are heated, and inclined cylinders revolve slowly as the raw materials are fed into the top. The materials gradually descend through the hotter firing zone to the cooler bottom.

Kilpatrick, William Heard

William Heard Kilpatrick, b. White Plains, Ga., Nov. 20, 1871, d. Feb. 13, 1965, was an American philosopher widely regarded as the father of PROGRESSIVE EDUCATION. After studying at Mercer and Johns Hopkins universities, Kilpatrick taught in the Georgia public schools and at Mercer. He taught at Teachers College, Columbia University, from 1909 until he retired in 1938. A colleague of the philosopher John DEWEY, whose ideas he popularized, Kilpatrick developed the project method of teaching, emphasizing a child-centered rather than subject-oriented approach. Over the course of his career he taught 34,000 graduate students.

Kim Il Sung

[keem eel sung]   Kim Il Sung, originally Kim Sung Chu, b. Apr. 15, 1912, became premier of the People's Republic of Korea (North Korea) on its establishment in 1948. Kim, who joined the Communist party in 1931, fought the Japanese occupation forces in the 1930s and commanded a Korean unit in the Soviet army in World War II. As premier, Kim directed the invasion of South Korea that led to the KOREAN WAR (1950–53). He became president in 1972 under a revised constitution. Promoting self-reliance, he has isolated his country from the outside world. Kim, known in North Korea as "Great Leader," has designated his eldest son, Kim Jong Il, as his successor.

Kimberley

[kim'-bur-lee]   Kimberley, a city of 74,061 (1985) in Cape province, central South Africa, is the nation's leading diamond center. Several diamond mines are located there, and all diamonds mined in South Africa are sold in Kimberley. Iron, manganese, and gypsum are also mined, and textiles and construction materials are manufactured. The city is an important rail junction. Kimberley was founded in 1871, after diamonds were discovered there. The mines were held by De Beers Consolidated Mines, headed by Cecil Rhodes.

kimberlite

[kim-bur-lite]   Kimberlites are fragmented IGNEOUS ROCKS of unusual composition that occur as narrow fissures, called pipes, that puncture plates of conti-

nental crust (see PLATE TECTONICS). Relatively low in silica, they apparently were explosively emplaced by forces deep within the Earth's mantle. In mineralogical terms, kimberlites are PERIDOTITES of serpentinized mica content (see SERPENTINE). They contain a variety of high-pressure minerals, including DIAMOND. The most notable are found in South Africa, Tanzania, Angola, and Siberia.

The kimberlite pipe at the famous Kimberley diamond mine in South Africa typifies the narrow surface area (approximately 40,000 m^2/450,000 ft^2) and great depth (from more than 1,000 m/3,500 ft below the present land surface to the limit of mining) of these subvolcanic features. At the time of the eruption, the Kimberley pipe extended an estimated additional 1,400 m (4,600 ft) through now-eroded layers of overlying sediments and formed a deep, narrow funnel of debris and kimberlite MAGMA.

Kincardine

[kin-kar'-din]   Kincardine, also known as The Mearns, is a former county on the North Sea coast of Scotland. To the west the rugged Grampians rise to more than 610 m (2,000 ft). Along the coast and in the river valleys potatoes and oats are grown; livestock raising is also important. Stonehaven (1981 pop., 7,885), the area's largest town, was once an important fishing village; now tourism and the wool industry are significant. The Picts were the first known inhabitants of the area, which also has some Roman remains. In 1296 a document was drawn up at Kincardine, turning over the Scottish crown to King Edward I, king of England. Kincardine became a part of the new administrative region of GRAMPIAN in 1975.

kindergarten

see PRESCHOOL EDUCATION

Kindi, al-

[kin'-dee, ahl]   Known as al-Arab because of his southern Arabian origins, al-Kindi, d. c.873, served as a translator and editor of Greek philosophical works at the court of the Abbasid caliphs al-Mamun and Mutasim. He was well versed in ancient learning and devoted his life to its dissemination in all areas of Muslim culture.

In his philosophical and scientific writings, al-Kindi was eclectic, although he regarded Neopythagorean mathematics as the foundation of all science; and like al-FARABI, he attempted to reconcile the views of Plato and Aristotle. According to al-Kindi, revealed and natural theology (philosophy) reached the same conclusions, but he maintained that philosophy was inferior to revelation.

kinematics

[kin-eh-mat'-iks]   Kinematics is the branch of physics concerned with the description of motion. (The analysis of the causes of motion is a separate subject called DYNAMICS.) The standard way to describe motion is to give the position of an object as a function of time. In one dimension, the displacement x from the origin is given in terms of the time t after zero time. The velocity v is the time rate of change of position. Similarly, acceleration is the time rate of change of velocity. When objects move in three dimensions, the speeds and accelerations in each perpendicular direction can be treated separately, since both velocity and acceleration are vectors.

See also: LAWS OF MOTION; MOTION, PLANAR.

kinetic art [kin-et'-ik] The term *kinetic art* is applied to sculpture in which physical motion plays an important role. The parts of a kinetic sculpture may be moved mechanically or by natural means. Kinetic art is a 20th-century phenomenon and was created by artists who saw it as valuable metaphor for the rhythms of a mechanical age. The Italian futurists (see FUTURISM) were the first to emphasize physical motion as the dominant element of an aesthetic theory. Similar ideas were put forward by Marcel DUCHAMP, whose *Mobile: Bicycle Wheel* (1913; Philadelphia Museum of Art) is thought to have been the first sculpture to use physical movement. After World War I, Soviet constructivist sculptors (see CONSTRUCTIVISM) incorporated the idea of motion into their dynamic works, and in the 1920s ideas of kinetic art were developed further by László MOHOLY-NAGY, who experimented with light and color. In 1932, Alexander CALDER created the first true MOBILE, whose parts move in air currents. Calder's mobiles inspired a resurgence of kinetic art in the 1950s and 1960s by such artists as Jean TINGUELY.

kinetic energy see ENERGY

kinetic theory of matter The kinetic theory of matter is an attempt to explain and predict all measurable properties of gases, liquids, and solids, based on a knowledge of their atomic and molecular compositions. This largely has been achieved for simple, low-density gases, and considerable progress is being made toward a similar understanding of more complex gases, liquids, and solids.

The kinetic theory of matter is based upon three fundamental assumptions. First, all matter is composed of atoms and molecules, even though other successful methods treat matter as uniform, continuous substances. Second, these atoms and molecules are not at rest but are in constant thermal motion, of which heat is a manifestation. Third, any macroscopic sample contains a large enough number of atoms or molecules so that statistical concepts can be used to determine their properties, eliminating the necessity of calculating the motion of each individual molecule. These postulates, in a more precise and mathematical form, are the basis of the kinetic theory of matter.

Development. The kinetic theory of gases was developed in the 19th century to explain a number of diverse experiments on gases carried out during the 17th and 18th centuries. (See GAS LAWS.) Among the first of these was the observation by Robert Boyle that, at constant temperature, a gas's pressure is proportional to its density. Jacques Charles and Joseph L. Gay-Lussac showed that if a gas is heated at constant volume, its pressure is proportional to the temperature measured from absolute zero, and the rate of increase of the pressure is independent of the gas studied. These two observations can be expressed in one form of the ideal gas law $PV = Nk_BT$, where P is the pressure, V the volume, N the number of atoms or molecules, T the absolute temperature, and k_B the BOLTZMANN CONSTANT.

Daniel Bernoulli explained (1738) Boyle's law on the basis of the molecular hypothesis; he assumed that pressure arises from collisions by gas molecules with the container walls. When the density is increased at constant temperature, the number of collisions increases and with it the pressure. Julius L. Mayer suggested (1842) that heat is simply a result of molecular motion; this equivalence of heat energy and molecular kinetic energy was verified experimentally (1843) by James P. Joule. Observations, during the 19th century, of BROWNIAN MOTION confirmed that the atoms and molecules in matter are in constant thermal motion.

Rudolf Clausius calculated (1857) that, if the molecules are all moving with the same speed, v, but in random directions, the rate of collisions with the wall can be calculated statistically, and the amount of momentum transferred during each collision is obtained from the laws of classical mechanics. The pressure is then found to be $PV = \frac{1}{3} Nmv^2$, where m is the mass of the molecules. Combining this with the ideal gas law gives the important relationship $\frac{1}{2}mv^2 = \frac{3}{2}k_BT$, showing that a gas's temperature is directly related to the velocities of the molecules that compose it.

James C. Maxwell showed that a gas's molecules have different velocities; he used probability theory to calculate their distribution. The relationship between temperature and velocity is still valid, but v^2 must be replaced by the average of the square of the velocity of the molecules. Ludwig Boltzmann used classical mechanics to put Maxwell's results on a more rigorous dynamical basis; he also derived the equation that describes the return of a dilute gas toward its equilibrium state. The Boltzmann equation is the basis of the kinetic theory of gases.

Josiah Willard Gibbs generalized Boltzmann's work and in so doing established the foundations of statistical mechanics; instead of restricting his attention to the dynamical evolution of dilute gases, he developed a formalism that is applicable as well to liquids and solids. His statistical description of matter not only satisfied the laws of thermodynamics, but also gave a prescription for calculating the thermodynamic properties of matter. The hypotheses that underlie his work have in recent years been given a more rigorous mathematical foundation and have been tested and verified by a wide variety of experiments.

Gases. The kinetic theory of gases has been extensively tested and verified experimentally. If the forces between atoms or molecules are known independently, such properties as the dependence of viscosity on temperature can be calculated using kinetic theory and compared with experiment, resulting in a high rate of agreement.

The reverse procedure is often used: forces between molecules can be determined from transport measurements on gases. The way in which light is scattered by a gas is also predicted correctly by kinetic theory.

Liquids and Solids. The kinetic theory of liquids and solids is at a much less developed state than that of gases. At low temperatures molecules form regular crystal-line lattices, and their motion can be described in terms of oscillations about equilibrium positions. As the temperature increases, these oscillations become larger in amplitude, defects form in the ordered lattice, and diffusion can occur. At the melting point the lattice structure disappears and the material forms a liquid, in which molecules can diffuse throughout the sample.

The kinetic theory of liquids is an area of active research that is particularly difficult, because a molecule in a liquid interacts simultaneously with many other molecules, rather than simply undergoing binary collisions as in a gas. Major advances in the understanding of the dynamics of simple liquids have been made since 1960 through the development of the method of molecular dynamics. High-speed computers are used to solve the equations of motion of a small number of molecules (typically 500–1,000). Many questions about liquid-state dynamics can be asked and answered through these computer simulations.

Billie Jean King, shown at Wimbledon in 1982, was one of the most highly regarded players in tennis during the 1960s and '70s. Off the court, King was probably the individual most responsible for women's tennis gaining monetary parity with men's.

kinetics   SEE CHEMICAL KINETICS AND EQUILIBRIUM

---

king   A king is a male ruler who reigns usually for life. Originally kings were often elected, although hereditary kingship generally became the rule. In some civilizations, such as ancient Egypt, the king was believed to be a god. Christian kings during the Middle Ages considered themselves representatives of God's will. Absolute monarchs, such as those of the 16th to the 18th century in Europe, claimed to rule by DIVINE RIGHT. Today the power of most kings is limited by constitutions, and they function mainly as symbols of national unity.

See also: MONARCHY; QUEEN.

King, B. B.   The blues singer and guitarist Riley "B. B." King, b. Itta Benna, Miss., Sept. 16, 1925, is acknowledged as a major influence on the development of ROCK MUSIC. At 16, King began to work as a Memphis, Tenn., disk jockey and as a singer in local clubs using his stage name, Blues Boy. He cut his first record in 1949 and by the mid-1960s had achieved wide recognition. His subsequent career has produced a long list of hits and a series of triumphal tours.

King, Billie Jean   Billie Jean Moffitt King, b. Long Beach, Calif., Nov. 22, 1943, is an American professional tennis star who became one of the most recognizable personalities in the sport. In 1979, King surpassed the record of Elizabeth Ryan (an outstanding doubles player of the 1920s) by accumulating 20 Wimbledon titles, 6 in singles (the latter total surpassed only by Helen Wills Moody and Martina Navratilova). King won the Wimbledon women's doubles title 10 times with 5 different partners in the period 1961–79. She was the U.S. Open singles champion 4 times, first as an amateur in 1967, then as a professional in 1971, 1972, and 1974. She won the French Open in 1972 and the Australian Open in 1968. King turned professional in 1968, and in 1971 she became the first woman athlete to earn $100,000 in a year. In 1973 she won a famous "mixed singles" victory over 1939 Wimbledon champion Bobby Riggs in the Houston Astrodome before a crowd of 30,472, at that time the largest ever to watch a tennis match.

King, Carole   Songwriter and recording artist Carole King, b. Carole Klein in Brooklyn, N.Y., Feb. 9, 1942, wrote the rhythm-and-blues ballad "Will You Love Me Tomorrow?" (1960) and over 100 other songs with her first husband, Gerry Goffin. King has composed in almost every pop style and, since her divorce in 1968, has been writing her own lyrics and performing her own songs. Her album *Tapestry* (1971) sold some 13 million copies and won four Grammy awards.

King, Ernest Joseph   Ernest Joseph King, b. Lorain, Ohio, Nov. 23, 1878, d. June 25, 1956, was a U.S. naval officer who began his career as a midshipman during the Spanish-American War (1898). In World War I he was assistant chief of staff to Adm. Henry T. Mayo, commander of the Atlantic Fleet. King was promoted to admiral in 1941. In World War II he became the first officer to serve as commander in chief of the U.S. Navy and chief of naval operations at the same time. In 1944 he was made a fleet (five-star) admiral and retired the next year.

King, Martin Luther, Jr.   Martin Luther King, Jr., was a man of impressive moral presence who devoted his life to the fight for full citizenship rights of the poor, dis-

Martin Luther King, Jr., a Baptist minister and the leading figure of the civil rights movement in the United States, employed the nonviolent tactics espoused by Mahatma Gandhi in his struggle to end discrimination against American blacks. King, who in 1964 became the youngest recipient of the Nobel Peace Prize, was assassinated in 1968.

advantaged, and racially oppressed in the United States. Born on Jan. 15, 1929, in Atlanta, Ga., he was the second of three children of the Reverend Michael (later Martin) and Mrs. Alberta Williams King. He received a bachelor's degree in sociology (1948) from Morehouse College, a B.D. (1951) from Crozer Theological Seminary, and a doctorate in philosophy (1955) from Boston University.

In 1954, King accepted his first pastorate—the Dexter Avenue Baptist Church in Montgomery, Ala. He and his wife, Coretta Scott King, whom he had met and married (June 1953) while at Boston University, had been resident in Montgomery less than a year when Mrs. Rosa Parks defied the ordinance concerning segregated seating on city buses (Dec. 1, 1955). King's successful organization of the year-long Montgomery bus boycott, with the assistance of Rev. Ralph ABERNATHY and Edward Nixon, catapulted him into national prominence as a leader of the CIVIL RIGHTS movement.

King studied the life and teachings of Mahatma Gandhi and further developed the Indian leader's doctrine of *satyagraha* ("holding to the truth"), or nonviolent civil disobedience. In the aftermath of Montgomery he traveled, delivered speeches, and wrote his first book, *Stride toward Freedom* (1958). In 1960 he accepted copastorship with his father of the Ebenezer Baptist Church in Atlanta and became president of the Southern Christian Leadership Conference (SCLC). Although he continued to travel and speak widely and firmly committed the SCLC to voter-registration campaigns throughout the South, King's major campaigns were those in Albany, Ga. (December 1961–August 1962), Birmingham, Ala. (April–May 1963), and Danville, Va. (July 1963). He organized the massive March on Washington (Aug. 28, 1963) where, in his brilliant "I Have a Dream" speech, he "subpoenaed the conscience of the nation before the judgment seat of morality." In January 1964, King was cho-

sen by *Time* magazine as Man of the Year, the first African American so honored. Later that year he became the youngest recipient of the Nobel Peace Prize.

After supporting desegregation efforts in Saint Augustine, Fla., in 1964, King concentrated his efforts on the voter-registration drive in Selma, Ala., leading a harrowing march from Selma to Montgomery in March 1965. Soon after, a tour of northern cities led him to assail conditions of economic as well as social discrimination. This marked a shift in SCLC strategy, one intended to "bring the Negro into the mainstream of American life as quickly as possible." Having begun to recognize the deeper relationships of economics and poverty to racism, King now called for a "reconstruction of the entire society, a revolution of values." Along with demands for stronger civil- and voting-rights legislation and for a meaningful poverty budget, he spoke out against the Vietnam War.

Early in 1968, King began to plan a multiracial poor people's march on Washington to demand an end to all forms of discrimination and the funding of a $12 billion "Economic Bill of Rights." In the midst of organizing this campaign, he flew to Memphis, Tenn., to assist striking sanitation workers. There, on Apr. 4, 1968, King was felled by an assassin's bullet. The violent death of this man of peace brought an immediate reaction of rioting in black ghettos around the country. Although one man, James Earl Ray, was convicted of King's murder, the question of whether he was the paid agent of conspirators has not been resolved. In 1983, King's birthday was designated a national holiday.

King, Rufus   Rufus King, b. Scarborough, Mass. (now in Maine), Mar. 24, 1755, d. Apr. 29, 1827, was an American political leader who took an active part in framing the federal Constitution. After graduating from Harvard in 1777, he practiced law in Newburyport, Mass., and was elected to the legislature in 1783. He was a leading delegate (1784–87) to the Continental Congress, and he introduced the prohibition on slavery in the Northwest Ordinance of 1787 (see NORTHWEST TERRITORY). An advocate of strong central government, he was an active member of the Constitutional Convention of 1787 and urged ratification of the Constitution by Massachusetts.

After settling in New York City, King worked closely with Alexander Hamilton in the formation of the FEDERALIST PARTY. He served as U.S. senator (1789–96) and minister to Great Britain (1796–1803) and was an unsuccessful vice-presidential candidate on the Federalist ticket in 1804 and 1808. Reelected to the U.S. Senate (1813–25), he ran as the Federalist presidential candidate in 1816 but lost by a wide margin to James Monroe. Because of his strong antislavery views, he took the lead in the Senate in 1820 in opposing the admission of Missouri as a slave state (see MISSOURI COMPROMISE).

King, Stephen   Stephen Edwin King, b. Portland, Maine, Sept. 21, 1949, a writer of supernatural horror novels who also writes under the pseudonym Richard

Bachman, has won both critical acclaim and enormous popular success. Many of his novels have been filmed, most notably *Carrie* (1974; film by Brian De Palma, 1976) and *The Shining* (1977; film by Stanley Kubrick, 1980). Among his other novels are *Firestarter* (1980), *Pet Sematary* (1983), *Misery* (1987), and *Four Past Midnight* (1990).

King, W. L. Mackenzie   William Lyon Mackenzie King, b. Berlin (now Kitchener), Ontario, Dec. 17, 1874, d. July 22, 1950, was three times prime minister of Canada (1921–26, 1926–30, 1935–48). He was named for his mother's father, William Lyon Mackenzie. Educated at the universities of Toronto, Chicago, and Harvard, he specialized in political economy. In 1909 he won a seat in the House of Commons; he became minister of labor the same year. King, one of the first Canadian politicians to recognize the importance of improving labor conditions, attempted to persuade management to recognize labor unions.

King lost his parliamentary seat when the Laurier government fell in 1911. In 1919, after the death of Laurier, he was chosen leader of the Liberal party and found a parliamentary constituency on Prince Edward Island. In the federal election of December 1921, King and his party won a plurality of seats and, with the support of some Progressives, were able to form a minority government. In 1925 the Liberals were narrowly defeated at the polls, but continued support from the Progressives enabled King's administration to survive until a scandal in the Customs Department brought it down in June 1926.

A general election in October 1926 returned King to power with a Liberal majority. He was defeated in 1930 and led the opposition to Richard Bedford Bennett's Conservative government until 1935. The Liberals won a clear victory in 1935, and King remained prime minister until he retired undefeated in 1948.

Mackenzie King, prime minister of Canada for a total of 21 years (1921–26, 1926–30, 1935–48) and the leader of Canada's Liberal party for nearly 30 years (1919–48), did much to solidify Canadian independence and to strengthen relations with the United States.

King was isolationist in thought and sympathy, and he underestimated the danger from the European Fascist powers. For much of his career he could also be described as anti-British. In the 1920s his governments pushed for total Canadian autonomy within the British Empire, the dominion status finally recognized by the Statute of Westminster in 1931. When World War II broke out, therefore, Canada entered the conflict on its own authority. Throughout the war, King sought to cooperate with Britain and the United States without allowing Canada to be taken for granted.

King was a prime minister who operated by consensus politics. He disliked hard, clear policies, and his thoughts often seemed to be expressed in woolly terms. He thought of himself as a rebel, like his grandfather Mackenzie, but to others he seemed a rather conventional liberal. Mild in manner, he could be, and was, politically ruthless.

King, William Rufus de Vane   William Rufus de Vane King, b. Sampson County, N.C., Apr. 7, 1786, d. Apr. 18, 1853, was briefly vice-president of the United States under President Franklin Pierce. After serving in Congress (1811–16) as a Democratic representative from North Carolina, he moved to Alabama and became (1819) one of that state's first senators. He resigned to serve as ambassador to France (1844–46) but returned to the Senate in 1848. Elected vice-president in 1852, King was sworn into office while in Cuba for his health.

King George's War   see French and Indian Wars

King Lear   [leer]   William Shakespeare's *Tragedy of King Lear* has affinities with classical Greek tragedy, as described in Aristotle's *Poetics*. *King Lear* has a lofty theme that pits man against the powers of nature and the gods and develops, in both the king and the duke of Gloucester, a tragic recognition of human frailty and folly. The main action, concerning Lear and his daughters, is paralleled by a second series of events involving Gloucester and his sons. The story is deeply rooted in folklore. Shakespeare used Raphael Holinshed's *Chronicles* (1577) as the basis for his setting in pre-Roman Britain and also relied on the old play *The True Chronicle History of King Leir* (publ. 1605). Shakespeare's play, probably written about 1605, was first performed in 1606 and published in 1608. The madness of King Lear leads him to tragic awareness. He is schooled in the ways of adversity by his acerbic, witty Fool.

King Philip's War   King Philip's War (1675–76) was the most destructive Indian war in New England's history. It was named for Philip (Metacom), the son of Massasoit and sachem (chief) of the Wampanoag tribe of Plymouth Colony from 1662. Philip deeply resented white intrusion and domination. After maintaining peace with the colonists for many years, he finally became a leader in open resistance. Fighting first broke out at the frontier settlement of Swansea in June 1675, after which the conflict between Indians and whites spread rapidly across southern New England, involving the colonies of Plymouth, Massachusetts, Connecticut, and, to a limited extent, Rhode Island. Indian raiding parties burned many New England towns and killed or captured hundreds of colonists. Eventually, colonial forces imposed even greater destruction on the Indians, until finally all resistance was crushed. Philip himself was trapped and killed in August 1676.

The prairie king snake lives in open woodlands and prairies. Some older snakes have a melanistic (dark) phase.

king snake   King snakes, genus *Lampropeltis*, in the family Colubridae, are moderately sized, powerful constrictors and have smooth scales and single anal plates (the scale in front of the vent). Their diet consists of a variety of vertebrates, including other snakes. Six species occur in the United States. The prairie king snake, or mole snake, *L. calligaster*, is distributed from Maryland westward to Nebraska and Texas and southward to Florida. It is brown or tan with darker blotches. Most subspecies of the common king snake, *L. getulus*, are dark brown or black with white or yellow bands, stripes, or spots. This species occurs from coast to coast. Two species, the Sonora mountain king snake, *L. pyromelana,* and the California mountain king snake, *L. zonata,* are restricted to mountainous regions in the western United States and Mexico. They are tricolored with red, black, and white. The Mexican king snake, *L. mexicana,* is marked with gray, black, and sometimes orange and is found in southwestern Texas and northern portions of the Mexican Plateau. Two species, *L. triangulum* and *L. doliata,* are often known as MILK SNAKES.

King William's War   see FRENCH AND INDIAN WARS

kingbird   The kingbird comprises the genus *Tyrannus* of the New World family, Tyrannidae, known as tyrant flycatchers. Despite their relatively small size, kingbirds are boldly aggressive against intruders, especially birds of prey. They measure 20–24 cm (8–9.5 in) in length and are brown- or gray-backed birds with white or yellowish undersides and gray heads. Some have a small crown spot of bright red, which is usually concealed. The eastern kingbird, *T. tyrannus,* has a dark gray back, a white underside, and a white band on its tail's tip. During the summer it ranges throughout the northern United States east of the Rocky Mountains to central Canada. It winters in tropical South America. In the Midwest its range overlaps that of the western kingbird (*T. verticalis*), which has a lighter gray back and yellow underside and has white on the sides of its tail. This bird winters in Central America.

kingfisher   Kingfisher is the common name for members of the cosmopolitan avian family Alcedinidae, order Coraciiformes. The greatest number of species are found in the tropics and subtropics. These birds measure 10 to 46 cm (4 to 18 in) in length and have a large, usually crested head and a compact body. The bill is usually straight, long, and powerful, and the front toes are characteristically fused at the base. Kingfisher plumages are green, blue, purple, reddish brown, or white; several species have iridescent feathers. The majority of species do not eat fish, but rather insects and other invertebrates. Many kingfishers hover in search of prey before they swoop to the ground or dive into the water. Most species are solitary. Their unlined nests are in tree cavities or in embankments.

The most familiar of the tree kingfishers, subfamily Daceloninae, is the Australian KOOKABURRA, *Dacelo gigas,* known for its variety of loud calls, some of which are reminiscent of human laughter.

The belted kingfisher is a common North American bird that lives near streams and rivers. The female (bottom) differs from the male (top) by a band of dark-colored feathers on its belly.

kinglet   The kinglet is a common name for birds of the genus *Regulus* of the Old World warbler family, Sylviidae, including two very small, active North American birds. Both measure about 10 cm (4 in) in length and have olive gray backs, light wing bars, and paler undersides. The golden-crowned kinglet, *R. satrapa*, has white stripes over its eyes and a bright cap—orange in the male, yellow in the female—that is bordered with black. The male ruby-crowned kinglet, *R. calendula*, has a small, bright red head spot. Kinglets feed almost exclusively on insects. Found from coast to coast, they nest in northern coniferous forests and winter south to Guatemala.

Kings, Books of   The two books of Kings, labeled 1–2 Kings in the Hebrew and English versions of the BIBLE, but 3–4 Kings in the Greek and Latin, are so designated because of their contents. They follow and are a continuation of the books of SAMUEL (1–2 Kings in Greek and Latin) and narrate the history of Israel and Judah from SOLOMON's accession to the destruction of Jerusalem and the exile of Judah in 587 BC. The Books of Kings give a detailed account of Solomon's wisdom and wealth and the building of the Temple at Jerusalem. They also narrate the decline that began during his reign and culminated in the exile. These books conclude the Deuteronomistic History, the name given to the books from DEUTERONOMY to Kings, all of which appear to have been compiled on the same principle. The hand of the Deuteronomistic editor or editors is evident in the stereotyped evaluation of each king by the often anachronistic standards of the Deuteronomic law; the editor(s) also composed the greater part of Solomon's Temple dedication prayer, as well as the long explanation for the fall of Israel. The compiler(s) did use earlier sources, however. These include lost works called the Acts of Solomon, the Chronicles of the Kings of Judah, and the Chronicles of the Kings of Israel; some official lists; an account of the Temple's construction; and a summary of the official annals of both Israel and Judah. The compiler(s) also incorporated a number of early prophetic legends, including the Elijah-Elisha cycles. The original work dates from *c.*615 BC, but it was updated and reedited *c.*550 BC.

Kingsley, Charles   The writer and social reformer Charles Kingsley, b. June 12, 1819, d. Jan. 23, 1875, was an Anglican country clergyman, canon of Westminster Abbey, and from 1860 to 1869 professor of modern history at Cambridge. An early supporter of Charles Darwin's theory of evolution, Kingsley had a remedy for the ills of society: "Christian Socialism," a call for cooperative enterprise and morality in social action. In the novel *Yeast* (1851), Kingsley described the distress of agricultural labor; in *Alton Locke* (1850) he attacked the exploitation of urban workers. *The Water Babies* (1863), a popular children's fantasy, was both a moralizing fable and a speculation on evolution. Of Kingsley's historical fiction, *Westward Ho!* (1855) and *Hereward the Wake* (1866) are the best known.

Kingston (Jamaica)   Kingston (1982 pop., 104,041), the capital and largest city of Jamaica, lies on the south-

eastern coast of the island. Its metropolitan-area population is 524,638. One of the leading ports of the West Indies, it exports sugar, rum, molasses, and bananas. Other industries include tourism, oil refining, shoe and clothing manufacturing, and food processing. The University of the West Indies (1962) is there.

Founded in 1692 after nearby Port Royal was destroyed by an earthquake, Kingston became the capital of Jamaica in 1872. Points of interest include Rockfort, a 17th-century fortress; the Church of Saint Thomas; and Headquarters House (18th century), once the seat of government.

Kingston (New York)   Kingston, the seat of Ulster County, N.Y., is located 145 km (90 mi) north of New York City in the fertile Hudson River valley. It has a population of 23,095 (1990). A distribution center for fruits and dairy products produced on the surrounding farms, Kingston is also a gateway to the summer and winter resorts of the upper CATSKILL MOUNTAINS. Light manufactures include computers and apparel.

Henry Hudson's party landed near the site of Kingston in 1609, and it was first settled by the Dutch about 1652 as Esopus. In 1664 it came under British control and was renamed Kingston (1669). In 1777 it was chosen as the first state capital, and the legislature met there once before the British burned the city during the American Revolution.

Kingston (Ontario)   Kingston, a Canadian city located in southeastern Ontario, has a population of 55,050 (1986). It is located on the north shore of Lake Ontario, where the St. Lawrence Seaway and Rideau Canal join the lake. It is a busy port and industrial city, where locomotives, ships, aluminum, synthetic fibers, and ceramics are manufactured. Queen's University (1841) and the Royal Military College (1876) are there. Fort Henry, built during the War of 1812, is now a military museum.

The city was founded (1673) as Fort Frontenac by Louis de Buade, comte de Frontenac. It was destroyed (1758) by the British and resettled (1784) by United Empire Loyalists, who renamed the city for King George III. From 1841 until 1844 the city served as the seat of government of the united provinces of Upper and Lower Canada.

kinkajou [kink'-uh-joo]   The kinkajou, *Potos flavus,* sometimes called a honey bear, is a member of the raccoon family, Procyonidae. Its slender, short-legged body may reach 58 cm (23 in) in length (plus a 56-cm/22-in prehensile tail) and 2.7 kg (6 lb) in weight. The kinkajou is one of only two carnivores (the other is the binturong) that have prehensile tails. Kinkajous are arboreal and inhabit forests from southern Mexico to Brazil. They are nocturnal and feed on fruit, insects, and small mammals.

Kinnock, Neil   Neil Gordon Kinnock, b. Mar. 28, 1942, is the leader of Britain's Labour party. The son of a

Welsh miner, he was educated at University College, Cardiff, and elected to Parliament in 1970. Kinnock was a close associate of former Labour leader Michael Foot, whom he succeeded in 1983. Taking charge of a party weakened by division, he moved to strengthen its position with moderate voters by disassociating himself from Labour's left wing. Labour was defeated in the 1987 general election, however.

Kino, Eusebio Francisco [kee'-noh, ay-oo-say'-byoh frahn-sees'-koh]   Eusebio Francisco Kino, b. Tyrol, c.1644, d. Mar. 15, 1711, was a Jesuit missionary and explorer who directed the establishment of Spanish missions among the PIMA Indians in Pimería Alta (in what is now northern Sonora, Mexico, and southern Arizona). Arriving in New Spain in 1681, he began his longtime mission to the Pima Indians. From headquarters established at Nuestra Señora de los Dolores in Sonora in 1687, he founded a number of missions. Explorations of the area around the mouth of the Colorado River in 1701 persuaded him that Baja California was a peninsula, not an island. His 1705 map was the standard reference for the area for more than a century.

Kinross [kin-raws']   Kinross is a former county in central Scotland. Farming and livestock raising are major activities. The principal cities are Kinross and Milnathort. Some coal is mined in the Benarty and Cleish hills, which border Loch Leven, noted for its trout fishing. Mary, Queen of Scots, was imprisoned on the island in the loch in 1567 but escaped the following year. In 1975, during the reorganization of local government in Scotland, Kinross became part of the TAYSIDE administrative region.

Kinsey reports [kin'-zee]   The Kinsey reports, *Sexual Behavior in the Human Male* (1948) by Alfred C. Kinsey, Wardell B. Pomeroy, and Clyde E. Martin, and *Sexual Behavior in the Human Female* (1953) by the same authors and Paul H. Gebhard, were the first large-scale empirical studies of sexual behavior. The Kinsey investigators questioned 5,300 white males and 5,490 white females from many different backgrounds about sexual behavior such as the frequency of masturbation, petting, marital and extra-marital intercourse, oral sex, and female orgasm. Today the Kinsey reports are not only respected for breaking new ground in sex research but are considered authoritative in most of their findings.

Kinshasa [keen-shah'-suh]   Kinshasa (formerly Leopoldville) is the capital and largest city of Zaire, with a population of 2,653,558 (1984 est.). It is located on the CONGO RIVER where the river widens to become Malebo Pool (formerly Stanley Pool) and at the point where upstream navigation becomes possible. A rail line, completed in 1898, links the city to the ocean port of Matadi. The leading industries are food processing and paper,

textile, and chemical manufacturing. Kinshasa was founded as a supply depot by Henry Morton Stanley in 1881 at the site of an African village. In 1923 it replaced Boma as the capital of the Belgian Congo. When the Congo gained its independence in 1960, Kinshasa became the new capital of Zaire.

kinship   Kinship is the network of human relationships created by genealogical connections as they are conceived of in particular societies and by social ties modeled after natural genealogical relations. Because kinship is universal, it plays an important role in regulating behavior and in the formation of social groups. The most important of these is the FAMILY, which provides children with emotional roots, socialization and training, and their initial position in and orientation to the social world. Kinship is often the basis for the formation of important social, political, and territorial groups, and it may be the basis for office holding of many kinds. The study of kinship is a major field of anthropological and sociological investigation.

Kin Terms. Kinship comprises two categories of relatives. The first are consanguines, often referred to as blood relatives, whose links to each other are rooted ultimately in the link between parents and children. Consanguines include descendants—persons of succeeding generations linked to an individual through his or her children, such as a grandchild—and ascendants—persons of preceding generations, such as a grandmother. Ascendants and descendants together are called lineal relatives. Collaterals, another type of consanguine, are the siblings of lineal relatives or their descendants, such as an uncle, an aunt, or a cousin by blood. The second major type of relative is an affine, a person related by marriage, such as a brother-in-law or an aunt by marriage.

Kinship does not depend on factual knowledge of conception and genetics; such knowledge, especially about the role of paternity, was unknown in most societies throughout most of history. A kinship system consists of a society's cultural beliefs about how the genealogical relationships of consanguinity and affinity are to be categorized and labeled and about what rights, duties, and expectations are linked with each kinship category.

Descent. Very common is the notion of unilineal descent, in which a person is counted as being descended from only one parent. If descent is traced through the male line (through the father), it is called patrilineal; if it is traced through the mother it is called matrilineal. Double unilineal descent is traced through the mother's mother and the father's father. Bilateral descent, used by U.S. society, is traced through both the mother and father.

Because the principle of unilineal descent assigns an individual unequivocally to a kinship group, it can be used to form corporate groups, such as a LINEAGE or a CLAN. Corporate groups often assume such functions as holding land or providing representatives for office on a village or tribal council. Societies in which kinship is used as a broad organizing principle for many aspects of life are sometimes called kin-dominated societies. They exist throughout the world, notably among preliterate, middle-range social groups, such as the pastoral nomads of Asia and the Middle East, traditional African agriculturalists, and the Australian Aborigines.

Unilineality is also used as a principle for the inheritance of property or position. In a patrilineal society, positions (such as head of the household) and major property (land, in many societies) are inherited by a man's patrilineal heir, usually his son or a younger brother. In matrilineal societies the heir will also be a male, but one with whom the link is traced matrilineally, usually a man's sister's son. Unilineal inheritance has the advantage of keeping the inherited position or property within the unilineal descent group.

Kinship has its origins in MARRIAGE, the socially recognized union of a man and a woman, and reflects the particular form of marriage practiced, whether POLYGAMY, MONOGAMY, or other kinds of unions (see CONCUBINAGE). Some forms of marriage, such as the sororate, the levirate, and ghost marriage, are based on the cultural belief that marriage extends beyond the lifetime of one of the partners.

Artificial or fictive kinship refers to customs in which a person is given kin status by attribution rather than by birth. The prime example is ADOPTION. In another type of pseudo-kinship, called figurative usage, kinship terms are extended to nonkin in order to stress an aspect of the person's role that is similar to that of a kinsperson. Children are taught, for example, to call a close female friend of their parents "aunt" because she plays an avuncular role. Ritual kinship, a third type of pseudo-kinship, entails a formalized relationship that is similar to but distinct from actual kinship, such as bloodbrotherhood.

Kintpuash [kint'-poo-ahsh] Kintpuash, c.1837–73, also called Captain Jack, was a MODOC headman and leader in the Modoc War (1872–73), a series of battles between the Modoc and the U.S. Army. Kintpuash and other Modoc left the Klamath reservation in Oregon and returned to their California homeland, requesting a reservation there. In late 1872 a detachment of U.S. troops attempted to force them to return to the Klamath reservation. The Indians resisted; several soldiers and Indians were killed. Kintpuash fled with his band to the nearby Lava-beds.

White authorities arranged a peace conference. Kintpuash, formerly an advocate of peace, was asked by other leaders to prove his commitment to resistance by killing white negotiators if they did not meet Indian demands. When the whites refused to compromise, Kintpuash shot Gen. Edward Canby and another commissioner and fled. A large military force besieged the Indians in the Lava-beds. Kintpuash skillfully directed the Indian defense; his 50-odd warriors and their families stood off nearly 1,000 U.S. troops for more than nine months. Kintpuash was finally captured, however, and he and three other headmen were summarily tried and hanged.

Kiowa [ky'-uh-wuh] The Kiowa are a North American tribe of Plains Indians who speak a Kiowa-Tanoan lan-

guage. Kiowa tradition speaks of a migration in the company of the Kiowa APACHE into the Plains from the headwaters of the Missouri River during the 18th century. At that time they were organized in 10 independent bands and numbered an estimated 3,000. The ARAPAHO, CHEYENNE, and Dakota (SIOUX) pushed them out of the Black Hills region southwestward into their historic range along the headwaters of the Arkansas, Cimarron, Canadian, and Red rivers. There they met and at first fought the COMANCHE, but, from c.1790, Kiowa and Comanche shared territories and together raided settlements in Texas and New Mexico. Their raids furnished horses and mules for trade with northern Plains tribes. Although the Kiowa accepted a restricted range at the Medicine Lodge Treaty of 1867, tribal resistance continued. Since 1875, however, the Kiowa have adapted to reservation life in Oklahoma. The Kiowa played an important role in the spread of the peyote religion (see NATIVE AMERICAN CHURCH). In 1989 their population was about 4,800 on or near the reservation.

Kipling, Rudyard [kip'-ling, ruhd'-yard] The English novelist, short-story writer, and poet Joseph Rudyard Kipling, b. Dec. 30, 1865, d. Jan. 18, 1936, was a literary giant. He is most widely known for his works for children, especially *The Jungle Book* (1894) and *The Second Jungle Book* (1895), and his celebration of British imperialism. He was, however, no crude jingoist and wrote on many subjects in a highly imaginative fashion.

Born in Bombay, India, Kipling was educated in England, where he spent several unhappy childhood years later described in the short story "Baa, Baa, Blacksheep" (1888) and in the autobiographical *Something of Myself* (1937). From 1882 to 1889 he worked for Indian newspapers but then returned to England where he gained rapid

Rudyard Kipling, who in 1907 became the first English writer to win the Nobel Prize for literature, strikes a pensive pose in this portrait by Sir Philip Burne-Jones. (National Portrait Gallery, London.)

acceptance by London literary society, initially with the semiautobiographical novel *The Light That Failed* (1890).

Many of Kipling's works came from his experience of India—among them the "Jungle Books," *Kim* (1901), and the *Just So Stories* (1902). He was most characteristic when, mainly through the short story, he used a variety of settings—India, London, the sea, the jungle—to convey ideals of duty and self-abnegation; the importance of law and action was shown in *Actions and Reactions* (1909), *Debits and Credits* (1926), and *Limits and Renewals* (1932). These themes also occur in *Captains Courageous* (1897), stimulated by a visit to America, and in the school story *Stalky & Co.* (1899).

Kipling gained a reputation as a humorist with "The Village That Voted the Earth Was Flat" (1913). In *Puck of Pook's Hill* (1906) and *Rewards and Fairies* (1910) he expressed his love of England's past. His collections of verse, including *Barrack Room Ballads* (1892), *The Seven Seas* (1896), and *The Five Nations* (1903), display a great range of technical achievement and a variety of subject matter.

Kirchhoff, Gustav Robert [kirk'-hawf] The German physicist Gustav Robert Kirchhoff, b. Mar. 12, 1824, d. Oct. 17, 1887, discovered (1859) a fundamental law of electromagnetic radiation: the emissive power of the radiation of a BLACKBODY is represented by a universal function of wavelength and temperature. The search for a theoretical explanation of this function later led to Planck's quantum hypothesis in 1900. Along with the experimental results obtained in collaboration with Robert Bunsen, Kirchhoff's discovery put spectroscopy on a firm scientific basis. In the 1860s, using spectral analysis, Kirchhoff and Bunsen detected new elements on the Earth and identified terrestrial elements in the solar atmosphere. The latter accomplishment signaled the birth of astrophysics.

Kirchner, Ernst Ludwig [kirsch'-nur] Ernst Ludwig Kirchner, b. May 6, 1880, d. June 15, 1938, was a leading German expressionist painter and a master of graphics, especially the woodcut. In 1905 he became a founding member of Die BRÜCKE (The Bridge) with Erich HECKEL and Karl SCHMIDT-ROTTLUFF. This group was strongly influenced by Vincent van Gogh's intense color and heavy impasto (thickness of paint) as well as the color experiments of the French Fauves (see FAUVISM).

Kirchner painted female nudes, mountainous landscapes, and city streets. His *Self-Portrait with Model* (1907; Kunsthalle, Hamburg) shows the artist wearing a brightly striped robe shadowed with green, and his expression violent and masklike. In *Five Women on the Street* (1913; Wallraf-Richartz Museum, Cologne) the expression of pain is even more aggressive. Kirchner transformed the long dresses and feather boas of the time into sinister, barbaric costumes. During this period he replaced his bright palette with a darkly shadowed range of

colors. Kirchner's bitter view of his world is expressed all the more sharply in his starkly savage and highly acclaimed woodcuts, lithographs, and etchings, of which he produced about 2,000. By the late 1920s, however, the emotional urgency of his earlier works had disappeared. In despair and poor health, he committed suicide.

Kirghizia [kir-gee'-zee-uh] Kirghizia was one of the 15 constituent republics of the USSR, but when it became independent in late 1991, it changed the form of its name to Kyrgyzstan. Located in Central Asia, the country borders China in the east and south, Tajikistan in the south and west, Uzbekistan in the west, and Kazakhstan in the north. The area is 198,500 km^2 (76,641 mi^2), and the population is 4,385,000 (1992 est.). The capital is Bishkek (formerly FRUNZE), with a population of 626,000 (1989).

Kirghizia is situated largely in the high mountain country of the TIAN SHAN, which rise to 7,437 m (24,400 ft) in Pobeda (Victory) Peak on the Chinese border. The Naryn River, a headstream of the Syr Darya, drains the region. A distinctive feature is a large mountain lake, Issyk-Kul, with an area of about 6,200 km^2 (2,400 mi^2).

The republic's population and economic activities are concentrated in the Zhu River valley in the north and in the west around the margins of the Fergana Valley, most of which lies in neighboring Uzbekistan. The Kirghiz, a Mongoloid people of short stature and stocky build, speak a Turkic language. They account for about 52% of the population. Russians, 22% of the population, live mainly in cities, and Uzbeks, 13%, are cotton farmers. Kirghizia is important mainly for its mineral production, including petroleum and natural gas, uranium, mercury, antimony, and coal. Traditional stock herding, food processing, and textile manufacturing are other economic activities.

The Kirghiz people began migrating to the region during the 16th century. It came under Russian control in the second half of the 19th century. After the Bolshevik Revolution it was constituted in 1924 as an autonomous oblast, initially called Kara-Kirghiz (the past name given to the Kirghiz people). It was renamed Kirghiz in 1925 and raised to the status of autonomous republic the following year. In 1936 it became a full soviet socialist republic. In 1990 tension between the Kirghiz and the Uzbek minority erupted into rioting in which more than 100 people were killed. Under the leadership of Askar Akayev, a proponent of radical economic change, the newly independent country is pursuing democratization and market-oriented reforms.

Kiribati [kir'-uh-bahs] The Republic of Kiribati, formerly the Gilbert Islands, straddles both the equator and the international date line in the Pacific Ocean. The national territory extends over 5 million km^2 (2 million mi^2), but the land area is less than that of New York City. Kiribati's 33 islands are grouped into the Gilbert Islands (including

REPUBLIC OF KIRIBATI

Land: Area: 712 km^2 (275 mi^2). Capital and largest city: Tarawa (1988 est. pop., 22,833).

People: Population (1990 est.): 70,012. Density: 98 persons per km^2 (255 per mi^2). Distribution (1985): 33% urban, 67% rural. Official language: English. Major religions: Roman Catholicism, Protestantism.

Government: Type: republic. Legislature: House of Assembly. Political subdivisions: 20 island councils.

Economy: GDP (1989): $34 million; $500 per capita. Labor distribution (1985): services and public administration—47%; construction—6%; trade—13%; transportation and communication—15%; agriculture—5%. Foreign trade (1988): imports—$21.5 million; exports—$5.1 million. Currency: 1 Australian dollar = 100 cents.

Education and Health: Literacy (1985): 90% of adult population. Universities (1990): none. Hospital beds (1986): 283. Physicians (1986): 16. Life expectancy (1990): women—57; men—52. Infant mortality (1990): 65 per 1,000 live births.

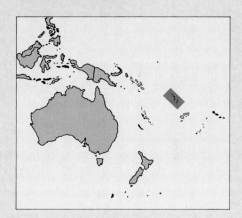

Tarawa, the capital, and Banaba, or Ocean Island), the Line Islands, and the PHOENIX ISLANDS. Kiribati was a part of the Gilbert and Ellice Islands colony until 1975, when the Ellice Islands gained independence as TUVALU.

Land and People

All of the islands except volcanic Banaba are low coralline structures with few elevations above 4 m (12 ft). The soil is poor, composed of coral sand and rocks. Vegetation is limited to coconut palms and pandanus trees. Temperatures in Kiribati vary more during a 24-hour period than during the year, with minima of 26° C (79° F) and maxima of 32° C (89° F). The mean annual rainfall near the equator is about 1,020 mm (40 in), whereas the extreme northern and southern islands average about 3,050 mm (120 in).

The I-Kiribati are overwhelmingly Micronesian, with some Polynesians and Europeans. Many inhabitants migrate to other Pacific island nations in search of employment.

Economy

Phosphate, mined on Banaba, was once the leading source of income; the economy suffered severely when phosphate mining ceased in 1979. Copra is now the leading export. Fishing, handicrafts, and small-scale businesses are being developed, and a causeway linking Tarawa's two main islands was completed in 1987. Kiribati's fishing rights are among its most valuable resources. Remittances from locally trained seamen working on overseas vessels provide additional income.

History and Government

Kiribati's earliest inhabitants are thought to have been Samoans, who sailed there in the 13th century. Britain established the High Commission for the Western Pacific in 1877 to oversee the islands and their European inhabitants. Gradually all the present islands were brought under the commission's jurisdiction. Kiribati was granted independence in 1979. Later that year the United States renounced its claims to the Line and Phoenix islands. Ieremia Tabai, Kiribati's first president, was reelected to successive terms.

Kirkcaldy [kur'-kaw'-dee] Kirkcaldy is a town in County Fife, eastern Scotland. Located on the Firth of Forth about 16 km (10 mi) north of Edinburgh, it has a population of 46,314 (1981). Coal mining is the area's most important economic activity. Linoleum, malt, textiles, rope and twine, farm machinery, and furniture are manufactured. It is the birthplace of the architect Robert Adam and the economist Adam Smith. Kirkcaldy dates from its grant in 1334 to nearby Dunfermline Abbey; it became a royal burgh in 1450 and grew rapidly as a commercial port.

Kirkcudbright [kur-koo'-bree] Kirkcudbright is a former county in southwestern Scotland. Castle Douglas and Kirkcudbright are the largest towns. The low coastal plain on the Irish Sea is fertile land for dairy farms and mixed agriculture. Inland, to the northwest, the terrain rises to a maximum elevation of 843 m (2,765 ft) at Merrick. Sheep and cattle graze in these highlands. Hydroelectric plants have been built on the River Dee where it flows out of the highlands. Tourism is growing in importance. As part of the reorganization of Scotland's local government in 1975, Kirkcudbright was incorporated into the administrative region of DUMFRIES AND GALLOWAY.

Kirke, Sir David   Sir David Kirke, b. c.1597, d. January or February 1654, was an English merchant and adventurer in Canada. In 1627 and 1629, Kirke and his four brothers led expeditions against the French at Quebec, forcing Samuel de CHAMPLAIN to surrender the colony in 1629. It was restored to France in 1632. Kirke was knighted (1633) and from 1639 to 1651 served as the first English governor of Newfoundland.

Kirkland, Gelsey [gel'-see]   Gelsey Kirkland, b. Bethlehem, Pa., Dec. 29, 1953, is a ballerina renowned for the technical purity of her dancing. Kirkland entered the New York City Ballet (NYCB) at the age of 15, was given her first principal role in *The Firebird* in 1970, and by 1972 was a principal dancer. She danced with American Ballet Theatre (1974–81, 1982–84), where she triumphed in *Giselle* and *The Sleeping Beauty.* Her autobiography, *Dancing on My Grave*, was published in 1986.

Kirkland, Lane   Joseph Lane Kirkland, b. Camden, S.C., Mar. 12, 1922, was elected president of the American Federation of Labor and Congress of Industrial Organizations (AFL-CIO) on Nov. 19, 1979. Kirkland joined the AFL staff in 1948 and for many years was chief assistant to AFL-CIO president George MEANY. As Meany's successor, he vigorously criticized the Reagan administration's economic policies. In 1984 and 1988 he led union support for the losing Democratic presidential candidates. In 1987 he welcomed the TEAMSTERS back to the AFL-CIO, followed by the United Mine Workers in 1989.

Kirkpatrick, Jeane   Jeane Jordan Kirkpatrick, b. Duncan, Okla., Nov. 19, 1926, served (1981–85) as U.S. ambassador to the United Nations under President Ronald Reagan. Educated at Columbia University and the University of Paris, Kirkpatrick has taught political science at Georgetown University. A forceful advocate of conservative positions, she caused controversy by her distinction between "authoritarian" (friendly right-wing) governments and "totalitarian" (hostile left-wing) regimes.

Kirlian photography [kur'-lee-uhn]   Kirlian photography, sometimes called electrophotography or corona discharge photography, uses high-voltage electricity to produce an image. The technique was known in the late 1800s but was perfected in the 1940s by Soviet electrician Semyon Kirlian. In a typical procedure the object being photographed is placed directly on an unexposed sheet of photographic film. The film rests on an electrode coated with a thin layer of a nonconductive material such as glass or plastic. When voltage is applied to the electrode, a corona discharge occurs between the electrode and the object. A corona discharge is an ionization phenomenon (see ION AND IONIZATION) that is invisible to the eye but is recorded on film.

In Kirlian photographs, objects appear to be surrounded by a glow or "aura." In photographs of living objects this glow is quite pronounced, leading some parapsychologists to claim that Kirlian photographs are evidence of the existence of "psychic" energy. The intensity of the glow, however, can be explained by the presence of moisture, which heightens the corona discharge effect. Researchers have attempted to develop Kirlian photography as an analytic tool, but the technique has proven to have little scientific usefulness.

Kirov [kee'-rawf]   Kirov is the capital of Kirov oblast in the Russian republic of the USSR. Located on the west bank of the Vyatka River in northern European Russia, the city has a population of 441,000 (1989).

Kirov is an important manufacturing center served by several railroads and by shipping on the Vyatka. Its principal industries are machine-building and metal-fabricating plants producing construction equipment, agricultural equipment, and heavy machinery. The city's location in the forested zone has given rise to a wood-products industry, including a large match factory. Kirov also has a tire plant. Artificial leather is also produced. A number of buildings dating from the 17th and 18th centuries have been preserved, including the Uspensky Cathedral.

Originally known as Khlynov, the city was renamed Vyatka in 1780. In 1934 its name was changed to Kirov in honor of Sergei M. Kirov, a high Soviet official, whose assassination that year formed the pretext for the Great Purge.

Kirov Ballet   The Kirov Ballet, of Leningrad (formerly Saint Petersburg), was the most important ballet company in Russia until 1944, when the Kirov's chief choreographer, Leonid Lavrovsky (1905–67), and its prima ballerina, Galina ULANOVA, were transferred to Moscow's Bolshoi Ballet. The company's weakened artistic standing gave eventual preeminence to Moscow.

Founded during the reign (1730–40) of Empress Anna as a ballet school for the children of court servants, the Imperial Ballet Company was originally housed in the Bolshoi Theater of Saint Petersburg. It moved in 1889 to the Maryinsky Theater, which was renamed Kirov Theater in 1935.

The company's first ballet masters and choreographers came from abroad. Although Russian artists gradually made their mark, it was a Frenchman—Marius PETIPA— who dominated ballet in Saint Petersburg from 1862 until his retirement in 1903, and it was a series of Italian virtuoso dancers who captured the public's admiration. Only toward the end of the 19th century did Russian dancers gain ascendancy. The first native choreographer acclaimed at the Maryinsky (Kirov) was Mikhail FOKINE.

After the 1917 Revolution the Kirov encouraged experimental ideas for a time but soon reverted to conservatism. In the 1960s and '70s the company lost some of its finest dancers, among them Mikhail BARYSHNIKOV, Natalia MAKAROVA, and Rudolf NUREYEV, who chose to live and work in the West. Despite such problems the Kirov has remained one of the world's finest classical ballet companies.

Kirstein, Lincoln [kur'-steen] Lincoln Edward Kirstein, b. Rochester, N.Y., May 4, 1907, is a renowned American dance writer and ballet administrator. He was responsible in 1933 for bringing choreographer George BALANCHINE to the United States. With Balanchine he established (1934) the School of American Ballet, the U.S. equivalent of the professional dance academies of Russia and Europe. This school was to become the base for a series of performing companies—including the American Ballet and Ballet Society—culminating in the NEW YORK CITY BALLET (founded 1948). The latter, with Balanchine as chief choreographer (until his death in 1983) and Kirstein as patron, policy maker, and policy defender (he was general director until his retirement in 1989) was probably the single most significant force in shaping the style of contemporary ballet.

Kisangani [kee-san-gah'-nee] Kisangani (previously Stanleyville) is a city in northeastern Zaire located on the Congo River. The population of the city is 315,511 (1990 est.). Kisangani owes its importance to its location at the base of Stanley Falls, making it the river's head of navigation. It is a busy port, and major industries are brewing, the manufacture of furniture and clothing, and food processing. The University of Zaire (1963) is there.

A settlement was established there in 1880 by Henry Morton Stanley. Patrice Lumumba, before becoming Zaire's first prime minister, made Kisangani his seat of power; it was also the seat of a Lumumbist government in exile (1960–61).

Kish Kish (modern Uhaimir), situated 14 km (9 mi) east of Babylon in Iraq, was the most important Sumerian city-state during the formative years of Mesopotamian civilization (c.2800–2370 BC). An ancient list of Sumerian kings records Kish as the first postdiluvian kingdom (c.2750–2370 BC). Although some of the kings mentioned are mythical, others, including Enmebaragesi and Mesilim, are known from contemporary inscriptions. Kish was occupied almost continuously from late prehistoric times (c.3500 BC) until the Sassanian period (AD c.600), but it was no longer paramount after the removal (c.2371 BC) of political power to the city of Agade.

The site, about 8 by 3 km (5 by 2 mi), contains the

mounds of twin cities: Kish and Hursagkalama (modern Ingharra), to the east. Remains of the flourishing 3d-millennium-BC city include three ziggurats, a temple, a residential palace, and chariot burials. Religious and secular buildings of the Old Babylonian (early 2d millennium) and neo-Assyrian (8th century BC) periods contained important collections of cuneiform tablets.

Kishinev [kish-in-yef'] Kishinev (1989 pop., 665,000) is the capital of Moldavia, a republic of the USSR. It is situated on the Byk River, a Dnestr tributary. Under Soviet rule, Kishinev developed into a diversified manufacturing center specializing in the processing of produce, particularly wines, canned goods, and tobacco, from the agriculturally rich hinterland.

First mentioned in 1466, Kishinev received the status of city during the 17th century. It developed into the economic and political center of the disputed historical province of Bessarabia, which was seized by Russia from the Ottoman Empire in 1812. Between the two world wars the city was part of Romania and was known as Chísinau.

Kissinger, Henry A. [kis'-in-jur] Henry Alfred Kissinger, b. Fürth, Germany, May 27, 1923, was chief foreign-policy advisor and secretary of state to Presidents Richard NIXON and Gerald FORD. Among his achievements were the restoration of U.S. relations with the People's Republic of China and the arrangement of a cease-fire between the Israelis and Arabs in the Arab-Israeli War of 1973. He also negotiated a cease-fire in Vietnam, sharing the Nobel Peace Prize for 1973 with the North Vietnamese negotiator Le Duc Tho.

Kissinger came to the United States in 1938 and in 1943 became a U.S. citizen. He served in the U.S. Army in World War II and in the U.S. military government of Germany in 1945–46. He studied political science at Harvard University and taught there from 1954 until 1969. His *Nuclear Weapons and Foreign Policy* (1957) brought him recognition as an expert on nuclear strategy. Kissinger served as a consultant on foreign policy for Presidents Kennedy and Johnson.

Henry Kissinger, a professor of government at Harvard, entered the Nixon administration in 1969 and was secretary of state from 1973 to 1977. During his tenure the United States entered a period of détente with the USSR, reestablished ties with China, and withdrew its forces from Vietnam.

As assistant to President Nixon for national-security affairs (1969–73), Kissinger gathered most of the reins of foreign policy into his own hands. He controlled the National Security Council; he outweighed the secretary of state (William P. Rogers) in discussions of policy; and he negotiated with heads of state and prime ministers. He succeeded Rogers as secretary of state in September 1973, continuing to hold the post of director of the National Security Council until 1975. He remained as secretary of state after Gerald Ford succeeded Richard Nixon in August 1974.

Kissinger was most successful in the period 1971–73, when new relationships were established with China and the USSR, the first strategic arms limitation agreement (SALT I) was signed, and U.S. troops were withdrawn from Vietnam.

After retiring (1977) as secretary of state, Kissinger remained active as a commentator on foreign affairs, a teacher, and a consultant. His memoirs, *White House Years* and *Years of Upheaval*, appeared in 1979 and 1982, respectively.

Kitakyushu

Kitakyushu [kee-tah'-kyoo-shoo]   Kitakyushu (1989 est. pop., 1,034,328) is a city located at the northernmost tip of Kyushu island, Japan, across a narrow strait from Honshu island. Kitakyushu was created in 1963 from the formerly independent cities of Moji, Kokura, Yawata, Tobata, and Wakamatsu.

Kitakyushu is one of Japan's major centers of heavy industry near the western end of the Tokaido megalopolis. Iron and steel, chemical fertilizers, paper and pulp products, machinery, and metal products are the leading products. Shipbuilding is another of the city's industries. Yawata is near the country's largest coal mine and is the site of Japan's first steel plant.

Kitchen Cabinet

Kitchen Cabinet   In U.S. history, Kitchen Cabinet was the name given by critics of President Andrew JACKSON to an informal group of advisors who influenced him on matters of policy. Before the cabinet reorganization of 1831, Jackson never held official cabinet meetings. Members of the Kitchen Cabinet included Martin VAN BUREN, John H. EATON, and Amos KENDALL.

Kitchener

Kitchener   Kitchener, a city in Canada with a population of 150,604 (1986), is located in southern Ontario in the Grand River Valley. It is the seat of Waterloo County. The economy is based on the meat-packing, brewing and distilling, and textile industries. It has close ties with its nearby twin city of Waterloo. Kitchener was settled about 1806 by German Amish and Mennonite farmers from Pennsylvania; it was known as Berlin until the name was changed (1916) during World War I.

Kitchener, Herbert Kitchener, 1st Earl

Kitchener, Herbert Kitchener, 1st Earl   Horatio Herbert Kitchener, 1st Earl Kitchener, b. June 24, 1850, d. June 5, 1916, was Britain's foremost general at the beginning of the 20th century. Commissioned in the Royal Engineers in 1871, he became commander in chief of the Egyptian army in 1892. He established his reputation by reconquering the Sudan from the Mahdists, winning the famous Battle of Omdurman in 1898. That same year his tactful handling of the FASHODA INCIDENT may have prevented a war with France.

After serving as governor of the Sudan, Kitchener became (1899) chief of staff to Frederick Sleigh ROBERTS in the SOUTH AFRICAN WAR and succeeded as commander in chief in 1900. He was much criticized for interning Afrikaner civilians in concentration camps. As commander in chief in India (1902–09), Kitchener quarreled with the viceroy, Lord CURZON, but the London government supported him. From 1911 to 1914 he was the virtual ruler of Egypt as British consul general.

At the start (1914) of World War I, Kitchener became secretary of state for war. He expanded the army from 20 divisions to 70, but he was blamed for the munitions shortage on the western front. Kitchener was drowned when his ship was torpedoed while on a mission to Russia.

kite (bird)

kite (bird)   Kite is the common name for about 30 species of typically lightly built birds of the hawk family, Accipitridae, widely distributed over warmer regions of the world. They are distinguished by their graceful, gliding flight and occur most commonly near water or wetlands. The swallow-tailed kite, *Elanoides forficatus,* found from the southeastern United States and the West Indies to northern Argentina, is slim, black above, and white below and has a white head and a long, deeply forked tail. It spends most of its time on the wing, feeding on the larger flying insects and skimming the water to bathe and drink. The Everglade kite, *Rostrhamus sociabilis,* found from southern Florida into Argentina, is heavier-bodied and dark, with a broad white band across the tail. It feeds exclusively on snails. Some Old World species are scavengers.

kite (object)

kite (object)   A kite consists of a lightweight frame that is covered with paper, plastic, or cloth; it is designed to be flown in the wind at the end of a long cord wound on a

This o-dako, *or giant fighting kite, is typical of those flown during the kite-dueling festivals,* tako-kichi matsuri, *held throughout Japan. The movements of these giant kites are controlled by 42 or 49 bridles, or ropes.*

A contestant in Baltimore's annual kite festival prepares a Rogallo kite for flight. This kite, developed by Francis Rogallo, is one of the most popular kite styles today. The principles governing the Rogallo kite have been successfully applied to aircraft designs.

stick or drum. In Eastern countries, kites have been flown since before recorded history and have deep-rooted cultural and historical associations. Although kites are used primarily for recreation, they have also been employed in war and in scientific research. In 1752, Benjamin Franklin, the U.S. statesman and inventor, flew a kite during a thunderstorm to demonstrate the electrical nature of lightning. Kites have been used for military observation and for meteorological experiments, but today airplanes and balloons have replaced the kite for such work.

Common kite shapes are the diamond, hexagon, box, and tetrahedron. The best wind for kite flying ranges between 13 and 32 km/h (8 and 20 mph) and is steady close to the ground.

kithara [kith'-uh-ruh]   The largest of the ancient Greek LYRES, the kithara was a wooden instrument with from three to usually seven strings. Its base was a sound box from which two upthrust arms, straight or curved, were connected at the top with a crossbar. The strings, which ran from top to bottom, crossed a bridge that provided tension, and they were plucked with a plectrum. Associated with the cult of Apollo, the instrument was used by professionals as a solo instrument and as an accompaniment for solo singers. It was usually heavy enough to require support by a strap or band. Its smaller counterpart, the lyre, was the instrument of amateurs. Plucked instruments of this variety are known to have existed in Egypt as early as 1500 BC.

Kitt Peak National Observatory   Kitt Peak National Observatory, located 84 km (52 mi) southwest of

Tucson, Ariz., on top of the 2,100-m (7,000-ft) Kitt Peak, is one of the world's major astronomical research centers. It was founded in 1958 by the Association of Universities for Research in Astronomy (AURA), a nonprofit consortium of 17 universities that operates the observatory under contract with the U.S. National Science Foundation.

The observatory does research in solar, planetary, stellar, galactic, and extragalactic astronomy. It has 15 telescopes, among them reflectors with apertures of 158 in (4 m), 84 in (2.1 m), and 51 in (1.3 m), the 60-in (1.5-m) Robert McMath solar telescope (the world's largest), and a 24-in (61-cm) solar vacuum telescope. The National Radio Astronomy Observatory also operates a 36-ft-diameter (11-m) radio telescope at Kitt Peak. Using INTERFEROMETERS and image-enhancement techniques (see IMAGE PROCESSING), astronomers at Kitt Peak photographed for the first time the surface of a star (Betelgeuse) other than the Sun.

kiva [kee'-vuh]   Kivas (Hopi for "old house") are sacred ceremonial chambers of the present-day PUEBLO Indians of Arizona and New Mexico; they are also found in the ruins of the prehistoric ANASAZI culture. The kivas traditionally belong to the religious fraternities in Pueblo society. Most kivas are semisubterranean, built along clefts on the edge of the mesa with the roof of the kiva level with the ground surface. These rectangular or circular stone rooms have no doors and can be entered only by hatchways, descending by ladders through the roof. In addition to being used for the performance of esoteric rituals, the kivas also traditionally serve as council chambers and workshops.

The common, or brown, kiwi, a strange-looking bird, lays an egg approximately 10 percent of its weight, the largest of any bird. The kiwi is the national emblem of New Zealand and is pictured on that country's coins, bills, and stamps.

kiwi (bird) [kee'-wee] The kiwi is a flightless, solitary, nocturnal bird found only in New Zealand. Three living species, all in the genus *Apteryx,* comprise the family Apterygidae. They are usually classified in their own order, Apterygiformes. Named for their cry, kiwis are brownish or grayish in color and may be streaked or barred. They have small heads, hairlike plumage, minute wings, and no external tail. The bill is long and slender, with nostrils near the tip. Kiwis range from 1.25 to 4 kg (2.75 to 9.0 lb) in weight and from 45 to 84 cm (18 to 33 in) in length and stand up to 30 cm (1 ft) high. They inhabit humid forests or swamps, where they feed on insects, snails, berries, and especially earthworms. Recent experiments confirm that kiwis locate food by smell, which is unusual for birds. The one or two very large eggs, each about 13 cm (5 in) in length and 400 g (14 oz) in weight, are laid in a burrow, and the smaller male incubates them for about 11 weeks. The little spotted kiwi, *A. oweni,* seems to be disappearing.

kiwi (fruit) The kiwi fruit is the fruit of a grapelike, deciduous vine, *Actinidia chinensis,* native to south central China, where it grows on trees to heights of 10 m (30 ft) or more. About 1906 it was introduced into New Zealand, which is now the principal producer of the fruit, although plantings have also been made in California. The small, round fruit has a fuzzy, greenish brown skin roughly resembling the plumage of the kiwi bird; its flesh is a translucent emerald green, with a refreshing limelike flavor. Kiwi fruit is eaten fresh or cooked, and, like the papaya, its juice may be used as a meat tenderizer.

Kiyomasu   see UKIYO-E

Kiyonaga [kee-yoh-nah'-gah] Kiyonaga, or Torii Kiyonaga, 1752–1815, a Japanese artist and the fourth titular head of the Torii school, is generally regarded as the greatest UKIYO-E master of the 1780s. He executed a wide range of paintings, prints, and illustrated books. The

elongated, idealized feminine beauty celebrated in his prints had a profound influence on contemporary Japanese artists. Later prints of Kabuki actors exhibit a new, realistic portrait style.

Kiyonobu I [kee-yoo-noh'-boo] Kiyonobu I, or Torii Kiyonobu I, 1664–1729, was a major Japanese painter and printmaker in the UKIYO-E style who specialized in illustrations of Kabuki actors for the three theaters of Edo (modern Tokyo). The son of an Osaka Kabuki actor, Kiyonabu I moved (1687) to Edo and came under the influence of MORONOBU, whose lively woodblock prints of populist genre subjects typified the Ukiyo-e style. Building on Moronobu's legacy, Kiyonobu I founded the Torii school of Ukiyo-e prints, which greatly advanced Japanese printmaking. His greatest works were two books (1700) dazzlingly illustrated in black and white, one portraying actors and the other depicting courtesans. The fluidly contoured and highly decorative style of these illustrations influenced Ukiyo-e masters for decades to come. One of his numerous pupils was his son, Kiyonobu II, who helped carry on his father's tradition.

Klamath [klam'-uhth] The Klamath are North American Indians who in the 19th century lived on the shores of Upper Klamath Lake, Klamath Marsh, and the lower Sprague and Williamson rivers in south central Oregon. Their language belongs to the Sahaptin stock of the Penutian linguistic family. More closely related to the Plateau than to the Great Basin or Californian culture areas, their economy was highly adapted to their lake and marsh environment. The Klamath built substantial semisubterranean earth lodges at their main village sites, mat lodges at temporary camps. They used dugout canoes for lake and river transport. The guardian spirit quest and associated dances were the principal religious activities, along with shamanistic curing. Traditionally aggressive, Klamath raided nearby California Indian villages for captives to be traded.

By the treaty of 1864 with the United States, a reservation was created comprising much of the original Klamath home area. Later the Modoc and some Paiute and Pit River Indians were forced onto the same reservation, and eventually merged with the Klamath to form a cohesive Klamath tribe; this body retained control of extensive timberlands until termination of the reservation in 1954. In 1986 the Klamath tribe was reorganized. Its population is about 2,500.

Klee, Paul [klay] A Swiss-born painter and graphic artist whose personal, often gently humorous works are replete with allusions to dreams, music, and poetry, Paul Klee, b. Dec. 18, 1879, d. June 29, 1940, is difficult to classify. Primitive art, surrealism, cubism, and children's art all seem blended into his small-scale, delicate paintings, watercolors, and drawings.

Klee's early works are mostly etchings and pen-and-ink drawings. These combine satirical, grotesque, and surreal elements and reveal the influence of Francisco de Goya and James Ensor, both of whom Klee admired. Two of his best-known etchings, dating from 1903, are *Virgin in a Tree* and *Two Men Meet, Each Believing the Other to Be of Higher Rank.* Such peculiar, evocative titles are characteristic of Klee and give his works an added dimension of meaning.

After his marriage in 1906 to the pianist Lili Stumpf, Klee settled in Munich, then an important center for avant-garde art. That same year he exhibited his etchings for the first time. His friendship with the painters Wassily Kandinsky and August Macke prompted him to join Der BLAUE REITER (The Blue Rider), an expressionist group that contributed much to the development of abstract art.

A turning point in Klee's career was his visit to Tunisia with Macke and Louis Molliet in 1914. He was so overwhelmed by the intense light there that he wrote: "Color has taken possession of me; no longer do I have to chase after it, I know that it has hold of me forever. That is the significance of this blessed moment. Color and I are one. I am a painter." He now built up compositions of colored squares that have the radiance of the mosaics he saw on his sojourn. *Red and White Domes* (1914; Collection of Clifford Odets, New York City) is distinctive of this period.

Klee often incorporated letters and numerals into his paintings, as in *Once Emerged from the Gray of Night* (1917–18; Klee Foundation, Berlin). These, part of Klee's complex language of symbols and signs, are drawn from the unconscious and are used to obtain a poetic amalgam of abstraction and reality.

Klee taught at the BAUHAUS school after World War I, and in 1925, in his *Pedagogical Sketchbook,* he tried to define and analyze the primary visual elements and the ways in which they could be applied. In 1931 he began teaching at Düsseldorf Academy but was dismissed by the Nazis, who termed his work "degenerate." Klee left Germa-

Paul Klee's Fish Magic *(1925) exemplifies the imagination, humor, and thematic use of small motifs characteristic of his work. (Philadelphia Museum of Art.)*

ny for Switzerland in 1933, where he developed the crippling collagen disease scleroderma, which forced him to develop a simpler style and eventually killed him. The late works, characterized by heavy black lines, are often reflections on death and war. *Still Life* (1940; Felix Klee collection, Bern), however, is a serene summation of his concerns as a creator.

Klein, Calvin   SEE FASHION DESIGN

———

Kleist, Heinrich von [klyst]   Bernd Heinrich Wilhelm von Kleist, b. Oct. 18, 1777, d. Nov. 21, 1811, driven to suicide largely because he failed to achieve fame as an author, ironically is today considered one of Germany's greatest poets. Kleist did not go unnoticed during his lifetime; his genius was recognized, with qualifications, by most of the leading German authors of the day, but his turbulent, self-expressive plays and stories were puzzling and disturbing to audiences more accustomed to moralistic and sentimental literature.

Kleist's principal dramatic works included the one-act comedy *The Broken Pitcher* (1806; pub. 1811; Eng. trans., 1961), the Amazon tragedy *Penthesilea* (1808; Eng. trans., 1959), and his masterpiece, *The Prince of Homburg* (1810; pub. 1821; Eng. trans., 1956). His best-known novellas are *Michael Kohlhaas* (1810; Eng. trans., 1913–15) and *The Marquise of O.* (1810; Eng. trans., 1960). Existentialists see in Kleist a forerunner of Kierkegaard and other philosophers of *Angst,* and Marxists claim him as an early critic of feudalism in his native Prussia. The intense erotic feeling that characterizes many of his portrayals has interested psychoanalytic critics, and there has been a renewed appreciation of the comic and ironically humorous elements in his works.

Partly because he was unable to support himself by his writing, Kleist never married. By 1811 the Prussian government had suppressed his journal, the *Berliner Abendblätter*, and his hopes of a German uprising against Napoleon became forlorn. His suicide fulfilled a promise to a friend's wife, who believed she was incurably ill, that he would kill her and join her in death whenever she wished.

———

Klemperer, Otto [klem'-pur-ur]   The German conductor Otto Klemperer, b. May 14, 1885, d. July 6, 1973, was only 22 when, on the recommendation of Gustav Mahler, he was named to conduct the German National Theater in Prague. After conducting opera in Hamburg, Bremen, Strasbourg, Cologne, and Wiesbaden, he joined (1927) the Kroll Opera in Berlin and in 1931 the State Opera. He left Germany in 1933 and became conductor (1933–39) of the Los Angeles Philharmonic; he also directed the reorganization of the Pittsburgh Symphony. In 1959 he was appointed principal conductor "for life" of the London Philharmonia (later New Philharmonia) Orchestra, with which he made many memorable recordings, particularly of the German repertoire. Klemperer was also the composer of six symphonies, nine string quartets, and a mass.

kleptomania   Kleptomania is the obsessive impulse to steal, in the absence of any need or desire for the articles stolen. According to psychoanalytic theory, the stolen objects have sexually symbolic value; other theories view kleptomania as revenge for emotional deprivation in infancy or an attempt to extend the limits of power.

See also: NEUROSIS.

Klimt, Gustav [kleemt]   The work of the painter and illustrator Gustav Klimt, b. July 14, 1862, d. Feb. 6, 1918, embodies the high-keyed erotic, psychological, and aesthetic preoccupations of turn-of-the-century Vienna's dazzling intellectual world. He has been called the preeminent exponent of ART NOUVEAU. Klimt was a cofounder and the first president of the Vienna Secession, a group of modernist architects and artists who organized their own exhibition society and gave rise to the SECESSION MOVEMENT, the Viennese version of Art Nouveau. He was also a frequent contributor to *Ver Sacrum,* the group's journal.

The primal forces of sexuality, regeneration, love, and death form the dominant themes of Klimt's work, as in the paintings *Judith I* (1901) and *The Kiss* (1907–08), both at the Österreichische Galerie, Vienna, and *Hope I* (1903; National Gallery, Ottawa).

The sensualism and originality of Klimt's art led to a hostile reaction to his three ceiling murals—*Philosophy* (1900), *Medicine* (1901), and *Jurisprudence* (1902)—for the University of Vienna. Other important decorative projects undertaken by Klimt were his celebrated *Beethoven frieze* (1902; Österreichische Galerie), a cycle of mosaic decorations for Josef Hofmann's Palais Stoclet in Brussels (1905–09), and numerous book illustrations.

Klimt's style drew upon an enormous range of sources: classical Greek, Byzantine, Egyptian, and Minoan art; late-medieval painting and woodcuts; photography and symbolist art. In synthesizing these diverse sources, Klimt's art achieved both individuality and extreme elegance.

Kline, Franz   Franz Kline, b. Wilkes-Barre, Pa., May 23, 1910, d. May 13, 1962, was an important member of the New York school of ABSTRACT EXPRESSIONISM. After studies (1930s) in Boston and London and a period of representational still lifes and cityscapes, he worked in New York City. Through most of the 1950s, Kline limited his vast nonobjective canvases to hurtling black streaks or bars surrounded by areas of white, for example, *Mahoning* (1956; Whitney Museum of American Art, New York City).

The critic Dore Ashton described Kline's black figures as energies or forces spanning an immeasurable wilderness, and he argued that their effectiveness lay in their refusal to take on a coherent compositional format. About

(Left) *The Austrian Secessionist painter Gustav Klimt painted the watercolor-gouache study* Fulfillment (The Kiss) *for a mosaic mural in a Brussels residence. (Musée d'Art Moderne, Strasbourg.)*

(Right) *The American artist Franz Kline's* Copper and Red *(1959) shows the vehemence and bold movement characteristic of his work. Kline, one of the leading exponents of abstract expressionism, is best known for his massively structured compositions. (Private collection.)*

1959, Kline abandoned his starkly simple scheme to add middle tones and color.

Klinefelter's syndrome   A congenital disease of males, Klinefelter's syndrome is characterized by small size and firmness of the testes, lack of sperm cells, breast development, and increased excretion of sex hormones; mental retardation often occurs. A relatively common syndrome, it occurs in about 1 out of 500 live male births. The plasma concentration of the male hormone testosterone is often low. The diagnosis is rarely made before puberty, and many affected males may still appear mentally and physically normal.

The fundamental abnormality is an excess of X-type (female) sex chromosomes in the body cells. A body cell in a normal male has an X chromosome and a Y chromosome, the latter determining maleness. Body cells in patients with Klinefelter's syndrome have more than one X chromosome along with the Y. The excess female chromosomes interfere with full development of male characteristics.

Klondike [klahn'-dyk]   The Klondike is a sparsely populated area in west central Yukon Territory in Canada, near the Alaskan border. It was the site of a great gold rush in the 1890s. The Klondike, which encompasses an area of about 2,070 km^2 (800 mi^2), takes its name from the Klondike River. Gold mining has continued on a small scale, along with lead, silver, and zinc extraction. The Alaska Highway passes through the southern part of the Klondike, offering a reliable overland connection with Alaska and other parts of Canada.

Gold was discovered at Rabbit Creek (later Bonanza Creek) in 1896, and a great gold rush began in 1897. More than 30,000 people streamed into the area. Dawson, still the major town of the Klondike, served the needs of the prospectors. By 1910, when the great strike was over, more than $100,000,000 worth of gold had been taken from the Klondike.

Klopstock, Friedrich Gottlieb [klawp'-shtawk]   A German epic, lyric, and dramatic poet, Friedrich Gottlieb Klopstock, b. July 2, 1724, d. Mar. 14, 1803, produced a literary landmark with his most substantial work, *The Messiah* (Eng. trans., 1788)—an epic on the Passion in 20 cantos, which appeared between 1748 and 1773. His plays include three on biblical themes and a trilogy (1769–87) the German national hero Hermann, but the influence of his *Odes* (1747–80; Eng. trans., 1848) was perhaps more lasting. Klopstock's use of language was individual: he coined words and exploited the resources of German word order. A major contributor to developments among the next generation of German poets, seen especially in Hölderlin's use of language and the melancholy devotion of Novalis, Klopstock was a link between German classicism and romanticism.

klystron   SEE ELECTRON TUBE

knee   see JOINT (in anatomy)

Kneller, Sir Godfrey [nel'-ur]   Sir Godfrey Kneller, b. Lübeck, Germany, Aug. 8, 1646, d. Oct. 26, 1723, was a prolific court painter to five monarchs of England. He was originally named Gottfried Kniller. In 1674 he arrived in England, where he met and painted a portrait of James Vernon (1677; National Portrait Gallery, London), secretary to the duke of Monmouth. Through Monmouth he obtained the opportunity to paint King Charles II, thus launching a highly successful career as a painter to the courts of Charles II, James II, William III, Queen Anne, and George I; he became court painter (1688) and principal painter (1692) and was knighted (1692) by William III.

Knickerbocker group [nik'-ur-bahk-ur]   Named after Diedrich Knickerbocker, a pseudonym assumed by Washington Irving in his *History of New York* (1809), the Knickerbocker group was a loose-knit school of writers in New York City during the first half of the 19th century. Its members shared similar literary tastes, writing more to entertain than to instruct, and a similar goal: to make New York an important literary center and to nurture a national literature. The principal figures, in addition to Irving, were James Fenimore Cooper and William Cullen Bryant.

Knidos   see CNIDUS

Knievel, Evel [kuh-neev'-ul, ee'-vul]   Robert Craig "Evel" Knievel, b. Butte, Mont., Oct. 17, 1938, was a professional motorcycle stuntman. A natural athlete, Knievel was a ski-jump champion and also played briefly with the Charlotte (N.C.) Clippers of the professional Eastern Hockey League. Knievel gained fame, however, under his assumed name, for zooming on his motorcycle up a ramp and over parked cars for distances of more than 45 m (150 ft). The daredevil sustained serious injuries in a crash landing after jumping over fountains at a Las Vegas hotel. He was unsuccessful in attempting (1974) to jump the Snake River Canyon, Idaho, in a rocket-powered motorcycle.

knife   see SWORD AND KNIFE

knife fish   Knife fish is the common name for members of the African and Asian fish family Notopteridae, also called featherbacks. The family consists of three genera (the Asian *Notopterus* and the African *Papyrocranus* and *Xenomystus*), with six species, all of which are characterized by a deep, thin, bladelike body, a long anal fin extending nearly the full length of the underside of the body, and a distinctly narrow or pointed tail. All but *Xenomystus* also have a small, slender dorsal fin in the center of the back (the "feather"). They range in size from 15 cm (6 in) to about 1 m (3 ft) and are typically freshwater fishes, but a few enter brackish water.

knight   In medieval Europe the term *knight* referred to a mounted warrior of secondary noble rank. The name is sometimes also applied to the *equites* of ancient Rome, a similar class of mounted soldiers who ranked below senators. The Roman class was formed to provide a means of advancement for men who were not born into a noble family (or *gens*). The medieval rank, however, probably originated with the barbarian tribes of northern Europe, and the English term was derived from the Old English

An artist's rendering of a knight in armor is based on the effigy of Sir Edmund de Thorpe, who fought under the English king Henry V and was killed in Normandy in 1418. A tunic worn over the knight's breastplate, or cuirass, bears his quarterly arms (A). For such ceremonial functions as jousting or for actual warfare, the knight might have worn a great helm (B), in which the basinet (pointed helmet) and visor were decorated with a panache of peacock feathers and a tassled mantle. The well-armed knight was equipped with several specialized weapons. The pointed face of the war hammer (C) was used to pierce an opponent's armor. The mace (D) was capable of shattering armor and incapacitating an enemy. The knight's war sword (E) was kept close at hand, worn in a sheath, or scabbard (F).

cniht, meaning "youth" or "military follower." Often the younger son of a hereditary peer, the knight began his training as a young boy by entering the service of an overlord. At age 15 or 16 he was raised to the rank of squire and began his period of trial. When his overlord considered him worthy, the prospective knight received his accolade, traditionally a tap on the shoulder with a sword, which proclaimed him a knight. Once knighted he was entitled to the honorific title "Sir."

As FEUDALISM developed, the rank of knight (in French, *chevalier;* in German, *Ritter*) became a landholding rank. The knight held his land by what was known as military tenure. That is, in return for a land grant the knight was expected to render military service to his overlord.

At the time of the CRUSADES the great military and religious orders of knighthood were established. They included the Knights of St. Lazarus (formed as early as the 4th century but militarized during the 12th century); the Knights HOSPITALERS (formed in the 12th century); the Knights TEMPLARS (1118); the TEUTONIC KNIGHTS (1190); and the Knights of the Sword (Livonian Order; 1204). The Spanish orders of Alcántara, Calatrava, and Santiago were founded in the 12th century, and the Portuguese Order of Saint Benedict of Avis evolved during the following century.

Later secular knightly orders were established in Europe. They included the Order of the Garter (*c.*1349) in England, the Order of Saint Michael (1469) in France, and the Burgundian Order of the Golden Fleece (*c.*1430; later split into Austrian and Spanish branches). As modern weapons and battle techniques diminished the military effectiveness of the armored knight, his title became primarily honorary. Increasingly, the military service required of a landholding knight was converted to money payments to the overlord.

In modern times many monarchies established purely honorific orders of knighthood. In Great Britain they included the Order of the Bath (1725) and the Order of the Thistle (for Scots; reformed in 1687). The French Legion of Honor was established by Napoleon I in 1802 and the Japanese Supreme Order of the Chrysanthemum in 1888.

Honorary knighthood still exists. In Britain the title of knight is not hereditary but is conferred by the monarch (with the advice of the government). The British feminine equivalent of knight is dame commander.

See also: CHIVALRY; HERALDRY.

Knight, Bobby   Robert Montgomery Knight, b. Orrville, Ohio, Oct. 25, 1940, became during the 1988–89 season the youngest collegiate basketball coach to attain 500 career victories. After being a successful defense-oriented head coach at Army (1966–71), Knight went on to Indiana University (1972–), where he has won a National Invitation Tournament title (1979), three National Collegiate Athletic Association titles (1976, 1981, 1987), and three College Coach of the Year awards (1975–76, 1989). When he led the U.S. team to a gold medal in the 1984 Olympics, Knight became only the second coach in history to win NIT, NCAA, and Olympic championships.

A   B   C   D   E   F

Knight, Etheridge   The poet and teacher Etheridge Knight, b. Corinth, Miss., Apr. 19, 1931, d. Mar. 10, 1991, was an inmate at Indiana State Prison when he began to write about the brutality of prison life. A Korean War veteran, Knight showed an impressive sensitivity to the psychological effects of a racially divided society. Among the best known of his books are *Poems from Prison* (1968) and *Black Voices from Prison,* which he edited in Italian in 1968 and published in English in 1970. Other verse is found in *Belly Song and Other Poems* (1973) and *The Essential Etheridge Knight* (1986).

Knights Hospitalers   see HOSPITALERS

Knights of Columbus   The Knights of Columbus (K. of C.), a U.S. fraternal order of Roman Catholic men, was founded in 1882 by Michael J. McGivney, a Connecticut priest. The K. of C. provides social activities, insurance, and other benefits for its members, sponsors athletic events, contributes to various charitable and educational projects, and works to promote Catholic interests. Its headquarters are in New Haven, Conn. The K. of C. magazine, *Columbia*, is published monthly.

Knights of Labor   The Knights of Labor was the major national workers' organization in the United States from about 1880 to 1890 and the first to try to bring all workers into one centralized LABOR UNION. It was founded in Philadelphia in 1869 by Uriah S. Stephens and other garment workers to protect its members against abuse from employers. When Terence V. Powderly replaced Stephens as master workman in 1879, membership was below 10,000. The Knights then attempted to draw together the entire labor movement. Successful strikes against railroads increased membership to 700,000 in 1886.

Unsuccessful strikes in 1886 and antilabor sentiment generated by the HAYMARKET RIOT brought setbacks. A more fundamental cause of the organization's decline was confusion over goals. On the one hand, the Knights favored a weekly pay law, an eight-hour workday, and industrial safety measures. On the other, the Knights of Labor was unreconciled to large-scale industrial enterprise and unwilling to make a clear distinction between capital and labor; the Knights established producers' cooperatives and even admitted the owners of small businesses as members. The national leadership opposed strikes, which were from time to time forced on it by rank-and-file action. By 1890 the organization had been overshadowed by the craft-union-oriented American Federation of Labor, and in 1893 membership was only 75,000. The Knights was formally dissolved in 1917.

knitting   Knitting is the making of fabric by using special needles to interlace yarn in a series of loops, or stitches. Knit patterns are produced with two basic stitches: the knit stitch and the purl stitch.

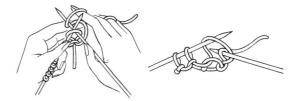

To form a knit stitch, the tip of the right-hand needle is inserted from left to right through the front of the first stitch on the left-hand needle and the yarn is looped under, then over, the tip of the right-hand needle (above left). This loop is then drawn through the stitch on the left-hand needle (above right), and the original stitch is slipped off the left-hand needle behind the new stitch on the right-hand needle. The stitches should be loose enough to slide easily along the needle and the tension consistent to maintain even size.

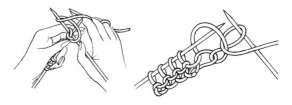

The purl stitch is the reverse of the knit stitch. To form a purl stitch, the right-hand needle is inserted from right to left through the front of the stitch on the left-hand needle; the yarn is then looped over and under the tip of the right-hand needle (above left). This loop is drawn through the stitch on the left-hand needle (above right), and the original stitch is slipped off the left-hand needle in front of the new stitch formed on the right-hand needle. Alternate rows of knit and purl stitches create the smooth surface known as stockinette. Alternating knit and purl stitches in the same row creates a ribbed effect.

Hand knitting, using two single-pointed needles for flat work and a flexible circular needle with points at each end or several double-pointed needles for circular work, remains a popular hobby. Most knit fabrics today, however, are produced by machine.

William Lee, an English clergyman, invented the first knitting machine in 1589. His "stocking frame," based on an early form of hand knitting that used hooked needles mounted side by side on a frame, allowed an operator to form an entire row of loops with a single stroke of a foot pedal. It remained essentially unaltered until the mid-18th century, when mechanisms were added for making ribbed knitting and even types of lace. The stocking frame produced a weft fabric, where the stitches were built up horizontally. The first warp-knitting machine, invented in 1775, knit yarn together vertically and could produce fabric far more quickly than the older machines.

Modern knitting machines belong to either the weft or warp category and may be controlled by computer. Weft machines are often circular—the needles are mounted on a rotating cylinder, and a tubular fabric is produced as the cylinder turns. Warp machines are usually flatbed, with the needles mounted in a straight line. These machines knit a flat fabric that is less elastic than fabrics knitted on weft machines and are used for knitting full-fashioned garments.

Knopf, Alfred A. [kuh-nahpf'] A noted American publisher, Alfred Abraham Knopf, b. New York City, Sept. 12, 1892, d. Aug. 11, 1984, began his career with Doubleday, Page & Company in 1912 and started his own firm three years later. Blanche Wolf, whom he married in 1916, was his copublisher until her death in 1966. The Knopf firm introduced to U.S. readers many foreign authors, among them André Gide, Thomas Mann, and Sigrid Undset. Among the American writers who were published by Knopf are Willa Cather, John Hersey, George Jean Nathan, and H. L. Mencken. After it was sold to Random House in 1960, the Knopf firm retained its own imprint.

Knossos [nahs'-uhs] Knossos, home of the legendary King MINOS and the MINOTAUR, was from earliest times the leading settlement of Crete and center of Minoan culture during the Aegean Bronze Age. It dominated the fertile central region of the island, of which its successor, Herakleion (Iráklion), remains the commercial capital. A hill west of the Kairatos stream was settled by a group of the first people to land in Crete at the end of the 7th millennium BC. The settlement gradually expanded, especially after the transition to the Bronze Age (c.3000 BC). From the end of the 3d millennium BC the original hill was occupied by a great palace, named the Palace of Minos by Sir Arthur EVANS, who excavated it in 1900–05. With its elaborate plan and winding corridors, this sprawling complex may have been the reality behind the myth of the labyrinth built by DAEDALUS for Minos. The finest surviving example of Minoan architecture, the palace has been extensively restored.

The Bronze Age city surrounding the palace, at its greatest extent in the 16th century BC, is thought to have covered an area of 600,000 m^2 (718,000 yd^2), with a population of about 20,000. By that time Knossos apparently exercised authority over the whole of Crete; it remained the chief center after the island was conquered by the Mycenaeans from the Greek mainland (c.1450 BC). The palace was destroyed in the 14th or early 13th century BC and never rebuilt, but the city continued to be inhabited until the end of the Bronze Age (c.1100 BC), and Knossos rivaled Gortyna for predominance among the Dorian Greek states of Crete from c.1000 BC until the Roman conquest in 67 BC. After the Battle of Actium in 31 BC, Augustus settled some of his veterans at Knossos, making it a Roman colony. Ruins of an aqueduct and Roman public buildings are still visible.

See also: AEGEAN CIVILIZATION.

The Great Palace, built on the debris of a Neolithic settlement, dominates the ancient site of Knossos, near modern Iráklion on Crete. Knossos, home of the legendary King Minos, was the largest Cretan city of the Bronze Age.

Know-Nothing party The Know-Nothing party was an antiforeign, anti-Roman Catholic political organization that flourished in the United States between 1852 and 1856. Nativism had been growing since the mid-1840s in response to massive immigration, especially from Ireland and Germany. Many of these immigrants had become part of urban Democratic political machines, much to the resentment of non-Democratic old-stock Americans. In the early 1850s, various secret, anti-immigrant organizations joined to form a new political party. Officially called the American party, it was popularly known as the Know-Nothing party because members answered "I know nothing" when asked about their exclusive, native-Protestant organization.

The Know Nothings advocated exclusion of Catholics and foreigners from public office and sought to increase the naturalization period from 5 to 21 years. The Know-Nothings won national prominence chiefly because the two major parties—Whigs and Democrats—were at that time breaking apart over the slavery issue. The party reached its zenith in 1854–55, but it too soon became factionalized over the slavery issue. In 1856 Millard FILLMORE, the American party presidential candidate, received 21 percent of the popular vote, but the party rapidly disintegrated thereafter. Most of its Northern members joined the ranks of the newly formed Republican party.

Knowth Knowth, a hamlet in County Meath, Ireland, is the site of a major Neolithic passage grave in the Boyne River valley. The principal burial mound measures 90 by 78 m (300 by 250 ft), stands 11 m (36 ft) high, and covers an area of nearly 6,500 m^2 (70,000 ft^2). This extensively excavated BARROW was found to contain two stone passages, 33 and 34 m (108 and 111 ft) long and larger than any others known in Europe. One of the passages terminated in a characteristically cruciform-shaped chamber with side recesses, in one of which was a large ornamental stone basin of presumed ritual purpose. Around the central tomb were grouped 16 satellite tombs of simpler construction. The whole group belongs to the later Neolithic Period of the 3d millennium BC.

Knox, Fort see FORT KNOX

Knox, Henry   Henry Knox, b. Boston, July 25, 1750, d. Oct. 25, 1806, a bookseller before the outbreak of war, served with distinction as an artillery officer in the American Revolution and later became secretary of war. In 1775, Knox helped save Boston from capture by the British when he brought 55 pieces of badly needed artillery from Fort Ticonderoga. He later commanded artillery forces in several operations, including the battles of Trenton, Monmouth, and Yorktown. Commander of West Point (1782–84), Knox also founded (1783) the Society of the Cincinnati, an organization for officers who were veterans of the Revolution. He served (1785–94) as secretary of war under the Articles of Confederation and also, in George Washington's administration, under the U.S. Constitution.

Knox, John   John Knox, b. c.1514, d. Nov. 24, 1572, was the key figure of the REFORMATION in Scotland as the founder of Scottish PRESBYTERIANISM. After serving briefly as a Roman Catholic priest, he became a Protestant through the efforts of the Scottish reformer George Wishart.

Upon the defeat of a Protestant rebellion, Knox was sentenced to serve on French galleys. After 19 months his release was secured by English Protestant influence. Knox then lived for four years in England, serving as a parish preacher in Berwick and Newcastle and becoming (1551) a chaplain to King Edward VI. His objections to the Second Book of Common Prayer in 1552 paved the way for the later Puritan movement in England.

Knox fled to the Continent in 1553 when the Catholic Mary I succeeded to the throne in England. He served as minister to English refugees in Frankfurt, met John CALVIN in Geneva, and returned for a 9-month preaching tour in Scotland before settling (1556) as the minister of the English refugee church in Geneva. Knox's theology, which stressed God's sovereignty, continued to develop along Calvinistic lines. He went well beyond Calvin in his political theory, however. In 1554, Knox had begun to justify resistance to faithless rulers who attack their dutiful subjects. While in Geneva, Knox published a notorious work, *The First Blast of the Trumpet against the Monstrous Regiment of Women* (1558), in which he denounced rule by women. It was directed at the queen regent of Scotland (Mary of Guise), MARY, QUEEN OF SCOTS (then also queen of France), and England's Mary I—all Catholic monarchs. The work's major effects, however, were to embarrass Calvin, to offend the Protestant Elizabeth I, who succeeded Mary I to the English throne in 1558, and to make Knox persona non grata in England.

Knox returned to Scotland in May 1559 at the height of conflict between Catholics and Protestants. His inspirational preaching and timely aid from England allowed Protestant forces to triumph. The return of the widowed Mary, Queen of Scots, in 1561 led to a famous series of face-to-face confrontations between the young queen and Scotland's foremost preacher. When Mary was forced to abdicate in 1567, Protestantism was secured in Scot-

John Knox, leader of the Scottish Reformation, was largely responsible for the establishment of Presbyterianism in Scotland.

land. Knox played the leading role in formulating the constitution of the reformed Church of Scotland (see SCOTLAND, CHURCH OF), and he remained an outspoken preacher until his death.

Knox, Philander Chase   Philander Chase Knox, b. Brownsville, Pa., May 6, 1853, d. Oct. 12, 1921, U.S. secretary of state (1909–13) under President William Howard Taft, is remembered for advancing "dollar diplomacy," whereby the protection of U.S. financial interests abroad became a major goal of the nation's foreign policy. A Pennsylvania lawyer, Knox served (1901–04) as U.S. attorney general and instituted several important antitrust actions under President Theodore Roosevelt. From 1904 to 1909, Knox, a Republican, sat in the U.S. Senate. After serving as secretary of state he returned to the Senate (1917–21), where he opposed U.S. membership in the League of Nations.

Knoxville   Knoxville is the seat of Knox County in eastern Tennessee. Located along the Tennessee River about 280 km (175 mi) east of Nashville, the city has a population of 165,121 (1990). Knoxville is a center for industry and agricultural trade and the headquarters of the Tennessee Valley Authority (TVA). Its manufacturing is concentrated in textiles and chemicals. Marble quarrying, zinc mining, and food processing are also important. A significant number of tourists come to Knoxville en route to the Great Smoky Mountains National Park, Cumberland Mountains, and several TVA lakes. The Oak Ridge National Laboratory is nearby. Knoxville is the site of the University of Tennessee (1794) and Knoxville College (1875).

Knoxville was settled permanently in 1785. It was named for Maj. Gen. Henry Knox, secretary of war, in 1791. Knoxville twice served as the state capital (1796–1812 and 1817–19).

Knyphausen, Wilhelm, Baron von [knip'-how-zen] Baron von Knyphausen, b. Nov. 4, 1716, d. Dec. 7, 1800, was a German general who commanded the Hessians in British service during the American Revolution. He fought at the battles of White Plains, Brandywine, and Monmouth and was temporarily British commander (1779–80) in New York. He returned to Germany in 1782.

koala [koh-ah'-luh]   The koala, *Phascolarctos cinereus,* is a marsupial mammal in the phalanger family, Phalangeridae. It is sometimes placed in a separate family, Phascolarctidae. It has a large head; hairy ears fringed with white; a large nose; dense, woolly, grayish white fur; and a vestigial tail. It grows up to 84 cm (33 in) long, and weighs up to 14 kg (30 lb). Selective eaters of eucalyptus leaves and young bark, koalas are solitary or live in small harems led by a single male. The young are born after a gestation period of 25 to 30 days and weigh about 5.5 g (0.2 oz) at birth. They spend about 6 months in the mother's pouch and are weaned on predigested eucalyptus leaves, devoid of fecal material, that have passed through the mother's digestive tract. Nearly exterminated by epidemics around the turn of the century, by massive slaughter for their fur into the 1920s, and by human-caused fires, koalas are presently found only in the eucalyptus forests of eastern Australia. They are now fully protected by law.

The koala is often found in eucalyptus trees, the leaves of which are its basic diet. The animals avoid young leaves, which are poisonous. Koalas are permeated with the pungent odor of eucalyptus.

koan [koh'-ahn]   In Zen Buddhism a koan (literally, a public case) is a theme for meditation used by masters to help their disciples break through the barriers of the intellect to achieve enlightenment. There are about 1,700 popular koans, which usually consist of a saying from a great Zen master or his answer to a question. For example, a monk asked Tung-shan "Who is Buddha?" and received the reply "Three *chin* of flax." By meditating on such a koan, which is nonrational, Zen students open their minds to spiritual intuition. Koan practice was developed in China and transmitted to Japan in the 13th century.

kob [kahb]   Kobs are ANTELOPES in the genus *Kobus,* of the ox and antelope family, Bovidae. The kob is a graceful, long-nosed animal 1 m (3 ft) high at the shoulder and weighing about 112.5 kg (250 lb). The coat is smooth and yellowish brown to almost black, with whitish underparts. The long horns of the male curve backward with an upward tip. The kob lives in Africa south of the Sahara and in the upper Nile valley. It favors high, dry plains, where it is found in small herds or singly.

Kobe [koh'-bay]   Kobe, a city in south central Honshu, Japan, lies on a coastal lowland facing the Inland Sea, about 32 km (20 mi) west of Osaka. The population is 1,447,557 (1988 est.). Kobe is one of the largest and busiest ports in Japan. It exports mostly manufactured or semimanufactured goods and imports raw materials and foodstuffs. It is also an industrial city with shipbuilding and steel, rubber, and textile manufacturing. Tourist attractions include the Municipal Museum of Arts, Suma Temple, Suma Aquarium, Minatozawa Shrine, and Sorakuen Park. Several universities and colleges are located there. A port since the 13th century, Kobe was opened to foreign trade and residence in 1868.

Koblenz [koh'-blents]   Koblenz, a city in the German state of Rhineland-Palatinate, lies between Bonn and Mainz at the confluence of the Mosel (Moselle) and Rhine rivers. Its population is 110,843 (1986 est.). Long a commercial and industrial center, Koblenz produces aluminum, machinery, chemicals, furniture, textiles, and clothing. It is also a popular tourist and conference site. The church of Saint Castor dates from AD 836. The Ehrenbreitstein Castle houses a Rhine museum.

The Romans fortified the site about 9 BC. It became the headquarters of the Franks in the 6th century AD and in the 11th century was presented to the archbishops of Trier by Holy Roman Emperor Henry II. France took control of the city in 1794 and held it until 1815, when it became part of Prussia. From 1824 to 1945, Koblenz was the capital of the Rhine province. It was heavily bombed during World War II, but most of its historic buildings have been restored.

Koch, Edward I. [kahch]   Edward Irving Koch, b. New York City, Dec. 12, 1924, was a three-term mayor (1978–90) of New York City. A lawyer, he entered New York City Democratic politics in 1962; he served on the city council (1967–68) and as a member of Congress (1969–77). Known for his brash, colorful manner, Koch maintained his popularity despite New York's problems of unemployment and steadily declining services. He was reelected in 1981 and again in 1985. His support had slipped among many minority voters, however, by 1989, when he was defeated in the Democratic primary election by David Dinkins. Koch wrote (with William Rauch) the autobiographical *Mayor* (1984) and *Politics* (1985) and, with John Cardinal O'Connor, *His Eminence and Hizzoner* (1989).

Koch, Marita [kohk] The career of East German sprinter Marita Koch, b. Feb. 18, 1957, was one of sustained excellence and versatility. From her first world record (200 m), in 1978, to her last (400 m), in 1985, Koch set 10 individual world marks at 200 m and 400 m, and took part in five others in all three sprint relays. Her best time for 200 m was 21.71 sec, and for 400 m, 47.60 sec, a record that still stands. Koch won the 1980 Olympic gold medal at 400 m. She retired in 1986.

Koch, Robert The German bacteriologist Robert Koch, b. Dec. 11, 1843, d. May 27, 1910, made many contributions to bacteriology, including his important discovery (1882) of the bacillus responsible for tuberculosis. He was awarded the 1905 Nobel Prize for physiology or medicine for his work. In 1876, Koch discovered the ANTHRAX bacillus and later found a way of preventing the disease through preventive inoculation. In the early 1900s, Koch worked in Africa, studying the transmission of several diseases, including African sleeping sickness. His many achievements also include his development of improved microscopic techniques and bacterial staining and culturing methods. Koch set forth four principles, known as Koch's Postulates, for locating disease-causing microorganisms; these are now considered fundamental in bacteriology.

Kodály, Zoltán [koh'-dy, zohl'-tahn] The Hungarian composer and teacher Zoltán Kodály, b. Dec. 16, 1882, d. Mar. 6, 1967, collected, arranged, and published Magyar folk songs—sometimes in collaboration with Béla Bartók—and wrote extensively about them. His techniques for teaching music to children have been organized into the widely used Kodály Method. In his compositions, Kodály used folk elements, harmony, and rhythm more conservatively than Bartók. One of Kodály's most popular works is the orchestral suite *Háry János* (1926). Others include a symphony, a concerto for orchestra, music for the stage, chamber music, solos for piano and other instruments, folk-song arrangements, choral music, songs, church music, and educational music. He is also the author of books on pedagogic and historical subjects.

Kodiak Island [koh'-dee-ak] Kodiak is an island located in the Gulf of Alaska, off the southern coast of Alaska. The island has an area of 13,895 km^2 (5,365 mi^2) and a population of 13,309 (1990). The city of Kodiak is the island's main commercial center. The eastern part of the island is mountainous and heavily forested; the western lowlands are covered by grasses. The island is volcanic in origin. Three-quarters of the area is a national wildlife refuge (established 1941) inhabited by the Kodiak brown bear. Due to the proximity of the Japan Current, the climate is warm and humid. Fishing, mining, grazing, and fur trapping are economic mainstays.

Discovered in 1763, Kodiak was settled in 1784 by Grigory Ivanovich Shelekhov, who founded a Russian colony at Three Saints Bay. It remained under Russian jurisdiction until 1867, when the United States purchased Alaska.

Koestler, Arthur [kest'-lur] Arthur Koestler, b. Budapest, Hungary, Sept. 5, 1905, d. Mar. 3, 1983, established his reputation with novels in English, such as *Darkness at Noon* (1940), which examine the totalitarian and revolutionary politics of the 20th century. Koestler became disillusioned with Communism after his membership in the German Communist party (1931–38) and became a British subject in 1945. Much of Koestler's work deals with psychology and the creative process and includes *The Sleepwalkers* (1959) and *The Act of Creation* (1964). More recent books are *The Thirteenth Tribe* (1976), *Janus: A Summing Up* (1978), *Bricks to Babel* (1980), and *Kaleidoscope* (1981).

Koetsu [koh'-ayt-soo] The Japanese artist Honnami Koetsu, 1558–1637, was one of the principal founders of Rimpa, a school of Japanese decorative art that emerged in the early Edo period (1615–1868). A distinguished calligrapher and tea master, he was also one of Japan's finest potters and designers of lacquer ware. In 1615 he was granted an estate at Takagamine, outside Kyoto, by the Tokugawa shogun Ieyasu. There various artisans worked together under Koetsu's direction.

Koetsu collaborated with the painter SOTATSU in revitalizing the ancient tradition of the decorated poem scroll: Koetsu inscribed classic poetry in his bold hand over Sotatsu's gold and silver designs, introducing a new decorative style into Japanese art. A notable example is the *Deer Scroll* (early 17th century; Seattle Art Museum, Wash.).

Koffka, Kurt [kohf'-kah] Kurt Koffka, b. Berlin, Mar. 18, 1886, d. Nov. 22, 1941, was one of the three major figures identified with the origin and spread of GESTALT PSYCHOLOGY. Together with Max Wertheimer and Wolfgang Köhler, Koffka elaborated the new Gestalt approach. From 1911 to 1924, Koffka taught at the University of Giessen, publishing many experimental studies within the Gestalt paradigm. He wrote a major Gestalt treatise on developmental psychology in 1921 (Eng. trans., 1924) and the first substantial paper on Gestalt theory in a U.S. journal (*Psychological Bulletin,* 1922). After teaching at Cornell University and the University of Wisconsin, Koffka became a professor of psychology in 1927 at Smith College, where he remained until his death. His *Principles of Gestalt Psychology,* the fullest and most systematic statement of the Gestalt approach to psychology, was published in 1935.

Kohl, Helmut　Helmut Kohl, b. April 3, 1930, is the Christian Democratic chancellor who presided over the reunification of Germany in 1990. Kohl succeeded Helmut Schmidt as West German chancellor in 1982, and won endorsement from the electorate in 1983 and 1987. When the Communist East German regime began to disintegrate early in 1990, he gained a following among East German voters as a champion of rapid and total German reunification within NATO. Overcoming strong opposition both at home and abroad, he achieved the incorporation of East Germany into the Federal Republic in a few months, thus greatly increasing the size and prestige of his country and ending more than four decades of German disunity.

Kohler, Kaufmann　[koh'-lur, kowf'-mahn]　Kaufmann Kohler, b. Bavaria, May 10, 1843, d. Jan. 28, 1926, was a rabbi and a leading theologian of Reform Judaism. The radicalism of his doctoral thesis, "The Blessing of Jacob," created such controversy that he was barred from the pulpit and emigrated (1869) to the United States. Kohler helped formulate (1885) the so-called Pittsburgh Platform, the original code of Reform Judaism. It emphasized moral teachings and social justice and rejected many traditional ideas, including sacrificial cults, resurrection, and the concept of a national restoration of Israel to Palestine. Between 1903 and 1921, Kohler served as president of Hebrew Union College, Cincinnati, Ohio, and as editor of the *Hebrew Union Annual.*

Köhler, Wolfgang　[ker'-lur]　The psychologist Wolfgang Köhler, b. Tallinn, Estonia, Jan. 21, 1887, d. June 11, 1967, was—with Kurt Koffka and Max Wertheimer—one of the originators of GESTALT PSYCHOLOGY. From 1913 to 1920, on Tenerife in the Canary Islands, Köhler undertook pioneering studies of intelligent problem solving ("insight learning") by chimpanzees, published as *The Mentality of Apes* (1917; Eng. trans., 1925). He directed the Psychological Institute at the University of Berlin from 1921 to 1935. Thereafter he taught at Swarthmore College until 1955 and at Dartmouth College from 1958 until his death.

Köhler was the natural scientist of the early Gestalt trio. He applied the Gestalt approach in physics, animal and human learning and problem solving, memory, perception, brain processes, and other areas.

Koko Nor　[koh'-koh nohr]　The Koko Nor (Chinese: Jing Hai), a large glacial lake in Central Asia, is located in the Nan Shan mountain system of west central China. It is approximately 105 km (65 mi) long and 64 km (40 mi) wide and has a maximum depth of 37 m (123 ft). Formed during the Pleistocene Epoch, the lake was originally filled with glacial meltwater; today it receives water from 23 rivers and streams. It has no outlet. The azure water is brackish and is frozen from November through March.

Kokoschka, Oskar　[koh-kohsh'-kuh, ohs'-kur]　Oskar Kokoschka, b. Mar. 1, 1886, d. Feb. 22, 1980, was a leading Austrian painter, printmaker, and writer. His early expressionist portraits reflected the anxious, decadent atmosphere of prewar Vienna, as in the nervous linearity and psychological intensity of *The Portrait of August Forel* (1909; Städtische Kunsthalle, Mannheim, Germany). A public performance (1909) of his sadistic play *Mörder, Hoffnung der Frauen* (Murder, the Hope of Women; 1907), about the battle of the sexes, provoked scandal, and in 1910, seeking a less hostile milieu, Kokoschka moved to Berlin. There he joined the artist group associated with the influential magazine *Der Sturm.*

After World War I, Kokoschka taught (1919–24) at the Dresden Academy. The work of this period is typified by *The Power of Music* (1919; Staatliche Gemäldegalerie, Dresden), with its bold colors and broad, crude forms. He then traveled through Europe, North Africa, and the Near East, painting spatially distorted, somewhat impressionistic cityscapes. When the Nazis included some of his works in the Exhibition of Degenerate Art (1937), Kokoschka responded with his *Self-Portrait of a Degenerate Artist* (1937; Emil Korner Collection, Port William, Scotland).

Vienna, State Opera *(1956) is an example of Kokoschka's later, decorative style. (Österreichische Galerie, Vienna.)*

kola nut　[koh'-luh]　Kola "nuts" are the edible, fleshy seeds of tropical trees of the *Cola* genus. The most important species, *Cola acuminata*, is native to rain forests of tropical West Africa. Wild trees, often preserved during forest clearance, have been a source of kola nuts up to modern times. Cultivation began in the late 19th century, principally in West Africa, although the trees were introduced into the New World during the 17th and 18th centuries and are now also cultivated in Brazil and Jamaica.

The nuts contain the stimulant CAFFEINE, and in Africa and South America they are chewed to dispel hunger and to alleviate fatigue. They are commercially valuable as a source of flavor and caffeine in cola drinks and medicines.

Kollantai, Aleksandra [kuh-luhn-ty'] The Russian Marxist feminist Aleksandra Kollantai, b. Apr. 1 (N.S.), 1872, d. Mar. 9, 1952, became the first woman accredited as a foreign ambassador. An advocate of free love and full equality for women, she served (1917–18) as Soviet commissar of social welfare but resigned in protest against the authoritarianism of the Bolshevik regime and joined the "Workers' Opposition." Later reconciled with the regime, she headed (1923–45) the Soviet diplomatic missions to Norway, Mexico, and Sweden; in 1944 she negotiated the Soviet-Finnish armistice.

Kollwitz, Käthe [kawl'-vits, kay'-te] The distinguished German graphic artist Käthe Kollwitz, b. July 8, 1867, d. Apr. 22, 1945, took as her theme the suffering caused by poverty, rebellion, war, and death. Kollwitz's urgent social and political concern is evident in her major print cycles: *The Weavers' Uprising* (1895–98), a series of three lithographs and three etchings based on a play by Gerhardt Hauptmann; *Peasants' War* (1902–08), etchings; *War* (1922–23) and *Proletariat* (1925), both comprising woodcuts in an expressionist style reminiscent of Ernst Barlach; and *Death* (1934–35), lithographs that combine the theme of mortality with self-portraiture. Kollwitz is also known for her sculpture, notably her war monument (unveiled 1933) in Belgium's Roggevelt Military Cemetery.

Käthe Kollwitz's lithograph Woman with a Blue Shawl (1903) exemplifies the realism and compassion of her moving portrayals of the poor and oppressed. (Wallraf-Richartz Museum, Cologne.)

Komodo dragon [kuh-moh'-doh] The largest living lizard, the Komodo dragon, *Varanus komodoensis*, attains a total length of up to 3 m (10 ft) and an average weight of 136 kg (300 lb). These giant lizards live only in the vicinity of Indonesia, for example, on Komodo island, for which they are named. They are representative of the MONITOR lizard family, Varanidae. Like other monitors,

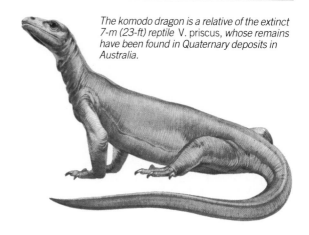

The komodo dragon is a relative of the extinct 7-m (23-ft) reptile V. priscus, whose remains have been found in Quaternary deposits in Australia.

Komodo dragons are carnivorous, feeding on animals as large as small deer and bush pigs. Like other large monitors, they can be formidable adversaries, even for humans, if actually cornered. Young Komodo dragons climb trees, but adults—far too large to be arboreal—dig burrows or spend hot daylight hours under bushes, coming out in the morning and evening. Like several other monitors, Komodo dragons swim well. These reptiles are endangered and are under strict protection by the Indonesian government.

Kon-Tiki see HEYERDAHL, THOR

Konarak [kohn-ah'-ruhk] The enormous black-granite temple of Konarak, dedicated to the sun-god Surya, was built along a remote stretch of beach on the eastern coast of India, about 380 km (240 mi) south of Calcutta, during the reign of Narasimhadeva (AD 1238–64). It was originally designed as a series of halls and pavilions ranged along a common axis and leading to a tower rising above the sanctum. The complex was never completed, and little survives except the massive assembly hall that stood in front of the sanctuary tower. A striking feature of the temple's design is that the hall and tower complex was intended as an architectural replica of Surya's solar chariot; around its high platform are placed 12 great wheels intricately carved in stone and, flanking the main approach to the platform, 7 colossal freestanding figures of horses, placed as though pulling the temple through space.

Kongo, Kingdom of The Kingdom of Kongo emerged as a centralized state during the late 14th and early 15th centuries in a large area around the lower course of the Congo River in what is modern Zaire and Angola. It was one of the first major African kingdoms contacted by the Portuguese (in 1482). During the first decades of relations between Portugal and the mani-kongos (Kongo monarchs), efforts were made by both sides to stimulate peaceful relations based on trade and missionary activity.

The mani-kongos themselves converted to Christianity and adopted Portuguese reign names beginning with Alfonso I (r. 1505–43). Commerce became increasingly centered on the slave trade, however, leading to deterioration of relations between the Kongo and Portugal. All efforts at collaboration ended by the middle of the 17th century when the Portuguese, from their base in nearby Angola, invaded the kingdom and killed the reigning monarch, Antonio I (r. 1661–65). Although claimants continued to assert their rights to the title of mani-kongo through the 19th century, the kingdom actually disintegrated into a number of small vassal states that eventually formed parts of the colonies of Portuguese West Africa and the Belgian Congo.

Konoe Fumimaro [kohn'-oh-ay foo'-mee-mah-roh]
Konoe Fumimaro, b. Oct. 12, 1891, d. Dec. 16, 1945, was twice prime minister of Japan (1937–39, 1940–41). As a prince he sat in the house of peers, becoming its president in 1933. Konoe became prime minister in 1937, a month before the outbreak (July 7) of the Second SINO-JAPANESE WAR. Thereafter he cooperated with the army in extending government controls in Japan. In 1938 he issued a statement expounding Japan's expansionist aims for a "new order in East Asia." When he returned to power in 1940, Konoe announced the formation of a New National Structure to create an "advanced national defense state"; political parties were replaced by the Imperial Rule Assistance Organization.

In September 1940, Konoe concluded a military alliance with Germany and Italy and in April 1941 a nonaggression pact with the USSR. Fearing American intervention, he then pursued negotiations with the United States. When these failed, he resigned in October 1941, to be replaced by Gen. TOJO HIDEKI. After Japan's defeat in August 1945, Konoe became a member of the nation's first postwar cabinet. He was issued an arrest warrant as a possible war criminal, however, and committed suicide late that year.

Konya [kohn'-yah]   Konya (1985 pop., 439,181) is the capital city of Konya province, central Turkey. Known as Iconium in ancient times, and for its handwoven carpets since the 13th century, Konya also produces sugar, flour, textiles, leather goods, and aluminum. Tourism is important.

One of the oldest cities in the world, Konya was settled by the Phrygians in the 3d century BC and was visited by Saint Paul. It became the capital of Lycaonia in the 4th century AD. In the late 11th century, the SELJUKS gained control of the area, and the city became the seat of the sultanate of Iconium or Rum. The city reached the peak of its prosperity in the 13th century. Konya was captured by the Il-Khan Mongols in the late 13th century and was part of the Turkoman principality of Karaman before it was annexed (1472) by the Ottoman Empire. After a period of decline, it grew with the construction (1896) of the Istanbul-Baghdad railroad.

Kook, Abraham Isaac [kohk]   Abraham Isaac Kook, b. Latvia, 1865, d. Sept. 1, 1935, a Jewish philosopher, mystic, and Zionist, was the first chief rabbi in British-mandated Palestine. He emigrated to Palestine in 1904. He was at a conference in Germany when World War I began; he made his way to England, where he spent the war years and stirred popular support for the BALFOUR DECLARATION. He returned to Palestine in 1919 and was elected chief rabbi in 1921, a post he held until his death.

Kook's form of Zionism was based on his mystical doctrine of inclusion; as he understood it, even secularist Jews working to build up the Jewish homeland were doing God's work. He held that the fire of Israel blazes in every Jew and that a Jew's imagination could only be "lucid and clear, clean and pure" in the Holy Land.

kookaburra [kook'-uh-bur-uh]   The kookaburra, or laughing jackass, *Dacelo gigas*, is a large and noisy bird of the Australian forests. Although a member of the KINGFISHER family, Alcedinidae, order Coraciiformes, the kookaburra does not eat fish but feeds mainly on large insects and small reptiles and amphibians. At a maximum of 47 cm (18.5 in) in length, and with a 10-cm (4-in) bill, the kookaburra is larger than most kingfishers, but its brown and tan plumage is drab by the standards of the family. Kookaburras nest during the spring and lay two to four white eggs in tree holes or termite nests. Their loud cries resemble human laughter and are typically chorused at dawn and dusk.

The kookaburra is also called the "bushman's clock" in Australia.

Koopmans, Tjalling C.   The Dutch-American economist Tjalling Charles Koopmans, b. 's Graveland, the Netherlands, Aug. 28, 1910, d. Feb. 26, 1985, shared

(1975) the Nobel Prize for economics with Leonid V. Kantorovich for his work in econometrics—the application of statistics, probability, and other quantitative techniques to economics. Koopmans received a doctorate from the University of Leiden in 1936, taught in Rotterdam (1936–38), and worked for the League of Nations (1938–40). He moved to the United States in 1940. He retired from Yale as a professor emeritus in 1981.

Kootenai   see KUTENAI

Köppen, Wladimir Peter [kur'-pen, vlahd'-ee-mir pay'-tur]   Wladimir Peter Köppen, b. St. Petersburg (now Leningrad), Russia, Sept. 25, 1846, d. June 22, 1940, was a German climatologist and meteorologist widely known for his classification and mapping of world climatic regions. As a young student in the Crimea, Köppen became interested in the influence of climate on vegetation. From 1875 to 1919 he served as director of meteorological services at the German Naval Observatory in Hamburg, where he organized weather warnings and upper-air observations. In 1900 he introduced his first version of a climatic classification based on vegetation. Recognizing that plants require more moisture under higher temperatures, he established numerical limits for five major climatic types and their subdivisions in terms of monthly values of temperature and precipitation.

Koran   The Koran, or Qur'an (Arabic for "recital"), is the Sacred Scripture of ISLAM. Muslims acknowledge it as the actual words of God revealed to the Prophet MUHAMMAD between c.610 and his death (632). The text contains 114 chapters (*suras*), arranged—except for the opening sura—approximately according to length, beginning with the longer chapters.

The Koran describes itself as a healing and mercy, as light and guidance from God (17:82; 27:77; 41:44; 42:52), as the absolute Truth (69:51), and as a perspicuous Book sent down from heaven in Arabic (12:1–2), part by part (17:106; 25:32), upon Muhammad. Announcing Judgment Day as the final fulfillment of God's threat and his promise (21:97–104), it warns evildoers and those who are ungrateful (17:89; 25:50) but brings good tidings to those who accept the guidance to the straightest path (17:9) and who live in accord with its message and its commandments (regarding marriage and divorce, children and inheritance, lawful foods, spoils of war, and so on). The text asserts that its message is neither a human invention (as its inimitability proves, 17:88) nor an innovation, because it confirms and clarifies the Scripture that Jews and Christians had received earlier (3:3; 5:15, 48; 35:31).

It is generally believed that the standard text of the Koran, adopted during the reign (644–56) of the caliph Uthman, is based on the compilation of one of Muhammad's secretaries, Zayd Ibn Thalbit. By calligraphic copying of its verses, and in many other ways as well, Muslims express their devotion to this Scripture.

The Soviet gymnast Olga Korbut demonstrates remarkable flexibility in a routine on the balance beam during the 1976 Olympic games in Montreal. Korbut's performance at the previous Olympics in Munich earned her three gold medals.

Korbut, Olga [kohr'-buht, ohl'-guh]   Olga Korbut, b. May 16, 1955, was a Soviet whose gymnastic mastery and vivacity impressed and charmed judges and spectators at the 1972 Olympics in Munich. Only 17 years old, she won three gold medals, one each for the team competition and the floor and balance-beam events. She also won a silver medal on the uneven parallel bars. She was selected Associated Press Female Athlete of the Year for 1972. At the 1976 Olympics in Montreal, Korbut garnered two additional medals—a silver for the balance beam and a gold as a member of the winning Soviet female team. Korbut retired in 1977.

Korda, Sir Alexander [kohr'-duh]   Alexander Korda, the professional name of Sándor Kellner, b. Sept. 16, 1893, d. Jan. 23, 1956, was a major figure in British cinema for almost 25 years. He began his producing and directing career in Hungary but left his native land in 1919 to embark on an international career in Europe and Hollywood. After establishing London Film Productions in Britain in 1932, Korda achieved world recognition with *The Private Life of Henry VIII* (1933). Specializing in historical films and using international directors, he turned out such successes as *Rembrandt* (1936), *The Four Feathers* (1939), *The Third Man* (1949), and *Richard III* (1956). Korda was knighted in 1942.

Kordofanian language   see AFRICAN LANGUAGES

Korea [kuh-ree'-uh]   Korea is a small, strategically important, and politically divided country occupying a nar-

DEMOCRATIC PEOPLE'S REPUBLIC OF KOREA (NORTH)

Land: Area: 120,538 km² (46,540 mi²). Capital and largest city: Pyongyang (1986 est. pop., 1,275,000).

People: Population (1990 est.): 21,292,649. Density: 177 persons per km² (458 per mi²). Distribution (1990): 64% urban, 36% rural. Official language: Korean. Major religions: Buddhism, Confucianism, shamanism, Chundo Kyo.

Government: Type: Communist state. Legislature: Supreme People's Assembly. Political subdivisions: 9 provinces, 3 cities.

Economy: GNP (1990): $21.5 billion; $1,069 per capita. Labor distribution (1990): manufacturing—39%; agriculture and fishing—43%; government and public authorities—18%. Foreign trade (1985): imports—$2.6 billion; exports—$2.1 billion. Currency: 1 won = 100 chon.

Education and Health: Literacy (1984): 95% of adult population. Universities (1986): 1. Hospital beds (1987): 289,000. Physicians (1987): 57,800. Life expectancy (1990): women—75; men—69. Infant mortality (1990): 27 per 1,000 live births.

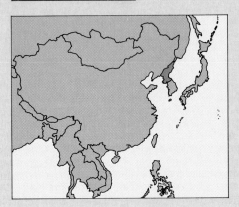

row peninsula of the East Asian mainland. It shares land borders with China on the north and with the USSR on the northeast, and it reaches to within 195 km (120 mi) of the largest Japanese island, Honshu. Formerly a united kingdom, Korea was divided (1948) at about the 38th parallel of latitude into the Communist-controlled Democratic People's Republic of Korea, otherwise known as North Korea, and the U.S.-supported Republic of Korea, or South Korea. Both republics seek eventual reunification of the peninsula through the political overthrow of the other. Seoul is the capital of South Korea, and Pyongyang is the capital of North Korea.

Korea has a long history as a cultural bridge across which Chinese culture was transmitted to Japan and Japanese influences reached the mainland. The country's name is derived from Koryo, the dynasty that ruled the peninsula from 918 to 1392. Following the devastation of the KOREAN WAR (1950–53), both nations had to rebuild their economies. South Korea looked outward, developing a successful export-oriented economy. North Korea, one of the world's most highly regimented and isolated societies, focused on economic self-sufficiency.

Land and Resources

Korea occupies a predominantly mountainous peninsula, about 320 km (200 mi) wide, that extends southward from the Asian mainland for about 965 km (600 mi). The peninsula is bordered by the Yellow Sea on the west and the Sea of Japan on the east. More than 3,000 islands, most of them small and uninhabited, border the irregular,

8,700-km-long (5,400-mi) coastline. Only about 20% of the Korean peninsula consists of lowlands suitable for settlement and cultivation; the remaining 80% is too rugged for cultivation.

The mountains drop steeply along the east coast, forming a narrow plain with few good harbors except in the northeast. To the west, the descent is gentler; along the coast are the largest and richest agricultural lands. The highest mountains are the Paektu-san (Ch'ang-pai Mountains), which reach 2,744 m (9,003 ft) at Mount Paektu, Korea's highest point.

To the east of the lowlands are the T'aebaek Mountains, the backbone of the peninsula, which extend southward from Wonsan to form the main watershed. These mountains rise steeply from a narrow coastal plain along the Sea of Japan and reach 1,709 m (5,604 ft) at Diamond Mountain. To the south, separating the western lowlands from the south coast and Pusan's Naktong Valley, is the Sobaek Range.

Soils. Korea's best agricultural soils are alluvial and are found in river valleys and coastal plains. Even these, however, tend to be somewhat infertile and sandy and require heavy fertilizing. Soils in the mountains are generally thin.

Climate. The climate is both continental and monsoonal. During the winter, the peninsula is usually swept by cold, dry north and northwest winds. As a result, North Korea has long, cold, and snowy winters, with an average January temperature of about –8° C (17° F) at Pyongyang; milder, shorter winters occur farther south, with an

REPUBLIC OF KOREA (SOUTH)

Land: Area: 98,484 km^2 (38,025 mi^2). Capital and largest city: Seoul (1989 est. pop., 10,513,000).

People: Population (1990 est.): 43,045,098. Density: 437 persons per km^2 (1,132 per mi^2). Distribution (1987): 69% urban, 31% rural. Official language: Korean. Major religions: Buddhism, Christianity, Confucianism, shamanism, Chundo Kyo.

Government: Type: republic. Legislature: National Assembly. Political subdivisions: 9 provinces, 6 cities.

Economy: GNP (1989): $211.9 billion; $4,968 per capita. Labor distribution (1990): commerce and services—42%; manufacturing—28%; agriculture and fishing—19%; construction—6%; government and public authorities—4%. Foreign trade (1990 est.): imports—$65.0 billion; exports—$63.5 billion. Currency: 1 won = 100 chon.

Education and Health: Literacy (1990): 98% of adult population. Universities (1986): 31. Hospital beds (1987): 85,327. Physicians (1987): 34,185. Life expectancy (1990): women—73; men—66. Infant mortality (1990): 23 per 1,000 live births.

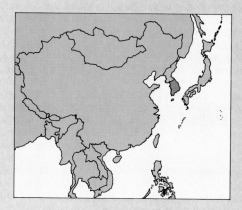

average January temperature of –5° C (23° F) at Seoul. During the summer, southerly monsoon winds, blowing onshore from the surrounding seas, predominate. Temperatures in July average 27° C (80° F) throughout the peninsula except in mountainous regions. Annual precipitation is heaviest in the south, which receives more than 1,525 mm (60 in), and decreases to about 510 mm (20 in) in the north. Most precipitation occurs in summer.

Drainage, Vegetation, and Animal Life. The rivers of Korea are short and swift. They are widely used for irrigation and for generation of hydroelectricity but are of limited value for navigation. The most important rivers are the YALU and T'umen in the north; the Taedong, Han, and Kum in central Korea; and the Naktong in the southeast.

Coniferous forests grow extensively in the north and at higher elevations farther south. Deciduous trees and pine forests predominate in warmer areas. Such wild animals as wolves, bears, leopards, and tigers are still found in some sparsely settled northern and peninsular upland areas.

Resources. Korea is well endowed with mineral resources, including large deposits of coal, iron ore, copper, gold, silver, and tungsten. Because of the political division at the 38th parallel, most coal and metals, as well as most of the commercial forests and hydroelectric power resources, are located in North Korea; South Korea, on the other hand, possesses the best agricultural land and a larger labor force.

People

Koreans are an ethnically homogenous Mongoloid people who have shared a common history, language, and culture since at least the 7th century AD, when the peninsula was first unified. The official language of both North and South is Korean (see KOREAN LANGUAGE), which is believed to have developed from a Tungusic base thousands of years ago, although many words have been borrowed from the Chinese and Japanese languages. The Korean alphabet, called *hangul,* was developed during the 15th century and is believed to have been the first phonetic alphabet in East Asia.

North Korea officially adheres to Marxism and *Juche* ("self-reliance") as the national ideology, and organized religion is reportedly suppressed. The majority of South Koreans profess (as did most North Koreans, until the Communists came to power) Buddhism and Confucianism; the latter was Korea's official religion from the 14th to the early 20th century. About 28% of South Koreans are Christians. Also important are shamanism, a widely practiced belief in natural spirits, and the nationalistic religion known as Chundo Kyo (Tonghak before 1905), which was founded in the 19th century and combines elements of Confucianism, Daoism, and Buddhism.

Demography of North Korea. About 34% of all Koreans now live in North Korea. The population density is greatest in the plains along the western coast. Although the population is growing rapidly, North Korea experiences a severe labor shortage, partly because of heavy casualties during the Korean War and also because of the migration of more than 3,000,000 persons from North to South Korea since 1948. The population is more urban than rural, and urban migration continues. The largest cities are Pyongyang (the capital), Kaesong, Chongjin, and Hungnam.

Demography of South Korea. About 66% of all Koreans now live in South Korea, which ranks among the world's most densely populated nations. As in North Korea, the lowlands along the western coast are the most densely populated areas. Although the overall rate of population growth has slowed, South Korea is experiencing an urban growth rate of 5% a year. The largest cities are Seoul (the capital, with about 23% of South Korea's total population), Pusan, Taegu, Inchon (Seoul's port), Kwangju, and Taejon.

Education and Health in North Korea. Education is free and compulsory for all students between the ages of 5 and 16, and about 20% pursue some form of higher education. The largest institution of higher learning is Kim Il Sung University (1946), in Pyongyang. Free medical treatment is available, and paramedics supplement the care provided by physicians.

Education and Health in South Korea. Elementary education is free and compulsory for all students between the ages of 6 and 11. More than 75% of all children also attend secondary school. Opportunities for higher education have been greatly expanded since 1948, as have healthcare facilities. Traditional medical treatment now complements Western medicine.

The Arts. Korea's rich artistic and cultural heritage has been strongly influenced by centuries of close contact with China. Buddhism, which dominated Korean life from the 7th to the 12th century, has influenced the arts. Buddhist temples, monasteries, shrines, palaces, fine metalwork, and other art treasures still bear witness to the achievements of this golden age. Under the Koryo dynasty (918–1392), delicate celadon ceramics of outstanding beauty were produced. Folk tales, music, poetry, and drama all draw heavily on the Buddhist and Confucian traditions. (See Korean art.)

Economic Activity

North Korea. After the North-South division, North Korea possessed most of the industrial plants, iron and other ores, coal reserves, and hydroelectric dams developed during the Japanese occupation (1910–45). Damage inflicted during the Korean War was rapidly repaired with assistance from the USSR and other Communist nations. By the end of the 1970s, however, economic growth had slowed, and the gross national product by the late 1980s was less than one-sixth that of South Korea. Under Communist control, all industry has been nationalized and agriculture collectivized.

Manufacturing and Power. In the early years of Communist control, expansion of the iron and steel, chemical, metallurgical, and machine industries was stressed in an effort to build an industrially self-sufficient and militarily strong economy. Since the 1970s the emphasis has shifted from heavy industries to the development of previously neglected consumer products. Major products currently include heavy machinery, trucks, tractors, bulldozers, farm implements, and electrical generators.

Electricity is produced at large hydroelectric installations on the Yalu River and its tributaries. Thermal elec-

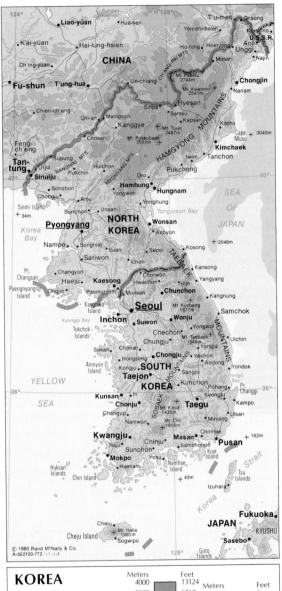

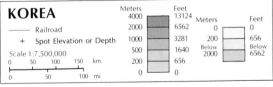

KOREA

	Meters	Feet
	4000	13124
—— Railroad	2000	6562
+ Spot Elevation or Depth	1000	3281
	500	1640
Scale 1:7,500,000	200	656
0 50 100 150 km	0	0
0 50 100 mi		

Meters	Feet
0	0
200	656
Below 2000	Below 6562

tric plants fueled by coal and imported oil supplement hydroelectric power. In 1989, 40.2 billion kW h of electricity were produced.

Agriculture, Fishing, and Forestry. It is estimated that less than half of the total labor force works in agriculture, reduced from 75% in 1948. The chief crop is rice. Agriculture is heavily mechanized, partly in response to the

(Left) *Pyongyang, the capital of North Korea, is located on the Taedong River. The city was almost completely destroyed during the Korean War but has since been rebuilt.* (Right) *Seoul, the capital and largest city of South Korea, lies in a basin flanked by low mountainous ridges. Founded in 1392 and rebuilt following the Korean War, the city is South Korea's major industrial, commercial, and cultural center.*

labor shortage, and irrigation is widely used. Commercial fishing is a major industry along the east coast, and marine products are an important export item. Commercial forestry is well developed.

Transportation. An extensive rail network links North Korea with China and also connects the country's major ports and cities; most freight and passengers are carried by rail. Road transportation is less well developed.

Trade. The principal imports are petroleum, coking coal, wheat, cotton, and machinery. The principal exports are rice, metals, cement, machinery, and chemicals. Efforts to develop trade with Western nations in the 1970s resulted in major balance-of-trade problems, and North Korea was forced to default or defer payments on many of its Western purchases. Since 1990, after several years of renewed emphasis on economic self-reliance, the government has again sought to develop trade and technical links with capitalist countries.

South Korea. Since the Korean War the South Korean economy has been revitalized and greatly expanded with the aid of capital investment from the United States and Japan. During the 1960s and 1970s the economy grew at a rate between 7% and 10% a year. Overall growth continued during most of the 1980s. Overseas construction contracts, particularly in the Middle East, also provided a significant source of income.

Manufacturing and Power. Early postwar industrial development focused on Korea's low labor costs and included such labor-intensive industries as electronics, footwear, and textile manufacturing. Today Korean-made televisions, videocassette recorders, and textiles successfully compete with those made in Japan. In addition, emphasis is now placed on industries producing high value-added items, such as petrochemicals, steel, ships, ce-

ment, and automobiles and trucks.

At the end of the Korean War, South Korea began a massive construction effort to develop electrical generating facilities, including nuclear power stations. In 1989, 80 billion kW h of electricity were produced (16 times the 1966 output).

Agriculture, Fishing, and Forestry. About 22% of the land is farmed. Agriculture provides less than 25% of the national income, and many foodstuffs are imported. Rice is the principal summer, or wet-season, crop; wheat, barley, corn, potatoes, and sweet potatoes are the major dry-season crops. South Korea's rice yields, among the highest in the world, are obtained through heavy use of fertilizers, hybrid seeds, irrigation, and mechanization, plus a strong system of cooperatives. Fish, a traditional part of the Korean diet, are abundant offshore and in the Sea of Japan. South Korea now ranks third (following Japan and China) among Asian fish producers. Forests cover about 66% of the total land area, but demand greatly exceeds the yearly wood output.

Transportation. The principal rail line connects Seoul, Taejon, Taegu, and Pusan. A second rail line runs from Seoul to the south and west, and a third serves the east coast. The construction of an extensive network of superhighways has led to a decline in the use of rail transportation.

Trade. The keystone of South Korea's growing prosperity is foreign trade. Exports include a wide range of manufactured goods from electronic goods to textiles. The country imports all of its petroleum and most of its industrial raw materials. Trade with China, the Soviet Union, and Eastern Europe has expanded dramatically since the late 1980s, although overall South Korean exports face increasing competition from other industrializing nations and are threatened by protectionist legislation in the United States and elsewhere.

Government

North Korea. North Korea is a Communist state in which political power rests with the leadership of the Korean Workers' party. According to the constitution of 1972, top policy-making power rests with the Central People's Committee. Legislative power nominally belongs to the Supreme People's Assembly, whose members are directly elected; this body, however, only ratifies decisions of the Central People's Committee. Executive power rests with the president and the State Administrative Council, headed by a premier named by the president.

South Korea. According to the 1987 constitution, the sixth since 1948, legislative power is vested in the mostly popularly elected National Assembly and executive power in a president elected to a single five-year term. The president appoints the cabinet, headed by a prime minister. The new constitution curtailed presidential powers, strengthened the legislature, and pledged military neutrality in politics.

History since 1945

Korea, one of the oldest nations in the world, was first unified in the 7th century AD (see KOREA, HISTORY OF). The country was occupied by Japan in 1905 and formally annexed by that state in 1910. During World War II, Korea was promised independence following the defeat of Japan. At the end of the war, however, it was divided at the 38th parallel of latitude; Soviet troops occupied Korea north of this line, and American forces were south of the parallel. Subsequent reunification efforts failed. In 1947 the United Nations agreed to supervise country-wide elections for a new government but was denied access to North Korea. Elections proceeded in the south, and on Aug. 15, 1948, the U.S. military government ended, and the Republic of Korea, with Syngman RHEE as president, was proclaimed. On Sept. 9, 1948, a Communist-controlled government in North Korea proclaimed the independence of the Democratic People's Republic of Korea under Premier KIM IL SUNG. Both governments claimed jurisdiction over the entire peninsula. In 1950, North Korea invaded the South in the first phase of the Korean War, and the United States quickly came to the aid of the South. In 1953 the war ended inconclusively, and the cease-fire line was placed at about the 38th parallel, with a 2,000-m-wide (6,560-ft) demilitarized zone (DMZ) on either side. The truce has been an uneasy one, marked by frequent border skirmishes. Reunification talks have been held and proposed periodically since 1972, without result.

North Korea since 1953. Chinese troops aided North Korea during the Korean War, but North Korea tried to disassociate itself from the dispute between China and the USSR during the 1960s; in 1966, North Korea declared its political independence. In 1968 tensions increased when the crew of the U.S. ship *Pueblo* were held and charged with spying, but neither Moscow nor Beijing intervened (see PUEBLO INCIDENT). Kim Il Sung, who became president under a new constitution in 1972, was raised to demigod status. He chose his eldest son, Kim Jong Il, as his eventual successor. Tensions between North and South increased in the late 1980s due to North Korea's construction of a giant dam on the North

Korean villages frequently are situated near foothills, which protect them from severe monsoon winds. Although Korea's terrain is quite mountainous and only about 20% of the land is suitable for agriculture, nearly half of all Koreans live in small villages.

Han River and its boycott of the 1988 Olympics (held in Seoul) when it was unable to host the event. The prime ministers of North and South Korea met for the first time since the Korean War in 1990; in 1991 the two countries signed a landmark treaty of reconciliation and nonaggression. That same year, both North and South Korea became members of the United Nations.

South Korea since 1953. In 1960 student-led riots forced the resignation of President Syngman Rhee. The new president, Chang Myun, was overthrown in 1961 in a military coup that brought Gen. PARK CHUNG HEE to power. Park, elected president in 1963, did much to restore economic prosperity. Rising protests against his authoritarian rule, however, led to the imposition of military rule in 1972. In 1975 all political opposition was banned. Park was assassinated by the head of the Korean Central Intelligence Agency in 1979. Premier Choi Kyu Hah was then elected president.

In May 1980 protests against the reimposition of martial law led to an uprising in Kwangju that was harshly suppressed by the army. Soon after, a military committee led by CHUN DOO HWAN assumed power. A new constitution was approved in October, and Chun became president in 1981. His army-backed Democratic Justice party (DJP) lost seats in the 1985 legislative elections, and in June 1987 the worst political protests since 1980 erupted. ROH TAE WOO, Chun's successor as head of the DJP, reached an agreement with opposition leaders Kim Dae Jung and Kim Young Sam in September on a new constitution providing for direct presidential elections. Roh won the December 1987 elections with only 37% of the vote over a divided opposition and assumed office on Feb. 25, 1988. In the April 1988 legislative elections, three opposition parties won 164 of the 299 seats. In November former premier Chun apologized for abuses of power by his regime. In 1990 the DJP and two leading opposition parties merged to form the Democratic Liberal party (DLP). In 1991 the DLP won a majority of seats in the first local elections since the 1961 coup; it captured 149 of 299 seats in the March 1992 legislative elections. South Korea established diplomatic relations with China, North Korea's only major ally, in 1992.

Korea, history of   Korean history is thought to have begun c.3000 BC with the settlement of the peninsula by Tungusic tribes, who spoke a Ural-Altaic language, followed shamanic religion, and had a paleolithic culture. Tangun, a legendary figure, is said to have established the first Korean "kingdom" of Choson in 2333 BC. The introduction of bronze tools from China and the establishment of Chinese military colonies in Korea in 108 BC led to the sinicization of Korea and the rapid development of agriculture.

Three Kingdoms. Meanwhile, three loosely organized Korean tribal federations, which emerged in the 3d century BC, were transformed into kingdoms. The establishment of the kingdoms of Silla in 57 BC, of Koguryo in 37 BC, and of Paekche in 18 BC (traditional dates) marked the beginning of the Three Kingdoms period in Korean

history. Koguryo, initially based in southern Manchuria, expanded southward and in AD 313 overthrew Lo-lang, the last Chinese stronghold in Korea.

During this period, the influence of CONFUCIANISM, DAOISM, and other forms of Chinese culture increased in Korea; BUDDHISM also grew, particularly in Paekche and Silla. Silla expelled (562) the Japanese—who had established a foothold on the coast in the 4th century—and between 660 and 668 destroyed both Paekche and Koguryo with Chinese help. Having unified Korea, Silla became a highly centralized state in which Buddhism and the arts flourished. In the 9th century, however, serious provincial rebellions broke out, and in 936 the kingdom was finally overthrown by rebels who had established the Koryo dynasty, with its capital at Kaesong, in 918.

Koryo. Under the Koryo dynasty power was initially wielded by civilian administrators, and the political, social, economic, and educational systems of Korea became increasingly sinicized. In 1170 the military seized control and suppressed Buddhism. By the end of the 12th century a military family, the Ch'oe, ruled the country. In 1258 the Ch'oe were deposed. Their civilian successor submitted to the MONGOLS, who had begun invasions of the peninsula in 1231.

A relatively peaceful period of Koryo rule under Mongol suzerainty followed. The invention (1234) of a new printing system with movable type allowed the ready dissemination of Buddhist and Confucian writings, and Korean potters manufactured high-quality green Koryo ware (see KOREAN ART). A revolt against Mongol rule in 1356 brought another period of disorder. Finally, in 1392, the Koryo king was overthrown by the Yi dynasty, aided by the new Ming dynasty in China, to whom the Yi swore allegiance.

Yi. The Yi dynasty, which established a new capital at Hanyang (now Seoul), rejected Buddhism and established Ju Xi Confucianism as a national orthodoxy. It also improved relations with its Chinese overlords and brought about economic and social reforms. A well-functioning Confucian bureaucracy, an orderly social structure, and rapid development of the educational system seemed to promise a bright future. The adoption of the Korean writing system, called *hangul,* by King Sejong (r. 1418–50) in 1443 marked the high point in cultural development.

From the early 16th century, however, growing factionalism among scholars, mismanagement of state affairs by officials, court intrigues and power struggles, usurpation of power and privileges by the landed gentry, decline of foreign trade, and increasing tax burdens brought about political instability as well as economic decline and social upheavals. A reform school known as Silhak arose among scholars and officials, but Confucian conservatism prevented change.

The devastating but unsuccessful invasions (1592–98) by the Japanese under HIDEYOSHI and the wars of conquest (1627–37) by the Manchu worsened the internal situation. Vassalage to the Manchu, who went on to overthrow the Ming and establish the Qing dynasty in China, fostered the antiforeign sentiments of the Koreans. The state of the nation continued to deteriorate as rebellions and peasant uprisings erupted.

Contact with the West and Japan. Roman Catholicism was brought to Korea from China in the 17th century, and what was called Western Learning developed. A new native religion called Tonghak (Eastern Learning) arose in 1860 and won the support of the underprivileged and mistreated peasantry. Persecution of the Christians and the destruction of a U.S. merchant ship in 1866 helped provoke Western assaults by the French in 1866 and the United States in 1871. The Koreans resisted these attacks, but in 1876 the Japanese took advantage of the governmental disruption within Korea to force a commercial treaty on the Yi. Six years later Korea, the "hermit kingdom," also opened its doors to the Western nations, beginning with a treaty with the United States.

After the opening of Korea, rivalries developed—particularly among China, Japan, and Russia—for predominance of influence over the weak Korean state. In 1894 followers of Tonghak revolted against the government, and China sent troops to suppress the rebellion. Japan also sent troops to Korea. The First SINO-JAPANESE WAR ensued (1894–95), and victorious Japan established hegemony over the nominally independent Korea. After defeating the Russians in the RUSSO-JAPANESE WAR (1904–05), Japan was strong enough to force Korea to become a protectorate. After some Korean resistance Japan formally annexed the country in 1910.

Modern History. During the Japanese colonial period (1905–45) the Koreans endured political suppression, economic exploitation, and social and educational discrimination, in addition to attempts to Japanize their culture. The so-called March movement of 1919 mounted massive demonstrations against colonial rule and was brutally suppressed. Subsequent independence movements were similarly treated. In the meantime, Korea became an important economic and military base for Japan's continental expansion.

The Japanese surrender to the Allies in 1945 liberated Korea from Japan, but the country was divided along the 38th parallel of latitude between the U.S. and Soviet occupation forces. In November 1947 the United Nations adopted a resolution to set up a unified independent Korean government, but the UN commission responsible was able to hold elections only in the southern (U.S.) zone. On Aug. 15, 1948, the Republic of Korea was inaugurated, ending U.S. military rule in the South. In North Korea the Communists established their own regime and inaugurated the Democratic People's Republic of Korea in September 1948. Thus, the temporary military demarcation line became the boundary between two Korean states. Since the devastating KOREAN WAR (1950–53), which resulted from a North Korean invasion of the South, there has been only an uneasy truce along the line.

For the history of North and South Korea since 1948, see KOREA.

Korean art   The arts of Korea, although a distinct entity, were profoundly influenced by Chinese art and architecture. Korean traditions in turn formed an important early link between Chinese and Japanese culture; it was

The Koryo period (918–1392) of Korean art is renowned for its porcelain wares. This 12th-century water bowl is typical of the uniquely Korean technique of inlaying black and white clay on celadon ware. (Museum of Fine Arts, Seoul.)

through Korea that Buddhist art forms first reached Japan during the 6th century.

The earliest Korean art, dating from about 3000 BC, appeared in the form of Neolithic pottery impressed with simple geometric decoration. Metalworking developed in Korea after the 10th century BC. From the 3d century BC on, cast-bronze mirrors and other utilitarian objects were made that attest to the marked influence of Chinese styles. Richly furnished burial chambers discovered at Lolang, near modern Pyongyang, North Korea, have revealed many of the finest surviving examples of decorative arts from the Han dynasty (206 BC–AD 220).

During the Three Kingdoms period (late 1st century BC–AD 668), the local powers of Koguryo in the north, Paekche in the southwest, and Silla in the southeast vied for control over the Korean peninsula. Koguryo art survives principally in the form of fresco-type mural paintings decorating 5th- and 6th-century tomb chambers—vigorous polychrome paintings depicting lively everyday scenes, real and fantastic animals, and other stylized motifs. The Paekche kingdom maintained close ties with Japan in the 6th and 7th centuries; its art is primarily known from gracefully sculpted Buddhist images preserved in Japan. Monumental tomb mounds surrounding Kyongju, the Silla capital, have yielded a striking array of uniquely Korean ornaments, including a group of gold crowns richly embellished with masses of comma-shaped jade pendants and gold discs.

Silla unified the Korean kingdoms into a single realm in 668, marking the start of the Great Silla period (668–918). Impressive granite monuments were erected, including the mid-8th-century pagoda of the Pulgaksa monastery and the cave-temple of Sukkalam (both near Kyongju). Silla-period metalworkers excelled in the creation of large bronze temple bells, which were often as high as 4 m (13 ft); also noteworthy are their elegant gilt-bronze figurines of Buddhist deities.

(Above) *Tombs of the Korean Koguryo dynasty were decorated with polychrome wall paintings. This hunting scene from the Tomb of the Dancing Figures (c.400) exemplifies the bold lines of this period.*

This ink-monochrome landscape painting by Chong Son (1676–1759) reflects the innovations in painting introduced during the later Yi period. (University Museum, Seoul.)

Royal patronage of Buddhism during the Koryo dynasty (918–1392) encouraged the renewed construction of temples and monasteries, the most important extant example being the Hall of Eternal Life at the 13th-century Pusoksa, believed to be the oldest wooden building in Korea. Although sculpture and stonework declined during the Koryo period, the aristocratic arts—precious metalwork, lacquer inlaid with mother-of-pearl, and above all, ceramics—reached new levels of quality and refinement. Porcelain making, introduced (late 11th century) from Zhejiang, China, was rapidly transformed by native artisans into a distinctly Korean variant—the "kingfisher-colored" Koryo celadons. These subtle blue green wares are regarded as among the most serenely beautiful Asian porcelains ever produced. In the 12th century the Koreans invented the technique of inlaying black or white clays into the celadon wares to produce delicate bird, flower, and cloud patterns.

With the founding of the Yi dynasty (1392–1910), Buddhism was replaced by a Chinese-inspired Neo-Confucianism. Not until the 18th century did distinctively Korean tendencies emerge in the work of a number of Yi artists. Genre painting in particular displayed typically Korean deftness and wit.

In Yi decorative arts, the delicate celadons of the preceding period were replaced by *pun-ch'ong*, a coarsely made pottery often enhanced by freely applied patterns in white or blue slip. Highly prized by collectors in Japan, the rustic Yi wares exhibit qualities of vitality and freshness that characterize much of Korean folk art, from inlaid lacquer objects to charming painted illustrations of Korean folk tales.

___

Korean language   Korean is the language spoken by approximately 65 million people living on the Korean peninsula: 43 million in the Republic of Korea (South Korea) and 22 million in the Democratic People's Republic (North Korea). The political partition of the country, along with the resulting different economic and social systems, has tended to strengthen long-standing linguistic divergences between north and south.

A member of the URAL-ALTAIC family of languages, Korean was brought down into the peninsula by early invaders who first entered the region during the diffusion of the Altaic peoples in Neolithic times. Each of the three kingdoms (18 BC–AD 935) of Silla, Koguryo, and Paekche appears to have had a different variety of Old Korean, but the sources for these earliest stages of the language are too fragmentary to make clear whether Old Korean was one language with three dialects or three different, but probably related, languages.

Middle Korean was apparently the final stage in the historical development of the variety of Old Korean used in the Silla kingdom, especially as that language had survived into the period of Unified Silla from the 7th to the 10th century. Not until late Middle Korean are there extensive records, written in *hangul,* an indigenous phonetic script of great precision and efficiency. The development of *hangul* about 1443–44 remains one of the major achievements of Korean civilization. Today the north employs *hangul* exclusively. In the south the use of borrowed Chinese characters to supplement *hangul* is discouraged but tolerated.

___

Korean War   In the Korean War (1950–53) a U.S.-dominated United Nations coalition came to the aid of South Korea in responding to an invasion by North Korea, which was aided by the USSR and allied with Communist China; the war ended in a military stalemate and the restoration of the political status quo. Concurrently, the United States was assuming increasing leadership of the Western nations against what were perceived as the expansionist intentions of its former ally, the USSR. As this COLD WAR heated up, it brought the United States into a military confrontation with Communist forces in Korea.

Background

The Korean peninsula was a Japanese possession from 1910 to 1945. When World War II ended in the Pacific in 1945, the USSR administered the surrender of Japanese forces north of the 38th parallel in Korea, and the United States supervised the surrender in the South. The two allies established a joint commission to form a provisional Korean government. The Soviets and the Americans soon disagreed, however, on the legitimacy of the competing political groups that sought to govern Korea, and mutual suspicions mounted.

In 1947 the United States asked the United Nations to attempt to unify the northern and southern halves of the country. The 38th parallel hardened ominously, however, into an international boundary in 1948 with the establishment of Syngman RHEE's Republic of Korea in the South and the Democratic People's Republic of Korea under KIM IL SUNG in the North. The arbitrarily set border split the peninsula both politically and economically into a Communist industrial North and a primarily agricultural South, which was dependent on U.S. aid. By 1949 both the USSR and the United States had withdrawn most of their troops, leaving behind small advisory groups. Increasing hostility led to sporadic border clashes between North and South Koreans throughout 1949 and into 1950. In September 1949 a UN commission, after trying unsuccessfully to unify the country, warned of the possibility of civil war.

The Invasion of South Korea

The withdrawal of U.S. forces and a speech (Jan. 12, 1950) by Secretary of State Dean ACHESON excluding South Korea from the U.S. defensive perimeter in the Pacific encouraged North Korea to attack South Korea on the morning of June 25. At 5:30 AM the main attack, consisting of North Korean infantry and tanks, advanced toward Seoul, the capital of South Korea. North Korean divisions also struck in the mountains of central Korea and along the east coast.

The United States immediately requested an emergency meeting of the UN Security Council to discuss the situation. The Security Council called on the North Korean government to cease hostilities. Because it seemed clear by June 27 that the North Koreans intended to disregard the UN request, the Security Council met again to consider a new resolution—one recommending that "the members of the United Nations furnish such assistance to the Republic of Korea as may be necessary to repel the armed attack and to restore international peace and security in the area." After some debate the resolution passed. The USSR was not represented in the Security Council, because it was boycotting that body in protest over the exclusion of Communist China from the United Nations.

In the meantime, U.S. President Harry S. TRUMAN conferred with Acheson and concluded that the USSR had directed the invasion. On June 27, Truman, without a congressional declaration of war, committed U.S. military supplies to South Korea and moved the U.S. Seventh Fleet into the Formosa Strait. Proceeding unilaterally, the U.S. Joint Chiefs of Staff (JCS) directed (June 30) General of the Army Douglas MACARTHUR, the American commander in East Asia, to commit his ground, air, and naval forces against the North Koreans. On July 7 the UN Security Council passed a resolution requesting that all member states wishing to aid South Korea make military forces and assistance available to the United States. By this resolution, President Truman became the executive agent for the UN on all matters affecting the war in Korea, and MacArthur became the commander in chief, UN Command. Although the United States ultimately contributed most of the air and sea power and about half of the ground forces (with South Korea supplying the bulk of the remainder), MacArthur controlled the allied war effort of a total of 17 combatant nations (the largest contributors, after the United States and South Korea, being Australia, Canada, Great Britain, and Turkey).

Delay and Defense

MacArthur's sole hope of saving the South Koreans from the superior Soviet- and Chinese-trained North Korean forces was to hold the port of PUSAN at the southern tip of the Korean peninsula until help arrived. He rushed reinforcements north to bolster the hard-pressed South Korean Army; on July 5, American units made contact with North Korean tanks and infantry just north of Osan. The Eighth Army, commanded by Lt. Gen. Walton H. Walker (1889–1950), delayed the North Koreans north and west of the Naktong River, the last natural barrier protecting Pusan. As the North Koreans pushed south toward the Naktong, however, Walker moved the Eighth Army into what came to be known as the Pusan Perimeter. Beginning on August 5 the North Koreans launched a series of violent attacks against the perimeter in an effort to capture Pusan. By September 12, however, reinforcements had greatly increased the combat power of the allies, and the North Korean offensive had spent itself.

The Inchon Landing

With virtually all enemy units concentrated against Pusan, MacArthur planned a counterstroke against the port of Inchon, on the west coast of Korea behind the North Korean line. He made a daring amphibious landing at Inchon on September 15, successfully cutting the North Korean supply lines. In the days that followed, the marines seized Kimpo Airport and the city of Seoul while the infantry turned south to meet the Eighth Army, which was pursuing a fleeing enemy north from the Pusan Perimeter. By Oct. 1, 1950, the North Koreans had been pushed out of South Korea, and the UN forces were poised south of the 38th parallel.

Crossing the 38th Parallel

In the meantime, the Joint Chiefs of Staff urged that MacArthur be allowed to pursue the North Korean Army into North Korea and destroy it. On September 11—four days before the Inchon landing—the president agreed but also adopted restraints recommended by the National Security Council to avoid provoking the Chinese and the Soviets: no UN troops should enter Manchuria or the USSR; only South Koreans should operate along international borders; and if the Soviets or Chinese intervened before the scheduled crossing, it should be canceled.

On October 7 the UN General Assembly authorized MacArthur to send his forces into North Korea. The North Korean capital of PYONGYANG fell on October 19, and the allied UN troops pushed the North Korean forces to the YALU RIVER, which formed the North Korean border with the Manchurian region of China. By the end of the month,

the fall of North Korea seemed imminent.

Chinese Intervention

Communist China had warned of possible Chinese intervention if UN forces crossed the border, and between October 14 and November 1 about 180,000 Communist "volunteers" had secretly crossed the Yalu. On November 25 the Chinese army struck quickly and with full force.

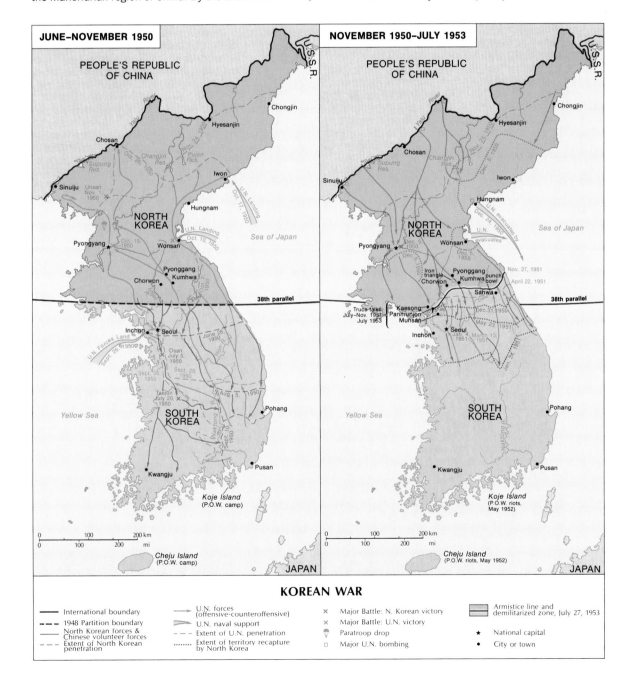

KOREAN WAR

—— International boundary	→ U.N. forces (offensive-counteroffensive)	✕ Major Battle: N. Korean victory		Armistice line and demilitarized zone, July 27, 1953
--- 1948 Partition boundary	▷ U.N. naval support	✕ Major Battle: U.N. victory		
—— North Korean forces & Chinese volunteer forces	--- Extent of U.N. penetration	⬤ Paratroop drop	★ National capital	
--- Extent of North Korean penetration	⋯⋯ Extent of territory recapture by North Korea	◻ Major U.N. bombing	• City or town	

Stunned, American and South Korean units began a long retreat that ended in early January 1951, only after the UN forces had recrossed the 38th parallel and the city of Seoul had once again fallen.

Changing War Aims

Lt. Gen. Matthew B. RIDGWAY, who took over the Eighth Army after General Walker died (Dec. 23, 1950) in a jeep accident near the front line, brought the UN withdrawal to a halt south of Seoul. Throughout January, February, and March, Ridgway's men pushed on relentlessly until they once again crossed the 38th parallel. In early April the UN advance slowed temporarily.

In the meantime the defeat in North Korea had forced the UN to reexamine its war aims in light of Chinese involvement. MacArthur quickly charged that he was facing "an entirely new war." He wanted more forces and a broader charter to retaliate against the Chinese, especially to conduct air operations against the "privileged sanctuary" of Manchuria. In this strategy, he was completely at odds with President Truman and other UN leaders who wanted a lesser commitment and a cease-fire. The UN General Assembly branded Communist China an aggressor in February 1951 and voted to subject it to economic sanctions. Its new war aim was to contain the Communist forces along the 38th parallel while negotiating an end to the conflict. Even in the darkest days before the Inchon landing, American leaders believed that restraint was necessary to avoid widening the war. Now that China was involved, the administration feared that it might invoke the Sino-Soviet treaty and cause the Soviets to unleash their nuclear capability against the United States or mount a conventional strike in Europe. MacArthur's proposals to expand his force and to retaliate against the Chinese were, therefore, not favorably considered by the administration. MacArthur openly appealed to the public and Congress in an attempt to reverse the new war policy. During this period of cold-war tensions many Americans agreed with MacArthur's stand.

The Dismissal of MacArthur

MacArthur had been a difficult subordinate. He had clashed with Truman over U.S. policy toward Taiwan early in the war and complained about the restrictions placed on his forces and his freedom to wage the war. He publicly suggested that the policies of the Truman administration had been responsible for military setbacks. On Mar. 25, 1951, just as President Truman put the finishing touches on a new initiative seeking a cease-fire, MacArthur broadcast a bellicose ultimatum to the enemy commander that undermined the president's plan. Truman was furious; MacArthur had pre-empted presidential prerogative and directly challenged the president's authority as commander in chief. On April 11, MacArthur was relieved of his command. On his return to the United States, he received a hero's welcome.

Stabilizing the Front

After MacArthur's dismissal Ridgway moved to Tokyo to replace him, and Lt. Gen. James A. VAN FLEET took command of the Eighth Army. On April 22, while Van Fleet's army edged north, the more than 450,000 Chinese opened a general offensive. Followed closely by this formidable force, Van Fleet withdrew below the 38th parallel.

On May 10, the Chinese launched a second offensive, concentrating their main effort on the eastern sector of the UN line. Van Fleet attacked in the west, north of Seoul. The surprised Communist units pulled back, suffering their heaviest casualties of the war, and by the end of May they were retreating into North Korea. By late June, a military stalemate had developed as the battle lines stabilized in the vicinity of the 38th parallel. Both sides dug into the hills and for the next two years waged a strange and frequently violent war over outposts between their lines.

Negotiations

On July 10, 1951, the armistice delegations met at Kaesong, with Vice Admiral C. Turner Joy representing the UN command and Gen. Nam Il of North Korea representing the Communists. On July 26 the two sides finally reached agreement on an agenda containing four major points: fixing a demarcation line and demilitarized zone, supervision of the truce, arrangements for prisoners of war, and recommendations to the governments involved in the war. Numerous problems arose, however, causing frequent suspensions of the talks, which in October resumed at a new site, Panmunjon.

One by one the issues were resolved until the only remaining obstacle was the handling of prisoners of war (POWs). The UN wanted the prisoners themselves to decide whether they would return home; the Communists insisted on forced repatriation. A lengthy stalemate developed. By April 1953 the POW deadlock was finally broken, and the first prisoners were exchanged at Panmunjon under a compromise that permitted prisoners to choose sides under supervision of a neutral commission. Not satisfied with a truce that did not result in the unification of Korea and totally voluntary repatriation, Syngman Rhee disrupted the proceedings on June 18 by releasing about 25,000 North Korean prisoners who wanted to live in the South. To gain Rhee's cooperation, the U.S. government promised him a mutual security pact, long-term economic aid, expansion of the South Korean Army, and coordination of goals and actions in the international conference to follow (see GENEVA CONFERENCES).

On July 27, 1953, an armistice was signed, without the participation of South Korea, and the shooting phase of the Korean War came to an end. Although the precise number of Chinese and North Korean casualties is unknown, estimates of total losses range between 1.5 and 2 million, plus perhaps a million civilians in the north. The UN command suffered a total of 88,000 killed, of whom 23,300 were American. Total casualties for the UN (killed, wounded, or missing) were 459,360, including 300,000 South Koreans. Another million civilian casualties were incurred in South Korea. In addition more than 40 percent of the industry and a third of the homes in that country were ruined.

Politically and militarily the war was inconclusive. For years the two armies continued watching each other over the demilitarized zone, a 4-km-wide (2.5-mi) band stretching 250 km (155 mi) across the Korean peninsula, waiting for the day when the fighting might begin again. Korea was no closer to unification; the war only served to intensify bitterness between North and South. The Korean War had other important results in the arena of international diplomacy. It contributed to the strained relations between Washington and Peking. In addition it added a new military dimension to the U.S. foreign policy of containment, which had heretofore been implemented by political and economic measures, including military aid. Originally formulated by George F. KENNAN, developed by Dean Acheson, and advanced by John Foster DULLES, the containment policy helped lead to U.S. military involvement in Vietnam during the 1960s.

Korin [koh'-reen] Japanese artist Ogata Korin, 1658–1716, crystallized the sophisticated taste of Kyoto's prosperous urban culture in his paintings, textile designs, fans, and lacquer ware. Heir to the artistic ideas of KOETSU and SOTATSU, he worked in the classical mode of those masters, eliminating superfluous decorative elements in favor of concise designs rendered in clear outline and brilliant color.

Korin painted the ceramics produced by his brother KENZAN. By 1701 his painting skill had been recognized officially by the award of the honorary title of *Hokkyo*, with which he signed all his paintings. During sojourns (1704–05 and 1707–09) in Edo (modern Tokyo) he developed an ink-painting style based on his study of SESSHU, Sesson, and Kaiho Yusho, earlier painters favored by the military class.

For his large-scale compositions Korin drew on the classical Japanese traditions as revitalized by Sotatsu—*Iris Screens* (Nezu Museum, Tokyo) exhibits a synthesis of Sotatsu's bold forms with an elegant simplicity. Korin's radically concise designs and his use of brilliant color patches set against gold leaf profoundly influenced Rimpa, the tradition of Japanese art that emerged in the early Edo period (1615–1868); it also had some influence on 19th-century European artists.

Kornilov, Lavr Georgiyevich [kur-nee'-luhf, lah'-vur gee-ohr'-gee-eh-vich] Lavr Georgiyevich Kornilov, b. July 30 (N.S.), 1870, d. Apr. 13, 1918, was a Russian general who led White Russian resistance to the Bolsheviks in the Russian Civil War (1918–20). He served in the Russo-Japanese War (1904–05) and commanded a division in World War I. After the RUSSIAN REVOLUTION of March 1917, Kornilov was made commander in chief by the provisional government. After the Bolshevik Revolution in November, he assumed command of a volunteer White Russian army on the Don River. He was killed while attacking Ekaterinodar (now Krasnodar).

Kosciusko, Mount [kah-zee-uhs'-koh] Mount Kosciusko, located in the Snowy Mountains (also called the Muniong Range) of the Australian Alps, in southeastern New South Wales, is Australia's highest peak (2,228 m/7,309 ft). From May to September it is a center for winter sports. The first European to discover the mountain was P. E. Strzelecki in 1840, who named the peak for his fellow Pole, Tadeusz Kościuszko.

Kościuszko, Tadeusz [kah-see-uhs'-koh, tuh-dush'] Tadeusz Andrzej Bonawentura Kościuszko, b. Feb. 4, 1746, d. Oct. 15, 1817, was a Polish military and national leader who also served in the Continental Army during the American Revolution. His fortification of Bemis Heights helped win the victory at Saratoga (see SARATOGA, BATTLES OF); he also fortified West Point.

Following the Second Partition (1793) of Poland, Kościuszko raised peasant armies and defeated a Russian army at Raclawice (Apr. 4, 1794). Defeated by Russian and Prussian forces six months later, he was imprisoned (1794–96) in St. Petersburg. After a visit to America in 1797–98 he lived in France and later in Switzerland. Kościuszko made Thomas Jefferson executor of his will, bequeathing his property to buy freedom and education for slaves. His *Manual on the Maneuvers of Horse Artillery* (1808) was used by the U.S. Army for many years.

kosher [koh'-shur] A rabbinic term, usually applied to food permitted to be eaten by traditionally observant Jews, *kosher* (or *kasher*) is a Hebrew word that means "fit, proper." The Jewish dietary laws, based on the Bible (Lev. 11; Deut. 14) as interpreted in the Talmud, concern animal products only. Kosher foods include barnyard fowl; the meat of cattle, sheep, and goats (and their milk); and such fish as have fins and scales—excluding shellfish, eels, and so on. Poultry and quadrupeds must be killed by specially trained and licensed slaughterers in accordance with detailed rules; the carcasses are drained of blood and inspected to ensure that the animals were not diseased. Unless it is to be broiled, meat must be thoroughly salted and later rinsed before cooking, to remove any remaining blood. The hindquarter of animals may be eaten only if certain nerves and sinews are first removed. Meat and milk products may not be cooked and eaten together or immediately after one another, and the use of the same utensils in their preparation and consumption is forbidden. The dietary laws were not hygienic in original intent, but they have probably been so in effect; the Bible describes them as a means of sanctification.

Košice [kaw'-shih-tsee] Košice, an industrial city in Czechoslovakia, is a regional capital of the Eastern Slovak republic. It lies on the Hornád River, about 310 km (195 mi) east-northeast of Bratislava, and has a population of 232,253 (1989 est.). Košice is an important metallurgical center and a major railroad junction. Its principal industries are petroleum refining and the manufacture of iron, steel, heavy machinery, magnesite, clothing, and wood products.

Settled in the 9th century, Košice was chartered in 1241 by Hungarians and was later occupied at various times by Austrians, Hungarians, Russians, and Turks. It was ceded to Czechoslovakia by Hungary in 1920. In the spring of 1945, Košice was a seat of the provisional Czechoslovak government.

Kosinski, Jerzy [kuh-zin'-skee, yur'-zee] A Polish-born novelist who wrote all his books in English, Jerzy Nikodem Kosinski, b. June 14, 1933, d. May 3, 1991, emigrated to the United States in 1957 and published the nonfictional *The Future Is Ours, Comrade* (1960) and *No Third Path* (1962), under the pseudonym Joseph Novak. *The Painted Bird* (1965), his bitter first novel, is a nightmarish depiction of childhood during World War II, reflecting the years he spent hiding from the Nazis in the Polish countryside. Its sequel, *Steps* (1968; National Book Award), is in a similar vein. His sardonic humor and grim pessimism are also evident in the novels *Being There* (1971; film, 1979), *The Devil Tree* (1973), *Blind Date* (1977), *Passion Play* (1979), and *Pinball* (1982). Kosinski died a suicide.

Kossuth, Lájos [koh-shoot, lah'-yohsh] Lájos Kossuth, b. Sept. 19, 1802, d. Mar. 20, 1894, was the foremost leader of the REVOLUTION OF 1848 in Hungary. Brought up in the anti-Habsburg Protestant traditions of northeastern Hungary, Kossuth emerged in the 1830s as one of the leaders of the liberal opposition against the Austrian rule. His main goal was the establishment of a liberal, independent Hungary. A brilliant orator, he became the idol of the Magyars, but his refusal to recognize the aspirations of the other nationalities of Hungary brought him into conflict with the non-Magyars.

After serving as the minister of finance in Hungary's first constitutional government (Apr. 7–Sept. 28, 1848), Kossuth assumed full control of the revolution. His declaration of Hungary's independence on Apr. 14, 1849, triggered Russian intervention, which brought about Hungary's defeat.

After his flight from Hungary on Aug. 11, 1849, and two years in Turkey, Kossuth toured Britain and the United States in a well-publicized but unsuccessful effort to gain Western support for Hungary's independence movement. When Ferenc DEÁK and the moderate Hungarian leaders concluded the Compromise of 1867, establishing the Dual Monarchy of Austria-Hungary, Kossuth's hopes faded altogether. Although he retained much influence over the Magyar masses, his political role ceased. He died in exile in Turin, Italy.

Kosygin, Aleksei N. [kuh-see'-gin] Aleksei Nikolayevich Kosygin, b. Saint Petersburg (now Leningrad), Feb. 20 (N.S.), 1904, d. Dec. 18, 1980, was premier of the USSR from October 1964 until his resignation in October 1980. He became a member of the ruling politburo in 1948. Stalin demoted him to candidate member in 1952, but Kosygin returned to the politburo in 1960, when he became first deputy premier under Nikita Khrushchev. After Khrushchev's downfall, in 1964, Kosygin took over as premier, while Leonid BREZHNEV succeeded Khrushchev as first party secretary. Together they dismantled many of the reforms of their predecessor and introduced a more steady and sophisticated foreign policy. Kosygin's diplomatic talents were used on numerous assignments, such as negotiating the India-Pakistan cease-fire in 1966 and meeting U.S. president Lyndon B. Johnson in Glassboro, N.J., in 1967.

koto [koh'-toh] The koto is a Japanese zither derived from the Chinese *qin* (or *chyn*). Its common use in Japan dates back to the 17th century, although its use at court began much earlier. When played, the 2-m-long (6-ft) instrument rests on the floor with the upper end raised a few centimeters above the lower. Its 13 strings are supported by individual movable bridges and plucked by three ivory plectra on the player's right hand. The koto is used for purely instrumental music or to accompany singing or dancing. The performer can raise the pitch of each string by a half step or whole step by applying pressure beyond the bridge. In this way the 12 half steps of the Pythagorean scale can be used over its two-octave range even though the instrument is tuned to a pentatonic (five-tone) scale.

Koufax, Sandy [koh'-faks] Sanford Koufax, b. Brooklyn, N.Y., Dec. 30, 1935, an American professional baseball player, was the most dominating pitcher of the mid-1960s. Many baseball authorities believe that he might have established himself as the greatest pitcher ever had not chronic arthritis in his left elbow forced his early retirement in 1966. From 1955 to 1960, Koufax, who played for 12 years with the Dodgers baseball organization, was an unimpressive pitcher. He changed his style, however, and in 1961 won 18 games and led the

Sandy Koufax delivers a pitch to a Minnesota Twins batter during the final game of the 1965 World Series. Relying on his blazing fastball and baffling curve, Koufax led the Los Angeles Dodgers to victory in the series.

National League in strikeouts with 269. For the next five years he had the lowest earned-run average in the league (1.97), won 111 games, lost 34, pitched 4 no-hit games (including one perfect game), and led the Los Angeles Dodgers to three pennants and two World Series titles. He also won three Cy Young Awards as baseball's best pitcher. In 1972, at age 36, he entered the Baseball Hall of Fame, the youngest inductee ever.

Koussevitzky, Serge [koo-suh-vits'-kee, serzh]   The Russian-born conductor Serge Koussevitzky, b. July 26, 1874, d. June 4, 1951, achieved his greatest fame as the director (1924–49) of the Boston Symphony Orchestra. He studied the double bass at the Moscow Conservatory and became a virtuoso on that neglected instrument. He composed several valuable solo works for double bass, including a concerto. Koussevitzky conducted the Berlin Philharmonic in 1908; thereafter, he soon established himself as a brilliant conductor in Russia and Europe (1909–20). In 1921 he moved to Paris, where he introduced a unique series of orchestral programs, the Concerts Koussevitzky, in which he introduced many important new works by French composers. He was named permanent conductor of the Boston Symphony in 1924, a post he held for 25 years. In 1940 he established a music school at the Berkshire Music Center (see TANGLEWOOD FESTIVAL), and in 1942 he founded the Koussevitzky Music Foundation, which continues to commission works and support contemporary music.

Kovacs, Ernie   Television comic Ernie Kovacs, b. Trenton, N.J., Jan. 23, 1919, d. Jan. 13, 1962, was the first comedian to put television's potential for sight effects to creative use. An actor and gag writer, Kovacs first appeared on Philadelphia TV as the chef in an unscripted cooking show. His mad goulash chatter aroused the notice of NBC-TV, and in 1951 he starred in the first of several short-lived comic series. Equipped with cigar and horn-rimmed glasses, Kovacs shrank and expanded, disappeared and zoomed back into focus, pantomimed to extraordinary effect, and, in fact, opened TV's visual possibilities for succeeding comic shows such as *Laugh-In*.

Kowloon   Kowloon (Zhoulong) is an urban area on the west shore of Kowloon Peninsula, southeastern China, in the British crown colony of HONG KONG. Kowloon is located 1.6 km (1 mi) from Hong Kong Island and is a free-trade area, manufacturing center, and tourist destination.

Kozintsev, Grigory [koh-zint'-sef]   Grigory Kozintsev, b. Mar. 22 (N.S.), 1905, d. May 11, 1973, was a noted Russian filmmaker. In 1921 he helped organize a theater workshop in Petrograd, called Factory of the Eccentric Actor (FEKS). A group from the workshop collaborated to make their first "politico-eccentric" film, *Adventures of Oktyabrina* (1924). Kozintsev's best-known collaborative efforts include *Shinel* (The Cloak, 1926, from Gogol's story); *S.V.D.* (1927, on the Decembrist revolt of 1825); and *The New Babylon* (1929, on the Paris Commune). The most notable films he made on his own were *Don Quixote* (1957), *Hamlet* (1964), and *King Lear* (1972).

Kraepelin, Emil [krep-uh-leen', ay'-mil]   Emil Kraepelin, b. Feb. 15, 1856, d. Oct. 7, 1926, was a German psychiatrist who developed an influential classification of psychoses into two types: dementia praecox, now called SCHIZOPHRENIA, and manic-depressive psychosis. Kraepelin was the first to use objective tests and measurements to study drug effects and mental disorders.

krait [krite]   Kraits are venomous South Asian snakes of the genus *Bungarus*, family Elapidae. There are about a dozen species, most of which reach 1.2 m (4 ft) in length, except for two species that reach 2.1 m (7 ft). Kraits are usually colorful, with alternating light and dark bands. They feed mainly on other snakes and have highly toxic venoms, for which antivenins are available.

Krak des Chevaliers [krahk day shev-ahl-yay']   The well-preserved Krak des Chevaliers (French for "Krak of the Knights") is a Crusader fortress in Syria near the northern border of Lebanon. It is one of the world's finest surviving monuments of medieval military architecture. Originally a Saracen castle, the Krak (from the Levantine Arabic *Karak*, meaning "fortress") was garrisoned by Kurds in 1031. In 1110, Crusaders took over the site, making it part of a chain of fortresses protecting approaches to their County of Tripoli. The HOSPITALERS manned the Krak from 1142 until its capture by the Mameluke sultan Baybars I in 1271.

Krak stands on a mountain spur with ravines on three sides. Gigantic taluses make it an artificial mountain, with walls faced with bossed masonry blocks. Rounded towers provided flanking fire from loopholes, and the main entrance is protected by a huge moat, drawbridge, and portcullis.

Krakatoa [krak-uh-toh'-uh]   Krakatoa is an active island volcano located in the Sunda Strait, south of Sumatra and west of Java, Indonesia. About 813 m (2,667 ft) above sea level at present, the cone is believed to have once reached 1,800 m (6,000 ft). The island is 3.2 km (2 mi) long and 6.5 km (4 mi) wide.

The earliest recorded eruptions on Krakatoa were in 1680–81. Activity next began on May 20, 1883, culminating in four gigantic explosions on August 27. The third of these, the most violent explosion on Earth in modern times, blew away the northern two-thirds of the island; produced tidal waves as high as 37 m (120 ft) that resulted in 36,000 deaths; and sent a dust cloud 80 km

(50 mi) into the atmosphere, causing atmospheric effects for more than a year. An estimated 21 km^3 (5 mi^3) of material was ejected; the total energy released was equivalent to 200 megatons of TNT.

Kraków [krah'-koof]   Kraków (English: Cracow), the capital of the Polish province of the same name, lies on the Vistula River about 260 km (160 mi) south of Warsaw. With a population of 744,000 (1988 est.), it is Poland's third largest city.

Kraków is today an important industrial (chemicals and metallurgy) and trading center as well as a major railroad junction, but it is known primarily because of its prominent role in Polish history and cultural life. Between 1320 and 1609 the city was Poland's capital; its cathedral served as the coronation and burial place of Polish kings until 1764. In 1364 the prestigious Jagiellonian University, the second oldest university in central Europe, was established there. In 1794 the famous Polish revolutionary hero Tadeusz KOŚCIUSZKO led an uprising against the Russians who had occupied the city; this unsuccessful revolt led to the third partition of Poland (1795), in which Kraków was given to Austria. In 1815, Kraków and the surrounding territory became a free republic. As the only independent part of Poland, Kraków became the focus of Polish national aspirations. In 1846, therefore, Austria, Prussia, and Russia decided that the Kraków free state should be incorporated into Austria. After World War I, Kraków became part of the reconstituted Polish state.

Kramer, Jack   The American John Albert Kramer, b. Las Vegas, Nev., Aug. 1, 1921, was a tennis champion who, more than anyone else, through his play and promotion elevated the status of the professional game when it was unfashionable to do so. After winning Wimbledon (1947) and Forest Hills (1946–47), Kramer successfully turned professional, witnessing the establishment (1968) of open play 10 years after retirement.

Krasner, Lee   The American painter Lee Krasner, b. Brooklyn, N.Y., Oct. 27, 1908, d. June 19, 1984, was a leading figure in ABSTRACT EXPRESSIONISM. Her chief contribution to post–World War II American painting was her distinctive use of surging, overlapping forms that charge the surfaces of her works with organic energy.

Krasnodar [kruhs'-nuh-dah]   Krasnodar, a town in the southwest of the Russian republic of the USSR, is situated on the north bank of the Kuban River, in the Northern Caucasus region. Its population is 620,000 (1989). An important manufacturing center, the city has food-processing industries; textile, machinery, furniture, and garment factories; and an oil refinery. Kuban State University (1970) is there. Founded in the 1790s by Cossacks, the city was known until 1920 as Yekaterinodar, named for Empress Catherine II.

Krasnoyarsk [kruhs-nuh-yarsk']   Krasnoyarsk is a city in Siberia, in the Russian republic of the USSR. The city's population is 912,000 (1989). It is situated at the junction of the Trans-Siberian Railroad and the Yenisei River. One of Siberia's largest cities, Krasnoyarsk produces heavy mining equipment, truck trailers, synthetic rubber, chemicals, tires, and aluminum. The city is the seat of Krasnoyarsk State University (1970).

Founded in 1628 as a fortified outpost during the Russian advance through Siberia, Krasnoyarsk became an administrative center in 1822. Its growth accelerated after 1895, when the railroad arrived, and again after World War II.

Krebs cycle   The Krebs cycle, or citric acid cycle, is a series of chemical reactions in cells for the oxidation of food. It is named for the German-British biochemist Sir Hans Adolf Krebs (1900–81), who shared the 1953 Nobel Prize for physiology or medicine for his discovery of the cycle. During the Krebs cycle, energy is removed bit by bit from cellular fuels and stored in chemical form in adenosine triphosphate (ATP), the chief storehouse of energy in all organisms.

As a result of oxidation reactions in the cycle, carbon-carbon bonds in fuel molecules are broken, and the energy that held the carbon atoms together is released. Fuel molecules—the carbohydrates, fats, and proteins in foodstuffs—are not fed directly into the Krebs cycle, however. They are first broken down to acetyl coenzyme A, which enters at the start of the cycle and, after reaction with oxaloacetic acid, is progressively transformed into CITRIC ACID (containing 6 carbons), ketoglutaric acid (5 carbons), succinic acid (4), and oxaloacetic acid (4). Acetyl coenzyme A then reenters the cycle and reacts with oxaloacetic acid, and the cycle "turns" again.

See also: ATP; METABOLISM.

Krefeld [kray'-felt]   Krefeld is a city in northwestern Germany in the state of North Rhine–Westphalia; the city has a population of 216,598 (1987 est.). When Uerdingen and several other nearby towns were annexed to Krefeld during the early 20th century, the city gained access to the Rhine River, about 8 km (5 mi) to the east. Until 1940 it was known as Krefeld-Uerdingen am Rhein. Noted for the production of silks and velvets, it maintains a textile school and textile museum. Other manufactures include steel, boilers, chemicals, rugs, clothing, and dyes. Chartered in 1373, Krefeld passed to Prussia in 1702. The city was heavily damaged during World War II.

Kreisky, Bruno [kry'-skee]   Bruno Kreisky, b. Jan. 22, 1911, d. July 29, 1990, was chancellor of Austria from 1970 to 1983. A socialist and a Jew, Kreisky fled to Sweden when Austria was annexed by Nazi Germany in 1938. Returning after the war, he helped negotiate (1955) Austrian independence and neutrality, was elected to the Nationalrat (parliament) in 1956, and served as foreign minister from 1959 to 1966. As chancellor he took a prominent part in international affairs.

Kreisler, Fritz [kry'-slur] Fritz Kreisler, b. Feb. 2, 1875, d. Jan. 29, 1962, was a celebrated Austrian violinist whose compositions for his instrument became popular showpieces for violin virtuosos. He entered the conservatory in Vienna at age 7 and won the gold medal at age 10. He subsequently studied in Paris with Lambert Joseph Massart (violin) and Léo Delibes (composition), and he made his American debut in New York in 1888. For a decade (1889–99) he retired from music to study medicine and art. When he resumed his musical career he toured extensively and settled (1940) in the United States, where he became a citizen in 1943. His best-known compositions include "Caprice Viennois," "Liebesfreud," and "Schön Rosmarin" for violin, and two operettas.

Kremlin [krem'-lin] In many old Russian cities, such as Novgorod, the fortified area, or kremlin (from the Russian *kreml*, meaning "fortress"), still stands; that of Moscow, occupying a hillside that abuts Red Square, is the largest and most famous. It was first mentioned in monastic chronicles in 1331. Its triangular area of 36.4 ha (90 acres) is enclosed by a 2.25-km-long (1.4-mi) brick wall built (1485–95) during the reign of Grand Duke IVAN III (r. 1462–1505); with the help of Italian architects, Ivan converted the Kremlin into the symbol of his power.

Within the walls the oldest ensemble is set around the Cathedral Square: the Assumption (Uspenski) Cathedral (1475–79), where rulers were crowned; the Annunciation (Blagoveshchenski) Cathedral (1484–89), the private church of the tsars; and the Archangel Cathedral (1505–08), burial place of the royal family until Tsar Peter I. The Hall of the Facets (Granovitaya Palata, 1487–91) is the sole remnant of the Grand Ducal Palace. The 81-m (266-

The Kremlin of Moscow, a triangular walled enclave on the Moskva River, contains the government offices of the Soviet Union. The complex of cathedrals and palaces, originally constructed as a citadel, housed the royal court of Russian tsars until the capital was moved to Saint Petersburg in 1712.

ft) Bell Tower of Ivan III completes the ensemble. In the 17th century, when the Kremlin ceased being a fortress, its defense towers were capped with tentlike cupolas.

After the Bolshevik Revolution the capital was moved back (1918) to Moscow, and the Soviet government was centered in the Kremlin. Lenin's apartment and office are preserved in the Senate building. Only two new buildings were added in the 20th century: the Presidium of the Supreme Soviet (1932–34) and the Palace of the Congresses (1959–61). After Stalin's death (1953) the grounds of the Kremlin were opened to the public.

Krenek, Ernst [kren'-ek] The Austrian composer Ernst Krenek, b. Aug. 23, 1900, gained international recognition with the success of his jazz-influenced opera, *Jonny spielt auf* (Johnny Strikes Up; 1925–26). Krenek emigrated to the United States in 1937 and became a U.S. citizen in 1945.

During the 1920s, Krenek's compositional style varied from the atonal to the neoclassical to an almost Schubertian romanticism. Since 1931 he has been composing SERIAL MUSIC and has also experimented with tape and electronic music. Krenek's works include five symphonies and four piano concertos, the choral work *Lamentations of Jeremiah* (1941–42), and eight string quartets.

krill Shrimplike marine crustaceans of the order Euphausiacea, krill comprise about 90 species; more particularly, the term *krill* refers to species of the genera *Euphausia, Thysanoessa,* and *Meganyctiphanes,* which constitute major elements in the diets of certain whales. Krill range from 8 to 80 mm (0.3 to 3 in) in length and are pelagic, inhabiting open seas from the surface to depths of about 2,000 m (6,500 ft). The krill's body is divided into a head, thorax, and abdomen, and, characteristically, the head and thorax are covered by a shallow, shieldlike carapace that does not enclose the featherlike gills protruding beneath it. None of the thoracic legs are modified into maxillipeds (chewing mouthparts), as in lobsters; instead, these legs commonly bear long, hairlike setae, which are used to strain the krill's food of microplankton from the water. *E. superba,* the common krill of the southern polar seas, feeds largely on tiny diatoms (algae).

Some species of krill live in huge swarms. Heavy concentrations may contain as many as 63,000 individuals per m^3 (48,000 per yd^3), weighing a total of about 20 kg (34 lb). It is upon these heavy concentrations that whales feed.

Krill are generally luminescent, having photophores that produce a brilliant blue green light. Luminescence is thought to be used as a form of communication in swarming and reproduction. During reproduction, eggs are typically freely released into the sea. A female may lay as many as 11,000 eggs.

Krishna [krish'-nuh] Perhaps the most popular god of Hinduism, Krishna is celebrated in literature, art, music, and dance throughout India. He may be depicted as the

Krishna, the eighth avatar (incarnation) of the Hindu god Vishnu, displays two distinct characters— one sensual, one wise and awe-inspiring. This Indian bronze statuette depicts the young Krishna as a cowherd playing the flute to amuse the cowmaidens.

blue, flute-playing beloved of the cowmaidens (*gopis*) of Brindaban, as a prince consorting with his lover Radha, or as a small child caught stealing butter. The basic source for this Krishna is the Puranas.

Connected in popular belief but of a quite different temperament is the Krishna of the BHAGAVAD GITA, an avatar (incarnation) of VISHNU, who discourses to the hero Arjuna on the battlefield of Kurukshetra. Although this Krishna is the focus of a number of devotional cults (see BHAKTI), the spirit is one of the awesome might and all-encompassing nature of God, displayed to Arjuna in a dazzling vision by Krishna, and devotion is taught as only one of three disciplines (the others are knowledge and nonattached action) leading to release.

Krishnamurti, Jiddu [krish-nu-mur'-tee, yid'-oo]

Jiddu Krishnamurti, b. May 22, 1895, d. Feb. 17, 1986, was an Indian Hindu religious philosopher. Annie BESANT, a leader of the Theosophical Society, met Krishnamurti in 1909 and proclaimed him an incarnation of Maitreya, the messianic Buddha. In 1911 he founded the World Order of the Star, based on the claim that he was Buddha reincarnated. He dissolved this movement in 1929, following a tour of the United States and England with Besant during which he repudiated her claim, Krishnamurti continued to write and lecture in India and the West.

Krivoi Rog [kree-voy' rawk]

Krivoi Rog, which means "crooked ravine," is a city of Dnepropetrovsk oblast in Ukraine, a Soviet republic. It is situated on the Ingulets River, a tributary of the Dnepr. The city has a population of 713,000 (1989). Krivoi Rog is the center of the USSR's largest iron-ore mining region, accounting for more than half of the nation's ore production. Iron ore is mined both underground and in huge open pits. A small steel plant dating from the 1930s has become one of the

nation's largest. Much of the ore is shipped to the DONETS BASIN. The city was founded by Zaporozhye Cossacks in the 17th century.

Kroeber, Alfred L. [kroh'-bur]

Alfred Louis Kroeber, b. Hoboken, N.J., June 11, 1876, d. Oct. 5, 1960, is generally considered the most influential American anthropologist after Franz BOAS, one of his teachers. During his tenure (1901–46) at the University of California at Berkeley, he advanced the study of California Indians and developed important theories about the nature of culture. A major figure in the emergence of anthropology as an academic discipline, he held that human culture could not be entirely explained by psychology, biology, or related sciences. Kroeber was immensely prolific, publishing continuously until the time of his death, in Paris at the age of 85.

Kronos   see CRONUS

Kropotkin, Pyotr Alekseyevich [kruh-poht'-kin, pyoh'-tur uhl-yik-syay'-eh-vich]

Prince Pyotr Alekseyevich Kropotkin, b. Moscow, Dec. 21 (N.S.), 1842, d. Feb. 8, 1921, was a Russian political philosopher and anarchist whose work inspired European anarchist groups in the late 19th century (see ANARCHISM). Kropotkin's early writing was on scientific subjects. From his study of zoology he developed a theory that cooperation, not competition, leads to evolution in the higher species. On the basis of this belief Kropotkin attacked Social Darwinism and developed a theory of nonviolent anarchistic social organization. Exiled from Russia in 1876 because of his political views, he lived in France, where he was imprisoned (1883–86), and then in England (1886–1917). Kropotkin returned to Russia at the beginning of the Russian Revolution (1917), but he was soon disillusioned with the authoritarian Bolshevik regime.

Kruger, Paul

The South African statesman Paul Kruger, b. Oct. 10, 1825, d. July 14, 1904, headed the Boer republic of the Transvaal in the confrontation with Great Britain that led to the SOUTH AFRICAN WAR. Born in Cape Colony, Stephanus Johannes Paulus Kruger moved north with his family on the GREAT TREK (1835, 1840) and settled in the Transvaal. He became commandant-general of the Transvaal in 1863. The Transvaal was temporarily annexed by Britain in 1877 but regained its independence after a brief war in 1880–81. In 1883, Kruger became president of the republic.

After the discovery of gold at the Witwatersrand (1886), Kruger welcomed European, especially British, immigrants to develop the mines, but he refused to grant political rights to these so-called *uitlanders* (foreigners). His anti-British sentiments were intensified by the unofficial British raid launched against the Transvaal by Leander Starr JAMESON in 1895.

Convinced that war with Britain was inevitable, Kruger struck the first blow in the South African War by invading the Cape Colony and Natal in 1899. When the fortunes of war turned against him, he vainly sought aid in Europe, where he died.

krummhorn [krum'-horn] The krummhorns (English, crumhorn; also known by various regional names) were a family of woodwinds bent at the lower end like a fishhook. They were popular in the 16th and 17th centuries. A double reed was enclosed by a wooden cap with a hole into which the player blew as on a recorder, the player's lips never touching the reed; the fingering also is similar to that of the recorder. Krummhorns accompanied shawms, trombones, and viols in secular and religious music.

Krupa, Gene The most famous drummer of the SWING era, Gene Krupa, b. Chicago, Jan. 15, 1909, d. Oct. 16, 1973, achieved international celebrity as a drum virtuoso with Benny GOODMAN's band during the 1930s. Krupa was the first who dared to use the bass drum on recordings in the 1920s. He formed his own band in 1938 but continued to perform occasionally with other jazz groups, including those of Goodman and Tommy Dorsey.

Krupp (family) [krup] The Krupp family were German steel and armament manufacturers based in Essen. **Friedrich Krupp**, b. July 17, 1787, d. Oct. 8, 1826, is considered to have founded the family business, although his ancestors had been in the armaments and iron business since the 16th century. The business expanded considerably under Friedrich's son **Alfred Krupp**, known as the "Cannon King," b. Apr. 26, 1812, d. July 14, 1887. An inventor and metallurgist, Alfred discovered how to cast steel in large masses. His son, **Friedrich Alfred Krupp**, b. Feb. 17, 1854, d. Nov. 22, 1902, focused on the financial side of the business and vastly increased the Krupp holdings. After his death, management of the Krupp works was taken over by **Gustav Krupp von Bohlen und Halbach**, b. Aug. 7, 1870, d. Jan. 16, 1950, a Prussian diplomat who married Friedrich's daughter Bertha (for whom the large World War I artillery pieces called "Big Berthas" were named) and assumed the family name.

After Hitler's assumption of power in 1933, the Krupp works provided the foundation for German rearmament. During World War II the company employed a large number of slave laborers, including Jews and prisoners of war. At the Nuremberg war crimes trials, Gustav was indicted as a major war criminal, but because of his failing health he was not tried. His son, **Alfried Krupp von Bohlen und Halbach**, b. Aug. 13, 1907, d. July 30, 1967, who had taken over the firm in 1943, was tried along with 11 leading members of the company. On July 31, 1948, he was sentenced to 12 years in prison and confiscation of all his property. He was released, following a general amnesty, on Feb. 3, 1951. His corporate property was returned to him, and he again took command of the Krupp works. By 1959 the company was acquiring new industries. In 1967, however, Alfried's son **Arndt von Bohlen**

und Halbach (d. 1986) renounced his rights to the succession, and in 1968 the company became a corporation owned by the stockholding public.

Krupskaya, Nadezhda Konstantinovna [krup'-skuh-yuh, nuh-dezh'-duh kuhn-stahn-tee-nohv'-nuh] Nadezhda Konstantinovna Krupskaya, b. Feb. 26 (N.S.), 1869, d. Feb. 27, 1939, was a Russian revolutionary and the wife of Vladimir Ilich LENIN, whom she married in 1898. After the Bolsheviks seized power (October 1917), she held various posts in the education commissariat. When Lenin died (1924), Krupskaya presented to the Politburo his so-called Testament, in which he recommended the removal of Joseph STALIN from the party leadership. No action was taken, but Krupskaya lost all influence.

Krylov, Ivan Andreyevich [krih-lawf', ee-vahn' uhn-dray'-uh-vich] Ivan Andreyevich Krylov, b. Feb. 13 (N.S.), 1769, d. Nov. 21 (N.S.), 1844, was Russia's greatest writer of fables. He began publishing them, together with translations of La Fontaine's fables, in 1809 and by 1843 had nine volumes in print. Krylov also wrote comic operas, comedies, and tragedies. His only play to achieve success, however, was *Modnaya lavka* (The Fashion Shop, 1806). Krylov's other outstanding literary enterprise was the satirical journal *Pochta dukhov* (The Spirit's Mail, 1789). Conceived in the same spirit was *Kaib* (1792), subtitled "An Eastern Tale," an allegory of the autocracy of Catherine II.

krypton [krip'-tahn] The chemical element krypton is the fourth member of the noble gases, Group 0 of the PERIODIC TABLE. The word *krypton* is derived from the Greek *kryptos,* meaning "hidden." Krypton's symbol is Kr, its atomic number is 36, and its atomic weight is 83.80. Krypton is a monatomic gas. Along with neon and xenon, it was discovered in 1898 by Sir William Ramsay and Morris W. Travers in the residue from the fractional distillation of liquid air. It is present in the Earth's atmosphere at concentrations of about 1 part per million by volume. Naturally occurring krypton is composed of six stable isotopes.

Krypton has a melting point of $-156.6°$ C, a boiling point of $-152.30°$ C, and a gas density of 3.733 g/l at $0°$ C. The electron configuration of krypton is [argon] $3d^{10} 4s^2 4p^6$. The element was originally believed to be truly inert, but a few compounds such as krypton difluoride, a hydrate, and clathrates have since been synthesized. The commercial separation of krypton from liquid air is the most difficult of the noble-gas separations, and consequently the high cost of the gas has limited its uses. Its principal use is in filling various fluorescent and incandescent lighting devices.

Krypton is characterized spectroscopically by brilliant green and orange lines. In 1960 it was internationally agreed that the fundamental unit of length, the meter, should be redefined so that 1 meter equals 1,650,763.73 wavelengths of the orange-red line of ^{86}Kr. This definition replaced the former standard, the platinum-iridium alloy bar kept in Paris.

Ku K'ai-chih   see GU KAIZHI

Ku Klux Klan [koo kluhks klan]   The Ku Klux Klan is the name of two distinct groups of white racists in U.S. history. During the RECONSTRUCTION era, when the votes of newly enfranchised black Southerners put Republicans in power in the Southern states, white Southerners resorted to force to preserve white supremacy. From 1866 to 1872 they organized into secret societies that terrorized local white and black Republican leaders and blacks whose behavior violated old ideas of black subordination. Especially strong in Tennessee and North and South Carolina, many of these organizations coalesced under the largest, the Ku Klux Klan, which was for a time led by former Confederate general Nathan B. FORREST. Sworn to secrecy, its members wore white robes and masks and adopted the burning cross as their symbol. They were most active during election campaigns, when their nighttime rides to murder, rape, beat, and warn were designed to overcome Republican majorities in their states.

By 1871 the violence was so serious that Republicans in Congress gave President Ulysses S. Grant authority to use national troops to restore order in affected districts. Faced with trained soldiers empowered to arrest suspects and hold them without trial, the Klan collapsed with surprising swiftness and disappeared by the end of 1872.

In the 1870s most Americans repudiated the methods of the Ku Klux Klan. However, at the turn of the century the story of the Klan was popularized in Thomas B. Dixon's *The Clansman* (1905) and D. W. GRIFFITH's powerful movie *The Birth of a Nation* (1915). This helped lead to the establishment of a new Ku Klux Klan, which spread throughout the nation and preached anti-Catholic, anti-Jewish, anti–African American, antisocialist, and anti-labor-union "Americanism." Often taking the law into their own hands, mobs of white-robed, white-hooded men punished "immorality" and terrorized "un-American" ele-

ments. At its height in the early 1920s, the Klan had more than 2 million adherents and exercised great political power in many states in the South, West, and Midwest.

In many ways a response to the great changes taking place in American society in the post–World War I years, the Klan began to wane as people adjusted to the new environment. By the 1930s it had lost nearly all of its power. Some remnants of the Klan continue to exist; there was a membership spurt in the South in response to the civil rights movement of the 1960s. Various independent Klan groups probably had fewer than 10,000 members by the early 1990s.

Kuala Lumpur [kwah'-luh lum-poor']   Kuala Lumpur (1985 est. pop., 1,103,200), the capital city of Malaysia, is located at the confluence of the Kelang and Gombak rivers. Its port city, Port Swettenham, is on the coast of the Malay Peninsula along the Strait of Malacca. Due to its central location, Kuala Lumpur is the commercial and transportation center for the surrounding tin-mining and rubber-plantation region. Industries include iron, tin, rubber and food processing, and railroad-equipment and cement manufacturing. Two universities are in the city.

Kuala Lumpur was settled in 1857 by Chinese tin miners and grew rapidly because of its location. It became the capital of Selangor state (1880), the capital of the British colony of the Federated Malay States (1896), the capital of the independent Malaya (1957), and the capital of Malaysia (1963). Kuala Lumpur was designated a separate federal territory in 1974; Shah Alam became the new capital of Selangor in 1977.

Kubin, Alfred   The Austrian graphic artist, writer, and philosopher Alfred Kubin, b. Apr. 10, 1877, d. Aug. 20, 1959, joined the BLAUE REITER group in 1911. The visionary pessimism of his fertile imagination, charged with a strong sense of the macabre and burlesque, is recorded in numerous drawings, prints, and book illustrations, for which he won considerable acclaim, including a prize at the 1952 Venice Biennale and the International Prize for Drawing at the 1955 São Paolo Biennale.

Kubitschek, Juscelino [koo'-buh-chek, zhoo-suh-lee'-no]   Juscelino Kubitschek de Oliveira, b. Sept. 12, 1902, d. Aug. 22, 1976, was president of Brazil from 1956 to 1961 and the person chiefly responsible for the construction of BRASÍLIA, the country's new modern capital. One of his aims in pushing for the development of Brasília was to open up the interior of the country to development. During his term as president he attempted to develop the country's industrial base and to increase food production. He also initiated public-works projects to improve transportation.

Kublai Khan, Mongol Emperor [koob'-ly khan]   Kublai Khan, b. 1215, d. February 1294, grandson of the

Members of the Ku Klux Klan, clad in their traditional white robes, parade through the streets of Washington, D.C., in 1925. The Klan, a secret terrorist society devoted to maintaining white supremacy, originated in 1866.

Kublai Khan, founder of the Mongol dynasty in China, receives the Venetian travelers Nicolò, Marco, and Maffeo Polo at his court in Beijing. (Bibliothèque Nationale, Paris.)

first great Mongol conqueror GENGHIS KHAN, established China's YUAN dynasty and extended the empire of the MONGOLS to its widest dimensions. The fourth son of Genghis Khan's son Tolui, he was proclaimed great khan in 1260 but did not consolidate his control over the eastern Mongol territories until 1266.

In 1279, Kublai Khan conquered the SONG dynasty in southern China, and he subsequently directed military expeditions against Indochina, Burma, the island of Java, and Malacca (Melaka) on the western coast of the Malay Peninsula. Attempted invasions of Japan in 1274 and 1281 failed partly because of bad weather. Kublai made no efforts to extend his rule to the west into territory ruled by other Mongols.

Kublai Khan moved his capital from Karakorum to Beijing, where his lavish court was visited by Marco POLO and other Europeans. Although educated by Confucian scholars, he adopted Buddhism, blending it with traditional shamanism into a type of Buddhism later known as Mongolian Lamaism.

Kubrick, Stanley [koob'-rik]   Stanley Kubrick, b. New York City, July 26, 1928, is an American film writer, director, and producer with a virtually legendary status as an idiosyncratic master. His early films include *Fear and Desire* (1953) and *Killer's Kiss* (1955). With *The Killing* (1956), critics began to take notice of his taut, brilliant style and bleakly cynical outlook. *Paths of Glory* (1957) solidified his reputation as a filmmaker interested in depicting the individual at the mercy of a hostile world. In *Spartacus* (1960; restored, 1991), Kubrick met the challenge of bringing a costume spectacle to the screen. *Lolita* (1962), based on the novel by Vladimir Nabokov, re-

ceived mixed reviews. But *Dr. Strangelove, or How I Learned to Stop Worrying and Love the Bomb* (1964) was enthusiastically hailed for its black-comedy vision of atomic-age apocalypse. His *2001: A Space Odyssey* (1968) and *A Clockwork Orange* (1971), both made in England where Kubrick has worked since 1961, engendered critical controversy, but *2001* has now become accepted as a landmark in modern cinema. His later films include *Barry Lyndon* (1975), a visually arresting adaptation of a minor Thackeray novel; *The Shining* (1980), a domestic horror tale based on a Stephen King novel; and *Full Metal Jacket* (1987), about the Vietnam War.

Kuibyshev [koo'-ib-ih-shef]   Kuibyshev (also Kuybyshev) is the capital of Kuibyshev oblast in the western Russian republic of the USSR. It is situated along the left bank of the Volga River at the mouth of the Samara River. Kuibyshev has a population of 1,257,000 (1989). A major river port, Kuibyshev is the largest city of the Volga River valley. Its diversified manufacturing industries produce equipment for the oil industry and for construction and ball bearings.

Kuibyshev, originally named Samara, was founded in 1586 as a Russian fortress guarding the eastern margins of the Russian state and the trade route along the Volga. Modern industrial development and urban growth began during World War II. Kuibyshev was the temporary capital of the USSR from 1941 until 1943. It was renamed in 1935 for Valerian Kuibyshev, an expert on economics.

Kuiper, Gerard [keh-oo'-pur, kay'-rard]   The Dutch-born American astronomer Gerard P. Kuiper, b. Dec. 7, 1905, d. Dec. 23, 1973, is best known for his study of the surface of the Moon. A graduate of the University of Leiden (1927, 1933), Kuiper went to the United States in 1933. He joined the faculty of the University of Chicago in 1936 and from 1947 to 1949 and again from 1957 to 1960 headed the university's YERKES OBSERVATORY and McDonald Observatory. Kuiper also founded (1960) and directed the Lunar and Planetary Laboratory of the University of Arizona. He discovered a satellite of Uranus in 1948 and one of Neptune in 1949, found an atmosphere on Titan, and advanced theories of planetary formation.

Kukenaam Falls [kur'-ken-ahm]   Kukenaam (Spanish: Cuquenán) Falls, on the Venezuela-Guyana border, are the second highest falls in South America. They spill 610 m (2,000 ft) down the sandstone face of Mount Kukenaam, a flat-topped 2,627-m (8,620-ft) mountain in the Guyana Highlands. The falls continue as the Kukenaam River, a tributary of the Caroni River in the Orinoco Basin.

Kula Ring [koo'-luh]   The Kula Ring is a route of ceremonial exchange established in southeastern Papua between the Trobriand Islanders and the Dobu-speaking people of the D'Entrecasteaux Islands. Two kinds of valuables symbolic of wealth and prestige—red-shell necklaces and white-shell armbands—were the customary Kula gifts passed in reciprocal exchange. The exchanges took place annually, with the objects circulating along a fixed trade route. The necklaces were passed clockwise from island to island, the armbands counterclockwise.

Magic, ritual, and mythology were associated with the Kula. An interisland Kula expedition was both a collective ritual and a competitive undertaking having political implications. All interisland trade was conducted under the auspices of the Kula exchange. Lifelong trade relationships were established between a man and his Kula partners. First studied by the anthropologist Bronislaw MALINOWSKI in the 1920s, the Kula exchange has declined somewhat in recent years with the introduction of a cash economy and other European influences.

---

kulaks [koo-laks'] In Russian history the term *kulaks* was used to connote relatively prosperous peasants. Under the NEW ECONOMIC POLICY (NEP) introduced in 1921, Soviet policy favored the kulaks for a time. Toward the end of the 1920s, however, the government placed increasing economic restrictions on them. In 1929, Soviet dictator Joseph STALIN launched a drive to "liquidate the kulaks as a class"—dekulakization—in order to collectivize agriculture. A kulak came to be defined as any peasant who opposed the system of socialism as defined by Stalin. Many kulaks forcibly resisted collectivization; countless numbers burned crops and slaughtered livestock. It is estimated that by the mid-1930s more than 5 million peasant households had been eliminated. Many kulaks were sent to forced labor camps in Siberia, and famine caused numerous deaths.

Kumin, Maxine American writer and teacher Maxine Winokur Kumin, b. Philadelphia, June 6, 1925, is best known for her poetry but writes novels, essays, and short stories as well. She has also authored 20 books for children, 3 of them with the poet Anne Sexton. *Up Country: Poems of New England* (1972) received the 1973 Pulitzer Prize for poetry. *Our Ground Time Here Will Be Brief* (1982) is a collection of new poems and others gathered from her 6 earlier books of verse.

---

kumquat [kuhm'-kwaht] The kumquat, genus *Fortunella* of the rue family, Rutaceae, is an evergreen shrub or tree belonging to the citrus group and native to eastern Asia and Malaysia. Its sweet-scented white flowers produce small, orange fruits, whose mildly acid-flavored pulp and rind are edible. Of the several kumquat varieties grown, the oval Nagami, *F. margarita*, is the most common. The Marumi, *F. japonica*, has acidic juice and a sweet rind. The egg-shaped Meiwa, *F. crassifolia*, is a sweet variety that is cultivated in China.

The kumquat is the hardiest of the CITRUS FRUITS and is grown for its fruit and as an ornamental shrub in areas

that may be too cold for oranges. The fruit is eaten fresh and is used as an ingredient in marmalades. Preserved in sugar syrup, it is a staple dessert in Chinese cookery.

Kun, Béla [koon, bay'-lah] Béla Kun, b. Feb. 20, 1886, d. Nov. 30, 1939, was one of the founders of the Hungarian Communist party and the de facto head of the short-lived Communist regime established in Hungary in 1919. On the fall of the government of Count Mihály Károlyi, Kun became commissar for war and foreign affairs in the Communist administration established on Mar. 22, 1919. His radical reforms and repression of dissent created both internal and external antagonism. The regime fell on Aug. 1, 1919, and Kun later went to Moscow, where he became a leader of the Comintern. Arrested (1936) during the Stalinist purges, he died in prison.

K'un-ming see KUNMING

Kundera, Milan [kun'-duh-ruh] The Czech writer Milan Kundera, b. Apr. 1, 1929, has lived in France since 1975, persuaded to self-exile by the censoring or suppression of his work by the Czech government. Kundera has long denied any political motivation in his writings, which are humorous, skeptical, and fundamentally pessimistic in describing the universal human condition, whether under Communism or not. *The Book of Laughter and Forgetting* (1979; Eng. trans., 1980) is Kundera's most celebrated novel. Other notable works include *The Joke* (1967; Eng. trans., 1982); *Laughable Loves*, a collection of short stories originally published in the 1960s (Eng. trans., 1974); *Life Is Elsewhere* (1969; Eng. trans., 1974); and *The Unbearable Lightness of Being* (1984; Eng. trans., 1984; film, 1987).

Küng, Hans [koong, hahns] Hans Küng, b. Mar. 19, 1928, is a Swiss Roman Catholic theologian who has been censured by The Vatican. Küng made his greatest impact upon the Roman Catholic church through the publication of his *The Council, Reform and Reunion* (1960; Eng. trans., 1961) on the eve of the Second Vatican Council. His later works include *The Church* (1967), *Infallible? An Inquiry* (1971), *On Being a Christian* (1976), and *Does God Exist?* (1980). At the insistence of Pope John Paul II, who objected to his questioning of basic Catholic doctrines, Küng was dismissed from the University of Tübingen's faculty of Catholic theology in 1979.

---

kung fu see MARTIAL ARTS

Kunitz, Stanley J. [kyoo'-nits] The American poet, scholar, and critic Stanley Jasspon Kunitz, b. Worcester, Mass., July 29, 1905, published his first book of poems, *Intellectual Things,* in 1930. He has compiled biographical dictionaries of English and American writers, served as editor of the Yale Series of Younger Poets, and collaborated with Max Hayward on translations of the works of the Russian poets Anna Akhmatova and Andrei Voznesensky. Kunitz's *Selected Poems 1928–58* won the Pulitzer Prize for poetry in 1959.

Kuniyoshi [kun-ee-yoh'-shee] The Japanese painter and printmaker Utagawa Kuniyoshi, 1798–1861, has been hailed as the last great master of the Japanese color print to work in the UKIYO-E tradition. After studying in Edo (modern Tokyo) under Katsukawa Shun'ei, he became a member of the Utagawa school. Reappraised in recent years as an artist of great originality, he depicted a wide range of subjects, including atmospheric landscapes, actors, and animals, as well as heroic episodes from Japanese history. His taste tended toward the dramatic and bizarre, and his later works are extraordinarily complex.

Kuniyoshi, Yasuo [yah-soo-oh'] The Japanese-born painter Yasuo Kuniyoshi, b. Sept. 1, 1893 or 1889, d. May 14, 1953, settled in the United States in 1906 and became a major figure in his field during the 1930s and '40s. He taught at the Art Students League for 20 years. His early paintings (1920s) were generally flattened, symbolic landscape fantasies containing animals and figures. During the 1930s he painted thickly impastoed still lifes and figures directly from life, his melancholy, reflective women were meant to be universal symbols, not portraits.

Kuniyoshi was deeply affected by World War II. His paintings of the 1940s were ominous, surrealistic fantasies, peopled by harshly modeled, garish carnival figures. He was the first living American to be given a retrospective exhibition (1948) at New York City's Whitney Museum.

Kunlun Mountains [kwen'-lwen'] The Kunlun Mountains (Kunlun Shan), the longest mountain chain in Asia, extend more than 2,400 km (1,500 mi) between the HIMALAYAS to the south and the TIAN SHAN to the north. Their western edge is the PAMIRS, in the USSR; as they stretch eastward through Tibet to Qinghai province, China (where they end), they become broader and higher. The highest peak, Ulugh Muztagh (7,724 m/25,340 ft), is in Tibet.

Although the main system was formed about 230 million years ago, seismic activity is common. The climate is extremely arid, but melting snow and glaciers during the summer months feed several major rivers, among them the HUANG HE (Yellow River), the MEKONG, and the CHANG JIANG (Yangtze).

Kunming (K'un-ming) [kwen-ming] A city in southwestern China on the northern shore of Dian Chi, Kunming is the capital of Yunnan province; it has a population of 1,550,000 (1988 est.). An important transportation and industrial center, it has iron and steel mills and industries producing textiles, chemicals, and machinery. Kunming is the site of China's major copper-smelting operations. Educational institutions include Yunnan University (1923).

Although Kunming is an ancient city, its modern development began with the completion of the railroad to Indochina (1910). Refugees from Japanese-occupied China moved their industries there during World War II. It was the eastern terminus of the Burma Road.

Kunstler, William The radical American lawyer William Moses Kunstler, b. New York City, July 7, 1919, is best known for his 1969–70 work in defending the "Chicago Seven," who were charged with conspiracy to incite a riot at the 1968 Democratic National Convention. Among other notable cases, Kunstler defended American Indian militants in the 1974 WOUNDED KNEE case and acted for the prisoner-defendants in the Attica prison riot trial (1975).

Kuo Mo-jo see GUO MORUO

Kuomintang (Guomindang) [kwoh'-min-tahng'] China's Kuomintang (Nationalist party, or KMT) played an active political role on the Chinese mainland for more than three decades; since 1949 it has been the ruling party in Taiwan. It was organized in 1912 by Song Qiaoren as the successor to the secret revolutionary league Dong Meng Hui (Together-Sworn Society), which had been founded in 1905 by SUN YAT-SEN to overthrow the QING (or Manchu) dynasty. Although Sun had been elected (1911) provisional president of the new Chinese republic, he reluctantly yielded the presidency to the north China military leader YUAN SHIKAI. After a KMT election victory, Yuan had Song, who had engineered the victory, killed and all Kuomintang members, including Sun, expelled from the assembly. By 1914, Yuan had become a virtual dictator.

After Yuan's death (1916), Sun's Kuomintang government assumed control (1917) at Guangzhou and accepted aid from Soviet advisors to help enlist mass support for the party. In 1924 the Kuomintang party congress, which included Communists, accepted Sun's "Three Principles of the People": nationalism, democracy (realized in stages), and livelihood (guaranteed through collectivization).

Such was the Kuomintang legacy when Sun died in 1925, leaving CHIANG KAI-SHEK in control. At the completion of Chiang's NORTHERN EXPEDITION (1926) against the Beijing warlords, he dismissed (1927) both the Soviet advisors and the Chinese leftists, thus beginning a long civil war between the two Chinese factions. In 1928 the Kuomintang captured Beijing and won diplomatic recognition for its government at Nanjing.

Chiang tolerated Japanese intervention to the north until Kuomintang forces clashed with the Japanese in July 1937 (see SINO-JAPANESE WARS). The Kuomintang governed China throughout World War II, although it was greatly weakened militarily by campaigns against the Chinese Communists. After the war, Chiang's exhausted and demoralized Kuomintang was unable to maintain control. The Communists, now led by MAO ZEDONG, took over the mainland in 1949, and the exiled Kuomintang retreated to the island of Formosa (now Taiwan).

Kupka, František [kup'-kah]   The Czech painter František Kupka, b. Sept. 23, 1871, d. June 24, 1957, explored the psychological effects of abstract color and is credited with painting the first totally abstract work, *Fugue in Red and Blue* (1912; National Gallery, Prague). After 1895, Kupka lived primarily in Paris, where he was greatly influenced by the Orphism of Robert DELAUNAY. Kupka exhibited his *Diagrams and Whirling Arabesques* paintings in 1924 and in 1936, but he was not widely recognized before a 1946 retrospective exhibition in Czechoslovakia.

Kurdistan [kur'-dis-tahn]   Kurdistan, which means "land of the Kurds," is a large, mountainous plateau region encompassing parts of eastern Turkey, northern Iraq, northwestern Iran, and areas of Syria and Azerbaijan. The area measures about 720 km (450 mi) from north to south and 600 km (375 mi) from east to west at the broadest part. The region is bounded by the ZAGROS MOUNTAINS in Iran and Iraq and by the TAURUS MOUNTAINS in eastern Turkey. The TIGRIS and EUPHRATES rivers rise in eastern Kurdistan, as do many other smaller rivers and streams. The average elevation is about 2,500 m (8,300 ft), but some peaks reach over 4,000 m (13,100 ft). The climate is extreme, with bitterly cold, harsh winters and hot, dry summers.

Kurds have lived in Kurdistan since about 2400 BC. Traditionally, the Kurds were nomads. In recent times, however, most of them have settled down because the separate governments have introduced sedentary agriculture and have forced Kurds to move their goat herds within national boundaries. Grain, cotton, and fruits are grown in the lowlands.

Kurdistan (Kordestan) is also the name of a mountainous province in western Iran, with an area of 24,998 km^2 (9,652 mi^2) and a population of 1,078,415 (1986). The capital is Sanandaj. Most of the inhabitants of the province are Kurds.

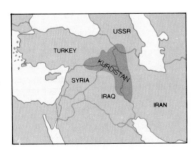

Kurdistan occupies portions of Turkey, Syria, Iraq, Iran, and Azerbaijan. The Kurds, who are ethnically closest to the Iranians, traditionally are nomadic herders. Saladin, the great opponent of the Crusaders, was of Kurdish descent.

Kurds [kurdz]   Kurd is the ethnic name of a number of tribal groups inhabiting the mountainous border regions of southeast Turkey, northwest Iran, north Iraq, northeast Syria, and Azerbaijan. These tribes speak various dialects of Kurdish, an Indo-Iranian language. Most Kurds are Sunni Muslims of the Shafi rite. Some are pastoral no-

mads, but most have become settled farmers due to the closing of national frontiers and the Kurdish political struggles of the last several decades. The greatest number of the estimated 10–20 million Kurds live in Turkey, Iraq, and Iran.

Although the Kurds have never been united politically, Kurdish autonomy has had a long history. Kurd as a collective name was first applied to the tribal groups in the 7th century AD when the Arabs converted them to Islam. Three short-lived Kurdish dynasties with more than local power existed in the 10th to 12th centuries; the 12th-century Kurdish warrior SALADIN, a prominent foe of the Christian Crusaders, founded another dynasty that lasted into the 13th century. Only in the late 19th and early 20th centuries did a nationalist movement emerge. With the breakup of the Ottoman Empire after World War I, Turkey agreed to the establishment of an independent Kurdistan under the Treaty of Sèvres (1920). This part of the treaty was never ratified, however, and the autonomy clause was completely eliminated from the Treaty of Lausanne (1923) through Turkish efforts under Kemal Atatürk.

Kurds staged an unsuccessful uprising in Iran after the 1979 Islamic revolution and Kurdish separatists remain active in Turkey, but most nationalist activity since 1946 has been in Iraq, where Kurds waged guerrilla warfare (1961–70) and staged an open rebellion (1974–75) against the government with covert Iranian support. Iraqi Kurdish separatists later backed Iran in the IRAN-IRAQ WAR (1980–88). In 1988 the Iraqi government was accused of using chemical weapons against the Kurds. Another Kurdish revolt in Iraq after the 1991 GULF WAR was brutally suppressed. In April 1992, Iraqi Kurds held their first elections free of Iraqi control to choose a leader and a national assembly, but the Kurdish region remained under an Iraqi economic blockade.

Kuril Islands [koo'-reel]   The Kuril (or Kurile) Islands, a chain of 30 major plus many smaller islands with a total land area of 15,600 km^2 (6,025 mi^2), extend 1,200 km (745 mi) from the KAMCHATKA PENINSULA, Russia, to Hokkaido, Japan. They are part of Russia. The chain separates the Pacific Ocean from the Sea of OKHOTSK. Most of the islands are of volcanic origin; 38 volcanoes are still active. Fishing, sulfur mining, whaling, and hunting are the chief occupations. The principal town is Kurilsk, on Iturup, the largest island. Dutch sailors sighted the Kurils in 1634. Japan and Russia penetrated the islands in the 18th century, and both claimed them in the 19th century. Japan acquired them in 1875 in exchange for Sakhalin. The USSR occupied them from 1945, claiming that they were ceded to the Soviet Union by the Yalta agreement, but Japan continued to claim several of the southern islands. Russia and Japan are negotiating the dispute, which is a major irritant in Russian-Japanese relations.

Kurosawa, Akira [koo-roh'-sah-wah, ah-kee'-rah]   The most famous Japanese film director in the West, Akira Kurosawa, b. Mar. 23, 1910, first achieved international recognition with *Rashomon* (1950), a brilliant study of a crime of violence told from four different points of view. His reputation soared with a series of sword-fight epics set in feudal times: such movies as *The Seven Samurai* (1954) inspired a host of Western imitations. Kurosawa has been equally influenced by Western themes and has made screen adaptations of Dostoyevsky's *The Idiot* (1951), Gorky's *The Lower Depths* (1957), and two of Shakespeare's blackest dramas—*Macbeth* (*Throne of Blood*, 1957); and *King Lear* (*Ran*, 1986). These are cinematic spectaculars; yet, despite their overwhelming physical beauty and the monumental cruelty they display, they demonstrate compassion and an awareness of human nobility as well as its weakness. Two modest but moving Kurosawa films are his *Ikiru* (1952), about a lonely, dying old man; and *Derzu Uzala* (1975), a story set in Russian Siberia.

Kutenai

[koot'-en-ay] The Kutenai (or Kootenay, a Blackfoot term) are North American Indians who inhabited northwest Montana and British Columbia in the 18th century. Their own name is Sanka. Upper Kutenai occupied territory around the Columbia River headwaters and adopted Plains traits when ranging eastward to hunt bison; Lower Kutenai maintained a distinct Plateau culture centered on fishing the Lower Kootenay River. Both Upper and Lower Kutenai used digging sticks to gather bitter root and camas bulbs; nuts and berries, deer, elks, and fish supplemented their food supply. After obtaining horses both groups exploited seasonal bison herds. Because of resistance from other Plains bison hunters, the Kutenai formalized war honors and gloried in acts of bravery. Slavery was practiced following the introduction of war captives, but the traditional social organization remained simple. Northwest Coast and Plains cultures influenced the religion of the Kutenai, who adopted a modified form of the SUN DANCE ritual.

When first contacted by white traders in the early 1800s, the Kutenai were scattered widely across their territory. The white threat united them briefly, but a series of misunderstandings led to their dispersion. One band joined the FLATHEAD; others took a reservation in Idaho. The majority scattered along the Kootenay River in British Columbia. The population of the Kootenai Reservation in Idaho was 118 in 1987.

Kutuzov, Mikhail Illarionovich

[koo'-too'-zuhf, mee-kuh-yeel' ee-luh-ryohn'-uh-vich] Mikhail Illarionovich Kutuzov, b. Sept. 16 (N.S.), 1745, d. Apr. 16 (N.S.), 1813, was the Russian military commander who repulsed NAPOLEON I's invasion of Russia in 1812. After service in the Russo-Turkish Wars, he rose to prominence as the Russian commander against the French at the Battle of AUSTERLITZ in 1805; he advised a retreat but was overruled by Russian emperor ALEXANDER I and was badly defeated. Thereafter, Alexander I disliked Kutuzov. When Napoleon began his invasion in 1812, however, Alexander recalled Kutuzov and appointed him field marshal.

After the Russian defeat at Borodino on Sept. 7 (N.S.), 1812, Kutuzov adopted his own tactics of retreat, evacuated Moscow, and saved his army. When Napoleon began his own retreat for lack of supplies, Kutuzov harried the French army out of Russia.

See also: NAPOLEONIC WARS.

kuvasz

[kuv'-ahs] The kuvasz is a Hungarian working breed of dog that generally resembles the Great Pyrenees. Both breeds are large, white, and heavily coated and were originally used as guard dogs, especially of flocks of sheep. The male kuvasz stands 76 cm (30 in) high at the shoulder and weighs up to 52 kg (115 lb), with females slightly smaller. It has a compact body, with a rather long head, close-hanging ears, and a long, thickly haired tail. Its coat is slightly wavy and reaches 13 cm (5 in) long. Although the kuvasz is Hungarian, its name is a corruption of Turkish and Arabic words for guardian, possibly reflecting an Asiatic origin for the breed.

Kuwait

(country) Kuwait, an oil-rich Arab sheikhdom in the northeastern corner of the Arabian Peninsula at the head of the Persian Gulf, is bordered on the north and west by Iraq, on the east by the Persian Gulf, and on the south by Saudi Arabia. It ranks fourth in proven oil reserves (after Saudi Arabia, the USSR, and Iraq) and was a founding member of the ORGANIZATION OF PETROLEUM EXPORTING COUNTRIES (OPEC). Its name is derived from *kut*, the Arabic word for fort. The capital, Kuwait, is located on an inlet of the Persian Gulf.

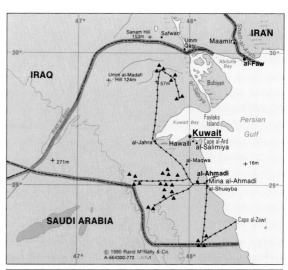

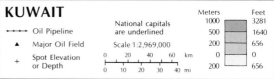

KUWAIT

+━━•━━ Oil Pipeline	National capitals are underlined
▲ Major Oil Field	Scale 1:2,969,000
+ Spot Elevation or Depth	

Meters	Feet
1000	3281
500	1640
200	656
0	0
200	656

AT A GLANCE

STATE OF KUWAIT

Land: Area: 17,818 km^2 (6,880 mi^2). Capital: Kuwait (1985 pop., 44,224). Largest city: al-Salimiya (1985 pop., 153,220).

People: Population (1990 est.): 2,123,711. Density: 119.2 persons per km^2 (308.7 per mi^2). Distribution (1989): 94% urban, 6% rural. Official language: Arabic. Major religion: Islam.

Government: Type: constitutional emirate. Legislature: National Assembly (suspended). Political subdivisions: 4 districts.

Economy: GNP (1988): $26.25 billion; $13,680 per capita. Labor distribution (1986): services—45%; construction—20%; trade—12%; manufacturing—9%; finance and real estate—3%. Foreign trade (1988): imports—$5.2 billion; exports—$7.1 billion. Currency: 1 Kuwaiti dinar = 1,000 fils.

Education and Health: Literacy (1990 est.): 71% of adult population. Universities (1990): 1. Hospital beds (1987): 5,503. Physicians (1987): 2,799. Life expectancy (1990): women—76; men—72. Infant mortality (1990): 15 per 1,000 live births.

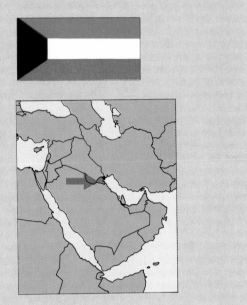

Land and People

Kuwait is a virtually flat desert; the highest point in the country is a hill in the south rising to 299 m (981 ft). Of its few oases, al-Jahrah is the largest. Nine offshore islands are included in the national territory, but only one, Failaka, is inhabited. Most of the nation lies below an elevation of 200 m (656 ft). The red desert soils do not favor agriculture. The average daily temperature is 33° C (91° F), with maxima of 52° C (126° F). Rainfall ranges from 25 to 175 mm (1 to 7 in) annually, falling mostly in winter, when cyclones occur. Fierce dust storms, called *kaus*, may last several days in winter. Most vegetation consists of low bushes and scrub. Less than 9% of the land is arable, and most water is obtained through massive desalination efforts.

Kuwaiti society is composed of five strata: the ruling family, old Kuwaiti merchant families, former Bedouins who have become city dwellers, Arabs from other countries who have obtained citizenship, and foreigners. Arabic is the official language, although many people speak English. Muslims (an estimated 30% of them Shiites) comprise 99% of the population and Christians less than 1%.

Prior to the August 1990 Iraqi invasion, Kuwait had one of the highest per capita incomes in the world, financed by petroleum revenues. Kuwaiti citizens made up less than 40% of the population and about 19% of the labor force. The population was growing at almost three times the world rate, a result of both natural increase and immigration. The non-Kuwaitis—mostly Palestinians, Egyptians, and South Asians—enjoyed most of the welfare benefits of Kuwaiti citizens (including free education and low-cost medical care) but could not own property or vote. After the invasion, nearly half of all Kuwaitis were in exile, mostly in Saudi Arabia and other Gulf states. Hundreds of thousands of foreign workers, many of whom lost everything they owned, also fled.

Economic Activity

The economy of modern Kuwait was based almost totally on petroleum. Agricultural activity was minimal, but some consumer goods and fertilizer were manufactured. By law, 10% of all petroleum revenues were deposited in a special reserve fund to provide for the time when oil reserves were exhausted. Exports from Iraqi-occupied Kuwait were halted by an international embargo. Kuwait's substantial overseas assets remained under control of its government in exile, which contributed to the cost of U.S. forces in the Gulf and aided poorer Arab nations backing the effort to liberate Kuwait.

The economy was devastated by the brutal eight-month-long Iraqi occupation. Basic services were systematically looted and destroyed, the population was brutalized, and hundreds of Kuwaiti oil wells were set ablaze by retreating Iraqi troops. The cost of rebuilding was estimated at $20 billion.

History and Government

The Sabah dynasty was established in 1756 after Arab tribes settled the area. Kuwait was nominally a province in the Ottoman Empire, but the sheikh received British

In late February 1991, Iraqis fleeing the advancing allied forces looted and set ablaze much of Kuwait City. Most buildings, including Sief Palace (pictured), escaped major structural damage, but the fires set at nearby oil installations shrouded the city in smoke. Limited oil exports resumed in July 1991, and the last oil-well fire was ceremonially extinguished by the emir on Nov. 6, 1991. Oil production was expected to return to its preinvasion level in late 1992.

protection in 1899 when the Turks threatened actual control. Kuwait achieved independence in 1961, but when Iraq claimed the area, it again received a British pledge of protection. Under the 1963 constitution, executive power is vested in the emir and exercised by a council of ministers. Sheikh Jabier al-Ahmad al-Sabah became emir in 1977. The legislature was suspended from 1976 to 1981 and again from 1986 to 1992; an interim council without legislative powers was elected in June 1990. In the 1980s, Kuwait was subject to terrorist attacks by Shiite Muslim extremists, including a 1985 attempt to assassinate the emir; it supported Iraq against Iran in the IRAN-IRAQ WAR (1980–88).

On Aug. 2, 1990, after a dispute over oil, money, and boundaries, Iraq invaded and annexed Kuwait. The world community condemned the Iraqi invasion. On Jan. 15, 1991, after international diplomatic efforts and sanctions had failed to force Iraq to withdraw, an international, UN-sanctioned coalition under U.S. field command launched the GULF WAR, recapturing Kuwait City on February 26. The emir returned on March 14 and imposed martial law until June 26. Later that year, Kuwait and the United States signed a 10-year security pact. Legislative elections held in October 1992 produced the first National Assembly in Kuwait's history with an opposition majority; secular and Islamic candidates calling for democratic reform captured 31 of 50 seats.

Kuznetsk Basin   The Kuznetsk Basin (abbreviated Kuzbas) is one of Russia's major coal fields. Extending along the Tom River in southwestern Siberia, between the Kuznetsk Ala-Tau and the Salair ranges, it has an area of about 26,000 km^2 (10,000 mi^2). The basin's immense coal reserves are among the highest-quality deposits in the world. The proximity of iron-ore deposits has made the Kuzbas one of Russia's leading industrial areas, producing iron and steel, chemicals, and heavy machinery. The region's many cities include Kemerovo and Novokuznetsk. Large-scale mining began in the mid-19th century. Industrial development began in the 1930s and continued during World War II to replace industrial areas held by the Germans.

Kwakiutl [kwah'-kee-oo'-tul]   The Kwakiutl are a group of closely related North American Indians who traditionally have occupied both Vancouver Island and the adjacent mainland shores and islands of southern British Columbia, Canada. Along Douglas and Gardner channels lived the Xaisla, Bella Bella, and Haihais, speakers of Heiltsuk dialects. The Kwakiutl language family (Kwakiutl and Heiltsuk/Xaisla), with NOOTKA, forms the Wakashan linguistic stock (see INDIAN LANGUAGES, AMERICAN). Before European contact the Kwakiutl numbered an estimated 7,000, the Heiltsuk/Xaisla–speakers about 10,000. With the introduction of European diseases in the 19th century, their combined population was reduced to less than 1,900. By the 1980s they numbered about 3,400.

With the aid of anthropologist Franz BOAS in the late 1800s, thousands of pages of information on Kwakiutl life were recorded in the Kwakiutl language and in English translation by George Hunt and his Kwakiutl-raised Tlingit wife. Thus Kwakiutl culture is among the most documented of all American Indian cultures. Skilled canoeists, fishers, and sea hunters, the Kwakiutl also excelled as carvers of TOTEM poles and other ritual objects. With their Heiltsuk kin they originated the most spectacular ceremonials of the Northwest Coast culture area. Although these ceremonies and the POTLATCH exchange were prohibited by Canada's much-amended Indian Act (1876), the Kwakiutl still staged them to preserve the formal ranked statuses valued by their society. Since repeal of the law in 1951, both institutions have been performed in modified form as affirmations of Kwakiutl identity.

Kwangsi   see GUANGXI

Kwangtung   see GUANGDONG

▬

kwashiorkor [kwash-ee-or'-kor]   Kwashiorkor is a form of malnutrition common in developing countries among those living on a diet inadequate in calories and grossly deficient in PROTEIN. The signs of this nutritional disease are anemia, edema (swelling), liver damage, muscle wasting, loss of appetite, and general apathy. The disease occurs mainly in children, especially those already suffering from parasitic disease or infectious diarrhea. The principal cause, however, is a mainly carbohydrate diet that provides inadequate protein. (The name *kwashiorkor* is derived from the Ga language of West Africa and means "the disease of the displaced child.") The disease is particularly prevalent in Africa, Latin America, and Asia. It is associated with poverty and diets of plantains or starchy roots, such as cassava. Treatment consists of a well-balanced, protein-rich diet; the disorder is often fatal, however. Those who survive may have physical stunting and mental retardation. A related disease, nutritional marasmus, results from a low intake of all nutrients and calories. The symptoms are similar to those of kwashiorkor, but edema is not present.

Kweichow   see GUIZHOU

▬

kyanite [ky'-uh-nyt]   The aluminum SILICATE MINERAL kyanite (derived from the Greek *kyanos,* meaning "blue") is used in the manufacture of spark plugs, porcelain, and other refractories; it has the same chemical composition (Al_2SiO_5) as ANDALUSITE and sillimanite. Its long-bladed, usually blue crystals (triclinic system) have perfect cleavage in one direction. Kyanite occurs in metamorphic rocks and granite PEGMATITES; it is an indicator of deep-seated, regional metamorphism of clay-rich sediments.

▬

Kyd, Thomas   The Elizabethan playwright Thomas Kyd (1558–94) was the author of *The Spanish Tragedy* (*c.*1586), the first revenge tragedy in English literature and easily the most popular play of the day. *The Spanish Tragedy* owes much to the Roman writer Seneca. Kyd was imprisoned in 1593 on a false charge of atheism and died soon after his release.

▬

Kyoto [kyoh'-toh]   Kyoto is one of Japan's largest cities. Located on south central Honshu, it has a population of 1,461,140 (1990) and an area of 611 km² (236 mi²).

Kyoto served as Japan's imperial capital for more than a thousand years (794–1868) and is still Japan's leading cultural center. Traditional handicrafts, such as silk, dyed fabric, damascene, porcelain, dolls, and lacquer ware are made there, and sake is brewed. Heavy manufacturing includes copper smelting, chemicals, and machinery. The city is located at the center of the vast urban and industrial region covering southern Honshu and has well-developed transportation links to Osaka, Tokyo, and Nagoya. Because of the numerous Buddhist temples, Shinto shrines, gardens, and traditional houses that preserve Kyoto's rich history, it is a leading tourism center visited by an estimated 20 million persons annually. The Kyoto National Museum, Imperial Palace, Yasaka Shrine, and Kinkakuji (Temple of the Golden Pavilion) are noted landmarks. The many universities and colleges include the prestigious Kyoto University (1897).

Adopted as the site of the imperial capital by the Emperor Kammu, Kyoto (or Heian) was built in 794. Like nearby Nara, the previous capital, the city was modeled after Chang'an, capital of the Tang dynasty in China. Before the rise of Edo (now Tokyo) as the capital of the Tokugawa shogunate (1603–1868), Kyoto enjoyed more than eight centuries of unrivaled glory among Japanese cities. Finally, in 1868, Tokyo became the imperial capital. Kyoto is so rich in historical relics that it was spared Allied bombing during World War II.

Kyrgyzstan   see KIRGHIZIA

▬

Kyushu [kyoo'-shoo]   Kyushu, the southernmost and most densely populated of the four main islands of Japan, encompasses 42,023 km² (16,225 mi²). It has a population of 13,296,054 (1990). The island's volcanic mountains, part of the Ryukyu range, reach a height of 1,788 m (5,866 ft) at Kuju-san. Abundant rainfall of more than 2,000 mm (80 in) annually and a mean average temperature of 15° C (60° F) enable cultivation of tropical fruits and vegetables as well as grains, soybeans, tea, and tobacco. Fishing, mining, and the production of raw silk and porcelain are also important industries. The chief cities include FUKUOKA, KITAKYUSHU, NAGASAKI, and Omuta. Inhabited at least since the Stone Age, Kyushu became the seat of the Yayoi civilization in the 1st century BC.

▬

Kyzyl Kum [kuh-zul' koom]   The Kyzyl Kum ("red sands") is a desert covering about half of Uzbekistan and a southern strip of Kazakhstan. Stretching 800 km (500 mi) east to west and 725 km (450 mi) north to south, it has an area of 300,000 km² (115,000 mi²).

Generally low, the Kyzyl Kum has scattered peaks more than 915 m (3,000 ft) in elevation. Rainfall averages only 100 mm (4 in) a year, so there is little vegetation to hold the shifting sand dunes. Shepherds tend Karakul sheep, and at oases along rivers—particularly the SYR DARYA and the AMU DARYA—cotton, rice, and wheat are grown. Sulfur, gold, and natural gas are extracted.

Ll

𝕴	Л	L	ᐯ	ᐁ	Λ	ꓘ	ᒪ	Ɩ	ᐯ
GERMAN-GOTHIC	RUSSIAN-CYRILLIC	CLASSICAL LATIN	EARLY LATIN	ETRUSCAN	CLASSICAL GREEK	EARLY GREEK	EARLY ARAMAIC	EARLY HEBREW	PHOENICIAN

L *L/l* is the 12th letter of the English alphabet. Both the letter and its position in the alphabet were derived from the Latin alphabet, which in turn are derived from the Greek by way of the Etruscan. The Greeks call the letter *lambda* and took its name, form, and position from a Semitic writing system, in which the name of the sign was *lamedh*.

L/l is a liquid consonant, that is, frictionless and able to be prolonged like a vowel. In English *L/l* is regularly voiced, as in *lip* and *fall*. When the letter is preceded by a voiceless consonant, voicing is normally delayed until the *l* sound has already begun, as in *please* or *slip*. In some words *L/l* is not pronounced, though it affects the pronunciation of the preceding vowel, as in *walk* and *should* (compare *shoulder*).

L'Amour, Louis One of the best-selling American authors ever, Louis Dearborn L'Amour, b. Jamestown, N.Dak., 1908, d. June 10, 1988, wrote 86 novels—almost all Westerns—that sold more than 160 million copies in his lifetime. He also wrote more than 400 short stories. Establishing his Western format early—*Hondo* (1953; film, 1954) is an example—L'Amour produced heroic action tales that reflect scrupulous historical research. *The Walking Drum* (1984), however, is set in medieval Europe, and *Last of the Breed* (1986) in contemporary Siberia.

L'Anse aux Meadows [lawnse oh med-doh'] L'Anse aux Meadows, on the northernmost tip of Newfoundland, is the site of a Viking settlement dating from about AD 1000; it may have been the VINLAND settlement described in the early Norse sagas about the explorer LEIF ERIKSSON. Excavation of the site, begun in 1961, revealed the remains of eight turf-walled houses, one of which was a longhouse 22 m by 15 m (72 ft by 50 ft) containing five rooms including a "great hall," and a smithy, where bog iron was smelted. Several of the houses had stone ember pits identical with those found in Norse houses in Greenland. Among the artifacts unearthed was a soapstone spindle whorl similar to those discovered in Norse ruins in Greenland, Iceland, and Scandinavia; this find suggests that women as well as men were present at the site. Other artifacts point to a brief, much earlier occupation of the site by Maritime Archaic Indians and a later occupation by Dorset Eskimo.

La Brea Tar Pit [bray'-uh] La Brea Tar Pit is a natural accumulation of tar that formed over the site of an ancient oil seep in what is now Los Angeles's Hancock Park. It formed when petroleum from rock strata deep beneath the ground oozed upward and collected in pools on the surface. With the passing of time, the oil lost its volatile elements and gradually became a thick deposit of as-

An artist's conception of the La Brea Tar Pit about 20,000 years ago depicts a probable scene of the period. Since 1906 archaeologists have found thousands of well-preserved, tar-impregnated bones and teeth of various extinct creatures that became mired.

phalt. Discovered by Spanish explorers, the asphalt was mined commercially for many years. Today, Rancho La Brea ("Ranch of the Tar") is better known for the FOSSIL RECORD of extinct vertebrate life it has yielded.

During Early Pleistocene time (over a million years ago; see GEOLOGIC TIME), animals coming to the seeps for water became mired in tar and preserved in this natural death trap. Larger herbivorous animals that have been found include extinct species of horses, bison, and camels, as well as MASTODONS and the giant ground sloth. Carnivores attracted by these animals include mountain lions, SABER-TOOTHED CATS, the giant California jaguar, and dire wolves. Bird fossils include a vulture with a 3.6-m (12-ft) wingspan and the California stork.

La Bruyère, Jean de [lah bru-yair']   The French moralist Jean de La Bruyère, b. Paris and baptized Aug. 17, 1645, d. May 10, 1696, became famous from one work, *The Characters, or the Manners of the Age, with the Characters of Theophrastus* (Eng. trans., 1699), in which he sarcastically depicted 17th-century Paris and the life of the French court. The tutor of the duc de Bourbon (grandson of the Great Condé), La Bruyère served (1686–96) as head of the Condé library at Chantilly.

La Coruña [lah kor-oon'-yah]   La Coruña is located on an inlet of the Atlantic Ocean in northwest Spain. A major commercial port for trade with North and South America, the city is also the capital of La Coruña province. Its population is 242,437 (1987 est.). La Coruña's port primarily exports agricultural products, and it has Spain's second largest fishing industry. There is also some light manufacturing. Historical landmarks include a lighthouse probably built by the Romans in the 1st century AD and the churches of Santiago (12th century) and Santa María del Campo (13th century). Called Brigantium by the Romans, La Coruña was ruled by the Moors (8th–10th century) and the Portuguese (14th century) until annexed to Spain in the 15th century. During the 16th century the port was the site of several battles between English and Spanish fleets.

La Crosse [luh kraws]   La Crosse (1990 pop., 51,003), a city in western Wisconsin on the Mississippi River at the influx of the Black and La Crosse rivers, is the seat of La Crosse County. Rubber footwear and air-conditioning equipment are manufactured, and lumber is milled there. The University of Wisconsin has a branch at La Crosse. Settled as a trading post in 1841, La Crosse became an important lumbering center after the railroad arrived in 1858.

La Farge, John [luh farzh]   John La Farge, b. New York City, Mar. 31, 1835, d. Nov. 14, 1910, was an American muralist, stained-glass designer, landscape painter, and writer. An offer to complete (1876) the mural decorations of Trinity Church in Boston led to a succession of important commissions for murals, such as his *Ascension* (1888; Church of the Ascension, New York City), and *Athens* (1898; Bowdoin College, Brunswick, Maine). He also experimented with stained glass, and, by eliminating much of the leading, he achieved a shimmering, incandescent effect that is best represented in his *Old Philosopher* window (1880; Crane Memorial Library, Quincy, Mass.). Most of his landscape paintings are topographically accurate, but some, such as his watercolor *The Strange Thing Little Kiosai Saw in the River* (1897; Metropolitan Museum of Art, New York City), take a visionary turn.

La Fayette, Comtesse de [lah fah-yet', kohn-tes' duh]   Marie Madeleine Pioche de La Vergne, comtesse de La Fayette, baptized Mar. 18, 1634, d. May 25, 1693, wrote the first analytical novel in French literature. Because of an aristocratic prejudice she never signed her works; they were published either anonymously or under the name of her friend and fellow writer Jean Segrais. Both LA ROCHEFOUCAULD, with whom she had a long liaison, and Segrais unquestionably were involved in the creation of her novels. All of them—*La Princesse de Montpensier* (1662), *Zaÿde* (1670), her masterpiece *La Princesse de Clèves* (1678), and the posthumous *La Comtesse de Tende* (1724)—deal with the dangers of passionate love. She also produced two historical works, the *Histoire de Madame Henriette d'Angleterre* (The Story of Henrietta of England, 1720) and *Mémoires de la Cour de France* (Reminiscences of the French Court, 1731).

La Follette, Robert M. [luh fahl'-et]   Robert Marion La Follette, Sr., b. Primrose, Wis., June 14, 1855, d. June 18, 1925, was one of the leading progressive politicians in the United States. He served as governor of Wisconsin and U.S. senator and was also a presidential candidate.

Robert "Fighting Bob" La Follette became a leader of reform-minded progressive Republicans during his three terms as governor of Wisconsin and later as a U.S. senator from that state.

An 1880 law graduate of the University of Wisconsin, La Follette won election that year as district attorney of Dane County. In 1884 he was elected to Congress and later was placed on the prestigious Ways and Means Committee, where he helped William McKinley draft the highly protective Tariff Act of 1890. Its unpopularity caused both of them to lose their seats in the 1890 election.

In the following years La Follette campaigned against the corrupt party machine in Wisconsin. Twice rejected (1896, 1898) for the Republican gubernatorial nomination, he took his campaign to the people, focusing on the novel idea of a direct primary for party nominations. Finally elected governor in 1900, La Follette enacted a program that included direct primaries, more equitable taxation, a more effective railroad commission, civil-service reform, conservation, control of lobbyists, a legislative reference library, and bank reform.

In 1905 the Wisconsin legislature elected La Follette to the U.S. Senate. He was a controversial senator almost from the beginning. In a long freshman speech he sought to strengthen the Hepburn bill (1906) regulating railroad rates. In 1908 he conducted a record, but unsuccessful, filibuster against the Aldrich-Vreeland bill, charging that one of its aims was to enrich bankers. After William Howard Taft became president, La Follette forged the progressive Republican opposition to the Payne-Aldrich Tariff and became a persistent critic of the administration. In 1911 he was chosen as the progressive Republican candidate to displace Taft, but he was superseded by Theodore Roosevelt in 1912.

La Follette supported most of the policies of Democratic President Woodrow Wilson until the question of U.S. entry into World War I arose. Vigorously opposed to entry, he was the victim of an unsuccessful attempt to expel him from the Senate for an antiwar speech. After the war he voted against ratification of the Treaty of Versailles because it failed to allow colonial self-determination and equity for weak nations. By this vote he also rejected U.S. participation in the League of Nations. In the postwar period La Follette resisted the anti-Communist scare and fought for the interests of workers and farmers against the business-oriented Republican administrations. He initiated the investigation into the TEAPOT DOME scandal in 1922. The following year he made an independent race for the presidency on the PROGRESSIVE PARTY ticket and received almost 5 million votes.

La Fontaine, Jean de [lah-fohn-ten', zhawn duh]
One of the world's greatest fabulists, the French writer Jean de La Fontaine, baptized July 8, 1621, d. Apr. 13, 1695, modeled himself after two classic predecessors, Aesop and Phaedrus, to create incomparable, deceptively simple poetic masterpieces of humor and penetrating psychological observation.

A native of Champagne, La Fontaine in 1652 bought a commission as inspector of forests and waterways and subsequently divided his time between Paris and the provinces. Thanks to his witty and pleasing personality, he received financial support from wealthy patrons, such

as Nicolas Fouquet, Louis XIV's minister of the treasury, and Madame de la Sablière. In the latter's salon he met philosophers, scientists, and writers. Because of his Nonconformist views he made friends with others in marginal religious, philosophical, and ethical groups, such as Jansenists and disciples of Gassendi.

La Fontaine's first literary piece was a comedy, *L' Eunuque* (The Eunuch, 1654), in imitation of Terence. It was followed by his well-known *Tales and Novels in Verse* (Eng. trans., 1898), short licentious tales adapted from Boccaccio and Ariosto, which, starting in 1664, La Fontaine continued to publish until his death. He then turned to his masterwork, *Fables* (pub. in 3 parts, 1668–94; Eng. trans., 1806), which depicts human vanity, stupidity, and aggressiveness in animal guise. La Fontaine also produced miscellaneous verse works, further comedies, and a narrative piece in prose and verse, *The Loves of Cupid and Psyche* (1669; Eng. trans., 1744).

La Guardia, Fiorello [luh gwar'-dee-uh, fee-oh-rel'-oh]
Fiorello Henry La Guardia, b. New York City, Dec. 11, 1882, d. Sept. 20, 1947, was an American political reformer, congressman, and mayor of New York City. Admitted to the bar in 1910, he was first elected to Congress as a Republican in 1916, and after service in the U.S. Air Force during World War I, he served again in the House of Representatives from 1923 to 1933. In Congress, La Guardia defended the interests of his predominantly immigrant, working-class constituency. He condemned legislation establishing national-origins quotas for the admission of immigrants, and he cosponsored the Norris–La Guardia Act (1932), which barred the use of injunctions to prevent strikes.

Elected mayor of New York City in 1933 on a Fusion ticket and reelected twice, he held that office until 1945. As mayor, La Guardia (known as "The Little Flower," from his name Fiorello) led a drive against political corruption, modernized the city's administrative structure, and introduced major improvements in the fields of health, hous-

Fiorello La Guardia distinguished himself during seven terms in Congress (1916–18; 1923–33) and three consecutive terms as mayor of New York (1934–45) by liberal legislation and wide-reaching reform.

ing, recreation, and the arts. He was equally well known for reading comic strips over the radio to entertain children during a newspaper strike. La Guardia served briefly as director of the Office of Civilian Defense (1941–42) and as head of the United Nations Relief and Rehabilitation Administration (1946).

La Guma, Alex [luh goo'-muh] The South African novelist Justin Alexander La Guma, b. Feb. 20, 1925, d. Oct. 11, 1985, was a critic of the political, economic, and social realities that exist for nonwhites in South Africa. His literary reputation was established with the novelette *A Walk in the Night* (1962), on ghetto life in a South African city. La Guma resided in London and later in Cuba, having been imprisoned in South Africa for his political activities and then exiled. His novels include *And a Threefold Cord* (1964), *The Stone Country* (1967), *In the Fog of the Season's End* (1972), and *Time of the Butcherbird* (1979). He also wrote short stories and edited *Apartheid: A Collection of Writings on South African Racism by South Africans* (1972).

La Meri [lah mair'-ee] La Meri, b. Russell Meriwether Hughes, Louisville, Ky., May 18, 1898, d. Jan. 7, 1988, was an ethnic dancer and one of the world's experts on the ethnologic or art dance. In 1928, La Meri embarked on world tours, performing solo ethnic dances and studying native dances to add to her repertory. She founded the School of Natya with Ruth St. Denis in New York in 1940. In 1941 she organized her own company and the next year renamed it the Ethnologic Dance Center and expanded the curriculum. In addition to teaching in the school until 1956, La Meri choreographed, lectured, and performed; she also toured with her company and served as a resident teacher at Jacob's Pillow (Mass.).

La Paz [lah pahs'] La Paz is the administrative capital and leading commercial center of Bolivia and the capital of La Paz department. It has a population of 1,033,288 (1986 est.). Located 3,658 m (12,001 ft) above sea level in a canyon carved out of the Altiplano (Bolivia's high plateau) by the La Paz River, it is the world's highest capital city.

In addition to its governmental function, La Paz serves as the Altiplano's major trade and market center. Its industries are food processing and light manufacturing. The center of city life is the Plaza Murillo, on the north side of the river. Facing its formal gardens are the huge cathedral, the presidential palace, the national congress building, and the national museum of art. La Paz is the site of the University of San Andrés (1830).

La Paz was founded by the Spaniards in 1548—on the site of an Inca village—as a way station along the caravan route from the silver mines at Potosí to Lima. The town's location, in the valley, was selected as a means of escaping the harsh climate of the Altiplano, and the town was named Nuestra Señora de La Paz to commemorate

La Paz, the administrative capital of Bolivia and the country's most populous city, lies in a narrow valley at the foot of the Cordillera Real. At an altitude of 3,658 m (12,001 ft), the city is the world's highest capital.

the peaceful conditions existing in Bolivia at that time. During the 18th and 19th centuries La Paz developed into a leading commercial center and supply point for the numerous mining activities carried out on the Altiplano. The importance of the city was further enhanced by the construction of railroads from La Paz to Chile and to Argentina and by the building of roads linking La Paz to other regions of Bolivia.

La Pérouse, Jean François de Galaup, Comte de [lah pay-rooz', zhawn frahn-swah' duh guh-loh, kohnt duh] The French navigator Jean François de Galaup, comte de La Pérouse, b. Aug. 22, 1741, d. c.1788, discovered the strait north of Japan named for him. In 1785 he was given command of two ships, *La Boussole* and *L'Astrolabe*, to find the Northwest Passage from the Pacific side. Sailing from France, he rounded Cape Horn and went on to Hawaii and other Pacific islands, Alaska, Macao, and the Philippines. After discovering (1787) La Pérouse Strait, he landed on Kamchatka and later sailed on to Australia. After leaving Botany Bay in March 1788 he disappeared. In 1826–27 a few remains from his ships were found on the Melanesian island of Vanikoro.

La Plata [lah plah'-tah] La Plata, the capital of the province of Buenos Aires, Argentina, is located 56 km (35 mi) south of Buenos Aires near the south shore of the Río

DE LA PLATA estuary. Its population is 564,750 (1980). La Plata is closer to the Atlantic Ocean than is Buenos Aires and has a deeper, artificial, nontidal port at Ensenada, thus making it the main outlet for the produce of the Pampas. Textile, chemical, meat-packing, refining, and packaging industries supplement the export-import trade.

A model of planned urban development, La Plata was laid out as the new capital of the province in 1882 after Buenos Aires was named the national capital (1880). The National University (1897) is there.

La Rochefoucauld, François, Duc de [lah rohsh-foo-koh'] François VI, duc de La Rochefoucauld, b. Sept. 15, 1613, d. Mar. 17, 1680, was a French classical moralist whose literary fame rests on one sparkling book, *The Maxims.* His early years, both in the army and at the French court and involving many fights and amorous escapades, participation in the Fronde (1648), and an attempt (1651) to assassinate Cardinal Retz, were recorded in his *Memoirs* (1662; Eng. trans., 1684).

In 1652, following his recovery from a severe head wound that kept him in retirement for three years, La Rochefoucauld returned to Paris and the literary salons. In the meantime, influenced by JANSENISM, he had begun to think seriously about the meaning of a Christian life. Encouraged to write out his thoughts, he did so in maxims. The maxim, a peculiarly French literary form of epigram, expresses in a clear, impersonal image an often paradoxical truth that surprises or shocks. The first edition of La Rochefoucauld's *Maxims* was published in 1665, after which he began a 15-year liaison with the novelist the comtesse de LA FAYETTE. He completed four later editions of the *Maxims*—revisions and expansions of his original work—in 1666, 1671, 1675, and 1678.

La Rochelle [lah roh-shel'] La Rochelle (1982 pop., 75,840) is the capital city of Charente-Maritime department in western France. Located on the Bay of Biscay, it is an important fishing port and a popular summer resort. Major industries include petroleum refining and chemical, aircraft, and automobile manufacturing.

La Rochelle was made a commune in 1199 when it was already a busy port. During the 16th century it was a center of HUGUENOT resistance to the crown. Conceded by treaty to the Huguenots in 1573, the city was besieged by Cardinal RICHELIEU in 1627–28. During the 18th century La Rochelle's port handled most of France's trade with Canada. The old section of the city contains the 16th-century town hall and 14th-century towers guarding the harbor entrance. Occupied by the Germans during World War II, La Rochelle withstood an Allied siege from September 1944 to May 1945.

La Salle, Robert Cavelier, Sieur de [lah sahl, roh-bair' kah-vul-yay', syur duh] The French fur trader and explorer René Robert Cavelier, sieur de La Salle, b. Rouen, France, Nov. 21, 1643, d. Mar. 19, 1687, was

LA SALLE'S ROUTE
1679-80, 1682

the European discoverer of the lower Mississippi. He spent nine years as a Jesuit novice, studying logic, physics, and mathematics. In 1667, however, he left the order and emigrated to Canada. There he became consumed with ambition to discover the elusive route to the Orient through the interior of North America. Many people with whom La Salle came in contact in succeeding years looked on him as a visionary— some even doubted his sanity—so obsessed was he with becoming famous as a discoverer.

La Salle's travels did not develop seriously until about 1673, when he became an instrument of the comte de FRONTENAC's policy of western commercial and military expansion for New France. He was appointed commandant of Fort Frontenac on Lake Ontario and charged with the development of the fur trade in that area. Under Frontenac's sponsorship he traveled in 1679 to Lake Michigan, in 1680 to the Illinois country, and in 1682 from the Illinois River down the Mississippi to its mouth. Four new forts—Niagara (1679), Saint Joseph and Crèvecoeur (1680), and St. Louis (1682)—were established in the northwest, and the first sailing vessel, the

Griffon, built (1679) by La Salle's associate Henri de TONTY, was launched on the Great Lakes above Niagara.

Supported by the French Court, La Salle was to lay claim, on behalf of France, to the territory that he had named Louisiana, stretching from the Illinois country to the Gulf of Mexico, and beyond into the interior of New Spain (Mexico). To this end he was supplied with ships and men to sail into the Gulf of Mexico, penetrate Spanish territory, and exploit the mines he was expected to find. The expedition, which set sail in 1684, was a failure. La Salle did not succeed in rediscovering the Mississippi delta from the Gulf, and he was finally murdered by mutineers in Texas.

La Scala [lah skah'-lah]   La Scala, or the Teatro alla Scala, in Milan, Italy, has been one of the world's most prestigious opera houses since the 18th century, when on Aug. 3, 1778, a new theater was built by order of the Empress Maria Theresa to replace one that had burned down. The theater was so named because it was built on the former site of Santa Maria alla Scala, a 14th-century church. An air raid in 1943 during World War II was responsible for the virtual destruction of the theater, but it was rebuilt after the war in 1946; it now seats an audience of 3,600.

La Spezia [lah spayt'-syah]   La Spezia (formerly Spezia), the capital of La Spezia province in Liguria, northwest Italy, lies southeast of Genoa on the Ligurian Sea at the eastern end of the Riviera. Its population is 107,435 (1988 est.). The area is a summer and winter resort. Along the Gulf of La Spezia near the city are the picturesque villages of Lerici and Portovenere.

Although the city has been inhabited since Roman times, it remained a small fishing village until it was fortified in the Middle Ages. La Spezia was badly damaged by Allied bombing in World War II, but the medieval Castel San Giorgio survived, and a 15th-century cathedral was rebuilt.

La Tène [lah ten]   La Tène is an important early Iron Age site on the east side of Lake Neuchâtel, Switzerland. Excavations at the site between 1907 and 1917 revealed that the CELTS had driven piles into the edge of the lake and constructed two timber causeways there. Numerous objects were also found in the shallow waters of the lake, including iron swords and other weapons and everyday ironwork and wood objects. Some of the finds were decorated with abstract, curvilinear patterns that appear in widely distributed examples of later CELTIC ART.

The site of La Tène has given its name to the second phase of the Celtic Iron Age in Europe, which followed the HALLSTATT period and lasted from the mid-5th century BC until the Roman conquest. Its earliest remains, found in the Marne and Middle Rhine region of west central Europe, consist of chariot burials accompanied by imported Etruscan and Greek drinking vessels, which reached Celt-

ic lands over the Alpine passes. During the La Tène phase, prehistoric Celtic culture was at its zenith. La Tène culture existed in France, Germany, Austria, Switzerland, Bohemia, Britain, Ireland, parts of Iberia, the Low Countries, and Italy north of the Po River. From the 5th century BC the La Tène Celts are mentioned by classical writers. They sacked Rome in 387 BC, raided the Carpathians, Bulgaria, and Macedonia, which they laid waste in 279 BC; and plundered Hellenistic Delphi.

Julius Caesar finally met a united force of Celts under Vercingetorix at Alesia in 52 BC where his victory meant the collapse of Celtic dominance of Gaul. Independent Celtic kingdoms were maintained in Ireland and parts of Scotland until the Middle Ages.

La Tour, Georges de [lah toor', zhorzh duh]   The paintings of the Lorraine artist Georges de La Tour, baptized in Vic-sur-Seille, Mar. 14, 1593, d. Jan. 30, 1652, are a unique and personal expression of the far-reaching influence of the Italian painter Caravaggio. His early style, as in *The Fortune Teller* (c.1621; Metropolitan Museum of Art, New York City), displays an interest in naturalistic detail and plastic form along with a concern for formal, large-scale composition with dramatic effects of light and color.

In the late 1630s a change occurred in his style. The early daylight compositions gave way to nocturnal scenes illuminated by candles or torches, a device popularized by the Utrecht Caravaggist, Gerrit van Honthorst. *The Flea Hunt* (c.1635; Museum of Lorraine, Nancy) is a typical example. The mundane subject is enhanced by a quiet intimacy achieved through disciplined reduction of detail and controlled color and lighting. The figure is reduced to a series of nearly geometric planes echoing the pattern of horizontals and verticals that dominates the painting.

In The New Born *(1646–49) by the French painter Georges de La Tour, sharp, simplified forms are illuminated dramatically by controlled artificial light. (Musée des Beaux-Arts, Rennes.)*

This abstracting tendency creates a serenity that is characteristically French and is developed further in La Tour's mature style.

La Tour's late style is remarkable for its subtlety, and his masterpiece, *Saint Irene Mourning Saint Sebastian* (c.1649; Staatliche Museen, Berlin), is an exquisitely balanced study of stylized figures arrested in a moment of intense, spiritual repose.

La Tour, Maurice Quentin de   Maurice Quentin de La Tour, b. Sept. 5, 1704, d. Feb. 17, 1788, was the most popular French portrait painter of his day. The majority of his portraits were done in pastels. A virtuoso technician with a flair for capturing the inner qualities of his sitters, La Tour quickly rose to prominence. His gifts are revealed fully in his *Self-Portrait* (1751; Amiens Museum). Although *Voltaire* (1736; National Museum, Stockholm) is only a preliminary study of the famous man's features, it succeeds in representing the tremendous energy and vitality of the sitter. A similar vivacity animates most of La Tour's lucid and well-composed portraits, among which his *Madame de Pompadour* (1755) and *Philibert Orry* (1745)—both in the Louvre, Paris—stand out.

La Venta [lah vayn'-tah]   La Venta, on an island in the Tonalá River near the Gulf coast in western Tabasco, Mexico, was one of the two great OLMEC capitals. Between 900 and 400 BC it was the most powerful center in Mesoamerica.

La Venta was a modest civic-ceremonial center between 1200 and 900 BC. With the collapse of SAN LORENZO, the first Olmec capital, La Venta flourished, dominating the Olmec world until 400 BC. Its political and economic influence spread far beyond the Gulf coast Olmec heartland, reaching almost every part of Mesoamerica. La Venta's architecture features clay platforms for temples and perhaps palaces. The main pyramid, which may be an effigy volcano, is more than 30 m (100 ft) tall. La Venta is best known for its monumental stone sculpture, especially colossal human heads, and for its many caches of jade figurines and ornaments.

La Vérendrye, Pierre Gaultier de Varennes, Sieur de [lah vay-rahn-dree', pyair goh-tyay' duh vah-ren', syur duh]   The soldier, fur trader, and explorer Pierre Gaultier de Varennes, sieur de La Vérendrye, b. Trois Rivières (now in Quebec), Nov. 17, 1685, d. Dec. 5, 1749, extended the frontiers of New France well into the present Canadian province of Manitoba, visited part of the area that is now the northern U.S. Plains states, and approached the foothills of the Rockies. The son of René Gaultier, sieur de Varennes, the longtime governor of Trois Rivières, he pursued a military career in New France and France until 1712. He subsequently became the partner of his brother Jacques René in the fur trade north of Lake Superior. There he met Indians whose reports convinced him that the water route to the fabled Western Sea led through the lakes and rivers to the northwest.

Between 1731 and 1738, accompanied by three of his sons and a nephew, he established posts at Rainy Lake, the Lake of the Woods, Lake Winnipeg, the Red River, and the Assiniboine River. Unable to discover a river flowing toward the western ocean, La Vérendrye reaped an impressive fur-trade harvest. In late 1738 he visited the Mandan Indian villages on the Missouri River in present North Dakota.

In the 1740s his sons claimed (1743) for France the area around modern Pierre, S.Dak., and added to the number of trading posts in the area that is now Manitoba. In spite of this expansion, La Vérendrye's operations were a financial failure; he resigned in 1744 and died at Montreal five years later.

La Vérendrye had failed to persevere westward to the mountains, but he had won new Indian tribes to the French allegiance, luring their trade away from the British HUDSON'S BAY COMPANY and toward Montreal.

Laban, Rudolf von [lah'-bahn, roo'-dohlf fuhn]   Rudolf von Laban, b. Dec. 15, 1879, d. July 1, 1958, was a Hungarian dancer, teacher, and theorist who codified the laws of physical expression and in 1928 invented a system of dance notation, *Kinetographie Laban*, now known as Labanotation. Born in Bratislava, Laban studied painting in Munich and ballet in Paris. In 1930 he was appointed director of movement in the Berlin State Opera and choreographed large productions. Reacting against what he saw as the artificiality of ballet, Laban sought freer methods of bodily expression in plastic rhythms and movement for its own sake. Working with his students Kurt JOOSS and Mary WIGMAN, he evolved eukinetics, a system of controlling the dynamics and expressiveness of human movement. Laban sought to spread his philosophy to a lay audience and set up teaching centers all over Europe. Hitler's rise to power forced him to go (1938) to England, where, during World War II, Laban adapted his work to teach factory workers corrective exercises.

Labiche, Eugène Marin [lah-beesh', u-zhen' mah-reen]   A writer of comedy and farce, Eugène Labiche, b. May 5, 1815, d. Jan 23, 1888, was one of the most prolific and popular 19th-century French dramatists. He produced many light, charming plays, which ranged from short sketches to full-length comedies, such as *The Italian Straw Hat* (1851; Eng. trans., 1956) and *Monsieur Perrichon's Journey* (1860; Eng. trans., 1957).

Labor, U.S. Department of   The U.S. Department of Labor, established in 1913, administers federal laws involving wages, hours, working conditions, unemployment insurance, workers' compensation, and freedom from discrimination in employment. It also publishes statistical information and engages in other activities concerned with jobs and labor unions.

The department's Employment and Training Administration assists the states in maintaining public employment services intended to help workers find jobs. It operates training programs and emergency job programs for the unemployed and sets standards for industrial training. The Labor-Management Services Administration administers laws that require regular reports from labor unions and private pension plans. It helps veterans exercise their reemployment rights and supervises labor-management relations in the federal government. The Employment Standards Administration administers the minimum-wage and hour laws and various other laws concerning the compensation of workers. In 1970 the OCCUPATIONAL SAFETY AND HEALTH ADMINISTRATION was established by Congress to enforce safety and health standards in industry. The Bureau of Labor Statistics compiles the Consumer Price Index and indexes of wholesale prices and publishes information on employment and earnings.

Labor Day   Labor Day is a holiday set aside to celebrate and honor working people. Inaugurated in 1882 by the Knights of Labor, it is now a legal holiday observed on the first Monday in September in the United States, Puerto Rico, and Canada. In Europe the day on which the history and accomplishments of labor are celebrated is May 1, MAY DAY.

Labor-Management Relations Act   The Labor-Management Relations Act of 1947, better known as the Taft-Hartley Act, was intended to limit some of the activities of labor unions in the United States. It amended the NATIONAL LABOR RELATIONS ACT of 1935 (the Wagner Act), which had defined unions' rights to organize and to bargain with employers. The Taft-Hartley Act was amended by the Labor-Management Reporting and Disclosure Act of 1959.

The Taft-Hartley Act forbade unions to force employees to become members. It also banned closed shops (requiring prior union membership as a condition of being hired) and secondary boycotts. The act placed other limitations on union activities. It authorized the president of the United States to impose an 80-day delay on any strike found to imperil the national health or safety; it required unions to provide information on their finances and to give a 60-day notice before striking; it allowed employers to replace striking workers; and it imposed a ban on union contributions to political campaigns. The ban on union contributions was virtually nullified later by court rulings that it infringed the constitutional right of citizens to free expression.

Labor-Management Reporting and Disclosure Act   The Labor-Management Reporting and Disclosure Act of 1959, also known as the Landrum-Griffin Act, undertakes to "eliminate or prevent improper practices on the part of labor organizations, employers, labor relations consultants and their officers or representatives." It was enacted after extensive congressional investigation into union racketeering, especially in the TEAMSTERS Union, and amends the Labor-Management Relations (Taft-Hartley) Act. The act has five principal titles.

Title I is a "bill of rights" for union members—specifically, protection against discrimination, the right to freedom of speech and assembly, and the right to sue. Procedures are established for setting dues and initiation fees, for disciplinary action, and for access to the collective-bargaining agreement.

Title II deals with disclosures of information: disclosure by the union of finances, disclosure by union officials of conflict-of-interest involvements, disclosure by employers and their consultants of payments to union officials and employees.

Title III protects trusteeships from abuse. In a trusteeship the national union typically sets aside the self-government of a subordinate body and installs a trustee. Title IV establishes standards for democratic union elections. Title V aims to protect union finances from mishandling, including bonding of financial officers. It prohibits bribes and payoffs in employer-union dealings.

labor union   A labor union is an organization of employees whose purpose is to bargain with an employer or a group of employers over pay and working conditions. In the United States about 16 percent of all nonagricultural employees belong to unions and employee associations. In other countries, especially in Western Europe, union membership is higher. It is not uncommon, as in the Scandinavian countries, for a large majority of all employees to belong to unions.

The four functions of unions in the United States are to recruit new members, negotiate with employers, occasionally conduct strikes to achieve their purposes, and engage in politics by supporting political candidates who are favorable to them and by working to influence legislation. Unions maintain professional staffs to manage these various operations.

In 1989 about 17 million nonagricultural workers belonged to unions and employee associations in the United States. They constituted 16 percent of the total nonagricultural labor force. Union membership has been generally increasing since the early 1960s, largely because of the growth of public employee unions. At the same time, the proportion of all workers and employees enrolled in unions has been declining. This decline is probably due to the shift of the labor force away from manufacturing and manual work—areas in which unions have always been strongest—and into service occupations.

Union Structure

Unions are classified either as craft unions, industrial unions, or public employee unions. Membership in a craft union is limited to those who practice an established craft or trade, for example, bricklayers, carpenters, and plasterers.

The membership of an industrial union is composed of skilled, semiskilled, or unskilled workers in a particular workplace, industry, or group of industries, primarily in the more technologically advanced industries.

Public employee unions are organizations of municipal employees such as fire fighters, teachers, and police. The major difference between unions in the private sector and those in the public sector is that the latter generally do not have the right to strike. They often strike anyway, or circumvent the ban on strikes by proclaiming that their members have been taken ill. One of the most important issues in union-management relations today concerns strikes in the public sector.

The typical union operates on five organizational levels. In the plant, a shop committee discusses day-to-day, on-the-job problems with management. One or more shop units make up a local union, which in urban industrial areas may have many members. The local union is the basic unit and has authority to levy dues or fees, discipline its members, and enter into written agreements with management. Sometimes local unions in a geographical or industrial area form an association (known as a district council, joint council, and so on) to coordinate their efforts on matters of common interest. The national union is composed of locals and intermediate bodies and is the kingpin in the trade union structure.

The federation of national unions is the top organizational body. The principal U.S. federation at present is the AMERICAN FEDERATION OF LABOR AND CONGRESS OF INDUSTRIAL ORGANIZATIONS (AFL-CIO), which is mainly an association of autonomous national unions and is financed ultimately by the dues of union members. Funds are disbursed in specified proportions to affiliated groups, with the national and local unions usually getting the largest shares.

Collective Bargaining

The major function of U.S. unions is collective bargaining, a process by which unions and employers negotiate terms of employment. The terms are set forth in a written agreement that the union and the employer promise to enforce. The collective agreement is a fairly large document that is divided into five main sections: (1) wages and wage supplements; (2) workers' rights on the job; (3) union rights in relation to the employer; (4) management rights in relation to the union; and (5) machinery for enforcing these rights, that is, the grievance procedure.

Wages and Wage Supplements. The wage provisions of the agreement specify how much the employees are to be paid in relation to particular job classifications and types of work. The provisions cover paid holidays, paid vacations, overtime rates, and hours of work. Most agreements specify minimum daily or weekly pay guarantees.

Among the most important provisions of collective bargaining agreements are those covering so-called fringe benefits, such as health insurance, sick leave, and pensions. These benefits are no longer "fringe" but are of central importance. The pay rate negotiated by unions and management is, therefore, not a matter of simply deciding on the hourly rate but a complex structure of wages, job classifications, and wage supplements.

Job Rights. Unions are also interested in workers' rights on the job, which give employees a voice in determining

"Breaker" boys employed (c.1900) in U.S. coal mines often worked 10-hour shifts, sorting coal under deplorable conditions. Labor unions were among the chief supporters of the earliest state and federal attempts to regulate child labor.

work conditions and protect them from arbitrary acts of their superiors. Workers have the right to complain to management without fear of reprisal if they have reason to believe that some provision of the collective agreement has been violated. Another important job right concerns discharge and discipline. In such cases, the employee must be given "just cause," or a good reason; if the employer fails to show just cause, the worker has the right of redress through the grievance machinery. Workers are also entitled to seniority rights; length of service must be considered in determining layoffs, transfers, promotions, and vacation time.

Union Rights. A collective bargaining agreement also contains union security provisions that establish the union's right to recognition as long as it represents a majority of the employees in a bargaining unit. Most agreements provide for a union shop, where workers are hired on the condition that they join the union and pay dues. (In a CLOSED SHOP, all persons hired must already be union members. OPEN SHOPS, which are mandatory in states that have RIGHT-TO-WORK LAWS, do not require union membership as a condition of employment.) Under federal law a union has exclusive representation in any collective bargaining unit where it has been selected by a majority of the employees. The employer may not bargain with any other union or employee group claiming to represent workers in that unit, which may be an occupation, craft, department, plant or plants, company, or companies, depending on the scope of the agreement.

Management Rights. An agreement will also contain provisions designed to protect "management's right to manage" from union penetration. A typical management rights provision will read, "The management of the plant and the direction of the working force, including the right to establish reasonable rules and regulations and production schedules, to hire, to promote outside the bargaining unit, and to discharge for just cause, shall be vested exclusively in the company, subject to the agreement."

Enforcement. Many unionists believe that enforcing the agreement is the most important part of the collective bargaining process and that without enforcement the written agreement is ineffective. Enforcement is administered through a functioning grievance procedure that culminates in ARBITRATION.

Political Action

Most unions have found that political and legislative activity are necessary complements to collective bargaining. They work to elect candidates for federal, state, and local offices who favor union positions. In the 1930s, Franklin D. Roosevelt turned to organized labor for political support, and in most presidential elections since then the unions have favored the Democratic nominee.

The legislative side of union activity consists of lobbying for union policies in the state legislatures and in Congress and of monitoring the enforcement of these policies. Full employment, improved Social Security benefits, fuller health-insurance coverage, protection from foreign imports, equal opportunity, taxation, occupational health and safety, minimum wages, and the reform of labor laws are some of the major legislative interests of unions. Legislation and politics are the primary concern of the staff of the AFL–CIO.

Samuel Gompers, who helped to found the American Federation of Labor in 1886, served as that organization's president for 37 years.

Development of Unions

In the Middle Ages the GUILDS—economic organizations of craftsmen—set price and quality standards and fended off competition. The 16th-century journeymen's societies carried out extensive lobbying and some strikes. The labor union in England developed in response to the changed conditions of the Industrial Revolution, but attempts to organize unions were largely unsuccessful until the formation (1868) of the TRADES UNION CONGRESS and the passage of the Trade Union Act. In the late 19th century British unions allied with socialists in the Independent Labour party (later the LABOUR PARTY). German unions began to organize after 1848 but attained no lasting significance until after World War II; in France labor union groups formed in the early 19th century. In Russia labor unions developed for a brief time in 1905 and again under state supervision after 1917. Developing countries in the second half of the 20th century have spawned politically important mass union movements.

Unions have existed in the United States since the late 18th century, when the growing distance between masters and workers encouraged the formation of unions. The early unions were local units organized by skilled craftsmen to protect themselves against the competition of half-trained workers ("green hands").

After about 1830 the unions became reform-minded and sought to change the economic and social system rather than simply to bargain with employers. The skilled craftsmen in the unions had not fully reconciled themselves to the status of wage earners; they clung to the ideal of self-employed artisan, which they saw being threatened by the growth of large industry. The spokesmen of this movement were middle-class intellectual reformers who, even before the time of Karl Marx, sought to direct the workers along anticapitalist and anti-industrialist lines. Producers' cooperatives, currency reform, temperance, and independent labor parties were popular causes. The KNIGHTS OF LABOR, which flourished between 1869 and 1886, marked the full flowering and then the rapid decline of this kind of reformism in the American labor movement. As the Industrial Revolution got fully under way in the post–Civil War period, the Knights of Labor gave way to the emerging craft unions. The American Federation of Labor, formed in 1886 under Samuel GOMPERS, became the symbol of the new unionism. The AFL unionists believed that industrial capitalism was here to stay and grow, that there was no retreat from the wage system, and that the primary purpose of the unions had to be improving the workers' lot through collective bargaining. This was called "pure and simple" or "bread and butter" unionism, in contrast with socialist or revolutionary unionism, the primary objective of which was transforming society. Although craft unions dominated this period, radical voices, both within and outside the AFL, argued that no permanent solution to the problems of the worker was possible in a capitalist society. The most dramatic challenges came from such socialist leaders as Eugene V. DEBS and Daniel DE LEON. Another radical was William D. (Big Bill) HAYWOOD, the leader of the militant INDUSTRIAL WORKERS OF THE WORLD (IWW).

George Meany, then president of the AFL, and Walter Reuther of the CIO join hands victoriously at the 1955 convention that proclaimed the merger of the two labor federations.

SELECTED U.S. LABOR ORGANIZATIONS, 1989

Name of Organization	Members
Teamsters, Chauffeurs, Warehousemen, and Helpers of America, International Brotherhood of	2,000,000
National Education Association	1,600,800
Food and Commercial Workers, United	1,300,000
State, County, and Municipal Employees, American Federation of	1,200,000
United Automobile, Aerospace, and Agricultural Implement Workers of America, International Union	1,197,000
Electrical Workers, International Brotherhood of	1,000,000
Service Employees' International Union	850,000
Machinists and Aerospace Workers, International Assoc. of	800,000
Steelworkers of America, United	750,000
Teachers, American Federation of	715,000
Carpenters and Joiners of America, United Brotherhood of	700,000
Communications Workers of America	650,000
Engineers, International Union of Operating	370,000
Hotel Employees and Restaurant Employees International Union	370,000
Postal Workers Union, American	320,000
Plumbing and Pipefitting Industry of the U.S. and Canada, United Association of Journeymen and Apprentices of the	320,000
Letter Carriers of the United States of America, National Association of	304,000
Printing Trades Association, International Allied	300,000
Clothing and Textile Workers Union, Amalgamated	272,669
Civil Service Employees Association	265,000
Government Employees, American Federation of	250,000
Mine Workers of America, United	240,000
Paperworkers International Union, United	240,000
Retail, Wholesale, and Department Store Union	225,000
Electronic, Electrical, Salaried, Machine, and Furniture Workers, International Union of	200,000
Graphic Communications International Union	200,000
Musicians of the U.S. and Canada, American Federation of	200,000
School Employees, American Association of Classified	200,000
Government Employees, National Association of	195,000
Transportation Communications International Union	175,000

SOURCE: *Encyclopedia of Associations 1991.*

New Deal Era. Trade unions reached their lowest point during the Great DEPRESSION that began in 1929 and continued into the early 1930s; however, Franklin D. Roosevelt's NEW DEAL (1933) changed their fortunes. The New Deal permitted government intervention in the economy, and much of it was designed to strengthen the unions and the workers. For the unions the most significant part of the New Deal was the NATIONAL LABOR RELATIONS ACT of 1935, better known as the Wagner Act, which strengthened the unions' rights to organize and bargain with employers. Leaders such as John L. LEWIS, Walter P. REUTHER, David DUBINSKY, and Sidney HILLMAN brought great personal abilities to the creation of new unions in the mass-production industries. These unions affiliated in the Congress of Industrial Organizations, which in 1955 merged with the American Federation of Labor under the leadership of George MEANY.

Labor Legislation. The Wagner Act and other laws, mostly federal laws reinforced by court interpretations, have protected and regulated labor unions. The Norris–La Guardia Act (1932) prohibited the granting of injunctions in labor disputes in federal courts. The LABOR-MANAGE-

UNION MEMBERSHIP IN THE UNITED STATES, 1955–89

Year	Union Membership	Union Membership as % of Nonagricultural Labor Force
1955	17,749,000	24.4
1960	18,177,000	23.6
1965	18,519,000	22.4
1970	20,752,000	22.6
1974	21,643,000	21.7
1978	21,784,000	19.7
1980	19,843,000	18.2
1983	17,717,000	20.1
1986	16,975,000	17.5
1989	16,960,000	16.4

SOURCE: U.S. Bureau of Labor Statistics.

MENT RELATIONS ACT (1947), more often called the Taft–Hartley Act, prohibited certain unfair practices by unions against employers. The LABOR-MANAGEMENT REPORTING AND DISCLOSURE ACT of 1959, called the Landrum–Griffin Act, protected the rights of union members as against union officers and sought to eliminate union racketeering. The CIVIL RIGHTS ACT of 1964 prohibited discrimination by unions and employers on the basis of race, sex, or age.

Recent federal laws and regulations determine not

only how bargaining is to be accomplished but what the parties should bargain about. Since World War II, the federal government has occasionally stepped in to restrict the wage increases that unions could ask for, in an effort to curb inflation. The federal government is increasingly setting standards for specified areas previously covered only by the collective agreement, for example, in occupational health and safety and in PENSION plans.

Labour party The Labour party, one of Great Britain's two major political parties, came into being in 1900 as the offspring of the British trade union and socialist movements of the late 19th century. The Reform Acts of 1867 and 1884, which enfranchised the workers, the founding (1868) of the TRADES UNION CONGRESS (TUC) to coordinate the burgeoning labor movement, and the formation of the socialist FABIAN SOCIETY (1883) and of the Independent Labour party (ILP, 1893) laid the groundwork for a viable Labour party. In 1900 the TUC and the ILP merged to form the Labour Representation Committee. In 1906 this organization was renamed the Labour party. In World War I the pacifist stand of the Labour party's leader Ramsay MacDONALD led to his replacement in 1914 by Arthur HENDERSON. The party joined in the coalition governments during the war, but it withdrew in 1918. By 1922, the Labour party had become the second strongest party in Great Britain.

The MacDonald Governments. In 1924, with Liberal support, the first Labour government was formed, led by Ramsay MacDonald, but the government fell before the year was out. Labour returned to power in 1929–31 with another minority government. Faced with the world economic crisis, MacDonald turned to conservative policies that were rejected by his own cabinet; he formed (1931) a new coalition with Liberals and Conservatives. Although the Labour party expelled him from its ranks, he continued as prime minister with support from other parties until 1935. Labour did not return to power until 1940, when it joined Winston Churchill's wartime coalition government.

The Attlee Era. By the 1940s the party had developed a broad program of social reform involving nationalization of key industries. In July 1945 it won a decisive victory at the polls, and Clement ATTLEE became prime minister in Labour's first majority government. Attlee's able cabinet included Ernest BEVIN as foreign secretary, Sir Stafford CRIPPS as chancellor of the exchequer, and Aneurin BEVAN as minister of health. The government passed a comprehensive national health bill and nationalized the Bank of England and major industries.

The 1950 elections severely reduced Labour's parliamentary majority, and in 1951 the Conservatives returned to power for 13 years. Ensuing years were marked by ideological conflict within Labour's ranks. Left-wingers, led by Bevan, advocated further nationalization of industry and a reduced dependence on the United States. They lost to those led by Hugh GAITSKELL, who wanted a less doctrinaire program. At the same time, many suburban and middle-class people were joining the party.

The 1960s and After. The Labour party was in power again from 1964 to 1970 under Harold WILSON and returned once more in 1974. The country's economic difficulties were a continuing burden. Great Britain's participation in the European Economic Community troubled many members, and inflationary wage demands by unions that form the core of the party caused considerable friction. James CALLAGHAN, who succeeded Harold Wilson in 1976, had some success in fighting inflation, but a series of strikes and renewed economic problems in the winter of 1978–79 led to Labour's losing a vote of confidence in the House of Commons (March 1979) and then to the party's crushing defeat by the Conservatives in May 1979. The split between the left- and right-wing factions of the party widened in 1980 over issues of party organization. In November Callaghan was succeeded by Michael FOOT, a left-wing moderate. In 1981 the party voted to adopt a system of choosing a leader in which representatives of the unions and local organizations participated as well as members of Parliament (who had previously been the sole electors). This left-wing victory caused four former cabinet members, including Roy JENKINS, to leave the party and form the new Social Democratic party. (The Social Democrats subsequently allied with the Liberal party.) Weakened by this defection, Labour was again defeated at the polls in the general elections of 1983 and 1987. In 1983, Neil KINNOCK replaced Foot as party leader.

Labrador [lab'-ruh-dohr] Labrador is the northeastern sector of mainland Canada encompassing parts of the provinces of Quebec and Newfoundland. It covers about 1,620,000 km^2 (625,000 mi^2). Labrador is bounded by Hudson Strait (north), Hudson Bay (west), the Gulf of St. Lawrence and Eastmain River (south), and the Atlantic Ocean (east). The name Labrador is often applied only to the Newfoundland coast, whereas the Quebec portion is called UNGAVA. The principal towns are Schefferville in Quebec and Labrador City and Wabush in Newfoundland.

Mining of iron ore along the Ungava-Newfoundland border is the main economic activity. Lumbering and its products are important, and some income is derived from fishing and fur trapping. Hydroelectric resources are being developed, with plants at Menihek and Churchill Falls.

By about the 10th century AD, Vikings who had sailed across the Atlantic established a settlement (L'ANSE AUX MEADOWS) on the Labrador coast. The settlement was subsequently deserted. In 1498, John Cabot visited Labrador. Political control of the region was not settled until 1927, when the border between Newfoundland and Quebec was established.

Labrador retriever A strongly built, medium-sized, all-purpose dog, the Labrador retriever has become one of the world's most popular breeds. Males stand 57.2–62.2 cm (22.5–24.5 in) at the shoulder and weigh 27–34 kg

The Labrador retriever is an accomplished swimmer. Originating in Newfoundland, it is used to retrieve waterfowl and to flush out and retrieve pheasant, grouse, and other upland game birds.

Arabian Sea about 320 km (200 mi) from the south Indian coast; they are a union territory of India. The 27 coral islands and numerous reefs have a total area of about 29 km² (11 mi²) and a population of 40,237 (1981). The main islands are Kavarrati, Minicoy, and Amindivi. The people, mostly Muslims, fish and produce copra and coconut fiber. The Portuguese sighted the islands in 1498.

lace True laces are decorative openwork fabrics made of very fine threads of linen, cotton, silk, or similar material. If the thread is worked with spools, or bobbins, the lace is called bobbin or pillow lace; lace made with a needle is called needle lace, point lace, or needlepoint lace. Composite laces are made using a combination of the two techniques. Almost all modern lace is made by

(60–75 lb); females are 54.6–59.7 cm (21.5–23.5 in) and weigh 25–31.7 kg (55–70 lb). The Labrador's tail is medium in length, thick at the base, and tapering toward the tip. The short, dense coat has no feathering and is black, yellow, or chocolate. The Labrador originated in Newfoundland, where it aided fishermen. The dogs' express job was to swim to shore with the drag ends of fishing nets in their mouths. The men then took over the nets and the dogs swam back to the boats.

Lacan, Jacques The French psychiatrist Jacques Marie Émile Lacan, b. Apr. 13, 1901, d. Sept. 9, 1981, was a controversial psychoanalyst. Considering himself a strict Freudian but taking ideas also from structuralist linguistics, he revived interest among French intellectuals in Freudian ideas. He held that a child's acquisition of language begins the repression of thoughts and emotions that later could result in mental illness. In 1953 he and his followers were expelled from the International Psychoanalytic Association for unorthodoxies that included using analytic sessions as short as five minutes.

Lacandón [lah-kahn-dohn'] The Lacandón are Maya Indians living in the mountainous, heavily forested area of eastern Chiapas, Mexico, near the Guatemalan border. Their history is relatively unknown, but there are indications that the Lacandón had a complex sociopolitical organization in pre-Columbian times. Today they number only about 200 and live in tiny, widely scattered villages practicing slash-and-burn agriculture. The Lacandón are noted for their fierce resistance to the introduction of Roman Catholicism. Each village contains a crudely built temple in which copal (incense) is burned to propitiate the traditional gods.

Laccadive Islands [lak'-uh-dive] The Laccadive Islands, renamed Lakshadweep in 1973, are located in the

(Left) *This Belgian handkerchief (late 19th century; Metropolitan Museum of Art, New York City) is of linen and Valenciennes bobbin lace.*

(Below) *The floral patterns of this early-18th-century cravat are typical of needle lace of the baroque period. (Cooper-Hewitt Museum, New York City.)*

machine and closely imitates the techniques and motifs of handmade types.

To make needle lace, one or more threads are laid down on parchment according to a pattern drawn on it. Some of the areas between the tacked-down threads are filled in to form the background, called the net ground or reseau. The remaining open areas are filled in with more ornamental needlework to produce the primary design elements (toile).

To make bobbin lace, individual threads, each wound on a bobbin, are twisted and plaited together around a network of pins in a paper pattern attached to a pillow.

lacertid [luh-surt'-id]   Lacertids are about 20 genera and 160 species of lizards of the family Lacertidae. They occur in Europe, Asia, and, most abundantly, in Africa. Characteristic of this family is a complete bar at the rear of the skull; bony plates (osteoderms) cover the opening above the bar and obscure its presence. Osteoderms fused to the skull also underlay the large scales (shields) on top of the head.

For the most part, lacertids are small, agile lizards. The largest species, the jeweled lizard, *Lacerta lepida*, reaches only about 75 cm (29.5 in) in total length. The viviparous lizard, *L. vivipara*, is live-bearing through most of its extensive range. The European fence lizard, *L. agilis*, is representative of many Eurasian species, breeding in the spring and laying eggs in early summer. Incubation takes two to three months. Lacertids eat mainly insects and other small invertebrates.

lacewing [lays'-wing]   Lacewings (family Chrysopidae) are common insects that are important predators of aphids. They are usually greenish, often with copper-colored eyes, and mostly 10–20 mm (0.4–0.8 in) in length. The common name refers to the lacy character of the wings, which at rest are held rooflike over the body. The eggs are laid on foliage, each at the end of a tiny stalk. Adult lacewings give off a disagreeable odor when handled.

The giant lacewings are the largest types of lacewing, with wingspans up to 75 mm (nearly 3 in).

Lachaise, Gaston [lah-shez', gahs-tohn']   The French American sculptor Gaston Lachaise, b. Paris, Mar. 1, 1882, d. Oct. 18, 1935, contributed a contemporary Venus—imperious, erotic, yet full of grace—to modern art.

The innovative *Standing Woman: Elevation* (1912–27; Albright-Knox Art Gallery, Buffalo, N.Y.) announces his mature style. His ornamental sculptures include work on the RCA Building and the International Building at Rockefeller Center in New York City. The voluptuous and iconic *Heroic Woman* (1932; Museum of Modern Art, New York City) marks the culmination of Lachaise's treatment of the monumental female nude.

Lachish [lay'-kish]   Lachish, identified at the mound of Tell ed-Duweir, in present-day Israel, southwest of Jerusalem, was a major city of ancient Palestine during the Bronze Age (2d millennium BC). Caves beneath the mound proper were occupied as early as the 4th millennium BC; they were subsequently used for burials. During the Middle Bronze Age (c.1900–1500 BC) the city was fortified with a glacis and provided with a moat. In the Late Bronze Age (c.1550–1200 BC) this moat was the location for three successive temples.

At the end of the 13th century BC, Lachish was destroyed, perhaps by the Israelites. The city was rebuilt (928–911 BC) by Rehoboam, and a palace was founded above the earlier buildings of the Late Bronze Age. The city was fortified with a double wall with buttresses and towers, and a rock-cut water system was started but was never completed. After the city's violent destruction by Sennacherib in 701 BC, the events of which are recorded on a relief from Nineveh, this palace was abandoned. The gateway of the succeeding 7th-century BC city contained rooms in which were found the famous Lachish Letters. Written (c.589 BC) in ink on potsherds, they vividly describe the conditions of the city immediately prior to its destruction by Nebuchadnezzar II in 587 BC.

Lackawanna River [lak-uh-wahn'-uh]   The Lackawanna River flows through northeastern Pennsylvania. Its east and west branches meet just south of Uniondale and flow 56 km (35 mi) southwest, crossing a major anthracite coal-mining region, to join the SUSQUEHANNA RIVER near Pittston. SCRANTON is the largest city on the Lackawanna's banks.

lacquer [lak'-ur]   Lacquer is a fast-drying, high-gloss varnish used as a protective and decorative coating on objects made, usually, of wood and known as lacquer ware. It is also used in industrial applications on metal, fabric, leather, and paper. Pigmented lacquers are generally considered to be a type of PAINT. Lacquers originated in China, perhaps as early as the Zhou dynasty, although the Ming period produced the most diverse and beautiful lacquered objects. Japanese lacquerers probably learned the art from the Chinese (see CHINESE ART AND ARCHITECTURE; JAPANESE ART AND ARCHITECTURE).

Although the word *lacquer* is derived from *lac*, a resin secreted by an insect (*Laccifer lacca*) found largely in Southeast Asia (see SHELLAC), the first true lacquers were

This early-15th-century red lacquer box was created during the Ming dynasty (1368–1644), when carved red lacquer ware attained full expression. The design is characteristic of lacquer ware of the period. (Smithsonian Institution, Freer Gallery of Art, Washington, D.C.)

exudates collected from the sap of a sumac tree, *Rhus vernicifera*, native to China, Japan, and the Himalayas. After being boiled down and mixed with coloring pigments, the sap would dry to a high, hard gloss when painted on a surface. A soft, smooth wood was usually used as the base of the lacquered object. The wood was coated with pastes made of starch, clay, and resin and then covered with a thin cloth, over which successive layers of lacquer were painted, allowed to dry, and then rubbed to a glossy, smooth polish.

Most modern lacquers are synthetic. Many industrial lacquers are made from cellulose compounds, especially nitrocellulose, with resins added for durability and adhesion and plasticizers added to improve flexibility. Cellulose-based lacquers are used in the manufacture of inks and furniture coatings.

lacrosse [luh-kraws'] Lacrosse is a team sport in which players use a netted stick, the crosse, to throw or bat a ball into a goal; players may also kick the ball into the goal. The game originated in contests among various North American Indians. The Indian game, baggataway, received its modern name from French Canadians who saw in the crosse's shaft a resemblance to a bishop's crosier (*la croix*). Intertribal Indian games used as many as 200 men to a side, and the goal area was designated by the place where the senior medicine man from each tribe stood. A modern lacrosse game with a set of rules was first played in an enclosed field by two Indian teams in 1834. Soon many whites played the game, and in 1867, Dr. George W. Beers, a native of Montreal, codified the first lacrosse rules. The game spread to other English-speaking countries, and in North America it remains a popular club and school sport.

The modern lacrosse field is 110 yd (100.58 m) long and from 60 to 70 yd (54.86 to 64 m) wide. The goals have 6-ft (1.82-m) square openings with net backings and are 80 yd (73.15 m) apart. Each goal is centered in a circle 18 ft (5.48 m) in diameter called the goal crease. A lacrosse ball is made of India rubber, is slightly smaller than a baseball, and weighs about 5 oz (141.74 g). A crosse is from 3 to 6 ft (.91 to 1.82 m) long, and its net is walled on either one or both sides to form a pocket in which a player carries the ball. The crosse face is 7 to 12 in (17.78 to 30.48 cm) wide, depending on the player's position.

A lacrosse team consists of 10 players—3 attackers, 3 mid-fielders, 3 defenders, and 1 goalie. Players try to move the ball in the direction of the opponents' goal by carrying the ball with the crosse, passing it to a teammate by using a wrist-flipping motion, or kicking it. Only the goalie may use his hands to stop shots at the goal. Games are divided into four 15-minute periods, and in the event of a tie at the end of regulation play, two 5-minute over-time periods are played.

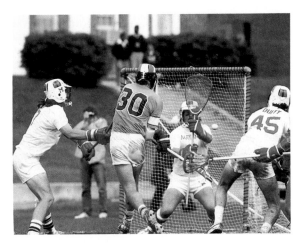

A goalkeeper tries to block a shot during a lacrosse match. Although the sport has been sponsored by the National Collegiate Athletic Association since 1971, its popularity in the United States has remained largely regional.

Lactantius, Lucius Caecilius Firmianus [lak-tan'-shuhs, loo'-shuhs ky-see'-lee-uhs furm-ee-ay'nuhs] Lucius Caecilius Firmianus Lactantius, *c*.240–*c*.320, a North African Christian apologist distinguished for his Latin prose style, was called the "Christian Cicero" by Renaissance scholars. Appointed (*c*.290) teacher of rhetoric at Nicomedia by the Roman emperor Diocletian, he resigned (*c*.305) his post when the emperor began persecuting Christians.

lactic acid [lak'-tik]   Lactic acid, or 2-hydroxypropionic acid, is an odorless, colorless liquid produced in metabolism by almost all living cells as an end product of fermentation, or anaerobic respiration. It is reconverted to glycogen in the liver, or it can be used directly for energy. Lactic acid is produced industrially for use in manufacturing drugs, plastics, and other products.

lactone [lak'-tohn]   Lactones are a class of organic compounds that can be described as intramolecular, cyclic ESTERS. Lactones are widely distributed in nature. Some, such as penicillic acid lactone, ascorbic acid (vitamin C), and mycin antibiotics, have physiological activity. The musk odor of large-ring lactones is important in perfumes.

lactose   see MILK; SUGAR

Ladewig, Marion [lad'-wig]   Marion Ladewig, b. Grand Rapids, Mich., Oct. 30, 1914, is generally regarded as the greatest woman bowler of all time. Ladewig won eight National All-Star Tournaments from 1949 to 1963, and from 1950 to 1963 she was named Woman Bowler of the Year a record nine times. She was elected to the National Bowling Hall of Fame in 1964, three years before retiring from national competition.

Ladislas I, King of Hungary [lad'-is-luhs]   Saint Ladislas I, b. c.1040, d. July 29, 1095, was one of the early Árpád kings of Hungary. The second son of Béla I (r. 1060–63) and successor to his brother Géza I (r. 1074–77), Ladislas is looked on as the embodiment of Christian knighthood and of effective political and military leadership. Internally, he resumed the work of STEPHEN I by consolidating royal power and further strengthening Hungary's nascent Christianity. In his foreign policy he supported the popes against the Holy Roman emperors. When his conquest of Croatia (1089–91) was opposed by Pope URBAN II, however, he did not hesitate to change sides. Ladislas also sought Byzantine connections, and his daughter Piroska (Irene) married the future Byzantine emperor JOHN II COMNENUS. Ladislas was canonized in 1192.

Ladoga, Lake [lah'-doh-guh]   Lake Ladoga, the largest lake in Europe, is located in the northwest European region of the USSR about 40 km (25 mi) east of Leningrad. Approximately 220 km (135 mi) long, it has a maximum width of 124 km (77 mi) and a maximum depth of 230 m (754 ft). Its area is 17,679 km^2 (6,826 mi^2).

Formed by glacial action, the lake's basin and northern shores are rocky and indented; its southern shores are low and marshy. The lake contains more than 650 islands. It is fed by many rivers and drains into the Gulf of Finland via the Neva River. The lake is part of the Volga-Baltic Waterway.

Lady Chatterley's Lover   *Lady Chatterley's Lover*, a novel by D. H. LAWRENCE first published (1928) in a privately printed edition in Italy, has been one of the most controversial books of the 20th century. Lady Chatterley is the wife of a British industrialist who, paralyzed below the waist by war wounds, serves as a metaphor for upper-class impotence. Constance Chatterley finds fulfillment in a sexual union with Mellors, her husband's gamekeeper, thus portraying the author's belief in the health of physical life freed from social constraint. Lawrence's explicit but lyrical descriptions of the sexual act led to expurgations and prosecution for obscenity in the United States, England, and Canada between 1959 and 1962.

ladybug   Ladybugs, or ladybird beetles, are insects of the family Coccinellidae, order Coleoptera. They are small, usually 10 mm (0.4 in) or less in length; oval to nearly circular in longitudinal cross section; and highly curved above and flat below. Although some ladybugs are unmarked, most are brightly marked and colored. Both adults and larvae are voracious eaters of aphids, scale insects, and other plant pests. With the exception of two plant-eating species, which are large and downy, ladybugs are extremely beneficial.

The seven-spot ladybug is one species of brightly colored beetle that fascinates children. The ladybug serves to rid gardens of aphids and other pests.

lady's slipper   Lady's slippers are a genus, *Cypripedium*, of flowers belonging to the orchid family, Orchidaceae. The approximately 50 species are found throughout the Northern Hemisphere. Flowers are often

Lady's slipper C. calceolus is a wild orchid commonly found in woodlands, especially under groves of pines.

large and showy and are characterized by the formation of the lower petal into an elongated pouchlike lip said to resemble a slipper or a moccasin. The leaves are broad and pleated and surround the stem at their bases. The stem of the showy lady's slipper, *C. reginae*, is covered with hairs containing a fatty acid that causes blistering similar to that caused by poison ivy.

Laënnec, René Théophile Hyacinthe   see
STETHOSCOPE

Iaetrile   Laetrile has been purported by some authorities to be an effective cure or remedy in cancer treatment. The name has been used incorrectly and interchangeably with amygdalin, the chief component of laetrile, which is found in the seeds of many fruits, notably apricots and bitter almonds. Laetrile as originally prepared and patented (1949) by the California physician Ernest T. Krebs, Sr., and his son, Ernest T. Krebs, Jr., was an extract of apricot pits. A less toxic, purified form was subsequently developed.

According to the Krebses, the chief proponents of laetrile as an anticancer drug, amygdalin is broken down in the body by enzymes known as beta glucosidases to yield dextrose and mandelonitrile, a compound containing hydrogen cyanide. Cyanide-containing compounds are the components allegedly active against cancer. Proponents claim that tumor cells are selectively killed by laetrile because they contain more of the beta glucosidase enzymes than do healthy tissues. They also claim that tumors contain less of the enzymes that convert toxic hydrogen cyanide to nontoxic compounds than do healthy tissues. Laetrile has also been claimed to be a vitamin—so-called vitamin B_{17}.

From the medical and scientific viewpoint, no objective, acceptable evidence is said to exist today to indicate that laetrile has any activity as an anticancer agent or as a vitamin. The U.S. Food and Drug Administration prohibited importation and interstate sale of laetrile in 1963, and use of the substance has been banned in Canada and Mexico since the mid-1970s. Despite these rulings and the negative scientific reports, numerous U.S. states have approved the manufacture and sale of laetrile, which is widely used.

Lafayette (Indiana) [lah-fee-et']   Lafayette (1990 pop., 43,764), a city on the Wabash River in west central Indiana, is the seat of Tippecanoe County. Surrounded by a livestock- and grain-producing region, Lafayette is a meat-packing and shipping center; metal products, pharmaceuticals, beer, and sponge-rubber products are manufactured there. Railroad shops serve three major lines. Purdue University (1865) is across the river in West Lafayette. Lafayette was laid out in 1825.

Lafayette (Louisiana)   Lafayette, a city on the Vermilion River in south central Louisiana, is the seat of Lafay-

ette Parish. Settled about 1770 by exiled Acadians from Nova Scotia, the city of 94,440 (1990) retains a Cajun character. It is a commercial and shipping center for an area that produces sugarcane, cotton, corn, livestock, and petroleum. Heymann Oil Center, headquarters for many oil companies, is in Lafayette, as is the University of Southwestern Louisiana (1898).

Lafayette, Marie Joseph Paul Yves Roch Gilbert du Motier, Marquis de [lah-fuh-yet', mah-ree' zhoh-zef pohl eev rawsh zheel-bair' dih moh-tyay']   The French general the marquis de Lafayette, b. Sept. 6, 1757, d. May 20, 1834, called the hero of two worlds, was prominent in the American and the French revolutions. Born to a noble family in the Auvergne, he crossed the Atlantic in 1777 to offer his services to the Continental Congress at Philadelphia. He was a friend of George Washington and served under him at the Battle of the Brandywine and at Valley Forge. In 1779 he went to France to expedite the dispatch of a French army, but he returned to fight at Yorktown (1781). Brave in battle, Lafayette won enduring popularity in America, and his fame did much to make liberal ideals acceptable in Europe.

As discontent in France mounted, Lafayette advocated the convocation of the STATES-GENERAL in 1789. He became a deputy, proposed a model Declaration of Rights, and was elected (July 15, 1789) commander of the National Guard. However, Lafayette had neither a realistic policy of his own nor the flexibility to support the more practical comte de MIRABEAU. Despised by the court as a renegade aristocrat whose bourgeois army was unable to protect the royal family, he was also hated by the populace for trying to suppress disorder.

In 1792, as an army commander, Lafayette made a futile attempt to save the monarchy and then deserted to the Austrians, who promptly imprisoned him as a dangerous revolutionary. Released in 1797 at Napoléon Bonaparte's insistence, Lafayette was allowed to return to

The marquis de Lafayette, hero of the American Revolution and a key figure in the early phase of the French Revolution, participated in the final defeat of the British at Yorktown (1781). Appointed (1789) commander of the National Guard at the beginning of the French Revolution, Lafayette sought a moderating role but lost popularity and was impeached in 1792.

France in 1799. In 1815 he was one of those who demanded NAPOLEON I's abdication.

In 1824, Lafayette made a triumphant U.S. tour. By then his home, La Grange, was a place of pilgrimage for liberals throughout the world. During the July Revolution of 1830 he was called on, as a symbol, to command the National Guard.

Lafitte, Jean [lah-feet', zhawn]   Born in France, Jean Lafitte, or Laffite, c.1780–c.1826, became a Louisiana privateer and smuggler. About 1810 he and his men settled in the area of Barataria Bay, near New Orleans, and preyed on Spanish ships in the Gulf of Mexico. In 1814, during the WAR OF 1812, the British attempted to buy Lafitte's aid in attacking New Orleans. Instead, he passed their plans on to the Americans and helped Andrew Jackson defend the city in January 1815. Lafitte later returned to privateering.

Lafleur, Guy [lah-flur, gee]   The professional ice hockey player Guy Damien Lafleur, b. Thurso, Quebec, Sept. 20, 1951, is one of the most prolific scorers in National Hockey League history. Playing for the Montreal Canadiens (1971–84), Lafleur led the NHL in scoring three times (1976–78), was league MVP twice (1977–78), and was a 1st-team All-Star six times. The Canadiens won six Stanley Cups—NHL titles—and he had amassed 1,246 career points (518 goals, 728 assists) when he retired in 1984. He returned in 1988, playing for the New York Rangers for one season and the Quebec Nordiques for two seasons. He retired for a second time in 1991 with a final total of 1,353 career points (560 goals, 793 assists).

Lafontaine, Sir Louis Hippolyte [lah-fohn-ten']   Sir Louis Hippolyte Lafontaine, b. near Boucherville, Lower Canada (now Quebec), Oct. 4, 1807, d. Feb. 26, 1864, was a Canadian political leader who helped establish responsible, or cabinet, government, the constitu-

Sir Louis Lafontaine, a leader of the French-Canadian Reform party, was joint prime minister of Canada with Robert Baldwin (1842–43; 1848–51). The second Baldwin-Lafontaine ministry, called the "great ministry," was noted for its reforms.

tional principle that allowed British colonies to evolve into self-governing nations. A lawyer, Lafontaine was elected to the Legislative Assembly of Lower Canada in 1830. He supported the reformer Louis Joseph PAPINEAU but opposed his call for an armed uprising in 1837. His association with Papineau led him to flee to Europe after the failure of the REBELLIONS OF 1837, but he returned in 1838. Lafontaine, now the leading French-speaking reformer, cooperated with Robert BALDWIN, who occupied a similar position in Upper Canada (now Ontario), to secure control of the executive by the elected house of the legislature.

In 1841, Upper and Lower Canada were united into one province, and the following year Lafontaine joined with Baldwin in the first reform ministry. It collapsed in 1843, but in 1848 a second Baldwin-Lafontaine ministry was formed, and this time it succeeded in establishing the principle that an appointed governor must accept the advice of a ministry holding the confidence of the legislature. A period of constructive legislation in the areas of municipal government, railroads, and education followed until 1851, when Lafontaine and Baldwin retired. Lafontaine was appointed chief justice of Canada East (the former Lower Canada) in 1853 and was made a baronet in 1854.

Laforgue, Jules [lah-forg', zhool]   The French symbolist poet Jules Laforgue, b. Uruguay, Aug. 16, 1860, d. Aug. 20, 1887, was, with Rimbaud, among the inventors of *vers libre* (free verse)—poetry composed to the rhythm of speech rather than to traditional regular metrical phrases. Despite his short life, Laforge had a significant influence on 20th-century poets such as Ezra Pound and T. S. Eliot. His *Complaints* (1885) and *The Imitation of Our Lady the Moon* (1886) with their plain speech and music-hall lyrics did much to change the course of poetry.

Lagash [lay'-gash]   The ancient Sumerian city of Lagash (modern al-Hiba) lies about 200 km (120 mi) northwest of Basra, Iraq, and 10 km (6 mi) southeast of ancient Girsu (modern Tello), which was earlier believed to have been Lagash. The Lagash mounds are among the largest in areal extent in all of Mesopotamia; the earliest known levels are prehistoric (c.4000 BC). During the Early Dynastic period (c.2800–2400 BC) the city became the largest in SUMER; its kings are known from contemporary inscriptions, including that of Girsu's famous *Stela of the Vultures* (Louvre, Paris). Subject to the Agade Empire (c.2371–2230 BC), Lagash revived under the governorship of Gudea (c.2130 BC), whose monuments and inscriptions reveal a flowering of economic and artistic wealth. The city had declined by the Old Babylonian period (c.1900–1600 BC) and may not have been occupied after the mid-2d millennium BC.

Lagerkvist, Pär [lah'-gur-kvist, pair]   Pär Fabian Lagerkvist, b. May 23, 1891, d. July 11, 1974, was a

Swedish novelist, poet, and dramatist. In *Ord-Konst och Bildkonst* (Literary and Pictorial Art, 1913) he argued for the literary development of a primitive vitality and an intellectual discipline characteristic of modern painting. His pessimism about the individual's place in a meaningless world deepened during World War I—a view found in *Ångest* (Anguish, 1916), considered the first collection of expressionist poems in Swedish literature, and in *Sista Människan* (The Last Man, 1917) and *The Secret of Heaven* (1919; Eng. trans., 1966), plays that show the influence of Strindberg. Lagerkvist's bleakness gave way in the 1920s to a more hopeful view seen in *Denilyckliges väg* (The Happy Man's Way, 1921), a collection of poems, and *Guest of Reality* (1925; Eng. trans., 1936), an idyllic description of his childhood.

A critic of totalitarianism in the 1930s, Lagerkvist protested against the brutality in the world in the novel *The Hangman* (1933; Eng. trans., 1936). *The Dwarf* (1944; Eng. trans., 1945) and *Barabbas* (1950; Eng. trans., 1951) are studies of the struggle between good and evil inherent in the human condition. *The Sibyl* (1956; Eng. trans., 1958) and *The Death of Ahasuerus* (1960; Eng. trans., 1962) speak of reconciliation with God. Lagerkvist was awarded the Nobel Prize for literature in 1951.

▬
Lagerlöf, Selma [lah'-gur-lurv, sel'-mah]   Selma Ottiliana Lovisa Lagerlöf, b. Nov. 20, 1858, d. Mar. 16, 1940, a Swedish novelist and short-story writer, was the first woman awarded the Nobel Prize for literature (1909). Her initial success was *The Story of Gösta Berling* (1891; Eng. trans., 1898), a saga written in a romantic style that characterizes all her later works. *The Miracles of Antichrist* (1897; Eng. trans., 1899) is a novel about socialism in Sicily. After a tour of Palestine, Lagerlöf published *Jerusalem* (1901–02; Eng. trans., 1915), a two-volume novel describing a settlement of Swedish farmers in Jerusalem. When school authorities commissioned her to write a Swedish geography, she produced *The Wonderful Adventures of Nils* (1907) and *Further Adventures of Nils* (1911), describing a boy's journey through Sweden.

▬
lagomorph [lag'-uh-morf]   Lagomorphs, once considered rodents, are members of the order Lagomorpha, which includes HARES, PIKAS, and RABBITS. They are small, gnawing animals readily distinguished from rodents by the presence of two pairs of upper incisors (front teeth), one behind the other. Serological (blood) tests suggest that lagomorphs are distantly related to hoofed animals.

▬
lagoon [luh-goon']   Lagoons are marginal marine water bodies protected and partially isolated from the open sea by sand-island barriers, coral reefs, or partially drowned preexisting topography.

   Types. Along sandy coastal plains (such as the central Atlantic coast of the United States), lagoons are linear water bodies paralleling the coast, protected from the

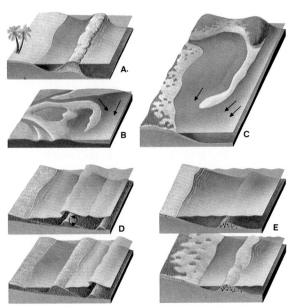

Lagoons are shallow bodies of seawater separated from the ocean by (A) coral barrier reefs; (B) curved, fingerlike extensions of deltas formed by sediment deposited from seaward-flowing rivers and ocean currents parallel to the shore; (C) shoreward-curving spits formed by extension of a headland by sediment deposition from longshore currents; (D) offshore bars build up above sea level by sediment-carrying waves that break well offshore; and (E) broad areas of seafloor brought up out of the water by an uplift of land or fall of sea level.

ocean by sand-island barriers but usually connected with the ocean by one or more tidal inlets. Shallower than ESTUARIES, coastal plain lagoons are valuable recreational and shellfish resources.

   In tropical regions lagoons may form behind CORAL REEFS. Such lagoons, which may be over 30 m (100 ft) in depth and dotted with pinnacle reefs, exchange a limited amount of water with the ocean by reef overwash. Reef barriers must generally be cut to make an artificial channel before the deeper lagoon behind can be reached by even small ships.

   Characteristics. Lagoons in tropical and temperate climates differ in two important aspects. First, sediments accumulating in most tropical lagoons are calcium-carbonate skeletal remains of organisms that lived in or near the lagoon. Temperate and some tropical lagoons, in contrast, receive largely terrigeneous, or land-derived, sediment carried into the lagoon through tidal inlets, and they have only minor amounts of locally produced skeletal remains (see SEDIMENT, MARINE). Second, tropical carbonate lagoons tend to be underlain and bounded by rigid topography—whether modern reef, preexisting limestone rock, or volcanic terrain. Temperate-climate lagoons, on the other hand, are mostly bounded and underlain by unconsolidated muds, sands, and gravels that can be remolded by waves and currents. Major storms can create new inlets in temperate lagoons, dramatically altering the size and shape of the lagoon.

Tidal currents actively scour lagoon bottoms only in the vicinity of inlets. Tides may dominate water circulation in lagoons that are subjected to a broad tidal range or that have multiple inlets. Tidal circulation is of limited influence in most other lagoons. Wind-generated waves dominate bottom agitation and circulation in most shallow lagoons. Lagoons may be gradually filled in by encroachment of marginal tidal flats, marshes, and swamps.

Lagos [lah'-gohs]   Lagos, the capital and industrial and commercial center of Nigeria, lies in the southwestern part of the country. Located on the Bight of Benin, an inlet of the Gulf of Guinea, it occupies four islands and parts of the mainland. The population is 1,274,000 (1989 est.). Population growth in Lagos has been overwhelming; transportation, utilities, housing, and port facilities are all seriously strained. Foodstuffs, automobiles, radios, metals, textiles, paints, soaps, and pharmaceuticals are manufactured in Lagos. Among many national institutions located there are the National Museum, the National Library, the University of Nigeria (1960), and the University of Lagos (1962).

The Portuguese, who first visited the site of Lagos in 1472, later established a slave-trading center there. The area was under the domination of the Kingdom of Benin from the late 16th to the mid-19th century, and in 1861 it was taken over by the British. The city became the capital of the Colony and Protectorate of Nigeria in 1914 and the capital of independent Nigeria in 1960. In 1976 the government announced that within about 20 years the national capital would be moved to a newly created federal territory near Abuja in the central part of the country.

Lagrange, Joseph Louis de [lah-grahnzh', zhohzef' lwee duh]   The French physicist Joseph Louis, comte de Lagrange, b. Jan. 25, 1736, d. Apr. 10, 1813, was one of the most important mathematical and physical scientists of the late 18th century. He invented and brought to maturity the calculus of variations and later applied the

Joseph Louis, comte de Lagrange, was the preeminent mathematician of his age. The range of his groundbreaking research included studies in celestial mechanics, analytical mechanics, number theory, and calculus of variations.

new discipline to CELESTIAL MECHANICS, especially to finding improved solutions to the THREE-BODY PROBLEM. He also contributed significantly to the numerical and algebraic solution of equations and to number theory. In his classic *Mécanique analytique* (Analytical Mechanics, 1788), he transformed mechanics into a branch of mathematical analysis. The treatise summarized the chief results in mechanics known in the 18th century and is notable for its use of the theory of differential equations. Another central concern of Lagrange was the foundations of calculus.

Lagrange served as professor of geometry at the Royal Artillery School in Turin, Italy (1755–66), and helped to found the Royal Academy of Science there in 1757. When Leonhard Euler quit the Berlin Academy of Science, Lagrange succeeded him as director of the mathematical section in 1766. In 1787 he left Berlin to become a member of the Paris Academy of Science, where he remained (through its new form as the National Institute from 1795) for the rest of his career.

A diplomatic and amenable man, Lagrange survived the French Revolution. During the 1790s he worked on the metric system and advocated a decimal base. He also taught at the École Polytechnique, which he helped to found. Napoleon named him to the Legion of Honor and Count of the Empire in 1808.

Lahore [luh-hor']   Lahore, the second largest city of Pakistan and the capital of Punjab province, is located in the northeastern part of the country on the Ravi River, about 25 km (15 mi) from the Indian border. Its population is 2,952,689 (1981), and it covers 332 km^2 (128 mi^2).

Nearly 20% of Pakistan's industrial establishments are located in Lahore, producing iron and steel, textiles, rubber, processed foods, and gold and silver handicrafts. Large railroad yards are there, and Lahore is the center of Pakistan's motion-picture industry. The traditional center of the Punjab, Lahore is a cultural and educational hub. The University of the Punjab (1882) is Pakistan's oldest university. Lahore has many important 17th-century landmarks, including several mosques, the palace and mausoleum of the Mogul emperor Jahangir, and the famous Shalimar gardens.

Little is known of Lahore's early history, but in 1036 its ruling Brahmin dynasty was overthrown by the Muslim Ghaznavids from Afghanistan, who made Lahore the capital of their empire in 1106. The city entered its most influential era following 1524, when it was taken by the Moguls and made one of their capitals. In 1767 it passed to the SIKHS, who made it the capital of their kingdom until 1849, when the British annexed the whole Punjab. Lahore was the scene of fighting during the 1965 India-Pakistan War.

Lahr, Bert   Bert Lahr, b. Irving Lahrheim in New York City, Aug. 13, 1895, d. Dec. 4, 1967, was a popular comic on vaudeville and Broadway stages, as well as in motion pictures. Perhaps his most memorable role was that of the Cowardly Lion in the 1939 film *The Wizard of Oz*.

Laika [ly'-kuh] The female dog Laika was the first living creature to be sent into outer space. She was launched by the USSR on Nov. 3, 1957, in the 508-kg (1,120-lb) *Sputnik 2* satellite. Laika traveled in a sealed, cylindrical cabin that contained equipment for recording her pulse, respiration, blood pressure, and heartbeat. The craft was not designed to return her to Earth.

Laika is also the name of a group of northern Eurasian dogs of the spitz type raised as pets and for hunting.

Laing, R. D. Psychiatrist Ronald David Laing, b. Glasgow, Scotland, Oct. 7, 1927, d. Aug. 23, 1989, applied existential philosophy to challenge prevailing conceptions of mental illness. Laing, through experiences in the British Army (1951–53) and Glasgow hospitals (1953–56), came to view SCHIZOPHRENIA, the most common PSYCHOSIS, as "a special strategy that a person invents in order to live in an unlivable situation." The medical model of mental illness, Laing claimed, strips a patient of power and dignity, subjects him or her to treatment devoid of compassion, and in labeling him or her "mad" may well be missing the point that the patient might be sane and the environment mad.

In 1957, Laing moved to the Tavistock Clinic in London, where he applied his theories. In later work Laing placed more stress on disturbed family environments as a cause, a view now widely discarded by the psychiatric community. In 1965 he helped found Kingsley Hall, a therapeutic community in London where patients and therapists live on an equal footing. Laing later withdrew many of his claims about the causes of and proper treatment for mental disorders, and he admitted that many of his own methods of treatment for schizophrenia had failed.

laissez-faire [les-ay-fair'] Laissez-faire (French, "leave alone"), in economics, is the doctrine that the best economic policy is to let businesses make their own decisions without government interference. This doctrine of noninterference was first enunciated by the French PHYSIOCRATS of the 18th century as a reaction against the restrictionist policies of MERCANTILISM. Linked with the concept of FREE TRADE, it became the basis of Adam SMITH's classical economics. Later, Jeremy BENTHAM and John Stuart MILL applied the economic notions of laissez-faire CAPITALISM to utilitarian, individualistic political theory, and the Manchester school economists John BRIGHT and Richard COBDEN used them for practical political purposes.

Modern proponents of laissez-faire stress the importance to economic growth of the profit incentive. The phrase, however, has been largely supplanted by such terms as *market economy* or *free enterprise*.

Lájos for Hungarian kings of this name, see LOUIS

lake (body of water) Lakes are inland bodies of standing water. They are important for water storage, regulation of streamflow, navigation, and recreation (see WATER RESOURCES). Depending on the purpose, lakes have been classified according to the origin of their basins, their age, their permanency, the frequency of their water circulation, and their salt content.

Origin

Lake basins may be formed in a variety of ways. Tectonically formed basins result from deformation of the Earth's crust—such as gentle crustal movements (for example, the CASPIAN SEA, a relict sea), folding (the Fählensee in Switzerland), or faulting (Lake BAIKAL). Basins of volcanic origin include those formed in extinct craters (such as CRATER LAKE in Oregon), and those located in basins either produced by volcanic collapse (Yellowstone Lake) or dammed by lava or MUDFLOWS (Snag Lake in Lassen National Park). The two main types of glacial-lake basins (see LAKE, GLACIAL) are those formed by the scouring out or deepening of basins in the native rock (for example, the English LAKE DISTRICT and the GREAT LAKES of North America), and those formed behind MORAINES (such as the FINGER LAKES of New York State).

Basins may form when limestone dissolves, as in the Karst regions of Yugoslavia. River-action lakes include basins formed by release of materials held in suspension when the water velocity is decreased, by abandoned river channels in mature floodplains, called OXBOW LAKES, and by the obstruction of a river by a LANDSLIDE.

Life Cycle and Water Circulation

Lakes are temporary features of the landscape (see LANDFORM EVOLUTION). Many lakes in arid regions are intermittent, existing only for a short period after heavy rains. But even the "permanent" lakes will eventually disappear because of infilling by sediments, erosion of the barrier forming the lake basin (see EROSION AND SEDIMENTATION), or changes in the drainage pattern. In addition, a change to a drier climate will lower the lake level and may cause it to disappear (see PLAYA).

In addition to movement from inflow to outlet, there are two other principal causes of water circulation in lakes. Wind stress causes surface waves and, more importantly, seiches, a rocking motion of the surface that occurs when a persistent wind leads to a piling up of water at one end of the lake, followed by flow in the opposite direction.

Horizontal and vertical DENSITY CURRENTS occur because most lake water is denser at cold temperatures. Lakes stratify into layers, with less-dense water on top and denser water below. Seasonal cooling of the upper layer increases its density and causes an annual or semi-annual overturning of the waters.

Composition

Ions, gases, and organic compounds occur in the water in a dissolved state. The salinity—the total concentration of ions present—is determined by the nature of the inflowing water, which in turn reflects the composition of the drainage basin. Generally, the salinity of open lakes (from which water is drained by outflow) will not change markedly over

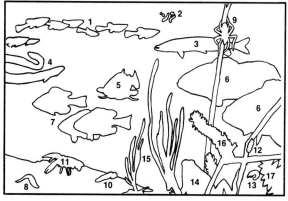

A North American lake harbors a closely interacting community of aquatic animals and plants. Mosquitofish (1) eat mosquito larvae (2). The northern pike (3) is a voracious predator. The American freshwater eel (4) is a true fish with a snakelike body. The brown bullhead catfish (5) ranges throughout all the United States and southern Canada. The largemouth black bass (6) is considered a challenge among sports enthusiasts because it is a good fighter when hooked. The pumpkinseed sunfish (7) enjoys sunny waters. A dog leech (8) attaches by its jaws to fishes or frogs. A fisher spider (9) catches aquatic insects and small fish. Insects and crustaceans that are important food for fishes include the caddisfly (10) and such crustaceans as the American crayfish (11), a freshwater isopod (12), and an amphipod, the scud (13). The common bullfrog (14) is the largest of North American frogs. Plant life includes water celery (15); waterweed (16); and water lobelia (17).

time, while the salinity of closed lakes (which have no outlet and lose water only through evaporation) will increase over time. Salt lakes are found only in arid regions, but they differ greatly in their degree of salinity. The GREAT SALT LAKE has about four times the dissolved solids content of seawater and the DEAD SEA about seven times.

All lake waters contain at least some suspended matter, which settles slowly to the bottom and accumulates as sediments (see SEDIMENTS, MARINE). These consist of inorganic matter (erosion products from the rocks in the watershed), organic compounds, and chemical precipitates. Deposits in saline lakes differ from those in freshwater lakes in the predominance of chemical precipitates

and the relatively small fraction of organic matter (see EVAPORITE).

Environmental Problems

Lakes face two basic kinds of environmental problems: threats to water quality and the deterioration of shoreland. Pollution (see POLLUTION, ENVIRONMENTAL) by municipalities, industries, shipping, and poor agricultural practice has led to poisoning of the water, changes in its temperature, and acceleration of the natural process of EUTROPHICATION. The last is due to the enrichment of lakes by agricultural fertilizers and various other nutrients, which promote the growth of so much algae that the

MAJOR LAKES OF THE WORLD

| Lake | Surface Area | | Volume | | Mean Depth | |
	km²	mi²	km³	mi³	m	ft
Caspian	371,000	148,000	79,340	19,035	182	597
Superior	82,100	31,700	12,088	2,900	149	489
Victoria	68,780	26,560	2,660	637	40	131
Huron	59,570	23,000	3,543	850	59	195
Michigan	57,750	22,300	4,918	1,180	85	279
Aral*	41,000	15,830	374	90	9	30
Tanganyika	33,990	13,120	19,420	4,659	572	1,876
Baikal	31,490	12,160	23,260	5,581	740	2,427
Nyasa (also Malawi)	30,790	11,890	8,370	2,009	273	895
Great Bear	30,400	11,740	2,200	529	72	238
Erie	25,670	9,910	480	116	19	62
Great Slave	25,390	9,800	1,550	373	62	204
Winnipeg	24,520	9,470	320	76	13	43
Ontario	19,554	7,550	1,640	393	86	283

*The fourth largest lake in area in 1960, the Aral Sea has shrunk 40% since then.

water's oxygen content is depleted. Some of the world's major lakes now suffer from such problems, including the Great Lakes of North America. Shorelines act as a buffer between the land and the water. Their development results in increased erosion, impairment of the WATER QUALITY, and scenic deterioration. Irrigation practices can likewise cause damage, as in the shrunken ARAL SEA, once the world's fourth largest lake.

Some researchers have also recommended the monitoring of volcanic lakes similar to Cameroon's Lake Nyos, the site of a 1986 disaster where the escape of carbon-dioxide gas killed 1,700 people.

See also: LIMNOLOGY.

---

lake (dye)   Lake is the name given to a class of dyestuffs that are made by combining a soluble dye with a mordant, a metallic salt that renders the DYE insoluble in water. Many organic substances—such as the carmine derived from cochineal insects or the violet color made from brazilwood—cannot be used as dyestuffs because, being soluble, they will wash out of the dyed material. Combined with a chromium, iron, or other metallic salt, however, these colors become the insoluble carmine lake and Vienna lake. Lakes are also made from synthetic, coal-tar–derived colors. Synthetic alizarin combined with an aluminum salt produces the color Turkey red.

---

lake, glacial [glay'-shul]   Glacial lakes include glaciogenic lakes, created by the action of glaciers (see GLACIER AND GLACIATION), and pluvial lakes (found today in desert and semidesert areas), whose depth and extent have fluctuated in response to worldwide climatic changes during glacial-interglacial cycles (see ICE AGES).

Glaciogenic Lakes

Four types of lakes originate directly from glacial action: glacier margin, glacial erosional, glacial depositional, and isostatic.

Glacier-Margin Lakes. A glacier may act as a dam to create a temporary lake along its margin. Long, narrow glacier-margin lakes are created when a valley glacier forms dams across tributary valleys, or when a glacier flowing out of a tributary valley blocks the main valley. The lakes in tributary valleys are generally small but numerous.

Glacier-margin lakes tend to be short lived; they fluctuate in level with the waxing and waning of the glacier that dams the lake, and the water level can fall rapidly if lake-outlet streams melt and erode the glacier. Buildup of hydrostatic pressure in a lake may float a glacier off its bed, creating an outlet that suddenly drains the lake through release of a catastrophic flood. Proglacial lakes along the continental ice sheets commonly overflowed land barriers to the south. Fed by large volumes of glacial meltwater, these flows created spectacular spillway channels.

Glacial-Erosion Lakes. Glaciers are better able than streams to "overdeepen" their beds by selectively removing weak rock, mostly by ice scour and plucking. Both continental ice sheets and mountain glaciers produce such depressions, which, until filled with sediment, are sites of ponds and lakes from less than one to as many as thousands of square kilometers in area. CIRQUE lakes—also known as tarns in England, corries in Scotland, and cwms in Wales—in mountainous areas, and paternoster (or stairstep) lakes, created by selective erosion in valleys, constitute the most common category.

Glacial-Deposition Lakes. The sediments left after a glacier melts can produce lake basins of several types. Moraine-dammed lakes are caused by end MORAINES—ridges of TILL deposited during stillstands of the retreating glacier—that dam either a mountain valley or a sloping continental surface. Classic examples such as Lakes GARDA and COMO in Italy, Lake Zurich in Switzerland, Chiemsee in Bavaria, and Jackson and Jenny Lakes in Grand Teton National Park in Wyoming, are generally found in the piedmonts and lower ends of glaciated valleys.

Outwash-dammed lakes, such as Lakes McDonald and

Kintla and the Lower Two Medicine Lakes in Glacier National Park, were created by plugs of glacial DRIFT—gravel and sand deposited by meltwater streams—in valleys. Finally, blocks of ice that have melted from within either a ground moraine—till deposited in irregular heaps by a stagnant, dying glacier—or an outwash plain beyond the ice margin may create small lakes, ponds, and swamps called kettles.

Isostatic Glacial Lakes. Isostatic glacial lakes occupy the lowest parts of large areas that have been weighted down by a large ice sheet (see ISOSTASY). During the last glaciation the Laurentide Ice Sheet depressed the land surface north of a line connecting Milwaukee, Cleveland, and New York by as much as 100 m (330 ft). Isostatic rebound from this depression has been in progress ever since the start of deglaciation about 17,000 years ago. The depression has tended to block drainage southward away from the ice sheets, especially along the southern margin of the Laurentide Ice Sheet, and it is still significant in impeding the drainage of ice-scoured lake basins in the Canadian Shield.

Lakes Associated with Continental Ice Sheets. The greatest concentrations of glacial lakes by far were created by the Laurentide and Scandinavian ice sheets of North America and Europe. Interior parts of these ice sheets scoured deeply into bedrock, mostly granitic and gneissic rock, producing myriad large and small lakes, especially in southeastern Canada and Finland.

In North America, just beyond the southern margin of the Laurentide Ice Sheet, a series of proglacial lakes developed during the waning of the last glaciation, between 14,000 and 10,000 years ago. These lakes fluctuated greatly in depth and extent but were often huge—much larger than the present GREAT LAKES. Most notable were Lake Agassiz (the largest), Lake Souris, and the ancestral Great Lakes, which at times extended most of the distance—more than 2,000 km (1,200 mi)—from Saskatchewan to the upper St. Lawrence River.

Pluvial Lakes

Pluvial lakes, although features of semiarid or arid areas, show evidence of large fluctuations in water level that were mainly in response to ice-age climatic changes, and so they are classed with glacial lakes. All known pluvial lakes are less than 2 million years old, that is, of Quaternary age (see GEOLOGIC TIME).

Today, pluvial lakes are either PLAYAS, which are lake beds that are usually dry, or saline lakes, such as the Great Salt Lake, which are shrunken remnants of the expanded ancient lakes.

Pluvial lakes occur in desert and semidesert regions, where the net runoff within their drainage basins is generally less than the annual precipitation. In North America they are numerous in the BASIN AND RANGE PROVINCE, especially the Great Basin, the site of Lake Bonneville and Lake Lahontan (the largest and second-largest pluvial lakes in the Western Hemisphere). The largest pluvial lake in the world is the ARAL SEA–CASPIAN SEA–BLACK SEA system in the USSR and central Asia. The stratigraphy of the shore and bottom sediments of such lakes yields a wealth of data on the climatic changes that caused the lakes to fluctuate.

Lake Charles

Lake Charles (1990 pop., 70,580), a city on the Calcasieu River in southwestern Louisiana, is the seat of Calcasieu Parish. A deepwater port of entry, it is connected to the Gulf of Mexico by a 48-km-long (30-mi) channel. McNeese State University (1939) is located there. Settled in 1852 as a lumbering town, Lake Charles became the center of a rice-growing area after the arrival of the railroads brought Midwestern settlers. With the discovery of petroleum and natural gas nearby, it became an important petrochemical producer.

Lake District

The Lake District is a region of mountains, lakes, and waterfalls, long famous for its beauty, in Cumbria, northwestern England. England's highest mountains, including the highest, Scafell Pike (978 m/ 3,210 ft), and largest lakes are there. The latter include Windermere (the largest), Ullswater, Bassenthwaite Lake, Derwent Water, and Coniston Water. The Lake District National Park, established in 1951, covers 2,243 km^2 (866 mi^2). Tourism is the principal source of income, but sheep, dairy cattle, and poultry are raised, and some slate and building stone are quarried. The poet William Wordsworth lived there, as did Samuel Taylor Coleridge and Robert Southey, who together are called the Lake Poets.

lake dwelling

Lake dwellings were villages or single houses built near the waters of a lake or a marsh, on platforms or artificial mounds. They have existed during several periods of human history. The most famous prehistoric lake dwellings are those of the late Neolithic and early Bronze Ages in Switzerland, France, and northern Italy.

The discovery of these lake villages occurred during the dry summer of 1853–54, when a drop in the level of the Lake of Zurich revealed the stumps of piles that had supported the platforms on which houses were built during the Neolithic Period. Because of the waterlogged conditions, materials not normally preserved at prehistoric sites, including wooden vessels and implements, were found intact. Subsequent research showed that these villages had been built on marshy ground at the edge of lakes, not in open water. The earliest villages are datable to the 4th millennium BC. Their pottery indicates that the lake dwellers belonged to a group of cultures usually designated the Western Neolithic. In France the lake villages belong to what is called the Chassey culture; in Switzerland they are characteristic of the Cortaillod culture; the north Italian variant is known as the Lagozza. Some lake villages of the Bronze and Iron Ages are also known, notably the Iron Age villages of Gastonbury and Meare in Somerset, England.

Lake dwellings in the form of single homesteads built on artificial islands are found in parts of Ireland and Scotland. Called *crannogs* (from the Irish *crann* or "tree"), they range in date from the late Bronze Age to the 17th century AD.

Lake of the Woods

Lake of the Woods, located on the borders of Minnesota, Manitoba, and Ontario, covers 3,846 km^2 (1,485 mi^2). The lake, shallow and irregularly shaped, has a heavily indented shoreline and more than 14,000 islands. Located in an area forested with pines, the lake and four provincial parks along its shores are used for recreation.

Lakeland terrier

The Lakeland terrier, one of the oldest English working terriers, has been known in the English lake districts for centuries. The breed was developed to hunt fox and otter. It had to be small enough to go to ground (burrowing) yet big enough to run down its quarry.

The Lakeland is a small, square dog, sturdily built, with small V-shaped ears, wiry coat, and docked tail. The ideal height for a mature male is 36.25 cm (about 14.5 in) with a weight of 7.65 kg (17 lb); females are slightly smaller. The undercoat is soft, the outer or guard coat hard and wiry. Lakelands may be white, blue, black, liver, black and tan, blue and tan, red, red grizzle, grizzle and tan, or wheaten.

A small working dog was the Lakeland terrier, developed in the Lake District of England to hunt foxes. Packs composed of hounds and a few of these terriers would pursue a fox to its hiding place, where a Lakeland would enter and kill the predator.

Lakshmi

[luhk'-shmee] Wife of the Hindu god VISHNU, and one of the incarnations of the Mother-Goddess, or *Devi,* Lakshmi is the goddess of fortune and prosperity as well as the epitome of feminine beauty. According to Hindu legend, she was born radiant and fully grown from the churning of the sea. Lakshmi is portrayed as sitting on a lotus, her traditional symbol.

See also: SHAKTI.

Lalique, René

[lah-leek', ruh-nay'] René Lalique, b. Apr. 6, 1860, d. May 5, 1945, was a French jewelry de-signer and glassmaker who is best known for his use of unusual materials and innovative styles in jewelry and glassware. An interest in glass resulted (1908) in his designs for mass-produced perfume bottles in molded forms. The success of these early designs allowed him to establish (1920) his own glass factory, where he developed a style that was initially called Art Moderne and is now known as ART DECO. The sleek, stylized formulations of Lalique's Art Deco designs exerted a profound influence on his contemporaries.

Lalique's innovative lighting fixtures were particularly influential in modern interior decoration. His most famous single commission (1931–35) was the palatial first-class dining salon of the S.S. *Normandie.*

Lalo, Édouard

[lah-loh'] The French composer Édouard Victor Antoine Lalo, b. Jan. 27, 1823, d. Apr. 22, 1892, is best known for his rhythmic and colorful *Symphonie espagnole* (1875) for violin and orchestra. He studied at the Lille and Paris conservatories, becoming a skilled violinist and violist, and in 1855 he became violist of the Armingaud-Jacquard string quartet. He achieved his first major success with the *Symphonie espagnole,* when Pablo de Sarasate performed the work in 1875. Lalo's Cello Concerto (1876) is one of the better-known concerti for that instrument. The melodious suites from his ballet *Namouna* (1882) as well as excerpts from his opera *Le Roi d'Ys* (The King of Ys; 1888) are occasionally performed. His other works include the Symphony in G minor, concerti for violin and piano, chamber music, and songs. Lalo was a skillful orchestrator whose music, written in the late-romantic idiom, foreshadows the impressionist style.

Lamaism

see TIBETAN BUDDHISM

Lamaist art and architecture

Lamaist art and architecture arose in areas that came under the influence of TIBETAN BUDDHISM (Lamaism) in addition to Tibet itself—Ladakh, Nepal, Sikkim, Bhutan, parts of Central Asia, Mongolia, parts of western China, and a small area

This 18th-century gilt-bronze statue of Avalokitesvara, the bodhisattva of infinite compassion and mercy, is representative of Lamaist art as it was interpreted in North China. (Philip Goldman Collection, London.)

This 18-century mandala is an example of Tibetan bardo painting and is attributed to the Nying-ma-pa sect of Tibet. The bardo is the intermediate state between death and rebirth. (Gulbenkian Museum, Durham, England.)

tures are in the form of deity groups (MANDALAS) or relic mounds (STUPAS). Building materials are generally of wood, stamped earth, stone, or sun-dried bricks; smooth surfaces (particularly on stupas) were often brightly painted.

Inward-tapering walls, flat roofs, and small windows are characteristic features of Tibetan architecture, a notable example being the magnificent Potala, former residence of the Dalai Lama, in Lhasa.

Sculpture and Painting. The images placed in Lamaist buildings as objects of worship are generally made of metal or stucco; some wood sculpture is also found, principally in Nepal, and a small amount of stone carving. Metal images are usually of cast copper, bronze, or brass, but some of the larger figures are also of embossed copper. Gilding is common, especially on Buddha statues, which are typically rendered as slender figures with delicate, youthful features. Figures in all materials are often painted and adorned with jewelry, crowns, scarves or complete sets of outer clothes.

Paintings, the other principal category of Lamaist image-making, are often in the form of elaborate wall paintings, designed to augment the ritual significance of the three-dimensional images. Based on texts such as the *Mahavairochanasutra*, they function as the visual realization of these sacred doctrines. They not only have served to teach the illiterate but also to heighten religious awareness within the temple. In addition to wall paintings, several forms of portable paintings are significant, of which temple banners, called tankas, are the most important. The aim of the Lamaist artist was not to be creative in the Western sense, but to follow the conventional Lamaist iconographic traditions as closely as possible in order to produce an object that was effective in its religious purpose.

Images of tantric deities abound in Lamaist art, both in painted and sculpted form. They are usually portrayed in their ferocious aspect and are often accompanied by their female counterparts. A characteristic example is the fantastic demonic mask, produced in brightly painted papier-mâché, wood, or leather. A host of uniquely Lamaist ritual objects such as prayer wheels and altar lamps were made, often of exquisite workmanship, as well as items for secular use including brass and copper teapots and bowls, often gilded or inlaid with silver, and distinctive rugs and saddlery.

in northern China near Beijing. It was almost entirely devoted to the service of religion, mainly Buddhist but also, in Tibet, to Bön-po, the indigenous shamanistic religion that was centered on nature spirits and magic.

The Lamaist artistic tradition is derived from several sources, the most important being India, China, and Central Asia. Probably the earliest influence came from India and was received in Tibet, together with Buddhism, about the 7th century AD. Close links based on this religious association continued between India and Tibet until the 12th century, when the Muslims invaded India. Nepal and China became important influences on Tibetan culture after the Mongol domination of both China and Tibet in the 13th century. Eventually, Tibet's position changed from that of an importer of religious ideas from India to that of a custodian of Buddhism north of India, with a consequent increase in the prestige of its art among other northern Buddhist countries. Conservative, regional art styles continued until about the 17th century, when Tibet developed its own national style.

Architecture. Some Lamaist religious buildings are based on secular Tibetan architecture, being rectangular and having a courtyard. The most characteristic struc-

Lamar, Lucius [luh-mar', loo'-shuhs]   Lucius Quintus Cincinnatus Lamar, b. Putnam County, Ga., Sept. 17, 1825, d. Jan. 23, 1893, was a Mississippi political leader and U.S. official whose career spanned the Civil War. He served as a U.S. representative from Mississippi (1857–60), drafted Mississippi's ordinance of secession from the Union (1860), and returned to Washington as representative (1873–77), senator (1877–85), secretary of the interior (1885–88), and associate justice of the Supreme Court (1888–93). After the Civil War he promoted North-South reconciliation.

Lamar, Mirabeau Buonaparte [luh-mar', mir'-uh-boh bwohn'-uh-parte] Mirabeau Buonaparte Lamar, b. Warren County, Ga., Aug. 16, 1798, d. Dec. 19, 1859, was the second president (1838–41) of the Republic of Texas. He distinguished himself in the TEXAS REVOLUTION and in 1836 was elected vice-president of the republic. Later, as president (1838–41), Lamar instituted the building of Austin, a system of public education, a law protecting homesteads from foreclosure, support for a Texas navy, and the much-criticized expulsion of the Cherokee Indians from East Texas. He later fought in the Mexican War and served (1857–59) as U.S. minister to Nicaragua.

Lamarck, Jean Baptiste [lah-mark', zhawn bahp'-teest] Jean Baptiste Pierre Antoine de Monet, Chevalier de Lamarck, b. Aug. 1, 1744, d. Dec. 18, 1829, was a French naturalist who became widely known for his theory of EVOLUTION. The theory, known as Lamarckism, was based on the idea, not unreasonable at the time, that plants and animals evolve by adjusting to changes in their environment. According to Lamarck, once a change occurred in a plant or animal, it could be passed on to the next generation. This theory, included in Lamarck's 2-volume *Zoological Philosophy* (1809; Eng. trans., 1914), was accepted by many contemporary scientists, but it was later proved to be incorrect. Today the generally accepted theory is that of Charles DARWIN, who proposed that changes in traits occur randomly, not directly in response to changes in the environment.

Originally interested in botany, Lamarck wrote a 3-volume text, *Flore française* (French Flora, 1778). He was appointed the royal botanist in 1781 and became a professor of invertebrate zoology in 1793 at the Museum of Natural History in Paris.

The first scientist to distinguish between animals with backbones (vertebrates) and without backbones (inverte-

The French naturalist Jean Baptiste Lamarck is best known for his erroneous theory that organisms acquire new characteristics in response to environmental factors and pass along these traits to succeeding generations. Lamarck also contributed to comparative anatomy and the study of invertebrates and originated the term biology.

brates), he classified many invertebrates into the categories of arachnids, crustaceans, and echinoderms. He also wrote a text on invertebrate systems, *Système des animaux sans vertèbres* (1801), and a 7-volume treatise on the natural history of invertebrates (1815–22).

See also: HEREDITY.

Lamartine, Alphonse de Alphonse de Lamartine, b. Oct. 21, 1790, d. Feb. 28, 1869, was a major French romantic poet and a distinguished orator who commanded a large popular following during the Revolution of 1848. Lamartine served briefly in the military guard of Louis XVIII and in 1820 obtained a diplomatic post in the French embassy at Naples. In the same year he published his first volume of verse, *Méditations poétiques* (1820). *Nouvelles Méditations poétiques* (1823) and *Mort de Socrate* (1823)—based on Plato's *Phaedo*—were less well received, but *Le Dernier Chant du pèlerinage d'Harold* (1825), a tribute to Lord Byron, was eagerly read by the English poet's French admirers. Lamartine was elected to the Académie Française in 1829 and in the following year published the plaintive *Harmonies poétiques et religieuses*.

Abandoning his diplomatic career in 1830, Lamartine tried unsuccessfully to win election as a deputy in the government. He was finally elected in 1833 after he had begun composing the long narrative poems *Jocelyn* (1836) and *La Chute d'un ange* (1838). His last volume of verse, *Les Recueillements poétiques* (1839), reflects compassion for the mass of humanity and regret for his own former egotism and isolation. During this period he made many of his finest speeches, which include discourses on political liberty and apologies for Napoleon. When Louis Philippe was deposed in 1848, Lamartine was an idol of the people, but he failed to win election in 1849 and retired from public affairs.

Lamb, Charles Charles Lamb, b. London, Feb. 10, 1775, d. Dec. 27, 1834, is best known as the author of the ingratiating *Essays of Elia* (1823, 1833). A small, stuttering man who devoted himself to a mentally unstable sister, Mary, and whose official career was clerking (1792–1825) for the East India Company, Lamb was a central figure in the first generation of British romantics (see ROMANTICISM).

In the mid-1790s, about the time Mary killed their mother during one of her seizures, he began writing poetry, the most reprinted being the tender "Old Familiar Faces" (1798). After a muted sentimental novelette, *A Tale of Rosamund Gray* (1798), he turned to drama. Of his five plays only one, *Mr. H: or Beware a Bad Name* (1806), was produced, and that failed. With Mary he wrote some children's books, the best known being *Tales From Shakespear* (1807). He was proud of his *Specimens of English Dramatic Poets* (1808), which led to other dramatic criticism, notably "On the Tragedies of Shakespeare," published (1811) in Leigh Hunt's *Reflec-*

Charles Lamb, a 19th-century English writer, achieved literary prominence through his critical dissertations on the works of Elizabethan dramatists and through satirical essays.

tor, and "On the Artificial Comedy of the Last Century," which appeared (1822) in the *London Magazine.*

When Lamb was 45 he began publishing in the *London Magazine* a series of personal essays signed "Elia"—observing that the name was an anagram for "a lie." These essays, which include the familiar "Dream Children," "A Dissertation upon Roast Pig," "The South-Sea House," and "Christ's Hospital," are protectedly autobiographical, sometimes deriving from his franker, more vigorous letters, which are among the best from the 19th century.

lame duck   In U.S. politics a lame duck is an officeholder who has not been reelected or who is prevented by law from running for office again. During the period between the election and the end of his or her term, the lame duck's political influence may be greatly reduced because the successor is not bound to follow the lame duck's policies and because the latter has few political levers, such as patronage, left to exercise.

Lamennais, Félicité Robert de [lahm-uh-nay', fay-lee-see-tay' roh-bair' duh]   Hugues Félicité Robert de Lamennais, b. June 19, 1782, d. Feb. 27, 1854, was a French priest and religious writer. His initial writings were conservative and ultramontane (that is, pro-papal), reacting to the French Revolution with a plea for the return of power to the clergy. In the 1820s, however, he evolved toward a belief in liberalism and the separation of church and state as the only means of achieving a religious revival. He and his friends elaborated their liberal ideas in the newspaper *L'Avenir,* founded in 1830. After being censored by the pope, Lamennais gradually left the church altogether, became an ardent proponent of republicanism, and died unreconciled with the church.

Lamentations, Book of [lam'-en-tay'-shuhnz]   The Book of Lamentations in the BIBLE is actually five poems that lament the destruction of Jerusalem in 586 BC. Often called "The Lamentations of Jeremiah," it is usually placed after the Book of JEREMIAH, despite its uncertain authorship. The poet vividly describes the devastation endured by Jerusalem. Although this recitation of laments faced the harsh realities of the present, the prayer-poems also stirred continuing hope in Yahweh's promises for the future.

Lamia [laym'-ee-uh]   In Greek mythology Lamia was a beautiful woman whose children were taken away in jealousy by HERA because ZEUS had loved her. In revenge Lamia began to steal and kill the children of others. Because Hera had condemned her to sleeplessness, Zeus gave Lamia the ability to remove her own eyes at will in order to sleep. In later legend the lamia was a vampire that seduced young men.

Lamont-Doherty Geological Observatory   The bequest (1948) of a large plot of land in Palisades, N.Y., to Columbia University by the widow of the financier Thomas W. Lamont, coupled with the need by a geology research group for a place to test sensitive seismic instruments, led to the establishment (1949) by the university of what later became known as the Lamont-Doherty Geological Observatory. Under the leadership of Maurice Ewing, the first director (1949–72), and his successor Manik Talwani, the observatory—with a current staff of about 600—has placed a major emphasis on the study of the ocean floor and what lies beneath it. Through the use of their two research ships and the development and improvement of geophysical instruments, observatory staff members have played a leading role in research on oceanic plate tectonics. They have established the continuity of the MID-OCEANIC RIDGE system and the association of earthquake epicenters with the crest of the system, and made noteworthy contributions to the theory of seafloor spreading.

lamp   A device for producing light by burning oils, fats, or combustible fluids, the lamp has been a part of all civilizations. In modern times, the term *lamp* has been extended to include various other devices producing light or heat, such as INCANDESCENT LAMPS; FLUORESCENT LIGHTS; and SUNLAMPS. The earliest lamps were shells or saucer-

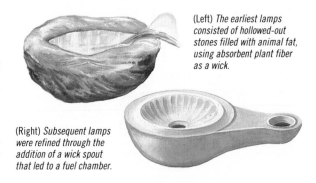

(Left) *The earliest lamps consisted of hollowed-out stones filled with animal fat, using absorbent plant fiber as a wick.*

(Right) *Subsequent lamps were refined through the addition of a wick spout that led to a fuel chamber.*

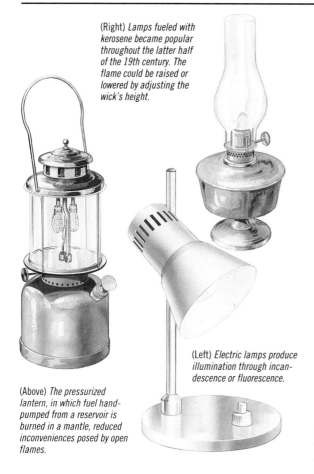

(Right) *Lamps fueled with kerosene became popular throughout the latter half of the 19th century. The flame could be raised or lowered by adjusting the wick's height.*

(Left) *Electric lamps produce illumination through incandescence or fluorescence.*

(Above) *The pressurized lantern, in which fuel hand-pumped from a reservoir is burned in a mantle, reduced inconveniences posed by open flames.*

shaped pieces of stone that held oil or animal fat with crude wicks of vegetable fiber. (Both the lamp and the candle seem to have had a common origin in the torch and the rushlight—a rush dipped in tallow. The oil lamp, however, was used long before the candle.) Later, stones were shaped specifically to serve as lamps, with oil reservoirs and grooved lips to hold the wicks. Many changes were made in the location of the wick, including the wick spout, which led from the oil chamber.

Not until the 18th century was the wick finally moved from the edge of the oil reservoir to its center. In the 1760s the first central burner, a flat woven wick encased in a metal sheath, was developed. Flat wicks burned far more efficiently than the round, solid wicks that had commonly been used. The first real improvement in lamp design, however, was the invention of a Swiss scientist, Aimé Argand (1753–1814). His oil lamp (1782) used a circular tubular wick that enabled air to reach the inner wick surface and a glass chimney that both sheltered the flame and improved its combustion.

Whale oil was an important source of lamp fuel during the early and middle 1800s; other fuels commonly used included various kinds of vegetable and fish oils and lard. After 1850, however, kerosene became the principal fuel.

The Welsbach mantle, which had been invented for the gas light (see LIGHTING DEVICES), was adapted for kerosene; suspended above the wick, the mantle burned the inflammable vapors produced by the wick flame.

Pressurized kerosene lamps were first used in the late 1860s and, in such forms as the Coleman lamp, are still popular. In these lamps hand-pumped air forces the oil through a coil that is heated by the flame; the heated oil is partially vaporized and burns with a bright light.

Lampedusa, Giuseppe di [lahm-pay-doo'-zah, joo-zep'-pay dee] Giuseppe Tomasi di Lampedusa, b. Dec. 23, 1896, d. July 23, 1957, was an Italian nobleman whose only novel *The Leopard* (1958; Eng. trans., 1960; film, 1963) won worldwide acclaim. Drawn from his own family history, the novel is a vast panorama of aristocratic Sicilian society and its changes during 1860–1910. *Two Stories and a Memory* (1961; Eng. trans., 1962) was also published posthumously.

lamprey [lamp'-ree] Lampreys, family Petromyzontidae, and hagfishes are the two surviving groups of jawless vertebrates (class Agnatha). The earliest known lampreys, genus *Mayomyzon*, are from the Pennsylvanian Period, about 300 million years ago, and are thought to be closely related to an extinct group of jawless fishes, the ostracoderms, which flourished earlier. Lampreys are eel-like in shape and lack scales and paired fins (pectorals and pelvics), but they do have a tail fin and one or two dorsal (top) fins. In place of jaws, lampreys have an oral sucking disk bearing teeth and a rasplike tongue. The internal body support consists of a notochord ("backbone") and a cartilaginous skeleton. Lampreys have seven separate gill openings on each side and a single nostril on the upper part of the head.

Some lampreys live only in fresh water. Other species are anadromous, living in marine waters but breeding in

Lampreys are fish without jaws. The mouth is a circular, toothed, sucking disk, and the body skeleton consists almost entirely of cartilage. Shown are a sea lamprey (top); a river lamprey (center); and a brook lamprey (bottom).

fresh water. Lampreys are found in cold to cool coastal and inland waters of both the Northern and Southern hemispheres, with the exception of all of Africa but the northwestern tip.

Although individuals within a single lamprey species may be either parasitic or nonparasitic, it is more usual for a species to be exclusively one or the other. When lampreys hatch they develop into small, blind, toothless, almost wormlike larvae called ammocetes, which burrow in the stream bottom. Ammocetes are filter feeders, straining tiny organisms from the water for food. After several years the ammocetes metamorphose, or change, into the adult form. If the species or individual is nonparasitic, the digestive system degenerates and the adult neither feeds nor grows, merely surviving long enough to reproduce. If parasitic, the adult will adhere to the bodies of other fish with its sucking disk and then rasp their flesh to feed on their blood and tissues.

lamp shell   see BRACHIOPOD

Lamy, Jean Baptiste [lah-mee', zhawn bap-teest'] The French missionary Jean Baptiste Lamy, b. Oct. 11, 1814, d. Feb. 13, 1888, was the first Roman Catholic bishop of Santa Fe, N.Mex. After several years of parish work in France, he labored among scattered American Catholics, principally in southern Ohio, until he was sent (1850) to the Southwest as vicar apostolic. He became bishop (1853) and later archbishop (1878) of Santa Fe, a desert diocese with Indian, Spanish, Mexican, and American traditions.

Lan-chou   see LANZHOU

Lanark [lan'-urk]   Lanark is a former county located in south central Scotland. The terrain rises from the Clyde River valley in the north to the hilly southern uplands. The major cities include GLASGOW; the former county town, also named Lanark; and Airdrie. Lanark is Scotland's most industrialized region; shipbuilding and textile, machinery, heavy-metals, and brick manufacturing take place there. During the Middle Ages, Lanark had prosperous market towns. Its growth was assured after the Industrial Revolution because it possessed large reserves of coal and iron and its rivers provided sources of power for the earliest factories. In 1975, during the reorganization of local government in Scotland, Lanark became part of the STRATHCLYDE administrative region.

Lancashire [lank'-uh-shur]   Lancashire is a county in northwestern England along the Irish Sea coast. Its population is 1,381,900 (1988 est.) and the county covers 3,043 km² (1,175 mi²). Lancaster is the county seat. Until 1974, Lancashire included the industrial cities of MANCHESTER and LIVERPOOL and adjoining coal deposits, which made it the most industrialized and populous county in England. In the local government reorganization

of 1974, however, these cities and their surrounds were constituted as separate metropolitan counties. Today Lancashire's principal industrial and commercial centers are Lancaster and Preston. Tourism is important at coastal resorts such as BLACKPOOL.

The Romans established military camps in Lancashire, which subsequently became part of the Anglo-Saxon kingdom of NORTHUMBRIA. The Industrial Revolution made Lancashire the world's leading producer of cotton textiles, a position it held until the end of the 19th century. Since then, the county has suffered an economic decline.

Lancaster (dynasty) [lank'-uh-stur]   Lancaster was the family name of the 15th-century English kings HENRY IV, HENRY V, and HENRY VI, who were descended from JOHN OF GAUNT, duke of Lancaster.

The title earl of Lancaster was first bestowed (1267) on **Edmund Crouchback**, 1245–96, the younger son of HENRY III and brother of King EDWARD I. Edmund's son **Thomas, earl of Lancaster**, c.1277–1322, who possessed vast estates, led the baronial opposition to EDWARD II and dominated the government from 1314 to 1318. Thomas was executed after defeat in the Battle of Boroughbridge (1322), and the title passed to his brother, **Henry**, c.1281–1345. Henry's son, **Henry of Grosmont**, c.1299–1361, was the first duke of Lancaster and an important commander in the HUNDRED YEARS' WAR. John of Gaunt, the fourth son of EDWARD III, acquired the title and the Lancastrian estates by his marriage to Duke Henry's heiress, Blanche.

The house of Lancaster acquired the throne when John's son Henry Bolingbroke overthrew RICHARD II in 1399. Crowned king as Henry IV, he sought legitimacy by claiming that Edmund Crouchback had actually been the elder son of Henry III—a clear fiction. Henry's eldest son, Henry V (r. 1413–22), was outlived by two brothers—John, duke of Bedford (1389–1435) and Humphrey, duke of GLOUCESTER—who played prominent roles during the long minority of Henry V's only son, Henry VI. The latter's rule was finally challenged by the rival royal house of YORK. Henry was overthrown (1461) by the Yorkist EDWARD IV during the Wars of the ROSES, and the Lancastrian line ended with the deaths of Henry VI and his son, Edward, in 1471.

Lancaster (Pennsylvania)   Lancaster, the seat of Lancaster County, is 95 km (60 mi) west of Philadelphia in southeastern Pennsylvania. It has a population of 55,551 (1990). Lancaster is the market center for the surrounding Piedmont plateau, where tobacco, grain, and dairy products are produced. Lancaster also has many small industries engaged in the manufacture of machinery, watches, building materials, and other electrical and metal products. It is the heart of the Pennsylvania Dutch region, and many residents belong to the Amish, Mennonite, and Dunkard sects. Tourists come to farmers' markets and "Wheatland" (1828), the home of President James Buchanan, a national shrine. The city was settled in 1709 and laid out as a town in 1730. From 1799 to 1812 it served as the state capital.

Lancaster, Burt   Burton Stephen Lancaster, b. New York City, Nov. 2, 1913, became in the 1950s a top Hollywood action star in such films as *Gunfight at the OK Corral* (1957). More demanding roles made him a critical success in *From Here to Eternity* (1955), *Elmer Gantry* (1960; Academy Award), and *1900* (1976), among others. In *Atlantic City* (1981) and *Local Hero* (1983) the mature Lancaster seemed at the height of his powers.

Lancaster, Joseph   The British educator Joseph Lancaster, b. Nov. 25, 1778, d. Oct. 24, 1838, was a developer of the monitorial system of education in the era preceding public education. While still in his teens, he began teaching poor children in London. To handle the large number of students his schools attracted, Lancaster had the more advanced pupils teach the others. Eventually 30,000 were enrolled in 95 Lancasterian schools before bankruptcy forced Lancaster to emigrate to the United States in 1818. There he founded schools in several cities before again overspending. Lancasterian schools were an important factor in the growth of mass education.

lancelet   see AMPHIOXUS

Lancelot, Sir   [lans'-uh-laht]   In the medieval stories about King Arthur (see ARTHUR AND ARTHURIAN LEGEND), Sir Lancelot of the Lake (du Lac) was King Arthur's bravest knight. As a baby he was rescued from a lake by Morgan le Fay, who prepared him to receive his surname—Lancelot. He was descended from kings named Galahad and was the father of Sir GALAHAD. When grown, Lancelot superseded Sir GAWAIN as Arthur's champion. In later versions of the legend, Lancelot committed adultery with Queen Guinevere. The legend of Lancelot seems to have originated in ancient Ireland, where he was the Gaelic sun-god of summer, known at Tara as Lugh (Lug) Lamfada.

lancet fish   Lancet fishes, family Alepisauridae, are large, slender-bodied, deep-sea fishes with long, high dorsal fins and large, daggerlike teeth. Two or three species are recognized. The Atlantic lancet fish, *Alepisaurus ferox*, is blackish in color and grows to 2 m (6 ft) long.

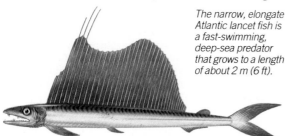

The narrow, elongate Atlantic lancet fish is a fast-swimming, deep-sea predator that grows to a length of about 2 m (6 ft).

land   The term *land* has various uses in different fields. In physical geography it may refer most broadly to the solid part of the Earth's surface. More commonly it refers to the portion of the Earth's surface that lies above sea level and consists of SOIL and ROCK, and to its mineral and other resources.

In economics, land is one of the productive factors, along with labor and capital—a commodity to be employed variously (agriculture, construction, and so on). In law, land is basically treated as a gift of nature; it applies to all natural surface areas that may be defined by boundaries and about which questions of ownership, right of use, inheritance, and so forth can be raised (see PROPERTY; PUBLIC DOMAIN).

Land, Edwin   Edwin Herbert Land, b. May 7, 1909, d. Mar. 1, 1991, was an American scientist and industrialist known for inventing the single-step (one-step) method of developing and printing photographs. As a student at Harvard University he became interested in POLARIZED LIGHT. By the mid-1930s he was able to apply polarization to antiglare automobile headlights, camera filters, reduced-glare sunglasses, and three-dimensional motion pictures. He founded the Polaroid Corporation in 1937.

After World War II, Land developed a camera that took and developed photographs in a single-step process. Known as the Polaroid Land Camera, it was first marketed in 1948. A camera that was able to take color photographs was marketed in 1963. His motion-picture system (Polavision), in which a movie could be viewed almost immediately after being taken, was being sold by 1978. Land also developed a theory of color perception that holds that at least three independent image-forming mechanisms work together to indicate the COLOR seen by the eye.

land-grant colleges   Land-grant colleges are institutions of higher education founded or expanded with the assistance of federal lands granted to the states. The Land-Grant Act of 1862, often called the MORRILL ACT, was introduced by Justin S. Morrill, a Republican congressman and later a senator from Vermont. It offered tracts of federal lands to states as an incentive for establishing college programs in scientific, agricultural, industrial, and military studies. Some states applied the grants to a single institution, others to several institutions. Most of the colleges developed higher-education programs in addition to those required by the act. Awards generally went to public institutions, but in a few cases private colleges such as the Massachusetts Institute of Technology won them. Occasionally a state changed its mind: in Connecticut, after farmer organizations protested the designation of Yale University as the grant recipient, the award was transferred to a state college that later became the University of Connecticut. The second Morrill Act, approved in 1890, continued to support land-grant colleges and required that states practicing racial segregation create black colleges as a precondition to receiving funds. In the 50 states, the District of Columbia, Guam, Puerto Rico, and the Virgin Islands, 72 land-grant colleges and universities have been established.

land reclamation Land reclamation makes inaccessible areas available for human use. Swamps, deserts, and submerged coastal lands are naturally inaccessible; surface mines, waste-disposal sites, and municipal landfills are waste areas created by human activity. Reclaimed land has been used for agriculture, forest, recreation, wildlife, and industrial or residential development.

Reclamation of Naturally Inaccessible Areas

Naturally inaccessible areas are frequently the result of moisture extremes. Wet areas must be either filled in or drained. Drainage (see DRAINAGE SYSTEMS) is accomplished in several ways: by building a system of channels, by laying drainage pipes, and by pumping. Filling in an area requires large quantities of suitable fill material such as sand, which is often obtained by DREDGING adjacent areas. Water is supplied to arid areas either by pumping it from underground sources or by transporting it through an irrigation system.

IRRIGATION of arid lands has been practiced for thousands of years in the Middle East. It has been most intensively developed in Israel, where conduits carry water from the Jordan River and other freshwater sources in northern Israel to the Negev Desert, more than 200 km (125 mi) away.

Reclamation of wetlands has significantly enhanced the well-being of several nations. Over a period of centuries the amount of arable land in the Netherlands has been significantly increased by the construction of dikes, enclosing portions of the shallow coastal waters, which are then drained off. The Zuider Zee project, begun in 1920, and the DELTA PLAN, started in 1958, have included dikes, dams, and a huge, movable storm-surge barrier, creating vast areas of polders (land reclaimed from the sea).

Considerable areas in salt marshes have also been reclaimed in eastern England by constructing embankments that separate the marshes from the sea, and draining the marshes both with ditches inside the embankments and through tidal sluices. Land reclaimed from the sea has such a high salt level that only salt-tolerant vegetation can be planted during the first few years; after several years, however, rain leaches out most of the salt.

An example of large-scale reclamation of freshwater marshes is the drainage in the 1930s of the Pontine Marshes of Italy, a 75,000-ha (195,000-acre) region of dunes and marshes.

Reclamation of wetlands has been less actively pursued in the United States, because such areas are highly productive habitats for fish, shellfish, birds, and wildlife. Reclamation of arid lands, however, has been a major goal of the U.S. Bureau of Reclamation. The Lower Colorado River Project has transformed desert areas, such as the Imperial Valley of California, into some of the most productive cropland in the world.

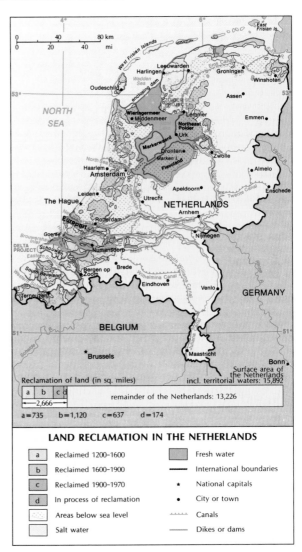

LAND RECLAMATION IN THE NETHERLANDS

Reclamation of land (in sq. miles)

a	b	c d	remainder of the Netherlands: 13,226

←—2,666—→

a = 735   b = 1,120   c = 637   d = 174

Surface area of the Netherlands incl. territorial waters: 15,892

a	Reclaimed 1200–1600	Fresh water
b	Reclaimed 1600–1900	International boundaries
c	Reclaimed 1900–1970	National capitals
d	In process of reclamation	City or town
	Areas below sea level	Canals
	Salt water	Dikes or dams

Nearly 17% of the present surface area of the Netherlands has been recovered from the sea by land-reclamation projects, many of which have been ongoing since the beginning of the 12th century.

Reclamation of Artificially Created Waste Areas

The major problems associated with waste areas that are the result of human activity—industry, mining, and waste disposal (see LANDFILL)—are slope instability, chemical leachates, and soil nutrient deficiencies. Such waste areas occupy only a small fraction of the land area, but they are frequently concentrated in highly populated regions and, in addition to their ugliness, often cause air and water pollution over widespread areas.

Slope instability can be reduced by reshaping the waste areas into landforms with gentler slopes that will conform with the surrounding landscape features. Erosion is prevented through water-control measures and the establishment of a vegetative cover.

The Aberfan disaster in Wales in 1966—in which 170 people, mostly schoolchildren, were killed when a coal-refuse bank collapsed—led to a large reclamation project. The piles of black wastes formerly so common in many of the urban areas of England and Wales have been transformed into landscaped parks and preserves.

Many waste piles of closed mines dot the landscapes of the older coal-mining regions of the United States, particularly in the East. Although most cause serious environmental problems, few have been reclaimed.

Reclamation of Surface-Mined Land. Of much greater magnitude in terms of the amount of land involved are the scars left by surface-mining operations, especially where coal has been mined. Federal and state laws now require the reclamation of land disturbed by strip-mining operations, and a concerted effort is underway to reclaim land disturbed by mining in the past. Mine operators are required to restore surface-mined land by using some or all of the following methods: stockpiling the upper soil layers, segregating and burying potentially toxic material, reshaping the piles to approximately the original contour, respreading the soil, and establishing a vegetative cover.

Reclamation of surface-mined areas in the western United States and Canada is difficult because of the arid climate and, in some cases, high elevations. Nevertheless, surface mining will probably expand rapidly there in the next few decades, not only for coal but also for oil shale and oil sands.

Reclamation of Chemically Polluted Land. Methods used in alleviating problems of chemical pollution vary, depending upon the nature of the chemicals involved. High concentrations of soluble salts can be reduced by leaching the salts from the surface layers of the soil with water. Acidity can be lessened by applying calcium-containing material, such as pulverized limestone, to the soil.

The chemical and physical properties of the waste are sometimes so adverse to plant growth that the only satisfactory reclamation measure is to cover the waste with a thick layer of soil material. In other cases it may be possible to improve conditions by applying another waste material, such as the fuel ash produced by coal-burning electric-generating stations or sewage sludge from municipal treatment plants.

Landfill Reclamation. The most common reclamation problem throughout the world involves the disposal of urban wastes. Although most such wastes are inert or biodegradable and seldom contain hazardous toxic materials, they can constitute public-health problems. Many attempts have been made to reclaim valuable materials from the waste and to produce energy or new products from it; nevertheless, most of it is still disposed of on land. Unfortunately, there is a shortage of suitable landfill sites, especially near large cities (SEE WASTE DISPOSAL SYSTEMS).

In addition to urban wastes, reclamation problems are created by highway and reservoir embankments, pulverized fuel ash, and wastes resulting from the removal and processing of such materials as sand, gravel, building stone, limestone, bauxite, china clay, iron ore, gold, and some heavy metals.

Reclamation usually involves the establishment of vegetation. Selection of species and strains that are tolerant of adverse conditions can reduce site-modification costs and improve the chances for positive results. Success is more likely if lime and fertilizer are incorporated into the upper layers, a seedbed is prepared, seed is drilled into the soil, and a mulch is applied.

Battery Park City, built on a landfill along the Hudson River in New York City, is considered a fine example of urban design.

Landau, Lev [luhn-dow', lef]   One of the most important Soviet scientists of the 20th century, Lev Davidovich Landau, b. Jan. 22 (N.S.), 1908, d. Apr. 1, 1968, made contributions to almost every field of theoretical physics. In 1931, Landau was appointed head of the Ukrainian Physico-Technical Institute of Kharkov, which under his leadership became the center for theoretical physics in the Soviet Union. At Kharkov he also began, in collaboration with his former student E. M. Lifshits, his multivolume treatise on theoretical physics, which even today remains an important work in the field. Landau received many honors in his own country, including the Stalin Prize, the Lenin Prize (1962), and the title Hero of Socialist Labor, but his critical statements outside the field of physics also made him many enemies. He was imprisoned in 1938, and only the personal intervention of the Soviet physicist Peter Kapitza saved him from deportation to a concentration camp. He subsequently received the Nobel Prize in 1962 for his pioneering work on the theory of liquids, especially liquid helium.

Landau's work in low-temperature physics includes a theory of superfluidity of liquid helium and a theoretical description of superconductivity. To solid-state physics Landau contributed the theory of diamagnetism and the theory of phase transitions. In plasma physics, which deals with the study of ionized matter, he gave a description of the motion of a system of charged particles. In astrophysics he predicted in the 1930s the existence of NEUTRON STARS, since confirmed by the discovery of pulsars. He also showed that when the mass of a star depleted of its nuclear fuel is greater than 1.5 solar masses, its material is subjected to pressures that the atomic forces can no longer overcome (see BLACK HOLE).

In nuclear physics Landau did important work on the scattering of mesons by nuclear forces and the scattering of light by mesons. He was also the first to describe how cosmic radiation in the Earth's atmosphere gives rise to electron "avalanches." Landau applied Heisenberg's uncertainty principle to relativistic quantum mechanics, contributed to the description of electron-positron annihilation, and studied quantum effects on the motion of electrons and mesons.

In 1962, Landau was severely injured in a car accident and was declared clinically dead several times. He lived until April 1968 but performed no further scientific work.

landfill   The sanitary landfill provides a way of safely disposing of solid wastes in a controlled manner. The landfill site is lined with an impermeable material such as clay, and soil is used to surround and contain the waste materials. Municipal solid wastes—the garbage collected from households—and, at times, certain industrial and agricultural wastes are spread in layers and compacted by heavy bulldozers to reduce their volume. At least once every 24 hours, a thin layer of soil (a minimum of 15 cm/6 in. in thickness) is spread on top of the compacted waste and is itself compacted before more waste is added. When the mound reaches a certain height, it is covered with a thicker layer of soil (at least 60 cm/2 ft thick) and is then revegetated. The water table under the site must be at least 2 m (6 ft) deep and the site not subject to flooding. Soils vary greatly in their ability to contain and renovate the ordinary decomposition products of solid waste, so only a small proportion of potential sites are suitable for use as sanitary landfills.

The decomposition of organic wastes generates biogas, a mixture of methane and carbon dioxide. A number of U.S. landfill sites are equipped to collect the gas, which can serve as a source of energy and be used to generate electricity.

The heterogeneousness of the material in landfills causes uneven settlement of the mound, and ordinarily a closed landfill cannot be used as a building site. It may be reclaimed, however, for recreational use.

Many of the nation's landfills have reached their capacities and were forced to close by the early 1990s. Today large incinerators have replaced landfills in many municipalities. Incinerators also have drawbacks, however, principally hazardous exhaust gases and a highly toxic ash, the final product of waste burning.

In the future it may be possible to reduce the total amount of solid waste requiring disposal. Metal, glass, paper, and many kinds of plastic are starting to be recycled (see RECYCLING OF MATERIALS) in more and more communities.

See also: POLLUTION, ENVIRONMENTAL; WASTE DISPOSAL SYSTEMS.

landform evolution   Landform evolution is a concept describing how landforms in various geographic settings change with the passage of time. Schemes of landform evolution have been worked out for areas that are humid, arid, or glacial, or for the alternation of two or more types of climate. Such schemes must also take into account the roles of crustal movements and mountain building

Effects of Humid Climates.   In humid areas where the Earth's crust remains stable for long periods of geologic time, cycles of EROSION AND SEDIMENTATION, driven largely by the action of running water, are thought to climax in creation of a low, featureless land surface. Such surfaces were named peneplains by the American geomorphologist William M. DAVIS. In areas where the crust is unstable and the land surface is rising while simultaneously being eroded, topographic relief caused by incising streams (see RIVER AND STREAM) becomes accentuated under conditions of prolonged humidity for as long as uplift continues. A ridge-ravine (selva) topography results, which resembles Davis's "mature" developmental stage. Individual hillslopes, beneath vegetal cover, tend to be shaped by gravity erosion and solutional effects of percolating GROUNDWATER, and thus incline toward watercourses. Landform evolution substantially slows down when a balance is reached between erosion and deposition.

Effects of Arid Climates.   In DESERT regions steady-state landforms tend to be represented by erosional plains (pediplains) and surfaces of alluviation generated by running water, which may be modified locally by formation of sand dunes and other features created by wind erosion and deposition. Such areas are found in parts of the Sahara and Australian deserts. Desert running water eventually evaporates and deposits sediment rather than eroding and extending drainage systems. Individual hillslopes in deserts tend to be worn back and down by a combination of gravity erosion and, where barren, by sheetwash erosion.

Effects of Climate Change.   Widespread changes in climate during the Quaternary, or most recent period of geologic time, restrict areas of possible steady-state landform evolution to little more than 10 percent of the Earth's land surface. In fact, landform evolution over most of the Earth has proceeded under a variety of alternating climates, and therefore tendencies toward steady-state morphologies are periodically interrupted, producing an array of polygenetic landforms. Valley cutting under humid conditions may give way to valley alluviation and pedimentation under aridity (see ALLUVIAL FANS), only to result in dissection of the alluvial deposits when humid conditions return and streamflow is renewed. Resulting landscapes often exhibit stair-stepped terrain that reflects alternating planation and valley deepening, as in the southern Ozark region of the United States.

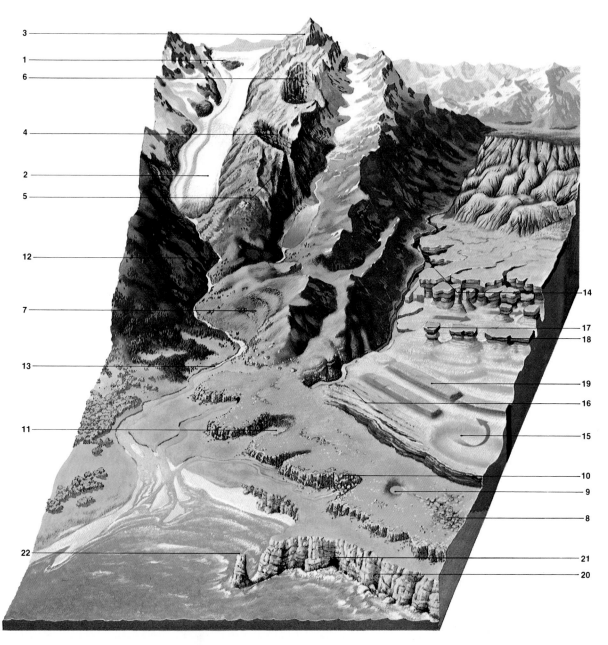

Processes of erosion, or the wearing away of land surfaces by ice, water, and wind, and of deposition have sculptured the land into various shapes called landforms. In mountainous areas, mass movements of ice caps (1) and glaciers (2) have abraded and carved out pyramidal peaks (3), hanging valleys (4), truncated spurs (5), and cirques (6), or bowl-shaped depressions. The impact of rain on surfaces with no protective vegetative cover causes slopewash (7), whereas the chemical action of rain and dissolved carbon dioxide on limestone results in grikes (8), or grooved surfaces, swallow holes (9), chasms (10), and dry valleys (11). A rapidly flowing river erodes its bed vertically and laterally (12) first to form steep and then wide river valleys (13) and canyons (14). Winds blowing across dry land create basinlike depressions, or deflation hollows (15). The sandblasting action of windblown soil particles may smooth pebbles and rocks and then fit them together closely to form a continuous layer, or desert pavement (16), or may abrade the base of a small rock mass to form a pedestal, or mushroom rock (17). It may also abrade larger rock masses to form zuegens (18), or may excavate long passageways between deeply undercut overhanging ridges, or yardangs (19). Along coastlines, wave action may result in cliffs (20), caves (21), and stacks (22).

The long-term evolution of terrain developed under changing climate may be determined by the intensity and duration of the various climate types. Thus, in a setting such as the North American High Plains, planation, or flattening, may eventually dominate and generate a plain, even with sporadic episodes of gully cutting. Alternatively, valley cutting may predominate despite sporadic intervals of alluviation, as recently occurred in west-central Tennessee.

Effects of Glaciation. Glacial conditions (see GLACIER AND GLACIATION), as in Antarctica and Greenland, may dominate landform evolution. More commonly, in the lower latitudes, they may alternate with humid or arid conditions. Thus, valley cutting under humid conditions occasionally gives way to ice scour and drift deposition (see DRIFT, GLACIAL). Drainage systems are periodically disrupted in this fashion, and isolated glacial depressions often contain lakes that may gradually fill with sediment and evolve into swamps (see SWAMP, MARSH, AND BOG) and then prairies (see LAKE, GLACIAL). Northern portions of North America and Eurasia show many landforms that are products of alternating glaciation and aridity or humidity.

Effects of Crustal Movements and Volcanism. Effects of various types of crustal movement and volcanism (see VOLCANO) can be imposed on those of climate to determine landform evolution. MOUNTAIN landforms commonly evolve in response to a combination of climatic effects and those of rock deformation. In newly formed mountains, the effect of climate may be slight. At lower latitudes, developing mountains initially experience arid or humid climates, but uplift to great elevations may induce sculpture by alpine glaciers.

Ultimately, not only climate but also the way rocks are deformed governs landform evolution in mountains. In mountains formed by collisions between continents (see PLATE TECTONICS), a mountain root is formed, which maintains the mountainous elevations in an isostatic crustal relationship. Erosion of the rising root eventually reduces such mountains to lower and lower levels. If uplift is not renewed, after the passage of many millions of years a plain begins to form.

Mountains that develop on the edge of an OCEANIC TRENCH, as in the case of the Andes, evolve in a characteristic way. Subduction of the crust near such trenches adds new volcanic rock to the mountain root and crestal peaks, thereby offsetting the effects of erosion.

Coastal Landform Evolution. Coastal landforms (see BEACH AND COAST) evolve in response to the exposure of shoreline rocks to erosion by waves and currents and to sediment accumulation. Deltas form and enlarge at river mouths as a result of the high influx of sediment that accompanies the onset of humid conditions on land. On the other hand, they are destroyed by marine erosion as sediment influx wanes. Sand beaches grow and dwindle largely in response to the same cycle. Shaping of coastal outlines and bedrock exposures varies with worldwide changes in sea level, which interrupt the normal cycles of evolution.

Landini, Francesco [lahn-dee'-nee, frahn-ches'-koh] Francesco Landini, b. *c.*1325, d. Sept. 2, 1397, was the most celebrated Italian poet-musician of the 14th century. Blinded at an early age by smallpox, he turned to music as a youth. He became the leading organist in Florence and was noted for his skill at the portative organ. Often compared in versatility and genius to his French contemporary Guillaume de MACHAUT, Landini wrote many of the texts he later set to music. Of his 154 preserved compositions, 140 are *ballate* and the rest are madrigals and *cacce*. Landini's music is characterized by free-flowing melody, consonant harmony, and technical refinement and sophistication.

Landis, Kenesaw Mountain Kenesaw Mountain Landis, b. Millville, Ohio, Nov. 20, 1866, d. Nov. 25, 1944, was an American judge (1905–22) and commissioner of professional baseball from 1921 until his death. As U.S. district judge for northern Illinois he fined (1907) Standard Oil of Indiana $29,240,000 for illegal rebates. Although the fine was overturned on appeal, Landis's harsh treatment of the corrupt company was very popular. Appointed baseball commissioner after the bribery scandals of 1919, in which the Chicago White Sox allegedly lost the World Series intentionally, he restored baseball's integrity. Upon his death a special committee elected him to the Baseball Hall of Fame.

landlord   see LEASE; TENANT

Landon, Alf Alfred Mossman Landon, b. West Middlesex, Pa., Sept. 9, 1887, d. Oct. 12, 1987, was a key figure in the U.S. Republican party in the 1930s and ran unsuccessfully for president in 1936. "Alf" Landon first entered the national political arena in 1912, campaigning for Theodore Roosevelt, who was the Progressive party candidate for president. Landon continued to be associated with progressive politics within the Republican party. In 1932 he was elected governor of Kansas, and two years later he was the only incumbent Republican governor to be reelected in a Democratic landslide. This success made Landon a strong candidate to oppose President Franklin D. Roosevelt in 1936. Although he won 17,000,000 votes, Landon carried only Maine and Vermont. Following his defeat Landon retired from national politics. His daughter Nancy Landon Kassebaum was elected U.S. senator from Kansas in 1978 and reelected in 1984 and 1990.

Landor, Walter Savage The English poet and essayist Walter Savage Landor, b. Warwick, Jan. 30, 1775, d. Sept. 17, 1864, won renown for his lengthy prose work, *Imaginary Conversations* (1824–53)—a series of 152 dialogues between celebrated writers, statesmen, and philosophers of ancient and modern times. His early poetry includes the epic *Gebir* (1798) and the verse drama *Count Julian* (1812). During a writing career that spanned 68 years Landor produced many fine short poems and epigrams that are terse, polished expressions of intense feeling. His violent republican beliefs made him an outcast from English society, and he lived in Spain and Italy for much of his life.

Landowska, Wanda   The harpsichordist and pianist Wanda Landowska, b. Warsaw, July 5, 1877, d. Aug. 16, 1959, was the leading figure in the 20th-century revival of the harpsichord and was particularly admired for her interpretations of Bach. She started her career as a pianist in 1891. She made her debut as harpsichordist in 1903 in Paris and first performed in the United States in 1923. In Saint-Len-la-Forêt, near Paris, she established (1925) a world-famous school for the study of early music. During World War II she settled permanently in the United States.

Landrum-Griffin Act   see LABOR-MANAGEMENT REPORTING AND DISCLOSURE ACT

Land's End   Land's End, a peninsula in Cornwall, is the westernmost point of England. Spectacular granite cliffs looming more than 20 m (60 ft) above the water make Land's End a popular tourist attraction. A lighthouse completed in 1797 warns ships of the many rocky reefs located offshore.

Landsat   Landsat, formerly Earth Resources Technology Satellite (ERTS), is a series of U.S. satellites designed to observe the Earth's surface in different regions of the electromagnetic spectrum. Their applications include forecasting crop production around the world, assisting in soil and forestry management, locating energy and mineral resources, and assessing urban population densities.

Landsat 1 (launched July 23, 1972; turned off January 1978), *Landsat 2* (Jan. 22, 1975; turned off February 1982), and *Landsat 3* (Mar. 5, 1978; turned off March 1983) provided a total of more than 1 million pictures. On July 16, 1982, *Landsat 4* was launched into an orbit that brought it over the same point on Earth every 16 days, and on Mar. 1, 1984, *Landsat 5* was sent into a circular polar orbit.

Each of the first three Landsats carried a Multi-Spectral Scanner (MSS) and a Return Beam Vidicom (RBV) camera system. The MSS "sees" the Earth in the green, red, and infrared spectral regions. It relays signals to Earth or to Tracking and Data Relay Satellites (TDRS; see TRACKING STATION), or stores them for later sending. The MSS has a resolution of 70 m (230 ft). The RBV is a backup sensor that distinguishes objects as small as 100 m (330 ft). The next two Landsats also carried a Thematic Mapper (TM), a device that scans in seven narrower spectral bands and provides nearly three times the resolution of the MSS.

Landsats are the property of the federal government. In 1984 their management was transferred to a private firm, the Earth Observational Satellite Company (EOSAT), a joint venture of RCA Corporation and Hughes Aircraft Company. In 1979 federal responsibility for and financial support of the satellites was transferred from the National Aeronautics and Space Administration (NASA) to the National Oceanographic and Atmospheric Administration (NOAA). NOAA felt that land surveys did not belong within its purview and tried to end Landsat funding in 1989, an attempt that was blocked by the Bush administration.

The first color photomosaic of the continental United States was compiled from 569 individual cloud-free photographs taken by an orbiting Landsat satellite. The Landsats, a series of spacecraft that transmit data to Earth-based stations, were launched by NASA but are now controlled by a private company.

landscape architecture

landscape architecture The art of landscape architecture is almost as old as that of architecture itself. In ancient Egypt, Mesopotamia, and Persia, immense efforts were devoted to creating verdant enclosures for temples and palaces, of which the most famous were the "Hanging Gardens" of Babylon, a complex of irrigated terraces erected *c*.605 BC by Nebuchadnezzar II (see MESOPOTAMIA; EGYPT, ANCIENT; PERSIAN ART AND ARCHITECTURE).

Ornamental horticulture first flourished in imperial Roman times in suburban villas around Rome. Excavations at Pompeii have also revealed formal courtyard gardens. The Romans seem to have regarded their gardens as unroofed living spaces and treated them as integral parts of domestic architecture.

The ancient tradition of the pleasure garden persisted in medieval Arab civilization (see MOORISH ART AND ARCHITECTURE). Some of the greatest Moorish gardens of Spain have partially survived at the Alhambra and Generalife palaces, dating from the 13th century, where plantings, fountains, pools, and canals occupy the richly decorated courtyards. In northern Europe tiny, formally planted, walled gardens containing bathing pools and marble tables provided settings for courtly life.

Italy. During the Italian Renaissance eminent architects took up the design of gardens under the patronage of the nobility and the popes. For Giovanni de'Medici (see MEDICI family), MICHELOZZO built one of the first great hillside villas with terraced gardens, at Fiesole, overlooking Florence, in 1458. The Medicis were also responsible for the most extensive gardens of Florence, the Boboli, which they developed over the course of 150 years behind the Pitti Palace.

By the latter half of the 16th century, Rome and its environs contained the finest achievements of Renaissance landscape architecture with gardens such as those of the Villa Medici, built about 1580, and the Villa d'Este at Tivoli, designed by Pirro Ligorio and begun *c*.1550. They combine formal beds, sculpture galleries, woodlands, and flowing water on hillside terraces. During the baroque period in Italy, complex patterns of planting and varied combinations of plant types became popular.

France. In 16th-century France the large terraces of Renaissance gardens were dominated by parterres, interlaced designs of low, clipped evergreens and flowers or colored earths; and by topiary, bushes trimmed in animal shapes. *Parterres de broderie*, or "embroidery plantings"—extremely complex, curvilinear patterns in dwarf evergreens and low-growing flowers—were identified with French gardens. Under Louis XIV, French gardeners began to work on a grander scale and in closer relationship with architecture. The foremost landscape architect of this time was André LE NÔTRE. At the Palace of VERSAILLES, he laid out a vast expanse of basins, fountains, parterres, and woodland alleys along a broad central axis whose terminus was the horizon.

French 18th-century garden design responded to English naturalism with romantic woodland landscapes dotted with grottos and pseudo-antique ruins. Perhaps the most famous garden complex of this type was the *Hameau* built at Versailles in 1782 for Marie Antoinette—an informal replica of a rustic farm.

England. English Renaissance gardens were characterized by intricate "knots" (a form of parterre), elaborate topiary, mazes, and areas of clipped lawn. Gardens such as those of HAMPTON COURT retained some of the intimacy of medieval gardens while incorporating Italian and French elements of design. By the late 17th century, however, a reaction against formal gardens had occurred.

In the 1740s the painter and architect William KENT produced a compromise between the formal, restricted garden and natural scenery, coordinating vistas of buildings, replicas of classical temples, and trees in the grounds of Stowe (1736), Rousham (1738–41), and

(Right) *The "natural" landscape of Blenheim Palace, designed during the late 18th century by Capability Brown, replaced the formal gardens created earlier by Benjamin Wise with carefully planned lakes, meadows, and groves.* (Below) *The sunken gardens adjoining London's Kensington Palace, a symmetrical arrangement of flower beds and lawns, contrast with the less formal gardens surrounding the palace grounds.*

(Above) *The gardens of the Château de Chenonceaux, influenced by the court style, form a brocade of elegant parterres.*
(Left) *Exquisite parterres of clipped shrubbery and flowers in the gardens at Versailles, designed by André Le Nôtre, contribute to the splendor of Louis XIV's palace.*

Kensington Gardens (*c.*1744). Many landowners then took up the style.

The idea of the natural garden reached complete expression in the work of a professional gardener, "Capability" BROWN. Brown's characteristic landscape design, applied throughout a long career that began in 1749, consisted of an irregular belt of trees surrounding the property; a curving walk providing views of the landscape; small clumps of trees irregularly placed about the lawn; and an expanse of water created by the damming of a stream.

Sir Uvedale Price, in his *An Essay on the Picturesque* (1794), asserted that Brown's theory of beauty was inappropriate to landscape gardening and advocated another quality, the "picturesque," which was rough, irregular, and strong in contrasts. Price felt that the gardener, instead of imposing a pattern on nature, should examine each site individually and work with its peculiarities, articulating and extending existing features while leaving the ground covered with rocks and weeds. This theory was partially applied by Humphry REPTON, who, with the architect John NASH, produced a celebrated series of castles and Italianate villas in picturesque settings.

In the 1880s, William Robinson (1838–1935) created the naturalistic flower garden of undulating perennial borders and woodland plantings of bulbs. His ideas were developed by Gertrude Jekyll (1843–1942) around the turn of the century, often with extraordinary effects of texture and color in very small gardens.

The United States. In the United States during the mid-19th century, the tradition of formal gardening gave way to natural landscaping in the manner of Repton. This development was primarily due to the influence of Andrew Jackson DOWNING, whose gardens, intended to provide settings for picturesque country houses, consisted of irregularly grouped trees of varying heights, massed flowers, undulating contours, and curving walks and lakes.

The English tradition, as interpreted by Downing, was the inspiration for the great public parks laid out by Frederick Law OLMSTED in the second half of the 19th century. Olmsted's greatest work, New York's Central Park, begun

in 1857, is a varied yet harmonious landscape of woods, meadows, lakes, and formal precincts dotted with pavilions and monuments: an ideal rural landscape in the center of the city.

The most notable landscape architecture of the 20th century is to be found in California. Many of the most characteristic of these were designed in the 1940s and '50s by Thomas Church. More recently, Lawrence Halprin has devised a dramatic landscaping technique at the California coastal development Sea Ranch, begun in 1962, and has revived the tradition of the water garden.

See also: FOUNTAIN; GARDEN.

landscape painting Landscape elements played almost no part in Western painting until panoramas of nature began to appear in Roman wall painting of the late 1st century BC. One of two surviving examples from this period, the *Odyssey Landscapes* (Museo Profano, The Vatican), gives a panoramic account of the adventures of Odysseus in eight compartments subdivided by pilasters. In the murals called *View of a Garden* (Villa Livia, Primaporta, Italy), the artist dispensed with the architectural framework to portray a lovely garden. Despite these early efforts, landscape painting did not achieve a prominent place in Western art until the mid-14th century.

In the great Eastern civilizations, on the other hand, a religious and mystical devotion to nature accorded landscape a leading role in painting. The era of the Tang and Song dynasties in China (*c.*618–1279) produced superb landscape views, particularly those by the great landscapist Fan Kuan in the late 10th and early 11th centuries. Landscape was also a primary element in Islamic art (see ISLAMIC ART AND ARCHITECTURE)—for example, in *Landscape Mosaic* (715; The Great Mosque, Damascus, Syria), in manuscript illuminations such as *Two Warriors Fighting in a Landscape* (1396; British Museum, London), and in *Summer Landscape*, from the famous *Album of the Conqueror* (15th century; Topkapi Palace Museum, Istanbul).

In European painting, landscape began to assume a more independent aspect from the first half of the 14th century. Ambrogio Lorenzetti's *Good and Bad Government* frescoes (1338–40; Palazzo Pubblico, Siena, Italy) and Simone MARTINI's frescoed *Guidoriccio da Fogliano* (1328; Palazzo Pubblico, Siena) contain the first landscape vistas seen in Western art since the Roman era. The LIMBOURG BROTHERS' series of views of life in nature in *Les Très Riches Heures du Duc de Berry* (*c*.1416; Musée Condé, Chantilly, France) unite landscape with architectural interiors and exteriors and display the first snow landscape in European painting. During the Renaissance, the study of PERSPECTIVE gave rise to further experimentation with landscape as a backdrop for human endeavors—the atmospheric settings of LEONARDO DA VINCI being a prime example. In some of the works by Venetian Renaissance painters, such as Giovanni Bellini's (see BELLINI family) *Saint Francis in Ecstasy* (*c*.1485; Frick Collection, New York City) and GIORGIONE's *The Tempest* (*c*.1505; Galleria dell'Accademia, Venice), the masterful pastoral vistas seem to overshadow the human characters.

In northern Europe, 15th-century Flemish artists had already established a tradition of meticulously detailed landscapes. After he visited (1494–95) Venice, Albrecht DÜRER produced landscape watercolors such as his *Alpine Landscape* (1495; Ashmolean Museum, Oxford, England). Dürer's landscapes, in turn, influenced the Danube valley painter Albrecht ALTDORFER, whose *Danube*

The power and beauty of the wilderness, a theme prevalent in German landscapes, was first expressed by Albrecht Altdorfer. Danube Landscape near Regensburg (c.1520–25) epitomizes the dramatic chiaroscuro and detail characteristic of Altdorfer's work. (Alte Pinakothek, Munich.)

Landscape near Regensburg (*c*.1520–25; Alte Pinakothek, Munich) is often called the first pure landscape painting in Western art. During the same period, Pieter Bruegel the Elder (see BRUEGEL family) was incorporating detailed views of fields and forests into diagonally organized compositions whose landscape planes unfold into the distance.

The merging of the Venetian and local traditions produced the unrivaled pictorial realism of 17th-century Dutch landscape painting, in which landscape for the first time emerged as one of the most influential forces in art. Jan van GOYEN's naturalistically painted scenes of canals, harbors, riverbanks, and winter recreation represent a revolutionary move away from pure detail and toward atmospheric effects and spatial breadth. The influence of Goyen is manifest in the dynamic, imaginative compositions of Jacob van RUISDAEL, whose *Jewish Graveyard* (one version *c*.1660; State Picture Gallery, Dresden) is one of the masterpieces of landscape art, and in the works of Meindert HOBBEMA, whose work profoundly influenced 18th- and 19th-century English landscape painting.

In France an idealized style of landscape painting that contrasted greatly with the naturalistic vein of Dutch art

Traveling amid Mountains and Streams, *a landscape scroll by the Chinese artist Fan Kuan, who flourished during the late 10th and early 11th centuries under the Song dynasty (960–1279), reflects the yin-yang principle of complementary opposites. (National Palace Museum, Taipei.)*

Hunters in the Snow (1565), by the Flemish artist Peter Bruegel the Elder, represents January in his series of landscapes devoted to the months of the year. The effect of deep space is enhanced by the pronounced diagonal that starts with the dogs and men in the lower left corner, extends down the steep hill with the row of trees, continues across the frozen ponds and through the village, and ends with the towering alpine crags at the upper right. (Kunsthistorisches Museum, Vienna.)

(Below) *Paul Cézanne's* Landscape with Viaduct: Mont Sainte-Victoire (c. 1885–87) *exemplifies the monumental and increasingly abstract forms in his topographical paintings of the late 19th century. (Metropolitan Museum of Art, New York City.)*

Albert Bierstadt, in The Rocky Mountains (1863), *sought to convey the beauty and grandeur of the American West. (Metropolitan Museum of Art, New York City.)*

evolved during the 17th century. Supreme masters of the idealized landscape were Claude LORRAIN, who executed serene pastoral scenes, and Nicolas POUSSIN, who set heroic scenes from antiquity in carefully structured landscapes.

Idealized pastoral scenes remained in vogue in the 18th century—in the paintings of Antoine WATTEAU and Thomas GAINSBOROUGH, for example—but toward the end of that century a new school of landscapists emerged in Britain, inaugurated by Gainsborough and Thomas GIRTIN, who was among the first to do naturalistic landscapes in watercolor. British landscape painting reached its peak in the early-19th-century works of John CONSTABLE and J. M. W. TURNER, who introduced a romantic and dramatic note to views of mountains and seas.

With the possible exception of German artist Caspar David FRIEDRICH, whose mystical and pantheistic landscapes represent an isolated and unique achievement, every important landscapist of the 19th century owed some debt to the British romantics, including the members of the American HUDSON RIVER SCHOOL (c.1825–75) and the French landscapists of the BARBIZON SCHOOL (c.1830–70). The French trend toward painting directly from nature, which was greatly advanced by the painterly landscapes of Camille COROT, eventually gave rise to IMPRESSIONISM and thus altered radically the entire course of Western art. The stylized landscapes of Japanese art also contributed to the birth of impressionism (see JAPANESE ART AND ARCHITECTURE).

Early in this century, innovative movements such as FAUVISM and CUBISM explored abstracted depictions of landscape, most of which reflect the impact of Paul CÉZANNE. Later, surrealists such as Salvador DALÍ created fantasy landscapes populated with nightmarish figures. At the opposite end of the artistic spectrum, Andrew WYETH and other American painters sought to render nature in photographic detail.

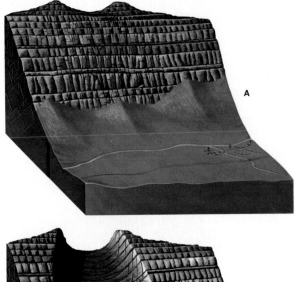

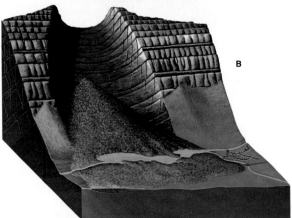

Landseer, Sir Edwin [lan'-seer] The English painter Sir Edwin Henry Landseer, b. Mar. 7, 1802, d. Oct. 1, 1873, was a renowned Victorian artist particularly admired for his animal subjects. Landseer became an associate of the Royal Academy in 1826 and a fellow in 1831. He was knighted in 1850 and became the favorite artist of Queen Victoria for such works as his popular *Monarch of the Glen* (1851; Dewar House, London). In 1858, however, he suffered a mental breakdown from which he never fully recovered. His four monumental bronze lions in Trafalgar Square, London, the result of one of his last bursts of creative energy, were put in place in January 1867. Although Landseer's anthropomorphic animal paintings may seem overly sentimental, the faultless technique is clearly evident; his small oil studies and his drawings, among the finest of the 19th century, reveal his superlative draftsmanship.

---

landslide and avalanche [av'-uh-lanch] Landslides and avalanches are massive gravitational movements of slope-forming materials. The term *landslide* is restricted to movement of rock and soil and includes a broad range of velocities, even slow movements that, although rarely a direct hazard to life, can destroy buildings or break buried utility lines. The term *avalanche* includes movement of snow and ice as well as rock and soil materials and applies only to movements rapid enough to threaten life.

Landslides. A landslide occurs when a portion of hillslope becomes too weak to support its own weight. The weakness is generally initiated when rainfall or some other source of water increases the water content of the slope, reducing the shear strength of the materials. Earthquakes also cause landslides. Landslides are especially common in areas of active erosion (see EROSION AND

One of the best-known landslides in history occurred in Alberta, Canada, on Apr. 19, 1903. An estimated 31 million m³ (40 million yd³) of limestone rock suddenly slid down between two peaks of Turtle Mountain (A, B). The sliding mass buried part of the town of Frank below, killing 70 persons; it also dammed the river forming a new lake. Coal excavation shafts had undermined the underlying rock foundation. Joints, or cracks, along the steep 50° sloping face had opened and fragmented the rock. An earthquake that had occurred two years before the fall had further loosened the rock fragments. Within the joints water from melting snows was frozen by a sudden cold spell, forcing the rock apart and starting the slide.

SEDIMENTATION). Many types of landslides move seasonally or sporadically and may lie dormant for years. Slow-moving landslides are distinguished from creep by having distinct boundaries with adjacent stable ground. Ground that is stable in its natural state may slide after human alteration. Grading for roads or buildings on hillsides facilitates landsliding, both by cutting into the slope—removing support from materials higher up the slope—and by overloading the slope below with the excavated materials. Many damaging landslides occur where development alters natural slopes or groundwater conditions, especially within dormant landslide masses that are barely stable in their natural state.

Landslides are generally classified into slides, falls, and flows. Slides move as largely coherent bodies by slippage along one or more failure surfaces. Falls of rock or soil originate on cliffs or steep slopes. Large rockfalls can be catastrophic events. An earthquake off the coast of Peru in 1970 started a rockfall from the northwest peak of HUASCARÁN. The descending mass, which incorporated material as it accelerated to more than 280 km/h (170 mph), buried more than 18,000 people.

Flows are landslides that behave as fluids. Many varieties are recognized. MUDFLOWS involve wet mud and debris. Earthflows involve wet clayey material. Slow earthflows are tongues of material up to hundreds of meters long that commonly move only a few meters a year. They are abundant on clayey hillslopes such as those in the California Coast Ranges. Rapid earthflows, in contrast, occur on very gentle slopes in sensitive silts and clays, as along Rivière Blanche, Quebec. A large, rapid flow of dry loess (wind-deposited silt) accompanying an earthquake (1920) in Gansu Province, China, killed 100,000 people. A rockfall avalanche is a form of dry flow in which enormous rockfalls flow rapidly for kilometers across gentle slopes. Rockfall avalanche deposits are also recognized on the Moon.

Avalanches. Snow avalanches are caused by the added weight of fresh snow or by gradual weakening of older snow. They are often triggered by the weight of a skier or the impact of small masses of snow or ice falling from above. Snow avalanches are a major danger in high mountain areas. In the Dolomites of Italy during World War I, 6,000 troops were killed in a single day by snow avalanches.

Two principal types of snow avalanche are distinguished. A loose snow avalanche gathers more and more snow as it descends a mountainside. A slab avalanche consists of more compact, cohesive snow and ice that breaks away from the slope in a discrete mass, much like a block-glide landslide; this type is responsible for the great majority of accidents.

Prevention and Damage Limitation. A number of methods are employed to prevent landslides, such as the capture and drainage of water before it reaches the potential slide area; the pumping of water from wells in the slide area; and the filling in of cracks that could be pervaded by precipitation or surface water. Damage to buildings and other structures is averted by conducting thorough examinations of the geology of construction sites before building begins and through the design and construction of earthworks.

The avalanche danger of unstable slope accumulations is reduced or prevented through detonation, by either launching grenadelike explosives or shooting artillery shells at the slope.

◼

Landsteiner, Karl [lahnt'-shty-nur]   The Austrian-American physician Karl Landsteiner, b. June 14, 1868, d. June 26, 1943, was a pioneer in the field of blood chemistry. His work led to the discovery of all four major blood groups (A, B, AB, and O), paving the way for the

safe use of blood transfusions. He was awarded the 1930 Nobel Prize for physiology or medicine. In 1940 he helped discover the Rh factor in blood.

◼

Lane, Fitz Hugh   The works of the American seascape painter Fitz Hugh Lane, b. Gloucester, Mass., Dec. 18, 1804, d. Aug. 13, 1865, are outstanding in the American movement now called LUMINISM. In his paintings of shore sites near his native Gloucester and on the coast of Maine, Lane sought to convey the purity of the air and the brilliance of the light while also retaining the distinctness and clarity of objects. Lane was crippled from infancy onward and confined to a wheelchair. Therefore, the vistas of his beautifully composed scenes are limited, enhancing the sense of almost magical concentration. An example is *Owl's Head, Penobscot Bay, Maine* (1862; Museum of Fine Arts, Boston).

◼

Lane, James Henry   James Henry Lane, b. Lawrenceburg, Ind., June 22, 1814, d. July 11, 1866, became known in U.S. history as the "liberator" of Kansas. As a U.S. congressman from Indiana (1853–55), he voted for the KANSAS-NEBRASKA ACT. Moving to Kansas, he presided over the Topeka convention (1855) that framed a free-state constitution and commanded the free-state militia in the ensuing guerrilla war against proslavery forces.

When Kansas was finally granted statehood under the free-state Wyandotte constitution, Lane became (1861) one of its U.S. senators. During the Civil War, he led the "Kansas brigade" in western Missouri and raised one of the first African-American regiments in the Union Army.

◼

Lanfranc [lan'-frank]   Appointed archbishop of Canterbury in 1070, Lanfranc of Bec, b. Pavia, c.1005, d. May 24, 1089, was a theologian and church reformer. Lanfranc defended the eucharistic doctrine of the church against Berengar of Tours.

In 1063, William, duke of Normandy, appointed Lanfranc abbot of St. Stephen in Caen. After William's conquest of England and assumption of the English crown as WILLIAM I, Lanfranc became archbishop of Canterbury. As archbishop he was particularly noted for his moral reform of the English clergy, for his strengthening of the monasteries, for the establishment of ecclesiastical courts, and for the transfer of sees from the towns to important cities.

◼

Lang, Andrew   Andrew Lang, b. Selkirk, Scotland, Mar. 31, 1844, d. July 20, 1912, was a journalist, translator, and poet but is best known as a folklorist and writer of fairy tales. In 1889 he published *The Blue Fairy Book*, an anthology of fairy tales for children. Lang responded to the immediate popularity of his book by producing a new collection of children's stories annually through 1913, among them *The Yellow Fairy Book*, *The Red Fairy Book*, and *The Green Fairy Book*. Lang was also known for his literary criticism and his *History of English Literature*

(1912). He collaborated with other scholars in the translations of Homer's *Odyssey* (1879) and *Iliad* (1883).

Lang, Fritz A long and distinguished career in Germany made Fritz Lang, b. Vienna, Dec. 5, 1890, d. Aug. 2, 1976, probably the most famous of the many European film directors who fled Hitler for Hollywood during the 1930s. Lang's early studies of painting and architecture clearly influenced the expressionist style and grand scale of such films as *Destiny* (1921), the two-part *Nibelung Saga* (1924), and his celebrated depiction of a futuristic slave society, *Metropolis* (1927). During the same period Lang was also making smaller-scaled studies of criminal society in *Dr. Mabuse the Gambler* (1922), *The Spy* (1928), and *The Last Will of Dr. Mabuse* (1932). Lang's interest in the criminal mind produced his masterpiece—the chilling portrait of a child killer, *M* (1931), his first sound film. Lang left Germany for France in 1933.

Lang made a highly successful American debut with *Fury* (1936), an indictment of mob violence, followed by a plea for social justice in *You Only Live Once* (1937). These films gave way to a succession of melodramas, most notably *The Ministry of Fear* (1944), *The Woman in the Window* (1944), and *Scarlet Street* (1945), that painted a picture of society less in terms of social issues than of a nameless, oppressive sense of dread. These expressionist nightmares, along with *M*, constitute the height of Lang's achievement. Thereafter, although he directed an offbeat Western in *Rancho Notorious* (1952), a first-rate police thriller in *The Big Heat* (1953), and a stylish costume drama in *Moonfleet* (1955), his films were of diminishing interest.

Langdell, Christopher Columbus [lang'-dul] Christopher Columbus Langdell, b. New Boston, N.H., May 22, 1826, d. July 6, 1906, was an American legal educator who originated the case-study method for teaching law. As dean of the Harvard Law School from 1870 to 1895, he transformed legal education by introducing required courses and examinations. His students became familiar with legal principles by studying important judicial decisions. His method eventually became standard law-school procedure.

Langdon, John [lang'-duhn] John Langdon, b. Portsmouth, N.H., June 5, 1741, d. Sept. 18, 1819, was a political leader in New Hampshire during and after the American Revolution. He represented his state at the Second Continental Congress and helped organize and finance the expeditions of John STARK and the New Hampshire militia against Gen. John BURGOYNE in 1777. A delegate to the Constitutional Convention (1787), Langdon campaigned vigorously in New Hampshire for ratification of the U.S. Constitution. He served in the U.S. Senate (1789–1801) and later as governor of New Hampshire (1805–09, 1810–12).

Lange, David [lahng-ee] David Lange, b. Aug. 4, 1942, became prime minister of New Zealand in 1984. A criminal lawyer, Lange entered parliament in 1977; in 1983 he became head of the Labour party. In July 1984 his party defeated the National party of Sir Robert MULDOON, and Lange became prime minister. After he forbade port visits from ships that might be nuclear armed, New Zealand was suspended from ANZUS. Lange remained prime minister after the 1987 elections but resigned in 1989.

Lange, Dorothea [lang] Dorothea Lange, b. Hoboken, N.J., May 26, 1895, d. Oct. 11, 1965, was a documentary photographer noted for the power and realism of her images. Her photographs for the Farm Security Administration, including *Migrant Mother, Nipomo, California* (1936), document the erosion of the land and people of rural America during the Great Depression and are her best-known images. Other significant projects included photo essays for *Life* magazine and a series of studies of justice in California. She often collaborated with her husband, the economist Paul Taylor.

Dorothea Lange's bleak, realistic portraits of migrant workers, such as Migrant Mother, Nipomo, California *(1936), helped win public support for federal relief programs during the Depression.*

Langer, Susanne K. [lang'-ur] Susanne Knauth Langer, b. New York City, Dec. 20, 1895, d. July 17, 1985, was an American philosopher primarily known as an aesthetician. A major influence on her thought was the philosophy of Ernst CASSIRER, which she developed into a logic of signs and symbols, initially applied to music and later extended to the whole range of the fine arts. Langer defined art as the creation of apparent forms expressive of human feelings and held that each art creates its own particular kind of appearance. In her study of the mind, she maintained that all mental phenomena are modes of feeling.

Langevin, André [lahn-zhuh-van'] With a series of novels that deal naturalistically with predestined losers, the French Canadian André Langevin, b. July 11, 1927, has gained a reputation as one of Canada's leading contemporary writers. For his first two novels, *Évadé de la nuit* (Fugitive of the Night, 1951) and *Dust over the City* (1953; Eng. trans., 1955), he won the Prix du Cercle du Livre de France. Later novels include *Le Temps des Hommes* (The Time of Men, 1956), *L'Élan d'Amérique* (The American Moose, 1972), and *Orphan Street* (1974; Eng. trans., 1976).

Langgaard, Rued Rued Immanuel Langgaard, b. July 28, 1893, d. July 10, 1952, a Danish composer and keyboard performer, made his debut as an organist in 1905 and as a composer in 1908. Rooted in late romanticism, his works advanced remarkably over the next two decades into the fields of polytonality and atonality. Although he later retreated to a less harmonically venturesome style, his music still exhibited a sometimes bizarrely idiosyncratic composing technique. His works include 16 symphonies, an opera, and many chamber and vocal compositions, often designed for liturgical use.

Langlade, Charles Michel de [lahng-lahd', sharl mee-shel' duh] Charles Michel de Langlade, b. Mackinac, Mich., May 1729, d. *c*.1801, was a pioneer of mixed French and Indian descent. In what is now Wisconsin he led an Indian detachment that took part in the defeat of British General Edward BRADDOCK near Fort Duquesne in 1755 during the FRENCH AND INDIAN WARS. He continued to lead Indian auxiliaries in aid of the French until 1761, when he surrendered the fort at Mackinac to the British and became a British subject. In 1763 he warned the British of PONTIAC'S REBELLION. During the American Revolution he fought George Rogers CLARK in the West.

Langland, William [lang'-luhnd] The 14th-century alliterative poet William Langland, *c*.1330–*c*.1400, author of the masterpiece PIERS PLOWMAN, is considered, along with Geoffrey Chaucer and the anonymous author of *Sir Gawain and the Green Knight*, one of the three Middle English writers of sustained genius. Langland probably came from the West Midlands, perhaps Ledbury in Shropshire. Two shorter poems, *Piers the Plowman's Creed* (*c*.1394) and *Richard Redeless* (*c*.1399), once attributed to Langland, are now thought to be the work of others.

Langley, Samuel Pierpont [lang'-lee, peer'-pahnt] The American astronomer Samuel Pierpont Langley, b. Boston, Aug. 22, 1834, d. Feb. 27, 1906, is most noted for his work on AERODYNAMICS and solar radiation. With only a high school education, he became professor of astronomy at the Western University of Pennsylvania (1867) and director of Allegheny Observatory in Pitts-

burgh. He served as secretary of the SMITHSONIAN INSTITUTION from 1887 and founded the Smithsonian Astrophysical Observatory in 1890. Langley's many attempts to build a full-size workable aircraft were all unsuccessful. He did, however, invent the heat-measuring bolometer, and he used it to advance knowledge of infrared solar radiation.

Langmuir, Irving [lang'-myoor] The American chemist Irving Langmuir, b. Brooklyn, N.Y., Jan. 31, 1881, d. Aug. 16, 1957, excelled in both theoretical contributions and their practical applications in many fields of science. He conducted (1909–50) his research at the General Electric Company in Schenectady, N.Y. Langmuir's studies of chemical reactions at high temperature and low pressure led to the gas-filled tungsten lamp. Other research by Langmuir shed light on the properties of atomic hydrogen and resulted in the manufacture of the atomic hydrogen torch used for welding. In atomic structure he contributed to the modern theory of electronic bonding. His work on thermionic emission resulted in the construction of many electron tubes. For his pioneer work in the fields of catalysis and adsorption Langmuir was awarded the 1932 Nobel Prize for chemistry.

Langton, Stephen [lang'-tuhn] A major statesman of the English church, Stephen Langton, b. *c*.1155, d. July 9, 1228, was instrumental in securing King JOHN's concession of the MAGNA CARTA in 1215. He was created (1206) a cardinal by Pope INNOCENT III and appointed (1207) archbishop of Canterbury. King John, however, did not recognize the appointment, and England was placed under interdict until 1213, when the king was reconciled with the papacy. Langton took his seat at Canterbury and from then on was active in English politics. His support of the barons against the king in securing the Magna Carta led to his suspension as archbishop, but he was restored to office in 1218.

Langtry, Lillie [lang'-tree] Emilie Charlotte Le Breton Langtry, b. Oct. 13, 1853, d. Feb. 12, 1929, better known as Lillie—or the Jersey Lily, a name bestowed by the painter John Millais because of her Channel Island origins—was the first of several women flaunted by the Prince of Wales, later Edward VII, as his mistress. She made her acting debut in 1881 and gained popular success through her beauty, style, and aura of scandal. Oscar Wilde wrote *Lady Windermere's Fan* (1892) for Langtry; her memoirs, *The Days I Knew*, appeared in 1925.

languages, artificial Artificial languages are languages that have been deliberately invented, unlike typical world languages that have developed naturally and, for the most part, without conscious planning. The planning that has gone into many natural languages, especially into standard forms taught in schools, has merely involved controlling or modifying natural languages already in use. Artificial languages, on the other hand, often introduce novel systems of symbols and are used in diverse fields—mathematics, formal logic, and computer science, for example. Such artificial languages are not to be compared with natural languages; they are designed to handle specific and special categories of subject matter and cannot serve to describe the whole range of human experience.

Less limited artificial languages have been proposed to create a more logical vehicle of thought than can be found in any natural language and to overcome the barriers to communication resulting from the multiplicity of languages spoken in the world. Although some natural languages have been widely used at various times as a common means of communication among speakers of different languages, it is uncertain that any one language will ever be adopted universally. English and French, the most widespread international languages, are difficult to learn and too closely identified with particular national groups. C. K. Ogden's *Basic English,* proposed in 1932, attempts to remedy the first impediment by reducing the vocabulary to a core of 850 words. For example, *enter* is replaced by *go into,* and *precede* by *go in front of.* It remains distinctly English, however.

The first major movement for an international artificial language, called *Volapük,* was initiated by Johann Martin Schleyer in 1880. The vocabulary of Volapük is based on English, but the words are so distorted in form that it neither looks nor sounds like English. This was deliberately done in order to give it a more neutral appearance. Volapük rapidly lost favor in competition with ESPERANTO, which was first presented by Ludwik Lazar Zamenhof in 1887. Esperanto has a highly regular system of word information with roots drawn from French, English, German, and other Indo-European languages. It is the most widely used artificial language today.

Of the various rival systems that have been proposed for international adoption in the 20th century, the most successful has been Alexander Gode's *Interlingua,* the culmination of a collaborative effort inspired in part by the Latin-based "interlingua" originally proposed in 1903 by the Italian mathematician Giuseppe Peano. Interlingua is based largely on the international vocabulary of science and technology and can be read with little difficulty by those familiar with English or a Romance language. It has been widely employed at medical conferences and in scientific journals.

languages, extinct   Extinct languages are not limited to ancient times. Dalmatian, a Romance language, died out in 1898 when Anthony Udina, the last known native speaker, was killed in a mine explosion; Cornish became extinct when Dolly Pentreath died in Mousehole, England, in 1777. An extinct language, however, is not necessarily a forgotten one. Many Dalmatian and Cornish texts survive, for example, and several languages of the ancient world are preserved on clay tablets or papyrus.

Sumerian. The oldest written language of Mesopotamia, Sumerian, has no known relatives. Its CUNEIFORM writing system evolved from a pictographic stage that began about 3100 BC. Sumerian was largely replaced by Akkadian after 2000 BC, but it survived for another two millennia as a religious language among the Babylonians and Assyrians—in much the way that Latin survived in medieval Europe.

Elamite. First written in pictographs (2500 BC) and later in cuneiform (1600–400 BC), Elamite was spoken in the eastern part of Mesopotamia and in southwest Iran. Some evidence suggests that the language descended ultimately from Akkadian.

Hattic. A language of central Anatolia, Hattic, often called Hattian, Khattish, or proto-Hittite, is preserved largely in Hittite records, where both Hattic words and whole Hattic sentences are found. It became extinct about 1400 BC and has no affinities with any known language.

Hurrian. A language of southeast Anatolia that was still alive at the beginning of the 1st millennium BC, Hurrian is preserved both in its own inscriptions and in Hittite texts. Hurrian is related to Urartian.

Urartian. Urartian, sometimes called Vannic or Chaldean, was spoken in eastern Anatolia around Lake Van and in what is now Soviet Armenia near Yerevan. Inscriptions have also been found in Persian Azerbaijan, and there is an important Urartian/Assyrian bilingual text. Written records date from 900–600 BC, after which time the Urartians suddenly disappeared, replaced almost immediately in the same area of eastern Anatolia by the Armenians. Urartian is closely related to Hurrian, though not derived from it.

Phrygian. Phrygian, a language of west central Anatolia, had two literary periods, Old Phrygian (730–430 BC) and New Phrygian (AD 100–350). The later used a Greek-like script, the earlier an eclectic alphabet based on Northwest Semitic models. Though of INDO-EUROPEAN origin, Phrygian is poorly understood, especially for the earlier period. It seems more closely related to Greek than to any other Indo-European language but also shows affinities with Armenian. An older theory, no longer tenable, related Phrygian to Thracian and posited a Thraco-Phrygian language family.

Thracian. Thracian was spoken along the west coast of the Black Sea, south of the Danube, in what is now Bulgaria, and in parts of Greece and Turkey. Although no significant inscriptions exist, numerous words are known from Greek and Roman texts. In addition, a large number of personal and place names have been recorded. Thracian is of Indo-European origin, but its affinities to any language other than Dacian and perhaps Phrygian are vague.

Dacian. Also referred to as Getic, Dacian was spoken in what is now Romania—on the west coast of the Black Sea, north of the Danube. Like Thracian, it is known from words mentioned in Greek and Latin texts and from proper names. It has recently been shown that Dacian became distinct from Thracian, but the differentiation took place probably only after 1500 BC. Some scholars believe that a Dacian layer underlies Albanian and that perhaps Dacian rather than Illyrian was the original form of that language.

Illyrian. Illyrian was spoken north and west of Greece during the Greco-Roman period. It is uncertain whether the term refers to one language or to many languages. Most evidence for Illyrian comes from proper names; the core of the material is now called Messapic. Traditionally, Illyrian has been considered an ancient form of Albanian, a view losing favor.

Etruscan. The Etruscans controlled large sections of the Italian peninsula, particularly in the northwest, from the 8th through the 4th century BC, before the rise of the Romans. Nearly 10,000 brief, often repetitious inscriptions, as well as a few longer examples, survive from their language. Etruscan was written in a Greek-like script, but the language itself does not have any relatives. Thus the etymological method so helpful with Indo-European languages is of no use in deciphering Etruscan. A few terms like *puia*, "wife," and *clan*, "son," are known, however, as are the numbers from one to six—*thu, zal, ci, śa, mach, huth*. The recovery of more Etruscan represents a great challenge to modern linguists.

The Hittite-Luwian Group

The six Anatolian languages that make up the Hittite-Luwian group show archaic Indo-European features. The languages are known from texts as early as 1800 BC and as recent as 200 BC. Hittite, Palaic, and Lydian form one subgroup; Cuneiform Luwian, Hieroglyphic Luwian, and Lycian form a second. Three other languages of southern Anatolia—Carian, Pisidian, and Sidetic—have been proposed as additions.

Hittite. The most important language of the Hittite-Luwian group is Hittite. It was translated early in this century by the Czech scholar Bedřich Hrozný, who showed, to the surprise of most linguists, that the language was Indo-European, although it maintained certain features that had been lost in all the other Indo-European languages. Hittite used a form of Akkadian cuneiform writing, the knowledge of which was most helpful to Hrozný in translating. The written language contains numerous loanwords from Luwian, Hattic, and Hurrian and also seems to use, in a random fashion, vocabulary from both Sumerian and Akkadian.

Palaic. Related to Hittite, but very poorly substantiated, Palaic has survived in fewer than 200 words, all known through a cuneiform writing system.

Lydian. Lydian was spoken on the west coast of Anatolia and written in the Greek script from 500 to 300 BC. An Aramaic/Lydian bilingual text has proved of great value in understanding the language. Besides inscriptions, about 50 words are found in the writings of Greek authors.

Cuneiform Luwian. The most thoroughly understood language of the Luwian subgroup, Cuneiform Luwian is known from 1400 BC in south central Anatolia. It is called "cuneiform" after the type of writing system in which it is preserved and to distinguish it from its very close relative, Hieroglyphic Luwian. It differs from Hittite both in vocabulary and in its phonological system.

Hieroglyphic Luwian. Often called Hieroglyphic Hittite, Hieroglyphic Luwian is not yet well understood, and its pictographic script has not been wholly deciphered. The language is clearly related to Cuneiform Luwian but probably represents a later stage of development. A breakthrough in decipherment came with the discovery of the Karatepe bilingual inscriptions, a parallel Phoenician translation of a Hieroglyphic Luwian text. The language is recorded from 1200 to 700 BC in what is now northern Syria and south central Turkey. Some of the vocabulary of Hieroglyphic Luwian may be preserved as loanwords in classical Armenian.

Lycian. Spoken in the southwest corner of Anatolia, Lycian is recorded from 500 to 200 BC in about 150 short inscriptions written with a West Greek alphabet.

Languedoc [lahng-dohk'] Languedoc is a historic province in southern France, bordering the Mediterranean Sea on the south and the Rhône River in the east. MONTPELLIER and TOULOUSE have long been the leading cities. The southern portion of the region, Bas Languedoc, is composed of a low limestone plain where wine is produced. In the north are the Cévennes Mountains.

In 121 BC the area was incorporated into the Roman province of Gallia Narbonensis. By AD 924 it came under the control of the powerful counts of Toulouse and developed a rich culture based on its distinctive French dialect, *langue d'oc*. Troubadour poetry in the dialect flowered from the 10th to the 12th century (see PROVENÇAL LITERATURE). During the same period, the ALBIGENSES, a religious sect, enjoyed a wide following in the area. In 1209, however, Pope INNOCENT III declared a crusade against the sect, and Languedoc was subsequently invaded by northern French troops. By the mid-13th century, Languedoc had been annexed by the French crown. During the French Revolution, Languedoc was divided into the departments of Ardèche, Gard, Hérault, and Aude and parts of Haute-Garonne, Lozère, Tarn-et-Garonne, Ariège, and Haute Loire.

Languedoc, a historic region bordering the Gulf of Lions in southern France, was occupied during ancient times by a succession of invading peoples because of its strategic location between Italy and the Iberian Peninsula.

---

langur [luhng-goor'] The langurs, genus *Presbytis*, also called leaf-eating or leaf monkeys, are a group of 14 species of long-tailed, tree-dwelling monkeys of southern Asia. Their habitats range from sea-level, dry-zone forests, through tropical rain forests, to snow-covered trees at altitudes of 4,000 m (13,000 ft). Langurs are 43 to 79 cm

The hanuman langur is considered in India a symbol of self-sacrifice. Folktales tell how this langur got its black face and hands by being scorched in a fire while helping a friend.

(17 to 31 in) long, have a tail 49.5 to 109 cm (19.5 to 43 in) long, and weigh from 3 to 21 kg (6.5 to 46 lb). The fur is rather long and often forms a crest or cap on the head and a prominent ridge above the eyes. Coloration is generally brownish, grayish, or blackish, with lighter underparts. Langurs subsist largely on a diet of leaves. They live in troops of 3 to 120 individuals. Four other species in the same family, Cercopithecidae, are also called langurs: the douc langur, *Pygathrix nemaeus*, of Indochina; the snub-nosed langurs, *Rhinopitecus roxellanae* of western China and *R. avunculus* of North Vietnam; and the Mentawi Islands langur, *Simias concolor*, from islands off the west coast of Sumatra.

Lanier, Sidney [luh-neer'] The American poet, novelist, critic, and musician Sidney Lanier, b. Macon, Ga., Feb. 3, 1842, d. Sept. 7, 1881, fought in the Confederate army and was captured (1864) and imprisoned. Sick and poor when released a year later, he published the novel *Tiger-Lilies* (1867) about his war experiences. In 1873 he became first flutist in the Peabody Orchestra in Baltimore. He augmented his income by delivering lectures—published posthumously in 1902 as *Shakspere and His Forerunners*—and these led (1879) to a teaching position at Johns Hopkins University. In 1880 he published *The Science of English Verse*.

lanolin [lan'-oh-lin] A soft, pale yellow wax, lanolin is a purified form of wool "grease," a by-product of the preparation of raw wool for spinning. Chemically, it is a mixture of cholesterol esters. Its resistance to rancidity, emulsifying properties, slightly antiseptic effect, and capability of forming a stable emulsion with water permit it to be widely used as a base for ointments, emollients, salves, cosmetics, soaps, and shampoos. Lanolin is extracted by washing raw wool in water or a soap solution

and then separating wax from water in a centrifuge. The crude wool wax is purified, bleached, and mixed with water to form an emulsion. Lanolin can be mixed with almost twice its weight in water.

Lansdowne, Henry Charles Keith Petty-Fitz-maurice, 5th Marquess of [lanz'-down, mar'-kwes] Lord Lansdowne, b. Jan. 14, 1845, d. June 3, 1927, was a British politician whose long career included service as governor general of Canada (1883–88), viceroy of India (1888–93), secretary of state for war (1895–1900), and foreign secretary (1900–05). While he was in Canada, the rebellion of Louis RIEL was suppressed (1885), the Canadian Pacific Railway was completed (1886), and negotiations were begun to settle the Newfoundland fisheries dispute with the United States.

Originally a Liberal, Lansdowne broke (1886) with that party over Irish Home Rule and aligned himself with the Conservatives. As foreign secretary in the Conservative government, he concluded an Anglo-Japanese alliance (1902) and the Entente Cordiale with France (1904; see TRIPLE ENTENTE). During World War I he served (1915–16) in the coalition government and in 1917 raised a storm of protest by publishing a letter calling for a negotiated peace.

Lansing Lansing, the capital of Michigan, is located at the junction of the Grand, Red Cedar, and Sycamore rivers in the southern part of the state. Lansing has a population of 127,321 (1990). In addition to being the seat of state government, the city is a major automobile production center and the commercial focus of a large agricultural area. Michigan State University (1857), the first agricultural college in the United States, is in East Lansing, which adjoins the city. The late-Renaissance-style capitol building, completed in 1878, stands in the center of the city.

Originally named Michigan, the city was settled in 1837 by settlers from New York State; it was renamed for Lansing, N.Y., when it was chosen state capital in 1847. Industrial growth was spurred by the arrival of the railroads in 1871. Ransom E. Olds began the automobile industry there in 1899.

Lansing, Robert Robert Lansing, b. Watertown, N.Y., Oct. 17, 1864, d. Oct. 30, 1928, was U.S. secretary of state (1915–20) under President Woodrow WILSON. He was admitted to the bar in 1889, and in 1892 he was asked to assist in the arbitration of the Bering Sea Controversy over fur seals. Thereafter he represented the United States in more international arbitrations than any other American lawyer of his time.

Appointed counselor of the Department of State in 1914, Lansing became its secretary after the German sinking of the LUSITANIA. Lansing proved more anti-German than President Woodrow Wilson and welcomed U.S. entry into World War I in 1917. He negotiated the Lansing-Ishii agreement (Nov. 2, 1917) with Japan, whereby the Unit-

The American lawyer and statesman Robert Lansing gained international recognition as secretary of state (1915–20) under President Woodrow Wilson. Lansing's misgivings about provisions of the Paris Peace Conference, including the establishment of the League of Nations, led to his resignation.

ed States recognized Japan's special interests in China.

At the PARIS PEACE CONFERENCE, Lansing found himself largely ignored by Wilson. He protested strongly when the president gave in to Japan's demands for extended rights in China. After the conference a disgruntled member of the U.S. delegation revealed that Lansing considered the Treaty of Versailles too harsh on Germany and that the secretary was not enthusiastic about the League of Nations. Several months later Wilson forced Lansing's resignation.

lantern fish   Lantern fishes, family Myctophidae, are about 200 species of small, abundant oceanic fishes with strings of pearllike photophores, or light organs, along their sides (see BIOLUMINESCENCE). They average less than 15 cm (6 in) long and inhabit the mid-depths of the ocean, down to almost 1 km (0.6 mi), making upward feeding migrations each night.

The lantern fish Myctophum punctatum, *found in the Mediterranean Sea and Atlantic Ocean, has light organs* (yellow) *on the lower body.*

lanthanide series [lan'-thuh-nide]   The lanthanide series is the group of chemical elements that follow lanthanum in Group IIIB in the periodic table. Their distinguishing feature is that they fill the $4f$ electronic subshell. Although only the elements cerium (atomic number 58) through lutetium (71) are lanthanide elements in principle, most chemists include yttrium (39) and lanthanum (57) in this group because they have similar

physical and chemical properties. They are also called the rare earths, because they were originally discovered together in rare minerals and isolated as oxides, or "earths." In comparison with many other elements, however, they are not really rare, except for promethium (61), which has only radioactive isotopes with short half-lives. Lanthanide elements are found in many minerals, principally MONAZITE; in igneous rocks on the Earth's surface, cerium is the most abundant lanthanide.

In their elemental form, the lanthanides are silvery metals with high melting points. They tarnish slowly in air, except for samarium, europium, and ytterbium, which are much more reactive toward oxygen or moisture. The metals are prepared from fluorides or oxides by treatment with strongly reducing metals such as calcium, or from molten chloride or fluoride salts by electrolysis at high temperatures. The lanthanides are typically isolated as a group by precipitating their insoluble hydroxides, oxalates, or phosphates. Until 1945, tedious, repetitive procedures such as fractional crystallization were required to separate these elements from one another. A much more effective separation technique, ion-exchange CHROMATOGRAPHY, has been used since 1945.

Until recently the only commercial use of the rare earths was as misch metal, an alloy consisting principally of cerium, lanthanum, and neodymium, which is pyrophoric (catching fire in air) when finely divided and is used to make cigarette-lighter flints. Commercial production of the rare earths is now growing by approximately 20% each year. They are used as alloying materials in metallurgy (to remove sulfur and oxygen) and to make strong permanent magnets, such as those from $SmCo_5$. Other modern uses are as magnetic oxides such as yttrium iron garnet, $Y_6Fe_{10}O_{24}$; as phosphors in television screens (Eu^3+ yields a red phosphor when "doped" into some oxides); as catalysts that decompose auto air pollutants, such as $La_{0.7}Sr_{0.3}MnO_3$; and as compounds that store hydrogen effectively, such as $LaNi_5H_6$.

lanthanum [lan'-thuh-nuhm]   Lanthanum is a chemical element, a white, malleable metal, and the first of the rare earths. Its symbol is La, its atomic number is 57, and its atomic weight is 138.9 (average weight of the two natural isotopes, ^{138}La and ^{139}La). ^{138}La is radioactive, with a half-life of 1.12×10^{11} years. Lanthanum is found with other lanthanides in monazite, bastnaesite, and other minerals. It was discovered in 1839 by the Swedish chemist Carl G. Mosander. Scientists have created many radioactive isotopes of lanthanum. Because lanthanum increases the refractive index of glass, it is used in manufacturing high-quality lenses. Lanthanum is also used as a reagent, as a phosphor in fluorescent lamps, and as a catalyst for cracking crude petroleum (its largest use).

Lanvin, Jeanne   see FASHION DESIGN

Lanzhou (Lan-chou) [lahn-jrow]   Lanzhou is the capital of Gansu province in north central China. It is located on the upper Huang He (Yellow River). With a population of 1,420,000 (1988 est.), it is the largest city, as well as the economic and cultural center, of the province, and it is connected by rail with all major parts of China. Since the Communist takeover in 1949, Lanzhou has been transformed from a small town into a thriving industrial city. Machine manufacturing, oil refining, metallurgy, textile weaving, and cement and chemical production are the major industries.

Lanzhou flourished as a caravan center during the Han dynasty (202 BC–AD 220). Strategically located between China proper and Central Asia and between northern and southwestern China, the city was used by successive dynasties as a stronghold for controlling Central Asia. It became the capital of Gansu in 1666.

Lao   see LAOS

Lao-tzu   see LAOZI

Laocoön [lay-ah'-koh-ahn]   The *Laocoön* is an ancient marble statue (n.d.; Cortile del Belvedere, Vatican) depicting Laocoön, the Trojan priest of Apollo, and his two sons being attacked by serpents. The Trojans saw the death of Laocoön not only as a portent for their city but also as Athena's punishment for the priest, who had hurled a spear at the wooden horse left behind by the Greeks on their feigned departure from Troy. The statue, which stands 2.4 m (8 ft) tall, was rediscovered in Rome in 1506 and was much admired and copied. In the late 16th century it was exalted as an example of unrestrained emotion. Pliny the Elder, in his *Historia Naturalis* (1st century AD), attributed the statue to the Rhodian sculptors Agesander, Athenodorus, and Polydorus. Its date is uncertain: if it is Hellenistic, it dates from the 2d or 1st century BC; if Roman (based on a Hellenistic prototype), from the first century of the Christian era.

The emotionalism of Hellenistic sculpture is epitomized in the Laocoön statue. Attributed to three Rhodian sculptors and believed to date from the 2d or 1st century BC, the sculpture portrays the death struggle of the Trojan priest Laocoön and his sons. (Cortile del Belvedere, Vatican, Rome.)

Laoighis [lay'-ish]   Laoighis (also Leix) is a county in Leinster province in central Ireland, covering an area of 1,720 km² (664 mi²); its population is 73,094 (1986). Major rivers are the Barrow and the Nore; the county town is Port Laoighis (Maryborough). The Slieve Bloom Mountains are in the northwest. Agriculture is the mainstay of the economy. A branch of the Grand Canal and the Cork-Dublin rail line pass through the county. Part of the kingdom of Ossory from the 1st to the 11th century, Laoighis came under the English crown in the 16th century and was developed as a major agricultural region.

Laos [lah'-ohs]   Laos is a small, landlocked country located in the interior of the Indochinese Peninsula. China lies to the north, Vietnam to the east, Cambodia to the south, and Burma and Thailand to the west. Laos was a part of French INDOCHINA after 1893 and was granted full independence in 1953. After the French departed, a protracted civil war ensued. In 1975 the Communist forces gained control, and Laos became a people's democratic republic.

Land

Laos is a predominantly mountainous land, with less than 10% of the total land area suitable for permanent agricultural settlement. The northern half of the country is occupied by rugged mountains, which include Mount Bia (2,820 m/9,252 ft), the highest point in the country. The southern half of the country—sometimes referred to as the panhandle because of its long, narrow shape—is dominated by the mountains of the Annamese Cordillera, which extend from north to south along the eastern border. The Annamese mountains are extremely rugged and are a major obstacle to travel and communication between Laos and Vietnam. The western half of the panhandle is occupied by most of the nation's principal lowlands, located on alluvial floodplains along the MEKONG RIVER and its tributaries.

Laos has a monsoonal climate. Winters (November to April) are relatively cool and dry, and summers (May to October) are hot and wet. During the summer rainy season the average daily temperature is about 27° C (80° F), and rainfall is between 1,270 mm (50 in) and 2,286 mm (90 in). Temperatures during the dry season average 16° to 21° C (61° to 70° F).

Forests cover almost two-thirds of Laos, but much of the valuable wood in the primary forest areas has been destroyed. Tin is mined, and deposits of coal, iron ore, copper, gold, lead, salt, and zinc await development. Laos's enormous hydroelectric potential is also undeveloped.

People

The population of Laos is ethnically complex, with each ethnic group more closely tied to related groups outside the country's borders than to the Laotian nation. The dominant group are the Lao, who account for nearly 50% of the total population and are concentrated in the alluvial floodplains. They practice a high-yielding wet-rice (paddy) form of agriculture. The Lao Teung, occupying middle elevations in the highlands, practice a low-yield-

AT A GLANCE

LAO PEOPLE'S DEMOCRATIC REPUBLIC

Land: Area: 236,800 km^2 (91,429 mi^2). Capital and largest city: Vientiane (1985 est. pop., 377,409).

People: Population (1990 est.): 4,023,726. Density: 17 persons per km^2 (44 per mi^2). Distribution (1987): 16% urban, 84% rural. Official language: Lao. Major religions: Buddhism, traditional religions.

Government: Type: Communist one-party state. Legislature: National Congress of People's Representatives. Political subdivisions: 16 provinces, 1 municipality.

Economy: GDP (1987): $696 million; $156 per capita. Labor distribution (1990): agriculture—80%; commerce and services—18%; manufacturing—2%. Foreign trade (1989): imports—$230 million; exports—$97 million. Currency: 1 new kip = 100 at.

Education and Health: Literacy (1990): 41% of adult population. Universities (1986): 1. Hospital beds (1985): 9,815. Physicians (1985): 558. Life expectancy (1990): women—51; men—48. Infant mortality (1990): 126 per 1,000 live births.

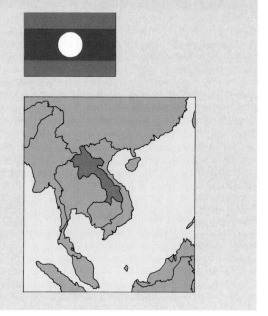

ing slash-and-burn form of agriculture. They are regarded as the original inhabitants and constitute about 25% of the total population. At higher elevations are the Meo (Hmong) and Man (YAO) hill tribes, which account for about 13% of the total population. Also separate are the tribal Tai, who practice a religion different from that of the lowland Lao. The official language is Lao, which is the language of the Lao ethnic group and is similar to Siamese. The Lao Teung all speak languages of the Mon-Khmer family, and the Meo and Man languages are regarded as belonging to the Miao-Yao language family. Theravada Buddhism remains an important part of Lao life under the Communists. The Lao Teung, tribal Tai, and other hill tribes practice various forms of animism and ancestor worship.

By Southeast Asian standards, Laos is sparsely populated, even in the alluvial lowlands where most people are concentrated. The largest urban area is VIENTIANE, the capital. The birthrate is high and unlikely to fall to the level of developed nations because of a government ban on birth-control practices. The death rate is also high, so the net population increase is moderate. Also, since 1975 an estimated 400,000 refugees, including most of the educated, wealthy elite and many tribespeople from the hills, have left the country.

Six years of schooling is compulsory. Since 1975, Lao has replaced French as the language of school instruction. Higher education is available at Sisavangvong University (1958) or may be sought abroad. Malaria and malnutrition are widespread, and infant mortality is high.

Economic Activity

Laos is economically underdeveloped, with one of the lowest per capita incomes in the world. Most of the people are dependent on subsistence farming. In 1979, in an attempt to revive the crippled economy, the ban on private trade was lifted and farmers were given incentives to increase production; further reforms were instituted in the late 1980s. By 1984 the government claimed to have achieved self-sufficiency in food, although shortages still exist in some areas. Rice is the chief food crop. The opium poppy is a major cash crop of the Meo and Man hill tribes. Fish from rivers and local fish ponds provide an important source of protein.

Manufacturing is virtually nonexistent, and economic development has been hampered by inadequate transportation. The main travel artery is the Mekong River, which is navigable between Savannakhet, Vientiane, and LUANG PRABANG.

Electricity from the Nam Ngum dam, exported to Thailand, is the leading source of foreign exchange. Laos has a chronic trade deficit and is heavily dependent on foreign aid.

Government

In 1975, King Savang Vatthana abdicated, and the coalition government led by Prince SOUVANNA PHOUMA was replaced by a Communist-controlled government led by Prime Minister Kaysone Phomvihan and President SOUPHANOUVONG, who retired in 1986. The Lao People's Revolutionary party is the only political party. In 1989, nationwide elections for an assembly to ratify a new constitution were held.

History

Laos was part of the KHMER EMPIRE before 1353 when the Laotian prince Fa Ngum assumed the throne of Muong Swa (Luang Prabang) and founded the kingdom of Lan Xang. Theravada Buddhism, adopted from the Khmers, became the state religion. The Lao kingdom reached its zenith under King Souligna Vongsa (r. 1637–94). After 1707, dynastic feuds divided the kingdom, and three competing kingdoms emerged—Vientiane, Luang Prabang, and Champasak. In the 19th century, annexation by Thailand was averted by an appeal for French protection. In 1893, Laos became part of French Indochina.

During World War II, Laos came under Japanese occupation. In April 1945, King Sisavang Vong of Luang Prabang proclaimed Laotian independence under Japanese protection. With the defeat of Japan, he accepted the French reassertion of control, despite the opposition of the Free Lao (Lao Issara) anti-French revolutionary movement, which formed a government in exile in Thailand. In 1949, Laos became a semiautonomous state within the French Union, and in 1953 it was granted full independence. By this time, however, the Free Lao movement, regrouped as the Communist-backed PATHET LAO, had established control of northern Laos. Prolonged civil war ensued between the Pathet Lao and the royal government. The struggle was actually three-way because control of the royal government in Vientiane passed back and forth between the pro-Western rightists led by Gen. Phoumi Nosavan and the neutralists led by Prince Souvanna Phouma.

In 1961 a 14-power nation conference in Geneva sought to defuse the conflict by establishing a neutralist coalition government under Souvanna Phouma. Fighting soon broke out again, however, and Laos increasingly became a side theater in the VIETNAM WAR. The final coalition government, led by Souvanna Phouma and including his half brother, the Pathet Lao leader Souphanouvong, was established in April 1974. After the fall of South Vietnam and Cambodia to the Communists in 1975, the Pathet Lao assumed full control in Laos. In December, Souvanna Phouma's government was terminated, and the monarchy abolished.

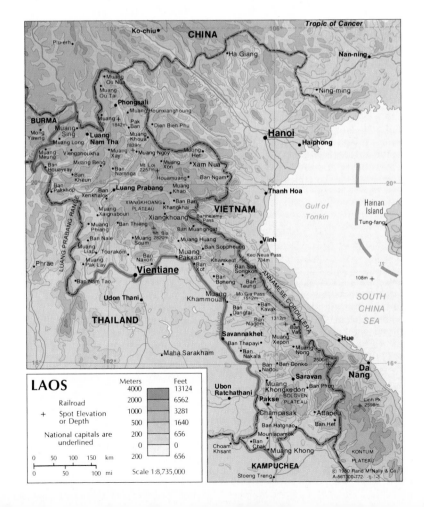

Women belonging to the Lao-Tai tribal group are differentiated as Red Tai and Black Tai by the color of their dress. Four major ethnic groups dominate the population of Laos.

Laos signed a treaty of peace and friendship (1977) and a border delineation treaty (1986) with Vietnam. By 1989, less than 2,000 Vietnamese soldiers remained in Laos, but their presence contributed to strained relations between Laos and Thailand and Laos and the United States.

Laozi (Lao-tzu) [low'-dzu]   Laozi, or Master Lao, is the name of the putative author of the Daoist classic *Daode Jing*. According to Daoist legend, Laozi, the founder of DAOISM, was named Li Erh and had the courtesy name Lao Dan. An older contemporary of Confucius (551–479 BC), he was keeper of the archives at the imperial court. In his 80th year he set out for the western border of China, toward what is now Tibet, saddened and disillusioned that men were unwilling to follow his path to natural goodness. At the border (Hank Pass), however, the guard Yin Xi requested that Laozi record his teachings before he left, whereupon he composed in 5,000 characters the famous *Daode Jing* (The Way and Its Power). The essential teaching of Laozi is the *Dao,* or Way, to ultimate reality—the way of the universe exemplified in Nature. The harmony of opposites (*Tai Chai*) is achieved through a blend of the *Yin* (feminine force) and the *Yang* (masculine force); this harmony can be cultivated through creative quietude (*wu wei*), an effortless action whose power (*de*) maintains equanimity and balance.

lapidary   see GEM CUTTING

lapis lazuli [lap'-is laz'-u-lee]   Lapis lazuli has long been valued both as a deep blue ornamental GEM and as a source of the pigment ultramarine. The color is due to lazurite, a blue variety of the FELDSPATHOID mineral sodalite. Usually intermixed are other minerals, including calcite, pyrite, amphibole, apatite, diopside, feldspar, sphene, and zircon. Lapis lazuli, a contact METAMORPHIC ROCK with variable composition and varying physical properties, usually occurs in altered limestones. Lapis lazuli is distinguished from artificially colored jasper by the presence of gold-colored flecks of pyrite and the absence of the tiny, colorless quartz crystals present in jasper. Major sources are at Badakhshan in Afghanistan, Lake Baikal in the USSR, and Ovalle in Chile.

Lapis lazuli, an opaque, deep-blue stone, has been valued for ornamental purposes for more than 6,000 years. Of variable composition, it consists essentially of lazurite mixed with small amounts of other aluminum silicates.

Laplace, Pierre Simon de [lah-plahs', pyair see-mohn' duh]   The French astronomer and mathematician Pierre Simon de Laplace, b. Mar. 28, 1749, d. Mar. 5, 1827, confirmed the long-term stability of the solar system by mathematically demonstrating the long-term periodicity of three apparently secular, or cumulative, sets of irregularities in the motions of solar-system bodies: the acceleration of the mean motions of the mutually perturbing planets Jupiter and Saturn; the acceleration of the mean motions of the mutually perturbing inner three Galilean satellites of Jupiter; and the acceleration of the mean motion of the Moon.

Laplace's monumental 5-volume work, *Traité de mécanique céleste* (Treatise on Celestial Mechanics, 1799–1825; Eng. trans., 1829–39), was the culmination of work devoted to the mathematical explanation, on the basis of gravitational theory, of the motions of the solar-system bodies. Earlier, in his popular-level *Exposition du système du monde* (Exposition of the System of the World, 1796), he presented his famous nebular hypothesis, which viewed the solar system as originating from the contracting and cooling of a large, flattened, and slowly rotating cloud of incandescent gas.

Laplace made important contributions to a number of mathematical and physical fields, such as analysis, probability, optics, and electricity and magnetism.

Laplace had a prosperous career. When he was 19, d'Alembert obtained an appointment for him as professor

The French mathematician and astronomer Pierre de Laplace made invaluable contributions to the development of probability theory and celestial mechanics.

of mathematics at the École Militaire in Paris. He became an associate (1773) and then a pensioner (1785) of the Paris Academy of Sciences. During the French Revolution he helped to establish the metric system, taught the calculus at the École Normale, and was a member of the French Institute (1795). Under Napoleon he was a member, then chancellor, of the Senate, received the Legion of Honor (1805), and became Count of the Empire (1806). With his political suppleness, he was named a marquis (1817) after the Bourbon restoration.

Lapland   Lapland (Finnish: Lappi; Swedish: Lappland), a vast area stretching across the northern part of Norway, Sweden, Finland, and the Kola Peninsula of the USSR, is the home of the Lapps. Lapland covers approximately 388,500 km^2 (150,000 mi^2). The region lies mainly within the Arctic Circle and is bordered on the east by the White Sea, on the north by the Barents Sea, and on the west by the Norwegian Sea. The eastern portion is close to sea level and is dotted with lakes. The northeast is largely tundra, but other sections are mountainous and forested, and good pasturelands are to be found in some areas. The highest point is Kebnekaise Peak, in Sweden, with an altitude of 2,123 m (6,965 ft).

The climate is arctic, and part of the region is under ice and snow all year. Minerals abound, and the iron ore deposits are among the world's richest. The Lapps arrived from east central Europe in the middle of the first millennium BC, and Finns and Swedes came to the area in the 9th and 14th centuries AD.

Lapps   The Lapps are a European people without a formal homeland of their own. Numbering about 43,000, they inhabit the arctic and subarctic regions of four countries: Norway, with around 20,000 Lapps; Sweden, with an estimated 17,000; Finland, with around 4,000; and the Soviet Union, with about 2,000. The name Lapp, from Finnish *lappalainen,* is a foreign term as far as these people are concerned. They prefer to be called Samit, their own name for themselves. The Lappish language belongs to the Finno-Ugric subfamily of the Ural-Altaic languages. It is thus unrelated to neighboring Scandinavian and Slavic languages with the exception of Finnish, Estonian, Latvian, and certain lesser-known tongues. Finnish is the closest of these to Lappish, but the two are not mutually intelligible. Lappish itself divides into three large language groups—east, central, and south Lappish.

The origins of the Samit are still uncertain, but they may be the oldest postglacial inhabitants in the Far North. Originally living as hunters, gatherers, and fishing people, some became pastoralists by the Middle Ages at the latest. They have been Christians since the 1600s. Reindeer herding remains their most distinctive occupation. Reindeer herders today may frequently be seen in the traditional costume of colorful, decorated tunic and tasseled hat. Most Samit today, however, dress like other Europeans and live mostly in permanent houses and communities rather than in the tents and camps of their seasonal herding migrations. Many Samit live in fishing communities along arctic coasts and inland waters. Others have lived for generations as settled farmers. Some work at mining or forestry.

The Lapps, shown in traditional costume, inhabit an area of northern Europe known as Lapland, which borders on and lies within the Arctic Circle, including parts of Norway, Sweden, Finland, and the USSR.

Laramie   [lair'-uh-mee]   Laramie, a city in southeastern Wyoming on the Laramie River, is the seat of Albany County. Its population is 26,687 (1990). It serves as the commercial, industrial, and transportation center for the surrounding sheep- and cattle-raising region. The University of Wyoming (1886) is there. Laramie is the headquarters of Medicine Bow National Forest. It was settled in 1868 as a tent and shanty town for workers building the Union Pacific Railroad. The railroad and ranching brought prosperity to the area.

larceny [lar'-sen-ee]   Larceny is the taking and carrying away of another's personal property without legal claim to that property, without the owner's consent, and with the intent permanently to deprive the rightful owner of its use. Carrying away has been held to mean any movement of the property, however slight. Personal property includes tangible goods, fixtures attached to the land, crops, and legal documents. Larceny has occurred if consent has not been freely given by the rightful owner or if it has been induced by trick or fraud. Larceny is commonly distinguished from robbery, in which force or violence is used or threatened.

Most states of the United States have statutes specifying what activities constitute larceny. Included among these are picking pockets, the receiving of stolen goods, the passing of checks drawn against insufficient funds or nonexistent bank accounts, the use of slugs in coin-operated machines, and, in some states, embezzlement. Laws generally distinguish among several kinds or degrees of larceny and punish them accordingly. Simple larceny, a MISDEMEANOR, is the taking of property; compound larceny, a FELONY, is the taking of property from a person or a person's business or dwelling. The value of the stolen property distinguishes grand larceny from petit, or petty, larceny; the former is generally a felony, the latter a misdemeanor.

larch   Larch is the common name for trees of the genus *Larix* of the pine family. Ten species occur naturally in cool, moist regions of the Northern Hemisphere. Two North American species—the eastern larch, or tamarack, *L. laricina*, and the western larch, *L. occidentalis*—have commercial value. The main distinguishing characteristic of larches is that although they are pines they are deciduous, losing their foliage in the winter. The bark is thick and scaly, and the needles are pale or bright green, turn-

The Japanese larch, like other larches, loses its leaves in winter. Larches are among the few deciduous conifers.

ing yellow in autumn. The European larch, *L. decidua*, is an important continental tree used for reforestation in the eastern United States. The Japanese larch, *L. kaempferi*, is used as a landscaping tree in the United States. Large forests of larch are sometimes destroyed by the larch sawfly.

Lardner, Ring   An American humorist who used the vernacular in his cynical short stories of ordinary people, Ringgold Wilmer Lardner, b. Niles, Mich., Mar. 6, 1885, d. Sept. 25, 1933, started his writing career as a columnist for the *Chicago Tribune*. A series of pieces for the *Saturday Evening Post* about a bush-league baseball pitcher turned pro became his first collection of short stories, *You Know Me, Al* (1916). Further collections, featuring prizefighters and other figures from the world of sports, secretaries, salesmen, Tin Pan Alley songsmiths, and Broadway chorus girls who revealed themselves in the idiom of their kind, included *Gullible's Travels* (1917), *Treat 'Em Rough* (1918), *How to Write Short Stories* (1924), and *The Love Nest* (1926). With George S. Kaufman, Lardner also wrote the comic play *June Moon* (1929). An unorthodox autobiography, *The Story of a Wonder Man*, appeared in 1927.

Laredo [luh-ray'-doh]   Laredo, Tex., stands on the Rio Grande opposite Nuevo Laredo, Mexico. It is the seat of Webb County and has a population of 122,899 (1990). A port of entry handling considerable trade, it is also the retail center for an extensive region of cattle ranches, irrigated farms, and petroleum and natural gas fields. Ceramics, electronics equipment, medical supplies, clothing, and leather goods are manufactured, and petroleum oil is refined. Tourism is also important.

Laredo was established in 1755 by Spanish settlers. After the Texas Revolution (1835–36), ownership of the city was disputed until the Treaty of Guadelupe Hidalgo (1848) established the Rio Grande as the border between Mexico and Texas.

large numbers, law of   The law of large numbers is a theorem in PROBABILITY theory that states that the average of the outcomes of independent repetitions of a chance phenomenon must approach the expected value of the outcome as the number of repetitions increases without limit, or approaches infinity. It is also called Chebyshev's Theorem or Bernoulli's Theorem. For example, the actual average winnings per play in a game of chance in the long run must approach the expected winnings per play. Gambling houses, insurance companies, and other industries base their business practices on this assurance that the average result of many independent chance trials is quite predictable—even if the result of one individual trial is not.

The law of large numbers, popularly known as "the law of averages," is often thought to require that future outcomes balance past outcomes, but this assumption is not correct. A roulette wheel that has produced ten straight "reds" has no memory and so is no more likely to produce "black" than at any other time. It is a gambler's fallacy to think that the ten reds in a row will be balanced by extra blacks. The odds remain the same for each repetition, regardless of the past outcomes.

Larionov, Mikhail Fyodorovich [luh-rih-yaw'-nawf, mee-kuh-yeel' fyoh-dor'-uh-vich] Mikhail Fyodorovich Larionov, b. Teraspol, Ukraine, May 22 (N.S.), 1881, d. Paris, May 10, 1964, was an early leader of the Russian avant-garde movement in painting. He was instrumental in introducing and interpreting French and Italian art and ideas to Russia and by 1910 was the accepted leader of advanced Russian painting. In 1912 he issued the manifesto of rayonism, a style of abstract expressionist painting based on the disintegration of form into radiating beams of light. Although rayonism was short-lived, it provided the intellectual basis for the foundation of SUPREMATISM by Kasimir MALEVICH in the same year.

lark Lark is the common name for about 70 species of terrestrial, robin-sized songbirds belonging to the family Alaudidae. These birds are distributed worldwide, although most species are found in Africa. Larks are noted for the elaborate song of the males, which is performed during flight. Larks measure 13 to 23 cm (5 to 9 in) in height. They have long legs; the hind toe has a large, straight claw, making perching difficult.

The horned lark, *Eremophila alpestris,* which ranges throughout most of the Northern Hemisphere, is the only species native to North America. It has brown plumage on its back, is paler below, and has a pair of small, dark head tufts, or "horns." In the New World, it nests from the Arctic to South America. The common skylark, *Alauda arvensis,* of Eurasia, has also been introduced into the New World.

The common skylark, one of the most populous birds of Europe, has long been celebrated for its song. It is approximately 18 cm (7 in) long.

Larkin, Philip Philip Arthur Larkin, b. Aug. 9, 1922, d. Dec. 2, 1985, was a highly regarded modern British poet. *The North Ship* (1945), a volume of his early verse, was followed by two novels, *Jill* (1946) and *A Girl in Winter* (1947). Larkin's fame as a poet was firmly established by *The Less Deceived* (1955). His portrayal of modern England concentrates on dejected and nondescript aspects of the industrial landscape, whose inhabitants he describes without sentiment but with unaffected compassion. Larkin's stoical, witty, and unpretentious style is seen to its greatest advantage in *The Whitsun Weddings* (1964) and *High Windows* (1974). His jazz criticism is collected in *All What Jazz* (1970), and he was the editor of *The Oxford Book of Twentieth-Century English Verse* (1973). Various essays are collected in *Required Writing: Miscellaneous Pieces, 1955–82* (1984).

larkspur Larkspur is the common name for about 40 species of annual herbs constituting the genus *Consolida* in the buttercup family, Ranunculaceae. Native to temperate regions of the Northern Hemisphere, larkspurs bear feathery leaves and loose racemes (clusters) of flowers, which range from purple to pink and white in color. The names larkspur and delphinium are sometimes used interchangeably, but botanists now place the DELPHINIUM—sometimes perennial—in a separate genus.

Larousse, Pierre [lah-roos'] Son of a village blacksmith, Pierre Athanase Larousse, b. Oct. 23, 1817, d. Jan. 3, 1875, became one of the most influential scholars and educators of 19th-century France. He published a series of reference works that in their revised and updated forms continue to be among the most popular in the world. His first book, a basic vocabulary list (1849), was followed by grammars and other school texts. In 1852, Larousse founded his own publishing house in Paris with Augustin Boyer. Four years later the firm published a compact dictionary. Larousse's masterwork, the comprehensive 15-volume encyclopedia the *Grand Dictionnaire,* came out in installments over a ten-year period from 1866 to 1876.

Lars Porsena, King of Clusium [lahrz-por-sen'-uh, klooz'-ee-uhm] Lars Porsena was a quasi-historical Etruscan ruler of the 6th century BC. According to Roman tradition, this chieftain of Clusium (modern Chiusi) sought to restore the exiled TARQUINIUS SUPERBUS to the Roman throne but was deterred by the bravery of HORATIUS. Historians give more credence to the Etruscan legend of Mastarna (identified with Porsena), who conquered and ruled Rome until vanquished by the federated forces of the Latin League.

Lartet, Édouard Armand [lahr-tay'] Édouard Armand Isidore Hippolyte Lartet, b. Apr. 15, 1801, d. Jan. 28, 1871, was one of the pioneers of modern paleontology. After his initial discovery (1834) of fossil remains in southwestern France, he began the first systematic investigation of French cave sites. During excavations at Aurignac he found evidence of human and extinct mammals existing in the same period. Beginning in 1863, Lartet and the English ethnologist Henry Christy worked together in the Dordogne area, where they excavated such famous prehistoric sites as Les Eyzies and La Madeleine. Lartet became (1869) professor of paleontology at the Musée d'Histoire Naturelle in Paris.

Lartigue, Jacques Henri [lahr-teeg'] Jacques Henri Lartigue, b. June 13, 1894, d. Sept. 12, 1986, is best known in his native France as a painter, his work having been exhibited in Paris, Marseilles, and Menton. But his photographs, which aim to capture the feeling of movement and to record the emotions of an era, are also highly acclaimed. Many of them appear in *Boyhood Photographs of J.-H. Lartigue: The Family Album of the Gilded Age* (1966); *Diary of a Century* (1970), edited by Richard Avedon; *Les Femmes* (1974); and *The Autochromes of J. H. Lartigue* (1981).

larva [lahr'-vuh] A larva is an immature animal that occurs in the life-cycle stage between the time certain animals hatch from eggs and the time they undergo development, or METAMORPHOSIS, into a markedly different form, the adult. Larval stages occur in many kinds of invertebrates and in fish and amphibians. One kind of amphibian, the AXOLOTL, never passes from the larval stage to the adult stage. Although it becomes sexually mature and reproduces, its outward form is still larval. This condition is called NEOTENY. Some insects first pass through a PUPA stage (seemingly inactive) before reaching the adult stage.

In contrast to adults, whose principal purpose is to reproduce, the principal purpose of larvae is to eat. For many insects the adult diet, if any, is completely different from the larval diet. Therefore, larvae and adults do not compete for the same food. For many marine species the larval stage is also a time of dispersal.

laryngitis [lar-in-jy'-tis] Laryngitis is an inflammation of the LARYNX, or voice box, usually associated with a common cold or overuse of the voice. It is commonly characterized by swelling, hoarseness, pain, dryness in the throat, coughing, and inability to speak above a whisper, if at all. Spasmodic laryngitis, most often seen in children with RICKETS, is characterized by crowing or whistling sounds while breathing in.

Complete recovery from common laryngitis can be expected within a few days if the patient refrains from speaking aloud. Chronic forms of laryngitis without respiratory infection or voice strain may be due to tuberculosis, syphilis, or tumors pressing on or in the larynx.

larynx [lair'-inks] The larynx, or voice box, is a muscular tube in the throat of all mammals and some reptiles and amphibians. It contains the vocal cords, which produce sound that is converted into speech and other utterances by the lips, teeth, and tongue. Birds do not have a larynx, but most have a modified portion of the windpipe called the syrinx with which they vocalize.

The larynx has several segments of firm, elastic cartilage held together by muscle and ligaments. The largest segment, the thyroid cartilage, consists of two plates that form a ridge, called the "Adam's apple." The larynx extends from the pharynx (throat) above to the trachea (windpipe) below.

In mammals, including humans, the larynx has a flap-like structure, the epiglottis, at its inlet. The epiglottis causes swallowed food to pass from the throat into the esophagus rather than into the trachea.

The vocal cords, located in the upper region of the larynx, are two muscularized folds of mucous membrane that extend from the larynx wall. The gap between the folds is the glottis. Each fold encloses an elastic vocal ligament and muscle, which controls the tension and rate of

The larynx regulates voice production and prevents material from entering the windpipe during swallowing. Located at the entrance to the trachea (A), it is a framework of cartilages with different shapes and functions. The vocal cords (1) are stretched between the large thyroid cartilage (2) and two smaller moving cartilages (3). A large cartilaginous ring (4) at the top of the trachea supports the larynx. During swallowing, the vocal cords move together to close the windpipe, and the epiglottis (5) drops over the larynx. The vocal cords move apart during breathing (B). During speech (C) they are drawn together, and air forced through the larynx makes them vibrate.

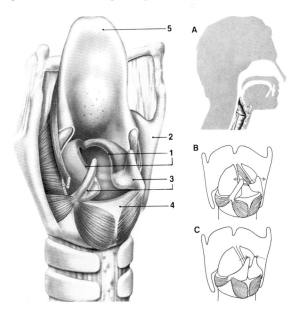

vibration of the cords as air passes through them. In normal breathing the vocal muscles are held slack, allowing air to pass in and out of a wide slit. The tighter the vocal muscles contract the vocal cords, the higher the tone of the sound produced.

Cancers or other growths sometimes necessitate removal of the larynx, an operation known as a laryngectomy. After such an operation a patient usually breathes through a surgically formed opening in the neck. The patient may be taught to use gullet tissues to produce sounds that are then modified by the mouth structures to yield recognizable speech.

Las Campanas Observatory [lahs kahm-pah'-nahs] Las Campanas Observatory, situated on a 2,500-m (8,250-ft) ridge in northern Chile, is operated by the Carnegie Institution of Washington. From 1970 to 1980 it was part of the Hale Observatories. The 2.5-m (100-in) Irenée du Pont telescope, opened in 1977, uses a complex optical system to reduce distortion and achieve an unusually wide field of view. It uses a deeply curved (f/3) primary mirror and a 74-cm (29-in) Gascoigne corrector to eliminate astigmatism. Also on the mountain are a 1-m (40-in) Swope reflector and the 61-cm (24-in) University of Toronto reflector, which was opened in 1971.

Las Casas, Bartolomé de [lahs kah'-sahs, bahr-toh'-loh-may] Known as the Apostle of the Indies, Bartolomé de Las Casas, b. 1474, d. July 1566, was one of the first Spanish missionaries in Latin America. His *Historia de las Indias* (History of the Indies) is a major source for the early period of colonization. Las Casas first went to Hispaniola in 1502, and about 1512 he became a priest. In 1514 he began a lifelong effort to improve conditions for the harshly treated Indians, securing (1542) enactment of the New Laws, by which the system of forced labor called the ENCOMIENDA was to be phased out.

Las Cruces [lahs kroo'-sis] Las Cruces, the seat of Dona Ana County, in southern New Mexico, is located on the Rio Grande, 60 km (37 mi) north of the Mexican border. Its population is 62,126 (1990). Las Cruces is the commercial center for an irrigated agricultural area growing vegetables, cotton, alfalfa, and pecans. New Mexico State University (1888) is there, and the White Sands Missile Range is to the northeast. Of interest are the nearby Organ Mountains, extinct volcanoes in the West Potrillo Mountains, and the small Indian community called Tortugas. Founded in 1848, the town was named for the wooden crosses (*Las Cruces*, in Spanish, "the crosses") marking the graves of an earlier band of settlers from Chihuahua, Mexico.

Las Palmas [lahs pahl'-mahs] Las Palmas, the largest city in Spain's Canary Islands, with a population of 358,272 (1987 est.), is the capital of Las Palmas prov-

ince on Grand Canary Island. It lies 7 km (4 mi) inland from the major port, Puerto de la Luz. Tourism, shipbuilding, fisheries, food processing, and export of agricultural products are important. Of interest is the Cathedral of Santa Ana (begun in 1497). Las Palmas was founded in 1478.

Las Vegas Las Vegas, a city in southeastern Nevada, is the seat of Clark County and, with a population of 258,295 (1990), is the largest city in the state. Because of its gambling casinos, it is a world-famous resort. Las Vegas is also the commercial center for a large mining and ranching area. The city lies at an altitude of 620 m (2,033 ft) on a desert plain surrounded by mountains. Income from luxury hotels, gambling casinos, and other entertainment forms the base of the city's economy. Livestock raising, mining, railroading, and the manufacture of beverages are also important industries. HOOVER DAM is nearby. A branch of the University of Nevada is in Las Vegas.

Artesian springs first attracted California-bound travelers to the site. Mormons from Utah settled there briefly (1855–57), and in 1864 the U.S. Army built Fort Baker. First part of Arizona Territory, Las Vegas was included in the state of Nevada in 1867. Arrival of the railroad in 1905 encouraged the town's growth. Gambling was legalized in Nevada in 1931, and the population burgeoned after 1940.

Lascaux [lahs-koh'] Lascaux, a cave site near Montignac in Dordogne, France, ranks with ALTAMIRA as one of the most spectacular and famous examples of PREHISTORIC ART yet discovered. Superb paintings and drawings in black, brown, red, and yellow pigments, as well as rock engravings, appear on the walls and ceilings of the central cavern and in several side chambers and galleries within the cave. The main cavern, known as the Great Hall of Bulls, is in itself a complete work of art, containing what appears to be a deliberately planned frieze over the entire extent of its walls. The frieze consists of huge polychrome bulls and horses—the largest 5.5 m (18 ft) in length—

This cave painting of a cow and horses from Lascaux in southwestern France dates from the Upper Paleolithic Period (15,000–10,000 BC).

and smaller bison, stags, a bear, and a curious, possibly mythical, spotted and two-horned animal. In the left gallery are the most famous paintings of polychrome animals, including the so-called Frieze of Little Horses and, on the vaulted roof, a beautiful composition with horses and cows. Inside a small side chamber are several engraved cave lions. In the so-called Shaft of the Dead Man is a scene unique in cave art, depicting a two-horned rhinoceros, a schematically drawn dead man, a wounded bison, and a bird on a hooked instrument, possibly a spear-thrower. The significance of the scene and of the many engraved and painted latticelike signs that alternate with the painted animals is obscure.

The art of Lascaux is dated to the early Magdalenian phases of the Upper Paleolithic Period (about 17,000 years ago). Lascaux was closed to the public in 1963; an exact replica of the famous cave, Lascaux II, opened nearby in 1983.

---

laser [lay'-zur] The laser is a device that generates "well-organized", or coherent, LIGHT (see also OPTICS). The mechanism relies on a process known as stimulated emission, and the word *laser* is derived from *L*ight *A*mplification by *S*timulated *E*mission of *R*adiation. The MASER uses the same principle to generate or amplify electromagnetic radiation in the longer-wavelength microwave region.

Characteristics of Laser Light

Light is a wave and as such can be characterized by its frequency or wavelength. Ordinary light is incoherent, but laser light is coherent, that is, all of it has the same wavelength and phase.

Information can be carried by electromagnetic radiation. Light, with a higher frequency than radio waves or microwaves, has a greater information-carrying capacity.

All beams of radiation spread out as they travel (unless they are confined within a pipe or an optical fiber); however, this spreading can be minimized for coherent radiation. Light has a shorter wavelength than radio waves or microwaves and therefore spreads less and can be usefully transmitted over longer distances. In addition, coherent light can be focused into a smaller point than can incoherent radiation. Pulsed lasers offer the possibility of power multiplication: energy can be stored relatively slowly (in the inverted population), and then some fraction can be retrieved in a very brief laser pulse—thus, the power (the rate at which energy is provided) can be much higher than that of the original energy source. Concentration of even modest amounts of energy in a very small area can produce intense heating.

Principles of Operation

The essential components of a typical laser are (1) the

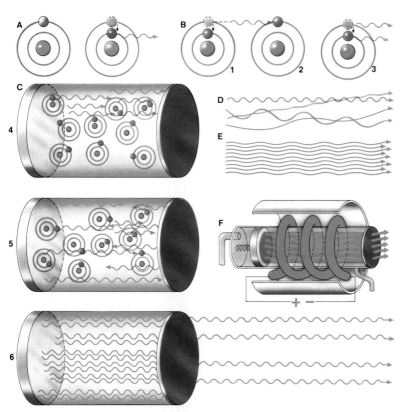

A laser is a device that produces an intense, highly concentrated beam of single-wavelength light. Most light is emitted by an excited atom (A) containing an electron in a higher-than-normal energy level. The electron soon returns spontaneously to its normal, or ground, state, releasing the excess energy in the form of light waves, or photons. In stimulated emission (B), a photon emitted from an atom (1) induces an electron in another excited atom (2) to fall immediately to a lower level and emit a photon identical to itself (3). Stimulated emission can thus be used to increase the number of emitted photons. Energy is first pumped into a laser material (C), raising most of the electrons to a level just above the ground state. Initially (4), only a few atoms will spontaneously radiate photons. Two silvered end mirrors, one partially transparent, reflect the radiation back and forth repeatedly (5), inducing a chain reaction of photon emission. All the electrons return to the ground state almost simultaneously, and a powerful pulse of laser light (6) emerges from the partially transparent end. Whereas light waves from conventional sources have a wide range of wavelengths and move in various directions (D), laser light waves have a single wavelength and are unidirectional and exactly in step with one another (E). A ruby laser (F) comprises a ruby rod with silver-coated ends spring-mounted in a liquid-cooled chamber. Energy for raising the atoms to the high-energy state is supplied by a coiled gas-discharge tube surrounded by a focusing reflector.

Above is one of the two power amplifiers of the huge carbon dioxide laser used in fusion research at Los Alamos National Laboratory. They deliver 20 trillion watts in pulses lasting a billionth of a second.

active medium, such as a ruby rod or carbon dioxide gas; (2) a method of introducing energy into the active medium, such as a flash lamp; and (3) a pair of mirrors placed on each side of the active medium, one of which transmits part of the radiation that strikes it.

The principles of operation of the laser are the same whether its active medium consists of atoms of a gas, molecules in a liquid, ions in a crystal, or any of several other possibilities. To be specific, however, these principles are here described in terms of a gas made up of atoms. Each atom is characterized by a set of energy states, or energy levels, in which it may exist. To simplify matters, consider a fictitious atom having only two energy states, and consider how this atom interacts with light. According to quantum mechanics, the atom interacts with light of only one frequency.

Three kinds of interaction are possible: absorption, stimulated emission, and spontaneous emission. An atom in the lower state can absorb light and be excited to the upper state; an atom in the upper state can fall spontaneously to the lower state, emitting light in the process; or the atom can be stimulated by the presence of light to jump down to the lower state and emit additional light while doing so. In stimulated emission the additional light that is emitted will have the same frequency and directional characteristics as the light that stimulates it. For the laser to work effectively, stimulated emission must predominate over both absorption and spontaneous emission.

For stimulated emission to dominate absorption, more atoms must be in the upper state than in the lower state. This unusual situation is called population inversion and can be achieved by supplying energy ("pumping" the laser) and carefully selecting the active medium. The sequence of events in generating a laser pulse is shown in the diagram.

History

Stimulated emission was proposed by Albert EINSTEIN in

1916, and population inversion was discussed by V. A. Fabrikant in 1940. The first maser was an ammonia maser, constructed in 1954 by J. P. Gordon, H. J. Zeiger, and Charles H. TOWNES. Over the next six years many workers, including Nikolai G. Basov, Aleksandr M. Prokhorov, Arthur L. Schawlow, and Townes, made important contributions that helped to extend these ideas from the microwave to the optical wavelength region. These efforts culminated in July 1960 when Theodore H. MAIMAN announced the generation of a pulse of coherent red light by means of a ruby crystal—the first laser. In 1964, Townes, Basov, and Prokhorov were jointly awarded the Nobel Prize for physics. Schawlow received a Nobel Prize in 1981.

Another aspect of laser history was finally resolved in 1987, when American physicist Gordon GOULD won his 30-year battle to obtain a patent for a gas-discharge laser he had conceived in 1957: he had failed to apply for the patent until 1959.

Laser Types

The helium-neon laser is an inexpensive, common type, costing less than $200. The diode laser is the smallest, being packaged in a transistorlike enclosure. Dye lasers have a broad, continuously variable wavelength capability. The carbon-dioxide laser is the most efficient, with a ratio of output light energy to input electrical energy of up to 30%. Many other types exist; for example, the free-electron laser uses a special magnet to produce a laser beam (ranging from infrared to visible wavelengths) from high-energy electrons emitted by a particle accelerator.

Many of these lasers may be operated so as to produce widely different pulse-duration, power, and wavelength characteristics. Pulse-duration times range from 40 picoseconds (1 psec = 10^{-12} sec) to continuous-wave (cw), which is essentially infinite.

The possible power levels cover a range of a million to a billion in magnitude. The lowest tabulated power—3 milliwatts (mW)—refers to a cw laser. By focusing high-power beams, enormous intensities can be reached for research purposes.

Applications

The ability to control thermonuclear fusion could be used to provide FUSION ENERGY. One approach involves heating and compressing a microscopic pellet of hydrogen-isotope (deuterium or tritium) fuel by placing it at the focus of a high-power, short-pulse laser beam.

Coded light pulses generated by lasers can be transmitted in glass fibers; such communications links are already in use (see FIBER OPTICS).

A laser beam can be used to heat-treat or coat a surface layer of a metal component or to melt and weld a pair of components without introducing sufficient heat to distort them.

Lasers have a number of medical applications. A laser beam can be used to seal capillaries in a shallow surface layer without damaging deeper tissues. Noninvasive surgery of the retina (laser light enters through the eye lens)

An excimer laser threaded into a human heart through a catheter is used to break apart built-up deposits of plaque with brief, intense bursts of energy.

and cauterization of stomach ulcers (light enters via an endoscopic fiber) are important applications.

A laser beam can be used as a straight line in SURVEY-ING. Distances can be measured by timing a light pulse traveling from the laser to a mirror and back to a detector near the laser.

Laser sources allow reproduction of three-dimensional images. This technique is known as HOLOGRAPHY.

Lasers are used by the military for range-finding and target designation and are being developed as both anti-satellite and ballistic-missile defense weapons (see STRA-TEGIC DEFENSE INITIATIVE).

Laser-etched discs are used for large-capacity audio, video, and data recording and playback (see COMPACT DISC; VIDEODISC).

Lashley, Karl S. [lash'-lee]

Karl Spencer Lashley, b. Davis, W.Va., June 7, 1890, d. Aug. 7, 1958, was a pioneer neuropsychologist in the United States especially known for his opposition to theories localizing complex psychological functions in the brain. In *Brain Mechanisms and Intelligence* (1929), Lashley proposed his theories of mass action (that learning involves the entire cortex) and equipotentiality (that parts of the cortex can take over the functions of other, damaged parts). Equally influential were his later papers, "The Problem of Serial Order in Behavior" (1951) and "In Search of the Engram" (1950).

Lassalle, Ferdinand [lah-sahl', fair'-dee-nahn]

Ferdinand Lassalle, b. Apr. 11, 1825, d. Aug. 31, 1864, was one of the founders of the German Social Democratic party. A Hegelian, Lassalle became a friend of Karl MARX but differed from Marx in believing that the Prussian state would aid workers in establishing producer cooperatives. He helped found the Universal German Workers' Associa-tion (1863), which became the Social Democratic party (1875). In conversations with Otto von BISMARCK, Lassalle tried to persuade the future chancellor to introduce universal suffrage, which Lassalle believed would lead to state socialism. He died in a duel.

Lassen Peak [las'-en]

Lassen Peak, an active volcano in the CASCADE RANGE in northeastern California, is 3,187 m (10,457 ft) high. It last erupted in 1921. The volcano's period of greatest recorded activity was in 1914–15, when massive mudflows and gaseous explosions destroyed large areas of forest. The Lassen Volcanic National Park, covering 430 km^2 (166 mi^2) and established in 1916, includes Lassen Peak, other volcanic cones, hot springs, mud pots, and fumaroles. Lassen Peak was discovered in 1821.

Lassus, Roland de [lah-sues']

Roland de Lassus, b. 1532, d. June 14, 1594, was a great Flemish composer. At the age of 21 he was appointed choirmaster at the basilica of Saint John Lateran in Rome. He relinquished the post a year and a half later to Giovanni Pierluigi da Palestrina, with whose music his own is often linked as embodying the ideals of Counter-Reformation polyphony. Lassus entered the service of Duke Albert V of Bavaria in 1556 and within a few years became chapelmaster at the court in Munich. He remained there, except for journeys to important musical centers including Venice, Paris, and Rome, until his death.

Lassus's surviving works, many of which were published during his lifetime, include approximately 175 madrigals and lighter works with Italian texts, 150 French chansons, 90 German lieder, about 50 masses, and more than 500 motets. The principal source of the motets is the *Magnum opus musicum*, a collection of 516 pieces for 2 to 12 voices printed posthumously in 1604. His secular music is by turns humorous, witty, noble, or sentimental, mirroring perfectly the mood of his chosen text. In his sacred music he sought out and expressed the inner meaning of the words through the use of ingenious and ever-changing musical means. A famous example of this expressive style is his setting of the *Seven Penitential Psalms*, completed in 1570.

Last Supper

The meal shared by JESUS CHRIST and his disciples on the night before he was crucified is called the Last Supper (Matt. 26:20–29; Mark 14:17–25; Luke 22:14–38; John 13:1–17:26). It was the occasion of his institution of the EUCHARIST, when he identified the broken bread with his body and the cup of wine with his blood of the new COVENANT. The ritual was that of a Jewish religious meal, which was given new meaning for Jesus' followers when they performed it in remembrance of him. Christians differ as to the meaning of the words of Jesus, the exact relationship of the bread and wine to his body and blood, and the frequency with which the rite is to be repeated.

Latakia [lat-uh-kee´-uh]   Latakia (1989 est. pop., 258,000) is the largest port of Syria and the capital of Latakia governorate. Situated on the Mediterranean in the northwest part of the country, Latakia is a market center and produces ceramics, asphalt, and cotton and tobacco products. Sponge fishing is important. Because of earthquakes, the city lacks old landmarks.

Of ancient origin, the city was called Ramitha by the Phoenicians. In the late 4th century BC it was named Laodicea by the Macedonian conqueror Seleucus I; this name was altered in time to the present name. Latakia was later held, successively, by the Romans, Arabs, Crusaders, Egyptian Ayyubids, and Ottoman Turks. After World War I it was the capital of the French territory of the Alawites until it was incorporated into the French mandate of Syria in 1926. Latakia became part of the independent republic of Syria in 1942.

Lateran councils [lat´-ur-uhn]   The Lateran councils were five ecumenical councils (see COUNCIL, ECUMENICAL) of the Roman Catholic church held during the 12th, 13th, and 16th centuries at the Lateran Palace in Rome. The First Lateran Council (1123) was called by Pope CALLISTUS II to ratify the Concordat of Worms (1122), which formally ended the lengthy INVESTITURE CONTROVERSY. The Second Lateran Council (1139) was convoked by Pope Innocent II to reaffirm the unity of the church after the schism (1130–38) of the antipope Anacletus II (d. 1138). It also condemned the teachings of ARNOLD OF BRESCIA. The Third Lateran Council (1179), convoked by Pope ALEXANDER III, ended the schism (1159–77) of the antipope Callistus III and his predecessors. It also limited papal electors to members of the College of Cardinals.

The Fourth Lateran Council (1215), convoked by Pope INNOCENT III, was attended by well over 1,000 churchmen from throughout Christendom. It sanctioned a definition of the EUCHARIST in which the word *transubstantiation* was used officially for the first time. The council also attempted to organize a new crusade to the Holy Land and to encourage crusading efforts against the ALBIGENSES and WALDENSES. Many precepts still binding on Roman Catholics (such as the Easter duty, or obligation, of annual confession and Holy Communion) were adopted at this council. The Fifth Lateran Council (1512–17), convened by Pope JULIUS II and continued by Pope LEO X, was convoked for the purpose of reform, but the main causes of the Reformation were left untouched. Its most significant decree was a condemnation of CONCILIARISM.

laterite [lat´-ur-ite]   The red, residual soil laterite is a weathering product comprised of a mixture of hydrated iron and aluminum oxides. Laterites are especially characteristic of the tropics and form under conditions of good drainage, high temperature, and extensive rainfall. The silica, alkalies, and alkaline earths of the parent rock are removed either by solution or colloidal processes. Iron tends to be oxidized and remains with the alumina. High-alumina laterites or high-iron laterites are sometimes mined as ores. The name is derived from the Latin word (*later*) for brick, which can be made from hardened laterite.

latex [lay´-teks]   A latex is a colloidal suspension of very small polymer particles (see POLYMERIZATION) in water. Many polymers can be produced as latex, but RUBBER latexes especially are of great commercial importance. Natural rubber comes from the tree as a latex; several synthetic rubbers are produced as latexes because the polymerization process takes place in water. In both cases the water is a soapy solution that helps the particles to remain separate. Products such as gloves or contraceptives are made directly from rubber latex. Latex paints are essentially a solution of colored pigment and rubber latex.

lathe   A lathe, or turning machine, is a MACHINE TOOL that removes unwanted material from a cylindrical workpiece by rotating it against a cutting tool. Common operations include shaping, boring, and threading. The lathe is the oldest and most important machine tool. Early wood-turning lathes, powered by a foot treadle, were used during the Middle Ages. The first screw-cutting lathe was developed by Jacques Besson in 1569, and the first

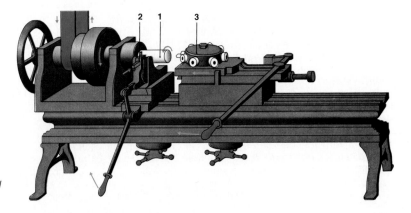

The invention of the turret lathe in 1850 was a major advance in mass production of metal components. Prior to that time a metal part (1) was machined by rotating it (red arrows) and slowly moving (blue arrows) a suitable cutting tool (2) against the work by means of a lever; a tool change required stopping the machine and replacing one tool with another, and then resetting the new tool before work could continue. The rotating turret (3) that was devised could hold up to eight different cutting tools. When the various tools were correctly adjusted in the turret by a skilled machinist, the lathe could be operated by an unskilled worker, who merely had to move the tool-feeding lever and turn the turret from one tool position to another according to a set procedure.

practical all-metal screw-cutting lathe was built by Henry MAUDSLAY about 1800. Maudslay's machine developed into the modern engine lathe, so named because it was first driven by James Watt's steam engine.

The engine lathe is one of the most useful machine tools. Its cutting tool can be power-driven along the edge and across the face of the workpiece for uniform cutting and to reproduce parts. Turret lathes provide a number of quickly indexed tools that can be used in sequence. Screw lathes synchronize the motion of the cutting tool with the rotation of the workpiece. Some turning machines have a vertical spindle (that is, the part that revolves with the workpiece) instead of a horizontal spindle and have a large rotating table, sometimes measuring a few meters across. Such a lathe is called a vertical boring mill and is capable of holding and turning huge castings or weldments. Speed lathes use a hand-manipulated cutting tool. These machines include metal-spinning lathes, used for forming and polishing.

The ancient Inca site of Machu Picchu (AD 1450–1532), located near Cuzco, Peru, contains superb examples of Inca masonry construction and agricultural terracing.

Lathrop, Rose Hawthorne [lay'-thruhp] Rose Hawthorne Lathrop, b. Lenox, Mass., May 20, 1851, d. July 9, 1926, the youngest child of Nathaniel Hawthorne, became a nun at the age of 49 and devoted herself to aiding the incurably ill.

Twenty years after her marriage, she and her husband, George P. Lathrop, became Roman Catholics in 1891. The couple separated, however, and, from 1896, Rose dedicated herself to caring for poverty-stricken cancer victims. Following her husband's death, she became a nun in 1900 and founded the Congregation of Saint Rose of Lima, a community of Dominican sisters. Taking the name Mary Alphonsa, she became superior of the nursing organization now known as the Servants of Relief for Incurable Cancer. A small house on New York's Lower East Side was formally constituted (1912) as Saint Rose's Free Home for Incurable Cancer.

Latimer, Hugh [lat'-ih-mur, hyoo] The English church reformer Hugh Latimer, b. *c.*1485, d. Oct. 16, 1555, was martyred with Nicholas RIDLEY under Queen MARY I. Ordained in 1522, he at first opposed Reformation ideas, but under the influence of the Cambridge reformer Thomas Bileny (*c.*1495–1531) he altered his opinions. He was twice imprisoned under HENRY VIII. His position improved with his defense of Henry's divorce and the king's subsequent break with Rome, following which Latimer was appointed (1535) bishop of Worcester. When the Roman Catholic Mary succeeded to the throne in 1553, he was confined to the Tower of London and, following a theological disputation, was burned at the stake.

Latin American art and architecture Latin American art and architecture refers to the artistic traditions developed by the European colonizers of Mexico, Central America, and South America, and their descen-

dants. Since the European discovery of the New World, the art and architecture of this vast area has evolved in two phases. The first was the colonial phase, beginning late in the 15th century and ending early in the 19th century, after the wars for independence were concluded. In Mexico the Revolution of the early 20th century marked the beginning of the second phase—the emergence of modern developments in architecture, painting, and sculpture. The rest of Latin America entered this phase at various times, although generally soon after it had begun in Mexico.

Highly developed civilizations existed in the New World thousands of years before the arrival of Europeans. Pre-Columbian American centers of great importance flourished in the Andes, central Mexico, and the MAYA area (Yucatán and Central America) up until the time of the Spanish conquest of the AZTECS (1519–21) and of the INCA (1531). On the desert coast of Peru the ruins of sun-dried mud-brick buildings carved with polychromed relief sculptures can still be seen at CHAN CHAN (AD 1200–1450) and other sites; remains of expertly cut stone constructions exist at CUZCO, MACHU PICCHU (AD 1450–1532), and elsewhere in the Andean highlands. In Mexico pyramids of earthen rubble faced with stone and finished with brilliantly painted plaster dominated the architecture of the pre-Columbian period. TEOTIHUACÁN, a great urban center of the central valley of Mexico (200 BC–AD 750), was larger in area than Imperial Rome.

Generally characteristic of PRE-COLUMBIAN ART AND ARCHITECTURE was its skillful integration of architecture, sculpture, and painting. This synthesizing tendency is also seen in the baroque style that appeared during the colonial period, and it is characteristic of much modern Latin American architecture.

Few of the native-American arts survived long after the conquest. In the manuscript painting practiced among the Indians of Mexico, earlier pre-Columbian styles with their abstract rendering of human figures gradually gave way to a more European approach to forms, the handling of the brush and pen, and even the use of European paper instead of tree bark and other native materials. Another survival of the pre-Columbian period in Mexico was the making of feather mosaics. Here the artists changed from making garments for the Aztec rulers and nobility to making decorations for bishops' miters and for other Christian ecclesiastical objects. In Peru the *keru*, a flared wooden drinking vessel decorated with carved and painted designs in the Inca tradition, continued into the colonial period with few changes except in subject matter.

Folk art traditions that began in the 16th century became widespread throughout Latin America. The Santos, polychrome paintings and sculptures of saints, executed in a notably reverential yet primitive style, are typical examples of folk art. Many church exteriors in the Andes region exhibit relief patterns resembling those found in local textiles. This distinctive folk style is sometimes called *mestizo* ("mixed") art because it combines traditional Indian features with Christian elements.

Colonial Period

During the colonial period cities of great architectural splendor as well as local schools of painting and sculpture arose, especially in those parts of Latin America where the pre-Hispanic civilizations had thrived at the time of the conquest. In Peru the main Inca center of Cuzco became in the colonial period a splendid city with great churches, monastic buildings, and palaces. The School of Cuzco, a major colonial painting tradition noted for its profuse use of gold leaf, also developed there. TENOCHTITLÁN, the Aztec capital, became Mexico City, the seat of the richest New World viceroyalty (that of New Spain) and an archbishopric; it is still sometimes called the City of Palaces, and its school of painting became the most important in the colonial world. Cities that became in effect cultural satellites of these two early capitals include Bogotá and Quito for Cuzco and Puebla and Oaxaca for Mexico City. Colonial Buenos Aires in Argentina, Santiago in Chile, Monterrey in Mexico, and Antigua in Guatemala were more or less frontier towns by comparison, depending primarily on mining, trade, or administration rather than cultural ascendancy for their importance in colonial times.

Unlike the other major New World colonies, the former Portuguese colony of Brazil was built upon no preexisting high Indian culture. Nevertheless, the architecture, painting, and sculpture of its principal colonial centers— Bahia, Recife, Belém—as well as of its mining towns in the province of Minas Gerais—all bear the imprint of having been created in a metropolitan environment rather than in provincial outposts. Perhaps strict ties to Lisbon kept Brazil abreast of European trends.

Sixteenth Century. The 16th century marked the construction of a wide range of public building (of which few are still standing); many monastic establishments, mainly by the Augustinian, Dominican, and Franciscan men's orders; and the beginnings of the great cathedrals. The early military conquerors and religious orders in the New

This 16th-century painted wooden figure of San Guillermo from Quito, Equador, exemplifies the statuary of the colonial period in Latin America.

World brought with them works of art—paintings and sculptures—as well as knowledge of the main architectural styles then current in Spain, particularly Late Gothic vaulted churches with pointed arches, buttresses, and traceried windows. The Late Gothic style, dominant in the early monastic establishments, was often conjoined with external facades and interior altarpieces designed in the Plateresque, or early Renaissance, style of Spain. This combination of styles appears in the cathedral of Santo Domingo on Hispaniola, the oldest cathedral in the New World, begun in 1512. By the end of the 16th century more advanced construction techniques appeared.

Another style the Spanish brought to their new colonies was called Mudéjar, meaning the style of Moorish artisans working for Christians. The most prevalent form of Mudéjar art to reach the New World, seen especially in South America and in the Carribean Islands, is the elaborate carved and painted coffered ceilings with exposed wooden beams. Modeled stucco decoration also using Moorish designs often appears on the outer walls of buildings. In Lima palaces having shuttered wooden balconies are reminiscent of the Moslem world of Spain or North Africa.

Throughout the colonial period, beginning with the first foundation of cities, an important role was played by forms of military architecture—castles, fortified city walls, and forts. City planning was also of great importance because so many new towns and villages had to be founded. In Mexico the Spaniards frequently relocated Indian villages from the low-lying hills to open and accessible locations so that they could be better controlled. When the new village or town was laid out it followed the regular European Renaissance plan—a gridiron of streets intersecting at right angles with a main plaza in the heart of the town. On this plaza were built the parish church or, depending on the importance of the town, cathedral, and other public buildings such as the city hall and jail, residences for important royal officials, and in the case of a

The architecture of Lima, Peru, the capital of Spain's New World empire until the 19th century, possesses a more profound Spanish influence than other Peruvian cities where Indian culture maintained its identity. The Palace of the Archbishop of Lima reflects Moorish architectural styles.

cathedral town, the palace of the bishop or archbishop.

In painting, frescoes decorating some of the earliest colonial buildings were executed in grisaille (shades of gray that create the illusion of sculpture). Sixteenth-century painters who migrated from Europe included Italian-born Bernardo Bitti (1548–1610) in South America, and in Mexico, Flemish-born Simón Pereyns (active second half of the 16th century). Both painted in the Mannerist style characterized by attenuated body proportions, small heads, and a kind of withdrawn facial expression. In the colonies as in Spain, the subject matter of painting was mainly of a religious nature; secular subjects were limited to portraits, and landscapes were unknown.

Seventeenth and Eighteenth Centuries. From the beginning of the 17th century to the end of the colonial period, the baroque styles dominated the artistic life of the Spanish and Portuguese colonies. Several phases of the baroque style are clearly evident in the monumental architecture and in the carved wooden retables (altarpieces) of the colonial church. The baroque retable is a painted and gilded screenlike construction placed behind the altar and often reaching from floor to ceiling. In the early 17th century appeared the so-called salamonic column, derived from the European Plateresque tradition. This spiral-shaped column, profusely carved with flower and fruit motifs, became a primary element in the 17th-century baroque altarpiece.

Colonial architectural projects were greatly expanded in the 18th century. Universities and other educational buildings were raised, as were numerous parish churches in the rich mining towns such as Taxco and Guanajuato in Mexico. Typically they were built on a cruciform plan with a dome over the crossing of nave and transepts. Golden altars were richly adorned with paintings and lifelike polychromed sculptures often garbed in silk, satin, or velvet garments.

In 1718, Jerónimo Balbás (fl. 1706–50) came from Spain to Mexico and introduced the sumptuous *estípite* columns in the Altar of the Kings in the Cathedral of Mexico City. The associated style of exuberant architectural decoration, commonly called Churrigueresque after the famous Spanish architect José de Churriguera (see CHURRIGUERA family), dominated colonial architecture for the rest of the century. *Estípite* columns are square in cross section and divided into three unequal parts by

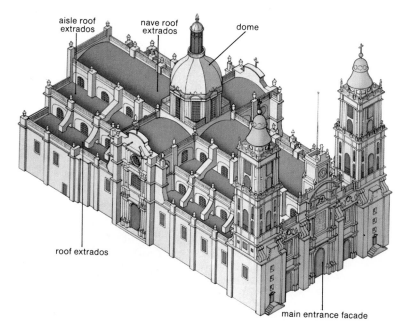

The Cathedral of Mexico City (1563–1667), built on the site of an ancient Aztec temple, is the largest church in Mexico. As master of architecture to King Philip II of Spain, Alonso Pérez de Castañeda based his design on the style of the 16th-century Jaén Cathedral in Spain. The plan is basilicalike and involves a fusion of architectural styles from Gothic to baroque. In the late 18th and early 19th centuries, the Spanish architect Manuel Tolsa designed the dome and lantern.

This 17th-century gilt-stucco relief of the Tree of Jesse is from the vault of Santo Domingo in Oaxaca, Mexico. Mexican art of this period was based on baroque styles, and interior design was characterized by ornamental facings.

deep horizontal moldings. They are usually covered with sculptured and gilded plants, fruits, and flowers. The entablature above is equally elaborated so that the visual effect is often dazzling, especially when it lines the entire side wall of a church or the main altar in the apse.

The erection of countless palaces in the cities and grand haciendas in the country marked the agricultural wealth of the colonists in the 18th century. As seen in the elegant house of the Marqués de Jaral de Berrio (c.1760; Mexico City), the city palace typically had a large formal patio in the front part of the building with an entrance from the street large enough to admit horses and carriages. The formal staircase of the first patio led to the formal rooms on the first floor—dining room, salon, sitting rooms, bedrooms, and in the most affluent houses, even a private chapel. Other patios followed in the plan, often one for the stables and carriage house, one for the kitchen, and another for the laundry and other services. The sculptural decoration on the palace walls followed generally that used in churches—salamonic columns in the 17th and estípite columns in the 18th century. In addition to architectural sculpture on the exterior facade the family coat of arms invariably appeared and often, in a niche, the patron saint of the builder.

Portrait painting became immensely popular in the late 17th and 18th centuries. Wealthy members of the colonial nobility posed in all of their most rich and formal finery—silks from China, pearls from the Pacific, and the insignias of knighthood and nobility from Spain or Portugal. The foreground of full-length or half-length portraits often includes a large painted shield or cartouche with the sitter's names and titles. Prominent painters of the

school of Mexico City were Baltasar de Echave Ibia (c.1585–c.1645), Cristobal de Villalpando (c.1652–1714), and Miguel Cabrera (1695–1768).

The main contribution of Brazil to the art of the baroque period was its magnificent churches and the sculptural creations of Antonio Francisco Lisboa, known as ALEIJADINHO. Brazilian architects endowed their churches with a forceful spatial expressiveness through the use of interconnecting oval interior spaces and contrasting concave and convex exterior walls. The octagonal nave was basic to much Brazilian church architecture.

Postcolonial Period

At the end of the 18th century the Spanish colonies received a royal order to cease building altarpieces in the opulent *estípite* style and also to destroy the ones in use and replace them with more chaste altars. Polychromed sculpture, lavish use of paintings, and the overwhelming profusion of gilding were all to be discontinued; the architectural elements were thenceforth to be made of white marble, alabaster, or of wood painted white to imitate marble. Columns were to be made in the simple forms associated with classical antiquity; the baroque predilection for carving plant decorations on the shaft was to be eliminated. This French-derived neoclassical style, reflected in such buildings as the College of Mines palace (1797–1813; Mexico City), emerged in both the Hispanic and Brazilian colonies in the late 18th and early 19th centuries, forming a bridge between the colonial period and the period of Latin American independence, which began in 1821.

Nineteenth Century. Architectural activity remained rather limited until the latter part of the 19th century, when the disturbances of the immediate postindepen-

The Prophet Daniel (1800–05) is one of the Twelve Prophets at Congohas do Campo created by the Brazilian architect and sculptor Antonio Francisco Lisboa, called o Aleijadinho ("The Little Cripple"). Aleijadinho was the most influential and widely acclaimed sculptor of colonial Brazil.

(Far left) *Mexico's folk art has flourished since ancient times. This scene of rural life, executed in bright colors on treated tree bark, epitomizes the vitality and originality of the Mexican folk art tradition.*

(Left) *The tradition of making handpainted wood and porcelain dolls has been part of Peruvian folk culture since the Spanish conquest. This elaborately costumed angel, depicted in a realistic style, was made by the 20-century folk artist Hilario Mendivil.*

dence period had abated and a new prosperity gained ground in Latin America. During the renewed period of building, new technologies such as plumbing, electrical equipment, and elevators were imported from Europe or the United States. Another import was the eclectic style associated with the École des Beaux Arts of Paris. Decorative detailing is rich and varied in this Beaux Arts style, as exemplified in the Venetian Gothic–styled post office in Mexico City and the baroque national theater (now the Palacio de Bellas Artes), both by the architect Adamo Boari. Bronze or wrought-iron balustrades, carved marble facades, and finely finished interior wood paneling were all part of the architectural program in the many Beaux Arts–inspired urban buildings of the late 19th century. The Art Nouveau style stemming from France was also widespread at the turn of the century.

Latin American painting in the 19th century can be divided into three major categories: academic painting sponsored by the government or by members of the ruling elite; folk art, continuing the strong currents of popular art that originated in the earliest days of the colonies; and a new element, the painting of everyday life in Latin America by European or North American artists traveling through the New World.

Academic painting in Mexico reflected the styles of academic painting that arose in Europe. Early in the 19th century neoclassicism was introduced, the foremost representative being the Mexican painter Rafael Jimeno y Planes (1759–1825), who decorated (1810) the dome of the cathedral of Mexico City. A revival of the baroque in the mid- and late 19th century was characterized by large, complex compositions depicting historical subjects. Whereas in Europe classical Greek or Roman subjects were generally portrayed, in Latin America subjects from its own past were favored, including scenes of Christopher Columbus, the Catholic kings, and other subjects from Spanish history. Uniquely New World subjects such as the invention of pulque (a Mexican fermented beverage) or the torture of Cuauhtemoc (an Aztec ruler) were also depicted, especially in Mexico.

Landscape painters also found much of their inspiration in European art styles. The landscapes of the great Mexican master José María Velasco Ibarra are among the most impressive paintings of their genre, on either side of the Atlantic.

Nineteenth-century folk art is represented not only by the continuation of rather stiff portraits but also by increasing numbers of *Ex-Votos*, a type of religious painting still being produced today. The *Ex-Voto* is rendered to offer thanks for a miraculous intervention by a particular saint or image of the Christ. Usually the account of what happened and the nature of the intercession is written out in detail, including the date and place in which the event occurred.

Among foreign artists who painted Latin American subjects was Frederick Catherwood, who excelled in making extraordinarily accurate views of Mayan ruins. The painters of the customs of the people, sometimes linked with native painters of similar subject matter who were called *costumbristas*, delighted in the picturesque character of country life.

Twentieth Century. Following the Mexican Revolution of 1910, an entirely new trend emerged in Latin American art and architecture—first in Mexico and at various times thereafter in other Latin American countries. The academic salon painting of Hispanic or pre-Hispanic historical subjects disappeared from the scene. In its place mural painting portraying the revolution emerged as the representative type. While the Parisian school was experimenting with cubism and collages and the Bauhaus group in Germany was creating abstract geometric exercises, the Mexicans were returning to representational traditions of Late Gothic and Renaissance Italy—paintings with didactic, humanistic meaning, now charged with clear political overtones. Like the great quatrocentro masters of the Italian Renaissance, the major Mexican

David Alfaro Siqueiros is one of the innovators in modern Mexican mural art. His abstract vision is depicted in The March of Humanity in Latin America. *(1971; Parque de Lama, Mexico City.)*

Diego Rivera's mural March to Tenochtitlan *(1929–35, 1944–50) is one of the scenes of Mexican history portrayed by the artist for the Palacio Nacional in Mexico City.*

muralists—Diego RIVERA, José Clemente OROZCO, and David Alfaro SIQUEIROS—painted large-scale figures using the fresco method, integrated painting into the framework of architecture, and recounted for the people large historical epics. The artistic energy represented by the work of these three men surfaced in an entire school of painters, all focusing on the human form as their main artistic motif, some in terms of history, some in terms of sociological significance, some as painters of scenes from Mexican life and lore, some even as surrealists.

Cándido Portinari is the most widely recognized of Brazil's recent painters. A true modernist, he did fresco murals as well as panel paintings of the Brazilian people, especially cowboys and city workers. Other well-known avant-garde painters include the Argentine Emilio Pettoruti, the Chilean Roberto MATTA ECHAURREN, and the Cuban Raúl Martinez.

Modern architecture in Latin America began as early as the 1920s with the functionalist principles of such Mexican architects as Juan O'GORMAN and José Villagrán Garcia. In Brazil the construction of the new Ministry of Education and Health building (1934–43; Rio de Janeiro) clearly signaled the inception of the modern international style. Among the participating architects were Lúcio COSTA and Oscar NIEMEYER; Le Corbusier came from France to act as consultant.

An almost baroque use of curving walls and dynamic definitions of internal and external space are found in much Latin American architecture, notably that of the Mexican architect Félix CANDELA. The combination of painted murals or mosaic-work with sculpture often forms an integral part of the architecture, as in O'Gorman's mo-

saic-filled Library Building at the University of Mexico (1953). The University City in Caracas, Venezuela, built (1950–57) by Carlos Raúl VILLANUEVA, is another example of the focused campus in place of the older tradition of the university occupying scattered buildings in the heart of a metropolis.

Perhaps the greatest urban design of this century in Latin America and one of the major examples of urban planning in the world is that of Brasília, the new inland

Alvorada Palace, the Brazilian presidential residence, is located in the inland capital city of Brasília. The palace is one of the many buildings designed for the city since 1960 by the architect Oscar Niemeyer.

capital of Brazil by Lúcio Costa (1957). Here an entire city, with all of its administrative, legislative, and executive functions clearly planned, was designed to bring the life of Brazil inland from the old coastal cities of the colonial period. Most of the individual buildings have been executed since 1960, by Oscar Niemeyer.

▬ Latin American literature

Latin American literature   As the result of a boom in novel writing during the 1960s, Latin American literature finally captured world attention. The novels, quickly translated into the major Western languages, caught the attention of critics and public alike both for the originality of their topics—all part of the present reality of Latin America—and for their rich, innovative styles.

Native and Early Colonial Writings. Except for the romances of chivalry they knew so well, and, to a lesser extent, the Bible, the Europeans who first came to Latin America in the 15th and 16th centuries had no literary models on which to base descriptions of what they found. The chronicles of the first conquerors and colonizers therefore contain accounts of feats of courage and bouts of despair that are half-real, half-imagined in the light of the books they had read at home. The land and its inhabitants were often described in idealized terms that suggested the influence of the popular European notion of the noble savage. In practice, however, the natives were enslaved through excessive labor, and their cultures were desecrated.

The degree of civilization represented by the indigenous tribes living in the New World varied widely. Some examples of the great Maya, Inca, and Aztec civilizations were preserved, thanks to the efforts of sympathetic friars. The Maya sacred book *Popol Vuh* (Eng. trans., 1950), containing their philosophy, cosmology, and history, is an example of this extraordinary culture. The Franciscan Fray Bernardino de Sahagún (c.1500–90) wrote a history of New Spain, as Mexico was then called, basing his observations on material in Nahuatl, the language of the Aztecs; and a mestizo from the viceroyalty of Peru, Garcilaso Inca de la Vega, wrote his *Royal Commentaries* (1609–17; Eng. trans., 1869–71) to record life in pre-Columbian Peru as well as the conquest and civil wars that followed.

Most Latin American literature in the 16th and 17th centuries attempted to describe the newly conquered lands for the European reader. Writers wavered between awestruck amazement and hyperbolic language when describing the exotic birds, the vibrant hues of tropical plants, the strange inhabitants, and their rites and temples; at the same time they recorded and sometimes enhanced their own major feat, the conquest. Perhaps the most engrossing account of this event is given by Bernal Díaz del Castillo (c.1492–1584) in *The True Story of the Conquest of Mexico* (1632; Eng. trans., 1956). This amazing chronicle vividly recalls the adventures of the author as a young soldier in the army of Cortés.

Although the largest number of works dealt with the conquest as a feat of courage and faith, critics of the enterprise were not lacking. Fray Bartolomé de LAS CASAS,

the most distinguished and successful critic, in his *Brevísima relación de la destrucción de las Indias* (1552; trans. 1953 as *The Tears of the Indians*) indicted the Spanish crown and its representatives for their maltreatment and eventual decimation of the native population. His advocacy prompted the king in Madrid to issue ordinances to temper the abuses.

Once colonization ended, picaresque accounts of travel and adventure, such as that written in 1690 by the Mexican Carlos de SIGÜENZA Y GÓNGORA, began to flourish. At the most sumptuous viceregal courts in Mexico and Lima baroque verse came into fashion in imitation of the style in vogue at the Spanish court. A Mexican nun, Sor JUANA INÉS DE LA CRUZ, became well known as the "tenth muse" at the Mexican court for her dramatic pieces, poetry, and sophisticated scientific and philosophical writings.

Literature of Independence. The 18th century and the beginning of the 19th saw the stirrings of a new pride among Latin Americans as independence approached. Most writers were by now members of the creole group, that is, descendants of Europeans born in the New World, with an allegiance to and sense of pride in their native land rather than Spain. After revolts against Spanish rule, independence was declared in Venezuela (1811), Mexico (1816), and Buenos Aires (1821). Not until later in the 1820s, however, did most of the continent free itself. With autonomy a variety of national literatures emerged, and attention was focused on both the land and the Indian, mulatto, or mestizo as its native inhabitant. Poets, realizing they had to establish their cultural identity, addressed themselves to the battles and heroes of independence, *La Victoria de Junín: a Bolívar* (The Victory of Junín: Hymn to Bolívar, 1825) of José Joaquín Olmedo (1790–1847) being the best-known example.

The Indian was the exalted topic of the poem *La Cautiva* (The Captive, 1837) by Esteban Echeverría and of the collection of poems *En el teocalli de Cholula* (On the Pyramid of Cholula, 1820) by José María Heredia (1803–39). Andrés BELLO and Domingo Faustino SARMIENTO both grappled with the problem of creating a grammar for the Spanish used in the New World; both also wrote works of description of the land, whereas Sarmiento alone, in his study of the native leader Juan Facundo Quiroga, attacked *caudillismo* (military dictatorship). It is at this point that barbarism and civilization come to be identified as coexisting and contending forces in Latin American life. To secure the victory of the latter was the task most writers set themselves; at the same time they evoked with a certain nostalgia the life of the gaucho and of the country dweller. The greatest work in this tradition, the epic *Martín Fierro* (1872) by José Hernández, became the national poem of Argentina.

Modernism. The last decade of the 19th century saw the emergence of a specifically Latin American literary movement, modernism. Its main exponent was the Nicaraguan Rubén DARÍO. Steeped in the French poetic tradition and in traditional Spanish verse, Darío managed to bring to Spanish verse a flexibility based on new combinations of sounds, kinesthesia, and evocation of moods. He also popularized the idea of Latin America as con-

Pablo Neruda (1904–73)

Carlos Fuentes (1928–)

Gabriel García Márquez (1928–)

stituting one homeland, having himself lived in several sister nations as well as in Paris and Spain. Darío's predecessor, the Cuban José MARTÍ, had introduced this notion while actively participating in the struggle to liberate his native land.

Literature of the Land and of the Mexican Revolution. At the start of the 20th century the so-called novel of the land emerged, undertaking to describe without idealization the land and its peoples and the ways of life specific to the geographic conditions. The gaucho in the pampas, the peon on the rubber plantation or in the sugarcane fields, the rancher of the Venezuelan plains, the Indian in his Andean hut—each was the subject of novels: *Raza de bronce* (A Race of Bronze, 1919) by Alcides Arguedas of Bolivia, *Don Segundo Sombra* (1926; trans. as *Shadows on the Pampas*, 1935) by Ricardo Güiraldes of Argentina, *Doña Bárbara* (1929; Eng. trans., 1931) by Rómulo GALLEGOS of Venezuela, *The Vortex* (1924; Eng. trans., 1935) by José Eustasio Rivera of Colombia, *Huasipungo* (1934; Eng. trans., 1962) by Jorge Icaza of Ecuador, and jungle stories by Horacio Quiroga of Argentina.

The Mexican Revolution (1910–20) received its own treatment in poetry and a series of novels. The most famous novel was *The Underdogs* (1915; Eng. trans., 1929) by Mariano AZUELA, who had fought in support of Francisco Madero, leader of the revolution. His work records the rise and fall of a peasant fighter for whom the revolution brings only suffering and devastation. Unlike the romantic writers, the novelists of the land no longer stood in awe of the landscape. They began to perceive that injustice was the prevailing order, that it had not disappeared with the coming of political independence. Their not-so-new social institutions, combined with what had been accepted unquestioningly in the previous century as the beneficent influence of European thought, began to seem inadequate to the American reality. These novelists, at times despairing of improving the lot of the downtrodden—even by violent, revolutionary means—ultimately stressed the innate purity of the people of the land, as revealed, for instance, by the peasant fighter in

The Underdogs and by the Indian characters in Icaza's works. Even *Shadows on the Pampas*, produced by a writer refined in the Parisian manner, suggests that spiritual renewal is to be found on the land rather than in salons.

The Brazilian Modernists. At the start of the 20th century the Brazilian modernist movement, centered on São Paulo, began to achieve a similar cultural independence. Brazil had gone through the same stages of development as the rest of Latin America, but its political and cultural independence came more gradually. The first emperor of Brazil, Pedro I, was a legitimate member of the royal Portuguese dynasty. Although he declared Brazil's independence from Portugal in 1822, the country remained under imperial rule and the dominance of the court in Rio de Janeiro until 1889.

With Brazil thus tied to Portuguese culture, Brazilian writers only little by little assumed responsibility for giving expression to their own landscape and ethnic mix of peoples. The presence of large numbers of former slaves added a distinctive African character to the culture, and subsequent infusions of immigrants of non-Portuguese origin helped the new nation to find its own voice.

Early in the century the novels of Joaquim Maria MACHADO DE ASSIS, such as *Dom Casmurro* (1899; Eng. trans., 1953), of Graça Aranna (1868–1931), and of Euclydes da Cunha (1866–1909) took stock of both urban and rural Brazilian life. About 1922 the modernist group (unrelated to the Spanish-language modernists of the 1890s) broke totally with this past, declaring themselves representatives of a new vanguard, and in numerous magazines and small publications experimented with verse and prose. A great deal of editorial and dramatic activity spread to areas remote from the coast, thus helping to upgrade the cultural validity of regions other than the largest urban centers. In the past the states of both Bahía and Minas Gerais had fostered active but relatively short-lived literary movements. Mário de ANDRADE was the foremost exponent of the modernist group.

Recent Latin American Literature. Brazil has given birth to a number of avant-garde schools since modernism, the best known being "concrete poetry," and both poetry and fiction have continued to develop under local and European influence. Recent Brazilian authors include Jorge AMADO, Érico Veríssimo (1905–75), Oswald de Andrade (1890–1954), Clarice Lispector (1925–77), João Guimãres Rosa (1908–67), and Raquel de Queiros in prose; and Carlos Drummond de Andrade, João Cabral de Melo Neto, Vinicius de Moraes (1913–80), and Jorge de Lima (1893–1953) in poetry.

Puerto Rican literature, particularly in response to nationalist and racial concerns, has come into its own only within recent decades. A vibrant indigenous theater movement has been distinguished by the work of Emilio Belaval, Manuel Méndez Ballester, Francisco Arriví, and René Marqués (1919–79)—the last known especially for his play *The Oxcart* (1951; Eng. trans., 1960). Enrique Laguerre and Pedro Juan Soto have dominated the field of fiction. In poetry, Luis Palés Matos (1898–1959) pioneered with the theme of "primitivism" versus the cultural imperialism of "civilization."

In the rest of Latin America many authors have had success in experimenting with such techniques as the "new novel," introduced by French novelists and literary critics, and with the innovations of such U.S. writers as Faulkner—while retaining a very personal style and a distinctly Latin American voice. Novelists or short-story writers in this vein include Carlos FUENTES and Juan Rulfo of Mexico; Alejo Carpentier of Cuba; Jorge Luis BORGES, Julio CORTÁZAR, and Manuel Puig of Argentina; Juan Carlos Onetti of Uruguay; Gabriel GARCÍA MÁRQUEZ of Colombia; Mario VARGAS LLOSA and José María Arguedas (1911–69) of Peru; and José Donoso of Chile. These writers have finally managed to fuse the persistent need for self-definition with the need for modernity and universality.

Many of their novels incorporate painful reassessments of the nation's immediate past as well as suggestions for new courses of action. These range from the creation of a new Latin America–wide consciousness, thus obviating the need for European models, to a return to an almost apocryphal native past. With every successful choice or error, Latin Americans have evolved their own sense of history, and writers have assumed an active role in forming this consciousness. The famous *Canto General* (1950) of Pablo NERUDA, for instance, is a summa of all Latin America: its land, its history, and its peoples. César VALLEJO in his poetry grieves for all the Christs of the continent; Nicanor Parra mocks the banality of ordinary experience; and Ernesto Cardenal exhorts Latin Americans to union and activism in the original Christian sense of setting all people free. Nicolás GUILLÉN is the poet who most successfully celebrates the infusion of African blood into the Hispanic cultural mainstream. Octavio PAZ, who has written lyric, surrealist, and even concrete poetry, remains the best-known exemplar of the cosmopolitan tradition.

Latin American music and dance The term *Latin American* as used here encompasses the Americas south of the United States, as well as the Caribbean.

During the colonial period in Latin America (16th–19th century) many Amerindian populations were decimated, and much traditional Amerindian musical culture was destroyed or syncretized with Iberian. Little concrete evidence remains as to the real nature of pre-Conquest music in the Aztec, Inca, and Maya civilizations apart from the testimony of 16th-century Spanish chroniclers and what can be seen of instruments depicted in hieroglyphs and pottery decorations. Drums, rattles, scrapers, slit drums (hollowed logs), whistles, vertical flutes, and panpipes were found, with almost total absence of stringed instruments. In performing the *yaraví* song, the *huayno* song and dance form, and other genres, modern Andean Amerindians still make extensive use of vertical flutes and panpipes, along with European instruments such as bass drums, harps, and guitars of different sizes. In Mesoamerica, Indians now play harps, fiddles, and guitars based upon archaic Spanish models, or MARIMBAS of African origin. Only in certain tropical areas (as the Amazon basin) are virtually unacculturated Amerindian musics found.

The Iberian origins of many song and dance forms are evident in a widespread predilection for alternating 3/4 and 6/8 meters (hemiola), the use of harps, fiddles, guitars, and many song types derived from Spanish verse structures such as the romanze or villancico. These include the corrido of Mexico, *desafio* of Brazil, *copla* of the Andean countries, and *décima* of South America, the Caribbean, and Mexico. Acculturated song and dance

The marimba is an upright percussion instrument featuring strips of hard wood mounted above resonating boxes. The Latin American marimba is distinguished from its African antecedent by the substitution of wooden boxes for gourds.

Since precolonial times, dance has been an important aspect of the arts in Latin America. The Ballet Folklórica of Mexico uses the rich Mexican cultural heritage in performances based on traditional themes and folklore.

genres are distinctly regional in text, structure, choreography, and spirit. They include the *zamba* of Argentina, cueca of Chile and Bolivia, bambuco of Colombia, joropo of Venezuela, jarabe and huapango of Mexico, and son and *punto* of Cuba. They are usually danced in couples, with shoe tapping or scarf waving.

The largest black populations are found in tropical coastal lowlands, as in the Caribbean, Eastern Central America, Venezuela, Brazil, and the Colombian-Ecuadorian coasts. African musical features commonly retained include call-and-response singing, polyrhythms, extensive use of ostinatos (persistently repeated musical figures), and improvisation based on recurring short phrases. African instruments found in both unaltered and adapted forms, with many regional names and variations, include long drums, often in "family" sets of three (congas), iron gongs, gourd scrapers (guiro), concussion sticks (claves), internal or external rattles (maracas, shekere), sanza (*marimbula*), and marimbas. The "steel drum" (tuned metal barrel) of Trinidad has no direct African equivalent but evolved from drum ensembles. The most African forms are usually associated with African-derived religions, such as the Yoruba-oriented candomblé of Brazil, lucumí of Cuba, and voodoo of Haiti. More acculturated Afro-American musics such as the urban *samba de morro* (carnival samba) of Brazil, merengue of the Dominican Republic and Haiti, *bomba* and *plena* of Puerto Rico, and rumba, conga, guaracha, son, and *són montuno* of Cuba have become national folk musics. SALSA has evolved from the rumba as a popular music of New York's pan-Hispanic Caribbean population.

Still more cosmopolitan forms have become popular on the "pan-Latin" and international level through their diffusion by mass media. These include the BOLERO and danzón of Cuba, the TANGO of Argentina, the cabaret samba and bossa nova of Brazil, the CALYPSO of Trinidad, and the *cumbia* of Colombia. The REGGAE of Jamaica is closer in style and spirit to "soul" music than to Latin musics of the Caribbean.

From the 16th through the 19th century, most Latin American "art" music reflected contemporary European models. Indian and Creole (those of European ancestry born in the colonies) composers and musicians composed and performed music much like that of their parent colonial cultures. In the 20th century, however, a number of composers discovered their "national voices," based partly upon traditional folk and tribal music (or their conception or reconstruction of it). These include Heitor VILLA-LOBOS in Brazil and Manuel Ponce, Carlos CHÁVEZ, Silvestre Revueltas, and Blas Galindo in Mexico. Other composers have tended to represent more universal, rather than nationalist, techniques: these include Alberto GINASTERA and Mauricio Kagel in Argentina, Camargo Guarnieri in Brazil, Domingo Santa Cruz Wilson and Juan Orrego-Salas in Chile, and Julián Carrillo in Mexico.

Latin language   Latin, originally the language spoken only in Rome and the surrounding region of LATIUM, gradually spread throughout the entire western Mediterranean region as more and more people came under Roman sway. Classical Latin was basically a learned language abstracted from the spoken vernacular by the educated upper classes in Rome. Regional varieties also existed, as did more popular forms, called Vulgar Latin, which can be seen on inscriptions and in the works of Plautus (2d century BC) and Petronius (1st century AD) and to some extent in the letters of Cicero (1st century BC).

Latin is a member of the INDO-EUROPEAN family of languages and retains many inherited features. Phonologically, initial syllables have shown the least change in Latin, no doubt because they are usually stressed. Various weakenings of articulation did occur, however, in interior syllables, in which the short vowels tended to be raised or lost, and the fricatives *f* and *s* became voiced as *b* or *d* and *r*. Long vowels, however, retained their pronunciation. In fact, their number was increased by the monophthongization of diphthongs, when *ei* became *ī* and *ou* became *ū*. The incidence of geminate consonants was increased by the simplification of consonant groups; *supmos*, for example, was simplified to *summos.*

Latin nouns were organized out of many earlier types into five basic declensions, and the number of cases, both singular and plural, also became fixed at five. Each noun incorporates a gender—masculine, feminine, or neuter—that governs the agreement of adjectives. Pronouns and adjectives are also declined, but adverbs, prepositions, and conjunctions are not. Because of these grammatical signals, the word order in a Latin sentence can vary widely, conveying emphasis rather than grammatical meaning.

The Latin verbal system was organized into four conjugations. The four principal parts—present, infinitive, perfect, past participle—provide all necessary information for deriving every form of the verb. Each finite verb expresses three persons in two numbers, actively and passively, in the indicative (real), subjunctive (ideal), or imperative mood and in the two aspects, imperfective and perfective. Infinitives, participles, and verbal nouns complete the system. Distinctions of tense are possible only in the indicative and display considerable symmetry, as seen in the indicative forms of the second person singular of *habeō*, "have":

	Imperfective	*Perfective*
Present	habē-s	habu-is-ti
Future	habē-b-is	habu-er-is
Past	habē-b-ās	habu-er-ās

Such clarity is not seen in the subjunctive, in which several original systems, including optative and subjunctive, seem to have coalesced:

Present or future	habe-ās	habu-er-is
Past	habē-r-ēs	habu-is-s-ēs

The major linguistic problem faced by the Romans was the creation of a vocabulary and syntax adequate to the requirements of world power and intellectual discourse. In this they were remarkably successful, and they created, partly on Greek models, a set of abstract nouns that continues to form the basis of learned discourse even today. Behind this vocabulary lies an earlier agricultural and military terminology that reflects the history of Roman institutions. For example, *grex*, "flock," became the root of both *congregatiō*, "association," and *ēgregius*, "outstanding." Syntactically, the Romans were able to subordinate ideas by giving each complex sentence only one indicative verb. All subordinate notions were conveyed by participles or subjunctives.

Although Latin is no longer a living language in its own right, it survives in various modified forms in the ROMANCE LANGUAGES. Latin also remains the official language of the Roman Catholic church, and scientists habitually turn to Latin roots when looking for names for their latest discoveries.

Latin literature

Although inscriptions and an assortment of laws and chants survive from as early as the 5th century BC, the formal beginnings of Latin literature are usually assigned to 240 BC, when LIVIUS ANDRONICUS presented at Rome his translations of two Greek plays, a tragedy and a comedy. He was followed by the epic poets Gnaeus Naevius and Quintus ENNIUS and the inventor of satire, Lucilius. The works of all four writers survive only in fragments. CATO the Elder, called the father of Latin prose, and the comic playwrights PLAUTUS and TERENCE fall within the same period.

The century following Marcus Tullius CICERO's first speech in 81 BC marked an extraordinary period of creativity. The philosophical poet LUCRETIUS and the lyricist CATULLUS both wrote during Cicero's lifetime. The next two generations—the Golden Age of Latin—saw the emergence of VERGIL, author of Rome's greatest epic, the AENEID; of HORACE, the master of satire and lyric poetry; of the elegists Sextus PROPERTIUS and Tibullus; of OVID, the cosmopolitan poet of the METAMORPHOSES; and of the historians of republican Rome, SALLUST and LIVY. Most of these authors' works appeared during the relatively benign reign (31 BC–AD 14) of Augustus.

The following period, often termed the Silver Age, was marked by a falling off in quality. Freedom of expression was circumscribed, and writing tended to become increasingly rhetorical. To this period belong the epic poets LUCAN, Statius, and Valerius Flaccus; the novelist PETRONIUS ARBITER; the satirists MARTIAL and JUVENAL; the tragedian Lucius Annaeus SENECA; the letter writer PLINY THE YOUNGER; the biographer of the emperors, SUETONIUS; and the towering historian of early imperial Rome, Cornelius TACITUS.

From the start Latin literature was permeated by the influence of ancient GREEK LITERATURE. Aside from satire the Romans produced no genre untouched by the Greeks, and even when not imitating them, the Romans tended to define themselves in terms of Greek writers. The greatest Latin authors—Cicero, Vergil, Horace—however, accepted imitation as a challenge. They deliberately recalled their Greek predecessors but often only to mark their departures from them.

latitude

[lat'-ih-tood]   The latitude of a point on the Earth's surface is its distance north or south of the equator. Lines of latitude, or parallels, extend east and west at precise intervals from the equator, which is the 0° parallel. Because the latitude lines are drawn around the Earth's sphere, they can be divided as a circle into degrees, minutes, and seconds. The latitude of Times Square in New York City, for example, is calculated to be 40°45'12" north. The length of a degree of latitude becomes larger as distance from the equator increases. When used in combination with lines of LONGITUDE, latitude lines give a unique designation to every point on the Earth.

Latium

[lay'-shuhm]   Latium (Italian: Lazio) is a region in west central Italy, stretching from the Tyrrhenian Sea to the Apennine Mountains and including Roma, Frosinone, Latina, Rieti, and Viterbo provinces. The population is 5,156,053 (1989 est.). ROME, the national capital, also serves as the capital of the region, and the main port is Civitavecchia. Agriculture is the region's economic mainstay. Industry is concentrated around Rome, and fishing and tourism are important.

In the 3d century BC, Rome conquered Latium. After the fall of Rome, the region was occupied, successively, by the Visigoths, the Vandals, and the Lombards. It came under the control of the popes in the 8th century AD and remained a part of the PAPAL STATES until 1870, when Italy was unified. In World War II, Latium was the site of intense fighting during the Allied push toward Rome (1944), especially at the battles at ANZIO and CASSINO.

Latrobe, Benjamin Henry [luh-trohb'] The leading figure in American architecture during the early 19th century, Benjamin Henry Latrobe, b. England, May 1, 1764, d. Sept. 3, 1820, adapted the styles of ancient Greece to his own time and place. After completing residential designs in Norfolk and the State Penitentiary in Richmond (1797–98), Va., Latrobe moved to Philadelphia, where he won the design competition for the Bank of Pennsylvania. His plan (1798) for this building initiated the GREEK REVIVAL movement in American architecture. At the same time (1798–99) he inaugurated the GOTHIC REVIVAL with his design for Sedgeley near Philadelphia, the first American mansion built in that style. In addition, he engineered Philadelphia's picturesque Waterworks, the first in America to employ steam pumps.

Latrobe's two most important commissions were the elegant, centrally domed Baltimore Cathedral (1804–18), the first Roman Catholic cathedral in the country, and the U.S. Capitol in Washington, D.C. For the cathedral, Latrobe submitted alternative designs—one classical and the other Gothic. Although the latter was not executed, it became a model for neo-Gothic church designs in America. In 1803, President Thomas Jefferson appointed Latrobe surveyor of buildings and thus new architect of the CAPITOL OF THE UNITED STATES, which had been started in the 1790s. He completed the South Wing with magnificent interiors and was called back to rebuild the structure (1815–17) after it was largely razed by the British.

Latter-Day Saints, Church of Jesus Christ of
see MORMONISM

Latvia [lat'-vee-uh] Located on the eastern shore of the Baltic Sea, the Republic of Latvia is bordered by Estonia on the north, Russia and Belarus on the east, and Lithuania on the south. With an area of 64,589 km² (24,938 mi²) and a population of 2,681,000 (1989), it is one of the smallest successor republics of the defunct USSR. The capital is RIGA, with a population of 917,000 (1989). On May 4, 1990, Latvia declared Soviet rule illegal and set a course for the gradual achievement of independence. Together with its two Baltic neighbors, Latvia became fully independent in September 1991.

Land and People. Latvia's major river is the Daugava, or Western Dvina (see DVINA RIVER, WESTERN), which flows for 360 km (224 mi) in Latvia. The rivers empty into the Gulf of Riga or the Baltic Sea. Their estuaries provide ice-free commercial and fishing harbors. Latvia has a moderate climate, with cool summers and mild winters. The highest elevation is under 300 m (984 ft).

The ethnic Latvians, or Letts, form 51.8% of the population (1989), down from 75% in 1923. Russians make up 34%, Belorussians 4.5%, Ukrainians 3.4%, and Poles 2.3%. The ethnic Latvians are mostly Lutheran and speak a Baltic language related to Lithuanian. Seventy-one per-

cent of Latvia's population live in cities, of which Riga is the largest. Others are the industrial centers of Daugavpils (1989 pop., 127,000), Liepaja (114,000), and Jelgava (72,000), and the oil and chemicals port of Ventspils (52,000). Jurmala (65,000), near Riga, is the best-known beach resort.

Economy. Latvia was the USSR's main producer of telephone equipment, railroad and street cars, generators, mopeds, and washing machines. Light industry includes food processing. The agricultural sector concentrates on meat and dairy production; grains and flax are grown. Most of Latvia's energy needs are supplied by Estonia and other former Soviet republics.

History. The Latvian people, along with the Lithuanians, have lived in the eastern Baltic region since ancient times. In the 13th century the Latvians were conquered and Christianized by the Germanic Knights of the Sword; their successors, the TEUTONIC KNIGHTS, founded the German-ruled state of LIVONIA, which dominated the area until the mid-16th century. In 1561–62, Latvia was divided between Poland and the duchy of Courland; the Swedes occupied part of the country in the 17th century, and between 1710 and 1721 the whole region was conquered by Russia under Peter the Great in the Great NORTHERN WAR.

The native German nobility continued to control Latvia under Russian rule, but a Latvian nationalist movement emerged in the 19th century, and independence was achieved (1918) after the collapse of the Russian Empire. Russian dominance was reestablished, however, when Latvia was annexed by the USSR in 1940. Under Soviet rule, which was extraordinarily harsh, the economy was industrialized, and Russian immigration reduced the Latvians almost to a minority in their own land.

The development of the PERESTROIKA reform movement of Soviet president Mikhail Gorbachev in the late 1980s

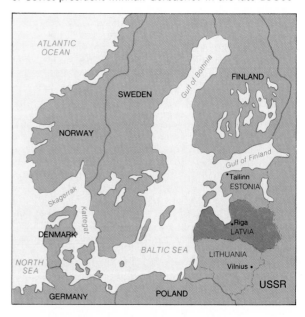

enabled the non-Communist Latvian People's Front, with wide popular support, to pressure the government into restoring Latvian as the official language and legalizing the use of the national symbols. Freedoms of speech, press, and religion were established, and private ownership of farms was legalized. In 1990, following the example of its Baltic neighbors, Lithuania and Estonia, Latvia began to move in the direction of independence. This met with opposition from the Soviet government, but gradually the Kremlin began negotiations with all three Baltic republics in search of a compromise solution. Following the failure of the August 1991 hard-liner coup, Latvia declared independence and was recognized by the USSR. It joined the United Nations later that year.

Latvian language   see Baltic languages

Latynina, Larisa [la-tee'-nee-nah]   Larisa Semyonovna Latynina, b. Dec. 27, 1935, was the dominant Soviet gymnast of her time and, as a world-class competitor from 1954 to 1966, won more Olympic medals than any athlete in any sport. In three Olympic Game, world, and European championship appearances she captured 9 gold, 15 silver, and 5 bronze medals. Her superb technique, beauty, and charm all contributed to her near invincibility in the 10 years after her debut at the world championships in 1954. She lost the combined exercises title at the 1964 Olympics to the Czech gymnast Vera Caslavska. Following her retirement, Latynina became the coach of the Soviet women's team.

Laud, William [lawd]   William Laud, b. Oct. 7, 1573, d. Jan. 10, 1645, was archbishop of Canterbury and a close advisor of King Charles I. Laud maintained a strong position against Puritan pressures for further church reform, insisted on the apostolic succession of bishops, and imposed his will by force and punishments. Increasingly, his administration became involved in political matters as he tried to carry his conservative program to Scotland and became identified with the Stuart royal cause. The notorious "etcetera oath," which he introduced at the Convocation of 1640, was designed to prescribe the doctrine of the divine right of kings and the hierarchical government of the church and brought a reaction against his policies. He was impeached (1641) by the Long Parliament, imprisoned in the Tower of London, tried (1644–45) under questionable judicial circumstances, and executed.

Lauda, Niki [low'-duh]   The Austrian Nikolaus-Andreas Lauda, b. Feb. 22, 1949, is one of only six men to win the Grand Prix car racing championship at least three times. Dedicated and fearless in pursuit of his sport, Lauda won his first title in 1975 and his second in 1977 (after a serious accident in 1976 left him close to death). He retired in 1979, returned to the circuit in 1982, and became three-time champion in 1984. He has since retired again.

Laudonnière, René Goulaine de [loh-dawn-yair', ruh-nay' goo-len' duh]   René Goulaine de Laudonnière, c.1529–c.1582, was a French Huguenot colonizer in Florida. After taking part in Jean Ribaut's expedition to Florida in 1562, he led a second expedition that established the French Protestant colony of Fort Caroline on the Saint John's River in 1564. In 1565, as the feuding colonists began to abandon the settlement, it was destroyed by the Spanish under Pedro Menéndez de Avilés. The wounded Laudonnière escaped to France.

laughing gas   see Anesthetics

Laughton, Charles [lawt'-uhn]   Charles Laughton, b. July 1, 1899, d. Dec. 15, 1962, was a distinguished British-born character actor of stage and screen, best remembered for his work in the 1930s. On stage he performed with the Sadler's Wells Company (1933–34), the Old Vic (1935), and the Comédie Française (1937). His many British and American films include *The Private Life of Henry VIII* (1933), for which he won an Academy Award in the title role; *Mutiny on the Bounty* (1935), in which he played Captain Bligh; *Rembrandt* (1936); *Jamaica Inn* (1938); *Witness for the Prosecution* (1957); *Spartacus* (1960); and *Advise and Consent* (1961). From 1929 he was married to actress Elsa Lanchester.

The British-born actor Charles Laughton is best known for his convincing character portrayals on the stage and in such films as Mutiny on the Bounty *(1935),* Witness for the Prosecution *(1957), and* The Private Life of Henry VIII *(1933), for which he received an Academy Award.*

Laurasia   see Plate Tectonics

laurel [lohr'-uhl]   Laurels are about 47 genera of mostly evergreen trees and shrubs in the laurel family, Lauraceae. They grow best in warm climates and are characterized by the aroma of their bark and their leathery, simple leaves. The true laurel, or sweet bay, *Laurus nobilis*, is native to Anatolia and has become naturalized in southern Europe. The dark green leaves of sweet bay are the bay leaf used in cookery. The flowers appear in yellow clusters, followed by black or dark purple berries. The other species of the genus, *L. canariensis*, is native to the

The sweet bay laurel (left) *was grown in ancient Roman temple gardens, and its leaves were fashioned into crowns symbolizing accomplishment. Its leaves are now used to flavor food. The California laurel* (right) *is an evergreen whose timber is used to make high-quality furniture. Both trees bear tiny flowers and olive-shaped fruit.*

Canary Islands. Members of other genera of the laurel family include the AVOCADO, the CINNAMON tree, the SASSA-FRAS, and the California laurel.

Certain other plants with similar leaves and bark are commonly referred to as laurels, but they do not belong to the laurel family. English laurel, *Prunus laurocerasus*, related to plum and cherry trees, is native from southeastern Europe to Iran. MOUNTAIN LAUREL, *Kalmia latifolia*, related to rhododendrons, grows naturally in the eastern United States. The Texas mountain laurel, or coral-bean tree, *Sophora secundiflora*, grows in the southwestern United States.

Laurel and Hardy [lor'-ul, har'-dee]   Masters of slapstick buffoonery, Stan Laurel, b. Arthur Stanley Jefferson in Lancashire, England, June 16, 1890, d. Feb. 23, 1965, and Oliver Hardy, b. Harlem, Ga., Jan. 18, 1892, d. Aug. 7, 1957, were one of Hollywood's greatest comedy teams, with the skinny, sad-eyed Laurel playing the sensitive underdog to the obese, peevish Hardy. Laurel, the more creative of the two, began his career as a music hall comedian before settling in America in 1911 and teaming in 1927 with Hardy, a former singer and film heavy. On screen the pair portrayed clumsy, genteel misfits who turned minor problems into major disasters. Their mayhem can be seen in such short films as *Putting Pants on Philip* (1927), *From Soup to Nuts* (1928), *Two Tars* (1928), and *Big Business* (1929), as well as in the features *Pack Up Your Troubles* (1932), *Sons of the Desert* (1934), *Babes in Toyland* (1934), and *Way Out West* (1937). Although they made a successful transition from silent to sound films, their popularity waned after their departure (1940) from the Hal Roach studio.

In this scene from the 1939 film The Flying Deuces, *the slapstick comedy team of Oliver Hardy* (left) *and Stan Laurel* (right) *face a dilemma typical of their zany misadventures.*

Laurence, Margaret [lor'-ens]   Margaret Laurence, b. Neepawa, Manitoba, July 18, 1926, d. Jan. 5, 1987, was considered by many critics the best novelist ever to write in Canada. A knowledgeable observer of African life and the author of books of short stories, travel, and translations, she has been most widely acclaimed for four linked novels of the Canadian west: *The Stone Angel* (1964), *A Jest of God* (1966; filmed as *Rachel, Rachel,* 1968), *The Fire-Dwellers* (1969), and *The Diviners* (1974). Her female protagonists are natives of a fictional prairie town called Manawaka; each is characterized sympathetically and compellingly, and each bespeaks courage in the face of adversity. Laurence has also published a volume of essays, *Heart of a Stranger* (1976).

Laurens, Henry [lor'-ens]   Henry Laurens, b. Charleston, S.C., Mar. 6, 1724, d. Dec. 8, 1792, was a leading patriot during the American Revolution. He was president of the Second Continental Congress from November 1777 until December 1778. In 1780 he was captured by the British while on his way to negotiate an agreement between the United States and Holland. Exchanged in 1782 for General CORNWALLIS, he became one of the commissioners sent to Paris to negotiate peace with the British.

Laurentian Mountains   The Laurentian Mountains, or Laurentides, located north of Montreal and the St. Lawrence River in southern Quebec, Canada, are part of the CANADIAN SHIELD. They are composed mainly of Precambrian igneous and metamorphic rocks and have deposits of valuable minerals. Worn down by Ice Age glaciers and time, the low, conifer-covered mountains are separated by streams and lakes. A popular ski and resort area, the Laurentides and Mount Tremblant provincial parks are there. Mount Tremblant, 960 m (3,150 ft), is the highest peak.

Laurentian Shield   see CANADIAN SHIELD

Laurier, Sir Wilfrid [law'-ree-ay]   Wilfrid Laurier, b. Saint-Lin, Quebec, Nov. 20, 1841, d. Feb. 17, 1919, was the first French-Canadian prime minister of Canada. A Liberal, he served first in the Legislative Assembly of Quebec (1871–74) and then in the Canadian House of Commons until his death.

Laurier was chosen leader of the Liberal party in 1887, and when his party won the election of 1896, he became prime minister. Laurier was returned to office in the elections of 1900, 1904, and 1908. He was finally defeated in 1911. The "age of Laurier" was a period of great economic development in Canada.

In the relations between English and French Canadians, Laurier tried to have diversity accepted as a characteristic of Canadian culture. He emphasized the need for cooperation and compromise. Laurier favored close ties with the British government, but after the French-Canadian outcry against the dispatch (1899) of Canadian troops to serve with the British forces in the South African War, he sought to balance imperial cooperation with the assertion of Canadianism. He therefore resisted the establishment of imperial defense forces but created in 1909 a

Sir Wilfrid Laurier, the first French-Canadian prime minister of Canada (1896–1911), worked to achieve "unity and harmony and amity" between French- and English-speaking Canadians. His tenure was marked by great economic development. Laurier was knighted in 1897.

separate Canadian Navy. In 1911 he concluded a tariff-reciprocity agreement with the United States, a further assertion of detachment from the British Empire.

These key issues formed the central focus of the important election of 1911, which brought Laurier's downfall. On tariff reciprocity, Laurier lost Ontario, where manufacturing industries needed national protection. On Canada's involvement in the British Empire, a realignment of the parties in Quebec occurred: the Conservatives, who opposed Laurier's Canadianism, coalesced with the French-Canadian nationalists, who opposed Laurier's imperial cooperation as antinational.

As leader of the opposition, Laurier supported Canada's entry (1914) into World War I. However, he condemned conscription, which the French-Canadian constituency vehemently opposed. To prevent a complete ethnic split, he refused to join Sir Robert BORDEN's Union government, formed in 1917 of Conservatives and an important group of English-speaking Liberals. The shattered Liberal party had begun to coalesce again before his death.

Lausanne [loh-zahn']   Lausanne is the capital of Vaud canton, western Switzerland, on Lake Geneva about 52 km (32 mi) northeast of Geneva. The population is 124,022 (1988 est.). An important tourist resort, rail center, port, and agricultural center, Lausanne also manufactures clothing, metalwork, leather goods, chocolate, and other products. The University of Lausanne (1891) was originally a theological school (1537) noted as a center for Calvinism. First settled by the Celts, Lausanne became the site of a Roman camp. A bishopric was established there in 590, and the city was ruled by prince-bishops until it came under Bernese rule in 1536 and the Reformation was introduced. Lausanne became the capital of Vaud in 1803.

Lausanne, Treaty of   The Treaty of Lausanne (1923) settled the boundaries of modern Turkey and resolved the territorial disputes raised in Anatolia by World

War I. At the end of the war the Allies imposed the Treaty of Sèvres (1920) on the defeated OTTOMAN EMPIRE; it effectively dismembered the empire, leaving only Anatolia (minus a Greek enclave at Smyrna, or IZMIR) under Turkish rule. This settlement was rejected by the Turkish nationalists led by Mustafa Kemal (later Kemal ÁTATÜRK), who objected to the loss of Smyrna to Greece. After driving the Greek troops out of Smyrna, Kemal's government forced the negotiation of a new treaty, which was finally concluded at Lausanne, Switzerland, on July 24, 1923.

According to the Treaty of Lausanne, Turkey regained not only Smyrna but also eastern Thrace and some Aegean islands. It also resumed control of the Dardanelles (internationalized under the previous treaty) on the condition that they were kept demilitarized and open to all nations in peacetime.

Streams of red-hot, molten lava flow down the sides of this volcano, which initially erupted underwater on Nov. 14, 1963, and within two days rose to form the new island of Surtsey off the coast of Iceland.

Lautaro [low-tah'-roh] Lautaro, c.1536–57, called the Hannibal of Chile, led warriors of the Mapuche group of ARAUCANIANS against invading Spanish troops in 1553. As a youthful captive of the Spaniards, he became Pedro de VALDIVIA's head groom. Lautaro escaped and joined the Mapuche south of the Bío-Bío River, informing them that Spaniards were human and not, as they believed, part of their horses. He was named *toki* (supreme military leader) in 1553. After defeating the Spaniards that year and killing Valdivia, he razed Concepción in 1554. In 1557 he was leading 800 Mapuche toward Santiago when he was killed. Lautaro became a hero immortalized in the epic poem *La Araucana* by Ercilla y Zúñiga (1533–94).

lava [lah'-vuh] Lava is a general term for molten rock at the Earth's surface. It generally erupts from the vents and fissures of a VOLCANO at temperatures ranging from 850° to 1,250° C (1,500° to 2,300° F). Lava usually includes at least some crystals floating in the melt, even before it is erupted. When lava cools rapidly, as by plunging into water, it may form OBSIDIAN, a volcanic glass. In lava that cools slowly, as in the Hawaiian lava lakes, crystals may have time to grow and produce medium or coarse-grain textures. Occasionally, large crystals may grow in the MAGMA before eruption, while fast cooling at the surface of a lava flow crystallizes the rest to a fine-grained matrix, giving rise to a PORPHYRY.

The composition of lavas varies widely, from silica-rich RHYOLITES to the iron- and magnesium-rich (silica-poor) alkali BASALTS and basanites. Volatile content ranges from very low, as in Hawaiian basalts, to very high, as in scorias and pumice.

The most fluid lavas are usually basaltic in composition and erupt at high temperatures. These basalts often form thin flows, called pahoehoe, of great lateral extent with relatively smooth surfaces. On the other hand, some basalt flows are jagged and blocky with very rough surfaces. These so-called aa flows form from more-viscous, lower-temperature lavas. In Hawaii some lava flows have been observed to start out as pahoehoe flows and then change to aa flows as they cool and become more vis-

cous. (Both pahoehoe and aa are Hawaiian terms now in general use.) The more viscous a lava is—because of either lower temperatures or higher silica content or both—the more blocky and fragmented the flow becomes. The most viscous lava flows, such as rhyolite domes, may move only imperceptibly and are often little more than steep-sided piles of volcanic rubble.

See also: IGNEOUS ROCK.

Laval [lah-vahl'] Laval (1986 pop., 284,164) is an industrial and suburban city of Canada in Quebec province. It occupies the entire 230-km² (90-mi²) Île Jésus, just north of the Île de Montréal in the St. Lawrence River. The island, settled in 1681, was named for the Society of Jesus. In 1965, Laval was created by merging the 14 towns on the island.

Laval, François de François de Laval, b. France, Apr. 30, 1623, d. May 6, 1708, was the first Roman Catholic bishop in Canada and laid the foundations for the Catholic church there. He founded (1663) a seminary in Quebec, which later became (1852) Laval University. He also organized an educational system that included a trade school and primary schools. His interest in Indian affairs and vigorous opposition to the sale of alcohol to Indians brought him into frequent conflict with the colonial authorities. In 1674, Laval succeeded in having Quebec declared a diocese and was named its first bishop. The case for his canonization was begun in 1878; he was beatified in 1960.

Laval, Pierre [lah-vahl'] Pierre Laval, b. June 28, 1883, d. Oct. 15, 1945, was a French statesman who figured significantly in the foreign and domestic affairs of the Third Republic and was vice-premier in the fascistic VICHY GOVERNMENT. Originally a leftist socialist, Laval entered in the Chamber of Deputies in 1914. In the 1920s he held a variety of governmental positions, but he was moving to the right and in 1926 was elected to the Senate as an independent.

Laval was premier in 1931–32 and both foreign minister and premier in 1935–36. In 1935 he formulated a plan with British foreign secretary Sir Samuel Hoare to halt the Italian invasion of Ethiopia by partitioning that country, giving much of it to Italy. Public indignation forced withdrawal of the plan, and Laval's government fell.

In 1940, Laval joined Marshal PÉTAIN's Vichy Government. Appointed vice-premier, he pressed for closer ties with Nazi Germany. In 1941, Pétain replaced the independent-minded Laval with Adm. Jean DARLAN. Returning to power in 1942, Laval maneuvered to avoid deeper commitment to Germany, but with minimal success. In 1944 he was arrested by the retreating Germans, but he escaped to Spain in 1945. He was returned to France and tried for treason, and after an abortive suicide attempt, he was executed.

Lavalleja, Juan Antonio [lah-vah-yay'-hah, hwahn ahn-tohn'-yoh]   Juan Antonio Lavalleja, b. June 24, 1784, d. Oct. 22, 1853, was a Uruguayan military officer and leader of the revolutionary group known as the Thirty-three Immortals who secured Uruguayan independence in 1828. The group precipitated a war (1825–28) between Brazil and Argentina that resulted in a British-imposed peace guaranteeing the independence of Uruguay as a buffer state.

Lavalleja was unable to translate his revolutionary successes into political power. A fellow Immortal, Fructoso RIVERA, became the first president and was succeeded by Manuel Oribe. Lavalleja sided with Oribe in the civil war that ensued (1843–51) between Rivera's faction, known as the Colorados (reds), and Oribe's faction, the Blancos (whites).

lavender [lav'-en-dur]   Lavender is the name given to 28 species of the genus *Lavandula,* a member of the MINT family. Grown for its fragrant flowers, it is used in perfumes, toilet preparations, and medicines. Lavender is native to the Mediterranean region and is commercially

French lavender is a shrub known for its fernlike leaves and purple flowers. Unlike some related species, it is not used to make perfume.

cultivated primarily in southern France and Italy. Important cultivated species include English or true lavender, *L. angustifolia,* with gray green foliage and small blue or white flowers; spike lavender, *L. latifolia,* a harsher-smelling, broader-leaved type; and lavandin, a hybrid of true and spike lavenders.

Laver, Rod [lay'-vur]   Rodney George Laver, b. Aug. 9, 1938, was an Australian tennis star who is considered by many experts to have been the greatest player in the game's history. Although he lacked an imposing physique, he was a spectacular shotmaker with an extremely effective topspin backhand. He is the only player in tennis history to win the Grand Slam of tennis (the Australian, British, French, and U.S. singles championships) twice, first as an amateur in 1962, then as a professional in 1969. He won 4 Wimbledon singles titles, 2 U.S. Open singles championships, and 3 Australian and 2 French singles titles between 1959 and 1969. He had a superb Davis Cup record, winning 10 of 12 Challenge Round matches. Laver virtually retired from tournament play after 1976.

Laveran, Charles [lah-vuh-rahn', sharl]   The French physician Charles Louis Alphonse Laveran, b. June 18, 1845, d. May 18, 1922, received the 1907 Nobel Prize for physiology or medicine for proving that certain diseases are caused by parasitic protozoans. He began his career as a French army doctor in 1867. In 1880, while stationed in Algeria, he discovered the causative organisms in the blood of malaria victims. Laveran also helped discover that kala-azar, African sleeping sickness (TRYPANOSOMIASIS), and other tropical diseases are caused by protozoans. In 1907 he founded the Laboratory of Tropical Diseases at the Pasteur Institute in Paris.

Lavoisier, Antoine Laurent [lah-vwahz-yay', ahn-twahn' loh-rahn']   The French chemist Antoine Laurent Lavoisier, b. Aug. 26, 1743, d. May 8, 1794, was the founder of modern chemistry. Although he discovered no new substances and devised few new preparations, he described his experiments and synthesized chemical knowledge in his revolutionary textbook *Elements of Chemistry* (1789; Eng. trans., 1790). In this textbook he presented a new system of chemistry that was based on an essentially modern concept of chemical elements and that made extensive use of the conservation of mass in chemical reactions. Formerly, chemical theory had been based on either three or four elements, and negative mass was considered a possibility by some chemists.

Lavoisier demonstrated experimentally that oxygen gas in the air is involved in combustion, calcination (rusting), and respiration, thus disproving George Ernst STAHL's PHLOGISTON THEORY. The basic principles of the new nomenclature, devised in collaboration with Claude Louis BERTHOLLET, Antoine de Fourcroy, and Guyton de Morveau, are still used. Among Lavoisier's major mistakes

The Frenchman Antoine Lavoisier was the founder of modern chemistry. He determined oxygen's role in combustion and respiration and was the first to distinguish between elements and compounds. He is shown here with his wife in a painting (1788) by J. L. David. (Rockefeller University, New York City.)

were the exaggerated importance he ascribed to the role of oxygen in acids and the inclusion of a weightless "heat substance" in his list of chemical elements.

Lavoisier was elected to the Academy of Sciences in 1768, the same year that he entered the Ferme Générale, a private firm that collected certain taxes for the government. He served (1775–91) on the Royal Gunpowder Administration and became a director of the Discount Bank and an administrator of the national treasury. During the period of the French Revolution Lavoisier served as an alternate deputy for the nobility—he had inherited a purchased title from his father in 1775—at the meeting of the Estates General; published reports on the state of French finances and on French agricultural resources; drafted with others a scheme for reforming the French educational system; and participated with other Academy members in establishing the metric system of weights and measures. Nevertheless, Lavoisier, a moderate constitutionalist, was subjected to attacks by radicals, such as Jean-Paul Marat, and his involvement with the unpopular Ferme Générale led to his execution by guillotine during the Reign of Terror.

---

law   Law can be defined broadly as a system of standards and rules of civil society: standards of human conduct that impose obligations and grant corresponding rights, and institutional rules regarding the ascertainment, creation, modification, and enforcement of these standards. The question "What is law?" has elicited a myriad of answers throughout human history, ranging from the Old Testament's assertion of law as the will of God to the thesis of Karl Marx and Friedrich Engels that law is an expression of class ideology.

Conceptions of Law

Notwithstanding the marked historical diversity in conceptions of law, many if not most of the conceptions of law can be placed in one of six broad categories: natural law, legal positivism, historical jurisprudence, sociological jurisprudence, Marxism, and legal realism.

Like Western philosophy in general, philosophy of law in particular first emerged in ancient Greece. In the 5th century BC the Sophists and Socrates, along with his followers, took up the question of the nature of law. Both recognized a distinction between things that exist by nature (*physis*) and those which exist by human-made convention (*nomos*). The Sophists, however, tended to place law in the latter category, whereas Socrates put it in the former, as did Plato and Aristotle. Thus began the debate that continues even today over whether the essence of law is nature and reason on the one hand or convention and will on the other hand. Thinkers who believe the former belong to what can be loosely called the tradition of NATURAL LAW, and those who assert the latter belong to the tradition of legal positivism.

Natural Law and Legal Positivism. All of the early political philosophers were deeply concerned with the nature of justice and good government. The idea of natural law can be found in Plato's concept of the just state—governed by the good and the wise—which in his view reflects the naturally hierarchical structure of human society. Governed by wisdom, the ideal state has no need of conventional law because wisdom itself is the recognition of the primacy of natural order. Marcus Tullius Cicero, a Roman statesman and politician who was also a Stoic (see Stoicism) legal philosopher, put forward the first full-blown theory of natural law, in his *Commonwealth* (51 BC): "True law is right reason in accord with nature; it is of universal application, unchanging and everlasting. ..."

Later, Saint Augustine combined Stoic legal thinking with Christian philosophy by identifying eternal, divine law with God's reason and will and by considering human law as being derived from and limited by divine law. The natural-law tradition culminated in the theory of Saint Thomas Aquinas, which synthesized Aristotelian, Stoic, Roman Law, and Christian elements. Aquinas formulated a fourfold classification of types of law: (1) eternal law—God's plan for the universe; (2) natural law—that part of the eternal law in which humans participate by their reason; (3) divine law—God's direct revelation to humankind through the scriptures; and (4) human law—particular determinations of certain matters arrived at through the use of reason from the general precepts of the natural law. Aquinas also argued—as Cicero had done—that an unjust law was not a genuine law but rather an act of violence. Later thinkers who may be placed in the natural-law tradition include Hugo Grotius, Thomas Hooker, Gottfried Leibniz, Baruch Spinoza, Jean Jacques Rousseau, and Jacques Maritain.

In marked contrast to natural-law jurists, legal positivists such as Thomas Hobbes argued that the essence of law is the command or will of the sovereign and that an "unjust law" is a contradiction in terms because the existing law is itself the standard of justice. Jean Bodin had anticipated Hobbes in the former respect when he claimed that "law is nothing else than the command of the sovereign in his exercise of sovereign power." Bodin had added, however, that the prince "has no power to exceed the law of nature," and he expected natural law to be found in constitutional restraints. Thus Bodin had not broken unequivocally from the natural-law tradition. John LOCKE's criticism of Hobbesian theory set the stage for modern theories of CIVIL DISOBEDIENCE and for independent government in the American colonies.

Many legal positivists after Hobbes have backed down from his extreme claims. For example, Jeremy BENTHAM and John Austin agreed that law was the command of the sovereign but rejected the idea that law was necessarily the standard of justice or morality. Bentham was more interested in the law's utility in providing the greatest happiness for the greatest number.

Historical Jurisprudence. In contrast with both natural-law jurists and legal positivists, members of the historical school of jurisprudence, most notably Friedrich Karl von SAVIGNY, maintained that "an organic connection [exists] between law and the nature and character of a people." In his view legislation is relatively unimportant except insofar as it declares customary law, which is the truly living law. Thus the spirit of the people and not the commands of the sovereign or right reason in accord with nature constitutes the essence of law.

Sociological Jurisprudence. Akin to historical jurisprudence is sociological jurisprudence, which can be traced to the writings of Rudolf von Jhering (1818–92). He rejected Savigny's theory on the ground that the latter, in viewing law as a spontaneous expression of subconscious forces, overlooked the importance of conscious human purposes and the pursuit of interests embodied in the law. Jhering also emphasized that law must be understood in the context of social life. He thus foreshadowed the jurisprudence-of-interests school of thought and sociological jurisprudence. Both strains of Jhering's thought influenced the jurisprudential theory of Roscoe POUND and other American sociological jurists, who focused on the notion of "social engineering" law as a means of social control and the relationship between law and society.

Marxism. In contrast to historical and sociological jurists, Marxist jurists stress the relationship between law and the economic aspects of society rather than society generally and emphasize the pursuit of class interests instead of interests generally. Responding to critics, Marx and Engels wrote in *The Communist Manifesto* (1848): "Your law is but the will of your class exalted into statutes, a will which acquires its content from the material conditions of [the] existence of your class."

Legal Realism. Legal realism, which has flourished in America, has been more of a movement than a school of thought. Its fundamental tenets were anticipated by Justice Oliver Wendell HOLMES, Jr., who remarked: "The life of the law has not been logic; it has been experience" and "Prophecies of what courts will do in fact, and nothing more pretentious, are what I mean by law." Like sociological jurists, legal realists revolted against analytic jurisprudence and formalism, or mechanical jurisprudence, but the realists were somewhat more extreme than the sociological jurists in their claims. They even went so far as to claim that legal rules are myths and that laws are really nothing more than particular judicial decisions.

Types of Law

Traditionally, law has been divided into public law and private law. Public and private laws that set forth the substance of rights and obligations are sometimes called substantive law in order to distinguish them from LEGAL PROCEDURE; the latter specifies the methods to be followed in adjudicating substantive law cases in order to ensure they are conducted in a manner protective of the rights of the participants. If procedural law relates to how the rights and duties of substantive law are to be vindicated and enforced, substantive law pertains to what the law is on a given matter.

Public Law. Public law concerns the structures, powers, and operations of a government, the rights and duties of citizens in relation to the government, and the relationships among nations. It can be divided further into constitutional law, administrative law, criminal law, and INTERNATIONAL LAW.

Constitutional law, the fundamental or paramount law of a nation, is derived from the nation's CONSTITUTION, which comprehends the body of rules in accordance with which the powers of government are exercised. Constitutions may be either written or unwritten—the United States's is an example of the former, Great Britain's of the latter. In some nations, courts have the power of JUDICIAL REVIEW, whereby they declare unconstitutional and therefore void laws that contravene the provisions or arrangements of the constitution.

Administrative law includes laws governing the organization and operation of agencies of the executive branch of government, the substantive and procedural rules that these agencies formulate and apply pursuant to their regulatory and other administrative functions, and COURT decisions involving public agencies and private citizens.

Criminal law consists of laws that impose obligations to do or forbear from doing certain things, the infraction of which is considered to be an offense not merely against the immediate victim but also against society. Most such laws are backed up by sanctions or punishments, which are applied in the event of conviction. Major breaches of the criminal law, usually defined as those punishable by imprisonment for more than 1 year, are termed FELONIES. Less serious crimes, called MISDEMEANORS, are punishable by imprisonment for a shorter period or by fines or both.

Finally, international law concerns the relationships among nations, including the use of the high seas, INTERNATIONAL TRADE, boundary disputes, warfare methods, and the like. Some legal theorists question whether international law is genuine law because it lacks an international legislature, centrally organized sanctions, and courts with involuntary jurisdiction, all of which characterize national legal systems.

Private Law. Unlike public law, private law does not involve government directly but rather indirectly as an adjudicator between disputing parties. Private law provides rules to be applied when one person claims that another has injured his or her person, property, or reputation or has failed to carry out a valid legal obligation.

On the basis of the types of legal rights and obligations involved, private law is conventionally subdivided into six main categories: (1) TORT law; (2) PROPERTY law; (3) CONTRACT and BUSINESS LAW; (4) CORPORATION law; (5) INHERITANCE law; and (6) family law.

Sources of Law. Laws can also be subdivided on the basis of the sources of law from which they derive. The various legal systems of the world recognize as valid and therefore binding on their subjects some or all of the following major sources: constitutions and administrative rules, such as those described above; legislative statutes; judicial precedents; and customary practice. Although when a person thinks of law, the concept of statutes comes most readily to mind, statutes are now outnumbered by the innumerable administrative rules and regulations that have accompanied the growth of administrative government in modern times. Judicial precedents (also known as case law), which are recognized as valid law that later courts must follow in COMMON LAW but not in CIVIL LAW systems, are prior cases decided by courts. Finally, customary practice is a minor source of law in the legal systems of advanced industrial nations, but it is the primary if not the only source in primitive legal systems and is inextricably linked with kinship, taboo, religion, and traditional authority systems.

Lawyers

The requirements for becoming a lawyer in the United States are set by each state (or the District of Columbia or Puerto Rico). In general, an individual must earn a bachelor's degree and then attend a recognized law school for either 3 years as a full-time day student or 4 years as a part-time evening student. In order to become an ATTORNEY the individual must also pass the state's bar examination. A person who wishes to work in the law but does not wish to pursue the program leading to a law degree may train to be a paralegal assistant to lawyers.

Most lawyers are in private practice. Because the law touches on all aspects of life, the work of lawyers is of infinite variety. Most lawyers specialize in a field such as tax law, estate planning, corporate law, workers-compensation law, and so forth. Some lawyers specialize in trial work. Many work for federal, state, or local government or for administrative agencies.

See also: DIVORCE; EQUITY (law); EVIDENCE; GERMANIC LAW; HAMMURABI, CODE OF; JURY; JUSTINIAN CODE; JUVENILE DELINQUENCY; MAGNA CARTA; NAPOLEONIC CODE; SEAS, FREEDOM OF THE; SPACE LAW.

---

law, history of Law is a system of rules of conduct and rights formally recognized by society or prescribed by the authority in a state. It distinguishes between what is permitted and what is prohibited. The appearance of an organized court system in Egypt around 4000 BC marked the beginning of legal history. Under this system, the word of the king was law. The palaces were centers of law with judges administering justice. Records of wills, contracts, titles, and boundaries to land were maintained, and all legal actions were filed in the palaces. The Egyp-

tian legal system endured until Egypt was conquered by Rome in the 1st century BC.

The oldest written code of law, the Code of Hammurabi (see HAMMURABI, CODE OF), came from the Mesopotamian legal system. Composed in approximately 2100 BC, the 285 provisions of the Code of Hammurabi controlled commerce, family, criminal, and civil law. Under the code, written pleadings began legal actions and testimony was given under oath.

Roman Law. The greatest contribution of the Roman Empire was the introduction of a legal system to the nations it conquered. The unified, written law of the Roman Empire—which at its height extended from England to Egypt—replaced unwritten native customs and rules.

ROMAN LAW had its recorded beginnings in the law of the Twelve Tables, formulated in 451–450 BC. These laws, primarily procedural, were cast in bronze and attached to the "Rostra," or orator's platform, in the Roman Forum so that all Roman citizens—especially the plebeians—might read and understand the law and be protected from arbitrary patrician justice.

Roman legal development ended with the codification known as the *Corpus Juris Civilis* (Body of Civil Law), which consolidated all existing law into a single written code. It was promulgated (AD 533–34) by the Byzantine emperor Justinian I and was known as the JUSTINIAN CODE. The code was a collection of past laws and opinions of Roman jurists and also included new laws enacted by Justinian. The Code of Justinian became the foundation of the present CIVIL LAW system. Civil law and COMMON LAW, formed in England, are the two major legal systems in the world today outside the Communist or socialist countries.

Other legal systems developed prior to the Middle Ages—the Chinese and Greek legal systems, for example. The Hebrew (see TALMUD), Islamic, Hindu (see MANU), and Roman Catholic canon (see CANON LAW) legal systems were rooted in religion, but their influence extended to the secular world. The Roman law system had, however, the greatest influence on Western legal development.

This 6th-century mosaic shows the Byzantine emperor Justinian I with members of his court. Justinian sponsored the compilation of Roman law into the Corpus Juris Civilis, *the basis of western civil law. (San Vitale, Ravenna, Italy.)*

The Dutch scholar Hugo Grotius, one of the most eminent jurists and humanists of the 17th century, is considered a founder of modern international law.

Law in the Middle Ages. The decline of the Roman Empire in Western Europe in the 5th century and the rise of the Germanic tribes suppressed legal development throughout much of Europe. The conquering Germanic tribes brought little to replace Roman law. GERMANIC LAW began as the unwritten custom of the tribe, not the enactment of any supreme authority in the state.

The early Middle Ages saw little progress in the development of law. Few schools of law existed. Learning was left to monks and clergy. The feudal system of land ownership, from the 8th century through the 14th century, was comprised of petty domains (see FEUDALISM). Systematic justice was destroyed. Each region administered, developed, and recorded its own local laws. The Roman Catholic church and its canon law system became increasingly influential during the Middle Ages in the vacuum of legal advancement.

Around the year 1100 scholars began to apply the principles of Roman law to Germanic and feudal customs, transforming Roman law into Italian law. During the 13th, 14th, and 15th centuries, faculties of law were founded in Spain, France, Germany, and the Netherlands. The studies conducted there were to form the basis of the modern civil law systems of these countries. Various interpretations of legal thought inevitably began to spring up. In the 16th century, for example, a school of law called legal humanism emphasized the importance and flexibility of classical Roman law. In the 17th and 18th centuries, legal scholars such as Hugo GROTIUS and Samuel von PUFENDORF put forward theories of NATURAL LAW, and advocated the use of reason in combination with tenets of Roman law.

Modern Civil Law. Despite the renewed respect for law, the weakness of royal governments and the strength of the feudal system in the Middle Ages militated against any unified national law. Royal absolutism and growing nationalism in the 16th, 17th, and 18th centuries, however, began to unite nations and thus provided the foundation for unified legal systems. The French Revolution in 1789 and the rise to power of Napoleon I gave birth to the French civil code, or NAPOLEONIC CODE, in 1804. Spread throughout Europe by Napoleon's conquests, it

became the most influential of the civil law national codes and was the basis of other national codes that followed: the Austrian Civil Code in 1811, the Italian Civil Code in 1865, the Spanish Civil Code in 1888, and the German Civil Code of 1900.

The modern civil law systems that arose from ancient Roman law are distinguished by codification—the systematic and comprehensive statutory treatment of the law. The civil law COURTS base their decisions on enactments rather than on judicial precedent; the latter is the basis of common law. If the civil court ruling is attacked, the attack is on the ground that the statute has been misinterpreted or misapplied.

Common Law. In England a second system of legal justice, known as common law, evolved. Unlike the civil law system, common law is not a written code but is based on written judicial decisions that constitute precedent. This doctrine of following precedents is called *stare decisis* (Latin, "to stand by decided matters"). Statutes modify the law rather than embody it as in the civil law systems.

English law was initially based on the Germanic tribal customs. When the Normans invaded England in 1066, they found a legal system more advanced than their own. The Normans under William I (r. 1066–87) and his successors Henry II (r. 1154–89) and Edward I (r. 1272–1307) consolidated the conflicting local customs into the common law. Their objective was to curb the power of the feudal landowners and ensure the supremacy of the king. Trial by JURY was instituted, and the MAGNA CARTA (1215) placed the king under the rule of law. Magistrates, or justices, traveled from town to town to hear cases. The office of judge became a full-time career. Admission to the bar was contingent upon legal knowledge. Pleas to the king's chancellor for fair solutions to wrongs not righted by common law courts created a separate body of law called EQUITY, which was not merged with common law in England until 1873, and which survives in the United States in a few states.

The Napoleonic Code Crowned by Time *(1833) celebrates the first modern codification of civil law, enacted (1804) by the French emperor as the Code Napoléon.*

Sir William Blackstone, the most eminent British jurist of the 18th century, is best known for the historical analysis and systematization of English law contained in his Commentaries on the Laws of England (1765–69). (National Portrait Gallery, London.)

Common law advanced through the teaching and writing of English legal scholars. Henry de Bracton (d. 1268) and Sir Edward COKE (1552–1634) advocated the common law system in their legal treatises. Sir William BLACKSTONE's *Commentaries on the Laws of England* (1765–69) analyzed English law and became the basis of legal education in the New World.

The common law system spread through English colonization and conquest. The United States was one of the first to adopt and defend this system. Common law also exists in the British Commonwealth nations and in former colonies such as India. Flexible and adaptable to change, common law proved a viable legal system.

Law in the North American Colonies. Because the majority of the colonists who first settled America came from England, the common law system was introduced in many colonies. More important was the reliance on Blackstone's *Commentaries*. The influence of this work, along with the lack of any law schools in America until 1784, a fact that necessitated the training of lawyers in England, established English common law in America.

Lawyers led the fight for independence and were instrumental in composing the CONSTITUTION OF THE UNITED STATES (1787) and the BILL OF RIGHTS (1791). Of the 56 signers of the DECLARATION OF INDEPENDENCE (1776), 25 were attorneys; so were 31 of the 55 members of the CONSTITUTIONAL CONVENTION (1787). After the Revolutionary War, common law survived despite prejudice against the English.

The United States Supreme Court. Before John MARSHALL's appointment as chief justice in 1801, the SUPREME COURT OF THE UNITED STATES was held in low esteem; it was disorganized and decided few cases. Marshall's concern was to establish a strong, independent judiciary. The decisions of his court did much to increase the power and prestige of the Court. In MARBURY V. MADISON (1803) the Supreme Court declared it had the power to determine the constitutionality of legislative acts.

In decisions such as MCCULLOCH V. MARYLAND (1819) and GIBBONS V. OGDEN (1824) the Marshall court shaped the future of the law and the country. These decisions gave the constitution the flexibility to meet the needs of a growing nation. As American society progressed, the functions of the Court expanded. An interesting and complicating feature of the U.S. legal system is the coexistence of two sets of law and jurisdictions—federal and state. The 14TH AMENDMENT (1868) had tremendous impact on the law and the future of the judicial system: it guaranteed EQUAL PROTECTION OF THE LAWS and DUE PROCESS of the law, allowing the federal courts to determine the constitutionality of state statutes that affect individual rights.

Civil Rights. The emphasis in U.S. law shifted from property rights in the late 19th and early 20th centuries to CIVIL RIGHTS and liberties in the middle and later part of the 20th century. The court outlawed segregation in public schools (BROWN V. BOARD OF EDUCATION OF TOPEKA, KANSAS, 1954); guaranteed the fundamental freedoms of religion, press, and speech (see FREEDOM OF THE PRESS; FREEDOM OF RELIGION; FREEDOM OF SPEECH); ensured the right to a trial by jury for criminal offenses; and added constitutional protections to those accused of crimes. The Court ruled that EVIDENCE obtained by illegal searches and seizures cannot be used in trials (*Weeks* v. *U.S.*, 1914, and *Mapp* v. *Ohio*, 1961), and it held that a criminal suspect must be informed of his or her right to remain silent (see SELF-INCRIMINATION) and to legal counsel (MIRANDA V. ARIZONA, 1966). The common law proved it could adapt to changing American society. An important function of the judiciary system has also been to protect the supremacy of law against abuses by the executive branch. In cases such as *Youngstown Sheet and Tube Company* v. *Sawyer* (1952) and *United States* v. *Richard M. Nixon* (1974), the Supreme Court respectively upheld the primacy of statutory authority and overruled the assertion of executive privilege when it was faced with the fundamental requirements of due process of law.

Corporate Law. U.S. law is called upon to deal with increasingly complex issues, such as how to regulate the ubiquitous corporation. Formed to conduct business for

During the 1950s the U.S. Supreme Court, under Chief Justice Earl Warren (1953–69), was composed of: (left to right, seated) William O. Douglas, Hugo L. Black, Earl Warren, Felix Frankfurter, Tom C. Clark; (standing) Charles E. Whittaker, John M. Harlan, William J. Brennan, Jr., and Potter Stewart. The Warren Court handed down landmark decisions in civil liberties and civil rights.

In September 1957, President Eisenhower ordered 1,000 federal troops to Little Rock, Ark., to effect the entrance of nine black students into the city's segregated Central High School. The unanimous 1954 decision of the U.S. Supreme Court in Brown v. Board of Education, Topeka, Kansas ruled that racially segregated educational facilities were unconstitutional.

profit, the corporation is a creation of the law. The ability of the U.S. legal system to adapt the common law to the requirements of a changing society is exemplified in BUSINESS LAW. Early Supreme Court decisions in DART-MOUTH COLLEGE v. WOODWARD (1819) and Bank of Augusta v. Earle (1839) provided impetus for corporate growth. As corporations grew in the late 19th and early 20th centuries, so did the demand for their control. Federal and state governments enacted legislation to regulate their development (see GOVERNMENT REGULATION).

Administrative Law. Another recent and increasingly important addition to the U.S. legal system is administrative law, which governs the proliferating activities of governmental agencies and officials whose function is to execute legislative mandates. Administrative law procedures differ substantially from traditional common law; but the fundamental principles of administrative law are at least in part derived from the U.S. Constitution.

American and other legal systems have been challenged by increasing demands. Aviation disasters can involve citizens and laws of many nations, and tremendous antitrust suits may involve multinational corporations. Larger law firms now have offices throughout the world to conduct INTERNATIONAL LAW.

See also: CONTRACT; CRIMINAL JUSTICE; LEGAL PROCEDURE; MARITIME LAW; MILITARY JUSTICE; PROPERTY; TORT.

Law, Andrew Bonar [bah'-nur] Andrew Bonar Law, b. Sept. 16, 1858, d. Oct. 30, 1923, led the British Conservative party for more than ten years and was briefly prime minister (1922–23). Born in Canada, he moved to Scotland as a boy and made a substantial fortune in the iron trade of Glasgow. Elected to Parliament in 1900, he became leader of the Conservatives in 1911 on the resignation of Arthur BALFOUR. Law excelled in the delivery of vigorous debating speeches, replete with facts and statistics.

During World War I, Law proved himself an excellent

administrator as colonial secretary (1915–16) in Herbert ASQUITH's coalition and as chancellor of the exchequer (1916–19) under David LLOYD GEORGE. In 1922, Law opposed the continuation of the coalition government, and he succeeded to the post of prime minister in October. Illness, however, forced him to resign after seven months.

Law, John John Law, b. Apr. 21, 1671, d. Mar. 21, 1729, was a Scottish financier whose brilliant but highly speculative banking and stock-market projects in France during LOUIS XV's minority created a spectacular but short-lived economic boom.

In 1716 Law's government-chartered General Bank began to issue paper currency and provide low-interest loans to businesses. At the same time, Law's Company of the West, organized in 1717, sold 100 million *livres* of stock based on the potential wealth of its monopoly over France's Louisiana Territory (see MISSISSIPPI SCHEME). In 1719 this company absorbed all other French trading companies. By 1720, Law was controller general of finance. In that year he merged his bank and company into a vast financial organization that assumed control of state debts, coinage, and taxation. Panic public selling later that year destroyed the entire scheme.

---

law, physical Physical laws give precise expression to observed regularities that occur in nature. They are necessary for describing, explaining, or predicting the development of natural phenomena. Classical physical laws, such as those of Kepler and Newton, however, lead to incorrect results when applied to atoms, nuclei, and elementary particles. Between 1900 and 1930 the laws of QUANTUM MECHANICS were discovered, developed, and successfully applied. Quantum laws can be written in the form of differential equations, which, as is true of the classical case, require that the initial data be specified. Heisenberg's UNCERTAINTY PRINCIPLE states that initial data cannot be specified with sufficient precision to apply classical laws; therefore, separate sets of laws apply to microscopic and macroscopic phenomena.

The basic physical laws share two surprising properties: they are all unproven and also unprovable. Developed from observation and experimentation, they are assumed valid as long as no natural violations of them can be found. It is presumed that natural physical laws exist and have always existed. It is the goal of scientists, mathematicians, and philosophers to discover and define those laws.

Law, William

Law, William William Law, b. 1686, d. Apr. 9, 1761, was an English theologian and mystic. Influenced by Jakob BÖHME, Law became a mystic after 1734. In 1740 he retired to his birthplace at Kings Cliffe, Northamptonshire, accompanied by two disciples. Their aim was to cultivate a saintly existence of devotion, study, and service. A powerful foe of deism and a mystical writer of note, Law is renowned for his devotional classic, *Serious Call to a Devout and Holy Life* (1728). His works were collected in nine volumes after his death.

Lawes, Sir John Bennett

Lawes, Sir John Bennett   see FERTILIZER

lawn bowls

lawn bowls [bohlz] Lawn bowls, or simply bowls, involves rolling balls, the bowls, down finely manicured grass lanes so that they stop in close proximity to a smaller ball. Bowls is a game played either indoors or outdoors by both men and women in teams of 1 to 4 and is most popular in English-speaking countries.

Prehistoric in origin, it was played in various forms by the Egyptians, Greeks, and Romans, who brought their version, BOCCIE, to northern Europe. It was popular in England by the 12th century, and the Scots codified the rules in 1849.

The standard bowling green is 120 ft (36.58 m) by

A player kneels to release a ball toward the jack, a smaller, white target ball, during a lawn bowling match in Sydney, Australia, the site of the first World Lawn Bowls Championship (1966).

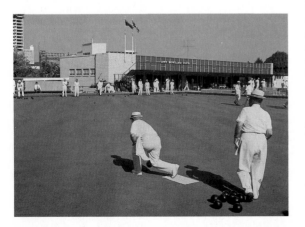

120 ft and is divided into 6 parallel rinks or lanes. The first player rolls the jack, a white ball 2.5 in. (6.35 cm) in diameter and weighing 10 oz (283 g), along the rink. Then the players each roll their bowls, which are 4.75–5.13 in. (12.1–13 cm) in diameter and weigh between 3 lb 2 oz and 3 lb 8 oz (1.42 and 1.59 kg), with the teams alternating turns. At the completion of a round, or end, each bowl closer to the jack than an opponent's scores 1 point. The game is over either after a specified number of ends (usually 21 for 4-person teams) or at a specified game point (21 in singles). A common tactic is to use the curved-path rolls of the biased, or eccentrically balanced, bowls to knock opponents' bowls aside.

Lawrence

Lawrence Lawrence (1990 pop., 70,207) is an industrial city in Essex County, northeastern Massachusetts, on the Merrimack River. First settled in 1655, it was chosen by Abbott Lawrence and other Boston entrepreneurs as the site of a planned industrial city, which was laid out in 1845. Lawrence soon became a major center for the manufacture of woolen textiles, its mills employing thousands of immigrant workers. In 1912 the Industrial Workers of the World led a famous strike of the Lawrence mill workers and won substantial concessions from the employers.

Lawrence, Abbott

Lawrence, Abbott Abbott Lawrence, b. Groton, Mass., Dec. 16, 1792, d. Aug. 18, 1855, was a promoter of the New England textile industry. In 1814 he and his brother Amos established A. & A. Lawrence, which imported textiles and manufactured goods. By 1830 the firm was one of the most prominent companies in Boston. Lawrence was also a founder (1845) of the industrial town of Lawrence, Mass. He served in Congress (1835–37, 1839–40), was a member of the Northeast Boundary Commission (1842), and was U.S. minister to Great Britain (1849–52). Lawrence founded the Lawrence Scientific School at Harvard University.

Lawrence, D. H.

Lawrence, D. H. In the course of 20 years D. H. Lawrence, b. Sept. 11, 1885, d. Mar. 2, 1930, published more than 40 volumes of narrative fiction, poetry, criticism, travel writing, and social commentary. He abandoned the traditional concerns of the English novel—worldly careers, courtship, and social manners—and regarded sexual relations as the decisive element in human behavior. For this reason two of his major novels—*The Rainbow* (1915) and LADY CHATTERLEY'S LOVER (1928)—were banned, but Lawrence's forthright portrayal of sexuality was an integral part of his crusade against the constricting and sterile values of modern civilization.

David Herbert Lawrence, the son of an illiterate coal miner and a schoolteacher, was born in England in the Nottinghamshire village of Eastwood. He attended Nottingham University, qualified as a teacher in 1908, and worked in a London school until 1912. In the same year Lawrence met Frieda Weekley (born von Richthofen), a

D. H. Lawrence, one of the outstanding British authors of the early 20th century, is best remembered for such novels as Women in Love *(1920) and* Lady Chatterley's Lover *(1928), which shocked readers and critics with their frank treatment of love and passion.*

married woman who left her husband and three children to live with him. For Lawrence their marriage (1914) exemplified many of the concerns of his fiction: the breaking down of social barriers, the flouting of moral conventions, and the conflict between the psychological and physical needs of men and women. The stresses of their relationship were portrayed in his volume of autobiographical verse *Look! We Have Come Through* (1917). Lawrence and his wife left England in 1919, returning only occasionally for brief visits. They traveled throughout Europe and also lived in Australia and New Mexico.

Lawrence's first novel, *The White Peacock* (1911), begun when he was 20, is modeled on his own boyhood and adolescence. Its style is romantic and owes something to Thomas Hardy and George Meredith, but the lyrical descriptions of rural England are all Lawrence's and prefigure the spirituality of his later work. *Sons and Lovers* (1913) is thought by some to be his finest novel. Certainly Lawrence never excelled the realism of this psychological portrayal of a young man's struggle to cast off the imprisoning emotional ties of his past and find fulfillment. The quest is continued in *The Rainbow*, the beginning of an account of several generations of women that concludes with *Women in Love* (1920). Both *The Rainbow* and *Women in Love* achieve unity of design and meaning through the use of symbolism—a device that Lawrence also exploited in his short stories. *Lady Chatterley's Lover*, Lawrence's last major novel, is an expression of his belief in the possibility of personal fulfillment through sexual relations.

Lawrence's short stories began to appear in 1909. The sermonizing tone that often mars his lesser novels, such as *The Plumed Serpent* (1926), is absent from his stories and novellas, which include the masterpieces "Odour of Chrysanthemums" (1914), "The Fox" (1923), and "The Man Who Died" (1931). Of his poems, published in a collected edition in 1932, many are merely autobiographical effusions; others, such as "Piano," are extremely fine.

Lawrence's long exile produced several fine volumes of travel writing—which include *Mornings in Mexico* (1927) and *Etruscan Places* (1932)—and a vast correspondence that provides insight into his irascible but generous nature. He suffered greatly from the hostility of a prudish public, who thought of him as a pornographer, and did not live to enjoy the praise that his books began to receive in the 1950s. He died of tuberculosis in France.

Lawrence, Ernest Orlando   The American physicist Ernest Orlando Lawrence, b. Canton, S.Dak., Aug. 8, 1901, d. Aug. 27, 1958, conceived (1929) and invented the cyclotron, a high-energy particle ACCELERATOR, for which he was awarded the 1939 Nobel Prize for physics. Lawrence built (1931) an 11-in-diameter (28-cm) cyclotron that accelerated protons to an energy of 1,250,000 electron volts; this energy enabled him to disintegrate (1932) lithium, the first artificial disintegration of matter in the Western Hemisphere. Lawrence was appointed (1936) director of Berkeley's Radiation Laboratory (since renamed the Lawrence Berkeley Laboratory), which was built to house the larger cyclotrons that he and his colleagues subsequently constructed. In the Manhattan Project, which produced the first atomic bomb, Lawrence was program chief in charge of developing an electromagnetic process for separating uranium 235.

Lawrence, Jacob   Jacob Lawrence, b. Atlantic City, N.J., Sept. 7, 1917, is a black American artist whose major works have chronicled the history and social progress of his race. Often using tempera, he favors a limited range of colors applied in flat areas; this technique, combined with a preference for angular, simplified forms, gives his paintings the look of posters. The social realism of his carefully researched works is well exemplified in his *Migration of the Negro* series (1940–41; Phillips Collection and the Museum of Modern Art, New York City).

Lawrence, John Laird Mair Lawrence, 1st Baron   John Laird Mair Lawrence, b. Mar. 4, 1811, d. June 27, 1879, was viceroy of British India (1864–69). He arrived in Calcutta in 1830 as a magistrate and for 19 years served in various positions in northwestern India. Lawrence restored order in the Punjab after the Sikh wars of the 1840s and welded the SIKHS into an army loyal and capable enough to stand behind the British during the INDIAN MUTINY of 1857. During the mutiny, his older brother, Sir Henry Lawrence (1806–57), was killed in the siege of Lucknow. As governor-general, John Lawrence expanded public works programs. He was made 1st Baron Lawrence in 1869.

Lawrence, T. E.   Colonel T. E. Lawrence, b. Aug. 15, 1888, d. May 19, 1935, known as Lawrence of Arabia, was a guerrilla leader in the Arab Revolt of 1916–18, which expelled the Turks from western Arabia and Syria during WORLD WAR I. Lawrence was an aloof, complex, somewhat arrogant genius. His exploits made him a popular, if enigmatic, hero in the Western world.

Lawrence, the son of an Anglo-Irish landowner and the family's governess, attended Oxford University, specializing in archaeology, architecture, and history. He began learning Arabic when he visited Syria and Palestine and worked as an archaeologist in the Middle East from 1910 until early 1914.

After the outbreak of World War I, Lawrence returned to Egypt in December 1914 as an intelligence officer. In October 1916 he accompanied a British mission to aid HUSAYN IBN ALI of Mecca, who had launched the Arab Revolt against Ottoman Turkish rule. Shortly thereafter, he joined Husayn's son and army commander, Faisal (later King FAISAL I of Iraq), as an advisor. Together, Faisal and Lawrence proceeded to push back the Ottoman forces. In October 1918 the Arabs took Damascus, and Lawrence returned to Britain.

As a member of the British delegation to the Paris Peace Conference (1919), Lawrence unsuccessfully championed the cause of Arab independence. He became a Middle Eastern advisor at the Colonial Office under Winston Churchill and succeeded in having Faisal appointed king of Iraq, but he tired of fame and what he termed "the shallow grave of public duty." Resigning from his post in 1922, he completed his famous account of his Arabian experiences, the *Seven Pillars of Wisdom* (printed privately, 1926; published, 1935). Under assumed names, he spent most of the remainder of his life as an enlisted man in the Royal Air Force and Tank Corps.

T. E. Lawrence, a British soldier, scholar, and writer, both promoted and resisted his almost legendary identity as Lawrence of Arabia.

Lawrence, Sir Thomas The British artist Sir Thomas Lawrence, b. Apr. 13, 1769, d. Jan. 7, 1830, was the most successful portrait painter during the romantic period in England. Lawrence's success as a professional portrait painter was immediate. He was commissioned to paint Queen Charlotte in 1789 and became painter to the king on the death of Sir Joshua Reynolds in 1792. His early portraits, such as the glittering *Eliza Farren* (1790; Metropolitan Museum of Art, New York City), are marked by a directness of vision and vivacity of handling that ex-

tended Reynolds's style and presaged the romantic era. In 1814 the prince regent (later George IV) selected him to paint what became a remarkable series of portraits of the leaders of the alliance against Napoleon, including the emperor of Russia, the king of Prussia, and Pope Pius VII. Lawrence was knighted in 1815 and succeeded (1820) Benjamin West as president of the Royal Academy.

This oil study, Charles William Lambton, typifies Sir Thomas Lawrence's darker and simpler late style. (1824–25; Collection Earl of Durham, London.)

Lawrence Berkeley and Lawrence Livermore laboratories [burk'-lee] The Lawrence Berkeley Laboratory is a multidisciplinary research center with activities in atomic and high-energy physics and in energy and environmental problems. It is the part of the center founded in 1931 as the Radiation Laboratory by Ernest LAWRENCE and is located in the Berkeley hills near San Francisco, Calif. The laboratory is operated by the University of California and funded by the U.S. Department of Energy. It was the location of the first cyclotron accelerators (see ACCELERATOR, PARTICLE) and played a distinguished part in the early days of high-energy physics research with the 6-GeV proton synchrotron, called the Bevatron, now converted for heavy-ion acceleration.

The Lawrence Livermore Laboratory, formerly part of the Radiation Laboratory, became a separate institution in 1952. Located in Livermore, Calif., the laboratory's applied research deals with nuclear explosives (for both weaponry and peaceful purposes), fusion reactions, and health problems caused by artificial radiation. The laboratory conducts underground nuclear-explosion tests at a site in Nevada.

lawrencium [luh-rens'-ee-uhm] Lawrencium is a synthetic radioactive metal, the last member of the ACTINIDE SERIES. Its symbol is Lr (originally Lw), its atomic number is 103, and its atomic weight is 260 (longest-lived isotope). Lawrencium does not occur naturally; it was first synthesized at the Radiation Laboratory in Berkeley, Calif., in 1961. By bombarding a mixture of californium isotopes with boron-II ions, Albert Ghiorso, T. Sikkeland, A. E. Larsh, and R. M. Latimer created ^{258}Lr, with a half-life of 4.2 seconds. The element was named for Ernest Lawrence, the inventor of the cyclotron. Other lawrencium isotopes have been created by bombarding other TRANSURANIUM ELEMENTS with heavy ions.

laws of motion   Newton's laws of motion are the three most fundamental natural laws of classical mechanics. Sir Isaac Newton stated them in his book *Principia Mathematica* (1686). Taken together, Newton's three laws of motion underlie all interactions of force, matter, and motion except those involving relativistic and quantum effects.

Newton's first law of motion is also known as the law of inertia, which states that any object in a state of rest or of uniform linear motion tends to remain in such a state unless acted upon by an unbalanced external force. In effect, this is a definition of equilibrium; the branch of physics that treats equilibrium situations is STATICS. The tendency for matter to maintain its state of motion is known as inertia.

Newton's second law of motion, the most important and useful of the three, establishes a relationship between the unbalanced force applied to an object and the resultant acceleration of the object. This relationship states that an unbalanced force acting on an object produces an acceleration that is in the direction of the force, directly proportional to the force, and inversely proportional to the mass of the object. In other words, force equals mass times acceleration, or $F = ma$. Thus, a given force will accelerate an object of small mass more rapidly than it will a massive object. Similarly, doubling the applied force produces twice the acceleration of an object of arbitrary mass.

According to Newton's third law of motion, which is also known as the principle of action and reaction, every action (or force) gives rise to a reaction (or opposing force) of equal strength but opposite direction. In other words, every object that exerts a force on another object is always acted upon by a reaction force. The recoil of a gun, the thrust of a rocket, and the rebound of a hammer from a struck nail are examples of motion due to reaction forces.

Lawton   Lawton (1990 pop., 80,561), a city in southwest Oklahoma, is the seat of Comanche County and a commercial center with diversified industries. The city is the site of Cameron University, and Fort Sill, the U.S. Army Field Artillery Center, is nearby. First inhabited by the Kiowa and Comanche, the area was opened to white settlement by lottery about 1901.

laxative   see CATHARTIC

Laxness, Halldór Kiljan [lahks'-nes]   Halldór Kiljan Laxness, b. Halldór Guðjonsson, in Reykjavik, Apr.

23, 1902, the most prominent figure in modern Icelandic literature, received the Nobel Prize in 1955. His first successful novel, *Vefarinn mikli frá Kasmír* (The Great Weaver from Kashmir, 1927), reflects his discomfort with Roman Catholicism and interest in expressionism and surrealism. In the 1930s, Laxness completed three sequences of novels: *Salka Valka* (1931–32; Eng. trans., 1936), about a small fishing community in transition; *Independent People* (1934–35; Eng. trans., 1945), about a poor farmer's struggle against injustice; and *World Light* (1937–40; Eng. trans., 1969), about a poet living among people unable to comprehend his genius. During World War II, Laxness wrote his finest novel, *Íslandsklukkan* (Iceland's Bell, 1943–46), a trilogy set in the late 17th and early 18th centuries. In *The Atom Station* (1948; Eng. trans., 1961) he gives a satirical account of the decline in Icelandic culture. Laxness also wrote an autobiography, *Skáldatími* (A Writer's Schooling, 1963), and a documentary novel, *Innansveitarkronika* (A Parish Chronicle, 1970).

Layamon [lay'-uh-muhn]   The English poet Layamon, a Worcestershire priest who flourished in the early 13th century, is known only for his 16,000-line poem *The Brut* (*c*.1205), which includes the first account in English of King Arthur and his knights. Brut, a shortened name for Brutus, was the mythical founder of Britain. Layamon's poem is based on the *Roman de Brut* by Robert Wace of Jersey, which in turn is an adaptation of GEOFFREY OF MONMOUTH's *Historia Regum Britanniae*.

Laye, Camara [lay, kam'-uh-ruh]   The Guinean author Camara Laye, b. Jan. 1, 1928, d. Feb. 4, 1980, was a leading French-language black-African writer. Educated in Islamic and French schools in Guinea, he lived for some years as an impoverished student in France. His first published work, *The African Child* (1953; Eng. trans., 1959), is a moving memoir of his village childhood. *The Radiance of the King* (1954; Eng. trans., 1956) renders in fictional terms Laye's belief that black and white cultures can achieve a positive synthesis. Laye's last work, *The Guardian of the Word* (1978; Eng. trans., 1984), is a "translation" of an African legend told by a *griot*, keeper of tribal history. A critic of Guinea's leader Sékou Touré, Laye died in exile in Senegal.

Lazarus [laz'-uh-ruhs]   In the New Testament, Lazarus, the brother of MARY AND MARTHA, was restored to life by Jesus (John 11–12) after four days in the tomb. This was one of the most striking miracles of Jesus recorded in the Gospels.

Lazarus, Emma   The American poet and essayist Emma Lazarus, b. New York City, July 22, 1849, d. Nov. 19, 1887, is particularly remembered as the author of the inscription on the Statue of Liberty. The sonnet, "The

New Colossus" (1883), is best known for the closing lines:

Give me your tired, your poor,
Your huddled masses yearning to breathe free,
The wretched refuse of your teeming shore,
Send these, the homeless, tempest-tost, to me,
I lift my lamp beside the golden door!

Among her other works are *Songs of a Semite* (1882) and *The Dance of Death*, a historical drama about medieval Hebrew life. An ardent champion of the Jews victimized in the Russian pogroms of the 1880s, Lazarus also translated Spanish, Hebrew, and German poetry.

Lazio   see LATIUM

lazurite   see LAPIS LAZULI

Le Brun, Charles [luh bruhn', sharl]   Charles Le Brun, b. Feb. 24, 1619, d. Feb. 2, 1690, a French painter, designer, politician, and courtier, held every important official post in the arts under Louis XIV. He was responsible for the creation of the characteristic Louis XIV style and exercised far-reaching authority over the arts in France until the death (1683) of his protector, Jean Baptiste COLBERT. One of the founders of the French Royal Academy in 1648, Le Brun was given complete authority as chancellor in 1663; his reform of the Academy converted it into a fully equipped school for the training of young artists. In 1663, Le Brun was made the first director of the GOBELINS tapestry factory, for which he not only furnished cartoons for tapestry series, such as the *Story of Alexander* (1664), but also provided designs for and supervised the work of the goldsmiths, cabinetmakers, bronze workers, and other artisans employed there. Le

The decorative classicism of "grand manner" painting is exemplified by The Chancellor Séguier in the Procession of Marie Thérèse's Entrance into Paris, 26 August 1660 *by Charles Le Brun. (Louvre, Paris.)*

Brun was responsible for the entire decorative program at the Palace of VERSAILLES (notably the Hall of Mirrors, 1678–84), including the sculptures in the park.

Son of a master sculptor, Le Brun was an apprentice in Paris to the painters François Perrier (from 1632) and Simon Vouet (from 1634) and studied in Italy (1642–45) with Nicholas Poussin. From Poussin and Italian masters such as Pietro da Cortona he learned a sober, classicizing baroque idiom of careful groupings, powerfully conceived figures, and concentration of dramatic focus that was to define the French classical style of the later 17th century.

Le Carré, John [luh kah-ray']   John Le Carré is the pseudonym of David Cornwell, b. Oct. 19, 1931, an English writer who won international recognition in 1963 with the novel *The Spy Who Came in from the Cold* (film, 1966), a critically acclaimed look at modern espionage. Le Carré served (1961–64) in the British Foreign Service, and all of his work is derived from that experience. His heroes—chief among them George Smiley, a much abused master of British intelligence—are organization men who operate in a frigid world in moral limbo and who are likely to be in greater danger from their superiors than from their enemies. Le Carré's novels include *The Looking Glass War* (1965; film, 1970); the trilogy comprising *Tinker, Tailor, Soldier, Spy* (1974; television adaptation, 1980), *The Honourable Schoolboy (1977),* and *Smiley's People* (1980; television adaptation, 1981); *The Russia House* (1989; film, 1990); and *The Secret Pilgrim* (1991).

Le Châtelier, Henri Louis [luh shaht-ul-yay', ahn-ree' lwee]   The French chemist and metallurgist Henri Louis Le Châtelier, b. Oct. 8, 1850, d. Sept. 17, 1936, discovered (1884) the thermodynamic principle that every change in a system in stable chemical equilibrium results in a rearrangement of the system so that the original change is minimized. This phenomenon, known as Le Châtelier's principle, helps predict the outcome of a chemical reaction. Le Châtelier also made reliable high-temperature thermometers using a thermocouple consisting of platinum and a platinum-rhodium alloy.

Le Corbusier [luh kor-boo-zyay']   Charles Édouard Jeanneret, known as Le Corbusier, b. La Chaux-de-fonds, Switzerland, Oct. 6, 1887, d. Aug. 27, 1965, was a Swiss-French architect who played a decisive role in the development of MODERN ARCHITECTURE. In 1910 he worked for several months in the Berlin studio of industrial designer Peter Behrens, where he met the future BAUHAUS leaders Ludwig Mies van der Rohe and Walter Gropius. Shortly after World War I, Jeanneret turned to painting and founded, with Amédée Ozenfant, the purist offshoot of cubism. With the publication (1923) of his influential collection of polemical essays, *Vers une architecture* (*Towards a New Architecture*, Eng. repr. 1970), he adopted the name Le Corbusier and devoted himself to creating a radically modern form of architectural expression.

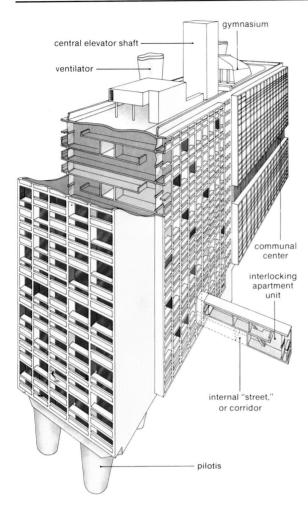

central elevator shaft

ventilator

gymnasium

communal center

interlocking apartment unit

internal "street," or corridor

pilotis

Le Corbusier's Unité d'Habitation *(1946-52) in Marseilles, France, reflects his "modulor" concept of scaling architecture to human proportions. The honeycombed facade, devised by Le Corbusier in 1933, became a standard feature in later apartment designs.*

In the 1920s and '30s, Le Corbusier's most significant work was in urban planning. In such published plans as *La Ville Contemporaine* (1922), the *Plan Voisin de Paris* (1925), and the several *Villes Radieuses* (1930–36), he advanced ideas dramatically different from the comfortable, low-rise communities proposed by earlier garden-city planners. During this 20-year span he also built many villas and several small apartment complexes and office buildings. In these hard-edged, smooth-surfaced, geometric volumes, he created a language of what he called "pure prisms"—rectangular blocks of concrete, steel, and glass, usually raised above the ground on stilts, or *pilotis*, and often endowed with roof gardens intended to compensate for the loss of usable floor area at ground level.

After World War II, Le Corbusier moved away from purism and toward the so-called New Brutalism, which utilized rough-hewn forms of concrete, stone, stucco, and glass. He was commissioned by the French government to plan and build his prototypical Vertical City in Marseilles. The result was the Unité d'Habitation (1946–52)—a huge block of 340 "superimposed villas" raised above the ground on massive pilotis, laced with two elevated thoroughfares of shops and other services and topped by a roof-garden community center that contained, among other things, a sculptured playground of concrete forms and a peripheral track for joggers.

His reputation led to a commission from the Indian government to plan the city of CHANDIGARH, the new capital of the Punjab, and to design and build the Government Center (1950–70) and several of the city's other structures. These handcrafted buildings represented a second, more humanistic phase in Le Corbusier's work that also was reflected in his lyrical Pilgrim Church of Notre Dame du Haut at Ronchamp (1950–54) in the Vosges Mountains of France; in his rugged monastery of La Tourette, France (1954–59); and in the several structures he designed (from 1958) at Ahmedabad, in India.

Le Guin, Ursula   Ursula Kroeber Le Guin, b. Berkeley, Calif., Oct. 21, 1929, is among the foremost writers of science fiction. Her most important work divides into two groups. The six novels of the "Hainish" cycle are concerned with earthly issues (for example, the distortions created by sexual role-playing, the ambiguities inherent in utopian idealism) as they might be played out on non-Earth worlds. Two of the novels, *The Left Hand of Darkness* (1969) and *The Dispossessed* (1974), won both the Hugo and the Nebula awards for best science fiction. The Earthsea trilogy (*The Wizard of Earthsea*, 1969; *The Tombs of Atuan*, 1971; and *The Farthest Shore*, 1972) are fantasies written for older children. *Always Coming Home* (1985) describes a future utopia in stories, essays, poems, and—on an accompanying tape—music and song.

Le Havre   [luh ahv']   Le Havre, the second largest seaport of France, is located in northern France on the English Channel at the estuary of the Seine River. The city has a population of 198,700 (1982); that of the conurbation is 255,000. Le Havre is France's principal Atlantic port. Although passenger-line traffic has declined, the cross-channel trade in cargo has increased rapidly. Much cargo destined for Paris via the Seine River is transshipped there. Le Havre has a variety of industries, including petroleum refining, shipbuilding, food processing, chemicals, wood products, and nonferrous metals.

Once a small fishing village, Le Havre took on added significance in 1517 when Francis I began harbor improvements. The port was an important military base during both world wars. Le Havre was occupied by the Germans and suffered much damage from Allied bombing during World War II. Postwar Le Havre is virtually a new city.

Le Mans [luh mahn']   Le Mans is a city in the Loire Valley in northwestern France, at the confluence of the Sarthe and Huisne rivers, about 185 km (115 mi) southwest of Paris. An industrial and marketing center, it has a population of 145,976 (1982). Manufactures include railroad and automobile machinery, textiles, plastics, and tobacco products. The Le Mans 24-hour Grand Prix automobile race is held just south of the city.

Le Mans was settled as early as the 5th century BC. The old walled city, fortified by the Romans, is the site of the Saint-Julien Cathedral (11th–15th century AD), the church of Notre-Dame-de-la-Couture (10th–13th century), and the Church of Sainte-Jeanne d'Arc (begun 11th century). During the Hundred Years' War the city was besieged by the English five times, and the city was occupied by the Germans in 1871.

Le Nain brothers [luh nan']   The three Le Nain brothers were French painters best known for their depictions of peasants and tradesmen in simple settings. All three brothers—Antoine, Louis, and Matthieu—were born in Laon, where they received their first training. From 1620 the brothers shared a studio in Paris. When they were received (March 1648) into the Royal Academy, Antoine and Louis were listed as *peintres de bambochades,* or painters of low-life—genre—scenes, and Matthieu was mentioned as portraitist. Early critics found the brothers' works so similar as to be virtually indistinguishable. Modern scholars, however, generally recognized three distinct groups within the Le Nain oeuvre, although the brothers' close association and their practice of signing works only with their surname make attribution difficult.

According to contemporary accounts, **Antoine Le Nain** (*c.*1588–1648) "excelled in miniatures and small por-

The French painter Louis Le Nain's The Traveller's Rest *marks a departure from previous portrayals of country people. In contrast to earlier painters, Le Nain rendered his peasants as dignified figures. (Louvre, Paris.)*

traits." Several of his small group portraits, such as the *Réunion de Famille* (1642; Louvre, Paris), show members of a bourgeois family placed before a neutral background. The diminutive, stiffly posed figures painted in strong, pure colors are naively arranged with little care for composition.

Louis Le Nain (*c.*1593–1648) was by far the most talented of the three brothers. The impressive large-scale paintings associated with his name are carefully constructed and well-ordered compositions in which the colors tend toward a narrow range of cool grays, gray browns, and gray greens. He took as his subject lowly French peasants, whom he portrayed without grotesque or comic qualities, as in *Peasants at Supper* (1645–48; Louvre, Paris).

Matthieu Le Nain (1607–77), in contrast, chose to portray the middle-class residents of Paris. His *Corps de Garde* (1643; private collection, Paris), for example, depicts a party of swaggering officers drinking in a candlelit interior. He became master painter to the city of Paris in 1633.

Le Nôtre, André [luh noht', ahn-dray']   The landscape architect André Le Nôtre, b. Mar. 12, 1613, d. Sept. 15, 1700, was the creator of the French formal garden.

His earliest royal post was first gardener to King Louis XIII at the TUILERIES in Paris, where he succeeded (1637) his father. Le Nôtre's best-known work is the immense park of the Palace of VERSAILLES (1661–90), commissioned by Louis XIV and imitated throughout Europe. The principles of the *jardin français,* however, can be seen more clearly at the Château de Vaux-le-Vicomte, where Le Nôtre worked (1656–61) in collaboration with the architect Louis Le Vau and the designer Charles Le Brun. Whereas the design of the typical Renaissance garden consisted of individual geometric units laid side by side, with a strong sense of compartmentalization, the gardens designed by Le Nôtre were unified by a dominant central axis that firmly controlled the movement of the spectator through the various lawns, gardens, and pools. His spacious, elegantly orchestrated works epitomized the opulent era of Louis XIV and played a key role in the development of LANDSCAPE ARCHITECTURE.

Le Vau, Louis [luh voh', lwee]   Louis Le Vau, b. 1612, d. Oct. 11, 1670, was a leading French architect who, in collaboration with other artists, created architectural ensembles in which the arts were fused in a typically baroque manner. Commissioned by Louis XIV's finance minister, Nicolas Fouquet, to build the Château de Vaux-le-Vicomte, Le Vau created (1657-61) a building that greatly influenced the subsequent design of country houses, particularly through the innovative placement of an oval salon in the center of the garden facade. Despite a characteristic misunderstanding of the classical orders, Le Vau brilliantly realized in Vaux-le-Vicomte an overall effect of opulence and theatricality. Louis XIV was so impressed with the complex, which included a decor by Charles LE BRUN and gardens by André LE NÔTRE, that Le

Vau soon was put to work (1669) on the enlargement of the Palace of VERSAILLES.

Le Vau's chief projects in Paris were the Collège des Quatres Nations (1661) and the completion of the LOUVRE Palace (1660s), for which Le Vau designed the colonnade of the east facade in collaboration with Le Brun and Claude Perrault.

---

lead Lead is a lustrous, silvery metal that tarnishes in the presence of air and becomes a dull bluish gray. Soft and malleable, it has a low melting point (327° C). Its chemical symbol, Pb, is derived from *plumbum,* the Latin word for waterworks, because of lead's extensive use in ancient water pipes. Its atomic number is 82; its atomic weight is 207.19.

Occurrence. The Earth's crust is about 15 parts per million (ppm) lead. Four stable lead isotopes exist in nature; three of them—^{206}Pb, ^{207}Pb, and ^{208}Pb—are end products of the radioactive decay of uranium and thorium. It is assumed that all of the fourth isotope, ^{204}Pb, that exists in rocks has been there since the rocks were formed. The most valuable lead ore is galena (lead sulfide, PbS), which is almost always mixed with other valuable ores. Much of the world production of bismuth, arsenic, antimony, and silver comes from the production of lead. Lead is also recycled from scrap metal.

Toxicity. Lead and lead compounds can be highly toxic when eaten or inhaled. Although lead is absorbed very slowly into the body, its rate of excretion is even slower. Thus, with constant exposure, lead accumulates gradually in the body. It is absorbed by the red blood cells and circulated through the body, becoming concentrated in the soft tissues, especially the liver and kidneys. Lead can cause lesions in the central nervous system and apparently can damage the cells making up the blood-brain barrier that protects the brain from many harmful chemicals (see BRAIN). Symptoms of lead poisoning include appetite loss, weakness, anemia, vomiting, and convulsions, sometimes leading to permanent brain damage or death. Children who ingest chips of old, lead-containing paint may exhibit such symptoms. The newborn of mothers who had been exposed to lead levels even considered safe for children appear to show signs of slowed mental growth. Levels of environmental lead considered nontoxic may also be involved in increased hypertension in a significant number of persons, according to studies released in the mid-1980s. As a result the U.S. Centers for Disease Control in recent years has been revising downward the levels of environmental lead that it would consider safe. At one time lead poisoning was common among those who worked with lead, but such workplace hazards have been largely curtailed (see POLLUTANTS, CHEMICAL).

Uses. Lead has been used by humans since ancient times. It was used in ancient Egypt in coins, weights, ornaments, utensils, ceramic glazes, and solder. Lead is mentioned in the Old Testament. The Romans conveyed drinking water in lead pipes, some of which are still in operation. Roman slaves extracted and prepared the lead, and Pliny describes a disease among the slaves that was clearly lead poisoning. Because of their potential toxicity, lead water pipes are no longer being installed. The greatest single use of lead metal today is in the plates of storage batteries for automobiles.

The protective oxidation layer formed by lead in contact with such substances as air, sulfuric acid, and fluorine makes it highly resistant to corrosion, so lead has been used to make drainage pipes and lead chambers in sulfuric acid factories. It is also used as a roofing material. The softness and malleability of lead make it useful for sheathing telephone and television cables, and it is used in solder because of its low melting point. When combined with tin, lead forms solder alloys that are stronger than lead alone, with melting points lower than those of either original metal.

Lead has the highest density of all metals in common use. Because of their high density, lead bullets and shot encounter little air resistance and thus achieve excellent striking power. Lead's density and softness also make it highly suitable for damping sound and vibrations. To isolate them from vibration, heavy machinery and even whole buildings are placed on lead blocks. Because the effectiveness of shielding against gamma and X rays depends largely on the density of the shield, lead is used in the protective shielding of X-ray machines and nuclear reactors.

Lead can be alloyed with many metals. Lead alloys are important because they resist attack by sulfuric acid and are harder than pure lead.

Lead Compounds. Lead exists in the divalent or tetravalent oxidation state in compounds. A number of lead compounds are important in the paint industry. At one time, lead pigments were often used in ceramic glazes and interior paints; but because lead pigments are toxic, their use is now restricted. White lead, $Pb(OH)_2 \cdot 2PbCO_3$, is the most important lead pigment. Lead dioxide, PbO_2, is a vigorous oxidizing agent that is sometimes used in match heads.

Tetraethyl lead or tetramethyl lead has often been added to gasoline to improve engine efficiency and reduce gasoline consumption in automobiles. Because of the toxic effect of lead on the environment, however, this use is being phased out (see GASOLINE). Lead azide, $Pb(N_3)_2$, is sensitive to striking and is highly explosive; it is frequently used as a detonator of explosives.

Leadbelly The black singer and guitarist Leadbelly, b. Huddie Ledbetter in Mooringsport, La., Jan. 21, 1888, d. Dec. 6, 1949, spent most of his life as an itinerant laborer and street singer in the small towns of the deep South. Accompanying himself on his 12-string guitar, Leadbelly sang the work songs, blues, hollers, and dance tunes of the black country people of his time. The folksong archivist John A. Lomax heard him in a Louisiana penitentiary, recorded his songs, and helped obtain his release. Leadbelly came to New York in 1934 and, from that year until his death, sang throughout the country and abroad, both in concert and on recordings. His posthumous influence on the folk music revival of the 1950s and '60s was enormous.

leadwort [led'-wurt]   Leadwort is a genus, *Plumbago*, of mostly tropical perennial herbs, sometimes shrubby or climbing, in the plumbago family, Plumbaginaceae. They produce spikelike clusters of slender-tubed flowers that are blue, reddish, or white. The cape leadwort, *P. auriculata,* from South Africa, is an evergreen shrub with short spikes of usually blue flowers. The Southeast Asian *P. indica* is a partially climbing evergreen shrub with branching stems and elongated clusters of red flowers.

Cape leadwort of South Africa is an evergreen shrub. Its blue or white flowers open in late summer or early fall.

leaf   see PLANT

leaf beetle   Leaf beetles, family Chrysomelidae, order Coleoptera, are a group of about 25,000 species of leaf-feeding insects that occur throughout the world. They have brightly colored, oval bodies that are usually less than 13 mm (0.5 in) long, with short antennae about half their body length. Adult leaf beetles feed on the leaves and flowers of various plants, and larvae eat the leaves and roots. Many leaf beetles, such as the Colorado potato beetle, *Leptinotarsa decemlineata*, are important agricultural pests.

leafhopper   Leafhoppers are a very large group of insects constituting the family Cicadellidae in the order Homoptera. Most of the more than 2,000 species in North America are small, less than 10 mm (0.4 in) long. Leafhoppers are usually slender, are often brightly colored, and have four wings and short hairlike antennae. They have piercing, sucking mouthparts and feed on plant juices; some species are economically important plant pests. A clear, sugary liquid called honeydew, composed of unused sap and excretory products, is expelled from the anus of many leafhoppers and may attract other insects and cause plant surfaces to become sticky.

League of Nations   The League of Nations was an organization established after World War I to promote international peace. Sixty-three nations were members, including all the major European powers at one time or another. The United States played an important role in setting it up but did not join. From its headquarters in Geneva, the league organized many social and economic welfare activities, although it concentrated on political matters. It was nominally responsible for the administration of many colonial territories under the mandate system.

An important instrument of diplomacy in the 1920s, the league was unable to fulfill its chief aims of disarmament and peacekeeping in the 1930s. It lost members and fell into disuse before World War II. The organization was formally terminated on Apr. 18, 1946, when it was succeeded by the newly organized UNITED NATIONS.

Creation.   The outbreak of World War I in 1914 led people in Britain, France, the United States, and several neutral countries to explore alternatives to traditional diplomatic methods for keeping the peace. Some government leaders, including U.S. president Woodrow WILSON and Jan SMUTS of South Africa, gave their support to the league ideal as a way to prevent future wars. This ideal was one of the FOURTEEN POINTS put forward by Wilson as the basis for a just peace, and by the time of the PARIS PEACE CONFERENCE it was a leading war aim of the victorious Allied powers.

The League of Nations was established on Jan. 10, 1920. Its Covenant, which was the basis for the league's operation, was included in the Treaty of Versailles imposed on defeated Germany. The U.S. Senate refused to ratify the peace treaty and, in a blow to President Wilson, also kept the country out of the league. The USSR was also not a member at first.

Organization.   The purpose and rules for the organization were set forward in the League of Nations Covenant. Outlined in the Covenant were three approaches to preventing war: arbitration in settling disputes, disarmament, and collective security.

Under the Covenant all member states were represented in an assembly, which held sessions at least once a year. Each nation had one vote, and unanimity was required for all decisions. The main political work of the league and the settlement of international disputes were delegated to another, smaller body—the council. Permanent seats on the council were reserved for Britain, France, Japan, Italy, and, later, Germany and the USSR; other countries were elected to temporary representation on the council to make a total of 8, later raised to 10, and then 14 members. The third main organ of the league was the secretariat, which administered league activities. In addition, the league was linked to several other bodies, most notably the Permanent INTERNATIONAL COURT OF JUSTICE, or World Court, and the INTERNATIONAL LABOR ORGANIZATION.

Activities.   By the late 1920s the league had gained in prestige because it had found peaceful solutions to a number of minor disputes and because the threat of war was remote. The LOCARNO PACT of 1925 reassured Germany's neighbors and paved the way for German admission to the league the following year. In addition, the league gained support through its nonpolitical work—

combating the spread of opium and other illicit drugs, contributing to child welfare, improving health conditions around the world, and lowering the barriers against international trade.

The DEPRESSION OF THE 1930s and a series of international crises changed the political climate. The crisis ensuing from the Japanese invasion of MANCHURIA in September 1931 is often seen in retrospect as the first decisive challenge to the league system. At the time, however, the European statesmen on the league council did not so perceive it. In 1932 they sent a commission of inquiry to study the rights and wrongs of the war between China and Japan (see SINO-JAPANESE WARS). Japan soon left the league, but no effort was made to force it to give back the territory it had conquered. This failure eroded confidence in collective security. Adolf HITLER's rise to power in Germany aggravated the crisis. In 1933 he pulled Germany out of the GENEVA CONFERENCE on disarmament and then out of the league itself. As Germany began to rearm and overturn the restrictions of the Treaty of Versailles, league supporters tried to win Hitler back to the organization rather than work to stop him.

Collective security was finally put to the test in 1935 when Italy attacked ETHIOPIA. After Ethiopia's emperor HAILE SELASSIE appealed for help, the league voted to impose economic sanctions against Italy until it stopped its aggression. Britain and France, whose cooperation was essential to this effort, acted timorously, as they did not want to antagonize the Italian dictator Benito MUSSOLINI. Italy was able to overcome this halfhearted sanctions policy and complete its conquest of Ethiopia. Italy withdrew from the league in 1937 and went on to further foreign intervention, along with Germany and the USSR, in the SPANISH CIVIL WAR.

The league never recovered from this setback and was all but ignored in the rush of events that led to the outbreak of World War II. It revived briefly in December 1939 to make the meaningless gesture of expelling the USSR for its attack on Finland.

Evaluation. Despite its eventual failure to halt the tide of war, the league was an important pioneering venture in international affairs. The recurrence of war only emphasized the world's need for an effective alternative to anarchy, and the United Nations followed the structure and methods of the league in its main outlines. The changes in emphasis in the new organization reflected some of the lessons of the league experience. The United Nations places more reliance on diplomacy and less on elaborate judicial procedures to prevent war. Moreover, the United Nations emphasizes nonpolitical work in economic development to a much greater degree than did the league. The United Nations is truly a worldwide group that tries to meet the needs of its members; the league was more limited in scope and membership.

League of Women Voters Founded in Chicago in 1920, the League of Women Voters is an organization that attempts to further the development of political awareness through political participation. The league, an offshoot of the National American Woman Suffrage Association, was organized in 1920, the year of national enfranchisement of women, to educate the female electorate in the use of their right to vote. The league voted in 1974 to extend membership to men. Its activities, no longer limited to issues involving women's rights, center on any important national political or social concern. The league conducts studies, distributes information on candidates and issues, runs voter-registration drives, and takes stands on pending legislation.

Leahy, William Daniel [lay'-hee] William Daniel Leahy, b. Hampton, Iowa, May 6, 1875, d. July 20, 1959, was an American admiral and diplomat. He graduated from Annapolis in 1897 and served in the Spanish-American War and World War I. In 1937, Leahy became chief of naval operations but retired two years later and became governor of Puerto Rico. In 1940, President Franklin D. Roosevelt named Leahy ambassador to Vichy France. Recalled to naval service in 1942, he was chief of staff to Roosevelt and to Harry S. Truman until 1949. In 1944, Leahy became the first fleet (five-star) admiral.

Leakey (family) [leek'-ee] The British anthropologists **Louis S. B. Leakey**, b. Aug. 7, 1903, d. Oct. 1, 1972, his wife **Mary**, b. Mary Nichol, Feb. 6, 1913, and their son **Richard**, b. Dec. 19, 1944, have made major contributions to the study of human evolution. Louis and Mary Leakey investigated early human campsites at OLDUVAI GORGE, Tanzania, and found important hominid fossils more than 1.75 million years old. Their son Richard has conducted research in the East Turkana area of Kenya and has discovered even earlier hominid fossils dating from as long as 3 million years ago.

Louis Seymour Bazett Leakey investigated Stone Age cultures in East Africa in the 1920s, then a pioneer field of research. From 1931 to 1959, Louis and his second wife, Mary, worked at Olduvai Gorge, reconstructing a long sequence of Stone Age cultures dating from approximately 2 million to 100,000 years ago. They documented the early history of stone technology from simple stone-chopping tools and flakes to relatively sophisticated, multipurpose hand axes. In 1959 the Leakeys discovered the skull of *Australopithecus boisei* (a species of the prehuman genus AUSTRALOPITHECUS). This skull was later dated at about 1.75 million years of age, using potassium-argon dating. The Leakeys also excavated another skull of a less robust individual in somewhat lower levels. Both new fossils were associated with stone chopping-tools. Louis Leakey claimed that the less robust hominid, which the Leakeys called HOMO HABILIS, was the earliest toolmaker and a direct ancestor of modern humans. Many scientists disagreed, largely because the fossil fragments were so small. By 1965 the Leakeys had found several other fossils at Olduvai, including a HOMO ERECTUS cranium that is about 1 million years old.

After Louis Leakey's death, Mary Leakey and their son Richard continued field research in East Africa. Mary

The Leakey family of British archaeologists and anthropologists has made many important contributions to the study of human origins. Pictured here are Louis Leakey and his wife Mary.

Leakey did much of the fieldwork at Olduvai, and in recent years she has discovered *Homo* fossils more than 3.75 million years old at Laetolil, located 40 km (25 mi) south of Olduvai. Richard Leakey has worked in the Omo area of southern Ethiopia and has discovered more than 388 km^2 (150 mi^2) of Lower Pleistocene deposits on the eastern shore of Lake Turkana (Rudolf) in northern Kenya. There he found traces of australopithecines, as well as fragments of a more advanced hominid, perhaps an early *Homo*. This fossil, known as Skull 1470, was dated by Leakey as 2.6 million years old. In 1984 he and his colleagues also found a nearly complete skeleton of a large *H. erectus*, dated as about 1.6 million years old.

Lean, David

David Lean, b. Mar. 25, 1908, d. Apr. 16, 1991, was one of contemporary Britain's most prominent film directors. A noted film editor during the 1930s, Lean collaborated with Noel Coward during the war to codirect such Coward vehicles as *In Which We Serve* (1942) and *Brief Encounter* (1946). He consolidated his reputation with two Dickens films—*Great Expectations* (1946) and *Oliver Twist* (1948)—and *The Sound Barrier* (1952). Lean became an outstandingly successful international producer-director with *Bridge on the River Kwai* (1957), for which he won an Academy Award; *Lawrence of Arabia* (1962), which won another Oscar; *Dr. Zhivago* (1966); *Ryan's Daughter* (1970); and *A Passage to India* (1984). Polished craftsmanship and highly disciplined editing were Lean's hallmarks.

leap year   see CALENDAR

Lear, Edward

The writer and artist Edward Lear, b. London, May 12, 1812, d. Jan. 29, 1888, is known both for his many nonsense LIMERICKS and songs and for his drawings and paintings of landscapes and birds. Having begun work as an artist before he was 16, he was commissioned to draw the menagerie of the earl of Derby.

While working on the estate he amused the earl's grandchildren with the limericks he later published as *A Book of Nonsense* in 1846. By that time he had also become a landscape painter, and he gave a series of lessons to Queen Victoria. He published collections of sketches of southern Italy, Greece, Palestine, and Turkey. An enlarged edition (1861) of *A Book of Nonsense* became very popular and was followed by four other humorous books containing such poems as "The Owl and the Pussy Cat" and "The Jumblies."

Lear, Norman

Writer, producer, and director in television and films, Norman Milton Lear, b. New Haven, Conn., July 22, 1922, changed U.S. situation comedy with his television series "All in the Family" (debut, 1971). Mainly through its central character—Archie Bunker, a realistic blue-collar, likable bigot from Queens, N.Y.—Lear challenged his audience by presenting areas of controversy with unprecedentedly strong language. The format spawned several other successful comedy series for Lear, among them "Maude" (debut, 1972), "Sanford and Son" (1972), and "The Jeffersons" (1975).

Lear began writing television comedy in the 1950s and moved into movies in the 1960s (*Come Blow Your Horn*, 1963, and *The Night They Raided Minsky's*, 1968, for example). In the 1980s he became increasingly active in liberal politics and environmental issues.

learning

Learning may be defined as a relatively permanent change, resulting from experience, in an organism's behavior. Its study is central to PSYCHOLOGY, interacting with such fields as PERCEPTION and PROBLEM SOLVING and fading imperceptibly into the study of MEMORY.

Historical Background. The study of learning began with ancient Greek philosophical speculations about how humans gain knowledge (see EPISTEMOLOGY). Modern learning study, however, began only with the acceptance of evolutionary theory, which pointed psychology in a new direction. Evolution suggests that mind, or CONSCIOUSNESS, has evolved because it aids survival. American philosopher and psychologist William JAMES, in his influential *Principles of Psychology* (1890), proposed that learning is the process by which animals gain new skills and adapt to changing environments.

A significant corollary of this view was the idea that animal behavior, and especially learning, can be studied with rigor and the results extended to humans. Influenced more by the English philosopher Herbert SPENCER than by James on this point, psychologists held that processes of human and animal learning differed only in complexity. Spencer accepted the thesis that learning proceeds by registering sensations and forming associations with them (see ASSOCIATIONISM).

Starting in the 1890s, psychologists put this program into practice and started studying association of ideas in animals. They expected their findings to illuminate human psychology. Because these studies were restricted to behavior and did not use introspection, they helped to start the movement called BEHAVIORISM. In standard psychological practice, the term *conditioning* has been used to designate the forms of behavioral learning that humans share with animals. From roughly 1920 to 1970, conditioning was the mainstay of research on learning in humans as well as animals. Later influenced by "mentalist" approaches to memory in humans, the study of animal learning now more nearly resembles the study of human memory. The basic types and phenomena of conditioning remain valid, however, whatever their theoretical interpretation.

Associative and Nonassociative Conditioning. Nonassociative conditioning, or learning, occurs when an organism's response to a single stimulus changes with repeated experience. In habituation (see HABIT), response decreases as a stimulus is repeated; in sensitization, it increases. Associative learning occurs when an organism learns to associate two or more stimuli, changing its response to one or more because of their being experienced together. All learning is considered associative to some degree, so associative learning has been the focus of most learning research.

Pavlovian and Instrumental Conditioning. Associative learning is usually divided into Pavlovian (classical, or respondent) conditioning and instrumental (operant) conditioning. The former primarily involves modification of innate REFLEXES. The latter involves modification of behavior by reward and punishment.

Pavlovian conditioning was first studied by the Russian physiologist Ivan PAVLOV. Pavlov would present two stimuli to his dog subjects at the same time. One, the unconditioned stimulus (US), was food, or a shock, that produced an unconditioned response (UR) such as salivation or avoidance. The other, conditioned stimulus (CS) was a tone, or light, that when presented alone evoked little response. Presenting it together with the US, however, gradually caused the CS by itself to evoke the UR, which would then be called the conditioned response (CR). Such conditioning was long treated as an example of simple associative learning. This is now known to be wrong. First, the main association thus formed is between the US and CS, not the CS and CR. Further, in the spirit of James, Pavlovian conditioning is now regarded as an adaptive process by which animals prepare for the immediate future by learning how to predict important coming events from patterns of current events. They learn to respond to CS's in order to prepare for the future (the US's).

At about the same time that Pavlov was working, the young American psychologist Edward THORNDIKE was describing instrumental conditioning. Here a behavior is followed by a reward or punishment, changing the frequency of the behavior as a result. Thorndike's basic law of instrumental learning, the law of effect, says that when a response is followed by a reward (now called a reinforcer), its probability of recurring in the same circumstances is increased. As for punishment, in psychology this means following a behavior with pain in order to eliminate it. The term *negative reinforcement* refers to applying pain and then removing it when a desired behavior occurs. Both

are forms of pain control, the effectiveness of which is debatable. Punishment is effective only if it is severe, immediate, and inescapable. It does not cause a habit to be unlearned but only to be suppressed. Because pain control causes ANXIETY and incites aggression, its use in BEHAVIOR MODIFICATION is mainly avoided.

Other Aspects of Learning. Psychologists have found that learning is more efficient when taking place in brief periods punctuated by rests, rather than in long sessions. They also distinguish declarative learning ("knowing how") from procedural learning ("knowing that"). When an organism learns that a CS predicts the appearance of a US, this is declarative learning. When it learns how to get a reinforcer through instrumental conditioning, this is procedural learning. The study of declarative learning—how organisms internally represent the world—becomes the study of memory.

The physiology of learning is a subject of ongoing research. Great progress has been made in recent years in locating the structures of the brain and the processes in the nervous system that make learning possible. In simple conditioning, learning depends on the synaptic connections between nerve cells. In more complex forms, larger structures are involved (see BRAIN).

---

learning disabilities
Learning disabilities, which may afflict children, youth, and adults, are disorders in the basic psychological processes involved in understanding or using language, and may be manifested in imperfect ability to listen, think, speak, read, write, spell, or do mathematical calculations. They include such conditions as perceptual handicaps, brain injury, minimal brain dysfunction, DYSLEXIA, and developmental aphasia, but exclude learning problems that result primarily from visual, hearing, or motor handicaps, or from mental retardation, emotional disturbance, or environmental, cultural, or economic deprivation.

The hundreds of different kinds of learning disabilities in children can be grouped into eight areas: oral expression, listening comprehension, written expression, basic reading skills, reading comprehension, mathematics calculation, mathematics reasoning, and spelling. There is little consensus on the precise characteristics of children with learning disabilities, although there is some agreement that these children can do certain things at or above the normal level of achievement while they can do other things only at a much lower level.

Several studies indicate that between 4 and 7 percent of the school-aged population need special education and related services because of learning disabilities. At present most states are serving significantly smaller percentages of the school-aged population as learning disabled, and some of these children might be better served in remedial programs.

The cause of learning disabilities is not known. Researchers have attempted to determine the role played by central-nervous-system dysfunction as a result of prenatal, perinatal, or postnatal trauma, malnutrition, biochemical imbalance, and infections. Genetic factors appear to play a part in some children whose learning disabilities may be characterized by specific symptoms such as reading disability or by a less-specific developmental delay or maturational lag. In general, teachers simply need to know the child's present level of performance in detail in order to set realistic goals in designing a program to remedy the deficits and improve the child's functioning in academic skills and adaptive behavior.

Though methods of instruction for children with learning disabilities vary widely, three major remedial strategies have been defined: task training, in which the task to be learned is simplified or modified; ability or process training, in which efforts are directed toward remediation of the disability that seems to be interfering with normal learning; and the combination process-task (or ability-task) approach, which integrates remediation of the process dysfunction with a task analysis of the sequence of skills required and attempts to bring about a precise match between the demand of the task and the particular pattern of learning in the child.

In addition to these educational approaches, a variety of other procedures such as eye-training exercises, diet control, motor training, sensory training, and medication, including antihistamines, stimulants, and vitamins, have been advocated by some professionals in the field.

The Association for Children with Learning Disabilities, founded in 1963 primarily for parents of such children, has become an influential national group that promotes the further development of programs catering to the learning disabled in every state.

lease   A lease is a grant by one person (the lessor or landlord) to another (the lessee or tenant) of the right to possess and use property for a specific period of time. Leases can be either oral or written, although most states of the United States require leases for one year or more to be written. The two most common types of leases are residential and commercial. Residential leases concern the rental of houses and apartments, and commercial leases involve the rental of land, offices, and other property for commercial purposes.

A valid lease must identify the parties by name and by status (such as landlord or tenant). It must describe the property with reasonable particularity. The commencement and duration of the leasehold must be specified, as must the amount of rent and when it is to be paid. A lease usually contains a series of covenants (promises) agreed upon by the parties concerned. In most jurisdictions these covenants are considered to be independent, that is, if one party does not perform his or her covenants, the other party is still liable to perform his or her own covenants. The only remedy for an aggrieved party is to sue the other party for breach of particular covenants. Express covenants are those written or orally agreed upon by the parties. Implied covenants are those covenants which the law treats as being usual and logical—for example, a tenant's duty to pay rent and a landlord's duty to provide quiet enjoyment of the property.

Residential leases tend to favor the landlord over the tenant. Although most reasonable lease provisions will be enforced by the courts, some states have enacted legislation protecting tenants against unreasonable lease clauses imposed upon them by landlords. In New Jersey, for example, the law provides that a security deposit may never exceed one and one-half month's rent, and that interest on it must be paid to the tenant.

A security deposit is usually required in a lease. This is an amount deposited by the tenant with the landlord to cover any damages to the property other than reasonable wear and tear, and to insure against rent default by the tenant. Late payment of rent penalty provisions are often included. Many leases contain clauses prohibiting assigning or subletting without the landlord's consent. These clauses are usually upheld by courts.

Lease, Mary Elizabeth [lees]   Mary Elizabeth Clyens Lease, b. Ridgway, Pa., Sept. 11, 1850, d. Oct. 29, 1933, was a populist who achieved fame by exhorting farmers to "raise less corn and more hell." The famous phrase, however, was probably not hers but that of a hostile reporter. A lawyer (by her own claim) in Kansas, Lease joined the Populist party and became a vigorous advocate of agrarian reform, woman suffrage, free silver, Prohibition, popular election of senators, government supervision of corporations, and nationalization of railroads. She was called Mary Yellin Lease by some opponents.

least-squares method   The least-squares method is a statistical procedure used to fit a set of measurements onto an approximate curve. It is a technique that allows researchers to identify trends based upon measurement values. Due to ERROR, measurement values generally deviate from their expected positions along a mathematical curve. Of the various curves based on correction formulas, the least-squares curve has the smallest sum of the squares of the individual measurement deviations.

German mathematician Carl Friedrich GAUSS developed the least-squares method in 1794. In 1801, Gauss successfully employed this method in an attempt to relocate the first known asteroid, Ceres, after it had been tracked for 41 days, then lost in the brightness of the Sun.

leather and hides   Leather is the hide or skin of a mammal, reptile, bird, or fish that has been made pliable and resistant to decay through tanning. The surface area of hides and skins contains the hair and oil glands and is known as the grain side. The arrangement of hair pockets and the texture of the surface give each type of leather its distinguishing character, or grain. The flesh side of the hide or skin is much thicker and softer.

One of the properties of animal hides and skins is their ability to absorb tannic acid, a plant extract, and other chemical substances that prevent them from decaying, make them resistant to wetting, and keep them supple and durable. In addition, the fibrous structure of hides and skins allows air and water vapor to pass through—thus, for example, perspiration will evaporate from leather shoes.

Properly treated leather is among the most long-lived of natural substances. Ancient pieces of leather clothing and utensils have been found throughout the world. The Athenian playwright Aristophanes referred (c.500 BC) to the tanner, who was already a well-established craftsman.

The Tanning Process. Before tanning, hides and skins must be cured to prevent putrefaction. Large hides are green salted: they are spread in layers for several days with salt between each layer. A faster process, used on smaller hides and skins, is brine-pickling—immersion in a salt-brine solution circulated by pumps or agitators.

At the tannery the hides and skins are trimmed, sorted into batches of the same size and thickness, and finally washed and soaked to remove excess salt and restore the fibers to a condition in which they can readily absorb tanning agents. Solutions of lime and enzyme materials are applied to loosen the hairs, and a dehairing machine leaves the surface smooth and the distinctive grain pattern visible.

Vegetable tanning with tannic acids is the oldest method. Used primarily for heavy cattle hides, the process may take a month or more. Tannin extracts come from the bark and wood of several trees. The hides are suspended in vats containing successively stronger tanning solutions. The tanned leather is then bleached and impregnated with natural oils and greases. The final product is a firm, water-resistant leather used chiefly in shoe soles but also in upholstery, luggage, saddlery, and industrial belting.

Almost all leather made from lighter-weight cattle hides and from the skin of other animals is chrome-tanned, using a process developed in the latter half of the 19th century. Hides and skins are tumbled in huge drums partially filled with chrome-salt solutions that produce a light blue green leather, which is then cleaned, dried, and smoothed by machine. The chrome-tanning process takes a matter of hours, rather than the days required by vegetable tanning, and produces leathers for shoe uppers, garments, handbags, gloves, and other small leather goods.

Finishing. After the leather is tanned, machines split it into flesh and grain layers. The leather must now be dried in a drying cabinet.

Various types of finishes are applied. Leathers are buffed with fine abrasives to produce a suede finish; waxed, shellacked, or treated with pigments, dyes, and resins to achieve a smooth, polished surface and the desired color; or lacquered with urethane for a glossy patent leather.

Sources of Leather. Cattle and calves are the largest single source of leather, and their hides and skins are used in almost every area where leather is needed. The United States, the USSR, Argentina, and Brazil are the largest cattle-hide producers. Other sources of leather are shown in the table.

The United States is the leading leather manufacturer, followed by the USSR, India, Brazil, and Argentina.

LEATHER TYPES AND USES

Source	Market Name	Uses
Cattle	Cattle hide	Shoe uppers and soles, luggage, upholstery, belts, clothing
	Untanned rawhide	Machine belts, bindings, luggage
	Calf leather	Shoe uppers, handbags, belts
Goat and kid	Goatskin and kidskin	Shoe uppers, purses, apparel, gloves
Sheep and lamb	Sheepskin and lambskin	Shoe uppers and linings, gloves, apparel, bookbindings, chamois
	Shearling (wool is clipped and left on hide)	Coats, boots, slippers
Wild hog (peccary) and domestic hog	Pigskin	Shoes, gloves, wallets, luggage
Asian water buffalo		Shoes, luggage, handbags
Reptile	Snakeskin	Shoe uppers, handbags
Deer	Deerskin and buckskin (grain surface removed)	Apparel, gloves, shoes
Shark	Sharkskin	Shoe uppers, small leather goods
Horse	Horsehide and cordovan	Shoe uppers, apparel, baseball covers

Synthetic Substitutes for Leather. Since the 1950s plastic materials have been developed that resemble leather, although they do not share leather's pliability and its ability to "breathe" and to retain its shape. Nevertheless, synthetic substitutes now constitute a sizable share of the products sold under the term *leather goods*, and up to 80 percent of shoe soling.

leatherback turtle The leatherback turtle, *Dermochelys coriacea*, is the largest living species of turtle and the sole surviving member of the family Dermochelyidae. It reaches 1.8 m (6 ft) in shell length and up to 680 kg (1,500 lb) in weight. The shell is covered with smooth, leathery skin and has seven prominent lengthwise ridges on the top. This species lives in the open sea, apparently going ashore only to lay eggs. The leatherback, threatened because of overhunting (particularly of its eggs), is scarce but worldwide in distribution, occurring mostly in tropical waters.

Largest of all turtles, the leatherback turtle is usually found singly in warm oceans worldwide. Its shell consists of bony plates embedded in its dark brown or black leathery skin.

Leatherstocking Tales, The   *The Leatherstocking Tales,* a series of five popular novels by James Fenimore COOPER, constitute an epic of the American wilderness. Natty BUMPPO, the central character, embodies the spirit of the frontier in The *Deerslayer* (1841), where he is an idealized youth, and in *The Prairie* (1827), in which, as an old man, he is transfigured and dies. The other novels in the series are *The Last of the Mohicans* (1826), *The Pathfinder* (1840), and *The Pioneers* (1823).

Leaves of Grass   *Leaves of Grass* (1855), Walt WHITMAN's first published volume of poetry, consisted of 12 poems written without regular meter or rhyme. Whitman revised and expanded his book until his death (1892); the ninth and final version contained hundreds of poems. Among the most famous are "Out of the Cradle Endlessly Rocking," "When Lilacs Last in the Dooryard Bloom'd," "O Captain! My Captain!" and "SONG OF MYSELF." The first edition contained a preface, later omitted, in which Whitman expounded a theory of the poet's vocation. The volume was not well received in the United States and found its first enthusiastic champions in England.

Leavis, F. R. [lee'-vis]   Frank Raymond Leavis, b. July 14, 1895, d. Apr. 17, 1978, was an influential British literary critic who profoundly affected the study of literature in British schools and universities. Unlike other major critics of his time, such as I. A. Richards, William Empson, or the American "New Critics" (see NEW CRITICISM), Leavis did not base his assessments on close verbal analysis. He evaluated authors according to their capacity to experience life with maturity and sensitivity. His first book, *New Bearings in English Poetry* (1932), praised the

work of T.S. Eliot, Ezra Pound, and Gerard Manley Hopkins but considered that of W. H. Auden and W. B. Yeats immature. His vehement judgments, often expressed with devastating scorn, found a wide audience through the journal *Scrutiny* (1932–53), which he edited with his wife, the scholar and critic Q. D. Leavis. *Revaluation* (1936) examined the tradition of English poetry, and *The Great Tradition* (1948) deemed the novelists Jane Austen, George Eliot, Henry James, Joseph Conrad, and D. H. Lawrence "significant in terms of the human awareness they promote." Many regard *The Common Pursuit* (1952) his finest book.

Leavitt, Henrietta Swan [lev'-it]   The American astronomer Henrietta Swan Leavitt, b. July 4, 1868, d. Dec. 12, 1921, established the period-luminosity relation for Cepheid variable stars. This led to the development of a new method for determining how far extremely distant stars and galaxies are from the Earth. She graduated from what is now Radcliffe College in 1892, and worked at Harvard College Observatory from 1902. There, her major task was conducting a program of photographic photometry initiated by Edward C. Pickering, to determine the brightnesses of selected stars. Her study of VARIABLE STARS, of which she discovered 2,400, led to the discovery of the relationship between the period of variability and the luminosity of Cepheid variables. Harlow Shapley later used this relationship to determine the distance of globular clusters.

Lebanon [leb'-uh-nuhn]   The Republic of Lebanon, a tiny country some 55 km (35 mi) wide and 215 km (135 mi) long, is located on the eastern shore of the Mediterranean Sea. It is bordered on the north and east by Syria and on the south by Israel. From earliest times (see PHOENICIA), Lebanon has been at the center of the tumultuous history of the Middle East. It was a French mandate from the end of World War I until 1943, when it gained full independence, and it gradually became the commercial and cultural hub of the Arab Middle East. Lebanon has long been known for its religious and cultural diversity. Its inhabitants generally coexisted peacefully until 1975, when a devastating civil war, broke out. Since that time the country's very existence has been threatened by domestic conflict and external pressures.

Land and Resources

Lebanon's narrow, fertile coastal plain is dominated by the foothills and peaks of the rugged Lebanon Mountains, which rise to 3,088 m (10,131 ft) at Qurnat al-Sawda, the highest point in the country. Behind the Lebanon Mountains lie successively the narrow, fertile al-Biqa (Bekaa) Valley (the northern extension of the GREAT RIFT VALLEY, some 915 m/3,000 ft above sea level) and the Anti-Lebanon Range. The latter forms Lebanon's eastern frontier with Syria and is often considered to include Mount HERMON. Lebanon's two major rivers, the Litani and the Orontes, rise in the al-Biqa Valley.

AT A GLANCE

REPUBLIC OF LEBANON

Land: Area: 10,452 km² (4,036 mi²). Capital and largest city: Beirut (1989 est. pop., 200,000).

People: Population (1990 est.): 3,339,331. Density: 319.5 persons per km² (827.4 per mi²). Distribution (1987): 80% urban, 20% rural. Official language: Arabic. Major religions: Islam, Christianity, Druze.

Government: Type: republic. Legislature: National Assembly. Political subdivisions: 5 governorates.

Economy: GDP (1989 est.): $2.3 billion; $700 per capita. Labor distribution (1986): agriculture—19%; manufacturing—18%; construction—6%; utilities, transportation, and communications—8%; finance—3%; trade—17%; public administration and services—29%. Foreign trade (1987): imports—$1.5 billion; exports—$1.0 billion. Currency: 1 Lebanese pound = 100 piastres.

Education and Health: Literacy (1985): 77% of adult population. Universities (1987): 5. Hospital beds (1982): 11,400. Physicians (1986): 3,509. Life expectancy (1990): women—70; men—66. Infant mortality (1990): 49 per 1,000 live births.

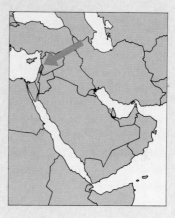

Climate. Lebanon's narrow coastal plain receives an average of 900 mm (about 35 in) of rainfall annually. Winters are mild and rainy; summers are warm, humid, and rainless. The foothills and mountains receive substantially more precipitation in the form of both rain and snow from October to April. Drier weather prevails in the al-Biqa Valley.

Soils, Vegetation, and Animal Life. Geologically, Lebanon is formed of three successive layers: limestone at the surface, sandstone, then limestone. Areas not cultivated—mostly above 1,200 m (4,000 ft)—are generally bare of vegetation due to overcutting and to overgrazing by goats, and the great forests of cedar celebrated in the Bible have largely disappeared. Indiscriminate hunting has greatly reduced a once rich and varied bird and animal population, and pollution in the Mediterranean threatens coastal fishing.

Resources. In ancient times Lebanon was famous for its wood, iron, and copper. All of these resources are now essentially exhausted. There are abundant limestone deposits.

People

Lebanon is an Arab country, and Arabic is the official language. French and English are widely spoken and taught in the schools, however. The people are ethnically diverse because of the area's long history of conquest and assimilation. Indeed, one of the fundamental principles of the social and political order is confessionalism—the proportionate sharing of power among the nation's various ethnic-religious communities. Among them, the principal Christian sects (several of which are EASTERN RITE CHURCHES) are the Maronites, Greek Orthodox, Greek Catholics, Protestant Evangelicals, Roman Catholics, Armenian Orthodox, Armenian Catholics, and Armenian Protestants. SUNNITES, SHIITES, and DRUZES (an offshoot of Shiite Islam) comprise the principal Muslim communities. In many ways, Lebanon today is less a nation than a collection of feudallike baronies organized along religious lines, and more than a decade of civil strife strengthened sectarian loyalties at the expense of national unity.

Demography. No official census has been taken since 1932, when Christians slightly outnumbered Muslims. The two most populous and prosperous sects, the Maronites and the Sunnites, used the 1932 census as the basis for the formula allocating political power along religious lines at independence; this unwritten agreement guaranteed the Maronites control of Lebanon. Since that time the Muslims, particularly the poorer Shiites, have had a substantially higher birthrate than the Christians. Recent estimates indicate that Muslims may constitute as much as 60% of the population—25% Sunnite, 25% Shiite, and 10% Druze—whereas Maronites comprise only an estimated 30% of the current total. The arrival of as many as 400,000 predominantly Muslim Palestinian refugees after 1948 further threatened Lebanon's delicate balance. After 1975, civil strife drove thousands of Lebanese from their homes. By the end of the 1980s, it was estimated that 35% of the population had become refugees. Many foreign investors and wealthy Lebanese left the country.

Education and Health. Lebanon long had one of the

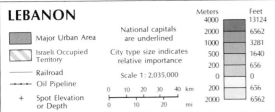

LEBANON

		Meters	Feet
		4000	13124
▨ Major Urban Area	National capitals are underlined	2000	6562
		1000	3281
▧ Israeli Occupied Territory	City type size indicates relative importance	500	1640
		200	656
——— Railroad	Scale 1: 2,035,000	0	0
·—·—· Oil Pipeline		200	656
+ Spot Elevation or Depth		2000	6562

0 10 20 30 40 km
0   10   20   mi

one-third of the wealth, a fact that contributed greatly to the subsequent conflict.

Agriculture. As recently as 1960 nearly half the population was rural, although only one-quarter of the land was cultivated and agriculture generated less than one-fifth of the GNP. Most farmers in the mountains are small freeholders; those in the al-Biqa Valley, southern Lebanon, and the extreme north are mostly tenant farmers or sharecroppers for absentee landlords. The coastal areas yield citrus fruits, bananas, and olives, and the lower slopes of the Lebanon Mountains are terraced for fruit production. Grains, potatoes, melons, and vegetables flourish in the al-Biqa Valley.

Manufacturing and Services. Lebanon's manufacturing sector, though small, is nonetheless significant. The principal manufactures are textiles, cement, ironwork, wood products, plastics, ceramics, pharmaceuticals, and processed foods; refineries at TRIPOLI and near SIDON process oil piped from Iraq and Saudi Arabia to meet domestic requirements. Manufacturing, concentrated in the Beirut area before the civil war, has since become decentralized.

Independent Lebanon prospered by attracting foreign investment. Its banking secrecy laws and uncontrolled foreign exchange market encouraged a strong banking sector. Some 80 major banks once served the Middle East from Beirut, which became the financial and commercial center of the region. Tourism, banking, finance, commerce, and other services were shattered by the civil war and later events.

Transportation. Lebanon's transportation system was one of its principal assets. Beirut is the country's leading port: Tripoli and Sidon are also important. After 1975 numerous illegal ports for smuggling weapons and contraband for the flourishing black market emerged. More recently, entire sections of the country were cut off by occupying foreign armies. Civil air transportation is confined to Beirut International Airport. A government-owned railway connects Beirut with Tripoli and Damascus. A good road system is now much in need of repair. Syria controls Lebanon's overland transportation links to other countries.

Trade. Lebanon's connections to the outside world are critical to its economic viability. For decades Lebanon's trade deficit was offset by the reexport trade and by remittances from Lebanese working abroad. A sharp decline in these remittances since 1983—particularly after the 1990 Iraqi invasion of Kuwait—contributed to the virtual collapse of the Lebanese pound on foreign exchange markets.

Government

The Lebanese republic, independent since 1943, was established under French mandate by the Constitution of 1926 (since amended). The constitution provides for an executive branch (president, prime minister, and cabinet) balanced by an independent judiciary and a unicameral legislature elected to a four-year term by universal adult suffrage. (The current legislature, elected in 1972, has extended its life by special legislation.) Until 1990 an unwritten agreement known as the National Pact was as important as the constitution. It specified that the presi-

best systems of private education in the Middle East, with private elementary and secondary schools serving about half the student population. Public education is insufficient to meet demand or to provide consistent quality. The most notable institution of higher education is the American University of Beirut (1866), in which about half the student body was once non-Lebanese. The Lebanese population's familiarity with foreign languages, high literacy rate, and relatively advanced educational level contribute to a still-vibrant cultural life. Before 1975, Lebanon's health-care system was one of the best in the region, although it concentrated services in urban areas. Since 1975 a growing refugee population has imposed great strains on community services.

Economic Activity

In modern times the Lebanese economy has been fundamentally transformed. Where once the majority of the population was engaged in agriculture, today a diversified economy is dominated by the service sector. The sharpest phase of economic transformation occurred after 1960 and benefited chiefly Christians and a few Sunni Muslims. By 1975 about 4% of the population controlled dent be a Maronite Christian, the prime minister a Sunni Muslim, and the speaker of the legislature a Shiite Muslim. Legislative seats were apportioned among the various sects in accordance with a 6:5 ratio of Christians to Muslims, as were posts in the cabinet, bureaucracy, judiciary, and military. Under constitutional reforms set forth in a 1989 Arab-brokered peace accord and signed into law in September 1990, many of the powers of the Christian president were shifted to the half-Christian, half-Muslim cabinet, and the Muslim prime minister was to countersign presidential decrees. The legislature was to be evenly divided between Christians and Muslims.

History

Lebanon has been in the mainstream of history since recorded history began. Its earliest inhabitants were a Semitic people related to the Canaanites who came to coastal Lebanon from the Arabian Peninsula about 3500 BC. The Greeks named these seafaring people Phoenicians, and they established city-states (including BYBLOS, TYRE, Sidon, Beirut, and BAALBEK) and spread their 22-letter alphabet throughout the Mediterranean region. After being successively ruled by the Egyptians, Assyrians, Neo-Babylonians, Persians, and Greeks, Lebanon came under Roman rule in 64 BC. Christianity was firmly established there before AD 395. Lebanon later became part of the Eastern Roman (or Byzantine) Empire.

Particularly during the early Christian era, when theological controversies bred numerous sects, Lebanon became a refuge for persecuted minorities fleeing imperial authority. In the 660s one of these sects, which later became the Maronite church, settled in the Lebanon Mountains to avoid forcible conversion to Islam by the Arabs, who had completed their conquest of the region by 640. The attractiveness of Lebanon as a refuge persisted into Islamic times. Shiites found a haven there during the 9th century, Druzes in the 11th century.

The coastal plain and Lebanon Mountains fell temporarily to the Crusaders (see CRUSADES) early in the 12th century. Many Lebanese Christians fought alongside the Crusaders, and thousands of them were slaughtered by Muslims once the Crusaders had been driven out in the late 13th century by the MAMELUKS of Egypt. Generally, however, the mosaic of religions that Lebanon had become offered semiautonomy or independence for its various groups, each of which concentrated in specific areas until modern times.

From 1516 to 1918, when Lebanon was formally part of the OTTOMAN EMPIRE, local leaders were granted relative autonomy as long as they paid taxes to their Ottoman rulers. One powerful Druze chieftain, Fakhr al-Din, gained control of Mount Lebanon and parts of Syria and Palestine. After his execution by the Turks in 1635, Druze power waned, paving the way for the rising influence of the Maronites, who established close ties with other Lebanese Christian sects. Under Ottoman rule, Lebanon developed commercial, educational, and religious ties with Europe. Open to the West, it became a center for political rivalries between various foreign powers, including France, England, and Russia. These powers assumed the protection of certain ethnic-religious groups, with France as the chief protector of the Maronites. Intermittent warfare between 1840 and 1860 cost both Maronite and Druze lives. A massacre of Maronites in 1860 prompted French and British intervention and the establishment (1864) by Turkey of a semiautonomous Christian-dominated province in Mount Lebanon.

After World War I, Lebanon became a French mandate, as promised by the secret Sykes-Picot Agreement of 1916. In 1920 the French created Lebanon's current boundaries by adding the al-Biqa Valley, the coastal cities, and areas to the north and south—with large Sunnite and Shiite populations—to predominantly Christian Mount Lebanon. The Republic of Lebanon, established by the Constitution of 1926, remained under French mandate until 1943, when it gained independence.

For a time, independent Lebanon was a model ecumenical society. Two grave weaknesses, however, eventually undid the Lebanese system. The first was the rigidity of the 1943 National Pact, which did not take into account changes in the demography and political consciousness of the various communities. The second was

Beirut, located on the Mediterranean Sea, is the capital and largest city of Lebanon. Since 1975 much of the city has been destroyed, and it has been divided by the so-called Green Line into predominantly Christian East Beirut and Muslim West Beirut.

The cedars of Lebanon, famous since biblical times, became the symbol of the country and are shown on the national flag. Today they are found only in a few protected groves.

Lebanon's gradual involvement in the Arab-Israeli conflict. Lebanon did not participate militarily in the ARAB-ISRAELI WARS, but the influx of predominantly Muslim Palestinian refugees after the 1948 war helped to change the country's internal balance of power. In addition, Lebanese Muslims who identified with the Pan-Arab nationalism of Egyptian president Gamal Abdel NASSER were alienated when President Camille Chamoun was the only Arab head of state who refused to break diplomatic ties with France and Britain during the 1956 Suez Crisis. Civil war broke out in 1958, ending only when U.S. Marines landed in Beirut. Muslim demands for more political and economic power and raids on Israel by PALESTINE LIBERATION ORGANIZATION (PLO) commandos operating a virtual state within a state in Lebanon continued, laying the groundwork for a new civil war.

The 1975–76 civil war pitted the Nationalist Movement (a mostly Muslim mixture of socialists, Communists, and Nasserites) against the Lebanese Front (a group dominated by the Maronite Phalange but including right-wing Muslims). The PLO joined the fighting on the side of the Nationalist Movement. In June 1976, with the Nationalist Movement near victory, Syria (which at various times had supported different groups) intervened on behalf of the Lebanese Front. The Syrian military action was ratified in October by the Arab League, which helped to arrange a cease-fire.

Despite the Syrian presence, sporadic communal strife and the cycle of Israeli-Palestinian violence on Lebanese soil continued. Israeli forces briefly invaded southern Lebanon in 1978 but withdrew after a United Nations peacekeeping force (UNIFIL) was sent into the area. In 1982, Israeli forces again invaded, occupying Beirut and forcing the PLO to evacuate its headquarters there. Phalangist leader Amin GEMAYEL took office as president in September; at his request, a multinational peace force was brought in to try to restore order. In May 1983, Gemayel concluded a security agreement with Israel that provided for a continuing Israeli role in southern Lebanon. Syria, which had refused to withdraw its troops when its Arab League mandate expired, rejected the accord. Meanwhile, the Lebanese army was unable to halt fighting between Lebanon's numerous armed militias (including rival Palestinian groups) or to stem terrorist bomb attacks on the multinational force, which was withdrawn in 1984. Gemayel then repudiated the unpopular Lebanese-Israeli security agreement and installed a new, pro-Syrian cabinet of national unity. The cabinet seldom met after Gemayel rejected a Syrian-brokered peace accord in January 1986, contributing to political and economic deterioration exacerbated by the activities of terrorist groups and by the 1987 assassination of Prime Minister Rashid Karami. Most Israeli forces left Lebanon by June 1985, but conflicting Israeli and Syrian interests still compounded Lebanon's formidable internal problems. In 1988 the legislature's inablility to agree on a successor to Gemayel led to the formation of rival Christian and Muslim governments.

In November 1989 the Lebanesse parliament accepted an Arab-brokered peace accord and elected Maronite René Moawad president. Moawad was assassinated on November 22; his successor was Elias Hrawi. The October 1990 surrender of Christian prime minister Gen. Michel Aoun (who had been battling the Syrian forces in Lebanon since 1989), coupled with the granting of political parity to Muslims and the later disarming of the Lebanese militias, raised new hopes for peace. Lebanon and Syria signed a cooperation pact on May 22, 1991. Communal tensions resurfaced in 1992, however, when Christians demanding a Syrian troop withdrawal boycotted Lebanon's first parliamentary elections in 20 years.

lecithin [les'-uh-thin]   Lecithin is a LIPID material that is found in all living cells, especially in nerve and brain tissue and in red blood cells. It is also a significant substance in egg yolk and in some vegetable oils and, for commercial use, is extracted from these substances and dried to form a waxy, colorless solid. Processed lecithin is used as an emulsifying agent in the manufacture of margarine, chocolate, and other foods.

Leclerc, Jacques Philippe [lu-klurk']   Jacques Philippe Leclerc, b. Nov. 22, 1902, d. Nov. 28, 1947, became famous as a commander of Free French forces in

World War II. Trained at Saint Cyr Military Academy, he escaped from Vichy France in 1940 and took command of Free French forces in Africa. In December 1942–January 1943 he led troops overland from Lake Chad to Tripoli to take part in the Tunisian campaign. Leclerc commanded French troops in the 1944 Normandy Invasion and led the first division into Paris. While on tour as inspector general of the French armies in North Africa, Leclerc died in an air accident in Algeria.

Lecompton Constitution [luh-kahmp'-tuhn] Drafted in October–November 1857 at Lecompton, capital of the Kansas Territory, the Lecompton Constitution was designed to bring Kansas into the United States as a slave state. The passage of the KANSAS-NEBRASKA ACT (1854), which allowed settlers in those territories to decide whether they should have slavery or not, had polarized Kansan politics. The proslavery elements controlled the territorial legislature at Lecompton, while free-state forces set up an extralegal government at Topeka. Guerrilla warfare erupted between the two sides, turning the territory into "bleeding Kansas."

When the Lecompton Constitution was presented to the electorate in 1857, the free-state forces boycotted the election, and it won. The House of Representatives, however, rejected the constitution. When it was resubmitted to Kansan voters in 1858, proslavery forces boycotted the election, and it was defeated. Kansas was admitted to the Union as a free state in 1861.

Leconte de Lisle, Charles Marie [luh-kohnt' duh leel'] Charles Marie René Leconte de Lisle, b. Oct. 22, 1818, d. July 17, 1894, was the leader and finest poet of the PARNASSIANS. His best work—*Poèmes antiques* (Poems of Ancient Times, 1852), *Poèmes barbares* (Poems on the Barbarian Races, 1862), and *Poèmes tragiques* (Tragic Poems, 1884)—depicting savage nature, reveals his profound nihilism. He succeeded Victor Hugo in the Académie Française in 1886.

Leda [lee'-duh] In Greek mythology Leda was the wife of Tyndareus, king of Sparta. ZEUS, who came to her as a swan, seduced her and was the father of one or more of her children. There are many variations of the legend. In one version Leda's daughter HELEN OF TROY was hatched from an egg. In another version Leda bore two eggs, from which came Helen and CLYTEMNESTRA and CASTOR AND POLLUX. Helen and Pollux are commonly thought to have been the children of Zeus, whereas Clytemnestra and Castor were those of Tyndareus.

Ledbetter, Huddie see LEADBELLY

Lederberg, Joshua [led'-ur-burg] The geneticist Joshua Lederberg, b. Montclair, N.J., May 23, 1925, expanded research in genetics through his studies of hered-

ity in bacteria. With Edward L. TATUM he discovered how bacterial genes are recombined, exchanged, and inherited. For this work both men shared the 1958 Nobel Prize for physiology or medicine with George BEADLE. Lederberg also showed how certain viruses could transfer genetic material from one bacterium to another, a process he called transduction.

Ledoux, Claude Nicolas [luh-doo', klohd nee-koh-lah'] The French architect and theorist Claude Nicolas Ledoux, b. Mar. 21, 1736, d. Nov. 19, 1806, was one of the three major proponents of what is termed *revolutionary*, or VISIONARY, ARCHITECTURE, along with Étienne Louis BOULLÉE and Jean Jacques Lequeu. His prophetic concepts prepared the way for modern architecture. Ledoux's early works, such as his Hôtel Hallwyl (1764–66; Paris) and Pavilion of Louveciennes (1770–71; Paris), were successful and popular designs in a traditional mode, although they contained the seeds of his more radical later works. A tendency toward austere and blocklike geometric forms in his late visionary work begins with his unexecuted plans for the utopian new town of Chaux. Among Ledoux's designs that actually were erected, the Palladian saltworks at Arc-et-Senans (1775–79), the Theater of Besançon (1778–94; Paris, only exterior intact), and the Tollhouse of la Villette (1785–89; Paris) stand out. His extravagant and innovative projects and his tendency to monumentalize proved to be his undoing, however, and all but four of his 16 unpopular tollhouses were sacked and burned in 1789.

Lee (family) The Lees of Virginia were among the most distinguished families of 18th- and 19th-century America. They traced their American roots to **Richard Lee**, d. 1664, who came to the colony about 1641, acquired land, and became a wealthy tobacco planter, shipowner, and merchant. In the tradition of the English gentry, he entered politics, holding both executive and legislative offices.

Richard Lee's great-grandsons were prominent in the next century. **Richard Henry Lee**, b. Jan. 20, 1732, d.

Richard Henry Lee, portrayed here by Charles Willson Peale, was an early American political leader. Both he and his brother, Francis Lightfoot Lee, signed the Declaration of Independence and served in the Continental Congress. (National Historical Park Collection, Philadelphia.)

June 19, 1794, and his brother **Francis Lightfoot Lee**, b. Oct. 14, 1734, d. Jan. 11, 1797, both served in the Continental Congress and signed the Declaration of Independence. As a U.S. senator from Virginia (1789–92), Richard Henry also played a major role in the adoption of the Bill of Rights. Two other brothers, **William Lee**, b. Aug. 31, 1739, d. June 27, 1795, and **Arthur Lee**, b. Dec. 21, 1740, d. Dec. 12, 1792, were diplomatic agents for the Continental Congress. The latter helped negotiate the 1778 pact with France, but he quarreled with fellow diplomats Benjamin Franklin and Silas Deane and brought about Deane's disgrace.

Henry "Light Horse Harry" Lee, b. Jan. 29, 1756, d. Mar. 25, 1818, a cousin of the four brothers named above, was a distinguished cavalry commander in the American Revolution, a close friend of George Washington, a member of the Continental Congress (1785–88), governor of Virginia (1791–94), commander of the forces that suppressed the WHISKEY REBELLION (1794), and a member of the U.S. Congress (1799–1801). His brother **Charles Lee**, b. 1758, d. June 24, 1815, was U.S. attorney general (1795–1801).

The best-known member of the family was Light Horse Harry's son, Robert E. LEE. His sons, **George Washington Custis Lee**, b. Sept. 16, 1832, d. Feb. 18, 1913, and **William Henry Fitzhugh Lee**, b. May 31, 1837, d. Oct. 15, 1891, both served as Confederate generals in the Civil War. The former was later president of Washington and Lee University (1871–97), and the latter was a member of the U.S. Congress (1887–91). Their cousin **Fitzhugh Lee**, b. Nov. 19, 1835, d. Apr. 28, 1905, was a Confederate cavalry general, governor of Virginia (1886–89), U.S. consul general in Havana (1896–98), and a general in the Spanish-American War.

▬

Lee, Ann   Ann Lee, b. Manchester, England, Feb. 29, 1736, d. Sept. 8, 1784, founded the SHAKERS in America. An illiterate cotton millworker and then a cook in Manchester, she married and had four children, all of whom died early. About 1758 she joined the Shakers, a faction of the Quakers. Personal experience and direct religious visions led her to embrace celibacy, which she believed could, in conjunction with attention to the spiritual promptings of God, bring those who accepted it to perfection. Her followers became convinced that the Second Coming was revealed in her.

Mother Lee and her small band of followers emigrated to America in 1774 and formed a community at Watervliet, N.Y., two years later. There she was heralded as both a prophetess and female messiah. The community that gathered around her welcomed everyone willing to share common property and seek release from bondage to the flesh.

▬

Lee, Charles   Charles Lee, b. 1731, d. Oct. 2, 1782, was a controversial general during the American Revolution. Born in England, he served in the British army in America during the French and Indian Wars of 1754–63. Lee settled in Virginia in 1773, and when the Revolution

began, Congress commissioned him a major general, second in rank only to George WASHINGTON.

Ambitious for supreme authority, Lee disregarded Washington's orders in December 1776 and was captured by the British in New Jersey. He was exchanged in 1778, but his tactics at the Battle of Monmouth in June 1778 nearly caused an American defeat (see MONMOUTH, BATTLE OF). He was court-martialed and suspended for a year. Lee's criticism of Washington continued, and Congress dismissed him from the service in 1780.

▬

Lee, Jesse   The Methodist preacher Jesse Lee, b. Virginia, Mar. 12, 1758, d. Sept. 12, 1816, is considered one of the most influential figures in early American Methodism. He began preaching in the South and Middle Atlantic States, but from 1789 to 1798 he was a circuit rider in New England, pioneering Methodism in that predominantly Congregationalist area. He became Bishop Francis Asbury's assistant in 1797 and, in 1801, presiding elder of the South District of Virginia. He served as chaplain in both the House of Representatives and the Senate, and his *Short History of Methodism in America* (1810) is the first history of the Methodists in the United States.

▬

Lee, John Doyle   John Doyle Lee, b. Kaskaskia, Ill., Sept. 12, 1812, d. Mar. 23, 1877, was an American executed for participating in the MOUNTAIN MEADOWS MASSACRE of 1857. He was converted to Mormonism in 1838 and devoted his life thereafter to church and community service. In 1850, Brigham YOUNG sent Lee to establish Mormon settlements in southern Utah. Among other functions, he served as an Indian agent, and his work with the Indians led to his involvement with a band of Paiute in the 1857 massacre of California-bound immigrants in a wagon train at Mountain Meadows. Lee continued his colonization work until 1875, when he was tried for the crime. After two trials he was executed at the ·site of the massacre.

▬

Lee, Robert E.   Robert E. Lee, the brilliant commander of Confederate forces during the U.S. CIVIL WAR, was one of the most famous and respected soldiers in American history. After the South lost the war, he served as a symbol of courage in defeat.

Early Life and Career. Robert Edward Lee was born on Jan. 19, 1807, at his family's home, "Stratford," in Westmoreland County, Va. His father, Henry "Light Horse Harry" Lee (see LEE family), had been a cavalry officer during the American Revolution and a close friend of George Washington. Lee grew up in genteel poverty in Alexandria, Va. Appointed to West Point in 1825, he graduated (1829) with an enviable academic record. In 1831, Lee married Mary Ann Randolph Custis, great-granddaughter of Martha Washington by her first marriage. During the next 30 years he often lived at Arlington, the Custis mansion near Washington, D.C.

Robert E. Lee, the outstanding Confederate general of the Civil War, refused an offer in 1861 to command Federal forces against his native South, becoming instead the commander of Confederate forces in Virginia and later of all Confederate forces. Lee was renowned for his bold strategies and gracious character.

Commissioned in the Corps of Engineers in 1829, Lee was made a captain in 1838. In the Mexican War he served as an engineering officer, and his outstanding work won for him praise and a brilliant reputation. From 1852 to 1855 he was superintendent at West Point, and in 1859 he commanded the force that suppressed the John BROWN raid on Harpers Ferry.

Role in the Civil War. Believing that he owed his first loyalty to his own state in the North-South controversy, he declined an offer to command the Federal army, resigned his commission in the U.S. Army, and offered his services to Virginia when it seceded in April 1861. Confederate president Jefferson DAVIS appointed Lee a general in the Southern army, and in March 1862 he became an advisor to Davis. That May, Lee was made commander of the main Confederate army in Virginia—a force that he soon named the Army of Northern Virginia.

When Lee took command, Federal troops were slowly gaining control of the Mississippi Valley, and a large enemy army was within sight of Richmond. In late June, Lee struck at the Unionists near Richmond and drove them away from the capital. In August he defeated a Northern army in the second Battle of BULL RUN and chased it into the defenses of Washington, D.C. Lee followed up this victory by invading Maryland. During the Battle of ANTIETAM (Sept. 17, 1862) he fought a drawn battle with the Federals. Lee then withdrew to Virginia, where he inflicted a costly defeat on his opponents at FREDERICKSBURG in December.

At CHANCELLORSVILLE (May 1863), Lee won his greatest victory and suffered his greatest loss. Boldly dividing his army into three parts, Lee assailed a larger Federal force. The Unionists were driven back with heavy casualties. Southern losses were also high, and among them was Lee's greatest general, Stonewall JACKSON, who died after the battle.

In the summer of 1863, Lee launched another invasion of the North. In early July he attacked a Federal army at Gettysburg, Pa., and was defeated in the greatest battle of the war (see GETTYSBURG, BATTLE OF). The Confederates fell back into Virginia, and there, in 1864, Lee led them into a series of bloody battles against the Northern army, now commanded by Ulysses S. GRANT. Lee maneuvered brilliantly against Grant and inflicted heavy losses on the Federals. Unable to seize the offensive, however, he was pushed back to Richmond and Petersburg and forced to defend those cities against a semisiege. Grant finally broke through the Southern lines in April 1865, and Lee was forced to surrender at APPOMATTOX COURT HOUSE on April 9. By then he had been appointed general in chief of all Confederate armies; when he surrendered, other Southern armies soon ceased fighting.

Postwar Life. After the war, Lee became president of Washington College (now Washington and Lee University) in Lexington, Va. Accepting the results of the war, he devoted himself to education and to helping rebuild the South. Lee died on Oct. 12, 1870.

Lee, Tsung Dao   see PARITY (physics)

Lee Kuan Yew   Lee Kuan Yew, b. Sept. 16, 1923, was the prime minister of Singapore from 1959 to 1990. He helped found Singapore's People's Action party in 1954 and in 1955 was elected to the legislative council. After becoming prime minister, he led (1963) Singapore into the Federation of Malaysia and remained prime minister of independent Singapore after it seceded (1965) from the federation. Lee, a staunch supporter of free-enterprise capitalism, is considered the architect of Singapore's remarkable postindependence economic growth. The rapid and orderly transformation of Singapore into a modern industrial state generated much popular support for Lee. His party's percentage of the popular vote in the 1985 and 1988 legislative elections declined, however, because of an economic slowdown and demands for political reform. Lee retired as prime minister in November 1990 (replaced by Goh Chok Tong) but remained in the cabinet and still headed the party.

Lee Teng-hui   Lee Teng-hui, b. Jan. 15, 1923, the first native-born president of Taiwan, assumed his post after the death of President CHIANG CHING-KUO on Jan. 15, 1988. Lee entered government in 1972, serving as mayor of Taipei (1978–81), governor of Taiwan province (1981–84), and vice-president (1984–88) before succeeding to the balance of Chiang's term. Later named chairman of the ruling KUOMINTANG and elected president in his own right in March 1990, Lee continued the reforms begun with the lifting of martial law in 1987.

leech   Leech is the common name for more than 300 species of aquatic or terrestrial annelid worms, phylum Annelida, class Hirudinea, that prey on small inverte-

This medicinal leech lives in ponds and swamps of Europe and Asia and grows to 10 cm (4 in) long.

The leek bears a single globelike flower and linear leaves. Its blanched leaf base (right) is eaten as a vegetable.

brates in fresh water or suck blood from vertebrate animals. Most leeches live in ponds and streams, where they feed on worms, snails, and insect larvae or wait for the chance to attach themselves to a fish, turtle, or wading bird or mammal to suck its blood. Some leeches are marine and get blood meals from fish or sea turtles. A few leeches inhabit tropical rain forests.

Leeches have flattened bodies and usually lack gills, breathing instead through their skin. They are generally black, brown, olive, or red in color and may be spotted or striped. Most leeches are from 2 to 5 cm (0.8 to 2 in) long, but they range from 1 cm (0.4 in) to 30 cm (12 in). Every leech has a muscular sucker at the rear end of the body; many have a second sucker around the mouth. These organs are used to hold the leech to a support or to a host while it is drawing blood.

Two types of feeding structures are found in leeches. Some leeches have an extendable, tubelike proboscis that is made rigid and forced into the tissues of the victim. Others lack the proboscis, having instead three knifelike jaws that slice through the host's skin. The wound area is anesthetized by an as yet unknown substance, so the victim feels no pain. Predatory worms feed rather frequently. Bloodsuckers feed only rarely but may consume many times their weight. The saliva of these leeches contains an ANTICOAGULANT called hirudin, which prevents blood clots and can dissolve them as well. Members of the genus *Hirudo*, called medicinal leeches, were once widely used for bloodletting and the relief of blood congestion; they are still employed by surgeons to maintain circulation in small blood vessels during delicate operations.

Leeds Leeds is a city of north central England located in West Yorkshire (see YORKSHIRE). Situated on the navigable River Aire with a canal connecting it with Liverpool, Leeds is a major inland port. The population is 709,600 (1988 est.). One of Britain's leading garment-manufacturing centers, Leeds also produces light machinery, electrical equipment, ceramics, leather, and paper. Kirkstall Abbey (1151) and Temple Newsam mansion (17th century) are landmarks. The city is the seat of the University of Leeds (1904).

The city was probably settled before Roman times, as the River Aire provides a strategic route through the Pennine mountain chain. It was a major woolen center from the 14th century until the Industrial Revolution. During the late 1700s it was renowned for pottery and linen manufacturing.

leek The vegetable leek, *Allium ampeloprasum*, family Amaryllidaceae, Porrum group, is a mild-flavored relative of the ONION. The plant produces a sheath of leaves about 4 cm (1.6 in) thick, but unlike the onion, it does not form a distinctive bulb. Plants are blanched by gradually building up the soil around their bases.

Leeuwenhoek, Antoni van [lay'-vuhn-hook, ahn'-tohn-ee vahn] Antoni van Leeuwenhoek, b. Oct. 24, 1632, d. Aug. 26, 1723, was a Dutch biologist and microscopist. He became interested in science when, as a Dutch businessman, he began grinding lenses and building simple microscopes as a hobby. Each microscope consisted of a flat brass or copper plate in which a small, single glass lens was mounted. The lens was held up to the eye, and the object to be studied was placed on the head of a movable pin just on the other side of the lens. Leeuwenhoek made more than 400 microscopes, many of which still exist. The most powerful of these instruments can magnify objects about 275 times.

Leeuwenhoek was the first person to observe single-celled animals (protozoans) with a microscope. He de-

Antoni van Leeuwenhoek, a self-taught Dutch scientist, built over 400 microscopes. With them, he observed and described diverse organic substances, including spermatozoa, blood, and bacteria.

scribed them in a letter to the Royal Society, which published his detailed pictures in 1683. Leeuwenhoek was also the first person, using a microscope, to observe clearly and to describe red blood cells in humans and other animals, as well as sperm cells. In addition, he studied the structure of plants and insects.

Leeward Islands

Leeward Islands [lee'-wurd]   The Leeward Islands, extending from Puerto Rico to Guadeloupe, are the northern group of the Lesser Antilles (see ANTILLES, GREATER AND LESSER) in the Caribbean Sea. (The WINDWARD ISLANDS lie to the south.) From 1871 to 1956 the name Leeward Islands was used for the collectively administered British colonies in the area. The VIRGIN ISLANDS are sometimes included in the island group.

Lefèvre d'Étaples, Jacques

Lefèvre d'Étaples, Jacques [luh-fev' day-tahp'luh, zhahk] Jacques Lefèvre d'Étaples, c.1455–1536, was one of the most famous scholars and Christian humanists of the French Renaissance. He traveled in Italy, where he met many of the prominent Italian humanists. He returned to Paris, where, as librarian of the abbey of Saint-Germain-des-Prés, he taught and wrote philosophy and began editing classical texts and producing his own commentaries on the Bible. He also translated portions of the Bible into French.

In 1520, Lefèvre was named vicar-general of Meaux, where he gathered about him an impressive group of younger scholars who joined him in working for reform in response to church abuses. He refused to break openly with the Catholic church, but many of his followers became Protestants.

left-handedness

left-handedness   see HANDEDNESS

legal aid

legal aid   Legal aid (sometimes called legal services) is the mechanism for providing legal counsel for poor people. The lawyers may be paid by the government or by charitable organizations or they may be appointed to serve without compensation.

Legal aid may be available in either civil or criminal cases. From its start in 1876 until the mid-1960s, civil legal aid was financed almost exclusively by private donations to local legal-aid societies. These societies generally hired a few full-time or part-time lawyers to help as many poor people as they could with the societies' very limited resources.

Legal aid for criminal defendants has evolved along different lines, with government assuming more responsibility. Some states and localities employ public defenders for people who cannot afford legal fees. Other jurisdictions rely on an assigned counsel system under which the judge appoints private lawyers to represent poor persons. In 1963 the U.S. Supreme Court provided new impetus when it declared, in *Gideon* v. *Wainwright*, that every poor defendant charged with a felony is entitled to free counsel as a matter of constitutional right. This decision com-

pelled every state and locality to make explicit provision for criminal legal aid. As a result, the number of public defenders multiplied several times as did government budgets for legal aid in criminal cases. In 1972 this right was extended to those charged with many kinds of misdemeanors.

Government neglect of civil representation ended in 1965 when the federal government started the Office of Economic Opportunity (OEO) Legal Services Program as part of the Johnson administration's "War on Poverty." During its first 18 months the OEO program increased eightfold the amount of civil legal aid available to poor people. In 1974, Congress created an independent public entity, the Legal Services Corporation, which assumed control of the OEO legal-aid program.

Although no constitutionally protected right to free counsel for poor people in civil cases exists as yet, there appears to be a slight tendency in that direction. Some state supreme courts recently have found a constitutional right to counsel for certain kinds of civil cases, such as paternity issues and child-dependency hearings.

legal procedure

legal procedure   Legal procedure consists of the methods used in enforcing legal rights and remedies. These include rules for initiating a lawsuit, conducting a trial, and appealing to a higher court and also the processes whereby one party secures redress or compensation from another.

American legal procedure is based on English COMMON LAW and equity (see EQUITY, law). All common-law countries, including the United States, Canada, and England, have modernized the traditional English procedure within the last century.

Preparation of a Legal Action. A lawsuit is initiated by the attorney for the plaintiff (the party bringing suit), who prepares a summons and a complaint. The summons is a notice to the defendant (the party against whom suit is brought) that he or she is being sued and specifies the time and place of the hearing and the nature of the demand being made. The complaint is a brief statement of the essentials of the plaintiff's case that is made under oath before an official who is empowered to charge people with offenses.

Normally the defendant will forward the complaint to an attorney, and the attorney will prepare a document called the answer, which will contradict one or more assertions contained in the complaint. The answer will then be served on the plaintiff.

The Trial. Following this exchange of information, the case will be tried. Either party may insist on a trial by JURY except for cases in equity. If neither party insists on a jury trial, the case will be heard solely by the judge.

The trial begins with opening statements by the plaintiff's attorney and the defendant's attorney; they both present a broad outline of what they intend to prove. Opening statements may be and often are waived. Following the opening statements, the plaintiff's attorney presents EVIDENCE, generally elicited through direct examination or questioning of witnesses under oath. After a witness is examined, the defendant's attorney may cross-examine to test the witness's accuracy and veracity. After all the plaintiff's witnesses have been examined and cross-examined, the defendant is given an opportunity to present witnesses. Each witness also may be cross-examined by the plaintiff's attorney.

After the evidence has been presented, the attorneys make their closing arguments in which they present their clients' positions as best they can based on their view of the evidence. In a trial by jury, the judge then instructs the jury in the rules of law applicable to the case. The jury's task is to decide the facts, to apply the law as contained in the instructions to the facts, and to reach a verdict. In many states a jury must reach a unanimous verdict. The losing party may request a new trial. The judge may grant such a request if, for example, new evidence is presented.

Appeals. The usual basis for APPEAL is that an error of law was committed during the original trial. The facts as established by the jury may not be challenged unless the court of appeals determines that no reasonable jury could have decided as it did.

The party bringing an appeal is called the appellant, and the opposite party—the winner in the lower court—is the appellee or respondent. Appellate courts are presided over by a panel of judges, usually at least three and sometimes as many as nine, depending on the particular court. No jury sits in an appeal because the findings of fact were determined by the trial court.

Both parties to an appeal submit written briefs containing legal authorities and arguments. The actual hearing consists of an exchange of oral presentations by the two attorneys. After the court has reached a decision, one of the judges prepares an opinion that states the facts of the case, the legal issues, how the case was decided, and why.

Judgment and Execution. Most civil (in other words, noncriminal) cases are brought to secure money damages. If a jury awards damages to the plaintiff, the court enters a judgment entitling the plaintiff to collect a sum of money from the defendant. Judgments are not, however, self-enforcing. If the defendant refuses to pay, the plaintiff must locate money or property belonging to the defendant and submit certain papers to the sheriff, who can seize the money or property. This action is called an execution on the judgment. If property is seized, the sheriff can have it sold at auction to satisfy the plaintiff's judgment.

See also: CRIMINAL JUSTICE.

legend   A legend originally was simply something to be read. The term may still be used in this restricted sense to refer to mottoes, titles, or inscriptions on coins and medals or elsewhere. The more general current meaning is illustrated by Washington Irving's title, "The Legend of Sleepy Hollow" (1820), in which the word denotes a tale of remarkable past exploits, whether fact or fiction.

Legendries, or lists of legends, were popularly accepted by their medieval readers as true histories. Many were lists of the lives of saints that detailed the wonders and miracles associated with each saint. The best known is the *Legenda Aurea,* or *Golden Legend,* written by Jacobus de Voragine, archbishop of Genoa, in the 13th century and translated into English by William Caxton in 1483. Geoffrey Chaucer's *Legend of Good Women* (1380–86) relates the stories of notable women of history whose lives or deaths witnessed to their passionate fidelity to love.

Many legendary figures are national heroes, such as King Arthur or Charlemagne, who attach to themselves cycles of legends, sometimes oral, sometimes written. These legends mix fact and fantasy and tell not only the bare deeds of the heroes' lives but also the marvelous exploits credited to them, each bearing the hallmarks of dedication to a particular credo, or belief. Thus Arthur and the Knights of the Round Table are renowned for their courtesy and valor, and Robin Hood and his men for their loyalty and defense of the downtrodden. Similarly, the United States has its heroes and folk figures in Paul BUNYAN, Long Barney Beal, "Oregon" Smith, and Johnny Appleseed (see CHAPMAN, JOHN).

See also: ARTHUR AND ARTHURIAN LEGEND; CHANSONS DE GESTE; FAUST; MYTHOLOGY; SAGA; WANDERING JEW.

Leger, Alexis Saint-Leger   see PERSE, SAINT-JOHN

Léger, Fernand [lay-zhay', fer-nahn']   The French painter Fernand Léger, b. Argentan, Feb. 4, 1881, d. Aug. 17, 1955, was a major figure in the development of CUBISM and a prime expositor of modern urban and technological culture. By 1911 he had become a key member of the evolving cubist movement. His personal style of cubism is characterized by tubular, fractured forms and bright colors highlighted by juxtaposition with cool whites to convey a sense of form in relief. Major works of this period include *La Noce* (1911–12; Musée National d'Art Moderne, Paris), *Woman in Blue* (1912; Oeffentliche Kunstsammlung, Basel), and *Contrasts of Forms* (1913; Philadelphia Museum of Art).

In The Great Parade *(1954), the French cubist painter Fernand Léger uses color as a technique of composition. (Guggenheim Museum, New York City.)*

Following World War I, Léger concentrated on urban and machine imagery, which led logically to his association (1919–c.1925) with the purism of Le Corbusier and Amédée Ozenfant. In paintings such as *The Mechanic* (1920; National Gallery of Canada, Ottawa) and *Three Women* (1921; Museum of Modern Art, New York City), he favored sharply delineated, flat shapes, unmodeled color areas, and combinations of human and machine forms. After 1930 he concentrated on scenes of proletarian life, such as his *Great Parade* (1954; Guggenheim Museum, New York City).

Léger, Paul Émile A Canadian cardinal and former archbishop of Montreal, Paul Émile Léger, b. Valleyfield, Quebec, Apr. 26, 1904, d. Nov. 13, 1991, was educated for the priesthood in Montreal, where he was ordained a priest in 1929. He continued his studies in France, where he joined the Sulpicians. From 1933 to 1939 he headed a Sulpician seminary in Japan that he had founded. In 1947 he was called to Rome as rector of the Canadian Pontifical College. Léger became archbishop of Montreal in 1950 and was named a cardinal in 1953. In 1967 he resigned as archbishop in order to do missionary work among lepers in Africa. Upon his return to Canada he worked as a parish priest in Montreal (1974–75).

Leghorn see LIVORNO

legion, Roman The legion was the basic combat unit of the ancient Roman army. By about 300 BC it had received its traditional form: a division of 3,000 to 6,000 men, consisting primarily of heavy infantry (*hoplites*), supported by light infantry (*velites*), and sometimes by cavalry. The hoplites were drawn up in three lines. The *hastati* (youngest men) were in the first, the *principes* (seasoned troops) in the second, and the *triarii* (oldest men) behind them, reinforced by velites. Each line was divided into ten maniples, consisting of two centuries (60 to 80 men per century) each. The cohort, which later superceded the maniple as the main tactical unit, was composed of one maniple from each line, plus the support forces. In 15 BC, 28 legions existed; under Septimius Severus, 200 years later, there were 33. The rigorously trained legions were the military key to the Roman conquest of the ancient world. From the 1st century AD on, the Romans relied increasingly on auxiliary forces of archers, light infantry, and cavalry to fend off the attacks of mounted barbarian armies.

Legion of Honor see MEDALS AND DECORATIONS

Legionnaires' disease Legionnaires' disease is a noninfectious respiratory illness that occurs as individual cases and sometimes in sporadic outbreaks. This disease, and a milder form known as Pontiac fever, are caused by several species of *Legionella* bacteria. The first recognized outbreak—caused by *L. pneumophila*—occurred at

an American Legion convention in Philadelphia in 1976, during which 221 people became ill, 34 of whom died. The bacteria contaminate such damp areas as large air-conditioning towers and hot-water systems and are spread on water droplets. People inhale the bacteria, which infect the lungs and are parasitic to certain white blood cells called monocytes; pneumonia, mental confusion, and kidney and liver damage result, with about a 15 percent mortality rate. Pontiac fever is not fatal and does not result in pneumonia. Treatment for both diseases includes such antibiotics as erythromycin.

legislature A legislature is a governmental decision-making body engaged in making law. Most legislators are popularly elected, although legislative bodies may contain some members who are appointed or who are entitled to membership because of their status in the society. Some legislatures, like the CONGRESS OF THE UNITED STATES, are full-fledged lawmaking bodies. Others, like the British House of Commons, largely follow the lead of the government of the day. Legislatures in authoritarian regimes have only the most formal and perfunctory role in lawmaking.

Representative assemblies like the senates of Greece and Rome have histories going back to ancient times, but the taproot of modern legislatures extends to the Middle Ages. The "mother of parliaments"—the British PARLIAMENT—began to take modern shape in the 13th century. Today, legislative bodies exist in about 140 countries.

A notable structural feature of legislatures is the number of houses that compose them. Almost two-thirds of the world's national legislatures are unicameral—one house. (One U.S. state legislature has a single house, that of Nebraska.) Other national legislatures are bicameral, including the U.S. Congress (made up of the HOUSE OF REPRESENTATIVES and the SENATE). Bicameral legislatures tend to develop in federal systems, where one chamber represents the people directly and the other represents the states or provinces.

The constitutional role of the world's legislatures varies greatly. In congressional systems like that of the United States the legislature is quite independent. In parliamentary systems the political executive is a member of the legislature and the leader of the dominant party; he or she must maintain the support of a majority of the legislature's members to stay in power.

In general, legislators are elected in two types of election systems. The first, the single-member district, plurality vote system, is common to English-speaking countries and others following their example. In this system a country is divided into a number of constituencies equal to the number of representatives to be elected; in each district, the election is won by a plurality of the vote. The second type of system is PROPORTIONAL REPRESENTATION. Here, seats in the legislature are allocated to political parties in proportion to their shares of votes in the election. Some legislative bodies include appointed, rather than elected, members. For instance, Canadian senators are appointed by the governor-general on the recommendation of the prime minister.

Legislatures perform three basic functions. First, legislatures endeavor to manage conflicts among diverse social, economic, or political groups. Often, managing conflict involves the passage of laws. Second, legislatures are involved in recruiting leaders. This function is limited in the United States, but the Senate does have the constitutional role of confirming presidential appointments. Third, legislatures provide important links between the government and the citizenry: legislators serve as representatives from their geographical areas to the central government.

See also: APPORTIONMENT; GOVERNMENT; REPRESENTATION.

legless lizard Legless lizards are two species of snakelike lizards, *Anniella pulchra* and *A. geronimensis,* in the family Anniellidae, inhabiting sandy areas in western California and Baja California. They are burrowing, blunt-tailed lizards reaching about 25 cm (10 in) in length. They feed on insects and are ovoviviparous, bearing one to four living young. Legless lizards possess movable eyelids but lack external ear openings, characteristics that distinguish them from the limbless worm lizards (amphisbaenians), which lack movable eyelids, and from the limbless glass snakes, *Ophisaurus,* and some European slowworms, *Anguis,* which have external ear openings.

legume [leg'-yoom] Legumes comprise a large family, Leguminosae, of flowering plants, ranging from trees (acacia, carob, tamarind) to vegetables (beans, lentils, peas) and forage crops (clover, alfalfa). All legumes are distinguished by their fruit, which grows in the form of a pod that splits along its seams when mature and opens to reveal the seeds. Many legumes have nodule-bearing roots that contain nitrogen-fixing bacteria, which transform nitrogen in the air into a form that can be utilized by plants. Nitrogen-fixing fodder crops such as clover and alfalfa are additionally important in agriculture as green manures that are planted to enrich the soil.

Lehár, Franz [leh'-har, frahnts] The Hungarian-born composer Franz Lehár, b. Apr. 30, 1870, d. Oct. 24, 1948, achieved international fame with his operettas. He worked first as an orchestral violinist, and then, as his father had before him, he became a military bandmaster, working in Trieste (1896), Budapest (1898), and Vienna (1899–1902). During this time he made some attempts at writing opera, but then turned to operetta, where he found success—particularly with *The Merry Widow* (1905), which established him among the foremost composers of the genre, the successor to von Suppé and Johann Strauss. Among Lehár's other operettas are *The Count of Luxembourg* (1909), *Gypsy Love* (1910), *Paganini* (1925), and *The Land of Smiles* (1929).

Lehman, Herbert H. [lee'-muhn] Herbert Henry Lehman, b. New York City, Mar. 28, 1878, d. Dec. 5, 1963, was an American banker and politician who became a leading spokesman for Democratic party liberals. In 1908 he joined the family investment firm Lehman Brothers. During World War I he held various posts, working for a time in the office of then Assistant Secretary of the Navy Franklin D. Roosevelt, with whom he was later closely associated. In 1928 he was elected lieutenant governor of New York, and in 1933 he succeeded Roosevelt as governor. From 1943 to 1946, Lehman was director of the United Nations Relief and Rehabilitation Administration. He later served (1949–57) in the U.S. Senate, where he was one of the few to oppose Sen. Joseph R. McCarthy.

Lehmann, Lotte One of the most acclaimed lyric-dramatic sopranos of her time, German-born Lotte Lehmann, b. July 2, 1885, d. Santa Barbara, Calif., Aug. 26, 1976, excelled in the operas of Richard Strauss, particularly in the role of the Marschallin in *Der Rosenkavalier.* She made her debut at the Hamburg Opera in 1909 and was a principal singer with the Vienna Opera from 1914 to 1938. There she created the roles of the composer in *Ariadne auf Naxos* and the dyer's wife in *Die Frau ohne Schatten,* both by Strauss. Lehmann sang at the Metropolitan Opera from 1934 to 1945, mostly in Wagnerian roles, and settled in California in 1938. She was an excellent pedagogue, and her masterclasses were attended by such singers as Marilyn Horne and Grace Bumbry.

Lehmbruck, Wilhelm [laym'-bruk, vil'-helm] Heinrich Wilhelm Lehmbruck, b. Duisburg, Germany, Jan. 4, 1881, d. Mar. 25, 1919, was a highly individualistic German sculptor and painter whose works addressed humanity's spiritual essence. The *Kneeling Woman* (1911; Museum of Modern Art, New York City), his first mature work, shows the attenuated forms and the austere and melancholic aura that would remain hallmarks of his sculptural style.

With the outbreak of World War I, Lehmbruck's themes became violent and sexual in nature, related indirectly to those of the German expressionist movement called Die Brücke and to those of the Norwegian expressionist painter Edvard Munch. The painting *Pietà I* (1916–17; Lehmbruck Museum, Duisburg) reveals his doleful state of mind during this period. In perhaps his most famous statue, *Seated Youth, or The Friend* (1918; Lehmbruck Museum), he created a poignant memorial to his dead compatriots and their foes. Burdened by despair for postwar Europe, he committed suicide after the end of the war at the age of 38.

Leibniz, Gottfried Wilhelm von [lyb'-nitz] The German philosopher and mathematician Gottfried Wilhelm von Leibniz, b. July 1, 1646, d. Nov. 14, 1716, was a universal genius and a founder of modern science. He anticipated the development of symbolic LOGIC and, independently of Newton, invented the calculus with a

Gottfried Leibniz was a pioneer in the advancement of intellectual and scientific thought that foreshadowed the German Enlightenment.

superior notation, including the symbols ∫ for integration and *dx* for differentiation. Leibniz also advocated Christian ecumenism in religion, codified Roman laws and introduced natural law in jurisprudence, and propounded the metaphysical law of optimism (satirized by Voltaire in *Candide*) that our universe is the "best of all possible worlds."

Leibniz was the son of a professor of moral philosophy at Leipzig. From 1661 to 1666 he majored in law at the University of Leipzig. He then went to the University of Altdorf, which awarded him the doctorate in jurisprudence in 1667.

Leibniz chose to pursue the active life of a courtier. After serving as secretary of the Rosicrucian Society in Nuremberg in 1667, he moved to Frankfurt to work on legal reform. From 1668 to 1673 he served the elector-archbishop of Mainz. He was in Paris from 1672 until 1676, where he practiced law, examined Cartesian thought with Nicolas de Malebranche and Antoine Arnauld, and studied mathematics and physics under Christiaan Huygens.

From 1676 until his death, Leibniz served the Brunswick family in Hanover as librarian, judge, and minister. After 1686 he served primarily as historian, preparing a genealogy of the Hanovers based on the critical examination of primary source materials.

In his later years Leibniz attempted to build an institutional framework for the sciences in central Europe and Russia. At his urging the Brandenburg Society (Berlin Academy of Science) was founded in 1700. He met several times with Peter the Great to recommend educational reforms in Russia and proposed what later became the Saint Petersburg Academy of Science.

Although shy and bookish, Leibniz knew no master in disputation. After 1700 he opposed John Locke's theory that the mind is a *tabula rasa* (blank tablet) at birth and that humans learn only through the senses.

Leibniz's most important works are the *Essais de Théodicée* (1710; Eng. trans., 1951), in which much of his general philosophy is found, and the *Monadology* (1714; trans. as *The Monadology and Other Philosophical Writings*, 1898), in which he propounds his theory of monads. His work was systematized and modified in the 18th century by the German philosopher Christian WOLFF.

Leicester [les'-tur]   Leicester, a city in central England on the River Soar, is the county town of Leicestershire. It lies about 160 km (100 mi) northwest of London and has a population of 278,500 (1988 est.). Leicester produces footwear, knitted goods, office machines, plastics, and dyes. Of historic interest are extensive Roman and Norman remains, several churches, the Guild Hall, and Trinity Hospital. The University of Leicester was founded in 1918.

Leicester was established, probably by the Romans, during the 1st century AD, at the site of a road crossing the Soar. The city's growth was slow until a railroad connected it to a nearby coal-mining region in the 19th century.

Leicester, Robert Dudley, Earl of   Robert Dudley, b. June 24, 1532 or 1533, d. Sept. 4, 1588, was a favorite of Queen ELIZABETH I of England, who made him earl of Leicester in 1564. With his father, John Dudley, duke of NORTHUMBERLAND, he tried to secure the succession to the throne of Lady Jane GREY in 1553. When the scheme failed, he was condemned to death but later pardoned.

Dudley's dashing personality and good looks made him Elizabeth's favorite courtier. She considered marrying him and might have done so had not his first wife, Amy Robsart, died under unusual circumstances in 1560. Many suspected that Dudley had murdered her, but there is no evidence to implicate him. In 1564, Elizabeth tried to marry him to MARY, QUEEN OF SCOTS, who rejected the proposal.

In 1578, Leicester alienated Elizabeth by marrying the widow of the 1st earl of Essex. From 1585 to 1587 he commanded English forces participating in the DUTCH REVOLT and again angered the Queen by becoming governor of the Low Countries. Leicester was also a notable patron of literature and drama.

Leicestershire [les'-tur-shir]   Leicestershire is a county in the Midlands region of central England. A rich agricultural area covering 2,553 km^2 (986 mi^2), it has a population of 885,500 (1988 est.). Leicester is the county town. Major rivers include the Avon, Soar, and Welland. Some coal is mined in the west. Industries include footwear, textile, and plastics manufacturing. Settled in Roman times, the county was invaded by the Angles and Danes; it became part of the Kingdom of Mercia in 653. Bosworth Field, the site of Richard III's defeat (1485) by the future Henry VII, is located there. The county was reorganized in 1974 to incorporate the former county of Rutland.

Leiden [ly'-den]   Leiden (also called Leyden) is a city in the South Holland province of the Netherlands, located close to the North Sea and about 15 km (10 mi) northeast of The Hague. Leiden's population is 107,893 (1988 est.). The State University of Leiden (1575), the first institution of higher learning in Holland, makes Leiden a prominent intellectual center. The food-processing and printing industries are important, as well as livestock marketing. The principal Dutch tulip fields are north of Leiden.

The city was founded near a 12th-century citadel at the confluence of the former Old and New branches of the Rhine River. A southward shift of the river's main channel curtailed shipping and stimulated creation of the canals for which Leiden is noted. The arrival of Flemish weavers brought prosperity from the 14th to the 16th century. The city was besieged by the Spanish (1574) during the Dutch Revolt.

Leif Eriksson [leef air'-ik-suhn] Leif Eriksson (or Ericsson), c.970–c.1020, was a Norse explorer who apparently reached North America c.1000. His exploits are known through the Icelandic SAGAS of the 13th century. Leif the Lucky was the son of ERIC THE RED, the colonizer of Greenland. He grew up in Greenland but c.999 visited Norway, where he was converted to Christianity. According to one saga, he was then commissioned by King OLAF I to convert the Greenlanders to Christianity, but he was blown off course, missed Greenland, and reached North America.

The other, more probable version describes Leif sailing on a planned voyage to lands to the west of Greenland that had been sighted 15 years earlier by Bjarne Herjulfsson. He landed at places called Helluland and Markland and wintered at VINLAND. These may well have been Baffin Island, Labrador, and Newfoundland, respectively, but historians differ in their identifications of the sites. Leif went back to Greenland, but an expedition led by THORFINN KARLSEFNI returned to settle Vinland. Leif may well have helped to Christianize Greenland.

See also: L'ANSE AUX MEADOWS.

Leinsdorf, Erich [lynz'-dorf, ay'-rik] The Austrian conductor Erich Leinsdorf, b. Feb. 4, 1912, is acclaimed for his versatility in traditional repertoire and as a champion of contemporary music. After an apprenticeship (1934) at the Salzburg Festival under Bruno Walter and Arturo Toscanini and subsequent appearances with European orchestras, he came to the United States and led (1938–43) the Metropolitan Opera, specializing in Wagner and the German repertoire. He went on to head the Cleveland Orchestra (1943) before serving in the U.S. Army, and afterward, the Rochester Philharmonic (1947–56), the New York City Opera (1956–62), and the Boston Symphony (1962–69). Since 1969 he has toured as a guest conductor. His writings include an autobiography, *Cadenza: A Musical Career* (1975), and *The Composer's Advocate* (1981), on the art of conducting.

Leinster [len'-stur] Leinster, a traditional province in southeastern Ireland, incorporates the areas of the ancient kingdoms of Leinster and Meath. It has an area of

19,632 km² (7,580 mi²) and a population of 1,852,649 (1986). Leinster contains the counties of Carlow, Dublin, Kildare, Kilkenny, Laoighis, Longford, Louth, Meath, Offaly, Westmeath, Wexford, and Wicklow; these are Ireland's most prosperous and populous counties. DUBLIN is the largest city. A dispute over the kingship of Leinster was the occasion for the first English invasion of Ireland in the 12th century, and in the later medieval period, Leinster—especially the area around Dublin, known as the Pale—was the only part of the country effectively under English control.

Leipzig [lipe'-tsik] Leipzig is a city in east central Germany in the state of Saxony, where the foothills of the central German mountains give way to the fertile North German plains. Leipzig's population is 549,230 (1988 est.).

Leipzig's old town is located between the Parthe, Elster, and Pleisse rivers. In the center is the old market, the 16th-century town hall, the Church of Saint Nicholas (first mentioned 1017), and the 13th-century Church of Saint Thomas. The walls encircling the old town were replaced in the 18th century by a ring of parks and promenades.

Leipzig is a commercial and industrial center and an important transportation hub. Its great trade fairs, which date back to the Middle Ages and attract businesspeople from all over the world, have acquired world renown. Factories in suburban industrial parks produce iron and steel, heavy machinery, scientific instruments, chemicals and plastics, musical instruments, textiles, and toys.

Leipzig's university, founded in 1409, was renamed Karl Marx University in 1952. The city also has a well-known conservatory of music, where both Johann Sebastian Bach and Felix Mendelssohn held positions.

Leipzig's name is derived from Lipsk, the original Slav settlement. During the 10th century the German king Henry I destroyed this settlement and erected a fort around which a new town began to grow. In 1174, Leip-

Leipzig, one of Germany's largest and most historic cities, lies at the confluence of three rivers in the Saxon lowlands.

zig received its charter from the margrave of Meissen, and it soon became a flourishing trade center. In 1519, Martin Luther held his momentous disputation with Johann Eck in Leipzig's citadel. The city suffered heavily during the Thirty Years' War. In October 1813, Napoleon I's army was defeated near Leipzig in the famous Battle of Leipzig (sometimes referred to as the Battle of the Nations). During World War II the city was heavily damaged by Allied bombing.

leishmaniasis [leesh-muh-ny'-uh-sis]   Leishmaniasis is a group of three conditions, each caused by a different species of a protozoan parasite of the genus *Leishmania*. Leishmaniasis normally affects canines and rodents and is transmitted to humans through the bite of sandflies of the genus *Phlebotomus* in regions where the disease is endemic. The parasites live and multiply inside certain tissue cells, called macrophages, in infected animals or humans. When multiplication causes these cells to burst, the released parasites invade fresh cells. Sandflies become infected when they feed on the blood of infected individuals.

Visceral leishmaniasis, or kala-azar, is caused by *L. donovani* and affects inhabitants mainly in the Mediterranean area, equatorial Africa, Ethiopia, central Asia and China, and South America. This form of leishmaniasis most severely affects the spleen, liver, lymph nodes, intestines, bone marrow, and skin. The rate of fatality is nearly 90 percent in untreated cases, but less than 10 percent when treated.

Cutaneous leishmaniasis, or Oriental sore, is caused by *L. tropica* and is found in the Mediterranean area, the Near East, China, and India. The infection normally remains localized in the region of the skin where the sandfly bite occurred—usually on the face, arms, or legs. Healing takes from 2 to 18 months, leaving depressed, often disfiguring, scars.

American leishmaniasis, or espundia, caused by *L. braziliensis*, occurs in southern Mexico and Central and South America but is most common in Brazil, Paraguay, and Peru. The disease causes disfiguring skin lesions that spread into the oral and nasal cavities; it may persist for years if untreated, resulting in death from secondary infection.

Leisler, Jacob [lyz'-lur]   Jacob Leisler, b. 1640, d. May 16, 1691, led a revolt against English authority in colonial New York in 1689–91. The German-born soldier arrived (1660) in the colony when it was still under Dutch rule. By the time the English took over in 1664, he had become a prosperous merchant.

The Glorious Revolution, which drove the Roman Catholic James II from the English throne in 1688, sparked American rebellion against Sir Edmund ANDROS, governor of the Dominion of New England, which included New York. In New York, Leisler assisted in the seizure of Fort James in May 1689 and assumed command of the rebel army after Lt. Gov. Francis Nicholson fled in

June. In December he proclaimed himself lieutenant governor. In March 1691 a new royal governor, Henry Sloughter, arrived in New York. Leisler was arrested, convicted of murder and treason, and hanged. The Protestant, antiaristocratic faction he represented in New York was a factor in the colony for another generation.

Leitrim [lee'-trim]   Leitrim is a county in Connacht province in the north of the Republic of Ireland. With an area of 1,525 km^2 (581 mi^2), it has a population of 27,035 (1986). The mountains in the north and wet lowlands in the south are divided by Lough Allen, a 36-km^2 (14-mi^2) lake. The county town is Carrick-on-Shannon. Livestock raising is the chief activity, and potatoes are the main crop; coal is mined in the north. Leitrim was owned by the O'Rourke family from the 12th to the 16th century.

Lely, Sir Peter [lee'-lee]   Sir Peter Lely, b. Pieter van der Faes, Sept. 14, 1618, d. Dec. 7, 1680, was the leading portrait painter at the court of Charles II, king of England. Of Dutch birth, Lely went to England in about 1641. Through hard work and the influence of Sir Anthony Van Dyck, he became the most popular portrait painter of his time. He confidently expressed the luxurious character of the court; this was typified in his series of *Beauties* (Royal Collection, Hampton Court) and in *The Duchess of Portsmouth* (c.1679; J. Paul Getty Museum, Malibu, Calif.) in which the subjects display a languishing air and are in a state of undress. However, Lely also made striking portraits of men of action and affairs—for example, the *Admirals* at the National Maritime Museum, Greenwich, England.

LEM   see LUNAR EXCURSION MODULE

Lem, Stanisław   Stanisław Lem, b. Sept. 12, 1921, is the most widely translated Polish writer since Henryk Sienkiewicz. In his fantasy-satires, philosophical essays, and science fiction, Lem probes moral questions involving modern science and technology. Perceiving human nature as flawed because intelligence is inherently limited and chained to a biology that is the product of evolutionary accidents, he is pessimistic about social improvement. Lem's fiction includes *Solaris* (1961; Eng. trans., 1970); *A Perfect Vacuum* (1971; Eng. trans., 1978–79), containing "perfect book reviews of nonexistent books" and first published in English in the *New Yorker; Memoirs Found in a Bathtub* (1971; Eng. trans., 1973); *The Chain of Chance* (1976; Eng. trans., 1978); *His Master's Voice* (1968; Eng. trans., 1983); and *Imaginary Magnitude* (1973; Eng. trans., 1984). He has also written such works of nonfiction as *Microworlds: Writings on Science Fiction and Fantasy* (1970; Eng. trans., 1986).

Lemaître, Georges Édouard [luh-metr']   The Belgian priest and astronomer Georges Lemaître, b. July 17,

1894, d. June 20, 1966, is known for his research on the origin of the universe, especially for his proposal (1927) of an expanding model of the universe, which was explained in 1931 by the assumption that the universe originated in an enormous explosion—an early version of the now widely accepted BIG BANG THEORY.

Lemercier, Jacques

Lemercier, Jacques [luh-mair-syay', zhahk] Jacques Lemercier, b. between 1580 and 1585, d. June 4, 1654, ranks with François MANSART as one of the great French classical architects of the 17th century. Lemercier studied (c.1607–14) in Rome under the architect Giacomo della Porta, and this Italian influence is fully evident in his early ecclesiastical designs in Paris: both the facade of the Church of the Sorbonne (begun 1635) and the portal of the Val-de-Grace—completed after Mansart's dismissal in 1646—are based on such Roman classical church facades as that of Il Gesù. Lemercier's major work for King Louis XIII was the enlargement of the LOUVRE Palace, to which he added the Pavillon de l'Horloge (1624).

After 1626 his chief patron was Cardinal Richelieu, from whom Lemercier received commissions for the Sorbonne (begun 1626), the château and church of Rueill (1630), the Palais Cardinal (1633; now the Palais Royal) in Paris, and the château, church, and town of Richelieu (from 1631). He also contributed to the field of domestic architecture.

lemming

lemming [lem'-ing] Lemmings, family Cricetidae, comprise four genera of rodents that are closely related to voles and meadow mice. They live in open grasslands or tundras in north temperate or arctic regions. Lemmings are 8–13 cm (3–5 in) long and weigh only a small fraction of a kilogram. The fur is reddish or grayish brown above and lighter-colored below; the tail is stubby. The animals burrow to make underground nests lined with grass or moss. They eat grass, roots, sprouts, and other plant matter. The mating season lasts from spring to fall; the female bears up to nine young after a 20-day gestation period.

The legend that lemmings deliberately join in a death march to the sea, where they drown, is untrue. Lemmings

The Norway lemming of Scandinavia is best known for its mass migrational behavior.

migrate periodically from their home area when their population begins to exceed the food supply. They swim across streams and rivers in order to find land with food. Sometimes, however, lemmings try to swim bodies of water that are too wide and may drown in great numbers.

lemon

lemon   Lemons, *Citrus limon*, of the Rutaceae family, are the most widely grown acid species belonging to the CITRUS group of fruits. They rank third among all citrus fruits in tonnage produced. The lemon is grown most successfully in mild, coastal climatic regions.

Lemon trees are similar in appearance and longevity to ORANGE trees but have a more upright growth habit. Propagation and cultivation are also roughly similar, although the lemon profits more from heavy pruning. Lemon fruits have an ellipsoid shape, often with a neck on the stem (peduncle) end and a nipple on the other (stylar) end. The rind is yellow when matured in a subtropical climate.

The fruit contains 30 to 45 percent juice depending on variety, climate, maturity, and storage. The acid in the juice is mostly citric. Much of the U.S. lemon crop is processed into frozen or concentrated juice and such byproducts as citric peel oil, pectin, and cattle feed.

The lemon is a small tropical tree with fragrant white flowers. Its yellow, acidic fruit is an important source of Vitamin C.

LeMond, Greg

LeMond, Greg   Gregory James LeMond, b. Lakewood, Calif., June 26, 1961, is a leading cyclist in world competition. LeMond was the 1983 world champion, and in 1986 he became the first American to win the prestigious Tour de France. In 1987, LeMond was shot in the back in a near-fatal hunting accident, but he returned to form, winning the Tour de France in both 1989 and 1990 and another world championship (1989).

Lemoyne, Jean Baptiste

Lemoyne, Jean Baptiste [luh-mwahn'] The sculptor Jean Baptiste Lemoyne the Younger, b. Feb. 19, 1704, d. May 25, 1778, represents the realist, nonclassical strain of French rococo art. From 1731 to 1774 he was the official portraitist of Louis XV, for whom he also produced monuments; most were destroyed during the French Revolution. Lemoyne's sculptures have a pictorial quality and were frequently polychromed. The vitality of his work lies in his direct, honest, sometimes stark manner of representation. An example is the spontaneous and expressive *Portrait of Voltaire* (c.1748; Château de Challis, Oise, France).

lemur [lee'mur]   Lemurs are approximately 15 species of monkeylike primates, grouped into 6 genera, making up the family Lemuridae. They are found only on Madagascar and on the Comoro Islands, northwest of Madagascar, and are generally slender-bodied and long-limbed, with thick, woolly fur and long tails. Lemurs range in size from the mouse lemurs, genera *Microcebus* and *Phaner*, which at about 60 g (2 oz) are among the smallest primates, to the gentle lemurs, genus *Hapolemur*, which are about the size of a large cat. (Some zoologists group the mouse lemurs and dwarf lemurs, genus *Cheirogaleus*, in a separate family, Cheirogaleidae.)

Some lemurs are nocturnal, others are active at dusk, and a few are diurnal. Lemurs are completely arboreal except for the ring-tailed lemur, *Lemur catta*, which spends about 15 percent of the daylight hours on the ground. Lemurs feed on leaves, flowers, fruits, or insects, and at least six species of nocturnal, flower-eating lemurs are significant pollinating agents for several Madagascar plants. Because of habitat loss, a number of lemur species are endangered.

The ring-tailed lemur, a highly social animal, is the most familiar of the lemurs because it can adapt well to life in zoos.

Lena River [lee'-nuh]   The Lena River rises in south central Siberia, USSR, west of Lake Baikal, and flows some 4,265 km (2,650 mi) north to the Laptev Sea, part of the Arctic Ocean. It is the third longest river in Asia and the seventh longest in the world. Over its early course it drops precipitously through a deep canyon. After it is joined by the Vitim River, the Lena becomes deep and slow-moving. Its delta is more than 160 km (100 mi) long and 400 km (250 mi) wide. Most of the Lena is navigable during the ice-free season. YAKUTSK, Osetrovo, and Peleduy are ports.

Lenca [leng'-kuh]   The Lenca are a Chibcha-speaking Indian people living in an isolated part of Honduras and estimated to number several thousand. They grow maize, beans, squash, and chili peppers and keep dogs, chickens, ducks, and pigs. They also hunt game and gather wild plants. Lenca villages are laid out in the Spanish colonial fashion around a central plaza lined with municipal buildings, stores, a church, and the houses of notables. Houses are adobe brick with thatch or tile roofs. Villages are virtually independent; each is headed by a *cacique* (chief) and town council. A family head may have as many as three wives. Although nominally Catholic, the Lenca have preserved their traditional beliefs in sacred mountains and hills.

Lend-Lease   The U.S. Congress passed the Lend-Lease Act, at President Franklin D. Roosevelt's request, in March 1941. Designed to allow Britain and China to draw on the industrial resources of the then nonbelligerent United States in World War II, the measure authorized the president to transfer, lease, or lend "any defense article" to "the government of any country whose defense the President deems vital to the defense of the United States." Though the bill was opposed by isolationists, it passed the House by a vote of 260 to 5 and the Senate, by 60 to 31. By Aug. 21, 1945, when the program was terminated, almost $50 billion in Lend-Lease aid had been shipped to Britain, the USSR, China, and other Allied nations. From September 1942 the United States received "reverse lend-lease" from the British Commonwealth and the Free French in the form of $8 billion worth of goods and services provided to U.S. forces overseas.

Lendl, Ivan [len'-duhl, ee-vahn']   Ivan Lendl, b. Mar. 7, 1960, is a Czechoslovakian tennis player who, in the early 1980s, became one of the world's best. Lendl led his country to the Davis Cup title in 1980. In 1985–87 he was top ranked in the world. With his powerful serve and forehand, Lendl has won 8 Grand Slam singles titles—the 1984 and 1986–87 French Opens, the 1985–87 U.S. Opens, and the 1989–90 Australian Opens.

L'Enfant, Pierre Charles [lahn-fahn', pyair sharl]   Pierre Charles L'Enfant, b. Aug. 2, 1754, d. June 14, 1852, was the French architect and engineer responsible for the design of Washington, D.C. The plan of the city is based on principles employed by André Le Nôtre in the palace and garden of Versailles, where L'Enfant's father had worked as a court painter, and on Domenico Fontana's scheme (1585) for the replanning of Rome under Pope Sixtus V. Through the use of long avenues joined at key points marked by important buildings or monuments, the city is a symbolic representation of power radiating from a central source.

When Congress decided (1791) to build a capital city on the Potomac, George Washington asked L'Enfant to prepare a design but dismissed him in the following year because of his high-handed and discourteous behavior. L'Enfant also designed the old City Hall in New York (c.1787).

Vladimir Ilich Lenin, the Russian revolutionary theorist, created the tightly organized Bolshevik party that won control in the October Revolution of 1917. Lenin is regarded as the founder of Russian communism.

Lenglen, Suzanne [lahn-glen', soo-zahn']   French tennis star Suzanne Lenglen, b. May 24, 1899, d. July 4, 1938, completely dominated women's tennis from 1919 to 1926, losing only one match. At Wimbledon, Lenglen won six singles titles (1919–23, 1925) and eight more in doubles. A brilliant strategist and groundstroker, she was nevertheless extremely cautious and rarely made an unforced error. Hampered by ill health and a moody temperament, Lenglen lost to champion Molla Mallory at the 1921 U.S. Championships and never played the tournament again.

Lenin, Vladimir Ilich [len'-in]   Vladimir Ilich Lenin, b. Apr. 22 (N.S.), 1870, d. Jan. 21, 1924, was founder of the Russian Communist party, leader of the Bolshevik Revolution of 1917, first head of state of the USSR, and a masterful political thinker whose theories shaped Communist thought.

Early Life. Lenin was born Vladimir Ilich Ulyanov in the provincial city of Simbirsk (now Ulyanovsk) on the Volga River. Lenin's father was a secondary-school teacher who rose to become a provincial director of elementary education. In 1887, shortly after the death of his father, Lenin's older brother Aleksandr was arrested in Saint Petersburg (now Leningrad) for plotting against the tsar. He was convicted and hanged. The tragic event affected young Vladimir deeply, and he immersed himself in radical writings, particularly those of Karl MARX and Nikolai Chernyshevsky. Graduating from high school with a gold medal, he entered the University of Kazan but was expelled and exiled because of his developing radical views. In 1891, however, he passed the law examinations at the University of Saint Petersburg and then briefly practiced law in Samara (now Kuibyshev).

Communist Theoretician. Between 1893 and 1902, Lenin worked out the essential features of what has come to be called Leninism. Troubled by the inability of Russian workers to develop spontaneously—as Marx had predicted—a radical consciousness capable of effective political action, Lenin came to believe that a radical consciousness had to be cultivated among workers through agitation by a well-organized revolutionary party.

It was during this period that he began using his pseudonym "Lenin" (sometimes "N. Lenin"). He also met and married Nadezhda Konstantinovna KRUPSKAYA. In 1900, Lenin went abroad and with Georgy Valentinovich PLEKHANOV and others organized the clandestine newspaper *Iskra* (The Spark), designed to "ignite" radical consciousness. This phase culminated with the publication of his pamphlet *What Is to Be Done?* (1902) and the organization of the Bolshevik (see BOLSHEVIKS AND MENSHEVIKS) wing of the Russian Social Democratic Labor party in the summer of 1903.

Organizing for the Revolution. After 1903, Lenin struggled to develop a revolutionary leadership party. Known for his absolute dedication to revolution and his complete lack of personal vanity, Lenin lashed out ruthlessly at opponents and castigated adversaries with biting sarcasm and scorn. He also showed himself a masterful political tactician. Although he was in forced exile until 1917 (except for a brief period—1905–07—during and after the RUSSIAN REVOLUTION OF 1905), he maneuvered for control over party committees and publications and condemned his Social Democratic opponents as Mensheviks (the Minority Group).

Masterminding the Revolution. In 1917, Lenin published *Imperialism, The Highest Stage of Capitalism* (Eng. trans., 1933, 1939, 1947). In it he denounced World War I as a fight among the imperialist powers for control of the markets, raw materials, and cheap labor of the underdeveloped world. Since neither the Allies nor the Central Powers offered any benefits to the working class, he urged all socialists to withhold their support from the war effort. The German government, looking to disrupt the Russian war efforts, allowed Lenin in early 1917 to return to his country from exile in Switzerland (traveling across Germany in a sealed train). Immediately on his return, Lenin denounced the liberal provisional government of Alexksandr KERENSKY and called for a socialist revolution. At this time he also gained the important support of Leon TROTSKY.

An abortive uprising against the government in July forced Lenin into exile once again (this time in Finland). In September, however, correctly perceiving the increasingly radical mood in Russia, he sent a famous letter to the party's central committee calling for armed insurrection. He slipped back into Russia and successfully brought the Bolsheviks to power. On November 7 (N.S.; Oct. 25, O.S.—hence the name October Revolution) the first Bolshevik government was formed and Lenin became its chairman (see RUSSIAN REVOLUTIONS OF 1917).

Head of Government. Lenin moved quickly to consolidate Bolshevik power. He reorganized the various party factions into the Russian Communist party, established a

secret police (the Cheka), and founded (1919) the COMIN-
TERN to ensure that the Russian Communist party would
remain in control of the Marxist movement. In order to
bring the country out of the war, he accepted the humiliating Treaty of Brest-Litovsk with Germany in 1918. That
same year civil war broke out, and he was forced to put a
Red Army in the field against the Whites, who were supported by the Allies and were not defeated until 1921.

By that time the Russian economy was in shambles,
and discontent among peasants and workers was danger-
ously widespread. In the face of these problems Lenin instituted the NEW ECONOMIC POLICY. He granted economic
concessions to foreign capitalists in order to encourage
trade; he placed some light industry and most retail operations back into private hands; and to appease the peasants he permitted them to sell their produce on the open
market.

On May 25, 1922, Lenin suffered a stroke that left
him partially paralyzed. After a series of other strokes he
died at the age of 53. Although dictatorial, Lenin was
never an absolute tyrannical ruler. Before his death he
foresaw the split between Trotsky and Joseph STALIN and
recommended that the latter be removed from power.

Lenin's mausoleum in Red Square, with his body em-
balmed and on display in a glass coffin, was turned into
the greatest shrine in the Communist world, and his writings, along with those of Marx, became the cornerstone of
Communist theory. Under the policy of GLASNOST in the
late 1980s, however, Lenin's supreme authority has been
increasingly challenged.

*The Grand Cascade, comprising gilt statues, fountains, and pools,
descends from the northern facade of Peterhof, the summer
home built for Peter the Great outside modern Saint Petersburg.*

Leningrad

Leningrad [len'-in-grad] Leningrad, renamed Saint
Petersburg in 1991, is Russia's second-largest city. It is
situated in the delta of the Neva River on the Gulf of Finland. The population of the city proper is 4,466,800
(1991 est.); including suburbs, it is 5,800,000 (1989).
Saint Petersburg spans more than 100 islands, connected by 635 bridges. Canals and waterways account for
one-sixth of the city's total area.

Built as a fortress in 1703 by PETER I (the Great), the
city was originally called Saint Petersburg. It became the
capital of Russia in 1712. When World War I broke out in
1914, its Germanic name was Russified to Petrograd; on
Lenin's death, in 1924, it was renamed Leningrad. Fol-

*Saint Petersburg's
Hermitage Museum
is housed in the
former Winter Pal-
ace, built for the
empress Elizabeth
in the 18th century.
The Hermitage has
one of the world's
finest collections of
European art and is
especially famous for
its French impres-
sionist paintings.*

lowing the failed coup of Soviet hard-liners in August
1991, the city reverted to its initial name. Despite the
changes in designation, from its founding Saint Petersburg has been a center of Russian economy and culture.
Its role in science and education was only slightly diminished when the capital of the USSR was moved to Moscow in 1918.

Contemporary City. Saint Petersburg's historical center
is situated on the left, or south, bank of the Neva River,
and the city spreads out over large delta islands to the
north bank. Due to the abundance of river channels and
canals, the city is subjected to flooding. Because of the
city's northern location, the sun descends only briefly below the horizon in June and July.

Saint Petersburg is connected by rail with foreign cities as well as with all parts of the former USSR. Commercial, cultural, and research institutions are concentrated
in the city center on the left bank. Most industries have
riverside locations upstream. The city is a highly diversified manufacturing center noted for the production of
power-generating equipment and electrical goods, industrial machinery, electronic components, chemicals and
allied products, rubber goods, and plastics. It is also a
major shipbuilding center and seaport, handling a large
portion of the former USSR's foreign trade.

Often regarded as one of the world's most beautiful
cities, Saint Petersburg is distinguished by its sumptuous
public buildings, designed for the tsars by Italian architects. Among the most prominent structures is the State
HERMITAGE MUSEUM (founded 1754), one of the world's

great art museums, which is housed in the tsar's former Winter Palace. Other landmarks include Saint Isaac's Cathedral (built 1818–1858) and the Fortress of Saints Peter and Paul (built 1703–80). Saint Petersburg's university was founded in 1819.

History. Peter the Great chose the coastal site for his new capital to give the isolated, inward-looking Russian state a "window on Europe." Saint Petersburg soon replaced Arkhangelsk as Russia's foreign-trade port. Industrialization began in the second half of the 18th century. Unrest among the city's large industrial labor force was a factor in the overthrow of the tsar and the assumption of power by the Bolsheviks in 1917. The city survived a 900-day siege (1941–44) by German forces in World War II.

Lenni-Lenape   see DELAWARE (Indian tribe)

Lennon, John   see BEATLES, THE

▬

Lenoir, Jean Joseph Étienne [luh-nwar' zhawn zhoh-zef' ay-tyen']   Jean Joseph Étienne Lenoir, b. Jan. 12, 1822, d. Aug. 4, 1900, is generally credited with designing the world's first INTERNAL-COMBUSTION ENGINE. Born in Belgium, he moved to Paris where his work with electroplating led him to other electrical inventions, among them a railway telegraph. Lenoir patented his first engine in 1860. Looking much like a double-acting STEAM ENGINE, it fired an uncompressed charge of air and illuminating gas with an ignition system of his own design. One of these engines powered a road vehicle in 1863; another ran a boat. Because of improved designs by Nikolaus Otto and other inventors, the Lenoir engine became obsolete, and only about 500 were built.

▬

lens   A lens, in OPTICS, is a piece of transparent material shaped to form an image by bending light rays (see REFRACTION). In ancient times lenses were called "burning glasses" because they could focus the Sun's rays to start fires. Their magnifying power has long been known (see EYEGLASSES; MICROSCOPE), but their use in TELESCOPES awaited the development of compound lenses. Other systems for focusing other kinds of beams are sometimes also called lenses (see ELECTRON MICROSCOPE). In astronomy, whole galaxies may function as lenses for more distant light (see GRAVITATIONAL LENS).

Optics of Lenses

A simple lens has two opposing faces, at least one of which is curved. Most lenses have spherical surfaces, but other curvatures are used for special purposes.

Lens Shapes. A lens is called converging, or positive, if light rays passing through it are deflected inward. It is called diverging, or negative, if the rays spread out. Converging lenses are thicker at the middle, whereas diverging lenses are thicker toward the edges. A lens surface is concave (curved inward), plane, or convex (curved outward). A meniscus lens has one concave and one convex surface.

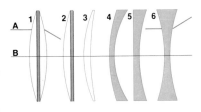

Converging lenses bend light (A) toward the axis (B); types include the double convex (1), plano-convex (2), and concavo-convex (3). Diverging lenses bend light outward; types inlcude the convexo-concave (4), plano-concave (5), and double concave (6).

Image Formation. The focal length of a single lens is the distance from the lens to the point at which incoming parallel rays focus. Light converged in this manner can produce a real image, that is, an image that can actually be projected onto a screen. In a negative lens, rays do not actually come to a real focus, but appear to originate from a point called the virtual focus. The focal length of a diverging lens is considered to be negative.

When the diverging rays from a point source, which may be an actual source of light or a point on an extended object, are passed through a lens, the emerging rays produce an image that will be either real or virtual, depending on the type of lens and the location of the source.

A simple convex lens, or magnifying glass, will produce a virtual image if the object is either at the focal point or between the focal point and the lens. Light from the object passes through the lens, and the eye focuses it onto the retina. The object appears enlarged behind the lens. If the object is beyond the focal point of the same lens, a real image can be formed. A magnifying glass held in front of a light bulb will cause an image of the filament to be projected onto a screen or wall across the room.

The Lens Equation. Whether real or virtual images are formed, the image distance q can be calculated from the lens equation when the distance of the object to the lens, p, is known: $1/p + 1/q = 1/f$. Here f is the focal length of the lens, positive for a converging lens and negative for a diverging lens. The equation also shows whether the image is real or virtual; positive values of q indicate a real image and negative values correspond to a virtual image.

Image Defects. The ability of a simple lens to form a perfect optical image is limited by certain inherent defects called ABERRATIONS. Chromatic (color) aberration is a defect caused by different wavelengths of light refracted at slightly different angles, so that the focal length is slightly different for each color. This results in a colored fringe around an image. The defect can be corrected by a two-component design made with different kinds of glass. Color-corrected lenses are called achromatic lenses and are used in all fine optical instruments. Astigmatism, coma, and spherical aberration are defects that cause an image to be blurred.

The f-Number. The f-number of a lens is the ratio of the focal length to the lens diameter. Lenses of large diameter have small f-numbers and hence greater light-gathering power than lenses of small diameter or large f-number. Aberrations generally become more serious as the f-number decreases. This factor is particularly important in the design of camera lenses.

Lens Materials. New kinds of optical glasses have been developed in recent years, such as rare-earth glass, having a relatively high index of refraction. Techniques for making good-quality plastic lenses have also been recently introduced. These lenses have advantages in special applications, such as spectacle lenses.

Lenses for use in the ultraviolet and infrared regions of the spectrum must be made of special materials, because ordinary optical glass is opaque to these wavelengths. Quartz is the most common material for ultraviolet-transmitting lenses. Infrared lenses are made with calcium fluoride, sodium chloride (salt) or other alkali halides, or silicon.

Lenses of Optical Instruments

The lens of a camera is a converging lens for forming a real image of the scene (object) that is to be recorded photographically. A simple convex lens theoretically focuses the incoming light beam, but in practice such a lens suffers from numerous aberrations, which cause blurring and distortion of the image.

A lens for an optical instrument such as a CAMERA, EN-LARGER, or PROJECTOR generally consists of up to eight or more simple lenses, or lens elements. These elements may be used either separately or cemented together in a group called a lens component. Such arrangements are designed to reduce aberrations to a minimum. The degree of reduction or enlargement of an image with respect to the size of the object depends on the focal length of the lens used.

Aperture. The brightness of the image is determined by the relative aperture, or *f*-number. In the same way that the amount of light falling on a wall opposite a circular window can be determined by calculating the ratio of the room length to the window diameter, the relative aperture is defined as the ratio of the focal length to the diameter of the effective aperture of the lens. This aperture can be varied by means of a diaphragm. For given lighting conditions, a lens of small aperture (large *f*-number) gives a dim image that requires a relatively long exposure. This shortcoming, however, is compensated by the decreased aberrations, and hence increased sharpness, of the image. On the other hand, wide-aperture (small *f*-number) lenses, which are required to give a bright and sharp image, need many lens elements to reduce aberrations and are therefore expensive and bulky.

Angle of View. The angle of view—the amount of the field that the lens will cover—depends on the lens's focal length. The field of a camera lens may be as small as about 15° or as large as about 140°. A standard lens may cover 60°; a wide-angle lens, 90°; and a telephoto lens, 30°.

Lens Grinding

Lens grinding is the process by which optical lenses are manufactured from glass. (Transparent plastics, which are used to produce certain types of lenses, are molded rather than ground.) Fine lenses are made from specially prepared optical glass, which must be free of metallic impurities that might cause discoloration.

Optical glass is often cast in blocks, although it is also available in strips, panes, and rods, or it may be molded roughly into lens shape. A lens blank is cut off the glass block and then rough-ground, using a diamond abrasive on a grinding wheel, to a shape approximating its final dimensions. Fine grinding, or lapping, is accomplished by using carborundum or emery abrasives in a convex or concave lapping tool made of a rigid material: iron, for mass-produced lenses such as those made for eyeglasses; or glass, for high-precision optical lenses. A number of small lenses may be mounted together on a spherical block and lapped simultaneously.

Lent   For Christians, Lent is a 40-day penitential period of prayer and fasting that precedes EASTER. In the Western church, observance of Lent begins 6½ weeks prior to Easter on ASH Wednesday; Sundays are excluded. In the Eastern church the period extends over 7 weeks because both Saturdays and Sundays are excluded. Formerly a severe fast was prescribed: only one full meal a day was allowed, and meat, fish, eggs, and milk products were forbidden. Today, however, prayer and works of charity are emphasized. Lent has been observed since the 4th century.

---

lentil [len'-tul]   An annual plant, the lentil, *Lens culinaris*, of the LEGUME family, Leguminosae, is among the most ancient of cultivated vegetables. It is believed to be indigenous to southwestern Asia and was cultivated in Egypt and Greece long before the biblical era. In the Bible it is probably the pottage vegetable that Esau traded for his inheritance. Today the vegetable is widely grown in temperate and subtropical climates. About 2 million ha (5 million acres) of lentils are grown worldwide; India is by far the largest producer. In the United States lentils

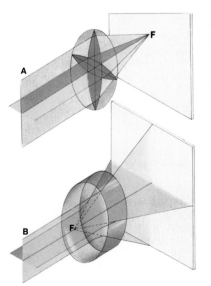

A simple lens consists of a piece of transparent material, such as glass, bounded by a curved surface—generally spherical—on one or both sides. Convex lenses (top) are positive lenses; light rays (A) entering parallel to the axis are converged at the focal point (F). Concave lenses (bottom) are negative lenses; light rays (B) entering parallel to the axis are spread out, appearing to originate from a negative focal point (F) called the virtual focus.

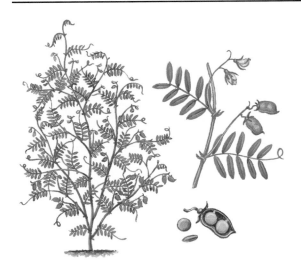

The lentil is a legume that is grown for its seeds, which are exceptionally rich in protein. Like beans, to which they are closely related, lentils vary widely in size and color.

are raised mainly in Washington and Idaho.

Lentils are grown for their seeds, which are rich in protein, and for animal forage (see PULSE CROP). The round, flattened seeds are contained in pods and must be threshed during harvesting. They range in size from 3 to 9 mm (0.118 to 0.354 in) and in color from white to green, brown, orange, and violet blue. Lentils can be dried and stored. They are eaten whole in soups and stews and are also ground into a flour.

Lenya, Lotte   The actress and singer Lotte Lenya, b. Karoline Blamauer in Vienna, Oct. 18, 1900, d. Nov. 27, 1981, popularized the songs of her husband, Kurt WEILL, especially those written in collaboration with playwright Bertolt Brecht. Lenya, a young dancer and actress in Germany, married Weill in 1926. She sang the lead in *The Little Mahagonny*, the first Weill-Brecht collaboration, in 1927, creating a sensation with her rendition of the "Alabama Song." She played her greatest role, that of the slavey Jenny in *The Threepenny Opera* (1928), and starred in the opera *The Rise and Fall of the City of Mahagonny* in 1930. In 1933, Lenya and Weill fled Germany for France and the United States. After Weill's death (1950), Lenya performed in a long-running revival of *The Threepenny Opera* in New York City and established herself as an actress in Hollywood and on Broadway—notably, in the 1966 production *Cabaret*.

Lenz's law [lents'-iz]   Lenz's law is a basic law in electromagnetic theory for determining the direction of flow of induced currents (see ELECTROMAGNETIC INDUCTION). It was first stated by the Estonian physicist Heinrich Lenz (1804–65). According to the law, when a current is caused to flow in an electrical conductor by a change in the external magnetic field surrounding the conductor, the direction of flow of the current is such as to produce a magnetic field opposing the original change. This law is a particular case of the more general principle of Henri Louis LE CHÂTELIER, which states that changes in systems displaced from equilibrium react to restore that equilibrium.

Lenz's law explains the behavior of the inductance coil, or INDUCTOR. In this device a changing current causes the inductor to develop its own electromotive force (emf) through self-inductance (see INDUCTANCE). If the current were decreasing, the induced emf would be in such a direction to sustain it. If the current were increasing, the emf would be in the reverse direction, opposing it. Thus an inductor tends to reduce or smooth out fluctuations in current. This is particularly the case with high-frequency components, which cause greater self-inductance than lower frequencies.

Leo   Leo (the Lion), the fifth constellation of the ZODIAC, is located between Cancer and Virgo and is best seen in the Northern Hemisphere in spring. The Sun passes southeastward through Leo from about August 23 to September 23, just prior to crossing the celestial equator at the autumnal equinox. Its brightest star is Regulus (Latin for "little king"), a blue-white star of magnitude 1.36 located 84 light-years from the Sun; Regulus has two dimmer companions, making it a triple star. Twice as close is the second brightest star, Denebola (Arabic for "tail of the lion"), which has a magnitude of 2.23. Leo is the apparent radiation point of the Leonid meteors, seen in November.

Leo III, Byzantine Emperor (Leo the Isaurian) [biz'-uhn-teen, ih-sor'-ee-uhn]   Leo III, b. *c.*685, d. June 18, 741, ruled (717–41) the BYZANTINE EMPIRE during a period of dire crisis. Of Isaurian, or Syrian, peasant stock, he rose through the imperial guard to military command and was brought to the throne by the army, displacing Theodosius III. A few months later, a large Muslim Arab army and fleet commenced a year-long siege of Constantinople (August 717–August 718). Leo's military ability and timely Bulgarian help saved the Byzantine capital.

Internally, Leo reformed the legal code and extended the *theme* system (military administration of civilian provinces). In 726 he inaugurated a policy of ICONOCLASM, or opposition to image worship, which marked the beginning of a long and bitter controversy in the empire. Leo was succeeded by his son, Constantine V.

Leo VI, Byzantine Emperor (Leo the Wise)   Leo VI, b. 866, d. May 12, 912, ruled the BYZANTINE EMPIRE from 886, in succession to his father, BASIL I. He completed his father's legal reforms by publishing the *Basilica* (Imperial Laws), the largest recodification since that of Justinian I. He also reorganized the imperial administration for greater efficiency. Leo's wars with the Bulgars and Arabs were unsuccessful: in 904 Arab corsairs sacked Thessalonika. His efforts to obtain an heir led him into a fourth marriage, which the Byzantine church vigorously opposed.

Leo I, Pope   Saint Leo I, called the Great, d. Nov. 10, 461, is acclaimed as one of the greatest popes in early Christian times. He assumed the pontificate in 440 and held it until his death. Leo had personal encounters with both ATTILA THE HUN (452) and GAISERIC, king of the Vandals (455), in which he persuaded the former not to attack Rome and the latter not to sack it.

The first pope to emphasize the divine origin of the power of the papacy, Leo was a strong-willed man of authority and government, as well as an extraordinary pastor, upholding discipline in faith. He defended the unity of the church against such heresies as MANICHAEISM, PELAGIANISM, and Priscillianism and defended Catholic teaching in the Nestorian-Monophysite Controversy. His *Letter (Tome) to Flavian* (449) provided the foundation for the Christological dogma of Chalcedon (see CHALCEDON, COUNCIL OF), defining the two natures and one person of Christ. He is a Doctor of the Church. Feast day: Nov. 10 (formerly Apr. 11).

Leo III, Pope   Saint Leo III was pope from 795 until his death in 816. He crowned the Frankish ruler CHARLEMAGNE emperor on Christmas Day, 800, an event of primary importance in Western history. The coronation had the dual effect of strengthening papal authority and creating in the West a ruler with status and prestige equal to that of the Byzantine emperor in the East. As pope, Leo first had to strengthen his position in Rome, which he did with Charlemagne's aid. The emperor also helped him defeat the Adoptionist heresy in Spain. In the controversy between the Eastern and Western churches over the doctrine of the procession of the Holy Spirit, Leo, while regarding the *Filioque* as dogmatically correct, refused Charlemagne's request to include it in the Nicene Creed (see CREED). He was canonized in 1673. Feast day: June 12.

Leo IX, Pope   Leo IX, b. June 21, 1002, d. Apr. 19, 1054, was pope from 1048 to 1054. He was an Alsatian named Bruno of Egisheim. After he was elected pope, Leo insisted on confirmation of the election by the people and clergy of Rome. He sponsored an extensive reform program, in which he was assisted by Hildebrand (later GREGORY VII), the statesman and reformer Humbert of Silva Candida, and PETER DAMIAN. During his pontificate, decrees were issued against simony, clerical marriage, and other abuses. In his campaign to enforce papal rights in southern Italy, however, Leo was defeated by the Normans at Civitate in 1053 and was taken prisoner for nine months. In 1054, Humbert, whom Leo had sent as legate to Constantinople, precipitated the final schism between the Eastern and Western churches by excommunicating the Patriarch MICHAEL CERULARIUS. Feast day: Apr. 19.

Leo X, Pope   Pope Leo X, b. Dec. 11, 1475, d. Dec. 1, 1521, was pope from 1513 to 1521. The second son of Lorenzo de'Medici, he was called Giovanni and made a cardinal in his boyhood. He became head of his family before he was 30. Although he was a pious man, Leo's mild disposition and his concern for the advancement of the Medicis made him, in fact, an ineffectual pope. A patron of Raphael, he continued great artistic projects begun by his predecessor, JULIUS II, but initiated little new work. Leo presided at the Fifth Lateran Council (see LATERAN COUNCILS), but it failed in its efforts to reform the church. Perhaps Leo's most famous act was his excommunication of Martin LUTHER on Jan. 3, 1521.

Leo XIII, Pope   Leo XIII, b. Mar. 2, 1810, d. July 20, 1903, was pope from 1878 to 1903. Born to a minor noble family at Carpineto, he was named Gioacchino Vincenzo Pecci. After his ordination in 1837, he entered the administrative service of the papacy and was appointed governor of Benevento (1838), governor of Perugia (1841), and nuncio to Brussels (1843). On diplomatic missions to other European cities, he gained a firsthand knowledge of modern social questions, an awareness that later characterized his pontificate.

Leo XIII reversed much of the conservative political policy of Pius IX. He improved relations with Germany, Great Britain, Russia, and Japan and established (1892) an apostolic delegation in Washington, D.C. His policy failed, however, in Italy. Italy refused to restore papal sovereignty over Rome, and Leo maintained the increasingly useless posture of "prisoner of the Vatican." He also failed to persuade French Roman Catholic leaders to support the Third Republic; his last years saw increasingly anti-Catholic French legislation.

The pontificate of Leo XIII was especially important for the leadership he gave on social questions. His most famous encyclical was *Rerum Novarum* (May 15, 1891), on the condition of workers in the modern world. The document outlined the duties of both employers and

Leo XIII, the former Cardinal Pecci, was elected to the papacy in 1878, succeeding Pius IX. Leo XIII is remembered for such diverse achievements as opening the Vatican archives to scholars, supporting social reform in various nations, and encouraging the growth of Catholic education.

workers, upholding the principles of collective bargaining, just wages, and private property.

León (Mexico) [lay-ohn'] León is the largest city in Guanajuato state in central Mexico. The city lies on the plain of the Gómez River about 50 km (30 mi) northwest of the city of Guanajuato, at an altitude of 1,884 m (6,182 ft). With 655,809 inhabitants (1980), it is the center of the fertile Bajío region. León is known primarily for its shoe industry, as well as for leatherwork and silver-decorated saddles produced by local artisans.

León (Nicaragua) León is the capital of León department in northwestern Nicaragua. The country's second largest city, with a population of 100,982 (1985 est.), it is an important commercial and agricultural center as well as the intellectual heart of Nicaragua, with a university (1812) and several museums and libraries. Rubén Darío, the famous poet, lived and studied in León and is buried in the city's cathedral. Until 1857, León served as the capital of Nicaragua.

León (Spanish city) León is the capital of León province in northwestern Spain, at the confluence of the Bernesga and Torio rivers. The city's population is 135,521 (1987 est.). Local industries include leather and brandy production, as well as lumbering, iron mining, and tourism. León is noted for its 13th-century Gothic cathedral with its 230 stained-glass windows, and for the 11th-century Romanesque Church of San Isidoro.

León (Spanish region) León, a historic region in northwestern Spain, comprised the provinces of León, Salamanca, and Zamora, which have a total area of 38,043 km^2 (14,688 mi^2) and a population of 1,133,749 (1988) est.). In 1983, León became part of the newly created autonomous community of Castile and León, which has its own elected parliament. It has an area of 94,193 km^2 (36,368 mi^2) and a population of 2,625,027 (1988 est.).

Much of León consists of arid plateaus. Livestock raising, farming, coal and iron mining, and textile manufacturing are of economic importance. The principal cities are León, SALAMANCA, Zamora, and Astorga.

In 217 BC, HANNIBAL captured the region for Carthage, and in the late 2d century BC most of the region was incorporated into the Roman province of Lusitania. In the early 8th century AD, León was conquered by the Moors. During the 9th century, Christians uniting to push the Moors out of Spain established their headquarters in León. Under King Ferdinand I of Castile, León and Castile were joined; this union lasted, with brief interruptions, from 1035 to 1157. During this period the powerful kingdom greatly expanded its holdings, and the Cortes, a parliament of local nobles, was established. In 1217, when FERDINAND III ascended to the throne, León was finally merged into Castile.

Leonard, Elmore A writer of Westerns and thrillers, Elmore Leonard, b. New Orleans, La., Oct. 11, 1925, won literary fame in the 1980s after three decades of modest commercial success with more than 20 novels and a substantial body of short stories and screenplays. His work is now compared with Hemingway's for the authenticity of its dialogue; his characters—usually men living at the margins of society—have an uncanny authenticity. *Hombre* (1961; film, 1967) is his most famous Western. His hard-boiled suspense thrillers include *Cat Chaser* (1982), *Glitz* (1985), and *Get Shorty* (1990).

Leonardo da Vinci [lay-oh-nar'-doh dah vin'-chee] The life and work of the great Italian Renaissance artist and scientist Leonardo da Vinci have proved endlessly fascinating for later generations. What most impresses people today, perhaps, is the immense scope of his achievement. In the past he was admired chiefly for his art and art theory. Leonardo's equally impressive contribution to science is a modern rediscovery, having been preserved in a vast quantity of notes that became widely known only in the 20th century.

Life

Leonardo was born on Apr. 15, 1452, near the town of Vinci, not far from Florence. He was the illegitimate son of a Florentine notary, Piero da Vinci, and a young woman named Caterina. His artistic talent must have revealed itself early, for he was soon apprenticed (c.1469) to Andrea del VERROCCHIO, a leading Renaissance master. He entered the painters' guild in 1472, and his earliest extant works date from this time. Leonardo worked for Duke Lodovico Sforza in Milan for nearly 18 years (1482–99). Although active as court artist, he also became deeply interested in nonartistic matters during this period, taking up scientific fields as diverse as anatomy, biology, mathematics, and physics. These activities, however, did not prevent him from completing his single most important painting, *The Last Supper.*

With the fall (1499) of his patron to the French, Leonardo left Milan to seek employment elsewhere. By April 1500 he was back in Florence. There he undertook several significant artistic projects, including the *Battle of Anghiari* mural for the council chamber of the Town Hall, the portrait of Mona Lisa, and the lost *Leda and the Swan.* His scientific interests deepened: his concern with anatomy led him to perform dissections, and he undertook a systematic study of the flight of birds.

Leonardo returned to Milan in June 1506, called there to work for the new French government. His scientific research began to dominate his other activities, so much so that his artistic gifts were directed toward scientific illustration; through drawing, he sought to convey his understanding of the structure of things. In 1513 he accompanied Pope Leo X's brother, Giuliano de'Medici, to Rome, where he stayed for 3 years, increasingly absorbed in theoretical research. In 1516–17, Leonardo left Italy forever to become architectural advisor to King Francis I of France, who greatly admired him. Leonardo died at the age of 67 on May 2, 1519, at Cloux, near Amboise, France.

Artistic Achievements

Early Work in Florence. The famous angel contributed by Leonardo to Verrocchio's *Baptism of Christ* (*c.*1475; Uffizi, Florence) was the young artist's first documented painting. Other examples of Leonardo's activity in Verroc-

chio's workshop are the *Annunciation* (*c.*1473; Uffizi); the beautiful portrait *Ginevra Benci* (*c.*1474; National Gallery, Washington, D.C.); and the *Madonna with a Carnation* (*c.*1475; Alte Pinakothek, Munich).

Other, slightly later works, such as the so-called *Benois Madonna* (*c.*1478–80; The Hermitage, Leningrad) and the unfinished *Saint Jerome* (*c.*1480; Vatican Gallery), already show two hallmarks of Leonardo's mature

(Left) Madonna of the Rocks *(begun 1490s; finished 1506–08) is a poetic vision of the infant John the Baptist adoring the infant Christ in the presence of the Virgin Mary and an angel. The work exemplifies Leonardo's technique of chiaroscuro, a method of painting in which three-dimensional modeling is achieved by means of light and shadow, creating a new unity between figures and their setting. (National Gallery, London.)*

(Below) *This drawing, a self-portrait of Leonardo as an elderly sage, was executed about 1512. The realism of the work testifies to the intensity of Leonardo's interest in the appearance and function of natural forms. (Royal Library, Turin.)*

Leonardo da Vinci's La Gioconda *(c.1503–05), or* Mona Lisa, *is probably the most famous of all paintings. The mysterious smile of this fashionable Florentine lady has never failed to puzzle and fascinate. (Louvre, Paris.)*

style: *contrapposto,* or twisting movement; and CHIAROSCURO, or emphatic modeling in light and shade. The unfinished *Adoration of the Magi* (1481–82; Uffizi) is the most important of all the early paintings. In it, Leonardo displays for the first time his method of organizing figures into a pyramid shape, so that interest is focused on the principal subject—in this case, the child held by his mother and adored by the three kings and their retinue.

Work in Milan. In 1483, soon after he arrived in Milan, Leonardo was asked to paint the *Madonna of the Rocks.* This altarpiece exists in two nearly identical versions, one (1483–85), entirely by Leonardo, in the Louvre, Paris, and the other (begun 1490s; finished 1506–08) in the National Gallery, London. Both versions depict a supposed meeting of the Christ Child and the infant Saint John. The figures, again grouped in a pyramid, are glimpsed in a dimly lit grotto setting of rocks and water that gives the work its name. In the great *The Last Supper* (42 × 910 cm/13 ft 10 in × 29 ft 7½ in), completed

in 1495–98 for the refectory of the ducal church of Santa Maria delle Grazie in Milan, Leonardo portrayed the apostles' reactions to Christ's startling announcement that one of them would betray him. Unfortunately, Leonardo experimented with a new fresco technique that was to show signs of decay as early as 1517. After repeated attempts at restoration, the mural survives only as an impressive ruin.

Late Work in Florence. When he returned to Florence in 1500, Leonardo took up the theme of the Madonna and Child with Saint Anne. He had already produced a splendid full-scale preparatory drawing (c.1498; National Gallery, London); he now treated the subject in a painting (begun c.1501; Louvre). It is known from Leonardo's recently discovered Madrid notebooks that he began to execute the ferocious *Battle of Anghiari* for the Great Hall of the Palazzo Vecchio in Florence on June 6, 1505. As a result of faulty technique the mural deteriorated almost at once, and Leonardo abandoned it; knowledge of this work comes from Leonardo's preparatory sketches and from several copies. The mysterious, evocative portrait Mona Lisa (begun 1503; Louvre), also known as *La Gioconda,* probably the most famous painting in the world, dates from this period, as does *Saint John the Baptist* (begun c.1503–05; Louvre).

Scientific Investigations

Written in a peculiar right-to-left script, Leonardo's manuscripts can be read with a mirror. The already vast corpus was significantly increased when two previously unknown notebooks were found in Madrid in 1965. The majority of Leonardo's technical notes and sketches make up the *Codex Atlanticus* in the Ambrosian Library in Milan. At an early date they were separated from the artistic drawings, some 600 of which belong to the British Royal Collection at Windsor Castle.

The manuscripts reveal that Leonardo explored virtually every field of science. They not only contain solutions to practical problems of the day—the grinding of lenses, for instance, and the construction of canals and fortifications—but they also envision such future possibilities as flying machines and automation.

Leonardo's observations and experiments into the workings of nature include the stratification of rocks, the flow of water, the growth of plants, and the action of light. The mechanical devices that he sketched and described were also concerned with the transmission of energy. Leonardo's solitary investigations took him from surface to structure, from catching the exact appearance of things in nature to visually analyzing how they function.

Leonardo's art and science are not separate, then, as was once believed, but belong to the same lifelong pursuit of knowledge. His paintings, drawings, and manuscripts show that he was the foremost creative mind of his time.

See also: ART; ITALIAN ART AND ARCHITECTURE; PAINTING; RENAISSANCE ART AND ARCHITECTURE.

Leonardo Pisano [lay-oh-nar'-doh pee-zah'-noh] Leonardo Pisano, b. c.1170, d. after 1240, also known as Leonardo of Pisa or Leonardo Fibonacci, was the first great mathematician of medieval Christian Europe. He played an important role in reviving ancient mathematics and made significant contributions of his own. *Liber abbaci* (Book of the Abacus, 1202), his treatise on arithmetic and elementary algebra, introduced the modern Hindu-Arabic system of numerals using ten symbols. His most important original work is in indeterminate analysis and number theory. The FIBONACCI SEQUENCE is named for him. *Mis practica geometriae* (Practice of Geometry, 1220) gave a compilation of the geometry of the time and also introduced some trigonometry.

Leoncavallo, Ruggero [lay-ohn-kah-vahl'-loh, rood-jay'-roh] Ruggero Leoncavallo, b. Mar. 8, 1858, d. Aug. 9, 1919, is known today for a single work, *I Pagliacci,* one of the masterpieces of Italian VERISMO opera. His study of music and literature prepared him to write both the music and librettos for his operas. In an effort to adapt Wagner's epical German manner to Italian opera, he composed the trilogy *Crepusculum,* depicting major figures of the Italian Renaissance. Unable to obtain either publication or performance for this work, and noting the success of Mascagni's short *verismo* opera *Cavalleria Rusticana* (1890), Leoncavallo composed a comparable work, *I Pagliacci* (1892). This work achieved immediate and lasting success. Of his 18 other operas, *La Bohème* (1897) and *Zazà* (1900) were received favorably when first presented, but are no longer staged.

Leonidas, King of Sparta [lee-ahn'-ih-duhs] Leonidas succeeded his half brother Cleomenes I as one of the two kings of Sparta about 488 BC. In 480, during the PERSIAN WARS, he led a small Greek army, including his royal guard of 300 Spartans, to hold the pass of THER-MOPYLAE against the Persian army of XERXES I. All the Spartans, including Leonidas, were killed.

Leonids see METEOR AND METEORITE

Leonov, Aleksei [lay-awn'-uhf, uhl-ek'-say] The Soviet cosmonaut Aleksei Leonov, b. May 30, 1934, was the first man to walk in space. A jet pilot, he became a cosmonaut in 1960 and was the copilot of VOSKHOD *2,* launched Mar. 18, 1965. During the flight he exited from the spacecraft and performed a space walk. Leonov was also commander of the Soviet part (July 15–21, 1975) of the APOLLO-SOYUZ TEST PROJECT, with flight engineer Valery Kubasov. Leonov has been called the "artist-cosmonaut" because of his paintings and caricatures.

leopard [lep'-urd] The leopard, *Panthera pardus,* is one of the largest members of the cat family, Felidae. A large male may weigh more than 91 kg (200 lb), may stand 70 cm (28 in) high at the shoulder, and may be 1.5 m (nearly 5 ft) long, plus a 90-cm (35-in) tail. Leopards occupy a great diversity of habitats, including dry grasslands, scrubland, mountains, and jungles. They have the greatest geographic distribution of any wild cat, being found over most of Africa south of the Sahara and from the Middle East and India north into central Asia and south into the East Indies. The leopard's color varies from a pale yellowish gray to a yellowish red, with whitish underparts. Spots are present over the entire body, but on the back and sides they are formed into circles, or rosettes. Black leopards, or panthers, occur in the same litter with yellowish leopards.

Leopards are chiefly nocturnal and solitary, but a male and female commonly hunt as a pair during and for a time after the mating season. Usually two to four young

The leopard is rarely seen, even by its prospective victims, because of its silent, wary habits. The black panther (left) *is actually a leopard with black coat pigmentation.*

are born after a gestation period of 90 to 105 days. Intensive hunting of leopards for their skins has eliminated or seriously reduced a number of subspecies and geographical races.

The snow leopard, or ounce, *Uncia uncia,* is similar in size and general appearance to the leopard. Its coat, however, has a dense, woolly underfur and a long, thick outer coat. It is generally light yellowish gray to cream colored, with black to grayish rosettes on the upper parts of the body. Snow leopards are found in the highlands of central Asia from the Altai Mountains into the Himalayas. They inhabit rocky grasslands above the tree line. Breeding occurs in late winter, and usually two to four young are born after a gestation period of about 98 days. The snow leopard has become quite scarce mainly because of overhunting for its beautiful fur.

The clouded leopard, *Neofelis nebulosa,* weighs up to 23 kg (50 lb) and may be 80 cm (32 in) high at the shoulder and 1 m (40 in) long, plus a 90-cm (35-in) tail. It is grayish or yellowish to brownish yellow in color, with black spots and dashes on the head, legs, and tail, and large, black-bordered, "cloudlike" blotches on its sides. Clouded leopards inhabit forests from India to Taiwan south into Borneo. Gestation is about 90 days, with apparently two young to a litter. The clouded leopard continues to be hunted, despite its rarity.

leopard frog Leopard frogs, family Ranidae, are medium-sized frogs, 5 to 10 cm (2 to 4 in) in body length, with distinct spots on the back. Once thought to be a single species, *Rana pipiens*, the leopard-frog complex is now divided into at least six different but closely related species. As a group, leopard frogs are one of the most widely distributed amphibians in North America, ranging from Canada to Costa Rica. They are usually the frogs that are dissected in elementary biology courses. Leopard frogs were previously used in pregnancy tests; when the male is injected with urine from a pregnant woman, it causes the frog to extrude spermatozoa within about two hours.

The leopard frog, a North American frog, is distinguished by its light-bordered spots and pointed head.

Leopardi, Giacomo, Conte [lay-oh-par'-dee, jah'-koh-moh, kohn'-tay] Count Giacomo Leopardi, poet, philologist, and prose writer, b. Recanati, in the Marches, June 29, 1798, d. June 14, 1837, was 19th-century Ita-

ly's greatest lyric voice. By the age of 15, Leopardi had mastered ancient Greek, Latin, Hebrew, and several European languages. In 1816 he produced an amazingly scholarly history of astronomy. Although his intense work had caused eye damage, he continued his studies and in 1819 began writing the lyrics *Canti* (Eng. trans., 1949). Love, sorrow, boredom, futility, patriotism, and the dire necessity for all men to be brothers so as to survive the pain of living and the brutality of nature are the major themes of his poetry. His major prose work, *Essays, Dialogues, and Thoughts* (1824–32; Eng. trans., 1905), is a series of dialogues and narratives whose main characters are mythological and historical figures.

Leopold, Aldo [lee'-uh-pohld, al'-doh] Naturalist Aldo Leopold, b. Burlington, Iowa, Jan. 11, 1886, d. Apr. 21, 1948, aroused the first great public interest in wilderness conservation. He believed that undisturbed wilderness is a valuable asset and felt that people should enjoy wilderness areas but disturb them as little as possible. Although Leopold received worldwide acclaim as an authority on wilderness conservation, he was also an expert on wildlife management.

Leopold I, King of the Belgians Leopold I, b. Dec. 16, 1790, d. Dec. 10, 1865, became the first king of the Belgians after Belgium had asserted its independence of the Netherlands in 1830. The youngest son of Duke Francis Frederick of Saxony-Coburg-Saalfeld, Leopold became a British subject when he married Charlotte (1796–1817), the only child of the future GEORGE IV of England. In 1831 he accepted the crown offered by the Belgian National Congress.

Leopold repelled the Dutch attempts to reconquer the country and finally secured Dutch recognition of Belgian

Leopold I, a German prince and uncle of Queen Victoria of England, was elected as the first king of the Belgians in 1831, shortly after Belgium had declared its independence from the Netherlands.

independence in 1839. He loyally observed the constitution and encouraged collaboration among the political parties. He was instrumental in arranging the marriage (1840) of his niece, Queen VICTORIA of England, to Albert of Saxe-Coburg-Gotha. His own daughter, Carlota, married (1857) MAXIMILIAN, the future emperor of Mexico.

Leopold II, King of the Belgians   Leopold II, b. Apr. 9, 1835, d. Dec. 17, 1909, succeeded his father, Leopold I, to the Belgian throne in 1865. A constitutional, if strong-willed, monarch in Belgium, he ruled the Congo Free State (now ZAIRE) as a personal domain.

Leopold sponsored Sir Henry STANLEY's 1879–84 expedition to the Congo, and in 1885 he was recognized by the United States and the European powers as personal sovereign of the Congo Free State. Reports of outrageous mistreatment of the native population led to an international protest movement, and in 1908 the Belgian parliament compelled the king to cede the Congo Free State to Belgium. In domestic politics Leopold emphasized military defense as the basis of neutrality.

Leopold III, King of the Belgians   Leopold III, b. Nov. 3, 1901, d. Sept. 25, 1983, succeeded his father, ALBERT I, to the Belgian throne in 1934. A strong-willed monarch, he refused to go into exile after the German conquest of Belgium in 1940 and became the target of criticism so bitter that he abdicated in 1951.

Leopold twice urged mediation of the conflict between Nazi Germany and the Western Allies just before and after the outbreak of war in 1939. After the German invasion in May 1940, he took command of the army and led its resistance for two weeks before surrendering. He refused to join the government-in-exile and stayed in Belgium as a self-proclaimed prisoner of war in his castle at Laken.

After the Allied invasion in June 1944, Leopold was taken to Germany and in May 1945 was liberated by American troops in Austria. He returned to Belgium in 1950 but met such fierce hostility that he abdicated on July 16, 1951, in favor of his son BAUDOUIN.

Leopold III, king of the Belgians, was forced to abdicate because of the controversy concerning his conduct during World War II.

Leopold I, Holy Roman Emperor   Leopold I, b. June 9, 1640, d. May 5, 1705, was the second son of the Holy Roman emperor FERDINAND III. After the sudden death of his older brother, Ferdinand, in 1654, Leopold inherited the Austrian Habsburg titles and lands. He was elected king of Hungary (1655) and king of Bohemia (1656) and succeeded his father as emperor in 1658. His efforts during his 47-year reign to strengthen the centralized authority of the Vienna court and to extend Counter-Reformation Catholicism throughout his domains provoked vigorous opposition from his Hungarian subjects, who periodically rebelled.

In foreign affairs Leopold had to contend with the French king LOUIS XIV and the OTTOMAN EMPIRE. Following the unsuccessful Ottoman siege of Vienna in 1683, Leopold's generals won a series of victories over the Turks, culminating in EUGENE OF SAVOY's triumph at Zenta in 1697. By the Treaty of Karlowitz (1699) most of Hungary was recovered from the Turks. Leopold joined (1686) the defensive League of Augsburg against France. Though preoccupied with the Turkish campaigns during the War of the GRAND ALLIANCE (1688–97), the imperial forces played a central role in the War of the SPANISH SUCCESSION (1701–13). Leopold left to his son JOSEPH I not only this war but also an expanded Austrian monarchy.

Leopold II, Holy Roman Emperor   Leopold II, b. May 5, 1747, d. Mar. 1, 1792, Holy Roman emperor from 1790 to 1792, was a ruler of vision and political skill who saved the HABSBURG monarchy from revolution and initiated war with revolutionary France. The third son of Emperor FRANCIS I and MARIA THERESA, he was brought up in Tuscany, succeeding his father as grand duke there in 1765. Influenced by the philosophical ENLIGHTENMENT, he reorganized Tuscan government, equalized taxes, abolished torture, and even drafted a constitution.

When he succeeded his brother JOSEPH II as emperor and ruler of the Habsburg lands in 1790, Leopold found the Austrian Netherlands and Hungary in rebellion, the imperial army tied down in a war with the Ottoman Turks, and the Prussians mobilized to exploit his troubles. Recognizing that Joseph's centralizing reforms had gone too far, the new emperor judiciously combined concession and force to restore order. In foreign affairs he thwarted Prussia by terminating (1791) the Turkish war and then enlisted Prussian aid in warning revolutionary France not to harm King Louis XVI and MARIE ANTOINETTE, Leopold's sister. The warning, though mild, led France to declare war one month after Leopold's death.

Léopoldville   see KINSHASA

Lepanto, Battle of   [lih-pant'-oh]   The naval Battle of Lepanto, fought off the coast of Greece on Oct. 7, 1571, was the first major defeat of the Ottoman Turks by the Christian states of western Europe. The allied fleet of Spain, Venice, and the papacy was commanded by Don JOHN OF AUSTRIA.

Lepidoptera   see BUTTERFLIES AND MOTHS

Lepidus, Marcus Aemilius [lep'-ih-duhs]   Marcus Aemilius Lepidus was the name of several notable figures in Roman history. The first, d. 152 BC, who held the offices of consul (187, 175), triumvir (183), and censor (179), founded several cities and instituted a notable building program. His descendant Marcus Aemilius Lepidus, d. 77 BC, was consul in 78 but the following year led an army against Quintus Lutatius CATULUS, who, with Pompey's help, defeated him. His son, Marcus Aemilius Lepidus, d. 13 BC, was consul with Julius CAESAR in 46. He was a member of the Second TRIUMVIRATE with Mark ANTONY and Octavian (later AUGUSTUS) and, after the Battle of Philippi (42), governed Africa. In 36 BC he laid claim to Sicily, but Octavian forced him to retire.

leprechaun   see FAIRY

leprosy [lep'-ruh-see]   Leprosy, a chronic infectious disease known for many centuries, affects an estimated 10 to 15 million people worldwide. It occurs mainly in tropical, subtropical, and temperate regions of Southeast Asia, Africa, and South America; of the approximately 6,000 persons in the United States who have leprosy, many came from these regions. In the early 1990s new U.S. cases amounted to about 300 per year, a 50 percent increase over 1980.

Cause. Once so dreaded that its victims were isolated in so-called leper colonies, leprosy is caused by the bacillus *Mycobacterium leprae.* (The bacillus was discovered in 1874 by a Norwegian physician, Gerhard Hansen, and leprosy is sometimes called Hansen's disease.) The agent is transmitted by skin-to-skin contact and nasal discharges. About 95 percent of the persons exposed to the bacterium are immune; thus, leprosy is not considered highly contagious. The bacterium invades the peripheral nerves, skin, and mucous membranes, damaging the nerves and causing anesthesia. The resulting insensitivity can lead to unnoticed and therefore neglected injuries; this accounts for many of the deformities—such as loss of fingers—that occur in leprosy. Paralysis may also result; in advanced cases, numbness of the eyes may lead to blindness.

Forms of Leprosy. Two main forms of the disease are known: tuberculoid and lepromatous. The tuberculoid form involves mainly the skin and nerves. Plaques—such as a red, raised rim surrounding a pale, flat center—occur most often on the arms and legs. Nerves under the plaques are damaged, and the areas become numb; contraction and wasting of muscles often occur. The lepromatous form is a more generalized infection that involves the skin, mouth, nasal passages, upper respiratory tract, eyes, nerves, adrenal glands, and testicles. Various skin eruptions may cover the entire body, but numbness is patchier and less severe than in tuberculoid leprosy. In advanced stages, however, lepromatous leprosy can cause ulcers, eyebrow loss, collapse of the nose, enlarged earlobes and facial features, and blindness.

Treatment. The drugs now available for treating leprosy, including thalidomide, can prevent the disfigurement and disability once associated with the disease. By the mid-1980s, scientists had developed cloning techniques to produce in quantity some of the antigens to the disease, for the potential development of a leprosy vaccine. Another vaccine, produced by older means, was already undergoing clinical trials by that time.

lepton [lep'-tahn]   A lepton is a class of FUNDAMENTAL PARTICLES that includes electrons, neutrinos, muons, and their antiparticles. The name is derived from a Greek word meaning light weight, although leptons are best characterized by their atomic interactions. The behavior of leptons is governed by the so-called weak interaction, and they are not affected by the strong interaction (see FUNDAMENTAL INTERACTIONS).

leptospirosis [lep-tuh-spy-roh'-sis]   Leptospirosis, or Weil's disease, is an acute fever caused by a spiral bacteria, *Leptospira* (see SPIROCHETE), communicated from animals to humans, commonly through skin contact with rat-infested water or sewage. It often takes a fatal form characterized by jaundice and bleeding. *Leptospira* may also cause MENINGITIS. Treatment is with penicillin.

Lermontov, Mikhail [lair'-muhn-tuf]   Mikhail Yurievich Lermontov, b. Moscow, Oct. 3 (O.S.), 1814, d. July 15 (O.S.), 1841, was one of Russia's greatest poets. Well tutored at home, Lermontov spent a short time at Moscow University and two years (1832–34) at the School of Cavalry Cadets in Saint Petersburg. He then received his commission in the Life Guard Hussars at Tsarskoye Selo.

Lermontov first attracted attention with "Death of a Poet" (1837), inspired by the death in a duel of Aleksandr Pushkin; the poem was an indictment of the court society that Lermontov blamed for the tragedy. This led to his exile to a regiment in the Caucasus, but his grandmother's influence made possible his return in 1838. In 1840 he was again exiled to the Caucasus for dueling, but he returned to Saint Petersburg in 1841. Exiled yet once more, he went to Pyatigorsk where he was killed in a duel at age 26.

Lermontov was preoccupied with the disillusioned Byronic hero. This is evident in his best-known narrative poem, *The Demon* (1841; Eng. trans., 1930), as well as in his novel, *A Hero of Our Time* (1840; Eng. trans., 1886). Lermontov's mature work, notably the *Song of the Merchant Kalashnikov* (1837), reveals his interest in folk poetry.

Lerner, Alan Jay, and Loewe, Frederick [loh]   Alan Jay Lerner, lyricist, b. New York City, Aug. 31, 1918, d. June 14, 1986, and Frederick Loewe, composer, b. Vienna, June 10, 1901, d. Feb. 14, 1988, created scores for many of the classic American musicals. Their supreme achievement was *My Fair Lady* (1956), a production based on George Bernard Shaw's *Pygmalion.* This popular work had a record-breaking run on Broadway and the London stage and was produced in many other countries. The pair's other classics are *Brigadoon* (1947), *Paint Your Wagon* (1951), *Camelot* (1960), and the Oscar-winning film *Gigi* (1958).

Les Combarelles [lay kohm-bah-rel']

Les Combarelles, a prehistoric cave site discovered (1901) near Les Eyzies in Dordogne, France, contains important examples of Ice Age cave art (see PREHISTORIC ART). The main gallery, a narrow, winding tunnel, contains an outstanding collection of engravings and, near the entrance, a few worn paintings. The animal engravings include not only the commonly depicted mammoth, bison, reindeer, horses, and ibex, but also cave lions, cave bears, and wolves. Several anthropomorphic figures, as well as masklike images, are also depicted. The site has been dated to the Middle Magdalenian phase of the Paleolithic (*c.*13,000–10,000 BC).

Lesage, Alain René [luh-sahzh', ah-lan' ruh-nay']

Alain René Lesage (or Le Sage), b. May 8, 1668, d. Nov. 17, 1747, was a French novelist and playwright whose popularization of the picaresque novel influenced Henry Fielding and Tobias Smollett. He authored or coauthored approximately 100 farces or comedies of manners for the popular fairground theaters of Paris. Many were adaptations of Spanish originals, but his *Turcaret* (1709; Eng. trans., 1933) was a genuine creation, satirizing the crooked practices of financiers. Lesage's masterpiece, however, is the picaresque novel *The Adventures of Gil Blas of Santillana* (Eng. trans., 1781), published in installments from 1715 to 1735.

lesbianism

Lesbianism is HOMOSEXUALITY in women. The name refers to the island of Lesbos, where the poet SAPPHO—whose love lyrics are often addressed to women—lived most of her life.

Lesbos [lez'-bahs]

Lesbos, a hilly Greek island in the Aegean Sea less than 25 km (15 mi) from the Turkish coast, covers 1,630 km^2 (630 mi^2) and has a population of 104,620 (1981). Olives, vines, grains, and fruits are grown. Mytilene is the largest city.

Lesbos was the site of Early Bronze Age settlements, and during the 2d millennium BC it was settled by the Aeolians. By the 7th century BC the island was a notable cultural center, home of the poets SAPPHO and ALCAEUS. Lesbos was captured by the Persians in 527 BC but joined the Delian League after the Persian defeat in 479. During the Peloponnesian War the island revolted (428–427 BC) unsuccessfully against Athens and later fell (405) to Sparta. It was later held successively by the Macedonians, Romans, Byzantines, Seljuks, Genoese, and Ottoman Turks. It became part of modern Greece in 1913.

Lesotho [luh-soh'-toh]

Lesotho is a small, landlocked country in southern Africa that is entirely surrounded by the Republic of South Africa. Until 1966 it was the British colony of Basutoland. With limited mineral and agricultural resources, little industry, and insufficient development capital, Lesotho is heavily dependent on South Africa for manufactured goods, transportation links, and employment.

Land and People

The eastern two-thirds of Lesotho is dominated by the rugged and sparsely populated DRAKENSBERG and Maloti ranges. These form a high plateau with an average elevation of almost 3,100 m (10,000 ft). The Orange (Senqu) and Tugela, two of southern Africa's most important rivers, rise near Thabana Ntlenyana (3,482 m/11,424 ft), Lesotho's highest mountain.

Western Lesotho is a narrow, lowland region at an average elevation of 1,700 m (5,500 ft). The area is densely populated, and most of the towns, including MASERU, the capital and largest town, are there. Temperatures throughout the country average 15° C (59° F) in January (the summer), and 3° C (37° F) in July (the winter). Average annual rainfall is 1,520 mm (60 in) in the east and 690 mm (27 in) in the west.

Lesotho is an ethnically homogeneous country. The Basuto tribal group constitutes more than 90% of the population. Coloureds, ZULUS, Tembus, and whites form small minorities. Non-Basutos are prohibited from owning land. Both English and Sesotho are official languages. More than 70% of the people are Christian, mostly Roman Catholic and Lesotho Evangelist. The remainder practice traditional animism.

Primary education is free, and about 67% of school-age children attend. Lesotho has one of the highest literacy rates in Africa, but few students advance beyond primary school. The National University of Lesotho is at Roma, near Maseru.

Economic Activity

Although only about 10% of Lesotho's land is suitable for agriculture, such activity provides about two-thirds of the domestic income, mostly in the form of subsistence farming. Maize (corn) is the leading crop, and wheat, sorghum, barley, and beans are important. Because agriculture suffers from severe soil erosion and poor farming practices, yields are low, and Lesotho must import food, primarily from South Africa. Cattle, ponies (used for transport), sheep, and goats are raised. Wool and mohair are the major agricultural exports.

The government is attempting to build up other sectors of the economy. The only major industries are light manufacturing (furniture, bricks, and cosmetics) and food processing (meat canning and beer brewing). Work on a giant water project began in 1988. Lesotho's beautiful, mountainous terrain has contributed to the growth of tourism. Because economic opportunities are scarce, about 140,000 Basutos, mostly men, leave Lesotho each year to work in South Africa.

KINGDOM OF LESOTHO

Land: Area: 30,355 km^2 (11,720 mi^2). Capital and largest city: Maseru (1986 est. pop., 106,000).

People: Population (1990 est.): 1,754,664. Density: 57.8 persons per km^2 (149.7 per mi^2). Distribution (1986): 16% urban, 84% rural. Official languages: English, Sesotho. Major religions: Roman Catholicism, Protestantism, Anglicanism.

Government: Type: titular monarchy, under military rule. Legislature: National Assembly (suspended 1970). Political subdivisions: 10 districts.

Economy: GNP (1989 est.): $412 million; $245 per capita. Labor force (1986): agriculture—66%; services—18%; trade—3%; public administration and defense—3%. Foreign trade (1989 est.): imports—$526 million; exports—$55 million. Currency: 1 loti = 100 lisente.

Education and Health: Literacy (1985): 60% of adult population. Universities (1990): 1. Hospital beds (1982): 2,300. Physicians (1982): 114. Life expectancy (1990): women—62; men—59. Infant mortality (1990): 80 per 1,000 live births.

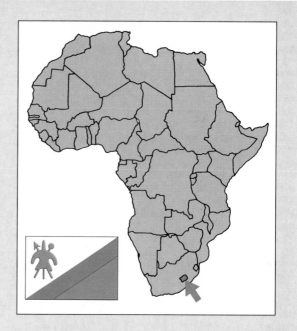

History and Government

Lesotho was sparsely populated by the SAN (Bushmen) until the late 16th century. During the 17th and 18th centuries refugees from tribal wars in the surrounding areas entered Lesotho. In the early 19th century, Paramount Chief MOSHESHWE, who ruled from about 1820 to 1870, welded the Basuto nation out of these diverse Bantu-speaking peoples. From 1858 to 1868 the Basuto were at war with the Boers. The latter won a large piece of Basuto land, and to prevent further loss, Mosheshwe requested British protection. Thus, in 1868 the kingdom became a British protectorate. From 1884 to 1959 it was, like Botswana and Swaziland, a British High Commission territory. On Oct. 4, 1966, independence was granted.

Until 1970, Lesotho was a constitutional monarchy, with a hereditary king who appointed the prime minister and cabinet. That year, following a disputed election, prime minister Dr. J. Leabua Jonathan declared a state of emergency and took away all political authority from the king, Mosheshwe II. When Lesotho, long a haven for black South African refugees, refused to sign a nonaggression pact with South Africa, South Africa severely restricted the flow of imports. The resultant economic crisis and discontent with Jonathan's policies led to a military coup on Jan. 20, 1986. Gen. Justin Lekhanya, head of the ruling military council, was more conciliatory toward South Africa. In January 1990, Lekhanya stripped King

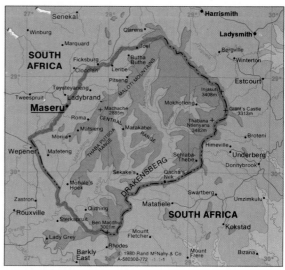

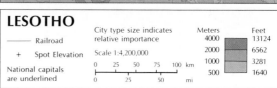

LESOTHO

		Meters	Feet
——— Railroad	City type size indicates relative importance	4000	13124
+ Spot Elevation		2000	6562
	Scale 1:4,200,000	1000	3281
National capitals are underlined	0 25 50 75 100 km	500	1640
	0 25 50 mi		

A Basuto shepherd watches over his flock on the hilly terrain of Lesotho, a small African nation completely surrounded by South Africa. Lesotho's economy is heavily dependent on livestock.

The 19th-century French diplomat Ferdinand de Lesseps promoted and organized the construction of the Suez Canal, which connected the Red and Mediterranean seas.

Mosheshwe II of his executive and legislative powers (restored in 1986). In November, Lekhanya deposed the king, then in exile in London. Mosheshwe II was succeeded as titular head of state by his son, Letsie David Bereng Seeiso (renamed King Letsie II). In April 1991, however, Lekhanya was overthrown in a military coup.

---

lespedeza [les-puh-dee'-zuh]   Lespedezas are several species of important crop plants, genus *Lespedeza*, widely grown for HAY and forage. Originally native to Asia, they are annual or perennial LEGUMES that generally stand about 30 cm (12 in) high, although some species are larger. The leaves consist of three leaflets marked by prominent veins or furrows. The inconspicuous flowers are usually bluish. Some species of lespedeza are also cultivated as ornamentals.

Lesseps, Ferdinand Marie, Vicomte de [leseps', fair-dee-nahn', vee-kohnt']   Ferdinand Marie de Lesseps, b. Nov. 19, 1805, d. Dec. 7, 1894, was responsible for building the SUEZ CANAL. He served (1825–49) as a diplomat in the overseas service of the French government in various cities, including Alexandria, Cairo, and Rome. In 1854 his friendship with Muhammad Said, made while in the diplomatic service, enabled him to secure an act of concession authorizing him to bridge the Isthmus of Suez with a canal from Port Said on the Mediterranean Sea to Suez on the Red Sea. The accession to the Egyptian throne of Muhammad Said made it possible

for him to bring forward the great scheme that he had long cherished. The international Suez Canal Company was incorporated in 1858. The French nation subscribed more than half the cost of construction, largely due to the enthusiasm and organizational ability of de Lesseps who was a superb administrator, politician, and public relations man. Construction of the canal began in 1859 and was completed in 1869; de Lesseps was acclaimed a national hero. For his role in the later transfer of the canal to British control, however, he suffered considerable temporary loss of popularity in France.

In 1879, de Lesseps, at age 74, began an attempt to carry out the construction of a canal across the Isthmus of Panama; the undertaking collapsed, however, and the company formed for the project was liquidated.

Lesser Antilles   see ANTILLES, GREATER AND LESSER

Lessing, Doris   The major British novelist and short-story writer Doris May Lessing, b. Oct. 22, 1919, has explored such themes as political commitment, the fundamental male-female dynamic, women's search for identity, and the relation between the artist and his or her work. She is probably best known for *The Golden Notebook* (1962), a long experimental novel about the lives of two talented professional women.

Although Lessing has lived in England since 1949, she was born in Persia and brought up in Rhodesia (Zimbabwe), the setting for her first novel, *The Grass Is Singing* (1950). Between 1952 and 1969 she published five novels centering on the character Martha Quest, collectively titled *The Children of Violence*, that traced Martha's search for an independent self against a background of impending global catastrophe. Later works such as *The Memoirs of a Survivor* (1974) continued the theme of apocalypse, whereas *Canopus in Argos* (1979) marked the start of a multivolume foray into science fiction. She returned to themes of contemporary society and the individual in *The Diaries of Jane Somers* (1984, originally published under the pseudonym Jane Somers), *The Good Terrorist* (1985), and *The Fifth Child* (1988).

Gotthold Ephraim Lessing, one of the most influential figures of the Enlightenment, is considered the creator of German literary criticism.

Lessing, Gotthold [gawt'-hohlt]   The German dramatist and critic Gotthold Ephraim Lessing, b. Jan. 22, 1729, d. Feb. 15, 1781, was the outstanding figure of the German ENLIGHTENMENT. Lessing studied theology and medicine at the University of Leipzig and received a degree in medicine from the University of Wittenberg (1752). His personal life was filled with disappointments. In 1776 he married but lost his wife in childbirth two years later. His hopes of becoming royal librarian in Berlin were dashed, and he failed in an attempt to establish a national theater in Hamburg. He finally became a librarian in Wolfenbüttel (1770) but there suffered censorship of his controversial theological opinions.

Lessing's writing career began at Leipzig, where his first comedy, *The Young Scholar* (1748; Eng. trans., 1878), was performed. Two others, *The Jews* (1749; Eng. trans., 1801) and *The Freethinker* (1749; Eng. trans., 1838), foreshadowed his later writings—the former a plea for racial and religious tolerance, the latter exposing a freethinker's intolerance. His finest comedy is *Minna von Barnhelm* (1767; Eng. trans., 1858).

In 1753, Lessing launched his *Briefe* (Critical Letters), containing a review of Samuel Gotthold Lange's translation of Horace. Lange's retort provoked Lessing to publish the annihilating *Ein Vademecum* (A Pocket Companion, 1754), establishing him as a controversialist. He continued to publish critical writings in his periodical *Theatralische Bibliothek* (Theatrical Library, 1754–58). Lessing provided a theoretical justification of middle-class tragedy in the *Hamburgische Dramaturgie* (Hamburg Dramaturgy, 1767–69). His own tragedy, *Emilia Galotti* (1772; Eng. trans., 1786), exerted a strong influence on the Sturm und Drang movement.

As an art critic Lessing made his mark with *Laocoön; or, The Limits of Poetry and Painting* (1766; Eng. trans., 1836). Taking issue with Johann WINCKELMANN, he defined coexisting objects as the field of painting and sculpture and consecutive events as that of poetry. Lessing again turned to drama with the parable of religious tolerance *Nathan the Wise* (1779; Eng. trans., 1781). His final work, *The Education of the Human Race* (1780; Eng. trans., 1938), propounds a rational religion progressing through Christianity to humanitarianism.

lethal injection   Lethal injection is a method of capital punishment by which a convicted criminal is administrated a deadly dose of barbiturates through an intravenous tube inserted into the arm. The procedure resembles the method used for a patient undergoing anesthesia before surgery. Although lethal injection has been adopted by several U.S. states since 1980, its first use (1982) stirred a debate over the ethics of employing medical procedures and medical professionals to end a life.

Lethbridge [leth'-brij]   Lethbridge, located on the Oldman River in southern Alberta, Canada, is Alberta's third largest city, with a population of 58,841 (1986). Long an important coal town, Lethbridge also serves as the commercial and food-processing center for the surrounding farming district. It also has diversified manufacturing and is the seat of the University of Lethbridge (1967). The city was settled about 1870 after extensive coal deposits were discovered in the area and originally called Coalbanks.

Lethe [lee'-thee]   In Greek mythology Lethe was one of the five rivers in HADES. Souls drank from it to forget their earthly sorrows before passing into the ELYSIAN FIELDS.

Leto [lee'-toh]   In Greek mythology Leto was the daughter of the Titans Coeus and Phoebe and the mother of ARTEMIS and APOLLO by Zeus. Leto wandered through many lands seeking a place to give birth to her children, because Hera, the wife of Zeus, had forbidden any place under the sun to receive her. In the most common version of the story, Leto gave birth while clinging to a palm tree on the island of Delos, which Poseidon had covered with waves to evade Hera's decree.

letter of credit   A letter of credit is a negotiable instrument issued by a bank, usually addressed to a correspondent bank, stating that it will accept drafts charged against it in the name of a person or company. Commercial letters of credit are often used by importers and exporters to finance the purchase of goods. A circular letter of credit is one not addressed to any particular bank. The TRAVELER'S CHECK is a form of letter of credit.

letterpress   Letterpress is the best known of the relief printing processes, in which the image is on a raised surface. It is the oldest printing process, with modern mechanical presses of this type going back to the presses of Johannes GUTENBERG (about 1450). In the letterpress process the image carriers can be cast-metal type, etched-metal plates, or photopolymer plates on which the image, or printing, areas are raised and the nonimage areas are below the surface of the printing areas. Printing is

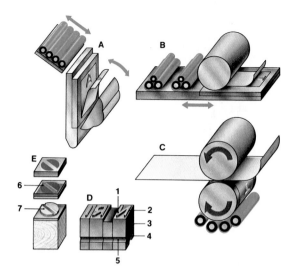

In letterpress printing an inked image is transferred directly from a raised type surface to paper. Paper may be pressed against the inked image by a flat platen (A) or, in a flatbed press, by a cylinder (B). A rotary press (C) feeds paper between an impression cylinder and a plate cylinder. Metal type (D) consists of a face (1), shoulder (2), body (3), foot (4), and a nick (5) that aids typesetting. Newly cast zinc blocks (E) have metal trimmed (6) from around the design (7).

done on a printing press, which provides means for inking the type or plates, transporting the substrate (usually paper), transferring the inked image directly to the substrate, and delivering the printed substrate as a sheet or folded signature. Presses suitable for letterpress printing include the platen press, the flatbed cylinder press, and the ROTARY PRESS. On platen and flatbed cylinder presses the cast-metal type or plates are mounted on a flat sur-

face that forms the printing bed of the press. Cast-metal type and flat metal plates cannot be used on rotary presses. The printing bed is a cylinder, so the image carriers must be curved. Printing can be done on sheets of paper using sheet-fed presses, or on rolls of paper using web-fed presses.

Sheet-fed letterpress on small platen and flatbed presses is used for short-run and medium-run job printing. Large sheet-fed letterpress is used for general commercial printing, books, catalogs, advertising, and packaging. Web letterpress is used for printing business forms, long-run magazines, and newspapers, especially the large metropolitan daily newspapers. Letterpress has the advantage that type can be either hand-set or machine-set (see TYPE AND TYPESETTING). It prints directly onto paper and is capable of long runs with reasonable consistency, high quality, and low paper waste. It has the disadvantage of high cost of photoengravings, time-consuming makeready (adjustments to compensate for high and low areas of type), and poor picture quality on rough papers such as newsprint. Because of these shortcomings and the advent of phototypesetting, letterpress is gradually being replaced by OFFSET LITHOGRAPHY for the short and medium runs and by gravure, a form of intaglio, for the long runs.

Lettish language   see BALTIC LANGUAGES

Letts   see LATVIA

lettuce [let'-uhs]   Lettuce, *Lactuca sativa,* of the family Compositae, is the most popular of all salad crops. It is a cool-season vegetable, growing best at temperatures between 15° and 18° C (59° and 64° F). It will often bolt, or produce seed prematurely, if it is grown in mid-

Of the many varieties of lettuce, the most popular include (left to right) *crisphead; oak leaf; butterhead; and cos, or romaine. Unlike the other types, the oak leaf is a loose-leaf variety and does not form a true head.*

summer heat. Of the four principal lettuce types, the most popular, the crisp-heading lettuces (iceberg is a well-known variety), have brittle, prominently veined leaves; butterhead types (Boston, for example) have softer leaves and a smooth texture; loose-leaf varieties (such as oak-leaf) do not form heads but grow as clusters or bunches of leaves; and cos lettuce, or romaine, forms a long, loaf-shaped head. Cos is slower to bolt than other lettuces and is therefore useful as a warm-weather crop. No cultivated lettuce variety has been found growing in the wild, although there are many wild lettuces, and it is assumed that domesticated varieties may be cultivars of the weed *L. serriola* (prickly lettuce).

Lettuce is usually propagated by seeding directly in the soil. Leaf lettuce is harvested about 40 days after seeding; head lettuce, from 70 to 90 days.

Leucippus [loo-sip'-uhs]   Leucippus, fl. 5th century BC, was a Greek philosopher and the founder of ATOMISM. He maintained that atoms and empty space are the ultimate realities. Atoms are imperceptible, individual particles that differ only in shape and position. The intermingling of these particles in space gives rise to the world of experience. DEMOCRITUS developed and popularized the ideas of Leucippus.

leukemia [loo-kee'-mee-uh]   Leukemia is a term given to a number of malignant, or cancerous, diseases of the BLOOD-forming organs. The acute and chronic leukemias, together with the other types of tumors of the blood, bone cells (myelomas), and lymph tissue (LYMPHOMAS), cause about 10% of all cancer deaths and about 50% of all cancer deaths in children and in adults under 30 years of age.

Leukemias are characterized by excessive amounts of white blood cells, with death resulting from the invasion of these cells into various tissues, particularly the bone marrow, spleen, and lymph nodes. The type of leukemia derives its name from the major type of white cell that has proliferated, for example, lymphoblastic and myeloblastic.

As with most human cancers, the exact cause of most leukemias has yet to be established. Some animal leukemias are induced by viruses, such as Rous chicken sarcoma, feline leukemia, and Rauscher mouse leukemia. More recently two RETROVIRUSES have been identified as causes of human T-cell leukemia. Certain chemicals, such as benzene, chloramphenicol, and procarbazine, as well as radiation, are also likely to be able to produce leukemia in humans. Genetic researchers, in addition, have been able to link certain chromosomal abnormalities with some forms of leukemia.

An individual with leukemia, more particularly the chronic rather than acute forms, may not be aware of it unless, for example, a blood count is done. As the condition progresses there may be weakness, fatigue, loss of appetite, weight loss, anemia, enlarged spleen, and bone pain. When untreated, acute leukemia is fatal in 1 to 2 years and often fatal within about 6 months of onset. Today's therapy produces 85% to 90% remissions for 3 or more years and apparent cure in 50% of the cases. Vigorous therapy is based on the premise that every leukemic cell must be destroyed.

In addition to radiation, various drugs, often in combinations with each other, are used to treat leukemias. Patients in remission are able to lead relatively normal lives. A rare form of leukemia, hairy-cell leukemia, responds to some degree to INTERFERON treatment.

leukocyte   see BLOOD

leukocytosis [loo-kuh-sy-toh'-sis]   An abnormally high number of leukocytes, or white BLOOD cells, is known as leukocytosis. This normally occurs in pregnant women but otherwise indicates a pathological condition, usually a bacterial infection such as staphylococcus or streptococcus. It also often follows a large loss of blood. Leukocytosis may be local (an abscess) or systemic (pneumonia). LEUKEMIA results in leukocytosis in the form of overproduction of immature leukocytes.

leukopenia [loo-kuh-peen'-yuh]   Leukopenia is a deficiency of circulating white blood cells, or leukocytes. If the white-blood-cell count falls below 2,500 per cubic millimeter of blood, the body may become more susceptible to disease. Diseases and other conditions that decrease the production of white cells by the bone marrow can cause leukopenia. These include viral infections (such as infectious MONONUCLEOSIS), tuberculosis, connective tissue diseases, toxic reactions to certain drugs, and the presence of malignant cells in bone marrow. Leukopenia can also result from increased destruction of leukocytes by the spleen during the occurrence of such conditions as rheumatoid arthritis or cirrhosis of the liver.

leukorrhea [loo-kuh-ree'-uh]   Leukorrhea, or vaginal discharge, is usually a symptom of infections of the vagina or cervix, or malignancies of the cervix, uterus, or vagina, or both. The major causes of vaginal infections are *Trichomonas vaginalis, Candida albicans,* and bacterial vaginitis. Trichomonads, protozoans commonly found in the urinary tract, do not cause infection unless they reach the vagina. There they can cause vaginitis with severe itching, ill smell, and painful urination. *C. albicans* is a fungus that causes CANDIDIASIS, the symptoms of which can include leukorrhea and itching. Bacterial vaginitis is commonly caused by *Hemophilus vaginalis.*

Any vaginal discharge that persists or is resistant to treatment, or both, should be investigated to rule out any evidence of malignancy in the genital tract.

Leutze, Emanuel [loyt'-suh, ay-mahn'-oo-el]   The German-American artist Emanuel Leutze, b. May 24, 1816, d. July 18, 1868, is best known for his large painting *Washington Crossing the Delaware* (1851; Metropolitan Museum of Art, New York City), one of the most familiar works in American art. His last major work was the enormous mural *Westward the Course of Empire Takes Its Way* (1862) for the Capitol in Washington, D.C.

Levalloisian [le-val-wah'-zee-uhn] Levalloisian (or Levallois), in archaeology, is a technique of PALEOLITHIC tool manufacture in which flakes are struck off a previously prepared stone core. First discovered in the 19th century at the Parisian suburb of Le Vallois-Perret, it was originally conceived of as a distinct tool culture. The Levalloisian is now known to have occurred in many middle and late sites of the Acheulean tradition and in several variations of the Mousterian in Africa, the Near East, and western Europe during the period from about 700,000 to 32,000 years ago.

Levant [luh-vant'] The Levant (from the Middle English *levaunt*, "east") is a name formerly applied to the areas along the eastern shore of the Mediterranean, including present-day Greece, Turkey, Syria, Lebanon, Israel, and Egypt; a more restricted definition includes only the non-European coastlands. The name is still sometimes used to refer to the former French mandates of Lebanon and Syria.

levee [lev'-ee] A levee is an earthen embankment constructed along the side of a river or stream to prevent flooding of the adjoining land (see FLOODS AND FLOOD CONTROL). The world's largest system of levees, covering a total of 5,741 km (3,566 mi), is constructed along the Mississippi River and its tributaries. Other rivers with important levee systems include the Sacramento; the Huang He (Yellow) and Chang Jiang (Yangtze) in China; the Rhône, Danube, and Rhine in Europe; and the Volga in the USSR. DIKES in the Netherlands are essentially levees.

When a levee alignment has been determined, the area is cleared of trees and brush. A muck ditch or cutoff trench is dug on the levee's river side, down to the more impervious subsoil layers. It is refilled with the most impervious soil available, such as clay or clayey gravel, in order to prevent seepage of water along the base of the levee. The levee embankment is then constructed and its slopes planted with grass to protect it from erosion.

The top of a levee is usually 1 to 1.5 m (3 to 5 ft) above the high-water mark and 1 to 3.5 m (3 to 12 ft) wide. The sides often have a slope of 1:2 or 1:3 on the land side and 1:3 or 1:4 on the river side; the lighter the construction material used, the flatter the slope.

Levellers The Levellers were members of an English radical political movement that arose in 1646–47 at the end of the first ENGLISH CIVIL WAR. Its leaders were John Lilburne (*c.*1614–1657) and Sir John Wildman (*c.*1621–1693), both gentry involved in trade. Its appeal, however, was to the lower middle classes.

The Levellers advocated a wider parliamentary fran-

chise, religious toleration, legal reform, and the abolition of tithes paid to the church. They also called for parliaments to be held every two years. This program, embodied in the Agreement of the People, was presented to the army's general council at the so-called Putney debates in October 1647. The army generals rejected the agreement out of hand.

After the execution of King CHARLES I (1649), the Levellers opposed the new oligarchy headed by Oliver CROMWELL, and Lilburne published a pamphlet entitled *England's New Chains*. Several Leveller mutinies within the army were broken, and the movement petered out. The Levellers' aims were essentially individualistic—unlike the communistic Diggers, an even shorter-lived movement of the same period.

lever [lev'-ur] The lever is a SIMPLE MACHINE used, in its most basic form, for magnifying the force that can be exerted on an object. An early lever, known as the shadoof, was used in ancient Egypt. It consisted of a long bar pivoted near one end that enabled a person pulling down on the long arm to raise a bucket of water, many times his or her own weight, attached to the short arm.

Three possible arrangements and effects can be produced with a lever, as seen in the illustration. All depend on the position of the pivot point, or fulcrum, relative to the points where the load and effort are applied. In the first two forms, the force used is multiplied.

In the third form, however, the lever is not a force-multiplying device, but rather a motion-multiplying device. This form of the lever is found on foot-operated sewing machines, in which a relatively large force applied by the foot of the operator through a small distance on the treadle results in a lesser force moving the sewing machine wheel through a large angular distance. In all levers what is gained in motion is lost in force, so that the larger force always moves through the smaller distance.

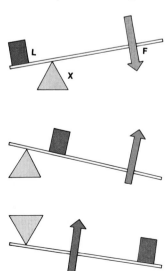

Three arrangements of levers are possible depending on where the force F is applied with respect to the fulcrum X, or point of support about which the lever turns, and the load L. In one case (top) the force and the load act on opposite sides of the fulcrum. In another case (center) the load lies between the fulcrum and the applied force. In a third arrangement (bottom) the force is applied between the load and the fulcrum. The amount of force required to move the load depends on the distance of each from the fulcrum.

Lever, William Hesketh, 1st Viscount Leverhulme [lee'-vur, hes'-keth, lee'-vur-hulm]

William Hesketh Lever, b. Sept. 19, 1851, d. May 7, 1925, turned a small soapworks in Warrington, England, into one of the most successful companies in Britain. The son of a grocer, Lever leased a soap factory in 1884 and with his brother built up the international firm Lever Brothers, which by 1925 had 250 associated firms. He created a model industrial village in Cheshire called Port Sunlight and embarked on a program of "prosperity-sharing" with his employees. Lever, who served in Parliament from 1906 to 1909, was made a baron in 1917 and a viscount in 1922.

Leverrier, Urbain Jean Joseph

see NEPTUNE (planet)

Levertov, Denise [lev'-ur-tawf]

The American poet Denise Levertov, b. Ilford, England, Oct. 24, 1923, became closely associated with the BLACK MOUNTAIN SCHOOL OF POETRY after moving to the United States in 1948. Her early volumes, such as *The Jacob's Ladder* (1961), describe everyday moments in a simple, idiomatic style. In the 1960s her poetry dealt primarily with her antiwar convictions, but she returned to earlier themes in *Life in the Forest* (1978), *Candles in Babylon* (1982), and *Breathing the Water* (1987).

Lévesque, René [lay-vek', ruh-nay']

The French-Canadian political leader René Lévesque, b. New Carlisle, Quebec, Aug. 24, 1922, d. Nov. 1, 1987, was elected premier of Quebec in November 1976. Formerly a broadcast journalist, he entered Quebec politics in 1960 as a member of the Liberal party. In 1967 he helped found the separatist Sovereignty Movement, which developed into the Parti Québécois in 1968. In May 1980, Quebec's voters rejected political sovereignty for the province, but Lévesque's party won again in general elections in April 1981. In June 1985, Lévesque resigned as party leader.

Levi, Primo [lay'-vee]

The Italian writer Primo Levi, b. July 31, 1919, d. Apr. 13, 1987, is remembered chiefly for his three-volume autobiography, which combines reminiscence, philosophy, and accounts of his experiences as an inmate of the Nazi concentration camp Auschwitz. Born into a middle-class Italian-Jewish family, Levi led a relatively placid life until the German occupation of Italy transformed him from chemist to partisan. Captured and sent to Auschwitz, Levi survived only because of his usefulness as a chemist. The autobiographical works are *Survival in Auschwitz* (1947; Eng. trans., 1959), *The Reawakening* (1958; Eng. trans., 1965), and *The Periodic Table* (1975; Eng. trans., 1984). Other works include the novels *The Monkey's Wrench* (1978;

Eng. trans., 1986) and *If Not Now, When?* (1982; Eng. trans., 1985), several posthumous gatherings of essays and short stories, and *Collected Poems* (1988).

Levi ben Gershon [lee'-vy ben gur'-shuhn]

The Jewish astronomer, mathematician, and philosopher Levi ben Gershon (also called Gersonides and Ralbag), b. Bagnols, France, 1288, d. Apr. 20, 1344, was a controversial commentator on Aristotelian philosophy, the Bible, and parts of the Talmud. His most important mathematical work (1342) dealt with trigonometry. As an astronomer he was an independent follower of the Ptolemaic tradition. Levi devised an instrument for measuring the angular separation between any two astronomical bodies, the JACOB'S STAFF, which was much used in navigation, especially in the 16th century.

Levi's major philosophic work, *Milhamot Adonai* (The Wars of the Lord, 1329), treats many of the critical philosophic problems of his time as an Averroist, that is, a follower of the Aristotelian commentator AVERROËS. Unlike Maimonides, who, when faced with an unresolvable contradiction between Aristotle and the Bible, accepted the biblical word as primary, Levi tried to accommodate biblical ideas to those of Aristotle. Because of this he was suspected of heresy.

Lévi-Strauss, Claude [lay-vee-strows', klohd]

Claude Lévi-Strauss, b. Nov. 28, 1908, a leading French philosopher, social theorist, and anthropologist, is associated with the development of STRUCTURALISM as a method in both the social sciences and humanities. Aside from a period spent teaching in Brazil before World War II and a few years as an academic and diplomat in the United States during and after the war, Lévi-Strauss has lived and taught in France. His researches have focused on the massive amount of ethnological materials collected by field-workers worldwide. By developing a sophisticated means of analyzing the cultural artifacts of preindustrial, nonliterate peoples, he has sought to discover underlying structures of thought that characterize not only so-called primitive societies—the anthropologist's specialty—but also the formal structures of human mentality generally.

Lévi-Strauss derived his structuralist method from structural linguistics. Considering the perspective of structural linguistics appropriate for culture and thought as well as for language, he attempted to demonstrate that the cultural features of tribal societies were assemblages of codes, in turn reflecting certain universal principles of human thought. Lévi-Strauss's first major work was *Elementary Structures of Kinship* (1949; Eng. trans., 1962), but his career project has been the structural study of mythology, realized in *Mythologiques* (4 vols., 1964–71; Eng. trans., 1970–81). Unlike previous analysts of myth, Lévi-Strauss holds that a myth's meaning is hidden in the underlying relationships of all its elements, which can be discovered only through structuralist analysis.

As Lévi-Strauss's works became available in English in

The French anthropologist Claude Lévi-Strauss is one of the leading exponents of structuralism. Widely respected for intellectual achievement, he was elected to the Académie Française in 1973.

the 1960s, his structuralist method gained popularity in the United States in such fields as sociology, architecture, literature, and art, as well as anthropology. His writings include *Tristes Tropiques* (1955; Eng. trans., 1964), *Structural Anthropology* (1958; Eng. trans. in 2 vols., 1963 and 1976), and *The Savage Mind* (1962; Eng. trans., 1966).

Leviathan   see HOBBES, THOMAS

Levine, Jack [luh-veen']   The American painter Jack Levine, b. Boston, Jan. 3, 1915, approaches social themes with a satirical and often angry outlook on the excesses and corruption inherent in modern society. A poverty-stricken childhood and early training in the socially conscious Federal Arts Project of the Depression years helped mold Levine's artistic attitude, evident in *The Feast of Pure Reason* (1937; Museum of Modern Art, New York City), *Welcome Home* (1946; Brooklyn Museum, N.Y.) and *The Gangster's Funeral* (1953; Whitney Museum of American Art, New York City).

Levine, James [luh-vyn']   The conductor and pianist James Levine, b. Cincinnati, Ohio, June 23, 1943, made his professional debut at the age of ten as piano soloist with the Cincinnati Symphony Orchestra. Hired by George Szell as apprentice conductor (1964) of the Cleveland Orchestra, he soon became assistant conductor and appeared with the orchestra as piano soloist. Following his conducting debut (1971) at the Metropolitan Opera, he became the company's principal conductor (1973), musical director (1976), and artistic director (1986). He was also appointed (1973) music director of the Ravinia festival, which includes a summer concert series by the Chicago Symphony Orchestra.

Levites [lee'-vyts]   Members of the Israelite tribe of Levi, descended by tradition from the third son of JACOB, were called Levites. MOSES belonged to this tribe. They were a religious caste, some or all of whose members acted as priests for Israel. Lacking their own territory, they lived among the other tribes in special settlements called Levitical cities. In early Israel the priesthood had a predominantly teaching function, because the laity then were considered competent to sacrifice. Later, especially in postexilic times, the sacrificial duties of the priests at the Jerusalem Temple were increased. Eventually the high priest and priests competent to sacrifice were traced back to the house of AARON, whereas Levite became the term for lower-rank cultic attendants who maintained the temple, taught, and provided music for worship.

Leviticus, Book of [luh-vit'-ih-kuhs]   Leviticus is the third book of the Pentateuch, or TORAH, the first five books of the BIBLE, which are traditionally ascribed to MOSES. Its name is derived from the tribe Levi (the Levites), which had the responsibility for overseeing Israel's ritual worship. Leviticus consists primarily of laws regulating such activity, including sacrificial offerings, the installation of priests, cultic purity (which includes the dietary laws), and a more general legal collection known as the Holiness Code because of its emphasis on God's holiness. These major collections, together with several shorter supplements, are part of the P source, normally dated to *c*.450 BC. Thus, as a book, Leviticus is postexilic, but the individual laws and various collections within the book differ in age, and some are quite ancient.

Levitt, William Jaird [lev'-it]   William Jaird Levitt, b. Brooklyn, N.Y., Feb. 11, 1907, introduced mass-production methods into the building of low-cost HOUSING tracts. In 1947–51 his company turned 480 ha (1,200 acres) of Long Island potato fields 16 km (10 mi) from New York City into a residential community named Levittown, N.Y. He followed this project with another Levittown in Pennsylvania halfway between Philadelphia and Trenton, N.J., built in 1951–55. Both communities were preplanned, consisting of thousands of simple homes built on concrete slabs, together with schools, shopping centers, playgrounds, and community centers. Other Levittown-type communities later were built in New Jersey, Maryland, Florida, and elsewhere.

Levittowns   see HOUSING

Lewes, George Henry [loo'-is]   George Henry Lewes, b. Apr. 18, 1817, d. Nov. 30, 1878, was an English literary critic, journalist, and scientific writer best known for his liaison with novelist George ELIOT (Mary Anne Evans). In 1840 he married and joined a communal marriage group in which he accepted his wife's affair with Thornton Hunt. He left his wife, however, when he learned in 1850 that his youngest son was Hunt's. Lewes met Evans in 1851, and they lived together from 1854 until his death.

An early Darwinian, he published books on physiological psychology and marine biology, as well as two novels and a number of philosophical and biographical works, most notably *The Life and Works of Goethe* (1855).

◾

Lewin, Kurt [le-veen'] The German-born American psychologist Kurt Lewin, b. Sept. 9, 1890, d. Feb. 12, 1947, developed field theory after doctoral studies in Gestalt psychology at the University of Berlin. His work subsequently influenced group dynamics and other areas of social psychology that study attitudes. Working in the United States from 1932 on, Lewin sought to combine theory and practical application.

Lewin's field theory maintains that an individual's behavior is determined by his or her contemporary life space. What constitutes the individual's life space is not the objective environment in itself but the way the individual perceives it. Lewin was one of the earliest psychologists to use mathematical models, presenting field theory in the language of topology and vector analysis.

Lewis, C. Day see DAY-LEWIS, C.

◾

Lewis, C. S. The English scholar and writer Clive Staples Lewis, b. Nov. 29, 1898, d. Nov. 22, 1963, led two virtually distinct—and equally successful—careers as an author. *The Allegory of Love* (1936) remains a standard work on medieval literature and the tradition of courtly love and was followed by *A Preface to Paradise Lost* (1942) and *English Literature in the 16th Century, Excluding Drama* (1954). Lewis was known to a large public, however, as a persuasive and passionate advocate of conservative Christianity. In a science-fiction trilogy—*Out of the Silent Planet* (1938), *Perelandra* (1943), and *That Hideous Strength* (1945)—he placed the idea of Christian pilgrimage in a cosmic setting. His most bril-

C. S. Lewis wrote numerous works about Christianity and a series of fantasy novels, The Chronicles of Narnia. *Lewis was also an acclaimed literary critic whose study of the conventions of allegory is considered a standard reference.*

liant work of Christian apologetics is perhaps *The Screwtape Letters* (1942; rev. ed., 1961), in which a seasoned old servant of the Devil instructs an apprentice in the art of capturing souls. Lewis also achieved success with *The Lion, the Witch, and the Wardrobe* (1950) and his other children's stories constituting *The Chronicles of Narnia.* He related his religious conversion in *Surprised by Joy* (1955).

◾

Lewis, Carl Hailed as the greatest track and field star since Jesse Owens, Frederick Carlton Lewis, b. Birmingham, Ala., July 1, 1961, at the 1984 Olympics in Los Angeles, won the same four gold medals as Owens did in 1936 (100 m, 200 m, long jump, 4 × 100-m relay). At the 1988 Olympics he repeated as gold medalist at 100 m and the long jump and earned a silver medal at 200 m. In 1981, Lewis received the Sullivan Award as the nation's finest amateur athlete.

◾

Lewis, Clarence Irving An American philosopher, Clarence Irving Lewis, b. Stoneham, Mass., Apr. 12, 1883, d. Feb. 3, 1964, combined studies in symbolic logic with epistemology and ethics. He received his B.A. (1906) and Ph.D. (1910) from Harvard University and began teaching philosophy at the University of California. In 1920 he returned to Harvard, where he taught until his retirement in 1953.

Lewis has greatly influenced academic philosophy, and more than any other thinker he serves as the link between American philosophy at the beginning of the 20th century and its current interests and directions. He was a critic of modern extensional systems of logic and developed a modal logic based on a new understanding of implication. In theory of knowledge, as well as in ethics, he developed a pragmatic position that reflects the influences of Josiah Royce and Immanuel Kant.

◾

Lewis, Gilbert Newton SEE ACIDS AND BASES

◾

Lewis, John L. John Llewellyn Lewis, b. Lucas County, Iowa, Feb. 12, 1880, d. June 11, 1969, was president of the UNITED MINE WORKERS OF AMERICA from 1920 to 1960 and a major force in organized labor in the 1930s and '40s. He was a prime mover in the organization of industrial unions in steel, rubber, automobiles, and other mass-production industries. He led them out of the American Federation of Labor (AFL) and formed the rival Committee for Industrial Organization (1935), later the Congress of Industrial Organizations (CIO), serving as its first president until 1940. The mine workers left the CIO in 1942. During World War II and afterward, Lewis led the miners in controversial strikes that won them substantial medical and retirement benefits.

◾

Lewis, Matthew Gregory Matthew Gregory Lewis, b. July 9, 1775, d. May 14, 1818, was an English writer whose sensationally popular GOTHIC ROMANCE *The Monk* (1796) was widely condemned for immorality. The novel, which earned its author the nickname "Monk" Lewis, is a melodramatic tale of sexual depravity and murder. Lewis repeated his success with a musical drama, *The Castle Spectre* (1798). He was also a diplomat and member of Parliament (1796–1802) and owned estates in the West Indies. His humane concern for the condition of slaves led him to write *Journal of a West India Proprietor* (1834).

Lewis, Meriwether Meriwether Lewis, b. near Charlottesville, Va., Aug. 18, 1774, d. Oct. 11, 1809, was cocommander, with William CLARK, of the LEWIS AND CLARK EXPEDITION, which made the first American crossing to the Pacific by an overland route. After a brief army career, he served as private secretary to President Thomas Jefferson from 1801 to 1803; during this time he planned the expedition, which began in 1804. On his successful return in 1806, Lewis was appointed governor of the Louisiana Territory and served until his death, which was either a murder or a suicide.

Lewis, Sinclair Sinclair Harry Lewis, b. Sauk Centre, Minn., Feb. 7, 1885, d. Jan. 10, 1951, was the first American to win the Nobel Prize for literature. He achieved an international reputation in the 1920s for his satirical portrayal of middle-class life in small midwestern American towns and cities in such novels as MAIN STREET, BABBITT, *Arrowsmith*, and *Dodsworth*. After graduating from Yale University in 1908, he started his career as a free-lance journalist and between 1914 and 1919 published five light romantic novels.

Lewis's first success came with *Main Street* (1920). Set in Gopher Prairie, modeled after Lewis's hometown, it was an exposure of the smug mediocrity of that legendary home of virtues, the small town, and as such burst like a bombshell on a war-weary, disillusioned audience. It was followed by another best-seller, *Babbitt* (1922), named

Sinclair Lewis, an American writer who won both the Nobel and Pulitzer prizes, chronicled the complacency and materialism of middle-class life in the United States. A succession of best-selling novels, including Main Street *(1920),* Babbitt *(1922), and* Arrowsmith *(1925), established him as a major 20th-century author.*

for a self-deluding realtor and community "booster." Lewis's next novel, *Arrowsmith* (1925), a bitter documentation of the obstacles a materialistic society puts in the path of an idealistic medical researcher, won him the Pulitzer Prize (1926), an honor he declined. *Elmer Gantry* (1927), a devastating portrait of opportunistic religious revivalists, and *Dodsworth* (1929), about a wealthy industrialist's late discovery of the pleasures of expatriate life, intensified both the attacks on Lewis's "disloyalty" and the praise for his work that culminated in the Nobel Prize awarded him in 1930. He had meanwhile divorced his first wife and married journalist Dorothy Thompson in 1928. This marriage ended in 1942. Although Lewis published ten more novels, only *It Can't Happen Here* (1935), a warning against the extension of fascism to the United States, and *Kingsblood Royal* (1947), a savage attack on racial discrimination in both the South and North, match the power of his earlier work.

Lewis, Wyndham Percy Wyndham Lewis, b. Nov. 18, 1882, d. Mar. 7, 1957, a British writer and painter of considerable distinction, was better known for his controversial, iconoclastic views than for any particular work of art. He was a founder of VORTICISM (1913–19), a movement that sought to break away from convention and develop a machine-age aesthetic, and the editor of the short-lived vorticist magazine *Blast* (1914–15).

After serving as a World War I artillery officer and war artist, Lewis produced hundreds of paintings and drawings in addition to stories, novels, poetry, criticism, and autobiography. He discussed politics in *The Art of Being Ruled* (1926) and philosophy in *Time and Western Man* (1927). Among his novels, *Tarr* (1918; rev. ed., 1928) and *The Revenge for Love* (1937) are fierce social satires that also reflect Lewis's anxiety about the difficulties of an artist's life.

Lewis and Clark Expedition The Lewis and Clark Expedition of 1804–06 was the first American exploring party to investigate the vast territory between the Mississippi River and the Pacific Ocean. It has often been mistakenly assumed that the purpose of the expedition was to explore the lands acquired in the LOUISIANA PURCHASE of 1803. In fact, the expedition had been planned and organized long before the purchase. President Thomas JEFFERSON, fascinated since childhood by the theory of a NORTHWEST PASSAGE or water route connecting the Mississippi with the Pacific, finally saw his dreams realized when the Congress, early in 1803, appropriated funds for the discovery of "the water communication across this continent." Selected to lead the expedition were two former army officers, Meriwether LEWIS, Jefferson's private secretary, and William CLARK, Lewis's close friend.

When the expedition left St. Louis on May 14, 1804, the captains' plans were to travel up the Missouri as far as the Rocky Mountains by winter, to cross the "short portage" from the Missouri to the Columbia and descend that stream to the Pacific in the spring of 1805, and then

The Lewis and Clark Expedition (1804–06) opened the American West. Led by Captains Meriwether Lewis and William Clark, members of the expedition traveled across the continent to reach the Pacific. (Gilcrease Institute, Tulsa.)

to retrace their steps to St. Louis by fall 1805. Navigation on the western rivers was harder than anticipated, however, and by November the party had traveled only as far as central North Dakota. They wintered there with the MANDAN Indians, gathering information on the land.

The captains still believed in a short portage when they left the Mandans in April 1805, now accompanied by the Shoshoni woman translator Sacajawea (c.1784–1812). On reaching the Three Forks of the Missouri in July 1805, they chose to follow the most westerly of the three rivers, which they called the Jefferson. This took them through difficult country, and their tortuous crossing of the Rockies—and the Continental Divide, reached

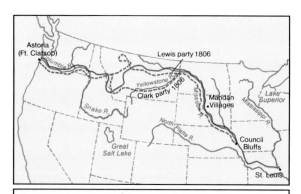

LEWIS AND CLARK EXPEDITION

——— Route 1804-05   ===== Route 1806

on August 12—convinced them that the fabled water route did not exist. In September the party reached the Clearwater River and descended it to the Snake, which they followed to the Columbia. The discouraged party did not reach the mouth of the Columbia until November 1805. Here they spent the second winter.

Leaving the Pacific shore in March 1806, the expedition retraced its steps to the Continental Divide and then split into two groups. Clark led one party down the Yellowstone River, while Lewis's group descended the Missouri River. They rejoined on Aug. 12, 1806, on the Missouri and returned to St. Louis on Sept. 23, 1806.

Lewiston   Lewiston (1990 pop., 39,757), on the Androscoggin River in southwestern Maine, is the second largest city in the state. Within the city limits the river drops 15 m (50 ft) over three falls, providing waterpower for industry. Lewiston's factories produce textiles, shoes, and electronic equipment. Bates College (1864) is there. The city was founded in 1770 by settlers from Massachusetts.

---

lexicology and lexicography [leks-ih-kahl'-uh-jee, leks-ih-kahg'-ruh-fee]   Lexicology is the study of the origin and meaning of words; lexicography is the practice of dictionary making. Lexicology is a theoretical science; lexicography is an applied science. Together they form the branch of LINGUISTICS that links the abstract discipline SEMANTICS and the tangible artifact the DICTIONARY.

The dictionary maker must first decide what vocabulary entries to include. Then each word's spelling (including capitalization), pronunciation, part of speech, inflection (if any), etymology, and meaning must be ascertained. A central concern is how prescriptive a dictionary should be. Should it record the language as it is spoken or as it "ought" to be spoken? Should it describe or prescribe?

The Selection of Lexical Items. No dictionary contains more than a fraction of all the words in a language. The largest unabridged English dictionary has more than half a million entries, but lexicographers have estimated that ten times as many words—6,000,000—could have been listed. Most dictionaries, for example, enter *storyteller*, but few include *storywriter* (or *story-writer*, or *story writer*), and probably no dictionary has an entry for *take-it-or-leave-it* as an adjective, as in the sentence *He is a take-it-or-leave-it kind of person.*

Spelling and Pronunciation. Lexicographers have become increasingly willing to indicate geographical and social varieties of pronunciation. So far, however, they have hesitated to follow the same policy with regard to spelling. Most dictionaries cite two or even three pronunciations for words like *tomato* or *economics* but give only one spelling for *millennium* or *memorandum*, although *millenium* and *memorandam* occur even among educated writers.

The two *n*'s of *millennium* and the *-um* ending of *memorandum* are certified by the Latin sources of the words. *Memorandum* is the neuter form of the Latin gerundive *memorandus*, and *millennium* combines Latin *mille*, "thousand," with an ending derived from the word *annus*, "year." Many other so-called correct English spellings, however, are incorrect from a Latin point of view. For instance, the British use the spelling *centre* for the word derived from Latin *centrum*, but ever since Noah Webster's time Americans have been writing *center*.

Parts of Speech and Inflections. Although linguists have suggested alternative analyses, dictionaries continue to class words according to the eight traditional PARTS OF SPEECH—noun, verb, adjective, adverb, pronoun, preposition, conjunction, and interjection. Most dictionaries also note whether a verb is transitive or intransitive, and some include labels such as "impersonal verb" or "auxiliary verb." Inflections (the changes in forms of words, like *fairies*, the plural of *fairy*, or *talked*, the past tense of *talk*) provide one of the most important indications of a word's part of speech. Some linguists even classify words strictly according to the inflections they take.

Etymology. A word's etymology is its history. A dictionary should indicate where each word came from—whether it was borrowed or invented or has always been in the language. Thousands of current English words can be traced to INDO-EUROPEAN via MIDDLE ENGLISH, OLD ENGLISH, and the GERMANIC LANGUAGES. Most words, however, are either generated within the language by combining familiar words or syllables (like *bookcase* from the nouns *book* and *case*, or *presently* from the adjective *present* and the adverbial suffix *-ly*) or are borrowed from other languages. Only a few common terms—*googol* is an example—are arbitrary creations.

Definitions. The process of determining and arranging definitions begins with collecting citations. The lexicographer assembles as many varied examples of each word's usage as possible—from written sources such as books, magazines, newspapers, and advertisements, and also from radio and television. The citations are then used to establish how many different meanings the word in question has. This step is perhaps the most subjective stage in lexicography; a check in any two dictionaries of comparable size will show that one lexicographer may distinguish three shades of meaning for a word, whereas another may find only two. Finally, when the definitions are written, each meaning must be expressed clearly and precisely.

Definitions may be listed either chronologically or in order of popularity—they may proceed either from the first meaning a word had in the language to the most recent or from the most common meaning to the least common. Under the entry *nice*, for example, a historical dictionary might begin with "foolish"—which is what *nice* meant when first used in English in the 13th century—and end with "agreeable"; another dictionary will place "agreeable" first—since that is currently the word's most prevalent sense—and then list the other meanings in descending order of popularity.

Placing a word's etymology before its definitions enables the reader to see quickly where the first meaning of the word came from. The English word *curious*, for instance, derives from Old French *curios*, which in turn descends from Latin *curiousus*, "careful." Thus the origin of the first sense—"solicitous"—borne by the word *curious* in English becomes immediately apparent.

Lexington   Lexington, a city in the Bluegrass region of central Kentucky, is the seat of Fayette County and the second largest city in the state. The population is 225,366 (1990). Noted as the center for Thoroughbred horse breeding, Lexington is also a major center for trade in burley tobacco, bluegrass seed, lamb, and beef. Its industries produce electronic equipment, bourbon whiskey, electric typewriters, automobile parts, and paper products. The city is the home of Transylvania University (1780) and the University of Kentucky (1865).

Lexington was settled in 1775 by an exploring party that had just heard of the Revolutionary War battle of Lexington in Massachusetts. The city owed its early prosperity to the sale of locally grown hemp to New England ship chandlers. After the Civil War tobacco became the cash crop, and Lexington's wealth grew. Many stately homes, notably those of Henry Clay, John Wesley Hunt, and Mary Todd Lincoln, are in Lexington.

Lexington and Concord, Battles of   The Battles of Lexington and Concord, fought in Massachusetts in April 1775, touched off the American Revolution. Because of the unrest that followed passage (1774) of the Intolerable Acts, British general Thomas Gage received orders to use force against the defiant colonials. Consequently, Lt. Col. Francis Smith led a British column from Boston to seize the gunpowder of the Massachusetts Provincial Congress at Concord. On the morning of April 19, Smith's redcoats scattered a company of local MINUTEMEN at Lexington, killing several when unauthorized firing occurred. At Concord, Smith managed to find only part of the gunpowder because news of his mission had been carried to the countryside by Paul REVERE and his associates. As they returned to Boston, the British were under constant assault from Massachusetts militiamen, who inflicted 273 casualties.

Leyden   see LEIDEN

Leyden jar [ly'-den]   The Leyden jar was an early apparatus for the storage of static electricity. It is named for the University of Leyden (Leiden) in the Netherlands, where it was first made in 1746. The earliest Leyden jar was a glass vial, partially filled with water and stoppered with a cork that was pierced with a wire or nail that dipped into the water. Static electricity was introduced into the jar through the wire. A person touching the wire would receive a shock, proving that electricity had been stored. The modern Leyden jar, which is used for laboratory demonstrations, is coated inside and out with metal foil. The outer covering is grounded; a brass rod touches the inner covering and extends out of the top of the jar through a rubber stopper. The Leyden jar is important as the ancestor of the modern CAPACITOR.

LH see HORMONE, ANIMAL; PITUITARY GLAND

Lhasa [lah'-suh] Lhasa is the capital of the Tibet Autonomous Region, China. It is located on the northern bank of the Kyi Zhu River, a tributary of the Zhangbo (upper Brahmaputra) River. The population is 105,000 (1982). Lhasa is the economic, cultural, and transportation center of the region. Long the religious center of Tibetan Buddhism (the name Lhasa means "holy land" in Tibetan), the city is dominated by the Potala Palace, former residence of the Dalai Lama (rebuilt in the 17th century), on Potala Hill. Other landmarks include the Jokhang (Great Cathedral), several monasteries, and the Norbulingka (the former summer palace of the Dalai Lama).

The recorded history of Lhasa dates back to the introduction of Buddhism in the 7th century, although settlement may have taken place as early as the 5th century. A trade center on the Silk Road between India and China, Lhasa became the capital of Tibet as early as the 9th century. Chinese Communists took over Tibet in 1951. Eight years later the Dalai Lama led a local revolt, which the Chinese soon crushed. Renewed Tibetan protests against Chinese rule led to the imposition of martial law in Lhasa from March 1989 to May 1990.

Lhasa apso [lah'-suh ap'-soh] The Lhasa apso, a small dog of Tibet with appealing hairy countenance, has become one of the more popular breeds in the United States. Short-legged, it stands 25–27.5 cm (10–11 in) at the shoulder and has pendant ears, and a tail curled over the back. The coat is heavy, straight, long, and very dense, with a profuse "fall" over the eyes. Lhasas come in a range of colors, with golden or lionlike colors being preferred.

The Lhasa apso is a small dog raised as an alarm dog and pet in its native Tibet. The Dalai Lama of Tibet customarily presented Lhasa apsos to visiting dignitaries as a gesture of friendship.

Li Bo (Li Po) [lee boh] Li Bo, also known by his courtesy name, Taibo, was the most brilliant of Chinese poets and one of China's most original personalities. Born in 701 in Central Asia, he grew up in what is now Sichuan; he died in central China in 762. After a period as court poet to the emperor Tang Xuandong, in 756–57 he served under the rebel Prince Lin and was subsequently imprisoned, released, exiled, and given amnesty.

Most of Li Bo's poems are in the traditional forms. Their principal themes are the grandeur of China's mountains and rivers, the poet's soaring journeys of the spirit, his legendary intoxication with wine and moonlight, and his friendships.

Li Hongzhang (Li Hung-chang) [lee hoong-jahng] Chinese political leader and general Li Hongzhang, b. Feb. 15, 1823, d. Nov. 7, 1901, became an active promoter of modernization for the Chinese military. As governor of the capital province of Zhili (1870–95), Li became the court advisor on foreign relations. He negotiated the Zhefu Convention (1876), establishing further European treaty ports; the Treaty of Shimonoseki (1895), which ended the First SINO-JAPANESE WAR; the Russo-Chinese alliance (1896); and the protocol (1901) compensating Westerners for losses during the BOXER UPRISING.

Li Peng (Li P'eng) [lee puhng'] Li Peng, b. October 1928, became acting premier of China, succeeding ZHAOU ZIYANG, in November 1987. The son of a revolutionary executed in 1930, Li Peng was raised in the household of ZHOU ENLAI. He joined the Communist party in 1945 and studied (1948–55) electrical engineering in Moscow. Returning to China, he became minister of power (1981), a party central committee member (1982), a deputy premier (1983), and minister of education and a member of the politburo (both 1985). Confirmed as premier in 1988, he backed the suppression of the student prodemocracy movement in June 1989.

Li Po see LI BO

Liang Kai (Liang K'ai) [lee-ahng' ky] Liang Kai, d. c.1246, and MUQI were the two great Chan (Zen) Buddhist monk-painters of 13th-century China. Liang left the Song academy for a Buddhist monastery. Known as Crazy Liang because of his eccentric personality, he developed a more subjective and intuitive approach to painting than that of the contemporary academic school. His celebrated *Huineng Chopping Bamboo* (Tokyo National Museum), a monochrome ink painting executed in the *qianbi* or abbreviated style, is regarded as the culmination of Chan painting.

Libby, Willard Frank The American chemist Willard Frank Libby, b. Grand Valley, Colo., Dec. 17, 1908, d. Sept. 8, 1980, won the 1960 Nobel Prize for chemistry for his RADIOMETRIC AGE-DATING technique (1947), which uses the isotope carbon-14 to date archaeological specimens. He described his work in his book *Radiocarbon Dating* (1952; 2d ed., 1955). He taught at the University of California at Berkeley (1933–45) and worked on the Manhattan Project (1941–45). He then joined the

Institute for Nuclear Studies at the University of Chicago (1945–59) and finally the University of California at Los Angeles (1959–80), where he directed the Institute for Geophysics and Planetary Physics. Libby twice served on the U.S. Atomic Energy Commission.

libel   see DEFAMATION

—

Liberal parties   Liberal parties exist in many countries and represent a variety of interests and viewpoints. This article considers the Liberal parties in Great Britain, Canada, Australia, and New York State.

The Liberal party in Great Britain, formed in the mid-19th century, supported such policies as free trade and freedom of the individual. In time it was responsible for important social legislation in such fields as education and labor. In their outlook the Liberals were heavily influenced by such thinkers as Jeremy Bentham, John Locke, John Stuart Mill, and Herbert Spencer. In politics they regarded the state in general and the crown in particular as the principal potential enemy of freedom. In economics they wanted to limit the government's role in the economy; they strongly favored competition.

The government formed in 1846 by Lord John Russell (later 1st Earl RUSSELL) is sometimes considered the first Liberal government. As an organized party, however, the Liberals made their appearance under William GLADSTONE, who was four times prime minister (1868–74, 1880–85, 1886, 1892–94). Gladstone's policies as prime minister included free trade, home rule for Ireland (see HOME RULE BILLS), and electoral reform (see REFORM ACTS). His advocacy of home rule split the party in 1886, when some of his supporters, led by Joseph CHAMBERLAIN, assumed the name Liberal Unionists and allied themselves with the Conservatives. The Liberal party, under such leaders as Sir Henry CAMPBELL-BANNERMAN, Herbert ASQUITH, and David LLOYD GEORGE, alternated in power with the Conservative party until shortly after World War I. The party's strength soon declined, however, and the Labour party became the chief opposition to the Conservatives. Except for coalition governments in 1931–32 and during World War II (1940–45), the Liberals remained out of power. During the 1980s they joined the Social Democratic party (SDP) in an electoral grouping called the Alliance, hoping to displace Labour as the main opposition party. The Alliance won 25.4% of the vote in the 1983 elections, and 22.6% in 1987. In 1988 the Liberals merged with the SDP to form the Social and Liberal Democrats.

The Liberal party in Canada has been close to its British counterpart in general philosophy. It was the opposition party in the 19th century from the time of Confederation in 1867 until it came to power in 1896. The architect of Liberal hegemony in Canada was Sir Wilfrid LAURIER, who became the party's leader in 1887. A French Canadian, he swung Quebec province to the Liberals; this considerable electoral advantage kept the party in power throughout most of the 20th century. Laurier was succeeded as prime minister by W. L. Mackenzie KING, who remained intermittently in office from 1921 until his retirement

in 1948. The next Liberal prime minister was Louis ST. LAURENT, who served from 1949 to 1957. Following a brief hiatus, the Liberals returned to power in 1963 under the leadership of Lester B. PEARSON, succeeded by Pierre Elliott TRUDEAU in 1968. Ousted by the Conservatives in 1979, Trudeau returned to power in 1980 and remained premier until his retirement in June 1984. His successor, John TURNER, was voted out of office in September 1984 and did not regain it, but continued to lead the Liberals until replaced by Jean CHRÉTIEN in 1990.

The Liberal party in Australia has been known by various names since its founding in 1910 as the Fusion party. It adopted the name Liberal in 1913 but merged during World War I with elements of the Labor party to form a government as the Nationalist party. Later it dropped the Labor elements and entered into an alliance with the Country party. The Nationalist-Country alliance remained in power until 1929. In the 1930s the Nationalists took the name United Australia party, governing in coalition with the Country party. They resumed the name Liberal in 1944; a Liberal-Country coalition governed Australia from 1949 until 1972, led by Robert MENZIES for most of that period. The Liberals under J. Malcolm FRASER again held power from 1975 to 1983. The party's policies generally have been conservative and probusiness.

The Liberal party in New York State was founded in 1944 by members who withdrew from the American Labor party. Those who withdrew included well-known New Deal liberals such as A. A. BERLE, David DUBINSKY, Reinhold NIEBUHR, and Alex Rose. They charged that the American Labor party contained a strong pro-Communist element. Since then the Liberal party has played an important balance-of-power role in New York politics. It generally supports liberal Democrats.

—

Liberal Republican party   The Liberal Republican party was founded in the United States in 1872 by a group of moderate Republicans who were disillusioned both with the aura of political corruption surrounding Ulysses S. GRANT's administration and with the RECONSTRUCTION policy of the Radical Republicans. Besides advocating an end to Radical Reconstruction, the party platform called for civil-service reform, local self-government, and the resumption of specie payment. Allied with the Democrats, the Liberal Republicans nominated Horace GREELEY for president and Benjamin Gratz Brown for vice-president in 1872, but Grant was reelected and the new party soon disbanded.

—

liberalism   Liberalism, a political philosophy that emphasizes individual freedom, arose in Europe in the period between the Reformation and the French Revolution. During the 16th, 17th, and 18th centuries the medieval feudal order gradually gave way as Protestantism, the nation-state, commerce, science, cities, and a middle class of traders and industrialists developed. The new liberal order—drawing on Enlightenment thought—began to place human beings rather than God at the center of things. Humans, with their rational minds, could comprehend all things and could improve themselves and society through systematic and rational action.

Liberal thinking favored freedom—a natural right—from traditional restraints. These notions did much to precipitate the American and French revolutions. Liberalism sought to expand civil liberties and to limit political authority in favor of constitutional representative government and promoted the rights to property and religious toleration. In the economic sphere, classical liberalism was opposed to direction by the state, arguing with Adam SMITH and David RICARDO that the forces of the marketplace were the best guide for the economy (see LAISSEZ-FAIRE).

One of the first thinkers to formulate a comprehensive liberal philosophy was the Englishman John LOCKE. Thomas Jefferson drew on Locke's ideas in framing the Declaration of Independence, and the French Enlightenment philosophers VOLTAIRE and MONTESQUIEU were indebted to him. Leading liberal voices in the 19th century included Jeremy BENTHAM, John Stuart MILL, Alexis de TOCQUEVILLE, and Thomas Hill Green.

In its full flower in the 19th century, liberalism stood for limited government and for free enterprise in the economy. In Britain the Liberal party, which espoused liberal doctrines, came into being (1846) under the leadership of Lord John Russell (later Earl Russell) and William GLADSTONE. In France, liberalism developed in opposition to the policies of the restored Bourbon kings and became a major force in the Third Republic; leading French liberals were Léon GAMBETTA and Georges CLEMENCEAU. In the United States the most characteristic representative of liberalism was Woodrow WILSON.

By the 20th century, political and economic thinking among liberals had started to shift in response to an expanding and complex economy. Liberals began to support the idea that the government can best promote individual dignity and freedom through intervention in the economy and by establishing a state concerned about the welfare of its people. With the rise of the WELFARE STATE, the new liberals also looked to government to correct some of the ills believed to be caused by unregulated capitalism. They favored TAXATION, MINIMUM WAGE legislation, SOCIAL SECURITY, ANTITRUST LAWS, public education, safety and health laws, and other measures to protect consumers and preserve the environment (see GOVERNMENT REGULATION).

liberation theology   Liberation theology, a term first used in 1973 by Gustavo Gutiérrez, a Peruvian Roman Catholic priest, is a school of thought among Latin American Catholics according to which the Gospel of Christ demands that the church concentrate its efforts on liberating the people of the world from poverty and oppression. Many Protestant churchmen and church bodies have adopted similar positions.

The liberation-theology movement was partly inspired by the Second Vatican Council and the 1967 papal encyclical *Populorum progressio*. Its leading exponents include Gutiérrez, Leonardo Boff of Brazil, and Juan Luis Segundo of Uruguay.

Liberia [ly-bir'-ee-uh]   The Republic of Liberia is located on the Atlantic coast of West Africa and is bordered by Sierra Leone, Guinea, and Ivory Coast. An independent nation since 1847, Liberia is the only nation in black Africa that was never under colonial rule. Partly settled by freed American slaves during the 19th century, Liberia long had close ties with the United States.

Land and Resources

Liberia's straight, sandy coast, 560 km (350 mi) long, is broken by lagoons and mangrove swamps and gives way to a low, rolling plain about 30 km (20 mi) wide. Further inland, foothills ranging in height from 200 to 300 m (600 to 1,000 ft) are found. They become mountains in the north and east. High plateaus are interspersed between the ranges. In the north is Mount Wutuvi, the highest point in the country, which rises to 1,381 m (4,531 ft). Liberian rivers are short, flowing from the mountains to the ocean.

Liberia's tropical climate is hot and humid. Average temperatures range from 17° C (63° F) to 31° C (87° F). Annual rainfall, as much as 4,500 mm (177 in) at the

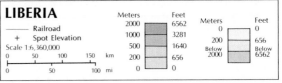

LIBERIA	Meters	Feet		Meters	Feet
—— Railroad	2000	6562		0	0
+ Spot Elevation	1000	3281			
Scale 1:6,360,000	500	1640		200	656
0 50 100 150 km	200	656		Below 2000	Below 6562
0 50 100 mi	0	0			

AT A GLANCE

REPUBLIC OF LIBERIA

Land: Area: 111,369 km² (43,000 mi²). Capital and largest city: Monrovia (1984 est. pop., 425,000).

People: Population (1990 est.): 2,639,809. Density: 23.7 persons per km² (61.4 per mi²). Distribution (1987): 42% urban, 58% rural. Official language: English. Major religions: traditional religions, Christianity, Isalm.

Government: Type: republic (rival governments proclaimed in 1990, none of which has effective control). Legislature: National Assembly (suspended). Political subdivisions: 13 counties.

Economy: GNP (1988): $988 million; $395 per capita. Labor distribution (1988): agriculture—71%; services—11%; industry and commerce—4%; other—14%. Foreign trade (1989): imports—$335 million; exports—$550 million. Currency: 1 Liberian dollar = 100 cents.

Education and Health: Literacy (1985): 35% of adult population. Universities (1990): 2. Hospital beds (1981): 3,000. Physicians (1983): 221. Life expectancy (1985–90): women—56; men—53. Infant mortality (1985–90): 87 per 1,000 live births.

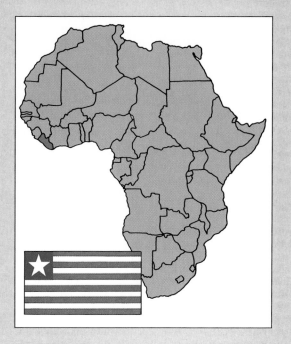

coast, gradually decreases inland to 1,750 mm (69 in). The monsoonal rainy season occurs between May and October. A dusty winter wind, the Harmattan, blows during December.

Liberia's vast timber resources include more than 90 commercially exploitable species. Mineral resources include substantial deposits of iron ore, diamonds, and gold.

People

The population consists of 16 indigenous ethnic groups, each with its own language, as well as the English-speaking Americo-Liberians. The largest groups are the Kpelle, the Bassa, and the Gio, Kru, Grebo, Mano, and Loma. The Americo-Liberians, who constitute only 5% of the population, are descendants of blacks who migrated to Liberia from the New World, mostly from the United States, between 1820 and 1865. They dominated Liberian society until the military coup of 1980. An earlier (1944) program of integration designed to reduce the imbalance had proved largely ineffective. After the coup, the government was dominated by the Krahn, allied with the Mandingo. After civil war began in late 1989, the army slaughtered many Gio and Mano, inflaming ethnic tensions. Liberia is officially Christian, but a majority practice traditional religions, and there is a Muslim minority.

Almost half of the urban population live in MONROVIA, the capital, which was badly damaged during the civil war. Earlier, Monrovia and mining centers in the interior experienced rapid growth due to internal migration from rural areas.

Education was formerly provided by Christian missions, but most schools are now government operated. Although education is free and compulsory from ages 6 to 16, fewer than half of all school-age children attend, partly because of a teacher shortage. The University of Liberia (1862) is in Monrovia.

Economic Activity

Most of Liberia's workers are engaged in subsistence agriculture. Commercial crops (most notably rubber) are grown primarily on plantations, which employ about half the wage earners. Fishing has always flourished along the coast, and mining and forestry are economically important. Iron ore replaced rubber as the leading export in 1961 and constituted about 57% of exports in 1987. Liberia also receives income from the registration of foreign ships, many of which fly the Liberian "flag of convenience" to avoid regulations and taxes. The industrial sector remains underdeveloped; machinery, transportation equipment, and food are imported.

Close economic relations are maintained with the United States. U.S. aid to Liberia totaled $500 million from 1980 to 1987—the largest amount per capita in sub-Saharan Africa—although economic mismanagement led to a subsequent reduction in assistance. Unable to pay its foreign debts for several years, Liberia was in a

A small clearing reveals workers' cottages on the 4,000-km² (1,500-mi²) rubber plantation leased by Harvey Samuel Firestone in 1926. Rubber is the chief agricultural product of Liberia and, together with iron ore, accounts for more than 75% of the country's exports.

state of virtual economic collapse by 1990 due to the civil war. Homes and businesses were destroyed, the planting and harvesting of crops were disrupted, and famine threatened much of the population.

History and Government

Liberia's tribal peoples migrated to the area between the 12th and 16th centuries. The Portuguese arrived in 1461 and began a trade in ivory and pepper, and later in slaves. In 1816 the AMERICAN COLONIZATION SOCIETY was founded in the United States to resettle former slaves in Africa. In 1820 the first colonists arrived, and their successful settlement was named Monrovia (for U.S. president James Monroe) in 1824. More colonists gradually arrived and established separate colonies. In 1847 the colonies amalgamated, and Liberia became the first independent republic in black Africa.

The new nation faced a variety of problems: resistance to the government by the indigenous tribes, decline in demand for Liberia's exports, and territorial encroachment by the British, French, and Germans. Liberia was able to maintain its independence only with U.S. support. In order to restore the languishing economy, a 99-year rubber-plantation concession was granted to the Firestone Company in 1926 in exchange for a large long-term loan from the U.S. government. After World War II, various development projects were constructed with U.S. financing. From 1878 to 1980, when the 1847 constitution was suspended after a military coup led by Sgt. Samuel K. DOE, politics were dominated by the Americo-

Liberian True Whig party. William V. S. TUBMAN served as president from 1944 until his death in 1971. His successor, William R. Tolbert, Jr., was killed in the 1980 coup. Liberian policies toward the United States and foreign business remained unchanged after the 1980 coup. In 1984 voters approved a new U.S.-style constitution. Doe remained head of the civilian government installed following elections in 1985 from which the main opposition parties were barred.

In December 1989, as political repression increased and the economy neared collapse, rebels launched a war against the Doe regime. Backers of rebel leader Charles Taylor and one of his allies, Prince Johnson, later split into rival factions. Taylor gained control of most of the countryside, while Johnson battled Doe's armed guard in Monrovia. In August 1990 a multinational West African force entered Liberia to try to end the bloody three-way civil war, which had caused at least 5,000 deaths (mostly among civilians as a result of tribal rivalries exacerbated by the war). Doe was killed by Johnson's forces on September 9, but a cease-fire accord was not reached until November 28. In early 1991 it was estimated that half of Liberia's population had become refugees (mostly in Guinea and Ivory Coast) or displaced persons. Prospects for a negotiated settlement remained dim.

Liberty Bell   The Liberty Bell is a pre–Revolutionary War relic that was first hung in 1753 in the newly finished Pennsylvania State House, the building that would eventually become Independence Hall. Cast in a London foundry, the bell was inscribed with the words *Proclaim Liberty throughout all the Land...* (Lev. 25:10). It was rung on the adoption of the Declaration of Independence in July 1776, inaugurating an Independence Day tradition that was observed until 1846. That year a small crack enlarged to the point where the bell could no longer be sounded. Perhaps the most famous symbol of the colonial struggle for independence, it is now housed in Philadelphia's Liberty Bell pavilion.

Liberty party   The first political party in U.S. history based exclusively on an antislavery platform, the Liberty party held its first convention in Albany, N.Y., on Apr. 1, 1840. James G. BIRNEY ran for the presidency on the Liberty party ticket in 1840 and 1844. The party was often strong enough in local elections to force major-party candidates to espouse abolitionism in order to win its backing. In 1848 it joined antislavery Whigs and Democrats in the new FREE-SOIL PARTY.

libido   see PSYCHOANALYSIS

Libra [leeb'-ruh]   Libra (the Balance), the seventh constellation of the ZODIAC, is located between Virgo and Scorpius and is best seen in the Northern Hemisphere in spring. The Sun passes southeastward through Libra from about October 24 to November 22, during its sojourn south of the celestial equator. Among Libra's stars are three binaries: the two stars of Alpha Librae are just barely resolvable to the naked eye; Beta Librae, with the unusual color of green, is a spectroscopic binary; and Delta Librae is an eclipsing binary.

library The library is a place where books, journals, microfilms, audio and visual materials, and computer data and terminals are kept and organized to support the cultural, informational, recreational, and educational needs of the general public or specific groups of users. Recent advances in computer and communication technologies have transformed the contemporary library: it is not only a repository but now also an active member in a vast network of libraries and databanks through which users have access to a worldwide store of recorded knowledge.

The most common kinds of libraries are public libraries and those of schools, colleges and universities, and government. Many specialized libraries also serve industry, commerce, the media, and the professions. In the United States and Canada alone more than 135,000 libraries exist, ranging in size from the LIBRARY OF CONGRESS to the smallest elementary school facilities. Currently American libraries face severe financial hardship from cutbacks in public funding and government support, escalating costs of materials and equipment, and a growing dependence on initially expensive technologies.

Classification Systems and the Catalog. Library classification systems permit users to look for a particular book by title or author or to discover what books on a particular subject are held by the library. Most libraries use one of three major classification systems: the Dewey Decimal System, invented by Melvil DEWEY; the Universal Decimal Classification, a European adaptation of Dewey; or a system developed by the Library of Congress.

The library's own catalog—either manual or electronic—is only one of the many forms in which bibliographic materials are available. Large libraries own the *Nation-*

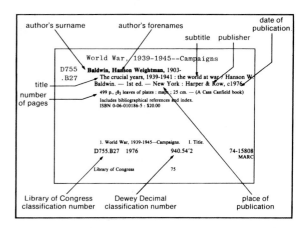

A subject card from the card catalog details information about a book in the listed subject area and provides the classification code that locates it in the library's collection. An up-to-date catalog is essential to efficient use of a library's resources.

The library of the University of Leiden, the Netherlands's oldest university, is portrayed in this Dutch engraving (1610). The upheavals of the Reformation led to the founding of many Protestant centers of learning, including university and town libraries, to replace monastic centers of learning.

Rare-book collections are housed in such diverse settings as Yale University's Beinicke Library (far right), *designed (1963) by Gordon Bunshaft, and the East Room of the Pierpont Morgan Library* (right), *New York City.*

Duke Humphrey's Library, founded by the Duke of Gloucester in 1489, is part of Oxford University's Bodleian Library.

(Below) *The reference desk of a public library provides professional assistance in locating information. Since the opening (1830s) of the first tax-supported library in the United States, public libraries have proliferated.*

al Union Catalog, for example—a cumulative listing of the resources of the Library of Congress and other major and specialized libraries in the United States and Canada—or can tap into it electronically. Libraries also may own or subscribe to such specialized catalogs as the *Eighteenth Century Short Title Catalog* (ESTC), a computerized database listing every publication—book, pamphlet, or single sheet—printed between 1701 and 1800 in English.

History. The earliest ancient libraries were clay-tablet repositories in ancient Mesopotamia. Ashurbanipal's library in Nineveh (7th century BC), for instance, consisted of thousands of inscribed clay tablets recording laws, astronomical data, commercial transactions, narrative poems, and royal happenings. The earliest large Greek library is attributed to Aristotle (4th century BC), but the greatest was established (3d century BC) by Ptolemy I in

the museum at Alexandria, Egypt. Scholars there copied, revised, collated, and edited works of the classical Greek writers. Their copies of ancient works became the standard editions on which other ancient copyists and libraries depended and, ultimately, the basis of most of the manuscripts in European libraries. The library flourished for several centuries and held about 500,000 papyrus scrolls.

Libraries in the Middle Ages were established in monasteries throughout Europe and in cathedrals that served as links between the monasteries and universities. Manuscripts were laboriously copied by hand on parchment pages that were assembled into woodbound codices (see BOOK).

In the Muslim world, Damascus, Baghdad, and many other cities had libraries, but most were destroyed by the 13th century. In China the first libraries were established

The John F. Kennedy Library in Dorchester, Mass., overlooking Boston Harbor, contains an extensive collection of tapes, documents, and studies concerning the late president's political career. This specialized library, designed by I. M. Pei, was dedicated in October 1979.

under the Chin dynasty (221–206 BC), when one copy of every book in the empire was placed in an imperial library and all other copies were burned. In the 1st century AD the Han-dynasty Imperial Library owned 677 works, of which 47 survive. The Sui-dynasty library (7th century AD) had over 5,000 titles and divided its holdings into four categories: Confucian classics, philosophy, history, and belles lettres.

In Europe the advent of printing in the 15th century brought down the cost of books. Private libraries became more common, and by the 17th century a few public libraries had come into being. Thereafter the number of libraries multiplied. Users remained few, however, until literacy became more widespread during the 18th century.

In the 17th century France's national library, the BIBLIOTHÈQUE NATIONALE, was founded in Paris. The British Library, originally a part of the BRITISH MUSEUM, was set up during the 18th century. The first academic library in the United States was established by John Harvard at Harvard College in 1638. In 1731, Benjamin Franklin founded the Library Company of Philadelphia, the first subscription library in America. The first U.S. public library was opened in Salisbury, Conn., in 1803 from a gift of 150 books by a resident.

Most countries have now established their own national libraries, but their oldest university libraries often have richer collections of rare materials. Harvard and Yale in the United States and Oxford (the BODLEIAN LIBRARY) and Cambridge in England are famous for their bibliographical treasures. Government libraries for the most part date from the 19th and 20th centuries; the great public libraries—those of New York, Boston, Philadelphia, Chicago—though older, did not develop into anything even approaching their present size until late in the 19th century.

Both public and private libraries have benefited from the generosity of individuals such as Andrew CARNEGIE, who helped establish more than 2,000 public libraries.

Notable private foundations in the United States include the FOLGER SHAKESPEARE LIBRARY, the Morgan Library, the Huntington Library, and the Newberry Library. In Europe, private collections such as the Ambrosian Library in Milan or the Laurentian Library in Florence can trace their origins to the Middle Ages or Renaissance.

Two national libraries, one in Beijing (People's Republic of China) and the other in Taipei (Taiwan), opened their new buildings in 1987 and 1988, respectively. The Beijing library is among the largest in the world, with holdings of 14 million items. The world's largest is the U.S. Library of Congress, with more than 88 million items in 1988, including 14.5 million books and 36.5 million manuscripts.

A librarian assists a student in the use of a microfilm reader. Such technological advances as microforms, which contain data on film, and computerized collections have greatly expanded the materials available to public libraries.

Library Trends. The trend of library policy is clearly toward the ideal of making all information available inexpensively and quickly to everyone. Because of the information explosion and the issues raised by the control, manipulation, encryption, and preservation of knowledge, accomplishment of this goal is difficult. For example, PAPER decay has plagued libraries for years. Microfilm copying was adopted as a makeshift way of maintaining decipherability, but now stress is being placed on conservation techniques to stem the decay of the volumes themselves. The problem of preserving not just the physical media (books, journals, film, and so on) but the transient information embodied in electronic form must now also be faced.

Library of Congress

The Library of Congress was created in 1800 to provide "such books as may be necessary for the use of Congress." Over the succeeding years it has grown to become the national library of the United States, serving all government branches and the public at large. Since the 1870s it has also administered the American copyright system. It publishes the *National Union Catalog*—a cumulative record of the books housed in 2,500 libraries in the United States and Canada—which serves as a basic bibliographic and catalog source (see LIBRARY), prints and distributes cataloging data for subscriber libraries, and has developed and popularized a system of subject classification. The library's Congressional Research Service prepares reports on any topic at the request of congressmen.

The library's collections contain more than 14 million books and 36 million manuscripts, including the personal papers of most U.S. presidents up to Calvin Coolidge. It also holds maps, music, art prints, photographs, motion pictures, videotapes, newspapers, pamphlets, recordings, and other materials—for a total of 88 million items. It receives a copy of every book copyrighted in the United States. The American Folklife Center, administered by the library, collects and preserves American folklore; it supports research projects and presents performances and exhibitions of folk music, arts, and crafts.

The library was originally housed in the Capitol; most of its books were destroyed when the British shelled the building during the War of 1812. The major step in rebuilding the collection was taken in 1815, when Congress purchased the 6,000-volume personal library of Thomas Jefferson. The main Library of Congress building was erected in 1897; the library also occupies the Thomas Jefferson building, formerly called the annex, and the new James Madison building. Recent Librarians of Congress include Archibald MacLeish (1939–44), L. Quincy Mumford (1954–74), Daniel J. Boorstin (1974–87), and James H. Billington (1987–).

The vast collection of the Library of Congress, the national library of the United States, includes all printed material subject to U.S. copyright laws, as well as recordings, artwork, and rare books and manuscripts.

libration

[ly-bray'-shun] A libration is a vibration around some equilibrium position (originally applied to a measuring balance). The word is often used in astronomy, as in the librations of the Trojan asteroids around their triangular equilibrium positions in the Sun-Jupiter-asteroid system (see THREE-BODY PROBLEM). For librations of the Moon, see MOON.

libretto

[lib-ret'-oh] A libretto (literally, "little book") is the text of an opera, operetta, or oratorio. (The libretto of a musical comedy is usually called the "book".) The author of a libretto often works in conjunction with the composer, as in the famous collaborations of Mozart and Lorenzo DA PONTE, Verdi and Arrigo Boito, Richard Strauss and Hugo von HOFMANNSTHAL, and GILBERT AND SULLIVAN. Some librettos have been set by more than one composer; some composers, such as Wagner, have written their own librettos to achieve a closer marriage of text and music.

Libreville

[lee-bruh-veel'] Libreville, the capital city of Gabon, lies on the Gabon Estuary, near the Gulf of Guinea. It has a population of 352,000 (1987 est.). The city is primarily an administrative center, but lumber, rubber, cacao, and palm products are shipped from its sheltered port, and an international airport is located 11 km (7 mi) north. It is the site of the National University of Gabon (1970). Settled by the Pongoue people in the 16th century, Libreville was colonized by the French in 1849, who settled freed slaves there.

POPULAR SOCIALIST LIBYAN ARAB JAMAHIRIYA

Land: Area: 1,759,540 km² (679,362 mi²). Capital and largest city: Tripoli (1988 pop., 1,083,000).

People: Population (1990 est.): 4,221,141. Density: 2.3 persons per km² (6 per mi²). Distribution (1985): 65% urban, 35% rural. Official language: Arabic. Major religion: Islam.

Government: Type: socialist state. Legislature: General People's Congress. Political subdivisions: 46 municipalities.

Economy: GNP (1988 est.): $20 billion; $5,410 per capita. Labor distribution (1985): construction—24%; services—17%; agriculture—17%; manufacturing—11%; transportation and communications—9%. Foreign trade (1988): imports—$5.0 billion; exports—$6.6 billion. Currency: 1 Libyan dinar = 1,000 dirhans.

Education and Health: Literacy (1985): 74% of adult population. Universities (1990): 3. Hospital beds (1985): 20,000. Physicians (1985): 5,450. Life expectancy (1990): women—70; men—65. Infant mortality (1990): 64 per 1,000 live births.

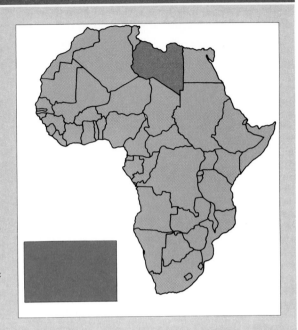

Libya [lib'-ee-uh]   Libya, a petroleum-rich Arab nation located in North Africa, is Africa's fourth largest country. After centuries of rule by Ottoman Turks, three decades as an Italian colonial possession, and post–World War II combined British and French administration, Libya gained independence in 1951 as the United Kingdom of Libya. In 1969, Col. Muammar al-QADDAFI led a military coup that ended the monarchy and proclaimed the Libyan Arab Republic. In 1977 its name was changed to the Popular Socialist Libyan Arab Jamahiriya (*Jamahiriya* means "state of the masses"). The Mediterranean Sea lies to the north, Egypt and Sudan to the east, Tunisia and Algeria to the west, and Chad and Niger to the south. Tripoli, on the Mediterranean coast, is the capital.

Land and Resources

The northwest region borders the Mediterranean Sea and rises southward in a series of steps from a narrow, often marshy, coastal plain to the Jaffara Plain and the shrub-covered plateau of Jabal Nafusah. The northeastern region, east of the Gulf of Sidra on the Mediterranean, rises southward from the narrow al Marj plain near the sea to the tree-covered slopes of the Jabal al Akhdar, or Green Mountains. To the south, covering more than 90% of the nation, stretch the semiarid and desert lands that are part of the SAHARA. Elevations range from below sea level in the northeast to 2,286 m (7,500 ft) in Bette Peak, Libya's highest point, near the border with Chad. Al-Kufrah,

Ghat, and Ghudamis, three of the large oases, are located in depressions where groundwater reaches the surface or where the drilling of wells is feasible.

Climate. Some areas along the coast have a Mediterranean climate with moderate temperatures and enough rain during the winter months for grain farming. In Tripoli average temperatures are 30° C (86° F) in summer and 8° C (46° F) in winter; annual precipitation averages 380 mm (15 in) and falls mainly in winter. Semiarid conditions predominate in the al Marj and Jaffara plains, and in the southern deserts frequent periods of drought occur. A scorching wind called the *ghibli* occasionally blows into the usually humid coastal towns.

Resources. Libya has no perennial rivers and is drained by intermittent water courses (wadis) that flow only after heavy rains. Most water is obtained from shallow wells that tap vast underground artesian aquifers (water-bearing rock layers). Only the Jabal al Akhdar, covering about 1% of the country, is forested. Steppe vegetation, including esparto and other short grasses, is characteristic of northern semiarid areas, and xerophytic, or drought-resistant, vegetation predominates in desert areas. Petroleum and natural gas constitute the principal mineral resources; iron ore and potash deposits are also present.

People

About 90% of Libya's population belong to the Arabic-speaking majority of mixed Arab-Berber ancestry. True BERBERS, who retain the Berber language and customs, are the largest non-Arab minority. Other minorities are the Arabic-speaking Harratin, of Negroid and West African ancestry and the Berber-related TUAREG and Tebu in the south. The Sunni branch of Islam is the official religion.

The Mediterranean coastal areas contain 90% of the population; other areas are only sparsely settled or uninhabited. TRIPOLI and BENGHAZI are the largest cities. About 20% of the population are nomadic, particularly in the east. Although population growth is rapid, Libya's development programs are hindered by a serious labor shortage; about 30% of the labor force is composed of foreigners. Primary education for children between the ages of 6 and 12 is compulsory. Libya's petroleum revenues have been used in part to finance construction of schools, hospitals, and clinics. The University of Garyounis (1955) in Benghazi and Tripoli's Alfateh University (1973) are among the higher-education institutes.

Economic Activity

Petroleum was discovered in 1959 and has since financed the transformation of Libya from a poor nation at the time of independence to a rich one that spends vast sums on social, agricultural, and military development. In 1987, Libya ranked 16th among world petroleum producers, with a governmentally regulated output of about 1.05 million barrels per day.

Manufacturing and other private-sector economic activities have been nationalized. The construction, food-processing, textile, petrochemical, and tanning industries, along with the production of traditional handicrafts, are the leading industrial activities. Land suitable for agriculture, located mainly in the coastal regions, constitutes less than 6% of the total area. Wheat, olives, and fruits and vegetables are the major crops. Livestock raising is the chief economic activity of the nomadic population. Libya remains dependent on imported foods. The drop in world oil prices in the 1980s forced Libya to scale back many development plans. In 1984, however, Qaddafi inaugurated the construction of a great artificial river to transport water from aquifers beneath the Libyan Desert to coastal cities.

A modern highway network connects the coastal towns with the desert oases and petroleum fields. Petroleum accounts for more than 95% of all export income, although the petroleum industry employs less than 10% of the labor force. The value of petroleum exports far ex-

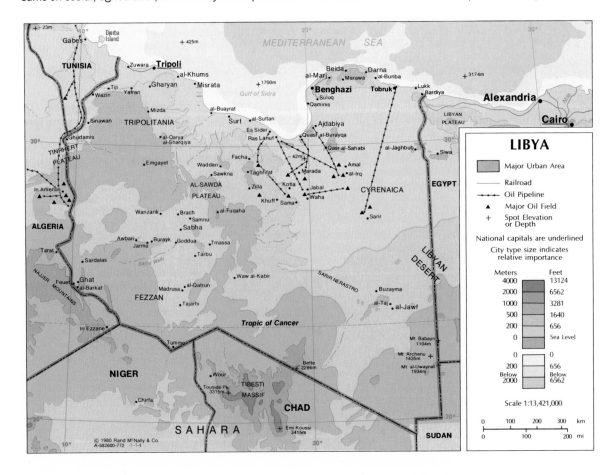

High-grade Libyan petroleum from the nation's interior is conveyed through pipelines to the Mediterranean coast for shipment to Western Europe and the United States. Libyan petroleum is particularly valued for its low sulfur content.

ceeds that of imports, dominated by machinery, foodstuffs, and armaments.

Government

Qaddafi has tried to transform Libya into an egalitarian, socialist state of the masses. In theory, there is no formal government. According to the 1977 constitution, the masses rule themselves through a network of people's committees that control virtually all governmental and nongovernmental activities. The highest of these bodies is the General People's Congress (GPC). Qaddafi, Libya's "Revolutionary Leader," has held no formal office since he resigned as head of the GPC in 1979.

History

Phoenicians, Greeks, and Romans established colonies in the area of present-day Libya. Arab domination began in the 7th century. In 1510, Spain conquered Tripoli and ruled until 1551, when Turkish forces made Libya part of the OTTOMAN EMPIRE. In 1711 the area became virtually autonomous and enjoyed 125 years of prosperity based on piracy directed by the Karamanli family; Ottoman rule was reasserted in 1835, however. In 1911, Italy declared war on Turkey (see ITALO-TURKISH WAR) and annexed Libya, making it a colony in 1934.

Italian settlement was opposed by the nationalist Sanusi (conservative Sunni Muslims; see SANUSI, AL-), whose leaders returned from exile to fight alongside the Allies and drive Italian and German forces out of Libya during World War II. After the war Libya was placed under British and French administration. Italy gave up attempts to regain control in 1947, and the United Nations granted Libya independence effective in 1951 as the United Kingdom of Libya; the Sanusi leader Muhammad Idris of Cyrenaica became King IDRIS.

In 1969, Idris was deposed, and Qaddafi and the Revolutionary Command Council seized power. Qaddafi, known for his radical Arab nationalism, has been a persistent foe of Israel and has attempted unsuccessfully to merge Libya with Egypt, Syria, Sudan, Tunisia, Chad, Morocco, and Algeria. Qaddafi has been accused of interfering in the internal affairs of a number of African states, most notably Chad. Qaddafi's activities also led to conflicts with the United States, France, and Great Britain. After U.S. air attacks on Libyan targets in 1986 in retaliation for his support of international terrorism, government agencies were moved from Tripoli to remote villages. Qaddafi survived coup attempts in 1970, 1975, and 1984. He released many political prisoners and moderated some of his economic policies in 1988. But popular discontent again mounted after the United Nations banned arms sales and airline flights to Libya in April 1992 when Qaddafi refused to turn over two Libyan security agents accused of involvement in the 1988 downing of Pan Am flight 103 over Lockerbie, Scotland, for trial outside Libya.

Libyan Desert   The Libyan Desert, the northeastern portion of the SAHARA, is located in northwestern Sudan, western Egypt, and eastern Libya. It covers about 1,950,000 km^2 (750,000 mi^2). Elevations vary from 133 m (436 ft) below sea level at the QATTARA DEPRESSION in northern Egypt, to 1,934 m (6,345 ft) at Jabal al-Uwaynat, where the three countries meet. The terrain is composed of sand-free, rocky plateaus and plains covered with sand dunes or gravel. The annual rainfall is less than 125 mm (5 in), and summer temperatures rise above 43° C (100° F). A few Berbers and Arabs live in the scattered oases, raising fruits and livestock. Potash, coal, salt, gypsum, and petroleum are extracted. The Egyptian portion of the desert was the scene of important battles during World War II.

---

lice   see LOUSE

---

lichen [ly'-kuhn]   Lichens are dual organisms composed of an alga and a fungus. The body, or thallus, of the lichen consists of algal cells mixed among the threadlike hyphae of the fungus; there are no true leaves, stems, or roots. The alga and the fungus live associated in a dependent symbiotic, or mutualistic, relationship; that is, they typically require each other to survive. Lichens are classified on the basis of the fungal component. The fungi are either Ascomycetes (sac fungi), Basidiomycetes (bracket fungi), or Deuteromycetes (fungi imperfecti). The algae are either green (Chlorophyta), blue-green (Cyanophyta), or yellow-green (Xanthophyta). Most lichens are composed of green algae and ascomycete fungi.

Lichens appear in a wide variety of habitats, including dry deserts, moist woods, mountaintops, under the soil, and in the ocean. They may be crustose (firmly attached to and encrusted on some surface); fruticose (projected out in upright, branched, or hanging stalks); or foliose (assuming leaflike shapes). Lichens are slow-growing, some enlarging as little as 1 mm (0.04 in) per year, and are generally long-lived, with some Arctic lichens claimed to be 4,000 years old. Lichens play a role in the establishment of plant colonies on bare areas by accumulating soil debris beneath them and by limiting rock disintegration, which aid in soil formation.

The alga manufactures and provides itself and the fungus with a carbohydrate, either a simple sugar, such as glucose, or a sugar alcohol, such as sorbitol; the fungus converts the carbohydrate into a sugar alcohol, mannitol, which may serve as a storage food. The alga also provides such vitamins as biotin and thiamine. Blue-green algae, in addition, are able to obtain, or fix, nitrogen from the air, which is also passed to the fungus. In turn, the fungus provides the alga with certain physical protection and obtains water vapor from the air, providing moisture for the alga. Few of the lichenized fungi or algae can survive alone; the green alga *Trebouxia*, found in about half of all lichen species, has never been found in the free-living state.

Reproduction occurs in several ways. The alga or fungus may reproduce separately, in a manner identical to free-living forms. The alga commonly does this by reproducing asexually within the lichen thallus. The lichen as a whole may reproduce vegetatively by fragmentation or by various special algal-fungal combinations, such as soredia and isidia. A soredium is a package of one or more algal cells and some fungal hyphae, which are commonly released in great numbers through openings in the surface of the thallus. The isidium is a small projection from the surface of the thallus containing algal cells; it may break off and reproduce vegetatively.

Lichens of the genus *Cladonia*, known as reindeer moss, are a staple of caribou diet in North America. Old-man's beard, *Usnea*, grows in long, gray green streamers from branches in moist northern woods. Dyes and medicinal substances are extracted from lichens, but only the dye orchil, which is used as a food colorant and the source of litmus (a pH indicator), is commercially important.

Lichtenstein, Roy [lik'-ten-steen]

Roy Lichtenstein, b. New York City, Oct. 27, 1923, is a pop artist well known for his painted enlargements of banal comic strips (see POP ART). After studying and teaching at Ohio State University, Lichtenstein taught (1960–63) at Rutgers University and held his first one-man show in New York City in 1962. Comic-strip paintings such as *Whaam* (1963; Tate Gallery, London) humorously transpose the simplified violence and sentimentality of popular culture into huge, almost abstract, images. More recently, Lichtenstein has applied his distinctive style of dots and lines

In Okay, Hot-Shot *(1963) and other comic-strip "frames" from the 1960s, the American Pop painter Roy Lichtenstein conveys a double irony: slick images, like the output of commercial printing presses, are produced using intricate hand techniques; dialogue balloons contain cryptic comments on popular culture. (Collection R. Morone, Turin.)*

to adaptations of works by modern masters such as Pablo Picasso, and has produced sculptural parodies of the decorative styles of the 1920s and '30s.

Lick Observatory

Lick Observatory, constructed through a gift from James Lick and opened in 1888, is situated on the peak of Mount Hamilton (elevation: 1,283 m/4,200 ft), 65 km (40 mi) from Santa Cruz, Calif. The main building houses the 36-in (91-cm) and 12-in (30-cm) refractors. (The first, built by Alvin Clark and installed in 1888, is the second largest refractor in the world.) Separate domes house the 36-in (91-cm) Crossley reflector, the 22-in (56-cm) Tauchman reflector, the 20-in (51-cm) Carnegie double astrograph, the 24-in (61-cm) reflector, and the 120-in (305-cm) Shane reflector. The observatory headquarters is located at the University of California at Santa Cruz.

licorice [lik'-uh-rish]

The word licorice refers both to the perennial herb *Glycyrrhiza glabra* of the legume fami-

Licorice, a Mediterranean herb, is related to the pea. Its root contains a substance that is 150 times sweeter than table sugar. Licorice-root extracts are used to flavor food, beverages, tobacco, and drugs such as cough syrup.

ly and to the flavoring produced from its roots. The plant grows to a height of about 1 m (3 ft) and has pealike blue flowers, flat pods (legumes), and long, soft, flexible roots that are bright yellow inside. The roots are crushed, ground, and boiled to extract the juice, which is then thickened to produce hard black sticks of paste known as black sugar. The bittersweet flavoring is used in candy and tobacco, as a soothing ingredient in cough lozenges and syrups, as a laxative, and in the manufacture of shoe polish. Spain is the largest producer of licorice, but the plant is grown throughout the Mediterranean area, in parts of Asia, and in California and Louisiana. A wild species, *G. lepidota*, is native to North America.

Lidice [lid'-yit-seh]   Lidice (est. pop., 500) is a coal-mining village in Bohemia, northwest Czechoslovakia. On June 10, 1942, German soldiers killed the adult male population, deported the women and children, and razed the village in retaliation for the assassination of Reinhard Heydrich, German administrator of Moravia and Bohemia. A new village was established in 1947 near the original site, which is now a national monument.

Lie, Trygve Halvdan [lee, troog'-veh hahlv'-dahn]   The Norwegian statesman Trygve Halvdan Lie, b. July 16, 1896, d. Dec. 30, 1968, became the first secretary-general of the United Nations. National secretary of the Norwegian Labor party from 1926 to 1946, he became minister of justice in 1935. During World War II he served in London as foreign minister for the Norwegian government in exile.

Lie attended the San Francisco conference that drafted the UN charter in 1945. The following year he was elected secretary-general of the new organization. Lie believed that UN membership should be universal and urged in 1950 that Communist China be admitted. That same year he condemned North Korean aggression against South Korea, and the Security Council voted to intervene in the Korean War. In 1953, Dag HAMMARSKJÖLD was elected to succeed Lie in the United Nations.

lie detector   *Lie detector* is the common name for the polygraph, an instrument used to record certain physiological changes that take place in response to questioning; these changes presumably indicate the truthfulness of the statements made by the person being questioned. The reliability of polygraphy depends heavily on the skill of the polygraph operator.

Attempts to correlate blood pressure and respiration rate with lying had been made since the late 19th century. The first practical polygraph was devised (1921) by John A. Larson, a medical student at the University of California. His instrument gave a continuous recording of blood pressure and respiration. Later, a technique was developed for measuring stress-induced variations in the electrical conductivity of the skin (galvanic skin reflex, or GSR).

Polygraph use has given rise to important civil-liberties

and legal questions—as well as the continuing question of reliability. In 1988, Congress prohibited private businesses from requiring workers and job applicants to take lie-detector tests, with some exceptions. The law banning polygraphs does not apply to federal, state, or local governments. Courts of law generally deny the admissibility of polygraph evidence except when agreed to by both defense and prosecution with the judge's concurrence.

Liebermann, Max [lee'-bur-mahn, mahks]   Considered the outstanding representative of German impressionist painting, Max Liebermann, b. July 20, 1847, d. Feb. 8, 1935, chose his subjects from the everyday world about him. He seems to have been more influenced by Dutch genre painting and the Barbizon school than by the French impressionists. His work shows little of the French interest in light and atmosphere, being more concerned with the depiction of the lives of the humble. Liebermann taught at the Berlin Academy and later became its president. His basic antagonism to academic art, however, led him to serve as the first president (1898–1911) of the Berlin Secession, a group of progressive artists. After the Nazis rose to power, he was forbidden, as a Jewish artist, to paint or to exhibit.

Liebig, Justus, Baron von [lee'-bik, yus'-tus]   Justus Liebig, b. May 12, 1803, d. Apr. 18, 1873, was a German chemist whose chief contributions were in the relatively new field of organic chemistry. They included the analysis and the establishment of the empirical formulas of many organic compounds, the discovery of new compounds, the theory of chemical RADICALS, the hydrogen theory of acids, and contributions to agricultural and physiological chemistry. Liebig became a full professor at the University of Giessen at the age of 23, and for the next 28 years the chemistry department there was famous throughout the world. Many of his students, such as August von HOFMANN, Friedrich KEKULÉ, and Charles Adolphe Wurtz, also became famous chemists.

Liebknecht (family) [leeb'-knekt]   The Liebknecht family played a prominent role in the development of German socialism in the late 19th and early 20th centuries. **Wilhelm Liebknecht**, b. Mar. 29, 1826, d. Aug. 7, 1900, took part in the Revolutions of 1848 and in 1869 formed a Marxian German socialist party with August BEBEL. This group subsequently merged (1875) with Ferdinand LASSALLE's party to form the Socialist Workers party. Elected to the Reichstag in 1874, Liebknecht was prominent in the Socialist INTERNATIONAL and edited the chief German Socialist newspaper, *Vorwärts*.

Karl Liebknecht, b. Aug. 13, 1871, d. Jan. 15, 1919, was Wilhelm's son. Elected to the Reichstag in 1912, he founded (1916) the radical Spartacist League with Rosa LUXEMBURG. In January 1919 the Spartacists—renamed the Communist party—attempted an uprising. Liebknecht and Luxemburg were arrested and murdered.

Liebling, A. J. [leeb'-ling] The American journalist Abbott Joseph Liebling, b. New York City, Oct. 18, 1904, d. Dec. 28, 1963, is remembered for his acerbic criticism of the press. His best criticism is collected in *The Wayward Pressman* (1947)—which also includes autobiographical accounts of his days as a journalist—and *The Press* (1961). Both contain many of his *New Yorker* articles. Other books include *The Earl of Louisiana* (1961), a portrait of Gov. Earl Long, and *The Most of A. J. Liebling* (1963).

Liechtenstein [lik'-ten-shtine] The Principality of Liechtenstein is in western Europe, bordered on the south and west by Switzerland and on the east by Austria. The country is approximately equal in size to Washington, D.C. The upper Rhine River flows along most of Liechtenstein's western border. The country maintains close relations with Switzerland, sharing customs, currency, and postal systems. This practice has enabled Liechtenstein to share in Switzerland's prosperity and, along with Liechtenstein's own industrial development, gives its citizens one of the world's highest per capita incomes.

Land and People

Liechtenstein is divided into two traditional regions, the Upper and Lower Country. The western portion, the Lower Country, is the flat plain of the Rhine. Most of Liechtenstein, however, is the mountainous Upper Country,

where the Alpine ranges run east-west. The highest point in the country is Vorder-Grauspitz (2,599 m/8,527 ft), in the south. Liechtenstein's 40 km² (16 mi²) of remaining forests are protected in preserves. Annual rainfall varies according to elevation, from an average of about 1,000 mm (40 in) in the lowlands to about 1,980 mm (78 in) in

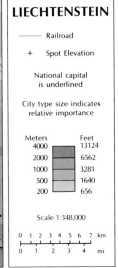

LIECHTENSTEIN

——— Railroad

+   Spot Elevation

National capital is underlined

City type size indicates relative importance

Meters	Feet
4000	13124
2000	6562
1000	3281
500	1640
200	656

Scale 1:348,000

0 1 2 3 4 5 6 7 km
0 1 2 3 4 mi

AT A GLANCE

PRINCIPALITY OF LIECHTENSTEIN

Land: Area: 160 km² (62 mi²). Capital and largest city: Vaduz (1990 est. pop., 4,874).

People: Population (1990 est.): 28,700. Density: 179 persons per km² (464 per mi²). Distribution (1984): 75% urban, 25% rural. Official language: German. Major religions: Roman Catholicism, Protestantism.

Government: Type: constitutional monarchy. Legislature: Diet (Landtag). Political subdivisions: 11 communes.

Economy: GNP (1987): $580 million; $21,000 per capita. Labor distribution (1988): manufacturing—33.8%; agriculture—2.5%; services—26.8%; trade—11.8%; construction—8.3%; other—16.8%. Foreign trade: imports (1987)—$330 million; exports (1988)—$1,216 million. Currency: 1 Swiss franc = 100 centimes.

Education and Health: Literacy (1990): 100% of adult population. Universities (1990): none. Hospital beds (1985): 100. Physicians (1987): 29. Life expectancy (1990): women—81; men—73. Infant mortality (1990): 5 per 1,000 live births.

Vaduz, the capital of Liechtenstein, is situated on the Rhine River floodplain at the foot of the central Alps. The castle of Vaduz, which serves as residence of Liechtenstein's prince, overlooks the town.

the mountains. Temperatures are mild—about –1° C (30° F) in January and 19° C (66° F) in July.

A homogeneous population, the residents speak Alemannish, a local dialect of German. The population is 90% Roman Catholic. Almost the entire population lives in the communities near the Rhine, with 20% of the total in VADUZ, the capital and largest city. Because of the employment opportunities in Liechtenstein, about one-third of the population is composed of resident foreigners. Liechtenstein's official literacy rate of 100% can be credited to its well-developed system of primary and secondary schools.

Economic Activity

Until the end of World War II, the economy of Liechtenstein was agricultural, but since 1945 an economic revolution has occurred. Today only a small percentage of the population are engaged in agriculture, specializing in dairying and stock breeding. Liechtenstein has a diversified industrial base, including the manufacture of machines and industrial equipment, precision instruments, dental supplies, textiles, ceramics, pharmaceuticals, and processed foods. More than 25,000 foreign businesses and banks have established nominal headquarters in Liechtenstein because of favorable tax policies. Tourism is important, especially during the winter skiing season.

Liechtenstein's postage stamps, sold to collectors, are a lucrative source of income.

History and Government

Once part of the Roman province of Rhaetia, the area was occupied by the Alemanni tribe during the 6th century. After 1396, Liechtenstein was an autonomous fief of the Holy Roman Empire, and in 1719 the independent principality was established. Between 1815 and 1866 it was a member of the German Confederation. Liechtenstein maintained close ties with Austria-Hungary until 1918 and since then has developed close ties with Switzerland, with whom it formed an economically important customs union in 1923.

According to the 1921 constitution, Liechtenstein is a constitutional monarchy, hereditary in the male line. Prince Hans Adam succeeded to the throne in 1989 on the death of his father, Francis Joseph II. A 5-member government is appointed by the prince on the recommendation of the Landtag (parliament), whose 25 members are elected every 4 years by direct universal suffrage; women won the right to vote in 1984. Liechtenstein's foreign affairs are handled by Switzerland.

Lieder   see SONG

Liège [lee-ezh']   Liège (Flemish: Luik), the capital of Liège province in eastern Belgium, is situated at the confluence of the Meuse and Ourthe rivers, about 100 km (60 mi) east of Brussels. The population is 200,312 (1988 est.). Home of the greatest concentration of French-speaking Belgians (Walloons), Liège is the cultural center of the region and has produced movements in defense of Walloon rights.

Linked by the Albert Canal with Antwerp, Liège is the third largest river port in Europe. Located in the center of Belgium's coal-mining region, Liège also produces steel, transportation equipment, chemicals, rubber, textiles, and glass. The University of Liège (1817) is located there.

Liège was ruled by prince-bishops from the 7th century until 1792, when French Revolutionary forces took the city. Liège suffered severe damage during both world wars.

lien [leen]   A lien is a claim on real or personal property used as security for a debt or other legal obligation. The possessor of a lien who properly records it in the appropriate public office is known as a secured creditor. Such a person has priority over general (or unsecured) creditors and is entitled to satisfy his or her claim regarding an unpaid debt from the sale of the secured property.

Liens are characterized as either general or particular. A general lien secures the creditor for all claims against the debtor. A specific lien secures a creditor only for claims arising from a particular transaction affecting a specific piece of property. Liens can be created by agreement, as with a MORTGAGE, or by operation of law. An example of the latter is the mechanic's lien, which gives a builder or contractor a claim on the property—both building and land—as security for payment for labor and materials.

Lifar, Serge [lee-fahr', sir-gay']   One of Serge DI-AGHILEV's later discoveries, Serge Lifar, b. Kiev, Russia, Apr. 2 (N.S.), 1905, d. Dec. 15, 1986, went on from his days as a star of the BALLETS RUSSES DE SERGE DIAGHILEV to help revitalize French dance through his leadership at the Paris Opéra. There he staged and danced in classics, such as *Giselle*, and choreographed and danced in original works, such as *Prométhée* (1929). From 1945 to 1947 he served as artistic director of the Nouveau Ballet de Monte Carlo. Lifar returned to the Paris Opéra from 1947 to 1958. In 1947 he founded the Institut Choréographique in Paris, called the Université de la Danse since 1957.

Life   A pioneer in American PHOTOJOURNALISM, *Life* magazine aimed, in the words of publisher Henry R. LUCE, "to see life; to see the world; to eyewitness great events." Originally published in 1883 as a magazine devoted to social satire, *Life* became a pictorial weekly when Luce purchased it in 1935. Outstanding staff photographers included Margaret BOURKE-WHITE, Robert CAPA, Alfred EISENSTAEDT, and W. Eugene Smith. The magazine broke circulation records in the 1960s, then declined and was forced to stop publishing in 1972 when advertisers shifted to television. Success of occasional special issues led to *Life*'s rebirth as a monthly in 1978.

---

life, extraterrestrial   The term *extraterrestrial life* encompasses all life, ranging from the lowest possible forms to those with suprahuman intelligences, that may exist beyond the Earth. In the most general sense such life may be based on principles far different from those which operate on Earth, thus extending the traditional definitions of life and providing insight into the nature of all living things. Although no compelling evidence has been presented to confirm the existence of extraterrestrial life, its possible occurrence has been the subject of debate since at least the 5th century BC.

Conditions for Life

Three conditions are important when considering the possibility of life on other planets: temperature, the existence of water, and the existence of an atmosphere. Although these conditions need not be precisely the same as those on Earth for life to exist, certain tolerance limits for life as it is normally understood can be established. (Totally different life chemistries lie only in the realm of conjecture.) An ecosphere for any star is that small range of distances from the star within which temperatures are suitable for life, water may exist in liquid form, and an atmosphere may be retained without boiling off into space.

   Within the Solar System. The ecosphere of the Sun includes the Moon and the planets Earth and Mars. The Moon and Mars present striking evidence that even with-

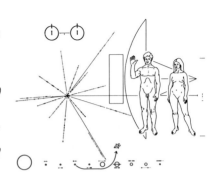

This drawing appeared on the plaques borne by the Pioneer 10 and 11 space probes. The plaque, interpreted through a measurement (in binary code) derived from the hydrogen atoms represented at the top, indicates the Earth's position in relation to 14 pulsars (left) and within our solar system (bottom).

in a star's ecosphere, planetary development may provide conditions inhospitable to life. The Moon lacks an atmosphere and water and is alternately scorched and frozen by temperatures ranging from 117° C (240° F) to −190° C (−310° F). Although small amounts of water may exist on Mars and temperatures at the equator may reach a comparatively mild 17° C (62° F), the average atmospheric pressure is only 6 millibars, compared to the standard atmospheric pressure of 1,013.25 millibars (about 14.7 psi) at mean sea level on the Earth, and the atmosphere is in the form of carbon dioxide.

   Outside of the ecosphere of the Sun, Mercury and Venus, with temperatures of 430° C (800° F) and 485° C (900° F) respectively, are ruled out as abodes of life, as are the outer planets, where temperatures fall below −140° C (−220° F) even in the upper cloud layers of the closest gas giant, Jupiter. Although internal heat sources might generate milder temperatures in the lower cloud layers of Jupiter or on the surface of a volcanic satellite such as Io, that life could exist under these conditions is difficult to conceive.

   Outside the Solar System. A large number of factors must be considered in attempting to estimate how many intelligent civilizations might have arisen throughout the Galaxy. One famous attempt at assessing these factors, originated by the radio astronomer Frank Drake, expresses the number of technical civilizations in the Milky Way Galaxy as $N = R_* f_p n_e f_l f_i f_c L$, where each of the letters on the right side of the equation represents a factor necessary to sustain intelligent life.

   The first three factors may be characterized as physical and take into account the rate of star formation (R_*), the fraction of stars with planetary systems (f_p), and the number of planets in each system with conditions favorable to life (n_e). The next two factors are biological and estimate the fraction of those planets on which life develops (f_l) and the fraction with intelligent life (f_i). The last two factors incorporate societal evolution and represent the fraction of those planets with intelligent life that evolve technical civilizations capable of interstellar communication (f_c), and the lifetime of such a civilization (L).

   Each of the factors in the Drake equation is extremely uncertain. Among the physical factors, for example, the most widely accepted theory of the origin of planetary systems asserts that planets condense out of a rotating nebula, of which the central star is itself the most prominent remnant, a circumstance that scientists have no reason to believe was unique to our solar system. Despite this theory, no other planets have ever been detected with certainty outside the solar system, in spite of claims made about perturbations of the motion of Barnard's star and others by possible planets. The cloud of material discovered around the star Vega in 1983, however, may indicate that a planetary system is forming there. As a result of such uncertainties, widely different numbers are used in the Drake equation, and scientists have estimated that as many as 10,000,000 technical civilizations exist in our galaxy or as few as 1, represented by the Earth.

Search for Life

The search for life in our solar system reached its highest point to date with the successful landing (1976) of two VI-KING spacecraft on Mars. Aboard were experiments designed to look for the biological processes of metabolism, photosynthesis, and respiration. Although the metabolism experiment gave positive results, a gas chromatograph failed to detect the presence of organic molecules, leading many to believe that the observed reactions were chemical rather than biological. The prevailing opinion is that Mars most likely does not support even low forms of life.

Because manned interstellar travel is not now feasible and because no evidence has established beyond doubt that Earth has been visited by interstellar travelers (despite persistent reports of UNIDENTIFIED FLYING OBJECTS), the search for extraterrestrial intelligence (SETI) outside the solar system must at present be carried out with radio telescopes (see RADIO ASTRONOMY). Such telescopes could detect radio signals transmitted by intelligent beings on distant planets. The central problem with this approach is deciding which stars to listen to and at what frequencies. In a landmark paper (1959) in *Nature*, Philip Morrison and Giuseppe Cocconi suggested a frequency of 1,420 mHz, corresponding to a wavelength of 21 cm, as a universally recognizable communication channel, because that frequency is emitted when an electron reverses its spin in an atom of hydrogen, the most abundant element in the universe. The very abundance of hydrogen, however, may make this channel too noisy, and thus other, supposedly fundamental frequencies might be used. Once a frequency is decided on, nearby Sun-like stars would be logical early targets.

The first attempt at radio communication with extraterrestrial intelligence was made by Frank Drake in 1960 at the National Radio Astronomy Observatory in Green Bank, W.Va. This pioneering attempt, known as Project Ozma, focused on the stars Epsilon Eridani and Tau Ceti at a frequency of 1,420 mHz. Since 1960 about 45 searches for extraterrestrial intelligence were initiated around the world, all of limited duration and concentrating on a few Sun-like stars, usually at the 1,420-mHz frequency. One SETI program begun at Harvard University's Oak Ridge Observatory in 1983 uses a 25.6-m (84-ft) radio telescope to scan about 68 percent of the sky. Originally employing a multichannel spectrum analyzer

that simultaneously scanned 131,072 channels (or frequency ranges), Oak Ridge's system was upgraded to 8.4 million channels in 1985. The National Aeronautics and Space Administration (NASA), in conjunction with Stanford University, is developing a 10–15 million-channel spectrum analyzer to be deployed by the early 1990s. NASA's effort will involve two approaches—a broad-band whole-sky survey that will utilize three existing 34-m (111.5-ft) antennas in Goldstone, Calif., Tidbinbilla, Australia, and Madrid; and a narrower-band "targeted search" of about 1,000 nearby stars that will use the same three antennas and several other antennas around the world.

———

life insurance Life insurance is a method by which numbers of individuals pool their funds so as to spread the risk of financial loss from death equally among them. Historically, the practice of life insurance dates back at least as far as the Romans whose burial clubs financed funeral expenses and made payments to families of the deceased.

Types of Life Insurance

The three basic types of life-insurance contracts are term, whole life, and endowment. A related type is the annuity.

Term Insurance. The simplest type of policy is term insurance, in which the policyholder buys protection only for the period of the contract, which may run from 1 to 20 years or more. Term insurance provides maximum protection for a minimum outlay at a given time. If the insured person dies within the period of the contract, the face value of the policy is paid to a beneficiary. The premium, or cost, of the term policy increases with the age of the insured.

Whole Life Insurance. A policy that is bought to cover the whole lifetime of the insured is called whole life, straight life, or ordinary life insurance. The younger the age when a person takes out a policy, the lower the rate of premium. This premium remains constant, since it is based on the expectation that the policy will be held for the person's lifetime. In early years the premium paid by the policyholder is more than the true cost of the insurance (the financial risk to the insurance company of a policyholder's death is more than covered by the premium rate), but in later years it is less. Thus in early years the policy builds up a cash value accruing from the difference between the premium paid in and the true cost of the insurance. The insured person can capture this cash value by borrowing on it or by discontinuing the policy and getting a refund. Since insurance companies invest the premiums paid in, they are required to guarantee the policyholder a certain rate of interest on the cash value; for this reason, whole life insurance requires lower cash outlay than other types of policies over a person's lifetime.

Variations on whole life insurance now include variable life schemes, where the policyholder has a choice of investment programs and cash value and death benefits (above a certain guaranteed minimum) change according to the performance of the program selected. The premium remains the same throughout. Universal life gives the policyholder the option of changing both premium and death benefit from time to time, adjusting them to his or her changing needs.

Endowment Insurance. An endowment policy is designed to accumulate savings over a period of years. Such a policy can be used to provide funds for a child's education or for retirement. However, it offers less protection in the event of early death than does a whole life policy. If the policyholder lives to a specific age he or she will be paid the face value of the policy, and if the policyholder dies within the period of the policy, the face value is also paid to a beneficiary.

Annuities. Closely related to life insurance is the ANNU-ITY. While life insurance may be said to protect against the risk of dying too young, an annuity protects against living too long. It assures that a person's accumulated funds will last for the remainder of his or her life. Thus a retired person with savings may decide to purchase an annuity that guarantees a specific income for as long as he or she lives. The price of the annuity is based on the average life expectancy for persons of a given age.

Costs of Life Insurance

The cost of a life insurance policy is affected by several factors: the amount and type of insurance being purchased, the age of the insured, the administrative and selling expenses of the insurance company, and the type of company from which it is purchased.

Whole life insurance requires the least cash outlay over a person's lifetime because part of its cost is paid from the interest on the accumulated value of the policy. Interest rates once were far lower than the rates obtainable from other forms of savings. Today, however, insurance companies compete with other financial organizations, and plans such as variable life offer the opportunity to invest in stock, bond, or money markets. Yields (minus fees) are therefore usually equivalent to those earned by direct investors. In addition, many policyholders appreciate the discipline of "forced" savings through regular premium payments.

Insurance companies vary in the amount of "loading"—the selling costs, administrative expenses, reserves, and profits that they add to the net insurance rate. For identical policies, premiums may vary as much as 50 percent.

Mutual insurance companies, in which the insured becomes a stockholder in the company, pay dividends from time to time that reduce the amount of the premiums over a period of years. For this reason a policy whereby the insured participates in a mutual company's earnings is generally less expensive, in the long run, than the nonparticipating policy sold by other companies.

Life of Samuel Johnson, The   see BOSWELL, JAMES

life span   Life span denotes the length of time between conception and death, during which organisms undergo remarkable changes in structure and function. In

MAXIMUM LIFE SPAN FOR SOME ANIMALS AND PLANTS

Organism	Life Span (years)	Organism	Life Span (years)
Mammals		**Fish**	
Humans	120	Eel	55
Indian elephant	78	Sea horse	6
Dog	29		
Brown bear	22	**Invertebrates**	
Guinea pig	14	American lobster	50
White laboratory rat	5	Earthworm	10
		Ant	5
Birds		Housefly	0.2
Condor	72		
Bald eagle	44	**Conifers**	
Domestic pigeon	35	Bristlecone pine	4,900
American robin	12	Sierra redwood	750
		Swiss stonepine	544
Reptiles and Amphibians		Common juniper	417
Galápagos tortoise	152	White spruce	300
Giant salamander	55		
Nile crocodile	40	**Flowering Plants**	
Bullfrog	16	English oak	1,500
		Linden	815
Fish		European beech	250
Sturgeon	82	Dwarf birch	80
Halibut	70		

the embryonic stage the fertilized egg differentiates into a highly complex multicellular organism. After birth the organism enters the juvenile phase, characterized by growth in size until sexual maturation, when growth slows down and eventually ceases. After the peak of the reproductive period, physiological capacities of various organs begin to decline, with a consequent increase in the probability of death for an organism.

All organisms have a finite and species-characteristic life span that reflects the underlying rates of AGING. There is a tremendous variation in life span among different groups of organisms. Differences in the longevity of species, hybrids, mutants, sexes, and strains lend support to the view that life span is genetically determined.

Life span is measured either as the maximum age achieved by a member or as an average among the population. The former reveals the genetic potential, whereas the average life span reflects the hospitality of the environment and is a more meaningful measure. In general, organisms live longer in captivity than in the wild. Females usually live 10–15 percent longer than males. The maximum natural life spans of organisms range from about 8 days in some rotifers to more than 150 years in tortoises and a few thousand years in some higher plants. Humans are the longest-living mammals and among the longest-living of all animals. As of the late 1980s, the highest authenticated human age was 120 years.

Plants. Plants age as animals do, but defining age in plants is more difficult because of the structural differences. For example, a plant may germinate from a seed that had been dormant for thousands of years. Also, the embryonic tissue sometimes functions for the life of the plant. Thus, a tree may continually add new cells while some parts die. A tree's age, however, may be at least roughly determined by counting its rings (new wood layers), which are added to the trunk with each growth period (see DENDROCHRONOLOGY). In addition, some plants propagate by developing offshoots that become genetically identical plants, or clones, whose ages, arguably, may be considered as extensions of the age of the original plant. On such terms, a stand of CREOSOTE BUSH clones has been dated as about 11,700 years old.

Single Cells. Unicellular organisms that reproduce asexually divide indefinitely and thus cannot be said to age. Any bacterial cell divides to produce two young cells; thus, division for such organisms is a process of rejuvenation. By contrast, individual cells in multicellular organisms normally die as part of the developmental sequence.

Recent experiments indicate that cells taken from animals and cultured in the laboratory also have a finite life span, and that death is an inherent property of cells themselves.

Evolution and Life Span. The limited life span of individuals appears to be necessary for ensuring survival of the species during evolution. The alternative, immortality, has three main disadvantages. First, it would be impossible for an immortal species to meet changes in the environment through trial changes in the organism. The necessary changes can arise only in organisms with new genetic combinations brought about by mutation and reproduction, so that the failures among the offspring die out, whereas those which succeed survive to reproduce the better-adapted genetic combinations.

Second, immortal parents would compete for food and mates with their offspring and thus threaten the survival of

future generations. Third, the constant presence of radiation from space often results in damaged genes and defective offspring. The probability of birth defects increases with the age of the mother; a population of immortal parents would reproduce many children unable to survive.

Limiting Factors. Senescence probably is due to an inability to fully restore damage inflicted at the molecular level. Whatever the nature of aging reactions may be, analysis of longevity in different mammals indicates a relationship between life span, brain weight, metabolic rate, and body weight. Animals with a higher brain-to-body-weight ratio tend to have a longer life span. Metabolic rate is inversely proportional to life span. Smaller mammals have a more intense metabolic rate and a shorter life span than do larger ones.

Another factor that exerts a significant effect on both the average and the maximum life span is the restriction of caloric intake. The maximum longevity of rats on restricted food intake is about 5 years, as compared to about 3 years in rats fed freely. Several environmental factors also have an effect on average life expectancy. They include diet, humidity, temperature, and population density. In humans, moderate exercise, relaxed life-style, and balanced diet tend to prolong life, whereas smoking, excessive drinking, and mental stress shorten the life span. Dietary supplements such as vitamins or drugs have not as yet proven to have any significant beneficial effect on the rate of aging.

life-support systems

life-support systems A life-support system is a system that provides, in surroundings hostile to life, a comfortable environment similar to that at the Earth's surface. Such systems range from the integrated group of subsystems characteristic of a spacecraft or an underwater vessel to individual devices such as scuba gear and the space suit. Multimanned life-support systems supply, at a minimum, air, water, food, and a controlled temperature and humidity. In addition, the system may collect, store, or dispose of bodily wastes and trash. In the future, particularly aboard very large multimanned space stations, the life-support system may also include a substitute for Earth's gravity. Underwater systems are discussed in articles on BATHYSCAPHE, SUBMARINE, OCEANOGRAPHY, and SCUBA DIVING; this article treats life-support systems in space.

Spacecraft Life-Support Systems

The three types of spacecraft life-support systems are open, semiclosed, and closed. The first type is now principally of historical interest, the second is used in all manned spacecraft, and the third is still a dream of the future.

Open Systems. The open system was used during the late 1940s and the 1950s when bacteria, insects, monkeys, and mice were sent in balloons, sounding rockets, and guided missiles to very high altitudes and into the lower fringes of space for relatively brief periods. They required little more than a supply of air. In a typical system supporting a monkey, temperature was controlled by means of metal foil and fiberglass materials. Oxygen was supplied from a compressed gas tank, and carbon dioxide

The graph shows survivorship curves of selected animal populations. White-tailed deer (A), display high mortality (low survival rate) in early years. The pigeon (B) and hydra (C) have a relatively constant death rate at different ages. Humans (D) and rotifers (E) have a very low mortality rate in early years.

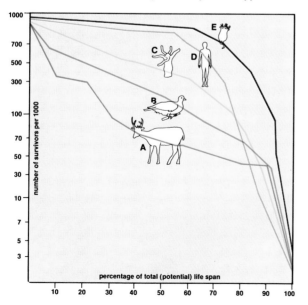

was removed by baralyme, a chemical used for the same purpose on submarines. Because of the length of the mission, which was only a matter of minutes, neither food nor water was required. The waste-management subsystem was simply a diaper.

Semiclosed Systems. The semiclosed system evolved from the open system during the preparation to enter space. It was subsequently used in the manned space programs of both the United States and the USSR. Its first appearance, in 1961, was with the Soviet VOSTOK satellite. Essentially the same system was used in the American Mercury spacecraft launched in the same year (see MERCURY PROGRAM). With technological refinement over the intervening years it was employed in the GEMINI PROGRAM, APOLLO PROGRAM, SOYUZ, SKYLAB, SALYUT, and SPACE SHUTTLE.

The life-support system of the *Skylab* space station is a good example of a semiclosed type. It was composed of an environmental-control subsystem, food-and-water-management subsystem, and waste-management subsystem. In addition, it had provisions for sleeping, personal hygiene, emergency medical attention, and monitoring astronaut vital signs.

Closed Systems. In the closed life-support system of the future, every atom within the closed system is accounted for and recycled. Thus, garbage cannot be dumped, and new supplies of food, air, and water cannot be brought from Earth as occurs with the Soviet Salyut space station. All such life-supporting elements must be provided continuously by the system. The obvious model for a closed system is the ecology of Earth. Such a system is closed only with respect to matter, not energy; because of the laws of thermodynamics, energy cannot be recycled and must be drawn from an outside source. The Sun, which is the ultimate source of energy on Earth, provides this source within the solar system.

Most models for a closed life-support system envision one based upon the exchange of metabolic products between human beings and lower forms of life. The heart of a typical system is a photosynthetic exchanger, in which a colony of algae suspended in water and exposed to light produces oxygen and takes up carbon dioxide produced by the crew. Nutrients for the algal colony are also provided by the liquid and solid wastes of the crew. Food for the crew comes from dried algae, which consist of 40 to 60% protein, 10 to 20% fat, 20% carbohydrate, and vitamins and amino acids.

Space Suits

The modern space suit permits an astronaut to leave the

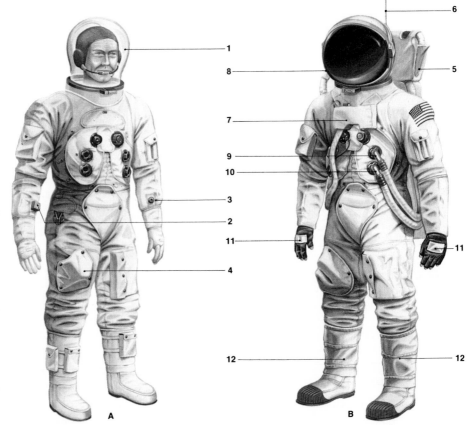

NASA developed two protective suits for astronauts on lunar missions. The space suit worn inside the vehicle (A) features an airtight helmet (1) to maintain necessary pressurization, which is monitored on an external pressure gauge (2) and regulated by a relief valve (3). A flap (4) on the upper leg houses tubing used for the elimination of waste fluid and permits access to the thigh for injections. The suit worn on the lunar surface (B) has its own environmental unit. The Portable Life-Support System, or PLSS (5), contains a radio transmitter and aerial (6), oxygen, and an air-conditioning unit. Its control panel (7) is located on the upper chest. The helmet's visor (8) shields against solar radiation. The wearer is supplied with air through an inlet tube (9), and an outlet tube (10) draws off exhaled carbon dioxide. Gloves (11) and boots (12) are insulated to protect against heat and micrometeorites.

spacecraft and function outside it, either in open space or on the surface of extraterrestrial bodies. Thus it must be reasonably airtight, thermally insulated, contain its own air and water supply, provide protection against micrometeoroids, and be flexible enough to permit a wide range of movements.

The space suits developed for the early astronauts of Mercury, Gemini, Apollo, Skylab, Vostok, and Soyuz were tailor-made and very expensive. They were designed for use inside the spacecraft during potentially hazardous periods of a mission such as reentry into the atmosphere, or for the limited periods of time outside the spacecraft.

The Apollo A–7 space suit, also used in a modified form on *Skylab*, is typical of the modern suit. It consisted of an innermost layer of heat-resistant nylon, a neoprene-coated nylon bladder with a nylon restraint layer to contain the bladder. This pressure garment covered the entire body except the hands and head. The head was protected by a polycarbonate plastic helmet that permitted a full range of vision. The gloves were made of the same material as the pressure garment and attached to it by means of a clamp and bellows that permitted limited manual dexterity. When the suit was used outside the spacecraft or on the Moon, a special garment was worn over it. It was essentially an envelope made of fireproof fiberglass cloth within which was a set of alternating layers of aluminized plastic and fireproof marquisette cloth. These ensured thermal and micrometeoroid protection. Thermally insulated gloves and boots were also worn.

The A–7 suit was pressurized with oxygen to 2.6 newtons/cm^2 (3.7 lb/in^2). In addition to providing the breathing gas for the astronaut, the oxygen also absorbed heat, water, vapor, and odors and transported them for removal. The oxygen entered the suit through a connector on the chest, flowed through ducts, and exited through another connector. The suit also had external connectors for a water-cooled undergarment used when the suit was worn outside the spacecraft. The garment was made of approximately 90 m (300 ft) of plastic tubing through which water circulated to remove heat generated by the body. External connectors on the suit also permitted cables from biosensors monitoring temperatures and heart rate of the astronaut to be attached.

A backpack containing sufficient water and oxygen for four hours made the suit independent of the spacecraft's life-support system. It was used for lunar-surface exploration and for retrieving film and experiments outside the Apollo command module on the return trip to Earth.

The United States and the USSR have also used a semirigid space suit in the Space Shuttle and the Salyut space station. It has a rigid plastic or metallic torso to which are attached fabric sleeves and legs similar to the Apollo suit. These space suits come in various sizes and use pure oxygen for breathing.

lifesaving and water safety Lifesaving is the act of rescuing a person who is in danger of DROWNING and, if necessary, reviving the person by using artificial respiration (see CARDIOPULMONARY RESUSCITATION). Lifesaving is an aspect of water safety—specifically, how to deal with potential dangers in the water. The Red Cross offers instruction in water safety and lifesaving; it also certifies competence in these areas.

Three basic methods are commonly used to rescue a drowning person. The safest and easiest method is for the rescuer to remain on shore and throw a rope or float or to extend an object such as a pole or tree limb to the victim. The victim may also be approached in a boat. Only if these two methods cannot be used should the rescuer attempt the third and most risky method—that of swimming to and seizing the person in danger and dragging him or her to shore while swimming with a special sidestroke. The danger is that the drowning person may grab the rescuer and drag them both down.

Water safety involves common sense about an individual's swimming stamina and about the condition of the water. It also requires certain acquired skills such as knowing how to swim with clothes and shoes on, how to disrobe in the water, and how to survive in rough water.

ligament [lig'-uh-ment] A ligament is a band of tough, flexible, dense, white, fibrous connective tissue that connects bones or cartilages, serving to support and strengthen joints. Ligaments are elastic only within narrow limits. One of the most important factors limiting joint movement is the tension of the ligaments, because they are designed to prevent excessive or abnormal joint movement. Most ligaments are within the joint capsule; a few accessory ligaments are extracapsular. Ligaments can also support organs. Certain folds of the peritoneum (the membrane lining the abdominal cavity) are also called ligaments.

When ligaments are stretched beyond their elastic limits, mild strains (sprains) or more severe tears result. Treatment of tears may involve the surgical grafting of TENDONS; in 1986 the Food and Drug Administration (FDA) approved the first synthetic ligament for the replacement of torn knee ligaments.

ligand SEE COORDINATION COMPOUNDS

Ligeti, György [lee'-get-ee, dyurd] The Hungarian composer György Ligeti, b. May 28, 1923, is a leader of the European musical avant-garde. Ligeti established his reputation with the orchestral *Atmosphères* (1961) in which he developed *Klangflächenkomposition,* music constructed with blocks of sound. In his mime-dramas *Aventures* (1962) and *Nouvelles Aventures* (1962–65) he used a meaningless language that resulted in a kind of musical theater of the absurd. An increasing interest in harmony can be discerned in the orchestral *Lontano* (1967), and beginning with his *Second String Quartet* (1968) he experimented with microtones. A subtle and complex polyphony characterizes most of Ligeti's music since the mid-1960s. His first opera, *The Grand Macabre,* was first performed in 1978. Music from his *Atmosphères* and *Requiem* (1963–65) was used in the film *2001: A Space Odyssey* (1968).

light   Light is ELECTROMAGNETIC RADIATION in the wavelength range extending from about 0.4 μ to about 0.7μ; or, perhaps more properly, the visual response to electromagnetic radiation in this range. By extension, the term is frequently applied to adjacent wavelength ranges that the eye cannot detect: ULTRAVIOLET LIGHT, infrared light (see INFRARED RADIATION), and black light. In addition to wavelength, FREQUENCY, in hertz, and wave number, in inverse units of length, are also used to specify and designate the character and quality of the radiation. Associated with wavelength or frequency is the visual response of COLOR. The term *monochromatic* is applied to the idealized situation in which the light in a beam is all of one wavelength.

Characterization of Light

Light is characterized not only by wavelength, essentially a temporal quality, but also by state and degree of polarization (see POLARIZED LIGHT), a geometric or directional quality, and by intensity, essentially a physical quality. The visual response to intensity is brightness. In the human visual system, at least, there is no counterpart response to the state and degree of polarization, but ample evidence exists that certain arthropods—bees in particular—are sensitive to the state of polarization of sky light.

Both a particle and a wave theory of light explain reflection and refraction, but only the wave hypothesis can account for diffraction and interference effects. Particles of light (A) would pass straight through a pinhole and form a point image on a rear screen. Light waves (B), however, would diffract, or spread out, and form a large circular image. The passage of light particles (C) through two slits would form two bright lines. A series of light and dark bands (D) are seen, however, which can only be explained in terms of waves. Bright lines result when light waves (E) arrive at the screen in phase. Dark bands occur when waves (F) are out of phase.

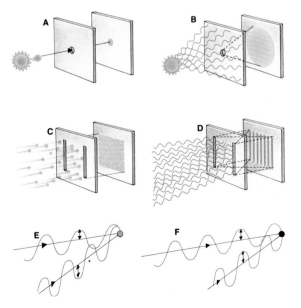

There is some speculation that certain migrating birds may also respond to this quality of light.

Light is further characterized by its degree of coherence. Coherence, closely related to the degree of polarization and to the degree of monochromaticity, refers to the ability of a beam of light to interfere (see INTERFERENCE) with itself. Coherence is therefore an interferometric property of light. By the use of a Michelson INTERFEROMETER, most light sources can be made to produce interference fringes. These are clearest when the length of the two arms of the interferometer are equal. As one arm is lengthened, however, the contrast of the fringes is seen to decrease until they are no longer visible. Unfiltered light from an incandescent source will barely produce fringes under any circumstances. Light from a mercury arc lamp will produce fringes over a range of one or two centimeters. On the other hand, light from a continuous-wave gas laser has produced fringes at a distance of more than 100 meters.

Light is moving energy that travels at a speed of 300,000 km/sec (186,000 mi/sec). It can be regarded both as a particulate flow and as a wave phenomenon. These two apparently diametrically opposed views have been brought together in a theory that combines the best features of each. The particulate unit is the PHOTON, which has associated with it a central frequency or wavelength that determines (or is determined by) the amount of energy it contains. In a so-called monochromatic beam, the photons are all of the same energy and therefore have the same frequency. They can be made to interfere, which indicates a high degree of coherence as well as a more or less uniform state of polarization. If the distribution of the energy in the photons is more random, however, the beam will be less coherent and will have a lower degree of polarization.

It is also convenient to think of light as propagating as wave fronts. These waves, like the crest of an ocean wave, are surfaces on which the phase relationship is constant. Unlike an ocean wave, a wave front or surface of constant phase is unobservable and undetectable. Light may be considered as energy being transported in a train of wave fronts. The direction of propagation (except for anisotropic media) is in a direction perpendicular to the wave front. Rays can be conceived as trajectories of photons.

Light Production

Light, like any other electromagnetic radiation, results from either an accelerating electric charge or a nuclear fusion or fission reaction. In nuclear reactions, a photon is created in the same manner as other elemental partial products of the reaction. With the exception of sunlight and starlight, however, light usually is the result of changes in the electronic structure of atoms and molecules as they absorb and readmit energy.

The incandescent electric light has as its light source the heat that results from the ohmic resistance of the filament to the electric current. A red-hot poker absorbs heat directly from the fire resulting from the liberation of chemical energy. As the material in the filament or poker heats up, the atoms and molecules gain kinetic energy,

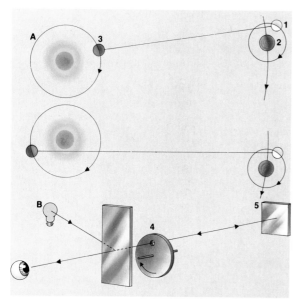

In 1675 a Danish astronomer, Olaus Roemer, was the first to find that light travels with a finite speed. The eclipse times (A) of Jupiter's moons (1) vary from the predicted times, depending on the distance between Jupiter (2) and Earth (3). Roemer calculated the velocity from the time difference and Earth's orbital diameter. In 1849 a French physicist, Armand Fizeau, determined the speed of light by sending a light beam (B) through a hole in a rotating disk (4) to a distant mirror (5). The disk's rotational speed was then adjusted until the reflected light could be seen through the hole. He calculated the speed of light from the disk's rotational speed and mirror distance.

which is realized by an increase in the number of collisions among the particles. The boiling off of some of the material is one mechanism that can be used to maintain an equilibrium temperature. Another mechanism is for the electrons associated with the various atoms in the metal to move to higher energy levels. When they drop back to lower energy levels they emit a photon, keeping the temperature of the material more or less constant despite the fact that energy is continually supplied. The excess energy is emitted as light.

Thermal production of light is essentially random and is idealized as BLACKBODY RADIATION. The light produced contains a mixture of wavelengths skewed around a central maximum λ_m, which is related to the temperature T of the material in degrees Kelvin. This relation, $\lambda_m T = $ constant, is known as the Wien displacement law. The spectrum produced by the light from such a source is continuous. Although there is a dominant wavelength, this light is not monochromatic. It is generally unpolarized and has a relatively short coherence length.

Another type of light source is energized plasma such as a flame or the gas in a discharge tube such as a neon bulb. Although light is produced by a mechanism similar to thermal emission, the atoms are in a gaseous phase and less random. The energy levels reached by the electrons depend more on the electronic structure of the atoms themselves, and therefore the photons emitted tend

to be clustered around specific wavelengths. The spectrum produced by such a source is not at all continuous but consists of lines or bands that are characteristic of the atoms or molecules in the gas. Highly monochromatic light can be obtained from this type of source, particularly if the light is filtered. The light has a much longer coherence length but is generally unpolarized.

A third type of source is the LASER. Two principles are involved in laser operation. First, the lasing material is composed of atoms, or mixtures of atoms, that have a peculiar energy level structure. As they absorb energy, their electrons move up to higher energy levels, tending to accumulate at certain metastable levels. This is called *population inversion*. There they remain until stimulated by a photon of the proper frequency. Then the electrons drop to a lower energy level, emitting a photon of the same frequency and traveling in the same direction as the incident, stimulating photon. Because a single photon may stimulate the release of a large number of additional photons, the total number of photons is increased, thus increasing the intensity of the light within the medium. The process is referred to as *gain*.

The second principle is the geometry of the laser itself. The laser can be regarded as a hollow tube, much like an organ pipe, which is tuned to the wavelength of the emitted photons. The process can be visualized as a wave front being reflected back and forth between the two ends of the laser, picking up more photons with each reflection. The portion of the light that is permitted to escape from the cavity is highly monochromatic, with a long coherence length. In some circumstances the laser output is highly polarized.

Relativity and the Dualistic Nature of Light

The historical development of a theory of light, at least from the 17th century on, involved two apparently contradictory descriptions. René Descartes and Pierre Fermat were both proponents of a corpuscular theory; Christiaan Huygens believed in a wave theory. He also obtained a proof of the refraction law in terms of the existence of wave fronts, a construction now called Huygens's principle.

If light is a wave phenomenon, however, then a medium is required. Sound waves travel through the air but not through a vacuum; ripples require a watery medium. Theorists chose to hypothesize the existence of a medium called the ETHER, a concept that led to unexpected results. It was postulated that if ether exists, then another observable phenomenon, ether "drift," must also exist. If both the Earth and light are moving through the ether, then the velocity of light observed on the Earth would depend on the direction of observation. The ether was regarded as stationary; the Earth and other planets, the Sun and the stars, and light moved through it. By measuring the apparent velocity of light in various directions, one could determine the absolute velocity and direction of motion of the Earth.

In the late 19th century A. A. Michelson and E. W. Morley attempted to measure the absolute motion of the Earth through the ether (see MICHELSON-MORLEY EXPERIMENT). No ether drift was observed. The conclusion was the inconceivable notion that the velocity of light was constant and independent of the motion of the observer. This paradox led to Einstein's special theory of RELATIVITY, a cosmological theory of major significance.

light horses see HORSE

light meter see ACTINOMETER

—

light-year A light-year is the distance light traverses in a vacuum in one year at the speed of 299,792 km/sec (186,282 mi/sec). With 31,557,600 seconds in a year, the light-year equals a distance of 9.46×10^{12} km (5.87×10^{12} mi). One parsec, the distance at which the semi-major axis of the Earth's orbit (1 astronomical unit) subtends one arc second, is equal to 3.26 light-years. Astronomers commonly use the parsec and the light-year to measure astronomical distances. Alpha Centauri, the nearest star to the Sun, has a parallax of 0.76 arc second, equivalent to a distance of 1.3 parsecs, or 4.3 light-years.

—

lighthouse A lighthouse is a structure designed to provide ships with a navigational point of reference by day and by night, and often to indicate dangerous rocks or shoals as well. Used since ancient times, lighthouses have evolved from beacon fires burning on hilltops to modern masonry or steel-frame towers that are capable of resisting the severest storms and are equipped with optical and sound signaling systems.

History

Although the Phoenicians and Egyptians are thought to have built lighthouses, there are no records of their accomplishments.

Construction. The first lighthouse for which a detailed account remains was the great Pharos of Alexandria, considered one of the SEVEN WONDERS OF THE WORLD. A stone structure about 107 m (350 ft) high with a wood fire at the top, the Pharos was built *c.*280 BC. The Romans built lighthouses along the European coastline, sometimes fortifying them for military use.

Among noteworthy medieval lighthouses were two on the commercially important Tyrrhenian Sea, the famous Lanterna of Genoa (built *c.*1161) and the slightly later tower on the island of Meloria.

In the 18th century rapid advances in equipment and construction occurred, and the first towers completely exposed to the sea were built. The Eddystone Light, off Plymouth, England, reflected in its successive forms increasingly scientific principles of design.

Illumination. Improvements over the old wood, coal, and oil illuminants were introduced at the end of the 18th century (see LIGHTING DEVICES). In 1782 the Swiss scientist Aimé Argand invented the Argand lamp—an oil lamp with a circular wick, protected by a glass chimney, and a central draft. The Argand lamp remained the principal lighthouse illuminant for over a century. The Welsbach gas-mantle lamp, which burned coal gas, was de-

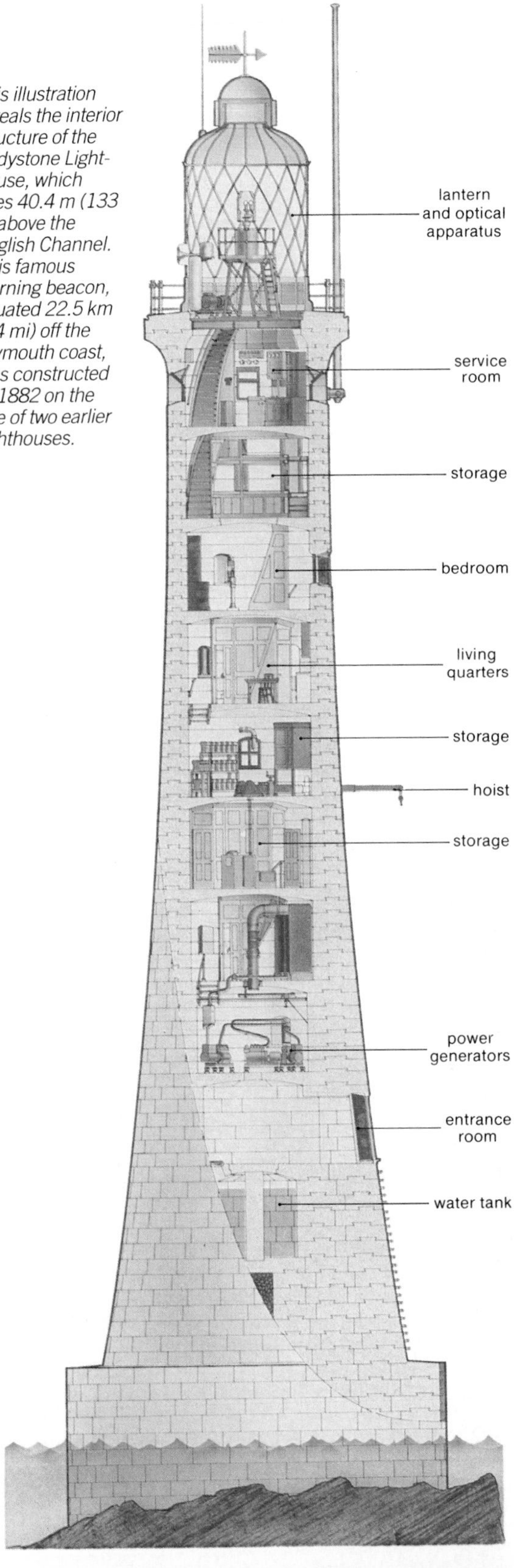

This illustration reveals the interior structure of the Eddystone Lighthouse, which rises 40.4 m (133 ft) above the English Channel. This famous warning beacon, situated 22.5 km (14 mi) off the Plymouth coast, was constructed in 1882 on the site of two earlier lighthouses.

lantern and optical apparatus

service room

storage

bedroom

living quarters

storage

hoist

storage

power generators

entrance room

water tank

veloped in the 1860s. Electric carbon-arc lamps were installed as early as 1858, in the South Forelands light on the English Channel.

The INCANDESCENT LAMP came into use in the 1920s and is standard lighthouse equipment today. An acetylene gas burner invented in 1906 by Nils Gustav Dalén of Sweden, and capable of automatic control, is still the normal illumination for unmanned lighthouses without electricity.

Optical Systems. At about the same time, reflectors and refractors were developed to focus, or concentrate, the light into a single powerful beam. A catoptric reflector invented in 1777, which consisted of hundreds of mirror sections set in a plaster mold in the form of a parabolic curve, was later replaced by parabolic silvered copper reflectors. The resulting beam had to be rotated so that it would be visible from any direction. The first revolving light, operated by clockwork, was installed at Carlsten, Sweden, in 1781.

The dioptric system, an improvement on the catoptric reflector, was designed by the physicist Augustin Fresnel in the 1820s; it consisted of a curtain of prisms around a bull's-eye lens; this arrangement refracted the light into a narrow, horizontal beam. Later Fresnel added reflecting prisms above and below, producing the catadioptric system, the basis of all lighthouse optical systems in use today.

Modern Developments

Modern construction methods include the sinking of steel CAISSONS. This approach was first tried on the foundations of the Rothersand Shoal light in the Weser estuary in Germany in the 1880s. Prefabricated concrete construction was pioneered in Sweden in the 1930s, culminating in the telescopic method of lighthouse construction that emerged in the late 1950s. According to this method, two or more sections of closed-bottom caissons are constructed, one inside the other, and are floated to the site. The entire structure is first sunk. The outer section forms the foundation, and the inner telescopic sections are then raised by hydraulic jacks and locked into position to form the tower.

New illuminants include the xenon high-pressure arc lamp, which incorporates a powerful electric arc in a quartz bulb filled with the inert gas xenon (see ARC, ELECTRIC). Where stationary towers cannot be built, BUOYS and lightships carry distinctive markings and, often, beacons.

---

lighting devices   Lighting, or artificial illumination, as opposed to the natural illumination of the Sun or Moon, was probably first furnished by campfires and by torches made of dried rushes or resinous wood. Crude stone LAMPS, in which light came from a flaming wick lying in a pool of oil or melting grease, were used by prehistoric peoples. CANDLES and oil-burning lamps remained the chief sources of artificial illumination until the middle of the 19th century, when kerosene lamps with flat, woven wicks and glass chimneys came into common use.

Gas for Lighting. Illuminating gas was produced first as the by-product of coal distillation in the production of tar.

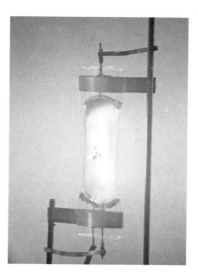

A xenon arc lamp, like the carbon arc lamp developed during the early 1800s, produces a brilliant bluish white light from current passing between two electrodes.

Its potential as an illuminant was recognized as early as the 1790s by the English engineer, William Murdock, and even earlier by a Frenchman, Philippe Lebon (1767–1804). In 1806–16, Murdock installed 1,000 gas lights in a Manchester cotton mill. The first gas generating station, the London Gas Light and Coke Company, was chartered in 1812, and by 1815, London possessed 42 km (26 mi) of gas line that supplied illuminant for street lamps and for a few homes. The first gas burners were simple iron or brass pipes with perforated tips, or orifices. Later, soapstone was used as the orifice. The invention of the Welsbach mantle in the 1890s greatly increased the brightness of the gas flame.

Electric Arc Lamps. Electric arc lamps consisting of electric arcs drawn between two carbon electrodes were one of the earliest lighting devices to make use of electrical energy. Invented around 1801, arc lamps were not used commercially until 1858, after one had been successfully installed in a LIGHTHOUSE in England.

The Incandescent Bulb. During the 1840s many experiments aimed at the development of a workable electrical INCANDESCENT LAMP were conducted. No practical advances took place, however, until 1879, when the American inventor Thomas Alva EDISON developed a successful carbon filament incandescent lamp. (Sir Joseph Wilson Swan had invented an earlier incandescent lamp.) Edison passed an electric current through thin filaments of carbonized threads that were tightly sealed inside a glass bulb from which all air had been removed by vacuum pumps.

Edison's invention marked the birth of electric lighting and the electric age. Edison also invented the first efficient electric generators as a means of supplying his lamps with current.

FLUORESCENT LIGHT came into popular use around 1939 and by 1950 had largely replaced incandescent lighting in commercial establishments. Fluorescent lamps emit more light per watt than incandescent bulbs.

Discharge Tubes. Fluorescent light belongs to the group of lighting devices known collectively as discharge

Thomas Edison's first commercially marketed incandescent bulb (left), a modified form of his original incandescent lamp (right), made possible the widespread use of electric lighting.

tubes—glass tubes filled with metal vapor, with electrodes at both tube ends. Electric current that is passed between the electrodes eventually ionizes the vapor, which begins to glow, producing light. Discharge tubes are widely used for street lighting. High pressure sodium vapor lamps produce a brilliant yellowish orange glow. Mercury vapor lamps, which operate at higher pressures, produce a greenish blue light. They are often enclosed in

tubes coated with a fluorescent material that creates a shift toward warmer colors in the radiated light.

Some discharge tubes emit flashes of high intensity light and are used in lighthouses and for directional beacons of various kinds.

Determining Optimal Light Levels. A footcandle is roughly the amount of illumination on a surface one foot away from a common candle. (The metric equivalent of footcandles, lumens per square meter, may be obtained by multiplying the number of footcandles by 10.763.) For many years lighting calculations for interiors were made to provide uniform illumination on working surfaces; recommendations ranged from 5 to 10 footcandles in the 1920s to 100 and upward in the 1960s, with much higher levels over small areas for critical seeing. Emphasis on energy conservation, which began in the 1970s, has led to more localized treatments of large offices.

lightning   Lightning is a natural, short-lived, high-current electrical discharge in the atmosphere. The path length of the discharge is normally several kilometers. The cumulonimbus clouds of THUNDERSTORMS are the most common source of lightning. Lightning also occasionally occurs in snowstorms, sandstorms, and clouds over erupting volcanoes.

At any one time as many as 2,000 thunderstorms occur over widely scattered locations around the Earth's surface. These thunderstorms produce cloud-to-ground lightning flashes at the rate of 100 per second. In an average year, approximately 100 to 200 persons are killed and several hundred injured by lightning in the United States alone, a death rate exceeding deaths caused by tornadoes and hur-

Lightning is a sudden atmospheric discharge of static electricity in the form of a long, luminous, multi-branched spark from one electrically charged area to an oppositely charged area. Thunderclouds are the most common producers of lightning. Such clouds typically are positively charged in the upper levels and negatively charged in the lower regions. Most spark discharges take place between oppositely charged regions within or between clouds.

Cloud-to-ground discharges, the most destructive form of lightning, commonly occur during thunderstorms. This photograph shows a flash of forked lightning over the town of Green River, Wyo.

ricanes. Estimates of total U.S. property losses due to lightning range as high as several hundred million dollars per year. Also, an estimated 10,000 forest fires are caused by lightning in the United States each year. When they occur away from human habitation, lightning-caused fires produce beneficial effects, such as reduction of fire-fuel accumulation, the propagation of seeds of certain plant species, and the recycling of nutrients.

Cause. Before lightning can occur, a charge separation large enough to cause electrical breakdown of the air must be developed. Theories of the mechanism of thunderstorm electrification fall into two main categories. One category holds that the principal mechanism for the separation of electric charge is the vertical separation of charged larger hydrometeors (that is, raindrops, graupel, or hailstones) from differentially charged smaller ones (that is, small cloud droplets or ice crystals) as a result of their different settling velocities in a cloud. These theories vary mainly in the way hydrometeors of different sizes become differentially charged. The other category of theories holds that small cloud particles and droplets are the principal charge carriers and that the main mechanism for the separation of charge is the variable convective air motions within the thundercloud, which carry some particles upward and others downward.

Formation. The most destructive lightning strokes, the cloud-to-ground flashes, originate near the bases of the clouds in the form of an invisible discharge called the stepped leader, which moves downward in discrete, microsecond steps about 50 m (165 ft) long. The stepped leader is believed to be initiated by a small discharge near the cloud base, releasing free electrons that move toward the ground. When the negatively charged stepped leader approaches to within 100 m (330 ft) or less of the ground, a leader moves up from the ground—especially from protruding objects such as buildings and trees—to meet it. Once the leaders have made contact, the visible lightning stroke, called the return stroke, propagates upward from the ground along the path of the stepped leader. Several subsequent strokes can occur along the original main channel in less than a second. These strokes

continue until the charge center in the lower part of the cloud is eliminated. The explosive heating and expansion of air along the leader path produces a shock wave that is heard as thunder.

Ball Lightning. Ball lightning, a little-understood phenomenon, is generally spherical, from 1 to more than 100 cm (0.4 to more than 40 in) in diameter; it usually lasts less than 5 seconds. The balls are reported to move at a few meters per second and to decay silently or with a small explosion.

Lightning Rods. In 1749, Benjamin Franklin first suggested the use of lightning rods for the protection of buildings and barns. A metal rod is placed at the apex of a structure and is grounded by a low-resistance cable. In theory, lightning strikes the rod and passes harmlessly into the ground; the rod's height must be sufficient, however, for lightning to strike at it rather than at the structure. The rod's area of protection is a cone-shaped space, with the base radius equal to the height of the rod. Lightning strikes within this area are not unknown, however.

lignin Lignin is a complex natural polymer that provides support and protects plant cells in woody plants. Dry WOOD consists of up to 30% lignin. The molecular weight of the polymer ranges from 2,000 to 15,000; its chemistry is not fully known, but among the constituents are the aromatic compounds coniferyl alcohol and syringin. A by-product of the paper and pulp industries, lignin is used in drilling muds, as an extender in phenolic plastics, as a rubber strengthener, and as a vanillin source, but much of it goes to waste because it is hard to break down chemically. Thus the discovery in a WHITE ROT FUNGUS of a lignin-attacking enzyme, lignase, may prove to be of great commercial significance.

lignite See COAL AND COAL MINING

Liguria [lee-goo'-ree-uh] Liguria, a region of northwest Italy with an area of 5,418 km² (2,092 mi²), extends along the Ligurian Sea between France and Tuscany, with the Ligurian Alps in the west and the APENNINES in the east. Its population is 1,749,272 (1988 est.); most of the people live in the coastal strip that includes the Italian Riviera. The region comprises Genoa, Imperia, La Spezia, and Savona provinces; GENOA (the capital) and LA SPEZIA are the leading ports.

Genoa struggled to dominate Liguria from the 11th century and was in firm control from the 16th century to the Napoleonic era. The Congress of Vienna (1815) awarded Liguria to Piedmont-Sardinia; its people were active in the Italian unification movement of the 1860s.

lilac [ly'-lahk] Lilacs are about 30 species of flowering, deciduous shrubs in the genus *Syringa* of the olive family, Oleaceae. Most species are cultivated, and their fragrant blooms range from white through shades of lilac to deep crimson.

The common lilac is valued for the strong, rich scent of its densely clustered flowers. Hybrids between this species and others are known as French lilacs and exhibit variety in the shape and color of the blooms but usually lack fragrance.

The common lilac, *S. vulgaris*, is native to southeastern Europe. It has been extensively used for landscaping as an ornamental throughout the temperate United States. A vigorous shrub that grows up to 6 m (20 ft) in height, it bears dense, pyramidal clusters of flowers in May and oblong, capsular fruit. The leaves are simple and ovate.

The Persian lilac, *S. persica*, another popular cultivated species, has long, tubular flowers that grow in loose clusters. The late lilac, *S. villosa*, native to China, has long, broad leaves and lilac or pinkish white flowers. A treelike lilac, *S. reticulata*, native to Japan, bears yellowish white flowers.

Lilienthal, Otto [leel'-yen-tahl, oht'-oh]   A German aviation pioneer of the 19th century, Otto Lilienthal, b. May 23, 1848, d. Aug. 10, 1896, helped lay the foundations for powered flight. Lilienthal founded (1880) a firm for the production of small steam engines and marine signal devices. After studying the flight of birds, he published the influential *Der Vogelflug als Grundlage der Fliegerkunst* (1889; trans. as *Birdflight as the Basis of Aviation*, 1911). Lilienthal designed and tested a series of 18 manned GLIDERS and in 1891 made the first of more than 2,000 glider flights. He crashed during one such flight and died the next day.

Lilith [lil'-ith]   In Jewish and Islamic tradition Lilith was the original wife of ADAM; she was turned out of Eden and replaced by EVE because she refused to submit to his authority. Lilith slept with Adam after his expulsion from the garden and gave birth to the evil spirits; in Islamic tradition she slept with the devil and gave birth to the jinn (see JINNI). In later legend she became a succubus, a demon who caused nocturnal emissions and the birth of witches and demons called *lilim*. She was also believed to steal and kill children, and charms were used to protect them from her.

Liliuokalani, Queen of Hawaii [lee-lee-oo'-oh-kah-lahn'-ee]   Liliuokalani, b. Sept. 2, 1838, d. Nov. 11, 1917, was the last reigning monarch of Hawaii. She succeeded her brother, Kalakaua, to the throne on Jan. 29, 1891. Liliuokalani resisted the curbing of royal power by the constitution of 1887. As a result, in 1893 a revolt inspired mainly by U.S.-born sugar planters led to her dethronement. She formally abdicated on Jan. 24, 1895. After the U.S. annexation of Hawaii in 1898, Liliuokalani unsuccessfully petitioned the federal government for property and other claims. She wrote many songs, notably "*Aloha Oe*" ("Farewell to Thee").

Lille [leel]   Lille, a leading industrial conurbation in northern France located 10 km (6 mi) from the Belgian border, is the capital of Nord department. The population of the city is 168,424; that of the metropolitan area is 1,012,000 (1982).

A leading textile producer since the 11th century, Lille also produces iron, steel, machinery, chemicals, and food products. The city is a transportation hub located on the canalized Deûle River. Its art museum is one of the best known in Europe. Many 15th-, 16th-, and 17th-century buildings are located in the old city, including the Flemish-style Bourse (stock exchange, begun 1652), the citadel (begun 1668), and the Church of St. Catherine.

The existence of Lille was first documented in 1066. During the Middle Ages, it was the chief city of the county of Flanders, but it subsequently changed hands numerous times before 1713, when it became part of France. It was occupied by Germany during both world wars.

Lillo, George [lil'-oh]   The English dramatist George Lillo, b. Feb. 4, 1693, d. Sept. 3, 1739, was the author of a popular tragic drama *The London Merchant* (1731). Lillo's play, which depicts bourgeois London life, made a break with contemporary theatrical convention in its realistic, although sentimental, portrayal of middle-class life. He also wrote the domestic dramas *The Christian Hero* (1735) and *Fatal Curiosity* (1736). His influence on the theater, which extended to France and Germany, is paralleled by that of Samuel Richardson on the English novel.

Lilongwe [lee-lawng'-way]   Lilongwe, the capital of Malawi, has a population of 220,300 (1987 est.). It is located on the inland plains of south central Malawi and is a commercial and transportation center for the surrounding fertile agricultural region. Some light industries are located there. Lilongwe was established in 1947 and became the nation's capital in 1975.

lily   The lily family, Liliaceae, is one of the largest families of flowering plants, containing more than 200 genera and about 3,000 species. It is worldwide in distribution, with most species occurring in temperate and subtropical

Lilies produce trumpet-shaped flowers (left to right): *The torch flower is named for its brilliantly hued flowers. The fragrant plantain lily is native to Japan. The Madonna lily is the oldest cultivated lily. The lily-of-the-nile, actually an amaryllis, has an appearance similar to lilies. The wonder flower has long-lasting blooms.*

regions. Members of this family, of the subclass Mono-cotyledonae, are mostly perennial herbs with storage rootstock in the form of bulbs, corms, rhizomes, or tubers. The flowers are usually bisexual—having both stamens and pistils—and possess regular symmetry; they are commonly tubular, with three petals and three sepals of similar appearance. The fruit is a capsule or a berry. The garden asparagus, *Asparagus officinalis,* is a member of the lily family. Among the popular ornamental plants that belong to the lily family are the aloe, genus *Aloe*; hyacinth, *Hyacinthus*; lily, *Lilium*; and tulip, *Tulipa.* In some classifications certain of these plants may be placed in other families, and some so-called lilies are not members of the Liliaceae.

The lily genus, *Lilium,* contains about 80 species native to the northern temperate regions. These erect perennial herbs usually possess a bulb-type rootstock, with solitary or clustered flowers in white, yellow, orange, purple, or maroon, but never blue. Most of today's popular lilies were developed since 1940. Many are hybrids of two Japanese species, *L. auratum* and *L. speciosum.*

lily of the valley   Lily of the valley, *Convallaria majalis,* is a perennial flowering plant in the lily family, Liliaceae. It is native to Eurasia and eastern North America and is grown worldwide in gardens in warm and temperate zones. The plants develop two or three shiny leaves and a graceful, one-sided group of fragrant bell-shaped flowers, white to pink in color.

Lima [lee'-muh]   Lima is the capital and largest city of Peru, with a metropolitan population of 5,493,900 (1988 est.). Situated between the Andean foothills and the Pacific Ocean at an elevation of 203 m (666 ft), it has grown to extend along the coast and now adjoins its

ocean port, CALLAO. It is the administrative, commercial, industrial, and cultural center of Peru. Among Lima's chief industries are textile, steel, and shoe manufacturing, petroleum refining, and food processing. Many businesses are headquartered in Lima. The city also has ten museums and a dozen universities, including the National University of San Marcos (1551), the nation's oldest.

Lima was founded by Francisco PIZARRO during Epiphany season (the Feast of the Three Kings) in 1535 and was accordingly named by him City of Kings. It came to be known, however, as Lima, a corruption of *Rimac,* the Indian word for the shallow local river. The central square built by Pizarro, the Plaza de Armas, remains the

Lima, the capital and commercial center of Peru, is located on the country's arid coastal strip, adjacent to the Pacific port of Callao. Founded in 1535, Lima has become Peru's most populous city and the center of the nation's industries.

heart of Lima. Located in the square are the presidential palace, completed in 1938, and the great cathedral planned by Pizarro (entirely rebuilt after the 1746 earthquake). Mummified remains displayed in the cathedral were long thought to be Pizarro's. In 1984, however, a skull found in the crypt in 1977 was verified as his. Lima was the capital of Spain's New World empire from 1535 until the early 19th century; during these 300 years it was the most prosperous city of Latin America. Subject to earthquakes, it was twice (1655, 1746) virtually destroyed and had to be rebuilt. Since World War II, Lima has undergone phenomenal industrialization and growth, leading to a variety of urban problems.

lima bean [ly'-muh] Lima beans, *Phaseolus limensis,* are vegetables belonging to the pulse family, Leguminosae, which also includes the closely related snap, or string, BEAN, *P. vulgaris.* Both the small, flat "baby" lima and the larger thick "potato" type are of tropical American origin. Both are grown in warmer areas throughout the United States.

Lima beans grow both as bushes and as climbing plants. They require warmer weather than snap beans and cannot tolerate frost. The beans are harvested when most of the seeds have reached maximum size but are still green and tender. Beans that will be dried and stored are left on the plant until they have become fully mature and white in color.

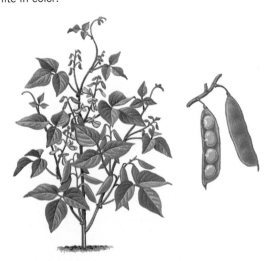

The lima bean grows on a vinelike shrub. Each pod contains four green beans, which turn white and hard if left unharvested.

Limbourg brothers [lam-bour'] The Limbourg brothers, Pol, Herman, and Jehanequin, fl. 1385–1416, were Flemish manuscript illuminators who received their initial training as goldsmiths. By 1402, Pol and Jehanequin were in France illuminating a Bible for Philip the Bold, duke of Burgundy. By 1410 they were working

for Philip's brother, the Duke of Berry, one of the foremost art patrons of his day. Pol, the oldest, painted a seminal manuscript, the *Belles Heures du Duc de Berry* (1410–13; The Cloisters, New York City), with which he may have been assisted by one of his younger brothers. In this work Pol showed his awareness of recent Italian art, then developing toward realistic representation and individualized portraiture.

All three brothers were engaged in painting the most important of all medieval illuminated manuscripts, the *Très Riches Heures du Duc de Berry* (Musée Condé, Chantilly) begun in 1413 and left unfinished at their death in 1416. It was completed by Jean Colombe about 1485. Of the 129 illustrations, 71 are by the Limbourgs. These are remarkable for the sensitivity and naturalism with which they portray daily life and are regarded as the supreme achievement of international Gothic style (see GOTHIC ART AND ARCHITECTURE).

See also: ILLUMINATED MANUSCRIPTS.

lime (chemical compound) Lime, quicklime, and burnt lime are common names for calcium oxide, CaO, a grayish-white powder. The manufacture of over 150 industrial chemicals requires lime. In fact only five other raw materials (salt, coal, sulfur, air, and water) are used in greater amounts. Lime is used in glass, cement, brick, and other building materials; in making steel, aluminum, and magesium; in poultry feed; and in processing cane and sugar beet juices. Lime is strongly caustic and can severely irritate human skin and mucous membranes.

lime (fruit) The lime, *Citrus aurantifolia,* is a small, evergreen tree of the Rutaceae, or RUE, family and also the tree's green fruit. Because it is the most frost-tender species of the CITRUS genus, most limes are grown in

The lime tree is a small, tropical tree whose green fruit is rich in vitamin C. British sailors of the 18th and 19th centuries ate limes during long voyages in order to prevent scurvy.

warmer climates, especially in Mexico, Egypt, Florida, and the West Indies. The tropical West Indian (Mexican, Key) lime has small, seedy fruit; the larger, seedless Persian, or Tahiti, type is also grown in subtropical regions such as southern Florida. Both are acid limes. A sweet lime is also grown, primarily in Egypt.

The fruit is small (diameter 3–6 cm/1½–2½ in), with a green to yellow rind when ripe and a juice that is more acid than that of the lemon. Limes have been used for centuries as a preventive against SCURVY (hence "limey," the slang name for a British sailor, whose diet aboard ship often included lime juice) and are a major source of citric acid.

Limerick [lim'-rik]   Limerick, the seat of County Limerick in west central Ireland, is the Republic of Ireland's third largest city, with a population of 56,279 (1986). Situated on the estuary of the River SHANNON, it is an important seaport. Industries include lace making, flour milling, brewing, and the manufacture of dairy products. Settled by Norse invaders in 812, the city was chartered in 1197; the fortress of King John, begun in 1210, still stands. Limerick was under siege by Oliver Cromwell in 1651 and by William III (William of Orange) in 1691.

County Limerick, in MUNSTER province in southwestern Ireland, has an area of 2,686 km² (1,037 mi²) and a population of 16,569 (1986). Primarily an agricultural region, it was made a shire in the early 13th century and came under control of the earls of Desmond in 1329.

---

limerick [lim'-rik]   A limerick is a form of comic verse, frequently nonsensical and often bawdy. Its five lines usually rhyme *a a b b a*, and the meter is basically anapestic (see VERSIFICATION). Limericks often contain puns and wordplay, as in the following example by Langford Reed:

> An indolent vicar of Bray
> His roses allowed to decay.
>   His wife, more alert,
>   Bought a powerful squirt
> And said to her spouse, "Let us spray."

---

limestone   Limestone is a SEDIMENTARY ROCK composed more than 50% by weight of calcium carbonate ($CaCO_3$).

Limestones are composed of a mixture of grains of calcium carbonate, clear crystalline calcite, and carbonate mud. Lime-secreting organisms, the major source of these components, produce carbonate sediment (both mud and coarser particles) and sedimentary structures—the latter by burrowing and boring activity. Other sources include calcareous algae and filamentous BLUE-GREEN ALGAE, which produce carbonate mud, grains, and mound-shaped structures called STROMATOLITES. Most limestones were deposited in subtropical to tropical zones, and sedimentation occurred in shallow water (less than 15 m/50 ft). It is in these areas that the variables that control life (temperature, light penetration, and nutrient supply) are most advantageous. In addition to the fossil content, the

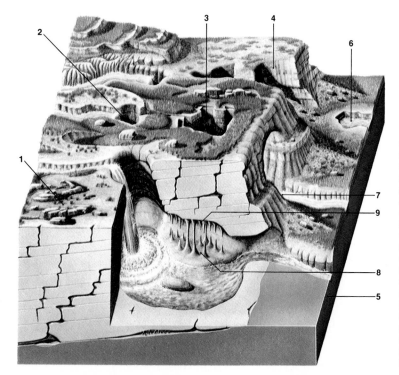

Limestone is slowly dissolved by water that contains carbon dioxide. Calcium carbonate is converted to water-soluble calcium bicarbonate. The removal of the latter by runoff surface water forms deeply grooved cracks, or grikes (1). In areas where water collects, the cracks enlarge to form funnel-shaped holes known as sink holes, or swallow holes (2). These holes may eventually enlarge by continued solution of limestone beneath them to create deep shafts, or chasms (3). Sometimes the roofs of long underground chasms or caves collapse and produce steep-sided ravines, or dry valleys (4). If the limestone rock rests on impermeable rock (5), water flowing from swallow holes through underground joints and caves will surface again as springs (6) or streams (7). The evaporation of water dripping from the roofs and sides of caves or chasms leaves deposits of calcium carbonate. These deposits accumulate and build up from floors of caves as stalagmites (8) or grow downward from the roofs to form stalactites (9).

clastic textures of some limestones, crossbedding, and other indicators of current action also imply the shallow-water origin of limestones.

Limestones differ greatly in texture and color, depending on the size of the shells or crystals composing them and the impurities they contain. Most limestones are light in color and contain fossils. Many are highly fossiliferous and represent ancient shell banks or CORAL REEFS. Minor constituents include silica (usually less than 5%), feldspar, clays, and pyrite. Limestones can form organically or inorganically. Organic rocks include CHALK, COQUINA, and other such FORAMINIFERA-containing deposits. Travertine is an inorganic limestone.

Limestones act as reservoirs for petroleum, natural gas, and groundwater and serve as hosts for ore deposits such as lead and zinc. Limestone is used for agricultural lime, cement, building stone, and concrete aggregate.

limit The study of the mathematical concept of a limit marks the transition from elementary mathematics to a large part of higher mathematics, including the CALCULUS. The most basic type of limit is the limit of a FUNCTION.

The Limit of a Function. A function can be regarded as a machine that is programmed to accept numerical input and produce numerical output. If a function is labeled f, and the input number, or independent variable, is x, then the corresponding output, or dependent variable, is designated $f(x)$, which is read *"f of x."* The statement

$$\lim_{x \to a} f(x) = L$$

is read "the limit of f of x as x approaches a is L." This statement means that the limit number L can be approximated by $f(x)$ to within any desired degree of accuracy by taking x sufficiently close to a. Notice that it is not required that x assume the value a, and in any case the number $f(a)$ need not be the same as L. More precisely, the above statement is an assertion that for any tolerance D on the distance between $f(x)$ and L, it is possible to prescribe a tolerance on d, the distance between x and a, such that $f(x)$ will be within distance D of L whenever x is within distance d of a.

The Limit of a Sequence. A mathematical SEQUENCE is a special type of function. A sequence is a list of mathematical quantities called members, or terms. The sequence 1, 4, 9, 16 is a finite sequence, since it has a finite number of terms (in this case, four). The sequence $a_1, a_2, a_3, a_4, \ldots, a_n, a_{n+1}, \ldots$ is an infinite sequence (it has an infinite number of terms). Infinite sequences may have limits; a finite sequence terminates and so does not approach any limiting value.

The statement

$$\lim_{n \to \infty} a_n = L$$

is read "the limit of a_n as n approaches infinity is L." It means that L can be approximated arbitrarily closely by a_n by taking n sufficiently large. More precisely, if a tolerance D is set for the distance from a_n to L, then it is possible to prescribe an integer N (dependent on D) such that for all n larger than N, the terms a_n lie within distance D of L.

Infinite sequences that have limits are called convergent sequences (see CONVERGENCE).

See also: CONTINUITY.

limitations, statute of   see STATUTE OF LIMITATIONS

limners [lim'-nur] The term *limners* commonly refers to the untutored, usually anonymous portrait painters of 17th-century New England and New York, who provide the earliest evidence of artistic impulses in British North America. After 1670, full-scale portraits were painted of a variety of sitters in the colonies; their names were usually used to identify the unknown artists: for example, the Freake Limner or the Gibbs and Mason limners painted members of those families. The simple, flat delineations of the limner portraits have a clarity and decorative charm that owe much to late medieval British art (see COLONIAL STYLES IN NORTH AMERICA). In the early 18th century the new fashion for baroque status images gradually replaced most of the primitive limner style throughout the colonies, although elements of it survived in the work of itinerant and folk artists in the 19th century.

limnology [lim-nahl'-uh-jee] Limnology (from the Greek prefix *limn-*, "marsh") is the science of the mutual relationships between freshwater organisms and the interactions between these organisms and their freshwater environments such as lakes, ponds, and streams. It is an interdisciplinary HYDROLOGIC SCIENCE combining aspects of meteorology, hydrobiology, hydrochemistry, hydrophysics, and geology.

Limoges [lee-mohzh'] Limoges is the capital city of Haute-Vienne department and an industrial and commercial center in south central France. The city's population is 140,400 (1982). Limoges is located on the Vienne River about 210 km (130 mi) northwest of Bordeaux, on the western edge of the Massif Central. The famous Limoges porcelain has been manufactured there since 1771. Electrical equipment, automobile parts, paper, and shoes are also made in the city. Uranium is mined nearby. The Gothic Cathedral of Saint Étienne, begun in 1273 and completed in 1520, is the most imposing building in the city. Cultural institutions include an excellent ceramic museum (opened 1867) and the University of Limoges (1808).

Limoges was originally the Roman city of Augustoritum. Two towns grew up there, one near the river and one on the hillside, where the Abbey of Saint Martial (9th century), a medieval pilgrimage center, was located. The two towns were united in 1792.

Limón, José [lih-mohn', hoh-zay'] The Mexican-American dancer José Limón, b. Jan. 12, 1908, d. Dec. 2, 1972, was a pioneer of MODERN DANCE and choreography. From 1930 to 1940 he studied dance with Doris Humphrey and Charles Weidman in New York City and performed with their company. Following military service Limón formed his own company in 1947 with Humphrey as artistic codirector. As the José Limón Dance Company it continues to present works by Humphrey and Limón. Limón's dances exhibit a direct, dramatically expressive style of movement. Limón's own roles featured his gifts as an intensely powerful mime, and were based on heroic sufferers, as in *The Moor's Pavane* (1949), drawn from Othello, and in *The Emperor Jones* (1956), adapted from Eugene O'Neill's tragic play.

---

limonite [ly'-muh-nite] The widespread and common hydrated iron OXIDE MINERAL limonite (Fe(OH)·nH_2O) is a minor ore of iron and a source of OCHER and umber pigments. Having no crystalline form and containing highly variable amounts of water, limonite forms yellowish earthy coatings or brown to blackish, stalactitic, grapelike, or fibrous masses and concretions. Hardness is 4–5½, luster is silky or earthy, streak is yellowish brown, and specific gravity is 2.7–4.3. Much of the material formerly thought to be limonite is now known to be a crystalline mineral GOETHITE. Limonite is common in the oxidized portions of SULFIDE MINERAL deposits and in marshes as bog iron ore.

The mineral limonite lacks a crystalline form and occurs in amorphous masses that may contain crystals of the related mineral goethite. Often called brown hematite, this common iron mineral forms the pigment ocher when mixed with clays.

Limosin, Léonard [lee-moo-zan', lay-oh-nar'] Léonard Limosin, or Limousin, c.1505–1576, was a celebrated French enamel painter of the 16th century. He executed enamels for Francis I and was appointed royal enameler to Henry II in 1548. In 1553, in collaboration with the Italian Mannerist painter Niccolo dell'Abbate, he executed a crucifixion altarpiece for Sainte-Chapelle, Paris (Louvre, Paris), which depicts Henry II and Catherine de Médicis as donors. In Paris, Limousin specialized in portraits and executed many for members of the court.

Limousin acquired an elegant and mannered style of portraiture, in which elongated forms are framed with jewellike decorative motifs that suited the sophisticated tastes of his patrons. He created rich and elaborate effects by combining a number of enameling techniques, using opaque enamels, gilding, and grisaille.

---

limpet Limpets are primitive snails of the class Gastropoda, phylum Mollusca. These rock-dwelling, usually intertidal forms are characterized by a flattened, conical shell, with no apparent spiraling. Keyhole limpets, family Fissurellidae, comprise three genera. These have a cleft at the front of the shell or a keyholelike opening at the top for the passage of ventilatory and excretory currents.

The true limpets, family Patellidae, comprise four genera. These limpets lack shell openings, and water currents enter and leave the shell between the foot and mantle cavity. Limpets generally feed by grazing on algal growths on rocks.

---

limpkin [limp'-kin] The limpkin, or courlan, is a long-legged wading bird found in open marshes of the New World, as far north as Georgia; it is the sole member (*Aramus guarauna*) of the family Aramidae. The limpkin's halting gait, resembling a limp, gives it its name. Approximately 64 cm (25 in) in length, it is olive brown, spotted and streaked with white; it has a long, slightly curved bill. Intermediate in size between the CRANE and the RAIL, it exhibits some of the behavioral and physical characteristics of each. It swims well, combing the marshes and waterways for freshwater snails, the staple of its diet.

Limpopo River [lim-poh'-poh] The Limpopo is a 1,600-km-long (1,000-mi) river in southeast Africa. It rises in the Witwatersrand, South Africa; flows in a large arc, first in a northeast direction, separating South Africa from Botswana and Zimbabwe, and then to the southeast across southern Mozambique; and empties into the Indian Ocean. The river's upper reaches, above the confluence with the Marico River, are also called the Krokodil, or Crocodile, and are often dry for several months of the year because much of the catchment area receives little rainfall. The only navigable portion of the Limpopo occurs after its confluence with the Olifants River, the major tributary.

Lin Biao (Lin Piao) [lin bee-ow] The Chinese general and master political strategist Lin Biao, c.1907–1971, played a leading role in the CULTURAL REVOLUTION of 1966–69. A graduate of Chiang Kai-shek's Huangpo (Whampoa) Military Academy, Lin joined (1927) the

Communist party soon after it split from the Kuomintang and served under ZHU DE (Chu Teh). Lin's decisive defeat of Chiang in Manchuria (1948) cleared the way for the Communist takeover of China in 1949. A supporter of MAO ZEDONG, Lin became minister of defense in 1959, compiling the *Quotations from Chairman Mao Zedong* (the famous "little red book"; Eng. trans., 1966) for use in the People's Liberation Army. He was named the successor-designate to Mao in 1969. The details of Lin's death are mysterious. In 1972 the government announced that he had tried to usurp power and had then been killed (September 1971) in the crash of a small jet fighter while fleeing to the USSR.

Lincoln (England)   Lincoln is the county town of Lincolnshire in eastern England. Located on the River Witham about 68 km (42 mi) southeast of Sheffield, it is a major industrial center and agricultural market for the surrounding farmlands. The population is 76,600 (1982 est.). The city manufactures diesel engines, automobile parts, agricultural equipment, and foodstuffs. Lincoln Castle was built (1068) by William the Conqueror; the beautiful Norman cathedral, built in 1075 and one of the most famous in Europe, has an 83-m (271-ft) bell tower called Great Tom. Several Roman ruins are in the vicinity. The Roman city of Lindum, Lincoln was successively settled by Saxons and Danes before being chartered in 1154. During the Middle Ages it was a major wool-trading center.

Lincoln (Nebraska)   Lincoln is the capital of Nebraska and the seat of Lancaster County. The second largest city in the state, it has a population of 191,972 (1990). It is situated in southeastern Nebraska, about 80 km (50 mi) west of the Missouri River. Lincoln is the transportation and manufacturing center of the surrounding grain-producing and livestock-raising region. Meat-packing, pharmaceutical and machinery manufacturing, and railroad shops are the major industries. More than 30 insurance companies are headquartered there. Government is significant in the economy. The state capitol (completed 1934), with its 122-m (400-ft) tower, is visible for miles. The Nebraska State Fair is an annual event. Colleges include the University of Nebraska (1869), Nebraska Wesleyan University (1887), and Union College (1891).

Originally known as Lancaster, Lincoln was founded in 1864. In 1867 the capital was moved from Omaha to Lancaster, which was renamed Lincoln. The city grew rapidly after the railroad arrived in 1870.

Lincoln, Abraham   Abraham Lincoln, the 16th president of the United States, guided his country through the most devastating experience in its national history—the CIVIL WAR. Many historians consider him the greatest American president.

Early Life. Lincoln was born on Feb. 12, 1809, in a log cabin in Hardin (now Larue) County, Ky. His father, Tho-

mas, was a skilled carpenter; little is known about Lincoln's mother, Nancy Hanks Lincoln. Abraham grew up with an older sister, Sarah.

Lincoln's father had purchased three farms in Kentucky before the family moved (1816) to Indiana, "partly on account of slavery," Abraham recalled, "but chiefly on account of difficulty in land titles in K[entuck]y." Land ownership was more secure in Indiana because the Land Ordinance of 1785 provided for surveys by the federal government; moreover, the Northwest Ordinance of 1787 forbade slavery in the area. Lincoln's parents belonged to a faction of the Baptist church that disapproved of slavery, which may account for Abraham's later statement that he was "naturally anti-slavery."

The Lincolns' life near Little Pigeon Creek, in Perry (now Spencer) County, was not easy. Lincoln "was raised to farm work" and recalled life in this "unbroken forest" as a fight "with trees and logs and grubs." Lincoln commented that "there was absolutely nothing to excite ambition for education." He attended "some schools, so called," but for less than a year altogether. "Still, somehow," he remembered, "I could read, write, and cipher to the Rule of Three; but that was all."

Lincoln's mother died in 1818, and the following year his father married a Kentucky widow, Sarah Bush Johnston. She "proved a good and kind mother." In 1828 he was able to make a flatboat trip to New Orleans.

In 1830 the Lincolns left Indiana for Illinois. Abraham made a second flatboat trip to New Orleans, and in 1831 he left home for New Salem, in Sangamon County near Springfield. In New Salem, Lincoln tried various occupations and served briefly in the BLACK HAWK WAR (1832). This military interlude was uneventful except for the fact that he was elected captain of his volunteer company, a distinction that gave him "much satisfaction." It opened new avenues for his life.

Illinois Legislator. Lincoln ran unsuccessfully for the Illinois legislature in 1832. Two years later he was elected to the lower house for the first of four successive terms (until 1841) as a Whig. His membership in the WHIG PARTY was natural. The party's ambitious program of national economic development was the perfect solution to the problems Lincoln had seen in his rural, hardscrabble Indiana past. His first platform (1832) announced: "Time and experience verified that the poorest and most thinly populated countries would be greatly benefitted by the opening of good roads, and in the clearing of navigable streams. There cannot justly be any objection to having rail roads and canals."

As a Whig, Lincoln supported the Second Bank of the United States, the Illinois State Bank, government-sponsored internal improvements (roads, canals, railroads, harbors), and protective tariffs. His Whig vision of the West was not at all pastoral. Unlike most successful American politicians, Lincoln was unsentimental about agriculture, calling farmers in 1859 "neither better nor worse than any other people." He remained conscious of his humble origins and was therefore sympathetic to labor as "prior to, and independent of, capital." He bore no an-

AT A GLANCE

ABRAHAM LINCOLN
16th President of the United States (1861–65)

Nicknames: "Honest Abe"; "Illinois Rail-Splitter"

Born: Feb. 12, 1809, Hardin (now Larue) County, Ky.

Profession: Lawyer

Religious Affiliation: None

Marriage: Nov. 4, 1842, to Mary Todd (1818–82)

Children: Robert Todd Lincoln (1843–1926); Edward Baker Lincoln (1846–50); William Wallace Lincoln (1850–62); Thomas "Tad" Lincoln (1853–71)

Political Affiliations: Whig; Republican

Writings: *Collected Works of Abraham Lincoln* (8 vols., 1953–55), ed. by Roy P. Basler

Died: Apr. 15, 1865, Washington, D.C.

Buried: Oak Ridge Cemetery, Springfield, Ill.

Vice-Presidents: Hannibal Hamlin (1861–65); Andrew Johnson (1865)

Abraham Lincoln

tagonism to capital, however, admiring the American system of economic opportunity in which the "man who labored for another last year, this year labors for himself, and next year he will hire others to labor for him." Slavery was the opposite of opportunity and mobility, and Lincoln stated his political opposition to it as early as 1837.

Lawyer and U.S. Representative. Encouraged by Whig legislator John Todd Stuart, Lincoln became a lawyer in 1836. In 1837 he moved to Springfield, where he built a successful practice. Lincoln courted Mary Todd, a Kentuckian of origins much more genteel than his. After a brief postponement of their engagement, which plummeted Lincoln into a deep spell of melancholy, they were married on Nov. 4, 1842. They had four sons. Mary Todd LINCOLN was a Presbyterian, but her husband was never a church member.

Lincoln served (1847–49) one term as a member of the U.S. House of Representatives, where he opposed the Mexican War, feeling that the Democratic president, James Polk, had violated the Constitution. Lincoln had been indifferent about the annexation of Texas, already a slave territory, but he opposed any expansion that would allow slavery into new areas; hence, he supported the WILMOT PROVISO, which would have barred slavery from any territory gained as a result of the Mexican War. He did not run for Congress again, returning instead to Springfield and the law.

The Slavery Issue and the Lincoln-Douglas Debates. Lincoln "was losing interest in politics" when the KANSAS-NEBRASKA ACT was passed by Congress in 1854. This legislation opened lands previously closed to slavery to the possibility of its spread by local option (popular sovereignty); Lincoln viewed the act as immoral. Although he was not an abolitionist and thought slavery unassailably protected by the Constitution in states where it already existed, Lincoln also thought that America's founders had put slavery on the way to "ultimate extinction" by preventing its spread to new territories. He saw this act, which had been sponsored by Democratic Senator Stephen A. DOUGLAS, as a new and alarming development.

In 1856, Lincoln joined the newly formed REPUBLICAN PARTY, and two years later he campaigned for the Senate against Douglas. In his speech at Springfield in acceptance of the Republican senatorial nomination (June 16, 1858) Lincoln suggested that Douglas, Chief Justice Roger B. Taney, and Democratic presidents Franklin Pierce and James Buchanan had conspired to nationalize slavery. In the same speech he expressed the view that the nation would become either all slave or all free: "A house divided against itself cannot stand."

The underdog in the senatorial campaign, Lincoln wished to share Douglas's fame by appearing with him in debates. Douglas agreed to seven debates: in Ottawa, Freeport, Jonesboro, Charleston, Galesburg, Quincy, and Alton, Ill. Lincoln's strategy was to stress the gulf of principle that separated Republican opposition to slavery as a moral wrong from the moral indifference of the Democrats, embodied in legislation allowing popular sovereignty to decide the fate of each territory. Douglas, Lincoln insisted, did not care whether slavery was "voted up or voted down." By his vigorous showing against the famous Douglas, Lincoln won the debates and his first considerable national fame. He did not win the Senate seat, however; the Illinois legislature, dominated by Democratic holdovers in the upper house, elected Douglas.

Election to the Presidency. In February 1860, Lincoln made his first major political appearance in the Northeast when he addressed a rally at Cooper Union in New York. He was now sufficiently well known to be a presidential candidate. At the Republican national convention in Chicago in May, Lincoln won the nomination, and he went on to win the presidential election. Lincoln selected a strong cabinet that included all of his major rivals for the Republican nomination: William H. SEWARD as secretary of state, Salmon P. CHASE as secretary of the treasury, and Edward Bates as attorney general.

By the time of Lincoln's inauguration in March 1861, seven states had seceded from the Union. His conciliatory inaugural address had no effect on the South, and against the advice of a majority of his cabinet, Lincoln decided to send provisions to FORT SUMTER in Charleston harbor. The fort was a symbol of federal authority—conspicuous in South Carolina, the state that had led secession—and it would soon have had to be evacuated for lack of supplies. On Apr. 12, 1861, South Carolina fired on the fort, and the Civil War began.

The Civil War. As a commander in chief Lincoln was soon noted for vigorous measures, sometimes at odds with the Constitution and often at odds with the ideas of his military commanders. After a period of initial support and enthusiasm for George B. McCLELLAN, Lincoln's conflicts with that Democratic general helped to turn the latter into his presidential rival in 1864. Above all, Lincoln sought a general who would fight, no matter what his politics. He found such a general in Ulysses S. GRANT, to whom he gave overall command in 1864. Thereafter, Lincoln took a less direct role in military planning.

Politics vied with war as Lincoln's major preoccupation in the presidency. The war required the deployment of huge numbers of men and quantities of matériel; for administrative assistance, therefore, Lincoln turned to the only large organization available for his use, the Republican party. With some rare but important exceptions (for example, Secretary of War Edwin M. STANTON), Republicans received the bulk of the civilian appointments from the cabinet to the local post offices. Lincoln tried throughout the war to keep the Republican party together and never consistently favored one faction in the party over another. Military appointments were divided between Republicans and Democrats.

Democrats accused Lincoln of being a tyrant because he proscribed civil liberties. For example, he suspended the writ of *habeas corpus* in some areas as early as Apr. 27, 1861, and throughout the nation on Sept. 24, 1862, and the administration made over 13,000 arbitrary arrests. On the other hand, Lincoln tolerated virulent criticism from the press and politicians, often restrained his commanders from overzealous arrests, and showed no

real tendencies toward becoming a dictator. There was never a hint that Lincoln might postpone the election of 1864, although he feared in August of that year that he would surely lose to McClellan.

The Constitution protected slavery in peace, but in war, Lincoln came to believe, the commander in chief could abolish slavery as a military necessity. The preliminary EMANCIPATION PROCLAMATION of Sept. 22, 1862, bore this military justification, as did all of Lincoln's racial measures, including especially his decision in the final proclamation of Jan. 1, 1863, to accept African Americans in the army. By 1864, Democrats and Republicans differed clearly in their platforms on the race issue: Lincoln's endorsed the 13th Amendment to the Constitution abolishing slavery, whereas McClellan's pledged to return to the South the rights it had had in 1860.

Lincoln's victory in that election thus changed the racial future of the United States. It also agitated the Southern sympathizer and Negrophobe John Wilkes Booth (see BOOTH family), who began to conspire first to abduct Lincoln and later to kill him. On Apr. 14, 1865, five days after Robert E. Lee's surrender to Grant at Appomattox Court House, Lincoln attended a performance of *Our American Cousin* at Ford's Theatre in Washington, D.C. There Booth entered the presidential box and shot Lincoln, who died at 7:22 the next morning.

Lincoln's achievements—saving the Union and freeing the slaves—and his martyrdom just at the war's end assured his continuing fame, as did his eloquent GETTYSBURG ADDRESS (Nov. 19, 1863) and his second inaugural address (Mar. 4, 1865), in which he urged "malice toward none" and "charity for all."

Lincoln, Benjamin   Benjamin Lincoln, b. Hingham, Mass., Jan. 24, 1733, d. May 9, 1810, an American general in the American Revolution, also served (1781–83) as secretary of war. Named (May 1776) a major general in the Continental Army, he won distinction in operations around New York City and in the Saratoga campaign (1777), during which he was wounded. Lincoln was later given command of the American army in the South but was trapped in Charleston, S.C., by the British. His surrender (May 12, 1780) was a serious setback to the American cause. Following a prisoner exchange, Lincoln became secretary of war. In 1787 he commanded the Massachusetts militia force that suppressed SHAYS'S REBELLION.

Lincoln, Mary Todd   Mary Todd Lincoln, b. Lexington, Ky., Dec. 13, 1818, d. July 16, 1882, was the wife of U.S. president Abraham Lincoln. Mary Todd came from a prominent family and was educated at a finishing school. In 1839 she moved to Springfield, Ill., where she met Lincoln, then a lawyer and member of the state legislature; they were married on Nov. 4, 1842.

William H. HERNDON, Lincoln's former law partner, wrote a biography of Lincoln (1889) that pictured a miserable domestic life, but most historians now agree that Herndon hated Mrs. Lincoln and that the marriage was

Mary Todd Lincoln appears in this photograph by Mathew B. Brady taken after Lincoln's death (1865). Her husband's assassination and the deaths of three of her four sons proved overwhelming for her already emotional, high-strung temperament.

not unusually stormy. The deaths of three of the Lincolns' four sons at early ages and the president's assassination at his wife's side in April 1865 made Mary Lincoln extremely unhappy in later life. She fretted needlessly about money, and her surviving son, Robert Todd Lincoln, had her committed to a sanitarium in 1875. After less than a year, however, she was declared sane.

Lincoln Center for the Performing Arts

Lincoln Center for the Performing Arts occupies four city blocks on Manhattan's West Side in New York City; it is bounded by 66th and 62d streets on the north and south and Columbus and Amsterdam avenues on the east and west. The center's seven glass-and-travertine buildings met with considerable criticism for what was regarded as their unimaginative monumentality, but they have proved popular with the public. The three well-designed plazas have been the most successful features of the center.

On the north side of the great central plaza is Avery Fisher Hall (1962; originally Philharmonic Hall), designed by Max Abramovitz, with a glass-walled exterior supported by a grid of thin, tapered columns. The concert hall within, cursed with poor acoustics, was gutted in 1976; the new rectangular hall, designed by Philip C. JOHNSON and John Burgee to the acoustical specifications of Cyril Harris, has been praised for its fine sound. It is the home of the NEW YORK PHILHARMONIC.

South across the plaza is the New York State Theater (1964), designed by Philip Johnson and Richard Foster. The sober exterior gives way to baroque grandeur in the lobby and in the spacious four-story grand foyer above the lobby. The lyre-shaped auditorium, lined with five shallow balconies, was directly inspired by Venice's rococo Teatro Fenice. It is the home of the NEW YORK CITY BALLET and the NEW YORK CITY OPERA.

Dominating the plaza is the gigantic Metropolitan Opera House (1966), designed by Wallace K. HARRISON. The heavily mullioned glass facade is framed by five barrel-vaulted arches. Much of the crowded lobby space is given over to the ungainly grand staircase, to the detriment of audience circulation and convenience. The enormous but acoustically successful auditorium, engineered by Cyril Harris, has four horseshoe-shaped tiers of boxes and balconies. The immense stage has the most modern theatrical equipment available (see METROPOLITAN OPERA).

The opera house is flanked on the south by Damrosch Park, with the onion-shaped Guggenheim Bandshell (1962). The other buildings in the Lincoln Center complex are the Library and Museum of the Performing Arts (1965), the Vivian Beaumont Theater (1965) and beneath it the smaller Mitzi I. Newhouse Theater for experimental works, and the JUILLIARD SCHOOL of Music (1968), which includes the Juilliard Opera House and the Alice Tully Hall for chamber music, as well as studios, classrooms, and offices.

Lincoln University

Established in 1854 as the Ashmun Institute and adopting its present name in 1866, Lincoln University is the oldest liberal arts college in the United States originally established for black education. The coeducational 4-year state school is located in Lincoln University, Pa.

Lincolnshire

Lincolnshire is a county in eastern England located on the North Sea, the River Humber estuary, and The Wash. It has an area of 5,884 km^2 (2,272 mi^2), and the population is 582,600 (1988 est). The county town is LINCOLN. Lincolnshire generally consists of fertile lowlands, where grains and vegetables are grown. Manufactures include heavy metals, chemicals, and agricultural equipment. Prehistoric relics found in the area indicate that settlement occurred as early as the Lower Paleolithic, or Old Stone Age. Lincolnshire was settled by the Romans and, during the Anglo-Saxon period, was under the control at different times of Mercia and Northumbria. Danish settlement took place in the 9th century.

Lind, Jenny

Jenny Lind, b. Sweden, Oct. 6, 1820, d. Nov. 2, 1887, was one of the most celebrated singers of her time. Between 1838 and 1849 she appeared at every major opera house in Europe and was known by her adoring public as "the Swedish nightingale." In 1850 she was brought to the United States by the circus impresario P. T. Barnum. The American public thronged to her recitals, and writers penned poems in her honor and newspaper articles by the hundreds. She left the United States in 1852 with a newly acquired fortune (most of which she donated to charities in Sweden) and a husband, her German accompanist Otto Goldschmidt. In 1856 she settled in England, where she continued her concert career until 1870. She also taught at the Royal College of Music.

Lindbergh, Anne Morrow

[lind'-burg]   An American writer and the wife of aviator Charles A. Lindbergh,

Anne Morrow Lindbergh, b. Englewood, N.J., 1906, received awards for helping her husband chart commercial air routes in 1933. She wrote about these flights in *North to the Orient* (1935) and *Listen! the Wind* (1938). Her best-known book is *Gift from the Sea* (1955), reflections on youth, marriage, age, and the need for privacy. In the 1970s four volumes of her diaries and letters appeared: *Bring Me a Unicorn* (1972); *Hour of Gold, Hour of Lead* (1973), covering the 1932 kidnapping of her infant son; *Locked Rooms and Open Doors* (1974); and *The Flower and the Nettle (1976)*, covering Charles's controversial trips to Germany in the late 1930s. Additional publications are *War Within and Without* (1980) and *The Worry Week* (1985).

Lindbergh, Charles A. Charles Augustus Lindbergh, b. Detroit, Feb. 4, 1902, d. Aug. 26, 1974, achieved fame in 1927 as the first person to fly alone across the Atlantic. This daring act made the pilot "the lone eagle" in the eyes of millions around the world.

After growing up in Little Falls, Minn., Lindbergh learned to fly at age 20. In 1926 he was flying a mail route between Chicago and St. Louis when he heard of a $25,000 prize offered for the first solo Atlantic flight. With the help of St. Louis businesspeople he set out to accomplish this feat in a specially built plane, the *Spirit of St. Louis.* Leaving Roosevelt Field in Long Island, N.Y., at 7:52 AM on May 20, 1927, he arrived at Le Bourget airport, Paris, at 10:22 PM (French time) on May 21. He had flown 5,800 km (3,600 mi) in 33½ hours.

Lindbergh spent much of his subsequent life as a consultant to the aircraft and airline industries. In 1929 he married Anne Spencer Morrow, daughter of the U.S. ambassador to Mexico, Dwight Morrow. Their life, however, was touched by tragedy in 1932 when their infant son was kidnapped from their New Jersey home and murdered. Soon thereafter Congress enacted the "Lindbergh law," making kidnapping a federal crime. After a sensa-

tional trial, Bruno Richard HAUPTMANN was convicted of the crime and executed (1936).

By 1940, Lindbergh had become politically controversial for speaking out in favor of American isolation as war in Europe intensified. Once the United States had entered World War II, however, he served as an aircraft consultant and even flew 50 missions against the Japanese. Lindbergh later used his influence to further U.S. space capabilities and conservation.

linden [lin'-duhn]   Lindens, comprising about 30 species of deciduous trees of the northern temperate regions, belong to the genus *Tilia* of the linden family, Tiliaceae. They are often called basswoods in North America. Lindens have saw-toothed, somewhat heart-shaped leaves and a tough, fibrous inner bark that has been used for cordage and mats. The small, fragrant yellow flowers of many species provide nectar for bees. The light, soft wood is used for containers, interior finish, and wood carving. *T. cordata,* the small-leaved European linden, is one of several European species planted as a shade tree in both Europe and North America.

The American basswood, a member of the linden family, grows in the northeastern and midwestern United States.

The American aviator Charles Lindbergh is shown standing next to The Spirit of St. Louis, *the monoplane he piloted on the first solo, nonstop transatlantic flight in May 1927.*

Lindner, Richard [lind'-nur]   The American painter and illustrator Richard Lindner, b. Hamburg, Germany, Nov. 11, 1901, d. Apr. 16, 1978, studied art in Nuremberg and Munich before emigrating first to France (1933) and then to the United States (1941). He worked as an illustrator for *Fortune, Harper's Bazaar,* and other leading periodicals, but in the 1950s he began to devote full time to painting the arresting, carefully shaded figures, usually of forceful women, that became his trademark—for example, *The Meeting* (1953; Museum of Modern Art, New York City). The solidity and vague sadism of these figures elicited comparisons with the art of the Weimar period in Germany, although analogies with POP ART have also been made.

Lindsay, Sir David [lin'-zee]

Sir David Lindsay (or Lyndsay) of the Mount, c.1490–c.1555, was a pre-Reformation Scottish poet and dramatist best known for his morality play *The Satyre of the Thrie Estatis*. First produced in 1540 and revised and expanded for a 1552 production, it is the only Scottish drama of its kind that survives intact. Lindsay's support for his contemporary John Knox and his fervent belief in the need for just government and religious reform are also reflected in his allegorical poem *A Dialogue between Experience and a Courtier* (1553).

Lindsay, Howard, and Crouse, Russel

Howard Lindsay, b. Waterford, N.Y., Mar. 29, 1889, d. Feb. 11, 1968, and Russel Crouse, b. Findlay, Ohio, Feb. 20, 1893, d. Apr. 3, 1966, collaborated on a number of highly successful Broadway plays. *Life with Father* (1939), with 3,224 performances, had the longest run up to then in Broadway history, while another joint effort, *State of the Union* (1945), won the Pulitzer Prize in 1946.

Lindsay, John V.

John Vliet Lindsay, b. New York City, Nov. 4, 1921, was mayor of New York City from 1966 to 1973. A graduate of Yale Law School, he was elected (1958) to Congress as a representative of Manhattan's "silk stocking" district. In 1965, Lindsay was elected mayor of New York City on the Republican and Liberal tickets. His first administration was beset with strikes by municipal service unions. Denied renomination in the 1969 Republican primary, Lindsay ran as the Liberal party nominee and won. In 1971, he switched to the Democratic party and in 1972 campaigned unsuccessfully to win nomination as the Democratic candidate.

Lindsay, Vachel [vay'-chul]

The poet Nicholas Vachel Lindsay, b. Springfield, Ill., Nov. 10, 1879, d. Dec. 5, 1931, first received recognition for the celebrated "General William Booth Enters Into Heaven" (1913). Between 1906 and 1912, he toured the United States on foot, giving readings of his poetry in return for food and lodging. In his strongly rhythmical verse he sought to revive the art of oral poetry. His publications include *Rhymes To Be Traded for Bread* (1912), *Adventures While Preaching the Gospel of Beauty* (1914), and one of the earliest works of film criticism, *Art of the Moving Picture* (1915).

line

A line, or straight line, is one type of plane curve. In geometry, it is impossible to define all terms; some must be left undefined—for example, *set, point, line*, and *plane*. Although line is ordinarily not defined, it is possible to list some properties of a line. For example, a line is straight, has infinite length (hence, no endpoints), has neither width nor thickness, and is determined uniquely by any two of its points. Line segments, rays, and half-lines are subsets of lines.

Any point on a line separates the line into two half-lines. Any line in a plane separates the plane into two half-planes. The set of points between and including two fixed points A and B is called the line segment AB. A ray is the set of points on a line that lie on one side of a fixed point (called the origin of the ray).

In mathematics a line that has a COORDINATE SYSTEM marked off on it is called a number line. Two perpendicular number lines that intersect at the zero points on both form a rectangular coordinate system. An equation of the form $ax + by + c = 0$, with a and b not both zero, is called a linear equation (equation of a line). Equations of lines can be written in other forms, depending on the information given or desired. The study of sets of points in terms of the coordinates of the points is called ANALYTIC GEOMETRY. If (x_1, y_1) and (x_2, y_2) are the coordinates of two points A and B, then the line AB through them has the equation

$$\frac{y - y_1}{x - x_1} = \frac{y_2 - y_1}{x_2 - x_1} \text{ where the expression } \frac{y_2 - y_1}{x_2 - x_1}$$

is called the slope of the line and is designated m. This is the two-point form of the equation of a line. The equation $y - y_1 = m(x - x_1)$ is called the point-slope form of the equation of the line through (x_1, y_1) having slope m.

lineage [lin'-ee-uhj]

A lineage, in anthropology, is a group of persons who trace their descent unilineally, or through one parent, back to a known ancestor, either male or female. In a matrilineage, descent is determined according to the ancestry of the mother; in a patrilineage, according to that of the father.

Lineages are characteristic both of large-scale cultures such as that of traditional China and India and of small-scale tribal societies such as that of the Ashanti of Ghana. As a form of KINSHIP, lineages have greater depth than the EXTENDED FAMILY, consisting normally of at least four generations. They are considered permanent, outlasting their members, who ultimately become ancestors.

Lineage membership, because it is reckoned by unilineal descent, is unambiguous, and the lineage often acts as a unified body within a given society, assuming group functions. Lineages commonly serve as property-holding groups and as legal groups, avenging wrongs or collecting and paying indemnities for wrongs committed. Often the lineage also has a political function; for example, chieftaincy or kingship often rests with a lineage. Political offices such as membership on a chief's council may also be vested in lineage.

Linear B

The Linear B script was first deciphered by British architect Michael G. F. Ventris, in 1952 and shown to represent a form of Greek about 500 years older

The syllabic script used from c.1500 to c.1400 BC for writing the Mycenaean Greek language is known as Linear B. Examples of Linear B have been found on clay tablets at Knossos on Crete and at Mycenae and Pylos on the Greek mainland.

than that used by Homer. Linear B was found initially at Knossos in central Crete but later also turned up at Mycenaean centers on the Greek mainland. Clay tablets were inscribed to form the archives of palaces at Pylos, Mycenae, and Tiryns in the Peloponnesus and at Thebes in Boeotia, as well as at Knossos. The Cretan tablets probably date from the early 14th century BC; those from the mainland, from the 13th. Some jars, probably Cretan, with short painted inscriptions have also been found.

Linear B consists of about 90 signs. Each sign represents a syllable, usually either a simple vowel or a consonant followed by a vowel. The interpretation is not straightforward, however, because the spelling gives only an outline of how the word was pronounced. The language clearly shows characteristic Greek features, and some Semitic and other loanwords are already present. The numerals operate on the decimal system, though the weights and measures show traces of the Babylonian division into 60 parts.

On Crete, Linear B superseded an earlier, Minoan script called Linear A, which had been in use since the 19th century BC. The identity of the language represented by Linear A remains an enigma. Although it has been assigned to either the Anatolian or Semitic group, convincing proof is lacking.

See also: AEGEAN CIVILIZATION.

linear equation   see EQUATION; LINE

linen   Linen is a yarn or a woven fabric made from the inner bark of the FLAX plant, *Linaceae usitatissimum*. Remnants of linen cloth that are many thousands of years old have been found. During the Middle Ages linen was the principal vegetable textile fiber, hence its name became the generic term for a large number of dress and household items—shirts, underwear, bedclothes, and tablecloths—that were then almost always made of linen.

Once the cotton gin made possible the manufacture of a large volume of cotton fabrics, linen began to lose its importance. Its use today is relatively minor in clothing, although it is still important as an upholstery and drapery fabric, and for fine handkerchiefs, tablecloths, and napkins.

Like cotton, linen consists principally of cellulose. It is resistant to sunlight and is stronger, cooler, absorbs moisture more readily, dries more quickly, has more luster, and soils less quickly than cotton. Aside from its cost—linen is still among the most expensive fibers because of the complexities of processing flax—a principal drawback in its use as a clothing fabric was its tendency to wrinkle. New finishing processes, however, have recently produced a wrinkle-resistant linen.

lingua franca   [lin'-gwuh fran'-kuh]   A lingua franca is any auxiliary language, usually rudimentary, used as a medium between speakers of different laguages. The term first described a mixture of Italian and other languages (*lingua franca*, Frankish tongue) used by traders in the Mediterranean during the Middle Ages. English, since it is spoken throughout the world, especially in its many PIDGIN forms, serves as a lingua franca. In countries where many languages or dialects are spoken one language may be chosen as the lingua franca of commerce and government. Examples include CREOLE, Mandarin Chinese, and SWAHILI, a Bantu language spoken throughout East Africa.

linguistic geography   see GEOGRAPHICAL LINGUISTICS

linguistics   [lin-gwis'-tiks]   Linguistics is the science of language—the pursuit of knowledge about the phenomenon of human language for its own sake. Most linguists also study foreign languages and frequently contribute to the development of materials and methods in language teaching, but these matters come under the rubric of *applied linguistics* and are by-products of linguistic analysis and research.

Implicit and Explicit Linguistic Knowledge. The acquisition of competence in foreign languages constitutes a tool of linguistics. The crucial distinction is between implicit and explicit knowledge. A competent speaker of a language has implicit knowledge of that language—in short, the ability to use the language whether or not its properties are consciously understood. A linguist seeks explicit knowledge—the conscious understanding of a language's properties.

Traditional Grammar. In the West speculation about language began with the Greeks. Although philosophers such as PLATO went no further than to suggest hundreds of fanciful etymologies, by the 1st century BC grammarians like Dionysius Thrax had worked out an elaborate system—later called traditional grammar—by and large faithful to the structure and properties of Greek. When the Roman grammarians Aelius Donatus (4th century AD) and Priscian (6th century) adopted this system for Latin, it worked well because Greek and Latin are genetically related as INDO-EUROPEAN LANGUAGES and structurally similar.

Difficulties with traditional grammar did not become evident until many centuries later when Latin had evolved into its descendant ROMANCE LANGUAGES such as Italian, French, and Spanish. The new languages were so different from Latin that the familiar analysis enshrined in the traditional grammars no longer had much relevance. Because of the esteem in which Latin was held, however, the notion arose that the emerging Romance languages represented corrupt forms of Latin. Scholars urged that

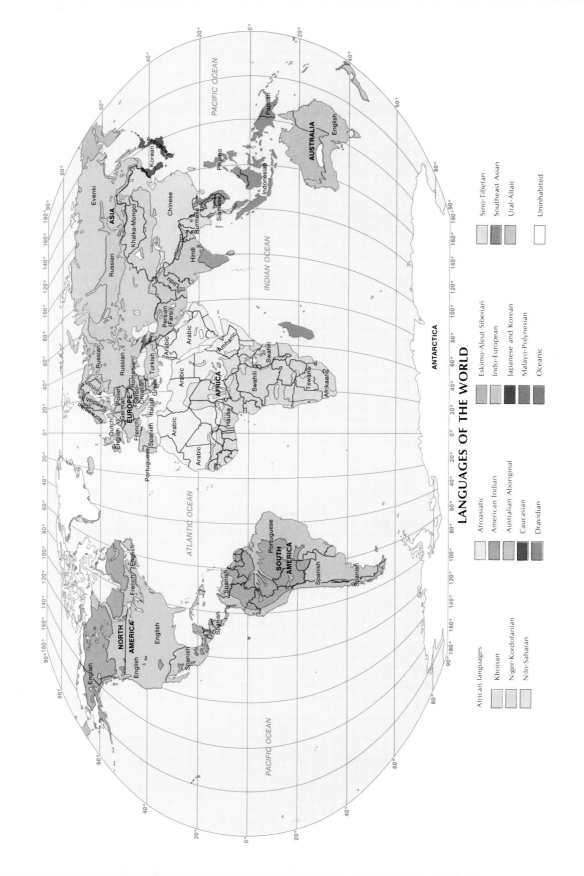

LANGUAGES OF THE WORLD

African languages

	Khoisan
	Niger-Kordofanian
	Nilo-Saharan

	Afroasiatic
	American Indian
	Australian Aboriginal
	Caucasian
	Dravidian

	Eskimo-Aleut-Siberian
	Indo-European
	Japanese and Korean
	Malayo-Polynesian
	Oceanic

	Sino-Tibetan
	Southeast Asian
	Ural-Altaic
	Uninhabited

this corruption should be countered by adherence to the archaic language forms and patterns found in Latin. This fundamentally mistaken view—that language change is inherently pathological and that hence a people's language should be kept immune from its normal course of development—is called linguistic prescriptivism.

With the Renaissance and the 15th-century boom in trade and exploration, information began to arrive in Europe about languages unrelated to and quite different from Greek and Latin. Not surprisingly, traditional grammar was unsuited to cope with the new, exotic languages. One consequence was the development of philosophical interest in properties common to all languages, particularly with reference to canons of universal logic. This movement culminated in the so-called general grammars of the 17th century.

The Beginnings of Modern Linguistics. The English colonization of India during the 18th century uncovered the existence of Sanskrit, an ancient language of religion, philosophy, and literature (see INDO-IRANIAN LANGUAGES). Among the Hindus, Sanskrit occupied a place of importance and esteem analogous to that once held in Christian Europe by Latin.

Linguists noticed almost immediately that Sanskrit bore a remarkable resemblance to Greek and Latin, not only in the shapes of individual words but equally in the organization of morphology and syntax. Sanskrit had also been the object of native grammatical investigation dating back three millennia and preeminently represented by the work of Panini. In 1786, Sir William JONES surmised that Sanskrit, Greek, and Latin may all "have sprung from some common source which, perhaps, no longer exists."

Jones's statement ignited the modern science of linguistics. For the next 100 years the interest was predominantly historical and comparative; linguists investigated the evolution and mutual relations of Sanskrit, Greek, and Latin, GERMANIC, CELTIC, and any additional Indo-European languages they could find. Other language families were also studied, notably URAL-ALTAIC; but it was not until the 20th century that the pale of historical linguistics was extended significantly beyond Europe.

Synchronic Linguistics. During the last years of the 19th century linguists began developing ways of studying a language independently of its history, as an object functioning at any given stage of its existence. An explicit and detailed exposition of the nonhistorical approach did not appear until the posthumous publication in 1916 of *Course in General Linguistics* by the Swiss linguist Ferdinand de Saussure. The new vantage on language came to be known as synchronic linguistics, in contradistinction to historical or diachronic linguistics.

In the two decades after World War I, the Geneva school of linguists continued Saussure's pioneering work; significant brands of linguistics also developed in Denmark under the direction of Otto JESPERSEN and Louis Hjelmslev, as well as in England in association with scholars like J. R. Firth. The most important European linguistic movement of the 1920s and '30s was Czechoslovakia's Prague school, led by Roman JAKOBSON, Nikolai Trubetzkoy, and others.

Behaviorism. During the 1920s, American interest was fueled by the study and analysis of the rich variety of American INDIAN LANGUAGES. Particularly in its formative period, American linguistics developed in close association with SOCIAL ANTHROPOLOGY—Franz BOAS, Edward SAPIR, and Alfred L. KROEBER, for example, were all anthropologists as well as linguists. By the early 1930s, however, descriptive work came more and more to be complemented by a search for theoretical foundations. Under the aegis of BEHAVIORISM, the sweeping, freshly formulated tenets of American linguistic thought were set down in 1933 by Leonard BLOOMFIELD in his book *Language*.

Because of its behaviorist foundations, American linguistics developed a variety of limitations to determine which phenomena might fall within the province of scientific inquiry. The limitations reflected the structuralist tenet that scientific inquiry must be implemented by totally explicit and automatically replicable analytic methods—the so-called discovery procedures—and that the objects discovered or postulated by these methods must be physically defined. In the case of language, this procedure was tantamount to requiring that the defining properties of sentences, verbs, vowels, and so on be manifested behaviorally—that is, in the external behavior of speakers.

Transformational Grammar. Perhaps the single most serious limitation that the structuralists imposed on themselves was derived from their belief that meaning could not be scientifically studied because it showed insufficient physical manifestation to pass the rigorous behaviorist requirements. In the early 1950s, however, one of the most influential structuralists, Zellig Harris of the University of Pennsylvania, began an important series of investigations that ultimately led not only to the development of techniques for the scientific study of meaning but also to a revolution in linguistics. Harris explored the possibility of extending structuralist analysis beyond the limits of the sentence and developed formulas to capture systematic linguistic relations between sentences of different types—formulas that he called transformations. For example, a sentence in the active voice like *Harry drank the beer* was analyzed as being transformationally related to its passive-voice counterpart, *The beer was drunk by Harry*. To the extent that the transformation could be structurally stated, this theory was a breakthrough into a new realm, the linguistic study of meaning.

Though Harris continued developing his own brand of transformational linguistics, probably the most important event in American linguistics since the appearance of Bloomfield's book was the publication in 1957 of *Syntactic Structures* by Noam CHOMSKY of the Massachusetts Institute of Technology. A former student of Harris's, Chomsky took over the concept of transformation and incorporated it into a new linguistic theory now known as transformational-generative, or simply generative, linguistics. The theory synthesizes theoretical and methodological elements from mathematics and the philosophy of language and abandons the structuralists' behaviorism for neorationalism, with roots going back to the 17-century concept of general grammar.

The Major Branches of Linguistics

Laypeople commonly believe that a language operates through the element called words, which are strung together into sentences to express thoughts. Although an oversimplification, this view does reflect fundamental truths about language.

According to the popular conception, words themselves have a dual role. First, they serve as building blocks for sentences; each individual word is viewed as having a meaning. Second, words have spellings, which are viewed as being more or less immutable and inviolable but which in turn are coupled with pronunciations that are characterized by considerable instability and have a tendency to degenerate. The first of these views seems to be essentially correct, except that the popular conception of *meaning* is fuzzy and inaccurate. The second conception, however, is backward, since both historically and functionally a word's pronunciation is primary, while its spelling not only is derivative but also is in fact dispensable. Even now many languages lack WRITING SYSTEMS, yet their words show no more variability or instability in pronunciation than do the words of English or any other language with an established orthography.

A word is an element coupling a meaning and a pronunciation, but comparisons between unrelated languages show the fundamental independence of meanings and pronunciations. For example, the English word *foot* may be compared with its nearest Hebrew equivalent, *regel*. The words differ in more than pronunciation; their meanings are not identical either. Both *regel* and *foot* designate the pedal extremity, but *regel* also designates the whole limb of which the pedal extremity is the end, a portion of the anatomy for which English uses the word *leg*.

Phonetics. PHONETICS studies the nature and mechanisms of human speech sounds independently of the meanings that those sounds are used to convey. The English word *mopper* ("one who mops"), for instance, is characterizable in phonetic terms as beginning with and containing segments formed by certain significant lip movements (spelled *m* and *pp* in this case); as being pronounced more loudly on the first syllable (*mop*) than on the second (*per*); as differing only in the first segment from the word *hopper*; and so on.

Semantics. SEMANTICS studies the nature and organization of the meanings conveyed by human language independently of the speech sounds used to symbolize those meanings. Thus aspects of the word *mopper* that are of interest to semanticists include delimitation of the set of entities designable by the term *mopper*; the contribution of the constituents *mopp-* and *-er* to the word's overall meaning; the fact that *mopper*, "one who mops," bears a semantically relevant relation to *hopper* in the sense "one who hops" but not also in the sense "a container for transferring loose material"; the fact that a *mopper* is a kind of *cleaner* and that other members of the same set include *sweeper* and *duster*; and so on.

Syntax. The relation between sentences and thoughts is not nearly so clear or foregone as was once assumed. The discipline of PSYCHOLINGUISTICS has shown that the term *thought* should be eschewed where possible in favor of more serviceable concepts. One such concept is *meaning*: human languages encode meanings into sounds through symbols called words, which enter into combinations called sentences.

The phonetic structure of a sentence is partially but not totally a sum of the phonetic structures of its component words. Likewise, the semantic structure of a sentence is partially but not completely determined by the meanings of its component words. As a result, when the phonetic and semantic variances are abstracted out of the comparable sentences in any two languages, an unaccounted-for residue of differences remains: elements present in one language but absent from the other, elements receiving multiple representation, and discrepancies in word order.

If these differences are neither phonetic nor semantic, what type of differences are they? Linguists tend to agree that the differences indicate the existence of a third level of language organization, the so-called syntactic level (see SYNTAX). Syntactic facets of the word *mopper* would include its derivational structure—that is, the PARTS OF SPEECH of both the word and its constituents *mopp-* and *-er*; its inflectional structure—for example, the fact that a plural form, *moppers*, exists; and its possible syntactic functions—for example, that of subject in the sentence "The mopper swabbed the deck."

Phonology. Evidence also exists for a fourth organizational level of language, phonology (see PHONOLOGY AND MORPHOLOGY), embracing aspects of both syntax and phonetics. Fundamentally, a language's phonological system specifies the deployment of its phonetic resources within the frames provided by the syntax. For example, the syntactic fact that the English nouns *mopper* and *mop* have plural forms *moppers* and *mops*, respectively, is complemented by the phonetic fact that *-s* is pronounced differently in each instance—voiced (vibration of the vocal cords) in *moppers* but voiceless (vocal cords at rest) in *mops*.

The phonological system provides the special relation between the voiced and voiceless sounds. This special relation is neither an exclusively phonetic fact—the final sounds of *moos* and *moose*, for instance, are phonetically identical with those of *moppers* and *mops*, respectively, yet lack the special relation found between the latter two sounds—nor an exclusively syntactic fact—the same special relation holds between the final sounds of the possessives *mopper's* and *mop's* and the verbs *slobbers* and *pops*, although these suffixes are syntactically distinct from the plural suffix.

Morphology and Lexicology. Most linguists recognize at least two additional organizational levels, morphology and lexicology (see LEXICOLOGY AND LEXICOGRAPHY). In traditional grammar a language's morphology gives the patterns internal to a word; syntax examines the relations among words in a sentence. Lexicology is the branch of theoretical linguistics that corresponds to the applied science of lexicography and is thus concerned with the question of a language's repertory of words and other lexical items. In contemporary usage, a language's lexicological inventory, or lexicon, is viewed as either complementary or parallel to its semantics, syntax, morphology, and phonology.

Language in Time and Space

Despite the importance of the distinction, the two modes of linguistic inquiry—the synchronic and the historical—were not kept sharply apart by linguists until the early part of the 20th century. An example of the difference between the synchronic and historical perspectives is provided by the English word *went*. Originally *went* was the past tense of the verb *wend*. In time, however, it came to replace the original past tense (*yede*, from Old English *eode*) of the verb *go*, and the verb *wend* itself developed a new regular past tense form, *wended*. Because of this development, Modern English *went* is synchronically the past tense of *go* but historically the past tense of *wend*.

Just as language change through time constitutes the subject matter of HISTORICAL LINGUISTICS, language variation in space provides the material for GEOGRAPHICAL LINGUISTICS, which includes both linguistic geography and dialectology. Linguistic geography studies differences of language usage in relation to differences of locality, with special attention to geographic and demographic conditions either favoring or hindering the diffusion of linguistic features. Dialectology is concerned with the development and mutual relations of regional and social varieties of a given language.

Language, Culture, Society, and the Individual

Since language is an exclusive property of human beings, the object of the science of linguistics—unlike the object of sciences such as chemistry or biology—is exclusively human. This fact might be sufficient to put linguistics in a special relation to the other social sciences, except that language interpenetrates the various human faculties and institutions so thoroughly that specific branches of linguistics have had to be developed to study each aspect. ANTHROPOLOGICAL LINGUISTICS and ethnolinguistics are the studies of the relation of language to culture, SOCIOLINGUISTICS deals with its relation to society, and psycholinguistics examines the interaction between language and mind. An especially close relation also exists between language and literature and between language and philosophy; these include the subdiscipline known as the philosophy of language.

The study of writing cannot be separated from linguistics; various other disciplines study language as a special case of broader concerns. In semiotics, for example, language is a special but particularly important case of a symbolic system. COMMUNICATIONS includes such paralinguistic fields as ANIMAL COMMUNICATION, SIGN LANGUAGE, and gesturemics. Several branches of mathematics, notably LOGIC, CALCULUS, and AUTOMATA THEORY, are also central to linguistics, as is CRYPTOLOGY, the analysis and decipherment of codes. Mathematical linguistics is dedicated to the study of the formal properties of language. Statistical linguistics refers to the application of probability theory to various analytical problems where quantitative significance must be reckoned with. Computational linguistics involves the computerization of linguistic data for practical or theoretical reasons. Neurolinguistics embraces the study of the anatomy and physiology of the brain as correlative with specific levels and patterns of language organization. Finally, onomastics is the linguistic study of names, particularly of persons and places.

Linlithgow, Victor Alexander John Hope, 2d Marquess of [lin-lith'-goh, mar'-kwes]   The 2d marquess of Linlithgow, b. Sept. 24, 1887, d. Jan. 5, 1952, was British viceroy of India from 1936 to 1943. Having served on commissions concerned with Indian affairs since 1926, he became viceroy shortly after passage of the Government of India Act (1935), which provided for provincial governments responsible to the Indian electorate. Linlithgow inaugurated the new system with skill. At the beginning of World War II (1939), however, he declared India a belligerent without consulting the Legislative Assembly. The offended Congress party leaders responded by resigning from the provincial ministries and later (1942) launching the "Quit India" movement. Linlithgow jailed the leaders of this civil disobedience campaign, including Mahatma GANDHI and Jawaharlal NEHRU. In 1943 he was replaced as viceroy by Lord WAVELL.

Linnaeus, Carolus [lin-ay'-uhs, kar-oh'-luhs]   The Swedish biologist Carolus Linnaeus, b. May 23, 1707, d. Jan. 10, 1778, made two major contributions to the field of natural science: the classification of all known plants and animals, and a system of assigning a single scientific name to each plant and animal. This system, called binomial nomenclature, assigns a two-word Latin name to each organism. The first word is the genus to which the organism belongs; the second, often descriptive, is the species name. The house cat, for example, has the scientific name *Felis domesticus.* Its relative the lion is *Felis leo.*

Linnaeus became interested in classification while studying the stamens and pistils (male and female sex structures) of flowers. He then used the numbers of these

Carolus Linnaeus, a Swedish botanist, developed the systematic use of two names for classifying plants, animals, and microorganisms. He coined the term Homo sapiens, *which means wise man, to classify humans.*

structures to classify all known flowering plants. Although earlier publications existed, his classification of plants achieved its final form in his book *Systema Plantarum* (1753). The book *Systema Naturae* (1758) comprises the classification of more than 4,000 animals, even human beings. It was Linnaeus in this book who first gave humans the scientific name *Homo sapiens.* He was also the first to use the signs ♂ and ♀ for male and female.

In recognition of his work, Linnaeus was knighted by the Swedish government in 1761. Shortly afterward, he officially changed his name to Carl von Linné.

Linotype [line'-uh-tipe] The Linotype is a mechanical type-composing machine that produces complete lines of type in solid metal (slugs). It was invented by Ottmar MERGENTHALER in the late 1880s and provided a quicker method of composition than typesetting by hand (see TYPE AND TYPESETTING).

The machine consists of four main sections—keyboard, magazine, casting mechanism, and distribution mechanism. The keyboard resembles that of a TYPEWRITER. When the operator presses the appropriate button, a matrix is released from a channel in a storage magazine and transferred to an assembler box, gradually building up a line of matrices. A character stamped in a recess on one of the vertical edges of each matrix serves as a mold for casting. Before casting, wedge-shaped spacebands are inserted between words to justify the line, or make the line fill the measure. The line of matrices and spacebands is brought into contact with a mold; molten metal is then pumped into the mold to cast the entire line of

A linotype operator sets the type for a weekly newspaper in this 1949 photograph. Invented during the 1880s, the linotype was among the earliest and most widely used mechanical typesetting devices.

type. (Hence, the name Linotype.) After casting, the line is automatically trimmed and then ejected onto a galley with other lines already set.

As soon as the line is cast, the spacebands are returned to their box and the matrices are transferred to a distributor bar suspended over the top of the magazine. The matrices move along this bar and drop into their correct channels according to combinations of teeth cut away on the matrices. The operation of the whole machine is entirely automatic. Slugs are more easily handled than individual letters, so Linotype saves a great deal of labor formerly spent in manually distributing type back into the type case. A disadvantage is the limited number of letters and symbols that can be set.

linseed oil Linseed oil, from the seeds of the FLAX plant, is used as a drying component in PAINTS and as a binder in INKS. Flax produces the LINEN fiber, and linseed oil was originally a by-product of the linen industry; but in the United States the plant is now grown solely for its oil. The oil changes from a thin liquid to a tough, clear, water-resistant yet flexible film when exposed to oxygen. It responds to heating or liming to produce a heavier-bodied oil that has a high gloss and a faster dry and is more adaptable to paint and ink use. When chemically or physically combined with synthetic or natural resin, the blend produced is known as VARNISH.

lintel see POST AND LINTEL

Linz Linz, the capital city of Upper Austria province, is in north central Austria on the Danube River, west of Vienna. Austria's third largest city, it has a population of 204,799 (1986 est.). A busy river port and rail junction, Linz manufactures iron and steel, machinery, and chemicals.

Originally the Roman fortress-settlement of Lentia (2d century AD), Linz became an important market town on the trade route from Italy to the Baltic during the Middle Ages. In the 15th century, during the residence of Holy Roman Emperor Frederick III, the city became a provincial capital. The Romanesque church of Saint Martin was begun in 799. Notable baroque structures include the cathedral (17th century), where Anton Bruckner was an organist (1855–68).

lion Lions, *Panthera leo*, are among the great or roaring cats of the family Felidae. Though the male lion is called the king of beasts, it is the less heavy and less majestic female lion that does most of the stalking and killing of prey and is the center of the lion pride (family). A male lion may be 1.8–2.4 m (6–8 ft) long, with the addition of a tufted tail of 58–89 cm (23–35 in), stand about 90 cm (3 ft) tall at the shoulder, and weigh 177–227 kg (390–500 lb). A lion's legs are short and massive, with large feet and heavy, sharp claws. In the male, the large head is usually framed with a ruff or mane. The coat is

The lion usually hunts in groups, one lion driving prey toward other lions lying in wait. The adult male (right) often takes no active role in the hunt but nevertheless will claim his portion of the kill. Lions live in groups called prides, each including several males, several females, and cubs. Common throughout central Africa, lions are in danger of extinction in India.

tawny yellow, with accents of black on the manes, ears, and tail tips of mature animals.

Within historic times the lion was common in many parts of Europe, Africa, and Asia. Today it is found only in protected areas south of the Sahara in Africa and in the Gir forest, a wildlife sanctuary in India. The Gir lions have some structural differences from the African lions. Lions favor open, grassy plains and thornbush country where water is available. They avoid dense forests. The prides are strongly territorial, defending against intrusion by other prides. Lions hunt at night and are a major factor in controlling the populations of grazing animals on the African savanna (see SAVANNA LIFE).

Lipchitz, Jacques [leep-sheets', zhahk] The French sculptor Chaim Jacob Lipchitz, known as Jacques Lipchitz, b. Lithuania, Aug. 22, 1891, d. May 26, 1973, was a vital figure in the development of modern sculpture. He achieved acclaim early in his long career for his cubist works, from which evolved the robust and solid forms characteristic of his mature style. His work is unified by several recurrent themes, including musicians, maternities, portraits, and improvisations.

Inspired by the aesthetic of CUBISM, Lipchitz executed such masterpieces as the pierced *Man with a Guitar* (1916; Museum of Modern Art, New York City). Although the flattened planes and angular masses remained prominent in his works of the 1920s and '30s, the *Bather*

(1923–25; Marlborough Gallery, New York City) marked the end of his purely cubist phase and the beginning of his exploration of a sculpture of themes and ideas rather than of formal relationships.

In *Figure* (1926–30; Museum of Modern Art, New

In the late 1920s and the 1930s, the Lithuanian-American sculptor Jacques Lipchitz began creating voluminous, undulating forms inspired by themes with strong religious or mythic meaning, such as his joyous Song of the Vowels. (Kunsthaus, Zurich.)

York City), Lipchitz synthesized his prior aesthetic examinations and made a decisive turn toward the monumentality expressed in his *Rape of Europa* (1941; Ingersoll Collection, Penllyn, Pa.), an allegorical comment on Hitler's conquest of Europe. After emigrating (1941) to the United States he developed a massive, vigorous style that culminated in his monument titled *Peace on Earth* (1967–69; Los Angeles Music Center).

lipid

lipid [lip'-id]   The term *lipid* describes a group of biological compounds that are insoluble in water but are relatively soluble in many organic solvents.

Classification

Lipids can be classified in three subgroups based on chemical composition: hydrocarbons, simple lipids, and complex lipids. Hydrocarbons contain carbon (C) and hydrogen (H) only. Simple lipids contain C, H, and oxygen (O). Complex lipids contain one or more additional elements, such as phosphorus (P), nitrogen (N), or sulfur (S).

Simple lipids can be segregated into structural types, which are fatty acids (FA), waxes, triglycerides (TG), and sterols. A fatty acid is a long-chain monocarboxylic acid. A wax is the ester of a long-chain alcohol and a fatty acid. A triglyceride is the ester of a glycerol that contains three FA molecules. Sterols are a special class of alcohols; they may combine with a fatty acid to form sterol esters.

Among the complex lipids, important structural types are phosphoglycerides, phosphosphingolipids, and glycolipids. The parent phosphoglyceride, phosphatidic acid (PA), is similar in structure to a triglyceride except that the 3-hydroxyl group of the glycerol moiety is esterified to phosphoric acid rather than to FA. Further esterification of the phosphoric acid of PA with a variety of small, hydroxyl-containing molecules leads to a series of derived phosphoglycerides, including phosphatidyl choline (PC), commonly known as lecithin, and phosphatidyl ethanolamine (PE).

The phosphosphingolipids are derived from sphingosine. The formation of an amide with an FA at the 2-position yields ceramide. Esterification of the 1-hydroxyl of ceramide with phosphorylcholine gives sphingomyelin, the major phosphosphingolipid. If the 1-hydroxyl group of ceramide is linked instead to a simple sugar, a cerebroside glycolipid is formed. The further addition of several amino sugars yields more complex glycolipids, the gangliosides.

Distribution and Function

Lipids are found in all organisms as structural components of the cell membrane. In most animals the major membrane lipids are lecithin, phosphatidyl ethanolamine, phosphatidyl serine, and a sterol, cholesterol. Cell membranes of the central nervous system contain, in addition to the above, sphingomyelin, cerebrosides, and gangliosides. In higher plant membranes, lecithin and PE predominate, although phosphatidyl glycerol (PG) and phosphatidyl inositol (PI) are also present. Cholesterol is absent, but other sterols, known as phytosterols, are commonly present.

Bacterial membranes are unique in that lecithin is rarely present and sterols are completely absent; PE and PG are usually the major lipids.

Although triglycerides are not important membrane lipids, they are stored in most animals and plants as a metabolic energy reserve. In vertebrates TG is located in adipose (fat) tissue. In insects TG is concentrated in a specific fat body that functions both as a depot and as a center for triglyceride metabolism. In higher plants TG is found in the seeds of most plants and is the source of most vegetable oils. In a few plants, such as the avocado, the palm, and the olive, the fruit also contains large amounts of triglycerides.

Lipids have a number of specialized functions. In mammals subcutaneous fat retards loss of body heat. Hydrocarbons and waxes on insect cuticle, as well as on plant leaves and fruit, aid in water retention. Certain cy-

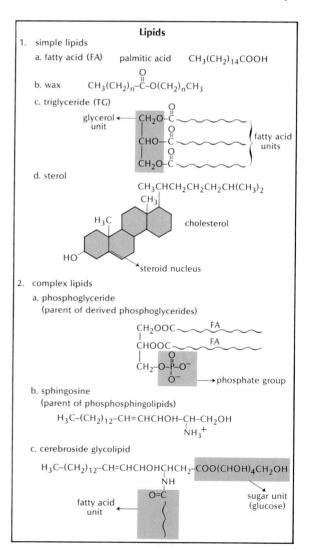

clic FA, the prostaglandins, are involved in blood clotting and hormonal responses in mammals, and a variety of other FA derivatives serve as sex attractants and growth regulators in insects. Sex hormones and the adrenal corticoids of higher animals are lipids derived from cholesterol. Essential dietary lipids include certain polyunsaturated fatty acids and the vitamins A, D, E, and K.

Metabolism

Triglycerides supply 30 to 50 percent of the calories of the average American diet. Ingested TG is hydrolyzed in the gut and absorbed as fatty acid and monoglyceride. Resynthesis of TG takes place within the intestinal cells and appears first in lymph and then in blood as the major component of chylomicrons, lipoproteins secreted by intestinal cells, which transport dietary lipid to adipose tissue and the liver.

Lipid manufactured in the liver, chiefly from carbohydrates, is transported in the blood by three other lipoproteins that are named according to their behavior in an ultracentrifuge: very low-density lipoproteins (VLDLs), involved in TG transport; low-density lipoproteins (LDLs), for cholesterol transport; and high-density lipoproteins (HDLs), the carriers of phosphoglycerides and cholesterol. In the capillaries of adipose tissue, the TG of chylomicrons and VLDLs are hydrolyzed to glycerol and FA. The FA is taken up by adipose cells and again converted to TG for deposition. At the same time, TG within the cells is hydrolyzed and released into the blood as FA and transported to other tissues for oxidation.

See also: FATS AND OILS; KREBS CYCLE; LYMPHATIC SYSTEM.

———

Lippi, Fra Filippo [lip'-pee, frah fee-lip'-poh] Fra Filippo Lippi, c.1406–1469, also called Lippo Lippi, was a leading painter of the Early Renaissance Florentine school. In his graceful portrayals of biblical personages and incidents he displayed the gifts of a superb draftsman and colorist as well as those of a natural storyteller.

Lippi, an orphan, was raised in a Carmelite monastery and became a monk at the age of 15. The religious life did not suit him, however, and he left the Carmelite order about 1431, later marrying Lucrezia Buti. Their son, Filippino Lippi, also became a prominent painter.

Lippi's earliest datable work is *Madonna Enthroned* (1437; National Gallery, Rome), in which, like Masaccio (who may have been his teacher), he achieved a sense of grandeur by using monumental figures, heavy draperies, and lighting designed to heighten the sculptural effect. The detailed domestic scenery in the background suggests a link with the Flemish masters; he may also have drawn inspiration from the relief sculptures of Donatello and Lorenzo Ghiberti, then key figures in Florentine art. Lippi's synthesis of these influences enabled him to bring new ideas to painting and to advance the work of his pupils, who included Sandro Botticelli and Il Pesellino.

Among Lippi's panel paintings is *Coronation of the Virgin* (1441–47; Uffizi, Florence); here, the crowded yet controlled pictorial surface displays the painter's lyrical

In Madonna and Child, *one of Filippo Lippi's soft-hued paintings from the 1440s, the solid and sober volumes of his earlier figures give way to a more colorful and decorative elaboration. (National Gallery of Art, Washington, D.C.)*

use of color. Lippi's frescoes in the Prato Cathedral (1452–65) show his mastery of the perspectival format, then relatively new.

Lippizaner see HORSE

———

Lippmann, Walter [lip'-mahn] The American journalist Walter Lippmann, b. New York City, Sept. 23, 1889, d. Dec. 14, 1974, was a major journalistic commentator of his time. Lippmann's education was broad. He was graduated from Harvard University in the famous class of 1909 and then worked as a graduate assistant to George Santayana. William James was one of his teachers; Lincoln Steffens became his mentor. With Herbert Croly he founded the *New Republic* in 1914, and after World War I he served as an aide to E. M. House preparing data for the Versailles peace conference. In 1921 he joined the *New York World* and was its editorial page edi-

Walter Lippmann was one of the most influential political commentators of the 20th century. His Pulitzer Prize-winning syndicated column, "Today and Tomorrow," analyzed social, political, and ethical issues for 36 years.

tor from 1929 to 1931. He then became a special writer for the *New York Herald Tribune*, and his column was syndicated in several newspapers.

Lippmann's early books, such as *A Preface to Politics* (1913) and *Public Opinion* (1922), displayed an astute understanding of politics. As a political commentator he took varying stands. *The Public Philosophy* (1955) was almost a document of "the new conservatism." Lippmann was, however, a strong backer of President John F. Kennedy and, until he became disillusioned with the war in Vietnam, of President Lyndon B. Johnson.

Lippold, Richard [lip'-ohld]   The American sculptor Richard Lippold, b. Milwaukee, Wis., May 3, 1915, is best known for his abstract wire pieces made in the tradition of constructivism. His first small sculptures were made (1942) from available junk metal, but after he moved (1944) to New York City he concentrated on large, elegant, geometrically designed wire works that express a preoccupation with delineating space. *Variation No. 7: Full Moon* (1949–50; Museum of Modern Art, New York City), a major work of this period, was intentionally in-

Richard Lippold's Variation No. 7: Full Moon *(1949–50) typifies his intricate constructions of wire and metal. (Museum of Modern Art, New York City.)*

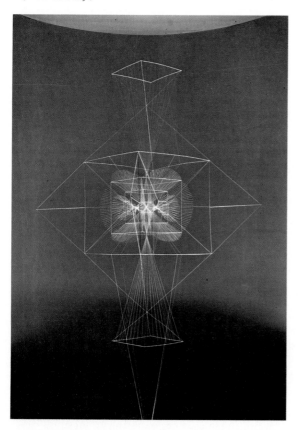

stalled in semidarkness with spotlights on the wires so as to seem to float in space. Since the 1960s, and continuing into the 1980s, Lippold's work has increased to monumental size, and he has collaborated with several architects on designing wire pieces for public buildings.

Lipton, Sir Thomas   Sir Thomas Johnstone Lipton, b. Glasgow, Scotland, May 10, 1850, d. Oct. 2, 1931, was the founder of the tea and provision company, Lipton, Ltd. Lipton made his fortune primarily on cured meats, eggs, butter, and cheeses. His small store in Glasgow grew to include a chain of shops throughout the United Kingdom; he also owned foreign tea, coffee, cocoa, and rubber plantations; fruit orchards, bakeries, and jam factories in England; and a meat-packing house in Chicago. Lipton was knighted in 1898 and made a baronet in 1902.

liquefied natural gas   see PETROLEUM INDUSTRY

liquefied petroleum gas   see PETROLEUM INDUSTRY

liquid   Liquid is the state of matter in which molecules or atoms have sufficient kinetic energy to flow, but insufficient kinetic energy to rise out of a container. Like gases, liquids are fluids. Given enough energy, a solid substance will usually melt, becoming a liquid; also, a liquid, when given enough energy, will boil (or vaporize), becoming a gas.

General Properties. The properties of a liquid are related to the properties of the same substance in the gaseous or solid state. Thus a liquid, being in a condensed state, has a density near that of the solid; it is usually somewhat less dense, but in a few cases, such as the water-ice system, the liquid is more dense. Like solids, liquids are difficult to compress. Because of their incompressibility and inability to support shear stress (sliding forces), liquids will transmit pressure in all directions (Pascal's law).

Depending on shape and the attractive forces present, the molecules of liquids are sometimes able to form loosely bound clusters. Long-chain molecules can form parallel alignments. Organic molecules with hydroxyl or amino groups are sometimes loosely joined by HYDROGEN BONDS, thereby creating a limited long-range order.

Surface Tension. The molecules in a liquid attract each other. A molecule in the interior is attracted equally in all directions, but a molecule at the surface is attracted only by other molecules beneath and beside it. This results in an unbalanced force at the surface called SURFACE TENSION. A combination of surface tension and adhesion (or nonadhesion) to the container causes the liquid surface to bend upward (or downward) at the edges, into a shape called a meniscus.

Electrical Conduction. Many liquids are conductors of electricity. If the liquid is a molten metal, conduction is by free electrons. Molten salts conduct current by the migration of the ions into which the salt has dissociated. A liquid that is a poor conductor when pure can be a solvent of substances that readily yield ions to transport the electricity. Water, for example, is a poor conductor when pure but is an excellent solvent for ion-producing substances.

Solutions. Without undergoing any chemical reaction, liquids can form solutions of solids, other liquids, and gases (see SOLUBILITY). The liquids alcohol and water are miscible. On the other hand, oil and water are immiscible. A carbonated beverage is an example of a solution of a gas in water.

See also: FLUID MECHANICS; KINETIC THEORY OF MATTER; PHASE EQUILIBRIUM; SUBLIMATION.

liquid crystal   Liquid crystals are substances that do not melt directly to the LIQUID phase but first pass through a paracrystalline stage in which the molecules are partially ordered. In this stage a liquid crystal is a cloudy or translucent fluid but has some of the optical properties of a solid CRYSTAL.

The three major types of liquid crystals—smectic, nematic, and cholesteric, or twisted nematic—are designated by the alignments of the rod-shaped molecules. Smectic liquid crystals have molecules parallel to one another, forming a layer, but within the layer no periodic pattern exists. Nematic types have the rodlike molecules oriented parallel to one another but have no layer structure. The cholesteric types have parallel molecules, and the layers are arranged in a helical, or spiral, fashion. The molecular structure can be altered easily by mechanical stress, electric and magnetic fields, pressure, and temperature. A liquid crystal also scatters light that shines on it, cholesteric types often in iridescent colors. Because of these properties, liquid crystals are often used to display letters and numbers on calculators and digital watches or to test for heat-sensitive areas on other materials.

A normally translucent liquid crystal can become turbulent in some regions when an electric field is applied to it. Light is scattered solely from the turbulent regions, and images are formed by controlling the size and shape of the turbulent areas. Flat, liquid-crystal television screens can replace bulky picture tubes but currently are confined to small applications (hand-held TVs) due to poor picture resolution.

liquor   see BRANDY; GIN; RUM; VODKA; WHISKEY

Lisboa, Antonio Francisco   see ALEIJADINHO

Lisbon   [liz'-buhn]   Lisbon (Portuguese: Lisboa) is the capital, largest city, and chief port of Portugal. The population of the city is 829,600 (1986 est.), and that of its metropolitan area is 2,119,600. More than 20% of Portugal's population live in Lisbon and its suburbs. The city lies on the northern shore of the Tagus River about 13 km (8 mi) from the Atlantic, on the westernmost piece of land in Europe. Its harbor is one of the finest in southern Europe.

Contemporary City.   The oldest part of Lisbon lies around a steep hill where the Castle of Saint George, built

Lisbon, the capital and largest city of Portugal, is situated along the Tagus River on the Atlantic Ocean. One of the world's great maritime cities, Lisbon was the center of a trading empire founded during the 15th and 16th centuries.

originally as a Moorish fortification, stands. On the lower ground to the west, the Baixa district was built after the earthquake of 1755, with straight, wide streets and spacious squares. The docks stretch along the waterfront, and modern residential quarters have been built on the hills to the north and west.

Up to two-thirds of Portugal's seaborne trade passes through Lisbon, some of it in transit from Spain. A manufacturing district has been developed to the south of the Tagus estuary, with petroleum refining, cement, steel, and consumer-goods industries.

Lisbon is the seat of the Portuguese government and is the country's chief cultural and educational center. The University of Lisbon (1290; reestablished 1911) is Portugal's largest university. Landmarks include the medieval cathedral, the Jéronimos Monastery, and the Tower of Belém.

History.   The origins of Lisbon are unknown, although it may have been founded (c.1200 BC) by the Phoenicians. Developed by the Romans during the 3d century BC as Felicitas Julia, it was captured by Germanic invaders in the 5th century AD. In the 8th century the city was taken by the Moors, who called it Lixbuna and held it until 1147, when it was taken by Christian Portuguese from the north. In 1256 the seat of government was transferred there from Coimbra.

Lisbon began to grow significantly with the discovery of the sea route to India and the development of oceanic trade. It became one of Europe's leading cities and the chief port serving the vast Portuguese Empire. The city declined, however, during the period of Spanish rule (1580–1640) over Portugal. In 1755 much of Lisbon was destroyed in one of the most disastrous earthquakes known in Europe. It was rebuilt under the direction of the crown minister, the marquês de POMBAL. During the Napoleonic Wars, Lisbon was occupied by the French (1807–08) and then by the British (1808–1820).

Lismer, Arthur [lis'-mur]

The Canadian landscape painter Arthur Lismer, b. Sheffield, England, June 27, 1885, d. Mar. 23, 1969, was a member of the GROUP OF SEVEN. After emigrating from England in 1911, he worked for several years as a commercial artist. In 1913, Lismer made his first trip to the Georgian Bay region; this rugged scenery of northern Canada inspired much of his work throughout his career. During World War I, while in Halifax, Nova Scotia, he painted scenes of naval life in the busy harbor. Lismer returned frequently to the Maritime Provinces after 1930, particularly Cape Breton Island. During these years he gained a wide reputation as a progressive teacher in the field of children's art education.

Lissitzky, El [lee-seet'-skee]

Eliezer Markovich Lissitzky, b. Nov. 10 (N.S.), 1890, d. Dec. 30, 1941, a Russian painter and designer, was one of the most enthusiastic advocates of ABSTRACT ART. It was largely through his efforts that suprematism and constructivism, both

El Lissitzky's sketch (1920) for his Story of Two Squares *is one diagram from a lithographic series (published 1922) of geometrical abstractions. (Museum of Modern Art, New York City.)*

early forms of abstraction, were first understood in western Europe. Around 1919 he began to paint what he called *Prouns*, geometrical abstractions influenced by the work of Kasimir MALEVICH, such as *Proun 2* (1920; Philadelphia Museum of Art). These convey an architectural feeling for clarity and order by the simple arrangement of lines, squares, and rectangles.

In 1922, as a result of the Bolshevik government's hostility to abstract art, Lissitzky went to Germany, where he contributed constructivist ideas to the Bauhaus and the Dada movement. He is also credited with the idea that modern abstract works should be viewed in a museum setting that is in accord with their style.

Lister, Joseph [lis'-tur]

The British surgeon Joseph Lister, b. Apr. 5, 1827, d. Feb. 10, 1912, was the first to use antiseptics to reduce infection after surgery (antisepsis). In 1865, Lister began dipping bandages and ligatures into carbolic acid and pouring the acid into wounds to sterilize them, greatly decreasing the rate of death from gangrene. His article "On the Antiseptic Principle in the Practice of Surgery" (1867), however, was not initially accepted in England or the United States. In 1897, Lister was made a baron by Queen Victoria, on whom he had once operated. Among his other contributions was the method of draining abscesses using a rubber tube.

Liszt, Franz [list, frahnts]

Franz (Ferencz) Liszt, b. Raiding, Hungary, Oct. 22, 1811, d. July 31, 1886, was the most celebrated pianist of the 19th century and one of its most innovative composers. As a small child he showed immense musical gifts. When he was 10, he and his family moved to Vienna, where he studied with Carl Czerny and Antonio Salieri and played for Beethoven. In 1823 his family moved to Paris, where Liszt studied composition with both Ferdinando Paër and Anton Reicha.

Liszt toured for several years as a recitalist before he settled (1834) in Geneva, Switzerland, with the Countess Marie d'Agoult. One of their three children, Cosima, married the conductor Hans von Bülow and then the composer Richard Wagner; another, Blandine, married Emile Ollivier, premier of France at the outbreak of the Franco-Prussian War of 1870–71. In 1839, Liszt resumed concert tours of Europe.

Appointed (1844) musical director in Weimar, he settled there in 1848 and devoted himself to conducting and composition, producing the two piano concertos, the *Totentanz* (Dance of Death) for piano and orchestra, the *Dante Symphony* (1856), and the monumental *Faust Symphony* (1854–57). Liszt also invented a new form, the SYMPHONIC POEM, an orchestral composition that follows a literary or other program; examples include *Tasso* and *Les Préludes*. Liszt unified his larger works by deriving their thematic materials from one or more short motifs. The *Hungarian Rhapsodies* are solo piano works that are based on Hungarian urban popular music rather than on folk music.

Liszt left Weimar for Rome in 1859 with the Princess

Franz Liszt, a 19th-century Hungarian composer, gave his first piano concert at the age of nine and eventually became the acknowledged master pianist of his day. A prolific composer, he produced more than 700 works, including the Faust Symphony *(1854–57) and his 20* Hungarian Rhapsodies.

Carolyne von Sayn-Wittgenstein, whom he met on a concert tour in Russia in 1847 and with whom he lived until 1863. After they separated, Liszt turned to writing religious music, including two masses, the *Legends* for piano, and the oratorio *Christus* (1863). In 1865 he received minor orders and was made an abbé by Pope Pius IX. Liszt returned to Weimar in 1869, but after his appointment as president of the New Hungarian Academy of Music in Budapest in 1875 he divided his time between Budapest, Weimar, and Rome.

The works of Liszt's late years, misunderstood by his contemporaries, are surprisingly modern in concept and anticipate many of the devices of Claude Debussy, Maurice Ravel, Béla Bartók, and the Austrian expressionists. He died while attending the Wagner festival in Bayreuth, Germany.

Liszt was one of the great altruists in the history of music: he performed the large piano works of Robert Schumann and Frédéric Chopin when they were physically unable to do so; he provided opportunities for Hector Berlioz, Wagner, and Camille Saint-Saëns to have their music performed; and he also arranged for piano much music in other media—from Bach's organ works to Wagner's operas. His piano writing incorporates both the orchestral style of Beethoven and the delicate pianistic effects of Chopin. He was also a distinguished piano teacher. Though many of Liszt's works contain passages of bombast or sentimentality, his innovations in harmony, musical form, and writing for the piano make him one of the most important and influential composers of the 19th century.

litany [lit'-uh-nee] The litany is a Christian prayer form consisting of a series of petitions sung or said by a deacon, priest, or cantor, to which the congregation repeats a fixed response. The form originated at Antioch in the 4th century and spread from there throughout the Eastern churches and then to the West. It has remained more important in the East, where litanies led by a deacon are the major form of participation by the congregation in the LITURGY. In the West the Litany of the Saints is the only li-turgical litany for Roman Catholics; the Book of Common Prayer contains a litany for Anglican churches.

litchi [lee'-chee] The litchi or lychee (*Litchi chinensis*) is a southeast Asian fruit tree of the Sapindaceae family, which includes the SOAPBERRY tree native to tropical America, the Akee tree, and the subtropical longan.

The plum-sized litchi fruit has a thin, tough, bright red peel and juicy, sweet-to-tart white flesh surrounding a single large, smooth seed. Although the seed is inedible, the dried fruit is often called a litchi nut.

The tree was introduced into India more than 200 years ago and more recently into South Africa, Florida, and other subtropical regions. It fruits regularly under subtropical conditions that include annual chilling (but not freezing) and also under tropical conditions at moderately high altitudes.

The tropical litchi fruit is usually eaten fresh or canned and is a common dessert in oriental restaurants in the West.

literacy and illiteracy Literacy is an ability to read and write. In the late 19th century the U.S. government defined literacy as the ability to read and write one's name. Today, UNESCO classifies it as the ability to understand and produce a simple statement on everyday life.

Literacy first arose in the ancient Near East, when about 3100 BC the Sumerians developed a system for representing speech—not ideas, as in earlier systems—by means of standardized visual symbols. The introduction of this script seems to have been in response to (and later helped promote) an increasingly complex commercial and administrative structure. Over the next 2,000 years similar requirements led to the introduction of writing systems in other countries, particularly Egypt and China.

Because these early scripts were cumbersome (having hundreds of symbols), ambiguous (not representing all speech sounds), or both, the number of people

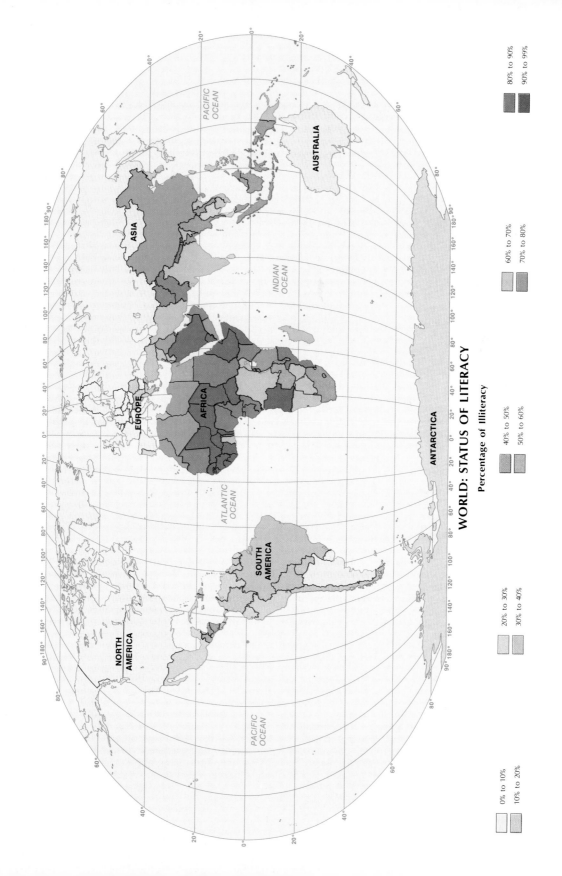

WORLD: STATUS OF LITERACY

Percentage of Illiteracy

0% to 10%

10% to 20%

20% to 30%

30% to 40%

40% to 50%

50% to 60%

60% to 70%

70% to 80%

80% to 90%

90% to 99%

NORTH AMERICA

SOUTH AMERICA

EUROPE

AFRICA

ASIA

AUSTRALIA

ANTARCTICA

PACIFIC OCEAN

ATLANTIC OCEAN

INDIAN OCEAN

who became literate was limited. (See WRITING SYSTEMS, EVOLUTION OF.)

The development of the Greek alphabet during the 9th and 8th centuries BC dramatically increased the potential of literacy. This alphabet, consisting of a small, easily mastered set of symbols that accurately represented all the sounds of the Greek language, spread throughout Greece, which became the world's first truly literate society.

Ancient Rome adopted the Greeks' appreciation and promotion of literacy. The Germanic and other tribes who assumed control of the empire from the 5th century AD, however, attached little value to literacy. Literacy was eradicated to such an extent that by the year 1000 that probably only 1 or 2 percent of Europe's population could read. The tradition of literacy and learning lasted longer in the Byzantine Empire, especially at Constantinople.

Like Judaism before it, Islam, from its beginnings in the 7th century AD, had a strong "tradition of the book." As Islam spread through Asia, North Africa, and Spain, this tradition was carried with it. Throughout the period of Europe's Dark Ages, literacy also continued to be esteemed in China and India.

The sole protector and nurturer of literacy in medieval Europe was the Roman Catholic church. In abbeys and monasteries across the continent, clerics carefully copied and studied religious texts. These were in Latin, however, not in the vernacular languages of the masses.

After 1000, literacy slowly began to reemerge in Europe, a tendency that was hastened in Italy by the advent of the Renaissance and the revival of humanistic learning in the 14th century. After the Reformation, Protestant countries encouraged people to read the Bible. By 1700, Europe's literacy rate ranged from 30 to 40 percent; by 1850, it was 50 to 55 percent; and by 1930, it had reached 90 percent.

The use of writing to convey a succession of revolutionary ideas, together with the establishment of universities and the invention of the printing press, resulted in the development of creative, analytical, and inferential literacy skills that could be used to understand and assess new ideas and put them into practice. At first, however, only elite groups gained such skills. Literacy instruction for the lower classes stressed rote learning, not analysis or evaluation. The industrialization of the 19th century made it necessary to teach more people to read and write, although until the 20th century most were taught only to comprehend, recall, and respect standard political or religious materials.

In the 20th century the more developed nations of the world virtually eliminated illiteracy. Moreover, many such countries made efforts to ensure that all people could do more than merely recite and minimally understand what they read. Several nations—including the USSR, Cuba, Mexico, China, and Argentina—which at the beginning of the 20th century had illiteracy rates of 70 percent or higher, have since 1945 greatly reduced or nearly eliminated illiteracy.

Most modern literacy programs in both developed and developing countries aim to make people *functionally* literate. This means bringing their reading and writing skills up to a level that enables them to perform effectively on the job. Some equate functional literacy with a sixth-grade reading achievement level. Others define functional literacy in terms of some external goal, such as economic improvement, that literacy can facilitate. The most common definition, however, equates functional literacy with the skills needed to perform everyday reading, writing, and arithmetic tasks. Various assessments conducted from this perspective have identified anywhere from 13 to more than 50 percent of American adults, especially those who are poor, undereducated, or members of minority groups, as being functionally illiterate. Although these results are controversial, it has nevertheless been established that millions of Americans read too poorly to function successfully in the everyday world.

The spread of literacy and the achievement of higher levels of literacy have been slow but generally steady. It is uncertain whether the increasing dependence on television and on electronic and computer technology will increase this diffusion or diminish the need for literacy and thus result in an oral culture overwhelming the present written one.

literary criticism   see CRITICISM, LITERARY

---

literary fraud   Literary fraud is the counterfeiting and disseminating of spurious manuscripts, printed works, or memorabilia. Such fabulous works as the *Travels of Sir John Mandeville*, composed in the mid-14th century—most probably by a French physician—were translated into many languages and their incredible tales accepted as true. Not until the 18th century, however, were there enough antiquarians and connoisseurs to make the forging of literary works profitable. The *Poems of Ossian* (1762), which its author, James MACPHERSON, claimed were translated from 3d-century Gaelic, were widely accepted as genuine.

Shakespeare has been a particularly fruitful subject for literary fraud. William H. V. Ireland (1777–1835) forged several Shakespearian manuscripts, including a complete play that was produced at Drury Lane. Ireland later published a confession, demonstrating how he had contrived the inks, seals, and signatures used in his bogus work. A more dangerous forger was the respected scholar John Payne Collier (1789–1883), whose fraudulent manuscript corrections and altered dates created a host of problems for later researchers. Another specialist in fraud was Thomas James Wise (1859–1937), who printed spurious first editions of major Victorian writers and used his own authority to certify and sell them.

Modern laboratory analysis and a more stringent scholarship have almost put an end to the common literary forgery, although faked letters of Byron, Poe, and others still confront autograph dealers. A spectacular contemporary hoax was the near acceptance by scholars and publishers of 60 handwritten volumes that surfaced in 1983 represented as Hitler's diaries but actually the work of a German dealer in Nazi memorabilia. Even more remarkable was the work of American Mark W. Hofmann, a scholar whose forgeries of Mormon documents fooled experts for years. Hofmann was jailed in 1987 for the murder of two accomplices who had threatened to reveal his forgeries.

literary modernism A general term describing an innovative style of literature of the first few decades of the 20th century, modernism meant, first of all, a rejection of the traditional literary forms and values of 19th-century literature. In many ways the modernist tendency in literature paralleled the various antitraditionalist movements in "modern" art, beginning with the CUBISM and ABSTRACT ART of the early 1900s. Both literary and artistic movements were profoundly influenced by the new psychologies of Freud and Jung and by anthropologist Sir James Frazer's *The Golden Bough* (1890). Both art and literature emphasized the central role of the unconscious mind, the importance of the irrational, the intuitive, and the primitive, and the use of myth. Many of the variant modernist movements were both literary and artistic: DADA, FUTURISM, SURREALISM, VORTICISM.

In rejecting traditional exposition, literary modernists often replaced it with STREAM OF CONSCIOUSNESS as a narrative mode. Internal experience was emphasized over outward "reality," and conventional chronology and causality frequently yielded to a more subjective order.

The 1920s were modernism's golden age, seeing the publication of its principal icons: PIRANDELLO's *Six Characters in Search of an Author* (1921), T. S. ELIOT's *The Waste Land* (1922), James JOYCE's *Ulysses* (1922), Ezra POUND's *A Draft of XVI Cantos* (1925), Franz KAFKA's *The Trial* (1925) and *The Castle* (1926), Thomas MANN's *The Magic Mountain* (1925), and William FAULKNER's *The Sound and the Fury* (1929). Though other major writers of the time and of the decades to follow may have been less obviously "modernist," all were children of the movement. It is impossible to conceive, for instance, of the works of Günter Grass, Thomas Pynchon, or Jorge Luis Borges within a context that does not include ideas and techniques of literary modernism.

literature The term *literature*, which originally designated all written language, is now restricted to examples of literary GENRES such as DRAMA, EPIC, LYRIC, NOVEL, and POETRY. For the literature of particular cultures and countries, see ARABIC LITERATURE, ENGLISH LITERATURE, and so forth. For literary theories and techniques, see CRITICISM, LITERARY; NARRATIVE AND DRAMATIC DEVICES; and VERSIFICATION.

literature for children see CHILDREN'S LITERATURE

lithium (drug) [lith'-ee-uhm] The term LITHIUM, in medicine, refers to the salts of the metal lithium that are used in preventing recurrent attacks of MANIC-DEPRESSIVE PSYCHOSIS and in correcting sleep disorders in manic patients. In the United States the salt approved for psychiatric use is lithium carbonate.

The salts are taken orally; careful control of dosage is necessary, because toxic levels can occur near the therapeutic levels. Early signs of lithium intoxication include diarrhea, lack of coordination, and vertigo; acute intoxication can lead to seizures and death.

lithium (element) Lithium is a chemical element of the ALKALI METALS, Group IA in the PERIODIC TABLE. Its chemical symbol is Li, its atomic number is 3, and its atomic weight is 6.941, the lowest weight of all metals. Soft and silvery-white, lithium quickly becomes covered with a gray oxidation layer when exposed to air. In nature, lithium is always found in bonded form. Lithium is found in the minerals spodumene, $LiAlS_2O_6$; petalite, $LiAlSi_4O_{10}$; and eucryptite, $LiAlSiO_4$. Lithium metal is prepared by electrolysis of molten lithium chloride, $LiCl$. In 1978 the world resources of lithium were estimated at more than 10 million metric tons.

Although a highly reactive element, lithium is less active than the other alkali metals. Like the others, it easily yields an electron, forming monovalent positive ions. Lithium reacts with water to form lithium hydroxide, $LiOH$, which is used as a carbon dioxide bonding agent in the ventilating systems of submarines and spaceships. Other important lithium compounds are lithium carbonate, Li_2CO_3, and lithium borate, $Li_2B_4O_7$, which are used in the ceramic industry as glaze constituents, and lithium perchlorate, $LiClO_4$, which like all perchlorates is a very powerful oxidizing agent. It has been suggested for use in solid fuels for rockets. Lithium salts are used as antidepressant drugs (see MANIC-DEPRESSIVE PSYCHOSIS).

Lithium hydride, LiH, is used to inflate lifeboats and balloons. It is also a powerful reducing agent. Lithium hydride, composed of the lithium-6 isotope and deuterium, is called lithium deuteride, LiD. LiD can be converted into helium in a nuclear fusion reaction. Lithium deuteride is the explosive material of the hydrogen bomb and may eventually be the fuel of controlled fusion reactors.

lithograph [lith'-oh-graf] A lithograph is a print made with a planographic (flat surface) process discovered in the 1790s by the German playwright Aloys Senefelder. To make a lithograph print in the original manner the artist uses a greasy crayon or an oily wash to draw on the surface of a limestone slab. After the stone is treated with an acid solution the areas touched by crayon or wash will reject water rubbed on the stone but retain ink. When the stone is placed on a press the inked design on its surface will print on a sheet of paper. By 1834 specially treated zinc plates began to replace the heavy stones in making lithographs, but limestone from Bavaria long remained the favored material.

Soon after its invention lithography came to be valued as an artistic medium as well as a convenient reproductive technique. Benjamin WEST made the first lithographs attributed to a well-known artist (a series titled *Specimens of Polyautography,* 1801–07). In the period 1815–30, romantic painters such as Francisco de GOYA and

The French artist Henri de Toulouse-Lautrec helped raise lithography from a commercial process to an art with bold, vivid posters such as La Goulue at the Moulin Rouge (1891). (Musée Toulouse-Lautrec, Albi, France.)

Eugène DELACROIX exploited lithography's advantages as a medium that preserved the liveliness of drawing without demanding the complicated preparation and slower execution of etching. Because lithographs were cheap to produce and an excellent vehicle for characterization, they also gained widespread favor among mid-19th-century newspaper and magazine illustrators. The French painter and illustrator Honoré DAUMIER was one of the first artists to reach a mass audience with his satiric lithographs.

The development of color lithography was perfected by Paul GAVARNI in his 12 color lithographs *Physiognomies of the Population of Paris* (1831). Henri de TOULOUSE-LAUTREC's dazzling, colorful posters played the most prominent role in gaining lithography an esteemed position among the art processes used in the late 19th century. His daring use of color lithography was widely emulated. Not all lithographic artists preferred to work in color, however. Monochrome lithography was popular with many German artists, and the Norwegian expressionist Edvard MUNCH worked with great originality in both color and black-and-white.

Chromolithography, a technique for printing color pictures using a separate plate for each color, produced an inexpensive and popular form of art from the mid-1700s. "Chromos," or oleographs, reproduced, sometimes garishly, many of the famous pictures of the time. CURRIER AND IVES prints were all oleographs, many printed with great skill.

In the 20th century, the development of photolithography and the use of lithography in combination with other graphic techniques have vastly increased the artistic range of the lithograph. Yet for contemporary artists, as much as for Delacroix and Toulouse-Lautrec, the attractiveness of lithography remains its flexibility and liveliness.

See also: GRAPHIC ARTS.

lithography, offset   see OFFSET LITHOGRAPHY

lithosphere [lith'-uhs-feer]   The lithosphere (from the Greek word *lithos,* "stone") is the solid portion of the Earth, as contrasted to the ATMOSPHERE and the HYDROSPHERE. In a more restricted sense, it is the crust, or outer, rigid shell, of the Earth, as opposed to the mantle and core, which together comprise the barysphere, or centrosphere (see EARTH, STRUCTURE AND COMPOSITION OF).

lithotripsy [lith'-uh-trip-see]   Lithotripsy is a widely used, noninvasive medical technique for crushing small KIDNEY STONES. Its full name is extracorporeal shockwave lithotripsy, or ESWL (see ULTRASONICS). ESWL is an alternative to surgery that eliminates the pain and risk associated with surgical incisions. The device used, called a lithotripter, was developed and first tested in West Germany in 1980. Clinical trials are also being conducted of ESWL use for gallstone crushing.

The anesthetized patient is placed in a water bath or on a water-filled cushion. The bath or cushion contains a small electrode that generates brief but numerous and noisy shock waves, typically over a one-hour period. The patient is positioned so that the waves focus on the kidney stone and cause it to fragment. The fragments are later passed naturally in the urine, and the patient usually returns to normal activity in a few days. Some physicians express concern, however, that ESWL has the potential of causing kidney damage in some patients, which in turn can lead to hypertension.

Lithuania [lith-oo-ayn'-ee-uh]   Located on the eastern shore of the Baltic Sea, Lithuania is bounded on the north by Latvia, on the east by Belarus, and on the southwest by Poland and the Russian enclave of Kaliningrad (Königsberg). Its area is about 65,200 km² (25,174 mi²), and its population is 3,754,000 (1991 est.). The capital is VILNIUS (1990 est. pop., 592,000). From 1940 to 1991, Lithuania was one of the 15 constituent republics of the USSR. It became the first Soviet republic to permit a multiparty system, leading the Baltics' push for sovereignty. In September 1991, Lithuania became fully independent.

Land and People. Lithuania's topography is of glacial origin, forming an extension of the East European plain. It is dotted with lakes and rivers. The highest elevation is about 300 m (960 ft). Most of the Baltic shoreline is separated from the open sea by a long narrow strip of sand dunes called the Courland Spit; the body of water behind the spit is the Courland Lagoon. Klaipeda, Lithuania's only commercial port, is situated where the lagoon meets the open sea. Lithuania has a moderate climate, with cool summers and mild winters. Precipitation ranges from 559 to 864 mm (22 to 34 in). The principal river is the Neman (Nemunas).

Ethnic Lithuanians constitute 79.6% of the population; 9.3% are Russians, and 7% are Poles (1989); most of the remainder are Belorussians, Ukrainians, and Jews. Lithuanians speak a Baltic language related to Latvian. Roman Catholicism is the predominant religion, but Protestant and Orthodox minorities also exist. Sixty-eight percent of the population are urban (1989). The principal cities, in addition to Vilnius and Klaipeda, are KAUNAS (an industrial center and the country's former capital), Siauliai, Panevezys, and Alytus.

Economy. Lithuania's natural resources include clays and sands that are used to make cement, glass, and ceramics. It also has modest deposits of oil and natural gas, but for most of its energy needs it is dependent on oil and natural-gas imports and on its giant nuclear power station near Ignalina. About 60% of Lithuania's gross national product is industrial, and about 25% agricultural. Industries include metalworking, oil refining, shipbuilding, machine construction, and the manufacture of paper, chemical products, construction materials, and furniture. Light industry concentrates on textiles and food processing. Lithuania has a large oceangoing fishing fleet. Its agriculture specializes in meat and dairy production; fodder crops, cereal grains, sugar beets, potatoes, vegetables, and flax are grown.

History. The Lithuanians, with the Latvians, are survivors of the Baltic family of peoples who lived in the region in ancient times. Lithuania emerged as a united nation under Grand Duke Mindaugas in the 13th century. Mindaugas's successors founded an empire extending as far south as the Black Sea. In 1386, Grand Duke Jagello (Jogaila; see JAGELLO dynasty) accepted the Polish crown, introduced Christianity, and established a personal union between Poland and Lithuania. In 1569 the two states were merged into a commonwealth, and Lithuania gradually was submerged into Poland as a province.

When Poland was partitioned in 1795, Lithuania was annexed by Russia. A Lithuanian nationalist movement developed during the 19th century, and after the collapse (1917) of the Russian Empire, Lithuania regained its independence (Feb. 18, 1918). It began its life as a democracy, but after a coup d'état in December 1926, authoritarian rule was set up under Antanas Smetona. Lithuania was forcibly annexed by the USSR in 1940.

Except for the German occupation of 1941–44, the country remained under Soviet rule for the next half-century. The Soviet regime was resisted by a partisan war (1944–52) that caused an estimated 40,000–60,000 casualties. More than 350,000 were deported or perished in Soviet labor camps. In the decades that followed the economy was industrialized, and an attempt was made to Russify the population.

In the late 1980s the advent of Mikhail Gorbachev's PERESTROIKA reform campaign brought an opportunity for change. In 1988 the non-Communist Sajudis (Lithuanian Reform) movement conducted a successful campaign to restore Lithuanian as the official language and to legalize the old national symbols. In February 1990, Sajudis won an overwhelming majority in free parliamentary elections, and in March independence was proclaimed and Vytautas Landsbergis was elected president. Moscow responded with an economic blockade that brought Lithuanian industry and transportation to a standstill. In June the Lithuanians agreed to suspend their independence declaration while negotiations were held to reach a solution. In January 1991, however, Soviet troops killed 15 Lithuanians during a crackdown on proindependence forces. Following the unsuccessful coup of Soviet hard-liners in August 1991, Lithuania was recognized by the USSR in September and shortly after that became a new member of the United Nations.

As with most of the former Soviet republics, Lithuania has experienced many difficulties in making the transition from authoritarianism to democracy and from a socialist to a market economy.

Lithuanian language   see BALTIC LANGUAGES

litotes   see FIGURES OF SPEECH

Little Bighorn, Battle of the   The Battle of the Little Bighorn (June 25, 1876), also called "Custer's Last Stand," was the last major Indian victory in the INDIAN WARS of the American West. The Sioux and Cheyenne peoples resisted incursions of whites prospecting for gold on Indian land in the Black Hills of Dakota beginning in 1874. In 1876 the U.S. Army sent an expedition to subdue the Sioux leaders, SITTING BULL and CRAZY HORSE. On June 24, Col. George Armstrong CUSTER, commanding the 7th Cavalry, located their camp on the Little Bighorn River in Montana. Underestimating his opponents' strength, he attacked them with a small force of about 225 men the following day. In the ensuing battle, Custer and all of his men were killed. Despite their victory, most of the Sioux had been expelled from the Black Hills by the end of 1876. The site of the battle is now a national monument.

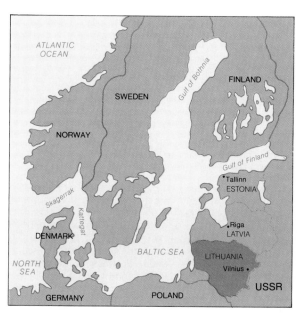

Little Dipper   A group of seven faint stars, the Little Dipper is part of a larger group, the constellation Ursa Minor, the Little Bear. The group contains POLARIS, the North Star, which lies very close to the celestial north pole at the end of the dipper's handle. The second brightest star in the group, Kochab, was closer to the pole about 2,000 years ago; hence its name is derived from the Arabic word meaning polestar.

Little Entente   [ahn-tahnt']   In 1920–21, Czechoslovakia, Romania, and Yugoslavia entered into a defensive alliance known as the Little Entente. These countries had emerged wholly or in part from the dismemberment of the Austrian Empire, which had occurred at the end of World War I. They joined together to preserve the postwar territorial settlement. Their alliance was aimed mainly at Hungary, but also at Germany and Italy. France was the major power most sympathetic to the Little Entente. In 1933 the members of the Little Entente concluded a new treaty setting up a permanent alliance organization. The resurgence of German power under the Nazis, however, weakened the Little Entente, and it collapsed after France and Britain agreed to the dismemberment of Czechoslovakia at the MUNICH CONFERENCE (1938).

Little League baseball   Little League baseball is an international program consisting of teams in leagues for children from ages 8 to 12. This network of approximately 7,500 leagues is managed by Little League Baseball, Inc., with operations in about 40 countries.

The first Little League was started by Carl E. Stotz in 1939, when three teams were established in Williamsport, Pa. The concept spread quickly in the United States, and by the 1950s teams were organized in other countries. Local leagues have 4 to 10 teams with 12 to 15 players each. In 1947 a Little League World Series was held at Williamsport. Today the champions from eight geographic regions—four from the United States and one each from the Far East, Europe, Latin America, and Canada—take part in the Series. In 1957 a team from Monterrey, Mexico, became the first Little League World Series champion from outside the United States. The following year they became the first team to win consecutive championships. Since 1969, teams from Taiwan have dominated.

Little League games are played on smaller-than-regulation-size fields, with bases 60 ft (18.3 m) apart and the pitcher's mound 44 ft (13.4 m) from home plate. In 1974 girls started playing on Little League teams.

Little Rock   Little Rock, a city in central Arkansas, is the capital and largest city of the state and the seat of Pulaski County. A port on the Arkansas River, it is the state's cultural, administrative, and economic center. Its population is 175,795 (1990). Little Rock is surrounded by farmland, and poultry, cattle, and a variety of agricultural products are processed in the city. Manufactures include lumber, concrete products, paper, clothes, and metal products. Bauxite and other minerals are mined nearby. The city is the site of the University of Arkansas at Little Rock (1927), Philander Smith College (1868), and Arkansas Baptist College (1884). Among Little Rock's landmarks are three capitol buildings: the restored territorial capitol, the Old State House, and the present capitol (completed 1916).

A French trader, Bernard de la Harpe, established a trading post on the site in 1722. Little Rock became the territorial capital in 1821 and the state capital in 1836. During the Civil War, the Battle of Little Rock was fought in 1863. The city drew wide attention in 1957 when federal troops enforced a Supreme Court ruling against segregation in public schools.

Little Turtle   Little Turtle, 1751?–1812, the great MIAMI Indian chief, led the Indians to victory over Gen. Josiah Harmar (1790) and Gen. Arthur St. Clair (1791), blocking American expansion into the Lake Michigan region. He later led his people against Gen. Anthony Wayne at the Battle of Fallen Timbers (1794) but was defeated by the Americans and deserted by his British allies. Thereafter he counseled peace and accommodation. While signing the Treaty of Greenville in August 1795, he proclaimed, "I am the last to sign it, and I will be the last to break it," and, true to his word, he refused to aid the Shawnee chief TECUMSEH in later years.

littoral zone   [lit'-uh-ruhl]   The littoral zone, the bottom environment on the perimeter of the ocean, extends from high water on the shoreline seaward to a depth of about 200 m (660 ft) at the CONTINENTAL SHELF break. It covers about 8 percent of the world's oceans and is subdivided into the eulittoral (nearshore) zone and sublittoral (shelf) zone. The eulittoral zone, usually considered to extend up to a depth of 50 m (165 ft), is the area most affected by waves, tides, and current action. Some scientists restrict the eulittoral to the zone between high- and low-tide levels. In areas of tectonic uplift, volcanism, or glacial scouring, the littoral substrate may be rocky and gravelly. Sand and gravel bottoms characterize the littoral zone along stable COASTAL PLAINS.

See also: BEACH AND COAST.

liturgy   [lit'-ur-jee]   Liturgy, from two Greek words meaning "people" and "work," refers to the formal public rituals of religious worship. In the Christian tradition, it is used as a specific title for the EUCHARIST and in general designates all formal services, including the DIVINE OFFICE. Both the written texts of the rites and their celebration constitute liturgy. Among Protestants the term describes a fixed rather than free form of worship. Outside the Christian church, liturgy is also used to designate the form of prayer recited in Jewish synagogues.

The historical Christian liturgies are divided into two principal families: Eastern and Western. The Eastern liturgies include the Alexandrian (attributed to Saint Mark), the Antiochene (Saint James, Saint Basil, Saint John Chrysostom), and the East Syrian (Assyrian) or Chaldean (Addai and Mari), as well as the Armenian and Maronite rites. The Byzantine liturgies (those attributed to Saint John Chrysostom and Saint Basil) are used today by all Orthodox Christians in communion with Constantinople. The Western liturgies are the Roman and the Gallican. The only Gallican liturgy still in use is the Ambrosian Rite of Milan, although the Mozarabic (Spanish), the Celtic, and the Franco-German Gallican were widely used until the 8th century.

Traditional Anglican and Lutheran liturgies have been based on the local uses of the Roman rite revised according to 16th-century Reformation principles. Reformed (Calvinist) churches attempted to replace historical liturgies with the forms of worship of the early Christian communities.

In the 20th century a movement has arisen among the Roman Catholic and Protestant churches to revise the liturgies to make them more contemporary and relevant while retaining the basic beliefs of the church. In the Roman Catholic church, the Constitution on the Sacred Liturgy of the Second VATICAN COUNCIL substituted the use of vernacular languages for Latin in the Mass and allowed the participation of the laity in public worship.

Litvinov, Maksim Maksimovich [leet-vee'-nuhf]

Maksim Litvinov, b. July 17 (N.S.), 1876, d. Dec. 31, 1951, was the Soviet commissar for foreign affairs from 1930 to 1939. A Jew from Russian Poland, originally named Meir Walach, he was associated with the Bolsheviks from 1903. In the 1920s, Litvinov was deputy to Foreign Affairs Commissar Georgy Vasilyevich Chicherin. Succeeding to Chicherin's office, he served (1932) as chief Soviet delegate at the Geneva conference on disarmament and conducted negotiations that led to the establishment of diplomatic relations with the United States (1933) and Soviet entry into the League of Nations (1934). Replaced by Vyacheslav Mikhailovich MOLOTOV in 1939, Litvinov was later (1941–43) Soviet ambassador to the United States.

Liu Shaoqi (Liu Shao-ch'i) [lyoo show-chee]

The Chinese Communist Liu Shaoqi, 1898–1969, served (1959–68) as head of state of the People's Republic. A stalwart of the Chinese Communist party from its founding in 1921, he became the party theoretician, second only to MAO ZEDONG in political authority. His manual *How to Be a Good Communist* (1939) was the orthodox text for the indoctrination of cadres. Liu, who had studied in Moscow and served as chief labor agitator for the party, succeeded Mao as head of state in 1959. Bitterly attacked during the CULTURAL REVOLUTION, he was purged from office in 1968 and imprisoned until his death. In 1980 he was posthumously rehabilitated.

liver   The liver, an organ found in all vertebrates, is the largest organ in the human body. It is a spongy, reddish brown gland that lies just below the diaphragm in the abdominal cavity. It serves to metabolize CARBOHYDRATES and store them as glycogen; metabolize LIPIDS (fats, including cholesterol and certain vitamins) and PROTEINS; manufacture a digestive fluid, bile; filter impurities and toxic material from the blood; produce blood-clotting factors; and destroy old, worn-out red blood cells (see CIRCULATORY SYSTEM).

Two large lobes, the right and the left, make up most of the liver; attached to the right lobe are the smaller quadrate and caudate lobes. The lobes are made up of lobules—six-sided cells arranged in sheets one cell thick—that are closely arranged around blood vessels, bile ducts, lymph vessels, and nerves. Certain reticuloendothelial cells (Kupffer cells) line these lobules and play a role in immunity.

Approximately three sides of each cell are in contact with a blood vessel, and three are adjacent to a bile duct. The bile manufactured by each lobule passes down a common duct, which connects to larger ducts that lead to the common hepatic duct. This duct joins with the cystic duct of the GALLBLADDER and enters the duodenum along with the pancreatic duct of Wirsung. In the intestines,

The liver (A) is situated in the upper abdomen below the diaphragm on the right side of the body. A part of the digestive system, it lies next to the stomach (B) and spleen (C) and above the duodenum (D) and pancreas (E). The liver performs at least 500 functions, more than any other organ. Oxygenated blood enters through the hepatic artery (1), and blood containing nutrients enters through the portal vein (2). After being processed by the liver, the blood exits through the hepatic vein (3). Bile is stored in the gallbladder (4) and is released into the duodenum through the bile duct (5). The relative positions of the liver and gallbladder are shown in front (F) and rear (G) views.

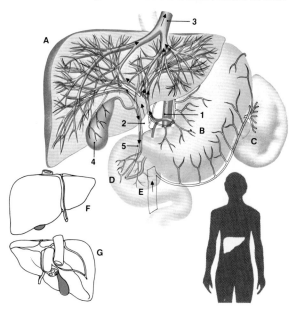

bile salts aid in emulsifying fats and enhancing the METABOLISM of fats and proteins.

The liver is a highly vascular tissue. It receives 25 percent of its blood from a hepatic artery. The other 75 percent of the blood supply comes from the portal vein, which transports digested nutrients and hormones from the intestines, hormones from the pancreas, and old red blood cells and bilirubin—a component of bile—from the spleen. Blood leaves the liver by the inferior vena cava, which goes to the heart.

The liver is able to regenerate itself after being injured or diseased; if, however, a disease progresses beyond the tissue's capacity to regenerate new cells, the body's entire metabolism is severely affected. Two common liver diseases are HEPATITIS (inflammation of the lobules) and CIRRHOSIS, or a scarring of the lobules. Many disorders can affect the liver and interfere with the blood supply, the hepatic and Kupffer cells, and the bile ducts. Bile consists of such substances as lecithin, bile salts, and cholesterol, the last two of which can form GALLSTONES under certain conditions and result in obstruction of bile ducts. JAUNDICE, a yellow skin discoloration, is a symptom of a variety of liver disorders. Liver cancer is fairly rare but generally incurable. Severely impaired livers are sometimes replaced (see TRANSPLANTATION, ORGAN).

Liverpool   Liverpool is an industrial city and major port in northwestern England on the northeastern shore of the Mersey Estuary. The population of the city is 469,600 (1988 est.); that of the metropolitan county of Merseyside is 1,448,100. The Mersey Estuary is linked by ship canal with Manchester and other industrial cities in the hinterland. The Queensway Tunnel under the Mersey links Liverpool with the industrial city of Birkenhead to the south.

As a port Liverpool is second only to London in national importance, and it is the main port for the highly industrialized north of England. Traditionally, it handles most of Britain's imported raw cotton and wool. Liverpool's manufacturing industries were at first those associated with its foreign commerce, such as grain milling and soap making, but automobile and electrical engineering, chemicals, and petroleum refining are now more important.

Liverpool is a cultural and educational center. The University of Liverpool was chartered in 1881, and the city's museums and galleries contain some of the finest collections in Great Britain. Liverpool is the seat of an Anglican bishopric and a Roman Catholic bishopric. The Roman Catholic cathedral was begun in 1933 according to a design by Sir Edwin LUTYENS. The Anglican cathedral (1904–79), a vast Gothic Revival building, was designed by Sir George Gilbert SCOTT.

Liverpool was settled in 1207, after King John granted a charter for a new, planned town. It developed during the mid-17th century as the main port linking England with Ireland. In the 17th and 18th centuries it became the center of the slave trade with Africa and North America. With the Industrial Revolution Liverpool became the port for the manufacturing region of Lancashire and West Yorkshire.

Liverpool, Robert Banks Jenkinson, 2d Earl of   The 2d earl of Liverpool, b. June 7, 1770, d. Dec. 4, 1828, served as prime minister of Great Britain from 1812 to 1827, years in which the British were victorious in the NAPOLEONIC WARS and experienced an aftermath of social and economic unrest. Entering the House of Commons as a Tory in 1790 and moving to the House of Lords in 1808, he was foreign secretary (1801–04), home secretary (1804–06, 1807–09), and secretary of war (1809–12) before succeeding the assassinated Spencer Perceval as prime minister.

Liverpool's talent lay in diplomatic handling of his cabinet colleagues and of the prince regent, who eventually became GEORGE IV, and in his acute sense of the changing political temper of the nation. Liverpool was thus able to work with both Lord CASTLEREAGH and the latter's enemy George CANNING, and in 1822 he replaced his reactionary home secretary Lord Sidmouth with the reformer Robert PEEL. The collapse of existing political alignments when a paralytic stroke forced his retirement in 1827 testifies to Liverpool's skills.

liverwort   Three hundred genera of green, terrestrial plants are known as liverworts; they comprise 10,000 species and belong to the class Hepaticae in the division Bryophyta. They play a definite role in stabilizing bare soils; they also promote soil formation from rock surfaces and downed logs by retaining water and breaking down minerals. Liverworts derive their name from a supposed resemblance of some species to lobes of the liver.

Liverworts are small plants, ranging in size from nearly microscopic to more than 20 cm (8 in) in length. Most abundant in the cool mountain forests of the tropics, liverworts inhabit all the continents, including Antarctica. Along with mosses and lichens, they form the dominant surface vegetation in many parts of the tundra. Some liverworts are entirely aquatic; most are restricted to regions of abundant moisture. They frequently are found growing along shady stream banks, over rocks, and on trunks of trees.

The plant body is relatively simple. Such complex tissues as xylem and phloem are absent. Two basic body types exist; one is characteristic of leafy liverworts, the other of thallose liverworts. Leafy liverworts are elongated and flattened and have two or three rows of leaves. They have structures that resemble stems (caulidia) and leaves (phyllidia). Thallose liverworts may grow in circular rosettes or, more typically, as elongated, lobed blades. They appear as straps or ribbons and are anchored to the substrate by one-celled rhizoids.

In reproduction the plant body often fragments, and leaves and stems regenerate. In addition, many species produce special cells (gemmae) that propagate asexually. In the sexual life cycle of liverworts the dominant phase, the gametophyte, is photosynthetic and alternates with the sporophyte, which is entirely dependent on the gametophyte for nutrition.

livestock   see ANIMAL HUSBANDRY

Livia Drusilla [liv'-ee-uh droo-sil'-uh]   Livia Drusilla, b. Jan. 30, 58 BC, d. AD 29, was the second wife of the Roman emperor AUGUSTUS. She first married (43 or 42) Tiberius Claudius Nero, by whom she had two sons: Tiberius and Nero Claudius Drusus. In 39, however, she divorced Nero to marry Octavian (later Augustus). Livia became Augustus's esteemed counselor and ran his domestic life with integrity and grace. She used her influence to ensure the succession of her son TIBERIUS in AD 14, but he thwarted her attempt to gain greater personal power during his reign.

Living Theatre   The Living Theatre is an American theater collective formed in 1947 by actors Judith Malina (b. 1926) and her husband Julian Beck (1925–85). At first dedicated to the text-oriented dramas of Brecht, García Lorca, Gertrude Stein, and Paul Goodman, the Living Theatre eventually evolved a performance style based on the nonverbal acting techniques of Antonin Artaud. Pioneers in the off-Broadway movement, the Living Theatre performed poetic dramas until 1956. In 1959 they presented Jack Gelber's play about drug addiction, *The Connection.* Ever since, their work has been largely dedicated to social and political issues reflecting their pacifist and anarchist beliefs. In 1963 the group produced Kenneth Brown's *The Brig,* which was set in a military prison. That same year the building in which the Living Theatre performed was closed for tax delinquency and the group went into exile. From 1964 to 1969 it performed throughout Europe, where it developed its most important pieces—*Antigone,* based on Sophocles and Brecht, *Frankenstein, Mysteries and Smaller Pieces,* and the revolutionary *Paradise Now.* In Brazil in 1970 the group began developing its epic work, *The Legacy of Cain.* Beck and Malina returned to New York in 1979. Their innovative performance techniques, mostly in the service of political and sexual ideologies, made the Living Theatre the most influential of the experimental groups of the 1960s and '70s.

Livingston (family)   The Livingston family was a dominant social and political force in 18th-century New York. The founder of the clan, **Robert Livingston**, 1654–1728, was born in Scotland and raised in the Netherlands. He arrived in New York in 1674 and soon married (1679) Alida Schuyler Van Rensselaer, thus merging the Livingstons with the prominent Schuyler and Van Rensselaer families. In 1686 he obtained the second largest manor in the colony, a 65,000-ha (160,000-acre) estate below Albany east of the Hudson River. Livingston Manor eventually passed to his son Philip; his son Robert received Clermont, 5,250 ha (13,000 acres) around the manor house.

Three of Philip's sons achieved distinction. **Philip**, b. Jan. 15, 1716, d. June 12, 1778, a politician and merchant, signed the Declaration of Independence. **Robert**, 1718–75, became third lord of the manor. **William**, b. Nov. 30, 1723, d. July 25, 1790, lawyer and member of

the Federal Convention of 1787, was the first governor of the state of New Jersey (1776–90). William's son, **Henry Brockholst Livingston**, b. Nov. 25, 1757, d. Mar. 18, 1823, was a Continental army officer, associate justice of the U.S. Supreme Court (1806–23), and founder (1805) of the New-York Historical Society.

The Clermont branch of the family also had its noteworthy members. **Robert R. Livingston**, b. Nov. 27, 1746, d. Feb. 26, 1813, a statesman and diplomat, served as chancellor of New York (1777–1801) and negotiated the LOUISIANA PURCHASE (1803). **Henry Beekman Livingston**, 1750–1831, was a Revolutionary War officer. **Edward Livingston**, b. May 28, 1764, d. May 23, 1836, was a lawyer, U.S. representative (1795–1801), and mayor of New York City (1801–03); after moving to New Orleans in 1803, he compiled a law code (1821) that made him famous and served as state legislator (1820–23), U.S. representative (1823–29), senator (1829–31), Andrew Jackson's secretary of state (1831–33), and minister to France (1833–35).

Livingstone, David   David Livingstone, b. Blantyre, Scotland, Mar. 19, 1813, d. May 1, 1873, made a series of journeys in the mid-19th century, thereby contributing more than any other single person to the opening of Africa to the West.

In 1838, Livingstone became a doctor of medicine and then an ordained minister in 1840. He was sent by the London Missionary Society to Kuruman (part of the modern Cape Province, South Africa), arriving in 1841. Never satisfied with the routine of missionary life, Livingstone began his dramatic explorations in 1849, when he guided the first successful European crossing of the Kalahari Desert to Lake Ngami.

Obsessed with a desire to open up inner Africa to new forms of commerce and religion in order to end the slave trade and advance civilization as he understood it, Livingstone investigated central Africa between 1853 and

The Scottish missionary David Livingstone explored Africa's interior in an attempt to introduce Christianity and eliminate slavery. He was the first European to sight the Zambezi River (1851) and Victoria Falls (1855), which he named.

1856. From the Chobe River (in modern Botswana) he traveled up the Zambezi River with a small group of Africans. Passing through Barotseland (modern Zambia), he followed African trade paths across the Cuango River into Portuguese Angola. He arrived at Luanda on the Atlantic coast in 1854. Livingstone then plunged back into the African interior. Following the Zambezi River downstream from the point of his earlier departure, he discovered (1855) and named the Victoria Falls. Continuing east across what is now Zambia and Mozambique until he emerged at Quelimane on the Indian Ocean in 1856, he became the first non-African to cross the continent from west to east.

Livingstone's return to London shortly thereafter set in motion efforts to introduce commercial and missionary enterprise into much of east and central Africa. The accounts of his experiences were best-sellers and stimulated the exploring endeavors of others such as Sir Richard BURTON and Sir Henry Morton STANLEY. Livingstone himself made another expedition in 1858–63, when he became the first Briton to describe Lake Nyasa and the Shire Highlands of what is now Malawi. From 1866 to 1873 he sought the source of the Nile and Congo rivers and investigated how the great African lakes related to each other and to the great rivers. In the process he reached the Lualaba tributary of the Congo River. In 1871, Stanley found the sick Livingstone at Ujiji on Lake Tanganyika. Livingstone insisted on continuing his explorations, however, and died in 1873 near Bangweulu.

▬

Livius Andronicus [liv'-ee-uhs an-druh-ny'-kuhs] Lucius Livius Andronicus, c.284 BC–c.204 BC, though non-Roman by birth and brought to Rome as a war captive from southern Italy, earned glory as the "father of Roman literature." Combining a mastery of earlier Greek poetry with a command of the Latin language, he produced (240 BC) the first Latin comedy and the first Latin tragedy. The development inaugurated the dynamic flourishing of Roman drama over the next century. His translation of Homer's *Odyssey* in Saturnian meter also influenced subsequent Roman epic poetry.

▬

Livonia [liv-oh'-nee-uh] Livonia is a historical region in the USSR, comprising the present-day areas of northern LATVIA and southern ESTONIA. Its original inhabitants were the Livs, a Finnic people who arrived between the 5th and 7th centuries.

At the beginning of the 13th century the German Order of the Brothers of the Sword (known as the Livonian Knights after they merged with the TEUTONIC KNIGHTS in 1237) conquered and Christianized the Livs, whose land they called Livonia. In 1207 the bishopric of Livonia became a principality of the Holy Roman Empire. Between 1558 and 1583, Russia fought the so-called Livonian Wars against the knights. Unable to defend themselves, the knights disbanded in 1561 and dismembered Livonia. Poland gained control of the area in 1569 but ceded most of it to Sweden in 1660. During the Great NORTHERN WAR, Russia conquered Livonia and in 1772 received Polish Livonia as part of the first Partition of Poland. In 1783, Livonia became a province of the Russian Empire. At the end of World War I, historic Livonia was divided between Estonia and Latvia. This division remained when the two countries were absorbed into the USSR in 1940.

▬

Livorno [lee-vor'-noh] Livorno (English: Leghorn) is the capital of Livorno province in the central Italian region of Tuscany. Situated on the Ligurian Sea and on the ancient Roman Aurelian Way, it is a thriving commercial, industrial, and tourist center and one of Italy's main ports. The city has a population of 173,114 (1988 est.). A canal completed in 1938 connects Livorno with Pisa. The city's plants produce chemicals, refined petroleum, and metals. The 16th-century cathedral and part of the 17th-century city walls are notable historic landmarks.

In the 16th century the original fishing village developed into a busy trading town when Cosimo I de'Medici began the construction of the Porto Mediceo (Medici Harbor) in 1571. Ferdinand I de'Medici, grand duke of Tuscany, made Livorno a free port in 1590 and opened the city to political and religious refugees. In 1860, Livorno became part of united Italy.

▬

Livy [liv'-ee] The ancient Roman historian Livy (Titus Livius), b. 64 or 59 BC, d. AD 17, wrote a history of Rome that was recognized as a classic during his lifetime. He was born in Patavium (Padua) but spent most of his life in Rome, where he witnessed civil wars, the fall of the republic, and the establishment of the principate by Augustus. Little else is known of his life. From his writings, it is evident that he read extensively in Greek and Latin literature and was influenced by Cicero.

Livy immersed himself in the past. His *History of Rome* covers the period from the arrival of Aeneas in Italy and the "foundation" of the city of Rome to 9 BC. Of the original 142 books, only 35 are extant—Books 1–10 and 21–45, dealing with the years 753–293 BC and 218–167 BC. Some fragments of other books remain, however, and summaries exist of all but one. Livy was not a critical historian; his genius lay in his vivid style and gift for dramatic composition. He followed an annalistic arrangement of events but focused on the characters of the leading figures in the episodes.

▬

lizard [liz'-urd] Lizards are reptiles that are closely related to snakes. Well adapted to life on land, lizards possess a dry, scaly body covering; limbs suited for rapid locomotion; internal fertilization; and hard-shelled eggs. Lizards feed mostly on insects, although a certain number of them eat plants. Only two species are venomous, the Gila monster (*Heloderma suspectum*) and the Mexican beaded lizard (*H. horridum*).

Lizards and Snakes

Lizards generally can be distinguished from snakes by the

When threatened by an enemy, the Australian frilled lizard rears on its hindlegs, whips its tail threateningly, opens its mouth and hisses, and unfolds its enormous neck frill—giving the impression of an adversary several times larger than its original size.

presence of two pairs of legs, external ear openings, and movable eyelids, but these convenient external diagnostic features, while absent in snakes, are also absent in some lizards. Lizards can be precisely separated from snakes, however, on the basis of certain internal characteristics. All lizards have at least a vestige of a pectoral girdle (skeletal supports for the front limbs) and sternum (breastbone). The lizard's brain is not totally enclosed in a bony case but has a small region at the front covered only by a membranous septum. The lizard's kidneys are positioned symmetrically and to the rear; in snakes the kidneys are far forward, with the right kidney placed farther front than the left. The lizard's ribs are never forked, as are one or two pairs in the snake.

Distribution and Habitat

There are more than 3,000 known species of lizards, making them one of the largest and most successful groups of reptiles. They are found on all the continents except Antarctica. The greatest diversity of species occurs in the tropics, but lizards range as far north as the Arctic Circle in Eurasia and as far south as southern Chile in South America. In North America lizards barely range into southern Canada. Lizards live at elevations exceeding 4,500 m (15,000 ft) in the Himalayas, in the Andes, and among the volcanoes of Mexico.

Although no living species of lizard can truly fly through the air, as did some reptiles of the past, lizards occupy practically every other habitat. Some lizards live in areas of rain and cloud forests soaked by daily rains. Others—such as the crocodile lizard, *Shinisaurus*, of China, which feeds on fish and tadpoles, and the snail-eating caiman lizard, *Dracaena*, of tidal marshlands in South America—have become semiaquatic. Conversely, some lizards have adapted to deserts that receive only 200 mm (about 8 in) or less of rainfall annually. The gecko, *Palmatogecko rangei*, has extensive webbing on its feet for walking over fine sand. Arboreal forms may exhibit various adaptations, including climbing pads, zygodactylous feet (having the toes arranged into two opposing groups), prehensile tails, and

strongly recurved claws. The flying dragons, *Draco*, of Southeast Asia have sheets of skin attached to their elongated ribs and are capable of gliding. Burrowing lizards often have reduced eyes and limbs, reduced head plates, smooth scales, and conical heads with rigid skulls to make for easier burrowing. The marine iguana, *Amblyrhynchus cristatus*, of the Galápagos Islands freely enters the ocean to feed on algae (seaweed).

General Features

Lizards range in size from 20 to 75 mm (0.75 to 3 in) in exceptionally small forms (*Brookesia*, *Sphaerodactylus*) to more than 3 m (10 ft) in the Komodo dragon (*Varanus komodoensis*), but most are closer to 400 mm (16 in) in length.

Limbs. Limbs are generally well developed, and some species demonstrate bipedalism, standing up and running on their hind legs. The racerunners, *Cnemidophorus*, are particularly quick and have been clocked at almost 30 km/h (19 mph). Burrowing forms often have degenerate limbs, and legless lizards move in the same manner as snakes. In some species, such as the marine iguana, the tail is vertically flattened, from side to side, an adaptation to swimming.

Skin and Teeth. The lizard's skin is dry and scaly. The scales, derived from the epidermis, vary from small granules, as in the gecko, to those bearing prominent spines, as in the horned lizard. Many lizards have osteoderms beneath the epidermal skin that provide internal support to the scales. The skin is shed periodically, usually in patches.

Skin glands are not numerous in lizards. Most lizards have scent glands at the base of the tail. Males often have

Like all chameleons, Jackson's chameleon catches prey by shooting out its tongue—longer than its body—trapping the prey on the tongue's sticky tip, and then quickly pulling in its catch.

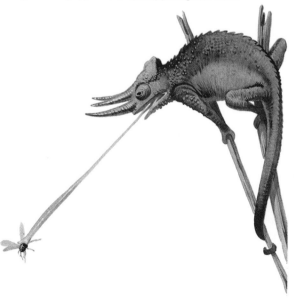

The Turkish gecko, like many lizards, can break off its tail to escape a predator—the violently thrashing tail distracts the enemy while the lizard escapes. The tail, which is severed by muscular contraction, will later regenerate.

glands in front of the anus or on the thigh that appear to play a role in courtship. The glands become filled with a hard, waxy, yellow substance, which may extend from the glands in hairlike columns that rub off on rocks and other surfaces.

Many species can darken or lighten their color in response to light, temperature, or emotional state. A few (chameleons) have developed the ability to alter their color to a remarkable degree. The green anole, *Anolis carolinensis*, called the American chameleon, can change from a bright green to brown.

A lizard's teeth are usually uniform in shape, but in certain species the teeth are more or less differentiated into conical and molar types. In general, there is little chewing of food. Many lizards simply seize their prey, bite it and move it about the mouth, and then swallow it.

Senses. Lizards recognize prey either by visual clues or by chemoreception (scent and taste). Nocturnal lizards usually have a vertical pupil, lack a fovea, and have numerous retinal rods (highly sensitive sensory cells) that distinguish different light intensities. Diurnal species generally have rounded pupils, a fovea, and retinal cones instead of rods; cones distinguish wavelengths of light (color) and hence provide more-detailed daytime vision. Many diurnal lizards have yellow oil in their retinal cones

that acts to filter out the shorter wavelengths of light, thereby reducing the amount of unequal refraction characteristic of these wavelengths. In addition to the pair of eyes possessed by most vertebrates, many lizards have a third, or parietal, eye located on the upper rear surface of the head. The parietal eye has been shown to act as a sort of light meter that helps to regulate the amount of time a lizard exposes itself to the sun.

The majority of lizards have eardrums (tympanic membranes), usually located nearly flush with the surface of the skin or just below it. Behind the eardrum is the middle ear cavity, which leads to the middle ear. The ear provides a sense of balance as well as hearing.

Jacobson's organs are paired chambers in the roof of the mouth that have a connection to the olfactory (scent) lobes of the brain. These chambers detect particles present in the mouth cavity and also particles brought to them by the tongue. By protruding its tongue, a lizard picks up airborne particles, which are then transferred by the tongue to the Jacobson's organs. This process is most efficient in lizards with deeply forked tongues, and in such lizards the sense of smell is relatively keen.

Internal Features. Lizards depend almost entirely on paired lungs to aerate the blood. The heart is three-chambered: the right atrium, which receives deoxygenated blood from the body, is separate from the left atrium, which receives oxygenated blood from the lungs; but the ventricle, which pumps blood to both the body and the lungs, is single. There is, however, an incomplete septum, or wall, across part of the ventricle that essentially separates the two bloodstreams.

Female lizards, like other reptiles, have saclike ovaries, and their eggs are large yolked. Males have two copulatory organs called hemipenes, one on each side of the base of the tail. Either one of the two hemipenes may be used in mating. The majority of lizards lay eggs, but at least half of the lizard families have species that bear live young, with varying degrees of placental formation.

Behavior

Parental care is unknown in lizards, but in some forms the female broods, or cares for, the eggs. Growth rates vary greatly, and sexual maturity may be reached in the first breeding season after birth in small species or not for several years in larger species. Life spans are poorly documented, but generally the small forms live short lives of

The lizard's skeleton includes a skull with two temporal openings separated by no more than one bony arch, and the brain is not completely enclosed by bone. The sternum and pectoral girdle are present in all lizards; many species also have special break points in the tail vertebrae.

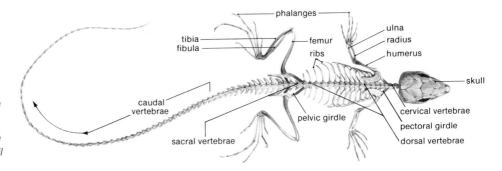

1 to 5 years, whereas larger forms may live for 10 to 20 years or even longer.

Temperature is one of the most important environmental factors influencing lizard behavior; it directly determines a lizard's metabolic rate. Lizards are ectothermic (cold-blooded) and thus depend primarily on an external heat source to regulate their body temperature. This does not mean, however, that a lizard's body temperature will be the same as that of its immediate environment. Lizards can control their temperature by various behaviors, such as by basking directly in the sun or by seeking shade.

Most lizards exhibit marked seasonal changes in activity. In order to avoid harsh weather conditions, lizards hibernate in temperate regions during the winter, generally seeking refuge beneath the frost line, or they may estivate

With more than 3,000 known species, lizards are one of the largest and most diverse groups of modern reptiles, ranging in size from 2-cm (0.75-in) geckos to Komodo dragons of more than 3 m (10 ft). Body form varies greatly. For example, marine iguanas have broad, flat tails for swimming; glass snakes are burrowing lizards with no legs; flying dragons use winglike flaps of skin to glide from tree to tree.

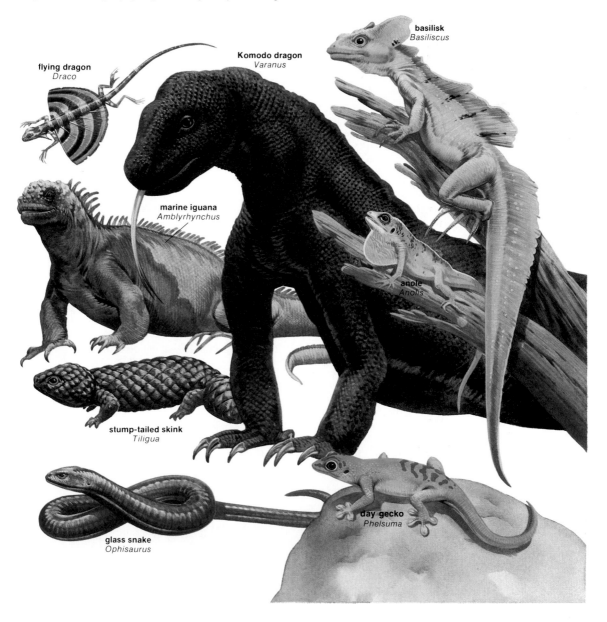

flying dragon
Draco

Komodo dragon
Varanus

basilisk
Basiliscus

marine iguana
Amblyrhynchus

anole
Anolis

stump-tailed skink
Tiligua

day gecko
Phelsuma

glass snake
Ophisaurus

during hot, dry conditions, often in deep crevices or fissures in the ground.

Many lizards are cryptically colored and thereby avoid detection. When disturbed, however, lizards have a variety of defensive actions that include threatening with an open mouth, hissing, inflating the body, positioning the body in such a fashion as to appear as large as possible, biting and scratching, and lashing with the tail. With few exceptions, only the geckos have a voice and can produce threat calls. Many species are equipped with spinelike scales that make it difficult for a predator to swallow them. Some forms expose brightly colored surfaces in an attempt to frighten enemies. Horned lizards, *Phrynosoma*, may eject blood from their eyes. Many lizards break their tails (autotomy) when confronted by an enemy or roughly handled. Predators are often attracted to the thrashing, dismembered tail, which allows the lizard to escape. A new tail is soon regenerated.

Evolution and Classification

Lizards probably arose from eosuchian reptiles that lived about 220 million years ago. About 100 million years ago certain lizards took to the sea and evolved into the giant MOSASAURS, some species reaching 9 m (30 ft) in length.

The lizards are classified in the order Squamata, suborder Sauria (or Lacertilia). The suborder is usually divided into four infraorders. The infraorder Gekkota contains three families: Gekkonidae, Pygopididae, and Xantusiidae (some authorities consider them a single family, Gekkonidae, with four subfamilies). The infraorder Iguania also contains three families: Iguanidae, Agamidae, and Chamaeleonidae. The Anguinomorpha comprises five families: Anguinidae, Xenosauridae, Helodermatidae, Lanthonotidae, and Varanidae. The Scrincomorpha is composed of four families: Cordylidae, Lacertidae, Scrincidae, and Teiidae.

Ljubljana [lee-oo-blee-ahn'-uh]   Ljubljana, the capital of the republic of Slovenia in northwest Yugoslavia, is situated on the Ljubljanica River near its junction with the Sava, about 50 km (30 mi) south of the Austrian border. The city of Ljubljana's population is 205,600 (1981). Manufactures include hydroelectric equipment, textiles, paper, footwear, drugs, and glass. Notable landmarks are a medieval fort and the Renaissance cathedral of Saint Nicholas. A university (1595) is located there.

In 34 BC the Romans founded a city called Emona on the site. It was destroyed by the Huns in 451, but the Slavs later built a new community, which was named Ljubljana in the 12th century. From 1277 until the creation of Yugoslavia in 1918 the city belonged to the Habsburg empire.

---

llama [lah'-muh]   The llama, *Lama peruana*, is a South American member of the CAMEL family, Camelidae. It stands 1.2 m (4 ft) high at the shoulder and may be more than 1.2 m (4 ft) long (plus a short tail) and 140 kg (300 lb) in weight. Its body is covered with a fine, fairly long

The llama, a relative of the camel, can carry loads of 45 kg (100 lb) for 16–32 km (10–20 mi) a day over rugged slopes at high altitudes. Besides being a means of transportation in parts of South America, the llama also furnishes wool used for clothing and blankets.

wool. The llama was domesticated as a wool and pack animal as long as 4,000 years ago by the Indians of Peru from either a now-extinct wild llama or from the guanaco, *L. guanacoe*.

Lloyd, Harold [loyd]   Harold Lloyd, b. Burchard, Nebr., Apr. 20, 1893, d. Mar. 8, 1971, was one of the most popular screen comedians of the 1920s, a living symbol of the shy but optimistic all-American boy. This ingratiating character started evolving in 1910–20 but crystallized only after he became a major star in such 1920s silent films as *Grandma's Boy* (1922) and *The*

In this scene from Safety Last (1923), Harold Lloyd finds himself in typically precarious circumstances. In his heyday in the 1920s, Lloyd was Hollywood's highest paid actor.

Freshman (1925). Lloyd's trademarks were a straw hat and horn-rimmed glasses, but he is perhaps best remembered for the "thrill comedy" of such films as *Safety Last* (1923). Snippets from his many early films appeared in two 1963 screen compilations: *Harold Lloyd's World of Comedy* and *Harold Lloyd's Funny Side of Life.* His unpretentious approach to comedy received wider attention after his "rediscovery" in the 1970s.

Lloyd, Henry Demarest   A leading opponent of business monopolies, Henry Demarest Lloyd, b. New York City, May 1, 1847, d. Sept. 28, 1903, was a pioneer MUCKRAKER of the late 19th century. He developed his antimonopoly theme as financial writer and editor (1872–85) at the *Chicago Tribune.* His *Wealth against Commonwealth* (1894) was a major denunciation of big business; later works included the reform tracts *Labour Copartnership* (1898), *A Country without Strikes* (1900), and *Newest England* (1900).

Lloyd George, David, 1st Earl Lloyd-George of Dwyfor [doo-ee'-vor]   David Lloyd George, b. Jan. 17, 1863, d. Mar. 26, 1945, was one of the commanding figures in 20th-century British politics and the only person of Welsh extraction to become prime minister. Born in Manchester, he was raised by his uncle, a village shoemaker and sectarian lay preacher in North Wales. In 1878 he was apprenticed to a solicitor (nontrial lawyer), and he opened his own law practice in 1884. In 1890 he was elected to Parliament as a Liberal.

Lloyd George acquired recognition speaking for the interests of Welsh Nonconformists—including temperance, disestablishment of the Anglican church in Wales, nondenominational education, and local autonomy. His reputation as an unorthodox, independent Liberal was enhanced by his opposition to the South African War (1899–1902). In 1905, Lloyd George was included in Sir Henry CAMPBELL-BANNERMAN's Liberal cabinet as a representative of Nonconformist interests, and in 1908, he was named chancellor of the exchequer by Herbert ASQUITH.

Lloyd George's "people's budget" of 1909, with its land taxes, provoked a clash with the Conservative-dominated House of Lords, ending in curtailment (1911) of the House of Lords' power to veto legislation. In 1911, Lloyd George guided through Parliament his pioneering National Health Insurance Act, which, together with his Old Age Pensions Act (1908), is often identified as the foundation of the British welfare state.

At first reluctant to approve Great Britain's entry (August 1914) into WORLD WAR I, Lloyd George soon advocated a knockout blow against Germany. He became minister of war shortly before he joined with the Conservative leaders to maneuver Asquith out of office in December 1916. Lloyd George then became prime minister and the dominant figure in the new five-member coalition war cabinet. He imposed an effective regime of "war socialism" on the British people, but he quarreled with his generals, particularly Douglas HAIG, and was unable to cut

David Lloyd George, a British statesman and prime minister (1916–22), led social reform efforts of the Liberal party before his controversial rise to the premiership. The varied achievements of his parliamentary career did much to shape the modern British state.

the heavy casualties on the western front. Nevertheless, he was popularly regarded as the man who won the war, and he exploited this reputation to win a huge election victory in 1918.

The last four years of Lloyd George's premiership (1918–22) were anticlimactic. He was the principal British negotiator at the PARIS PEACE CONFERENCE and five subsequent international parleys, but his "conference diplomacy" failed to mitigate postwar tensions. His government's housing program was a disaster; there was mounting unemployment and labor unrest; and a major recession began in 1921. He negotiated the treaty (1921) that established the Irish Free State, but this damaged his relations with the Conservatives. They withdrew their support after the Chanak Crisis (1922), in which Lloyd George brought Britain to the brink of war with Turkey.

Lloyd George succeeded Asquith as Liberal party leader (1926–31), but with the decline of Liberalism his fortunes waned. He never again held office, although he was a leading parliamentary critic of Labour and, more so, Conservative foreign and domestic policies.

Lloyd's of London [loydz]   Lloyd's of London is an association of insurance underwriters who provide all types of insurance coverage throughout the world. Lloyd's is actually a market in which members form several hundred syndicates specializing in such categories as marine, motor, and aviation insurance. A person wishing to insure with Lloyd's approaches a Lloyd's broker, who in turn approaches one or more syndicates. Lloyd's takes its name from the late-17th-century London coffee house of Edward Lloyd, where marine insurers met to do business. Lloyd's began to handle nonmarine insurance in the late 1880s. Hanging in Lloyd's headquarters is the Lutine bell, which was salvaged (1857) from a shipwreck; it tolls once for good news and twice for bad news.

loach [lohch]   Loaches are small, often slim, elongated fishes making up the family Cobitidae in the minnow order Cypriniformes. They have tiny scales, 6 to 12 barbels around the mouth, soft-rayed fins, and usually teeth in the pharynx (throat) but never on the jaws. In some species there is a movable spine located either below or in front of each eye. Many loaches are about 10 cm (4 in) in length. Some species have an unusual accessory breathing adaptation: they gulp and swallow air, and the intestinal walls absorb oxygen; carbon dioxide and unused gases are then expelled through the anus. One species, *Misgurnus fossilis,* appears to be so sensitive to weather that its increased activity is said to indicate a change in the weather, hence the name weatherfish. Loaches are common throughout Europe and Asia and locally in Morocco and Ethiopia. Many are spectacularly colored and are popular aquarium fishes.

loam   see SOIL

Lobachevsky, Nikolai Ivanovich [luh-buh-chef'-skee]   Nikolai Ivanovich Lobachevsky, b. Dec. 1 (N.S.), 1792, d. Feb. 24 (N.S.), 1856, was a Russian mathematician who is best noted for his work in the field of NON-EUCLIDEAN GEOMETRY, sometimes called Lobachevskian geometry. His major work, "Geometriya," completed in 1823, was not published in its original form until 1909. Since the time of Euclid, mathematicians had been trying to prove Euclid's fifth postulate as a theorem, either by assuming implicitly an equivalent statement or by directly substituting another postulate for the statement that, given a line and point not on it, *only one* coplanar line may be drawn through the point not intersecting the given line. Lobachevsky's geometry derives from the concept that a GEOMETRY in which all of Euclid's axioms except the fifth postulate are demonstrably true is not in itself contradictory. Lobachevsky categorized Euclidean geometry as a special case of a more general system.

lobbyist   A lobbyist is a person who attempts to influence legislators in favor of SPECIAL-INTEREST GROUPS. The word was originally used in the 1830s to describe individuals who frequented the lobbies of U.S. public buildings, particularly those of federal and state governments, and talked with legislators. Organizations that maintain lobbyists in Washington, D.C., and state capitals range from large business corporations to citizens' groups such as the AMERICAN CIVIL LIBERTIES UNION, COMMON CAUSE, and the NATIONAL RIFLE ASSOCIATION OF AMERICA. They may be concerned with a specific law or amendment or with an array of laws and regulations.

Lobbyists attempt to influence decision makers by direct contact, by affecting public opinion through the use of the media, and by mailing campaigns. Although its reputation has been frequently marred by such practices as bribery—the Korean lobby scandal of the late 1970s, for example—lobbying has become a familiar and accepted political activity. It is regarded by many as essential to the modern, complex process of government. Lobbyists, for instance, provide the busy legislator with prac-

tical information that helps in the drafting of technical legislation, and they work with administrative agencies to obtain clarifications and rulings on regulations.

Lobbying is protected by the U.S. Constitution, especially by the 1st Amendment's guarantees against interference with freedom of speech and the right to petition. Under the Federal Regulation of Lobbying Act (1946), persons who receive remuneration for such activities, as their principal purpose, must register with the secretary of the Senate and the clerk of the House of Representatives and file quarterly reports, which are then printed in the *Congressional Record*. These reports disclose on whose behalf lobbyists are acting, their objectives, and the amounts they receive and spend.

lobelia [loh-beel'-yuh]   *Lobelia* is a genus of about 375 species of herbs, shrubs, and some trees in the lobelia family, Lobeliaceae. In many classifications it is placed in the bellflower family, Campanulaceae. More than 250 varieties of annual and perennial lobelias are grown as ornamentals. Lobelia flowers are blue, violet, red, yellow, or white in color and commonly have petals formed into two projecting lips. The flowers are borne mostly in elongated spires (racemes).

The cardinal flower, *L. cardinalis*, is a perennial found in moist meadows and along streams throughout the eastern half of Canada and the United States. It produces short offshoots at its base and bears terminal spikes of cardinal-red flowers. The giant lobelia, *L. gibberoa*, native to Central and East Africa, is a treelike form reaching 9 m (30 ft) in height. It sends up solitary, hollow stalks bearing 60-cm (2-ft) leaves and long, spikelike clusters of tiny greenish white flowers.

Lobengula, King of the Ndebele [loh-beng-goo'-luh, en-duh-bee'-lee]   Lobengula, b. *c.*1836, d. January 1894, was the second and last king of the Ndebele, or Matabele, an African people who inhabited Matabeleland, now part of Zimbabwe. After the death (1868) of his father, Mzilikazi, the founder of the Ndebele kingdom, Lobengula's claim to the throne was challenged by a half brother, Nkulumane. Lobengula, who succeeded to the throne in 1870, granted (1888) rights to the minerals of his kingdom to agents of Cecil RHODES, who soon received a royal charter creating the British South Africa Company. Rhodes interpreted the concession as granting his company territorial rights over all Ndebele lands. Many conflicts then followed. By the early 1890s, Lobengula's army—formerly much feared—had grown weak and dispirited. He died of smallpox while fleeing the advancing British forces.

lobster   Lobsters are large marine crustaceans in the order Decapoda; they are closely related to crayfish and shrimp. The tasty white meat of the lobster is widely prized as a delicacy. In some areas, lobster fishing is an important industry.

The Norway lobster, a small species of lobster with slender pincers, is found along the northeastern Atlantic coast.

The lobster's body is made up of two main parts: the front section (cephalothorax) and the tail (abdomen). Several pairs of appendages perform a variety of functions. Two pairs are antennae, or feelers, and five pairs are legs. In most lobsters, one pair forms two large and differently shaped claws. One claw, the narrower one, is called the cutter because it is used to slice dead fish, one of the lobster's favorite foods. The heavier claw, called the crusher, has toothlike bumps used for crushing clam shells and other hard objects. The only lobsters without these large claws are the spiny lobsters, which have sharp body spines instead.

Perhaps the largest lobster is the American lobster, *Homarus americanus*, which lives along the Atlantic coast from Labrador to Virginia. It has been known to reach a length of 90 cm (3 ft) and a weight of 20 kg (44 lb). A popular European lobster is the Norway lobster, *Nephrops norvegicus*. Spiny lobsters in the family Palinuridae are caught off the coasts of California, Florida, Australia, New Zealand, and South Africa.

Local Group of galaxies The Local Group of galaxies is the small cluster of galaxies that surrounds our galaxy to distances within about one million parsecs (3,260,000 light-years). At least 28 members of the group are known. The exact number is unknown because of difficulties in identifying dim galaxies, especially dwarf galaxies, that are close to the galactic plane with its heavy interstellar absorption. Even some of the accepted members in the Local Group have still not been adequately studied.

The two giant members of the Local Group are our Milky Way Galaxy and the ANDROMEDA GALAXY (M 31).

There is a subclustering about these two giants: 13 galaxies in the Milky Way group and 9 galaxies in the M 31 group, with 5 galaxies outside both groups. Aside from the two giant galaxies, the Local Group also includes an average spiral (M 33); the Large MAGELLANIC CLOUD; more than a half dozen dwarf Magellanic irregular galaxies, including the Small Magellanic Cloud and its recently determined offshoot, the Mini Magellanic Cloud; and perhaps a dozen dwarf ellipticals. The total mass of the Local Group is about 700 billion solar masses.

See also: EXTRAGALACTIC SYSTEMS.

Locarno [loh-kar'-noh] Locarno is a town in the Italian-speaking canton of Ticino in southern Switzerland. It has a population of 14,103 (1980). Located on the northern shore of Lake MAGGIORE, it is a popular holiday and health resort. Industries include machinery and electrochemicals. Notable among the historic buildings are the Church of Madonna del Sasso (1480) and the castle of the dukes of Milan (14th century). Settled in prehistoric times, Locarno was under Milanese rule from 1342 to 1512, when it was taken over by the Swiss.

Locarno Pact The Locarno Pact was a group of treaties signed in 1925 at Locarno, Switzerland, by representatives of Belgium, Britain, Czechoslovakia, France, Germany, Italy, and Poland. These agreements were an attempt to settle security problems left unresolved at the end of World War I. The main treaty confirmed Germany's western borders with France and Belgium. Germany also signed treaties with its eastern neighbors, Poland and Czechoslovakia, and France concluded an agreement with the latter countries, promising to help them if Germany broke its commitment to settle any future disputes with them peacefully. The Locarno Pact made Germany's entry into the LEAGUE OF NATIONS possible and was followed by a short era of international harmony.

Loch Ness see NESS, LOCH

Loch Ness monster [lahk nes] The Loch Ness monster is a legendary animal said to live in the depths of Loch Ness in northern Scotland. Belief that a mysterious creature lives in the lake goes back to the Middle Ages and the legend of the water horse, or kelpie, which lured travelers to their deaths. The first recorded sighting dates back to AD 565, when Saint COLUMBA came upon the burial of a man said to have been bitten to death by a monster while he was swimming in Loch Ness. According to one writer, Saint Columba himself later saw the monster.

Although many sightings have been reported in the subsequent centuries, not until 1933 did the Loch Ness monster become a subject of worldwide fascination. In that year a man and woman driving along a road at the side of the lake noticed a great surging of water, and for several minutes they watched "an enormous animal rolling and plunging."

Since then many investigators have attempted to get evidence of the creature's existence, using equipment ranging from telescopes and cameras to sonar and even a submarine. Many purported photographs of the monster have turned out to be inconclusive or outright hoaxes. Most scientists remain skeptical of the existence of the "monster."

lock and key   A lock is a fastening contrivance consisting of a bolt and the mechanisms for propelling it. Locks are opened by keys designed to fit and move the bolt mechanism.

Early Development. The oldest known lock, found in the ruins of the Near-Eastern palace of Khorsabad near ancient Ninevah, dates from about 2000 BC. A forerunner of the modern pin-tumbler lock, this so-called Egyptian lock consists of a large wooden bolt pierced with holes; pins from the lock housing drop through the holes to secure the bolt. The key, a long wooden bar fitted on one end with a pattern of pegs corresponding to the pins in the bolt, lifts the pins and permits the bolt to slide.

Other ancient Mediterranean cultures produced their own versions of locking devices. The early Greeks are credited with first employing keyholes. Roman contributions include the first metal locks, the earliest padlocks, the introduction of small keys, and the development of warded locks. The warded lock employs projections (wards) inside the lock casing that obstruct any key except one cut with notches that correspond to the projecting ward.

Warded construction, although fairly easy to open with a picklock, continued as the standard lock design until the late 1700s. In medieval and Renaissance Europe skilled locksmiths devised ingenious variations and adorned them with elaborate decorations. The principle of the combination lock probably originated in China; it appeared in southern Germany in the 16th century and resurfaced in England in the following century. This keyless

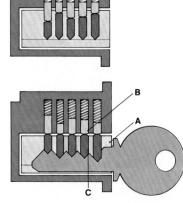

The cutaway diagram illustrates the process by which a key opens its corresponding lock. When the key is inserted until it meets the shear point (A), spring-loaded drivers (B) force the pins (C) to align with the grooves along the key. This permits the key to turn, opening the lock.

device depends on the correct alignment of numbers or letters on a dial to actuate the unlocking mechanism.

Modern History. In 1784, Joseph Bramah received a British patent for a lock that required a cylindrical key to push down and turn aside an arrangement of thin metal slides set in a barrel-shaped plug holding the bolt in place. Bramah and his assistant Henry MAUDSLAY are credited with successfully introducing mass-production techniques to 18th-century industry.

The modern pin-tumbler lock was invented by Linus Yale and Linus Yale, Jr. The senior Yale patented (1851) a lock with radial pin tumblers; his son patented improvements and began manufacturing the lock. Housed in a cylindrical plug, the pin tumblers stood in a row along the cylinder's turning axis. Use of the correct flat, serrated key lifted all the pins to the proper height, permitting the key to turn the bolt mechanism.

Today, new security technologies threaten the dominance of the metal lock and key. The keycard, developed in the early 1980s for use in hotels, has a magnetically imprinted code allowing a guest to enter the rented room. The code is changed when the person checks out. Newer technologies depend on the identification of person rather than the card. Sophisticated sensor-computer systems can scan and identify the unique patterns of blood cells inside a person's eye; recognize fingerprints; or respond to a voice whose digitized sound was previously stored in the system.

Locke, Alain   An American educator, critic, and anthologist, Alain LeRoy Locke, b. Philadelphia, Sept. 13, 1886, d. June 9, 1954, gained recognition as an authority on the cultural achievements of African Americans with his anthology *The New Negro* (1925; repr. 1968). Locke was active in the HARLEM RENAISSANCE movement, which he helped broaden to encompass artists and musicians and to include persons outside New York City. The first African-American Rhodes scholar, Locke completed (1918) his Ph.D. at Harvard and taught philosophy at Howard University for 36 years. His later anthologies were *The Negro and His Music* (1936; repr. 1968), *Negro Art—Past and Present* (1936; repr. 1969), and *The Negro in Art* (1940; repr. 1971).

Locke, David Ross   see NASBY, PETROLEUM V.

Locke, John   John Locke, b. Aug. 29, 1632, d. Oct. 28, 1704, was an English philosopher and political theorist, the founder of British EMPIRICISM. He joined the household of Anthony Ashley Cooper, later 1st earl of SHAFTESBURY, as a personal physician and became Shaftesbury's advisor and friend. Through him, Locke held minor government posts and became involved in the turbulent politics of the period. Because he was closely allied with Shaftesbury, Locke fled (1683) with him to Holland after Shaftesbury was tried for treason; he lived there until the overthrow (1688) of James II. His friendships with prominent government officers and scholars

John Locke, an English philosopher of the 17th century, is best known as an advocate of civil and religious liberties. He denied the divine right of kings, arguing that government is based on the consent of the people.

made him one of the most influential men of the 17th century.

Locke's *Essay Concerning Human Understanding* (1690) is one of the classical documents of British empirical philosophy. The essay had its origin in a series of discussions with friends that led Locke to the conclusion that the principal subject of philosophy had to be the extent of the mind's ability to know (see EPISTEMOLOGY). He set out "to examine our abilities and to see what objects our understandings were or were not fitted to deal with." The *Essay* is a principal statement of empiricism and, broadly speaking, was an effort to formulate a view of knowledge consistent with the findings of Newtonian science.

Locke began the *Essay* with a critique of the rationalistic idea that the mind is equipped with INNATE IDEAS, ideas that do not arise from experience. He then turned to the elaboration of his own empiricism: "Let us suppose the mind to be, as we say, white paper, void of all characters, without any ideas; how comes this to be furnished?... whence has it all the materials of reason and knowledge? To this I answer, in a word, from experience." What experience provides is ideas, which Locke defined as "the object of the understanding when a man thinks." He held that ideas come from two sources: sensation, which provides ideas about the external world, and reflection, or introspection, which provides the ideas of the internal workings of the mind.

Locke's view that experience produces ideas, which are the immediate objects of thought, led him to adopt a causal or representative view of human knowledge. In perception, according to this view, people are not directly aware of physical objects. Rather, they are directly aware of the ideas that objects "cause" in them and that "represent" the objects in their consciousness. A similar view of perception was presented by earlier thinkers such as Galileo and Descartes.

Locke's view raised the question of the extent to which ideas are like the objects that cause them. His answer was that only some qualities of objects are like ideas. He held that primary qualities of objects, or the mathematically determinable qualities of an object, such as shape, motion, weight, and number, exist in the world, and that ideas copy them. Secondary qualities, those which arise from the senses, do not exist in objects as they exist in ideas. According to Locke, secondary qualities, such as taste, "are nothing in the objects themselves but powers to produce ideas in use by their primary qualities." Thus, when an object is perceived, a person's ideas of its shape and weight represent qualities to be found in the object itself. Color and taste, however, are not copies of anything in the object.

As the first systematic theorist of the philosophy of LIBERALISM, Locke exercised enormous influence in both England and America. In his *Two Treatises of Government* (1690), Locke set forth the view that the state exists to preserve the natural rights of its citizens. When governments fail in that task, citizens have the right—and sometimes the duty—to withdraw their support and even to rebel. Locke opposed Thomas HOBBES's view that the original state of nature is "nasty, brutish, and short," and that individuals through a SOCIAL CONTRACT surrender—for the sake of self-preservation—their rights to a supreme sovereign who is the source of all morality and law. Locke maintained that the state of nature is a happy and tolerant one, that the social contract preserves the preexistent natural rights of the individual to life, liberty, and property, and that the enjoyment of private rights—the pursuit of happiness—leads, in civil society, to the common good. Locke's notion of government was a limited one: the checks and balances among branches of government (later reflected in the U.S. Constitution) and true representation in the legislature would maintain limited government and individual liberties.

lockjaw   see TETANUS

---

lockout   A lockout is the closing of a place of business by management in order to prevent employees from working and thus to pressure a labor union into settling a dispute in management's favor. The lockout is analogous to the STRIKE; it is a last resort. In U.S. labor history, lockouts were sometimes used to frustrate union organizers. This use of a lockout was outlawed by the National Labor Relations Act of 1935, which requires employers to bargain "in good faith" with representatives of their employees. An employer is not required under the law to agree to demands made by a union and may decide to endure a strike until the union comes to terms. For this reason a strike is sometimes called a lockout by workers involved in a dispute. During a lockout, an employer may continue to do business by hiring temporary replacements.

Lockwood, Belva Ann Bennett   Belva Lockwood, b. Royalton, N.Y., Oct. 24, 1830, d. May 19, 1917, was the first woman lawyer admitted to practice before the U.S. Supreme Court and the first woman candidate for the U.S. presidency. Rejected by many law schools on the ground that she was a woman, she finally entered the National University Law School and was admitted to the District of Columbia bar in 1873. She won the right to present cases before the Supreme Court in 1879. Lockwood was a leading litigator and lobbyist on behalf of women's rights. In 1884 and 1888 she was nominated as the presidential candidate of the National Equal Rights party.

locomotion, biological   see BIOLOGICAL LOCOMOTION

---

locomotive   A locomotive is a vehicle that runs on rails and is self-propelled by any of several forms of energy for the purpose of moving railroad cars. During its long history the railroad locomotive has experienced a complex technical development moving in turn from steam to electric and finally to diesel power.

History

Some of the first RAILROADS (called railways in Britain) used horses for motive power.

Steam Locomotive. England was the birthplace of the steam locomotive, which is essentially a STEAM ENGINE mounted on and used to propel a wheeled vehicle on rails. The first steam locomotive was built in 1804 by Richard TREVITHICK for the Penydarren Iron Works in Wales. It was able to haul a sizable load (25 tons) but was too heavy for the track and was converted to a stationary steam engine. George STEPHENSON built the engine *Locomotion* for the Stockton and Darlington Railway, which was opened in 1825. This engine, with a single flue and outside coupling rods, had insufficient boiler capacity. Far more powerful was the ROCKET, an engine designed primarily by George Stephenson's son Robert. The *Rocket* was the winning entry in the 1829 Rainhill Trials, a locomotive competition; the *Rocket*'s performance confirmed the practicability of steam motive power.

Because the United States then had such a limited manufacturing capacity, U.S. railways imported many English locomotives between 1829 and 1841. One of the first was the *Stourbridge Lion*; it was imported in 1829 by the Delaware & Hudson Railroad but was found to be too heavy and rigid for American track. More successful was the *John Bull*, which the Camden & Amboy Railroad imported in 1831.

The Americans soon began building their own locomotives. In 1830, Peter Cooper's tiny (1.43 hp) *Tom Thumb* lost its famous race against a horse-drawn coach but still convinced officials of the Baltimore & Ohio Railroad that they should use steam power. On Christmas Day, 1830, in South Carolina, the *Best Friend of Charleston*—the first locomotive built for sale in the United States—carried 141 passengers on the first scheduled steam railroad train in America. The *Stourbridge Lion*, the *John Bull*, and the *Best Friend of Charleston* all had four drivers, a connected pair on each side. John B. Jervis, a civil engineer who worked for the Mohawk & Hudson Railroad, was not happy with the rigid front axle and poor turning characteristics of such engines. In 1832 he built the *Experiment*, an engine with a single pair of drivers and a four-wheeled bogie (a swivel truck under the front of the locomotive). The new engine negotiated curves more easily and at much higher speeds.

Other U.S. innovations quickly followed. In 1836, Henry Campbell of Philadelphia designed an eight-wheeled engine (bogie truck plus four drivers); it was known as the American-type locomotive, and this type was to dominate U.S. locomotive design for half a century. Earlier in the decade, Isaac Dripps, of the Camden & Amboy, invented the pilot, or "cowcatcher," and placed the first one on the *John Bull*. Night rail travel was fairly common within 12 years, and by the 1840s the conventional large headlight, burning kerosene in front of tin reflectors, was quite common. The sandbox (to provide better driver traction) was first used in Pennsylvania in 1836. Both locomotive bells and whistles were soon found on most engines as a warning signal at railroad crossings; the whistle was later also used for signaling the train crew.

By the 1850s, British and U.S. locomotives tended to differ considerably. British engines were shorter, with generally smaller tenders and cabs. They rarely used the bogie or pony swivel truck in front, and the U.S.-type pilot was never seen on English engines.

Western & Atlanta's General, *built in 1855, typifies American locomotives of that vintage. It had 4 leading wheels, 4 drivers, and no trailing wheels; hence it was designated 4-4-0. The* General *was built by Thomas Rogers, a carpenter turned locomotive builder, who was the first to use a steam whistle in an American engine. Rogers was largely responsible for making Paterson, N.J., known as "The City of Iron Horses."*

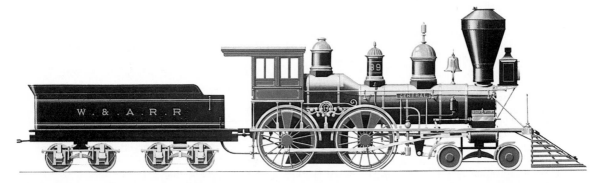

Great Northern Railway's single-driver locomotive, designed by Patrick Stirling, operated on Great Britain's east-coast line between King's Cross and York. These famous engines pulled London-Southend expresses in the 1890s.

The London and North Eastern Railway's Pacific Mallard, designed by Sir Nigel Gresley, broke the world speed record for a steam locomotive in 1938 by reaching a speed of 202 km/h (126 mph).

The Santa Fé Class 2900 is a good example of a large American fast freight locomotive. A 4-8-4 (four wheels in front, eight drivers, four wheels under the cab), it was built in 1943.

The French National Railway's Class CC 7100 electric locomotive broke the world rail speed record in March 1955 by reaching 331 km/h (205 mph).

Great Northern's diesel engine, built by General Motors, is a typical large American general-purpose diesel locomotive. Diesel power began to replace steam power in the 1950s, and soon most major rail lines owned no steam engines at all.

The New Tokaido Line, a high-speed electric line, runs between Tokyo and Osaka, Japan. It completes the 512-km (320-mi) journey in about three hours.

By the eve of the Civil War, the favorite U.S. locomotive design was the eight-wheel American type. This was known as a 4-4-0 (four wheels in front, four drivers, no wheels under the cab), according to the Frederic M. Whyte system of engine classification. In 1860 the average American-type locomotive had a functional cowcatcher, large headlight, balloon smokestack, and a name rather than a number; cost $8,000 to $10,000 to build; and used wood, or possibly coal, for fuel. By 1870 most of them were heavier, more powerful, and coal-burning, and they were providing about 85% of the motive power in the United States.

In the half century between the Civil War and World War I, a new emphasis was placed on strength, bulk, and power in the manufacture of American locomotives. One change was the increase in the number of drivers. The Baltimore & Ohio increasingly turned to Ten-Wheelers (4-6-0, according to the Whyte classification), and still more tractive power was possible when the Lehigh Valley introduced the Consolidation type (2-8-0). The need for a larger firebox was met by moving the firebox from between the rear pair of drivers, making it broader, and placing it over a trailing truck of smaller wheels. This resulted in the Atlantic type (4-4-2) in 1895. A few years later the Missouri Pacific achieved still greater power with its Pacific locomotive (4-6-2).

Improvements in U.S. steam locomotives continued during the first half of the 20th century. During World War I, the U.S. Railroad Administration purchased 1,930 locomotives, all built to standard specifications, with about half of the engines being Mikado (2-8-2) freight locomotives. In the prosperous 1920s, 15,000 new locomotives were purchased by American railroads, some of the largest being the huge mallet or articulated models, steam engines with two sets of drivers powered by a single firebox and boiler. During World War II, the Union Pacific commissioned 25 giant "Big Boys," huge articulated engines 35.1 m (117 ft) in length, with 170-cm (68-in) drivers, and capable of producing 7,000 hp.

Electric Locomotive. Late in the 19th century, steam motive power was challenged by electric locomotives, in both Europe and the United States. By the turn of the century the Baltimore & Ohio and the New York, New Haven & Hartford lines had successfully installed short electrified routes. Later the Milwaukee electrified much of its mountain line as it built west to the Pacific. In the 1920s and '30s the Pennsylvania did the same for some of its lines. By the mid-1950s, U.S. railroads were operating a total of 3,900 km (2,400 mi) of electrified route. The increasing popularity of the diesel locomotive, however, has led to a reduction in electrified sections of railroads.

Diesel Locomotive. The invention of the diesel locomotive made possible great increases in operating efficiency. The DIESEL ENGINE was invented in the 1890s by Rudolf Diesel, a French-born German mechanical engineer. The first diesel-electric locomotive was used by the Central Railroad of New Jersey for switching operations in New York City in the mid-1920s. In the mid-1930s diesel power began to be used for passenger trains, and in 1941 diesels were used for freight service. During and after World War II, the conversion to diesel power was rapid. By 1945, diesels powered 7% of the freight, 10% of the passenger, and 25% of the yard-switching service; by 1957 the now dominant form of locomotive power performed 92% of the freight, 93% of the passenger, and 96% of the switching service in the United States. A similar trend was occurring worldwide.

Comparison of Operation of Locomotive Types

The history of the steam locomotive accompanied the birth and growth of a viable rail industry that tended to peak in many industrial nations in the second quarter of the 20th century. In contrast the appearance of both electric and diesel power came at a time when the railroad industry was near, or even past, its peak in mileage and economic importance. Without doubt the greater efficiency of the diesels eased the financial strain that accompanied the decline of the industry. Today most railroads in industrial nations use either electric or diesel locomotives. Steam is still quite extensively used, however, in many underdeveloped countries in Africa, Asia, and South America.

In the diesel locomotive an oil-burning diesel engine supplies the power. It is possible to transmit this power to the driving wheels by using a mechanical or hydraulic transmission, but the indirect, flexible electric transmission is more commonly used, and such a locomotive is called a diesel-electric. In this type, the diesel engine turns electric GENERATORS; these, in turn, power several electric MOTORS, normally one for each axle. This form of power offers several advantages over the steam locomotive. Although diesels are expensive (costing probably double the price of steam engines of comparable horsepower) the higher initial costs are offset by the economic advantages of high fuel efficiency, low maintenance costs, and a high degree of availability of the diesel. While the average steamer requires extensive daily attention to its firebox and boiler, the diesel can run thousands of miles with only incidental maintenance. The diesel-electric transmits power to the wheels smoothly, without the reciprocating motion of the steam-engine drivers that subjects the track to heavy pounding. Like electric locomotives, the diesel can also reverse its motors to act as brakes on downgrades. Diesels are more flexible in usage, in that extra units can be added to the lead diesel unit, all the units being controlled by a single engine crew.

Many of the advantages of the diesel are also found in the electric locomotive. In addition, electric units are cleaner, because electric motors do not pollute the environment, and power is supplied from a large generating plant, which produces its power more efficiently and cleanly than individual diesel locomotives do. Electric locomotives are relatively simple in construction, have a low maintenance cost, and may have a longer economic life than diesel units. The major disadvantage of electrified service is the high original capital cost of the necessary facilities and equipment.

locoweed   Locoweed is the name given to a number of poisonous plants causing erratic behavior and sometimes death when eaten by livestock. Horses are the most susceptible. Commonly the name locoweed is applied to species of *Astragalus* in the pea family, Leguminosae; among the more toxic are the purple loco, *A. mollissimus*, and the western loco, *A. wootonii*. Another locoweed, *Oxytropis lambertii*, of the same family, is similar and is sometimes classified in *Astragalus*. The poison larkspur, *Delphinium glaucum*, and closely related species have a similar effect and are sometimes called locoweeds.

locust (insect)   Locust is the common name for about nine GRASSHOPPER species in the short-horned grasshopper superfamily, Acridoidea. These species are distinguished from other grasshoppers by sometimes swarming and taking part in mass migrations. The swarms are difficult to control and can devastate crops and vegetation. The species mentioned in the Old Testament, the desert locust (*Schistocerca gregaria*, family Catantopidae), roams over central and north Africa, the Middle East, and India. Other *Schistocerca* species also swarm in these regions and in South America. In North America the best-known swarming

Locust is the name given to a few species of grasshopper that migrate in huge swarms, ruining vegetation in the course of their flight. In its solitary phase (A), a locust is light colored and behaves like any other grasshopper. When an area is overpopulated with locusts or food is scarce, solitary locusts undergo a gregarious change (B); their skin turns dark and they swarm. A female is shown laying her eggs underground (bottom).

locust is *Melanoplus sanguinipes*. Swarms of *Locusta* and *Locustana* species, family Acrididae, occur from Europe through Africa and Asia and in New Zealand.

When populations of locusts are sparse in a region, the individuals live solitary lives and migrate singly at night, like other grasshoppers. As their numbers increase, however, they respond to more frequent encounters with each other by becoming more and more gregarious, active, and conspicuous. They form mobs of "hoppers" (nymphs) and adults, which migrate by day in a uniquely itinerant mode of life. The solitary phase is always present, whereas the gregarious phase appears only sporadically. Under sufficiently crowded conditions, a solitary hopper will mature into a gregarious adult, with longer wings, shorter legs, and other identifiable features. As more and more of the gregarious types appear, migratory swarms build up. Once started, a locust plague may last for several years. The swarms eventually die off and scatter, leaving only the solitary phase.

lodestone   see MAGNETITE

Lodge (family)   Members of the Lodge family of New England have held prominent public office as Republicans and have played leading roles in American foreign affairs. **Henry Cabot Lodge**, b. Boston, May 12, 1850, d. Nov. 9, 1924, wrote several historical biographies before becoming a Republican representative from Massachusetts (1887–93). He championed civil-service reform and helped write the SHERMAN ANTI-TRUST ACT (1890). Lodge subsequently served in the U.S. Senate (1893–1924), where he favored a strong navy and endorsed President Theodore Roosevelt's aggressive nationalism. As Senate majority leader (1918–24) and chairman of the Foreign Relations Committee (1918–24), he led the successful opposition to U.S. membership in the League of Nations in 1919. His grandson, **Henry Cabot Lodge, Jr.**, b. Nahant, Mass., July 5, 1902, d. Feb. 27, 1985, was also a Republican senator from Massachusetts (1937–44, 1947–53). He served as U.S. ambassador to the United Nations (1953–60) and was the unsuccessful Republican vice-presidential nominee in 1960. He was ambassador to South Vietnam (1963–64, 1965–67), ambassador-at-large (1967–68), and ambassador to West Germany (1968–69). He also led (1969) the American delegation to the Vietnam peace talks in Paris.

Lodge, Thomas   Thomas Lodge, *c.*1557–1625, was an English poet, dramatist, and writer of prose romances. He received a degree from Oxford in 1578 and went on to study law but abandoned it for a literary career. Sometime between 1584 and 1589, Lodge joined an expedition to the Canaries and the Azores. On the voyage he completed *Rosalynde*, a pastoral romance modeled on the style of his contemporary John Lyly; it was later used by William Shakespeare as the source for *As You Like It*. Lodge subsequently became an eminent physician.

Łódź [looj]   Łódź, the capital of Łódź province and the second largest city in Poland, lies about 120 km (75 mi) southwest of Warsaw. The population is 852,000 (1988 est.). An important transportation and industrial center, Łódź is primarily known for its textiles. The city has several colleges. Dating from the 14th century, Łódź was a small village until the 19th century, when it developed into an industrial city.

loess [loh'-es]   Loess (German for "loose") is a loose, fine-grained sediment deposited by wind during the Pleistocene ICE AGES. Details of its origin remain in dispute. Widespread deposits of loess 10 to 15 m (33 to 49 ft) thick are not uncommon; on the Loess Plateau of China, thicknesses reach 180 m (about 590 ft). Loess usually lacks internal layering, but some deposits display multiple strata, perhaps indicating episodic emplacement. Its gray or yellowish color is caused by iron-oxide minerals. Loess contains silt-size grains (0.01–0.05 mm/ 0.004–0.02 in), mostly of quartz but also smaller amounts of clay and other minerals. CARBONATE MINERALS may amount to 40 percent but are not invariably present. The silt in the deposits may have come from broad areas of barren till (see TILL AND TILLITE) and glacial outwash before they were stabilized by vegetation. Often highly porous, loess is always stable, holding clifflike walls in which birds dig nests.

Major deposits of loess are found in North America, Eurasia, and Argentina. In North America, loess occurs in an area extending east from the Rocky Mountains to

Loess cliffs along the Yukon River in Canada are thick, unstratified deposits of yellow-brown, fine-grained silt, sand, and clay. The sediments are believed to have been formed by windblown dust from dried-up beds of ice-age lakes and streams.

Pennsylvania and south to the Mississippi Delta. In Europe, it occurs from the Atlantic coast to the Ural Mountains but most extensively in Eastern Europe. In Asia, loess covers large areas of northern China.

Loewe, Frederick   see LERNER, ALAN JAY, AND LOEWE, FREDERICK

Loewy, Raymond [loh'-ee]   Raymond Loewy, b. Nov. 5, 1893, d. July 14, 1986, was an engineer and industrial designer known for his promotion of the "streamlined look." Born in France, he emigrated to the United States after World War I and founded his own INDUSTRIAL DESIGN firm in 1927. Loewy's first major success was the award-winning Coldspot refrigerator, commissioned by Sears Roebuck in 1935. He subsequently designed everything from automobiles, ocean liners, and locomotives to furniture, toothbrushes, and electric shavers, dramatically changing the appearance of the industrial products used by the American consumer.

Logan, James   James Logan, b. Ireland, Oct. 20, 1674, d. Oct. 31, 1751, was an associate of William Penn, the founder of Pennsylvania, who brought him to America in 1699. He held a number of government posts in colonial Pennsylvania, including provincial secretary (1701–17), councilor (1702–47), mayor of Philadelphia (1722), and chief justice of the Pennsylvania Supreme Court (1731–39). Logan wrote extensively—especially on botany and mathematics; on his death, his 3,000-volume library greatly augmented the collections of the Library Company of Philadelphia, an important cultural institution in that city.

Logan, John   Captain John Logan, c.1725–80, also known as James Logan or as Tahgahjute, was a leader of the Mingo, bands of Iroquois-speaking Indians who lived near the headwaters of the Ohio River in western Pennsylvania. Born a CAYUGA on the Susquehanna River, Logan became a vigorous defender of whites after moving to the Ohio region. Embittered when his kin were slaughtered by colonists during the Yellow Creek Massacre of 1774, Logan, with the blessings of the British, made numerous retaliatory raids against American settlers. After his defeat (1774) at the Battle of Point Pleasant, Pa., he delivered an eloquent speech that was much admired at the time and later cited by Thomas Jefferson.

Logan, John Alexander   John Alexander Logan, b. Murphysboro, Ill., Feb. 9, 1826, d. Dec. 26, 1886, was an American politician and Union general in the Civil War. After studying law, he served in the Illinois legislature and in 1858 and 1860 was elected Democratic representative from Illinois. In 1861 he resigned his House seat and entered the Union army as colonel of the 31st Illinois Infantry, which he organized. A good combat leader, Logan served at Fort Donelson (1862) and in the Vicksburg campaign (1862–63). By 1862 he was a general, and in 1864 he briefly commanded the Army of the Tennessee.

After the war, Logan returned to Illinois and reentered politics. He was elected to the U.S. Congress as a Republican, serving in the House (1867–71) and Senate (1871–77 and 1879–86). In 1884 he was the Republican candidate for vice-president. In 1868, Logan inaugurated the observance of Memorial Day to commemorate the Civil War dead.

Logan, Mount　Mount Logan, the highest mountain in Canada and the second highest in North America (after Mount McKinley), is situated in the southwestern Yukon in the St. Elias Mountains. The tallest of its several peaks reaches an altitude of 6,050 m (19,850 ft). Mount Logan is difficult to climb because of glaciers; the central peak was first ascended in 1925 by A. H. MacCarthy and his Canadian-American team.

logarithm　[lawg'-uh-rithm]　A logarithm is an exponent. The properties of logarithms can be used to simplify computations that might otherwise be very long and cumbersome, but such computations are now usually carried out with calculators (see CALCULATOR, ELECTRONIC).

The exponential equation $y = b^x$ can be equivalently expressed by the logarithmic equation $\log_b y = x$, which can be read, "the logarithm to the base b of y is x." Because logarithms are EXPONENTS, they satisfy the same properties as exponents, including the following:

1. $\log_b (xy) = \log_b x + \log_b y$
2. $\log_b (x/y) = \log_b x - \log_b y$
3. $\log_b x^y = y \log_b x$
4. $\log_b \sqrt[y]{x} = (1/y) \log_b x$

Any positive number other than 1 can be used as a base for a logarithm. The bases used most often are base 10 (because the ordinary number system uses base 10) and base e ($e = 2.7182818284590\ldots$), which simplifies many scientific calculations (see separate article on e). Logarithms to base 10 are called common logarithms, and logarithms to base e are called natural logarithms. When common logarithms are used, it is customary to dispense with any mention of the base. For example, log 100 = 2 means that the logarithm to the base 10, or common logarithm, of 100 is 2. In other words, $10^2 = 100$.

Each common logarithm has two parts, a characteristic and a mantissa. The characteristic is the number to the left of the decimal point in the logarithm and represents the greatest power of 10 that is less than the number whose logarithm is being found. The mantissa of a logarithm is the part that follows (is to the right of) the decimal point. It is normally determined by referring to a mathematical table of logarithms.

The discovery of logarithms (c.1614) is attributed to John NAPIER of Scotland and Jobst Biirgi of Switzerland.

Logarithmic tables were developed in the early 1600s by Henry Briggs of England and Adriaen Ulacq of the Netherlands.

loggerhead turtle　The loggerhead turtle, *Caretta caretta*, in the family Cheloniidae, is the most common sea turtle in North American waters and appears to be less tropical than others in its family. Characteristically, it has a large head and a reddish brown upper shell, which has five or more large scales, or laminae, on each side of the midline. Two subspecies are recognized: the Atlantic loggerhead, *C. c. caretta*, found in the Atlantic Ocean from Nova Scotia and Scotland to Argentina and South Africa and in the Mediterranean Sea; and the Pacific loggerhead, *C. c. gigas*, found in the Pacific and Indian oceans from Japan and southern California to South Africa, Australia, and Chile. Loggerheads feed on marine organisms such as mollusks and crustaceans and also eat seaweed. They are the largest hard-shelled turtles and are second in size only to the leatherback turtle. Records of specimens reaching 2.1 m (7 ft) long and 450 kg (1,000 lb) exist, but individuals of 140 kg (300 lb) are considered large.

The loggerhead turtle, like other sea turtles, has large, oarlike flippers as forelimbs. It is primarily aquatic.

logging　see LUMBER

logic　Logic is the systematic study of reasoning that provides standards by which valid reasoning can be recognized. It clarifies the reasoning process and provides a means for analyzing the consistency of basic concepts. Logic has played an important role in the history of PHILOSOPHY.

Traditional Logic

The history of Western logic can be traced to ancient Greece. ARISTOTLE is usually considered the first major Western logician, although earlier contributions to logic were made by PLATO, SOCRATES, ZENO OF ELEA, and others. Aristotle's logical system treated the categorical SYLLOGISM and the laws of logic. His many books on logic became the basis for its study up to the 19th century. The next school of logicians, the Megarians, flourished in the 4th century BC. Rather than study categorical inferences, they sought to define the conditions under which a conditional, "if A, then B," is true. The Stoics, especially one of their leaders, Chrysippus, took over and developed the logical ideas of the Megarians (see STOICISM). Aristotle had set forth a logic of terms; Chrysippus worked out a logic of propositions. Other late Greek and Roman logicians mainly codified the work of their predecessors, although Galen (AD 129–199) added some theories about special kinds of syllogisms.

The logic of the Greeks endured in the Middle East after the fall of Rome and the conquest of western Europe by the barbarian tribes. In the Middle Ages logic was again brought to the attention of the Western world by logicians of the Islamic empire. Many of Aristotle's writings as well as commentaries preserved by heretical Christian sects were available to these logicians. Al-Farabi (870–950), one of the greatest Muslim logicians, wrote commentaries on most of Aristotle's logical works. Other logicians translated other Greek works on logic into Arabic. (From Arabic they were usually translated by Jewish scholars into Hebrew, and then from Hebrew into Latin.) The great Muslim philosopher AVICENNA made logic independent of the teachings of Aristotle and the Stoics. By the 14th century, intellectuals were reading handbooks on logic by various Muslim scholars, instead of the classics.

Meanwhile, the logical materials that were being studied in the Islamic empire became known in Christian Europe. The Christians had previously had only a few of Aristotle's works and a few commentaries. The first significant logician of the Christian Middle Ages, Peter ABELARD, wrote before most of the Aristotelian materials became available but developed detailed and critical evaluations of the material that had been preserved in the West. The rest of Aristotle's logical writings became available by about 1200, resulting in the emergence of the *logica moderna,* a "new logic." Perhaps the greatest of the modern logicians was WILLIAM OF OCCAM, who wrote the *Summa Logicae* (1326?). Other logicians incorporated the Aristotelian heritage into a broader logic.

As the renaissance began, so did an attack on medieval (scholastic) thought and on the Aristotelian theories that provided its basis. The major Renaissance opponent of Aristotelian logic was the 16th-century French Protestant thinker Petrus RAMUS. Ramus attacked nearly all of Aristotle's logical doctrines and proposed instead that there be a logic of invention or discovery and a logic of judgment.

With the rejection of Aristotle's metaphysics by the great 17th-century thinkers Francis Bacon, René Descartes, Baruch Spinoza, and John Locke, a search began for a new logic that would fit with a new picture of reality. Gottfried Wilhelm von LEIBNIZ made major contributions to this new logic, although most of his logical work did not become generally available until the end of the 19th century. Leibniz tried to work out a universal logical language, and he also developed a logical calculus. He was apparently not ready to reject Aristotelian logic, but his examinations of other possibilities when discovered at the end of the 19th century nevertheless aided in the development of modern logic.

Mathematical Logic

Mathematical logic is that branch of logic which uses exacting formal methods to achieve precision and objectivity in explaining what it is to be logical in argument and reasoning. It concentrates on the explanation and development of proof and on the nature of formal systems used in constructing proofs. Although its greatest successes have been in application to mathematics and computers, its generality makes it potentially applicable to virtually any field. Different branches of mathematical logic treat different types of questions. Alethic modal logics have been applied to such diverse questions as the nature of God and the structure of scientific laws; deontic logics, to normative systems of legal and moral behavior.

Mathematical logic developed from the desire to provide systematic foundations for the practice of mathematics, explaining the nature of numbers and the laws of arithmetic and replacing intuition with rigorous proof. Noteworthy among its founders is the Italian mathematician Giuseppe Peano (1858–1932), but the German mathematical philosopher Gottlob FREGE (1848–1925) is considered the father of mathematical logic. Their early work was advanced by Bertrand RUSSELL and Alfred North WHITEHEAD in *Principia Mathematica* (3 vols., 1910–13), and by many others, including Alonzo Church, Kurt Gödel, David Hilbert, Emil Post, and Alfred Tarski.

Valid argument is basic to mathematical logic. An argument is composed of a *conclusion*, which is argued for, and *premises*, which are the reasons for the conclusion. In a valid argument the conclusion follows from the premises: the argument is of such a form that no argument having that form can have true premises and a false conclusion. Thus, the following argument is valid, and its corresponding form exemplifies a logical way of thinking.

Argument I	Form I
No one putting profits first is putting human rights first	No F is G
This person is putting profits first	This H is F
Therefore:	Therefore:
This person is not putting human rights first	This H is not G

In contrast, the following argument and corresponding form are invalid, as is shown by the counterexample.

Argument II	Form II	Counterexample II
All communists are dissenters	All F are G	All tigers are cats
All communists are subversives	All F are H	All tigers are striped
Therefore:	Therefore:	Therefore:
All dissenters are subversive	All G are H	All cats are striped

Counterexample II shows Form II to constitute an illogical way of thinking, in which truth can lead to falsehood. Arguments I and II are deductive: certainty of the premises would be intended to make the conclusion certain (see DEDUCTION). In contrast, inductive arguments seek probability rather than certainty (see INDUCTION).

Mathematical logic achieves precision, clarity, and manipulability through the use of artificial languages (see LANGUAGES, ARTIFICIAL), symbol systems deliberately constructed for use in logic. Sentences of such a system may represent sentences of natural languages like English, directly representing logical words such as *no* or *all* and suppressing structures considered irrelevant.

Formation rules, analogous to grammatical rules in natural languages, explain the forms of the sentences. Transformation rules (or rules of proof or of inference) state which forms may be validly concluded from others. Proofs string together valid arguments in accordance with such formal rules. In this way, formal methods free proofs of appeals to intuition and make assumptions explicit and open to debate.

Formation and transformation rules deal only with form and so are purely syntactic. SEMANTICS relates forms to the world via rules of valuation, which determine how logical operators like quantifiers and conditionals affect truth and falsehood and thus how form affects content. A rule of valuation states that the truth value of an atomic sentence like *"Dn"* is determined by whether the predicate *"D"* truly applies to the thing referred to by the name *n*; the sentence is true if the predicate applies, and otherwise false. Another rule for conditionals states that a conditional is false in case its left constituent (such as *"Cn"*) is true and its right constituent (such as *"Dn"*) is false; in any other case the conditional is true. Another rule handles the universal quantifier, and so on. These rules explain how complex sentences may be understood on the basis of simpler ones and bring out the conditions required for the proper application of the formal system to a given subject matter. They also make it possible to study the logical properties of the system.

Because validity is the formal impossibility of true premises and false conclusion, the semantics yields an explanation of validity independent of the transformation rules. The consistency (validity of the rules) and completeness (capacity to prove all valid arguments that are expressible) may thus be studied in a metalogic (logical theory of a logical system). These and other systemic properties have been successfully investigated by Hilbert, Post, Tarski, Church, Gödel, Leopold Löwenheim, Thoraf Skolem, and other philosophers.

Relational logic treats many-place predicates, which have more than one place for a name or variable. Examples are "*x* is between *y* and *z*" and "*x* spoke to *y*." The inclusion of relational predicates greatly increases the scope of the system, far surpassing the traditional syllogism of Aristotle. A special relation is identity, expressing the idea that something is one and the same thing as something. This concept is essential to expressing the concept of another—one thing different from the first— and is thus essential to counting.

SET THEORY, or the theory of classes, is often considered a step beyond elementary logic. It adds a relation of class membership to the basis already described. "*m ε* the class of presidents" would say that Carter is a member of the class of presidents. Such a class is an abstract grouping independent of physical proximity. With the relation of class membership and systemic expressions for referring to classes, all the basic concepts of arithmetic have been explained, including the kinds of numbers and arithmetic operations in general, without appeal to any undefined arithmetic concept. Such an explanation was what Russell and Whitehead first accomplished, based on Frege's work.

Modal logics deal with necessity and possibility, or "must" and "can." They have recently been given a rigorous semantics that has stimulated discussion of their application to such concepts as essential natures (METAPHYSICS); laws of nature (philosophy of science); what *would* be true if something that is not true *were* to be true (subjunctive conditionals); what ought to be done (ETHICS); what was or will be true (time and tense); and what is known (EPISTEMOLOGY). The assumptions involved are deeply controversial, however.

logical positivism

Logical positivism was a 20th-century philosophical movement in the tradition of ANALYTIC AND LINGUISTIC PHILOSOPHY. Like earlier forms of POSITIVISM, it had close ties to British EMPIRICISM and was marked by respect for natural science and hostility to metaphysical speculation.

The movement originated with a group of German and Austrian philosophers known as the Vienna Circle. At first just a discussion group, the Vienna Circle later became a more formal organization, publishing its own philosophical journal. Organized by Moritz Schlick (1882–1936), who came to the University of Vienna as professor of philosophy in 1922, it also included Herbert Feigl, Kurt GÖDEL, Hans Hahn, Friedrich Waismann, and, after 1926, Rudolf CARNAP.

The Circle was decisively influenced by Ludwig WITTGENSTEIN, though he was never really a member of it. In his *Tractatus Logico-Philosophicus* (1921), Wittgenstein put forward a general theory of linguistic representation, according to which propositions are "logical pictures" of possible facts. This implied that a proposition is not meaningful unless it determines a precise range of circumstances in which it is true. In metaphysics, however, philosophers have often tried to say something about reality as a whole, making claims supposedly so general and fundamental as to be indifferent to the particular facts of the world. On Wittgenstein's theory of language, such claims are literally nonsensical, words without meaning.

Although Wittgenstein had distinguished in an abstract way between elementary and complex propositions, the positivists took his elementary propositions to be reports of observations. This was the origin of their central idea, the verification principle, which said that any meaningful proposition, other than the tautological or, as they came to be called, "analytic" propositions of logic and pure mathematics, had to be verifiable by means of observation. Propositions belonging to traditional metaphysics—such as those about the existence of God, for example—were deemed not to meet this condition and were declared meaningless. Metaphysical statements were not the only ones to fail the test. Ordinary moral judgments seemed to fail it, too.

With the elimination of metaphysics, the business of philosophy was seen as the logical clarification of scientific statements and theories—for example, putting informally stated theories in strict axiomatic form, so as to distinguish clearly their analytic from their empirical elements.

Nevertheless, a good deal of controversy centered on the interpretation of the principles of logical positivism itself. One problem concerned observation statements: were they about an individual's private perceptual experiences, as Schlick thought, or about publicly accessible events? Another concerned the verification of scientific laws that, because they apply to a potentially infinite number of instances, cannot be verified with absolute conclusiveness. Eventually, the original strong notion of verification gave way to a weaker notion of confirmation.

With the advent of Nazism, most members of the Vienna Circle chose exile, many settling in the United States. Logical positivism's subsequent influence was strongest in the United States. In contemporary philosophy, especially in the United States, the spirit of logical positivism can be seen in the respect for science, distrust of high-flown jargon (or what is thought to be such), and insistence on clarity and rigorous argument. Its specific theoretical ideas are no longer accepted in their original form.

LOGO see COMPUTER LANGUAGES

logos The word *logos* (from the root of the Greek verb *lego*, "to say") figures prominently in a number of Greek and Christian philosophical doctrines. Although the word's earliest meaning probably was "connected discourse," by the classical period it already had a wide variety of other meanings, among them "argument," "rational principle," "reason," "proportion," and "measure."

HERACLITUS was the earliest Greek thinker to make logos a central concept. He urges that attention be paid to the logos, which "governs all things" and yet is also something people "encounter every day." In efforts to understand the world, one should look to language and the order embodied in it rather than to scientific or religious views that neglect this.

In the 3d century BC the proponents of STOICISM borrowed the idea of logos from Heraclitus (neither Plato nor Aristotle had given the term prominence) and used it for the immanent ordering principle of the universe—represented, at the level of language, by humankind's ordered discourse. Nature and logos are often treated as one and the same, but logos is nature's overall rational structure, and not all natural creatures have logos, or reason, within them. Humans are urged to "live consistently with logos."

In the New Testament, the Gospel According to Saint JOHN gives a central place to logos; the biblical author describes the Logos as God, the Creative Word, who took on flesh in the man Jesus Christ. The Old Testament also contains a doctrine of the Word of God, and in Aramaic paraphrases the "Word of God" takes on some of the functions of God.

■

Loire River [lwar] The Loire River, with a length of 1,006 km (625 mi), making it the longest river in France, rises on Mont Gerbier de Jonc in the MASSIF CENTRAL. Initially, it flows north toward the Paris Basin, but at OR-LÉANS it arcs toward the west, passing Blois, TOURS, and NANTES before flowing through a 56-km (35-mi) estuary to the Atlantic Ocean at Saint Nazaire on the Bay of BISCAY. Its tributaries include the Maine, Vienne, Cher, Allier, and Indre rivers, and its drainage area is 116,550 km² (45,000 mi²), more than a fifth of France.

The Loire has an irregular flow and is subject to sudden floods. Much of the river is lined by levees. Formerly, commercial navigation along the Loire and the canals that connect it with the Rhône and Seine river systems was very important. Today, however, the valley of the Loire is famous for its châteaus, especially those of Chambord, Chenonceaux, Amboise, Azay-le-Rideau, and Chinon.

■

Loisy, Alfred Firmin [lwah-zee'] Alfred Firmin Loisy, b. Feb. 28, 1857, d. June 1, 1940, was a French Roman Catholic modernist theologian and a biblical scholar. In 1881 he became professor of Hebrew at the Institute Catholique. Dismissed 12 years later and accused of heresy during a controversy over the inerrancy of the Bible, he began a long struggle with the church. Loisy became a leader of the MODERNISM movement, which applied the tools of scientific and historical criticism to the Bible. In 1903 five of his books were placed on the Index of Forbidden Books; later the body of his work was condemned by the Holy See.

■

Loki [loh'-kee] In Norse mythology Loki was the spirit of fire, strife, and envy. The son of a giant, he lived among the gods at ASGARD, where he continually caused them trouble but aided them with his cunning. After he contrived the death of BALDER, however, the gods chained him to a rock below a serpent whose mouth dripped venom. Loki was to remain bound until the final battle of RAGNAROK, in which he would lead the forces of evil against the gods.

■

Lollards [lahl-urdz] The Lollards, followers of the English religious reformer John WYCLIFFE, were members of a widespread Christian movement of the late 14th and early 15th centuries that was highly critical of the power and wealth of the church. The Lollards were led by Wycliffe's "poor priests," who used an English translation of the Bible and preached a nonsacramental Christianity that minimized clerical authority and emphasized poverty, ethical purity, and devotional intensity. The movement spread rapidly during the decade following Wycliffe's death (1384), enjoying the support of Oxford scholars, powerful nobles and country gentlemen, wealthy merchants, and masses of common people. Its preachers based their teachings on personal faith, divine election, and the Bible. They taught that the commonly held doctrines of transubstantiation (see EUCHARIST), INDULGENCES, and hierarchical church organization were unscriptural.

After the usurpation of the English throne by HENRY IV in 1399, the Lollards were subject to increasing persecution. HENRY V, determined to break the support of Lollardism by rural aristocrats, brought his friend, the popular Sir John Oldcastle (c.1378–1417), to trial and, finally, to the stake. Meanwhile, the Council of Constance (1414–18) officially condemned Wycliffe, and the Lollards were driven underground.

Lomax (family) [loh'-maks]

The field of American folksong study is founded in the work of **John Avery Lomax**, b. Goodman, Miss., Sept. 23, 1875, d. Jan. 26, 1948, and his son, **Alan Lomax**, b. Austin, Tex., Jan. 31, 1915. John was an English professor and banker who studied folklore as an avocation. In the early 1900s, equipped with an Ediphone cylinder recording machine, he traveled the back roads of the Southwest, collecting songs for his book, *Cowboy Songs and Other Frontier Ballads* (1910). In 1933, with his son, Alan, Lomax collected more songs, published as *American Ballads and Folk Songs* (1934). The materials were given to the newly formed Archive of American Folksong of the Library of Congress, and Lomax was made honorary curator—a post later filled by Alan, who continues to collect and record both in America and in Europe.

Lombardi, Vince [lahm-bard'-ee, vins]

Vincent Thomas Lombardi, b. Brooklyn, N.Y., June 11, 1913, d. Sept.

Vince Lombardi, himself an outstanding football player at Fordham University, compiled an enviable record of success as a coach of high school, collegiate, and professional football teams. During a nine-year span, Lombardi guided the Green Bay Packers to five NFL championships.

3, 1970, was head coach of the Green Bay Packers of the National Football League (NFL) from 1959 to 1967; he won 89 games, lost 29, and tied 4. His disciplined approach to football fundamentals became the standard training method used by contemporary coaches. The Packers, while coached by Lombardi, won five NFL titles (1961, 1962, 1965–67) and the first two Super Bowls (1967, 1968).

Lombardi played as a lineman on Fordham University's famed "Seven Blocks of Granite" team in the mid-1930s. He later served as an assistant coach at Fordham University and the United States Military Academy and as offensive coach for the professional New York Giants before joining the Packers in 1959. In 1968 he resigned as coach of the Packers but remained for another year as general manager. He also coached (1969) the Washington Redskins to their first winning season in 14 years. In 1971, Lombardi was inducted into the Pro Football Hall of Fame.

Lombards [lahm'-bardz]

The Lombards, a Germanic people, were first mentioned by classical writers in the 1st century AD. In the 4th century they moved southeastward from their home on the lower Elbe River. By the 6th century the Lombards had converted to Arian Christianity (see ARIANISM), and about 547 the emperor JUSTINIAN I gave them land in Pannonia and Noricum (modern Hungary and eastern Austria).

In 568 the Lombards, under King Alboin, invaded Italy, and by 572 they held the north as well as Spoleto and Benevento to the south. During the 7th and much of the 8th century the Lombards strengthened their hold on Italy and fought off the Franks, the Byzantines, and several coalitions raised against them by the popes. The kingdom reached its zenith under Liutprand (r. 712–44), who accepted Roman Christianity and made notable changes in the law and administration.

In 754–56, Pope Stephen II allied himself with the Frankish king PEPIN THE SHORT, who forced the Lombards to return a considerable amount of territory—the so-called Donation of Pepin—to the papacy. In 773–74 the Lombard king Desiderius (r. 756–74) was defeated by CHARLEMAGNE, and the kingship passed to the Frankish monarch.

Lombardy [lahm'-bar-dee]

Lombardy (Italian: Lombardia), an Italian region that borders on Switzerland in the north, is Italy's chief commercial and industrial region. With an area of 23,857 km^2 (9,211 mi^2) and 8,886,420 inhabitants (1988 est.), it is the country's most populous region. The capital is MILAN, and other major cities and provincial capitals are BERGAMO, BRESCIA, COMO, CREMONA, PAVIA, Mantua, Sondrio, and Varese. Lombardy's manufactures include iron and steel, automobiles, machinery, textiles, and furniture. The Alpine lakes COMO, GARDA, and MAGGIORE are well-known tourist attractions.

After the 3d century BC, Lombardy formed part of the

Roman Empire. From 568 to 774 it was the center of the kingdom of the Lombards, a Germanic people, and in the 8th century it was conquered by the Franks. Free city-states, first established in the 11th century, formed the Lombard League in 1167 and subsequently defeated Holy Roman Emperor FREDERICK I. Lombardy was ruled by Spain (1535–1700), Austria (1714–97), France (1797–1814), and again by Austria (1814–59).

Lombroso, Cesare   see CRIME

Lomé
[loh-may']   Lomé is the capital and primary city of Togo. Located on the Gulf of Guinea in western Africa, Lomé has a population of 366,476 (1983 est.). The city's excellent deepwater harbor is used for the export of raw cotton, cocoa, coffee, copra, palm nuts, and phosphates. The University of Benin (1965) is located there. As the capital of German Togoland (1897–1914), Lomé quickly became a prosperous colonial capital with an elaborate rail and road system. Lomé remained the capital while under Anglo-French rule (1914–22) and French rule (1922–60) and after Togo achieved independence in 1960.

Loménie de Brienne, Étienne Charles de
[loh-may-nee' duh bree-en', ay-tyen' sharl]   In the months immediately preceding the French Revolution the government of LOUIS XVI was headed by the French ecclesiastic Étienne Charles de Loménie de Brienne, b. Oct. 9, 1727, d. Feb. 19, 1794. In 1787 he led the opposition to finance minister Charles Alexandre de CALONNE's tax reforms, forcing him out of office and then replacing him. Loménie de Brienne's own efforts at fiscal reform caused such an uproar in the Paris PARLEMENT that the king was forced to convoke the STATES-GENERAL. That body quickly became radicalized, and its actions led to revolution. Loménie de Brienne was dismissed from office in 1788. He died in prison.

Lomonosov, Mikhail Vasilevich
[luh-muh-naw'-suhf]   The Russian scientist and man of letters Mikhail Vasilevich Lomonosov, b. Nov. 19 (N.S.), 1711, d. Apr. 15 (N.S.), 1765, made many discoveries in chemistry and physics and simplified the Russian of his time into a suitable vehicle for literary expression. He won a scholarship (1736–41) to the University of Marburg, where he began to write lyric poetry. After his return to Saint Petersburg, Lomonosov was appointed (1745) professor of chemistry at the university and in 1757 became a councillor of Moscow University, which he had helped found.

Lomonosov Ridge
Lomonosov Ridge is the major topographic feature of the Arctic Ocean basin. Extending for 1,800 km (1,100 mi) between the New Siberian Islands and Ellesmere Island, Canada, it separates the Arctic Ocean floor into the Canadian and the Eurasian basins. The ridge is about 3 km (2 mi) high. Its rather flat summit, lying at water depths of between 1,000 and 1,600 m (3,300 and 5,300 ft), appears to have been planed off by wave erosion during a period when sea level was much lower. The ridge displays neither seismic activity nor unusual magnetic anomalies, so it is not a mid-oceanic ridge. It appears instead to be a fragment that was formerly part of the Siberian continental shelf. The Lomonosov Ridge was discovered by Soviet scientists, who set up stations on drifting ice islands in the 1950s.

Lon Nol
[lahn nohl]   The Cambodian military and political leader Lon Nol, b. Nov. 13, 1913, d. Nov. 17, 1985, was ousted as president of the Khmer Republic (now Cambodia) by Communist forces in 1975. He served as a provincial governor and army district commander before becoming chief of general staff and minister of national defense, posts he held from 1955 to 1966. He became commander in chief (1960), deputy prime minister (1963), and then prime minister (1966–67, 1969–72). In 1970 pro-Western Cambodian officers led by Lon Nol overthrew Prince NORODOM SIHANOUK and proclaimed the Khmer Republic. In 1972, Lon Nol became president of the Khmer Republic and suspended the constitution. His attempts to eliminate Communist influence in Cambodia with the aid of the United States led to civil war. In May 1975 the Communist KHMER ROUGE defeated Lon Nol's forces and captured the capital city of Phnom Penh. Lon Nol went into exile in Hawaii.

London
(England)   London is the capital and largest city of the United Kingdom. The city (coterminous with the county of Greater London) covers 1,580 km^2 (610 mi^2) and has a population of 6,735,400 (1988 est.). It is located on the River Thames, 64 km (40 mi) from its estuary on the North Sea. London's size and population mirror the city's economic importance; it is one of the world's leading financial and insurance centers as well as an important industrial city.

Contemporary City

London is a multiracial city, with a large immigrant population from Britain's former colonies, especially from South Asia and the West Indies. Some quarters of the city are dominated by specific ethnic groups, for example, Paddington, Notting Hill, and Brixton.

Economy and Transportation. London is Great Britain's foremost manufacturing center, with light and consumer-goods industries predominating. Food processing is important, as are electronics, light metals, pharmaceuticals, and printing. Most heavy industry is located to the east, near the docks. London is also the country's main banking and financial center and one of the largest ports in the United Kingdom. Tourism, especially in the summer, is a major contributor to the economy.

London is linked with all parts of the country by roads and railroads. Transportation within the city is by means of a complex but efficient system of subways—the Un-

A famous London landmark is the clock tower of the Houses of Parliament, containing the bell known as Big Ben. This complex of buildings, properly known as Westminster Palace, dates from the mid-1800s.

derground—and by an even more complex system of surface transportation by bus. The principal airport is at Heathrow, west of the city center; it is supplemented by Gatwick and Stansted.

Government. Since 1965 the city of London has been coterminous with the county of Greater London, which is composed of the Corporation of the City of London (the historic core of the city); the 12 inner boroughs surrounding the City; and the 20 outer boroughs. Each borough elects its own government council. From 1963 to 1986, the elected Greater London Council (GLC) coordinated regional planning and services. With the abolition of the GLC, most of its functions went to centrally appointed boards.

Education and Culture. Because of London's long history as Britain's leading city, it abounds with major educational and cultural institutions. The University of London (see LONDON, UNIVERSITY OF) is the largest institution of higher education in the United Kingdom. The British Library houses one of the finest general collections in the world. Museums and galleries are of exceptional importance, notably the BRITISH MUSEUM, the TATE GALLERY, the National Gallery, and the Victoria and Albert Museum. Orchestras and other musical groups as well as ballet, opera, and theater companies perform in the city's many halls. The famed Wimbledon tennis championships are played in the city.

Historic Sites. One of London's oldest landmarks is the TOWER OF LONDON. The former royal residence located along the Thames was begun by William I (the Conquerer) about 1079 and later served as a prison. Tower Bridge, a distinctive Victorian structure, crosses the Thames beside the Tower. To the west lies the City, the heart of London and its financial district. The 17th-century SAINT PAUL'S CATHEDRAL is located there, as are the Bank of England, Mansion House (residence of the lord mayor), and many other landmarks. One of the bridges flanking the City is LONDON BRIDGE; the original wooden bridge (built 963–75) has been replaced many times, and it is now a six-lane concrete structure. West of the City, the Thames bends about 90° to the south, where the borough of Westminster is located on the west bank. The Houses of Parliament (see WESTMINSTER PALACE) are topped by the famous clock tower, Big Ben. WESTMINSTER ABBEY stands beside them. Many government buildings, including 10 Downing Street, the residence of the British prime minister, are nearby. Trafalgar Square contains the famous statue of Lord Nelson, commemorating his victory at the Battle of Trafalgar. The Mall, a long road cutting through Saint James's Park, ends at BUCKINGHAM PALACE, the residence of the royal family.

History

London was founded as the Roman town of Londinium in AD 43. The importance of London declined following the 5th century, during the period of Anglo-Saxon and Scandinavian invasions. Gradually, however, the city's strategic location along the Thames reasserted itself, and it became a prosperous trade center. In the early 11th century London became the seat of government of the last Anglo-Saxon kings, and in 1066, when the Normans invaded Britain, William the Conqueror granted London its charter and made the city his capital.

Throughout the Middle Ages London was the political center, largest city, and chief port of England. New palaces replaced the Tower as the royal residence—notably Westminster, SAINT JAMES'S, and Whitehall. The royal court was located in London much of the time, and the city became a great cultural center. London reached a new level of preeminence during the reign (1558–1603) of Queen ELIZABETH I. William Shakespeare's plays were first performed in the Globe Theatre, book publishing began, and London became the center of England's newly emerging foreign trade.

By the 17th century London was a crowded city of narrow and twisting streets. Outbreaks of the plague between 1625 and 1665 claimed more than 75,000 lives. Buildings were largely of wood, and a disastrous fire in 1666 consumed much of the city. The rebuilding of the city was distinguished by the work of the architect Sir Christopher WREN, who rebuilt Saint Paul's Cathedral and more than 50 city churches.

In the 18th century the city again began to grow, becoming the focus not only of politics but also of literary and artistic society. Building activity continued during the 19th century, especially in the inner boroughs, with industrial suburbs spreading to the northeast and east of

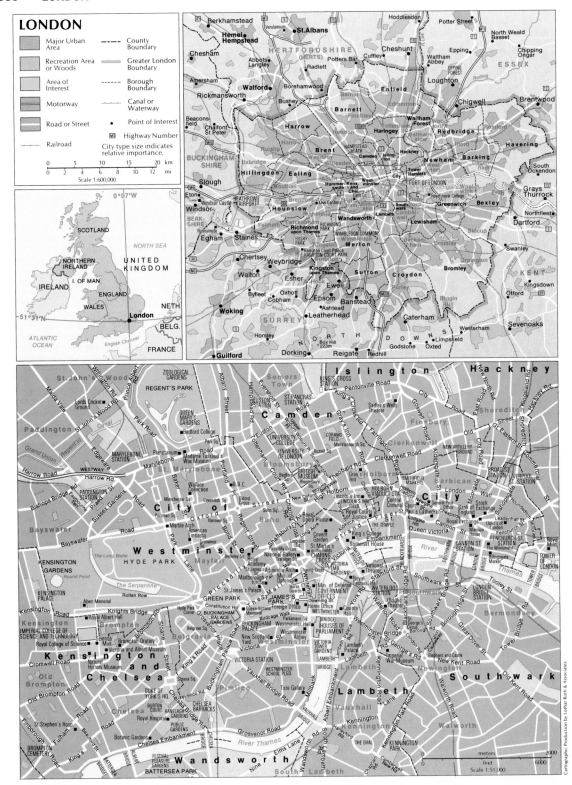

the city and the docks and dock-related industries spreading downriver. At the same time, straight, elegant streets were constructed through the congested inner city and open spaces such as Trafalgar Square were created. The 19th century was also a period of reform and establishment of municipal services: in 1829, Sir Robert PEEL established the Metropolitan Police Force, whose "bobbies" were named for him; in 1890 the world's first electric underground railroad was built.

During the 20th century the suburbs continued to grow until 1935, when a Green Belt law was instituted to control further growth beyond a ring of parks. During World War II, London suffered heavy bombing, resulting in about 30,000 casualties and the destruction of entire sections of the city. The greatest change of recent years has come from the subsequent rebuilding; the London skyline is today one of tower blocks rather than of spires and church towers.

London (Ontario) London, a Canadian city with a population of 269,140 (1986), is located in southeastern Ontario about 250 km (105 mi) southwest of Toronto. London is a rail and highway junction and an important distribution center for the surrounding agricultural valley. Its manufactures include beer and wine, flour, breakfast cereals, textiles, furniture, machinery, and transportation equipment. The University of Western Ontario (1878) is located there. The site was chosen in 1792 as the planned capital of Upper Canada, but it was not settled until 1826. Subsequently it served as a British military post.

London, Jack John Griffith London, b. San Francisco, Jan. 12, 1876, d. Nov. 22, 1916, was easily the most successful and best-known writer in America in the first decade of the 20th century. His vigorous tales of men and animals at odds with each other and with their environment—in Alaska, the South Seas, and elsewhere—made him an early Hemingway, a writer whose adventurous personal life seemed as exciting as his books.

An illegitimate child who later adopted his stepfather's name, London grew up in poverty and deprivation in the Oakland slums and poor farms nearby. While still in his teens he became an oyster pirate and gang leader in the Oakland docks, experiences behind such boys' adventure stories as *The Cruise of the Dazzler* (1902) and *Tales of the Fish Patrol* (1905). At 17 he ran away to sea on a sealing ship bound for the North Pacific; his brutal experiences on this voyage were the material for his best novel, *The Sea-Wolf* (1904). Afterward he became a hobo and spent 30 days in jail. His passionate concern for outcasts found expression in *The People of the Abyss* (1903), which pictured London slum life, and *The Road* (1907), the first of the vagrant novels in a tradition subsequently taken up by John Steinbeck and Jack Kerouac.

London worked his way through high school and the Oakland public library, taking jobs in canneries and laundries. His overwork to become a self-taught writer is recorded in his autobiographical novel, *Martin Eden*

Jack London, one of the most widely read American authors of the early 20th century, is best known for moving novels of conflict and adventure, such as The Call of the Wild *(1903) and* The Sea-Wolf *(1904).*

(1909); his hatred of the exploitation of factory labor, in his short story "The Apostate" (1906). London's year in the Klondike, where he participated in the Gold Rush of 1897–98, yielded no gold but did give him the raw material for his best short stories. Many were collected in *The Son of the Wolf* (1900), *The God of His Fathers* (1901), *Children of the Frost* (1902), *Love of Life* (1907), and *Smoke Bellew* (1912). His two short novels of dogs and wolves in the northland, *The Call of the Wild* (1903) and *White Fang* (1906), are classics.

London, treaties and conferences of London, the capital of Great Britain, has been the site of many international conferences and treaty negotiations.

At the London Conference of 1827–32 the major European powers determined the status and boundaries of the newly independent Greece. When the Belgians rebelled against Dutch rule in 1830, the conference also recognized Belgian independence. By the Treaty of London of 1839, the Netherlands confirmed that independence and the European powers guaranteed Belgian neutrality. The Germans, however, derided this treaty as a "scrap of paper" when they violated (1914) Belgian neutrality at the beginning of World War I.

The Treaty of London of 1852 recognized the disputed region of SCHLESWIG-HOLSTEIN as an autonomous province under the Danish crown, although this settlement proved short-lived. Another Treaty of London (1867) guaranteed the independence and neutrality of the Grand Duchy of Luxembourg.

During the BALKAN WARS delegates of the major powers met in London and produced (May 30, 1913) a preliminary peace treaty, under which Turkey agreed to surrender its Balkan territories and a state of Albania was to be created. This peace lasted less than a month, however. In World War I the Entente powers concluded (Apr. 26, 1915) the secret Treaty of London with Italy, which pledged to enter the war in exchange for territorial concessions. Although Italy fulfilled its obligation, it received only part of the territories promised when peace was concluded (1918–19).

Subsequent conferences held in London include the 1930 Naval Conference, at which Britain, France, Italy,

Japan, and the United States agreed to regulate submarine warfare and to limit ship construction until 1936. Britain, Japan, and the United States also accepted a treaty limiting the size of battleships. In 1933 a World Monetary and Economic Conference met in London but failed to reach agreement on methods needed to halt the worldwide depression.

London, University of   Established by royal charter in 1836, the University of London in London, England, is a federation of educational institutions, each with its own residence hall and library. These include University College (established 1826), King's College (1829), the London School of Economics and Political Science (1895), the Imperial College of Science and Technology (1907), the School of Oriental and African Studies (1916), the School of Slavonic and East European Studies (1915), the Courtauld Institute of Art (1932), and the Warburg Institute (1944). Also forming part of the university system are the London School of Hygiene and Tropical Medicine (1924) and 13 of the city's teaching hospitals. Located outside London are the Centre of International and Area Studies, a marine biological station in Scotland, and a nuclear reactor center in Berkshire. The Athlone Press (1949) is the university's publishing arm.

The university originally offered no instruction but granted degrees by examination to students of approved British universities. In 1868 it became the first university in the United Kingdom to admit women to its degree program. After 1900 the university was reorganized so as to incorporate as constituent schools private university-level colleges in London; thereafter it became a teaching as well as an examining body. Before 1949 all universities and colleges in England and Wales were part of the university's external degree system. As a result, their curricula strongly resembled London's. The university became the model for many Commonwealth universities.

Two types of students receive degrees from the university. The internal student, registered at one of the constituent colleges, receives university instruction. The external student takes courses on a part-time basis or at a private institution in the United Kingdom but is examined by the university in London or at centers elsewhere.

The University of London's executive and governing body in all academic affairs is the senate, consisting of the chancellor, vice-chancellor, chairman of convocation, principal, and representatives of faculties and heads of some schools. The senate appoints professors and readers.

London Bridge   At least three permanent structures known as London Bridge have spanned the Thames River. Old London Bridge (begun 1176) was designed by Peter

Old London Bridge was not just a means of crossing the Thames; for centuries it was a thriving business and residential area as well. Constructed on broad piers, the bridge so constricted the river's flow that at high tide the water rushed through with a loud noise.

of Colechurch, who had been in charge of the last of the timber bridges built (1163) over the Thames. Consisting of 19 pointed masonry arches varying in span from 4.6 to 10.4 m (15 to 34 ft) and founded on wide, protected piers, Old London Bridge was the first of its kind to be built over a swiftly flowing river with such a large tidal range (5 m/16 ft).

Although its wooden shops and houses were damaged by fire many times and were finally removed in 1763, Old London Bridge survived until 1831, when it was replaced by a five-arched, masonry structure designed by John Rennie. Upon being dismantled in 1967, the masonry facade of Rennie's bridge was sold to a private developer and reerected at Lake Havasu City, Ariz. The present London Bridge (completed 1972) is a six-lane, prestressed concrete structure.

London Company

The London Company, properly called the Virginia Company of London, was chartered by King James I of England in 1606 for the purpose of establishing a colony in North America between 34° and 41° north latitudes. It founded JAMESTOWN in Virginia in 1607.

The London Company was a joint-stock trading company, and its principal objective was to turn a profit for its investors. Plagued with difficulties, however, the company underwent a series of reorganizations. In 1609 the bounds of its jurisdiction were redefined, the company and its council were given authority to appoint a governor, and the colonists were offered stock in the company. The colony of Jamestown still did not prosper, however, and a new charter—designed to attract settlers and fresh capital—was issued in 1612. The company's governance of the colony was altered in 1619, when a "grand charter of liberty," creating an elected assembly, was issued. Factional quarrels among the leaders of the company, continued conflict with the Indians in Virginia, and the uncertain progress of Virginia's tobacco economy all worked to undermine the authority of the company. A commission of inquiry finally ruled that the management of both the company and the colony had been mishandled, and in 1624 the charter of the London Company was recalled. Virginia then became a royal colony. The PILGRIMS received their original settlement authorization from the London Company, but because they landed (1620) to the north of its jurisdiction, they were lost to it.

Londonderry

Londonderry, seat of the former County Londonderry in northwestern Northern Ireland, lies at the head of Lough Foyle on the Foyle River, about 150 km (95 mi) northwest of Belfast. It has a population of 95,100 (1982 est.). A shipbuilding and textile-manufacturing city, Londonderry also serves as the commercial center for local agricultural products. Magee University College (1865) is located there.

The town grew around a monastery founded by Saint Columba in 546. Following an unsuccessful Irish revolt against the English in the early 17th century, James I gave (1613) the town as a land grant to the City of Lon-

don; the original name, Derry, then became Londonderry. In 1689 the city withstood a 105-day siege by the army of JAMES II; the event is commemorated every year. Londonderry was a center of violence in the religious and political strife that plagued Northern Ireland from the late 1960s into the 1990s.

Remains of prehistoric settlements dating from at least 2000 BC are scattered over much of the hilly former county of Londonderry. Part of the ancient kingdom of ULSTER, Londonderry came under English control in 1609. It was a county from 1613 until the local government reorganization of 1974.

Long

Long (family)   The Long family of Louisiana has dominated the political life of that state for more than 50 years. The founder of the political dynasty was **Huey Pierce Long, Jr.**, b. Winnfield, La., Aug. 30, 1893, d. Sept. 10, 1935. After studying law at Tulane University and gaining admission to the bar (1915), Long became a member of the state's public service commission, making a reputation as a foe of corporate interests. A Democrat, he served as governor from 1928 to 1932. Long sponsored reforms that endeared him to the rural poor. He provided free textbooks for schoolchildren, built roads and bridges, and repealed the poll tax. Ruthless, cynical, and ambitious, Long ruled Louisiana in a dictatorial fashion and created a powerful political machine. In 1932 he left the governorship to serve in the U.S. Senate, where he gained a large following outside Louisiana by his advocacy of the "share-our-wealth" plan. By imposing high taxes on the rich, he promised to provide every family with a $5,000 homestead allowance and a guaranteed annual income of at least $2,000. By 1935 the Kingfish, as he was called, was a vitriolic critic of the New Deal, and he was considered a possible third-party candidate for the 1936 presidential election. On Sept. 8, 1935, however, he was shot by an assassin; he died two days later.

Earl Kemp Long, b. Winnfield, La., Aug. 26, 1895, d. Sept. 5, 1960, inherited his brother Huey's mantle. Elected lieutenant governor in 1936, Earl Long served

Huey Long, governor of Louisiana (1928–32) and a U.S. senator (1932–35), rose to prominence as a spokesman for the poor and established dictatorial control over the state of Louisiana. Long had begun to campaign for the presidency when he was assassinated in 1935.

briefly as governor in 1939–40 and was elected to four-year terms in 1948 and 1956. Although he padded the state payroll with political cronies, he also delivered free lunches to schoolchildren, provided pensions for the elderly, and equalized the pay of white and black school-teachers.

Huey's son, **Russell B. Long**, b. Shreveport, La., Nov. 3, 1918, was educated at Louisiana State University, receiving a law degree in 1942, and served in World War II. In 1948 he was elected as a Democrat to fill a two-year vacancy in the U.S. Senate. Reelected six times, he served until 1987. Russell Long was chairman of the Senate Finance Committee from 1966 to 1980. He was thus an influential figure in all legislation pertaining to taxation.

Long, Stephen H.   Longs Peak, in northern Colorado, one of the tallest of the Rocky Mountains, was first sighted (1820) and named by the American explorer Stephen Harriman Long, b. Hopkinton, N.H., Dec. 30, 1784, d. Sept. 4, 1864. Long became a U.S. Army engineer in 1814 and three years later was sent to explore the upper Mississippi and the portage of the Fox and Wisconsin rivers. In 1820 he headed a Rocky Mountains expedition and, like Zebulon Montgomery Pike before him, reported that the area that is now Colorado was uninhabitable. This view influenced U.S. expansion for almost four decades. Long examined the sources of the Minnesota River and the adjacent northern boundary of the United States in 1823.

Long Beach   Long Beach, a suburban port city located in southern California, is situated on San Pedro Bay about 30 km (19 mi) south of Los Angeles. The city has a population of 429,433 (1990). Long Beach is an oil production center; the oil, discovered in 1921, is pumped from both land-based and offshore wells. Other industries include canning and the manufacture of aircraft, electronic equipment, missiles, automobile parts, and chemicals. Tourism and conventions are also important. Connected to Los Angeles harbor by a channel, Long Beach is the site of a large naval station, a shipyard, and a dry dock. Points of interest include 14 km (9 mi) of beaches; the Long Beach Museum of Art; La Casa de Rancho Los Cerritos (1834), a preserved adobe ranch house; and the ocean liner *Queen Mary*, bought by the city in 1967 and docked there.

The site of Long Beach was originally an Indian trading camp and in 1784 became part of Rancho Nieto. The city was first called Willmore City for W. E. Willmore, who laid it out in 1881 and promoted it as a seaside resort. The name was changed to Long Beach in 1888.

Long Day's Journey into Night   The four-act drama *Long Day's Journey into Night* was written by American playwright Eugene O'NEILL in 1941 but not produced until 1956 (film, 1962), three years after his death. It is regarded as his greatest work. O'Neill had originally requested that no performance be given of this autobiographical work until 25 years after he died. It follows the course of 18 tortured hours in the life of Edmund Tyrone (O'Neill) as he and his family—a miserly actor father, a delicate mother who has returned to drug addiction, an alcoholic elder brother—vent their guilts and frustrations on one another.

Long Island   Long Island (1990 pop., 6,861,475), in southeastern New York, extends about 190 km (120 mi) east from the mouth of the Hudson River into the Atlantic Ocean; it is separated from the New York and Connecticut shores by Long Island Sound. The island's 3,615-km^2 (1,396-mi^2) area is divided into four counties: Kings (Brooklyn) and Queens (both boroughs of New York City), Nassau, and Suffolk. Of glacial origin, Long Island is dominated by two east-west ridges. At the eastern end these form two narrow peninsulas—Orient Point and Montauk Point—divided by Peconic Bay.

Long Island has experienced enormous urban and suburban growth since World War II. Agriculture (truck farming, potato growing, and duck raising) and fishing are still important in the east, and many tourists are attracted by its beaches.

Delaware Indians inhabited the island when the Dutch arrived in the 1630s. English settlement followed soon after, and the English took control in 1664. The 1776 Battle of Long Island took place in Brooklyn.

Long Island, Battle of   The Battle of Long Island, fought between the forces of George WASHINGTON and William HOWE on Aug. 27, 1776, opened the British campaign to seize New York City during the American Revolution. It was the first large-scale battle of the war. From American headquarters on Manhattan Island, Washington had sent about a third of his troops across the East River to Brooklyn Heights, where they constructed strong entrenchments. He erred, however, by sending forward 4,000 men and then failing to protect their left flank adequately. On August 22, Howe arrived from Staten Island with 20,000 men, whom he landed at Gravesend Bay, an inlet of lower New York Bay. In the early morning of August 27, Howe made a thrust against the American right. Simultaneously, he dispatched a column that passed undetected around the American left flank under Israel PUTNAM and attacked the Americans' rear position. The Americans lost more than 1,000 men; Howe lost 400. The American troops retreated and during the night of August 29–30 were ferried back to Manhattan.

Long Island Sound   Long Island Sound, a part of the Atlantic INTRACOASTAL WATERWAY, is a partially enclosed inlet of the Atlantic Ocean that separates Long Island, N.Y., from the Connecticut shore. The sound is 145 km (90 mi) long and 32 km (20 mi) across at its widest point. In the west it narrows to a tidal strait, the East River, which runs into the Upper New York Bay along the eastern side of Manhattan Island. BRIDGEPORT, NEW HAVEN, and NEW LONDON, located on the Connecticut shore, are Long Island Sound's main ports.

long jump see TRACK AND FIELD

Long March Sometimes called the most extraordinary march in human history, the Long March was the 10,000-km (6,000-mi) epic journey across China undertaken by the Chinese Communists in 1934–35. In October 1934 about 85,000 troops and another 15,000 auxiliary personnel of the Red Army escaped from a Nationalist cordon in Jiangsi province, in southeastern China. Beginning in January, the army, led by MAO ZEDONG, marched across mountains and rivers in a circuitous westerly route through the wilderness of southwest China, arriving in a remote area of Shaanxi province in October 1935. Thousands perished, but the Long March inspired many Chinese to join the Communist party, which established its headquarters in Yanan, Shaanxi province, in December 1936. From the survivors came the Chinese Communist leadership group—ZHOU ENLAI, ZHU DE, LIN BIAO, and Peng Dehuai—who, with Mao, shaped the first quarter century of the People's Republic of China.

longevity see LIFE SPAN

Longfellow, Henry Wadsworth Henry Wadsworth Longfellow, b. Portland, Maine, Feb. 27, 1807, d. Mar. 24, 1882, was the most popular American poet of the 19th century and had the widest range and greatest technical skill of all the poets of "the flowering of New England." Combining gentility with the common touch, he was equally successful in lyric and narrative poetry and during his later years became a master of the sonnet. Ballads like "The Wreck of the Hesperus" and "Paul Revere's Ride" were familiar to every schoolchild, and *Evangeline* (1847) became the first enduringly successful long poem written in the United States. His exploration of Indian lore in *The Song of Hiawatha* (1855) showed his skill with American subject matter.

Longfellow was educated at Bowdoin College, from which he graduated in 1825. He then pursued further studies in Europe and in 1829 became a professor at Bowdoin. From 1835 to 1854 he was Smith Professor of Modern Languages at Harvard. Longfellow's last visit to Europe (1868–69) was a triumphal tour, during which he received honorary degrees from both Oxford and Cambridge. In 1884, two years after his death, he became the first American to be honored with a bust in the Poets' Corner of Westminster Abbey.

For contemporaries Longfellow was a "new poet" sometimes reproached for lacking the didacticism modern readers now complain of in his work. A learned man, he valued simplicity and believed that the purpose of the imagination was not "to devise what has no existence, but rather to perceive what really exists, not creation but insight." A Christian humanist, he avoided the sentimental

Henry Wadsworth Longfellow was one of the most widely read poets of the 19th century. Longfellow's scholarly translations of European literature acquainted him with a variety of styles; his incorporation of these styles into his own work helped familiarize the American public with foreign verse forms.

nature pantheism popular in his time, and his essay "The Defence of Poetry," published in the *North American Review* (1832), anticipated much of what Ralph Waldo EMERSON would say five years later in his address "The American Scholar."

longhaired cats All longhaired cats are frequently, but incorrectly, called Persian or Angora cats because those are two of the oldest and best-known types. The Persian-type longhair is believed to have originated in Persia (Iran), but the evidence is inconclusive. A Persian-type longhair has a short, compact body, a short tail, and a large, rounded head with a short nose and small ears. Its coat tends to stand away from its body. Persian cats, officially called longhairs in Britain, are bred in a wide variety of coat colors and patterns. The Angora-type longhair is believed to have originated in Turkey and is presumably named for the superficial resemblance of its coat

The most popular of the longhaired breeds, the Persian cat has a massive head with large, widely spaced eyes. The Persian requires regular grooming to maintain its long coat.

to that of the Angora goat. The Angora is finer boned and longer bodied than the Persian, with longer legs and a longer tail. Its head is relatively smaller and more tapered, and it has larger ears. Its coat is usually white and not quite as long or as dense as that of the Persian, and it tends to lie closer to the body.

Another longhaired breed from Turkey is the Van cat or Turkish cat. Its white coat lacks an underfur and is not as dense as that of the Persian. Its head is wedge shaped, with large ears and a medium-length nose. A fourth Asiatic breed is the Birman cat of Burma. It is somewhat heavy bodied like the Persian but has a longer head and tail. Its coloring is unique. Like the Siamese, it has dark points—face, ears, legs, and tail—but its body is cream colored and its paws white.

A relatively old U.S. longhaired breed is the Maine coon cat, believed to be derived from random breedings (late 1800s) of Angora-type cats, particularly in Maine. It is large and Angora-like, with a variety of coat patterns. A new breed of longhair is the Balinese, which is essentially a longhaired Siamese. It differs from the Himalayan, which is a Persian-type cat.

Longhi, Pietro

Longhi, Pietro [lohng'-gee, pee-ay'-troh] Pietro Longhi, b. 1702, d. May 8, 1785, was the primary artis-

The 18th-century Venetian painter Pietro Longhi was a keen observer of his social milieu. His genre scenes, such as Viewing the Rhinoceros, *depicted boudoir and salon activities as well as worldly diversions. (Palazzo Ca' Rezzonico, Venice.)*

tic chronicler of the bourgeois character of 18th-century Venetian society through the genre known as the conversation piece. He studied with Antonio Balestra in Venice, and his early works were influenced by his study in Bologna with Giuseppe Maria Crespi. Although he began his career as a painter in the grand manner, Longhi did not devote himself to large-scale works; he chose the small cabinet format for his pleasant if somewhat bland depictions of polite society. *The Concert* (1741; Accademia, Venice), his first Venetian genre scene, displays the poetic intimacy he achieved through a combination of frankness and sympathy toward his subject. During the 1740s he executed a religious series, *The Seven Sacraments* (Pinacoteca Quirini Stampalia, Venice). After 1760 he depicted brothels, gambling houses, and other diversions.

longhorn cattle

longhorn cattle　see CATTLE AND CATTLE RAISING

Longinus

Longinus [lahn-jy'-nuhs]　Cassius Longinus, c.213–273, was a Greek Neoplatonist philosopher, a teacher of rhetoric in Athens, and a counselor to Zenobia, Queen of Palmyra. When his policies failed, Zenobia delivered him to the Romans, who executed him as a traitor. A work of literary criticism entitled *On the Sublime*, long attributed to Longinus, had actually been written by an unknown author two centuries earlier. It became popular in Europe in the French translation by Nicolas Boileau-Despreux (1674) and during the 18th century helped inspire the romantic movement in poetry and painting.

longitude

longitude [lawn'-jih-tood]　Longitude is a position on the Earth's surface indicating the distance east or west of Greenwich, England, the PRIME MERIDIAN. The distance—expressed in degrees, minutes, and seconds—is measured along a LATITUDE line. The imaginary half-circles connecting the points of the same longitude, from the North Pole to the South Pole, are called MERIDIANS. On the opposite side of the globe from Greenwich is the international date line, 180° West or East. At the equator, one degree of longitude equals 111.32 km (69.17 mi)—at the poles, it is zero.

Longmen

Longmen (Lung-men)　At Longmen, 16 km (10 mi) south of Luoyang, in Henan province, China, is a complex of Buddhist cave temples decorated with stone sculptures ranging in date from AD 494 to the mid-8th century. Sculptures in the Binyang cave (completed 523), which contains the finest examples dating from the Northern Wei period (386–535), are characterized by highly spiritualized, ethereal-looking figures robed in elegant cascading drapery.

A colossal group measuring more than 15 m (50 ft) high and located in the Fengxiang temple (built 672–75), is the most significant sculptural group of the 7th century. These figures, modeled in the sensuous forms and clinging draperies typical of the Tang period (618–907), reveal affinities with the Gupta style of India.

longshore drift See BEACH AND COAST; COASTAL PROTECTION

Longshoremen's Union See INTERNATIONAL LONGSHOREMEN'S UNION

■
longspur Longspurs are any of four species of small, seed-eating birds of the genus *Calcarius*, in the finch family, Fringillidae, named for their unusually long hind claw. Longspurs are migratory, ground-nesting birds, about 15 cm (6 in) long, inhabiting open country in North America. One species, the Lapland longspur, *C. lapponicus*, also occurs in Eurasia; it may be the most abundant nesting bird on the Arctic tundra. The longspur's upper body plumage is streaked in dead-grass colors, and in breeding season the males develop bold markings around the head. Females lay three to six eggs, which they incubate for 10 to 13 days. Both parents feed insects to the young.

■
Longstreet, James After the American Civil War, James Longstreet, b. Edgefield District, S.C., Jan. 8, 1821, d. Jan. 2, 1904, became embroiled in a lengthy controversy about his conduct as a Confederate general during the war. After graduating from West Point in 1842, Longstreet served in the U.S. Army until 1861, when he joined the Confederate Army. Commissioned a general, he led troops in most of the major battles in the Virginia theater—including the two Battles of BULL RUN and the Battle of FREDERICKSBURG—and at CHICKAMAUGA in Georgia before he was wounded (1864) in the WILDERNESS CAMPAIGN. When he recovered, Longstreet returned to duty and fought until the war ended in 1865. He was a solid, usually dependable subordinate, but he performed poorly in independent command in Virginia and Tennessee in 1863.

After the war, Longstreet became a Republican and was appointed to several federal posts by his friend President Ulysses S. Grant and by later Republican presidents.

James Longstreet, like many West Point graduates, elected to serve the Confederacy at the outbreak of the Civil War and became one of Robert E. Lee's most able subordinate generals despite his reputation as an overly cautious tactician.

This political connection hurt him in the eyes of ex-Confederates, as did his criticism of Robert E. Lee. Longstreet was blamed (unjustly it now seems) by Gen. Jubal A. Early and others for the Southern defeat at the Battle of GETTYSBURG.

■
Longueuil, Charles Le Moyne, Sieur de [lohn-gur'-yuh, sharl luh mwahn, sur duh] Charles Le Moyne, b. Aug. 2, 1626, d. February 1685, was a leading French colonist in Canada. Arriving in Canada in 1641, he worked with the Jesuits among the Huron Indians and became expert in Indian languages. He settled (1646) at Montreal, where he served both as an interpreter and as a soldier against the Iroquois Indians. As a reward he was made seigneur of Longueuil and of Châteauguay. Several of his children became famous, notably Sieur d'IBERVILLE, founder of Louisiana, and Sieur de BIENVILLE, founder of New Orleans.

■
loom A loom is a device for WEAVING, the interlacing of threads or yarns to form a fabric. The earliest looms were probably simple stick frames on which was wound a series of parallel lengthwise threads, the warp. The weaver used fingers or a needle to lace the filling threads, called the weft, over and under alternate warps. Only when a means was found to lift alternate warp threads mechanically did looms become capable of weaving significant quantities of cloth. A simple loom, such as the one illustrated here, has several such devices, called heddles— wooden slats with holes through which alternate warp threads are strung. When a heddle is lifted, its load of warp threads is lifted at the same time, and an open area, the shed, is created, through which the weft thread is passed. It is pressed tight, or beaten in, against the previous rows of weft by a batten, or reed. By using a number of heddles, the order of lifted warp threads can be varied, and different patterns created.

Early Looms. The earliest known loom was that used by the ancient Egyptians. It was a horizontal loom consisting of two beams (the warp, or back beam, and the breast, or front beam, of a modern hand loom) mounted on four posts that lifted the beams off ground level.

Early looms were often vertical. The warp hung down from an upper beam suspended from rope. When lengths of cloth were to be made longer than the length of the loom, the additional warp lengths were wound around a bottom beam, to be unwound as weaving progressed. Some vertical looms had no bottom beam; instead, groups of warp threads were tied onto stone weights. The vertical loom continued in use in Europe until late medieval times and is still used by carpet weavers in the Middle and Far East.

The Draw Loom. By the 1500s in Europe the heddle and shed operation was controlled by treadles, and intricate patterns could be produced by working several heddles in varied order or by operating two or more in unison. With the development of the draw loom, silk weaving, perfected long before in China, became a

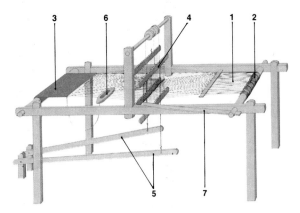

(Above) *Although the loom originated thousands of years ago, the basic method of interlacing warp and weft remains the same. Parallel threads, known collectively as the warp (1), are strung tautly between two rollers, originating with the warp beam (2) and terminating with the breast beam (3). As the warp traverses the loom it passes through the two or more frames known as heddles (4), which are activated by treadles (5) causing the warp to move alternately up and down. The shuttle (6), carrying the cross thread (weft), passes through the "shed," the open space between the warps. The newly laid weft is compressed against the previously laid weft with a toothed comb, called a reed or beater. When the lever (7) is depressed, more warp is fed out from the warp beam as fabric accumulates on the breast beam.*

(Below) *A craftsman demonstrates a treadle loom patterned after those used in early American household industry. The simple treadle loom may have been introduced in Europe as early as the 13th century and was widely used until the invention of automated looms during the 1800s.*

Western art as well. In the draw loom, certain warp threads in each heddle group were tied to overhead slip cords. Operated by a drawboy, who sat on top of the loom, the cords with their attached warp threads could be drawn up whenever the complexities of the pattern required it. The first automated loom, the Jacquard loom (1805; see JACQUARD, JOSEPH MARIE), used hooks instead of slip cords. The hooks were activated at each weft insertion by being pressed against a revolving chain of punched cards. Jacquard cards adapted for power looms are in use today.

The Flying Shuttle. In 1733, John KAY, an English broadcloth weaver, invented the flying shuttle. Broadcloth—so called because it was woven on a wide loom—required two weavers to operate the shuttle. Kay designed a driver mechanism that allowed the weaver, by pulling a cord, to send the shuttle mechanically across the width of the loom. Kay's son, Robert, later invented the drop box, in which several shuttles, each with a different weft, could be stored and retrieved automatically.

Power Looms. Mechanical devices to operate the heddles, the beating in, and the movement of the shuttle were invented in large numbers, and by the 19th century many of the looms that incorporated these devices were being powered by steam. Modern powered looms, although far more complex than even the late-19th-century versions, still carry out the same basic operations. The most significant advances have been (1) a device that senses when the weft on a bobbin is about to run out and replaces it with a full bobbin; and (2) the use of shuttleless looms, which carry the weft thread at enormous speed, either via a small steel projectile (a dummy shuttle), or via a flexible steel tape that reels out and in, or on a jet of air or water.

See also: INDUSTRIAL REVOLUTION; TEXTILE INDUSTRY.

loon Loons, also known as divers, belong to a single genus, *Gavia*, of the bird family Gaviidae, order Gavi-

The common loon, shown in summer (foreground) *and winter* (background) *plumage, is found in North America and Iceland.*

iformes. All four species are found in northern areas of the Northern Hemisphere and are migratory. Loons measure 61–102 cm (24–40 in) in length and have an elongated body and sharp, pointed bill. They are strong swimmers and propel themselves when diving by using their webbed feet. The legs are attached far back on the body, a characteristic that permits ease of movement when swimming but causes great difficulty when the loon walks on land. Loons are good fliers but become airborne only after an extensive run along the top of the water. Nests are placed on land near the water's edge, often on small islands. Usually two eggs are laid, and both sexes, which are similar in color, incubate the eggs and care for the young.

The common loon, *G. immer*, inhabits northern lakes of the New World and rivers throughout the world. The three other species are the yellow-billed loon, *G. adamsii*; the red-throated loon, *G. stellata*; and the arctic loon, *G. arctica*.

Loos, Adolf [lohs, ah'-dawlf]

The Austrian architect Adolf Loos, b. Dec. 10, 1870, d. Aug. 23, 1933, played a seminal role in the development of modern European architecture. Trained as an architect in Dresden, Loos spent several years in the United States, where he was impressed by the functional design of American industrial buildings. He returned to Vienna in 1896. The buildings he subsequently designed were primarily residences. Reacting against the excessive use of ART NOUVEAU, Loos condemned the use of ornament insofar as it had no useful purpose and was not an organic outgrowth of contemporary culture. The exteriors of his buildings, which were often built of the new, reinforced concrete, were spare and unadorned, but his interiors were sumptuous and visually delightful.

Loos, Anita [loos]

Actress, screenwriter, and playwright Anita Loos, b. Mount Shasta, Calif., Apr. 26, 1893, d. Aug. 18, 1981, won instant fame with her novel *Gentlemen Prefer Blondes* (1926). Its heroine, flapper Lorelei Lee, is remembered for her fractured grammar and hard-nosed romanticism. A play, two musicals, and two movies are based on the book. Loos' screenwriting career spanned the film industry's history from the earliest silents to sound hits of the 1930s and '40s. She wrote several successful plays, notably *Happy Birthday* (1946), three volumes of autobiography, and many humorous books, including the posthumous collection *Fate Keeps On Happening* (1984).

loosestrife

Loosestrifes are typically moisture-loving, sometimes slender plants of several different genera. They include 165 or more species classified in the genus *Lysimachia*, in the primrose family, Primulaceae. These are mostly leafy-stemmed perennial herbs of wide distribution in temperate regions. *L. vulgaris*, the common or garden loosestrife, is native to Eurasia but now grows wild in North America. It is a coarse, bushy plant, growing to 1 m (3 ft) or more in height, and bears leafy clusters of dark-margined yellow flowers.

Purple loosestrife, *Lythrum salicaria*, family Lythraceae, superficially resembles several species of *Lysimachia*. Native to Eurasia, it has become naturalized in North America. It is an erect perennial, growing to 1.8 m (6 ft) in height, with narrow leaves and spikes of red purple flowers. The water willow, *Decodon verticillatus*, of the same family, is sometimes called swamp loosestrife. The 75 species of aquatic or marsh plants of the genus *Ludwigia*, in the evening primrose family, Onagraceae, are called false loosestrifes.

Lop Nor [lahp nohr]

Lop Nor, an area of salt marshes and occasional lakes, is the lowest spot (elevation, 760 m/2,493 ft) in the Tarim Basin of southern Xinjiang Uygur Autonomous Region, China. It is surrounded by sparsely populated semidesert. The People's Republic of China tests its nuclear weapons at Lop Nor. The first Chinese-made atom bomb (a fission device) was tested there on Oct. 16, 1964; the first guided missile on Oct. 27, 1966; and the first thermonuclear (fusion) device on Dec. 28, 1966. In the early 20th century the area was visited by the explorers Sir Aurel Stein and Sven Hedin.

Lope de Vega   see VEGA, LOPE DE

López, Francisco Solano [loh'-pays, frahn-sees'-koh soh-lah'-noh]

Francisco Solano López, b. July 24, 1827, d. Mar. 1, 1870, the president of Paraguay from 1862 to 1870, pursued a disastrous course of military adventurism but is considered a national hero in Paraguay.

The son of President Carlos Antônio López, Francisco López became a brigadier general at the age of 19, then a special envoy to Europe (1853–54), minister of war (1855), and vice-president. After succeeding (1862) his father in office, he forged a despotism that enabled him to pursue his whims without opposition. He built the army into one of the largest in the Southern Hemisphere and tried to play a power broker in the Río de la Plata area. After Brazil sent (1864) its troops into Uruguay, López invaded southwestern Brazil. During the invasion Paraguay violated Argentina's border and was soon embroiled in war with that country as well as Brazil and Uruguay. During this War of the TRIPLE ALLIANCE (1865–70), much of Paraguay's male population was killed or died of disease, and its economy was ruined. López himself fell in battle.

Lopez, Nancy

Hall of Fame member Nancy Lopez, b. Torrance, Calif., Jan. 6, 1957, emerged in the late 1970s as the fastest rising woman professional golfer in history. After an outstanding collegiate and amateur record, Lopez joined the Ladies' Professional Golf Association (LPGA) tour in mid-1977. In 1978 she won nine tournaments, including a record five straight and the LPGA championship tournament, and her earnings totaled $189,813, then an LPGA record. In 1979 she won eight tournaments and $197,488. In 1978, 1979, and 1985, Lopez was named Player of the Year, in addition to winning the Vare Trophy, awarded annually to the player with the best average score per round. In 1985 and 1989 she won LPGA championships again, and in 1988, another Player of the Year award. By the early 1990s, Lopez had won more than $3 million and over 40 tournaments.

López Portillo y Pacheco, José [loh'-pays por-teel'-yoh ee pah-chay'-koh, hoh-say'] José López Portillo y Pacheco, b. June 16, 1920, was president of Mexico from 1976 to 1982. In foreign affairs he became one of the leading spokespersons of the Third World countries and was critical of U.S. policies. In the early years of his administration the Mexican economy benefited from the exploitation of the country's vast petroleum resources. When oil prices fell in the early 1980s, however, the boom ended, and the government was faced with a serious financial crisis. During his last year in office, López Portillo was forced to devalue the peso and nationalize Mexico's banks. He was succeeded by Miguel de la Madrid Hurtado.

Under President José López Portillo, Mexico gained new prestige as a leading petroleum producer. His moderately conservative policies appealed to both business interests and opposition parties.

loquat The loquat, *Eriobotrya japonica*, is a small evergreen tree of the rose family, Rosaceae, native to warm and temperate parts of China and Japan. It grows to 9 m (30 ft) tall and bears large, coarsely toothed, glossy green leaves with rusty, woolly undersides. The fragrant white flowers mature into clusters of yellow or orange pearlike fruits with a pleasant, slightly tart taste. Loquat fruits are juicy, with white or orange flesh surrounding smooth, brown seeds. The tree has been introduced into many parts of the tropics and warm-temperate areas.

LORAN see NAVIGATION

Lorca, Federico García see GARCÍA LORCA, FEDERICO

Lord of the Flies see GOLDING, WILLIAM

Lords, House of see PARLIAMENT

Lord's Prayer The Lord's Prayer, or Our Father, is the only formula of PRAYER attributed to JESUS CHRIST. It appears twice in the New Testament: in Matthew 6:9–13 and in a shorter version in Luke 11:2–4. In Matthew the prayer is composed of an invocation and seven petitions, the first three asking for God's glorification, the last four requesting divine help and guidance. A final doxology, "For thine is the kingdom...," is found in some ancient manuscripts. Protestants customarily include the doxology in their recitation of the prayer; Roman Catholics do not, although it is added in the new order of Mass. The prayer, known in Latin as the Paternoster, is the principal prayer and a unifying bond of Christians.

Lord's Supper see EUCHARIST

Loren, Sophia [luh-ren', suh-fee'-uh] Beautiful, sensuous, and stately, the Italian film star Sophia Loren, b. Sophia Scicolone, Sept. 20, 1934, first came to international attention in *Woman of the River* (1955). Quickly adopted by Hollywood for such films as *The Pride and the Passion* (1957), *Desire under the Elms* (1958), and *El Cid* (1961), Loren enjoyed greater critical success in the Italian comedies *Yesterday, Today and Tomorrow* (1963) and *Marriage Italian Style* (1964) and in the dramatic roles afforded by *The Key* (1958), *Two Women* (1961), for which she won an Academy Award, and *A Special Day* (1977). Since 1957 she has been married to producer Carlo Ponti.

The Italian film actress Sophia Loren appears here in a scene from Two Women *(1961), a film for which she received an Academy Award. Although her early films exploited her reputation as one of the world's most beautiful women, Sophia Loren is recognized as a talented performer.*

Lorentz, Hendrik Antoon [lohr'-ents, hen'-drik ahn'-tohn] The Dutch theoretical physicist Hendrik Antoon Lorentz, b. July 18, 1853, d. Feb. 4, 1928, made significant contributions to the theory of electromagnetic radiation, for which he received the 1902 Nobel Prize for physics jointly with Pieter ZEEMAN. His postulation that there are contractions in the lengths of objects at relativistic speeds is now known as the FITZGERALD-LORENTZ CONTRACTION.

Lorentz received his doctorate from the University of Leiden in 1875 and in 1877 accepted the newly created chair in theoretical physics at Leiden. Even before Joseph J. THOMSON proved the existence of electrons, Lorentz proposed that light waves were due to oscillations of an electric charge in the atom. From 1892 to 1904, Lorentz developed his electron theory, which mathematically distinguished the electromagnetic fields from matter. He attracted large numbers of physicists to Leiden with his Monday lectures on current problems in physics, and he served as president of the Solvay Congresses—a series of international science conferences sponsored by the Belgian industrial chemist Ernest Solvay—from the first in 1911 until 1927.

Lorenz, Konrad [lohr'-ents, kohn'-raht] Austrian ethologist Konrad Zacharias Lorenz, b. Nov. 7, 1903, d. Feb. 27, 1989, is often called the founder of ETHOLOGY, the comparative study of behavior in human beings and other animals. It was for his pioneering work in this field that Lorenz shared the 1973 Nobel Prize for physiology or medicine with animal behaviorists Karl von Frisch and Nikolaas Tinbergen.

Lorenz received his medical degree (1928) and his Ph.D. in zoology (1933) at the University of Vienna. In the early 1930s he and his colleague Oskar Heinroth studied and described the process of IMPRINTING that occurs at a very early age in some animals. He found, for example, that when goslings hatched in his presence and their mother's absence, they learned to follow him about and came to identify him as their mother in that way, even when they later saw their real mother. Lorenz found that some instinctive behavior patterns of this sort occur in all members of a species (see INSTINCT).

Lorenz later turned his attention to human behavior, particularly aggression. Although he found aggressive behavior patterns instinctive to some degree, he maintained that they were no longer necessary for survival and could

Konrad Lorenz, a founder of modern ethology, described imprinting in geese during the 1930s. He is known for comparative studies of behavior—especially instinct—in birds, fish, and other animals.

be altered to become socially useful behavior. His views, presented in *On Aggression* (1963; Eng. trans., 1966), aroused controversy but received wide attention.

Loricifera Loriciferans, microscopic invertebrate animals that live in marine sands and gravels, were first observed in 1974 but were not established as a separate phylum, Loricifera, until 1983. Both larval and adult loriciferans have a flexible mouth cone, surrounded by a mass of spines, that can be withdrawn into the body along with the head. The larvae also have swimming appendages, but the adults are apparently sedentary and may live as ectoparasites. The name Loricifera, which means "girdle wearer," refers to the series of cuticle platelets surrounding the midsections of the animals.

loris [lor'-is] A loris is one of three species of small, nocturnal, tree-dwelling primates of southern Asia characterized by extremely slow movements. The slender loris, *Loris tardigradus*, grows to about 26 cm (10 in) in length and weighs about 350 g (12 oz). The slow loris, *Nycticebus coucang*, grows to 38 cm (15 in) in length and weighs about 1.5 kg (3.5 lb). The lesser slow loris, *N. pygmaeus*, reaches only 20 cm (8 in) in length. Lorises feed on insects, lizards, birds and bird eggs, and fruit.

The slow loris is a primitive primate native to the jungles of Southeast Asia. It tightly grips tree branches as it slowly moves in search of food at night.

Lorrain, Claude [loh-ren', klohd] The French landscape painter Claude Gelée, b. Chamagne, Lorraine, 1600, d. Rome, 1682, is also known as Claude Lorrain, or simply as Claude. He moved to Rome as an adolescent and, but for a brief spell in Nancy, northeast France (1625–26), remained in Italy for the rest of his life. Not surprisingly, his work is more Italian than French in style.

Claude began his career as a fresco painter in Rome and Naples, but by the mid-1630s was producing small, finely detailed landscapes such as *View of Rome with the Trinità dei Monti* (1632; National Gallery, London). By the late 1630s he was the most celebrated landscape painter in Italy.

Claude may be said to have established the European tradition of LANDSCAPE PAINTING, but the true subject of his art was the beauty and variety of natural light. His intense interest in light led, in many of his early paintings, to the relegation of human figures and physical objects such as trees and classical ruins to a position of secondary importance. Typically, the light in his earlier work emanates from a point low in the sky, flooding through the composition and suffusing it with a radiant glow. In later classical and biblical landscapes, such as *The Marriage of Isaac and Rebekah* (1648; National Gallery, London) and the *Embarkation of Saint Ursula* (1644; National Gallery, London), light is more diffused and imparts an idyllic atmosphere to the pastoral scene. Human figures are rarely the focus of interest in Claude's landscapes, but *The Sermon on the Mount* (1656; Frick Collection, New York City) is an exception. Although Claude's works were executed in the studio, their details were based on the numerous sketches that he made in the countryside near Rome. Nearly 1,000 of these are preserved in collections—notably that of the British Museum.

Lorraine   see ALSACE-LORRAINE

Los Alamos National Scientific Laboratory
see ATOMIC BOMB

Los Angeles

Los Angeles [laws an'-juh-les]   Los Angeles, located on the Pacific coast of southern California, is the seat of Los Angeles County. With 3,485,398 (1990) inhabitants, Los Angeles is the second most populous city in the United States. Metropolitan Los Angeles County, with a population of 8,863,164, stretches eastward for about 160 km (100 mi) to the San Gabriel Mountains and includes LONG BEACH, PASADENA, SANTA MONICA, Beverly Hills, and about 100 other independent cities.

Numerous geologic faults cause periodic tremors. The climate of Los Angeles is Mediterranean, with long, dry summers and rain from occasional winter storms. In summer, cool sea air drawn in under hotter air creates a temperature inversion, trapping air pollutants and causing smog.

Contemporary City. The city is marked by shopping centers and industrial parks scattered among tract housing, with the whole tied together by freeways. Public transportation is poorly developed; the private automobile is almost the sole means of mobility. The original Los Angeles, "Downtown L.A.," is only one of many commercial centers.

The population is composed of many minorities set in a basic matrix of Anglo-Americans. African Americans are the primary occupants of the area from Watts and Huntington Park to Culver City. The Chicano group is growing rapidly as a result of heavy emigration from Mexico. The Japanese Americans have been integrated into the Anglo-American society and economy. Other groups include Koreans, Filipinos, Cubans, Chinese, and Vietnamese.

Modern Los Angeles industry falls largely into two groups: cinema-recording-advertising and aerospace-electronics-engineering-research. Manufactures include automobiles, farm machinery, chemicals, and textiles. Food processing, printing, and furniture making are also important. Petroleum, first discovered in 1892, is produced from several fields. The port of Los Angeles is one of the world's largest artificial harbors.

Included among the many institutions of higher education in the area are the CALIFORNIA INSTITUTE OF TECHNOLOGY (1891), the University of Southern California (1880), Occidental College (1887), and the University of California at Los Angeles (1919; see CALIFORNIA, UNIVERSITY OF). Among the numerous public parks are DISNEYLAND, Griffith Park, and Magic Mountain. The missions of San Gabriel (1771) and San Fernando (1797), El Pueblo de Los Angeles Historical Monument, and the Watts Towers are notable landmarks. The GETTY MUSEUM, the Los Angeles County Museum of Art, the Museum of Contem-

Part of the vast urban agglomeration of Los Angeles is surveyed in an aerial photograph. "Downtown L.A." (center) is the site of major banks, hotels, and high-rise office and shopping complexes, but the area is only one of several major commercial centers. To the north, the Santa Monica Hills and San Gabriel Mountains (background) extend in an east-west direction above the Los Angeles basin.

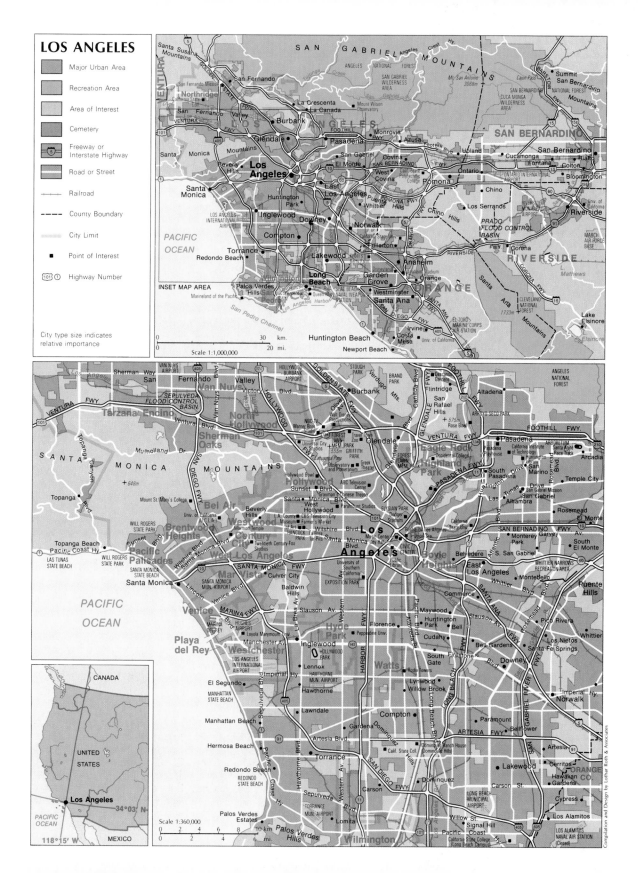

porary Art, and the Norton Simon Museum attract many visitors, as do the Hollywood Bowl and the Music Center for the Performing Arts.

History. The Spaniard Gaspar de PORTOLÁ camped near the site of Los Angeles in 1769. The settlement itself was founded in 1781 by Felipe de Neve, who named it El Pueblo de Nuestra Señora la Reina de los Angeles de Porciúncula (The Town of Our Lady, the Queen of the Angels of Porciúncula). U.S. forces won the city—then all of California—in 1847 during the Mexican War.

The arrival of two railroads—the Southern Pacific in 1876 and the Santa Fe in 1885—encouraged immigration. Los Angeles's rapid growth continued into the 20th century, and the city's population tripled between 1900 and 1910. During World War II defense industries underwent great expansion. The postwar years have brought Los Angeles face to face with the problems of older cities, epitomized by the Watts riots of 1965. Despite its success as host of the 1984 Summer Olympics, Los Angeles continued to be plagued by urban malaise, exacerbated by the recession of the late 1980s and early 1990s. Notwithstanding the 18-year tenure of black mayor Tom BRADLEY, the city exploded again in racial violence in 1992 following the acquittal of four white policemen charged in the videotaped beating-arrest of a black motorist, Rodney King. (See also RACE RIOTS.)

Los Millares [lohs meel-yar'-ays] Situated on a promontory above the Andarax River in southeast Spain, the prehistoric site at Los Millares consists of circular and rectangular huts inside an enclosure wall, four stone-built circular forts, and a cemetery of about 80 burials of passage-grave type (see MEGALITH), some set within beehive-shaped stone structures called *tholos* tombs. Rich in copper tools and painted pottery, Los Millares is regarded as the type site for the Chalcolithic (Copper Age) Millaran culture. Radiocarbon dating indicates that Los Millares was built before 3000 BC.

Losey, Joseph [loh'-zee] Although forced to abandon his career in the United States when blacklisted in the 1950s, Joseph Losey, b. La Crosse, Wis., Jan. 14, 1909, d. June 22, 1984, went on to become an important director in the British film industry. After extensive stage experience, Losey made his first feature film, *The Boy with Green Hair*, in 1948. This was followed by several taut melodramas—*The Lawless* (1950), *The Prowler* (1951), *M* (1951; a remake of Fritz Lang's classic), and *The Big Night* (1951)—that some still consider his best work. In 1952, during a period in which he was forced to work pseudonymously, he moved to London. There Losey gained international recognition with *The Servant* (1963), a film that marked the beginning of a fruitful collaboration with playwright Harold PINTER, (also *Accident*, 1967, and *The Go-Between,* 1971). The charged atmospherics of these films also characterized such later Losey efforts without Pinter as *The Romantic Englishwoman* (1975) and *Mr. Klein* (1977).

Lost Generation "You are all a lost generation," Gertrude Stein said to Ernest Hemingway. The epithet refers to a group of American writers who came of age during World War I and has been taken to mean that these authors were alienated from both traditional prewar values and their roots in the United States: many (John Dos Passos, Hart Crane, F. Scott Fitzgerald) lived in Europe. Hemingway used the phrase as the epigraph of his novel *The Sun Also Rises* (1926), whose characters have indeed lost their moral bearings. The words mean little, however, when applied to the work of the postwar generation: a body of writing of extraordinary originality and vitality.

lost-wax process The lost-wax process, also known as the investment casting process and by its French name *cire perdue*, is a precision casting method in which a pattern of wax or some other expendable material is used. The pattern is surrounded by a refractory slurry, commonly plaster; after the slurry mold has set, the wax is melted or vaporized out of the mold cavity. The metal is then poured into the space where the wax had been, and when the metal has cooled the slurry mold is removed. The method is a very old one and has been used for many years in casting bronze dental inlays, dentures, and jewelry. New techniques and materials have been devised to adapt the process to the casting of high-melting-point alloys such as those used in superchargers and gas turbines.

Lot [laht] In the Bible, Lot was the son of Abraham's brother Haran and lived in Sodom until it was destroyed by God (Gen. 19). He and his family escaped, but his wife turned into a pillar of salt when she looked back at the burning city. Through incestuous relations with his daughters, Lot was an ancestor of the Moabites and Ammonites.

Lothair, King of Lotharingia [loh-thair', lahth-uh-rin'-juh] Lothair, b. *c.*835, d. Aug. 8, 869, was the second son of Frankish Emperor Lothair I. When the latter abdicated in 855 he left his namesake the northern part of the Frankish Middle Kingdom, which came to be called LOTHARINGIA. Most of Lothair's energy seems to have been spent in the effort to divorce his childless wife, Teutberga, and marry his mistress, Waldrada, so that his son by the latter would be recognized as his heir. This ploy failed because of the opposition of Pope NICHOLAS I.

Lothair I, Frankish Emperor Lothair, b. 775, d. Sept. 29, 855, the eldest son of Emperor LOUIS I, came to rule the Middle Frankish Kingdom, which included most of what is now the Netherlands, Alsace-Lorraine, Switzerland, and northern Italy. Lothair was designated to succeed his father as emperor in 817. In 822 he became king of Italy, and the next year he was crowned coemperor by the pope.

When Louis I died in 840, civil war erupted between Lothair, his brother LOUIS THE GERMAN, and his half brother, Charles (later Emperor CHARLES II). Lothair was defeated at the Battle of Fontenoy (841), and in 843 he concluded the Treaty of Verdun (see VERDUN, TREATY OF), by which the Frankish empire was divided into three parts. Lothair received the Middle Kingdom and the imperial title. After dividing his kingdom among his three sons, Lothair entered the monastery of Prüm in 855.

Lothair II, King of Germany and Holy Roman Emperor

Lothair II (sometimes called Lothair III), b. 1075, d. Dec. 4, 1137, was German king (1125–37) and Holy Roman emperor (1133–37). The son of Gebhard, count of Supplinburg, Lothair was made duke of Saxony by Holy Roman Emperor HENRY V in 1106. When Henry died in 1125, the electors chose Lothair as his successor rather than Henry's nephew, which represented a victory of princely independence over heredity. Lothair encouraged the eastward expansion of Germany (see DRANG NACH OSTEN) and the spread of Christianity. Compliant toward the church and his advisor BERNARD OF CLAIRVAUX, Lothair supported Innocent II after the disputed papal election of 1130. On his deathbed, Lothair designated Henry as his successor, but the princes chose instead his former rival CONRAD III of HOHENSTAUFEN.

Lotharingia

[lahth-uh-rin'-juh] Lotharingia was a region in early medieval Europe that comprised much of the present-day Low Countries and ALSACE-LORRAINE. When the Frankish empire was divided by the Treaty of Verdun in 843, Emperor LOTHAIR I received the portion called the Middle Kingdom. Shortly before his death in 855, however, he divided his kingdom, giving to his son Lothair (see LOTHAIR, KING OF LOTHARINGIA) the northern segment, which came to be known as Lotharingia.

After the younger Lothair's death (869) without an heir, his uncles the future Emperor CHARLES II and LOUIS THE GERMAN divided Lotharingia between them by the Treaty of Mersen (870). The western parts in general went to Charles and the West Frankish Kingdom, and the more easterly areas were taken by Louis and his East Frankish Kingdom. The East Frankish king Louis the Younger won control of all Lotharingia in 879-80, but during the next half-century Lotharingia passed from East Frankish domination to West Frankish domination and then back to the East in 925. Finally, Archbishop Bruno of Cologne, brother of Holy Roman Emperor Otto I, divided (959) Lotharingia into two duchies: Upper and Lower Lorraine. The latter broke up, but Upper Lorraine, soon known simply as Lorraine, continued as a duchy until 1776.

Lothian

[loh'-thee-un] Lothian is an administrative region in southern Scotland. Bordered by the rivers Tweed and Forth, the region has an area of 1,753 km^2 (677 mi^2) and a population of 741,200 (1988 est.). A highly developed region, Lothian is a major agricultural and industrial center. The principal cities are EDINBURGH, Haddington, and Linlithgow.

Lothian was a part of the English shire of Northumberland before coming under the influence of the Scots in the 11th century. In 1333 the region was taken by Edward III of England, but it was eventually returned to the Scots. In 1975, during the reorganization of local government in Scotland, Lothian was created from parts of the former counties of East and West Lothian and Midlothian.

lottery

A lottery is a popular form of GAMBLING in which the players pay to participate, and the winners are determined by chance. In most lotteries, players buy numbered tickets at fixed prices. At a subsequent drawing, the winning numbers are picked at random (by lot) or are selected on some other unpredictable basis.

Governments have frequently used lotteries as a source of revenue or as a supplement to, or substitute for, taxation. The earliest state lotteries were organized in France in 1520. In 1680, England held a historic lottery to raise funds for improving London's water supply equipment. Spain developed the *gordo*, and Ireland, the sweepstakes. Lotteries were popular in the United States, although dishonest practices in both private and public lotteries eventually forced the federal government to prohibit (1890) the transportation of lottery tickets by mail or in interstate commerce. The states also took prohibitive action, and between the 1890s and 1963, no government-sponsored lotteries were held in the United States.

In 1963, however, New Hampshire authorized a sweepstakes lottery and designated a proportion of the moneys made to be spent on education. The lottery proved so profitable that, by the end of the 1980s, more than half the states (and the District of Columbia) had approved lotteries—among them, California, Massachusetts, New Jersey, New York, and Pennsylvania. The practice of the states is to reserve a certain percentage of the lottery take for expenses, a large percentage for the state itself, and a lesser percentage for prizes.

Lotto, Lorenzo

[loht'-toh, loh-rent'-soh] Lorenzo Lotto, b. c.1480, d. 1556, was one of the first great Venetian artists of the High Renaissance. His austere and elegant religious pictures, such as the *Madonna and Child with Saints* (c.1520s; Kunsthistorisches Museum, Vienna), are founded on a strong base of 15th-century religiosity. His use of strong, clear lighting is patterned after that in Giovanni Bellini's work, and he always used a perspectival grid overlaid with ornamental detail.

Lotto produced highly original works, such as his *Portrait of Andrea Odoni* (1527; Royal Collections, Hampton Court Palace), which could be mistaken for a much later Mannerist painting. He painted his last masterpiece, *The Presentation of Christ in the Temple* (after 1552; Palazzo Apostolico, Loreto), after becoming an oblate at the Sanctuary of the Holy House in Loreto. Lotto's long sequence of portraits done in the ¾-length Venetian mode are among the most riveting images of the 16th century.

The lotus Nymphaea lotus *bears many-seeded, berrylike fruit and leathery, floating leaves that may reach 50 cm (20 in) across. The cup-shaped flowers of the lotus were often represented in ancient Egyptian art and architecture.*

lotus [loh'-tuhs]   Lotuses are five species of water lilies, three in the genus *Nymphaea* and two in *Nelumbo*; both genera are members of the water-lily family, Nymphaeaceae. *Lotus* is also the name of a genus in the pea family, Leguminosae, which contains such plants as the bird's-foot trefoil, *L. corniculatus.*

Nymphaea lotus, the Egyptian white lotus, is believed to be the original sacred lotus of ancient Egypt. It and the Egyptian blue lotus, *N. caerulea*, were often pictured in ancient Egyptian art. The white lotus is a shallow-water, night-blooming plant with a creeping rootstock (rhizome) that sends up long-stalked, nearly circular, dark green leathery leaves, which float on the surface. The flowers, up to 25 cm (10 in) across, remain open until midday. The blue lotus is a smaller, less showy, day-blooming plant. The Indian blue lotus, *N. stellata*, differs from the blue Egyptian species largely in its leaves.

Nelumbo contains but two species. The American lotus, *N. lutea*, is found in the eastern half of the United States into southern Canada. It has a thick, spreading rootstock and large, circular, bluish green leaves that are usually raised above the surface of the water. The pale-yellow flowers usually open on three successive days. The East Indian lotus, *N. nucifera*, of southern Asia, has been a sacred symbol in many cultures.

Lotus-Eaters   In Greek mythology the Lotus-Eaters (or Lotophagi) were a North African people who subsisted on the fruit of the lotus tree, which made them forget the past and live in blissful indolence. In the *Odyssey*, some of ODYSSEUS's crew tasted the lotus fruit, forgot their homes and families, and had to be forcibly carried back to the ships by their companions.

Lotze, Rudolf Hermann [loht'-seh]   Rudolf Hermann Lotze, b. May 21, 1817, d. July 1, 1881, was a German philosopher who attempted to reconcile the concepts of mechanistic science with the principles of romantic idealism. Lotze combined a firm belief in the universality of scientific law with a conviction of the need for metaphysics. He insisted that philosophy be rooted in the natural sciences, because human beings are subject to the same natural laws as are inanimate objects. He protested against attempts to deduce reality from mere principles; knowledge, he held, is the result of observation and experimentation, not of logical dialectic. The task of metaphysics is therefore to analyze and systematize concepts that the sciences produce.

According to Lotze, nature is governed by mechanical law, but the system of nature is a set of means to a divinely appointed end. He considered all things as immanent in God; what the scientist sees as mechanical causality is simply the expression of the divine activity.

loudspeaker   A loudspeaker, or speaker, is one of several devices that convert electrical energy into mechanical energy. Such devices are called electromechanical TRANSDUCERS. In a loudspeaker the mechanical energy is in the form of vibrations that are transmitted to the surrounding air, producing sound (see SOUND AND ACOUSTICS).

Types of Speakers. Theoretically, a number of operating principles can be used for a loudspeaker. In practice, however, one particular type is most popular because of its efficiency and wide-range response; it is known as an electrodynamic, dynamic, magnetic, or magnetodynamic loudspeaker. Less popular, but also in use, is the electrostatic loudspeaker.

Operation. In the electrodynamic loudspeaker an electromagnet or permanent magnet produces a magnetic field. A voice coil situated within or surrounding the magnetic field is energized by the electrical signal. Hence a variable magnetic field is generated in the coil, and the coil is alternately attracted to and repelled from the magnet. The coil is linked to a diaphragm, which vibrates and causes the surrounding air to vibrate, re-creating the original sound. In the electrostatic loudspeaker the diaphragm is a conducting plate. Surrounding it are two

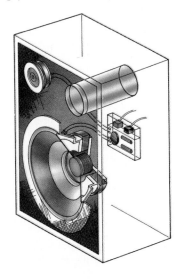

A bass reflex speaker, with its large woofer and small tweeter, also contains a port, or vent—the cylinder directly above the woofer—which enhances bass tones. The box on the cabinet's rear contains terminals for the wires connecting speaker and amplifier and the electronics for the crossover network.

fixed grids. When the signal voltage is applied to the grids, the electrostatic force produced causes the diaphragm to vibrate.

Most speaker transducers, known as drivers, require a surrounding structure called an enclosure to efficiently transfer sound energy to the surrounding air. A large driver, or woofer, with a diaphragm up to 76 cm (30 in) in diameter, and large enclosure are required for efficient low-frequency reproduction; at high frequencies a small driver, the tweeter (as small as 2.5 cm/1 in) is more efficient. Many speaker systems also have a midrange speaker, intermediate in size, that operates most efficiently at the middle frequencies. An electrical network called a crossover divides the audio spectrum into frequency bands suitable for each driver, which is then driven in the appropriate frequency band.

Types of Speaker Systems. In theaters, stadiums, and similar locations, driver/radiator combinations are often large, free-standing components. In high-fidelity systems for the home, however, all elements of the speaker system are usually contained in one multipurpose radiator called an enclosure.

Narrow-band speakers have been developed specifically to reproduce the narrow frequency band of speech; such speakers are used in public-address systems. The other extreme is the single speaker designed to cover the widest possible frequency band, as in small radios, televisions, and headphones.

Two sound channels are used to create stereophonic sound, a technique where sound is recorded simultaneously on right and left bands to fabricate the illusion of hearing the sounds live. To reproduce stereo sound, two speakers are needed.

Louganis, Greg Diver Gregory Louganis, b. San Diego, Calif., Jan. 29, 1960, was only 16 when he won a silver medal in the platform dive at the 1976 Olympics. Since then his accomplishments in both platform and springboard competition are unapproached: 4 of 4 Olympic gold medals (1984, 1988), 6 of 6 Pan American Games gold medals (1979, 1983, 1987), 5 of 6 world championships (1978, 1982, 1986), and 47 U.S. titles. Louganis was awarded the 1984 Sullivan Award as the finest U.S. amateur athlete.

Louis, Joe Joe Louis Barrow, b. Lafayette, Ala., May 13, 1914, d. Apr. 12, 1981, who fought as Joe Louis—nicknamed "the Brown Bomber"—was the longest-reigning world heavyweight boxing champion in history. Louis fought his first amateur bout in 1932, and two years later he won the Amateur Athletic Union (AAU) light-heavyweight title. He turned professional in 1934 and won the heavyweight title on June 22, 1937, by knocking out James J. Braddock in 8 rounds. On Mar. 1, 1949, he retired as champion after holding the title 11 years 8 months and defending it 25 times, a record for any division. He returned to the ring in financial straits in 1950 and lost a 15-round decision to Ezzard Charles in another

Joe Louis, a former national amateur champion, won the world heavyweight boxing championship in 1937 and defended his title 25 times before retiring in 1949.

title bout. After being knocked out in the 8th round the following year by Rocky Marciano, Louis retired permanently. He was a dexterous two-fisted fighter and is regarded by some as the greatest heavyweight ever. His only loss prior to his first retirement was in 1936 to Max Schmeling of Germany in a nontitle fight. In 1938, after he had become champion, Louis avenged the loss and knocked out Schmeling in the first round in one of the most famous fights in history; many sport fans saw the fight as a symbolic showdown between American democracy and German dictatorship. Louis defeated such fighters as Primo Carnera, Billy Conn, Lou Nova, Jack Sharkey, and Jersey Joe Walcott. During his professional career he recorded 68 victories (54 by knockout) and lost only 3 fights.

Louis, Morris Morris Louis, originally named Morris Bernstein, b. Baltimore, Md., Nov. 28, 1912, d. Sept. 7, 1962, was an abstract color-field painter and one of the leading members of the Washington Color School. The trademark of Louis's mature color-field style was his technique of pouring thinned, acrylic paint onto unprimed canvas to create soft, glowing effects, an idea inspired in 1953 by Helen FRANKENTHALER's work. His 1954 paintings, called "veils," consisted of layers of transparent paint. These were followed by "florals," composed of bursts of color that radiate from the center of the painting. His later, "unfurled," works exhibit large central areas of raw canvas, with stripes of color flowing diagonally across the lower corners. Louis's last paintings, called "stripes," were more formal, exhibiting only parallel lines of bright color.

Louis the German, East Frankish King One of the sons of Frankish emperor LOUIS I, Louis the German, b. *c*.804, d. Aug. 28, 876, was involved in the civil wars of his father's reign, which culminated in the Treaty of Verdun (843; see VERDUN, TREATY OF). This agreement divided the Carolingian state into three parts: Louis received the lands of the German-speaking peoples; his half brother, Charles the Bald (later Frankish Emperor CHARLES

II), the French-speaking areas; and his brother Emperor LOTHAIR I, a middle kingdom comprising Italy and the area later called LOTHARINGIA.

Much of Louis's reign was devoted to gaining control of the lands assigned to his brothers. In 860 he was promised Alsace, and in 870 he and Charles partitioned the remainder of Lotharingia by the Treaty of Mersen. Louis worked in vain to acquire the imperial crown and Italy for his son Carloman.

Louis Napoléon   see NAPOLEON III, EMPEROR OF THE FRENCH

Louis Philippe, King of France   Louis Philippe, b. Oct. 6, 1773, d. Aug. 26, 1850, was the last king of France. A member of the ORLÉANS family, the younger branch of the ruling Bourbon house, he fought in the republican army in early battles of the French Revolutionary Wars. In 1793, suspected of involvement in a conspiracy to restore the monarchy, he fled the country. While in Sicily for a time, Louis Philippe married (1809) Marie Amélie, daughter of Ferdinand IV of Naples and a descendant of LOUIS XIV of France.

In 1814, Louis Philippe returned to France. His political sympathies were with the liberal opposition to the restored Bourbon regime, but he was not significantly involved in politics. In 1830, however, when the July Revolution drove CHARLES X from Paris, Orléanist supporters elevated Louis Philippe to the throne.

As king, Louis Philippe observed the forms of parliamentary government but at the same time achieved a high degree of personal rule. He resisted all attempts to make the government more representative and responsive, and his rule became increasingly ill adapted to the needs and expectations of the country. On Feb. 23, 1848, a minor demonstration turned into insurrection, and Louis Philippe found himself without support. On

The reign of Louis Philippe, the "citizen king" of France, marked the triumph of the wealthy bourgeoisie over the aristocracy. Assuming power after the July Revolution (1830), Louis sought friendship with Britain and supported colonial expansion; France conquered Algeria during his reign. (Portrait by F. X. Winterhalter, Versailles.)

February 24, the Orléanist monarchy ended with his abdication and the proclamation of the Second Republic. Louis Philippe fled to England, where he died.

Louis I, King of Bavaria   Louis, or Ludwig, I, b. Aug. 25, 1786, d. Feb. 29, 1868, ruled Bavaria from 1825 until 1848, when he was forced to abdicate. A patron of the arts, he made Munich, his capital, one of the world's major art centers. Succeeding his father, MAXIMILIAN I, Louis initially pursued moderate, liberal policies. He aided the Greek revolt against the Ottoman Empire; his second son became king of Greece as OTTO I in 1832. Louis rapidly turned reactionary, however, and his unpopularity was increased by his affair with Lola MONTEZ. The REVOLUTIONS OF 1848 displaced him in favor of his son Maximilian II.

Louis II, King of Bavaria   Louis, or Ludwig, II of Bavaria, b. Aug. 25, 1845, d. June 13, 1886, called "Mad Ludwig," is remembered for his patronage of the composer Richard WAGNER, for his lavish buildings, and for his eccentricities.

Succeeding his father, Maximilian II, as king in 1864, Louis supported Austria in the SEVEN WEEKS' WAR (1866) but allied with Prussia in the FRANCO-PRUSSIAN WAR (1870–71) and joined the new German Empire in 1871. Soon disillusioned with the Prussian-dominated empire, he abandoned politics and involved himself totally in his cultural pursuits and his homosexual love life.

In 1864, Louis had invited Wagner to Munich, giving him a pension to complete his opera cycle *The Ring of the Nibelungs.* Although public hostility soon forced Louis to renounce his friendship with the composer, he continued his financial support of Wagner. Increasingly cut off from reality, the king developed a mania for building elaborate castles and palaces, where he created a fantasy world. Pronounced insane in 1886, he drowned himself a few days later. Louis's three country palaces are among Bavaria's most popular and profitable tourist attractions. Schloss Neuschwanstein (begun 1869), a many-turreted mock castle perched on a crag near Füssen in the Bavarian Alps, was built as a shrine to three of Wagner's operas: *Lohengrin, Parsifal,* and *Tannhäuser.* Schloss Linderhof (1870–79), Louis's only completed project, was his favorite residence. The diminutive palace is a white rococo confection set in a rugged alpine valley near Neuschwanstein. Schloss Herrenchiemsee (begun 1878), on an island in the Chiemsee, was intended as a full-scale facsimile of Versailles (see VERSAILLES, PALACE OF), but only the great central block was completed before Louis's death in 1886.

Louis I, King of France   see LOUIS I, FRANKISH EMPEROR (Louis the Pious)

Louis VI, King of France (Louis the Fat)   Louis VI, b. 1081, d. Aug. 1, 1137, succeeded his father, PHILIP I, as king of France in 1108. As early as 1100, however, he had begun to take over the military leadership of the monarchy. During this period the French princes were virtually independent, and the king had effective power only in the royal domain consisting of the Île-de-France, but even this region was infested with unruly barons. With strong support from the clergy, Louis VI forced these barons to accept his discipline, won the respect of the princes, and laid the foundations for the future growth in monarchical power. Louis had good relations with the popes, one of whom was his wife's uncle. He held his own against such dangerous and powerful neighbors as the duke of Normandy, who was HENRY I of England, and the count of Blois. He also repelled a German invasion in 1124, although he was less successful when he tried to intervene in Flanders in 1127. One of his advisors was SUGER, abbot of Saint-Denis, who later became his biographer. Shortly before Louis's death in 1137, ELEANOR OF AQUITAINE became his ward and married his son and successor, Louis VII.

Louis IX (Saint Louis), a Capetian king of France, appears at prayer in this medieval miniature. He led the Seventh Crusade to the Holy Land in 1248 and died during a later crusade. Louis was canonized in 1297 by Pope Boniface VIII. (Bibliothèque Nationale, Paris.)

Louis VII, King of France (Louis the Young)   Louis VII, b. 1121, d. Sept. 18, 1180, the second son of Louis VI of France, became heir to the throne on the death (1131) of his elder brother. He succeeded his father in 1137, a few days after marrying ELEANOR OF AQUITAINE. Louis inherited not only a prosperous, well-pacified royal domain, but also two experienced counselors, Raoul of Vermandois and SUGER. Louis's participation in the Second CRUSADE (1147–49), which turned out to be a military disaster, enhanced the visibility and prestige of the French crown. In 1152 the royal marriage was annulled, and Eleanor promptly married Henry, count of Anjou and duke of Normandy, who became HENRY II of England in 1154.

With Suger and Raoul both dead by the end of 1152, Louis had to reconstruct his government around new advisors. He established close ties with the counts of Flanders and Champagne, collaborated with the church, and encouraged the growing towns. To check Henry II and the Holy Roman emperor FREDERICK I, he reestablished strong royal influence in Burgundy and Languedoc. He also supported the intrigues of Henry's rebellious sons. In 1165, Louis's third wife, Adèle of Champagne, gave birth to a long-desired male heir, who was to succeed to the throne as PHILIP II.

Louis VIII, King of France   Louis VIII, b. Sept. 5, 1187, d. Nov. 8, 1226, was the son of PHILIP II of France and Isabella of Hainaut. He married (1200) Blanche of Castile, niece of King JOHN of England. In 1214, Louis blocked John's Poitou campaign, and in 1216 he invaded England, supporting the rebellious barons and laying claim to the throne. After a defeat at Lincoln he was persuaded to leave in 1217. Louis succeeded to the French throne in 1223 and conquered Poitou from the English in 1224. Throughout his career he was also heavily involved in the crusade against the ALBIGENSES. He made expeditions to southern France in 1215 and 1219 and returned as king in 1226 to pacify the region.

Louis IX, King of France (Saint Louis)   Louis IX of France, later known as Saint Louis, b. Apr. 25, 1214, d. Aug. 25, 1270, most closely approached the medieval ideal of chivalric kingship. The oldest son of the future king LOUIS VIII and Blanche of Castile, he came to the throne as a child in 1226. The queen mother, Blanche, successfully overcame several princely uprisings and in 1229 concluded a treaty with the count of Toulouse that gave the crown a foothold on the Mediterranean and terminated the crusade against the ALBIGENSES. Louis himself removed the last threat to royal authority in Poitou by defeating the English at Taillebourg in 1242.

A man of great piety and a strong pacifist in dealing with fellow Christians, Louis was bitterly intolerant of heretics and non-Christians. In 1245, while recovering from a serious illness, he resolved to lead a CRUSADE to the Middle East. He departed for the Levant in 1248, leaving Blanche as regent. He was accompanied on the crusade by Jean, sire de Joinville, whose biography of Louis remains an important historical source. The Crusaders captured the Egyptian port of Damietta, but later Louis was defeated and captured at Mansura in 1250. After his release he remained in the Middle East for several years before returning to France in 1254.

In his later years, Louis promoted internal reforms and concluded treaties with Aragon (1258) and England (1259). Before the end of the century, however, France fought wars with both these countries, and Louis was subsequently criticized for being too conciliatory. In 1270 he undertook a crusade against Tunis, during which he died. Admired for his prowess, his piety, and his strong sense of justice, Louis was revered as a saint well before his canonization by the church in 1297. Feast day: Aug. 25.

Louis XI, King of France   Louis XI, b. July 3, 1423, d. Aug. 30, 1483, was a highly successful French monarch whose enemies dubbed him the Spider. Louis did not get along with his father, CHARLES VII, and at the age of 17 he joined an unsuccessful princely revolt called the Praguerie. In 1447 he retired to the Dauphiné, the province that he held as heir to the throne (see DAUPHIN). He ruled efficiently there until Charles drove him into exile in 1456. Louis's continuing feud with his father was partly the product of misunderstandings purposely encouraged by their respective advisors.

Louis returned from exile in 1461 to succeed Charles as king. He soon realized that an effective monarchy required the weakening of the princes and that this goal could be achieved more easily by capitalizing on their mutual jealousies than by resorting to force. In general he endeavored to cooperate with the families of Bourbon and Anjou, to isolate Brittany, to crush the dissident Gascon lords, and to break the power of the duke of Burgundy. Louis's greatest successes—largely a matter of luck—derived from the death of CHARLES THE BOLD, duke of Burgundy, in 1477 and the extinction of the princely house of Anjou in 1481, both of which brought the crown substantial territory and eliminated dangerous rivals.

Louis XI's reign is rich in narrative sources—mainly chronicles, memoirs, and the reports of Italian ambassadors—which portray a king with many bizarre characteristics who enhanced the greatness of his realm through guile and cunning; he earned the hatred of his subjects by tripling taxes but was able to liquidate serious threats to the monarchy without recourse to costly wars. The vast administrative documents of Louis's reign have not been carefully studied, and the memoirs of Philippe de Commynes, long the most respected narrative source, has been discredited by recent scholarship. Louis XI remains an enigma.

Louis XII, King of France

Throughout his reign, Louis XII, b. June 27, 1462, d. Jan. 1, 1515, who ruled France from 1498 to 1515, was involved in foreign wars, most notably the ITALIAN WARS. The son of Charles, duc d'ORLÉANS and thus the great-grandson of king Charles V, he succeeded his cousin CHARLES VIII as king in 1498. He had his first marriage annulled in order to marry (1499) Charles's widow, ANNE OF BRITTANY, by whom he had two daughters. Brittany, however, was not incorporated into the royal domain until the reign of FRANCIS I, Louis's cousin and successor, who married Louis and Anne's older daughter, Claude, in 1514.

Louis XII inherited Charles VIII's claim to the throne of Naples and had a much stronger claim of his own to Milan, derived from his grandmother Valentina Visconti. These French claims in Italy had already alarmed FERDINAND II of Aragon, inducing that Spanish monarch to conclude marriage alliances with the Austrian Habsburg dynasty. The wars of Louis's reign were waged against this backdrop of complex dynastic politics and territorial claims.

First invading Italy in 1499, Louis was generally successful in the north, holding Milan from 1500 to 1512. He and Ferdinand agreed in 1500 to divide the kingdom of Naples. They then quarreled, however, and in 1503, Louis had to abandon Naples. In 1508, Louis joined the League of Cambrai against Venice and defeated the latter at Agnadello (1509). Pope JULIUS II subsequently organized (1511) a Holy League against France, comprising the papacy, Aragon, Venice, the Swiss Confederation, England, and the Holy Roman Empire. Defeated at Novara and Guinegate in 1513, Louis lost all his Italian conquests. Despite his defeats, Louis was a popular king because he did not demand excessive taxes and provided the nobles with military employment and opportunities for glory.

Louis XIII, King of France

Louis XIII, b. Sept. 27, 1601, d. May 14, 1643, allowed his minister Cardinal RICHELIEU to rule France for most of his reign. The son of HENRY IV and MARIE DE MÉDICIS, he succeeded to the throne in 1610 at the age of eight. Louis grew up to be proud, secretive, and devout, but he was determined to be just and showed genuine concern for his subjects. In 1615, while still under his mother's regency, the young king married ANNE OF AUSTRIA, daughter of Philip III of Spain. Two years later he ended the regency, exiling his mother to Blois. In 1620, Louis annexed the formerly autonomous and largely Protestant province of Béarn and led his troops in several campaigns to reimpose Catholicism there and in French Navarre.

In 1624, Louis entrusted Richelieu with total authority. While the cardinal crushed the French Protestants (HUGUENOTS), he allied France with the Protestant powers against Spain during the THIRTY YEARS' WAR. Richelieu made himself so indispensable that he survived the many plots to undermine his influence with the king.

Louis largely ignored his wife, who for a time dallied with the English duke of BUCKINGHAM—the incident fictionalized in Alexandre Dumas père's The Three Musketeers. The king formed close friendships with several other women and, from 1639, with the young marquis de Cinq-Mars. In 1642, however, he sanctioned the latter's execution when Richelieu proved that Cinq-Mars was plotting with Spain. Louis was succeeded by his young son, Louis XIV.

Louis XIV, King of France

Louis XIV, b. Sept. 5, 1638, d. Sept. 1, 1715, France's Sun King, had the longest reign in European history (1643–1715). He brought absolute monarchy to its height, established a glittering court at VERSAILLES, and fought most of the other European countries in four wars. The early part of his reign (1643–61) was dominated by the chief minister, Cardinal MAZARIN. In the middle period (1661–85), Louis reigned personally and innovatively, but the last years of his rule (1685–1715) were beset by problems.

Minority. The first child of the long-married Louis XIII and his Habsburg wife, ANNE OF AUSTRIA, Louis succeeded his father on the throne at the age of four. While Louis's mother was regent, Mazarin suppressed the FRONDE revolts (1648–53) and restored internal order. The Peace of Westphalia (1648; see WESTPHALIA, PEACE OF), which ended the Thirty Years' War, together with the Peace of the Pyrenees (1659), which concluded prolonged warfare with Spain, made France the leading European power. The latter treaty was sealed by Louis XIV's marriage (1660) to Marie Thérèse (1638–83), the daughter of PHILIP IV of Spain.

Personal Administration. On Mazarin's death in 1661, Louis astounded his court by becoming his own chief minister. A sensational three-year trial (1661–64) of the powerful and corrupt finance minister Nicolas FOUQUET sent the would-be chief minister to prison for life. The king thereafter ruled through his high state council (*conseil d'en haut*) and a few select ministers, the most famous and powerful of whom were Jean Baptiste COLBERT in internal affairs and the marquis de LOUVOIS in military matters.

Breaking with tradition, Louis excluded from his council members of his immediate family, great princes, and others of the old military nobility (*noblesse d'épee*), and relied on the newer judicial nobility (*noblesse de robe*). Local government was increasingly placed under removable intendants.

Period of Glory. The early personal reign of Louis was highly successful in both internal and foreign affairs. At home the PARLEMENTS lost their traditional power to obstruct legislation, and the judicial structure was reformed. Urban law enforcement was improved by creation (1667) of the office of lieutenant general of police for Paris, later imitated in other towns. Under Colbert, commerce, industry, and overseas colonies were developed by state subsidies, tight control over standards of quality, and high protective tariffs.

Colbert and the king shared the idea of glorifying the monarch and monarchy through the arts. Louis was a discriminating patron of the great literary and artistic figures of France's classical age, including MOLIÈRE, Charles Lebrun, Louis LE VAU, Jules Mansart, and Jean Baptiste LULLY. His state established or developed in rapid succession academies for painting and sculpture (1663), inscriptions (1663), French artists at Rome (1666), and science (1666), followed by the Paris Observatory (1667) and the academies of architecture (1671) and music (1672). The literary Académie Française also came under formal royal control in 1671.

Money was lavished on buildings. In Paris the LOUVRE was essentially completed with the classical colonnade by Claude Perrault. At Versailles, Louis XIII's hunting lodge was transformed into a remarkable palace and park. When the king moved permanently to Versailles in 1682, an elaborate court etiquette was established that had the aristocracy, including former rebel princes, vying to participate in Louis's rising (*levé*) and retiring (*couché*).

In foreign affairs, the young Louis XIV launched the War of DEVOLUTION (1667–68) against the Spanish Netherlands, claiming that those provinces had "devolved" by succession to his Spanish wife rather than to her half brother, the Spanish king CHARLES II. The war brought him some valuable frontier towns in Flanders. Louis turned next against the United Provinces of the Netherlands in the third ANGLO-DUTCH WAR (1672–78). By the

Louis XIV, the French "Sun King," epitomized absolutism in his long (1643–1715) reign. Louis's strong personal rule brought the extension of France's boundaries, the decline of the power of the nobility, and the promotion of industry and art. (Louvre, Paris.)

Peace of Nijmegen (1678–79) he gained more territory in Flanders, and the formerly Spanish FRANCHE-COMTÉ was added to France's eastern frontier, now fortified by the great siege expert, Sébastien Le Prestre de VAUBAN. Louis also annexed a series of towns along the Franco-German border, and in 1681 seized the Alsatian city of Strasbourg and Casale in northern Italy.

Period of Decline. The turning point in Louis's reign came after Colbert's death (1683). In 1685 the king took the disastrous step of revoking the Protestant (HUGUENOT) minority's right to worship by his Edict of Fontainebleau, often called the revocation of the Edict of Nantes (see NANTES, EDICT OF). Many Huguenots—who constituted an industrious segment of French society—left the country, taking with them considerable capital as well as skills.

In September 1688, Louis sent French troops into the Palatinate, thus initiating the nine-year War of the GRAND ALLIANCE. France barely held its own against the United Provinces and England, both under WILLIAM III, as well as Austria, Spain, and minor powers; but the Treaty of Rijswijk (1697) preserved Strasbourg and Louis's acquisitions along the Franco-German border.

In the disastrous War of the SPANISH SUCCESSION (1701–14), Louis defended his grandson PHILIP V's inheritance of Spain and its empire on the death of Charles II. The genius of the English general the duke of MARLBOROUGH and his Austrian counterpart, EUGENE OF SAVOY, was almost too much for the ducs de VILLARS, BERWICK, and VENDÔME, who were Louis's principal generals. By the Peace of Utrecht, France retained most of its earlier conquests, and the Spanish empire was divided between Philip V, who received Spain and its overseas colonies, and Holy Roman Emperor CHARLES VI, who acquired the Spanish Netherlands and Spain's Italian possessions.

During the post-1685 period the monarchy became increasingly bureaucratized. A bitter quarrel (1673–93) with the pope was concluded when the king withdrew the French clergy's Four Gallican Articles of 1682, in which they had claimed quasi-independence from the papacy for the French church (see GALLICANISM). Reconciliation with the papacy aided Louis's attempt to suppress JANSENISM. The Jansenist convents of Port-Royal were closed (1709–10), and in 1713 the pope issued, at Louis's request, the anti-Jansenist bull *Unigenitus*.

After a series of celebrated liaisons with mistresses, notably Louise de la Vallière and Madame de MONTESPAN, Louis settled down to a more sedate life with Madame de MAINTENON, whom he secretly married about 1683. She shared with Louis the grief of lost battles and the successive deaths of all but two of his direct descendants. The two who survived him were his grandson Philip V of Spain and a great-grandson who became Louis XV when the Sun King died.

Louis XV, King of France

Louis XV, King of France   Louis XV, b. Feb. 15, 1710, d. May 10, 1774, who succeeded his great-grandfather Louis XIV as king of France in 1715, was dominated by court factions, his own sensual pleasures, and his mistresses, notably the marquise de POMPADOUR and the comtesse DU BARRY. His reign's disastrous wars, mounting fiscal crisis, and conflicts with JANSENISM and the PARLEMENTS prepared the way for the French Revolution of 1789.

Born to the duc de Bourgogne (Burgundy) and Marie Adélaide of Savoy, Louis was a minor under the regency of the duc d'Orléans (see ORLÉANS, PHILIPPE II, DUC D') from 1715 to 1723. From 1726 to 1743 the young king was guided by his former tutor, André Hercule de FLEURY, who governed cautiously and economically. In the War of the POLISH SUCCESSION (1733–38), France backed the former Polish king STANISŁAW I, who was the father of Louis's wife Maria Leszczyńska. After the war Stanisław acquired Lorraine, which passed to France in 1766.

French participation in the War of the AUSTRIAN SUCCESSION (1740–48) proved costly and territorially unrewarding, and the king failed to back Controller-General Jean Baptiste de Machault's attempt to raise government funds by including the clergy, nobles, and parlementary judges in a new universal tax. In the SEVEN YEARS' WAR (1756–63), France lost most of its overseas empire (including its North American colonies; see FRENCH AND INDIAN WARS) to Britain.

The naval and army reforms of the duc de CHOISEUL and the acquisition (1768) of Corsica were not enough to restore the king's plummeting popularity. Belatedly, Louis moved to support the reform efforts of his chancellor,

René de Maupeou, who secured abolition of the parlements' tax-vetoing power in 1771. The reform was promptly overturned when the king died and was succeeded by his grandson, Louis XVI.

Louis XVI, King of France

Louis XVI, King of France   Louis XVI, b. Aug. 23, 1754, d. Jan. 21, 1793, grandson and successor of Louis XV as king of France, was neither interested in politics nor capable of dealing with the FRENCH REVOLUTION, which engulfed his reign. Absorbed in eating, hunting, and mechanical arts, he allowed a mounting financial crisis to culminate in the destruction of the once powerful absolute monarchy, and he lost his own life to the revolution.

Born to the Dauphin Louis and Maria Josepha of Saxony, Louis became heir to the French throne on his father's death in 1765. In 1770 he married the Austrian archduchess MARIE ANTOINETTE, and in 1774 he succeeded to the throne.

Louis's first fateful act as king was to restore the political power of the reactionary PARLEMENTS. He appointed (1774) the fiscal reformer Baron TURGOT as controller-general of finance but dismissed (1776) him in the face of parlementary opposition. Jacques NECKER, the next director of finances, was also dismissed (1781). French participation (1778–83) in the American Revolution increased the government's debts and fueled demands for liberty at home.

After the failure of Charles CALONNE, controller-general from 1783 to 1787, to steer tax reform past a royally appointed Assembly of Notables, Louis gave in to the popular demand for an elected STATES-GENERAL to discuss the financial crisis. When it met in 1789, the revolutionary middle-class delegates soon dominated events and declared themselves a National Assembly. When Louis half-heartedly summoned troops against the assembly, a Parisian mob stormed the BASTILLE (July 14).

In October 1789 a mob forced the royal family to leave Versailles for Paris. Although Louis had publicly accepted the revolutionary changes, he remained under

Louis XVI, the last Bourbon monarch of France with absolute powers, was a well-intentioned but weak-willed and indecisive ruler. Engulfed by the French Revolution (1789), Louis was convicted of treason and on Jan. 21, 1793, was guillotined in Paris. (Portrait by J. S. Duplessis, Versailles.)

suspicion because of footdragging on revolutionary legislation. An abortive attempt to flee France (the so-called Flight to Varennes, June 1791) and popular fear of Louis's collusion with the Austrians and Prussians, who invaded France in 1792, led to a mob uprising against the monarchy in August 1792. A republic was declared on September 21. Evidence that Louis had intrigued with the Austrians was used in his trial for treason in December. He was condemned by a close multiple vote in the republic's Convention and executed by guillotine.

Louis XVII, King of France   Although Louis XVII, b. Mar. 27, 1785, d. June 8, 1795, was proclaimed king of France by royalist exiles after the execution (January 1793) of his father, Louis XVI, he remained a prisoner until his death. The second son of Louis and MARIE ANTOINETTE, he became heir to the throne on the death (1789) of his elder brother. After the overthrow of the monarchy in 1792, he was first imprisoned with his family. In July 1793 he was removed from his mother and placed for a time in the care of a shoemaker, Antoine Simon. Neglected, he became ill and died. Rumors that he had escaped enabled a number of people to claim later that they were Louis XVII.

Louis XVIII, King of France   Louis XVIII, b. Nov. 17, 1755, d. Sept. 16, 1824, became king of France in 1814, when the Bourbon monarchy was restored following the Revolutionary and Napoleonic period. A younger brother of Louis XVI, he fled France early in the French Revolution, and in 1795, on the death of his nephew, Louis XVII, he proclaimed himself king of France. He did not recover the throne, however, until after the abdication of NAPOLEON I in 1814, and he was forced into exile again during Napoleon's brief return to power (1814–15).

When he came back to France in 1814, Louis understood that there could be no turning back. He granted (June 4, 1814) a constitution that guaranteed parliamentary government, a free press, and essential legal and social reforms. In the 1820s, however, he yielded increasingly to pressures from the Ultraroyalists and sanctioned policies favoring the nobility and the clergy. He was succeeded by his younger brother, CHARLES X.

Louis IV, King of Germany and Holy Roman Emperor (Louis the Bavarian)   Louis, or Ludwig, IV, b. Apr. 1, 1282, d. Oct. 11, 1347, was involved in the last major medieval church-state conflict. When Emperor HENRY VII of the house of Luxemburg died, the German electors were divided between Louis, who was duke of Bavaria and a member of the WITTELSBACH family, and the Habsburg Frederick the Fair of Austria. Both were elected king in 1314, and a long war ensued. Louis finally won in 1322.

At this point Pope JOHN XXII, living in Avignon, intervened, claiming the right to veto Louis's election. When Louis denied this right, John excommunicated him. Supported by philosophers MARSILIUS OF PADUA and John of

Jandun, as well as by some disaffected Franciscan friars, Louis entered Italy in 1327. He had himself crowned emperor by lay officials in Rome in 1328 and set up an antipope, Nicholas V. In 1338, by the Declaration of Rense, the German electors asserted that they alone had the power to elect the German kings, who automatically became emperors-elect. Louis's decree *Licet juris* enacted that statement as law.

Louis continued to negotiate, to no avail, with John's successors, Benedict XII and Clement VI. In the meantime he alienated his German supporters by his expansion of his family's domains. In 1346 the electors finally accepted the papal deposition of Louis and elected CHARLES IV of the house of Luxemburg as king. Louis was preparing to fight when he died while hunting.

Louis I, King of Hungary (Louis the Great)   Louis the Great, b. Mar. 5, 1326, d. Sept. 10, 1382, was king of Hungary (1342–82) and of Poland (1370–82). One of the greatest and most beloved rulers of Hungary, he made that country into a significant power in Central Europe. The son and successor of CHARLES I (Charles Robert), Louis was the second ANGEVIN king of Hungary. Louis's expansive foreign policy brought him considerable success in the Balkans (Dalmatia, Serbia, Bulgaria, Walachia). Because of papal opposition, however, his efforts to gain control over the Kingdom of Naples, where his family had come from, were doomed to failure. After the death of his maternal uncle CASIMIR III of Poland (1370), Louis also gained the Polish throne. Of his two surviving daughters, Maria inherited Hungary and JADWIGA ascended to the Polish throne.

Louis II, King of Hungary   Louis, or Lájos, II, b. July 1, 1506, d. Aug. 29, 1526, was the last king of the JAGELLO dynasty to rule Hungary and Bohemia. The son of Ulászló II, he succeeded to the throne as a minor in 1516. Sickly and frivolous, he remained under control of the Hungarian magnates after he was declared of age in 1521. In 1522 he married the Habsburg Maria of Austria. When the Ottoman Turks invaded Hungary, Louis led a force of 20,000 against them in 1526. His army was crushed in the Battle of Mohács, and Louis himself drowned during the retreat. His crowns then passed to his wife's brother Archduke Ferdinand (later Holy Roman Emperor FERDINAND I).

Louis I, Frankish Emperor (Louis the Pious)   Although Louis I, b. 778, d. June 20, 840, was an able ruler and energetic military commander, his reputation has suffered because he was not as successful as his father, CHARLEMAGNE. After reaching his majority, he established a vigorous Carolingian presence in Spain. His brothers having died, he was crowned coemperor in 813, and in 814 he succeeded Charlemagne as sole ruler of the Frankish empire.

Louis sought to develop the imperial ideal, working

closely with the church. In 817 he made his eldest son, LOTHAIR I, coemperor and allocated parts of the empire to his other sons, LOUIS THE GERMAN and Pepin. The birth of another son, the future Emperor CHARLES II, to Louis's second wife, Judith of Bavaria, started the trouble. The emperor's attempts to provide for Charles precipitated a series of revolts by the older sons. By the time of Louis's death the empire was in serious decline.

Louis II, Frankish Emperor   Louis II, b. c.822, d. Aug. 12, 875, was the eldest son of the emperor LOTHAIR I. Designated to rule Italy in 839, Louis was crowned king by the pope in 844, and in 850 he was made coemperor with his father. He became sole emperor in 855 after his father's abdication, although his rule was confined to Italy. Louis spent most of his career trying to expel the Saracens (Arabs) from southern Italy, but despite victories at Bari (871) and Capua (872), he failed to win control of the south. On the death (863) of his brother Charles, Louis gained much of the Provence. When his other brother, LOTHAIR II, died in 869, however, Louis received no part of Lotharingia, which was partitioned by his uncles LOUIS THE GERMAN and Charles the Bald (later Emperor CHARLES II).

Louisbourg   [loo'-is-burg]   Louisbourg (1986 pop., 1,355) is a town on Cape Breton Island, northeastern Nova Scotia. Fish processing and packing is the economic mainstay. Louisbourg was settled in 1713 by the French, who constructed (1720–40) there a great fortress designed by Sébastien le Prestre de VAUBAN. The town was taken by the British in 1745 during King George's War (see FRENCH AND INDIAN WARS) but was restored to France by the Treaty of Aix-La-Chapelle in 1748. During the final French and Indian War the British again captured (1758) the fortress; they evacuated the French and used Louisbourg as a base for capturing much of Canada. The old fortress has been extensively restored and is now a national historic park.

Louise, Lake   Lake Louise is a picturesque lake in the Canadian Rockies in southwest Alberta. Within Banff National Park, the small (2.4-km-long/1.5-mi) lake lies at an altitude of 1,728 m (5,670 ft) and is framed by tall, glacier-topped peaks. It drains eastward to the Bow River. Discovered in 1882, Lake Louise is a popular year-round resort.

Louisiana   Located in the southeastern United States, Louisiana lies entirely within the Gulf Coastal Plain. It is shaped like a capital *L,* approximately 530 km (330 mi) at its widest, and about 450 km (280 mi) from north to south. Louisiana is bordered by Mississippi on the east, the Gulf of Mexico on the south, Texas on the west, and Arkansas on the north. Sighted by the Spanish in 1519,

Louisiana was first explored by Pánfilo de NARVÁEZ of Spain, who navigated its coast in 1528. Later, Robert Cavelier, sieur de LA SALLE, named the region Louisiane in honor of the French king Louis XIV, claiming it for France in 1682. The state's long and varied history, diverse population, abundant energy resources, and strategic location at the mouth of the Mississippi River are valued attributes. The problems that exist in Louisiana stem from its prolonged recovery after the Civil War, its relatively slow industrial growth, and its heavy dependence on extractive industries.

Land

Louisiana is part of a sedimentary plain that slopes gently toward the Gulf of Mexico. The tilted strata that constitute this plain are pierced in the northwest and coastal area by enormous plugs of salt called salt domes. The most pronounced relief in the land surface is found in the northern hills and the area north of Lake Pontchartrain. The flattest terrain is on the coastal marshes. The dominant physical feature of the state is the Mississippi River.

Five natural regions are recognizable. The coastal marshes either have a firm surface or are soft, depending on the salt content. The gently sloping alluvial valley of the Mississippi lies toward the east, with its channels forming a bird-foot-shaped delta. The Red River valley, running northwest to southeast, follows the Mississippi's pattern on a much smaller scale. The terraces comprise the prairies in the southwest and the flatwoods to their north. The loessial bluffs flanking the Mississippi and containing moderate relief are also part of the terraces. The hill region, found in the northwest, is the oldest and highest part of the state.

Drainage.   The most important rivers in Louisiana are the MISSISSIPPI, RED, Atchafalaya, and Ouachita. The Mississippi flood plain is lower than the natural levees along the main watercourse, and water therefore drains away from the river. Much of Louisiana's terrain is related to the Mississippi.

Lakes, including an increasing number of artificial reservoirs such as Toledo Bend, are found throughout the state. Along the Mississippi and Red are a number of bayous or oxbows, formed as the rivers cut across their own meanders or when channels were cut off for flood control. False River and Raccourci Old River on the Mississippi are examples. Some larger lakes such as PONTCHARTRAIN and Maurepas are the result of subsurface faulting. In the west, shallow lagoons that formed behind beach ridges eventually created Sabine and Calcasieu lakes. To the east, subsidence of deltaic sediments formed round lakes.

Soils.   Louisiana's alluvial soils comprise the most fertile land. They are associated with the Mississippi and Red River flood plains. The organic marsh soils are high in natural fertility but poorly drained and subject to flooding.

Residual soils of the uplands are sandy and infertile. They are used primarily for grazing and forestland. The finely grained terrace soils of the prairies are alluvial soils underlain by a claypan layer. This stratum of clay, cou-

AT A GLANCE

LOUISIANA

Land: Area: 134,274 km^2 (51,845 mi^2); rank: 31st. Capital: Baton Rouge (1990 pop., 219,531). Largest city: New Orleans (1990 pop., 496,938). County equivalents (parishes): 64. Elevations: highest—163 m (535 ft), at Driskill Mountain; lowest— -2.4 m (-8 ft), at New Orleans.

People: Population (1990): 4,238,216; rank: 21st; density: 37.4 persons per km^2 (96.9 per mi^2). Distribution (1990): 68.1% urban, 31.9% rural. Average annual change (1980–90): -0.08%.

Government (1993): Governor: Edwin W. Edwards, Democrat. U.S. Congress: Senate—2 Democrats; House—4 Democrats, 3 Republicans. Electoral college votes: 9. State legislature: 39 senators, 105 representatives.

Economy: State personal income (1989): $56.6 billion; rank: 23d. Median family income (1989): $26,313; rank: 47th. Agriculture: income (1989)—$1.66 billion. Fishing: value (1989)—$265 million. Lumber production (1991): 870 million board feet. Mining (nonfuel): value (1988)—$435 million. Manufacturing: value added (1987)—$16.4 billion. Services: value (1987)—$14.9 billion.

Miscellany: Statehood: Apr. 30, 1812; the 18th state. Nickname: Pelican State; tree: bald cypress; motto: Union, Justice, Confidence; songs: "Give Me Louisiana" and "You Are My Sunshine."

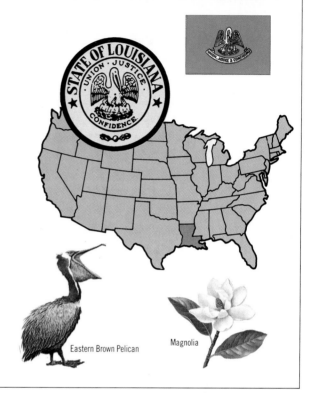

Eastern Brown Pelican

Magnolia

---

pled with low relief, causes slow drainage. Flatwoods soils are of low fertility.

Climate. Louisiana's humid subtropical climate is relatively uniform throughout the state. Annual average precipitation ranges from 1,175 mm (46 in) in the northwest to more than 1,625 mm (64 in) in the southeast. Diurnal summer temperatures range from 29° to 35° C (84° to 95° F) in the afternoons to 16° to 24° C (61° to 75° F) in the early morning. Temperatures of at least 38° C (100° F) occur in almost all years. Louisiana is subject to tropical storms in summer and hurricanes in summer and fall, often accompanied by tornadoes. The cooler seasons are more variable, influenced by both cold polar air and warm tropical air. Winter temperatures drop as low as 5° C (41° F).

Vegetation and Animal Life. The number of plant species in the state is estimated at 4,500. Treeless plains fringe the Gulf of Mexico, while freshwater marshes support floating plants. At slightly higher elevations stands of moss-festooned live oaks characterize the landscape. The prairie grasses in the southwest, inland from the marsh, are divided by gallery forests growing along streams. Longleaf pines grow north of the prairies in the west and north of Lake Pontchartrain in the east. The

northwestern corner of the state supports drought-resistant loblolly pine, oak, and hickory. Along smaller streams dogwood, redbud, and hackberry can be found. The floodplains of the major rivers have hardwoods on the well-drained soils and cypress in the swamps. In the lower swamps, black gum, red maple, and palmetto grow with the cypress. Bluff-land hardwoods include oak, maple, dogwood, tulip, and hickory.

Squirrels, turkeys, beavers, muskrat, mink, raccoon, opossums, and alligators are common. Nutrias have increased following their introduction in the 1930s, and large numbers of armadillos have migrated from the Southwest. A variety of fish is found inland and in the adjacent Gulf waters.

Resources. Louisiana's mineral resources are few in number but are economically important. Deposits of petroleum are found in the Mississippi delta area. To the west, increasing amounts of natural gas occur with petroleum. Large quantities of these minerals have also been extracted to the north, but since the 1940s drilling has moved offshore. Much of Louisiana's petroleum is associated with coastal salt domes. Extraction of salt is now mostly from the domes in the southern part of the state.

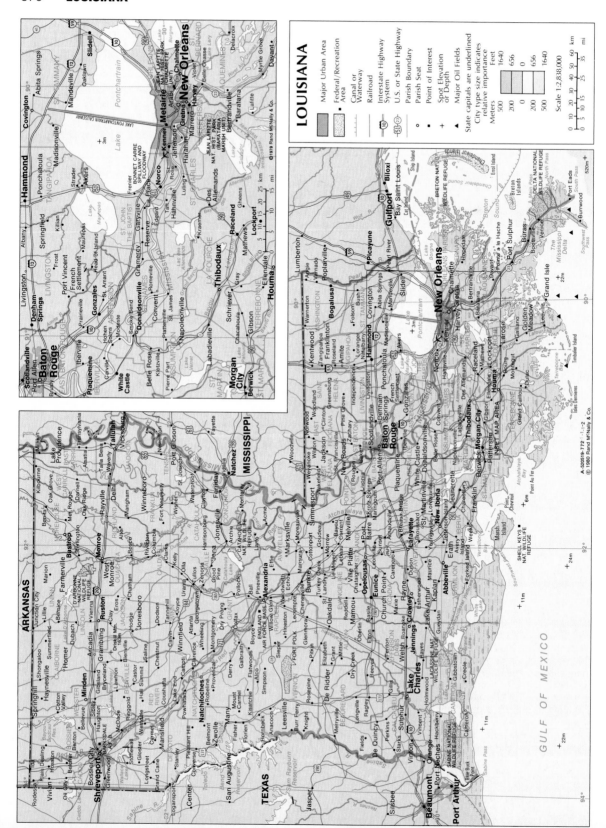

LOUISIANA

Major Urban Area

Federal/Recreation Area

Canal or Waterway

Railroad

Interstate Highway System

U.S. or State Highway

Parish Boundary

Parish Seat

Point of Interest

Spot Elevation or Depth

Major Oil Fields

State capitals are underlined

City type size indicates relative importance

Meters	Feet
500	1640
200	656
0	0
200	656
500	1640

Scale 1:2,838,000

© 1979 Rand McNally & Co.

A-500519-772 -1.1-2
© 1980 Rand McNally & Co.

GULF OF MEXICO

Louisiana's many swamp areas, such as this swamp near the Pearl River on the Mississippi border, are excellent hunting and fishing grounds. Water oaks, cypresses, tupelo gum, wild turkeys, deer, frogs, and various species of fish are found in these regions.

Sulfur, sand, gravel, clays, lime, shell, and gypsum are also extracted. Lignite occurs in the northwest.

People

Louisiana's population increased 15.4% from 1970 to 1980; from 1980 to 1990 it increased only 0.8%. The state has become more urban; the largest cities are NEW ORLEANS, BATON ROUGE, SHREVEPORT, and Metairie. During the period 1980–88, Louisiana experienced a net total out-migration of 162,000. A relatively small number of persons are foreign-born; most of these live in New Orleans.

Culturally, Louisiana is one of the most diverse states, having grown from settlement by French, Spanish, English, and American populations. Early French traits have been retained by CREOLES and CAJUNS in southern Louisiana. A Spanish influence was added to this culture in the southern and western portions of the state. People of Anglo-Saxon descent migrated to eastern and northern Louisiana, and blacks were brought into the plantation areas. Although French is no longer widely spoken as a first language, the French Roman Catholic core of southern Louisiana may still be distinguished from the English-speaking Protestant majority of northern Louisiana and the east. Baptists form the largest Protestant denomination.

Education. The first school in the state is believed to have been the Ursuline Convent for girls in New Orleans, dating from 1728. Public schools developed slowly until 1841, when New Orleans established free public schools. There are more than 30 public and private institutions of higher education operating in Louisiana. The Louisiana State University system includes Louisiana State University and Agricultural and Mechanical College (1855), with the main campus at Baton Rouge, and the University of New Orleans (1956). The state's per capita expenditures on public education perpetually lag behind the national annual average. Possibly reflecting this fact, Louisiana's literacy rate ranks among the lowest of all the states.

Culture. Louisiana maintains a number of cultural institutions—primarily in New Orleans, Baton Rouge, and Shreveport—which include art galleries, historical museums, and historical sites. The Louisiana State Museum, housed in the Cabildo in New Orleans, is probably the most famous. Other museums include the Louisiana State Exhibit Building and R. W. Norton Art Gallery in Shreveport, and the art gallery of the Louisiana Art Commission in Baton Rouge. Orchestras of note include the

The Mississippi River branches out into channels in the Delta region of Louisiana before ending its winding, 10-state journey at the Gulf of Mexico.

These trawlers are a small segment of the fleet of Louisiana shrimping boats that fish the Gulf coastal waters. Louisiana's fishing industry is among the most productive in the United States.

New Orleans Philharmonic, the Baton Rouge Civic Symphony, and the Shreveport Symphony.

Several historic sites have been designated, including the prehistoric Indian areas of Poverty Point, northeast of Monroe, and Marksville, southeast of ALEXANDRIA; the Mansfield Battle Park and Museum; and the Acadian House and Museum at Longfellow-Evangeline State Park in Saint Martinville near New Iberia. Chalmette National Historical Park is at the site of the Battle of New Orleans (1815). The most notable arena for sports is the Superdome in New Orleans; when completed (1975), it was the largest U.S. structure of its kind.

The most famous of Louisiana's daily newspapers is the *New Orleans Times-Picayune*; it is also the paper with the widest circulation. The state has ample numbers of television as well as AM and FM radio stations.

Economic Activities

Manufacturing. The leading industries in value added by manufacture are chemicals and allied products, petroleum products, and food and food products. The principal centers for manufacturing in Louisiana are the largest urban hubs, particularly New Orleans, Baton Rouge, and Shreveport. The state's leading manufactured or processed products, in addition to those based on petroleum, coal, and natural gas, include salt, drugs, fertilizers, processed rice, and sugar.

Energy. Louisiana generates almost all its power from hydrocarbons (petroleum and natural gas) extracted from within the state. There is a small nuclear-power capacity. In 1988, Louisiana's production of electricity was 56.8 billion kW h.

Agriculture, Forestry, and Fishing. Until World War II, Louisiana was basically an agricultural state. Since then, although agriculture remains a significant factor in the economy, the number of farms in operation has greatly decreased. Major agricultural commodities include soybeans, sugar and sugarcane, rice, and cotton, along with dairy products, cattle, and calves. Specialty crops include

hot peppers grown on Avery Island, which are made into Tabasco sauce, and the world's supply of pungent perique tobacco. By the 1930s the virgin forests had been depleted and the landscape scarred. Although the huge cypress and hardwood stands of the past are gone, Louisiana's climate has allowed the reforestation of rapid-growing pines to take place.

Louisiana leads all other states in volume of fish caught. Menhaden is most important, and buffalo, catfish, flounder, and spotted sea trout are commercially significant. Crabs, crayfish, oysters, and shrimp are important in both volume and value. Louisiana's fur industry has grown in recent years with the development of a stable market for nutria (an aquatic rodent that resembles a miniature beaver).

Tourism. Tourism is generally focused on the metropolitan centers, with New Orleans most important. The city attracts large numbers of Mardi Gras visitors. About 7.3 million people visited the New Orleans World's Fair between May and November 1984. The Acadian, or Cajun, country of the southwest is also a popular tourist area.

Transportation and Trade. Several thousand miles of railway track cross the state, serving primarily to move freight. Approximately 300 airports serve Louisianans. The highway and road network is extensive.

Foreign trade is important to Louisiana's economy; New Orleans handles the bulk of this trade. Louisiana is a principal U.S. exporter of chemicals, petroleum, primary metals, rice, cotton, and fish products. Imports include animal, fish, and vegetable oils and fats, foodstuffs, and crude rubber.

Government and Politics

Since 1812, Louisiana has operated under 11 constitutions, the most recent dating from 1974. The Louisiana legislature is composed of two houses—a 39-member senate and a 105-member house of representatives. Legislative sessions are annual. Legislators are elected for

New Orleans is the second largest port in the United States and an important shipbuilding center. Wharves line the Mississippi River as it loops around the city.

concurrent terms of 4 years. Judicial power is vested in the supreme court, the courts of appeals, and the district courts. The executive branch is headed by a governor elected to a 4-year term. The state is divided into 64 parishes which, with a few exceptions, are governed by elected bodies called police juries.

From 1877 until after World War II, Louisiana was controlled by Democrats. Since the 1950s, however, Republican U.S. presidential candidates have frequently won the state's electoral votes. In 1964, for the first time in this century, two Republicans were elected to the state legislature (others followed). In 1979, David C. Treen became the first Republican to be elected governor since Reconstruction.

History

The earliest known Indian occupancy dates to perhaps 10,000 years ago. A reasonable estimate of the Indian population in AD 1700 would be 15,000, formed of six linguistic groups: CADDO in the northwest, NATCHEZ near the middle Mississippi, Atakapa on the prairies of the southwest, Chitimachan in the Atchafalaya Basin, Muskogean east of the Mississippi, and Tunican in the northeast. Most were sedentary village farmers who also hunted and fished.

Permanent European settlement was begun by France almost 200 years after the Spanish had entered the area. Robert Cavelier, Sieur de La Salle, explored the Mississippi downstream to its mouth, and he claimed the entire drainage basin for France in 1682. La Salle's efforts at colonization failed, but the French continued in their attempt to establish a permanent settlement. Eventually, the colony, which had also failed at BILOXI, moved upstream on the Mississippi to the foot of the Great Raft on the Red River, establishing the first permanent settlement in the Louisiana Territory at Natchitoches in 1714. Colonization proceeded under the direction of Pierre Le Moyne, Sieur d' IBERVILLE and his brother, Jean Baptiste Le Moyne, Sieur de BIENVILLE.

The early history of the colony is a tragic one, as the first settlers were ill-suited to the rigors of frontier life. In 1717, France granted a monopoly on commerce to John LAW in order to promote development of the territory. His MISSISSIPPI SCHEME was designed to entice investment in what he claimed was a land of fabulous mineral wealth. The scheme fell apart in 1720, with no financial rewards to the investors, but the territory gained population as a result of Law's promotion.

German peasants from the Upper Rhine area contributed to the betterment of the region when they began to settle land upstream from New Orleans in the 1720s. Louisiana became a French crown colony in 1731. Crops, grown on plantations, included indigo, rice, and tobacco.

In 1762, Louisiana was ceded to Spain as a result of the French and Indian War, and Great Britain gained control of Florida, which extended to the east bank of the Mississippi. At the same time, Acadians, driven from Nova Scotia by the British, began migrating to Louisiana. The Acadians settled in the eastern prairies around the

The French Quarter of New Orleans is distinguished by its narrow streets and grillwork balconies. Also known as the Vieux Carré, *or* Old Square, *it was the original settlement at New Orleans and is now noted for nightlife and restaurants.*

present site of Saint Martinville and later along the Lower Mississippi and Bayou Lafourche.

The Spanish made feeble attempts to offset the growing French population but were eventually absorbed themselves. In 1800 they returned Louisiana to France by the Treaty of San Ildefonso. Although Napoleon I originally intended to establish a new empire in America, he sold Louisiana to the United States in 1803. The $15-million LOUISIANA PURCHASE represented about 4 cents an acre. Louisiana became the 18th state on Apr. 12, 1812, comprising the territory south of 33° north latitude, which had been the Territory of Orleans. The rest became the Missouri Territory. Not until 1819, however, was West Florida added to form the present state boundaries.

During the WAR OF 1812, British ships moved up the Mississippi River to New Orleans. On Jan. 8, 1815, Gen. Andrew Jackson's troops defeated the British at New Orleans. The battle ended 15 days after the Treaty of Ghent was signed, ending the war. Jean LAFITTE aided the American cause.

By 1860 the population exceeded 700,000, and a class system based on plantations with slave labor had developed. At the same time, yeoman farmers were practicing subsistence farming—Anglo-Saxons in the hills and Acadians to the south. During the Civil War, the importance of the port of New Orleans and Louisiana's strategic position on the Mississippi made it an early Union target; the state's economy was devastated.

Streams had been the major routes since the beginning of settlement. By the 1860 peak of steamboat travel, nearly all of the state could be reached by these craft. As railroads improved, steamboat traffic declined. Rail travel grew in the early 20th century. Much of the modern settlement of the prairies is attributable to the access rail travel gave the area. Highway development began after the 1920s.

Louisiana had come a long way from the earliest Spanish explorers and French settlers, through the Civil War and Reconstruction. In 1928 a Winnfield lawyer, Huey Pierce Long, Jr. (see LONG family), had obtained the governorship, and from 1930 to 1935 he served as a U.S. senator. His program of road building and free schoolbooks, based on tax revenue from petroleum, appealed to the grass-roots population, but his methods became increasingly suspect. Scandals, which had begun by the mid-1930s, accelerated after Long was assassinated in 1935, but his career marked a turning point in Louisiana history. For much of the period since World War II the petroleum industry sparked the economic development of the state; since the mid-1980s there has been an oil slump, however. Urgent environmental problems that emerged in the 1980s—industrial pollution, toxic-waste disposal, coastline erosion—continued in the 1990s. In 1992, Hurricane Andrew, one of the most intense U.S. storms of the century, severely damaged much cropland and several small coastal towns.

Louisiana Purchase   By a treaty signed on Apr. 30, 1803, the United States purchased from France the Louisiana Territory, more than 2 million km^2 (800,000 mi^2) of land extending from the Mississippi River to the Rocky Mountains. The price was 60 million francs, about $15 million; $11,250,000 was to be paid directly, with the

LOUISIANA PURCHASE

Troops fire a salute as the American flag is raised, replacing the tricolor of Napoleonic France, during the ceremonies on Dec. 20, 1803, marking the transfer of the vast Louisiana Territory from France to the United States.

balance to be covered by the assumption by the United States of French debts to American citizens.

In 1762, France had ceded Louisiana to Spain, but by the secret Treaty of San Ildefonso (1800) the French had regained the area. Napoléon Bonaparte (the future Emperor Napoleon I) envisioned a great French empire in the New World. By 1803, however, he faced renewed war with Great Britain, and he needed funds to support his military ventures in Europe. Accordingly, that April he offered to sell Louisiana to the United States.

Concerned about French intentions, President Thomas Jefferson had already sent James Monroe and Robert R. Livingston to Paris to negotiate the purchase of a tract of land on the lower Mississippi or, at least, a guarantee of free navigation on the river. Surprised and delighted by the French offer of the whole territory, they immediately negotiated the treaty.

Jefferson was jubilant. At one stroke the United States would double its size, an enormous tract of land would be open to settlement, and the free navigation of the Mississippi would be assured. Although the Constitution did not specifically empower the federal government to acquire new territory by treaty, Jefferson concluded that the practical benefits to the nation far outweighed the possible violation of the Constitution. The Senate concurred with this decision and voted ratification on Oct. 20, 1803. The Spanish, who had never given up physical possession of Louisiana to the French, did so at New Orleans on Nov. 30, 1803. In a second ceremony, on Dec. 20, 1803, the French turned Louisiana over to the United States. Disputes with Britain and Spain over the boundaries of the purchase took years to resolve.

Louisville [loo'-ee-vil] Louisville, the largest city in Kentucky, is located in the north central part of the state at the falls of the Ohio River. It is the seat of Jefferson County and has a population of 269,063 (1990). The city is a major river port and one of the South's leading industrial, commercial, and shipping centers. Whiskey, tobacco products, and appliances are among its chief manufactures. Louisville's orchestra and theater group have won national acclaim for commissioning and performing new works. The homes of George Rogers Clark and President Zachary Taylor are of historic interest. The University of Louisville (1798) is the oldest municipal university in the nation. The KENTUCKY DERBY, held annually at Churchill Downs since 1875, draws an international crowd of racing fans.

Louisville was settled in 1778, when George Rogers CLARK built a fort as a base of operations against the British and Indians. After a canal bypassing the falls was built (1830) and the Louisville and Nashville Railroad was extended (1880s) to Florida, Louisville developed as a major transportation center. During the Civil War it was a military and supply depot for Union forces. The city was torn by racial rioting in 1968 and again in 1975 by antibusing disturbances. FORT KNOX, the national gold depository, is nearby.

Lourdes [loord] Lourdes is a town in southwestern France in the foothills of the Pyrenees on the Gave du Pau (river). It has a population of 17,425 (1982). The town has been a pilgrimage center known for its miraculous cures since 1858, when 14-year-old Bernadette Soubirous (see BERNADETTE, SAINT) had numerous religious visions in a nearby grotto. A basilica was built on the site in 1876, and nearly 3 million tourists visit the shrine annually. An underground church was completed in 1958. The fortified town was a medieval stronghold.

Lourenço Marques see MAPUTO

louse [lows] Louse (pl. lice) is a name applied to several different invertebrates that are either external parasites (harmful to the host) or commensals (not harmful). Included are certain crustaceans, such as the parasitic fish louse, *Argulus*. Most commonly, however, the name refers to two groups of flattened, wingless insects living on warm-blooded animals. They are usually regarded as separate orders: Mallophaga, or chewing lice, and Anoplura, or sucking lice. Chewing lice are found on mammals but mostly inhabit birds. They chew feathers, hair, and skin and sometimes draw blood. Most species of chewing lice are limited to a single host species. Sucking lice feed only on the blood of mammals, most commonly rodents. The crab louse and the head and body louse are sucking lice and the only lice that parasitize humans. Both lice glue their eggs, or nits, to hair, but the body louse may also fasten its eggs to clothing. The immature lice look like tiny adults.

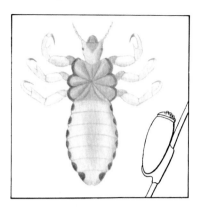

A body louse is a small, wingless insect that lives on humans, sucking its host's blood. A louse egg, or nit (lower right), is shown attached to hair.

In addition to the uncomfortable itching caused by its bites, the body louse may transmit the pathogens that cause typhus, relapsing fever, or trench fever. The spread of these diseases, and of lice themselves, is closely associated with crowded, unsanitary conditions.

Louvain [loo-van'] Louvain (Flemish: Leuven) is a university town in Brabant province, Belgium, about 24 km (15 mi) east of Brussels. Its population is 84,583 (1987 est.). In medieval times Louvain was a textile center and capital of the duchy of Brabant. Today its main industry is brewing. The Catholic University of Louvain, originally founded in 1425, was closed during the French Revolution and reestablished in 1834. Beginning in the late 19th century it was a leading center in the revival of SCHOLASTICISM. In 1970 it was divided into two universities, one for Flemish-speaking and one for French-speaking students.

Louvois, François Michel Le Tellier, Marquis de [loo-vwah', frahn-swah' mee-shel luh tel-yay'] The marquis de Louvois, b. *c*.1639, d. July 16, 1691, the second of three members of the Le Tellier family to serve as French war minister under LOUIS XIV, was the dominant figure in the royal council from 1683 to 1691. Le Tellier was groomed for the war ministry by his father, Michel Le Tellier (1603–85), who held that office from 1643. He assisted his father officially after 1662 and formally succeeded to the post when his father became chancellor in 1677. In 1683, with the death of his rival Jean Baptiste COLBERT, he became superintendent of buildings, arts, and manufactures.

Louvois was a harsh disciplinarian who controlled the army created by his father, established unprecedented civilian dominance over noble officers, and ensured adequate army supplies. His name is associated with implacable persecution of French HUGUENOTS and the brutal French devastation (1688) of the Palatinate, which triggered the War of the GRAND ALLIANCE. Military defeats after 1689 diminished royal favor, but Louvois's secretarial post passed to his son, the marquis de Barbézieux, after his sudden death.

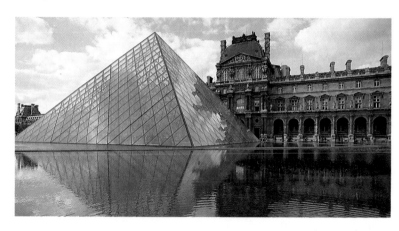

The glass pyramid in the central courtyard of the Louvre was opened in March 1989; it contrasts dramatically with the adjacent 19th-century portions of the museum complex. The pyramid, designed by the U.S. architect I. M. Pei, serves as the main public entrance to the Louvre. Also, it is a skylight for the main hall of the vast new underground Louvre. This subterranean addition contains cafeterias, an auditorium, and information and education facilities.

Louvre [loovr]   The Louvre, one the world's great art museums, houses many works of fundamental importance in Western cultures, including the Victory of Samothrace and Leonardo da Vinci's Mona Lisa. Originally a royal fortress and palace built (12th century) for Philip II, the Louvre is an immense complex of buildings erected in Paris over a span of four centuries. Most of the structures that constitute the museum follow the French Renaissance style of the architect Pierre Lescot, who in 1546 was commissioned by King Francis I to erect what is now the west wing. In founding the Louvre's collection, Francis I was guided by the Italian artists Andrea del Sarto and Francesco Primaticcio, whose works, along with those of their fellow expatriate Leonardo da Vinci, formed the nucleus of the museum's original holdings. The Louvre complex grew as the royal collections expanded.

Throughout the 17th century, as France assumed a dominant role in Europe, the Louvre's holdings increased dramatically. In the 18th century the annual SALON exhibitions were established. The first state museum was opened in the Louvre in 1793. The central position held by the Louvre in artistic life was magnified by Napoleon I, who began its Egyptian collection. The overall museum complex was completed under Napoleon III (r. 1852–70). Subsequently, the Louvre expanded its collections greatly through gifts and bequests.

In 1984 the French government launched a decade-long expansion and modernization program for the Louvre, under the direction of the U.S. architect I. M. PEI.

lovage [luhv'-ij]   Lovage, *Levisticum officinale*, is a branching perennial herb growing to 1.8 m (6 ft) in height, native to the mountains of southern Europe but now found wild across the United States from New Jersey to New Mexico. A member of the parsley family, Umbelliferae, lovage is cultivated as an ornamental and for its celery-flavored leaves; for its aromatic fruits, which are used as a flavoring; and for its oil, which is used in perfumes, liqueurs, and tobacco blends.

Love Canal   see POLLUTANTS, CHEMICAL

Lovecraft, H. P.   The writer Howard Phillips Lovecraft, b. Providence, R.I., Aug. 20, 1890, d. Mar. 13, 1937, was remarkable for the macabre imagination displayed in his fantasy and horror tales. A reclusive man, Lovecraft wrote of dislocations in the web of time and space that exposed unspeakable monsters. Some of his best writing is found in *The Dunwich Horror and Other Weird Tales* (1939; repr. as *The Dunwich Horror*, 1945) and *Best Supernatural Stories of H. P. Lovecraft* (1945). Five volumes of *Selected Letters* (1965–76) have appeared.

Lovelace, Richard [luhv'-luhs]   Richard Lovelace, 1618–58, an English CAVALIER POET, is remembered for two exquisite love lyrics: "To Lucasta, Going to the Wars" and "To Althea, from Prison." Lovelace, who remained loyal to the deposed King Charles I, was twice imprisoned for his royalist beliefs and died in poverty, having spent his fortune in the king's cause. Lovelace published *Lucasta* (1649), the only volume of his poems to appear during his life, while in prison. A second volume with the same title was published by his brother the year after his death.

Lovell, Sir Bernard [luhv'-ul]   The English astronomer Sir Alfred Charles Bernard Lovell, b. Aug. 31, 1913, is known for his work leading to the construction of the 76-m (250-ft) radio telescope at the Jodrell Bank Experimental Station (now called the NUFFIELD RADIO ASTRONOMY LABORATORIES), which he founded in Cheshire, 32 km (20 mi) south of Manchester.

After graduation from the University of Bristol, Lovell joined the staff of Manchester University and was appointed (1951) professor of radio astronomy and director of Jodrell Bank. There he began work on the 250-ft (76-m) radio telescope, at the time the world's largest fully steerable dish.

Low, Seth Seth Low, b. Brooklyn, N.Y., Jan. 18, 1850, d. Sept. 17, 1916, was an American political reformer and educator. A well-to-do merchant, Low became interested in municipal reform; he was elected mayor of Brooklyn in 1881 and served until 1885. He became president of Columbia College in 1890 and greatly expanded the institution and effected its move to its present site in Morningside Heights. In 1901 he was elected mayor of New York City, which by then included Brooklyn, as a fusion, anti-Tammany candidate. As mayor, Low instituted numerous reforms but was defeated for reelection in 1903.

low-pressure region A portion of the ATMOSPHERE with fewer molecules than adjacent portions is called a low-pressure region, area, or cell, or simply a low. In such a region a column of air exerts less pressure on the Earth's surface than do nearby columns. Because air is generally rising in such systems, they are cloudy, usually rainy, and often stormy. Low-pressure cells may be less than 1 km (0.6 mi) across in a TORNADO, about 100 km (60 mi) across in a hurricane (see HURRICANE AND TYPHOON), or more than 1,000 km (600 mi) across in a mature midlatitude CYCLONE. The largest are the semipermanent lows around Iceland and the Aleutian Islands, the low-pressure belt encircling Antarctica, and the region (variously called the DOLDRUMS, the tropical rainy belt, or the intertropical convergence zone) where the TRADE WINDS end in a region of warm, rising air near the equator.

Lowell [loh'-ul] Lowell, a city in northeastern Massachusetts, is located about 48 km (30 mi) northwest of Boston, at the confluence of the Merrimack and Concord rivers. One of two county seats of Middlesex County (the other is Cambridge), Lowell has a population of 103,439 (1990). The city has electronics, chemical, and plastics industries. The birthplace of the painter James McNeill Whistler, Lowell is also the seat of the University of Lowell—established by the 1975 merger of Lowell State College (1894) and Lowell Technological Institute (1895). First settled in 1653, Lowell became an important textile center in the 19th century when the waters of the Merrimack were harnessed to provide power for the mills and the Middlesex Canal system was completed.

Lowell, Abbott Lawrence Abbott Lawrence Lowell, b. Boston, Dec. 13, 1856, d. Jan. 6, 1943, was an influential president (1909–33) of Harvard University. A graduate of Harvard (1877) and its law school (1880), he practiced law before returning to Harvard in 1897 as a professor of government. He was appointed president in 1909, succeeding Charles William Eliot, who had replaced a required curriculum with a system of free electives. Lowell partially returned to a structured curriculum by having students concentrate on a major subject. He introduced a general examination and a system of tutori-

als. He also created the Harvard system of residential "houses." The enrollment doubled, endowment increased dramatically, and several professional schools were added during Lowell's tenure. Lowell is also known as a defender of academic freedom.

Lowell, Amy Amy Lawrence Lowell, b. Brookline, Mass., Feb. 9, 1874, d. May 12, 1925, a descendant of a distinguished New England family, is best known as the leading American advocate of IMAGISM in poetry. With untiring energy and shrewdness she created a reputation as a discerning critic of modern poetry, as a literary biographer—her massive study, *John Keats*, was published in 1925—and as a poet. Lowell wrote her first poems, published in *A Dome of Many-Coloured Glass* (1912), in the tradition of English romanticism. Her acquaintance with the experimental verse of Ezra Pound and F. S. Flint is reflected in the free-verse sections of *Sword Blades and Poppy Seed* (1914). Subsequent volumes included the popular "Patterns," "Lilacs," and other poems imagistic in their concreteness, particularity, and absence of direct message. In *Fir Flower Tablets* (1921; publ. 1946), Lowell tried to outdo Pound by translating some ancient Chinese poems. Among her critical works are *Six French Poets* (1915), *Tendencies in Modern American Poetry* (1917), and *A Critical Fable* (1922). *The Complete Poetical Works* of Amy Lowell, edited by Louis Untermeyer, appeared in 1955.

Amy Lowell, an American poet of the early 20th century, became a leading advocate of imagism through her collections of poetry, lectures, and literary criticism.

Lowell, Francis Cabot Francis Cabot Lowell, b. Newburyport, Mass., Apr. 7, 1775, d. Aug. 10, 1817, was a Boston merchant who helped launch the U.S. textile industry. In 1810–12 he visited England, where he observed the workings of the Lancashire cotton mills; on returning home he began building a cotton mill in

Waltham, Mass. Lowell worked with designer Paul Moody to construct the first American power loom and other equipment required to turn raw cotton into cloth. After his death, his brother-in-law, Patrick T. Jackson, built mills on land which in 1826 became Lowell, Mass.

Robert Lowell, a leading poet of post-World War II America, voiced his dismay at the spiritual impotence of individuals and society in such poems as "For the Union Dead" and "Skunk Hour."

Photo Jill Krementz © 1975

Lowell, James Russell   James Russell Lowell, b. Cambridge, Mass., Feb. 22, 1819, d. Aug. 12, 1891, was one of the finest New England poets of the 19th century and a distinguished literary critic. His *The Biglow Papers* (1848) is a noted example of dialect humor; *The Vision of Sir Launfal* (1848) combines medievalism with modern social consciousness; *A Fable for Critics* (1848) tempers criticism with humor; and *The Cathedral* (1870) is one of the important religious poems of the century, in some ways anticipating Henry Adams's *Mont-Saint-Michel and Chartres* (1913). Among the finest of his critical essays are the studies of Chaucer, Dante, Shakespeare, and Spenser.

Lowell graduated from Harvard Law School in 1840 but gave law up in 1843. He held the Smith Professorship at Harvard, succeeding Henry Wadsworth Longfellow; was the first editor (1857–61) of *The Atlantic Monthly* and the coeditor (1863–72) of *The North American Review* with Charles Eliot Norton; and served as minister to Spain (1877–80) and to England (1880–85).

Lowell, Percival   The American astronomer Percival Lowell, b. Boston, Mar. 13, 1855, d. Nov. 12, 1916, is best known for his belief in the existence of artificial canals on MARS. Lowell was a businessman and traveler in the Far East before becoming obsessed with Giovanni Schiaparelli's report (1877) of *canali* ("channels") on Mars. He founded (1894) the Lowell Observatory near Flagstaff, Ariz., especially for studying the Martian surface, and for more than a decade he charted the apparently crisscross markings of Mars. Although other astronomers vehemently denied the existence of canals on Mars, Lowell maintained that not only did they exist, they had also been built by intelligent beings. Not until the Mars probes of the 1960s were Lowell's claims conclusively disproved.

Despite the controversy over the Martian canals, Lowell Observatory has contributed substantially to studies of the planets and the stars. Lowell himself predicted the position of a perturbing planet beyond Neptune, later discovered by Clyde TOMBAUGH and named Pluto.

Lowell, Robert, Jr.   Robert Traill Spence Lowell, Jr., b. Boston, Mar. 1, 1917, d. Sept. 12, 1977, was the spokesperson for a generation of American poets who came to prominence during World War II. Lowell felt that individuals must not become depersonalized by war and by the constant pressure of violence in society.

Lowell was descended from several prominent American families. While a student he came under the influence of Elizabeth Drew's *Discovering Poetry* (1933). An interest in Roman Catholicism dominates his earlier volumes *Land of Unlikeness* (1944), *Lord Weary's Castle* (1946), and *The Mills of the Kavanaughs* (1951). Lowell attended (1935–37) Harvard University before transferring to Kenyon College to complete an undergraduate degree in classics. His teachers at Kenyon included the distinguished poet John Crowe Ransom. In 1940 he married the writer Jean Stafford and was converted to Catholicism. They were divorced in 1948, and Lowell married another prominent writer, Elizabeth Hardwick. After college, Lowell worked as an editor and teacher. During World War II he refused military service and was imprisoned for five months. *Land of Unlikeness*, which appeared shortly after his imprisonment, was greeted by mixed reviews. With *Lord Weary's Castle*, for which he won a Pulitzer Prize, Lowell was acknowledged as America's foremost young poet. His next important work, *Life Studies* (1959), broke with traditional poetic form and diction and introduced a personal, less declaratory tone to his work.

During the 1960s, Lowell remained preoccupied with social issues. In 1965 he refused to attend a White House Arts Festival because of American policies abroad, and in 1970, by way of protest, he took up residence in England. His output during these years was prolific: two books of translations; *The Old Glory* (1965), a trilogy of plays; and such verse works as *For the Union Dead* (1964), *Near the Ocean* (1967), and *Notebook* (1969). *The Dolphin* (1973) won him a second Pulitzer Prize. His final work, *Day by Day* (1977), was published shortly before he had a fatal heart attack.

Lowry, Malcolm   [low'-ree]   Malcolm Lowry, b. July 28, 1909, d. June 27, 1957, was a British novelist whose major work, *Under the Volcano* (1947), expresses many of the problems of his own life, generation, and educated class. A victim of chronic alcoholism, several mental breakdowns, and alienation from his country and family, Lowry had a grand scheme for a trilogy of novels on hell, purgatory, and heaven. *Volcano*, which Lowry called "a drunken Divine Comedy," is his inferno, the story of an ex-consul to Mexico named Geoffrey Firmin. Lowry's other writings, edited posthumously by his second wife, Marjorie Bonner, include the novel *Lunar Caustic* (1968) and the short stories in *Hear Us O Lord From Heaven Thy Dwelling Place* (1961) and *Dark As The Grave Wherein My Friend Is Laid* (1968).

Loyalists   In American history, the Loyalists, or Tories, were the men and women who refused to renounce allegiance to the British crown after July 1776; they demonstrated that the AMERICAN REVOLUTION was a civil war as well as a quest for independence. Approximately 500,000 persons, 20 percent of the white population, actively opposed independence; probably a like number were passive Loyalists. There were Loyalists in every colony, but they were most numerous in the Mid-Atlantic states and in the South.

Although the incidence of loyalism was greatest among crown officials, Anglican clergy, social and economic elites, and cultural minorities, the king's friends came from all racial, religious, ethnic, economic, class, and occupational groups. Vested interest, temperament, or political philosophy could separate Patriot from Loyalist.

As much as the Patriots did, the Loyalists put their lives, fortunes, and honor on the line during the Revolution. Besides those who served in the regular British Army, about 19,000 men fought in more than 40 Loyalist units, the largest of which was Cortlandt Skinner's New Jersey Volunteers. Refugees gathered in British-occupied New York City, where the Board of Associated Loyalists helped direct military activities. During the war, crown supporters suffered physical abuse, ostracism, disenfranchisement, confiscation of property, imprisonment, banishment, and even death. However, only 4,118 Loyalists requested compensation from Britain's Royal Claims Commission after the war.

The Revolution forced approximately 100,000 persons, 2.4 percent of the population into exile. Some refugees

This cartoon, printed in London in 1774, depicts a Loyalist in the American colonies being tarred and feathered by Patriots. Crown supporters, about one-fifth of the white population, suffered physical violence and loss of property throughout the Revolutionary War period.

went to England, others to Florida or the Caribbean; at least half went to Canada, where the colony of NEW BRUNSWICK was created (1784) to meet their demands for lands and recognition. The United Empire Loyalists, a hereditary organization created by the Canadian government in 1789 to honor those who rallied to the crown before the peace of 1783, remains today the Loyalist counterpart to the Sons and Daughters of the American Revolution.

LSD   LSD, or D-lysergic acid diethylamide, also known as LSD-25 and "acid," is a prototype of the hallucinogenic drug class. The mental effects of LSD were discovered in 1943 when a small amount was accidentally ingested by the Swiss chemist Albert Hofmann. The first to synthesize the drug, Hofmann did so while studying derivatives of alkaloids from the ERGOT fungus. LSD's action is complex and as yet not fully known. It produces dilation of the pupils and increases in pulse rate, blood pressure, and temperature. Acting on the brain, LSD can cause sensory distortions, with vivid hallucinations. Emotional and subjective responses vary widely and may include difficulty in concentration, loss of identity, feelings of unreality, seemingly magical insights, depression, anxiety, and sometimes panic and terror. LSD does not produce physical dependence, but psychological dependence and tolerance can develop. LSD is potent in very small doses; as little as 35μ can produce measurable effects. At present LSD has no proven and accepted medical use, and its general use, manufacture, and sale are illegal in the United States (see DRUG ABUSE).

Lu Hsün   see LU XUN

Lü-shun   see LÜSHUN

Lü-ta   see LÜDA

Lu Xun (Lu Hsün) [loo sheun]   Chinese writer Lu Xun (pseudonym of Zhou Shuren), 1881–1936, is known for stories and essays that humorously censure social and moral values. During the literary revolution launched by Hu Shi in 1917, Lu Xun won acclaim for short stories set in his native Zhejiang province and written in colloquial language. These include *Huangren Ruji* (Diary of a Madman, 1918), based on a work by Gogol in which a lunatic suspects that he alone is sane, and Lu Xun's most famous work, *A Q Zhengzhuan* (1921; trans. as *The True Story of Ah Q*, 1956), in which the hero, a village bum able to face reality only through self-deception, symbolizes reactionary forces in Chinese society. His later stories, collected in *Gushi Xinbian* (Old Tales Retold, 1935), are more ideological than his earlier work.

Luanda [loo-ahn'-duh]   Luanda, the capital of Angola and of Luanda district, is a port located on the Atlantic Ocean. Connected by rail to Quela, Luanda exports cotton, coffee, sugar, diamonds, and manganese ore. The city has a population of 1,134,000 (1988 est.). Industries include an oil refinery, fisheries, and factories that manufacture foodstuffs, beverages, textiles, motor vehicles, and construction materials. Luanda has an international airport, and it is the seat of an archdiocese and of the University of Angola (1963). Founded by the Portuguese in 1576, Luanda was the site of a large slave market from the mid-16th to the mid-19th century.

Luang Prabang [lwahng pruh-bahng']

Luang Prabang (Louangphrabang), a city in Laos, is the religious center of the country and the former royal capital. It lies on the Mekong River, about 200 km (125 mi) northwest of Vientiane. The population is 46,000 (1975 est.). The city is an important river port and a market town for fish, agricultural and forest produce, and some handicrafts. The Gold Buddha (Prabang), a sacred Sinhalese carving, was probably brought to the city in 1356.

Established as the capital of Laos by King Ngoun in 1353, the city was originally named Moung Swa. Its present name dates from 1563. It continued to serve as the royal residence until 1975, when the People's Democratic Republic of Laos was established. The royal palace is now is a museum.

Luba [loo'-buh]

The Luba, a Bantu-speaking people in Zaire related to the Lunda and Bemba peoples, have for many centuries been at the forefront of ethnic politics in the region. Their home area in the province of Shaba (formerly Katanga) may have been one of the central areas from which Bantu-speakers spread across Africa. By the 9th century AD the Luba were prominent in long-distance trade and had attained considerable technical skill and elegance in making pottery and in working copper, ivory, and iron. The forms of political organization that they developed by the 16th century were widely imitated by their neighbors. Their empire, governed through subordinate rulers under a powerful king, was extensive before the onset of European colonial rule in the 19th century. Among the earliest labor migrants to Upper Katanga, the Luba were also among the first to form voluntary ethnic associations. The Luba numbered more than 5 million in the 1980s.

Lubbers, Ruud

Rudolph Frans Marie Lubbers, b. May 7, 1939, is prime minister of the Netherlands. A wealthy industrialist, Lubbers entered parliament as a member of the Catholic People's party in 1972 and served as economics minister in the government of Johannes den Uyl from 1973 to 1977. A Christian Democrat after 1980, he became prime minister as head of a center-right coalition in 1982, winning endorsements from the voters in 1986 and 1989.

Lubbock [luhb'-uhk]

Lubbock, a city in northwest Texas, is the seat of Lubbock County. The trade center for the cotton- and grain-producing South Plains region, it has a population of 186,206 (1990). Manufactures include cottonseed oil, heavy agricultural and petroleum equipment, irrigation pipe and pumps, mobile homes, and electronic components. Texas Tech University is located in the city, and Reese Air Force Base is nearby. Quakers settled in the area in the 1870s. Present-day Lubbock was formed from the merger of Old Lubbock and Monterey in 1890.

Lübeck [lue'-bek]

Lübeck is a city in the German state of Schleswig-Holstein, on the Trave River near the Baltic Sea. The most important Baltic seaport of the country, it has a population of 209,159 (1987 est.). The economy is heavily concentrated on port activities. Manufactures include ships, iron and steel, cement, machinery, furniture, rugs, and food products. Among the city's landmarks are the Romanesque cathedral (begun 1173) and the 13th-century Rathaus (city hall).

Founded on the site of a ruined Slavic settlement, Lübeck was destroyed by fire in 1157. The present city dates from 1159, when it was rebuilt. It developed as an important economic and cultural center for the entire Baltic area; in 1358 it was chosen as the administrative headquarters for the HANSEATIC LEAGUE. Its importance lasted until the 15th century, when the league began to crumble. Napoleon I made it part of his empire in 1806, and after 1815 it was part of the German Confederation. Lübeck later became part of the North German Confederation and, in 1871, part of the German Empire. The Elbe-Lübeck Canal, opened in 1900, brought new prosperity. In 1937, Lübeck was attached to Schleswig-Holstein. During World War II the city was heavily bombed, but much of the devastated area has been rebuilt.

Lubitsch, Ernst [loo'-bich, airnst]

Ernst Lubitsch, b. Berlin, Jan. 28, 1892, d. Nov. 30, 1947, was a German-American film director known for his sophisticated comedies of manners. He had already achieved success as an actor and director in Europe when Mary Pickford brought him to Hollywood to direct her in *Rosita* (1923); Lubitsch's subsequent silent films—*The Marriage Circle* (1924), *Forbidden Paradise* (1924), *Lady Windermere's Fan* (1925), and *So This Is Paris* (1926)—established his reputation as a master of urbane, sardonic humor. The cynical wit that was his trademark was especially evident in his sound films, particularly *Trouble in Paradise* (1932); *Ninotchka* (1939), starring Greta Garbo; and *To Be Or Not To Be* (1942), which satirized Nazism. He departed from his usual brand of humor in *The Shop around the Corner* (1940), another comedy directed at the Nazi threat.

Lublin [loo'-blin]

Lublin, an industrial and commercial city in southeastern Poland, lies about 160 km (100 mi) southeast of Warsaw. The population is 333,000 (1988 est.). Manufactures include motor vehicles, farming equipment, and food products. Lublin has a Roman

Catholic university and many museums.

Founded in the late 9th century, the city grew around a 12th-century castle and was chartered in 1317. It was already a prosperous commercial center in 1569, when the Union of Lublin (between the Kingdom of Poland and the Grand Duchy of Lithuania) was signed there. Under Austrian rule from 1795, Lublin passed to Russian Poland in 1815 and to the Polish republic in 1918. In 1941 the Germans established the Majdanek concentration camp on the outskirts of the city; the camp is now a museum.

lubrication   Lubrication is the introduction of a substance, called a lubricant, between two moving surfaces in contact in order to reduce FRICTION. This reduction of friction greatly reduces the wear of the surfaces and thus lengthens their service life. It also reduces the energy required for the motion.

Functions of a Lubricant

Although the basic function of a lubricant is to reduce friction and wear, a lubricant may also perform a number of other functions. It may carry off heat that is generated, thus functioning as a coolant. This function is its primary purpose in some machine-tool operations, especially in grinding. It may help to control corrosion by coating parts with a protective film; this protection can be enhanced by adding a corrosion inhibitor to the lubricant. It may also help remove contaminants. In metalworking this flushing action is used to remove chips of metal. In automobile engines a detergent additive removes sludge deposits from inside the engine.

Types of Lubricants

Petroleum lubricants are predominantly hydrocarbons that are refined from crude petroleum by various methods, including distillation. Solid lubricants include inorganic compounds such as graphite, molybdenum disulfide, and talc; and organic compounds such as metallic soaps and animal waxes. Synthetic lubricants have been developed to meet the more demanding requirements of modern machinery. Examples are polymer films and silicones. A lubricating grease consists of a liquid lubricant with a thickening agent added to it. A grease is sometimes preferable to an oil, because grease acts as a seal to keep the lubricant in and contaminants out, and it requires less frequent applications.

Systems for Applying Lubricants

Modern machinery requires not only a proper lubricant but also an effective system for applying it. At first, lubricants were applied by hand or by the use of an oil can. (Oil is simply a lubricant that is a liquid.) Although simple, this method was not precise. Mechanical devices called lubricators were developed to apply the lubricant. A simple type is a small container with a hole or valve placed over the part to be lubricated. This arrangement is called drop-feed lubrication. In wick-feed lubrication a wick immersed in an oil reservoir is pressed against the moving part; the wick supplies the oil by capillary action.

Bath lubrication or splash lubrication may be used for gears, chains, bearings, and other moving parts that can be partly submerged in an oil reservoir. In the bath system the part picks up oil as it dips into the reservoir and carries it to other parts along its path. The splash system increases the efficiency by attaching a special splash ring to a moving part so that the oil is splashed against other parts. In oil-mist lubrication the oil is atomized in a stream of air. Force-feed lubrication uses an oil pump to force the oil under pressure to the parts. Some parts are self-lubricating and require no external lubrication; the lubricant may be sealed in, as in sealed ball bearings, or a porous material such as porous bronze can be used so that oil impregnated in the material can penetrate to the

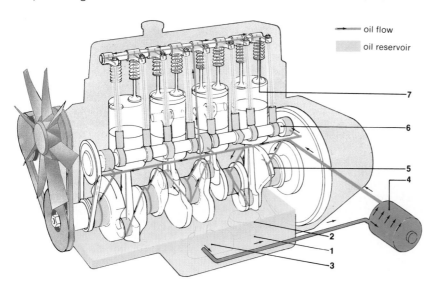

oil flow

oil reservoir

The lubrication system of an automobile engine furnishes clean, cool oil to moving parts to reduce friction and wear and to help remove heat. The oil in a sump (1) is sucked through a screened oil intake (2) into an oil pump (3). The pump forces the oil through a filter (4) to a main gallery line from which branch passages conduct it to moving parts, such as main crankshaft (5) and camshaft (6) bearings, valve rockers (7), and connecting rod bearings. Cylinder walls are sprayed with oil from rotating parts. The oil returns by gravity to the sump.

point of contact of the moving parts. In small two-stroke gasoline engines the oil is mixed in with the fuel to bring it to the moving parts inside the engine.

In automotive INTERNAL-COMBUSTION ENGINES, the engine crankcase is filled with oil. An oil pump, which is powered by the engine, forces oil from the crankcase under pressure to the cylinder block. Passages in the engine channel the oil to various moving parts, and the oil eventually drains back down in the crankcase. An oil filter is inserted in the oil circuit to filter out metal shavings, carbon deposits, and dirt. Because the filter is not completely effective, the oil eventually becomes contaminated, breaks down (decomposes), and loses its effectiveness. That is why routine auto maintenance calls for changing the oil and the oil filter periodically.

Lubumbashi [loo-boom-bah'-shee]   Lubumbashi (until 1966, Elisabethville) is the second largest city in Zaire, with a population of 543,268 (1984 est.), and the capital of Shaba (formerly Katanga) province. It lies in the southern part of the country, near the border with Zambia, in the heart of a rich copper-mining region where cobalt, zinc, and cadmium deposits are found. Lubumbashi is the administrative seat of the state-owned mining concern. A railway links it with Angola and with South Africa through Zimbabwe. A branch of the National University of Zaire is there.

Founded in 1910, Lubumbashi became the administrative capital of the Katanga region. In 1960–63 the city was the capital of the secessionist state of Katanga.

Lucan [loo'-kuhn]   Marcus Annaeus Lucanus, or Lucan, b. Nov. 3, 39, d. Apr. 30, 65, was a Latin epic poet and nephew of the philosopher Seneca. Lucan committed suicide at the age of 26, when detected in a conspiracy against the emperor Nero. His only surviving work, the *Bellum Civile,* sometimes called the *Pharsalia,* is an account of the Roman civil wars that pitted Julius Caesar against the senatorial class.

Lucas, George   The American film director, screenwriter, and producer George Lucas, b. Modesto, Calif., May 14, 1944, is best known for his trilogy of space-fantasy movies—*Star Wars* (1977), *The Empire Strikes Back* (1980), and *Return of the Jedi* (1983). After his first feature, *THX-1138* (1971), Lucas was successful with *American Graffiti* (1973), a nostalgic look at adolescence in 1962. He collaborated with filmmaker Steven Spielberg on the Indiana Jones trilogy—*Raiders of the Lost Ark* (1981), *Indiana Jones and the Temple of Doom* (1984), and *Indiana Jones and the Last Crusade* (1989).

Lucas van Leyden [loo'-kahs vahn ly'-duhn]   Lucas van Leyden, also known as Lucas Hugensz, 1494–1533, was one of the greatest engravers of the Netherlandish Renaissance. Although he began his career as a painter,

In his painting Lot and His Daughters *(c.1509), the Netherlandish Renaissance artist Lucas van Leyden uses the sinuous line of his engraving to create a dramatic composition to the night scene. (Louvre, Paris.)*

Lucas's work in this medium is completely overshadowed by his proficiency in ENGRAVING. His earliest-known engraving, *Mohammed and the Monk Sergius* (1508), displays a precocious mastery of technique and expertise in the handling of detail and pictorial space. In the so-called Circular Passion series (1510), he adopted a tondo, or round, format to depict scenes from the life of Christ in landscape settings.

The work of Albrecht Dürer inspired Lucas's two most celebrated engravings, *The Milkmaid* and *Ecce Homo* (both 1510). Lucas is thought to have learned the technique of etching from Dürer, whom he met in Antwerp in 1521, and it is certain that Lucas, after this meeting, began to engrave on copper, rather than on steel plates—a technique that allowed him to achieve the effects of engraving and etching in the same work. Among Lucas's finest paintings are *The Last Judgment* (1526; Stedelijk Museum, Leiden) and *Moses Striking the Rock* (1527; Museum of Fine Arts, Boston).

Lucca [luc'-cah]   Lucca (1981 pop., 91,097), the capital of Lucca province in the region of Tuscany, Italy, lies about 16 km (10 mi) northeast of Pisa. A market center for the nearby farming region, Lucca produces flour, olive oil, tobacco products, silk, and wine.

Of Ligurian origin, Lucca became a Roman Latin colony in 180 BC and the seat of a Lombard duchy in the 6th century. A commune from the 12th century, it was a prosperous commercial and artistic center. From 1322 to 1328 the city was ruled by the mercenary Castruccio Castracani. A period of rule by Florence and Pisa ended in 1369, when Lucca bought its independence. It remained an independent republic until taken by the French in 1799. Lucca became a principality under Napoleon's sister Élisa in 1805, an independent duchy under the Spanish infanta María Luisa in 1815, and a part of Tuscany in 1847. It was annexed to the Kingdom of Italy in 1860.

Henry Luce, an American editor and publishing magnate, founded a financial empire based on successful magazines he had established, including Time (1923), Fortune (1930), Life (1936), and Sports Illustrated (1954).

Luce, Clare Boothe [loos]   The playwright, journalist, and politician Clare Boothe Luce, b. New York City, Apr. 10, 1903, d. Oct. 9, 1987, started her career in publishing in 1930, working first on *Vogue* and then as a top editor (1931–34) of *Vanity Fair*. Following her marriage in 1935 to publishing magnate Henry R. Luce, she wrote three successful Broadway plays: *The Women* (1936; film, 1939), a satire; *Kiss the Boys Goodbye* (1938; film, 1941), a comedy; and *Margin for Error* (1940; film, 1943), an anti-Fascist melodrama. Luce served two terms (1943–47) as Republican congresswoman from Connecticut. Her appointment by President Eisenhower as U.S. ambassador to Italy (1953–57) made her the first American woman ever to hold a major diplomatic post. With the one-act play *Slam the Door Softly* (1970), Luce returned to her earlier interest in feminism.

Clare Boothe Luce, an American writer and public official, became the first American woman to hold a major diplomatic post with her appointment (1953) as ambassador to Italy. Luce, also a successful playwright and journalist, served two terms (1943–47) as a congresswoman from Connecticut.

Luce, Henry Robinson   Henry Robinson Luce, b. Apr. 3, 1898, to missionaries in Tengchow (now Penglai), China, d. Feb. 28, 1967, was the leading innovator and publisher of magazine journalism in this century. With fellow Yale graduate Briton Hadden (1898–1929), Luce

founded TIME (1923) as a weekly news summary. Its approach was adapted to radio and film under the *March of Time* title. Despite the Depression, a second magazine, *Fortune* (1930), soon became profitable. LIFE, which Luce began in 1936, grew into the most popular weekly picture magazine and was revived as a monthly in 1978 after a six-year absence. *Sports Illustrated* (1954) likewise became the foremost periodical of its type.

A fervent anti-Communist, Luce used his publications and prestige to influence U.S. policy favorably toward Chiang Kai-shek on the mainland of China and later on Taiwan. Luce was influential in Republican party policy and in drafting Eisenhower as a presidential candidate.

Luce, Stephen B.   Stephen Bleecker Luce, b. Albany, N.Y., Mar. 25, 1827, d. July 28, 1917, an American naval officer, inspired the establishment of the Naval War College at Newport, R.I. While teaching at the Naval Academy at Newport during the Civil War, he wrote *Seamanship* (1863), which became a standard text. After the war Luce lobbied for improved training of enlisted men, higher standards for the merchant marine, and a postgraduate college for naval officers. On Oct. 6, 1884, the secretary of the navy created the Naval War College and appointed Luce its first president. He retired as a rear admiral in 1889.

Lucerne [loo-surn']   Lucerne (German: Luzern), the capital of the Swiss canton of Lucerne, lies about 40 km (25 mi) southwest of Zurich on the Reuss River at Lake Lucerne. The city is an important tourist resort and textile center. The population is 59,574 (1988 est.). Notable structures include the Hofkirche (cathedral; 8th century), the town hall (built 1601–06), Am Rhyn House (1617), and the Mariahilf Church (1676–81). An international music festival is an annual summer event.

Lucerne was settled around the monastery of Saint Leodegar in the 8th century. It flourished as a trade center under Habsburg rule (1291–1332) and then joined the Swiss Confederation. It led the Catholic cantons of Switzerland in the civil wars of the Reformation (1529–31) and the *Sonderbund* (1847) and served (1798–1803) as the capital of the Helvetic Republic.

Lucerne, Lake Lake Lucerne (German: Vierwaldstätter See) is a mountain-ringed lake in central Switzerland. At an altitude of 434 m (1,424 ft), the lake is 39 km (24 mi) long and 3 km (2 mi) wide. Its outlet and principal tributary is the Reuss River. The lake is one of Switzerland's most popular resort areas.

Luchow see HEFEI

Lucian [loo'-shuhn] Lucian, *c*.120–*c*.180, was a Greek satirist of the Roman period who worked in a variety of genres. Typical of Lucian's innovative satirical works are the *Dialogues of the Gods* and *Dialogues of the Dead,* in which he ridicules Greek philosophy, religion, and mythology and pictures humankind as hypocritical and foolish. In the dialogue *Timon* the characters include an Athenian misanthrope, Zeus, Wealth, and Poverty. It is not clear that Lucian's satire, bitter as it is, reflects a deep-seated skepticism on his part; his objective may have been literary: to attract and startle his readers. In any case, he is often considered the forerunner of such biting, latter-day satirists as Swift and Voltaire.

Lucifer see SATAN

lucite see PLASTICS

Luckman, Sid Hall of Fame football player Sidney Luckman, b. Brooklyn, N.Y., Nov. 21, 1916, played quarterback when he starred both in college (Columbia, 1935–39) and as a professional in the National Football League (Chicago Bears, 1939–50). Considered one of the NFL's greatest passers, Luckman completed 904 of 1,744 passes for 14,683 yd and 139 touchdowns while leading the Bears to four NFL titles. He was the NFL's MVP in 1943, first-team All-League five times, and the leader in average gain per pass attempt seven times (unapproached). Luckman still shares the NFL record of seven touchdown passes thrown in a single game.

Lucknow [luhk'-now] Lucknow is the capital of Uttar Pradesh state, northern India. Situated on the Upper Ganges Plain, it is about 420 km (260 mi) southeast of New Delhi. The population is 895,721 (1981). Industries include food processing, sugar refining, distilling, cotton weaving, handicrafts, and paper milling. An administrative and cultural center, Lucknow is the site of Lucknow University, founded in 1921. Points of interest include the Great Imambara, a courthouse (1784); the Husainabad Imambara (1837), which contains several tombs and a mosque; and the State Museum (1863).

The legendary founder of Lucknow was Lakshman, famous from the RAMAYANA epic. In the 13th century the sheikhs of Bijnor built a fortress on the site. Modern Lucknow, however, is largely the creation of the nawabs of Oudh, who ruled from 1724 to 1856. During the Indian Mutiny, Lucknow was besieged for 12 weeks (June–November 1857) by Indian rebels. By the time it was relieved about 500 British had been killed.

Lucretia [loo-kree'-shuh] In Roman legend Lucretia was a virtuous and beautiful Roman matron, whose rape by Sextus, son of TARQUINIUS SUPERBUS, led to the overthrow of the Tarquin dynasty in Rome and the establishment of a republic (traditionally 509 BC). Lucretia made her husband and father vow to avenge her dishonor before she committed suicide. The story is the subject of William Shakespeare's *Rape of Lucrece.*

Lucretius [loo-kree'-shuhs] Titus Lucretius Carus, *c*.95–55 BC, Rome's most distinguished philosopher-poet, achieved his place in Latin literature on the basis of one work, *De Rerum Natura (On the Nature of Things),* a didactic poem in dactylic hexameter comprising six books. This made available to a Latin audience the ideas of the Greek philosopher Epicurus.

The object of Epicureanism was pleasure, but pleasure of an austere kind involving primarily freedom from fear of the gods and of an afterlife. According to Epicurus, although the gods did exist they had no concern for humans, either to punish or to reward them. Furthermore, because the soul was mortal, dying with the body, to fear the torments of an afterlife was unnecessary.

A good part of *De Rerum Natura* deals with the physical nature of the universe, which Lucretius explained in terms that approximate modern atomic theory and that were based on the theories of DEMOCRITUS. The purpose of his physical arguments, however, is ethical: to present a universe explicable in scientific terms and so banish fear of the unknown and free people's minds from superstition.

Lucullus, Lucius Licinius [loo-kuhl'-uhs, loo'-shuhs ly-sin'-ee-uhs] A leading Roman noble, Lucius Licinius Lucullus, *c*.117–56 BC, began his political career in 88 or 87 BC as quaestor under Lucius Cornelius SULLA. Elected consul in 74, Lucullus obtained command in the renewed war against MITHRADATES VI of Pontus. Although he occupied much of Pontus and invaded Armenia, taking its capital in 69, a series of mutinies among his troops weakened his political position. He also came under attack from powerful interests in Rome whose hopes of profit from the Asian conquests had been frustrated by Lucullus's judicious handling of financial matters. POMPEY THE GREAT began to intrigue for the Asian command, and in 66 finally received it. With CATO THE YOUNGER, and for a while with Marcus CRASSUS, Lucullus led the opposition to Pompey until the latter proved too powerful. After 59 BC he retired to a life of self-indulgent luxury.

Lüda (Lü-ta) [lue-dah] Lüda (1988 est. pop., 2,280,-000), an autonomous subprovincial municipality, occupies the tip of the Liaodong Peninsula in Liaoning province, China. The component cities of Lüda are LÜSHUN and DALIEN, once known as Port Arthur and Dairen, respectively. Lüda serves as an ice-free port for southern Manchuria and is a leading industrial center.

Luddites [luhd'-yts] To protest unemployment caused by the Industrial Revolution in the early 19th century, English workers known as Luddites resorted to a campaign of breaking machinery, especially knitting machines. Their name probably came from a legendary boy named Ludlam, who, to spite his father, broke a knitting frame. The Luddites revived the name by signing their proclamations "General Ludd," "King Ludd," or "Ned Ludd." The movement began in the hosiery and lace industries around Nottingham in 1811 and spread to the wool and cotton mills of Yorkshire and Lancashire. The government dealt harshly with the Luddites—14 were hanged in January 1813 in York. Although sporadic outbreaks of violence continued until 1816, the movement soon died out.

Ludendorff, Erich [loo-den-dorf, ay'-rik] Erich Friedrich Wilhelm Ludendorff, b. Apr. 9, 1865, d. Dec. 20, 1937, was a German general in WORLD WAR I. A career officer in the elite Prussian general staff, he distinguished himself in the opening days of the war by capturing the Belgian fortress-city of Liège. He was thereupon made chief of staff to Gen. Paul von HINDENBURG. Stunning victories at Tannenberg and the Masurian Lakes in the late summer of 1914 saved the eastern front and made the two generals national heroes.

In 1916, Emperor William II gave Hindenburg and Ludendorff virtually dictatorial control of the German supreme command. They consolidated the German lines on the stalemated western front and in 1917 commenced unrestricted submarine warfare, which resulted in the entry of the United States into the war against Germany. When their last great offensive failed in 1918, Hindenburg and Ludendorff insisted on an armistice. It was finally granted on Nov. 11, 1918, but on terms that caused Ludendorff to resign in protest.

In 1923, Ludendorff participated in Adolf HITLER's abortive MUNICH PUTSCH. He was a National Socialist member of the Reichstag (1924–1928), but played no part in the Third Reich.

Ludlow, Roger Roger Ludlow, b. 1590, d. after 1664, was one of the founders of colonial Connecticut. A director of the Massachusetts Bay Company, he left England for Massachusetts in 1630. He served (1634) briefly as deputy governor there, and in 1635 he joined in the organization of a new colony on the Connecticut River. In 1636, Ludlow presided over Connecticut's first court (held at Windsor), and in 1639 he founded the town of Fairfield, on Long Island Sound. He is credited with drafting the Fundamental Orders, a constitution adopted in January 1638 or 1639, that remained the basis of Connecticut's government until 1818, and Ludlow's Code, or the Code of 1650, a compilation of the colony's laws. In 1654, Ludlow went to Ireland in the service of the Cromwellian government and remained there, probably until his death.

Ludwig, Christa Christa Ludwig, a mezzo-soprano, b. Berlin, Mar. 16, 1928, grew up backstage in opera houses where her parents were singing. She has been a star of the Vienna Opera since 1955 and of the Metropolitan Opera since 1959. Her wide vocal range, from contralto to dramatic soprano, encompasses a varied repertoire, from soubrette (a light, comic role) to Wagnerian music drama. Among her roles are Kundry in *Parsifal*, Octavian in *Der Rosenkavalier,* and Cherubino in *The Marriage of Figaro.*

Ludwig for German kings of this name, see LOUIS

Lug In ancient Celtic mythology Lug was a major divinity, often identified with the Roman god MERCURY. According to Irish legend, he was a member of the Tuatha Dé Danann (people of the Goddess Danann), a divine race from which the Irish people are descended. He ensured the triumph of the Tuatha over their rivals, the Fomoire, by slaying Balor, the Fomoire chief, who was his own grandfather.

Lugano, Lake [loo-gah'-noh] Lake Lugano lies astride the border of Ticino canton, Switzerland, and the Lombardy region of Italy. Located in the Alps at an altitude of 271 m (889 ft), it is 35 km (22 mi) long, approximately 3 km (2 mi) wide, and reaches a maximum depth of 288 m (945 ft). Fed by mountain streams, it is drained by the Tresa River into Lake MAGGIORE.

Lugard, Frederick John Dealtry Lugard, 1st Baron [lou-gard'] The British colonial administrator Frederick Lugard, b. Jan. 22, 1858, d. Apr. 11, 1945, played an important role in opening Africa to European influence. After briefly attending the Royal Military College, Sandhurst, he served as an army officer in India, Afghanistan, the Sudan, Burma, and Nyasaland (now Malawi). In 1889 he entered the service of the Imperial British East Africa Company. He not only secured British supremacy in Uganda but also helped persuade the British government to declare Uganda a protectorate in 1894.

In 1900, Lugard was appointed high commissioner of Northern Nigeria, where he introduced a system of indirect rule through traditional tribal rulers. Between 1907 and 1912 he served as governor of Hong Kong, but in 1912 he returned to Nigeria, where he combined Northern and Southern Nigeria into a single country (1914), staying as governor-general until 1919. He was made Baron Lugard of Abinger in 1928.

luge   A luge is a small sled for one or two riders used for a type of TOBOGGANING in recreational and competitive settings. Its main portion, or shell, is made of fiberglass and wood; the two runners are made of fiberglass, wood, plastic, and steel. Riders are usually supine, feet first. Steering is accomplished with subtle movements of the body and feet. In competition, luge speeds can exceed 97 km/h (60 mph). The first European lugeing championship was held in 1914. A Winter Olympics sport since 1964 (one- and two-man and one-woman), luge is governed worldwide by the Fédération Internationale de Luge de Course (founded 1957).

Lugosi, Bela   [luh-gohs'-see, bel'-uh]   A respected Hungarian stage actor who made a hit in Hollywood as the Transylvanian vampire Count Dracula in the film *Dracula* (1931) after creating the role on Broadway (1927), Bela Lugosi, b. Béla Blaskó, Oct. 20, 1882, d. Aug. 16, 1956, failed through his imperfect command of English to utilize his full range and became typecast in cheap horror films. He was at his best in *White Zombie* (1932), *The Black Cat* (1934), *Son of Frankenstein* (1939), and *Abbott and Costello Meet Frankenstein* (1948).

Bela Lugosi stares malevolently while abducting the heroine in the classic horror film Dracula *(1931). Because of his vivid performance, the Hungarian-born actor was typecast in a series of horror films.*

Luisetti, Hank   Angelo "Hank" Luisetti, b. San Francisco, Calif., June 16, 1916, changed the character of basketball in the 1930s when he popularized the one-handed jump-shot, which is now standard. He played for Stanford University, which became a powerhouse and broke with the old style of setting up players for two-handed shots, a time-consuming procedure. Luisetti, who was 1 m 90.5 cm (6 ft 3 in) tall, led Stanford to a stunning upset of Long Island University in December 1936, stopping LIU's 43-game winning streak. He was elected to the Naismith Memorial Basketball Hall of Fame in 1959.

Lukács, György   [loo'-kahch]   György Lukács, b. Apr. 13, 1885, d. June 4, 1971, was a Hungarian Marxist philosopher, literary critic, and writer. His earliest works—such as *The Soul and the Forms* (1910; Eng. trans., 1978) and *The Theory of the Novel* (1920; Eng. trans., 1971)—were heavily influenced by sociologist Max WEBER as well as Karl Marx.

After moving to Vienna, Lukács wrote his major reevaluation of Marxism, *History of Class Consciousness* (1923; Eng. trans., 1971), and was promptly labeled a revisionist. After Hitler's rise to power in 1933 he lived in Moscow, where he worked at the Marx-Engels Institute and at the Institute of Philosophy of the Soviet Academy of Sciences. Following World War II, Lukács returned to Hungary to become a professor of philosophy and aesthetics in Budapest. His involvement in the revolution of 1956 pushed him into the background, but in 1965 he was rehabilitated.

György Lukács, a Hungarian philosopher and critic, sought to define a humanistic Marxist aesthetic in his essays and critical studies. His works, including History of Class Consciousness *(1923), were viewed with suspicion by some Marxists.*

Luke, Gospel According to   The Gospel According to Luke is the third book of the New Testament of the BIBLE. Because of its similarities to the Gospels According to Mark and Matthew, it is classified with them as the synoptic Gospels. Although the Gospel was traditionally ascribed to Luke, a companion of Paul (Philem. 24; 2 Tim. 4:11), most modern scholars think that it was written between AD 80 and 90 by a Gentile Christian who wrote the ACTS OF THE APOSTLES as a sequel. The Gospel characteristically teaches a message of universal salvation addressed to all people, not only to the Jews.

Luke's Gospel can be divided into five major sections: a prologue (1:1–4); infancy narrative (1:5–2:52); ministry in Galilee (3:1–9:50); journey to Jerusalem (9:51–21:38); and the passion and resurrection (22:1–24:53). The conclusion sets the scene for the spread of the Christian word, as recounted in the Acts.

In common with the other Gospels, Luke relates the principal events of Christ's public life. Passages peculiar to Luke include the parables of the good Samaritan (10:25–37) and the prodigal son (15:11–32), and Christ's words to the women of Jerusalem and to the good thief (23:27–31, 43). Commentators point out the prominence given to women. Examples include the story of Elizabeth (1:5–66), Mary's part in the infancy narrative (1:5–2:52), and the story of the widow of Naim (7:11–17). Luke also contains three hymns that have become an important part of liturgy: the Magnificat (1:46–55), the Benedictus (1:68–79), and the Nunc Dimittis (2:29–32).

Luke, Saint Saint Luke, traditionally considered to be the author of the third Gospel and the Acts of the Apostles, was a companion and fellow worker of Saint PAUL. According to Colossians 4:11–14, he was a Gentile and a physician. Later legend made him an artist, and during the Middle Ages the picture of the Virgin Mary in Santa Maria Maggiore, Rome, was ascribed to him. He is the patron saint of physicians and artists. Feast day: Oct. 18.

Luks, George [looks] A member of the Ashcan school, George Luks, b. Williamsport, Pa., Aug. 13, 1867, d. Oct. 29, 1933, was an American painter and graphic artist noted for his vigorous studies of New York City life. He worked as a newspaper illustrator, first for the Philadelphia *Press* and in 1896 as a cartoonist for the New York *World*.

Luks began painting scenes of urban life, specializing in lively figure and character studies in a vigorous style inspired partly by the work of Frans Hals, for example, *The Spielers* (1905; Addison Gallery of American Art, Phillips Academy, Andover, Mass.). He also produced a number of fine portraits, including *Otis Skinner as Col. Bridau in "The Honor of the Family"* (1919; The Phillips Collection, Washington, D.C.).

Lull, Raymond Raymond Lull (also called Llull or Lully), *c.*1235–1316, was a Catalan poet, philosopher, and Christian mystic. At the age of 30 he claimed to have a vision of Christ crucified. He abandoned his life at the court of Majorca and dedicated himself to the conversion of Muslims in North Africa after studying Arabic, Oriental mysticism, theology, and philosophy.

The author of almost 300 works, Lull was important in the development of the Catalan language. His interest in finding a common ground between Christianity, Islam, and Judaism made him one of the earliest ecumenists. Lull's principal work, *Ars magna* (The Great Art, 1305–08), was a philosophic defense of Christianity against the teachings of AVERROËS.

Jean Baptiste Lully was one of the most influential figures in the development of opera in France. Lully, who controlled French operatic production during the latter half of the 17th century, introduced the "French overture," influenced the form of French recitative, and produced a brilliant body of compositions.

Lully, Jean Baptiste [lue-lee'] Although Italian by birth, Jean Baptiste Lully, b. Nov. 28, 1632, d. Mar. 22, 1687, became one of the most significant French composers in history. In 1652 he entered the service of the 14-year-old Louis XIV to play the violin and later to compose court ballets and dance in them. He also organized Les Petits-Violons du Roi, which became the king's personal orchestra. Through musical and managerial talent, enormous ambition, and shrewdness, Lully rose quickly in position and authority. Between 1663 and 1671 he collaborated with Molière and produced comic masterpieces such as *Le Bourgeois Gentilhomme*. In 1672, having been given almost sole authority to develop French opera, he turned from ballet to the *tragédie-lyrique*, a term Lully applied to all his operas. He produced, in collaboration with his librettist Quinault, 20 operas in 14 years. Lully developed unprecedented standards of performance that became a model for all of Europe. He also raised the quality of declaiming French to music, and he reshaped traditional dry recitative to an orchestrally accompanied style. In 1687, while conducting a concert and beating time with a heavy baton, he accidentally struck his foot; the resulting gangrene caused his death.

---

lumbago [luhm-bay'-goh] Lumbago is a general term for low backache characterized by pain and tenderness originating in the fibromuscular tissue. The pain may be due to local inflammations in the spine, its ligaments, or its muscles, or it may be reflected to the back in disorders of the pelvic or abdominal organs. One common cause of lumbago is having legs of unequal length; even the smallest discrepancy in length causes the back muscles to work harder. If such a person is employed in an occupation that requires long periods of standing, the back muscles may become excessively strained and go into a painful spastic condition. Lumbago is common in women and is usually due to gynecologic causes. Osteoporosis, a degeneration of bone that may involve the spine, may also be a cause of lumbago in postmenopausal women and in very old people of either sex.

lumber   Lumber is timber that is cut from forests and prepared for use in the construction of buildings, furniture, and a wide variety of other products. More than 30 percent of the world's commercial timberland is in the USSR, and about 18 percent is in North America. Both regions predominate in softwoods, those relatively nonporous woods that are derived from conifers, or cone-bearing TREES. Some countries, such as Japan, support a lumber industry largely dependent on softwoods imported from the United States, Canada, and the USSR. Others, such as India, export valuable hardwoods, those usually derived from deciduous trees that lose their leaves in autumn. These include rosewood, mahogany, sandalwood, ebony, and teak. Softwood lumber, which constitutes 80 percent of U.S. production, is used mostly for building houses; hardwood lumber is used primarily for furniture and floors (see also WOOD).

Development of the Lumber Industry

The first steam-powered sawmill, built in 1663 in London, caused riots among sawyers who feared that such a machine would deprive them of jobs. Steam-powered sawmills did not come into general use until the early 1800s. Most early sawmills were water powered and situated on rivers and streams where logs could easily be floated or rafted.

The U.S. lumber industry began in New England, and by 1675 there were over 50 water-powered sawmills—called "gang mills" after the gang saws they used—in northern Massachusetts, New Hampshire, and Maine, producing barrel staves and board lumber. The best Northeastern white pines were not sawed but were marked by the British as property of the king and were used for ships' masts.

Timbering in the South began later, and after independence the U.S. Navy reserved much of the southern forest lands for ship lumber.

After the Civil War, the lumber industry shifted to the lake states of Michigan, Wisconsin, and Minnesota. From 1870 to 1900 these states led the nation in lumber production. The huge tracts of white pine found in the lake states, however, were eventually logged over and converted to farmland. In addition, despite the considerable forests that remained unlogged, the lake states could be

Walnut, a native American and European hardwood timber, is highly valued for its hardness, strength, elasticity, and velvety surfce. It is used in making furniture, cabinets, and gun stocks. Pine is a widely distributed softwood timber. Although low in strength and elasticity, its availability, smooth surface, and ability to take paints and varnishes well have led to its extensive use in paneling, cabinetmaking, and construction. Rosewood is an important hardwood timber from tropical countries. It has an attractive combination of hardness, elasticity, strength, and extremely high resistance to decay. Uses include the manufacture of fine furniture, ships, and handles for tools. Lime, a smooth, soft, and lightweight hardwood timber, is found in Europe and America; it is of little commercial value.

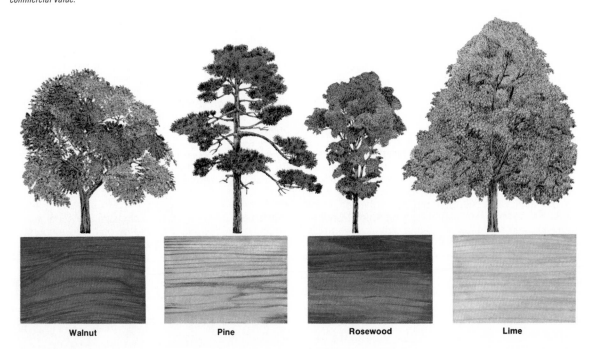

Walnut   Pine   Rosewood   Lime

Beech　　**Teak**　　**Oak**　　**Spruce**

(Above) *Beech is a hardwood timber from northern temperate regions. The wood, which is of even texture, dense, strong, and hard, is used in the manufacture of underwater piles, chairs, and furniture. Teak is a hardwood timber from Burma and neighboring countries. Noted for its hardness, dimensional stability, strength, resistance to decay, and pleasing appearance, it is used in making fine furniture, cabinets, and interior trim. Oak is among the world's most important timbers. A widespread hardwood that is tough, elastic, and decay resistant, it is widely used for shipbuilding, flooring, interior woodwork, and furniture. Spruce, a major softwood timber of Europe and North America, is used mainly as a source of pulpwood in the manufacture of paper. Small amounts are used for construction joists and boxes. (Below) Cedar, a widely used softwood, is grown in Europe and the Americas. Although low in strength and elasticity, it is prized for its high resistance to insects and decay and is used in making posts, lawn furniture, shingles, and storage chests. Mahogany, a hardwood timber from tropical America, is one of the most valuable of woods. An excellent combination of strength, toughness, durability, and luster make it an ideal lumber for use in high-quality cabinets, furniture, and ships. Fir is one of the most valuable softwood timbers in the Americas. Hard, strong, and available in long lengths, it is used for heavy structures, poles, fences, and plywood. Ash is a hardwood native to North America and Europe. Outstanding in strength, toughness, and elasticity, it is used mainly for sports equipment and tool handles.*

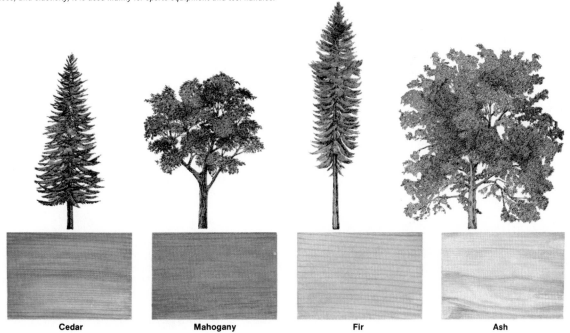

Cedar　　**Mahogany**　　**Fir**　　**Ash**

logged only on a seasonal basis, with cutting done in the fall and early winter, hauling during the winter, and transportation to mills in the spring when the rivers were at their fullest.

In the South forests could be harvested and logs moved to mills almost year-round, and huge, fast-growing stands of timber were available for conversion to lumber. By 1930, however, the best timber had been cut, and the lumber industry shifted to the West. Today the major lumber-producing states are Oregon, California, Washington, and Idaho.

The development of the lumber industry in Canada closely parallels that of the United States. The first Canadian lumber was exported to France in 1653 in the form of timbers up to 9 m (30 ft) long, hand hewed and squared with a broadax.

Important U.S. Timber Species

The major U.S. timber species now used for lumber are Douglas fir, loblolly and other southern pines, ponderosa pine, fir, hemlock, and spruce. These and other softwoods account for nearly two-thirds of the U.S. production.

In the West, Douglas fir, ponderosa pine, sugar pine, redwood, fir, cedar, hemlock, and spruce are the primary timber species supplied to sawmills. In the South, loblolly pine, longleaf pine, shortleaf pine, and slash pine are used extensively for lumber. Southern hardwoods, such

As logs are drawn along a conveyor, they pass through a debarking machine before reaching the first saws. The machine removes bark with scraping blades or high-pressure jets of water.

as the sweet gum, tupelo, and bald cypress, are also important lumber species. In the lake states, maple, beech, birch, elm, ash, cottonwood, and aspen are the dominant lumber species. Many of the more valuable hardwoods, such as cherry, yellow poplar, hickory, and walnut are in relatively short supply.

The Lumber-Making Process

In the forest trees are cut with large power saws, loaded onto trucks, and transported to sawmills. The old method of floating logs to the mill is now impractical for the most part and has been replaced by truck and rail transportation. Many of the old logging rivers have been dammed to produce hydroelectric power. In addition many of the forests near watercourses were logged first, forcing modern loggers to shift to forests that are not near navigable rivers and streams.

Because rafting is no longer used, most of today's lumber mills do not have millponds for log storage. Instead, logs delivered by truck and rail are stacked in yards, or decks, outside the mill, where they are usually sprayed with water to prevent insect damage. Once inside the sawmill, logs are processed into board.

A machine first strips the bark from the wood either by grinding or by high-pressure water jets. Stripped logs go to a headsaw where they are squared. Whenever possible, the slabs removed in this process are trimmed and sawed into boards. The squared log, called a cant, is then sent through a series of saws to be cut into boards of desired thickness. These boards are trimmed to desired length and width and placed on a moving belt, called a green chain, to be sorted for later drying.

Boards are dried either in open-air sheds or in large ovens called KILNS. The rough surfaces are smoothed by planing or sanding, and smoothed boards are then ready to be transported to markets. Sawmills also produce waste products in the form of sawdust, trimmings, and slabs. These manufacturing residues are reused to make PAPER, particle board, hardboard, and chipboard. These last three products are sheets of wood chips or particles of varying sizes that are bonded together by glue or resins and molded into large sheets.

See also: FORESTS AND FORESTRY.

lumen [loo'-men]   In photometry, the lumen is the SI unit of luminous flux, the rate at which radiant energy reaches a surface. It is defined as the flux emitted by a uniform point source of one candela intensity in a cone having a solid angle of one steradian.

Lumet, Sidney   Sidney Lumet, b. Philadelphia, June 25, 1924, is one of several prominent television directors who made the transition to films in the 1950s. Lumet's first film, *Twelve Angry Men* (1957), was a successful version of a play he had directed for television, and his subsequent films included *A View from the Bridge* (1961), *Long Day's Journey into Night* (1962), *Fail Safe*

(1964), and *The Pawnbroker* (1965).

Later, Lumet departed from the rough look and small-scale concentration of such work for the greater polish and bigger budgets of *The Anderson Tapes* (1971), *Serpico* (1974), *Murder on the Orient Express* (1974), and, with livelier results, *Dog Day Afternoon* (1975) and *Network* (1976). Lumet has comfortably worked in several different genres, directing slick entertainment vehicles such as *The Wiz* (1978), *Deathtrap* (1981), and *The Morning After* (1986), while also exploring social issues in such films as *Prince of the City* (1981), *The Verdict* (1982), and *Running on Empty* (1988).

Lumière, Louis and Auguste [loo-mee-air']   Louis Jean Lumière, b. Oct. 5, 1864, d. June 6, 1948, and Auguste Marie Lumière, b. Oct. 19, 1862, d. Apr. 10, 1954, were French inventors of an early motion-picture projector and pioneer filmmakers. The two brothers took over management of their father's photographic supply factory in Lyons in 1893. There Louis developed (1895) the Cinématographe, a single machine that functioned both as camera and projector. Its unique feature was a system of claws that moved the film mechanically but held each frame long enough for viewers to perceive the image.

The Cinématographe was first demonstrated before a paying audience in Paris on Dec. 28, 1895, with the showing of 10 of the brothers' films, including *Workers Leaving a Factory* and a comic sequence, *The Sprinkler Sprinkled*. The public exhibition marked the beginning of cinema history. In the next few years the Lumières continued to produce short, 2-minute films that were records of everyday life; they also made documentaries, newsreels, and a historical film, *The Life and Passion of Jesus Christ* (1897).

luminescence   Luminescence is the emission of light by relatively cold materials. It is distinct from incandescence, in which materials emit light as a result of their high temperatures. Luminescence includes the phenomena of FLUORESCENCE (prompt radiation-stimulated emission of light) and PHOSPHORESCENCE (radiation-stimulated emission of light that continues to occur for prolonged periods after the stimulation is removed).

Luminescent emission arises from atoms and molecules that have been energized in some manner without appreciably heating the bulk material, and that release the excess energy in the form of light. Excitation can be caused by absorption of visible light, ultraviolet radiation, X rays, and gamma rays, by collision with charged particles, by chemical reactions, and by other means.

The earliest observed forms of luminescence were the natural phenomena of ELECTROLUMINESCENCE, such as the AURORAS, and BIOLUMINESCENCE, the light produced by fireflies, glowworms, and many varieties of marine life. Bioluminescence is a form of chemiluminescence, which is the emission of light as a result of a chemical reaction.

Many elements, chemical compounds, and minerals can demonstrate fluorescence. NEON and other gases will fluoresce when a beam of electrons is passed through them. Solid material that will fluoresce—such as the coatings of fluorescent light tubes and television picture tubes—are known as PHOSPHORS. Certain minerals fluoresce in vivid colors when irradiated.

Luminism   A recent term of art historians, coined by John I. H. Baur in 1954, *Luminism* describes the work of a group of American landscape painters active between 1848 and 1876. Their spacious compositions, most of which emphasize the horizontal and infinite aspects of nature, usually portray the coastal wetlands and rocky shorelines of New England and the frontier wilderness of North, and later of South, America. A suffused, incandescent light floods their vistas, which symbolize a reasoned awareness of, and faith in, the physical grandeur and moral potential of the American continent. In exploring the effects of light, the Luminists made full use of new, intense cadmium pigments.

The Luminists include Fitz Hugh LANE (their first representative), Frederick Edwin CHURCH, John Frederick KENSETT, Martin Johnson Heade, and Sanford Gifford. Some of these painters, such as Church and Kensett, are also included in the HUDSON RIVER SCHOOL, the culmination of which is now seen to be Luminism.

lumpy jaw   SEE FUNGUS DISEASES

Lumumba, Patrice [loo-moom'-bah]   Patrice Emergy Lumumba, b. July 2, 1925, d. early 1961, the first prime minister of the independent Democratic Republic of the Congo (now Zaire), was born in Kasai province in what was then the Belgian Congo. Originally pro-Belgian in politics, Lumumba became an increasingly militant nationalist; in 1958 he helped to form the Congolese National Movement, aiming at an independent and uni-

Although his tenure as the first prime minister of the independent Republic of the Congo was brief (June–September 1960), Patrice Lumumba achieved enduring fame for his defiance of the West in seeking armed suppression of the secession of Katanga. Dismissed from office, he was subsequently murdered in Katanga.

tary Congolese state. Lumumba participated in the 1960 Belgo-Congolese conference at Brussels that led to independence, and in June 1960 he was appointed prime minister by President Joseph KASAVUBU.

The Congo was immediately engulfed in crisis when Moise Kapenda TSHOMBE launched a Belgian-backed separatist movement in Katanga province (now Shaba). Lumumba was determined to crush the secession. On Sept. 5, 1960, however, he was dismissed from office by Kasavubu, and within days the army leader Col. Joseph Mobutu (later MOBUTU SESE SEKO) seized power.

Still claiming to head the government, Lumumba was captured by Kasavubu's troops on December 2. He was turned over to the Katanga regime, which announced on Feb. 13, 1961, that he had been killed by villagers; his supporters believed that the Congolese government was responsible for his murder.

Luna (spacecraft) Luna, a series of Soviet space probes (see SPACE EXPLORATION) developed for the exploration of the Moon, produced the first probes to pass near, to impact, and to photograph the Earth's only natural satellite, and the first spacecraft to land on, to orbit around, and to automatically return samples from this celestial object. The first three achievements were accomplished in 1959 by *Lunas 1, 2,* and *3.* Each of these spacecraft weighed about 275 kg (600 lb).

A series of heavier Luna probes, each weighing about 900 kg (2,000 lb), began in 1963 with the goal of a hard but survivable landing on the Moon. After an agonizing series of failures and near misses, *Luna 9* made a landing on Feb. 3, 1966, and several television images of the surface were sent back to the Earth. *Luna 10* was placed into orbit around the Moon in 1966, becoming the first artificial lunar satellite. The newest and heaviest versions of Luna, each weighing about 4,500 kg (10,000 lb), began flight-testing in 1969, but a long series of booster and spacecraft failures plagued this program. The heavy spacecraft were designed for particular tasks: *Lunas 16, 20,* and *24* picked up samples of lunar soil and returned them to the Earth; *Lunas 17* and *21* carried LUNOKHOD "moon jeeps" that traversed the Moon's surface under remote control; and *Lunas 19* and *22* carried out extended lunar orbital surveys.

Lunar Excursion Module The Lunar Excursion Module (LEM), better known as the Lunar Module (LM), was the transport vehicle used in the APOLLO PROGRAM to ferry two astronauts between the command module in lunar orbit and the surface of the Moon. The lunar-orbit rendezvous eliminated the need to land the entire Apollo spacecraft on the Moon on a direct ascent flight path from Earth orbit, and thus made possible a lighter load of fuel. Nine LMs were flown during the Apollo program, and six landed on the Moon.

The two-stage LM was designed and built by the Grumman Aircraft Engineering Corporation under a $1.6-billion contract with the National Aeronautics and

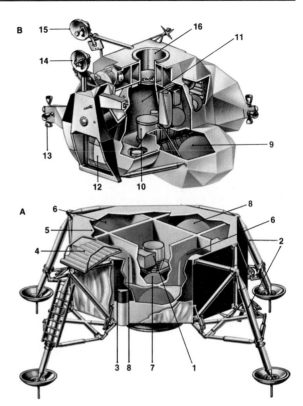

The Apollo lunar excursion module comprised two sections. The descent stage (A) contained the main engine (1), landing gear (2), scientific equipment bay (3), egress platform (4), and water (5), fuel (6), oxygen (7), and oxidizer (8) tanks. The ascent stage (B) contained a pressurized two-man cabin (11), ascent engine (10), fuel tank (9), forward hatch (12) for lunar egress and ingress, thruster assembly (13), rendezvous radar antenna (14), steerable radio antenna (15), and overhead hatch and tunnel (16) to the command module.

Space Administration. Because little was known about the lunar surface when construction began in 1962, engineers designed the cantilever landing gear—consisting of four sets of legs, each ending in a dish-shaped pod—so that the vehicle could land safely and remain upright on a variety of surfaces. With its legs extended, the LM was 7 m (23 ft) high and 4.3 m (14 ft) across. The descent stage, which stood slightly more than 3 m (10 ft) high, had an engine whose thrust could be controlled within a range of 44,500 to 4,600 newtons (4,530 to 475 kg, or 10,000 to 1,050 lb). To ensure a soft landing, the engine was fired continuously during descent from lunar orbit. The crew rode in the ascent stage. Both descent and ascent were made with the aid of a sophisticated guidance and navigation system that included a radar altimeter.

At launch, the LM was carried atop the third stage of a Saturn V rocket. As the vehicle system left Earth orbit on a translunar trajectory, the pilot of the Apollo Command and Service Module turned the spacecraft around and docked it nose to nose with the LM. In lunar orbit, two crew members transferred from the Apollo Command Module to the LM ascent stage through a docking tunnel, undocked the LM, and landed on the Moon. To leave the Moon, the crew fired the ascent-stage engine (using the descent stage as a launch platform), ascended to lunar orbit, and docked with the Apollo spacecraft. The descent stage was left on the Moon and the ascent stage was jettisoned in lunar orbit.

Lunar Orbiter   The Lunar Orbiter program was a series of five U.S. spacecraft used for a broad-scale lunar mapping effort, in contrast to the preceding RANGER spacecraft, which zeroed in on specific targets on their way to crash landings. The five Orbiter missions, all of them successful, were launched at approximately three-month intervals from Aug. 10, 1966, through Aug. 1, 1967.

The general area of interest for Apollo (see APOLLO PROGRAM) landing sites was a rectangle extending 5° north and south of the lunar equator and 45° east and west of the lunar prime (essentially earth-centered) meridian. *Lunar Orbiter 1* was launched to photograph the southern part of the rectangle, while *Lunar Orbiter 2* was concerned with the northern half. A dozen promising Apollo landing sites were selected from these batches of images, and the third probe in the series was used for additional photos of the chosen sites. *Lunar Orbiter 4* was placed in a higher-altitude orbit around the Moon, giving wider coverage while still showing the surface from a near-vertical aspect that cannot be seen from Earth except near the center of the lunar disk. *Lunar Orbiter 5* was also used to complete Apollo site studies, but the success of the four previous Lunar Orbiters enabled much of the photography of the fifth mission to be devoted to targets of primarily scientific interest. Altogether, 95 percent of the Moon's surface was photographed by the Lunar Orbiters.

Some of the photos were also used to help pinpoint the locations of some of the unmanned SURVEYOR landing craft, and *Lunar Orbiters 1* and *5* took pictures of the Earth. The Orbiters also discovered mascons (mass concentrations) on the Moon.

Lunar Rover   The Lunar Rover, or Lunar Roving Vehicle, was a wire-wheeled, battery-powered vehicle used by

The Lunar Orbiter, 1.7 m (5.5 ft) tall, carried a 69-kg (152-lb) photographic laboratory to assist in the selection of landing sites for the United States Apollo Program. Orbiter's major structures were: 454-kg (1,000-lb) thrust velocity control engine (1); attitude control thrusters (2); upper structural module weighing 321 kg (708 lb) (3); oxidant tank (4); micrometeoroid detectors (5); omnidirectional, low-gain antenna (6); flight programmer (7); Canopus star tracker (8), for orientation; inertial reference unit (9); Sun sensor (10), beneath instrument deck; lower structural module, photographic laboratory (11); solar panel (12); telephoto and wide-angle cameras (13), each with film for 212 exposures; high-gain dish antenna (14); attitude control thrusters (15); fuel tank (16); and heat shield (17).

Lunar roving vehicles were used by the Apollo 15, 16, and 17 astronauts to carry scientific equipment, tools, and lunar rocks across the Moon's surface. Each rover was powered by two 36-volt batteries (1) and equipped with a hand controller (2) for steering and braking, a 16-mm camera (3), a low-gain antenna (4), a high-gain antenna (5) for direct transmission to Earth, and a color television camera (6).

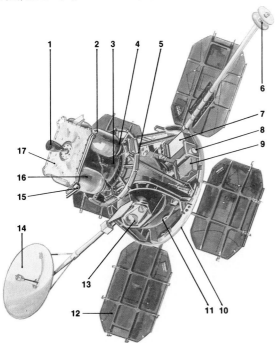

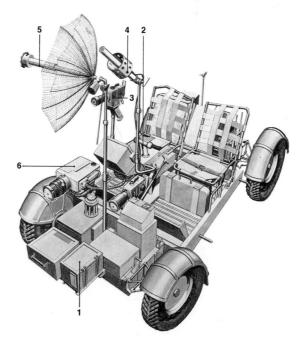

the *Apollo 15, 16,* and *17* astronauts to explore the Moon's surface at greater distances than previously possible from the landing sites (see APOLLO PROGRAM). Built by the Boeing Company, the 310-cm-long (122-in), 114-cm-high (45-in), 218-kg (480-lb) vehicle was stored folded in the Lunar Module's descent stage. Capable of supporting twice its own weight, the Lunar Rover could move at a speed of 13 km/h (8 mph), ascend slopes of up to 20°, and pass over 0.3-m-high (1-ft) obstacles and 0.6-m (2-ft) crevices.

Lundy, Benjamin

Benjamin Lundy, b. Sussex County, N.J., Jan. 4, 1789, d. Aug. 22, 1839, was an American Quaker abolitionist during the early years of the republic. A saddlemaker who settled in Ohio in 1815, he founded (1821) *The Genius of Universal Emancipation,* an abolitionist journal that circulated principally among Scotch-Irish, Moravian, and Quaker freeholders in the upper South. In 1828 he persuaded William Lloyd GARRISON to become a coeditor of the *Genius* and thus helped to launch the career of that leading abolitionist.

lung, artificial
see HEART-LUNG MACHINE; IRON LUNG

Lung-men
see LONGMEN

lungfish

Lungfishes are members of an ancient group of fishes and are characterized by functional lungs, a direct circulatory connection from the lung to the heart (as in mammals), a partial division of the atrium and ventricle of the heart into double chambers, and nostrils opening into the mouth cavity. Lungfishes are generally placed in a subclass of their own, Dipnoi.

The most primitive lungfish is the Australian lungfish, *Neoceratodus forsteri.* It grows to 1.8 m (6 ft) long and 45 kg (100 lb) in weight. It has a compressed body, flipperlike paired fins, large scales, four pairs of holobranchs (complete gills), and a single lung. It is not dependent on its lung for survival, nor does it estivate, or become dormant, during the dry season. The South American lungfish, *Lepidosiren paradoxa,* grows to about 1.2 m (4 ft) long. It has threadlike pectoral fins, somewhat featherlike pelvic fins, and three pairs of holobranchs. The African lungfishes, *Protopterus,* consist of four species, which may reach 2.1 m (7 ft) in length.

Both the South American and African lungfishes have cylindrical bodies, small scales, and paired lungs. They

The African lungfish *Protopterus* (shown) *may be descended from the extinct lungfish* Dipterus, *which lived about 275 million years ago.*

obtain more than 95 percent of their oxygen supply from their lungs and will drown if denied access to air. Both the South American and African lungfishes build breeding nests by burrowing into the mud, and both estivate at the bottom of a mud burrow during the dry season.

Lungfishes first appeared in the middle of the Devonian Period, about 370 million years ago. They are important in biogeography. Their present distribution in Australia, Africa, and South America are thought to represent the scattered remnants of a once-continuous lungfish distribution on the ancient landmass Gondwanaland.

lungs

The lung is an organ of the RESPIRATORY SYSTEM of air-breathing vertebrates and some fishes and amphibians that takes in atmospheric oxygen, needed for energy production, and at the same time expires carbon dioxide, a waste product of this metabolism. The lungs of most animals consist of two elastic chambers, usually located in the thorax, with thin linings across which oxygen and carbon dioxide are exchanged between blood capillaries and the air within the chamber.

In evolutionary terms, lungs are the counterparts of the gills of fish and crustaceans, which are adapted for extracting oxygen from water, and the tracheae of insects, which pipe oxygen directly to the tissues. The development of the lung permitted the eventual evolution of air-breathing mammals, which need large amounts of oxygen, which can be extracted more quickly from air than from water.

The greatly increased surface area of the lung in higher vertebrates results from a subdivision of the inner surface into pockets, or folds. The mammalian lung is honeycombed with almost a half billion tiny sacs, called alveoli, each of which is less than 1 mm (0.04 in) in diameter. Gas exchange takes place in the alveoli. The total exchange surface area in humans is about 70 m^2 (750 ft^2), thus ensuring great efficiency.

In humans, air first passes into the nose or mouth, through the pharynx (throat) and the larynx (voice box), and then into the trachea (windpipe). The generous blood supply of the nose, mouth, and pharynx brings incoming air to body temperature and humidity. The trachea splits into two branches called bronchi, each bronchus leading into one lung. Successive branchings of the bronchi are called bronchial tubes. These subdivide into still smaller tubes, or bronchioles, which lead into clusters of alveoli.

If greater than 1 mm in diameter, the airways have walls made of smooth muscle that expand or contract in response to the nervous system and are supported by discontinuous rings of CARTILAGE. Both the muscle and the cartilage are incorporated into a framework of connective tissue. Their inner surfaces are covered by ciliated epithelium interspersed with mucus-secreting goblet cells. The mucus acts as an escalator, on which particles that have passed into the bronchial tree are carried upward by the beating of the cilia and toward the throat, where they are cleared. Foreign bodies that do reach the alveoli are engulfed and disposed of by ameboid cells, the alveolar macrophages. In bronchioles smaller than 1 mm in diam-

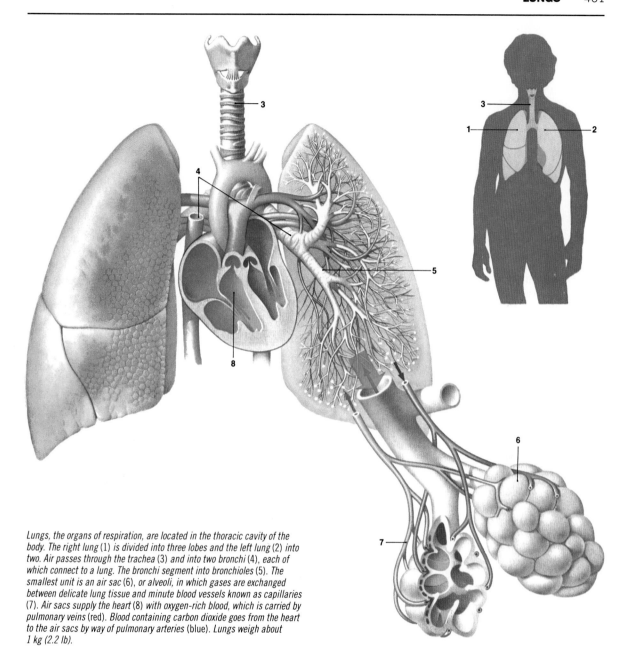

Lungs, the organs of respiration, are located in the thoracic cavity of the body. The right lung (1) is divided into three lobes and the left lung (2) into two. Air passes through the trachea (3) and into two bronchi (4), each of which connect to a lung. The bronchi segment into bronchioles (5). The smallest unit is an air sac (6), or alveoli, in which gases are exchanged between delicate lung tissue and minute blood vessels known as capillaries (7). Air sacs supply the heart (8) with oxygen-rich blood, which is carried by pulmonary veins (red). Blood containing carbon dioxide goes from the heart to the air sacs by way of pulmonary arteries (blue). Lungs weigh about 1 kg (2.2 lb).

eter, cartilage, ciliated cells, and goblet cells gradually disappear. The walls of the smallest airways and the entrance to the alveoli receive their support from an external network of connective tissue.

The capillaries permeating the walls of the alveoli arise from multiple branching of the pulmonary artery, which carries venous blood from the heart. As the capillaries leave the lung they rejoin to form the pulmonary veins, which return oxygenated blood to the heart. The pulmonary vessels are accompanied by lymph vessels, which return plasma water lost through the capillaries to the circulation.

The lobes of the lung are contained within the chest cavity and are separated from each other and the chest wall by a double membrane called the pleura.

See also: RESPIRATORY SYSTEM DISORDERS.

Lunokhod [loo-noh-koht'] The Lunokhods were remote-controlled moon rovers that the Soviet LUNA spacecraft successfully carried to the Moon's surface in 1970 and again in 1973. The purpose of the vehicles was to roll across the Moon's surface, sending back panoramic stereoscopic television images and making soil measurements. In shape and size the Lunokhods resembled bathtubs with four wheels on each long side. Total weight was about 900 kg (2,000 lb). A lid over the roof was raised in the daytime to expose solar power cells. A small radioisotope unit was used to maintain a survivable temperature.

The first successful Lunokhod (carried by *Luna 17*) landed in the Mare Imbrium on Nov. 17, 1970. It operated for 11 months under the control of a 5-man team at a communications center near Moscow and covered a total of 10 km (6 mi) while crisscrossing the landing site. The second Lunokhod (carried by *Luna 21*) landed on the Moon on Jan. 16, 1973, inside the crater Le Monnier in the Mare Serenitatis. It covered 35 km (22 mi) in 5 months before apparently becoming stuck while exploring a deep ravine.

Lunt, Alfred, and Fontanne, Lynn [luhnt, fahn-tan'] The actors Alfred Lunt, b. Milwaukee, Wis., Aug. 19, 1892, d. Aug. 3, 1977, and Lynn Fontanne, b. Woodford, England, Dec. 6, 1887, d. July 30, 1983, married in 1922 and during their 40-year professional career together gained the reputation of being the best acting couple on the American stage. They joined the Theatre Guild in 1924 and became famous for their wit and sophistication in such comedies as Molnár's *The Guardsman* (1924), Shaw's *Pygmalion* (1926), Noel Coward's *Design for Living* (1933) and *Quadrille* (1952), Shakespeare's *Taming of the Shrew* (1935), and Robert Sherwood's *Idiot's Delight* (1936). Their final stage appearance was in 1958–60, in Friedrich Dürrenmatt's chilling drama *The Visit*.

Alfred Lunt and Lynn Fontanne, a celebrated team in the American theater, entertained audiences for more than 40 years with their sophisticated light comedies.

Lupercalia [loo-pur-kay'-lee-uh] The Lupercalia was a Roman festival believed to have been in honor of FAUNUS, the god of flocks and fertility. Celebrated on February 15, it was intended to ensure the fertility of people, fields, and flocks for the new year. After sacrificing goats and a dog on the Palatine Hill, young men called Luperci raced around the borders of the hill, striking those they met with whips made of the goatskins. Women who were struck were ensured of fertility and of easy delivery of children. The festival survived until the 5th century AD.

lupine [loo'-pin] Lupine is the common name for about 200 species of annual and perennial flowering herbs, members of the genus *Lupinus* of the PEA family, Leguminoseae. They are characterized by deeply cut leaves with lancelike leaflets radiating from the tip of the leaf stalk. The flowers are predominantly blue, yellow, white, or rose in color and are borne on long-stemmed spikes in May and June. Mostly native to the United States, lupines are cultivated chiefly as ornamentals in gardens; some, however, are grown as cover and forage crops.

The annual lupine is an ornamental herb native to the northwest United States. Its flowers grow in tall, colorful spires.

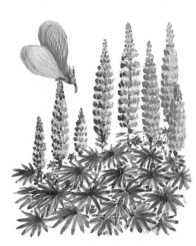

lupus erythematosus [loo'-puhs air-uh-theem-uh-toh'-suhs] Lupus erythematosus is a disease of the connective tissue. The immune system appears to react to the body's own tissues as if they were harmful invaders. Discoid lupus erythematosus (DLE), one form of the disease, is a skin disorder, forming red lesions usually on the face and scalp. In systemic lupus erythematosus (SLE), the other form of the disorder, the abnormal immune reaction can damage the kidneys, heart, lungs, liver, nervous system, joints, and skin. Lupus erythematosus cells, white blood cells that destroy other white cells, appear in the majority of cases, and their appearance is a diagnostic aid.

Lupus erythematosus occurs five to ten times more frequently in females than males, predominantly in the 15-to-55-year age group. The most frequent cause of death is uremia (buildup of toxic wastes due to kidney failure), followed by bacterial infection, heart failure, and hemorrhage.

Some patients have spontaneous remissions, whereas others respond favorably to treatment with corticosteroids, or agents that inhibit the body's immune reactions. Anti-inflammatory drugs and analgesics are also prescribed.

Luray Caverns [lur-ay'] The Luray Caverns cover 26 ha (64 acres) near the town of Luray in the Shenandoah Valley of northern Virginia. Many of the limestone chambers in the caverns surpass heights of 43 m (140 ft), and most are studded with colorful stalagmites, stalactites and columns formed by underground rivers and dripping water. The caverns were discovered by William and Andrew Campbell in 1878 and are a major tourist attraction.

Lurçat, Jean   see TAPESTRY

Luria, Aleksandr Romanovich [lur'-ee-uh] A. R. Luria, b. July 16, 1902, d. Aug. 14, 1977, was a noted Soviet psychologist and a founder of neuropsychology. Luria graduated from Kazan University in 1921 and from the First Moscow Medical Institute in 1937. In 1945 he became a professor at Moscow State University. Among other honors, he received the Order of Lenin, the Order of the Badge of Honor, and the Lomonosov Prize.

Luria's psychological studies of the 1920s and '30s centered on the function of speech. He was especially concerned with the role of language in controlling the affective processes, and with the relationship between speech and the mental development of children. According to Luria, the development of speech is inextricably linked to a child's intellectual development.

While studying the relationship between language and thought, Luria became interested in types of speech pathology, including aphasia. His work on aphasia led him to investigate brain correlates of aphasia and then to study the brain in general. During World War II, Luria made important advances in the rehabilitation of brain-injured casualties.

As in the work of most Soviet psychologists, Luria's studies show a bias toward materialist and behaviorist explanations. For example, his explanation of mental retardation stresses damage to the central nervous system and rejects genetic and cultural causes.

Luria, Isaac ben Solomon Isaac ben Solomon Luria, b. 1534, d. Aug. 5, 1572, a Jewish mystic, led the development of later KABBALAH, a school of Jewish mysticism. He was born in Jerusalem, the son of immigrant German parents.

Luria's thought was a combination of kabbalistic mysticism and messianism. He held a form of emanationism, teaching that, by voluntary self-contraction (*tsimtsum*), God made room for creation, which took the form of an emanation, or "overflowing," of the divine light. When the divine light was enclosed in finite "vessels" (*kelim*), they shattered (*shevirat ha-kelim*), and darkness (evil) came into creation and mingled with the light. Before the Mes-

siah comes, humankind must release the divine sparks from this mixture so that there may be a restoration (*tikkun*) of the pure light of God. This can be achieved by practicing saintliness and asceticism.

Lurie, Alison [lur'-ee] An American novelist and university professor, Alison Lurie, b. Chicago, Sept. 3, 1926, writes ironic fiction generally focused on the beleaguered, out-of-step relations between the sexes. Lurie's works zero in on contemporary events and fads. They include *The Nowhere City* (1965), *Imaginary Friends* (1967), *Real People* (1969), the highly successful *The War Between the Tates* (1974), *Only Children* (1979), and *Foreign Affairs* (1984), which won the 1985 Pulitzer Prize for fiction. Lurie also writes about children's literature.

Lusaka [loo-sah'-kah] Lusaka is the capital and largest city of Zambia, with a population of 870,030 (1988 est.). It is in the south central part of the country, about 95 km (60 mi) from the border with Zimbabwe. An important rail junction, it is a trading center for corn, wheat, tobacco, potatoes, and dairy cattle and produces building materials, tobacco products, foodstuffs, footwear, and textiles. The University of Zambia (1965) is there. Lusaka was founded by Europeans in 1905 as a railroad depot and named for the leader of a nearby African village. It replaced Livingstone as the capital of Northern Rhodesia (now Zambia) in 1935 because of its pleasant climate.

Lüshun (Lü-shun) [lue shoon] Lüshun, formerly Port Arthur, is an important port and naval base in China's northeast (formerly called Manchuria). Located at the southern tip of the Liaodong Peninsula, Lüshun guards the entrance to the Bohai (Gulf of Chihli). Lüshun and DALIEN, which lies 32 km (20 mi) to the northeast, form one urban center called LÜDA. The twin cities are connected by rail and a highway. Because of warm offshore currents the harbor stays ice free all year.

Although the site was used as a Chinese military post from the 2d century BC, modern Lüshun dates from the mid-19th century. The British occupied the area in the 1850s, and the Russians developed the settlement into a seaport in the late 19th century. The Russians obtained a lease on the port in 1898, but after their defeat in the Russo-Japanese War (1904–05) they were forced to cede it to Japan, which held it until 1945.

Lusitania (Roman province) see PORTUGAL

Lusitania (ship) The *Lusitania* was a British passenger ship that was sunk by a German submarine in the Atlantic on May 7, 1915. About 1,200 people were drowned, including 128 Americans. The sinking provoked a massive outcry in the United States, and President Woodrow Wilson protested strongly to Germany, demand-

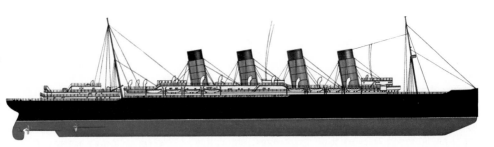

On May 7, 1915, the Lusitania, a British passenger ship, was torpedoed by a German submarine off the Irish coast. Of the more than 1,900 people aboard, 1,198 drowned. The incident contributed to sentiment in favor of U.S. entry into World War I.

ing reparations and the cessation of unrestricted submarine warfare. The German government justified the action on the grounds that the *Lusitania* carried munitions, but it privately ordered German submarines not to sink passenger ships without warning. The incident contributed to the deterioration in U.S.-German relations that eventually led the United States to enter World War I.

luster   Luster is the appearance of a mineral's surface in reflected light. Minerals such as pyrite and galena have a metallic luster; such minerals are frequently dark and opaque, even on thin edges. Light-colored minerals have various nonmetallic lusters: adamantine or brilliant (diamond), greasy (nepheline), resinous (sphalerite), silky (asbestos minerals), pearly (the micas), and vitreous, or glassy (quartz).

lute   *Lute,* a generic name for stringed instruments composed of a body and of a neck that serves as a handle and holds strings stretched across the instrument, is also the specific name of the European short-necked instrument of the Renaissance, for which a vast and significant musical literature was composed in the 16th and 17th centuries. Appearing early in antiquity, the lute had little impact on Europe until the late Middle Ages. By 1500 the classic lute was formed with six courses of strings stretching across its pear-shaped body and a fretted fin-

A small, 16th-century lute with 12 strings has intricate inlay work on its back. Lutes were popular instruments in Renaissance Europe.

gerboard to a pegbox tilted back at a sharp angle. About 1600, in order to adapt to new musical styles, an enlarged range was obtained by additional low strings, usually unstopped and suspended from a separate and higher pegbox (*theorbo* and *chittarone*), and tunings were often altered. By the end of the baroque period (about 1750), the lute was largely abandoned.

Few unaltered historic instruments remain, but many printed volumes of lute tablature testify to the lute's popularity and the high level of skill demanded of its performers. The recent revival of old music has produced many fine modern makers and players. The delicacy and finely shaded tone of the lute make it essentially an instrument for intimate performance.

luteinizing hormone   see HORMONE, ANIMAL; PITUITARY GLAND

lutetium   [loo-tee'-shee-uhm]   Lutetium is a chemical element, a silvery white metal of the LANTHANIDE SERIES. Its symbol is Lu, its atomic number is 71, and its atomic weight is 174.97 (the average weight of the two natural isotopes, ^{175}Lu and ^{176}Lu). ^{176}Lu is radioactive, with a half-life of 2.2×10^{10} years. Lutetium was discovered in 1907 by Georges Urbain, who called it Lutetia after the ancient Roman name for Paris.

Luther, Martin   Martin Luther, b. Nov. 10, 1483, d. Feb. 18, 1546, was a German theologian and a major leader of the Protestant REFORMATION. He is sometimes called the father of Protestantism, and one of the major branches of Protestantism—Lutheranism—is named for him.

Early Life. Luther, the son of a Saxon miner, was born in Eisleben. He entered the Augustinian monastery at Erfurt in 1505 and was ordained in 1507. In 1510, Luther visited Rome on business for the order and was shocked to find corruption in high ecclesiastical places. His theological studies led him to the conclusion that Christ was the sole mediator between God and man and that forgiveness of sin and salvation are effected by God's GRACE alone and are received by faith alone on the part of man. This point of view turned him against scholastic theology, which had emphasized man's role in his own salvation, and against many church practices that emphasized justification by good works.

Dispute over Indulgences. The doctrine of INDULGENCES aroused Luther's indignation. The sale by the church of indulgences—the remission of temporal punishments for sins committed and confessed to a priest—brought in much revenue. The archbishop of Mainz, Albert of Brandenburg, sponsored such a sale in 1517. When his representative arrived in Saxony, Luther posted his famous 95 theses on the door of the castle church at Wittenberg on Oct. 31, 1517. Although some of the theses directly criticized papal policies, they were put forward as tentative objections for discussion.

Copies of the 95 theses were quickly spread throughout Europe and unleashed a storm of controversy. The Saxon Dominican provincial charged him with heresy, and he was summoned to appear in Augsburg before the papal legate, Cardinal Cajetan. Refusing to recant, he fled to Wittenberg, seeking the protection of the elector FREDERICK III of Saxony. When the Wittenberg faculty sent a letter to Frederick declaring its solidarity with Luther, the elector refused to send Luther to Rome, where he would certainly meet imprisonment or death.

Reforms. In 1520, Luther completed three celebrated works in which he stated his views. In his _Address to the Christian Nobility of the German Nation,_ he invited the German princes to take the reform of the church into their own hands; in _A Prelude Concerning the Babylonian Captivity of the Church,_ he attacked the papacy and the current theology of sacraments; and in _On the Freedom of a Christian Man,_ he stated his position on justification and good works. The bull of Pope LEO X, _Exsurge Domine,_ issued on June 15 that same year, gave Luther 60 days to recant, and _Decet Romanum Pontificem_ of Jan. 3, 1521, excommunicated him.

In subsequent years Luther wrote the Small and Large Catechisms, sermon books, more than a dozen hymns,

Martin Luther, whose 95 theses of 1517 catalyzed the events of the Protestant Reformation, intended to provoke reform within the Catholic church when he nailed his assertions to the Wittenberg church door.

over 100 volumes of tracts, treatises, biblical commentaries, and thousands of letters, and translated the Bible into German.

With Philipp MELANCHTHON and others, Luther organized the Evangelical churches in the German territories whose princes supported him. He abolished many traditional practices, including confession and private mass. Priests married; convents and monasteries were abandoned. Luther lost some popular support when he urged suppression of the Knights' Revolt (1522) and the PEASANTS' WAR (1524–26); his failure to reach doctrinal accord with Ulrich ZWINGLI on the nature of the EUCHARIST (1529) split the Reform movement. Nonetheless, Luther found personal solace in his marriage (1525) to a former Cistercian nun, Katherina von Bora; they raised six children.

Late in 1545, Luther was asked to arbitrate a dispute in Eisleben; despite the icy winter weather, he traveled there. The quarrel was settled on Feb. 17, 1546, but the strain had been great and Luther died the next day.

Lutheranism Lutheranism is the branch of PROTESTANTISM that generally follows the teachings of the 16th-century reformer Martin LUTHER. The Lutheran movement diffused after 1517 from Saxony through many other German territories into Scandinavia. In the 18th century it spread to America and, thereafter, into many nations of the world. Lutheranism soon became more than the experience of Luther, but it never deviated from his theme that people are made right with God _sola gratia_ and _sola fide_—that is, only by the divine initiative of grace as received through God's gift of faith. Because Luther came across his discoveries by reading the Bible, he also liked to add to his motto the exhortation _sola scriptura,_ which means that Lutherans are to use the Bible alone as the source and norm for their teachings.

The Lutheran movement gained popularity quickly in Germany at a time of rising nationalism among people who resented sending their wealth to Rome. The early Lutherans were strongly based in the universities and used their learning to spread the faith among an international community of scholars. By 1530 they were formulating their own CONFESSIONS OF FAITH and proceeding independently amid the non-Lutheran reform parties that proliferated across most of northern Europe. By 1580 and through the next century, these confessions became increasingly rigid scholastic expressions, designed to define the church in formal terms. Ever since, Lutheranism has been known as a doctrinal and even dogmatic church.

Lutheranism did not and could not live only by the teaching of its professors. In the late 17th century its more gentle side, which grew out of the piety of Luther, appeared in the form of a movement called PIETISM. Nominally orthodox in belief and practice, the Pietists stressed Bible reading, circles of prayer and devotion, and the works of love. This pietism was somewhat unstable; in its downgrading of doctrine it helped prepare Lutherans for the age of Enlightenment, when many leaders and some of the faithful turned to rationalism. Subsequently, theology under Lutheran influence has often taken on a radical character, especially in Germany. As a result, there is often a considerable gap between intellectual expressions of Lutheranism and the liturgy and preaching of its congregations.

From the beginning, Lutheranism had to wrestle with the problem of its relation to civil authorities. Although Luther was a rebel against papal teaching, he was docile about reforming the civil order and rejected radical revolts by the peasants (see PEASANTS' WAR). Lutherans have been more ready than many other Christians to see the permanence of evil in the powers of the created and fallen world, that is, the world under the influence of sin. Consequently, they have put more of their energies into works of welfare and charity—into orphanages, hospitals, and deaconesses' movements—than into social schemes to transform the world.

In Europe most Lutheran churches are episcopal, that is, ruled by bishops, and the churches of Denmark, Finland, Iceland, Norway, and Sweden are established. In North America and elsewhere Lutherans prefer congregational and synodical forms of government, in which local churches link together for common purposes. In the United States, Lutherans have united in three main bodies: the Lutheran Church in America, the Lutheran Church–Missouri Synod, and the American Lutheran Church. The American Lutheran Church, the Lutheran Church in America, and a third group, the Association of Evangelical Lutheran Churches, united in 1987 to form the Evangelical Lutheran Church in America.

Luthuli, Albert John [luh-thoo'-lee]

The South African civil rights leader Albert Luthuli (or Lutuli), b. 1898, d. July 21, 1967, was the first African to receive the Nobel Peace Prize (1960). After attending Adams College, an American Board of Missions teacher-training institution, he taught there for 15 years. In 1936, Luthuli was elected chief of a Zulu community in Natal province. He joined the AFRICAN NATIONAL CONGRESS in 1945, advocating full citizenship for all South Africans. In 1952 he became the group's president-general. Luthuli was

The South African religious and political leader Albert Luthuli is shown here at a 1966 meeting with Robert F. Kennedy. Luthuli gained worldwide recognition and a Nobel Peace Prize for his work in seeking a nonviolent path to end apartheid.

strongly influenced by his religious convictions and by the American civil rights struggle. He opposed armed insurrection, putting his trust in passive resistance.

Repeatedly arrested and finally confined (1959) by the government to his own rural neighborhood for promoting "hostilities," he was allowed to leave the country briefly to receive the Nobel Prize, awarded to him for his peaceful struggle against racial discrimination. When he returned to South Africa he faced even stricter limitations on his freedom. In 1960 the African National Congress was outlawed and forced to operate underground or in exile. Luthuli's autobiography, *Let My People Go*, was published in 1962.

Lutosławski, Witold [loo-toh-swav'-skee]

Witold Lutosławski, b. Jan. 25, 1913, is one of Poland's most celebrated composers. After World War II, as his works became known, he was invited to give seminars in Western Europe and in the United States. His music through the 1950s—such as his Concerto for Orchestra (1954) and *Musique funèbre* (1958)—merges Polish folk elements with techniques introduced by Béla Bartók. As Lutosławski became more familiar with Western European styles, he experimented with the twelve-tone system and with aleatory music, of which *Jeux vénitiens* (Venetian Games, 1961) is an outstanding example. Such later works as the Second Symphony (1967) are rich in orchestral scoring. The Double Concerto for Oboe, Harp, and Chamber Orchestra (1980) draws upon his entire orchestral idiom of the preceding three decades.

Lutyens, Sir Edwin Landseer [luh'-chanz]

The British architect Sir Edwin Landseer Lutyens, b. Mar. 29, 1869, d. Jan. 1, 1944, is considered the last major architect to create significant works using traditional styles. Self-taught in architecture, Lutyens began his career by designing several distinguished country homes, such as the Deanery Garden, Sonning, Berkshire (1900–01), that reflect the influence of Philip Webb (1831–1915) and the Arts and Crafts movement. Lutyens's designs demanded a high level of craftsmanship, for which his domestic architecture is noted.

As he moved from domestic to public architecture, Lutyens developed a style that was classical in outline and inspiration yet stamped with his own personality. His largest public project was the planning (1912–14) of NEW DELHI, India, which came to include one of his most notable designs, the Viceroy's House (1920–31). In great demand following the New Delhi project, Lutyens designed several war memorials noted for their classical simplicity, such as the Cenotaph in London (1920) and the Thiepval Memorial Arch in France (1924).

Lutyens, Elisabeth

Elisabeth Lutyens, b. London, July 9, 1906, d. Apr. 14, 1983, was one of the few women of her generation to establish an international reputation as a composer. She studied at the Royal College of Music in London and at the École Normale in Paris. Her composi-

AT A GLANCE

GRAND DUCHY OF LUXEMBOURG

Land: Area: 2,586 km^2 (999 mi^2). Capital and largest city: Luxembourg (1988 est. pop., 75,500).

People: Population (1990 est.): 383,813. Density: 148 persons per km^2 (385 per mi^2). Distribution (1985): 78% urban, 22% rural. Official languages: French, German. Major religion: Roman Catholicism.

Government: Type: constitutional monarchy. Legislature: Chamber of Deputies. Political subdivisions: 3 districts.

Economy: GNP (1988): $8.4 billion; $22,600 per capita. Labor distribution (1987): agriculture—3.2%; industry and commerce—39.4%; services—26.8%; finance—10.1%; construction—8.8%; other—11.7%. Foreign trade (1988): imports—$5.9 billion; exports—$4.7 billion. Currency: 1 franc = 100 centimes.

Education and Health: Literacy (1990): 100% of adult population. Universities (1984): 1. Hospital beds (1987): 4,661. Physicians (1987): 666. Life expectancy (1990): women—80; men—72. Infant mortality (1990): 7 per 1,000 live births.

tional style progressed from romanticism to expressionism, in which she cultivated the twelve-tone technique; with this change she discarded everything she wrote before 1935. Her works include operas, chamber concertos, string quartets, choral and piano music, a dramatic scene, *The Pit* (1949), and the choral work *Essence of Our Happiness* (1970). She also composed for films and radio.

Luxembourg (city)   Luxembourg (1988 est. pop., 75,500) is the capital city of the Grand Duchy of Luxembourg. The city is a transportation, financial, and banking center, and its industries manufacture clothing, electrical machinery, chemicals, and processed foods. The Romans built a fort on the site, because of its strategic location overlooking the Alzette River; by the 10th century Luxembourg was one of Europe's strongest walled towns. The fortress was razed according to the terms of the Treaty of London (1867). During both world wars the city was occupied by Germany.

Luxembourg (country)   The Grand Duchy of Luxembourg is an independent European country. It is bordered on the north and west by Belgium, on the east by Germany, and on the south by France. Because of its central location, Luxembourg has been subject to foreign invasions and domination for much of its history. During the 20th century Luxembourg has been one of the strongest supporters of economic and political cooperation with other Western European countries. At the same time the people maintain a strong national identity.

Land and People

The northern third of Luxembourg, called Oesling, is an extension of the forested, gently rolling Belgian ARDENNES. At the northern tip is the Burgplatz, at 559 m (1,835 ft) the country's highest elevation. The southern portion, called Gutland or Bon Pays ("good earth" in German and French, respectively), is an extension of the French Lorraine Plateau. Luxembourg is laced with rivers and streams; most drain eastward into the two major rivers, the MOSELLE and the Sûre (German: Sauer). The climate is cool, with mean temperatures of about 1° C (30° F) in January and 17° C (62° F) in July. Average annual rainfall varies by region from 1,015 mm (40 in) to 685 mm (27 in).

Luxembourg's native population is primarily of French and German descent. Approximately one-quarter of the population are foreign workers, who come to the country because of employment opportunities. The predominant spoken language is Letzeburgesch, of German origin, but French and German are the two official languages. About 97% of the population are Roman Catholic. Education is free and compulsory from the ages of 6 to 15.

Economic Activity

A heavily industrialized economy gives Luxembourg one of the highest standards of living in Europe. Industry is concentrated in the southern portion of the country,

LUXEMBOURG

			Meters	Feet
——	Railroad	City type size indicates relative importance	1000	3281
+	Spot Elevation		500	1640
Scale 1:1,087,000		National capitals are underlined	200	656
0 5 10 15 20 25 km			0	0
0 5 10 15 mi.				

today chemicals, plastics, rubber, and synthetic fibers are produced. Agriculture, which employs only a tiny fraction of the labor force, is concentrated in central Luxembourg. Tourism, also important to the economy, is centered in the north, because of the scenic landscape and castle ruins. In 1948, Luxembourg joined the Benelux customs union, and in 1958, the EUROPEAN COMMUNITY.

History and Government

Luxembourg (or Luxemburg) emerged as a separate political entity during the Middle Ages, when it was a powerful fief of the Holy Roman Empire. In 1308 its ruling count was elected German king (later Holy Roman emperor) as HENRY VII. His son, John of Luxemburg (1296–1346), became king of Bohemia in 1310; although blind, John died fighting on the French side in the Battle of Crécy. John's grandson, the Holy Roman Emperor CHARLES IV, made (1354) Luxembourg a duchy under his brother Wenceslas. (Bohemia and the imperial crown passed to Charles's sons, first Wenceslas and later Sigismund.)

In 1443, Luxembourg was seized by Philip the Good of Burgundy. It subsequently passed (1477) to the HABSBURG dynasty and was under Spanish and (after 1714) Austrian rule. It was twice (1684–97 and 1795–1814) annexed by France. The Congress of Vienna (1814–15) made Luxembourg a grand duchy but bestowed the ruling title on WILLIAM I, king of the Netherlands, and provided for a Prussian garrison in the city of Luxembourg.

When Belgium gained its independence from the Netherlands, it received (1839) a portion of the grand duchy (now the Belgian province of Luxembourg). Finally, the London Conference of 1867 recognized the independence and neutrality of the grand duchy.

where extensive iron deposits are mined. The iron-and-steel industry, the economic heart of Luxembourg, accounts for almost half of the industrial production. In recent years industry has become more diversified, and

The historic city of Luxembourg is a center of trade, industry, and transportation. The capital of the Grand Duchy of Luxembourg, the city originally was the site of a Roman fort. By the 10th century, it was one of Europe's strongest and most strategic walled towns.

When Queen WILHELMINA succeeded to the Dutch throne in 1890, Luxembourg passed to a collateral branch of the house of Nassau. Germany violated the neutrality of Luxembourg and occupied the duchy in both world wars. The present grand duke is Jean, who succeeded on the abdication of his mother, Charlotte (r. 1919–64).

Luxembourg is a constitutional monarchy headed by the grand duke. He appoints the 7-member council of ministers. The council, however, is responsible to the 59-member Chamber of Deputies, elected by universal suffrage. A 21-member advisory council of state, whose members are appointed by the grand duke and serve for life, is required to review and advise on all legislation before it comes before the Chamber of Deputies.

Luxemburg, Rosa   Rosa Luxemburg, b. Mar. 5, 1871, d. Jan. 15, 1919, was a leading socialist theorist and founder of the German Communist party. Born into a prosperous Jewish business family in Russian Poland, she engaged in revolutionary activity from 1887. Acquiring German citizenship by marriage, Luxemburg became a leader of the extreme left wing of the German Social Democratic party. Active in the Second INTERNATIONAL, she fought the growing nationalism within the socialist movement.

While in prison (1916–18) for revolutionary activity during World War I, Luxemburg wrote the so-called Spartacus Letters. With Karl Liebknecht (see LIEBKNECHT family) she founded (1916) the radical Spartacus League, which, on Dec. 30, 1918, became the German Communist party. Liebknecht and Luxemburg were murdered by German troops after the abortive Spartacist uprising of January 1919. Luxemburg's chief work was *Accumulation of Capital* (1913; Eng. trans., 1951).

Luxor   [luhk'-sohr]   Luxor (1983 est. pop., 113,400), a city in upper Egypt, is located at the site of ancient THEBES. Located 740 km (460 mi) south of Cairo on the Nile River, it was the capital of ancient Egypt during the 11th dynasty (c.2130–1990 BC) but particularly in the New Kingdom (c.1570–1085 BC). In ancient times Luxor was called Waset, or No, meaning "the city" (Ezek. 30:14 and Nah. 3:8). Nothing can be seen of the ancient city except two of Egypt's finest pharaonic temples, those of Luxor and KARNAK, which stand on the east side of the river. On the west are the famous colossi of Amenhotep III (c.1417–1379 BC), the VALLEY OF THE KINGS and Valley of the Queens, the Ramesseum and other royal mortuary temples, and the finely decorated tombs of high officials.

Luzon   [loo-sohn']   Luzon is the northernmost and largest (104,688 km^2/40,420 mi^2) of the Philippine Islands. With 22,598,000 inhabitants (1980), Luzon is also the most populous island of the nation. MANILA, the largest city, capital, and chief port of the Philippines, is located on Luzon. The fertile central plain north of Manila is the largest tract of arable land in the archipelago. The southernmost part of Luzon consists of a series of elongated peninsulas, whereas the mountainous north has a more even coastline.

Aside from manufacturing centered in Manila, Luzon is largely agricultural. Leading crops include rice, corn, coconuts, sugarcane, tobacco, and abaca. Tropical hardwoods, iron, gold, manganese, copper, and chrome are exported.

Ferdinand Magellan was the first European to discover the archipelago, in 1521. The Spaniards established Manila in 1570. During World War II the battles of Bataan and Corregidor took place on Luzon.

Luzzatto, Moses Hayyim   [lut-saht'-toh]   Moses Hayyim Luzzatto, b. Padua, Italy, 1707, d. 1746, was a Jewish writer who ranks as one of the founders of modern Hebrew literature. His writings—chiefly his ethical treatise *Mesillat Yesharim* (1740; The Path of the Upright, 1936)—were notable for the clarity of their language, a departure from the complex style of contemporary literary Hebrew. During his lifetime, however, Luzzatto was known principally as a charismatic mystic and interpreter of the KABBALAH. Alarmed by his messianic pronouncements and fearing a repetition of the furor caused by the false Messiah SABBATAI ZEVI, the Italian rabbinate expelled Luzzatto, who died in Palestine.

Lvov   [lyuh-vawf']   Lvov is the capital of Lvov oblast in western Ukraine, USSR. The city has a population of 790,000 (1989). Lvov is a transportation center; its industries, based primarily on its skilled labor force, produce motor vehicles, light bulbs, television sets, and gas ranges. A petroleum refinery processes crude petroleum from the nearby Carpathian petroleum fields. The Lvov Ivan Franko State University, one of the oldest in the USSR, dates from 1661.

The history of Lvov is complex. Founded about 1256, it was named for Lev, a ruler of the early Russian principality of Galich. Together with the rest of the surrounding region of GALICIA, the city was transferred in the 14th century to Poland and was called Lwów. In 1772 it became part of Austria and was renamed Lemberg. Much of Lvov's modern development dates from the Austrian period. The city reverted to Poland in the period 1918–39, between the two world wars, and, with the rest of the western Ukraine, was then absorbed by the USSR.

Lyautey, Louis Hubert   [lee-oh-tay', lwee ue-bair']   The French statesman and soldier Louis Hubert Gonzalve Lyautey, b. Nov. 17, 1854, d. July 21, 1934, administered French Morocco as its first resident general. Lyautey served in Algeria, Indochina, Madagascar, and France before 1904, when he was sent back to French Algeria—

soon after France and Spain had secretly agreed to partition neighboring Morocco. As commandant at Aïn Sefra and later at Oran, Lyautey extended Algeria's territory by pushing the frontier westward into Morocco—especially after the Algeciras Conference of 1906, which allowed France to patrol the border. He returned to France in 1910 but in 1912 was appointed resident general of the new French protectorate of Morocco. Except for 1916–17, when he served as French war minister, Lyautey administered the protectorate until 1925.

lycée [lee-say']   In France the lycée is a state secondary school for students from the age of 11 to 18 or 19. First established in 1802 and reformed in 1959 to be more democratic and comprehensive, lycées, which can be for boys or for girls, prepare students for the *baccalauréat*, the degree required for university admission. Classical, modern, and technical studies aim at developing the students' critical thinking.

lyceum   Lyceum was a 19th-century movement organized in the United States to provide town and village audiences with literary and scientific knowledge. Founded at Millbury, Mass., in 1826 by Josiah Holbrook, the movement sponsored lectures, debates, concerts, and publications. Local community leaders as well as such luminaries as Ralph Waldo Emerson, Henry David Thoreau, and Daniel Webster were among the participants. A forerunner of the CHAUTAUQUA and other adult education programs, the lyceum was named for the ancient Athenian gymnasium where Aristotle taught.

Lycurgus [ly-kur'-guhs]   According to tradition, Lycurgus was the founder of the constitution of SPARTA and the lawgiver who designed that city-state's unique social and military structure. If Lycurgus was a real person rather than a myth, he was probably associated with the governmental and social reforms that followed the revolt of the enslaved population of Messenia in the mid–7th century BC.

Another Lycurgus, c.390–c.324 BC, was an Athenian orator and statesman in the period following Athens's defeat by Macedonia (338). He administered the state finances and an extensive building program.

Lydgate, John [lid'-gayt]   John Lydgate, c.1370–c.1450, a monk of Bury Saint Edmunds, was the most prolific Middle English poet. Two of his best early works, *A Complaint of a Lover's Life* (c.1400) and *The Temple of Glass* (c.1403), closely imitate poems by Geoffrey Chaucer. Lydgate's later works include the encyclopedic *Troy Book* (1412–20) and *Fall of Princes* (c.1431–39).

Lydia [lid'-ee-uh]   In ancient times Lydia was the name of a fertile and geologically wealthy region of western Anatolia. It extended from Caria on the south to Mysia on the north and was bounded by Phrygia on the east and by the Aegean on the west. Lydia first achieved prominence under the rule of the Mermnadae in the early 7th century BC. It is best known as the first ancient state to use coinage. In 547 BC, CROESUS, the powerful king of Lydia, was defeated by CYRUS THE GREAT of Persia; the Lydian capital Sardis then became the seat of a Persian satrap (governor). Lydia absorbed and reflected both Oriental and Greek culture and interacted politically with Greek cities throughout the Persian period. The country passed to the Romans in 133 BC.

lye   SEE CAUSTIC CHEMICALS

Lyell, Sir Charles [ly'-ul]   The British geologist Sir Charles Lyell, b. Nov. 14, 1797, d. Feb. 22, 1875, was the author of texts that were required reading in geology throughout the 19th century. The first volume (1830) of his *Principles of Geology* contained a vigorous indictment of CATASTROPHISM, the then-popular view that most of the Earth's history could be relegated to a short period of violent upheaval and flooding. Lyell argued instead that geological phenomena were explicable in terms of contemporary natural processes operating gradually over long periods of time, a concept termed UNIFORMITARIANISM. The second volume (1832) dealt with physical processes and introduced a number of new terms, including *metamorphic* to describe sedimentary rocks changed by high temperatures adjacent to igneous rocks. By the time the third volume—emphasizing stratigraphy and paleontology—appeared in 1833, second editions of the first two volumes had already been published. Lyell prepared many additional editions, the twelfth and last appearing in 1875.

Born to well-to-do Scottish parents, Lyell studied law at Oxford. His interest in geology was kindled by the lectures (1817) of William Buckland, one of the leading geologists of his day. Observations made during travels to Europe and the United States provided Lyell with the basis for a unified view of Earth history. Lyell was also a skilled zoologist. He drew on both geology and zoology in classifying the Tertiary rocks of northern Italy according to the FOSSIL RECORD these rocks revealed.

Lyell's *Principles* was avidly read by Charles Darwin prior to his voyage (1831–36) on the *Beagle*. Lyell's depiction of the vastness of geologic time helped pave the way for Darwin to develop the theory of evolution. After Darwin's return he and Lyell became friends, Lyell helping to get the ideas of both Darwin and Alfred Russel WALLACE published simultaneously. Lyell himself was a late (although enthusiastic) convert to Darwin's ideas, primarily because of doubts about the mechanism of progressive biologic change.

Lyly, John [lil'-ee]   John Lyly, c.1554–1606, was an ELIZABETHAN dramatist and author of *Euphues, the Anatomy of Wit* (1578) and *Euphues and his England* (1580). These popular romances created a fashion for elaborate, polished rhetoric (euphuism) and brought a new elegance to English prose. Lyly's comedies are likewise in the tradition of courtly, refined wit and based on classical mythology. Shakespeare caricatured Lyly's artificial style in his early comedy *Love's Labour's Lost.*

Lyman, Theodore [ly'-muhn]   The American experimental physicist Theodore Lyman, b. Brookline, Mass., Nov. 23, 1874, d. Oct. 11, 1954, investigated the far ultraviolet region of the electromagnetic spectrum. Lyman spent six years constructing a vacuum spectrometer for this work. In 1906 he obtained accurate measurements of lines below 2,000 angstroms (Å) and in 1917 he extended his ultraviolet research to 500 Å. He discovered (1914) a fundamental series of ultraviolet hydrogen lines, which were named in his honor. The discovery played a major role in supporting Niels Bohr's quantum theory of the atom.

lyme disease   Lyme disease is a mild to serious bacterial disease that is transmitted by ticks. It was first recognized in the northeastern United States (it is named for Lyme, Conn.) and is now known to occur in midwestern and western states as well as in many other countries. The tiny ticks, genus *Ixodes*, infest animals such as white-footed mice and white-tailed deer. When a human is bitten by a tick, the minute spirochete *Borrelia burgdorferi* enters the bloodstream. Within a month a painless rash may appear, often accompanied by severe headaches, fatigue, chills, and fever. Severe inflammation of the heart muscle or nervous system may follow in the next few months, causing heart problems, meningitis, and severe migratory pains. In some cases, neither of these stages is observed. Within two years, however, arthritic attacks may develop that can become chronic if untreated. Scientists have recently found that humans may have a genetic predisposition that increases their susceptibility to chronic arthritis. Antibiotics used in the early stages of the disease are effective treatments.

lymphatic system [lim-fat'-ik]   The lymphatic system, composed of widely spread and structurally distinct tissues, provides vertebrates, including humans, with immune defenses, filters foreign substances and cell debris from blood and destroys them, and produces lymphocytes, which circulate in blood and lymph vessels.

The lymph vessels comprise a network of capillaries, which filter blood impurities; they contain a clear, colorless fluid (lymph). Lymph passes from capillaries to lymph vessels and flows through lymph nodes that are located along the course of these vessels. Cells of the lymph nodes phagocytize, or ingest, such impurities as bacteria, old red blood cells, and toxic and cellular waste. Finally, lymph flows into the thoracic duct, a large vessel that runs parallel to the spinal column, or into the right

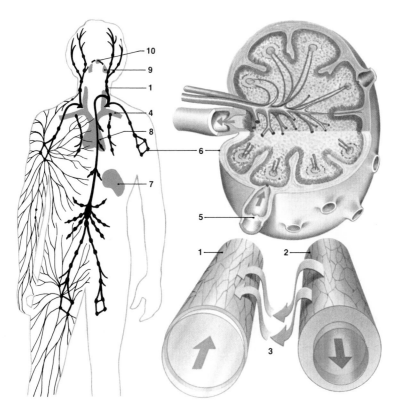

Lymph, or lymphatic fluid, which transports nutrients to tissues and collects tissue wastes, is carried by the lymphatic system, a network of interconnecting vessels (1). The pressure of blood circulating through the capillaries (2) forces lymph out into tissue spaces (3). This fluid is collected by the lymphatic vessels and eventually returned to the bloodstream through ducts that empty into large veins near the collarbones (4). Lymph is moved by contractions of body muscles and of the vessels themselves, which have valves (5) to prevent backflow. Lymph nodes (6), which are distributed throughout the system, remove wastes and other particles and contain large concentrations of white blood cells, which attack invaders such as bacteria and viruses. The spleen (7), thymus (8), tonsils (9), and adenoids (10), all composed of lymphoid tissue, are also part of the immune system.

lymphatic duct, both of which transport the lymph back into veins of the shoulder areas.

Tissues of the lymphatic system include the spleen, thymus, bone marrow, and aggregates of lymphatic tissue located in the intestines, tonsils, and adenoids. The spleen, thymus, and bone marrow manufacture lymphocytes. The spleen also destroys old blood cells and other substances, and plays a role in immune responses. The thymus controls lymphocyte production and antibody formation. Lymphatic tissues of the intestines, called lacteals, absorb digested fat (lipids).

Lymph nodes have an outer cortex and an inner medulla. The cortex contains a dense mass of lymphocytes; the medulla has lymphocytes and plasma cells arranged in cordlike structures. Lymph vessels that bring fluid into the node are called afferent vessels; efferent vessels drain the node.

The most common cell of the system is the lymphocyte. Lymphocytes can be classified as T cells (thymus-derived) or as B cells (bone-marrow-derived). T cells are active in cell-mediated immunity and are responsible for delayed hypersensitivity reactions, rejection of tissue grafts, and rejection of antigenically altered tissue within the organism itself. B lymphocytes are responsible for immunoglobulin secretion.

The lymphatic system can be affected by several disorders. Low white-blood-cell levels (LEUKOPENIA) and high white-blood-cell levels (LEUKEMIA) sometimes are disorders related to abnormal production of lymphocytes. Lymphedema, or obstruction of lymph circulation, may result from the presence of a tumor or an infection such as FILARIASIS. Degeneration of the lymph nodes, spleen, thymus, intestinal tissue, tonsils, and adenoids will impair the function of the lymphatic system. LYMPHOMAS, or cancers of the lymphatic system, include such disorders as HODGKIN'S DISEASE.

See also: BLOOD; CIRCULATORY SYSTEM; IMMUNITY (biology).

lymphocyte   see BLOOD; LYMPHATIC SYSTEM

lymphoma [lim-foh'-muh]   A lymphoma is a tumor of lymphatic tissue, which is the principal tissue in the lymph nodes, spleen, tonsils, and thymus gland. The benign or malignant tumor may involve any one of the various kinds of specialized cells of lymphatic tissue. The major sign of lymphoma is a painless enlargement of one or more lymph nodes. Patients may also experience fever, weight loss, nighttime sweating, liver and spleen enlargement, and gastrointestinal and kidney disturbances. One major type of lymphoma is HODGKIN'S DISEASE.

Lynch, Charles   Charles Lynch, b. near Lynchburg, Va., 1736, d. Oct. 29, 1796, a patriot leader in Bedford County, Va., during the American Revolution, supposedly gave his name to the practice of LYNCHING. A colonel in the militia, he set up his own court to try and sentence Loyalists accused of aiding the British. Lynch did not execute people; his usual sentence was flogging.

Lynch, John   The Irish political leader John Mary "Jack" Lynch, b. Blackpool, Aug. 15, 1917, was prime minister of the Republic of Ireland from 1966 to 1973 and again from 1977 to 1979. Before entering the field of law in 1945, Lynch had been a famous hurling athlete. He was elected (1948) to the Dail (parliament) as a Fianna Fáil party member, became (1957) a minister for education in Eamon de Valera's cabinet, and later became (1959) minister for industry and commerce. Made minister of finance in 1965, he succeeded Sean Lemass as prime minister of Ireland in November 1966. Lynch led Ireland into the Common Market in 1973 and sought, without success, to play a peacemaking role in the sectarian conflict in Northern Ireland.

Lynchburg   Lynchburg (1990 pop., 66,049) is a city on the James River in the foothills of the Blue Ridge Mountains in central Virginia. Its economy is balanced between manufacturing (shoes, textiles, paper, and metal products) and agriculture (tobacco and grains). Several colleges are located in the city. Founded by Quakers in 1757, Lynchburg flourished economically after the completion of the Kanawha Canal (1840) and the arrival of the railroad (1850).

lynching   Lynching is the unlawful killing of a person by a mob, usually by hanging. The term is thought to have been derived from the activities of Charles LYNCH, a Virginia patriot in the American Revolution who tried and punished suspected Loyalists in his own court. The practice of lynching in relatively recent times is most closely associated with the southern United States, both before the Civil War, when abolitionists and others aiding escaped slaves were the most common victims, and beginning again during Reconstruction (1865–77), when the KU KLUX KLAN and other white supremacist groups attempted to disenfranchise blacks through intimidation and violence. Victims were usually blacks accused of murdering or raping whites. Lynching was also a common form of frontier justice in the American West of the 19th century.

Lynching reached its peak in the South in the late 19th century and declined sharply after 1935. Increased news coverage and public awareness of lynching incidents, combined with progress in civil rights, may have ended the practice.

Lynn   Lynn is a city in northeastern Massachusetts, on Massachusetts Bay, about 18 km (11 mi) northeast of Boston. Its population is 81,245 (1990). Once an important shoe-manufacturing center and site of the country's first ironworks (1643), it now supports a wide range of industries, producing electrical equipment, jet engines, and machinery. Lynn has more than 5 km (3 mi) of beaches and a 809-ha (2,000-acre) park, Lynn Woods. The town was the home of Mary Baker Eddy, founder of Christian Science.

Settled in 1629 as Saugus, it was laid out in 1631 and named for King's Lynn, England, in 1637. Shoemaking developed from 1635 as a cottage industry. In 1848 the first shoe-sewing machine was introduced, and the factory system of production began.

▬

lynx [links]   The lynx, *Felis lynx*, is a small member of the cat family, Felidae. It weighs up to 18 kg (40 lb), measures 1.1 m (3.5 ft) in length, and stands about 61 cm (24 in) high at the shoulder. It has black ear tufts and a stumpy tail. The lynx has a tawny or grayish brown coat with darker spots and stripes. Its winter coat, much prized by furriers, is dense, silky, and long. The lynx lives in forested areas of Europe, Asia, and northern North America. It usually hunts at night, killing foxes, rabbits, rodents, deer, and some domestic animals. It is a good climber and swimmer.

The oldest section of Lyon, France's third largest city, includes the medieval Cathedral of Saint Jean (foreground) and the Place Bellecour, between the Rhône and Saône rivers.

The Spanish lynx, a subspecies of the European lynx, is distinguished by its prominent spots. The lynx's large, padded paws and long legs enable it to move easily in snow and ice.

▬

Lyon [lee-ohn']   Located at the confluence of the Rhône and Saône rivers, about 274 km (170 mi) north of Marseille, Lyon (or Lyons) is the third largest city in France. The city has a population of 418,476; the population of the metropolitan area is 1,173,000 (1982).

Lyon is a significant inland port connected with Marseille by both canal and river. Synthetic textile, chemical, and charcoal manufacturing, food processing, and metallurgy are leading industries. The University of Lyon (1896) and several museums and theaters are located in the city. The city is compartmentalized by its hills and the rivers. To the west is the Fourvière Ridge, on which Notre Dame Basilica (built 1871–94) is located. Nearby are the Roman odeon and theater. The central business district is on the peninsula formed by the juncture of the two rivers.

Lyon originated as a fishing village during the Roman period and, as Lugdunum, became the capital of Gaul. After the introduction of Christianity into Gaul, Lyon became a major ecclesiastical center. The powerful archbishop of Lyon controlled the city until 1307; two important ecumenical councils were held in Lyon, in 1245 and 1274. Lyon was annexed to the French crown in 1312 and quickly began to prosper as a cultural and commercial center. By the 16th century it was an important silk manufacturing center. It suffered economically during the French Revolution and did not emerge as a prominent city again until the early 20th century. During World War II, Lyon was an anti-German resistance center and consequently suffered much damage. It was freed from German control by the joint efforts of the resistance leaders and the French and U.S. armies in 1944.

Lyon, Matthew The Irish immigrant Matthew Lyon, b. July 14, 1750, d. Aug. 1, 1822, became prominent in Vermont and, later, Kentucky politics. After settling in Vermont he served with Ethan Allen during the American Revolution.

As a U.S. representative from Vermont (1797–1801), Lyon strongly opposed the policies of the Federalist party and was sentenced to a four-month prison term under the Sedition Act for criticizing President John Adams. Lyon later moved to Kentucky and represented that state in Congress (1803–11).

Lyon, Nathaniel Nathaniel Lyon, b. Ashford, Conn., July 14, 1818, d. Aug. 10, 1861, was a Union general in the U.S. Civil War. Assigned (March 1861) command of the St. Louis arsenal, he successfully attacked Camp Jackson, where Missouri's secessionist governor, Claiborne F. Jackson, had garrisoned the state militia. In June 1861 the pro-Southern militia under Sterling PRICE was reinforced by Confederate troops from Arkansas. Lyon attacked them at Wilson's Creek on August 10 but was killed in the battle.

Lyons, Joseph Aloysius [ly'-uhnz, al-oh-wish'-uhs] Joseph Aloysius Lyons, b. Sept. 15, 1879, d. Apr. 7, 1939, was prime minister of Australia from 1931 to 1939. A school teacher, he entered the Tasmanian legislature in 1909, served as Tasmania's first Labor premier (1923–28), and was elected to the federal Parliament in 1929.

Lyons held office in the Labor government until 1931, when he broke away to form the more conservative United Australia party in coalition with former Nationalists. As prime minister he was able to restore some economic stability as the Depression of the 1930s began to wane. He also expanded Australia's forces in response to the threat of Japanese aggression. He died in office.

Lyra [ly'-ruh] Lyra (the Harp) is a small but important northern constellation located between Hercules and Cygnus. Its brightest star, Vega (magnitude 0.04), is the fifth brightest in the heavens. Located 26 light-years from the Sun, Vega will be the pole star in about 12,000 years because of the precession of the Earth's axis. The second-brightest star, Sheliak (from the Arabic *al-shalyaq*, meaning "harp"), is an eclipsing binary. Another object in the constellation, Epsilon Lyrae, is resolvable, with keen eyesight or binoculars, into two stars; a telescope reveals that each of them in turn is double. Other important objects include the Ring Nebula in Lyra (M 57, or NGC 6720)—a planetary nebula shaped like an elliptical smoke ring—and the prototype RR Lyrae variable star.

lyre [lire] The lyre is a stringed instrument consisting of a resonance box or bowl with strings suspended from

The Greek lyra, one of the two types of lyre played in ancient Greece, was an instrument of the amateur musician. Lighter than the kithara, it had a bowl-shaped resonator and seven strings and was generally used to accompany vocal music. Popular in the ancient Middle East and medieval Europe, the lyre is known today in parts of East Africa and Siberia.

the base to a crossbar supported by two arms parallel to its surface. The earliest-known instruments were box lyres about three and a half feet in length found in Sumerian civilization about 3000 BC. The instrument spread throughout the eastern Mediterranean; Homer and other bards used it to accompany their epic poems.

The research of the musicologist Curt Sachs reveals a basic pentatonic (5-tone) tuning even when the number of strings had reached 11, as in the Greek kithara of the 5th century BC. The lyre was played by plucking the strings, either with a large plectrum while the fingers of the left hand damped unwanted strings, or with both plectrum and bare fingers. The lyre spread southward to Ethiopia and the headwaters of the Nile and Congo, where it is still played, and from Greece across Europe. A bowed instrument after 1000 BC, the lyre was ubiquitous during the Middle Ages and survived until recently in Wales, Estonia, and Finland.

lyric A lyric (from the Greek *lyrikos*) was originally a song written for musical accompaniment by a lyre. The term now refers to poems that, though not necessarily intended to be sung, are melodious in meter and rhythm. Lyrics tend to be subjective and emotional rather than intellectually complex and are generally written in the first person. The genres of elegy and ode are both lyrical in expression. The lyric is often distinguished from two other broad categories of poetry—the narrative and the dramatic—but both long narrative poems and verse plays frequently resort to lyric devices.

Lyrical Ballads The *Lyrical Ballads* (1798) is a volume of poetry by Samuel Taylor COLERIDGE and William WORDSWORTH that includes Wordsworth's "Lines Composed a Few Miles above Tintern Abbey" and Coleridge's RIME OF THE ANCIENT MARINER. The preface, which Wordsworth added to a second edition (1800), is regarded as the earliest and most important theoretical statement of the principles of English ROMANTICISM. In the preface Wordsworth rejected the artificial, consciously poetic diction of his predecessors and proposed to write in the "language really used by men," to illustrate "the primary laws of our nature" in the lives of humble, rustic people. His celebrated definition of poetry as "the spontaneous overflow of powerful feelings" is too personal to be inclusive but aptly describes the movingly introspective "Tintern Abbey."

Lysander [ly-san'-dur]   The Spartan general Lysander, d. 395 BC, was largely responsible for Sparta's ultimate victory in the PELOPONNESIAN WAR. As admiral of the Peloponnesian fleet in 408–407 BC he improved its condition with the assistance of CYRUS THE YOUNGER, son of Darius II of Persia. Lysander won the important Battle of Notium (406), causing ALCIBIADES to leave Athenian service. In 405, Lysander crushed the Athenian fleet at Aegospotami. By blockading Athens he helped establish the rule of the Thirty Tyrants after Athens capitulated.

Regarded at first as the savior of the Greeks, Lysander won their enmity and that of the Spartan authorities by arbitrarily arranging the governments of the cities he had liberated from Athens.

After failing to make the Spartan kingship an elective monarchy, Lysander made a bid for power by supporting (399) the succession of AGESILAUS II to a disputed kingship. Once in power, however, Agesilaus ignored Lysander. Lysander died in the Corinthian War.

Lysenko, Trofim Denisovich [lih-seng'-koh, truhfeem' duh-nees'-uh-vich]   Soviet agronomist Trofim Denisovich Lysenko, b. Sept. 29, 1898, d. Nov. 20, 1976, is best remembered for his adverse influence over Soviet biological and agricultural research.

Lysenko believed that he could improve the spring wheat crop by vernalization—keeping the seeds cool and moist before sowing them. He came to support the Lamarckian theory that acquired characteristics can be inherited, and he rejected the widely accepted Mendelian theory of heredity.

Although Lysenko was opposed by many Soviet scientists, he was noticed and supported by Joseph Stalin. In 1940 he became director of the Institute of Genetics of the Soviet Academy of Sciences. He then banished many scientists and insisted that only his views be taught in the schools.

After Stalin's death, in 1953, Lysenko's career began to wane. In 1965, after the retirement of Nikita Khrushchev, Stalin's successor, Lysenko lost favor completely.

Lysimachus, Macedonian King [ly-sim'-uhkuhs]   Lysimachus, c.360–281 BC, a senior Macedonian officer under ALEXANDER THE GREAT, was assigned rule over Thrace after Alexander's death in 323. He pacified the natives, then joined the alliance against ANTIGONUS I, and in 306–305 assumed the royal title.

After expanding his power to the north, Lysimachus took part in the final victory (301) over Antigonus and gained most of Anatolia. In alliance with PYRRHUS of Epirus, he drove DEMETRIUS I POLIORCETES from Macedonia, then expelled Pyrrhus and won sole control of Macedonia and northern Greece. Weakened by court intrigues, Lysimachus was attacked by SELEUCUS I NICATOR and died in battle.

Lysippus [ly-sip'-uhs]   The career of the Greek sculptor Lysippus, who helped pave the way from pure classical to Hellenistic sculpture, spanned the latter half of the 4th century BC. He is said to have made about 1,500 bronze statues of athletes, divinities, and notable personages, including Alexander the Great, who reportedly preferred him to all other sculptors. Of his works not a single known original remains, although some of Lysippus's athletes may be preserved in Roman marble copies. One such work in the Vatican museums is probably the *Apoxyomenos*, or *The Scraper*; another, the *Agias* in the Museum of Delphi, may be a contemporary replica. These statues, together with some comments by the Roman writer Pliny the Elder, suggest something of Lysippus's style, which introduced naturalism to the sculpture of his time.

He changed the system of proportions, elongating the body and reducing the size of the head to one-eighth the total height of the figure. More important, he departed from the principle of a uniform frontal plane for statuary, letting the limbs of his statues project in various directions, thus giving depth and a feeling of motion to his figures.

See also: GREEK ART.

Lysistrata [lis-is-trah'-tuh]   *Lysistrata*, an antiwar play by the Greek comic dramatist ARISTOPHANES, is built around the idea that the women of Greece can put an end to the Peloponnesian War if they but deny the men fighting it their sexual favors. In the play, first performed in 411 BC, when Greece was torn by civil war, the women, led by the proud Lysistrata, unite in chastity against their husbands and lovers until the love-starved men succumb and peace is restored. The plot of *Lysistrata* is simple, the language ribald, and the situations often hilarious, yet the play has remained a powerful statement against war through the ages. In modern times it is an often-revived favorite with antiwar and feminist groups.

lysosome [lis'-uh-sohm]   The lysosome is an intracellular organelle consisting of a membrane-enclosed sac containing ENZYMES, such as lysozymes, that catalyze the digestion of most substances in living cells, including proteins, nucleic acids, some carbohydrates, and possibly fats. Disruption of the lysosomal membrane and release of the enzymes results in rapid digestion and dissolution of the cell. Lysosomes normally digest food stored in the cell or break down foreign particles engulfed by white blood cells (phagocytes). They also destroy aged cells and dissolve the structures surrounding the egg cell during the act of fertilization by sperm.

ILLUSTRATION CREDITS

4 Mirèille Vautier
5 Wide World Photos
10 Stedlijk Museum, Amsterdam
14 Rand McNally & Company
15 Grant Heilman Photography/John Colwell
16 Photo Researchers/Van Bucher; Courtesy Kansas Department of Economic Development
17 Superstock/Shostal/Charles May
18 Photo Researchers/Charles Belinky
19 Kant-Gymnasium
22 Photo Researchers/Diane Rawson
24 © Karsh, Ottawa
27 Brown Brothers
29 Culver Pictures
30 Het Spectrum
31 The Bettmann Archive
32 UPI/Bettmann Newsphotos; Brown Brothers
34 J. Lampert Promotions, Inc.
36 UPI/Bettmann Newsphotos
37 White House Historical Society
38 UPI/Bettmann Newsphotos
41 Rand McNally & Company
42 Courtesy Kentucky Division of Tourism
43 Courtesy Kentucky Division of Tourism
44 Courtesy Kentucky Division of Tourism
47 Rand McNally & Company; AGE World Photo Service
49 Photo Researchers/Georg Gerster
50 Gamma/Liaison/Diane Walker
51 Aldus Books/Courtesy The Foundation Saint-Thomas, Strasbourg
53 © André Kertesz
55 Brown Brothers; The Bettmann Archive
58 Wide World Photos
59 Wide World Photos
65 The Bettmann Archive
69 All-Sport/Tony Duffy
70 Magnum Photos/Bob Adelman
71 The Bettmann Archive
75 National Portrait Gallery, London
79 UPI/Bettmann Newsphotos
80 TAL Streeter
81 TAL Streeter
83 Philadelphia Museum of Art, The Louise and Walter Arensberg Collection
88 Art Resource/Scala
89 The Bettmann Archive
92 Fotostudio Otto
95 ANP-Foto

98 Rand McNally & Company
99 Magnum Photos/Hiroji Kubota; Photo Researchers/Diane Rawson
100 Photo Researchers/Carl Purcell
102 Museum of Fine Arts, Seoul
103 University Museum, Seoul
108 Wide World Photos
111 Photo Researchers/Paolo Koch
112 Het Spectrum
114 UPI/Bettmann Newsphotos
115 Snark International
119 Rand McNally & Company
121 © J. Langevin/Sygma
124 The Bettmann Archive
125 The Bettmann Archive
126 Photo Researchers/Stephanie Dinkins
131 Courtesy Library of Congress
132 AFL-CIO Library
133 AFL-CIO Library
135 Cooper-Hewitt Museum, The Smithsonian Institution's National Museum of Design; Metropolitan Museum of Art, New York, Bequest of Catherine D. Wentworth
137 Smithsonian Institution, Washington, D.C., Freer Gallery of Art; Sports Illustrated/James Drake
139 The Bettmann Archive
140 National Archives of Canada
142 The Bettmann Archive
147 Scala, Florence
149 The Bettmann Archive
150 National Portrait Gallery, London
151 Piet Eggen
155 © Stan Ries Photography
159 NASA
160 Photo Researchers/Hans Namuth; The Image Bank/Michael Camp
161 Photo Researchers/Linda Bartlett; Photo Researchers/Louis Renault
166 Courtesy Library of Congress
171 The Bettmann Archive
174 Rand McNally & Company
175 Explorer; Photo Researchers/George Whitely
176 Culver Pictures; Photo Researchers/ M. Serrailler
182 Los Alamos National Laboratory
183 Photo Researchers/Alexander Tsiaras/Science Source
185 AGE/World Photo Service
186 Mirèille Vautier
187 Mirèille Vautier
188 Mirèille Vautier

189 Mirèille Vautier; Mirèille Vautier
190 Mirèille Vautier; Photo Researchers/George Holton
192 Arthur Sirdofsky; Courtesy Harper and Row Publishers, Inc.
194 Fred Fehl
197 Brown Brothers
198 Foto-Archief Spaarnestad
199 The Bettmann Archive
200 Photo Researchers/Ragnar Larusson
202 The Bettmann Archive
204 Scala, Florence
205 The Bettmann Archive; Photographie Giraudon
206 Professional Picture Service; UPI/ Bettmann Newsphotos
207 UPI/Bettmann Newsphotos
208 Picturepoint, London
209 National Portrait Gallery, London
210 Foto-Archief Spaarnestad
218 Bruce Coleman Ltd./J. & D. Bartlett
224 Rand McNally & Company
225 Photo Researchers/Harold Kinne
226 Picturepoint, London
227 Eastern National Park and Monument Association: Independence National Historical Park Collection
229 The Bettmann Archive
230 Het Spectrum
235 Bildarchiv Preussicher Kulturbesitz
236 Bruce Coleman Inc./Messerschmidt
240 Sovfoto
241 Servizio Editoriale Fotografico; Spectrum Color Library
245 The Bettmann Archive
250 Belgisch Instituut voor Voorlichting en Documentatie
251 Belgisch Instituut voor Voorlichting en Documentatie
254 Rand McNally & Company
255 Explorer; The Bettmann Archive
256 Bildarchiv Preussicher Kulturbesitz
261 Magnum Photos/Henri Cartier-Bresson
262 BBC—Hulton Picture Library
263 Brown Brothers
264 The Thomas Gilcrease Institute of American History and Art/Tulsa, Okla.
268 Rand McNally & Company
270 Photo Researchers/Bernard Pierre Wolff
271 Professional Picture Service
272 Pierpont Morgan Library, New York; Esto Photographics; Bodleian Library, Oxford; Esto Photographics
273 Courtesy Nathaniel Lieberman—I. M. Pei and Partners; Photo Researchers/ Russ Kinne
274 Courtesy Library of Congress
276 Rand McNally & Company
277 Agence De Presse Photografique Rapho
280 Rand McNally & Company
281 Sem Presser

282 Aldus Archives
291 Het Spectrum
292 Scala, Florence
293 Photo Researchers/Lowell Georgia
295 Photo Researchers/Tom McHugh
299 Photo Researchers/Russ Kinne
301 White House Historical Society
303 The Bettmann Archive
304 The Bettmann Archive
306 Aldus Archives
310 Het Spectrum
311 UPI/Bettmann Newsphotos
314 Brown Brothers
316 Bruce Coleman Inc./George Rockwin
318 The Bettmann Archive
327 The Bettmann Archive
332 The Bettmann Archive
333 Culver Pictures
337 Culver Pictures
342 Photo Researchers/Russ Kinne
347 Wide World Photos
349 Art Resource/Scala
350 Lothar Roth and Associates
351 Brown Brothers
353 The Bettmann Archive
355 Brown Brothers
357 The Bettmann Archive
358 Lowell Georgia
360 UPI/Bettmann Newsphotos; The Hark Group Ltd./Slidemakers
361 UPI/Bettmann Newsphotos
362 Photo Researchers/Tom McHugh
363 Lothar Roth and Associates
367 Courtesy Ring Magazine
368 Photographie Giraudon
369 Bibliothèque Nationale, Paris
371 Scala, Florence
372 Photographie Giraudon
376 Rand McNally & Company
377 Photo Researchers/Dennis Cipnik; Courtesy Tourist Development Commission/Baton Rouge, La.
378 Photo Researchers/Esther Henderson; Photo Researchers/Bradley Smith
379 Photo Researchers/Victor Englebert
380 Aldus Archives
382 Magnum Photos/Erich Hartmann
383 Brown Brothers
385 The Bettmann Archive
389 UPI/Bettmann Newsphotos; UPI/ Bettmann Newsphotos
392 The Hark Group Ltd./Slidemakers; Sovfoto/Eastfoto
393 J. E. Bulloz
396 Grant Heilman Photography/John Colwell
397 Wide World Photos
402 Brown Brothers
405 The Bettmann Archive
406 UPI/Bettmann Newsphotos
408 Rand McNally & Company; Superstock/Shostal
413 Agence De Presse Photografique Rapho